WOMEN'S AMERICA

Women's America

Refocusing the Past

SEVENTH EDITION

Edited by

Linda K. Kerber
University of Iowa

Jane Sherron De Hart
University of California, Santa Barbara

Cornelia Hughes Dayton
University of Connecticut

New York Oxford
Oxford University Press
2011

Oxford University Press, Inc., publishes works that further Oxford University's objective of excellence in research, scholarship, and education.

Oxford New York
Auckland Cape Town Dar es Salaam Hong Kong Karachi
Kuala Lumpur Madrid Melbourne Mexico City Nairobi
New Delhi Shanghai Taipei Toronto

With offices in
Argentina Austria Brazil Chile Czech Republic France Greece
Guatemala Hungary Italy Japan Poland Portugal Singapore
South Korea Switzerland Thailand Turkey Ukraine Vietnam

Published by Oxford University Press, Inc.
198 Madison Avenue, New York, New York 10016
http://www.oup.com

Library of Congress Cataloging-in-Publication Data

Women's America: refocusing the past/edited by Linda K. Kerber, Jane Sherron De Hart, Cornelia Hughes Dayton. — 7th ed.
v. cm.
Includes bibliographical references and index.
ISBN 978-0-19-538832-9—ISBN 978-0-19-538833-6 (v. 1)—ISBN 978-0-19-538834-3 (v. 2)
1. Women—United States—History—Sources. 2. Women—Employment—United States—History—Sources. 3. Women—Political activity—United States—History—Sources. 4. Women—Health and hygiene—United States—History—Sources. 5. Feminism—United States—History—Sources. I. Kerber, Linda K. II. De Hart, Jane Sherron. III. Dayton, Cornelia Hughes.
HQ1426.W663 2011
305.40973—dc22

2010021711

Printing number: 9 8 7 6

Printed in the United States of America on acid-free paper

To Gerda Lerner and Anne Firor Scott

who shaped the new women's history of this generation

and

to *Women's America* student collaborators since 1982

who herald the next generation of innovative teachers and scholars:

Patrick Blythe
Rachel Bohlmann
Sarah Case
JoAnn Castagna
Catherine Denial
Jillian Dowling
Gary Eblen
Malinda Ellwood
Eric Fure-Slocum
Daniel Gomes
Harlan Gradin
Kristina Groover
Cynthia Hamilton
Jill Harsin
Karissa Haugeberg
Charles Hawley
Michael Hevel
Kimberly Jensen
Barbara Ladd
Sharon Lake
Jennifer Lettieri
Carolyn Herbst Lewis
Doris Malkmus
David Manderscheid
Kim Nielsen
Kathryn Penningroth
Alexander Rondon
Jane Roules
Catherine Rymph
Roseanne Sizer
Kendall Staggs
Leslie Taylor
Sharon Wood

Contents

Preface

To our readers:

We are delighted that for the first time, *Women's America* is available both as a single, integrated book and in two volumes. This change is a testimony to the flourishing of scholarship about women in the last decade. The expansion of the range and scope of *Women's America* also reflects the significance and intensity of debates on issues of women and gender in our public culture and the media.

The two photo essays are the newest feature of this book, and one that we have had a great deal of pleasure developing. Each essay ranges over the full sweep of U.S. history; in this way, we aim to underscore themes that percolate through the narrative of American women's experience. The term *photo essay* is a convenient shorthand: photographs predominate, but lithographs and late eighteenth-century woodcuts are also included. We hope that the contextual material and reflections that accompany each image will help readers to look hard at the details and spur discussion. The essays can serve simultaneously as independent readings and as supplements to other items in *Women's America*. Note that we have placed cross-references throughout the book to individual images in the photo essays in the hope of encouraging readers to move back and forth.

We have placed the photo essay "Women in Public" in the context of the 1848 Seneca Falls convention in which women articulated clearly and strongly their commitment to reshaping the public order. A student who reads the full photo essay at that point will get glimpses of the tensions involving women in public before 1848 and after, all the way to the present moment, including objections to current wars in which the United States is engaged. We have paired the second photo essay, "Adorning the Body," with Joan Jacobs Brumberg's essay on the imposition of dress sizes which conveyed to women that they needed to reshape themselves. We have noticed in developing the essay that styles that are painful to wear—corsets and girdles, stiletto heels—have recurred from time to time in the last two centuries, often understood to be indicators either of respectability or of playful design that accentuates feminine sexual allure. Fashion carried other signifiers: the middle-class women wearing corsets would not be mistaken for working-class women whose physical labor required looser garments.

We have expanded the document component of *Women's America*. Documents appear from the founding years of women's studies programs, including notes from one of the very first women's history courses offered in the United States. We have added legal materials that deserve to be far better known, such as a nineteenth-century law that required Chinese women seeking to enter the United States to demonstrate that they were not prostitutes. Readers will find substantially expanded document essays on major subjects such as the law of slavery and freedom, Title IX, reproductive rights, and marriage (including same-sex marriage).

The seventh edition pays increasing attention to transnational elements of American women's lives. Among the additions, one can now read about the freighted ways in which indigenous African women were pictured in European travel accounts, Sally Hemings negotiating with Thomas Jefferson in Paris, New England girls captured by native Americans and brought to French Canada, young women entering convents in Ireland and then moving to New York City, and, in our own time, U.S. participation in the international women's rights movement against trafficking. For the nineteenth century, women's political agency is highlighted in several new essays. For the twentieth century, readers will discover essays on young Latinas' dating practices, television and radio portrayals of Jewish women during the cold war, urban African American women's strategies to sustain their families in the 1950s, and changes experienced by military servicewomen since the end of the Vietnam War.

Linda K. Kerber
Jane Sherron De Hart
Cornelia Hughes Dayton

ACKNOWLEDGMENTS

We've had a whirlwind year as Cornelia Hughes Dayton joins us in the making of *Women's America.* Meeting serendipitously in interesting places (Tempe, New York City, Wellfleet, Ottawa, Iowa City), continuing our conversations on e-mail and speakerphone, sending photo images and scans of text back and forth in cyberspace: through it all, shaping this seventh edition has been invigorating. We have been lucky to have the advice of nearly fifty users of previous editions, who anonymously provided forthright, critical assessments that helped us in our selections. This particular edition benefited from the reviews and insights of Nan Enstad, University of Wisconsin; Cynthia Harrison, George Washington University; Laura L. Lovett, University of Massachusetts; Jean A. Stuntz, West Texas A&M University; Cindy Wilkey, University of Virginia's College at Wise; Catherine Oglesby, Valdosta State University; Nina Silber, Boston University; Cynthia Kierner, University of North Carolina at Charlotte; Julie K. Berebitsky, Sewanne; Beth Robinson, University of Wisconsin, Milwaukee; Kimberly Jensen, Western Oregon University; Sylvie Coulibaly, Kenyon College; Nicholas Syrett, Northern Colorado University; Cynthia Culver Prescott, University of North Dakota; Landon Storrs, University of Houston; Elaine Frantz Parsons, Duquesne University; Karen Leroux, Drake University; Barbara Berglund, University of South Florida; Robert Hill, American University; Sherry Katz, UC San Francisco; Lara Vapnek, St. John's University; Catherine Kerrison, Villanova University; Steven Reschly, Truman State University; Patricia Cooper, University of Kentucky; Mary Ann Wynkoop, University of Missouri–Kansas City; Victoria Brown, Grinnell College; Janet Allured, McNeese State University; Dana Cooper, Stephen F. Austin; Chad David Cover, Framingham State College; Amy Richter, Clark University; Michelle M. Morgan, University of Wisconsin, Whitewater; Linzy Brekke-Aloise, Stonehill College; Laura Bier, Georgia Institute of Technology; Amy Bix, Iowa State University; and Anne Boylan, University of Delaware.

We are grateful, too, for the good counsel of friends and colleagues, among them Rachel Bohlmann, Patricia Bonomi, Catherine Denial, Ann Estin, Jennifer Glass, Linda Gordon, Elizabeth Liltillman, David Hollinger, Frederick Hoxie, Katherine Jellison, James C. Mohr, Elizabeth Israels Perry, Catherine Rymph, Terri Snyder, Sheila Skemp, and Judy Temple. We have turned to archivists and curators, often on tight deadlines, and been grateful for their enthusiastic responsiveness: among them are Sherill Redmon and Maida Goodwin of the Sophia Smith Collection at Smith College, Mary J. Bennett of the State Historical Society of Iowa, and Elizabeth Dunn and Kelly Wooten of the Sallie Bingham Center for Women's History and Culture in the Duke University Libraries.

Leandra Zarnow of the University of California, Santa Barbara, and Michael Hevel of the University of Iowa stepped in at crucial points in the editorial process. Patrick Blythe of the University of Connecticut did some early scouting for us. In the crucial months of compilation, Karissa Haugeberg and Sharon Lake of the University of Iowa have been a remarkable team, effectively serving as managing editors for this enterprise. Karissa Haugeberg has been photo editor, identifying images for the photo essays, tracking down their copyright holders (not always easy to do!), and drafting captions. Sharon Lake prepared the text for the press and wrote the essay on Title IX. Together they conducted much of the correspondence. Throughout they have brought their own rich resources of good judgment to bear on the shaping of this book, and they have done it with equanimity and infectious good spirits. They now know all too well how this particular manuscript moves into print, and we look forward to reading the books that they are now writing.

That *Women's America* appears in two volumes as well as a single volume is a result of the initiative of our editor, Brian Wheel. It has been a joy to work with him and with his assistants, Laura Lancaster and Danniel Schoonebeek. The book has been guided into print by the shrewd copyediting of Joan Gieseke and the production skills of Barbara Mathieu.

Women's America can only be as strong as the field of women's history, and we are awed by the power and force of the latest scholarship. The selection process has always been difficult; this time the challenges were unusually severe. Our understanding of the distinctive elements of women's experience is now expanded by studies that take into account the international dimensions of U.S. history and which root new developments in American law, politics, and culture in historical experience that we had not fully appreciated. We end with admiration for the many thousands of historians who are probing the archives that women and men have left behind—from first-year students writing term papers to winners of the National Book Award—all introducing us to women who have, one way or another, shaped the world in which we live.

Linda, Jane, Nina

INTRODUCTION

Gender and the New Women's History

Linda K. Kerber
Jane Sherron De Hart
Cornelia Hughes Dayton

One of the most effective ways in which dominant groups maintain their power is by depriving the people they dominate of the knowledge of their own history. The Martiniquian psychiatrist Frantz Fanon, a leader of the Algerian resistance against the French in the 1950s, understood this well. In *The Wretched of the Earth,* his classic attack on colonialism, Fanon observed that "colonialism is not satisfied merely with holding a people in its grip . . . [but] by a kind of perverted logic, it turns to the past of an oppressed people, and distorts, disfigures and destroys it." Lacking an appreciation of their own historical experience and the dignity, even glory, of the actions of their own people, the colonized are encouraged to think that they have no alternative to oppressive conditions. "The effect consciously sought . . . [is] to drive into the natives' heads the idea that if the settlers were to leave, they would at once fall back into barbarism, degradation and bestiality."[1]

Throughout history, certain women have understood this. When, in 1404, Christine de Pizan undertook to write the earliest modern chronicle of the lives of great women of the past, she explained to her readers that she hoped to bring them "out of the ignorance which so blinds your own intellect." Although they knew "for a certainty" from their own experience that women were capable of virtue and fortitude, they were vulnerable to "philosophers" who defined women as trivial. Pizan described her contemporaries as "valiant women" who, denied a knowledge of their own history, had been "abandoned . . . exposed like a field without a surrounding hedge, without finding a champion to afford them an adequate defense. . . . Where is there a city so strong which could not be taken immediately if no resistance were forthcoming . . . ?" To provide women with their history was to build "a city wall, strongly constructed and well founded."[2]

WOMEN'S HISTORY AS A FIELD OF RESEARCH

A fictional woman in Jane Austen's novel *Northanger Abbey* (1818) complains that she reads history only a little, "as a duty, but it tells me little that does not either vex or weary me. The quarrels of popes and kings, with wars or pestilences, in every page; the men all so good for nothing, and hardly any women at all."[3] As recently as twenty years ago, students in high school and college history classes could examine the index of their American history survey texts and reach the same conclusion.

In mid-nineteenth-century America, women activists self-consciously created a historical archive. Fearing that women would be denied knowledge of their own history, knowing that the actions of women were little regarded by historians, and predicting that pioneering activists on behalf of women's rights would die before their experiences had been recorded, Elizabeth Cady Stanton and Susan B. Anthony energetically collected evidence of the women's movement of their own time. The rich collection of documents that they published—six large volumes, entitled *History of Woman Suffrage*—was intended to be "an arsenal of facts" for the next generation of activists and historians.[4] But most historians ignored it. Ralph Henry Gabriel's *The Course of American Democratic Thought,* the standard text widely used throughout the 1940s and 1950s in college history courses, failed to cite a single work by a woman, not even the massive *History of Woman Suffrage.* "[I]f women were doing any thinking . . . ," the historian Mary Beard acidly observed in 1946, "it is difficult to find out from this treatise what it was."[5] In 1933 she herself edited a documentary collection, *America through Women's Eyes,* in which she argued that an accurate understanding of the past required that women's experience be analyzed with as much care as historians normally devote to the experience of men. Our perspective and our goals in this book are similar to hers. We offer essays that we not only enjoy reading and rereading but that represent some of the best work done during the past four decades in which women's history emerged as a research field.

Surveying those decades, the historian Gerda Lerner suggested that the writing of women's history can be arranged in four stages of development, each stage more complex and sophisticated than the last, but all useful and necessary.[6] The first stage she called "compensatory history," in which the historian wanders, like Diogenes with a lantern, seeking to identify women and their activities. In the decade of the 1970s, some historians began to search for women whose work and experiences deserved to be more widely known. The accomplishments of these women ranged from feats of exploration and endurance to scientific discoveries, artistic achievements, and humanitarian reforms. They included such pioneers as Amelia Earhart, the pilot whose solo flight across the Atlantic in 1933 dramatically demonstrated women's courage and daring; Alice Hamilton, the social reformer and physician whose innovative work in the 1920s on lead poisoning and other toxins made her a world authority on industrial disease and a strong critic of American industry; Maria Goeppert-Mayer, the brilliant theoretical physicist whose research on the structure of the atom and its nucleus won her the Nobel Prize; and Zora Neale Hurston, the novelist and folklorist who mastered African American folk idiom and depicted independent black women. One result of this search has been the publication of *Notable American Women,* four volumes of fascinating biographies of 1,800 remarkable individuals.[7]

"The next level of conceptualizing women's history," Lerner suggested, has been "contribution history." In this stage, historians describe women's contribution to topics, issues, and themes that have already been determined to be important. The main actors in the historical narrative remain men; women are subordinate, "helping" or "contributing" to the work of male activists. If the tone of "compensatory history" is delighted discovery of previously unknown women, the tone of contributory history can often be reproachful: how is it that men did not acknowledge women's help? Still, the work of contributory history can be very important in connecting women to major movements in the past: the women of Hull House "contribute" to Progressive reforms, the women in cotton factories in Lowell, Massachusetts, are an important part of the story of the industrialization of America. Pioneering historians in the late 1920s and 1930s, among them Julia Cherry Spruill, Mary Beard, and Caroline Ware, wrote important books that firmly established women's participation in and contribution to significant developments in American history: frontier settlement, abolition, urbanization and industrialization, populism and progressivism.

It could be said that a third stage of women's history—which developed as a vigorous field of study and research in the 1970s and 1980s—is to move past a recounting of women's "contributions" and to seek to test familiar generalizations and to rewrite the historical narrative. Things we thought we "knew" about American history turn out to be more complex than we had suspected. For example, most textbooks suggest that the frontier meant opportunity for Americans, "a gate of escape from the bondage of the past." But it was men who more readily found on the frontier compensation for their hard work; many women found only drudgery. (In fact, women were more likely to find economic opportunity in cities than on the frontier.) Other generalizations turn out to be equally suspect. We have often assumed that American slaves were provided with at least adequate diets, but the generalization holds better for male slaves than for pregnant women and nursing mothers; for them, the slaves' diet meant semistarvation. The new women's history challenges us to reexamine the social relations of the sexes, to *reconstruct* many historical generalizations, and to *reconfigure* the historical narrative.

Finally, women's history challenges us to understand that gender itself is a social construction. Historians increasingly ask questions about how people construct meaning for their historical experience, and how perceived difference between the sexes operates to shape the construction of meaning.[8] Women's history also suggests a more complex understanding of traditional categories of historical interpretation. Conventional periodization has used presidential administrations or wars as major guideposts in organizing our description of the past: the Revolutionary Era, the Age of Jackson, the Civil War, the Eisenhower Years. Conventional interpretations have tended to emphasize the accomplishments of men, whether they be presidents, generals, farmers, or ranch hands. But all men had women for contemporaries, and women experienced the same great social phenomena that men did.

This book is divided into four major chronological sections. Because dates that mark major turning points in traditional historical accounts do not automatically coincide with those dates that mark significant changes in the lives of American women, women's history challenges us to re-examine conventional periodization. Our sections are generally congruent with familiar periodization; they also reflect changing realities in women's experience. The dividing date between early and industrializing America is 1820, by which time forces were in motion that would erode the domestic economy of an agrarian society, slowly transforming women's lives in the process. The long period of industrialization that followed 1820 may be broken at 1880, by which time large-scale industries in which women were employed were firmly established. By this time, too, women's rights leaders had come to recognize that suffrage would not be granted by the courts on the basis of a fresh interpretation of the Constitution, and they demanded a specific constitutional amendment. Gerda Lerner has identified the necessary preconditions for women's emancipation as "urbanization; industrialization with technology permitting society to remove food preparation and care of the sick from the home; the mechanization of heating and laundry; spread of health and medical care sufficient to lower infant mortality and protect maternal health; birth control; . . . and availability of education on all levels to all children."[9] These conditions existed in varying measure by 1880.

It should be noted, however, that industrialization was never a uniform process occurring simultaneously in all of the United States. Industrialized areas in the East and upper Midwest coexisted with frontier conditions in the West. There, encounters between Anglos, Native Americans, and Hispanics accentuated disparities just as had earlier contact in the East among British immigrants, Native Americans, and Africans, prompting us to call this section "The Many Frontiers of Industrializing America, 1820–1880." Although the frontiers of industrializing America extended throughout the nineteenth century and beyond, 1880 marks a convenient break. In the next half century, American life would be reshaped by an influx of immigrants, increasing urbanization, severe racial segregation, rapid technological advances, and a growing consumer culture. In the midst of these changes, Progressives at the turn of the century and New Dealers during the 1930s worked to redefine the federal government's responsibility to its citizens, spurred by major events with seismic impacts—a crippling depression and two world wars. We have headed this third section "Creating the State in an Industrialized Nation, 1880–1945." Women were in the forefront of state-building just as they played an indispensable role in the struggle to organize unions, to hold their families together amid the onslaught of depression at home and Nazism in Europe, to keep production lines rolling so as to keep the troops fighting abroad, and—not least—to achieve full citizenship for themselves. For some women, however, a war waged in the name of freedom did not mean freedom in their own country. The state could be an instrument of injustice, as Japanese Americans discovered during World War II when they were forced out of their homes on the West Coast and placed in internment camps inland because of concerns about their loyalties. However misguided specific policies such as internment were, the United States emerged from World War II a true superpower. What we discover in this third section is how the perspective of women's history allows us to reexamine male-dominated structures such as the state, gaining new insights into the role women played in its creation. We also see once again how the perspectives of women of color and their communities call into question old notions about citizenship and about the nation as an organic entity.

The second half of the twentieth century consisted of decades dominated by the cold war, the rights revolution, and the resurgence of conservatism. It stands as a separate section, the fourth, and is titled "Struggles against Injustice, 1945–2010." While these struggles involving racial justice, civil rights, welfare rights, workers' rights, women's rights (including reproductive rights), and the nuclear arms race took place within the United States, they cannot be separated from those waged on an international stage. For those women engaged, politicization and participation in movement-building reached new heights during this period. Movements bred counter-movements as pro-choice women found themselves confronted by pro-life women.

However historical experience is periodized, women shared that experience. The history of industrialization, for example, is a history that involves female workers quite as much as it does male. Like their male counterparts, most women workers relied on their wages for their own support and that of their families. In the first factory labor force—the mill hands of Samuel Slater's first textile factory in Pawtucket, Rhode Island, in 1790—women and children actually outnumbered men. Extensively employed in manufacturing by the nineteenth century, they worked in a wide variety of trades as bookbinders, printers, shoemakers, seamstresses, laundresses, glass painters, button makers. In the twentieth century they worked in shipyards, airplane factories, and automobile plants turning out the military equipment essential to Allied victory in two world wars.

Women were at the forefront of working-class protest. Women weavers in Pawtucket, Rhode Island, who walked off work in 1824 were among the first American workers to strike against low wages and long hours; a significant number of strikes by women workers followed in the 1830s.[10] Women at the textile mills in Lowell, Massachusetts, in the 1840s were the first industrial workers in the nation to demand state regulation of the length of the workday. In the twentieth century, large-scale strikes organized by men in mines and railroads had their counterparts in large-scale strikes organized by women in textile mills and garment factories.[11]

Similarly, enslaved workers—primarily Africans but also, in the early centuries, Indians—were as likely to be women as men. Enslaved women workers were to be found in the fields, toiling alongside men, in the same jobs.

THE DIFFERENT HISTORICAL EXPERIENCE OF WOMEN AND MEN

The historical experience of the two sexes, for all its similarities, was in many important ways profoundly different. Difference itself is a comparative term. As legal scholar Martha Minow writes, "I am no more different from you than you are from me. A short person is different only in relation to a tall one." While making distinctions helps people cope with complexity, descriptions of difference usually carry with them unstated assumptions of value and hierarchy. As Minow puts it, "Women are compared to the unstated norm of men, 'minority' races to white, handicapped persons to the able-bodied, and 'minority' religions to 'majorities.'"[12] Difference, therefore, is not a neutral term.

Differences among women are also multiple. Differences of culture, nationality, and historical memory are exacerbated by distinctions of race, class, ethnicity, and sexual preference. Because women are apt to live with men—husbands, fathers, sons—who share their racial, class, and ethnic identities, commonalities with women who don't share that identity are often obscured. Because each of these differences carries with it implications of hierarchy, further distancing can develop. Affluent women may feel superior to poor women; white women may feel hostile to black women; Asian American women may feel that they have little in common with Hispanic women.

Hispanic women, who are often identified as a single ethnic group, are in fact people of many nationalities: Puerto Ricans, Cubans, Mexicans, Brazilians—to name a few. Moreover, most are of Central American Indian descent and share the gene pool of North American Indians. They learned to speak Spanish—hence the name "Hispanic"—only because their original land was conquered by Spain. "Hispanic" women differ from each other with respect to not only ethnicity but also class. Affluent women who are part of the Miami Cuban community may feel that they have little in common with migrant agricultural workers from Mexico. By the same token, Asian American women who came from such countries as China, Japan, the Philippines, Korea, Thailand, or Vietnam are separated by diverse heritages, various languages, and disparate economic resources. So are white women who are separated by multiple ethnic backgrounds, religious affiliations, and class positions.

Differences in sexual preference further divide women, which in the past has stigmatized lesbians and obscured the commonalities they share with heterosexual women. Women who are able to tolerate same-sex relationships as long as they remain discreetly hidden are often uncomfortable with open displays of homosexual preference and distance themselves from the women involved. Lesbians who have struggled for self-validation and a life-style that allows them to express same-sex love, affection, and sexuality feel no less alienated from women whose discomfort is a measure of their identification with a system that has stigmatized and oppressed other women.

That the factors which women share with men and which separate them from other women have been so powerful and persistent should not blind us to fundamental divergence in the historical experience of women and men. Gender differences in life cycles and family experiences have been a central factor in that divergence. Employment patterns of white women in a large New England textile factory make this clear. As young single women at the turn of the century, they went into the mill to supplement family income, often allowing brothers to improve their job prospects by staying in school; as wives, they withdrew when children were born and returned as mothers of small children when the perilous state of family finances required them to do so. As mothers of grown children, they returned to stay. Thus family responsibilities were a crucial factor not only in determining at what stage in their life cycle women were gainfully employed but also in explaining why their employment patterns differed from those of male workers.

Once in the work force, the jobs to which women were assigned, the wages they were paid, the opportunities for unionization they encountered, and the relationship they forged with governmental regulators all reinforced fundamental differences between the sexes. Even when they entered the factory together, with comparable skills, men and women were assigned by management to different tasks at markedly different pay scales. Despite the low wages, which should have made them ripe recruits for unionization, most unions were loath to organize women workers. In part because women lacked the leverage that unions afforded skilled male workers, federal and state governments reluctantly agreed to regulate women's hours, wages, and working conditions long before they regulated men's.

Most people, male and female, particularly if they were white and middle class, understood difference to mean advantage. They assumed that women were spared heavy physical labor and fierce competitive pressures. Excused from primary responsibility for family support, wives and daughters could spend most of their adult lives at home rather than in the work force, devoting their time to such congenial tasks as caring for children, doing charitable deeds, and socializing with friends. Those who were employed outside the home were thought to work for "pin money," which they could use to indulge their whims as consumers.

Recent research makes clear that most of these "advantages" were class-specific and illusory. Exhausting labor performed in hazardous conditions characterized many women's jobs. Responsibility for supporting other family members was not limited to men, especially among the working class. Unmarried women often returned their wages to their parents, who relied on daughters' wages for essentials. Most adult women—whether they were single, widows, or wives—worked to feed and shelter themselves, their children, other members of their families. Their expenditure of money was rarely capricious; in fact they accepted low wages in nonunionized jobs because they were so likely to be in desperate need.

The notion that the home protected working-class housewives from the competitive pressures of the marketplace and all housewives from real work was also an illusion. The home has always been less a haven than a workplace. It was the site of housework—heavy physical labor and unremitting toil—work that was no less strenuous for all the denial that it was work at all, since it was performed for love of family rather than for wages. Even the middle-class housewife who enjoyed the conveniences of nineteenth-century town life and possibly a servant to help with the laundry and cooking struggled with an exhausting array of tasks that included washing, starching, ironing, sorting, and putting away laundry; scrubbing, sweeping, and dusting floors, walls, windows, furniture, and accessories; growing, pickling, preserving, and baking food; sewing, mending, and knitting clothes, towels, pillowcases, quilts, curtains, carpets, and rugs; birthing, nursing, tending, instructing, and disciplining children. According to one harried antebellum housewife, every day was "hurry, hurry, hurry, and drive, drive, drive."[13] For rural women the workload was even heavier. There were farm-related chores to perform and raw materials such as soap and cloth to produce in addition to core household tasks. Through much of the nineteenth century, rural black women were enslaved; after the Civil War most lived in sharecropping families in which the level of subsistence was scarcely higher and the physical workload almost as heavy, although the psychological conditions were generally better. Reflecting on the workload of her mother's generation, a nineteenth-century daughter spoke for millions when she lamented that her mother had been robbed of "her health, her strength, and her life."[14] In some respects, little has changed. In the 1980s, a farm woman in northern Iowa told an interviewer, "I plant the garden, I feed the chickens, I sell the eggs, I put up a year's worth of vegetables. I don't have *time* to work!"[15]

Although twentieth-century technology has lightened the onerous physical burden, the equation of homemaking with leisure remains an illusion carefully nurtured by the advertising industry. From the introduction of the electric washing machine in the 1920s—"an entire new day will be added to your week"—to the dishwashers, ranges, and microwave ovens of the 1990s that will do the work "whether you are at home or not," promises of relief from drudgery through the purchase of new products have been accompanied by new expectations that entailed more work.[16] Laundry—and there was more of it—had to be done more frequently; cooking demanded more creativity; clothing necessitated hours spent shopping; child care involved properly sterilized bottles, regular feeding schedules, greater attention to toilet training, nutrition, hygiene, and properly supervised play. If the nature of housework had changed, the time spent doing it did not. In 1960, nonemployed urban women were spending fifty-five hours per week in housework—three hours more than rural homemakers in the 1920s. Fully employed women in the 1970s each week packed an additional twenty-five hours of work—housework—into evenings and weekends. While there is evidence that some men are doing considerably more, the gender disparity in terms of housework persists in the twenty-first century.[17]

If women seldom found the home that tranquil center of repose depicted in popular literature, they had equal difficulty finding in it the much celebrated "haven" from the competitive pressures of a "heartless world." We have long understood that severe downturns in the market have enormous economic and psychic impact on family life. During the Great Depression of the 1930s, for example, many homemakers were thrust into the work force, joining the long lines of men desperate for work. Refusing to sit by passively when their families lacked basic necessities, others opened their homes to boarders and applied their sewing skills to piecework—measures that wives of laborers had long used to supplement family income even in periods of prosperity. Resorting to the home production that had engaged their grandmothers, middle- and working-class women alike raised and canned vegetables and patched, mended, and recycled clothes in order to keep cash outlays at a minimum.

What historians have only begun to appreciate is the extent to which in more prosperous times such enterprise and frugality benefited not only the household economy but the national economy as well. By helping out husbands in shops, buying in bulk, taking in boarders, doing piecework, taking in wash, peddling goods on the street, scavenging for food and fuel, wives in laboring-class households throughout the nineteenth and early twentieth century managed to transform a husband's wages below subsistence level into subsistence wages. Because of such efforts, businesses employing those husbands were able to stay afloat in an undercapitalized and volatile economy. Among the emerging middle class where a husband's income was sufficient for maintenance, it was the value of the wife's labor that frequently provided the kind of savings and investments that buffered the family against market vicissitudes and fueled economic growth in an industrializing nation. In sum, even in the nineteenth century, the boundaries between home and market, domestic sphere and public sphere, were far more permeable than once assumed.

GENDER AS A SOCIAL CONSTRUCTION

The adverse economic implications for women associated with the old perception that housework was not real work suggest that in this instance, as in many others, difference has meant disadvantage. Women's historians have not only documented this disadvantage, but have sought to explain it. The factors involved in this explanation are very complex and still imperfectly understood. The explanation traditionally offered has been a variant of biological essentialism. As Supreme Court Justice David Brewer put it in 1908, "The two sexes differ in the structure of the body, in the functions to be performed by each, in the amount of physical strength, in the capacity for long continuing labor . . . , [in] the self reliance which enables one to assert full rights, and in the capacity to maintain the struggle for subsistence." Woman's "physical structure and a proper discharge of her maternal functions" place her at a disadvantage in that struggle, he continued, and justify legislation to protect her.[18] (See p. 415.)

Justice Brewer's statement reveals a common confusion of sex and gender. To the extent that his view of difference is based on anatomical and hormonal features that differentiate males and females biologically, he is talking about *sexual* difference. When, however, he speaks of "the self-reliance that enables . . . [men] to assert full rights," "the capacity [of men] to maintain the struggle for subsistence," and the "proper discharge of [woman's] maternal functions," he is referring to *gender* difference. The assumption that men are self-reliant and that women are not, that men struggle for subsistence and women do not, that women nurture their children and men cannot, reflects the ways in which Justice Brewer and most of his generation understood the implications of being male or female.

In antebellum America, for example, white southern males, whether members of the low-country planter class or the backcountry working class, identified masculinity with a concept of personal honor, in defense of which duels were fought and fists flew. In the cities of the North, many young working-class males shared their southern counterparts' obsession with physical prowess and bellicosity. So synonymous were masculinity and toughness for those New Yorkers known as "Bowery boys" that when the Bowery boy was represented on stage, he was immediately recognizable by his swaggering gait and aggressive persona. Although the black abolitionist Frederick Douglass would not have been comfortable with the flamboyant aggressiveness and virility flaunted by the Bowery boys as a badge of working-class masculinity, the identification of force and power with manhood was a concept he well understood. In *Narrative of the Life of Frederick Douglass* (1845), Douglass's autobiographical account of his life as a slave and his escape to freedom, the author prefaced a description of his brutal fight with the vicious slave breaker Covey with a single sentence: "You have seen how a man was made a slave; you shall see how a slave was made a man."

Not all social groups defined masculinity in this fashion, even in antebellum America. Although aggressiveness, self-reliance, and competitiveness were cultivated in most boys because these traits were needed in the work world of adult males, families whose values were shaped by evangelical Protestantism emphasized that manliness also involved self-restraint, moral self-discipline, and sobriety. These qualities became even more important in the new urban bourgeois culture of the late nineteenth century. A bureaucratized corporate capitalism would require of the middle class a model of masculinity different from the rougher, more "macho" ideal characteristic of the frontier. A "real" man, while projecting a virile and, if necessary, tough demeanor, also needed to be a "team player"—an attribute cultivated in boyhood games and team sports. Indeed, competitive sports, virility, and masculinity became so intertwined in the twentieth century . . . that "the boy or man who dislikes competitive sports or virile postures has little choice but to affect 'manly' interests and behavior and to hope these affectations will not be exposed."[19] To behave otherwise was to risk being called a "sissy" or a "queer." Such labels reflected popular assumptions that "real" men were sportsmen and that nonathletes, whether heterosexual or not, were males who wished to have sexual relations only with males, were effeminate, and/or wished to be women. In other words, sex refers to biological differences that are unchanging; gender involves the *meaning* that a particular society and culture attach to sexual difference. Because that meaning varies over time and among cultures, gender differences are both socially constructed and subject to change. Definitions of what is masculine and feminine are learned as each society instructs its members from infancy through adulthood as to what behavior and personality attributes are appropriate for males and females of that generation.

Sexuality is also socially constructed. Anatomical and hormonal characteristics set certain boundaries within which we operate. Within those boundaries, socially constructed scripts provide cues as to how we respond sexually—what or who arouses our desire. How sexual preference is first determined or chosen—and when—is a matter experts do not fully understand. But here, too, culture plays a part. It is helpful, writes historian Carroll Smith-Rosenberg, to "view sexual and emotional impulses as part of a continuum or spectrum. . . . At one end of the continuum lies committed heterosexuality, at the other uncompromising homosexuality; between, a wide latitude of emotions and sexual feelings."[20] Where we place ourselves on that continuum and whether we move within it is affected by cultural norms as well as by a strong biological component.

Sexuality has its own history. Conceptions of sexuality, attitudes as to how sexual feelings should be expressed, with whom, and where, have been continually reshaped by the changing nature of the economy and politics. In the seventeenth century, for example, women were believed to be more lustful and carnal than men. Female sexuality was seen as a source of power and corruption to be feared and controlled. By the nineteenth century, when sexual restraints had to be internalized, sexuality was redefined. Women—at least white, native-born, middle- and upper-class women—were viewed as having weaker sexual desires than men. Sensuality was attached to poor or "darker" women—who, by definition, "invited" male advances.

As we begin to uncover the history of sexuality, we can better understand what part sexuality played in women's subordination. We can also see how women tried to devise ways to enhance sexual control and expression. In the nineteenth century, for example, some married women used the concept of women as passionless to reduce the frequency of sexual intercourse so as to reduce the likelihood of pregnancy and enhance sexual pleasure. Women who wished to express themselves sexually as well as emotionally in single-sex relationships constructed life-styles that opened up new realms of freedom. Indeed, we are just beginning to understand the ways in which these private relationships sustained the public activism of women such as Jane Addams.

Like gender and sexuality, race, too, is a social construction, despite the fact that we have long believed it to be an indisputable biological marker. Indeed, it was not until the nineteenth century that the idea of race was fully conceptualized in the way we understand it: human beings connected to or separated from other human beings by virtue of physical characteristics that are presumably genetic, such as skin pigmentation, hair texture, proportion, facial structure, and so on. In fact, however, there are no genetic characteristics possessed by all blacks but not non-blacks; similarly, there is no gene or cluster of genes common to all whites but not to non-whites. It is law and custom that are critical determinants of how individuals are classified with respect to race. In colonial Virginia, for example, a child born of a black mother and white father was classified as black. In the wake of the American Revolution, the legal definition changed so that a person was defined as black if he or she had a black parent or grandparent; anyone less than one-quarter black was white. In practice, however, even a more distant black member in one's family tree resulted in the classification "black." In 1910, Virginians changed the law to define as black anyone who was one-sixteenth black. Twenty years later, the state adopted the notorious "one-drop" law, which defined as black anyone with one drop of African blood, however that might have been determined.

Mexican Americans have also been subject to changing classifications. In the early nineteenth century, the term referred to nationality, not to race. Those persons who lived in Mexico might be white, Native American, black, or Asian. Once land that had originally belonged to Mexico became a part of the southwestern United States, "Mexican" became a racial category. In 1855, the California legislature defined Mexicans as people with Spanish and Indian blood. Called a "mixed breed," they were seen as an indolent, cowardly people—an inferior "mongrel" race. Yet in the twentieth century, the Supreme Court determined that Mexican Americans were "white."

Just how arbitrary and confusing racial classification could become is illustrated in the case of people from India. Uniformly classified as Caucasian by anthropologists, which should have earned them the designation "white," many were dark-skinned and therefore regarded by the American public as "non-white." In a 1922 Supreme Court decision, *United States* v. *Thind,*[21] the justices, reasoning that "the average well informed white American would learn with some degree of astonishment that the race to which he belongs is made up of such heterogenous elements," concluded that common knowledge rather than science prevailed. Bhagat Singh Thind, the plaintiff in the case, was not, as he claimed, "white." That a concept with no scientific significance that has been understood in such varied and often irrational ways retains such force as a source of meaning, identity, and (dis)advantage is a reminder of how powerfully social constructions function in how we organize and understand our social world.

Class is yet another category that is socially constructed. Differences in wealth and property are transformed into class by a set of institutional practices that allows a small propertied elite to retain property within that group. For example, the practice of restricting marriages to people within the same propertied group assured the retention of wealth within that group. Arranged marriages served this function, as did the internalization of cultural definitions of who might be a suitable marriage partner. Consider the example of Eliza Lucas, who at the age of seventeen ran her father's South Carolina plantation while he served as royal governor of Antigua, a small island in the Caribbean. Rejecting the first two suitors her father selected, she made her own decision as to whom to marry. She chose a wealthy planter, Charles Pinckney—a choice consistent with the marital strategy of her class.

Miscegenation laws that prohibited intermarriage between "whites" and others and, therefore, transmission of property to heirs of "mixed blood" have been a device designed to preserve property of a particular racial group. The interpenetration of class and race was most evident in the South, where, in the decades after the Civil War, lynching and other forms of terror were often directed at black men who managed to secure some degree of economic independence. When race and class intersected, as it did for those black women who had the financial resources to purchase a ticket entitling them to sit in the "Ladies" car of the train, race trumped class. Women such as Ida Wells Barnett and Charlotte Hawkins Brown suffered the humiliation of being physically ejected—a reminder of how spatial segregation can reinforce social distinctions. For upper-class Mexican American women, on the other hand, class could trump race. When marriage brought with it significant property, Anglo suitors, eager to consolidate their own class position, could easily be persuaded that the young woman was of "pure" Spanish ancestry. Such practices exemplify the meaning of the phrase "money whitens."

Understanding how differences associated with gender, sexuality, race, and class interacted—and continue to interact—in the lives of women to privilege as well as to exclude and oppress is key to understanding the varied experiences of American women. The place to begin is with gender.

GENDER AND ITS IMPLICATIONS

Understanding the difference between sex and gender provides a key to understanding the differences in men's and women's historical experience. In the workplace, for example, women and men were assigned jobs that reflected the employers' beliefs about the kind of work each sex should do. In a society whose understanding of gender included the conviction that women's primary obligations were familial and their basic talents domestic, female wage earners were persistently channeled into jobs that corresponded with the kind of work done in the domestic sphere or with characteristics long associated with women.

In the preindustrial domestic economy, women did both heavy physical labor—hauling water, slaughtering chickens—and skilled tasks—spinning, weaving, nursing. When women sought new avenues through which to gain economic independence they followed these chores into the marketplace. As slaves and as "hired help" they toiled on other people's farms; as "mill girls" they tended dangerous spinning machinery for twelve hours a day; as packinghouse workers they labored amid stench and slime. Upwardly mobile women laid claim to the teaching and nursing professions by emphasizing that the personality characteristics and skills required for such work were precisely those believed to be unique to the female sex. Thus nursing, considered in pre–Civil War years an occupation no respectable woman would enter, was eventually touted as a profession eminently suited to women. Providence, after all, had endowed the fairer sex with that "compassion which penetrate[s] the heart, that instinct which divines and anticipates the wants of the sick, and the patience which pliantly bends to all their caprices."[22] As the economy grew more complex, middle-class women infiltrated the ranks of librarians and secretaries. These occupations had been primarily male, but, like teaching and nursing, were redefined so as to emphasize the nurturing, service-oriented qualities ascribed to women—with a corresponding decrease in pay. Newer industries provided new job titles but old work categories. Receptionists and social workers were hired by employers still convinced that the tasks required in these jobs were consistent with the personality characteristics and skills traditionally associated with women. New white-collar jobs were also segregated by race, even in the North where segregation was not officially practiced. White women were overwhelmingly hired as flight attendants on national airlines until after the civil rights legislation of the 1960s. Because gender rather than individual talent or inclination has been the primary consideration, the result of this kind of stereotyping has been to segregate women into certain kinds of work, whether in the professions or in industry. Most women workers are still employed in predominantly female occupations in retail, clerical, and service sectors of the economy.

Once a form of work has been identified with women, it has invariably become associated with low pay and minimal prestige. "Theoretically, the market treats men and women neutrally, judging only the characteristics of their labor," writes the historian Alice Kessler-Harris. "In the world of economists, the wage is rooted in the play of supply and demand." In practice, she continues, "the wage is neither neutral nor natural, but reveals a set of social constructs . . . that convey messages about the nature of the world, and about . . . men and women and . . . the relations between them."[23] Low pay was appropriate for people assumed to be marginal workers, whose place was in the home where purity and virtue could be protected and family duties fulfilled. In this way the home subsidized the factory.

Gender was embedded not only in economic relations but in legal relations as well. In the legal tradition English colonists brought to America, the husband was understood to be the head of the family and to represent it in its dealings with the world. Upon marriage, the woman lost her separate civil identity; it was assumed that she had voluntarily forsworn the claim to make choices at odds with those of her husband. In a powerful legal fiction, man and wife were understood to be one person; the married woman was the *feme covert,* "covered" with her husband's legal identity for virtually all purposes except crime.[24] All personal property she brought to the marriage became her husband's; he could sell her jewelry, gamble away her money. He could not sell her real estate unless she consented, but he could decide how it was to be used: whether land was to be farmed, rented out, planted in corn or vegetables, whether trees on it were to be cultivated or cut down. Since married women did not own property, they could not make legal contracts affecting it; they could not buy and sell without their husbands' consent. A married woman could not decide whether their children were to be kept at home or apprenticed or, if apprenticed, who their masters would be. She could not sign a contract independently; not until she was a widow could she leave a will. So powerful was the fiction that husband and wife are one person that marital rape was inconceivable. Indeed, marital rape was not outlawed anywhere in the world until 1978, when New York State passed a statute prohibiting forced sexual intercourse whether by a stranger, an acquaintance, or a spouse.[25]

Gender also defined political relationships. In Anglo-American tradition, the right to participate in political activities—voting, officeholding, jury duty—was conditioned on the holding of property. Since married women could not direct the use of their property, it seemed to follow that they could be neither jurors, nor voters, nor officeholders. That politics was considered a male domain, that women were not political beings, is an understanding as old as Western civilization. Aristotle, whose classic work provided the basic terms by which Westerners have understood politics, said that men alone realized themselves as citizens. It is no accident that the civic *virtue* he extolled derives from the same root as the word *virile.* Women, Aristotle maintained, realized themselves only within the confines of the household. Their relationship to the world of politics, like their legal status, was derivative—through fathers, husbands, and sons.

This derivative relationship forced women to carve out a political role that rested upon their ability to influence those who held political power. A time-honored tradition, this use of influence was employed in the interests of a wide range of important social issues and philanthropic causes in the years before 1920. Women found that the wielding of influence benefited their communities and enlarged their political skills. The uses of influence continued to be exploited by American women even after they got the vote. As primary adviser to Al Smith, governor of New York and presidential candidate in the 1920s, Belle Moskowitz had enormous impact both on the policies of his administration and on the politics of the Democratic Party. But she was uncomfortable claiming power for herself and never ran for political office. Mary McLeod Bethune, a prominent African American educator, was equally adept in the uses of influence. As president of the National Association of Colored Women and the National Council of Negro Women, Bethune met Eleanor Roosevelt. The First Lady, admiring the effectiveness with which this forceful black woman championed the needs of her people, used her own influence to secure for Bethune appointments to a number of positions, notably in the National Youth Administration. From her position within the administration, Bethune in turn organized the Federal Council on Negro Affairs, a group of black leaders who worked effectively to focus the attention of the media as well as the administration on the desperate problems facing blacks in the Depression.

The gendering of politics forced women to clothe their political claims in domestic language. Deflecting male hostility to their entry into the political arena, they argued that women should have the vote in order to elect city officials who would see to it that rotting garbage was removed from homes, decaying meat taken out of markets, and polluted water purified; otherwise, the best efforts of mothers to assure their children clean homes and wholesome food were to no avail. Women in the nuclear disarmament movement also used gendered language, naming their organization "Women Strike for Peace."

THE DIFFICULTIES OF UNDERSTANDING GENDER AS A SYSTEM

Economics, law, politics—each, as we have seen, was permeated by assumptions, practices, and expectations that were deeply gendered. So widely shared were these assumptions, practices, and expectations and so much a part of the ordinary, everyday experience that they acquired an aura of naturalness, rightness, even inevitability. Common sense dictated that "this is simply the way things are." But "common sense," as anthropologist Clifford Geertz has shrewdly observed, "is not what the mind cleared of cant spontaneously apprehends; it is what the mind filled with presuppositions . . . concludes."[26] The consequence of comprehending the world in this way—whether in the nineteenth century or in our own time—is that it obscures the workings of a system in which economic, political, and cultural forces interact and reinforce each other in ways that benefit some groups and disadvantage others. Unable to recognize the system, failing to understand that what shapes and defines our lives has been constructed piece by interlocking piece over time by other human beings, we constantly reproduce the world we know believing we have no other choice. As a result the inequities persist, becoming more difficult to challenge because they, too, seem as natural and inevitable as the system that has produced them.

To develop a way of looking that allows one to "see" economic and social relationships, which are presumed to be neutral and natural, as socially constructed arrangements which in fact benefit one group at the expense of others is always a difficult task. That task is made even more difficult by the fact that language itself has embedded within it the values, norms, and assumptions of the dominant group. Consequently it reflects and re-creates reality as it is perceived by that group. Using language that is not one's own to expose unequal relationships or to create an alternative to those relationships challenges the ingenuity and analytical abilities of even the most clearheaded and imaginative thinkers.

Analytical skills, however, are not inborn. They are developed slowly and painfully within an educational process that values and encourages those skills as contrasted, for example, with simple memorization or rote learning. Throughout history, women have been explicitly excluded from the intellectual community. Prior to the seventeenth century when most people were illiterate, elite families in which sons learned to read and write rarely provided such opportunities for their daughters. A major literacy gap existed until well into the nineteenth century throughout the world and, in many underdeveloped countries, persists today. At the time of the American Revolution, when it has been estimated that 70 percent of the men in northern cities could read, only 35 percent of their female counterparts could do so. Slaves were denied by law access to instruction in reading and writing lest they learn about alternatives to slavery. Not until the second half of the nineteenth century were white women admitted to major state universities. Between 1870 and 1890, a few elite colleges were founded that were designed to provide upper middle-class young women an education equivalent to that which their brothers were receiving at Harvard, Yale, and Princeton universities. These new women's colleges reluctantly admitted a few black students. It was left to black women with meager resources in a rigidly segregated society—notably Mary McLeod Bethune and Charlotte Hawkins Brown—to develop their own institutions. Because public schools served black children so badly, these private institutions often began not as colleges, but as elementary or secondary schools and later grew into larger and higher-level colleges. Only in recent generations have women in substantial numbers been able to acquire not only a basic education, but also the rigorous training that would facilitate their ability to analyze and question the social and cultural arangements within which they lived.

Another consequence of women's educational deprivation was their ignorance of history and, therefore, their lack of an intimate acquaintance with other historical actors—male or female—who had faced challenges that in some way resembled their own. Lacking a history of their own, they had few models—heroes to emulate or strategies to adopt. The lack of a history in which women were actors made it particularly difficult for even educated women to envision a world other than one in which men—their experiences and needs—were the norm. Marginality in the past thus confirmed and reinforced marginality in the present.

Understanding economic and social relationships that benefit one sex at the expense of another, developing language with which to critique those hierarchical relationships and articulate an alternative vision, and forging the group solidarity necessary to realize that vision have been the tasks of feminism. The term *feminism* came into use in the United States around 1910 at a time when women were engaged in the fight for suffrage as well as a host of other reforms. As historian Nancy Cott has pointed out, feminism included suffrage and other measures to promote women's welfare that had emerged out of the nineteenth-century women's movement.[27] However, feminism encompassed a wider range of fundamental changes, amounting to a revolution in the relation of the sexes. "As an *ism* (an ideology)," Cott notes, "[feminism] presupposed a set of principles not necessarily belonging to every woman—nor limited to women."[28] In other words, not all women would oppose a sex hierarchy that privileged men as a group, nor would they feel compelled to struggle for sexual equality. Some men would, joining feminist women in their efforts to dismantle a system that conferred on one sex the power to define the other. While this system has been partially dismantled—the goal of suffrage was realized in law in 1920[29]—the wider revolution remains to be accomplished.

RETHINKING THE SOCIAL CONSTRUCTION OF GENDER

Embracing the goals of their feminist predecessors and enriched by current scholarship on gender, contemporary feminists seek to reconstruct social relations between the sexes. To do so, they believe, requires change in both public life and private behavior. This double agenda has a long history.

In 1848, when American feminists drafted their first manifesto, Elizabeth Cady Stanton demanded change in both law and custom. She called for legal change in the form of property rights for married women and voting rights for all women. Recognizing the ways in which women's self-esteem and autonomy were undermined, she also urged women to work for wide-ranging cultural change, such as equal standards of sexual behavior and equal roles in churches.

When twentieth-century feminists began to understand gender as a social construction, they too realized that the feminist revolution had to be waged in personal life as well as public life; in home as well as in workplace; in the most intimate relationships as well as in the most remote. "It must be womanly as well as manly to earn your own living, to stand on your own feet," observed the feminist Crystal Eastman shortly after the national suffrage amendment was passed in 1920. "And it must be manly as well as womanly to know how to cook and sew and clean and take care of yourself in the ordinary exigencies of life. . . . [T]he second part of this revolution will be more passionately resisted than the first. Men will not give up their privilege of helplessness without a struggle. The average man has a carefully cultivated ignorance about household matters . . . a sort of cheerful inefficiency."[30] But it was fifty years before Eastman's insights became an agenda for action.

Feminists of the 1970s captured national attention with bitter criticisms of parents who gave nurses' kits to their daughters and doctors' bags to their sons and of guidance counselors who urged mathematically talented girls to become bookkeepers and boys to become engineers. Feminists condemned stereotypes that fit children to conventional roles in their adult life and encouraged the publication of books and toys designed to demonstrate to both boys and girls that they need not shape their aspirations to gendered stereotypes. (The popular TV show, record, and book *Free to Be You and Me* encapsulated these themes.) Feminists also urged a new set of private decisions in the family, so that both sexes would share more equitably the burdens and pleasures associated with earning a living, maintaining a household, and rearing a family. But gender stereotypes turned out to be more resilient than many had anticipated; socialization is a lifetime process.

Feminists themselves had to wrestle with a culture that maintained a hierarchy of values, reserving strength, competence, independence, and rationality for men and nurture, supportiveness, and empathy for women. Questioning both the hierarchy and the dualisms embedded in this gendering of values, feminists argued that these should be viewed as shared human qualities that are not sex-specific.

Sexual hierarchy was not the only cultural hierarchy that posed problems. There were also hierarchies of race and class. White feminists in the 1970s were criticized for promoting a vision of feminism that ignored black women and assumed that all women who were impatient with contemporary culture were white and middle-class. The upwardly mobile vision was a contested vision; the priorities of women of different classes and races did not necessarily converge. Many black women supported many elements of the agenda of middle-class white feminists of the 1970s—equal pay for equal work, access to jobs—but they disagreed on priorities. They were skeptical of those who placed the needs of middle-class women ahead of the needs of working women. Middle-class white women, the employers of domestic workers, were markedly more enthusiastic about the elimination of quotas for female students in law and medical schools than they were about the establishment of minimum wage and social security protection for domestic workers. The first generation of white radical feminists fought vigorously for the repeal of all abortion laws and for safe access to birth control; for black feminists the need for access to abortion was only one of a wide range of medical services for which many black women struggled.[31]

Differences in sexual preference also posed problems for this generation of feminists. Challenges to traditional gender arrangements have always inspired charges of sexual deviance from those seeking to discredit the movement and trivialize grievances; the 1960s were no exception. Concerned about the movement's image, many feminists, rejecting the charge, attempted to push lesbians out of sight. They insisted that equality, not sexual preference, was the issue. Lesbian feminists disagreed, arguing that autonomy in sexual matters involved more than access to reproductive control. In time, tensions eased as many heterosexual feminists accepted the legitimacy of lesbian involvement and the validity of their contention that straight/gay divisions also constituted a form of cultural hierarchy that reinforced male supremacy.

THE COMPLEXITY OF CREATING EQUALITY

Recognizing the magnitude of cultural and personal change required if each woman was to realize her full human potential, feminists of the 1970s simultaneously challenged the institutions and the laws that denied women equal treatment. They launched a barrage of test cases in state and federal courts challenging practices of unequal responsibility for jury service, unequal benefits for dependents, unequal age requirements for drinking and marriage. In 1971, in an Idaho case testing who was to be the administrator of a will, feminists persuaded the Supreme Court for the first time in American history to treat discrimination on the basis of sex as a denial of equal protection under the law.[32] But the Supreme Court was reluctant to build on this precedent in subsequent cases. The Court's refusal to apply as strict a standard to sex discrimination as to racial discrimination prompted feminists to try to insert a ban on sex discrimination in the Constitution. The Equal Rights Amendment, passed overwhelmingly by Congress in 1972, failed to garner the last three states necessary for the three-quarter majority required for ratification. A contributing factor in its failure was basic disagreement on whether equality under law requires equality of military obligation.

Lobbying vigorously with both Congress and the executive branch, feminists won guarantees of equal pay for equal work, equal employment opportunities, equal access to credit and to education.[33] Building on the tactics and achievements of the civil rights movement, feminists secured major gains in the 1960s and 1970s. In the process, however, they discovered that guarantees of equality in a system structured with men's needs as the norm does not always produce a gender-neutral result. In many professions, for example, there is enormous pressure to demonstrate mastery of one's field in the early stages of a career, precisely at the stage in their life cycle when it would be safest to bear children. Although the standard appears to be gender-neutral, it presents young women with excruciating choices that do not confront their male peers.

Nowhere was the challenge of achieving gender neutrality in the workplace greater than on the matter of pregnancy. Aware of the long history of discrimination against pregnant employees, feminists successfully attacked regulations that prevented women from making their own decisions about whether and how long to work when pregnant. But initial legislative "solutions" raised new complexities challenging the assumption that equality always requires identical treatment. If employers could no longer fire pregnant women, they could still exclude from the company's disability program those temporarily unable to work during some portion of their pregnancy or at childbirth. Pregnancy, according to the Supreme Court, was not temporary disability but a "voluntary physical condition."[34] Outraged by the Court's ruling, feminists and their allies demanded congressional action that would require pregnancy and childbirth be treated like any other physical event that befalls workers. Responding in 1978 with model legislation mandating *equal* treatment in the workplace, Congress required employers to give physically disabled pregnant workers the same benefits given to other disabled workers. The problem, however, was not yet resolved.

If employers denied disability leave to all employees as a matter of company policy, federal legislation mandating equal treatment for both sexes with respect to pregnancy disability would, in effect, penalize female employees unable to work because of pregnancy-related illness. Equality, in this instance, seemed to require *special* treatment. Lawmakers in California and a few other states agreed and required employers to provide pregnant workers disability coverage even if no other illnesses were covered. Employers complained that this constituted "preferential treatment" for women. Some feminists, aware of the ways in which legislation designating women as a special class of employees because of their reproductive capacity had penalized female workers in the past, questioned whether such legislation was in the best interests of women. Would it reinforce sexist stereotypes of men as "natural" breadwinners and women as "natural" childbearers and rearers, making employers reluctant to hire married women of childbearing age and further marginalizing women as workers? Wouldn't it be a better strategy to concentrate on extending disability benefits to workers of both sexes? Other feminists were untroubled. Pregnancy is unique to women, they argued, and calls for "special treatment" in recognition of that uniqueness. Such legislation, they insisted, acknowledges reality at a time when growing numbers of women become pregnant within one year of their employment.

Writing for the majority in a 1987 decision upholding a controversial California law on pregnancy disability benefits, Justice Thurgood Marshall went to the heart of the equality/difference dilemma. He noted that "while federal law mandates the same treatment of pregnant and non-pregnant employees, it would be violating the spirit of the law to read it as barring preferential treatment of pregnancy." The California law, he reasoned, "promotes equal employment opportunities because it allows women as well as men to have families without losing their jobs."[35]

The difficulty of determining what is fair treatment for pregnant women dramatically illustrates the complexities involved in reconciling equality and sexual difference. Part of the difficulty has to do with the meaning of equality. Is equality to be thought of, as it has been throughout American history, as equality of opportunity? Or is equality to be defined as equality of results? In either case, do the methods used to achieve equality demand the same treatment or different treatment? The stakes in this debate are high, as the debate over pregnancy in the workplace illustrates, because childbearing impacts so directly on women's struggle for economic independence.

Childbearing is only one aspect of sexual difference that complicates efforts to achieve equality between the sexes. Closely related are other issues surrounding reproduction. In the first half of the twentieth century, access to birth control was the contested issue. Feminists argued that the right to choose if and when to bear children was the foundation on which authentic equality between men and women must rest. The debate was intense and emotionally charged because reproductive issues involve sexuality, ethical and religious values, medical technology, constitutional rights to privacy, as well as matters of economic dependence, physical vulnerability, and state power. In the second half of the twentieth century, particularly in the wake of the Supreme Court's decision in *Roe* v. *Wade* (1973), these issues were fought out over policies governing access to abortion. Issues of race, class, and gender intersected. For many white middle-class feminists, preserving abortion rights was a top priority. Advocates of birth control, they saw abortion as a measure of last resort. Without that option, women's efforts to plan their lives, to set priorities, and to make choices were severely constrained, and constrained in ways that men's were not. For poor women and women of color who had been the subject of involuntary sterilization and who lacked access to a wide range of medical services, abortion was only one among many essential needs, and not necessarily the most pressing one. For many other women, abortion was not an essential need at all. Believing that the fetus is a human being from the moment of conception and that motherhood is women's key reason for being, they denied any connection between equality and access to abortion. They rejected the feminist contention that denying women access to abortion is a way in which men use the power of the state to reinforce their own power over women. Whether the state should permit and/or fund abortions for teenage victims of incest is the most dramatic of the issues in conflict.

Incest is only one aspect of the larger problem of sexual violence that feminists contend is the ultimate expression of male dominance. Sexual violence, they insist, is violence, not sex, and it is a public, not a private, matter. Rape crisis centers, battered women's shelters, and "Take Back the Night" marches are expressions of their insistence that government respond to male violence against women. Feminists also attack directly the notion that female victims of violence are in some measure to blame by virtue of provocative dress and behavior or prior sexual experience. In the late 1970s they convinced policymakers that sexual harassment was a form of economic discrimination and that those who maintained workplaces were legally obliged to take action to prevent it.

Feminists also exposed the link between sexual violence and pornography. Many of them argued that material that objectifies women and equates violence against them with sexual pleasure is an invasion of their civil liberties. This interpretation represents a radical reformulation of traditional civil liberties arguments and a willingness on the part of some feminists to entertain reconsideration of the boundaries of protected speech. Other feminists strenuously object. They argue that some pornography can give people pleasure and enable them to learn about their sexuality, that causes of male violence against women are multiple, and that the likely effects of real-world enforcement of restrictions on pornography would serve neither the interests of women nor the cause of free speech. They fear, for example, that laws would be so vaguely written as to ensnare sexually explicit material that all feminists would agree should not be censored.

THE ANGUISH OF FUNDAMENTAL CHANGE

Reconciling equality and difference, equity and justice, involves feminists in a task as consequential as any in human history. Relationships assumed to be the result of choice, even of love, were now exposed as hierarchical relationships involving power and control. Such exposures are always traumatic. "All the decent drapery of life is . . . rudely torn off," complained the British legislator Edmund Burke when revolutionaries in France challenged the divine right of kings 200 years ago. "When ancient opinions and rules of life are taken away, the loss cannot possibly be estimated. From that moment we have no compass to govern us; nor can we know distinctly to what port we steer."[36]

Even those in the vanguard of change can appreciate its difficulty; old habits are hard to break even for those determined to break them. For those who are not the initiators, challenges to long-standing beliefs and behaviors, whether issued now or in the past, can be, at best, unwelcome and, at worst, profoundly threatening. Feminism is no exception. Demands for equality in terms of power, resources, and prestige are usually seen as redistributive. Giving one party its share of the pie may result in a smaller share for the others. Even individuals who believe in equality in the abstract may find themselves loath to share power and privileges in practice, especially when their own lives are affected intimately. Moreover, new governmental policies designed to provide women equal protection in the law, equity in the workplace, and parity in politics were only part of what feminists were about. Cultural values as well as social institutions were under scrutiny. Even the definition of family was being tampered with as the 1980 White House Conference on Families made clear. Family had always meant that members were related by blood, marriage, or adoption. The term was now being applied to two mothers with children or an unmarried heterosexual couple who were childless; "anybody living under the same roof that provides support for each other *regardless* of blood, marriage, or adoption" seemed to qualify. To recognize these arrangements as multiple family forms, which many feminists did, was to legitimate people who, from the viewpoint of traditionalists, were living "illegitimate lifestyles."[37]

From this perspective, it is hardly surprising that gender changes that feminists saw as expanding options for women and men alike were seen by traditionalists as rejecting cherished beliefs and practices—"neuterizing society."[38] Women who believe they have lived useful and admirable lives by the old rules often regard feminists' attacks on traditional gender roles as an attack on a way of life they have mastered—and hence an attack on them personally. They fear that "a woman who has been a good wife and homemaker for decades" will be "turned out to pasture with impunity" by "a new, militant breed of women's liberationist" prepared to sacrifice justice for equality.[39] At issue are not just the economic security and personal identity of individuals but the larger social order. Convinced that biological differences between the sexes dictate "natural" roles, traditionalists see the maintenance of these roles as socially and morally necessary—a source of stability in a world of flux. Thus feminist insistence that women should be able to seek fulfillment in the public world of work and power as well as in the private world of home and family is viewed by traditionalists as an egocentric demand that places personal gratification above familial duty. "Feminists praise self-centeredness and call it liberation," observed activist Connie Marshner.[40] By the same token, the demand that women themselves be the ultimate judge of whether and when to bear children is seen by some not as a legitimate desire to ensure a good life for those children who are born but as an escape from maternal obligations that threatens the future of the family and ultimately, therefore, society itself.

To suggest that some women find feminism an essential part of their identity and that other women define themselves and their lives in terms of traditionalism is not to suggest that the ideological history of women is bipolar. It embraces many variants. Nor do we suggest that there is little on which the two groups agree. Traditionalist women may be as suspicious of male-controlled institutions as feminists. Traditionalists may also be as vocal and publicly active on behalf of their goals. Feminists may be just as dedicated to family as traditionalists. Both groups identify with "sisterhood" and see "women's issues" as special ones, although they do not consistently agree on what they are or how they should be addressed. Partisans of these issues may unite or divide along class, occupational, or political lines. But no matter where they fall on the ideological spectrum, *all* women are a part of women's history.

"Woman has always been acting and thinking . . . at the center of life," wrote Mary Beard three-quarters of a century ago;[41] but the significance of women's activities has, until recent years, often been discounted and rarely been understood. The scholarship of the past decades has spotlighted much that has lain in the shadows of history unnoticed and unappreciated. As we have examined that scholarship, we find ourselves less impressed by gender-based constraints—which were very real—than by the vigor and subtlety with which women have defined the terms of their existence. These creative experiences show how the private lives of historical persons can help us understand the rich complexities of change. To study women's history, then, is to take part in a bold enterprise that can eventually lead us to a new history, one that, by taking into account both sexes, should tell us more about each other and, therefore, our collective selves.

Notes

1. Frantz Fanon, *The Wretched of the Earth,* trans. Constance Farrington (New York: Grove Press, 1963), p. 170.

2. Christine de Pizan, *The Book of the City of Ladies,* trans. Earl Jeffrey Richards (New York: Persea Books, 1982), pp. 6–8, 10–11.

3. Jane Austen, *Northanger Abbey and Persuasion,* ed. John Davie (London: Oxford University Press, 1971), pp. 97–99.

4. Elizabeth Cady Stanton, Susan B. Anthony, and Matilda Joslyn Gage, *History of Woman Suffrage,* vol. 1 (New York: Fowler & Wells, 1881), pp. 7–8.

5. Mary R. Beard, *Woman as Force in History: A Study in Traditions and Realities* (New York: Macmillan, 1946), pp. 59–60.

6. "Placing Women in History: Definitions and Challenges," *Feminist Studies* 3 (1975): 5–14; reprinted in Gerda Lerner, *The Majority Finds Its Past: Placing Women in History* (New York: Oxford University Press, 1979), pp. 145–59.

7. Edward T. James, Janet Wilson James, and Paul Boyer, eds., *Notable American Women, 1607–1950: A Biographical Dictionary,* 3 vols. (Cambridge, Mass.: Belknap Press of Harvard University Press, 1971); and Barbara Sicherman and Carol Hurd Green, eds., *Notable American Women: The Modern Period* (Cambridge, Mass. Belknap Press of Harvard University Press, 1980).

8. Joan Wallach Scott, "Gender: A Useful Category of Historical Analysis," *American Historical Review* 91 (Dec. 1986): 1053–75.

9. Lerner, *The Majority Finds Its Past,* pp. 49–50.

10. Alice Kessler-Harris, *Out to Work: A History of Wage-Earning Women in the United States* (New York: Oxford University Press, 1982), p. 40.

11. For detailed essays on the wave of garment workers' strikes of the early twentieth century, see Joan M. Jensen and Sue Davidson, eds., *A Needle, a Bobbin, a Strike: Women Needleworkers in America* (Philadelphia: Temple University Press, 1984), pp. 81–182.

12. Martha Minow, "The Supreme Court—1986 Term. Foreword: Justice Engendered," *Harvard Law Review* 101 (1987): 13. Minow points out that "'Minority' itself is a relative term. . . . Only in relation to white Westerners are [people of color] minorities."

13. Quoted from Harriet Beecher Stowe in Jeanne Boydston, *Home and Work: Housework, Wages, and the Ideology of Labor in the Early Republic* (New York: Oxford University Press, 1991), ch. 4.

14. *Reminiscences and Letters of Caroline C. Briggs,* ed. George S. Merriam (New York: Houghton Mifflin, 1897), pp. 21–23. Quoted in Boydston, *Home and Work,* ch. 4.

15. See Deborah Fink, *Open Country, Iowa: Rural Women, Tradition and Change* (Albany: State University of New York Press, 1986), pp. 62–65.

16. Quoted in Susan Strasser, *Never Done: A History of American Housework* (New York: Pantheon Books, 1982), pp. 268, 278.

17. Joann Vanek, "Time Spent in Housework," *Scientific American* 231 (1974): 116–20.

18. Mueller v. Oregon, 208 U.S. 412.

19. Mark C. Carnes and Clyde Griffin, eds., *Meanings for Manhood: Constructions of Masculinity in Victorian America* (Chicago: University of Chicago Press, 1990), p. 203.

20. Carroll Smith-Rosenberg, "The Female World of Love and Ritual: Relations between Women in Nineteenth Century America," *Signs: Journal of Women in Culture and Society* 1 (1975): 29–30.

21. On *United States* v. *Thind,* see Ian F. Haney Lopez, "White by Law," in *Critical Race Theory: The Cutting Edge,* ed. Richard Delgado (Philadelphia: Temple University Press, 1995), pp. 542–50.

22. For purposes of these calculations, predominantly female occupations were defined as those hiring 70 percent or more women; predominantly male occupations were defined as those hiring 30 percent or fewer women. The calculations were made by Jennifer Lettieri on the basis of materials supplied by the U.S. Department of Labor, Bureau of Labor Statistics. See especially *Employment and Earnings* (Washington, D.C., January 1989), pp. 183–88.

23. Alice Kessler-Harris, *A Woman's Wage* (Lexington: University Press of Kentucky, 1990).

24. If, however, she committed a crime under his direction or surveillance, it was understood that he was the culprit. In most elements of criminal law, however, even married women were understood to have independent moral and ethical responsibilities; women could be charged with murder or treason.

25. New York Penal Law, sec. 130.00 (1978). *McKinney's Consolidated Laws of New York Annotated* (Buffalo, N.Y.: W. S. Heint, 1987). For a basic review of the laws, see Herma Hill Kay, ed., *Sex-Based Discrimination* (St. Paul: West, 1988), pp. 239–62; and Raquel Kennedy Bergen, *Wife Rape: Understanding the Response of Survivors and Service Providers* (Thousand Oaks, Calif.: Sage Publications, 1996), p. 150.

Most of the remaining states waited until 1993, when criminalizing partner rape would allow them to qualify for funds under the pending Violence Against Women Act, which finally passed in 1994 and was reauthorized in 2000 and 2005. See *Violence Against Women Act*, Public Law 103–322, *U.S. Statutes at Large* 108 (1994): 1796, recodified at 42 *U.S. Code* §13981.

26. Clifford Geertz, *Local Knowledge: Further Essays in Interpretive Anthropology* (New York: Basic Books, 1983), p. 84.

27. Nancy F. Cott, *The Grounding of Modern Feminism* (New Haven, Conn.: Yale University Press, 1987), pp. 13–16.

28. Ibid., p. 3.

29. But in a segregated South, poll taxes and other devices barred black women (as well as men) from voting; not until the civil rights movement of the 1950s and 1960s did suffrage slowly and irregularly become available.

30. "Now We Can Begin," in Blanche Weisen Cook, ed., *Crystal Eastman on Women and Revolution* (New York: Oxford University Press, 1978), pp. 54–55. Originally published in *The Liberator* (December 1920).

31. Jennifer A. Nelson, *Women of Color and the Reproductive Rights Movement* (New York: New York University Press, 2003).

32. *Reed* v. *Reed*, 404 U.S. 71 (1971).

33. Equal Pay Act of 1963; Equal Credit Opportunity Act of 1974; Title VII of the Civil Rights Act of 1964; .Title IX of the Educational Amendments Act of 1974.

34. *Geduldig* v. *Aielo*, 417 U.S. 484 (1974); and *General Electric* v. *Martha Gilbert*, 97 S.Ct. 401 (1976).

35. *California Federal Savings and Loan Association* v. *Guerra*, 479 U.S. 272 (1987). "Promoting equal employment opportunities" requires new child-care policies. Giving men and women equal access to a workplace that lacks provisions for child care is not gender-neutral in its results when over 50 percent of these women have children under six. Working mothers, whatever the ages of their children and whatever their income level, currently spend twenty-five hours per week on domestic work, compared with only eleven hours spent by their male partners. With less time and energy available for the kind of job-related activities and training programs that would improve their economic position, many are penalized with respect to both pay and promotion. Others who accept low-paying jobs for which they are overqualified because the hours or location allows them to more easily integrate wage work and family responsibilities find themselves similarly immobilized. For women who are single parents and heads of household, the penalties are especially severe.

36. Edmund Burke, *Reflections on the Revolution in France* (London, 1910), pp. 74–75.

37. Paul Weyrich, "Debate with Michael Lerner," speech presented at the Family Forum II conference, Washington, D.C., July 28, 1982. Quoted in Rebecca Klatch, *Women of the New Right* (Philadelphia: Temple University Press, 1987), pp. 125–26.

38. Phyllis Schlafly, *The Power of the Positive Woman* (New Rochelle, N.Y.: Arlington House, 1977), p 25.

39. Ibid., p. 81.

40. Connaught Coyne Marshner, *The New Traditional Woman* (Washington, D.C.: Free Congress Research & Education Foundation, 1982), pp. 1, 3–4, 12. See also Klatch, *Women of the New Right*, p. 129.

41. Mary R. Beard, ed., *America through Women's Eyes* (New York: Macmillan, 1933), pp. 4–5.

I

Early America

1600–1820

Traditionally, American histories treated the colonial period as a time when government and order were imposed upon a wilderness. Today, college textbooks acknowledge that North America was not a "virgin land" by opening with a chapter on the extent and diversity of indigenous peoples. And yet, old habits persist. The first woman likely to be mentioned by name is Pocahontas, the innocent Indian "princess" who allegedly saved the life of the hero of Jamestown, Captain John Smith. The second woman who appears is often Anne Hutchinson, who was banished from the Massachusetts Bay Colony for heresy. Both met premature and unpleasant deaths. Unaccustomed to the climate of England, where she had been taken to be shown to Queen Anne, Pocahontas died of pneumonia. Hutchinson was massacred by Indians during a raid on her lonely dwelling in what is now Westchester County, New York. The reader may be pardoned for concluding from these examples that the few women we remember are likely to have been troublesome and to have come to a bad end.

But suppose we ask Mary Beard's question: What did early America look like, seen through women's eyes? Native women encountered dramatic disruptions in the guise of devastating diseases, displacement from traditional lands, and a new vulnerability to rape. If they lived near the eastern seaboard, they were often coerced into servitude or slavery. They found their gender ways mocked and challenged by Europeans. Over time, they adopted a wide range of survival strategies, including taking leadership roles in conserving cultural knowledge, marketing their own products (pottery, baskets, blankets) to white settlers, and forging strategic intermarriages with selected newcomers to aid diplomatic efforts or ensure access to trade goods. European settler women would have described themselves collectivly as "helpmeets" not hindrances in the work of founding overseas colonies. Indeed, a settlement counted itself as having passed the stage of a temporary camp only after it had attracted a reasonable number of women. A sex ratio approaching 100 (that is, 100 women to every 100 men) was taken to be evidence that the settlement was here to stay. Once founded, communities were maintained in large part by women's labor. The productivity of housekeepers is not easily measured, but over sixty years ago Julia Cherry Spruill established the complexity of the tasks performed in frontier households.[1]

It may be that North America seemed to European women less radical a change from the Old World than it did to men. The terrors of the ocean crossing and of the wilderness were shared by all. In the newly established farming communities, daily tasks proceeded in the manner of England. The rituals of childbirth were transmitted intact from Old World to New, although it appears that the rate of survival for mothers and infants was better in the American countryside, where the dangers of infection were far fewer than in the towns and cities of Europe. By contrast, the innovations that made the colonies most distinctive from the Old World—especially governmental institutions like town meetings and provincial legislatures—were settings from which women were barred.

For African women, in sharp contrast, America meant violence and vulnerability. Slavery and the slave trade to the Americas had been established by the Spanish and the Dutch long before Virginians bought their first African slaves in 1619. In an era in which white working people often sold their labor for a term of years, African workers in the English colonies seem at first to have been treated not very differently from European indentured servants. But by the mid-seventeenth century, Africans were increasingly being treated as property, equated with slavery, and denied civil and human rights.

New England was largely settled by Protestant dissenters, and in the earliest days of their formation, radical Protestant groups often welcomed women as equals to men—not only in their moral selves but also in some of their social roles. For example, in Puritan New World settlements, women as well as men signed covenants establishing new churches; women as well as men made public professions of faith when they joined. (By the second generation of settlement, however, women's profession of faith was likely to be made privately or read out loud by the minister.) Peripheral churches retained participatory, even disruptive roles for women longer; among the Quakers it was established that women could prophesy, that women would speak in public, and that women would have a significant role in the institutional decisions of the community. Among Baptists and Methodists in the eighteenth century, radical evangelical faith also could translate into shared governance and public participation.

But despite repeated quotation of St. Paul's rule that "in Christ there is neither man nor woman," believers of every faith were very conscious of gender distinctions. Anne Hutchinson's heresy was compounded by the fact that it was formulated by a woman. Many of the questions in her trial were grounded in the objection that she had stepped out of her proper place. As Baptist and Methodist communities became more solidly established, more "mainstream," they narrowed the space they offered "disorderly" women.[2]

English colonists brought with them English legal practices, including the English system of domestic law. The old law of domestic relations began from the principle that at marriage the husband controlled the physical body of the wife. (There was no concept of marital rape in American statutes until the mid-1970s; only in the last few years has it been recognized in all states. In some, differences from the treatment of nonspousal rape still persist.) If he controlled her body, then he could easily force her into agreement with him on every other aspect of their lives. There followed from this premise the elaborate system of coverture. The practice of coverture transferred a woman's civic identity to her husband at marriage, giving him the use and direction of her property throughout the marriage.

When the United States purchased the Louisiana Territory in 1803, it acquired vast expanses of land that had been ruled by Spanish and French law, systems not marked by coverture, in which the property husbands and wives brought to their marriage became "community property." Although husbands were "head and master" of their households and had wide discretion in their use of family property, married women could keep separate property in their own names and pass it on to whomever they chose as heirs. These practices were not erased when the land passed to the United States. Louisiana, Texas, and New Mexico, as well as Arizona, Idaho, Nevada, California, and Washington, would be community property states, offering significant legal advantages to married women deep into the twentieth century.[3]

The right to participate in the political system was conditioned on holding property outright. Since married women normally did not hold property outright, it seemed logical to colonists that political rights be granted only to men. (Even this logic would not have explained the practice of excluding single women and widows from political rights.) Since girls could not grow up to be legislators or ministers or lawyers, little care was taken to provide them with any but the most elementary forms of schooling. "How many female minds, rich with native genius and noble sentiment, have been lost to the world, and all their mental treasures buried in oblivion?" mourned one writer.[4]

Despite formal exclusions, women by their actions and choices constrained men's options. A good example is George Washington's Revolutionary army. Lacking an effective quartermaster corps, it was dependent on women for nursing, cooking, and cleaning. The army, in turn, could not move as quickly as Washington would have liked because provision had to be made for the "woemin of the army." The task of the recruiting officer was eased when men could rely on their female relatives to keep family farms and mills in operation, fend off squatters, and protect family property by their heavy labor, often at grave physical risk. We have no simple calculus for measuring the extent to which women's services made it possible for men to act in certain ways during the Revolution, but it is clear that women's work provided the civilian context in which the war was carried on.

When the war was over and the political structure of the new nation was being reshaped in federal and state constitutions, legislators made many radical changes in the system of government they had inherited from England. The new republic promised to protect "life, liberty and property," but it maintained the old law that deprived a married woman of her property and her earnings, and the liberties that stemmed from property owning. If women had had the vote in 1789, they might well have used it to claim independent property rights for themselves or to claim custody of their children in the event of divorce. Almost certainly they would have used the vote to establish pensions for widows of veterans. But women's distinctive needs continued to be discounted as trivial. It was left to women of succeeding generations to accomplish for themselves what the Revolution had not.

Notes

1. Julia Cherry Spruill, *Women's Life and Work in the Southern Colonies* (Chapel Hill: University of North Carolina Press, 1938).
2. Mary Maples Dunn, "Saints and Sisters: Congregational and Quaker Women in the Early Colonial Period" in Janet Wilson James, ed., *Women in American Religion* (Philadelphia: University of Pennsylvania Press, 1980), pp. 27-46. For Methodists, see Donald Mathews, *Religion in the Old South* (Chicago: University of Chicago Press, 1977), chs. 1 and 2; for Baptists, see Susan Juster, *Disorderly Women: Sexual Politics and Evangelicalism in Revolutionary New England* (Ithaca, N.Y.: Cornell University Press, 1994).
3. See Deborah Rosen, "Women and Property across Colonial America: A Comparison of Legal Systems in New Mexico and New York," *William and Mary Quarterly*, 3rd ser. 60 (April 2003): 355–82.
4. Clio [pseud.], "Thoughts on Female Education," *Royal American Magazine*, Jan. 1774, pp. 9–10.

SARA EVANS

The First American Women

The first American women were Native American women. The religious, economic, and political roles that they played within their own societies prior to the arrival of Europeans suggest that Europeans and Native Americans held dramatically different ideas about what women and men should be and should do. The difficulty that Europeans had in understanding the alternative gender realities to which they were exposed tells us how strong is the impulse to view established gender definitions in one's own culture as natural rather than socially constructed.

Note the importance Evans attaches to Native American women's religious functions. How did the sexual division of labor within Native American tribes she describes affect women's economic importance in a subsistence economy? If you were assigned to do research in this vast area of Indian women and gender relations, what questions and sources would you pursue?

According to the Iroquois, the creation of the earth began when a woman came from heaven and fluttered above the sea, unable to find a resting place for her feet. The fish and animals of the sea, having compassion on her, debated in council about which of them should help her. The tortoise offered his back, which became the land, and the woman made her home there. A spirit noticed her loneliness and with her begot three children to provide her company. The quarrels of her two sons can still be heard in the thunder. But her daughter became the mother of the great nations of the Iroquois.[1]

Women appear frequently at the cosmic center of native American myths and legends, tales that are undoubtedly very ancient. The history of women on the North American continent began 20,000 years ago with the migration of people from the Asian continent across the land bridge that now is the Bering Strait. These early ancestors of contemporary native Americans gradually created a great diversity of cultures as they adapted to varied environmental circumstances and conditions over time. The archaeological record indicates that 2,000 years ago some North American cultures lived nomadically, hunting and gathering plants and animals. Others settled in villages and subsisted on domesticated plants as well as wild resources. Still others built complex, hierarchically organized societies centered in relatively large cities or towns. In these latter groups, archaeological remains reveal widespread trade relations and religious systems uniting people over vast areas of the continent. When the first Europeans reached North America in the fifteenth and sixteenth centuries, there were some 2,000 native American languages in use, a cultural diversity that made Europe look homogeneous.[2]

GATHERERS AND NURTURERS, TRADERS AND SHAMANS

Among the peoples of North America whose tribes lived in the woods, along the rivers, and on the edges of the plains, women were essential to group survival. In a subsistence economy, daily life revolved around finding food for the next meal or, at the most, the next season. Women's work as gatherers and processors of food and as nurturers of small children was not only visible to the whole community,

Reprinted from ch. 1 of *Born for Liberty: A History of Women in America* by Sara M. Evans (New York: Free Press, 1989, 1997) by permission of the author and publisher. Notes have been edited.

This portrait of an Algonquin woman was drawn at her home settlement during the summer of 1585 by John White, the official artist of the English expedition to Roanoke. His drawings are rare representations of Algonquin life before extensive European contact. The woman, who looks skeptically at the viewer, is the wife of a leading male chief or counselor. Her body is decorated with gray, brown, and blue tattoos on the face, neck, arms, and legs. Women's tattoos simulated elaborate necklaces and other ornamentation; men used body paint for ceremonial purposes. (Courtesy of The British Museum. See also Paul Hulton, America 1585: The Complete Drawings of John White *[Chapel Hill: University of North Carolina Press and British Museum Publications, 1984].)*

but it also shaped ritual life and processes of community decision making.

Women's activities were sharply divided from those of men in most Indian societies. Women gathered seeds, roots, fruits, and other wild plants. And in horticultural groups they cultivated crops such as corn, beans, and squash. Women were also typically responsible for cooking, preserving foods, and making household utensils and furnishings. In addition, they built and maintained dwellings, such as earth or bark lodges and tepees, and associated household facilities like storage pits, benches, mats, wooden racks, and scaffolds. In groups that moved on a seasonal basis, women were often responsible for transporting all household goods from one location to the next.

Male activities in many groups centered on hunting and warfare. After the hunts, Indian women played an important role in processing the hides of deer or buffalo into clothing, blankets, floor coverings, tepees, or trade goods; preserving the meat; and manufacturing a variety of bone implements from the remains of the animals.

Indian societies differed in their definitions of which tasks were appropriate for women or men and in their degree of flexibility or rigidity. In some groups pople would be ridiculed and shamed for engaging in tasks inappropriate for their gender, while other groups were more tolerant. Sometimes men and women performed separate, but complementary tasks. Among the Iroquois, for example, men cleared the fields so women could plant them. In other cases men and women performed the same tasks but the work was still segregated on the basis of sex. For example, many Plains Indian tribes divided the task of tanning hides according to the animal, some being assigned exclusively to women, others to men.

These differences shaped the relationships among women and between women and men. Societies with a clear sexual division of labor and cooperative modes of production, for example, encouraged gender solidarity. The Pawnee, a Plains society, lived in lodges large enough for several families, or about fifty people. Women shared cooking responsibilities among themselves, alternating between those on the north and those on the south sides of the lodge. Among the Hidatsa, another Plains group, female labor was organized by the household of female kin while male activities, ranging from individual vision quests to sporadic hunting parties, were organized by age and by village. Groups of female kin built and maintained their homes, gathered seeds and edible plants, raised crops, and processed the meat and skins of animals killed by the men.[3]

In Iroquois society, where men were frequently away for prolonged periods of time, women farmed in a highly organized way. A white woman adopted in 1758 by the Seneca (one of the six tribes of the Iroquois Confederacy) described their work:

> In the summer season, we planted, tended, and harvested our corn, and generally had all of our children with us; but had no master to oversee or drive us, so that we could work as leisurely as we pleased. . . . We pursued our farming business according to the general custom of Indian women, which is as follows: In order to expedite their business, and at the same time enjoy each other's company, they all work together in one field, or at whatever job they may have on hand. In the spring, they choose an old active squaw to be their driver and overseer, when at labor, for the ensuing year. She accepts the honor, and they consider themselves bound to obey her.
>
> When the time for planting arrives, and the soil is prepared, the squaws are assembled in the morning, and conducted into a field where each plants one row. They then go into the next field and plant once across, and so on till they have gone through the tribe.[4]

As they gathered, cultivated, and produced food, tools, and housing, some women also actively participated in trade. Algonkian women on the Atlantic coast traded with whites from the earliest days. In 1609 John Juet, Henry Hudson's first mate, recorded an incident in New York Harbor: "There came eight and twentie Canoes full of men, women and children to betray us: but we saw their intent, and suffered none of them to come aboord us. . . . They brought with them Oysters and Beanes, whereof we bought some."[5] In later years many observers noted both transactions with women and the high proportion of trade goods that were particularly interesting to women. Far to the northwest, on the Alaskan coast, the Tlingit built their economy on fishing for plentiful salmon and on trading with neighboring groups. Tlingit women not only dried and processed the salmon but they were also entrusted with managing and dispensing the family wealth. White traders were continually struck by the skill and sophistication of these women, who frequently stepped in to cancel unwise deals made by their husbands. These shrewd dealings paid off in that society where status could be gained by impressive displays of gift-giving.[6]

Religious myths and rituals offered women additional sources of power and status in their villages and tribes as they reflected in a symbolic realm the relations between people and nature.[7] In most North American Indian creation myths, females played critical roles as mediators between supernatural powers and earth. Many horticultural societies ritually celebrated the seasonal powers of Earth Mother—whose body produced the sacred foods of corn, beans, and squash. Groups primarily oriented to hunting more frequently conceptualized sacred powers as male, but in some cases the Keeper of the Game appeared as a woman. She observed humans' failures to address proper ritual prayers to the spirits of the animals and to treat the animal world on which they depended with proper respect; she could also inflict punishments of disease and famine.

American Indians perceived their world as sacred and alive. Power and mystery infused all living things, inspiring awe and fear. Women, like men, sought spiritual understanding and power by engaging in individual quests for visions. Quests involved a period of seclusion, fasting, and performance of prescribed rituals. Women's quests drew on the fasting and seclusion accompanying menstruation.

In most societies menstruating women were believed to be dangerously powerful, capable of harming crops or hunts and draining the spiritual powers of men. To avoid such harm they withdrew to menstrual huts outside the villages. Did women interpret this experience in terms of pollution and taboo, seeing it as a banishment, as many observers assumed? More likely they welcomed the occasional respite from daily responsibilities as an opportunity for meditation, spiritual growth, and the company of other women. The power that visions conferred allowed some women to serve as herbalists, midwives, medicine women, and shamans.

Marriage practices in some societies granted women considerable control in choosing their partners. In others, marriages were arranged by elders (often women) as a means of building economic alliances through kinship. Divorce, on the other hand, was common and easy to accomplish. A woman could simply leave her husband or, if the house was hers, she could order him out on grounds of sterility, adultery, laziness, cruelty, or bad temper. Women's autonomy often had a further sexual dimension: Although the male-dominated groups prized female chastity, most Indian groups encouraged sexual expressiveness and did not enforce strict monogamy. Female power in marital and sexual relations could also be shaped by the proximity of a woman to her own kin.

Women's political power was rooted in kinship relations and economics. The scale of clan and village life meant that people knew one another primarily through kinship designators (daughter, husband, mother's brother, grandmother), and in many cases the most important level of sociopolitical organization was the local kin group. It seems likely that female power was most salient at the level of the village group, where it would shape many facets of daily life. In many tribes, however, there were some (often transitory or temporary) public forums, such as a council of elders, where decisions could be made for the community as a whole. Women held proportionately few of these public roles, but a recent reevaluation of ethnographic evidence shows that despite most scholars' belief that women had no significant political roles, there were numerous female chiefs, shamans, and traders.[8]

Iroquois women represented the apex of female political power. The land was theirs; the women worked it cooperatively and controlled the distribution of all food whether originally procured by women or by men. This gave them essential control over the economic organization of their tribe; they could withhold food at any point—in the household, the council of elders, war parties, or religious celebrations.[9] The Iroquois institutionalized female power in the rights of matrons, or older women, to nominate council elders and to depose chiefs. As one missionary wrote: "They did not hesitate, when the occasion required, to 'knock off the horns' as it was technically called, from the head of a chief and send him back to the ranks of the warriors. The original nomination of the chiefs also always rested with them."[10] When the council met, the matrons would lobby with the elders to make their views known. Though women did not sit in formal or public positions of power, as heads of households they were empowered *as a group*. This, in turn, reflected their considerable autonomy within their households.[11]

GENDER AND CHANGE: THE IMPACT OF EUROPEAN CONTACT

When Europeans began to invade the Americas in the 1500s, the most devastating assault on Indian life initially came from the unseen bacteria and viruses Europeans brought with them. Within a century raging epidemics of typhoid, diphtheria, influenza, measles, chicken pox, whooping cough, tuberculosis, smallpox, scarlet fever, strep, and yellow fever reduced the population of Mexico to only 5 to 10 percent of its former level of 25 million. The population of the northern areas which later became the United States suffered similar fates.[12]

As cultural, economic, and military contacts grew, the differences between women and men in each group began to change. In some cases women appropriated new sources of wealth and power; in others they lost both skills and autonomy. These various changes were shaped by the sexual division of labor in indigenous cultures, the demographic composition of European colonizers, and the nature of the economic relations between Indians and Europeans.

For example, when the Aztec empire fell before the superior military technology of the Spanish, women were booty in the military victory. The demographic facts of a dense Indian population and Spanish conquerors who were almost exclusively male shaped a continuing sexual interaction between Spanish men and Indian women. Seeking stability, the Spanish soon began to encourage marriages with Christianized Indian women. These Indian mothers of the mestizo (mixed-bloods) were historically stigmatized both by a racial caste system and by association with illegitimacy. Nevertheless, they fashioned for their children a new culture blending Christianity and the Spanish language with cultural concepts and practices from their Indian heritage. Contemporary Mexican culture is the result of their creative survival.[13]

On the Atlantic coast of North America, by contrast, English colonizers emigrated in family groups, and sexual liaisons with Indians were rare. Algonkian Indian women quickly seized the opportunity to trade for European goods such as metal kettles, tools, and needles and put them to use in their daily work. Although quick to appropriate European technology, they and their people actively resisted European domination. They fought back militarily, politically, and culturally. One key form of resistance was the Indian insistence on continuing women's prominent roles in politics, religious ritual, and trade despite the inability of Englishmen to recognize or deal with them.[14]

The impact of Europeans was more indirect for inland Indians. The European market for furs represented an opportunity for tribes eager to procure European trade goods. In all likelihood the men's increased emphasis on hunting and warfare sharpened the separation of men's and women's lives. The Iroquois, for example, quickly became dependent on trade goods and lost traditional crafts such as making pottery, stone axes, knives, and arrowheads. Yet by the 1640s they had depleted the beaver supply and had to compete with neighboring tribes for hunting grounds. One result of their longer and longer hunting expeditions was that the village itself became a female space. As hunters, traders, and fighters, men had to travel most of the year while women stayed at home, maintaining villages and cornfields generation after generation.[15] One consequence, then, of the fur trade in the first two centuries after contact was increased power for Iroquois women as they controlled local resources and local affairs.

Lacking a similar strong base in highly productive local agriculture, however, women in other tribes did not gain the power and influence that Iroquois women did. Among the Montagnais-Naskapi in the upper St. Lawrence valley, the fur trade gradually shifted the economic balance toward dependence on income provided by the men's trap lines or wages.[16] In some tribes, polygamy increased when a single hunter could provide more carcasses than a single woman could process.[17]

One group of Indian women—those who married fur traders—created an altogether new cultural and economic pattern. European fur traders, principally the French and later the

English and Dutch, were almost exclusively male. As they traveled thousands of miles inland, traders depended on the Indians for their immediate survival and for long-term trade relations; thus, they began to marry Indian women. Indeed, Indian women provided the knowledge, skills, and labor that made it possible for many traders to survive in an unfamiliar environment. On the basis of such relationships, over the course of two centuries a fur trade society emerged, bound together by economics, kinship, rituals, and religion.[18]

Essentially traders adopted an indigenous way of life. Indian women prepared hides, made clothing and moccasins; manufactured snowshoes; prepared and preserved foods such as pemmican—a buffalo meat and fat mixture that could be carried on long trips; caught and dried fish; and gathered local fruits and vegetables such as wild rice, maple sugar, and berries. Stories abound of trading posts saved from starvation by the fishing or gathering or snaring skills of Indian women.

Indian women's ability to dress furs, build canoes, and travel in the wilderness rendered them invaluable to traders. A Chipewyan guide argued that the Hudson's Bay Company's failed expeditions were caused by a lack of women:

> in case they meet with success in hunting, who is to carry the produce of their labour? Women . . . also pitch our tents, make and mend our clothing, keep us warm at night; and, in fact, there is no such thing as travelling any considerable distance, or for any length of time, in this country, without their assistance.[19]

Indian women were active participants in the trade itself: They served as interpreters on whose linguistic and diplomatic abilities much depended. They trapped small animals and sold their pelts, as did many of their sisters who remained in traditional Indian society.

There is considerable evidence that some marriages between Indian women and fur traders resulted in long-lasting and apparently caring alliances. William McNeil, ship captain for the Hudson's Bay Company, mourned the loss of his Haida wife in childbirth: "The deceased has been a good and faithful partner for me for twenty years and we had twelve children together . . . [she] was a most kind mother to her children, and no Woman could have done her duty better, although an Indian.[20]

Despite their importance, many Indian women involved in the fur trade were exploited. As guides or as wives, they lived in a social and economic structure organized around the needs of male European traders.[21] When they decided to return to Europe, traders were notorious for abandoning wives of many years, sometimes simply passing them on to their successors. Such practices contributed to the increased reluctance of Indian women to have any relations with white men. According to observers in the early nineteenth century, the fertility of traders' wives, who commonly had eight to twelve children, was sharply higher than that of traditional Indian women, who bore only four children on average. Traders did not observe traditional practices that restricted fertility, such as lengthy hunting expeditions and ritually prescribed abstinence. And unlike their traditional sisters who had virtual control over their offspring, traders' wives experienced the assertion of patriarchal authority most painfully when their children—especially their sons—were sent away to receive a "civilized education."[22]

The daughters of such marriages eventually replaced Indian women as the wives of traders. Their mothers' training in language and domestic skills and their ongoing relations with Indian kin fitted them to continue the role of "women-in-between" and their marriages settled into more permanent, lifelong patterns. At the same time, these mixed-blood, or metis, daughters lacked many of the sources of power and autonomy of their Indian mothers. They were less likely to choose their marriage partners and they married at a much younger age. Also, they did not have strong kinship networks to which to escape if their marriages proved unhappy or abusive. The absorption of European norms meant a far more polarized notion of men's public and women's private spheres along with the explicit subordination of women in both. The ultimate burden for the Indian wives of European traders came with the arrival of increased numbers of white women to the wilderness in the nineteenth century. Indian and mixed-blood wives experienced a growing racial prejudice that was not abated by even the highest degree of acculturation.[23]

The fur trade collapsed in the middle of the nineteenth century, as did the society that had grown up around it. Sizable towns in the Great Lakes region were populated by metis people who spoke a common language used in trade, shared the Catholic religion, and grounded their lives in the economics of the fur trade. The disappearance of the fur trade and the emergence of reservation policies in the United States forcing persons of Indian descent to register as Indians defined out of existence a people whose unique culture was built on the lives and activities of Indian "women-in-between."

By contrast, in the sixteenth and seventeenth centuries a very different set of circumstances strengthened the influence of women in some tribes on the Great Plains while marginalizing their power in others. These changes were less a product of trading relationships than of new technologies and economic possibilities inadvertently introduced by Europeans. Navaho women, for example, owned and managed livestock, enabling them to develop broad social and economic powers and a position of high prestige based on their economic independence. Sheep and goats, originally introduced by Spanish explorers, rapidly became the principal livestock, greatly expanding women's resources.[24]

Farther north, the introduction of horses in the early 1700s transformed the technology of hunting and, therefore, the Indians' way of life on the Plains.[25] Nomadic tribes previously had traveled slowly, depending principally on women's gathering for subsistence and engaging in highly organized collective hunts that often failed. Early in the eighteenth century, however, Plains tribes gained access to horses descended from those brought by early Spanish explorers. Horses enabled bands of hunters to range over a far wider territory and transformed buffalo hunting. An individual hunter could ride into a herd, choose as prey the largest rather than the weakest animals, and shoot his arrows at point-blank range. The consequence for the material life of Plains people was sudden, unprecedented wealth: more meat protein than they could consume, with plentiful hides for tepees, clothing, and finally, for trade.

More individualized hunting styles placed a premium on skill and prowess while encouraging the accumulation of wealth. The fact that a single hunter could easily supply several women with hides to dress and meat to cure encouraged polygamy. And the chronic shortage of horses led to institutionalized raiding and continuous intertribal warfare. The lifestyle that emerged under such circumstances has become in some respects the center of American mythology about the Indian. Mythical images of warlike braves galloping across the Plains in full headdress or engaging in rituals like the famed sundance leave little place for Indian women except as passive squaws waiting in the background.

The myths themselves reflect the heightened emphasis on male domination and concurrent loss of female power that accompanied the social and economic revolution brought by the use of horses. Certainly men's and women's life experiences diverged substantially. Frequently women traveled with hunting parties, charged with the care of tepees, children, food preparation, and clothing manufacture, as well as the processing of the huge carcasses. Though the women continued to do the bulk of the work, the romance and daring of war and hunting dominated the ritual life of the group. Male bonding grew with such ritual occasions and the development of military societies.[26]

By the nineteenth century the Lakota culture had incorporated an emphasis on sexual differences into all aspects of daily life. Cultural symbols sharply emphasized the distinction between aggressive maleness and passive femaleness. The sexual division of labor defined these differences concretely.[27] Extreme distinctions in demeanor, personality, and even language flowed from this rigid division. Men went on vision quests, directed religious rituals, and served as shamans and medicine men. Though women were economically dependent, their work remained essential to group survival, and their importance found ritual expression in female societies and in some women's individual visions that gave them access to sacred powers. The most important female society was made up of quill and beadwork specialists devoted to the mythic Double Woman Dreamer. The Lakota believed that dreams of the Double Woman caused women to behave in aggressive masculine ways: "They possessed the power to cast spells on men and seduce them.

They were said to be very promiscuous, to live alone, and on occasion to perform the Double Woman Dreamer ceremony publically."[28]

The Double Woman Dreamer enabled the Lakota and other Plains Indians to incorporate specific social roles for women whose behavior violated feminine norms. Another was the widespread role of a "warrior woman" or "manly hearted woman" who acted as a man in both hunting and warfare. The manly hearted woman is a parallel role to the male "berdache," a man who could assume the dress and roles of a woman and was presumed to have special powers. Thus, although women lost both economic and cultural power as Plains tribes began using horses to hunt, to some degree women and men could move outside the boundaries of strictly defined feminine and masculine roles.

This fluidity allowed a few women quite literally to live the lives of men. In some societies manly hearted women were noticed very young and raised with extreme favoritism and license. In others the shift in gender roles received validation at a later age through dreams or visions. A trader on the Upper Missouri River told the story of one such woman, a member of the Gros Ventres captured at the age of 12.

> Already exhibiting manly interests, her adopted father encouraged these inclinations and trained her in a wide variety of male occupational skills. Although she dressed as a woman throughout her life, she pursued the role of a male in her adult years. She was a proficient hunter and chased big game on horseback and on foot. She was a skilled warrior, leading many successful war parties. In time, she sat on the council and ranked as the third leading warrior in a band of 160 lodges. After achieving success in manly pursuits, she took four wives whose hide-processing work brought considerable wealth to her lodge.[29]

WHAT THE EUROPEANS THOUGHT THEY SAW

At the time of the American Revolution, the existence of Indian societies, and in particular the highly democratic Iroquois Confederacy, provided for white Americans a living proof of the possibility of self-rule. Their virtues furnished a useful contrast to the corruption and tyranny against which Americans saw themselves struggling. For example, Thomas Jefferson wrote that the Europeans "have divided their nations into two classes, wolves and sheep." But for the Indians, "controls are in their manners and their moral sense of right and wrong." As a result, Indians "enjoy . . . an infinitely greater degree of happiness than those who live under European governments."[30]

What the founding fathers did not explore, however, was that the Iroquois model included considerably more political and economic power for women than any Europeans considered possible. Many white observers overlooked the cultural complexity of Indian societies and the great range of women's economic, social, and religious roles. From the sixteenth to the nineteenth century both male and female writers persisted in describing Indian women—if they described them at all—as slaves, degraded and abused. A sixteenth-century Jesuit outlined the many tasks of Montagnais-Naskapi women, contrasted them with the observation that "the men concern themselves with nothing but the more laborious hunting and waging of war," and concluded that "their wives are regarded and treated as slaves."[31] An English fur trader, exploring the Canadian forests in the 1690s, described the status of Cree women: "Now as for a woman they do not so much mind her for they reckon she is like a Slead dog or Bitch when she is living & when she dies they think she departs to Eternity but a man they think departs to another world & lives again."[32]

Similarly, Europeans failed to comprehend women's political power. Early contacts with the coastal Algonkians, for example, produced elaborate descriptions of villages, tribes, and occasional confederacies headed by "chiefs" or "kings." Because Europeans looked for social organizations similar to the cities and states they knew, they could not imagine that the most significant political and economic unit of these people was the matrilineal-matrilocal clan in which women had considerable power and autonomy.[33]

What these observers saw was a division of labor in which women performed many tasks that European culture assigned to men. They were especially outraged to see women chopping wood, building houses, carrying heavy loads, and engaging in agriculture—jobs that in their view constituted the very definition of manly work. Missionaries, for example, persistently defined their goal as civilizing the Indians, by which they meant not only urging them to accept Christian doctrine and sacraments but also to adopt a way of life based on female domesticity and male-dominated, settled agriculture. Not surprisingly, their ideas met sharp resistance.

Iroquois women by the late eighteenth century, for example, were eager to obtain information about the agricultural practices of Quaker missionaries, but they wanted to use it themselves. When Quakers insisted on teaching men, the women ridiculed them as transvestites. "If a Man took hold of a Hoe to use it the Women would get down his gun by way of derision & would laugh & say such a warrior is a timid woman."[34]

In the long run, the Iroquois example held deep implications not only for self-rule but also for an inclusive democracy that sanctioned female participation. The latter, however, was something that revolutionary founding fathers could not fathom. Their definitions of "public" and "private," "masculine" and "feminine" did not allow them to see the more fluid, democratic, and simply different realities of Indian life. Yet over the course of American history, an understanding of public, political life built on an inclusive definition of citizenship proved to be a powerful idea, one capable of subverting even the ancient hierarchies of gender.

Notes

1. Louis Hennepin, A *Description of Louisiana*, trans. John Gilmary Shea (New York: John G. Shea, 1880), pp. 278–80, in *The Colonial and Revolutionary Periods*, vol. 2 of *Women and Religion in America*, ed. Rosemary Radford Reuther and Rosemary Skinner Keller (San Francisco: Harper & Row, 1983), pp. 20-21.

2. See Carolyn Niethammer, *Daughters of the Earth: The Lives and Legends of American Indian Women* (New York: Collier Books, 1977); Ferdinand Anton, *Women in Pre-Columbian America* (New York: Abner Scham, 1973); and Gary B. Nash, *Red, White, and Black: The Peoples of Early America* (Englewood Cliffs, N.J.: Prentice-Hall, 1974). . . .

3. Janet D. Spector, "Male/Female Task Differentiation among the Hidatsa: Toward the Development of an Archeological Approach to the Study of Gender," in *The Hidden Half: Studies of Plains Indian Women*, ed. Patricia Albers and Beatrice Medicine (Washington, D.C.: University Press of America, 1983), pp. 77–99.

4. James Seaver, *Life of Mary Jemison: Deh-he-wamis* (1880), pp. 69–71, quoted in Judith Brown, "Economic Organization and the Position of Women among the Iroquois," *Ethnohistory* 17 (1970):151–67, quote on p. 158. . . .

5. Quoted in Robert Grumet, "Sunksquaws, Shamans, and Tradeswomen: Middle Atlantic Coastal Algonkian Women during the 17th and 18th Centuries," in *Women and Colonization: Anthropological Perspectives*, ed. Mona Etienne and Eleanor Leacock (New York: Praeger, 1980), p. 57.

6. Laura F. Klein, "Contending with Colonization: Tlingit Men and Women in Change," in Etienne and Leacock, *Women and Colonization*, pp. 88–108.

7. This section draws heavily on Jacqueline Peterson and Mary Druke, "American Indian Women and Religion," in Reuther and Keller, *Women and Religion*, pp. 1–41; see also Niethammer, *Daughters*, chap. 10.

8. Grumet, "Sunksquaws, Shamans, and Tradeswomen," pp. 43–62; see also Niethammer, *Daughters*, chap. 6.

9. Brown, "Economic Organization"; Diane Rothenberg, "The Mothers of the Nation: Seneca Resistance to a Quaker Intervention," in Etienne and Leacock, *Women and Colonization*, pp. 66–72.

10. Quoted in Brown, "Economic Organization," p. 154.

11. . . . [S]ee Elizabeth Tooker, 'Women in Iroquois Society," in *Extending the Rafters: Interdisciplinary Approaches to Iroquois Studies*, ed. Michael K. Foster, Jack Campisi, and Marianne Mithun (Albany: State University of New York Press, 1984), pp. 109–23; . . . and Daniel K. Richter, "War and Culture: the Iroquois Experience," *William and Mary Quarterly* 40 (1983): 528–59.

12. . . . See Henry Dobyns, "Estimating Aboriginal American Population: An Appraisal of Techniques with a New Hemispheric Estimate," *Current Anthropology* 7 (1966):395–412; . . . and Russell Thornton, *American Indian Holocaust and Survival: A Population History since 1492* (Norman: University of Oklahoma Press, 1987); . . .

13. See June Nash, "Aztec Women: The Transition from Status to Class in Empire and Colony," in Etienne and Leacock, *Women and Colonization*, pp. 134–48.

14. Niethammer, *Daughters*, chaps. 5–6.

15. Anthony F. C. Wallace, *The Death and Rebirth of the Seneca* (New York: Alfred A. Knopf, 1970), p. 28.

16. Leacock, "Montagnais Women and the Jesuit Program for Colonization," in Etienne and Leacock, *Women and Colonization*, p. 27. . . .

17. . . . See Carol Devens, "Separate Confrontations: Gender as a Factor in Indian Adaptation to European Colonization in New France," *American Quarterly* 38 (1986):461–80.

18. See Sylvia Van Kirk, *"Many Tender Ties": Women in Fur Trade Society in Western Canada, 1700–1850* (Winnipeg: Watson & Dwyer, 1980); Jennifer S. Brown, *Strangers in the Blood: Fur Trade Company Families in Indian Country* (Vancouver: University of British Columbia Press, 1980); . . .

19. Quoted in Van Kirk, *"Many Tender Ties,"* p. 63.

20. Ibid., p. 33.

21. Ibid., p. 88.

22. Ibid., chap. 4.

23. [Ibid.,] . . . p. 145. See also chaps. 5–10.

24. Niethammer, *Daughters*, pp. 127–29.

25. Alan Klein, "The Political-Economy of Gender: A 19th Century Plains Indian Case Study," in Albers and Medicine, *The Hidden Half*, pp. 143–73; Niethammer, *Daughters*, pp. 111–18.

26. See Klein, "The Political-Economy of Gender."

27. See, for example, quote from Geo. Sword, *Manuscript Writings of Geo Sword*, vol. 1 (ca. 1909), quoted in Raymond J. DeMallie, "Male and Female in Traditional Lakota Culture," in Albers and Medicine, *The Hidden Half*, p. 238.

28. Ibid., pp. 241–47, quote from p. 245; also Niethammer, *Daughters*, pp. 132–37.

29. In Beatrice Medicine, "Warrior Women—Sex Role Alternatives for Plains Indian Women," in Albers and Medicine, *The Hidden Half*, p. 273, see also pp. 267-80.

30. Thomas Jefferson quoted in Bruce Johansen, *Forgotten Founders: Benjamin Franklin, the Iroquois and the Rationale for the American Revolution* (Ipswich, Mass.: Gambit, 1982), pp. 112, 114.

31. Quoted in Leacock, "Montagnais Women," in Etienne and Leacock, *Women and Colonization*, p. 27.

32. Quoted in Van Kirk, *"Many Tender Ties,"* p. 17.

33. Grumet, "Sunksquaws, Shamans, and Tradeswomen."

34. "Journal of William Allinson of Burlington" (1809) quoted in Rothenberg, "Mothers of the Nation," in Etienne and Leacock, *Women and Colonization*, p. 77.

JENNIFER L. MORGAN

"Some Could Suckle over Their Shoulder": European Depictions of Indigenous Women, 1492–1750

Of all the women who crossed the Atlantic east to west between 1492 and 1800, four-fifths made the journey from African homelands. They were fully one-third of the Africans compelled to embark on the infamous Middle Passage. White European women were a small proportion of female migrants—forced or voluntary—because of the insatiable demand of New World planters, especially in Brazil and the Caribbean (then referred to as the West Indies), for laborers to harvest profitable crops like sugarcane. These taskmasters were not averse to using girls and women as laborers.* Thus, while middling-status European women were likely to experience the hope, anxiety, and exhilaration that could come with establishing a homestead in a new land, far more African women were fated to associate the American continent with severe trauma, ongoing despair, and cultural loss.

The merchant capitalists, investors, and planters who promoted New World colonization had little compunction about subjecting poor, uneducated European working men, women, and children to a host of exploitative, coercive labor systems. But they forced upon the eight million Africans carried off in the transatlantic

*Jennifer L. Morgan, "Slavery and the Slave Trade," in *A Companion to American Women's History*, ed. Nancy A. Hewitt (Malden, Mass.: Blackwell Publishers, 2002), pp. 20–34.

Excerpted from the introduction and "'Some Could Suckle over Their Shoulder': Male Travelers, Female Bodies, and the Gendering of Racial Ideology," ch. 1 of *Laboring Women: Reproduction and Gender in New World Slavery* by Jennifer L. Morgan (Philadelphia: University of Pennsylvania Press, 2004). Reprinted by permission of the author and publisher. Notes have been edited and renumbered.

slave trade even more degrading conditions—both on slave ships and on American plantations. How did they justify this behavior to themselves? We cannot point simply to racism, because a concept of race as a biologically hereditable set of traits congealed only in the nineteenth century. In the sixteenth century, educated Europeans believed that all humans descended from a common ancestor and thus shared a common humanity. "Race" was used mostly to indicate national origin or lineage. Skin color was not seen as an immutable marker of difference; many believed one's complexion would change according to how close one lived to the equator. Jennifer Morgan's essay forces us to grapple with how Europeans and Africans alike called into being the categories of blackness and whiteness.

To understand the process, Morgan argues, we must pay attention to Europeans' depictions of women's bodies and sexuality in the travel narratives of the time. The narratives' authors, European adventurers of the sixteenth to eighteenth centuries, can be thought of as early ethnographers in that they engaged in the close description of human cultures. Travelers to Africa borrowed tropes (i.e., significant themes or motifs) from earlier accounts written about indigenous American women. How did European depictions of African women change between the 1550s and the 1770s? Do you agree that these imaginary presentations amounted to "porno-tropical writings"? Does Morgan convince you about their boundary-making power? Morgan's analysis helps us to understand not only the impact of these texts and their accompanying pictures on English readers, but also the enduring legacy they created for African and African-descended women and men in the Americas.*

Ideas about black sexuality and misconceptions about black female sexual behavior formed the cornerstone of Europeans' and Euro-Americans' general attitudes toward slavery.[1] Arguably, the sexual stereotypes levied against African-American women in the nineteenth and twentieth centuries were so powerful because of the depth and utility of their roots. Before they came into contact with enslaved women either in West Africa or on American plantations, slaveowners' images and beliefs about race and savagery were indelibly marked on the women's bodies. . . . For European travelers, both those who settled in the Americas and those who did not, the enslavement of African laborers required a sense of moral and social distance over those they would enslave. They acquired that distance in part through manipulating symbolic representations of African women's sexuality. In so doing, European men gradually brought African women into focus—women whose pain-free reproduction (at least to European men) indicated that they did not descend from Eve and who illustrated their proclivity for hard work through their ability to simultaneously till the soil and birth a child. Such imaginary women suggested an immutable difference between Africans and Europeans, a difference ultimately codified as race. . . .

Prior to their entry onto the stage of New World conquests, women of African descent lived in bodies unmarked by what would emerge as Europe's preoccupation with physiognomy—skin color, hair texture, and facial features presumed to be evidence of cultural deficiency. Not until the gaze of European travelers fell upon them would African women see themselves, or indeed one another, as defined by "racial" characteristics. During the decades after European arrival to the Americas, as various nations gained and lost footholds, followed fairytale rivers of

*A set of the illustrations analyzed by Morgan appears in an earlier version of this essay, "'Some Could Suckle over Their Shoulder': Male Travelers, Female Bodies, and the Gendering of Racial Ideology, 1500–1770," *William and Mary Quarterly*, 3rd ser., 54 (Jan. 1997): 167–92 (accessible on-line in some college libraries via the database JSTOR).

gold, traded with and decimated Native inhabitants, and ignored and mobilized Christian notions of conversion and just wars, English settlers constructed an elaborate edifice of forced labor on the foundation of emerging categories of race and reproduction. The process of calling blackness into being and causing it to become inextricable from brute labor took place in legislative acts, laws, wills, bills of sale, and plantation inventories just as it did in journals and adventurers' tales of travels. Indeed, the gap between intimate experience (the Africans with whom one lived and worked) and ideology (monstrous, barely human savages) would be bridged in the hearts and minds of prosaic settlers rather than in the tales of worldly adventurers. . . . I turn here to travel narratives to explore developing categories of race and racial slavery. . . .

The connections between forced labor and race became increasingly important. . . . A concept of "race" rooted firmly in biology is primarily a late eighteenth- and early nineteenth-century phenomenon. . . . As travelers and men of letters thought through the thorny entanglements of skin color, complexion, features, and hair texture [over the course of the sixteenth and seventeenth centuries], they constructed weighty notions of civility, nationhood, citizenship, and manliness on the foundation of the amalgam of nature and culture. Given the ways in which appearance became a trope for civility and morality, it is no surprise to find gender located at the heart of Europeans' encounter with and musings over the connection between bodies and Atlantic economies.

In June 1647, Englishman Richard Ligon left London on the ship *Achilles* to establish himself as a planter in the newly settled colony of Barbados. En route, Ligon's ship stopped in the Cape Verde islands for provisions and trade. There Ligon saw a black woman for the first time. He recorded the encounter in his *True and Exact History of Barbadoes*: she was a "Negro of the greatest beauty and majesty together: that ever I saw in one woman. Her stature large, and excellently shap'd, well favour'd, full eye'd, and admirably grac'd . . . [I] awaited her comming out, which was with far greater Majesty and gracefulness, than I have seen Queen Anne, descend from the Chaire of State." Ligon's rhetoric must have surprised his English readers, for seventeenth-century images of black women did not usually evoke the monarchy as the referent. . . .[2]

[But] over the course of his journey, Richard Ligon came to another view of black women. He wrote that their breasts "hang down below their Navels, so that when they stoop at their common work of weeding, they hang almost to the ground, that at a distance you would think they had six legs." In this context, black women's monstrous bodies symbolized their sole utility—the ability to produce both crops and other laborers.[3] It is this dual value, sometimes explicit and sometimes lurking in the background of slaveowners' decision-making processes, that would come to define women's experience of enslavement most critically. . . .

As Ligon penned his manuscript while in debtors prison in 1653, he constructed a layered narrative in which the discovery of African women's monstrosity helped to assure the work's success. Taking the female body as a symbol of the deceptive beauty and ultimate savagery of blackness, Ligon allowed his readers to dally with him among beautiful black women, only to seductively disclose their monstrosity over the course of the narrative. Ligon's narrative is a microcosm of a much-larger ideological maneuver that juxtaposed the familiar with the unfamiliar—the beautiful woman who is also the monstrous laboring beast. As the tenacious and historically deep roots of racialist ideology become more evident, it becomes clear also that, through the rubric of monstrously "raced" African women, Europeans found a way to articulate shifting perceptions of themselves as religiously, culturally, and phenotypically superior to the black or brown persons they sought to define. In the discourse used to justify the slave trade, Ligon's beautiful Negro woman was as important as her "six-legged" counterpart. Both imaginary women marked a gendered. . . .whiteness on which European colonial expansionism depended. . . .[4]

Travel accounts produced in Europe and available in England provided a corpus from which subsequent writers borrowed freely, reproducing images of Native American and African women that resonated with readers. Over the course of the second half of the seventeenth century, some eighteen new collections with descriptions of Africa and the West Indies were published and reissued in England; by the eighteenth century, more than fifty new synthetic works, reissued again and again, found audiences in England.[5] Both the writers and the readers of these texts learned to dismiss the idea that women in the Americas and Africa might be innocuous or unremarkable. Rather, indigenous women bore an enormous symbolic burden, as writers from Walter Ralegh to Edward Long used them to mark metaphorically the symbiotic boundaries of European national identities and white supremacy. The conflict between perceptions of beauty and assertions of monstrosity such as Ligon's exemplified a much larger process through which the familiar became unfamiliar as beauty became beastliness and mothers became monstrous, all of which ultimately buttressed racial distinctions. Writers who articulated religious and moral justifications for the slave trade simultaneously grappled with the character of a contradictory female African body—a body both desirable and repulsive, available and untouchable, productive and reproductive, beautiful and black. By the time an eighteenth-century Carolina slaveowner could look at an African woman with the detached gaze of an investor, travelers and philosophers had already subjected her to a host of taxonomic calculations.

Europe had a long tradition of identifying Others through the monstrous physiognomy or sexual behavior of women. Armchair adventurers might shelve Pliny the Elder's ancient collection of monstrous races, *Historia Naturalis*, which catalogued the long-breasted wild woman, alongside Herodotus's *History*, in which Indian and Ethiopian tribal women bore only one child in a lifetime. They may have read Julian's arguments with Augustine in which he wrote that "barbarian and nomadic women give birth with ease, scarcely interrupting their travels to bear children." . . . Images of female devils included sagging breasts as part of the iconography of danger and monstrosity. The medieval wild woman, whose breasts dragged on the ground when she walked and could be thrown over her shoulder, was believed to disguise herself with youth and beauty in order to enact seductions. . . .[6]

Writers . . . easily applied similar modifiers to Others in Africa and the Americas in order to mark European boundaries. According to *The Travels of Sir John Mandeville*, "in Ethiopia and in many other countries [in Africa] the folk lie all naked . . . and the women have no shame of the men." Furthermore, "they wed there no wives, for all the women there be common . . . and when [women] have children they may give them to what man they will that hath companied with them." Deviant sexual behavior reflected the breakdown of natural laws—the absence of shame, the inability to identify lines of heredity and descent. This concern with deviant sexuality, articulated almost always through descriptions of women, is a constant theme in the travel writings of early modern Europe. . . . Indeed, Columbus used his reliance on the female body to articulate the colonial venture at the very outset of his voyage when he wrote that the earth was shaped like a breast with the Indies composing the nipple; his urge for discovery of new lands was inextricable from the language of sexual conquest.[7]

Richard Eden's 1553 English translation of Sebastian Münster's *A Treatyse of the Newe India* presented Amerigo Vespucci's 1502 voyage to English readers for the first time. Vespucci did not use color to mark the difference of the people he encountered; rather, he described them in terms of their lack of social institutions ("they fight not for the enlargeing of theyr dominion for asmuch as they have no Magistrates") and social niceties ("at theyr meate they use rude and barberous fashions, lying on the ground without any table clothe or coverlet"). Nonetheless, his descriptions are not without positive attributes, and when he turned his attention to women his language bristled with illuminating contradiction:

> Theyr bodies are verye smothe and clene by reason of theyr often washinge. They are in other thinges fylthy and withoute shame. Thei use no lawful coniunccion of mariage, and but every one hath as many women as him liketh, and leaveth them agayn at his pleasure. The women are very fruiteful, and refuse no laboure al the whyle they are with childe. They travayle in maner withoute payne, so that the nexte day they are cherefull and able to walke. Neyther have they theyr bellies wimpeled or loose, and hanginge pappes, by reason of bearinge manye chyldren.[8]

The passage conveys admiration for indigenous women's strength in pregnancy and their ability to maintain aesthetically pleasing bodies, but it also illustrates the conflict at the heart of European discourse on gender and difference. It hinges on both a veiled critique of European female weakness and a dismissal of Amerindian women's pain. Once English men and women were firmly settled in New World colonies, they too would struggle with the notion of female weakness; they needed both white and black women for hard manual labor, but they also needed to preserve a notion of white gentlewomen's unsuitability for physical labor. . . .

Despite his respect for female reproductive hardiness, at the end of the volume Vespucci fixed the indigenous woman as a dangerous cannibal:

> There came sodeynly a woman downe from a mountayne, bringing with her secretly a great stake with which she [killed a Spaniard.] The other wommene foorthwith toke him by the legges, and drewe him to the mountayne. . . . The women also which had slayne the yong man, cut him in pieces even in the sight of the Spaniardes, shewinge them the pieces, and rosting them at a greate fyre.

Vespucci later made manifest the latent sexualized danger inherent in the man-slaying woman in a letter in which he wrote of women biting off the penises of their sexual partners, thus linking cannibalism—an absolute indicator of savagery and distance from European norms—to female sexual insatiability.[9]

The label "savage" was not uniformly applied to Amerindian people. Indeed, in the context of European national rivalries, the indigenous woman became somewhat less savage. In the mid to late sixteenth century, the bodies of women figured at the borders of national identities. . . .

In "Discoverie of the . . . Empire of Guiana" (1598), [Sir Walter] Ralegh stated that he "suffered not any man to . . . touch any of [the natives'] wives or daughters: which course so contrary to the Spaniards (who tyrannize over them in all things) drewe them to admire her [English] majestie." Although he permitted himself and his men to gaze upon naked Indian women, Ralegh accentuated the restraint they exercised. In doing so, he used the untouched bodies of Native American women to mark national boundaries and signal the civility and superiority of English colonizers in contrast to the sexually violent Spaniards. Moreover, in linking the eroticism of indigenous women to the sexual attention of Spanish men, Ralegh signaled the Spaniards' "lapse into savagery."[10] . . .

[Visual depictions of Native women were always in flux]. . . . [E]arly volumes of Theodor de Bry's *Grand Voyages* (1590) depicted the Algonkians of Virginia and the Timucuas of Florida as classical Europeans: Amerindian bodies mirrored ancient Greek and Roman statuary, modest virgins covered their breasts, and infants suckled at the high, small breasts of young attractive women. . . .

In the third de Bry volume, *Voyages to Brazil*, published in 1592, the Indian was portrayed as aggressive and savage, and the representation of women's bodies changed. The new woman is a cannibal with breasts that fell below her waist. She licks the juices of grilled human flesh from her fingers. . . . The absence of a suckling child in these . . . depictions . . . signified the women's cannibalism—they consumed rather than produced. Although women alone did not exemplify cannibalism, women with long breasts came to mark such savagery in Native Americans for English readers. As depictions of Native Americans traversed the gamut of savage to noble, the long-breasted women became a clear signpost of savagery in contrast to her high-breasted counterpart . . .[11]

English travelers to West Africa drew on American narrative traditions as they too worked to establish a clearly demarcated line that would ultimately define them. Richard Hakluyt's collection of travel narratives, *Principal Navigations* (1589), brought Africa into the purview of English readers. *Principal Navigations* portrayed Africa and Africans in both positive and negative terms. . . . In response, Hakluyt presented texts that, through an often-conflicted depiction of African peoples, ultimately differentiated between Africa and England and erected a boundary that made English expansion in the face of confused and uncivilized peoples reasonable, profitable, and moral. . . . [12] [To] write of sex was also to define and expand the boundaries of profit through productive and reproductive labor.

The symbolic weight of indigenous women's sexual, childbearing, and childrearing practices moved from the Americas to Africa and continued to be brought to bear on England's literary imagination in ways that rallied familiar notions of gendered difference for English readers. John Lok's account of his 1554 voyage to Guinea, published forty years later in Hakluyt's collection, . . . described all Africans as "people of beastly living." He located the proof of this in *women's* behavior: among the Garamantes, women "are common: for they contract no matrimonie, neither have respect to chastitie." This description of the Garamantes first appeared in Pliny, was reproduced again by Iulius Solinus's sixth century *Polyhistor* and can be found in travel accounts through the Middle Ages and into the sixteenth and seventeenth centuries. . . . [13]

William Towrson's narrative of his 1555 voyage to Guinea, also published by Hakluyt in 1589, further exhibits this kind of distillation. Towrson depicted women and men as largely indistinguishable. They "goe so alike, that one cannot know a man from a woman but by their breastes, which in the most part be very foule and long, hanging downe low like the udder of a goate." This was, perhaps, the first time an Englishman in Africa explicitly used breasts as an identifying trait of beastliness and difference. He went on to maintain that "diverse of the women have such exceeding long breasts, that some of them will lay the same upon the ground and lie downe by them."[14] Lok and Towrson represented African women's bodies and sexual behavior in order to distinguish Africa from Europe. Towrson in particular gave readers only two analogies through which to view and understand African women—beasts and monsters. . . .

. . . After Hakluyt died, Samuel Purchas took up the mantle of editor and published twenty additional volumes in Hakluyt's series beginning in 1624.[15] . . . [including] a translation of Pieter de Marees's *A description and historicall declaration of the golden Kingedome of Guinea*. This narrative was first published in Dutch in 1602, was translated into German and Latin for the de Bry volumes (1603–1634), and appeared in French in 1605. Plagiarism by seventeenth- and eighteenth-century writers gave it still wider circulation. Here, too, black women embody African savagery. De Marees began by describing the people at Sierra Leone as "very greedie eaters, and no lesse drinkers, and very lecherous, and theevish, and much addicted to uncleanenesse; one man hath as many wives as hee is able to keepe and maintaine. The women also are much addicted to leacherie, specially, with strange Countrey people . . . [and] are also great Lyers, and not to be credited." As did most of his contemporaries, de Marees invoked women's sexuality to castigate the incivility of both men and women. Women's savagery does not stand apart. Rather, it indicts the whole: all Africans were savage. The passage displays African males' savagery alongside their access to multiple women. Similarly, de Marees located evidence of African women's savagery in their sexual desire. . . .

[He] further castigated West African women: they delivered children surrounded by men, women, and youngsters "in most shamelesse manner . . . before them all." This absence of shame (evoked explicitly, as here, or implicitly in the constant references to nakedness in other narratives) worked to establish distance. Readers, titillated by the topics discussed and thus tacitly shamed, found themselves further distanced from the shameless subject of the narrative. De Marees dwelled on the brute nature of shameless African women. He marveled that "when the child is borne [the mother] goes to the water to wash and make cleane her selfe, not once dreaming of a moneths lying-in . . . as women here with us use to doe; they use no Nurses to helpe them when they lie in child-bed, neither seeke to lie dainty and soft. . . . The next day after, they goe abroad in the streets, to doe their businesse."[16] . . .

De Marees goes on to inscribe an image of women's reproductive identity whose influence persisted long after his original publication. "When [the child] is two or three monethes old, the mother ties the childe with a peece of cloth at her backe. . . . When the child crieth to sucke, the mother casteth one of her dugs backeward over her shoulder, and so the child suckes it as it hangs."[17] Frontispieces for the de Marees narrative and the African narratives in de Bry approximate the over-the-shoulder breastfeeding de Marees described, thereby creating an image that could symbolize the continent . . .

The image, in more or less extreme form, remained a compelling one, offering in a single narrative-visual moment evidence that black women's difference was both cultural (in this strange *habit*) and physical (in this strange *ability*). The word "dug," which by the early seventeenth century meant both a woman's breasts and an animal's teats, connoted a brute animality that de Marees reinforced through his description of small children "lying downe in their house, like Dogges, [and] rooting in

Appearing in a much-reproduced travel narrative, this engraving purported to show representative examples of women's clothing and personal decoration in four regions of western Africa. (Women in Africa, *From* Verum et Historicam Descriptionem Avriferi Regni Guineaa, *in* Small Voyages, *vol. 6, by Theodor de Bry [Frankfurt am Main, 1604], p. 3. Courtesy of the John Work Garrett Library, Johns Hopkins University.)*

the ground like Hogges" and of "boyes and girles [that] goe starke naked as they were borne, with their privie members all open, without any shame or civilitie.[18] . . .

As Englishmen traversed the uncertain ground of nature and culture, African women became a touchstone for physical and behavioral curiosity both within Africa and in the Americas and Europe. Fynes Moryson wrote of Irish women in 1617 that they "have very great Dugges, some so big as they give their children suck over their Shoulders." But it is important that he connects this to being "not laced at all," or to the lack of corsetry.[19] While nudity—a state in which the absence of corsetry is certainly implicit—is constantly at play in descriptions of African women, the overwhelming physicality of the image is disaggregated from culture and instead becomes part of African female nature; something no amount of corsetry would set right . . .

African women's Africanness became contingent on the linkages between sexuality and a savagery that fitted them for both productive and reproductive labor. . . . [D]escriptions of African women in the Americas almost always highlighted their fecundity along with their capacity for manual labor. Erroneous observations about African women's propensity for easy birth and breast-feeding reassured colonizers that these women could easily perform hard labor in the Americas; at the same time, such observations erected a barrier of difference between Africa and England. Seventeenth-century English medical writers, both men and women, equated breast-feeding and tending to children with difficult work, and the practice of wealthy women forgoing breastfeeding in favor of sending their children to wet nurses was widespread. English women and men anticipated pregnancy and childbirth with extreme uneasiness and fear of death, but they knew that the experience of pain in childbirth marked women as members of a Christian community.[20] . . .

. . . By about the turn of the seventeenth century, however, as England joined in the transatlantic slave trade, assertions of African savagery began to be predicated less on consumption and cannibalism and more on production and reproduction. African women came into the conversation in the context of England's need for productivity. Descriptions of these women that highlighted the apparent ease and indifference of their reproductive lives created a mechanistic image. . . . Whereas English women's reproductive work took place solely in the domestic economy, African women's reproductive work embodied the developing discourses of extraction and forced labor at the heart of England's design for the Americas. . . .

By the eighteenth century, English writers rarely used black women's breasts or behavior for anything but concrete evidence of barbarism in Africa. In *A Description of the Coasts of North and South-Guinea*, begun in the 1680s and completed and published almost forty years later, John Barbot "admired the quietness of the poor babes, so carr'd about at their mothers' backs . . . and how freely they suck the breasts, which are always full of milk, over their mothers' shoulders, and sleep soundly in that odd posture." William Snelgrave introduced his *New Account of Some Parts of Guinea and the Slave-trade* with an anecdote designed to illustrate the benevolence of the trade. He described himself rescuing an infant from human sacrifice and reuniting the child with its mother, who "had much Milk in her Breasts." He accented the barbarism of those who had attempted to sacrifice the child and claimed that the reunion cemented his goodwill in the eyes of the enslaved, who, thus convinced of the "good notion of White Men," caused no problems during the voyage to Antigua.[21] . . .

Eighteenth-century abolitionist John Atkins similarly adopted the icon of black female bodies in his writings on Guinea. "Childing, and their Breasts always pendulous, stretches them to so unseemly a length and Bigness that some . . . could suckle over their shoulder." Atkins then considered the idea of African women copulating with apes. He noted that "at some places the Negroes have been suspected of Bestiality." . . . The evidence lay mostly in apes' resemblance to humans but was bolstered by "the Ignorance and Stupidity [of black women unable] to guide or controll lust." Abolitionists and antiabolitionists alike accepted the connections between race and black women's monstrous and fecund bodies . . .

The visual shorthand of the sagging-breasted African savage held sway for decades . . . When William Smith embarked on a voyage to map the Gold Coast for the Royal Africa Company in 1727, he was initially disinterested in ethnography. His first description of people comes more than halfway through the narrative when he writes "but before I describe the Vegetables, I shall take Notice of the Animals of this Country; beginning with the Natives, who are generally speaking a lusty strong-bodied People, but are mostly of a lazy idle Disposition." His short description, followed by a section on "Quadrepedes," is organized primarily around accusations of polygamy and promiscuity in which "hot constitution'd Ladies" are put to work by husbands who treat them like slaves. As the narrative continues, his ethnographic passages, while always brief, are also always organized around sexually available African women. In Whydah, for example, the reader encounters female Priests inclined to whoredom, and he tells of an anomalous Queen in Agonna who satisfies her sexual needs with male slaves, hands down her crown to the resulting female progeny and sells any male children into slavery.[23] . . .

One of a very few English women in late eighteenth-century West Africa, abolitionist Anna Falconbridge . . . noted that women's breasts in Sierra Leone were "disgusting to Europeans, though considered *beautiful* and ornamental here." But such weak claims of sisterly sympathy could hardly interrupt 300 years of porno-tropical writing. By the 1770s, Edward Long's *History of Jamaica* presented readers with African women whose savagery was total, for whom enslavement was the only means of civilization. . . . Long used women's bodies and behavior to justify and promote the mass enslavement of Africans. By the time he wrote, the Jamaican economy was fully invested in slave labor and was contributing more than half of the profits obtained by England from the West Indies as a whole. The association of black people with beasts—via African women—had been cemented: "Their women are delivered with little or no labour; they have therefore no more occasion for midwifes than the female oran-outang, or any other wild animall. . . . Thus they seem exempted from the course inflicted upon Eve *and her daughters*."[24] If African women gave birth without pain, they somehow sidestepped God's curse upon Eve. If they were not Eve's descendants, they were not related to Europeans and could therefore be forced to labor on England's overseas plantations with impunity. . . . [25]

When [Richard] Ligon arrived in Barbados and settled on 500-acre sugar plantation with 100 slaves, his notion of African beauty—if it had ever really existed—dissolved in the face of racial slavery. He saw African men and women carrying bunches of plantains: "Tis a lovely sight to see a hundred handsom Negroes, men and women, with every one a grasse-green bunch of these fruits on their heads . . . the black and green so well becoming one another." Here in the context of the sugar plantation, where he saw African women working as he had never seen English woman do, Ligon struggled to situate African women as workers. Their innate unfamiliarity as laborers caused him to cast about for a useful metaphor. He compares African people to vegetation; now they are only passively and abstractly beautiful as blocks of color. Ligon attested to their passivity with their servitude: They made "very good servants, if they be not spoyled by the English."[26]

But . . . he ultimately equated black people with animals. He declared that planters bought slaves so that the "sexes may be equall . . . [because] they cannot live without Wives," although the enslaved choose their partners much "as Cows do . . . for, the most of them are as near beasts as may be." Like his predecessors, Ligon offered further proof of Africans' capacity for physical labor—their aptitude for slavery—through ease of childbearing. "In a fortnight [after giving birth] this woman is at worke with her Pickaninny at her back, as merry a soule as any is there."[27] In the Americas, African women's purportedly pain-free childbearing thus continued to be central. When Ligon reinforced African women's animality with descriptions of breasts "hang[ing] down below their Navels," he tethered his narrative to familiar images of black women that—for readers nourished on Hakluyt and de Bry—effectively naturalized the enslavement of Africans . . .

By the time the English made their way to the West Indies, decades of ideas and information about brown and black women predated the actual encounter. In many ways, the encounter had already taken place in parlors and reading rooms on English soil, assuring that colonists would arrive with a battery of assumptions and predispositions about race, femininity, sexuality, and civilization. Confronted with an Africa they needed to exploit, European writers turned to black women as evidence of a cultural inferiority that ultimately became encoded as racial difference. Monstrous bodies became enmeshed with savage behavior as the icon of women's breasts became evidence of tangible barbarism. African women's "unwomanly" behavior evoked an immutable distance between Europe and Africa on which the development of racial slavery depended. By the mid-seventeenth century, what had initially marked African women as unfamiliar—their sexually and reproductively bound savagery—had become familiar. To invoke it was to conjure a gendered and racialized figure that marked the boundaries of English civility even as she naturalized the subjugation of Africans and their descendants in the Americas.

Notes

1. Deborah Gray White, *Ar'n't I A Woman? Female Slaves in the Plantation South* (New York and London: W.W. Norton, 1985), 29–46; Barbara Bush, *Slave Women in Caribbean Society, 1650–1838* (Bloomington: Indiana University Press, 1990), 11–12.

2. Richard Ligon, *A True and Exact History of the Island of Barbados* (London, 1657), 12–13.

3. Ligon, *True and Exact History of Barbados*, 51.

4. Kim F. Hall, *Things of Darkness: Economies of Race and Gender in Early Modern England* (Ithaca, N.Y.: Cornell University Press, 1995), 29–61.

5. Anthony J. Barker, *The African Link: British Attitudes to the Negro in the Era of the Atlantic Slave Trade, 1550–1807* (London: Frank Cass, 1978), 22.

6. Pliny the Elder, *Natural History*, 10 vols., trans. H. Rackham (Cambridge, Mass., Harvard University Press, 1938–63), 2: 509–27; Herodotus, *The History*, trans. David Grene (Chicago: University of Chicago

Press, 1987), 4, 180, 191; Elizabeth A. Clark, "Generation, Degeneration, Regeneration: Original Sin and the Conception of Jesus in the Polemic Between Augustine and Julian of Eclanum," in *Generation and Degeneration: Tropes of Reproduction in Literature and History from Antiquity to Early Modern Europe*, ed. Valeria Finucci and Kevin Brownlee (Durham, N.C.: Duke University Press, 2001), 30; Richard Bernheimer, *Wild Men in the Middle Ages: A Study in Art, Sentiment, and Demonology* (Cambridge, Mass.: Harvard University Press, 1952), 33–41, 34.

7. *The Travels of Sir John Mandeville: The Version of the Cotton Manuscript in Modern Spelling*, ed. A.W. Pollard (London: Macmillan, 1915), 109, 119; Sharon W. Tiffany and Kathleen J. Adams, *The Wild Woman: An Inquiry into the Anthropology of an Idea* (Cambridge: Schenkman, 1985), 63.

8. *A Treatyse of the Newe India by Sebastian Münster* (1553), trans. Richard Eden (microprint) (Ann Arbor, Mich., 1966), 57.

9. Münster, *Treatyse*, trans. Eden, quoted in Louis Montrose, "The Work of Gender in the Discourse of Discovery," *Representations* 33 (1991): 1–41, 4, 5.

10. Ralegh, "The Discoverie of the large rich and beautifull Empire of Guiana," in Richard Hakluyt, *The Principal Navigations Voyages Traffiques & Discoveries of the English Nation*, 12 vols. (1598–1600; reprint Glasgow, 1903–5), 10: 39; Karen Robertson, "Pocahantas at the Masque," *Signs* 21 (1996): 561.

11. Theodore de Bry, ed., *Grand Voyages*, 13 vols. (Frankfurt am Main, 1590–1627); Bernadette Bucher, *Icon and Conquest: A Structural Analysis of the Illustrations of de Bry's Great Voyages*, trans. Basia Miller Gulati (Chicago: University of Chicago Press, 1981).

12. Emily C. Bartels, "Imperialist Beginnings: Richard Hakluyt and the Construction of Africa," *Criticism* 34 (1992): 517–38, 519.

13. "The second voyage [of Master John Lok] to Guinea . . . 1554," in Richard Hakluyt, *The Principal Navigations, Voiages, Traffiques, and Discoueries of the English Nation*, 12 vols. (London, 1598-1600), 6: 167, 168; Barker, *African Link*, 121.

14. "The first voyage made by Master William Towrson Marchant of London, to the coast of Guinea . . . in the yeere 1555," in Hakluyt, *Principal Navigations*, 6: 184, 187.

15. Samuel Purchas, *Hakluytus Posthumus, or Purchas His Pilgrimes: Contayning a History of the World in Sea Voyages and Land Travells by Englishmen and Others*, 20 vols. (1624; reprint Glasgow: J. MacLehose and Sons, 1905).

16. De Marees, "Description and historicall declaration of the golden Kingdome of Guinea," in *Purchas His Pilgrimes*, 6: 251, 258–59. This testimony to African women's physical strength and emotional indifference is even more emphatic in the original Dutch. In the most recent translation from the Dutch, the passage continues: "This shows that the women here are of a cruder nature and stronger posture than the Females in our Lands in Europe." Pieter de Marees, *Description and Historical Account of the Gold Kingdom of Guinea*, trans, and ed. Albert van Dantzig and Adam Jones (1602; reprint Oxford: Oxford University Press, 1987), 23.

17. De Marees, "Description and Historicall declaration of the Golden Kingdome," 259.

18. De Marees, "Description and historicall declaration of the Golden Kingdome," 261. Oxford English Dictionary, 2nd ed., 1989.

19 Fynes Moryson, *Shakespeare's Europe: A survey of the Condition of Europe at the end of the Sixteenth Century, Being unpublished chapters of Fynes Moryson's Itinerary*, 2nd ed. (1617; reprint New York: Benjamin Blom, 1967), 485.

20. Jordan, *White over Black*, 39; Marylynn Salmon, "The Cultural Significance of Breastfeeding and Infant Care in Early Modern England and America," *Journal of Social History* 28 (1994): 247–70; Linda Pollock, "Embarking on a Rough Passage: The Experience of Pregnancy in Early Modern Society," in *Women as Mothers in Pre-Industrial England*, ed. Valerie Fildes (New York: Routledge, 1990), 45.

21. Barbot, *A Description of the Coasts of North and South-Guinea*, in *A Collection of Voyages*, ed. A. Churchill (London, 1732), 36; William Snelgrave, "Introduction," *A New Account of Some Parts of Guinea and the Slave Trade* (1734; reprint London: Cass, 1971).

22. John Atkins, *A Voyage to Guinea, Brazil, and the West-Indies* (1735; reprint London: Cass, 1970), 50, 108.

23. William Smith, *A New Voyage to Guinea* (London, 1744), 142–43, 195, 208.

24. Anna Maria Falconbridge, *Two Voyages to Sierra Leone, During the Years 1791-2-3*, in *Maiden Voyages and Infant Colonies: Two Women's Travel Narratives of the 1790s*, ed. Deirdre Coleman (London: Leicester University Press, 1999), 45–168, 74, emphasis in the original; Edward Long, "History of Jamaica, 2, with notes and corrections by the Author" (1774), Add. Ms., 12405, p364/f295, p380/f304; Robin Blackburn, *The Making of New World Slavery: From the Baroque to the Modern, 1492–1800* (London: Verso, 1997), 527–45.

25. Early modern European women were so defined by their experience of pain in childbirth that an inability to feel pain was considered evidence of witchcraft. Lyndal Roper, *Oedipus and the Devil: Witchcraft, Sexuality and Religion in Early Modern Europe* (London: Routledge, 1994), 203–4.

26. Ligon, *True and Exact History of Barbadoes*, 44, 47, 51.

27. Ligon, *True and Exact History of Barbadoes*, 47, 51.

LAUREL THATCHER ULRICH

The Ways of Her Household

One of the greatest barriers to an accurate assessment of women's role in the community has been the habit of assuming that what women did was not very important. Housekeeping has long been women's work, and housework has long been regarded as trivial. Laurel Thatcher Ulrich shows, however, that housekeeping can be a complex task and that real skill and intelligence might be exercised in performing it. The services housekeepers perform, in early as well as in contemporary America, are an important part of the economic arrangements that sustain the family and need to be taken into account when describing any community or society. Note the differences Ulrich finds between rural and urban women, and between middle-class and impoverished women.

By English tradition, a woman's environment was the family dwelling and the yard or yards surrounding it. Though the exact composition of her setting obviously depended upon the occupation and economic status of her husband, its general outlines were surprisingly similar regardless of where it was located. The difference between an urban "houselot" and a rural "homelot" was not as dramatic as one might suppose.

If we were to draw a line around the housewife's domain, it would extend from the kitchen and its appendages, the cellars, pantries, brewhouses, milkhouses, washhouses, and butteries which appear in various combinations in household inventories, to the exterior of the house, where, even in the city, a mélange of animal and vegetable life flourished among the straw, husks, clutter, and muck. Encircling the pigpen, such a line would surround the garden, the milkyard, the well, the hen-house, and perhaps the orchard itself—though husbands pruned and planted trees and eventually supervised the making of cider, good housewives strung their wash between the trees and in season harvested fruit for pies and conserves.

The line demarking the housewife's realm would not cross the fences which defined outlying fields of Indian corn or barley, nor would it stretch to fishing stages, mills, or wharves, but in berry or mushroom season it would extend into nearby woods or marsh and in spells of dearth or leisure reach to the shore. Of necessity, the boundaries of each woman's world would also extend into the houses of neighbors and into the cartways of a village or town. Housewives commanded a limited domain. But they were neither isolated nor self-sufficient. Even in farming settlements, families found it essential to bargain for needed goods and services. For prosperous and socially prominent women, interdependence took on another meaning as well. Prosperity meant charity, and in early New England charity meant personal responsibility for nearby neighbors. . . .

. . . For most historians, as for almost all antiquarians, the quintessential early American woman has been a churner of cream and a spinner of wool. Because home manufacturing has all but disappeared from modern housekeeping, many scholars have assumed that the key change in female economic life has been a shift from "production" to "consumption," a shift precipitated by the industrial revolution.[1] This is far too simple, obscuring the variety which existed even in the preindustrial world. . . .

Excerpted from ch. 1 of *Good Wives: Image and Reality in the Lives of Women in Northern New England, 1650–1750*, by Laurel Thatcher Ulrich (New York: Alfred A. Knopf, 1982). Reprinted by permission of the author and publisher. Notes have been edited and renumbered.

. . . Beatrice Plummer, Hannah Grafton, and Magdalen Wear lived and died in New England in the years before 1750. One of them lived on the frontier, another on a farm, and a third in town. Because they were real women, however, and not hypothetical examples, the ways of their households were shaped by personal as well as geographic factors. A careful examination of the contents of their kitchens and chambers suggests the varied complexity as well as the underlying unity in the lives of early American women.

Let us begin with Beatrice Plummer of Newbury, Massachusetts.[2] Forgetting that death brought her neighbors into the house on January 24, 1672, we can use the probate inventory which they prepared to reconstruct the normal pattern of her work.

With a clear estate of £343, Francis Plummer had belonged to the "middling sort" who were the church members and freeholders of the Puritan settlement of Newbury. As an immigrant of 1653, he had listed himself as a "linnen weaver," but he soon became a farmer as well.[3] At his death, his loom and tackling stood in the "shop" with his pitchforks, his hoes, and his tools for smithing and carpentry. Plummer had integrated four smaller plots to form one continuous sixteen-acre farm. An additional twenty acres of salt marsh and meadow provided hay and forage for his small herd of cows and sheep. His farm provided a comfortable living for his family, which at this stage of his life included only his second wife, Beatrice, and her grandchild by a previous marriage. . . .

The house over which Beatrice presided must have looked much like surviving dwellings from seventeenth-century New England, with its "Hall" and "Parlor" on the ground floor and two "chambers" above. A space designated in the inventory only as "another Roome" held the family's collection of pots, kettles, dripping pans, trays, buckets, and earthenware. . . . The upstairs chambers were not bedrooms but storage rooms for foodstuffs and out-of-season equipment. The best bed with its bolster, pillows, blanket, and coverlet stood in the parlor; a second bed occupied one corner of the kitchen, while a cupboard, a "great chest," a table, and a backless bench called a "form" furnished the hall. More food was found in the "cellar" and in the "dairy house," a room which may have stood at the coolest end of the kitchen lean-to.[4]

The Plummer house was devoid of ornament, but its contents bespeak such comforts as conscientious yeomanry and good huswifery afforded. On this winter morning the dairy house held four and a half "flitches" or sides of bacon, a quarter of a barrel of salt pork, twenty-eight pounds of cheese, and four pounds of butter. Upstairs in a chamber were more than twenty-five bushels of "English" grain—barley, oats, wheat, and rye. (The Plummers apparently reserved their Indian corn, stored in another location, for their animals.) When made into malt by a village specialist, barley would become the basis for beer. Two bushels of malt were already stored in the house. The oats might appear in a variety of dishes, from plain breakfast porridge to "flummery," a gelatinous dish flavored with spices and dried fruit.[5] But the wheat and rye were almost certainly reserved for bread and pies. The fine hair sieves stored with the grain in the hall chamber suggest that Beatrice Plummer was particular about her baking, preferring a finer flour than came directly from the miller. A "bushell of pease & beans" found near the grain and a full barrel of cider in the cellar are the only vegetables and fruits listed in the inventory, though small quantities of pickles, preserves, or dried herbs might have escaped notice. Perhaps the Plummers added variety to their diet by trading some of their abundant supply of grain for cabbages, turnips, sugar, molasses, and spices. . . .

Since wives were involved with early-morning milking, breakfast of necessity featured prepared foods or leftovers—toasted bread, cheese, and perhaps meat and turnips kept from the day before, any of this washed down with cider or beer in winter, with milk in summer. Only on special occasions would there be pie or doughnuts. Dinner was the main meal of the day. Here a housewife with culinary aspirations and an ample larder could display her specialities. After harvest Beatrice Plummer might have served roast pork or goose with apples, in spring an eel pie flavored with parsley and winter savory, and in summer a leek soup or gooseberry cream; but for ordinary days the most common menu was boiled meat with whatever "sauce" the season provided—dried peas or beans, parsnips, turnips, onions, cabbage, or garden greens. A heavy pudding stuffed into a cloth bag could steam atop the vegetables and meat. The broth from this boiled dinner might reappear at supper as "pottage" with the addition of minced herbs and some oatmeal or barley for thickening. Supper, like breakfast, was a simple meal. Bread, cheese, and beer were as welcome at the end of a winter day as at the beginning. . . .

Preparing the simplest of these meals required both judgment and skill. . . . The most basic of the housewife's skills was building and regulating fires—a task so fundamental that it must have appeared more as habit than craft. Summer and winter, day and night, she kept a few brands smoldering, ready to stir into flame as needed. The cavernous fireplaces of early New England were but a century removed from the open fires of medieval houses, and they retained some of the characteristics of the latter. Standing inside one of these huge openings today, a person can see the sky above. Seventeenth-century housewives did stand in their fireplaces, which were conceived less as enclosed spaces for a single blaze than as accessible working surfaces upon which a number of small fires might be built. Preparing several dishes simultaneously, a cook could move from one fire to another, turning a spit, checking the state of the embers under a skillet, adjusting the height of a pot hung from the lug-pole by its adjustable trammel. The complexity of firetending, as much as anything else, encouraged the one-pot meal.[6]

The contents of her inventory suggest that Beatrice Plummer was adept not only at roasting, frying, and boiling but also at baking, the most difficult branch of cookery. Judging from the grain in the upstairs chamber, the bread which she baked was "maslin," a common type made from a mixture of wheat and other grains, usually rye. She began with the sieves stored nearby, carefully sifting out the coarser pieces of grain and bran. Soon after supper she could have mixed the "sponge," a thin dough made from warm water, yeast, and flour. Her yeast might have come from the foamy "barm" found on top of fermenting ale or beer, from a piece of dough saved from an earlier baking, or even from the crevices in an unwashed kneading trough. Like fire-building, bread-making was based upon a self-perpetuating chain, an organic sequence which if once interrupted was difficult to begin again. Warmth from the banked fire would raise the sponge by morning, when Beatrice could work in more flour, knead the finished dough, and shape the loaves, leaving them to rise again.

Even in twentieth-century kitchens with standardized yeast and thermostatically controlled temperatures, bread dough is subject to wide variations in consistency and behavior. In a drafty house with an uncertain supply of yeast, bread-making was indeed "an art, craft, and mystery." Not the least of the problem was regulating the fire so that the oven was ready at the same time as the risen loaves. Small cakes or biscuits could be baked in a skillet or directly on the hearth under an upside-down pot covered with coals. But to produce bread in any quantity required an oven. Before 1650 these were frequently constructed in dooryards, but in the last decades of the century they were built into the rear of the kitchen fireplace, as Beatrice Plummer's must have been. Since her oven would have had no flue, she would have left the door open once she kindled a fire inside, allowing the smoke to escape through the fireplace chimney. Moving about her kitchen, she would have kept an eye on this fire, occasionally raking the coals to distribute the heat evenly, testing periodically with her hand to see if the oven had reached the right temperature. When she determined that it had, she would have scraped out the coals and inserted the bread—assuming that it had risen enough by this time or had not risen too much and collapsed waiting for the oven to heat.[7]

Cooking and baking were year-round tasks. Inserted into these day-by-day routines were seasonal specialities which allowed a housewife to bridge the dearth of one period with the bounty of another. In the preservation calendar, dairying came first, beginning with the first calves of early spring. In colonial New England cows were all-purpose creatures, raised for meat as well as for milk. Even in new settlements they could survive by browsing on rough land; their meat was a hedge against famine. But only in areas with abundant meadow (and even there only in certain months) would they produce milk with sufficient butterfat for serious dairying.[8] Newbury was such a place.

We can imagine Beatrice Plummer some morning in early summer processing the milk which would appear as cheese in a January breakfast. Slowly she heated several gallons with rennet dried and saved from the autumn's slaughtering. Within an hour or two the curd had formed. She broke it, drained off the whey, then worked in a little of her own fresh butter. Packing this rich mixture into a mold, she turned it in her wooden press for an hour or more, changing and washing the cheesecloth frequently as the whey dripped out. Repacking it in dry cloth, she left it in the press for another thirty or forty hours before washing it once more with whey, drying it, and placing it in the cellar or dairy house to age. As a young girl she would have learned from her mother or a mistress the importance of thorough pressing and the virtues of cleanliness. . . .

The Plummer inventory gives little evidence of the second stage of preservation in the housewife's year, the season of gardening and gathering which followed quickly upon the dairy months. But there is ample evidence of the autumn slaughtering. Beatrice could well have killed the smaller pigs herself, holding their "hinder parts between her legs," as one observer described the process,"and taking the snout in her left hand" while she stuck the animal through the heart with a long knife. Once the bleeding stopped, she would have submerged the pig in boiling water for a few minutes, then rubbed it with rosin, stripped off the hair, and disemboweled it. Nothing was lost. She reserved the organ meats for immediate use, then cleaned the intestines for later service as sausage casing. Stuffed with meat scraps and herbs and smoked, these "links" were a treasured delicacy. The larger cuts could be roasted at once or preserved in several ways.[9] . . .

Fall was also the season for cider-making. The mildly alcoholic beverage produced by natural fermentation of apple juice was a staple of the New England diet and was practically the only method of preserving the fruit harvest. With the addition of sugar, the alcoholic content could be raised from five to about seven percent, as it usually was in taverns and for export. . . .

Prosaic beer was even more important to the Plummer diet. Although some housewives brewed a winter's supply of strong beer in October, storing it in the cellar, Beatrice seems to have been content with "small beer," a mild beverage usually brewed weekly or bi-weekly and used almost at once. Malting—the process of sprouting and drying barley to increase its sugar content—was wisely left to the village expert. Beatrice started with cracked malt or grist, processing her beer in three stages. "Mashing" required slow steeping at just below the boiling point, a sensitive and smelly process which largely determined the success of the beverage. Experienced brewers knew by taste whether the enzymes were working. If it was too hot, acetic acid developed which would sour the finished product. The next stage, "brewing," was relatively simple. Herbs and hops were boiled with the malted liquid. In the final step this liquor was cooled and mixed with yeast saved from last week's beer or bread. Within twenty-four hours—if all had gone well—the beer was bubbling actively.[10]

. . . A wife who knew how to manage the ticklish chemical processes which changed milk into cheese, meal into bread, malt into beer, and flesh into bacon was a valuable asset, though some men were too churlish to admit it. After her husband's death, Beatrice married a man who not only refused to provide her with provisions, but insisted on doing his own cooking. He took his meat "out of ye pickle" and broiled it directly on the coals, and when she offered him "a cup of my owne Sugar & Bear," he refused it. When the neighbors testified that she had been a dutiful wife, the Quarterly Court fined him for "abusive carriages and speeches." Even the unhappy marriage that thrust Beatrice Plummer into court helps to document the central position of huswifery in her life.[11] . . .

Beatrice Plummer represents one type of early American housewife. Hannah Grafton represents another.[12] Chronology, geography, and personal biography created differences between the household inventories of the two women, but there are obvious similarities as well. Like Beatrice Plummer, Hannah Grafton lived in a house with two major rooms on the ground floor and two chambers above. At various locations near the ground-floor rooms were service areas—a washhouse with its own loft or chamber, a shop, a lean-to, and two cellars. The central rooms in the Grafton house were the "parlour," with the expected featherbed, and the "kitchen," which included much of the same collection of utensils and iron pots which appeared in the Plummer house. Standing in the corner of the kitchen were a spade and a hoe, two implements useful only for chipping away ice and snow on the December day on which the inventory was taken, though apparently destined for another purpose come spring. With a garden, a cow, and three pigs, Hannah Grafton clearly had agricultural responsibilities, but these were performed in a strikingly different context than on the Plummer farm. The Grafton homelot was a single acre of land standing just a few feet from shoreline in the urban center of Salem.[13]

Joshua Grafton was a mariner like his father before him. His estate of £236 was modest, but he was still a young man and he had firm connections with the seafaring elite who were transforming the economy of Salem. When he died late in 1699, Hannah had three living children—Hannah, eight; Joshua, six; and Priscilla, who was just ten months.[14] This young family used their space quite differently than had the Plummers. The upstairs chambers which served as storage areas in the Newbury farmhouse were sleeping quarters here. In addition to the bed in the parlor and the cradle in the kitchen, there were two beds in each of the upstairs rooms. One of these, designated as "smaller," may have been used by young Joshua. It would be interesting to know whether the mother carried the two chamber pots kept in the parlor upstairs to the bedrooms at night or whether the children found their way in the dark to their parents' sides as necessity demanded. But adults were probably never far away. Because there are more bedsteads in the Grafton house than members of the immediate family, they may have shared their living quarters with unmarried relatives or servants.

Ten chairs and two stools furnished the kitchen, while no fewer than fifteen chairs, in two separate sets, crowded the parlor with its curtained bed. The presence of a punch bowl on a square table in the parlor reinforces the notion that sociability was an important value in this Salem household. Thirteen ounces of plate, a pair of gold buttons, and a silverheaded cane suggest a measure of luxury as well—all of this in stark contrast to the Plummers, who had only two chairs and a backless bench and no discernible ornamentation at all. Yet the Grafton house was only slightly more specialized than the Newbury farmhouse. It had no servants' quarters, no sharp segregation of public and private spaces, no real separation of sleeping, eating, and work. A cradle in the kitchen and a go-cart kept with the spinning wheels in the upstairs chamber show that little Priscilla was very much a part of this workaday world.

How then might the pattern of Hannah Grafton's work have differed from that of Beatrice Plummer? Certainly cooking remained central. Hannah's menus probably varied only slightly from those prepared in the Plummer kitchen, and her cooking techniques must have been identical. But one dramatic difference is apparent in the two inventories. The Grafton house contained no provisions worth listing on that December day when Isaac Foot and Samuel Willard appeared to take inventory. Hannah had brewing vessels, but no malt; sieves and a meal trough, but no grain; and a cow, but no cheese. What little milk her cow gave in winter probably went directly into the children's mugs. Perhaps she would continue to breastfeed Priscilla until spring brought a more secure supply. . . . Trade, rather than manufacturing or agriculture, was the dominant motif in her meal preparations.

In colonial New England most food went directly from processer or producer to consumer. Joshua may have purchased grain or flour from the mill near the shipbuilding center called Knocker's Hole, about a mile away from their house. Or Hannah may have eschewed bread-making altogether, walking or sending a servant the half-mile to Elizabeth Haskett's bakery near the North River. Fresh meat for the spits in her washhouse may have come from John Cromwell's slaughterhouse on Main Street near the Congregational meetinghouse, and soap for her washtubs from the soap-boiler farther up the street near the Quaker meetinghouse.[15] Salem, like other colonial towns, was laid out helter-skelter, with the residences of the wealthy interspersed with the small houses of carpenters or fishermen. Because there was no center of retail trade, assembling the ingredients of a dinner involved many transactions. Sugar, wine, and spice came by sea; fresh lamb, veal, eggs, butter, gooseberries, and parsnips came by land. Merchants retailed their goods in shops or warehouses near their wharves and houses. Farmers or their wives often hawked their produce door to door.[16] . . .

In such a setting, trading for food might require as much energy and skill as manufacturing or growing it. One key to success was simply knowing where to go. Keeping abreast of the arrival of ships in the harbor or establishing personal contact with just the right farmwife from nearby Salem village required time and attention. Equally important was the ability to evaluate the variety of unstandardized goods offered. An apparently sound cheese might teem with maggots when cut.[17] Since cash was scarce, a third necessity was the establishment of credit, a problem which ultimately devolved upon husbands. But petty haggling over direct exchanges was also a feature of this barter economy.

Hannah Grafton was involved in trade on more than one level. The "shop" attached to her house was not the all-purpose storage shed and workroom it seems to have been for Francis Plummer. It was a retail store, offering door locks, nails, hammers, gimlets, and other hardware as well as English cloth, pins, needles, and thread. As a mariner, Joshua Grafton may well have sailed the ship which brought these goods to Salem. In his absence, Hannah was not only a mother and a housewife but, like many other Salem women, a shopkeeper as well.

There is another highly visible activity in the Grafton inventory which was not immediately apparent in the Plummer's—care of clothing. Presumably, Beatrice Plummer washed occasionally, but she did not have a "wash-house." Hannah did. The arrangement of this unusual room is far from clear. On December 2, 1699, it contained two spits, two "bouldishes," a gridiron, and "other things." Whether those other things included washtubs, soap, or a beating staff is impossible to determine. . . .

But on any morning in December the wash-house could . . . have been hung with the family wash. Dark woolen jackets and petticoats went from year to year without seeing a kettle of suds, but linen shifts, aprons, shirts, and handkerchiefs required washing. Laundering might not have been a weekly affair in most colonial households, but it was a well-defined if infrequent necessity even for transient seamen and laborers. One can only speculate on its frequency in a house with a child under a year. When her baby was only a few months old, Hannah may have learned to hold little Priscilla over the chamber pot at frequent intervals, but in early infancy, tightly wrapped in her cradle, the baby could easily have used five dozen "clouts" and almost as many "belly bands" from one washing to another. Even with the use of a "pilch," a thick square of flannel securely bound over the diaper, blankets and coverlets occasionally needed sudsing as well.[18]

Joshua's shirts and Hannah's own aprons and shifts would require careful ironing. Hannah's "smoothing irons" fitted into their own heaters, which she filled with coals from the fire. As the embers waned and the irons cooled, she would have made frequent trips from her table to the hearth to the fire and back to the table again. At least two of these heavy instruments were essential. A dampened apron could dry and wrinkle while a single flatiron replenished its heat.

As frequent a task as washing was sewing. Joshua's coats and breeches went to a tailor, but his shirts were probably made at home. Certainly Hannah stitched and unstitched the tucks which altered Priscilla's simple gowns and petticoats as she grew. The little dresses which the baby trailed in her go-cart had once clothed her brother. Gender identity in childhood was less important in this society than economy of effort. It was not that boys were seen as identical to girls, only that all-purpose garments could be handed from one child to another regardless of sex, and dresses were more easily altered than breeches and more adaptable to diapering and toileting. At eight years of age little Hannah had probably begun to imitate her mother's even stitches, helping with the continual mending, altering, and knitting which kept this growing family clothed.[19]

In some ways the most interesting items in the Grafton inventory are the two spinning wheels kept in the upstairs chamber. Beatrice Plummer's wheel and reel had been key components in an intricate production chain. The Plummers had twenty-five sheep in the fold and a loom in the shed. The Graftons had neither. Children—not sheep—put wheels in Hannah's house. The mechanical nature of spinning made it a perfect occupation for women whose attention was engrossed by young children. This is one reason why the ownership of wheels in both York and Essex counties had a constancy over time unrelated to the ownership of sheep or looms. In the dozen inventories taken in urban Salem about the time of Joshua Grafton's death, the six non-spinners averaged one minor child each, the six spinners had almost four. Instruction at the wheel was part of the almost ritualistic preparation mothers offered their daughters.[20] Spinning was a useful craft, easily picked up, easily put down, and even small quantities of yarn could be knitted into caps, stockings, dishcloths, and mittens.

. . . a cluster of objects in the chamber over Hannah Grafton's kitchen suggests a fanciful but by no means improbable vignette. Imagine her gathered with her two daughters in this upstairs room on a New England winter's day. Little Priscilla navigates around the end of the bedstead in her go-cart while her mother sits at one spinning wheel and her sister at the other. Young Hannah is spinning "oakum," the coarsest and least expensive part of the flax. As her mother leans over to help her wind the uneven thread on the bobbin, she catches a troublesome scent from downstairs. Have the turnips caught on the bottom of the pot? Has the maid scorched Joshua's best shirt? Or has a family servant returned from the wharf and spread his wet clothes by the fire? Hastening down the narrow stairs to the kitchen, Hannah hears the shop bell ring. Just then little Priscilla, left upstairs with her sister, begins to cry. In such pivotal but unrecorded moments much of the history of women lies hidden.

The third inventory can be more quickly described.[21] Elias Wear of York, Maine, left an estate totaling £92, of which less than £7 was in household goods—including some old pewter, a pot, two bedsteads, bedding, one chest, and a box. Wear also owned a saddle, three guns, and a river craft called a gundalow. But his wealth, such as it was, consisted of land (£40) and livestock (£36). It is not just relative poverty which distinguished Elias Wear's inventory from that of Joshua Grafton or Francis Plummer. Every settlement in northern New England had men who owned only a pot, a bed, and a chest. Their children crowded in with them or slept on straw. These men and their sons provided some of the labor which harvested barley for farmers like Francis Plummer or stepped masts for mariners like Joshua Grafton. Their wives and their daughters carded wool or kneaded bread in other women's kitchens. No, Elias Wear was distinguished by a special sort of frontier poverty.

His father had come to northern New England in the 1640s, exploring and trading for furs as far inland in New Hampshire as Lake Winnipesaukee. By 1650 he had settled in York, a then hopeful site for establishing a patrimony. Forty years later he died in the York Massacre, an assault by French and Indians which virtually destroyed the town, bringing death or captivity to fully half of the inhabitants. Almost continuous warfare between 1689 and 1713 created prosperity for the merchant community of Portsmouth and Kittery, but it kept most of the inhabitants of outlying settlements in a state of impecunious insecurity.[22]

In 1696, established on a small homestead in the same neighborhood in which his father had been killed, Elias Wear married a young widow with the fitting name of Magdalen. When their first child was born "too soon," the couple found themselves in York County court owning a presentment for fornication. Although New England courts were still sentencing couples in similar circumstances to "nine stripes a piece upon the Naked back," most of the defendants, like the Wears, managed to pay the not inconsequential fine. The fifty-nine shillings which Elias and Magdalen pledged the court amounted to almost half of the total value of two steers. A presentment for fornication was expensive as well as inconvenient, but it did not carry a permanent onus. Within seven years of their conviction Elias was himself serving on the "Jury of Tryalls" for the county, while Magdalen had proved herself a dutiful and productive wife.[23]

Every other winter she gave birth, producing four sons—Elias, Jeremiah, John, and Joseph—in addition to the untimely Ruth. A sixth child, Mary, was just five months old when her father met his own death by Indians in August of 1707 while traveling between their Cape Neddick home and the more densely settled York village. Without the benefits of a cradle, a go-cart, a spinning wheel, or even a secure supply of grain, Magdalen raised these six children. Unfortunately, there is little in her inventory and nothing in any other record to document the specific strategies which she used, though the general circumstances of her life can be imagined.

Chopping and hauling for a local timber merchant, Elias could have filled Magdalen's porridge pot with grain shipped from the port of Salem or Boston. During the spring corn famine, an almost yearly occurrence on the

Maine frontier, she might have gone herself with other wives of her settlement to dig on the clam flats, hedging against the day when relief would come by sea.[24] Like Beatrice Plummer and Hannah Grafton, she would have spent some hours cooking, washing, hoeing cabbages, bargaining with neighbors, and, in season, herding and milking a cow. But poverty, short summers, and rough land also made gathering an essential part of her work. We may imagine her cutting pine splinters for lights and "cattails" and "silkgrass" for beds. Long before her small garden began to produce, she would have searched out a wild "sallet" in the nearby woods, in summer turning to streams and barrens for other delicacies congenial to English taste—eels, salmon, berries, and plums. She would have embarked on such excursions with caution, however, remembering the wives of nearby Exeter who took their children into the woods for strawberries "without any Guard" and narrowly avoided capture.[25] . . .

. . . The Wears probably lived in a single-story cottage which may or may not have been subdivided into more than one room. A loft above provided extra space for storage or sleeping. With the addition of a lean-to, this house could have sheltered animals as well as humans, especially in harsh weather or in periods of Indian alarm. Housing a pig or a calf in the next room would have simplified Magdalen's chores in the winter. If she managed to raise a few chickens, these too would have thrived better near the kitchen fire.[26]

Thus, penury erased the elaborate demarcation of "houses" and "yards" evident in yeoman inventories. It also blurred distinctions between the work of a husbandman and the work of his wife. At planting time and at harvest Magdalen Wear undoubtedly went into the fields to help Elias, taking her babies with her or leaving Ruth to watch them as best she could.[27] A century later an elderly Maine woman bragged that she "had dropped corn many a day with two governors: a judge in her arms and a general on her back."[28] None of the Wear children grew up to such prominence, but all six of them survived to adulthood and four married and founded families of their own. Six children did not prevent Magdalen Wear from remarrying within two years of her husband's death. Whatever her assets—a pleasant face, a strong back, or lifetime possession of £40 in land—she was soon wed to the unmarried son of a neighboring millowner.[29]

Magdalen Wear, Hannah Grafton, and Beatrice Plummer were all "typical" New England housewives of the period 1650–1750. Magdalen's iron pot represents the housekeeping minimum which often characterized frontier life. Hannah's punch bowl and her hardware shop exemplify both the commerce and the self-conscious civilization of coastal towns. Beatrice's brewing tubs and churn epitomize home manufacturing and agrarian self-sufficiency as they existed in established villages. Each type of housekeeping could be found somewhere in northern New England in any decade of the century. Yet these three women should not be placed in rigidly separate categories. Wealth, geography, occupation, and age determined that some women in any decade would be more heavily involved in one aspect of housekeeping than another, yet all three women shared a common vocation. Each understood the rhythms of the seasons, the technology of fire-building, the persistence of the daily demands of cooking, the complexity of home production, and the dexterity demanded from the often conflicting roles of housekeeper, mother, and wife.

The thing which distinguished these women from their counterparts in modern America was not, as some historians have suggested, that their work was essential to survival. "Survival," after all, is a minimal concept. Individual men and women have never needed each other for mere survival but for far more complex reasons, and women were essential in the seventeenth century for the very same reasons they are essential today—for the perpetuation of the race. . . . Nor was it the narrowness of their choices which really set them apart. Women in industrial cities have lived monotonous and confining lives, and they may have worked even harder than early American women. The really striking differences are social.

. . . [T]he lives of early American housewives were distinguished less by the tasks they performed than by forms of social organization which linked economic responsibilities to family responsibilities and which tied each woman's household to the larger world of her village or town.

For centuries the industrious Bathsheba has been pictured sitting at a spinning wheel—"She

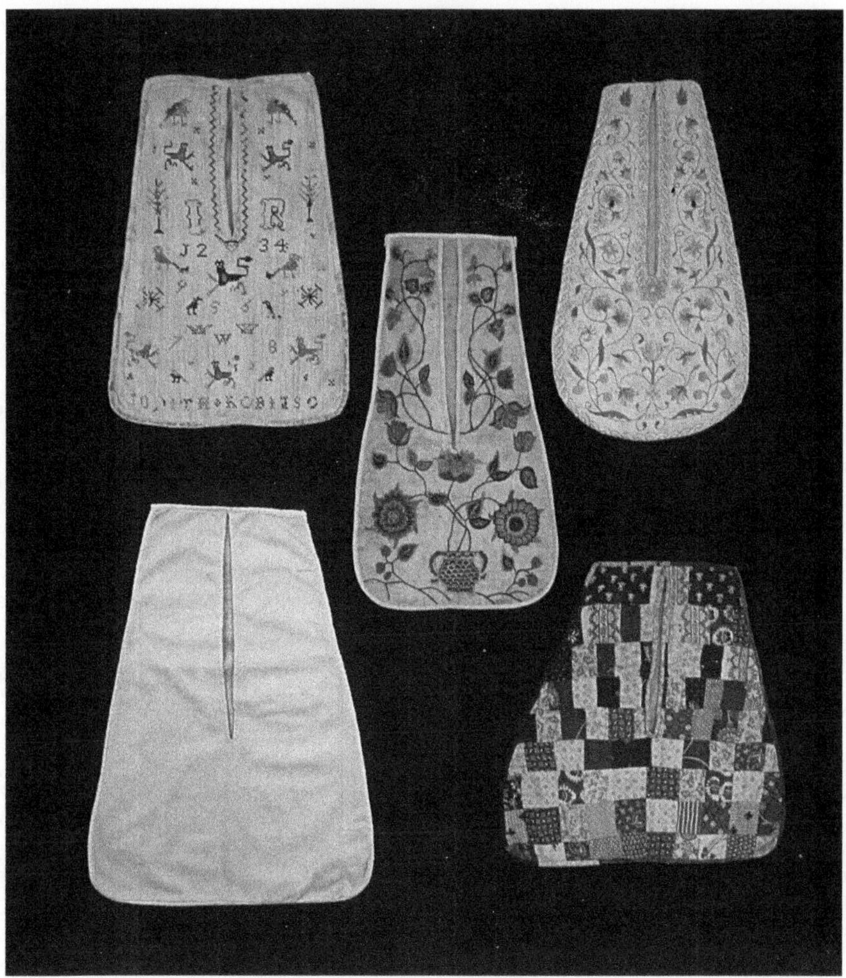

Laurel Thatcher Ulrich suggests that the pocket, not the spinning wheel, is the best icon for colonial European women. Pockets were tied around the waist, and hidden between the skirt and the petticoat. They were handy for carrying small objects on one's daily circuit. Women typically made their own pockets—sometimes in a plain style and sometimes embroidered or pieced. Here are five examples ranging in date from roughly the 1720s to the 1820s. Clockwise from top left: Pocket with lions, made by Judith Robinson, Pennsylvania, 1780–1820; Pocket with flowers and vase, New England, 1720–1750; Floral pocket, Britain, 1737; Pieced pocket, New York, probably Albany, ca. 1810; White pocket, New York, Scotia area, 1780–1820. (Courtesy, The Colonial Williamsburg Foundation.)

layeth her hands to the spindle, and her hands hold the distaff." Perhaps it is time to suggest a new icon for women's history. Certainly spinning was an important female craft in northern New England, linked not only to housework but to mothering, but it was one enterprise among many. Spinning wheels are such intriguing and picturesque objects, so resonant with antiquity, that they tend to obscure rather than clarify the nature of female economic life, making home production the essential element in early American huswifery and the era of industrialization the period of crucial change. Challenging the symbolism of the wheel not only undermines the popular stereotype, it questions a prevailing emphasis in women's history.

An alternate symbol might be the pocket. In early America a woman's pocket was not attached to her clothing, but tied around her waist with a string or tape. (When "Lucy Locket lost her pocket, Kitty Fisher found it.") Much better than a spinning wheel, this homely object symbolizes the obscurity, the versatility, and the personal nature of the housekeeping role. A woman sat at a wheel, but she carried her pocket with her from room to room, from house to yard, from yard to street. The items which it contained would shift from day to day and from year to year, but they would of necessity be small, easily lost, yet precious. A pocket could be a mended and patched pouch of plain homespun or a rich personal ornament boldly embroidered in crewel. It reflected the status as well as the skills of its owner. Whether it contained cellar keys or a paper of pins, a packet of seeds or a baby's bib, a hank of yarn, or a Testament, it characterized the social complexity as well as the demanding diversity of women's work.

Notes

1. [See] William H. Chafe, *Women and Equality: Changing Patterns in American Culture* (New York: Oxford University Press, 1977), p. 17; . . . and Nancy F. Cott, *The Bonds of Womanhood* (New Haven and London: Yale University Press, 1977), p. 21.

2. Unless otherwise noted, the information which follows comes from the Francis Plummer will and inventory, *The Probate Records of Essex County* (hereafter *EPR*) (Salem, Mass.: Essex Institute, 1916–1920), II:319–22.

3. Joshua Coffin, *A Sketch of the History of Newbury, Newburyport, and West Newbury* (Boston, 1845; Hampton, N.H.: Peter E. Randall, 1977), p. 315.

4. Abbott Lowell Cummings, *The Framed Houses of Massachusetts Bay, 1625–1725* (Cambridge, Mass., and London: Harvard University Press, 1979), pp. 29–32.

5. Darrett B. Rutman, *Husbandmen of Plymouth* (Boston: Beacon Press, 1967), pp. 10–11. . . . *Records and Files of the Quarterly Courts of Essex County, Massachusetts* (hereafter *ECR*) (Salem, Mass.: Essex Institute, 1911–1975), III:50; . . . Massachusetts Historical Society (hereafter MHS) *Collections,* 5th Ser., I:97; and Jay Allen Anderson, "A Solid Sufficiency: An Ethnography of Yeoman Foodways in Stuart England" (Ph.D. diss., University of Pennsylvania, 1971), pp. 171, 203–04, 265, 267, 268.

6. Cummings, *Framed Houses,* pp. 4, 120–22; . . . Jane Carson, *Colonial Virginia Cookery* (Charlottesville: University Press of Virginia, 1968), p. 104; . . .

7. Carson, *Colonial Virginia Cookery,* pp. 104–06.

8. Anderson, "Solid Sufficiency," pp. 63, 65, 118; . . . New Hampshire Historical Society *Collections,* V (1837), p. 225.

9. Anderson, "Solid Sufficiency," pp. 99–108, 120–32.

10. Sanborn C. Brown, *Wines and Beers of Old New England* (Hanover, N.H.: University Press of New England, 1978). . . .

11. ECR, IV:194–95, 297–98.

12. Unless otherwise noted, the information which follows comes from the Joshua Grafton will and inventory, Manuscript Probate Records, Essex County Probate Court, Salem, Mass. (hereafter Essex Probate), vol. CCCVII, pp. 58–59.

13. "Part of Salem in 1700," pocket map in James Duncan Phillips, *Salem in the Seventeenth Century* (Boston: Houghton Mifflin, 1933), H-6.

14. Sidney Perley, *The History of Salem, Massachusetts* (Salem, 1924), I:435, 441.

15. Phillips, *Salem in the Seventeenth Century,* pp. 328, 314, 318, 317; and James Duncan Phillips, *Salem in the Eighteenth Century* (Boston: Houghton Mifflin, 1937), pp. 20–21.

16. [See] Karen Friedman, "Victualling Colonial Boston," *Agricultural History* XLVII (July 1973): 189–205, and . . . Benjamin Coleman, *Some Reasons and Arguments Offered to the Good People of Boston and Adjacent Places, for the Setting Up Markets in Boston* (Boston, 1719), pp. 5–9.

17. . . . *The Salem Witchcraft Papers,* ed. Paul Boyer and Stephen Nissenbaum (New York: Da Capo Press, 1977), I:117–29.

18. [See] . . . e.g., *Province and Court Records of Maine* (hereafter *MPCR*) (Portland: Maine Historical Society, 1928–1975), IV:205–06; . . . and Essex Probate, CCCXXI:96. . . .

19. Susan Burrows Swan, *Plain and Fancy: American Women and Their Needlework,* 1700–1850 (New York: Holt, Rinehart and Winston, 1977), pp. 18–19, 34–38.

20. "Letter-Book of Samuel Sewall," MHS *Collections,* 6th Ser., I:19. . . .

21. Unless otherwise noted, the information which follows comes from the Elias Wear will and inventory, Manuscript Probate Records, York County Probate Court, Alfred, Me., . . . II:26.

22. Charles Clark, *The Eastern Frontier* (New York: Alfred A. Knopf, 1970), pp. 67–72.

23. *MPCR,* IV:91–92, 175, 176, 206, 263, 307, 310.

24. Maine Historical Society *Collections,* IX:58–59, 457, 566; MHS *Collections,* 6th Ser., I:126–65, 182–84, 186–89; . . .

25. Cotton Mather, *Decennium Luctuosum* (Boston, 1699), reprint Charles H. Lincoln, ed., *Narratives of the Indian Wars* (New York: Charles Scribner's Sons, 1913), pp. 266–67.

26. Richard M. Candee, "Wooden Buildings in Early Maine and New Hampshire: A Technological and Cultural History, 1600–1720" (Ph.D. diss., University of Pennsylvania, 1976), pp. 18, 42–48. . . .

27. . . . MHS *Proceedings* (1876), p. 129. Also see *ECR,* II:372–73, 22, 442; . . .

28. Sarah Orne Jewett, *The Old Town of Berwick* (Berwick, Me.: Old Berwick Historical Society, 1967), n.p., . . .

29. Sybil Noyes, Charles Thornton Libby, and Walter Goodwin Davis, *A Genealogical Dictionary of Maine and New Hampshire* (Portland, Me.: Southworth-Anthoensen Press, 1928), pp. 726, 729.

DOCUMENT

The Law of Domestic Relations: Marriage, Divorce, Dower

Examples from Colonial Connecticut

Marriage is an intimate relationship that is a result of private choice. But marriage is also a public act and has important social, political, and legal implications for both women and men. Indeed, deep into our own time, the law of marriage has shaped how men and women relate to each other and how they act in the world; when people want to change those relationships, they often begin by challenging the rules of marriage. If we want to understand the systems of gender in a culture, the rules of marriage are the place to begin.

Europeans were startled by the patterns of intimate relations among Native Americans. Although there were many differences among native cultures, marriage was generally situated within complex matrifocal systems of kinship in which husbands moved into the dwellings of the wife's kin; in which sisters and brothers remained close even in adulthood; and in which uncles and aunts could play important roles in the upbringing of nieces and nephews. In these kin networks, premarital sex, polygamy, marital separation, and divorce were not necessarily frowned upon, and there was often a space for a third gender or homosexual practice. For Europeans, such different rules of intimacy were signs of weakness and lack of civilization.

"Husband and wife are one person in law, that is, the very being or legal existence of the woman is suspended during the marriage, or at least is incorporated and consolidated into that of the husband; under whose wing, protection, and *cover*, she performs every thing; and is therefore called . . . *a feme covert.*" This understanding, known as *coverture,* was the foundation of the English law of domestic relations. When an Englishwoman married, her husband became the owner of all the movable things she possessed and of all the property or wages she might earn during their marriage. He also received the right to manage and collect the rents and profits on any real estate she owned; if they had a child, the child could not inherit the dead mother's lands until after the death of the father (For more details of the system of coverture, see Kerber, pp. 147–153.)

All colonies placed in their statutes a law regulating marriage. This step reflected a concern that marriage be celebrated publicly in order to guard against bigamy. Connecticut did not forbid interracial marriage, but many other colonies did. Laws also defined incest; note the large number of relatives prohibited from marrying in the statute from colonial Connecticut that follows. Over the course of the next century, the list of prohibited relatives was gradually reduced. Note that the Connecticut marriage law included a provision against cross-dressing.

An Act for Regulating and Orderly Celebrating of Marriages. . . . 1640, with revisions 1672, 1702

Forasmuch as the ordinance of marriage is honourable amongst all; so it is meet it should be orderly and decently solemnized:

Be it therefore enacted . . . That no persons shall be joined in marriage, before the purpose or intention of the parties proceeding therein, hath been sufficiently published in some public meeting or congregation on the Lord's day, or on some public fast, thanksgiving, or lecture-day, in the town, parish, or society where the parties, or either of them do ordinarily reside; or such purpose or intention be set up in fair writing, upon some post or door of their meeting-house, or near the same, in public view, there to stand so as it may be read, eight days before such marriage.

. . . And in order to prevent incestuous and unlawful marriages, be it further enacted, That no man shall marry . . . his grand-father's wife, wife's grandmother, father's sister, mother's sister, father's brother's wife, mother's brother's wife, wife's father's sister, wife's mother's sister, father's wife, wife's mother, daughter, wife's daughter, son's wife, sister, brother's wife, son's daughter, daughter's daughter, son's son's wife, daughter's son's wife, wife's son's daughter, wife's daughter's daughter, brother's daughter, sister's daughter, brother's son's wife, sister's son's wife.

And if any man shall hereafter marry, or have carnal copulation with any woman who is within the degrees before recited in this act, every such marriage shall be . . . null and void; And all children that shall hereafter be born of such incestuous marriage or copulation, shall be forever disabled to inherit by descent, or by being generally named in any deed or will, by father or mother. . . .

And that if any man shall wear women's apparel, or if any woman shall wear men's apparel, and be thereof duly convicted; such offenders shall be corporally punished or fined at the discretion of the county court, not exceeding *seventeen* dollars . . .

Early America was a divorceless society. South Carolina boasted that it granted no divorce until 1868. Most colonies followed the British practice of treating marriage as a moral obligation for life. Occasional special dissolutions of a marriage were granted by legislatures in response to individual petitions or by courts of equity, but these were separations from bed and board, which normally did not carry with them freedom to marry again.

The Puritan settlers of Massachusetts and Connecticut were unusual in treating marriage as a civil contract, which might be broken if its terms were not carried out. Connecticut enacted the earliest divorce law in the colonies. It made divorce available after a simple petition to the superior court under certain circumstances. People who did not fit these circumstances were able to present special petitions to the legislature.

Most petitioners for divorce in early America were women. What sorts of troubled marriages could women in colonial Connecticut exit by getting a judicial divorce? If you were a legislator, what grounds for divorce would you add? Scholars call the eighteenth and nineteenth centuries a period of "fault divorce." One spouse was seen as guilty of having breached the contract, while the other was innocent; thus, divorce due to incompatibility or irreconcilable differences was not available. Identify the language in the Connecticut statute that reflects this outlook.

An Act Relating to Bills of Divorce, 1667

Be it enacted . . . that no bill of divorce shall be granted to any man or woman, lawfully married, but in case of adultery, or fraudulent contract, or wilful desertion for three years with total neglect of duty; or in case of seven years absence of one party not heard of: after due enquiry is made, and the matter certified to the superior court, in which case the other party may be deemed and accounted single and unmarried. And in that case, and in all other cases aforementioned, a bill of divorce may be granted by the superior court to the aggrieved party; who may then lawfully marry or be married again.

Perhaps no statutes were more important to women in the first 250 years after settlement of the English colonies than the laws protecting their claims to dower. The "widow's dower" should be distinguished from the dowry a bride might bring with her into marriage. "The widow's dower" or the "widow's third" was the right of a widow to use one-third of the real estate that her husband held at the time of his death. She was also entitled to one-third of the personal property he had owned, after the debts were paid. It was an old English tradition that he might leave her more in his will, but he could not leave her less. If a man died without a will, the courts would ensure that his widow received her "thirds."

It is important to note that she only had the right to use the land and buildings. She might live on this property, rent it out, farm the land, and sell the produce. But she could not sell or bequeath it. If the real estate was simply the family home and her children were adults, she had a claim only to a *portion* of the house. (Occasionally husbands wrote that they intended the widow to have the "best" bedroom, a sign that they could not always trust their own sons to care well for their mothers.) After the widow's death, the property reverted to her husband's heirs, who normally would be their children, but in the event of a childless marriage was likely to revert to his brothers or nephews.

A contrasting situation existed in the community property jurisdictions, including Louisiana, New Mexico, and California (see pp. 26–27). There, "dotal" property, or dowry, was intended to help with the expenses of the marriage; the husband could manage this property and spend its income, but at the end of the marriage it was restored to the wife or her heirs, thus keeping it in her own family line of succession. She also kept her own "paraphernalia"—personal clothing and other items—which she could trade as a merchant without her husband's consent or dispose of in her own will.

In the Connecticut statute, which follows, note the provisions protecting the widow's interests. Normally colonial courts were scrupulous about assigning the widow's portion. Observe, however, that widows could not claim dower in "movable" property, which might represent a larger share of their husband's wealth than real estate. As time passed and the American economy became more complex, it became increasingly likely that a man's property would not be held in the form of land. If the land were heavily mortgaged, the widow's prior right to her "third" became a barrier to creditors seeking to collect their portion of a husband's debts. By the early nineteenth century, courts were losing their enthusiasm for protecting widows' thirds.

By the middle of the century, the married women's property acts began to reformulate a definition of the terms by which married women could claim their share of the property of wife and husband. But between 1790 and 1840, when the right to dower was more and more laxly enforced and the new married women's property acts had not yet been devised, married women were in a particularly vulnerable position. (See Keziah Kendall, pp. 238–240.)

An Act Concerning the Dowry of Widows, 1672

That there may be suitable provision made for the maintenance and comfortable support of widows, after the decease of their husbands, Be it enacted . . . that every married woman, living with her husband in this state, or absent elsewhere from him with his consent, or through his mere default, or by inevitable providence; or in case of divorce where she is the innocent party, that shall not before marriage be estated by way of jointure in some houses, lands, tenements or hereditaments for term of life . . . shall immediately upon, and after the death of her husband, have right, title and interest by way of dower, in and unto one third part of the real estate of her said deceased husband, in houses and lands which he stood possessed of in his own right, at the time of his decease, to be to her during her natural life: the remainder of the estate shall be disposed of according to the will of the deceased. . . .

And for the more easy, and speedy ascertaining such rights of dower, It is further enacted, That upon the death of any man possessed of any real estate . . . which his widow . . . hath a right of dower in, if the person, or persons that by law have a right to inherit said estate, do not within sixty days next after the death of such husband, by three sufficient freeholders of the same county; to be appointed by the judge of probate . . . and sworn for that purpose, set out, and ascertain such right of dower, that then such widow may make her complaint to the judge of probate . . . which judge shall decree, and order that such woman's dowry shall be set out, and ascertained by three sufficient freeholders of the county . . . and upon approbation thereof by said judge, such dower shall remain fixed and certain. . . .

And every widow so endowed . . . shall maintain all such houses, buildings, fences, and inclosures as shall be assigned, and set out to her for her dowry; and shall leave the same in good and sufficient repair.

MARY BETH NORTON

"Searchers again Assembled": Gender Distinctions in Seventeenth-Century America

The story that Mary Beth Norton tells is one that demonstrates that gender is a social as well as a biological construction. It is very rare that a newborn is hermaphrodite, or intersexed, displaying "some combination of 'female' and 'male' reproductive and sexual features." Later in life, hormonal abnormalities may mask clear distinctions between male and female. In our own time, "sexual reassignment" surgery is generally performed while an intersexed child is an infant; for adults, hormonal treatments, sometimes accompanied by surgery, can be used to clarify the gender identity of an individual.*

In one seventeenth-century Virginia community, the presence of a person who dressed as a man and also as a woman, who behaved alternately like a woman and like a man, and whose physical formation was vulnerable to multiple interpretations was deeply disconcerting. How did T. Hall's neighbors respond to gossip that this person's sex was unclear? What authority did women claim in assessing the situation? What authority did men claim? What does the struggle to mark T. Hall's gender identity suggest about the structure of community life and the roles of men and women?

On April 8, 1629, a person named Hall was brought before the General Court of the colony of Virginia. Hall was not formally charged with a crime, although witnesses alluded to a rumor about fornication. Yet Hall's case is one of the most remarkable to be found in the court records of any colony. If no crime was involved, why was Hall in court?

Hall had been reported to the authorities for one simple reason: people were confused about Hall's sexual identity. At times Hall dressed as a man; at other times, evidently, as a woman. What sex was this person? other colonists wanted to know. The vigor with which they pursued their concerns dramatically underscores the significance of gender distinctions in seventeenth-century Anglo-America. The case also provides excellent illustrations of the powerful role the community could play in individuals' lives and of the potential influence of ordinary folk, both men and women, on the official actions of colonial governments.

The Hall case offers compelling insights into the process of defining gender in early American society. Hall was an anomalous individual, and focusing on such anomalies can help to expose fundamental belief systems. Since in this case sex was difficult to determine, so too was gender identity. Persons of indeterminate sex, such as the subject of this discussion, pose perplexing questions for any society. The process through which the culture categorizes these people is both complex and revealing. The analysis here will examine the

*Suzanne Kessler, "The Medical Construction of Gender: Case Management of Intersexed Infants," *Signs: Journal of Women in Culture and Society* 16 (1990): 3–26.

Excerpted from the prologue to sec. 2 of *Founding Mothers and Fathers: Gendered Power and the Forming of American Society* by Mary Beth Norton (New York: Alfred A. Knopf, 1996). Reprinted by permission of the author and publisher. Notes have been edited and renumbered.

ways in which seventeenth-century Virginians attempted to come to grips with the problems presented to them by a sexually ambiguous person.[1] . . .

Describing my usage of personal pronouns and names is essential to the analysis that follows. The other historians who have dealt with the case have referred to Hall as "Thomas" and "he," as do the court records (with one significant exception). Yet the details of the case, including Hall's testimony, make such usage problematic. Therefore the practice here shall be the following: when Hall is acting as a female, the name "Thomasine" and the pronoun "she" will be used. Conversely, when Hall is acting as a male, "Thomas" and "he" are just as obviously called for. In moments of ambiguity or generalization (as now) "Hall," or the simple initial "T" will be employed (the latter as an ungendered pronoun).

Thomasine Hall was born "at or neere" the northeastern English city of Newcastle upon Tyne.[2] As the name suggests, Hall was christened and raised as a girl. At the age of twelve, Thomasine went to London to stay with her aunt, and she lived there for ten years. But in 1625 her brother was pressed into the army to serve in an expedition against Cadiz. Perhaps encouraged by her brother's experience (or perhaps taking his place after his death, for that expedition incurred many casualties), Hall subsequently adopted a new gender identity. Thomas told the court that he "Cut of[f] his heire and Changed his apparell into the fashion of man and went over as a souldier in the Isle of Ree being in the habit of a man."[3] Upon returning to Plymouth from army service in France, probably in the autumn of 1627, Hall resumed a feminine identity. Thomasine donned women's clothing and supported herself briefly by making "bone lace" and doing other needlework. That she did so suggests that Thomasine had been taught these valuable female skills by her aunt during her earlier sojourn in London.

Plymouth was one of the major points of embarkation for the American colonies, and Hall recounted that "shortly after" arriving in the city Thomasine learned that a ship was being made ready for a voyage to Virginia. Once again, Hall decided to become a man, so he put on men's clothing and sailed to the fledgling colony. Thomas was then approximately twenty-five years old, comparable in age to many of the immigrants to Virginia, and like most of his fellows he seems to have gone to the Chesapeake as an indentured servant.

By December, Hall was settled in Virginia, for on January 21, 1627/8, a man named Thomas Hall, living with John and Jane Tyos (T's master and mistress), was convicted along with them for receiving stolen goods from William Mills, a servant of one of their neighbors. According to the testimony, Hall and the Tyoses had encouraged Mills in a series of thefts that began before Christmas 1627. Some of the purloined items—which included tobacco, chickens, currants, a shirt, and several pairs of shoes—were still in the possession of Hall and the Tyoses at the time their house was searched by the authorities on January 14. Although Thomas Hall is a common name (indeed, John Tyos knew another Thomas Hall, who had arrived with him on the ship Bona Nova in 1620), a significant piece of evidence suggests that T and the man charged with this crime were one and the same. William Mills had difficulty carrying the currants, which he piled into his cap during his initial theft. Since that was clearly an unsatisfactory conveyance, when Mills was about to make a second foray after the desirable dried fruits he asked his accomplices to supply him with a better container. Thomas Hall testified that Jane Tyos then "did bring a napkin unto him and willed him to sowe it & make a bagg of it to carry currants." It is highly unlikely that an ordinary male servant would have had better seamstressing skills than his mistress, but Thomasine was an expert at such tasks.[4]

Although thus far in Hall's tale the chronology and the sequence of gender switches have been clear—for T specifically recounted the first part of the tale to the Virginia General Court, and the timing of the thefts and their prosecution is clearly described in court testimony—the next phase of the story must be pieced together from the muddled testimony of two witnesses and some logical surmises.

A key question not definitively answered in the records is: what happened to raise questions in people's minds about Hall's sexual identity? Two possibilities suggest themselves. One is that John and Jane Tyos, who obviously recognized that Hall had "feminine" skills shortly after T came to live with them, spoke of that fact to others, or perhaps visitors to their plantation observed Hall's activities and drew their own conclusions. Another possibility is that, after traveling to Virginia as a man, Hall reverted to the female clothing and role that T appears to have found more comfortable. The court records imply that Hall did choose to dress as a woman in Virginia, for Francis England, a witness, reported overhearing a conversation in which another man asked T directly: why do you wear women's clothing? T's reply—"I goe in weomans aparell to gett a bitt for my Catt"—is difficult to interpret and will be analyzed later. In any event, a Mr. Stacy (who cannot be further identified) seems to have first raised the issue of T's anomalous sexual character by asserting to other colonists that Hall was "as hee thought a man and woman." Just when Mr. Stacy made this statement is not clear, but he probably voiced his opinion about a year after T arrived in the colony.

In the aftermath of Mr. Stacy's statement, a significant incident occurred at the home of Nicholas Eyres, perhaps a relative of Robert Eyres, who had recently become John Tyos's partner. "Uppon [Mr Stacy's] report," three women—Alice Longe, Dorothy Rodes, and Barbara Hall—scrutinized Hall's body. Their action implied that T was at the time dressed as a woman, for women regularly searched other women's bodies (often at the direction of a court) to look for signs of illicit pregnancy or perhaps witchcraft. They never, however, performed the same function with respect to men—or anyone dressed like a man. Moreover, John Tyos both then and later told Dorothy Rodes that Hall was a woman. Even so, the female searchers, having examined Hall, declared that T was a man. As a result of the disagreement between Tyos and the women about T's sex, T was brought before the commander of the region, Captain Nathaniel Basse, for further examination.[5]

Questioned by Mr. Basse, T responded with a description of a unique anatomy with ambiguous physical characteristics. (The text of the testimony is mutilated, and the remaining fragments are too incomplete to provide a clear description of T's body.) Hall then refused to choose a gender identity, instead declaring that T was "both man and woeman." Captain Basse nevertheless decided that Hall was female and ordered T "to bee putt in weomans apparell"—thus implying that T was, at that moment at least, dressed as a man. The three women who had previously searched T's body were shaken by the official ruling that contradicted their own judgment; after being informed of the commander's decision, they reportedly "stood in doubte of what they had formerly affirmed."

John Tyos then sold Hall, now legally a maidservant named Thomasine, to John Atkins, who was present when Captain Basse questioned T. Atkins must have fully concurred with Mr. Basse's decision; surely he would not have purchased a female servant about whose sex he had any doubts. Yet on February 12, 1628/9, questions were again raised about T, for Alice Longe and her two friends went to Atkins's house to scrutinize Thomasine's body for a second time. They covertly examined her while she slept and once more decided that the servant was male. But Atkins, though summoned by the searchers to look at his maid's anatomy, was unable to do so, for Hall's "seeming to starre as if shee had beene awake" caused Atkins to leave without viewing her body.

The next Sunday, the three women returned with two additional female helpers.[6] On this occasion, the searchers had the active cooperation and participation of John Atkins, who ordered Thomasine to show her body to them. For a third time the women concluded that Hall was a man. Atkins thereupon ordered his servant to don men's clothing and informed Captain Basse of his decision.

By this time not only Hall but also everyone else was undoubtedly confused. Since Hall was now deemed to be male, the next curiosity-seekers to examine T's body were also male. One of them was Roger Rodes, probably the husband of Dorothy, who had joined in all the previous searches of Hall's body. Before forcefully throwing Thomas onto his back and checking his anatomy, Roger told Hall, "thou hast beene reported to be a woman and now thou art proved to bee a man, i will see what thou carriest." Like the female searchers before them, Roger and his associate Francis England concluded that T was male.

A rumor that Hall "did ly with a maid of Mr Richard Bennetts called greate Besse" must have added considerably to the uncertainty. Hall accused Alice Longe, one of the persistent female searchers, of spreading the tale. She denied the charge, blaming the slander instead on an unnamed male servant of John Tyos's. If the story was true, what did it imply about Hall's sexual identity? Whether Hall was male or female would obviously have a bearing on the interpretation of any relationship with Bennett's maid Bess. Clearly, Virginians now had reason to seek a firm resolution of the conflict. Since Captain Basse, the local commander, had been unable to find an acceptable solution, there was just one remaining alternative—referring the dilemma to the General Court.

That court, composed of the governor and council, was the highest judicial authority in the small colony. The judges heard from Hall and considered the sworn depositions of two male witnesses (Francis England and John Atkins), who described the events just outlined. Remarkably, the court accepted T's own self-definition and, although using the male personal pronoun, declared that Hall was "a man and a woman, that all the Inhabitants there may take notice thereof and that hee shall goe Clothed in mans apparell, only his head to bee attired in a Coyfe and Crosecloth with an Apron before him." Ordering Hall to post bond for good behavior until formally released from that obligation, the court also told Captain Basse to see that its directives were carried out. Since most court records for subsequent years have been lost (they were burned during the Civil War), it is impossible to trace Hall's story further.

What can this tale reveal about gender definitions and the role of the community in the formative years of American society? Six different but related issues emerge from the analysis of Hall's case.

First, the relationship of sexual characteristics and gender identity. All those who examined T, be they male or female, insisted T was male. Thus T's external sex organs resembled male genitals. Roger Rodes and Francis England, for example, pronounced Thomas "a perfect man" after they had "pulled out his members." Still, T informed Captain Basse "hee had not the use of the mans parte" and told John Atkins that "I have a peece of an hole" (a vulva). Since T was identified as a girl at birth, christened Thomasine, and raised accordingly, T probably fell into that category of human beings who appear female in infancy but at puberty develop what seem to be male genitalia. Such individuals were the subjects of many stories in early modern Europe, the most famous of which involved a French peasant girl, Marie, who suddenly developed male sex organs while chasing pigs when she was fifteen, and who in adulthood became a shepherd named Germain. It is not clear whether early Virginians were aware of such tales, but if they understood contemporary explanations of sexual difference, the narrative of Marie-Germain would not have surprised them. Women were viewed as inferior types of men, and their sexual organs were regarded as internal versions of male genitalia. In the best scientific understanding of the day, there was just one sex, and under certain circumstances women could turn into men.[7]

What, then, in the eyes of Virginia's English residents, constituted sufficient evidence of sexual identity? For the male and female searchers of T's body, genitalia that appeared to be normally masculine provided the answer. But that was not the only possible contemporary response to the question. Leaving aside for the moment the persons who saw T as a combination of male and female (they will be considered later), it is useful to focus on those who at different times indicated that they thought T was female. There were three such individuals, all of them men: Captain Nathaniel Basse, who ordered T to wear women's clothing after T had appeared before him; John Atkins, T's second master, who purchased Thomasine as a maidservant and referred to T as "shee" before bowing to the contrary opinion of the female searchers and changing the pronoun to "him"; and, most important of all, T's first master, John Tyos.

It is not clear from the trial record why Captain Basse directed T to dress as a woman, for T asserted a dual sexual identity in response to questioning and never claimed to be exclusively female. Perhaps the crucial fact was T's admission that "hee had not the use of the mans parte." Another possibility was that Mr. Basse interpreted T's anatomy as insufficiently masculine. As was already indicated, the partial physical description of T included in this portion of the record survives only in fragmentary form and so is impossible to interpret, especially in light of the certainty of all the searchers.

John Atkins acquired T as a servant after Captain Basse had issued his order, and he at first accepted Thomasine as a woman, referring to how "shee" seemed to awaken from sleep. Yet Atkins changed his mind about his servant after he and the five women subjected T's body to the most thorough examination described in the case record. It involved a physical search by the women, then questioning by Atkins, followed by an order from Atkins to Hall to "lye on his backe and shew" the "peece of an hole" that T claimed to have. When the women "did again find him to bee a man," Atkins issued the directive that contradicted Captain Basse's, ordering T to put on men's clothes. For Atkins, Hall's anatomy (which he saw with his own eyes) and the women's testimony were together decisive in overriding his initial belief that T was female, a belief presumably based at least in part on his presence at Mr. Basse's interrogation of T.

Unlike Atkins, John Tyos had purchased T as Thomas—a man. And for him the interpretive process was reversed. After just a brief acquaintance with Thomas, John and his wife learned that he had female skills. Approximately a year later Tyos "swore" to Dorothy Rodes that Hall "was a woman," a conclusion that contradicted the opinion of the female searchers. It also seemingly flew in the face of what must have been his own intimate knowledge of Hall's physical being. The lack of space in the small houses of the seventeenth-century Chesapeake is well known to scholars.[8] It is difficult to imagine that Tyos had never seen Hall's naked body—the same body that convinced searchers of both sexes that T was male. So why would Tyos insist that T was Thomasine, even to Dorothy Rodes, who forcefully asserted the contrary? The answer must lie not in T's sexual organs but in T's gender—that is, in the feminine skills and mannerisms that would have been exhibited by a person born, raised, and living as a female until reaching the age of twenty-two, and which would have been immediately evident to anyone who, like John Tyos, lived with T for any length of time.

Thus, for these colonists, sex had two possible determinants. One was physical: the nature of one's genitalia. The other was cultural: the character of one's knowledge and one's manner of behaving. The female and male searchers used the former criterion, John Tyos, the latter. John Atkins initially adopted the second approach, but later switched to the first. Nathaniel Basse may have agreed with Tyos, or he may have refused to interpret T's anatomy as unambiguously as did the searchers: it is not clear which. But it is clear that two quite distinct tests of sexual identity existed in tandem in early Virginia. One relied on physical characteristics, the other on learned, gendered behavior. On most occasions, of course, results of the two tests would accord with each other. Persons raised as females would physically appear to be females; persons raised as males would look like other males. Hall acted like a woman and physically resembled a man. Thus in T's case the results of the two independent criteria clashed, and that was the source of the confusion.

Second, the importance of clothing. Many of the key questions about Hall were couched in terms of what clothing T should wear, men's or women's. Captain Basse and John Atkins did not say to T, "you are a man," or "you are a woman," but instead issued instructions about what sort of apparel T was to put on. Likewise, although the General Court declared explicitly that Hall was both male and female, its decision also described the clothing T was to wear in specific detail. Why was clothing so important?

The answer lies in the fact that in the seventeenth century clothing was a crucial identifier of persons. Not only did males and females wear very different garb, but persons of different ranks also were expected to reveal their social status in their dress. In short, one was supposed to display visually one's sex and rank to everyone else in the society. Thus, ideally, new acquaintances would know how to categorize each other even before exchanging a word of greeting. In a fundamental sense, seventeenth-century people's identity was expressed in their apparel. Virginia never went so far as Massachusetts, which passed laws regulating what clothing people of different ranks could wear, but the Virginia colonists were clearly determined to uphold the same sorts of rules.[9]

Clothing, which was sharply distinguished by the sex of its wearer, served as a visual trope for gender. And gender was one of the two most basic determinants of role in the early modern world (the other was rank, which was never at issue in Hall's case—T was always a servant). People who wore skirts nurtured children; people who wore pants did not. People who wore aprons could take no role in governing the colony, whereas other people could, if they were of appropriate status. People who wore headdresses performed certain sorts of jobs in the household; people who wore hats did other types of jobs in the fields. It is hardly surprising, therefore, that Virginians had difficulty dealing with a person who sometimes dressed as a man and other times as a woman—and who, on different occasions, did both at the direction of superiors. Nor, in light of this context, is it surprising that decisions about T's sexual identity were stated in terms of clothing.[10]

Third, the absence of a sense of personal privacy throughout the proceedings. To a modern sensibility, two aspects of the case stand out. First, seventeenth-century Virginians appear to have had few hesitations about their right to examine the genitalia of another colonist, with or without official authorization from a court and regardless of whether that activity occurred forcibly, clandestinely, or openly. The physical examinations were nominally by same-sex individuals (women when T was thought to be female, men when T had been declared to be male), with one key exception: John Atkins joined the women in scrutinizing the body of his maidservant. A master's authority over the household, in other words, extended to the bodies of his dependents. If a master like Atkins chose to search the body of a subordinate of either sex, no barrier would stand in his way.

Second, Hall seems not to have objected to any of the intrusive searches of T's body nor to the intimate questioning to which T was subjected by Captain Basse and the General Court. Hall too appears to have assumed that T's sexual identity was a matter of concern for the community at large. Such an attitude on Hall's part was congruent with a society in which the existing minimal privacy rights were seen as accruing to households as a unit or perhaps to their heads alone. Subordinates like Hall neither expected nor received any right to privacy of any sort.

Fourth, the involvement of the community, especially women, in the process of determining sexual identity. One of the most significant aspects of Hall's story is the initiative taken throughout by Hall's fellow colonists. They not only brought their doubts about Hall's sex to the attention of the authorities, they also refused to accept Captain Basse's determination that Hall was female. Both men and women joined in the effort to convince Virginia's leaders that T was male. Nearly uniformly rejecting T's self-characterization as "both" (the only exception outside the General Court being Mr. Stacy), Virginians insisted that Hall had to be either female or male, with most favoring the latter definition. They wanted a sexual category into which to fit T, and they did not hesitate to express their opinions about which category was the more appropriate.

Women in particular were active in this regard. Three times groups of women scrutinized T's body, whereas a group of men did so only once. After each examination, women rejected T as one of their number. Because of the vigorous and persistent efforts of female Virginians, Hall was deprived of the possibility of adopting unambiguously the role with which T seemed most comfortable, that of Thomasine. Here Hall's physical characteristics determined the outcome. Accustomed to searching the bodies of other females, women thought T did not physically qualify as feminine—regardless of the gendered skills T possessed—and they repeatedly asserted that to any man who would listen. For them, T's anatomy (sex) was more important than T's feminine qualities (gender).

Male opinion, on the other hand, was divided. The three male searchers of T's body—Roger Rodes, Francis England, and John Atkins—agreed with the women's conclusion. Other men were not so sure. John Tyos and Nathaniel Basse thought T more appropriately classified as a woman, while Mr. Stacy and the members of the General Court said T displayed aspects of both sexes. It seems plausible to infer from their lack of agreement about T's sex that men as a group were not entirely certain about what criteria to apply to create the categories "male" and "female." Some relied on physical appearance, others on behavior.

Moreover, the complacency of the male searchers can be interpreted as quite remarkable. They failed to police the boundaries of their sex with the same militance as did women. That T, if a man, was a very unusual sort of man indeed did not seem to bother Rodes, Atkins, and England. For them, T's physical resemblance to other men was adequate evidence of masculinity, despite their knowledge of T's feminine skills and occasional feminine dress. That opinion was, however, in the end overridden by the doubts of higher-ranking men on the General Court, who were not so willing to overlook T's peculiarities.

Fifth, the relationship among sex, gender, and sexuality. Twice, and in quite different ways, the case record raises issues of sexuality rather than of biological sex or of gendered behavior. Both references have been alluded to briefly: the rumor of Thomas's having committed fornication with "greate Besse," and T's explanation for wearing women's clothing—"to gett a bitt for my Catt."

A judgment about T's body would imply a judgment about T's sexuality as well. Yet was it possible to reach a definitive conclusion about T's sexuality? If T were Thomas, then he could potentially be guilty of fornicating with the maidservant Bess; if T were Thomasine, then being in the same bed with Bess might mean nothing—or it could imply "unnatural" acts, the sort of same-sex coupling universally condemned when it occurred between men. The rumor about Bess, which for an ordinary male servant might have led to a fistfight (with the supposed slanderer, Tyos's servant), a defamation suit, or a fornication presentment, thus raised perplexing questions because of T's ambiguous sexual identity, questions that had to be resolved in court.[11]

T's phrase "to gett a bitt for my Catt," as reported by Francis England, was even more troubling. What did it mean, and was that meaning evident to England and the members of the General Court? As an explanation for wearing female apparel, it could have been straightforward and innocent. One historian reads it literally, as indicating that Hall wore women's clothing to beg scraps for a pet cat. Hall might also have been saying that because T's skills were feminine, dressing as a woman was the best way for T to earn a living, "to get a bit (morsel) to eat." But some scholars have read erotic connotations into the statement. Could T, speaking as a man, have been saying that wearing women's clothing allowed T to get close to women, to—in modern slang—"get a piece of pussy" by masquerading as a female?[12]

There is another more likely and even more intriguing erotic possibility. Since Hall had served in the English army on an expedition to France, T could well have learned a contemporary French slang phrase—"pour avoir une bite pour mon chat"—or, crudely put in English, "to get a penis for my cunt." Translating the key words literally into English equivalents (bite=bit, chat=cat) rather than into their metaphorical meanings produced an answer that was probably as opaque and confusing to seventeenth-century Virginians as it has proved to be to subsequent historians.[13] Since much of Francis England's testimony (with the exception of his report of this statement and the account of his and Roger Rodes's examination of T's anatomy) duplicated John Atkins's deposition, England could have been called as a witness primarily to repeat such a mysterious conversation to the court.

If T was indeed employing a deliberately misleading Anglicized version of contemporary French slang, as appears probable, two conclusions are warranted. First, the response confirms T's predominantly feminine gender, for it describes sexual intercourse from a woman's perspective. In light of the shortage of women in early Virginia, it moreover would have accurately represented T's experience: donning women's garb unquestionably opened sexual possibilities to Thomasine that Thomas lacked. Second, at the same time, Hall was playing with T's listeners, answering the question about wearing women's apparel truthfully, but in such an obscure way that it was unlikely anyone would comprehend T's meaning. In other words, Hall was having a private joke at the expense of the formal and informal publics in the colony. Hall's sly reply thus discloses a mischievous aspect of T's character otherwise hidden by the flat prose of the legal record.

Sixth, the court's decision. At first glance, the most surprising aspect of the case is the General Court's acceptance of Hall's self-definition as both man and woman. By specifying that T's basic apparel should be masculine, but with feminine signs—the apron and the coif and cross-cloth, a headdress commonly worn by women at the time—Virginia officials formally recognized that Hall contained elements of both sexes. The elite men who sat as judges thereby demonstrated their ability to transcend the dichotomous sexual categories that determined the thinking of ordinary Virginians. But their superficially astonishing verdict becomes explicable when the judges' options are analyzed in terms of contemporary understandings of sex and gender.

First, consider T's sexual identity. Could the court have declared Hall to be female? That alternative was effectively foreclosed. Women had repeatedly scrutinized T's anatomy and had consistently concluded that T was male. Their initial determination that T was a man (in the wake of Mr. Stacy's comment that T was both) first brought the question before Captain Basse. Subsequently, their adamant rejection of Captain Basse's contrary opinion and their ability to convince John Atkins that they were correct, coupled with the similar assessment reached by two men, were the key elements forcing the General Court to consider the case. A small community could not tolerate a situation in which groups of men and women alternately stripped and searched the body of one of its residents, or in which the decisions of the local commander were so openly disobeyed. Declaring T to be female was impossible; ordinary Virginians of both sexes would not accept such a verdict.

Yet, at the same time, could anyone assert unconditionally that Hall was sexually a man? Francis England, Roger Rodes, John Atkins, and the five female searchers thought so, on the basis of anatomy; but John Tyos, who was probably better acquainted with T than anyone else, declared unequivocally that Hall was a woman. And T had testified about not having "the use of the mans parte." Hall, in other words, revealed that although T had what appeared to be male genitalia, T did not function sexually as a man and presumably could not have an erection. To Captain Basse and the members of the General Court, that meant that (whatever T's physical description) Hall would not be able to father children or be a proper husband to a wife.

. . . The ability to impregnate a woman was a key indicator of manhood in seventeenth-century Anglo-America. Childless men were the objects of gossip, and impotence served as adequate grounds for divorce. A person who could not father a child was by that criterion alone an unsatisfactory male. T had admitted being incapable of male orgasm. Given that admitted physical incapacity and its implications, declaring Hall to be a man was as impossible as declaring T to be a woman.[14]

Second, consider T's gender identity. In seventeenth-century Anglo-America, as in all other known societies, sexual characteristics carried with them gendered consequences. In Hall's life history those consequences were especially evident, because what T did and how T did it were deeply affected by whether T chose to be Thomas or Thomasine.

Whenever Hall traveled far from home, to France in the army or to Virginia, T became Thomas. Men had much more freedom of movement than did women. Unlike other persons raised as females, Hall's unusual anatomy gave T the opportunity to live as a male when there was an advantage to doing so. Even though T seemed more comfortable being Thomasine—to judge by frequent reversions to that role—the option of becoming Thomas must have been a welcome one. It permitted Hall to escape the normal strictures that governed early modern English women's lives and allowed T to pursue a more adventurous lifestyle.[15]

Thus whether T chose to be male or female made a great difference in T's life. As Thomas, Hall joined the army and emigrated to the colonies; as Thomasine, Hall lived quietly in London with an aunt, did fancy needlework in Plymouth, and presumably performed tasks normally assigned to women in Virginia. T's most highly developed skills were feminine ones, so T was undoubtedly more expert at and familiar with "women's work" in general, not just seamstressing.

It was, indeed, Hall's feminine skills that convinced some men that T was female; and those qualities, coupled with Hall's physical appearance, must have combined to lead to the court's decision. T's gender was feminine but T's sex seemed to be masculine—with the crucial exception of sexual functioning. Given T's sexual incapacity, all indications pointed to a feminine identity—to Thomasine. But Virginia women's refusal to accept T as Thomasine precluded that verdict. On the other hand, the judges could not declare a person to be male who had admitted to Captain Basse an inability to consummate a marriage. Ordinary men might possibly make a decision on the basis of physical appearance alone, but the members of the General Court had a responsibility to maintain the wider social order. If they said Hall was a man, then Thomas theoretically could marry and become a household head once his term of service was complete. That alternative was simply not acceptable for a person of T's description.

So, considering sex (incompletely masculine) and gender (primarily feminine), the Virginia General Court's solution to the dilemma posed by Hall was to create a unique category that combined sex and gender for T alone. Unable to fit Hall into the standard male/female dichotomy, the judges preferred to develop a singular definition that enshrined T's dual identity by prescribing clothing that simultaneously carried conflicting messages.

The court's decision to make Hall unique in terms of clothing—and thus gender identity—did not assist the community in classifying or dealing with T. After the verdict, Virginians were forced to cope with someone who by official sanction straddled the dichotomous roles of male and female. By court order, Hall was now a dual-sexed person. T's identity had no counterpart or precedent; paradoxically, a society in which gender—the outward manifestation of sex—served as a fundamental dividing line had formally designated a person as belonging to both sexes. Yet at the same time it was precisely because gender was so basic a concern to seventeenth-century society that no other solution was possible.

Hall's life after the court verdict must have been lonely. Marked as T was by unique clothing, unable to adopt the gender switches that had previously given T unparalleled flexibility in choosing a way of life, Hall must have had a very difficult time. T, like other publicly marked deviants—persons branded for theft or adultery or mutilated for perjury or forgery—was perhaps the target of insults or assaults. The verdict in T's case, in its insistence that T be constantly clothed as both sexes rather than alternating between them, was therefore harsh, though it nominally accorded with T's own self-definition. Hall's identity as "both" allowed movement back and forth across gender lines. The court's verdict had quite a different meaning, insisting not on the either/or sexual ambiguity T had employed to such great advantage, but rather on a definition of "both" that required duality and allowed for no flexibility.

It is essential to re-emphasize here what necessitated this unusual ending to a remarkable case: the opinions and actions of the female neighbors of John Tyos and John Atkins. Captain Nathaniel Basse, confronted with basically the same information that the General Court later considered, concluded that Hall should be dressed and treated as a woman. In a sexual belief system that hypothesized that women were inferior men, any inferior man—that is, one who could not function adequately in sexual terms—was a woman. Thus, charged the women at an Accomack cow pen in 1637, John Waltham "hade his Mounthly Courses as Women have" because his wife had not become pregnant.[16] Undoubtedly the General Court's first impulse would have been the same as Captain Basse's: to declare that T, an inferior man, was female and should wear women's clothing. But Virginia women had already demonstrated forcefully that they would not accept such a verdict. Hall's fate therefore was determined as much by a decision reached by ordinary women as it was by a verdict formally rendered by the elite men who served on the General Court.

Notes

1. Anthropologists have been in the forefront of the investigation of the various relationships of sex and gender. A good introduction to such work is Sherry Ortner and Harriet Whitehead, eds., *Sexual Meanings: The Cultural Construction of Gender and Sexuality* (New York: Cambridge University Press, 1981).... For an account of how contemporary American society handles sexually ambiguous babies at birth, see Suzanne J. Kessler, "The Medical Construction of Gender: Case Management of Intersexed Infants," *Signs*, XVI (1990), 3–26.

2. Unless otherwise indicated, all quotations and details in the account that follows are taken from the record in the case, *Va Ct Recs*, 194–95.

3. The expedition in which Thomas took part was an ill-fated English attack on the Isle de Ré during the summer of 1627. The troops who futilely tried to relieve the French Protestants besieged in the city of La Rochelle embarked on July 10, 1627; most of them returned to Plymouth in early November.

4. *Va Ct Recs*, 159, 162–64 (quotation 163). Yet it is possible that the Thomas Hall in this case was the other man, the one who came to Virginia in 1620. (For him, see Virginia M. Meyer and John F. Dorman, eds., *Adventurers of Purse and Person Virginia 1607–1624/5*, 3d ed. [Richmond: Order of First Families of Virginia, 1987]. The Virginia muster of 1624/5 [ibid., 42] lists Thomas Hall and John Tyos as residents of George Sandys's plantation in James City....

5. Little can be discovered about the three women....

6. The two newcomers were the wife of Allen Kinaston and the wife of Ambrose Griffen....

7. The best discussion of the one-sex model of humanity and its implications is Thomas Laqueur, *Making Sex: Body and Gender from the Greeks to Freud* (Cambridge, Mass.: Harvard University Press, 1990). See 126–30 for an analysis of Marie-Germain....

8. See Lois Green Carr et al., *Robert Cole's World: Agriculture & Society in Early Maryland* (Chapel Hill: University of North Carolina Press, 1991), 90–114, on "the standard of life" in the early Chesapeake.

9. See *Mass Col Recs,* IV, pt 1, 60–61, IV, pt 2, 41–42. . . .

10. Laqueur observes, in *Making Sex,* 124–25, that "in the absence of a purportedly stable system of two sexes, strict sumptuary laws of the body attempted to stabilize gender—woman as woman and man as man—and punishments for transgression were quite severe." A relevant recent study is Marjorie Garber, *Vested Interests: Cross-Dressing and Cultural Anxiety* (New York: Routledge, 1991).

11. A good general discussion of the colonists' attitudes toward sexuality is John D'Emilio and Estelle B. Freedman, *Intimate Matters: A History of Sexuality in America* (New York: Harper & Row, 1988), 1–52, especially (on the regulation of deviance) 27–38.

12. Brown interprets the statement literally in her "Gender and the Genesis of Race and Class System," I, 88. The suggestion that the phrase might have meant "earning a living" is mine, developed after consulting the *OED* (q.v. "bit"). Katz speculates that T's phrase had the erotic meaning suggested here, though he recognizes that such an interpretation is problematic (*Gay/Lesbian Almanac,* 72).

13. I owe the identification of the probable French origin of this phrase to Marina Warner and, through her, to Julian Barnes, whom she consulted (personal communication, 1993). My colleague Steven Kaplan, a specialist in the history of early modern France (and scholars he consulted in Paris), confirmed that "bite" and "chat" were used thus in the late sixteenth century and that the interpretation appears plausible.

14. On the importance of marital sexuality in the colonies: D'Emilio and Freedman, *Intimate Matters,* 16–27.

15. See, on this point, Rudolf M. Dekker and Lotte C. van de Pol, *The Tradition of Female Transvestism in Early Modern Europe* (London: Macmillan, 1989).

16. Susie M. Ames, ed., *County Court Records of Accomack-Northampton, Virginia, 1632–1640* (American Legal Records, VII), (Washington, D.C., 1954), p. 85.

DOCUMENT

The Trial of Anne Hutchinson, 1637

"What law have I broken?"

In 1989, in a solemn ceremony soaked with irony and bitter humor, the leaders of the Newport Rhode Island Congregational Church announced that injustice had been done more than 350 years before when Anne Hutchinson had been expelled from Boston's Congregational Church for blasphemy and perjury. The minister who took the initiative, and who coincidentally bore the same name as the John Wilson who had read the formal excommunication in the seventeenth century, thought that the Hutchinson affair raised questions that remained central to religion in the present: questions "of spiritual freedom, the role of women in the church, the issue of individual freedom versus being part of a covenant community, and the church-state issue." In a public ceremony, the president of the Rhode Island Conference of the United Church of Christ burned a copy of the writ of excommunication.*

The Antinomian heresy of 1637–38 threw the Puritan colony of Massachusetts Bay into turmoil for years and forced its leaders to reconsider the nature of their experiment. Antinomians placed greater emphasis on religious feeling than did orthodox Puritans. They tended to be suspicious (*anti*) of law (*nomos*) or formal rules and came close to asserting that individuals had access to direct revelation from the Holy Spirit. They criticized ministers who seemed to argue that it was possible to earn salvation by good deeds rather than leaving it to God freely to decide who was to be saved by their faith, a distinction between the "covenant of works" and a "covenant of faith" which they thought separated authentic Puritans from ones who remained too close to the Anglican Church.

One such Antinomian critic, clergyman John Wheelwright (Anne Hutchinson's brother-in-law) was tried in early 1637 for giving a controversial sermon, found guilty of sedition, and banished. The close relationship between church and state in early New England meant that such challenges to the majority's theological views were interpreted as threatening to established authority of all kinds.

One leading dissenter was Anne Hutchinson, a high-status, well-educated woman in her mid-forties who had migrated to the colony with her merchant husband in 1634, four years after its founding, and who commanded great

*Madeline Pecora Nugent, "Apologizing to Anne Hutchinson," *Christian Century* 106 (Mar. 22, 1989): 304–5.

respect for her competence as a midwife. At meetings held in her home after Sunday church services, she summarized, discussed, and criticized ministers' sermons. Initially attended by five or six women, the meetings became very popular; soon Hutchinson was holding separate gatherings for men and women. The women who followed Hutchinson were often those who respected her medical knowledge and shared her theological ideas. The men who attended were often those who were critical of the colony's leadership on political and economic as well as religious grounds. Tensions were high in Massachusetts Bay through 1636 and 1637 as colonists violently attacked the Pequot Indians, decimating the tribe and capturing and enslaving the women and children. In a context in which pastor John Wilson linked the destruction of "barbarous Indians" with God's will, religious and political dissent seemed to merge easily. Rumor spread that criticism of the governor and council, the majority of ministers, and the Pequot War had been voiced in the Hutchinsons' house. This led to Anne's being grilled, first by a convocation of ministers and then, in November 1637, by the magistrates and legislators of the colony, in a court held in Newtown (now Cambridge).

The proceedings were not a trial in the contemporary sense with due process safeguards; instead they followed the format of the early modern magisterial examination, an inquisition without a jury. Hutchinson, who was pregnant, had no lawyer. Her trial was conducted by the governor of the colony, John Winthrop. (His house was directly across the path from the Hutchinsons' dwelling; he could not have avoided seeing the people coming and going to her meetings.) Winthrop was joined in his questioning by the deputy governor and other members of the legislature (called the General Court). Only very late in the interrogation did Anne make an incautious statement—that God had directly revealed things to her—which provided her judges with a rationale to convict her of heresy and sentence her banishment from the colony.

Hutchinson's secular trial was followed by a disciplinary hearing in the Boston church to which she belonged. This second trial covered much of the same ground as the first; one of the ministers present spoke for many of the men in the room when he declared: "You have stept out of your place, you have rather bine a Husband than a Wife and a preacher than a Hearer; and a Magistrate than a Subject." After the members voted to excommunicate her, pastor Wilson pronounced the judgment: "Forasmuch as you, Mistress Hutchinson, have highly transgressed and offended and forasmuch as you have so many ways troubled the Church with your Errors and have drawn away many a poor soul and have upheld your Revelations: . . . I command you . . . as a Leper to withdraw your self out of the Congregation." At this, Hutchinson rose, walked to the meetinghouse door, turned, and spoke directly to her accusers: "The lord judgeth not as man judgeth, better to be cast out of the Church then [than] to deny Christ."

After Hutchinson was exiled, at least ten more women were banished or excommunicated for being outspoken. Thus, a clear message was sent that explicit dissent by women was not to be tolerated in the Massachusetts Bay Colony. In Winthrop's memoir of the events, published in 1644, miscarriages suffered by Hutchinson and her closest colleague, Mary Dyer, were interpreted as evidence of God's "displeasure against their opinions and practices, as clearly as if he had pointed with his finger, in causing the two fomenting women in the time of the height of the Opinions to produce out of their wombs, as before they had out of their braines, such monstrous births as no Chronicle . . . hardly ever recorded the like."*

Hutchinson and her husband fled to Rhode Island, a colony with a policy of religious toleration. Several years later, they moved to Dutch territory north of what is now New York City. Widowed, Anne Hutchinson died in an Indian raid on her settlement, in 1643.

In reading this excerpt from Anne Hutchinson's 1637 trial, note the extent to which criticism of her religious and political behavior merges with the complaint that she is challenging gender roles. It will help to know that by "rule," Protestants of the era meant a biblical passage that stipulated how Christians should behave. What strategies did Hutchinson use to defend her actions and challenge the proceedings? Which points of the dialogue best reveal colonial leaders' fear of independent women?

NOVEMBER 1637

The Examination of Mrs. Ann Hutchinson at the Court at Newtown

Mr. Winthrop, governor. Mrs. Hutchinson, you are called here as one of those that have troubled the peace of the commonwealth and the churches here; you are known to be a woman that hath had a great share in the promoting and divulging of those opinions that are causes of this trouble, and to be nearly joined not only in affinity and affection with some of those the court had taken notice of and passed censure upon, but you have spoken divers things as we have been informed very prejudicial to the honour of the churches and ministers thereof, and you have maintained a meeting and an assembly in your house that hath been condemned by the general assembly as a thing not tolerable nor comely in the sight of God nor fitting for your sex, and notwith standing that was cried down you have continued the same, therefore we have thought good to send for you to understand how things are, that if you be in an erroneous way we may reduce you that so you may become a profitable member here among us, otherwise (if you be obstinate in your course that then the court may take such course that you may trouble us no further) therefore I would intreat you to express whether you do not hold and assent in practice to those opinions and factions that have been handled in court already, that is to say, whether you do not justify Mr. Wheelwright's sermon and the petition.[1]

Mrs. Hutchinson. I am called here to answer before you but I hear no things laid to my charge.

Gov. I have told you some already and more I can tell you.

Mrs. H. Name one, Sir.

Gov. Have I not named some already?

Mrs. H. What have I said or done?

Gov. Why for your doings, this you did harbour and countenance those that are parties in this faction that you have heard of.

Mrs. H. That's matter of conscience, Sir.

Gov. Your conscience you must keep or it must be kept for you. . . . Say that one brother should commit felony or treason and come to his other brother's house, if he knows him guilty and conceals him he is guilty of the same. It is his conscience to entertain him, but if his conscience comes into act in giving countenance and entertainment to him that hath broken the law he is guilty too. So if you do countenance those that are transgressors of the law you are in the same fact.

Mrs. H. What law do they transgress?

Gov. The law of God and of the state.

Mrs. H. In what particular?

Gov. Why in this among the rest, whereas the Lord doth say honour thy father and thy mother.

Mrs. H. Ey Sir in the Lord.

Gov. This honour you have broke in giving countenance to them. . . .

Mrs. H. What law have I broken?

*Sandra F. VanBurkleo, "'To Bee Rooted Out of Her Station': The Ordeal of Anne Hutchinson," in *American Political Trials*, rev. ed., ed. Michael R. Belknap (Westport, Conn.: Greenwood Press, 1994), pp. 1–24; *The Antinomian Controversy, 1636–1638: A Documentary History*, ed. David D. Hall (quotes on pp. 382–83, 388, 214); and *Winthrop's Journal, "History of New England": 1630–1649*, vol. 1, ed. James Kendall Hosmer (New York: Charles Scribner's Sons, 1908), p. 251.

Gov. Why the fifth commandment.

Mrs. H. I deny that for [Mr. Wheelwright] saith in the Lord.

Gov. You have joined with them in the faction.

Mrs. H. In what faction have I joined with them?

Gov. In presenting the petition . . .

Mrs. H. But I had not my hand to the petition.

Gov. You have councelled them.

Mrs. H. Wherein?

Gov. Why in entertaining them.

Mrs. H. What breach of law is that Sir?

Gov. Why dishonouring of parents.

Mrs. H. But put the case Sir that I do fear the Lord and my parents, may not I entertain them that fear the Lord because my parents will not give me leave?

Gov. If they be the fathers of the commonwealth, and they of another religion, if you entertain them then you dishonour your parents and are justly punishable.

Mrs. H. If I entertain them, as they have dishonoured their parents I do.

Gov. No but you by countenancing them above others put honor upon them.

Mrs. H. I may put honor upon them as the children of God and as they do honor the Lord.

Gov. We do not mean to discourse with those of your sex but only this; you do adhere unto them and do endeavour to set forward this faction and so you do dishonour us.

Mrs. H. I do acknowledge no such thing neither do I think that I ever put any dishonour upon you.

Gov. Why do you keep such a meeting at your house as you do every week upon a set day?

Mrs. H. It is lawful for me so to do, as it is all your practices and can you find a warrant for yourself and condemn me for the same thing? [I]t was in practice before I came therefore I was not the first.

Gov. For this, that you appeal to our practice you need no confutation. If your meeting had answered to the former it had not been offensive, but I will say that there was no meeting of women alone, but your meeting is of another sort for there are sometimes men among you.

Mrs. H. There was never any man with us.

Gov. Well, admit there was no man at your meeting and that you was sorry for it, there is no warrant for your doings, and by what warrant do you continue such a course?

Mrs. H. I conceive there lyes a clear rule in Titus, that the elder women should instruct the younger[2] and then I must have a time wherein I must do it.

Gov. All this I grant you, I grant you a time for it, but what is this to the purpose that you Mrs. Hutchinson must call a company together from their callings to come to be taught of you?

Mrs. H. Will it please you to answer me this and to give me a rule for then I will willingly submit to any truth. If any come to my house to be instructed in the ways of God what rule have I to put them away?

Gov. But suppose that a hundred men come unto you to be instructed will you forbear to instruct them?

Mrs. H. As far as I conceive I cross a rule in it.

Gov. Very well and do you not so here?

Mrs. H. No Sir for my ground is they are men.

Gov. Men and women all is one for that, but suppose that a man should come and say Mrs. Hutchinson I hear that you are a woman that God hath given his grace unto and you have knowledge in the word of God I pray instruct me a little, ought you not to instruct this man?

Mrs. H. I think I may.—Do you think it not lawful for me to teach women and why do you call me to teach the court?

Gov. We do not call you to teach the court but to lay open yourself.

Mrs. H. I desire you that you would then set me down a rule by which I may put them away that come unto me and so have peace in so doing.

Gov. You must shew your rule to receive them.

Mrs. H. I have done it.

Gov. I deny it because I have brought more arguments than you have.

Mrs. H. I say, to me it is a rule.

Mr. Endicot. You say there are some rules unto you. I think there is a contradiction in your own words. What rule for your practice do you bring, only a custom in Boston.

Mrs. H. No Sir that was no rule to me but if you look upon the rule in Titus it is a rule to me. If you convince me that it is no rule I shall yield.

Gov. . . . [T]his rule crosses that in the Corinthians.[3] But you must take it in this sense that elder women must instruct the younger about their business, and to love their husbands and not to make them to clash.

Mrs. H. I do not conceive but that it is meant for some publick times.

Gov. Well, have you no more to say but this?

Mrs. H. I have said sufficient for my practice.

Gov. Your course is not to be suffered for, besides that we find such a course as this to be greatly prejudicial to the state, besides the occasion that it is to seduce many honest persons that are called to those meetings and your opinions being known to be different from the word of God may seduce many simple souls that resort unto you, besides that the occasion which hath come of late hath come from none but such as have frequented your meetings, so that now they are flown off from magistrates and ministers and this since they have come to you, and besides that it will not well stand with the commonwealth that families should be neglected for so many neighbours and dames and so much time spent, we see no rule of God for this, we see not that any should have authority to set up any other exercises besides what authority hath already set up and so what hurt comes of this you will be guilty of and we for suffering you.

Mrs. H. Sir I do not believe that to be so.

Gov. Well, we see how it is we must therefore put it away from you, or restrain you from maintaining this course.

Mrs. H. If you have a rule for it from God's word you may.

Gov. We are your judges, and not you ours and we must compel you to it.

Mrs. H. If it please you by authority to put it down I freely let you for I am subject to your authority.

Notes

1. The petition the Antinomian party presented to the General Court in March 1637.
2. Titus 2.3, 4, 5.
3. 1 Corinthians 14.34, 35.

CAROL F. KARLSEN

The Devil in the Shape of a Woman: The Economic Basis of Witchcraft

Puritan ministers stressed the equality of each soul in the eyes of God and the responsibility of each believer to read the Bible. They urged women as well as men toward literacy and taking responsibility for their own salvation. One distinguished minister, Cotton Mather, writing at the end of the seventeenth century, observed that since women came close to the experience of death in repeated childbirth, their religiosity was likely to be greater than that of men. In being "helpmeets" to their husbands, women were encouraged to strengthen their ability to be competent and capable. There was much in Puritan thought that could be appealing to women.

But, as we have seen in the case of Anne Hutchinson, the Puritan community was unforgiving to women who failed to serve the needs of godly men in their strictly hierarchical community. Lurking in their imagination—as it lurked throughout the Judeo-Christian tradition—was the cautionary biblical story of Eve, who, by her disobedience, brought evil into the world. (Puritans paid no attention to other elements of that complicated tale: Eve's disobedience, after all, was in quest of Knowledge; the biology of birth is reversed, with Eve emerging from Adam's body.) Witchcraft prosecutions were rare in English colonies outside of New England; there, they occurred individually or in small clusters, numbering under 100 until the famous outbreak in and near Salem, Massachusetts, in 1692, during which nearly 200 people, three-quarters of whom were women, were accused, and 13 women and 6 men were executed. Carol F. Karlsen argues that in early colonial New England culture, an older view of women as a necessary evil had been only superficially superseded by a new, Protestant view of women as a necessary good. Note that fear of women-as-witches was endemic at this time in Europe, where between 1450 and 1750 roughly 90,000 trials occurred, including 3,000 in the British Isles.

In her essay, Karlsen provides in-depth, biographical profiles of several women who faced accusations both prior to and during the Salem witch-hunt. This research technique led her to make a startling and truly innovative discovery involving the category of "inheriting women." Her findings help to answer a frequently asked question: even though everyone in the society believed that witches existed and supernatural forces were operating in their lives, *why* did neighbors and aquaintances launch accusations against particular persons?

Anthropologists have long understood that communities define as witches people whose behavior enacts the things the community most fears; witchcraft beliefs, wrote Monica Hunter Wilson, are "the standardized nightmare of a group,

Excerpted from "The Economic Basis of Witchcraft," ch. 3 of *The Devil in the Shape of a Woman: Witchcraft in Colonial New England* by Carol F. Karlsen (New York: W. W. Norton, 1987). Reprinted by permission of the author and publisher. Notes have been revised and renumbered and tables renumbered.

and . . . the comparative analysis of such nightmares . . . [is] one of the keys to the understanding of society."* Have witch-hunts (using the word metaphorically) occurred in your lifetime or the lifetimes of your parents or grandparents?

Most observers now agree that witches in the villages and towns of late sixteenth- and early seventeenth-century England tended to be poor. They were not usually the poorest women in their communities, one historian has argued; they were the "moderately poor." Rarely were relief recipients suspect; rather it was those just above them on the economic ladder, "like the woman who felt she ought to get poor relief, but was denied it."[1] This example brings to mind New England's Eunice Cole, who once berated Hampton selectmen for refusing her aid when, she insisted, a man no worse off than she was receiving it.[2]

Eunice Cole's experience also suggests the difficulty in evaluating the class position of the accused. Commonly used class indicators such as the amount of property owned, yearly income, occupation, and political offices held are almost useless in analyzing the positions of women during the colonial period. While early New England women surely shared in the material benefits and social status of their fathers, husbands, and even sons, most were economically dependent on the male members of their families throughout their lives. Only a small proportion of these women owned property outright, and even though they participated actively in the productive work of their communities, their labor did not translate into financial independence or economic power. Any income generated by married women belonged by law to their husbands, and because occupations open to women were few and wages meager, women alone could only rarely support themselves. Their material condition, moreover, could easily change with an alteration in their marital status. William Cole, with an estate at his death of £41 after debts, might be counted among the "moderately poor," as might Eunice Cole when he was alive. But the refusal of the authorities to recognize the earlier transfer of this estate from husband to wife ensured, among other things, that as a widow Eunice Cole was among the poorest of New England's poor. . . .

Despite conceptual problems and sparse evidence, it is clear that poor women, both the destitute and those with access to some resources, were surely represented, and very probably overrepresented, among the New England accused. Perhaps 20 percent of accused women . . . were either impoverished or living at a level of bare subsistence when they were accused.[3] Some, like thirty-seven-year-old Abigail Somes, worked as servants a substantial portion of their adult lives. Some supported themselves and their families with various kinds of temporary labor such as nursing infants, caring for sick neighbors, taking in washing and sewing, or harvesting crops. A few, most notably Tituba, the first person accused during the Salem outbreak, were slaves. Others, like the once-prosperous Sarah Good of Wenham and Salem, and the never-very-well-off Ruth Wilford of Haverhill, found themselves reduced to abject poverty by the death of a parent or a change in their own marital status.[4] Accused witches came before local magistrates requesting permission to sell family land in order to support themselves, to submit claims against their children or executors of their former husbands' estates for nonpayment of the widow's lawful share of the estate, or simply to ask for food and fuel from the town selectmen. Because they could not pay the costs of their trials or jail terms, several were forced to remain in prison after courts acquitted them. The familiar stereotype of the witch as an indigent woman who resorted to begging for her survival is hardly an inaccurate picture of some of New England's accused.

Still, the poor account for only a minority of the women accused. Even without precise economic indicators, it is clear that women from all levels of society were vulnerable to accusation. . . . Wives, daughters, and widows of "middling" farmers, artisans, and mariners were regularly accused, and (although much less often) so too were women belonging to the gentry class. The accused were addressed as Goodwife (or Goody) and as the more

*Quoted in Carol F. Karlsen, *The Devil in the Shape of a Woman* (New York: W. W. Norton, 1987), p. 181.

honorific Mrs. or Mistress, as well as by their first names.

Prosecution was a different matter. Unless they were single or widowed, accused women from wealthy families—families with estates valued at more than £500—could be fairly confident that the accusations would be ignored by the authorities or deflected by their husbands through suits for slander against their accusers. Even during the Salem outbreak, when several women married to wealthy men were arrested, most managed to escape to the safety of other colonies through their husbands' influence. Married women from moderately well-off families—families with estates valued at between roughly £200 and £500—did not always escape prosecution so easily, but neither do they seem, as a group, to have been as vulnerable as their less prosperous counterparts. When only married women are considered, women in families with estates worth less than £200 seem significantly overrepresented among convicted witches—a pattern which suggests that economic position was a more important factor to judges and juries than to the community as a whole in its role as accuser.[5]

Without a husband to act on behalf of the accused, wealth alone rarely provided women with protection against prosecution. Boston's Ann Hibbens, New Haven's Elizabeth Godman, and Wethersfield's Katherine Harrison, all women alone, were tried as witches despite sizable estates. In contrast, the accusations against women like Hannah Griswold of Saybrook, Connecticut, Elizabeth Blackleach of Hartford, and Margaret Gifford of Salem, all wives of prosperous men when they were accused, were simply not taken seriously by the courts.[6] . . .

Economic considerations, then, do appear to have been at work in the New England witchcraft cases. But the issue was not simply the relative poverty—or wealth—of accused witches or their families. It was the special position of most accused witches vis-à-vis their society's rules for transferring wealth from one generation to another. To explain why their position was so unusual, we must turn first to New England's system of inheritance.

Inheritance is normally thought of as the transmission of property at death, but in New England, as in other agricultural societies, adult children received part of their father's accumulated estates prior to his death, usually at the time they married.[7] Thus the inheritance system included both pre-mortem endowments and post-mortem distributions. While no laws compelled fathers to settle part of their estates on their children as marriage portions, it was customary to do so. Marriages were, among other things, economic arrangements, and young people could not benefit from these arrangements unless their fathers provided them with the means to set up households and earn their livelihoods. Sons' portions tended to be land, whereas daughters commonly received movable goods and/or money. The exact value of these endowments varied to a father's wealth and inclination, but it appears that as a general rule the father of the young woman settled on the couple roughly half as much as the father of the young man.[8]

Custom, not law, also guided the distribution of a man's property at his death, but with two important exceptions. First, a man's widow, if he left one, was legally entitled "by way of dower" to one-third part of his real property, "to have and injoy for term of her natural life." She was expected to support herself with the profits of this property, but since she held only a life interest in it, she had to see that she did not "strip or waste" it.[9] None of the immovable estate could be sold, unless necessary for her or her children's maintenance, and then only with the permission of the court. A man might will his wife more than a third of his real property—but not less. Only if the woman came before the court to renounce her dower right publicly, and then only if the court approved, could this principle be waived. In the form of her "thirds," dower was meant to provide for a woman's support in widowhood. The inviolability of dower protected the widow from the claims of her children against the estate and protected the community from the potential burden of her care.

The second way in which law determined inheritance patterns had to do specifically with intestate cases.[10] If a man died without leaving a will, several principles governed the division of his property. The widow's thirds, of course, were to be laid out first. Unless "just cause" could be shown for some other distribution, the other two-thirds were to be divided among the surviving children, both male and female.[11] A double portion was to go to the eldest son, and single portions to his sisters and younger brothers. If there were no sons, the law stipulated that the estate was to be shared equally by the daughters. In cases where any or all of the children had not yet come of age, their portions were to be held by their mother or by a court-appointed guardian until they reached their majorities[12] or married. What remained of the widow's thirds at her death was to be divided among the surviving children, in the same proportions as the other two-thirds.

Although bound to conform to laws concerning the widow's thirds, men who wrote wills were not legally required to follow the principles of inheritance laid out in intestate cases. Individual men had the right to decide for themselves who would ultimately inherit their property. . . . [T]he majority seem to have adhered closely (though not always precisely) to the custom of leaving a double portion to the eldest son. Beyond that, New England men seem generally to have agreed to a system of partible inheritance, with both sons and daughters inheriting.

When these rules were followed, property ownership and control generally devolved upon men. Neither the widow's dower nor, for the most part, the daughter's right to inherit signified more than access to property. For widows, the law was clear that dower allowed for "use" only. For inheriting daughters who were married, the separate but inheritance-related principle of coverture applied. Under English common law, "feme covert" stipulated that married women had no right to own property—indeed, upon marriage, "the very being or legal existence of the woman is suspended."[13] Personal property which a married daughter inherited from her father, either as dowry or as a post-mortem bequest, immediately became the legal possession of her husband, who could exert full powers of ownership over it. A married daughter who inherited land from her father retained title to the land, which her husband could not sell without her consent. On her husband's death such land became the property of her children, but during his life her husband was entitled to the use and profits of it, and his wife could not devise it to her children by will.[14] The property of an inheriting daughter who was single seems to have been held "for improvement" for her until she was married, when it became her dowry.[15]

This is not to say that women did not benefit when they inherited property. A sizable inheritance could provide a woman with a materially better life; if single or widowed, inheriting women enjoyed better chances for an economically advantageous marriage or remarriage. But inheritance did not normally bring women the independent economic power it brought men.

The rules of inheritance were not always followed, however. In some cases, individual men decided not to conform to customary practices; instead, they employed one of several legal devices to give much larger shares of their estates to their wives or daughters, many times for disposal at their own discretion. Occasionally, the magistrates themselves allowed the estate to be distributed in some other fashion. Or, most commonly, the absence of male heirs in families made conformity impossible. In all three exceptions to inheritance customs, but most particularly the last, the women who stood to benefit economically also assumed a position of unusual vulnerability. They, and in many instances their daughters, became prime targets for witchcraft accusations.

Consider first the experience of witches who came from families without male heirs. . . . [T]hese histories begin to illuminate the subtle and often intricate manner in which anxieties about inheritance lay at the heart of most witchcraft accusations.

KATHERINE HARRISON

Katherine Harrison first appears in the Connecticut colonial records in the early 1650s, as the wife of John Harrison, a wealthy Wethersfield landowner.[16] Her age is unknown[17] and her family background is obscure. We know that she called John, Jonathan, and Josiah Gilbert, three prominent Connecticut Valley settlers, her cousins, but her actual relationship to them is ambiguous.[18] . . . She may have been the daughter or niece of Lydia Gilbert, who was executed as a witch in Hartford in 1654, but we can be reasonably certain only that the two women were members of the same Connecticut family.[19] . . .

It has been said that Katherine Harrison was first tried as a witch in October 1668.[20] If so, then she must have been acquitted, because she was indicted in the Court of Assistants in Hartford on 25 May 1669, on the same charge.[21] The jury was unable to agree upon a verdict, however, and the court adjourned to the next session. Meantime, Harrison was supposed to remain in jail, but for some reason she was released in the summer or early fall, and she returned home to Wethersfield. Shortly thereafter, thirty-eight Wethersfield townsmen filed a petition, complaining that "shee was suffered to be at libertie," since she "was lately prooved to be Deaply guiltie of *suspicion* of Wichcrafte" and that "the Juerie (the greater part of them) judged or beleaved that she was guilty of such high crimes" and "ought to be put to death." Among the petition's signers were several of the town's most prominent citizens, including John Blackleach, Sr., who had "taken much paines in the prosecution of this cause from the beginninge," and John Chester, who was then involved in a legal controversy with Harrison concerning a parcel of land.[22] When the Court of Assistants met again in October, all of the jury members found her guilty of witchcraft.[23]

The Hartford magistrates, however, were reluctant to accept the verdict. Perhaps remembering how accusations had gotten out of hand during the Hartford outbreak seven years before, they put Harrison back in prison and appealed to local ministers for advice on the use of evidence. The response was ambiguous enough to forestall execution.[24] At a special session of the Court of Assistants the following May, the magistrates reconsidered the verdict, determined that they were not able to concur with the jury "so as to sentance her to death or to a longer continuance in restraynt," and ordered Harrison to pay her fees and leave the colony for good.[25]

If witnesses testifying against her in her 1669 trial can be believed, Katherine Harrison's neighbors had suspected that she was a witch sixteen or eighteen years earlier. Elizabeth Simon deposed that as a single woman, Harrison was noted to be "a great or notorious liar, a Sabbath breaker and one that told fortunes"—and that her predictions frequently came to pass. Simon was also suspicious of Harrison for another reason: because she "did often spin so great a quantity of fine linen yarn as the said Elizabeth did never know nor hear of any other woman that could spin so much."[26] Other witnesses testified to the more recent damage she did to individuals and their property. Harrison was also a healer, and although many of her neighbors called upon her skills, over the years some of them came to suspect her of killing as well as curing.[27] Or so they said in 1668–69; she was not formally accused of any witchcraft crimes until after her husband's death.

John Harrison had died in 1666, leaving his wife one of the wealthiest, if not *the* wealthiest woman in Wethersfield. In his will he bequeathed his entire estate of £929 to his wife and three daughters. Rebecca, age twelve, was to have £60, and his two younger daughters, eleven-year-old Mary and nine-year-old Sarah, were to have £40 each. The remaining £789 was to go to his widow.[28] Unlike many widows in colonial New England, Katherine Harrison chose not to remarry. Instead she lived alone, managing her extensive holdings herself, with the advice and assistance of her Hartford kinsman, Jonathan Gilbert.

In October 1668, not long after her adversaries began gathering their witchcraft evidence against her, Harrison submitted a lengthy petition to "the Fathers of the Comonweale" asking for relief for the extensive vandalism of her estate since her husband's death. Among other damage, she spoke of oxen beaten and bruised to the point of being "altogether unserviceable"; of a hole bored into the side of her cow; of a three-year-old heifer slashed to death; and of the back of a two-year-old steer broken. Her corn crop was destroyed, she said, "damnified with horses, they being staked upon it," and "30 poles of hops cutt and spoyled." Twelve of her relatives and neighbors, she said, including Jonathan and Josiah Gilbert, could testify to the damage done. The response of the court went unrecorded, but there is no indication that provision was made for the "due recompense" Harrison requested or that her grievances were even investigated.[29]

The Court of Assistants also seems to have been unsympathetic to another petition Harrison submitted in the fall of 1668, in which she complained that the actions of the magistrates themselves were depleting her estate.[30] Indeed, the local court had recently fined her £40 for slandering her neighbors, Michael and Ann Griswold—a fine greatly in excess of the normal punishment in such cases.[31] The exact circumstances of the incident are unknown, but the

Griswolds were among Harrison's witchcraft accusers, and she apparently considered Michael Griswold central in the recruiting of additional witnesses against her, for she said that "the sayd Michael Griswold would Hang her though he damned a thousand soules," adding that "as for his own soule it was damned long agoe." Griswold, a member of Wethersfield's elite, but not as wealthy as Harrison, sued her for these slanderous remarks and for calling his wife Ann "a savadge whore."[32] Besides levying the fine, the court ordered Harrison to confess her sins publicly.[33] She made the required confession, but she appealed the exorbitant fine.

Harrison's petition, which she filed within the month, was a peculiar mixture of justification for her actions, concession to the magistrates' insistence on deference in women, determination in her convictions, and desperation in her attempt to salvage her estate. Acknowledging herself to be "a female, a weaker vessell, subject to passion," she pleaded as the source of her frustration and anger the vicious abuse to which she had been subjected since her husband's death. She admitted her "corruption," but pointed out that it was well known that she had made "a full and free confession of [her] fault" and had offered "to repaire the wound that [she] had given to [the Griswolds'] names by a plaster as broad as the sore, at any time and in any place where it should content them." At the same time, she indicated Michael Griswold for being less interested in the reparation of his name than in her estate and did not hesitate to call the fine oppressive, citing the laws of God and the laws of the commonwealth as providing "that noe mans estate shal be deminished or taken away by any colony or pretence of Authority" in such an arbitrary manner. In her final statements, however, she returned to a more conciliatory stance: "I speake not to excuse my fault," she said, "but to save my estate as far as Righteousness will permit for a distressed Widow and Orphanes."[34]

Fear of losing her estate is a recurring theme in the records of Harrison's life during this period. Almost immediately after her husband's death in 1666, she petitioned the court to change the terms of her husband's will. Arguing that the bequests to the children were "inconsiderate" (by which she probably meant inconsiderable), she asked that the magistrates settle on her eldest daughter £210, and £200 on each of her younger daughters, reserving the house and lot for herself during her lifetime.[35] Since her husband had left her full ownership of most of his estate, she could simply have given her daughters larger portions, but she must have felt that the court's sanction rendered the inheritances less vulnerable. Several months later, she appealed directly to Connecticut's governor, John Winthrop, Jr., requesting that Hartford's John and Jonathan Gilbert, and John Riley of Wethersfield, be appointed overseers of her estate.[36] Winthrop must not have granted her request, because in 1668 Harrison signed over the rest of the estate she had inherited from her husband to her daughters and appointed Jonathan and John Gilbert her daughters' guardians.[37] By the following year, her neighbors reported, she had "disposed of great part of her estate to others in trust."[38]

In June 1670, Katherine Harrison moved to Westchester, New York, to begin her life anew. Her reputation for witchcraft followed her, however, in the form of a complaint, filed in July by two of her new neighbors, that she had been allowed to resettle in Westchester. Noting that suspicion of her in Connecticut "hath given some cause of apprehension" to the townspeople, in order to "end their jealousyes and feares" a local New York magistrate told her to leave the jurisdiction.[39] Harrison refused. Before any action could be taken against her, her eldest daughter was fortuitously betrothed to Josiah Hunt, a son of Thomas Hunt, one of the men who had protested her presence in Westchester. The elder Hunt became a supporter and appeared in court on her behalf, with his son and three other influential men. Though she was required to give security for her "Civill carriage and good behaviour," the General Court of Assizes in New York ordered "that in regard there is nothing appears against her deserving the continuance of that obligacion shee is to bee releast from it, and hath Liberty to remaine in the Towne of Westchester where shee now resides, or any where else in the Government during her pleasure."[40]

Evidently Harrison continued to live with recurring witchcraft suspicion, but after 1670 there is no further evidence of official harassment.[41] Early in 1672, she reappeared in Hartford to sue eleven of her old Connecticut Valley neighbors, in most cases for debt, and to release her "intrusted overseer" Jonathan Gilbert from his responsibilities for her estate (although he continued to act as guardian to her two younger daughters).[42] A month later, she signed at least some of her remaining Wethersfield land over to Gilbert.[43] After that, she fades from view. She may have returned to Connecticut for good at that time, for some evidence suggests that she died at Dividend, then an outlying section of Wethersfield, in October 1682.[44]

SUSANNA MARTIN

Born in England in 1625, Susanna North was the youngest of three daughters of Richard North. Her mother died when Susanna was young and her father subsequently remarried. The family migrated to New England in or just prior to 1639, the year in which Richard North was listed as one of the first proprietors of Salisbury, Massachusetts. Susanna's sister Mary had married Thomas Jones and was living in Gloucester by 1642. Of her sister Sarah we know only that she married a man named Oldham, had a daughter named Ann, and died before the child was grown. In August 1646, at the age of twenty-one, Susanna married George Martin, a Salisbury man whose first wife had recently died. In June of the following year, she gave birth to her son Richard, the first of nine children. One of these children, a son, died in infancy.[45] . . .

Early in 1668, less than a year after the birth of her last child, Susanna Martin's father died, leaving a modest estate of about £150. As the only surviving children, the then forty-three-year-old Susanna and her sister Mary anticipated receiving a major portion of the property, to posses either immediately or after the death of their stepmother, Ursula North. They were disappointed. According to the will probated shortly after he died, Richard North had voided all previous wills and written a new one—*nearly two decades* before his death. In this document, dated January 1649, he left all but £22 of his estate directly to his wife. Twenty-one pounds was to be divided among Mary Jones, Susanna Martin, and Ann Bates (Sarah Oldham's daughter). Susanna's share was 20 shillings and the cancellation of a £10 debt George Martin owed his father-in-law. Listed as witnesses to this will were Thomas Bradbury of Salisbury and Mary Jones's daughter, Mary Winsley.[46] But the will raised problems. In 1649, Ann Bates was still Ann Oldham (she did not marry Francis Bates until 1661) and the Mary Winsley listed as witness to the will was still Mary Jones, at most eleven or twelve years old when it was allegedly written.[47] Despite the obvious irregularities, Thomas Bradbury and Mary Winsley attested in court that this was indeed Richard North's last will and testament.

Whether Susanna Martin and her sister saw or protested this will when it was probated cannot be determined. Susanna, at least, may have had more pressing concerns on her mind. In April 1669, a bond of £100 was posted for her appearance at the next Court of Assistants "upon suspicion of witchcraft." That was the same day that George Martin sued William Sargent for slandering his wife. According to George Martin, Sargent had not only said that Susanna "was a witch, and he would call her witch," but also accused her of having "had a child" while still single and of "wringing its neck" shortly after. George Martin also sued William Sargent's brother Thomas for saying "that his son George Marttin was a bastard and that Richard Marttin was Goodwife Marttin's imp."[48] . . .

Meanwhile, the magistrates bound Susanna Martin over to the higher court to be tried for witchcraft. Although the records have not survived, she must have been acquitted, because several months later she was at liberty. In October 1669, George Martin was again bound for his wife's appearance in court, not for witchcraft this time but for calling one of her neighbors a liar and a thief.[49]

By April 1671, George and Susanna Martin (Susanna's sister Mary Jones would later join them) were involved in what would become protracted litigation over the estate of Susanna's father. Ursula North had died a month or two before, leaving a will, dated shortly after her husband's death, that effectively disinherited her two stepdaughters by awarding them 40 shillings apiece. She left the rest of the original North estate first to her granddaughter, Mary Winsley, and secondarily to Mary and Nathaniel Winsley's only child, Hepzibah.[50]

The exact sequence of the numerous court hearings that followed is less clear. Evidently, Susanna and George Martin initiated legal proceedings against Mary and Nathaniel

Winsley in April 1671, for unwarranted possession of the North estate. . . . In October 1672, the General Court responded, giving Susanna Martin liberty to sue for her inheritance a second time at the local level.

In April 1673, the recently widowed Mary Jones and George Martin, acting for his wife, sued Nathaniel Winsley "for withholding the inheritance of housing, lands and other estate . . . under color of a feigned or confused writing like the handwriting of Mr. Thomas Bradbury and seemingly attested by him, and Mary Winsly." The court declared the case nonsuited, and again Susanna Martin appealed to the General Court, requesting that the case be reheard at the local level. The General Court consented in May 1673, and the following October, Susanna and George Martin instituted proceedings against the Winsleys for the third time. Again the county court decided for the defendants, and the Martins appealed to the Court of Assistants. For a while it looked as though things were finally going their way. The higher court, which "found for the plaintiff there being no legall prooffe of Richard North's will," ordered that "the estate the said North left be left to the dispossall of the county court." . . .

[In 1674] Susanna, George, and Mary appealed a final time to the General Court, this time for "a hearing of the whole case" by the highest court itself. The magistrates agreed to hear the case, remitting the usual court fees, as they had done before, on the basis of Susanna's pleas of poverty. But in October 1674, after "perusall of what hath binn heard and alleadged by both parties," the court found for Nathaniel Winsley.[51] In what Susanna Martin and Mary Jones believed was a flagrant miscarriage of justice, they had lost what they considered their rightful inheritances.

For almost the next two decades, Susanna Martin's name rarely appears in the public records of the colony. Her sister Mary died in 1682, followed by her husband George in 1686.[52] Early in 1692, she was again accused of witchcraft, this time by several of the possessed females in Salem. They claimed that her apparition "greviously affected" them, urging them to become witches themselves. Summoned before the court as witnesses against her were eleven men and four women, all old neighbors of the now sixty-seven-year-old widow.[53]

Unnerved by neither the agonies of the possessed or the magistrates' obvious belief in her guilt, Martin insisted that she was innocent. To Cotton Mather, she "was one of the most impudent, scurrilous, wicked Creatures in the World," who had the effrontery to claim "that she had lead a most virtuous and holy life."[54] Years of living as a reputed witch had left Martin well-versed on the subject of the Devil's powers. "He that appeared in sam[uel]s shape, a glorifyed saint," she said, citing the Bible in her own defense, "can appear in any ones shape." She laughed at the fits of her young accusers, explaining: "Well I may at such folly." When asked what she thought the possessed were experiencing, she said she did not know. Pressed to speculate on it, she retorted: "I do not desire to spend my judgment upon it" and added (revealing what must have been her long-standing opinion of the magistrates' bias), "my thoughts are my own, when they are in, but when they are out they are anothers."[55] . .

Susanna Martin was found guilty of witch-craft and was one of five women executed on 19 July 1692. One week later, another Salisbury woman was indicted on the same charge. She was Mary Bradbury, the now elderly wife of the man Susanna Martin believed had written her father's "will" nearly twenty-five years before. Mary Bradbury was sentenced to hang too, but friends helped her to escape. No explicit connection between the accusations of the two women is discernible. Rumors circulated, however, that because Thomas Bradbury had friends in positions of authority, there had been little real effort to capture his fugitive wife.[56] . . .

These . . . short histories . . . suggest the diverse economic circumstances of witches in early New England. . . . The . . . women featured in these histories were either (1) daughters of parents who had no sons (or whose sons had died), (2) women in marriages which brought forth only daughters (or in which the sons had died), or (3) women in marriages with no children at all. These patterns had significant economic implications. Because there were no legitimate male heirs in their immediate families, each of these . . . women stood to inherit, did inherit, or were denied their apparent right to inherit substantially larger portions of their fathers' or husbands' accumulated estates than women in families with male heirs. Whatever actually happened to the property in question—and in some cases we simply do not know—these women were aberrations in a society with an inheritance system designed to keep property in the hands of men.

These . . . cases also illustrate fertility and mortality patterns widely shared among the families of accused witches. A substantial majority of New England's accused females were women without brothers, women with daughters but no sons, or women in marriages with no children at all (see Table 1). Of the 267 accused females, enough is known about 158 to identify them as either having or not having brothers or sons to inherit: only 62 of the 158 (39 percent) did, whereas 96 (61 percent) did not. More striking, *once accused,* women without brothers or sons were even more likely than women with brothers or sons to be tried, convicted, and executed: women from families without male heirs made up 64 percent of the females prosecuted, 76 percent of those who were found guilty, and 89 percent of those who were executed.

These figures must be read with care, however, for two reasons. First, eighteen of the sixty-two accused females who *had* brothers or sons to inherit were themselves daughters and granddaughters of women who did not. It appears that these eighteen females, most of whom were young women or girls, were accused because their neighbors believed that their mothers and grandmothers passed their witchcraft on to them. Therefore they form a somewhat ambiguous group. Since they all had brothers to inherit, it would be inaccurate to exclude them from this category in Table 1, yet including them understates the extent to which inheritance-related concerns were at issue in witchcraft accusations. At the same time, the large number of cases in which the fertility and mortality patterns of witches' families are unknown (109 of the 267 accused females in New England) makes it impossible to assess precisely the proportion of women among the accused who did not have brothers or sons.

Table 2 helps clarify the point. It includes as a separate category the daughters and granddaughters of women without brothers or sons and incorporates the cases for which this information is unknown. Although inclusion of the unknowns renders the overall percentages meaningless, this way of representing the available information shows clearly the particular vulnerability of women without brothers or sons. Even if *all* the unknown cases involved women from families *with* male heirs—a highly unlikely possibility—women from families without males to inherit would still form a majority of convicted and executed witches. Were the complete picture visible, I suspect that it would not differ substantially from that presented earlier in Table 1—which is based on data reflecting 60 percent of New England's witches and which indicates that women without brothers and sons were more vulnerable than other women at all stages of the process.

Numbers alone, however, do not tell the whole story. More remains to be said about what happened to these inheriting or potentially inheriting women, both before and after they were accused of witchcraft.

It was not unusual for women in families without male heirs to be accused of witchcraft shortly after the deaths of fathers, husbands, brothers, or sons. Katherine Harrison [and] Susanna Martin . . . exemplify this pattern. So too does elderly Ann Hibbens of Boston, whose execution in 1656 seems to have had a profound enough effect on some of her peers to influence the outcome of subsequent trials for years to come. Hibbens had three sons from her first marriage, all of whom lived in England; but she had no children by her husband William Hibbens, with whom she had come to Massachusetts in the 1630s. William died in 1654; Ann was brought to trial two years later. Although her husband's will has not survived, he apparently left a substantial portion (if not all) of his property directly to her: when she wrote her own will shortly before her execution, Ann Hibbens

TABLE 1. Female Witches by Presence or Absence of Brothers or Sons, New England, 1620–1725 (A)

Action	Women without Brothers or Sons	Women with Brothers or Sons	Total
Accused	96 (61%)	62 (39%)	158
Tried	41 (64%)	23 (36%)	64
Convicted	25 (76%)	8 (24%)	33
Executed	17 (89%)	2 (11%)	19

TABLE 2. Female Witches by Presence or Absence of Brothers or Sons, New England, 1620–1725 (B)

Action	Women without Brothers or Sons	Daughters and Granddaughters of Women without Brothers or Sons	Women with Brothers or Sons	Unknown Cases	Total
Accused	96 (36%)	18 (7%)	44 (16%)	109 (41%)	267
Tried	41 (48%)	6 (7%)	17 (20%)	22 (26%)	86
Convicted	25 (56%)	0 (0%)	6 (13%)	12 (27%)	45
Executed	17 (61%)	0 (0%)	2 (7%)	9 (32%)	28

was in full possession of a £344 estate, most of which she bequeathed to her sons in England.[57]

Similarly, less than two years elapsed between the death of Gloucester's William Vinson and the imprisonment of his widow Rachel in 1692. Two children, a son and a daughter, had been born to the marriage, but the son had died in 1675. Though William Vinson had had four sons (and three daughters) by a previous marriage, the sons were all dead by 1683. In his will, which he wrote in 1684, before he was certain that his last son had been lost at sea, William left his whole £180 estate to Rachel for her life, stipulating that she could sell part of the lands and cattle if she found herself in need of resources. After Rachel's death, "in Case" his son John "be Living and returne home agayne," William said, most of the estate was to be divided between John and their daughter Abigail. If John did not return, both shares were to be Abigail's.[58] . . .

In other cases, many years passed between the death of the crucial male relative and the moment when a formal witchcraft complaint was filed.

. . . Mary English of Salem was charged with witchcraft seven years after she came into her inheritance. Her father, merchant William Hollingworth, had been declared lost at sea in 1677, but at that time Mary's brother William was still alive. Possibly because the younger William was handling the family's interests in other colonies, or possibly because the father's estate was in debt for more than it was worth, the magistrates gave the widow Elinor Hollingworth power of attorney to salvage what she could. With her "owne labor," as she put it, "but making use of other mens estates," the aggressive and outspoken Mistress Hollingworth soon had her deceased husband's debts paid and his wharf, warehouse, and tavern solvent again.[59] She had no sooner done so, however, than she was accused of witchcraft by the wife of a Gloucester mariner.[60] Though the magistrates gave little credence to the charge at the time, they may have had second thoughts later. In 1685, her son William died, and Elinor subsequently conveyed the whole Hollingworth estate over to Mary English, who was probably her only surviving child.[61]

Elinor Hollingworth had died by 1692, but Mary English was one of the women cried out upon early in the Salem outbreak. Her husband, the merchant Philip English, was accused soon after. Knowing their lives were in grave danger, the Englishes fled to the safety of New York. But as one historian of witchcraft has pointed out, flight was "the legal equivalent of conviction."[62] No sooner had they left than close to £1200 of their property was confiscated under the law providing attainder for witchcraft.[63]

Not all witches from families without male heirs were accused of conspiring with the Devil *after* they had come into their inheritances. On the contrary, some were accused prior to the death of the crucial male relative, many times before it was clear who would inherit. . . . [O]ne of these women . . . was Martha Corey of Salem, who was accused of witchcraft in 1692 while her husband was still alive. Giles Corey had been married twice before and had several daughters by the time he married the widow Martha Rich, probably in the 1680s. With no sons to inherit, Giles's substantial land holdings would, his neighbors might have assumed, be passed on to his wife and daughters. Alice Parker, who may have been Giles's daughter from a former marriage, also came before the magistrates as a witch in 1692, as did Giles himself. Martha Corey and Alice Parker maintained their innocence and were hanged. Giles Corey, in an apparently futile attempt to preserve his whole estate for his heirs, refused to respond to the indictment. To force him to enter a plea, he was tortured: successively heavier weights were placed on his body until he was pressed to death.[64]

What seems especially significant here is that most accused witches whose husbands were still alive were, like their counterparts who were widows and spinsters, over forty years of age—and therefore unlikely if not unable to produce male heirs. Indeed, the fact that witchcraft accusations were rarely taken seriously by the community until the accused stopped bearing children takes on a special meaning when it is juxtaposed with the anomalous position of inheriting women or potentially inheriting women in New England's social structure.

Witches in families without male heirs sometimes had been dispossessed of part or all of their inheritances before—sometimes long before—they were formally charged with witchcraft. Few of these women, however, accepted disinheritance with equanimity. Rather, like Susanna Martin, they took their battles to court, casting themselves in the role of public challengers to the system of male inheritance. In most instances, the authorities sided with their antagonists. . . .

. . . The property of women in families without male heirs was vulnerable to loss in a variety of ways, from deliberate destruction by neighbors (as Katherine Harrison experienced) to official sequestering by local magistrates. In nearly every case, the authorities themselves seem hostile or at best indifferent to the property claims of these women. One final example deserves mention here, not only because it indicates how reluctant magistrates were to leave property in the control of women, but because it shows that the property of convicted witches was liable to seizure even without the benefit of an attainder law.

Rebecca Greensmith had been widowed twice before her marriage to Nathaniel Greensmith. Her first husband, Abraham Elsen of Wethersfield, had died intestate in 1648, leaving an estate £99. After checking the birth dates of the Elsens' two children, three-year-old Sarah and one-year-old Hannah, the court initially left the whole estate with the widow. When Rebecca married Wethersfield's Jarvis Mudge the following year, the local magistrates sequestered the house and land Abraham Elsen had left, worth £40, stating their intention to rent it out "for the Use and Benefit of the two daughters."[65] The family moved to New London shortly after, but Jarvis Mudge died in 1652 and Rebecca moved with Hannah and Sarah to Hartford. Since Rebecca was unable to support herself and her two daughters, the court allowed her to sell the small amount of land owned by her second husband (with whom she had had no children) "for the paing of debts and the Bettering the Childrens portyons."[66]

Sometime prior to 1660, Rebecca married Nathaniel Greensmith. During the Hartford outbreak, Rebecca came under suspicion of witchcraft. After Nathaniel sued his wife's accuser for slander, Nathaniel himself was named. Both husband and wife were convicted and executed.[67]

Respecting Nathaniel's £182 estate, £44 of which was claimed by the then eighteen-year-old Sarah and seventeen-year-old Hannah Elsen, the court ordered the three overseers "to preserve the estate from Waste" and to pay "any just debts," the only one recorded being the Greensmiths' jail fees. Except for allowing the overseers "to dispose of the 2 daughters," presumably to service, the magistrates postponed until the next court any decision concerning the young women's portions. First, however, they deducted £40 to go "to the Treasurer for the County."[68] No reason was given for this substantial appropriation and no record of further distribution of the estate has survived.

Aside from these many women who lived or had lived in families without male heirs, there were at least a dozen other witches who, despite the presence of brothers and sons, came into much larger shares of estates than their neighbors would have expected. In some cases, these women gained full control over the disposition of property. We know about these women because their fathers, husbands, or other relatives left wills, because the women themselves wrote wills, or because male relatives who felt cheated out of their customary shares fought in the courts for more favorable arrangements.

Grace Boulter of Hampton, one of several children of Richard Swain, is one of these women. Grace was accused of witchcraft in 1680, along with her thirty-two-year-old daughter, Mary Prescott. Twenty years earlier, in 1660, just prior to his removal to Nantucket, Grace's father had deeded a substantial portion of his Hampton property to her and her husband Nathaniel, some of which he gave directly to her.[69]

Another witch in this group is Jane James of Marblehead, who left an estate at her death in 1669 which was valued at £85. While it is not clear how she came into possession of it, the property had not belonged to her husband Erasmus, who had died in 1660, though it did play a significant role in a controversy between her son and son-in-law over their rightful shares of both Erasmus's and Jane's estates. Between 1650 and her death in 1669, Jane was accused of witchcraft at least three times by her Marblehead neighbors.[70] . . .

Looking back over the lives of these many women—most particularly those who did not have brothers or sons to inherit—we begin to understand the complexity of the economic dimension of New England witchcraft. Only rarely does the actual trial testimony indicate that economic power was even at issue. Nevertheless it is there, recurring with a telling persistence once we look beyond what was explicitly said about these women as witches. Inheritance disputes surface frequently enough in witchcraft cases, cropping up as part of the general context even when no direct link between the dispute and the charge is discernible, to suggest the fears that underlay most accusations. No matter how deeply entrenched the principle of male inheritance, no matter how carefully written the laws that protected it, it was impossible to insure that all families had male offspring. The women who stood to benefit from these demographic "accidents" account for most of New England's female witches.

The amount of property in question was not the crucial factor in the way these women were viewed or treated by their neighbors, however. Women of widely varying economic circumstances were vulnerable to accusation and even to conviction. Neither was there a direct line from accuser to material beneficiary of the accusation: others in the community did sometimes profit personally from the losses sustained by these women . . . , but only rarely did the gain accrue to the accusers themselves. Indeed, occasionally there was no direct temporal connection: in some instances several decades passed between the creation of the key economic conditions and the charge of witchcraft; the charge in other cases even anticipated the development of those conditions.

Finally, inheriting or potentially inheriting women were vulnerable to witchcraft accusations not only during the Salem outbreak, but from the time of the first formal accusations in New England at least until the end of the century. . . . The Salem outbreak created only a slight wrinkle in this established fabric of suspicion. If daughters, husbands, and sons of witches were more vulnerable to danger in 1692 than they had been previously, they were mostly the daughters, husbands, and sons of inheriting or potentially inheriting women. As the outbreak spread, it drew into its orbit increasing numbers of women, "unlikely" witches in that they were married to well-off and influential men, but familiar figures to some of their neighbors nonetheless. What the impoverished Sarah Good had in common with Mary Phips, wife of Massachusetts's governor, was what Eunice Cole had in common with Katherine Harrison. . . . However varied their backgrounds and economic positions, as women without brothers or women without sons, they stood in the way of the orderly transmission of property from one generation of males to another.

Notes

1. Alan Macfarlane, *Witchcraft in Tudor and Stuart England: A Regional and Comparative Study* (New York, 1970), pp. 149–51. See also Keith Thomas, *Religion and the Decline of Magic* (New York, 1971), pp. 457, 520–21, 560–68.

2. See Trials for Witchcraft in New England (unpaged), dated 5 September 1656 (manuscript volume, Houghton Library, Harvard University, Cambridge, Mass.).

3. Relying on very general indicators (a married woman who worked as a servant, a widow whose husband had left an estate of £39, and so forth), I was able to make rough estimates about the economic position of 150 accused women. Twenty-nine of these women seem to have been poor. . . .

4. For Abigail Somes, see *The Salem Witchcraft Papers: Verbatim Transcripts of the Legal Documents of the Salem Witchcraft Outbreak of 1692*, 3 vols., ed. Paul Boyer and Stephen Nissenbaum (New York, 1977), 3:733–37 (hereafter cited as *Witchcraft Papers*). For Tituba, see *Witchcraft Papers* 3:745–57. Documents relating to Ruth Wilford are in *Witchcraft Papers* 2:459; 3:961; *The Probate Records of Essex*

County, Massachusetts, 1635–1681, 3 vols. (Salem, 1916–20), 3:93–95 (hereafter cited as *Essex Probate Records*).

5. Most families in seventeenth-century New England had estates worth less than £200. However, since only a very small proportion of convicted witches who were married seem to have come from families with estates worth *more* than £200, it seems reasonable to conclude that married women from families with less than £200 estates were overrepresented among the accused. Nearly all of the convictions of married women from families with estates worth more than £200 occurred during the Salem outbreak. . . .

6. For accusations against Hannah Griswold and Margaret Gifford, see Norbert B. Lacy, "The Records of the Court of Assistants of Connecticut, 1665–1701" (M.A. thesis, Yale University, 1937), pp. 6–7 (hereafter cited as "Conn. Assistants Records"); and *Records and Files of the Quarterly Courts of Essex County, Massachusetts,* 9 vols. (Salem, 1912–75), 7:405; 8:23 (hereafter cited as *Essex Court Records*).

7. This discussion of the inheritance system of seventeenth-century New England is drawn from the following sources: *The Book of the General Lawes and Libertyes Concerning the Inhabitants of the Massachusetts,* ed. Thomas G. Barnes (facsimile from the 1648 edition, San Marino, Calif., 1975); *The Colonial Laws of Massachusetts. Reprinted from the Edition of 1672, with the Supplements through 1686,* ed. William H. Whitmore (Boston, 1887); John D. Cushing, comp., *The Laws and Liberties of Massachusetts, 1641–91: A Facsimile Edition,* 3 vols. (Wilmington, Del., 1976); *Massachusetts Province Laws, 1692–1699,* ed. John D. Cushing (Wilmington, Del., 1978); *New Hampshire Probate Records; Essex Probate Records: A Digest of the Early Connecticut Probate Records,* vol. 1, ed. Charles W. Manwaring (Hartford, 1904) (hereafter cited as *Conn. Probate Records*); Marylynn Salmon, *Women and the Law of Property in Early America* (Chapel Hill, 1986); George L. Haskins, "The Beginnings of Partible Inheritance in the American Colonies," in *Essays in the History of American Law,* ed. David H. Flaherty (Chapel Hill, 1969); Edmund S. Morgan, *The Puritan Family: Religion and Domestic Relations in Seventeenth-Century New England* (1944; reprint New York, 1966).

8. See Morgan, *The Puritan Family,* pp. 81–82.

9. Barnes, *Book of the General Lawes,* pp. 17–18. . . .

10. Since only a small proportion of men left wills during the colonial period, intestacy law played a significant role in determining inheritance practices. See Salmon, *Women and the Law of Property,* p. 141.

11. Barnes, *The Book of the General Lawes,* p. 53.

12. Young women officially came of age in New England when they reached 18; young men when they reached 21.

13. William Blackstone, *Commentaries on the Laws of England,* 4 vols. (Oxford, 1765–69), 1:433.

14. Once widowed, a woman who inherited land from her father (or who had bought land with her husband in both of their names) could make a will of her own, as could a single woman who came into possession of land. . . . See Salmon, *Women and the Law of Property,* pp. 144–45 and passim.

15. Evidence suggests that in seventeenth-century New England, daughters of fathers who died relatively young (and possibly most sons) did not normally come into their inheritances until they married. If daughters had received their shares when they came of age, we would expect to find probate records for single women who died before they had the opportunity to marry. Though there are many existing intestate records and wills for single men who died in early adulthood, I have located only one record involving a young, single woman.

16. Wethersfield Land Records (manuscript volume, Town Clerk's Office, Town Hall, Wethersfield, Conn.) 1:19, 38.

17. Given the ages of her children, Katherine Harrison had to have been between her late twenties and her mid-fifties when she was first accused of witchcraft in 1668. I suspect that she was in her forties.

18. See Wethersfield Land Records 2:149; Katherine Harrison to John Winthrop, Jr., undated letter (probably early 1667), and Katherine Harrison's Testimony, undated document (probably October 1669), in the Winthrop Papers, Massachusetts Historical Society, Boston (hereafter cited as Winthrop Papers). . . .

19. Samuel Wyllys Papers: Depositions on Cases of Witchcraft, Assault, Theft, Drunkenness and Other Crimes, Tried in Connecticut, 1663–1728 (manuscript volume, Archives, History and Genealogy Unit, Connecticut State Library, Hartford, doc. 15) (hereafter cited as Wyllys Papers).

20. See Sherman W. Adams and Henry R. Stiles, *The History of Ancient Wethersfield,* 2 vols. (New York, 1904), 1:682; and Lacy, "Conn. Assistants Records," p. 12.

21. Lacy, "Conn. Assistants Records," p. 13.

22. Petition for the Investigation of Katherine Harrison, Recently Released after Imprisonment, Signed by John Chester and Thirty-Eight Other Citizens of Wethersfield (Manuscript Collections, Connecticut Historical Society, Hartford [hereafter cited as Petition for the Investigation of Katherine Harrison]) (emphasis mine). See also Order about Katherine Harrison's Land, in the Winthrop Papers. . . .

23. Lacy, "Conn. Assistants Records," pp. 13–14, 18–19.

24. "The Answers of Some Ministers to the Questions Propounded to Them by the Honored Magistrates," dated 20 October 1669, Samuel Wyllys Papers, Supplement: Depositions on Cases of Witchcraft Tried in Connecticut, 1662–1693, photostat copies of original documents from the Wyllys Papers, Annmary Brown Memorial Brown University Library, Providence, R.I. . . .

25. Lacy, "Conn. Assistants Records," p. 23. . . .

26. Wyllys Papers Supplement, p. 11.

27. Depositions submitted against Harrison in 1668 and 1669 are in the Wyllys Papers, docs. 6–17; Wyllys Papers Supplement, pp. 46–63. . . . For Harrison's response to these accusations, see Katherine Harrison's Testimony, Winthrop Papers.

28. Manwaring, *Conn. Probate Records* 1:206.

29. "A Complaint of Severall Greevances of the Widdow Harrison's," Wyllys Papers Supplement, p. 53.

30. "The Declaration of Katherine Harrison in Her Appeal to This Court of Assistants," dated September 1668, in Connecticut Archives, Crimes and Misdemeanors, 1st ser. (1662–1789) (manuscript volume, Archives, History and Genealogy Unit, Connecticut State Library, Hartford), vol. 1 (pt. 1):34 (hereafter cited as Crimes and Misdemeanors).

31. Connecticut Colonial Probate Records 56:80; Records of the Colony of Connecticut, Connecticut Colonial Probate Records, County Court, vol. 56, 1663–77 (Archives, History and Genealogy Unit, Connecticut State Library, Hartford, 56:79–81 (hereafter cited as Connecticut Colonial Probate Records).

32. Ibid., pp. 78–79. For the Griswolds as accusers, see Katherine Harrison's Testimony, Winthrop Papers.

33. Connecticut Colonial Probate Records 56:80.

34. "The Declaration of Katherine Harrison," Crimes and Misdemeanors, 1 (pt. 1):34.

35. Manwaring, *Connecticut Probate Records,* p. 206.

36. Katherine Harrison to John Winthrop, Jr., "Letter," Winthrop Papers.

37. Wethersfield Land Records 2:149.

38. Petition for the Investigation of Katherine Harrison.

39. See "The Cases of Hall and Harrison," in *Narratives of the Witchcraft Cases, 1648–1706,* ed. Charles Lincoln Burr (New York, 1914), pp. 48–49.

40. Ibid., pp. 48–52.

41. See Samuel D. Drake, *Annals of Witchcraft in New England* (New York, 1869), pp. 133–34.

42. Connecticut Colonial Probate Records 56:118; Wethersfield Land Records 2:249.

43. Wethersfield Land Records 2:210.

44. See Gilbert Collection.

45. See Joseph Merrill, *History of Amesbury, Including the First Seventeen Years of Salisbury. . . .* (Haverhill, Mass., 1880), pp. 11–13, 28; *Vital Records of Salisbury . . .* (Topsfield, Mass., 1915), pp. 151, 415.

46. *Essex Probate Records* 2:125–27.

47. James Savage, *A Genealogical Dictionary of the First Settlers of New England,* 4 vols. (Boston, 1860–62), 1:138; 4:483.

48. See *Essex Court Records* 4:129, 133.

49. *Essex Court Records* 4:184, 187, 239.

50. *Essex Probate Records* 2:223–24.

51. See *Records of the Governor and Company of the Massachusetts Bay in New England,* 6 vols., ed. Nathaniel B. Shurtleff (Boston, 1853–54), 5:6, 26–27.

52. Savage, *Genealogical Dictionary* 2:566. . . . When he died, George Martin left an estate valued at £75, most of which he left to Susanna "during her Widowhood."

53. See *Witchcraft Papers* 2:549–79.

54. Cotton Mather, *The Wonders of the Invisible World* (1693; facsimile of the 1862 London edition, Ann Arbor, Mich., 1974), p. 148.

55. *Witchcraft Papers* 2:551.

56. *Witchcraft Papers* 1:115–29.

57. Ann Hibbens' will is reprinted in *New England Historical and Genealogical Register,* vol. 6 (1852), pp. 287–88.

58. See *Witchcraft Papers* 3:880–81.

59. *Essex Probate Records* 3:191–93.

60. *Essex Court Records* 7:238.

61. *New England Historical and Genealogical Register,* vol. 3 (1849), p. 129.

62. Marion L. Starkey, *The Devil in Massachusetts* (New York, 1949), p. 185.

63. *Witchcraft Papers* 3:988–91.

64. For Martha and Giles Corey and Alice Parker, see *Witchcraft Papers* 1:239–66; 2:623–28, 632–33; 3:985–86, 1018–19.

65. Manwaring, *Conn. Probate Records* 1:7–8.

66. *Records of the Particular Court of Connecticut, 1639–1663, Collections of the Connecticut Historical Society,* vol. 22 (1928), p. 119.

67. Ibid., p. 258.

68. Manwaring, *Conn. Probate Records* 1:121–22.

69. Norfolk Deeds (manuscript volume, Registry of Deeds, Essex County Courthouse, Salem, Mass.), 1:116, 154.

70. *Essex Probate Records* 1:314–16; 2:160; *Essex Court Records* 1:199, 204, 229; 2:213; 3:292, 342, 413.

CAROL BERKIN

African American Women in Colonial Society

There was much in the slave experience that women and men shared. Denied any legal ability to control the conditions of their lives, both men and women labored according to their masters' demands. Both women and men were vulnerable to brutal punishment and to the separation of families; neither men nor women had any choice but to accept marginal food and clothing. Enslaved men and women were part of the productive system of the colonial economy; they were found on tobacco plantations, in rice fields, in urban households in Charleston and Savannah, and, though in fewer numbers, throughout farms and towns in the North.

But women also did reproductive work. By this we mean not only the actual bearing and nurturing of children but also the domestic work within slave quarters that fed husbands, fathers, and children and gave them the strength to persevere at the productive work of the masters' economy. As childbearing women, they were physically vulnerable in ways that men were not; indeed, slaves suffered a heavy proportion of deaths due to sudden infant death syndrome because of the malnutrition and overwork of mothers.* The law did not protect enslaved women against rape or seduction. Because the children of enslaved women followed "the condition of the mother," the legal system actually offered advantages to men of the master class who seduced or raped them. In the lives of enslaved women, economics and biology intersected in complex, forceful, and sorrowful ways.

Still, as Carol Berkin shows, enslaved women built strong bonds of family and community. Note the wide range of work that slave women did. Compare and contrast the work they did on plantations and in cities, North as well as South. Consider the pervasiveness of slavery throughout the colonies.

Mary came to Virginia aboard the *Margrett and John* in the spring of 1622, soon after the Powhatan Indians launched an attack on the English tidewater settlers. She entered a community still reeling from the violent death of 350 colonists killed in a single morning. That the slaughter took place on Good Friday added to the horror these colonial survivors felt, but the day carried no special meaning for Mary. She was, after all, neither English nor Christian. She was one of a handful of Africans brought against her will to this struggling Chesapeake colony.

We can say very little about Mary; her age when she arrived in Virginia, her physical appearance, her temperament, her abilities are all unknown. Yet her experiences before arriving in Virginia could not have differed greatly from those of other Africans wrenched from their homeland and carried to America. The accounts we have of the brutality of the slave traders, from both black and white witnesses,

*Michael P. Johnson, "Smothered Slave Infants: Were Slave Mothers at Fault?" *Journal of Southern History* 47 (1981): 495–509.

Excerpted from "The Rhythms of Labor: African American Women in Colonial Society," ch. 5 of *First Generations: Women in Colonial America* by Carol Berkin (New York: Hill & Wang, 1996). Reprinted by permission of the author and publisher.

of the painful forced march to the Atlantic coast of Africa in which women and men were chained together, of the humiliation of branding, and of the horrors of the "middle passage" allow us to envision her distress even if we lack her personal testimony on such matters. The knowledge we have of her adjustment to America—mastering a foreign tongue, adapting to a new climate, to strange clothing and food, a new physical environment, and a culture whose customs and values were alien—make the loneliness and isolation of her situation certain even if it is undocumented. Her circumstances, then, are more vivid than her personality.

Mary was taken to Richard Bennett's large tobacco plantation on the south side of the James River. Here she witnessed the full consequences of hostile relations between the English and the Indians, for only five of the fifty-seven servants who worked Bennett's Warresquioake plantation had survived the Good Friday assault. Although her English master needed every able-bodied worker he could muster, Bennett may not have set Mary to work in the tobacco fields. His culture identified agriculture with masculinity, and in these earliest decades of Chesapeake society, some masters may have been unwilling to overturn the gendered division of labor they held to be natural. Mary surely demurred from such notions, for in most West African societies women dominated agriculture. These very different traditions produced a surprising harmony in the matter of slave importation. Faced with demands for captives, African villages preferred to surrender up their males and protect their female agriculturists; faced with a need for fieldworkers, Europeans preferred to purchase men.

What we do know of Mary's life in the colonies is that she had good fortune. Despite the scarcity of Africans of either sex in the Chesapeake, one of Warresquioake's five lucky survivors of the Good Friday attack was a black man named Antonio. Mary took him as her husband, in fact if not in English law. In a society where early deaths routinely interrupted marriages, Mary and Antonio enjoyed a forty-year relationship. Together they made the transition from bound service to freedom, although how and when is unclear, and together they raised four children, whom they baptized in the Christian faith.

Like most freed servants, Mary and her husband—known in their freedom as Mary and Anthony Johnson—migrated from Bennett's plantation, seeking arable land of their own. The Johnsons settled on the Pungoteague River, in a small farming community that included black and white families. By mid-century, they had accumulated an estate of over 250 acres on which they raised cattle and pigs. In 1653, their good luck was threatened by a fire which ravaged their plantation and brought the Johnson family close to ruin. Mary's neighbors responded with sympathy, and local authorities helped by granting the Johnsons' petition that Mary and her two daughters be exempt from local taxes for their lifetimes.

This considerate act by the courts is the first concrete evidence that race set Mary and her family apart from their English neighbors. In seventeenth-century Virginia, taxes were assessed on people rather than on possessions, and Virginia's taxable citizens were those "that worke in the grounde." Such a definition was intended to exempt the wives and daughters of Virginia planters, whose proper occupation was domestic. By the time of the Johnsons' devastating fire, however, the earlier unity of gender had been severed by race and "Negro women" were denied this exemption. And yet the racial distinction was not so rigid, the practice was not so uniform that Mary's neighbors could not embrace her as a proper woman if they chose. . . .

In the 1660s, the Johnsons, like other eastern shore colonists, pulled up stakes and moved to Maryland in search of fresh land. The Johnsons may have arranged to have someone else finance their move, for they were claimed as the headrights of two wealthy planters. They were not, however, claimed as servants. Instead, Anthony was a tenant, leasing a 300-acre farm in Somerset County, Maryland, which he named Tonies Vineyard. Anthony and Mary's now grown sons and daughters soon joined them in Maryland, establishing farms nearby. Thus when Anthony died shortly after the move, Mary Johnson was surrounded by her family.

In 1672, when Mary sat down to write her will, a new generation of Johnsons was making its mark in this farming community. But a new generation of English colonists was making their task harder. Bad signs were everywhere: in a new colonial policy that forbade free blacks to employ white indentured servants, and in the Virginia and Maryland laws that lengthened terms for servants without indenture, a category to which almost every new African immigrant belonged. Mary's grandchildren, to whom she lovingly willed her cows and their calves, would grow to adulthood in a strikingly biracial society, for the number of African immigrants was rapidly growing. But few of these Africans would enter the world of free men and women as Mary and Anthony had done. The society that had once found room for "Mary a Negro," to become the matriarch of a comfortable family, could spare no such space for Mary's descendants. If it was accidental, it is apt that when Mary's grandson John died in 1706, the Johnson family disappeared from the historical record. . . .

In 1623 Mary Johnson was one of only twenty-three Africans in Virginia. By 1650, she was one of perhaps three hundred. . . . In the decade of Mary Johnson's death, the African population in the Chesapeake began to rise sharply, reaching 3,000 in Virginia by 1680 and continuing to grow until, by 1700, the colony had almost 6,000 black settlers. African population growth in Maryland was no less dramatic: in 1658 there were only 100 blacks in four Maryland counties, but by 1710 the number had risen to over 3,500, or almost one-quarter of the local population. Nearly 8,000 of Maryland's 43,000 colonists that year were black. Yet the mass involuntary migration of Africans had only begun. Between 1700 and 1740, 54,000 blacks reached the Chesapeake, the overwhelming majority imported directly to these colonies from Biafra and Angola rather than coming by way of the West Indies. Immigrants from the west, or "windward," coast of Africa poured into South Carolina as well. By the time of the American Revolution, over 100,000 Africans had been brought to the mainland colonies. For the overwhelming majority, their destination was the plantation fields of the upper and lower South.

The relentless demand for cheap agricultural labor spurred this great forced migration. As the English economy improved in the 1680s and 1690s, the steady supply of desperate young men and women willing to enter indentured servitude in the colonies dwindled. . . . Planters were forced to abide by customs that prevented labor after sunset, allotted five hours' rest in the heat of the day during the summer months, and forbade work on Saturday, Sunday, and many religious holidays. On the other hand, local courts would not acknowledge or uphold any claims to such "customary rights" by African servants . . .

Slavery—as a permanent and inheritable condition—developed unevenly across the colonies and within individual colonies. In the Chesapeake, the laws that sharply distinguished black bound labor from white were accompanied by laws that limited the economic and social opportunity of free blacks. Together, these laws established race as a primary social boundary. The process began before the greatest influx of Africans to the region. The 1672 law forbidding free black planters to purchase the labor of white servants squeezed those planters out of the competitive tobacco market. This disarming of African Americans in the economic sphere was echoed in Chesapeake laws that forbade blacks to carry or possess firearms or other weapons. In 1691, Chesapeake colonial assemblies passed a series of laws regulating basic social interaction and preventing the transition from servitude, or slavery, to freedom. Marriage between a white woman and a free black man was declared a criminal offense, and the illegitimate offspring of interracial unions were forced into bound service until they were thirty years old. A master could still choose to manumit a slave, but after 1691 he was required to bear the cost of removing the freed woman or man from the colony. Such laws discouraged intimacy across racial lines and etched into social consciousness the notion that African origins were synonymous with the enslaved condition. By 1705, political and legal discrimination further degraded African immigrants and their descendants, excluding them from officeholding, making it a criminal offense to strike a white colonist under any circumstances, and denying them the right to testify in courts of law. While Mary Johnson had never enjoyed the rights of citizenship available to her husband, Anthony, eighteenth-century African-American men of the Chesapeake lost their legal and political identity as well. Thus, the history of most African Americans in the Chesapeake region, as in the lower South, is the history of women and men defined by slavery, even in their freedom.

Much of a newly arrived slave woman's energy was devoted to learning the language of her masters, acquiring the skills of an agriculture foreign to her, and adjusting to the climate and environment of the Chesapeake. Weakened by the transatlantic voyage, often sick, disoriented, and coping with the impact of capture and enslavement to an alien culture, many women as well as men died before they could adjust to America. Until well into the eighteenth century, a woman who survived this adjustment faced the possibility of a lifetime as the solitary African on a farm, or as the solitary woman among the planter's African slaves. . . .

Under such circumstances, African women found it difficult to re-create the family and kinship relations that played as central a part in African identity as they did in Native American identity. In fact, the skewed sex ratio—roughly two to one into the early eighteenth century—and the wide scattering of the slave population, as much as the heterogeneity of African cultures and languages, often prevented any satisfactory form of stable family. Until the 1740s, those women and men who did become parents rarely belonged to the same master and could not rear their children together. The burden of these problems led many African-born women to delay childbearing until several years after their arrival in America. Most bore only three children, and of these, only two were likely to survive. With twice as many male slaves as female, delayed childbearing, and high mortality among both adults and infants, there was no natural increase among the Chesapeake slaves in the late seventeenth or early eighteenth century.

There was little any Chesapeake slave woman could do to rectify the circumstances of her personal life. While women of any race or class in colonial society lacked broad control over their person or their actions, the restraints of slavery were especially powerful. A woman deprived of physical mobility and unable to allocate the use of her time could take few effective steps to establish her own social world.

Although Mary Johnson may never have worked the fields at Warresquioake plantation, the slave women who came to the Chesapeake after 1650 were regularly assigned to field labor. Organized into mixed-sex work gangs of anywhere from two to a rare dozen laborers, slave women and men worked six days a week and often into the night. Daylight work included planting, tending, and harvesting tobacco and corn by hand, without the use of draft animals. In the evening, male and female slaves stripped the harvested tobacco leaves from stems or shucked and shelled corn. The crops were foreign to most African-born slave women, but the collective organization of workers was not. Indeed, slaves resisted any effort to deny them this familiar, cooperative form of labor.

By the middle of the eighteenth century, slave women on the largest Chesapeake plantations would wake to a day of labor that segregated them from men. As the great planters shifted from cultivation by the hoe to the plow, and as they branched out into wheat and rye production, lumbering, milling, and fishing, they reinstituted a gendered division of labor. Male slaves were assigned to the new skilled and semi-skilled tasks. While men plowed and mastered crafts, women remained in the fields, left to hoe by hand what the plows could not reach, to weed and worm the tobacco, and to carry the harvested grain to the barns on their heads or backs. When new tasks were added to women's work repertoire, they proved to be the least desirable: building fences, grubbing swamps in the winter, cleaning seed out of winnowed grain, breaking new ground too rough for the plow, cleaning stables, and spreading manure.

If many male slaves were drawn out of the fields and into the workshops or iron mills, few black women in their prime were assigned to domestic duty in the planter's house or taught housewifery skills. Instead, throughout the eighteenth century, young girls not yet strong enough for field labor and elderly women past their productive years in the hoeing gang were assigned to cleaning, child care, and other domestic tasks in the planter's home. Thus, much of the work done by Chesapeake slave women in 1750 differed little from the work done by slave women a half century earlier.

Slave women's work may have remained constant, but other aspects of their lives did not. By 1750, some of these women had the opportunity to create stable families and to participate in a cohesive slave community. These opportunities were linked to changes in the size of plantations and in the composition of their labor forces. Throughout the eighteenth century, great plantations developed, and the number of slaves on these plantations grew, too, ending the isolation the earliest generations had experienced. Many of these slaves were native-born rather than "saltwater," and their energies were not drained by the efforts of adjustment and acculturation. As English-speakers, they shared a common language, and in Christianity, many shared a common religion as well. Both were factors in helping creole slaves begin to create a distinctive community. The gradual equalization of the sex ratio among creoles also helped, and, so did the lower mortality rate. Finally, the evolution of this slave community and slave culture in the Chesapeake was aided by a growing opportunity for slaves to live away from the intrusive eyes of their white masters. The retreat from contact was mutual: many white colonists sought relief from the alien impact of Africanisms by creating separate slave quarters. In these slave quarters blacks acquired a social as well as a physical space in which to organize everyday domestic activities, establish rituals, and develop shared values and norms. Most important, they were able to establish families through which to sustain and uphold this shared culture. . . .

Black women delivered their children in the company of other women, just as English colonists continued to do throughout most of the eighteenth century, and midwives saw the mother through these births. The differences are perhaps more telling than the similarities, however. African nursing customs, retained by many slave women, produced wider intervals between children than English weaning

Although white masters seem to have hesitated to require field work of indentured white women servants, they felt no hesitancy in requiring enslaved women to work in the fields at heavy labor. In this rare eyewitness testimony, Benjamin Henry Latrobe's watercolor documents the practice in late-eighteenth-century Virginia. He gave it the ironic title An Overseer Doing His Duty. *(Watercolor, ink, and ink wash on paper, 1798. Papers of Benjamin Henry Latrobe. Courtesy of the Maryland Historical Society, Baltimore, Maryland.)*

patterns. Slave women bore an average of nine children, giving birth every twenty-seven to twenty-nine months. The power of masters to separate wives and husbands—through hiring-out practices or sales—led to wide gaps in many slave women's childbearing histories. Conception and birth cycles in King William Parish, Virginia, reveal other ways in which race interposed upon gender. Two-thirds of the black births in King William Parish occurred between February and July, while white women bore their children in the fall and early winter months. For black women, this meant that the most disabling months of pregnancy often fell in the midst of heavy spring planting chores. Perhaps this accounts for the greater risk of childbirth for slave mothers and the higher infant mortality rate among slave children. . . .

Thus, after 1750, a Chesapeake slave woman might be able to live out her life in the company of her family, as Mary Johnson had done. Yet she knew that powerful obstacles stood in her way. Husbands often lived on other plantations. Children between the ages of ten and fourteen, especially sons, were commonly sold. Sisters and brothers were moved to different slave quarters. And on a master's death, slaves were often dispensed along with other property to his heirs. A master who might never separate a family during his lifetime thought it his obligation to his survivors to divide them at his death. Hard times could prompt a master to sell a slave woman's family members in order to provide for his own. A planter's widow might keep her family intact by hiring out her slave's sons or daughters. Even the wedding celebration of a planter's daughter might mean the tragic separation of a slave woman and her own young daughter, sent to serve in the bride's new home. In the 1770s, the westward expansion of agriculture into the Piedmont and beyond led to mass dispersal of slave families among the new farms and plantations. Slave women, and their men, could succeed in creating effective family structures despite the many demands of slavery, but they could not ensure their permanence. . . .

The planters of the Lower South also relied on an African slave-labor force. Indeed, the slave-based agriculture of this region developed with remarkable speed in the early eighteenth century. . . . Despite clear laws against slaveholding, the Georgia settlers were, as one observer put it, "stark Mad after Negroes." Illegal sale of slaves took place right under the nose of colonial authorities, eventually forcing the ban to be lifted. Between 1751 and 1770, the slave population of Georgia rose from 349 to 16,000; these slaves were imported directly from Africa or purchased from traders in South Carolina.

In the region's showplace city, Charleston, a largely creole population of African Americans swelled to over half the population, filling positions as house servants, boatmen, dockworkers, and artisans of all kinds. The highly acculturated Charleston slave women shared little in common with their rural sisters, for the slaves who worked the large rice plantations had almost no contact with white society. The plantation slave society that developed was the product of an isolation more pronounced than in the Chesapeake. And because of the steady importation of Africans throughout the eighteenth century, this community differed significantly from the creole-dominated world of the Chesapeake slaves. West African traditions shaped the rice and indigo culture in fundamental ways. Plantation slaves spoke Gullah, a language which combined English and several West African dialects, and they preserved the African custom of naming children for the day of the week on which they were born. Chesapeake girls and boys came to recognize themselves in the diminutives of English names—Lizzie, Betty, or Billy—but among slave children in the Lower South names like Quaco, Juba, and Cuba linked them to their African past.

Like Chesapeake slave women, Lower South women worked the fields. But as rice growers, the women of Carolina and Georgia labored under a task system rather than in gangs. This system assigned specific tasks to each slave but did not regulate the time in which it was to be completed. Thus, slaves on the rice plantations controlled the pace of their workday. The task system did provide a measure of autonomy, but no slave who worked the rice plantations would call their occupation an enviable one. "The labor required for the cultivation [of rice] is fit only for slaves," wrote one frank observer, "and I think the hardest work I have seen them engaged in." The most grueling of all the tasks was the pounding of grain with mortar and pestle—and this was a woman's job. It was also the deadliest; mortality rates were higher in the Lower South than in the Chesapeake, and the women who beat the rice were more likely to die than the men who spent hours stooping in the stagnant rice-paddy waters.

By the middle-of the eighteenth century, each slave was responsible for a quarter of an acre. Other activities on the plantation—pounding the rice, making fences, and later, in tidal rice cultivation, digging critical irrigation systems—were tasked as well. . . . The task system was not designed-to-accommodate the women and men who worked in the rice fields or paddies, of course. Its logic lay in the fact that effective rice cultivation did not require the constant supervision of workers. Yet the task system allowed slaves to develop a lively domestic or internal economy. South Carolina and Georgia slaves were given land on which to grow a variety of crops, including corn, potatoes, tobacco, peanuts, melons, and pumpkins, all of which they marketed. This agriculture within an agriculture quickly became entrenched, despite efforts by lawmakers to curtail it. By 1751 Lower South authorities were fighting a staying action, insisting that slaves could sell their rice, corn, or garden crops only to their own masters. These restrictions were ignored. Slave women and men continued to sell everything from corn to catfish, baskets, canoes, and poultry products. But here, unlike in the Piedmont, slave agriculture reflected the community's active African tradition, for Low Country slaves grew tania, bene, peppers, and other African crops. When local slave crops reached Charleston, slave women took charge of their marketing. These female traders were known for their shrewdness in bargaining with customers of both races, to whom they hawked poultry, eggs, and fruit at sometimes shocking prices. Slave women willingly paid their masters a fee for the privilege of selling the pies, cakes, handicrafts, or dry goods they made or brokered, for any profits after the fee was met belonged to them. These women drew on a West African tradition of female traders not unlike the female market-town traders of England. . . .

Slavery in the North was an accepted tradition but not a widespread habit. The Dutch had employed slave labor extensively when New York was New Netherlands, using African labor to compensate for the scarcity of colonists from Holland. The small farmers of New England, on the other hand, had little practical use for slave labor, and where slaves were employed it was often because of their master's close tie to the transatlantic slave trade. For example, the merchant-landowners of Rhode Island who made their riches in trade liked to flaunt their prosperity by retaining anywhere from five to forty slaves. One merchant magnate boasted a holding of 238 slaves. But the majority of New England slaves, like the slaves of the middle colonies, were found in the cities, where shortages of white labor in artisan shops, on the docks, and in household or personal service were a periodic problem. The greatest influx of African slaves to Pennsylvania, for example, came during the Seven Years War, when the flow of English and other European servants was seriously disrupted. By mid-century, roughly 10 percent of the population of Boston, Philadelphia, and New York was black, although only one out of every five families owned a slave.

A slave woman in these Northern cities spent her days engaged in housework—cooking, cleaning, washing and ironing, tending the fires and the gardens, and looking after her master's children. She passed her nights sleeping in the garret or the kitchen. She might be hired out to nurse the sick, to put in a neighbor's garden, to preserve food or wait on tables for a special occasion, but few urban slave women were ever hired out to learn a craft. Colonial artisans considered their shops a male domain. Ironically, the "black mammy" so often associated with plantation life was not an authentic figure of the colonial South, but she could be found in the fashionable homes of Philadelphia and New York. Slaves in the countryside also did housework, but more of their time was spent tending larger gardens, raising poultry, milking cows, and spinning cloth than in cooking, cleaning, or serving as personal maids to farm family members. At harvest time, these women were assigned to fieldwork.

As they worked in the wheat fields of southern Pennsylvania or in the kitchens of Boston, Northern slave women experienced constant, intimate contact with white society. Whether their owners were kind or callous, their values and customs were ever present, and a solitary black servant, working, eating, sleeping in a crowded Pennsylvania farmhouse, or in the close quarters of a merchant's home, lacked the steady reinforcement of her African heritage. Not surprisingly, Northern slave women were more likely to acculturate than their sisters in the plantation South.

Urban slave women had little hope of creating a family that could remain intact. Slaveholdings were too small for a woman to choose a husband from the household, and few urban colonists were willing to shoulder the costs of raising a slave child in their midst. Rural slaveholders could set a slave's child to work in the garden or field, but in the cities youngsters were simply a drain on resources and living space. At least one master preferred to sell his pregnant slave rather than suffer having her child underfoot. Other masters solved the problem of an extra mouth to feed by selling infants—or, in one case, giving his slave's baby away. Slave women who dared to start or add to their families were sometimes separated from the men who fathered their children. In Boston, a pregnant woman and her husband chose to commit suicide rather than endure the dissolution of their family. Urban slave women who were allowed to keep their children often lost them quickly. Communicable diseases and cramped quarters combined in deadly fashion in every household in eighteenth-century colonial cities, but black infant mortality rates were two to three times higher than white.

A slave woman's life—like a slave man's—could be enriched by a family, an independent culture and community, and the autonomous spaces created by the task system or wrested from the gang-labor system of the Chesapeake. In a sense, these were all forms of resistance to enslavement. But there were other forms of resistance as well—rebellion, suicide, murder, escape, self-mutilation, disobedience, the destruction of tools and equipment, arson, theft of supplies, feigned illness, feigned pregnancy, and feigned ignorance or stupidity. Colonial English society rarely assumed that slaves were docile or content, and slaveholders preferred to rely on repressive laws, a show of force, and harsh reprisals rather than a belief in the passivity or contentedness of their slaves. . . .

The work demanded of Northern slave women was less grueling than the work done with mortar and pestle in the Carolinas or with hoes and hands in the Chesapeake tobacco fields. Indeed, slavery in the North was generally less brutal than in the Southern colonies. Yet enslaved women in the middle colonies and New England also resisted, ran away, and rebelled. Here, too, women fled their master's home, determined to reunite with their husband or children. And here, too, women participated in the rare but violent uprisings of slaves seeking to overthrow their oppressors. When authorities moved against participants in the 1712 Slave Revolt in New York City, several women were among those arrested and convicted. And when a slave presented the first petition for freedom to the newly formed state legislature of Massachusetts in 1782, she was a woman. The woman, Belinda, pressed these Revolutionaries to make good on their state constitution's pledge to discontinue slavery, stating her case with eloquence: "I have not yet enjoyed the benefits of creation . . . I beg freedom."

DOCUMENTS

The Law of Slavery and Freedom

Virginia Establishes a Double Standard in Tax Law

Tax policy was the site of one of the earliest and most significant interventions made by English colonial lawmakers to cordon off black women from white, practically and symbolically. In the 1643 law that follows, the Virginia Assembly made one of its first discriminations according to race. The provision clarified the tithing system—by which Anglican ministers in each parish would be paid. European colonists paid a variety of taxes based not on income but "per poll" (per person) or according to the property they owned. Given the scarcity of circulating coins or paper currency, taxes were typically paid in goods including foodstuffs. From 1643 forward, heads of household would be required to pay annually the designated amount for each male over fifteen in the household (whether free, indentured, or enslaved)—and for what other category of person? We can think of the distinction that the law silently made between "negro" and other women as a continuation, or a second act, in the process of sexual stereotyping described by Jennifer L. Morgan (pp. 37–46). The Virginia law not only placed an extra financial burden on free black families, but also broadcast the ruling class's dictum that African and African-descended women were assumed to be field laborers, thus denying their domesticity.

The 1643 statute was tested in the colony's lower courts. Would authorities permit any exceptions to be made? Two examples are given here. In the first case, white male colonist Francis Stripes had recently married; probably a neighbor or tax assessor complained to the court that Stripes had not been paying the proper tithe. In Susannah's case, we do not know how the petitioner made a living, but it was not necessarily as a farm laborer. What do you imagine she argued in her plea (which was likely made orally) to the bench of local gentlemen who served as justices? How did they justify their ruling to themselves and to her? The court clerk's omission of Susannah's surname reflected a common colonial tendency to erase the chosen identities of people of color.

Be it further enacted and confirmed That there be tenn pounds of tob[acco]o per poll & a bushel of corne per poll paid to the ministers within the severall parishes of the colony for all tithable persons, that is to say, as well for all youths of sixteen years of age as upwards, as also for all negro women at the age of sixteen years.

Assembly of Virginia, act 1, March 1643, in William Waller Hening, *The Statutes at Large: Being a Collection of All the Laws of Virginia, from the First Session of the Legislature, in the Year 1619*, 13 vols. (New York: R & W & G Bartow, 1823), 1:242; Lower Norfolk County Order Book, 1665–75, fol. 73, and Charles City County Order Book, 1677–79, 216, reproduced in *The Old Dominion in the Seventeenth Century: A Documentary History of Virginia, 1606–1689*, rev. ed., ed. Warren M. Billings (Chapel Hill: University of North Carolina Press, 2007), p. 183. The cases are reprinted with the kind permission of the author and publisher.

1671 case, Lower Norfolk County: It is the opinion and Judgement of the Court that francis Stripes ought to pay Leavyes and tythes for his wife (shee being a negro) It being according to Law; and therefore ordered that he pay the Same for the Last year past, as well as this present [year] and so for the future.

1677 case, Charles City County: Upon the petition of Susannah a free Negro-Woman that she may be Exempted from paying Levyes, And Whereas the Worshipful Courte is informed of her strength and ability It is thereupon thought fit that she be not Exempted but pay Levyes.

"According to the condition of the mother . . ."

The North American system of slavery relied heavily on marking differences of status (slave or free)—by visible bodily difference (black or white). Free black people and enslaved mulattoes undermined the simplicity of these signals, displaying in their very beings the fact that it was power, not nature, that placed any particular individual in one status or another.

In defining slavery—a condition not then recognized in English law—colonial lawmakers faced the question of how to interpret the status of children born to parents who were not married to each other, and whose fathers were white and mothers were black. Might such offspring claim free status? Could white fathers be obliged to take responsibility for the children's upbringing? In Spanish colonies in Central and South America, a complex system of godparenting made it possible for white fathers to maintain a wide variety of relationships with their mixed-blood children.

The Virginia law of 1662 shows how English colonists settled the question (Maryland had passed a similar statute two years earlier). Along with other laws passed at mid-century, it marked a turning point—from a period when blacks' status was often ambiguous and freedom was not foreclosed to a long era in which the default assumption would be that African-descended persons were enslaved and had few opportunities to become free. The Latin phrase for the rule enshrined in the colonial slave codes was *partus sequitur ventrem*, meaning that the status of the child (slave or free) would follow the mother's status. How did the 1662 law conflict with traditional English inheritance practices? What do the statute's two sections reveal about how Virginia legislators wished to shape interracial sexual relations? (With regard to the second section, note that the usual fine for fornication was 500 pounds of tobacco.) What are the implications of the law for children whose fathers were free black men and whose mothers were enslaved?

Whereas some doubts have arrisen whether children got by any Englishman upon a negro woman should be slave or free, *Be it therefore enacted and declared by this present grand assembly*, that all children borne in this country shalbe held bond or free only according to the condition of the mother, *And* that if any christian shall committ fornication with a negro man or woman hee or shee soe offending shall pay double the [usual] fines. . . .

Assembly of Virginia, act 16, December 1691, in William Waller Hening, *The Statutes at Large: Being a Collection of All the Laws of Virginia, from the First Session of the Legislature, in the Year 1619*, 13 vols. (New York: R & W & G Bartow, 1823), 2:170.

"For prevention of that abominable mixture . . ."

Late in the seventeenth century, Virginia and Maryland lawmakers imposed harsh disincentives for whites and blacks who wished to marry (such as Francis Stripes and his wife in the earlier document extract, stopping just short of an outright ban like the one that would later be enacted and would stand until the 1967 U.S. Supreme Court ruling in *Loving* v. *Virginia* (pp. 767–768). What interracial relationships are omitted in Virginia's 1691 law? How would you characterize the legal status of mixed-race children born out of wedlock to free white women? Why did legislators think this set of laws would be self-enforcing?

[1691] . . . for prevention of that abominable mixture and spurious issue which hereafter may encrease in this dominion, as well by negroes, mulattoes, and Indians intermarrying with English, or other white women, as by their unlawful accompanying with one another, *Be it enacted* . . . that . . . whatsoever English or other white man or woman being free shall intermarry with a negroe, mulatto or Indian man or woman bond or free shall within three months after such marriage be banished and removed from this dominion forever. . . .

And be it further enacted . . . That if any English woman being free shall have a bastard child by any negro or mulatto, she pay the sume of fifteen pounds sterling, within one moneth after such bastard child shall be born, to the Church wardens of the parish . . . and in default of such payment she shall be taken into the possession of the said Church wardens and disposed of for five yeares, and the said fine of fifteen pounds, or whatever the woman shall be disposed of for, shall be paid, one third part to their majesties . . . and one other third part to the use of the parish. . . and the other third part to the informer, and that such bastard child be bound out as a servant by the said Church wardens untill he or she shall attaine the age of thirty yeares, and in case such English woman that shall have such bastard child be a servant, she shall be sold by the said church wardens, (after her time is expired that she ought by law to serve her master) for five yeares, and the money she shall be sold for divided as is before appointed, and the child to serve as aforesaid.

[1705] *And be it further enacted*, That no minister of the church of England, or other minister, or person whatsoever, within this colony and dominion, shall hereafter wittingly presume to marry a white man with a negro or mulatto woman; or to marry a white woman with a negro or mulatto man, upon pain of forfeiting or paying, for every such marriage the sum of ten thousand pounds of tobacco; one half to our sovereign lady the Queen . . . and the other half to the informer. . . .

Assembly of Virginia, act 16, April 1691, in William Waller Hening, *The Statutes at Large: Being a Collection of All the Laws of Virginia, from the First Session of the Legislature, in the Year 1619*, 13 vols. (New York: R & W & G Bartow, 1823), 3: 86–87; and Assembly of Virginia, ch. 49, sec. 20, October 1705 in Hening, *Statutes at Large*, 3:453.

A Massachusetts Minister's Slave Marriage Vows

Although Africans and African-descended people made up a much smaller proportion of the population and labor force in northern than in southern colonies, few white northerners took issue with the assumptions that undergirded the slave system. In fact, the merchants of Newport, Rhode Island, made enormous profits as the most active slave traders in the English colonies. For a gentleman, having one or two enslaved persons among his dependents was seen as a status symbol. Clergymen—who were respected for their learnedness, but were rarely wealthy—were sometimes presented with the gift of an enslaved youth or adult by their wealthy parishioners. By the eighteenth century, New England elites did not hesitate to encourage enslaved men and women to acculturate by embracing Christianity. Church records contain scattered entries for blacks—free and enslaved—receiving baptism, owning the covenant, marrying, having their children baptized, and being buried.

This is the "form of a Negro-Marriage" used by Congregational clergyman Samuel Phillips of Andover, Massachusetts, when enslaved men and women came to him, asking to be wed, during his sixty-year pastorate (1710–71). Similar vows were used in other churches. Read the vows aloud, and imagine what the marriage ceremony was like. How would you characterize the marriage contract that is being made? Which Christian rules is the Reverend Phillips selectively invoking? Some years later, in the famous *Jennison* v. *Walker* case that is often cited as ending slavery in Massachusetts, attorney Levi Lincoln confirmed and challenged the paradox at the core of these vows: "The master has a right to separate the Husband and wife—is this consistent with the law of nature[?] Is it consistent with the law of nature to separate what God has joined and no man can put asunder?"*

Minister: "You,____do now in the Presence of God, and these Witnesses, Take____:to be your Wife; Promising that so far as shall be consistent with the Relations which you now sustain, as a Servant, you will Perform the Part of an Husband towards her; And in particular, you Promise, that you will Love her: And that, as you shall have the Opportunity & Ability, you will take a proper Care of her in Sickness and Health, in Prosperity & Adversity: And that you will be True & Faithfull to her, and will Cleave to her only, so long as God, in his Providence, shall continue your and her abode in Such Place (or Places) as that you can conveniently come together:—Do you thus Promise?"

Then the same Vow was declared for the woman to agree to.

Minister: "I then agreeable to your Request, and with the Consent of your Masters &

*"Brief of Levi Lincoln in the Slave Case Tried 1781," *Collections of the Massachusetts Historical Society*, 5th ser., 3 (1877): 441.

George E. Howard, *A History of Matrimonial Institutions* . . . (London, 1904), vol. 2, pp. 225–26, quoting George H. Moore, "Slave Marriages in Massachusetts," *Dawson's Historical Magazine*, 2nd ser., 5 (1869): 137. We have modernized spelling and expanded abbreviated words.

Mistresses, do Declare, that you have Licence given you to be conversant and familiar together, as Husband and Wife, so long as God shall continue your Places of abode as aforesaid; and so long as you shall behave yourselves as it becomes Servants to doe: For you must, both of you, bear in mind, that you Remain Still, as really and truly as ever, your Master's Property, and therefore it will be justly expected, both by God and Man, that you behave and conduct your-selves, as Obedient and faithfull Servants towards your respective Masters & Mistresses for the Time being. . . ."

"I shall now conclude with Prayer for you, that you may become good Christians, and that you may be enabled to conduct as such; and in particular, that you may have Grace to behave suitably towards each Other, as also dutifully towards your Masters & Mistresses, not with Eye-Service, as Men-pleasers, but as the Servants of Christ, doing the will of God from the heart."

ANN M. LITTLE

Captivity and Conversion: Daughters of New England in French Canada

Ann Little's essay introduces us to the geopolitics of the second half of the colonial period. Protestant England and Catholic France, along with their independent-minded Indian allies, engaged in a succession of imperial wars involving North American territory from the late seventeenth century through the Seven Years' War of 1756–63. In 1700, English settlers far outnumbered the 15,000 French soldiers, missionaries, fur traders, and *habitants* (farmers) clustered chiefly in settlements along the St. Lawrence River. However, the English occupied only a narrow sliver along the eastern seaboard, while the French claimed authority (and established mutually advantageous relations with native groups) from Louisiana to Canada along the Mississippi River and around the Great Lakes. It was not at all clear if one European power (France, Spain, or England) could gain ascendancy over the continent as a whole.

The author takes us on a detective's journey to recover the voices of and find out what happened to the children, teenagers, and grown women who were captured from New England towns and farms in wartime raids by Abenaki allies of the French. On arrival in Canada, English girls were typically schooled at Ursuline convents in New France's principal northern towns, Montreal, Québec (City), and Trois Rivières. Finding these New England women in the thorough records kept by French notaries—baptisms, marriages, deaths—means that they converted to Catholicism. Letters exchanged with their birth families in New England confirm that a high proportion of them chose not to be redeemed or ransomed so as to return to their onetime homes.

A good way to assess the author's evidence is to construct a list or table profiling the life courses of the captives who stayed. What do you find are the most compelling factors explaining why New England women remained in New France?

In the 1690s in the midst of the first war with New France, English depictions of frontier warfare and captivity shifted dramatically from identifying Indians as the primary danger to New England to portraying the French and their Catholicism as the chief threat to the New England way. While Indians were still formidable opponents in the battle, in New England they came to be feared more as agents of the French than as actors in their own right . . . Even more threatening . . . were European enemies who had studied the tactics of their Native allies so well. French Catholics proved more successful than Indians at encouraging English people to cross cultural borders and live among them for the rest of their lives. European Catholics were perhaps even more disturbing than Indian enemies

Excerpted from Ann M. Little, "'A Jesuit will ruin your Body & Soul!': Daughters of New England in Canada," ch. 4 of *Abraham in Arms: War and Gender in Colonial New England* by Ann M. Little (Philadelphia: University of Pennsylvania Press, 2007). Reprinted by permission of the author and publisher. Notes have been edited and renumbered.

because they were not all that different from English Protestants. They dressed the same, they did the same work, they ate the same food, they worshipped the same God—and thus they could be plotting and scheming just about anywhere and at any time. . . . Thus New Englanders began to worry less about Indian captivity and more about the vulnerability of captives in the hands of dedicated missionaries like the Jesuits, Ursulines, Sulpicians, and the Sisters of the Congregation of Notre Dame. Captivity narratives began to discuss the dedicated efforts that French priests and nuns made to convert their English prisoners of war, a theme that was . . . a feature of the genre through the Seven Years' War (1756–63).[1]

What was perhaps additionally disturbing about French successes in getting and keeping English captives is that the majority of the captives were New England's daughters, sisters, wives, and widows. While male captives always comprised the majority of New Englanders in captivity (mostly as prisoners of war, sometimes as adopted captives), female captives were vastly more likely to remain in Canada, convert to Catholicism, and marry.[2] This apparent danger to female captives jibed with long-standing puritan fears of women's greater vulnerability to spiritual corruption, as well as their specific susceptibility to the seductions of Catholicism. The sensually rich experiences of the Mass were believed to be powerfully attractive to unlearned, undisciplined women, as they had already proved to be to the Indians living in the French mission villages like Odanak (St. Francis), Kahnawake, La Montaigne, and Lorette.[3] Girls and women who remained in Canada became the focus of a great deal of familial and cultural anxiety in New England, as they lived lives that openly rejected the faith, language, and laws of their fathers. The following pages offer some explanations for their decisions to stay in Canada, choices that so baffled, wounded, and disturbed their families and communities in New England.

While for a time they were the subjects of intense diplomacy and worry on the part of their families and New England officials alike, these girls and women have been largely forgotten in the histories of the northeastern borderlands. This is partly because they did not write narratives about their experiences the way returned captives did, but it may also be due in part to their families' shame of daughters or sisters who stayed in Canada even when they were free to return to New England, and even in the face of parental and brotherly pleading and admonitions to come home. Because these women chose to remain in Canada, the sources for understanding their motivations and their lives in Canada are very thin. Furthermore, once these girls and women decided to remain in Canada, their New England families apparently had very little to say about them. . . . [M]ost New England families evidently disinherited and turned their backs on their disobedient daughters. . . .

Why is it that the usually prolific, expansive, and furious New England writers like Cotton Mather had so little to say about these girls and women who did not come home? Perhaps the shame and anger they felt both at being bested by the French, as well as because of their daughters' defiance, explains why these women's stories have been largely deleted from the family histories of New England.

New England's paranoia about the designs of the French and their successful alliances with Indians emerged in local writings and publications as early as King Philip's War (1675–78). Reports on the war's progress on the Maine and western Massachusetts frontiers note the presence and influence of the French among the Indians. By the time of the first war with New France, the English came to see the French as their major—if not yet their only—rivals for the control of North America.[4] The clear success of the French in creating political and diplomatic alliances with Indians (particularly with the Eastern Abenaki and the mission Iroquois) made a formidable European foe truly frightening to the English living in the northeastern borderlands at the end of the seventeenth century.

Fear and loathing of the French as enemies went hand-in-glove with the strong anti-Catholicism that was a foundational part of New England's sense of its historical and religious mission. Because religion and nationalism were so intertwined for English Protestants in the early modern era, it is impossible to separate New Englanders' fears of French political and military victories and their fear of being compelled to embrace Catholicism. . . . New England was founded by people who were especially zealous adherents to several versions of reformed Protestantism. They and their descendants believed that warfare and Indian captivity in the northeastern borderlands were evidence, variously, of God's disfavor or his willingness to test their faith. New Englanders who saw Indian warfare as an opportunity to test and prove their faith were even more willing to see wars against Catholic New France as an extension of Christ's struggle against the Devil for worldwide dominations.[5]

. . . [A]nti-Catholicism in Old and New England was . . . a strongly gendered phenomenon. Ever since the struggles between Elizabeth and Mary Queen of Scots for the English throne in the 1560s and 1570s, Protestant propagandists had effectively linked Catholicism with femininity and claimed that this feminization was both the cause and result of political and spiritual corruption. By the seventeenth century, xenophobia and misogyny were knit into the fabric of transatlantic English nationalism. All English people were in theory united by their collective struggle against the "Scarlet Whore of Babylon," the foreign and feminized Roman church.[6]

With King William's War under way (1688–97), New England writers and publishers of the 1690s produced some of its first virulently anti-French and anti-Catholic books and pamphlets. . . . [The Puritan minister] Cotton Mather was one of the most enterprising purveyors of this propaganda. . . . Mather's books and other contemporary pamphlets show that both the Roman empire and the Church of Rome represented despotic power in the minds of New Englanders and stood only for the power to compel people of the true faith to worship false gods.[7]

. . . [W]e cannot dismiss Mather's fears as mere paranoia, as the French had purposefully and determinedly sought to bring their religion to the Indians. Led chiefly by the energetic Catholic Reformation orders of the Jesuits and the Ursulines, religious men traveled down the St. Lawrence River to the Great Lakes, up to Hudson's Bay, and down the Mississippi to spread their faith, and they established successful Indian missions throughout New France and its borderlands from modern-day Maine and Nova Scotia westward to Ontario, Michigan, and the Mississippi River valley. Religious women established schools in Québec, Montreal, and Three Rivers that served as vital centers for the preservation and transmission of French language and culture as well as religion. The work of these French men and women stood in direct contrast to the distinctly underfunded efforts of the English to convert Indians and establish "praying towns." Only a minority of English ministers and settlers expended any efforts whatsoever on preaching to and converting Native Americans. . . .[8]

Cotton Mather agreed with other frontier observers that New England had failed grievously in its neglect of the souls of the Indians, and he argued that King William's War was in part God's punishment of New England for failing their duty to spread the gospel as energetically as French priests had brought their religion to the New World: "*This is the Vengeance of God upon you, because you did no more, for the Conversion of those Miserable Heathen.*" But Mather's concern about Protestant missionary work was not simply for fear of the Lord's judgment; he also saw how French missionary work had paid off in their strong military alliances with the Eastern and Western Abenaki in particular. "Had we done, but half so much as the *French Papists* have done, to Proselyte the *Indians* of our East, unto the *Christian Faith*, instead of being, *Snares and Traps* unto us, *and Scourges in our Sides, and Thorns in our Eyes* they would have been, *A wall unto us, both by Night and Day.*" Mather supports this observation with the claim that English captives of the Indians had been told by their captors that "*had the English been as careful to Instruct us, as the French, we had been of your Religion*!" While at other times in the same book Mather scorns the close association between the French and the Indians, disdaining the "*Frenchified Indians*" and "*Indianized French*" that were the result of such New World alliances, in the end he recognizes the advantage of their cooperation and blames New England for not reaching out to the Indians. "[I]f the Salvages had been Enlightened with *The Christian Faith*, from us, the *French Papists* could never have instill'd into them those *French Poisons*."[9]

. . . Mather played a key role in introducing explicitly anti-Catholic themes to captivity narratives with the publication of Hannah Swarton's story in 1697. Even amidst her difficult removes with the Indians after her capture from Casco in 1690, she reports, "yet

I dreaded going to *Canada*, to the *French*, for fear lest I should be overcome by them, to yield to their Religion; which I had *Vowed* unto God, *That I would not do*. But the Extremity of my Sufferings were such, that at length I was willing to go, to preserve my Life." Like many New England captives who were brought to Canada, she was relieved to receive the hospitality of the French and gloried in eating familiar foods and dressing in European clothing once again. But this was the danger of consorting with the French—their way of life was so comfortable to English captives, especially after months or even years with the Indians, that it made captives all the more susceptible to seduction by "popery." After being taken to Québec and so "kindly Entertained" and "courteously provided for . . . so that I wanted nothing for my Bodily Comfort, which they could help me unto," she was inevitably cast into a conflict that caused her intense spiritual discomfort. (Many readers might have assumed that as a woman, she was naturally more easily seduced by creature comforts that appealed to her carnal nature.) But Swarton, as we hear her through Mather's pen, was all too aware of the dangers that faced her: "Here was a great and comfortable Change, as to my *Outward man*, in my *Freedom* from my former Hardships, and Hard hearted Oppressors. But here began a greater Snare and Trouble to my Soul and Danger to my *Inward man*." Her mistress in Québec, and several priests and nuns "set upon me . . . to perswade me to Turn *Papist*." Swarton, through Mather's narrative, claims that they sometimes used scriptural arguments, "which they pressed with very much Zeal, Love, Intreaties, and *Promises*," and sometimes "Hard Usages," even threatening to send her "to *France*, and there I should be *Burned*, because I would not Turn to them." This kind of rhetoric served two purposes: it would stir up the emotions of the New England reading public to hear of the allegedly barbarous methods of French proselytizers, but it also gave Swarton and Mather the opportunity to demonstrate the steadfastness of her faith and prove herself a worthy model for other New Englanders to emulate . . . Through her ordeal [Swarton] . . . was comforted by Psalm 118:17–18, "*I shall not Dy but live, and Declare the works of the Lord*.". . .[10]

. . . The gaping hole in Swarton's narrative of triumph over French priestly designs is the fact that Swarton's own daughter Mary remained in Montreal after she herself returned to New England. She and Mather end her narrative with an earnest request for the "prayers of my Christian Friends, that the Lord will deliver" her [daughter]. Captured with her mother when she was fourteen, at the age of twenty-two Mary married an Irish fellow convert, John Lahey (more often rendered in the French records as Jean LaHaye) in 1697, the same year Mather published her mother's narrative. They presented eleven children for baptism over the next twenty years, three of whom had New England-born godmothers, Christine Otis, Freedom French, and Mary Silver. As eloquent as Mather and Swarton are about her heroic efforts to resist conversion, they are silent about the decision her daughter made to become a French *bonne femme* instead of an English goodwife.[11]

As Swarton's narrative and personal experiences with captivity suggest, children (and especially daughters) were more vulnerable to the various cultural and religious conversions that might be required of them in captivity. Elizabeth Hanson was grateful when she was purchased by the French in 1725, whom she reports "were civil beyond what I could either desire or expect." "But," she reports with some alarm, "the next Day after I was redeemed, the *Romish* Priests took my Babe from me, and according to their custom, they baptized it." The priests explained that "if it died before [baptism], it would be damned, like some of our modern pretended reformed Priests." Hanson, a Quaker, worked in an insult aimed at other Protestants in her discussion of priestly intervention. Significantly, Hanson also reports that the priests gave her daughter a new Catholic name: "Mary Ann Frossways" (actually *Françoise*, or French).[12]

The captivity narrative of John Gyles, published in 1736, nearly fifty years after his boyhood capture and captivity among the Maliseet (Eastern Abenaki) in 1689, illustrates how completely French Catholics had replaced Indians as the enemies of New England and highlights particular fears of the vulnerability of children to conversion. After his initial capture, his Indian "master" shows him to a Jesuit missionary, who Gyles says "had a great mind to buy me. . . . I saw the Jesuit shew him Pieces of Gold, and understood afterward, that he tendered them for me." The politics of the mid-eighteenth century surely shaped his memories of 1689, as he reports a great deal of anxiety about conversion. "The Jesuit gave me a Bisket, which I put into my Pocket, and dare not eat; but buried it under a Log, fearing that he had put something in it, to make me Love him: for I was very Young, and had heard much of the Papists torturing the Protestants &c. so that I hated the sight of a Jesuit."

Fear of being made to "love" a priest may also reflect other dangers Catholic clergy represented in the minds of English people: their sexual ambiguity, and the possibility that they may replace English mothers and fathers, as Indian men and women had for many captives. Just as Catholicism itself was suspect because of its allegedly feminized nature and its greater appeal to women, so priests were often held in suspicion by Protestants as "unnatural" or feminized men. Men who lived intimately together and shunned marriage were suspect in a culture that elevated heterosexuality to a near-sacrament and regularly depicted Catholicism as a shield for all manner of sexual improprieties. Additionally, New Englanders may have feared that French priests (or nuns) might offer their captive children another alternative family. . . .

A poignant moment in Gyles's narrative suggests that priests might represent both of these kinds of danger, sexual and familial, at the same time. The last time Gyles saw his mother alive, he told her that he might be sold to a Jesuit, and he reports that she reacted with great alarm: "Oh! my dear Child! If it were GOD's Will, I had rather follow you to your Grave! Or never see you more in this World, than you should be Sold to a Jesuit: for a Jesuit will ruin you Body & Soul!". . .[13]

. . . [W]e have almost no direct testimony from captives who remained in Canada. What little evidence we have of these people, their lives in Canada, and their reasons for remaining there comes from their slight communications with their New England families and their chance encounters with other captives who returned to New England to author narratives of their captivity among the Indians and the French. The numbers and demography of those who remained in Canada speak powerfully to the notion that their fates were not accidental. While they were always in the minority of those taken during the border wars (approximately 392 of 1,579 total captives, or less than a quarter .of the captive population), girls and women were much likelier to remain in Canada, convert to Catholicism, marry French men, and (presumably) fill Canada's need for European housewifery. Of ninety-five captives taken between 1689 and 1755 who can be reliably traced through the Canadian notarial records, sixty-five (nearly 70 percent) were girls and women. While overall only about one captive in twenty stayed in Canada, female captives were nearly seven times as likely to stay in Canada as their male peers. . . . [A] bare majority of the female captives who remain in Canada were abducted as children; almost a third of them were adolescents or adults—a few women were even married mothers or widows in their thirties and forties. . . . [14]

What made these (mostly) girls and young women remain in Canada? More than half of them (thirty-four out of sixty-five) were taken into captivity before their thirteenth birthday, many of them as very young children. These captives, who frequently lost all memories of their English families and mother tongue, were the most easily assimilated into Canadian life. William Pote tells the sad story of Rachael Quackenbush, whom he saw while in prison in Québec during King George's War (1744–48). "This Child had been with ye French Ever since she was Taken with her Parents which is about 18 months. There was her Father & mother, Grandfather and Grandmother In this prison. They Endeavour'd to make her speak with ym, But she would not Speak a word Neither in Dutch nor English." Even for those captive girls who remembered their families and their native language, after spending several years in Canada, learning French, converting to Catholicism, and marrying a French man, it may have been simply unimaginable to return to a home a family they no longer knew nor remembered well. However, twenty of these captives were adolescents or adults when taken into captivity, young women who were almost fully grown and fully acculturated as English-speaking Protestants, and who would have been unlikely candidates to forget their native language and homeland. The choices of these twenty women are difficult to untangle, although given their age, it is appropriate to call their remaining in Canada a choice. [By the time they were free to return to New England], many of these older captives—especially the older teenagers—had probably adapted to life in Canada and perhaps had already converted to Catholicism. Many may have met a French man they fancied . . . Some of them may have resented or disliked their natal families; surviving court records indicate that at least one of them was eager to escape an abusive home in New England, as we will see.[15] . . .

There are some broad economic and legal facts that might have made New France a more attractive place for women. In stark contrast to the English common law tradition, French Canadian laws governing the "communauté de biens," or the "marriage community" of husband and wife, followed the Custom of Paris, which said that except for wealth in land owned by either partner prior to marriage, husbands and wives owned marital property equally. Although husbands were designated "masters of the community," neither husbands nor their wives could sell, mortgage, or alienate their joint property without the written consent of the other. . . . Upon the death of either spouse, the widow or widower inherited half of all real and personal property, as well as half the debts; the other half of the property and debts went to the children. Thus, women in French Canada were not economically disenfranchised in marriage as were their sisters in the English colonies. We will never know the extent to which French marital laws were major factors in these women's decisions to turn their backs on New England. However, these property laws may be indicative of a culture that was generally more welcoming and tolerant of women as economic producers and decision makers. This autonomy might have been especially attractive to former captives, as many of them would have spent significant time among Indians before they were purchased by French masters, and they may have come to expect the authority over family resources exercised by their Indian mothers.[16]

Beyond this legal framework, it is clear that New France had very good reasons to want to recruit and retain New England girls and women in the late seventeenth and early eighteenth centuries. French agricultural settlments in the St. Lawrence River valley had long suffered from an imbalanced sex ratio and they were desperate for women trained in European housewifery skills like dairying, baking, and working with textiles (spinning, knitting, weaving, and sewing). Censuses of seventeenth-century New France are unreliable and vary greatly, but they indicate that the scarcity of women was a problem in colonial New France. One historian has put the overall percentage of women among French immigrants to Canada at 12.3 percent for the seventeenth century. . . .[17]

Women skilled in European housewifery would have made the lives of male *habitants* more comfortable, to be sure, but these skills were also central to European identity in a place that was dominated by other people and other cultural ways. Indians in the colonial northeastern borderlands did not keep cows or consume dairy products; they did not bake European bread; and they did not produce their own thread or cloth. Furthermore, in the later seventeenth century, French officials came to see that the more obvious fruits of marriage might be important to the colony's political future. Observing the rapidly increasing English population along the Atlantic seaboard and in the Connecticut and Hudson River valleys, Canadian officials concluded that recruiting and retaining women with strong bodies and European skills was not just a personal convenience for male *habitants*; it was a political necessity if the French were going to best their rivals for the control of North America.[18]

Officials in New France spent considerable money and energy recruiting French women for Canadian settlement or, alternatively, training Indian girls to become like French wives and mothers, and religious women played a key role in these efforts in the 1670s and 1680s. Teaching not just French girls but English captives and Indian girls and women in their convent schools, the nuns instructed them in academic subjects, religion, and women's domestic skills that were in such scarce supply in early New France. This dedication to girls' education resulted in a literacy rate higher among French women than men before the British conquest, although in the end few Indian girls and women crossed over to become French housewives—the majority of Native women trained in French schools assumed Indian ways when they returned to their villages and married there. . . . [19]

One of the most striking things about the treatment of English female captives in Canada was the attention and personal involvement of the colony's highest officials.

Governor of Montreal (1698–1703) and then governor general of New France from 1703 to his death in 1725, Philippe de Rigaud, Marquis de Vaudreuil, was a powerful central player in the politics and diplomacy of the first two intercolonial wars. Thus it is revealing that he took a personal interest in several female captives during his governorship, even bringing some of them into his household and looking after their educations. He was the godfather of Mary Silver when she was baptized in 1710 among the Sisters of the Congregation of Notre Dame in Ville-Marie (near Montreal), and he placed Mary Scammon among the Ursulines in Three Rivers in 1725. . . . [T]he girls and women that Vaudreuil took such a personal interest in were high-status captives. In order to preserve diplomatic relations, he would have had a strong interest in ensuring these young women's health and happiness as much as possible, given their circumstances. However, the measures he took—putting them into convent schools and witnessing their baptisms and marriages—doubtlessly served to bind them closer to their adopted home. Other officials of New France also served as godfathers and witnesses at the marriages of English captives, as the notarial records are full of references to "Intendants" performing these duties. In contrast, no New England governors ever expended equal funds or political capital to get these young women back.[20]

Vaudreuil's son Pierre de Rigaud, Marquis de Vaudreuil-Cavagnal, who was governor of Three Rivers and then Louisiana before he became governor general of New France in 1755, carried on his father's tradition of looking after English captives, especially the girls. He witnessed their baptisms, put them into convent schools, and took them into his home. He placed Jemima Howe's daughters Mary and Submit Phipps in the Ursuline convent school in Québec during the Seven Years' War with the instructions that "they should both of them together, be well looked after, and carefully educated, as his adopted children." When he brought Mary Phipps to France with him after the French capitulation in 1760, her mother reports that she was married there "to a French gentleman, whose name is Cron Lewis." Submit became so enthusiastic about her new faith that she refused to leave her convent. "[S]he absolutely refused," wrote her frustrated mother, "and all the persuasions and arguments I could use with her, were to no effect." Only because the younger Vaudreuil himself insisted that she be returned to her mother did Submit finally live up to her name, but she returned to her mother quite unwillingly. This very personal touch was doubtessly influential in the lives of the young women taken in by the Vaudreuil family over a half-century, but perhaps more significantly, it suggests how important these girls and women were to their new country.[21]

Beyond this personal and official encouragement of English captives, the French crown also directly assisted their assimilation into Canadian society by offering naturalization and even cash payments to male and female captives alike. In 1702, Canadian officials secured two thousand livres of crown support for thirty-eight Catholicized English captives (twenty-one women and seventeen men). In May of 1710, Louis XIV naturalized twenty-eight male and thirty-eight female war captives, and again in 1713 he naturalized another thirty-four men and four women. . . .

The interest of government officials in the fates of these captive girls and women was important, but they relied heavily on Church officials to bring the young women over to French language, culture, and religion. While priests alone had the power to administer the sacraments of baptism and marriage that were so important to bringing ex-captives into Canadian society, much of the daily hard work of these multiple conversions was done by the nuns of Québec, Montreal, and Three Rivers through their convent schools. As we have seen, these female-run institutions were central to seventeenth-century efforts to bring Native girls and women into French society, so adding English girls to their lists of pupils required little adjustment on the part of the sisters who gloried in their evangelical work.[22]

We know that all of the captives who stayed to make lives in Canada were persuaded by this evangelism—or, at least that they accepted the necessity of converting to Catholicism in order to be naturalized. There is too little evidence on the religious opinions of former captives in Canada for us to generalize about their religious experiences. Renouncing Protestantism and converting to Catholicism was an enormous ideological leap, as religion and nationalism were so tightly bound to each other in New England.

Even English families on the far borderlands of New England had a strong sense of the moral and intellectual superiority of English Protestantism versus their perceptions of the so-called despotism and corruption of French Catholicism, although they may not have appreciated the finer points of doctrinal difference. Nevertheless, many former captives may have become earnestly devout Catholics. . . . For those who had spent months or years among Indian families who were not living in mission towns, they may have felt a welcome familiarity upon seeing a cross, hearing European music sung, or taking communion again. Some might have come to Catholicism through the practice of Indian families who adopted them. . . .

While officials of both the church and the state clearly played an important role in acculturating English captives, the girls and women themselves established bonds with one another that appear to have eased their adoption into Canadian society. The fact that English captives created and maintained their own networks that lasted decades is further evidence that remaining in New France was a choice, not a fate, for most of them. Canadian notarial records show that ex-captives witnessed one another's baptisms, weddings, and children's baptisms; . . . these women were friends and neighbors who continued to support one another through their lives. . . .

We get only a haphazard picture of these networks through the captivity narratives of returned New Englanders . . . Susanna Johnson reports being approached by two ex-captives turned Ursuline nuns when Johnson and her sister as captives went to the Ursuline convent in Québec to visit Jemimah Howe's daughters, Mary and Submit Phipps. "We here found two aged English ladies, who had been taken in former wars." One of them was Esther Wheelwright (now La Mère Marie-Joseph de l'Enfant Jésus), and the other perhaps Sarah Davis, who took the name Marie-Anne Davis de Saint-Benoit. Mother Esther (as she called herself) was taken in the same 1703 raid on Wells, Maine, along with the Storer cousins Mary and Priscilla, including Priscilla's sister Rachael who also married a French man but settled in Québec rather than Montreal. Mother Esther too expressed interest in the English visitors to her convent, and she told Johnson that she had "a brother in Boston, on whom she requested me to call, if ever I went to that place." After she was redeemed and returned to New England, Johnson followed up on the connection. "I complied with her request afterwards, and received many civilities from her brother." Mother Esther, Mary St. Germaine, and other captives clearly had the connections to go home if they wanted to. They were interested in and affectionate toward their New England friends and families, but they had made their home in Canada. . . .[23]

[A]t least one of the women who stayed in Canada fled some of the more dramatic consequences of New England patriarchy. Abigail Willey (or Willy) stands out . . . because of her age and her marital status: taken in 1689 from Oyster River, New Hampshire, she was a married woman of 32 with two daughters who were about thirteen and eight. Her young daughters were prime candidates to stay in Canada, but why would someone of such a relatively advanced age, and with a husband and other children remaining in New Hampshire, choose baptism and (eventually) remarriage in New France? In a 1683 statement to the New Hampshire colony court, Abigail Willey outlined the harsh reality of her life as an English goodwife. She complained of her husband's chronic violence against her and her isolation as an abused woman: "I have for several years past lived and spent, without making my addresses to any in authority, with Stephen Willy, my husband, often suffering much by sore and heavy blows received from his hand, too much for any weak woman to bear." She also related his frequent threats "to take away my life by the evil disposition of his own mind, seeing that neither his own relations, neither my own natural brothers, dare countenance in any way of natural friendship [with Stephen]." Abigail Willey described herself, in short, as "the suffering subject of his insatial jealousy." Her claims in this petition were supported by an accompanying deposition by a neighbor, Joseph Hill, who one night heard Stephen Willey yell, "I will kill her or whore." (Perhaps Hill meant to indicate that Willey said either, "I will kill her," or "I will kill the whore.") He apparently went into the Willey home to intervene in the violent affair, and found "John Willy, his brother, standing between the said Stephen and his wife, to prevent them from danger."

She had not brought her situation to the attention of local officials and instead suffered for years in silence, perhaps because she believed herself to be the victim of the English courts as well as of her husband. An earlier experience before the bar was grievously humiliating: when Stephen Willey brought her before Judge Edgerly, Willey reports that her husband "at his own request procured of said judge the shameful sentence of ten strips, to be laid upon me at a post." The judge later reversed himself and cancelled the whipping, accepting a twenty-shilling fine instead. But then, when Willey went to visit her sister in Kittery, she reports "said judge sent after me as a runaway, to be procured; the second time to be dealt with according to law." . . . Clearly, she saw this English magistrate and English law as operating at the whim of her disreputable and abusive husband. Perhaps she chose to remain in Canada because she saw an opportunity to escape not just a despotic husband but a legal system that did not operate in her interest.[24]

Colonial Anglo-American women's historians have shown how difficult it was for woman to procure a divorce on any grounds other than desertion, [adultery,] or sexual insufficiency on the part of the husband. Catholic Canada was hardly a libertine's playground—in fact, divorce was nonexistent—but French Canadian women could claim greater economic self-sufficiency when their marriages broke down, and for a wider variety of reasons. There were two types of legal separation available to aggrieved couples: division of the marital property without physical separation, or a separation of bed and board in addition to the division of all assets. Of 149 petitions for separation in the seventeenth- and eighteenth-century St. Lawrence Valley, most were filed by wives, and most focused on the profligacy of the husband and his inability to manage domestic affairs, situations that were frequently linked to drunkenness and domestic violence. . . . New France, like New England, tolerated wife-beating, but evidence from separation petitions suggests that repeated spousal abuse, death threats, insanity, and venereal infection could gain wives a bed and board separation from men like Stephen Willey. The differences between the New France and New England legal systems are telling, with Canada offering women more flexibility and control in both happy and unhappy marriages. New France's legal tradition offered abused wives more economic rights and autonomy in marital separations than . . . New England.[25]

We know comparatively little of Willey's life in Canada and can glean only a few details from the notarial records that note her transformation from English wife and mother, to French servant, and eventually to wife of a Montreal *habitant*. Willey was baptized as a Catholic in 1693, took the name Marie Louise Pilman (presumably a transcription error, after her maiden name Pitman), and was described as a servant to Hector de Callières, a Montreal official; apparently even servitude was preferable to her life as an abused New England wife. Her husband Stephen's 1696 will made no mention of her name or her existence whatsoever; neither did he recognize or remember his two daughters in Canada. He died sometime in or before 1700; Mary Louise Pilman married Edouard de Flecheur in 1710 and was naturalized the same year, at the age of fifty-three. Her two daughters had preceded her in marriage to French men . . .[26]

English families used inheritances and inheritance law to compel their captive children and siblings to return to New England, although this tactic was used differently depending on the sex of the captive. Based on the fragmentary evidence available in wills and probate records, it appears that daughters' inheritances were more likely to be contingent upon their return to New England, while New England's captive sons were twice as likely to receive their inheritances without returning to New England. . . . The fact that female captives in Canada fared worse than their male counterparts when it came to their inheritances may be unsurprising, given the patriarchal nature of inheritance law in general: eldest sons reaped great privileges that eldest daughters did not. Furthermore, property ownership was itself a gendered phenomenon, because the law of coverture meant that Anglo-American women might easily spend the majority of their lives as *femes couverts*, and thus not as property owners. But even beyond this, evidence indicates that parents of children who remained in Canada of their own choice used the power of inheritance to communicate disapproval of their children's decisions, or to compel a return to New England, especially when it came to their daughters. . . . [T]he legal structures of Anglo-American society communicated very clearly whose work was valued and whose was not; and whose interests were directly represented and whose were not. We will never know to what extent the concepts of coverture versus the marriage community (in New France) influenced the thinking of captive girls and women, but it was a difference that they were likely aware of, especially those daughters who were threatened with disinheritance.

The way in which William and Mary Moore's parents' estate was settled in 1694 reveals a clear double standard of male and female captives' inheritance. Whereas brother William could receive his portion of the estate "provided said William be alive & demand it," sister Mary could receive hers only if she returned to New England: "if Mary More doo not return from captivity, then her redemption money and her portion to be equally devided among the rest of her brethren and sisters." . . . The language parents used could be very specific: daughters could not simply come home to claim their inheritance (like William Moore would have been permitted to); they had to renounce French law, language, and religion, and come home to stay. Joseph Storer wrote in his 1721 will: "I Give & Bequeath to my beloved Daughter Mary St. Germain Fifty pounds in good Contrey pay upon Condition that She return from under the French Government & Settle in New England.". . . Esther Wheelwright was . . . disinherited by her mother's 1750 will, unless she "by the Wonder working Providence of God be returned to her Native Land and tarry & dwell in it."[27]

Captive sons fared much better. . . . Even when their claims on inheritance were disputed, returned male captives had good luck in court, especially with the help of a mother's testimony. William Hutchins, taken from Kittery, Maine, in 1705 when he was nine, was apparently presumed dead when the state ordered the division of his late father's estate in 1721, as he was left entirely out of the proceedings. When he returned to Maine in 1733 to claim his inheritance, . . . his brothers denied his identity, so he decided to sue them for his inheritance. Many neighbors testified that he was in fact the real William Hutchins; in the end his mother's judgment that "he is the first born of my Body" prevailed. Hutchins not only received an inheritance, he won the double portion due him as the eldest brother. Conveniently settled, he married a New England woman in 1734 and remained for some time in Kittery. Clearly, English male captives who remained in French Canada were still seen as legitimate heirs, by their families and by the courts, even decades after they had left New England. Their sisters were not so lucky. . . .[28]

The case of Mary Storer and her contested relationship with her English family bears close examination, both for what it suggests about the female captives who remained in Canada and for one family's reaction to this exercise of daughterly will and determination. The surviving correspondence of Mary Storer St. Germaine consists of nine letters to her eldest brother, Ebenezer, one letter each to her mother and another brother, five letters from her husband, Jean St. Germaine, to Ebenezer, and two letters from Ebenezer, one addressed to Mary, the other to her husband, a total of eighteen letters that span nearly thirty years, from 1725 to 1754. Read together, these letters offer valuable glimpses into family relationships in colonial New England. More importantly, they are almost the only direct words we have from a female captive who remained in Canada, and thus offer us some insight into the mind of one captive as she attempts to reconcile the English and the French sides of her family and her own identity. Mary's brother Ebenezer seems to have functioned as the go-between for his sister and the rest of their family in these letters, performing as the executor of not only his father's will but also his family's wishes regarding Mary in general.[29]

The correspondence begins twenty-two years after Mary was taken by the Indians, when both she and Ebenezer were middle-aged parents. Mary Storer was taken in the 1703 Abenaki raid on Wells, Maine, when she and her cousins Rachael and Priscilla Storer were taken in the same attack as Aaron Littlefield and Esther Wheelwright. . . . [T]he Storer girls were teenagers: Mary was eighteen, Priscilla nineteen, and Rachael about sixteen. All three Storers were therefore young women at the time of their captivity, not children, which may have contributed to greater resentment among the Storer family of their daughters' choices. All three married French men and remained in Canada—Mary and Priscilla . . . lived near each other in Montreal the rest of their lives, and Rachael (baptized "Marie Françoise") settied in Québec with her husband, Jean Berger.

The occasion for what seems to have been a new or renewed epistolary relationship with Mary's brother Ebenezer was a visit she made to Boston in the late spring and summer of 1725, as the first letters she writes are posted from Newport, Rhode Island, where she was awaiting the ship that would return her to Montreal. These first letters, all but one addressed to Ebenezer, communicate her distress at having been so long separated from her birth family and indicate that like the Williams family, her family wanted to return her and her children to New England and thus to the Protestant faith. In her own handwriting and crude spelling, she assures brother Ebenezer, "my harte is alwais full of sorey and my eyes full of ters to think that I have toke sech a grate jorney to come to se my deare father and mother and had no coumforte to staye longe with them." In another letter she repeats the same sentiments in similar language: "[While] I am not with you my harte and tender love is alwaise with you I shall never for git what every good peple has sead to me becaus I know that is for my good and I pray to god onley that it maie be so an if I can sende one of my childrine I will." Another letter, which was probably intended for her brother Seth, a congregational minister in Watertown, Massachusetts, also gives thanks for some good counsel she received during her visit: "I had but a litel time with you who I thought woulde show and teach me more then aney bodey [sir?] but what you have saide to me I will not forgett it and I hope god will in able me in all my aflections and that it may be for the best and good of my soule deare brother." Clearly, Mary's natal family had urged her to the Protestant fold, as well as tried to convince her to return to New England. Her notation to Ebenezer that "if I can sende one of my childrine I will" seems to indicate that the Storers were interested in taking in and evangelizing her Catholic children as well. . . .

Although Mary wrote that she understood that the Storer family's counsel to return to New England and to puritanism was "for the goode of my soule and bodey," she had no intention of remaining with them. Her continuing correspondence with Ebenezer suggests that she was adept at shifting between identifying with her natal family in Boston and with her husband and children in Montreal. Continuing to address herself to Ebenezer before her return home, she writes, "Dear brother it grievs me to thinke of my father and mother that I had soe litel time to staye with theme but I finde the time very longe with strangers and longe to be with my famelie." Thus by calling her natal family "strangers," as opposed to her "famelie" in Montreal, she makes it clear that her family of first allegiance was in Montreal, not in Boston. And while she implies that her Boston family are "strangers" to her, her emotional attachment to them was quite powerful immediately after her 1725 visit. "Deare brother I remember what you have saide to me I thanke you and all that has spoke for my goode." Then again using formulaic language, she writes, "I desier your prayers for me who is youre sister til death with a harte full of sorey and my eyes full of tears fearewell my deare brother and sister I remaine your loving and sorrowful sister," and signs herself, as she did through most of their correspondence, "Mary St. Germaine, Mary Storer," as though to signify her awareness of her two families and her two identities. With only a few notable exceptions, however, her married name was written above her maiden name.

. . . For eight years after her visit to Boston, Mary and Ebenezer continued to exchange letters every year or two, updating each other on family news and sending along formulaic but apparently warm good wishes. When Ebenezer sent news of their father's death, Mary [wrote]. . . "I pray to god to comforte us all wee are father les children [while] I am hear [in Montreal], you may beleive my harte love is with you all we are al the same blode you can not denie it."

. . . In a letter to her mother, she writes that Ebenezer told her, "my dear father maide his will that I [might?] be equal to my sisters you may believe my dear mother [while] I am far of[f] from you and my deare familei I belave that is not cappable to kep it frome me in conseonc that is for me who is youre [own] child." Regarding her father's command that she remove herself from "French government" in order to receive her inheritance, Mary then claims it is impossible for her even to visit Boston: "wee have a governer & he will nat give any permission to goe in [New] England to our contre[y]," she writes, and names the merchant in Boston whom she had designated to receive and convey her inheritance. . . . [S]he signs her letter, "your dutifull daughter," a departure from her usual practice, and a maneuver that suggests an effort to recast herself as a properly obedient and submissive daughter.

There exists no letter of reply from Mary's mother, but brother Ebenezer's reply underscores the differences her New England family drew between Mary and her siblings. . . . Ebenezer does not promise [her] her inheritance, but he writes that he will remind their mother of her request, and assures Mary, "I know she will do any thing yt is proper & it be not against ye will of our Father deceas'd." The problem was that what Mary was requesting was clearly against her father's will. Joseph Storer had decreed that "if She doth not returne [to New England] Then I Give & bequeath to her the Sum of Tenn Shillings in Countrey pay." This paltry remembrance stood as a rebuke to Mary's resistance of her father's will, and her mother and brother were apparently willing to let the rebuke stand. Legally they could not have directly sent Mary St. Germaine her portion directly from her father's estate, but they could have chosen to give her her portion out of their own fortunes.

Perhaps not surprisingly, there is no record of Mary St. Germaine ever receiving her inheritance, and the surviving correspondence between her and her brother ceases for several years. Only in the autumn of 1739, nearly six and a half years since her last surviving letter to Ebenezer, Mary wrote to him, and the tone of that letter suggests that she is still annoyed with him and his role in her non-inheritance. Whereas before she had always written him in English in her own hand, this letter appears to have been written by an amanuensis; it is also, significantly, written in French. She opens this letter with a standard, if cooler, salutation to Ebenezer, and then quickly announces the purpose of her letter: "I desire the favour to Let me hear from you & your family for as I have not heard any knews of mother I dont know whether she is on the Land of the Living which obliges me to adress my self to you to lett me hear from her." Notice how her language has changed since her fervent correspondence around the time of her father's death. . . . "If you still have any Love for me I hope you will not refuse me that Comfort," she adds, in further confirmation of her alienation from her natal family. She passes on news of her family, briefly reporting her children's marriages and sadly noting the death of her youngest son the previous year. We do not know if she ever received a reply. . . .

This may well have been the last letter Mary St. Germaine wrote to her brother Ebenezer, for the next letter in the collection is by her husband, Jean, dated eight and a half years after Mary's last letter. Like Mary's last letter, it too is written in French. Seven months after the fact, he wrote the man he addressed as his "very dear brother" to let Ebenezer know of his sister's death. "She died with all possible resignation to the will of God, that is to say as a perfect Christian, and as she had been here 39 years that we were together we had a blessed union and we never had a single difficulty. You know well my dear brother that her death is a great affliction to me, but I must submit to the will of our Creator, as it was he who gave me one of the best women in the world.". . .

Stories like that of Mary Storer St. Germaine show the effects that choices like hers had on the workings of patriarchal power within New England families. The Storer family was typical of other New England families, . . . who also went to great lengths to recover their daughters and save them from the twin evils of French government and Catholicism, or to punish them for their rejection of New England government and Protestantism, or both. Any captives who turned their backs on New England by converting to Catholicism and remaining in Canada represented a painful and shameful failure of the New England way, boys and men as well as girls and women. But New England communities and colonial governments actively courted the return of male ex-captives by offering them cash and jobs, whereas former female captives were offered little if any incentive to return. Instead, it was the government of New France that went out of its way to retain female captives from New England, especially in the years 1689–1713. Mary Storer St. Germaine's story demonstrates that New England families interpreted their daughters' conversion to Catholicism and marriage to French men and Indians as a rejection of New England patriarchal authority. Instead of dutiful obedience and submission to their fathers' (or brothers') household government, women like Mary Storer St. Germaine set themselves against New England's prescribed gender roles when they refused to come home and return to puritanism. While their own decision to abandon New England is no doubt part of the reason they have been written out of New England history, perhaps their families' shame and desire to forget these daughters are also responsible for the fact that so many of them have disappeared from the New England record.

Notes

1. Frances E. Dolan, *Whores of Babylon: Catholicism, Gender, and Seventeenth-Century Print Culture* (Ithaca, NY.: Cornell University Press, 1999).

2. James Axtell, *The Invasion Within: The Contest of Cultures in Colonial North America* (New York: Oxford University Press, 1985), 287–301; Barbara E. Austen, "Captured . . . Never Came Back: Social Networks Among New England Female Captives in Canada, 1689–1763," and Alice N. Nash, "Two Stories of New England Captives: Grizel and Christine Otis of Dover, New Hampshire," both in *New England/New France, 1600–1850*, ed. Peter Benes (Boston: Boston University, 1992), 28–48; William Foster, *The Captors' Narrative: Catholic Women and Their Puritan Men on the Early American Frontier* (Ithaca, N.Y.: Cornell University Press, 2003).

3. On women's alleged vulnerability to the devil's blandishments, see Carol Karlsen, *The Devil in the Shape of a Woman: Witchcraft in Colonial New England* (New York: Norton, 1987), especially chs. 4 and 5; Elizabeth Reis, *Damned Women: Sinners and Witches in Puritan New England* (Ithaca, N.Y.: Cornell University Press, 1997).

4. For reports of French collaboration with the Abenaki during King Philip's War, see Henry Jocelyn and Joshua Scottow to Gov. John Leverett, September 15, 1676, Coll. S-888, misc. box 33/21, Maine Historical Society, Portland, Maine; *Documentary History of the State of Maine* (Portland, Maine: Lefavor-Tower, 1869–1916), 4:377–79.

5. Francis D. Cogliano, *No King, No Popery: Anti-Catholicism in Revolutionary New England* (Westport, Conn.: Greenwood Press, 1995), introduction and chs. 1–2.

6. Anne McLaren, "Gender, Religion, and Early Modern Nationalism: Elizabeth I, Mary Queen of Scots, and the Genesis of English Anti-Catholicism," *American Historical Review* 107 (June 2002): 739–67; Dolan, 6–27.

7. Cotton Mather, *Humiliations follow'd with Deliverances* (Boston, 1697), 30–31. He made the same historical argument a few years later in *Decennium Luctuosum: an History of Remarkable Occurences in the long war which New England hath had with the Indian Salvages, 1688–1698* (Boston, 1699).

8. Francis Jennings, *The Invasion of America: Indians, Colonialism, and the Cant of Conquest* (Chapel Hill: University of North Carolina Press, 1975), 228–53. On the praying Indians more generally, see Ann Marie Plane, *Colonial Intimacies: Indian Marriage in Early New England* (Ithaca, N.Y.: Cornell University Press, 2000).

9. Mather, *Decennium Luctuosum*, 81, 215–16.

10. Mather, *Humiliations follow'd with Deliverances*, 59–71; Emma Lewis Coleman, *New England Captives Carried to Canada* (Portland, Maine: The Southworth Press, 1925; reprint, Bowie, Md.: Heritage Books, 1989), vols. 1 and 2.

11. Mather, *Humiliations follow'd with Deliverances*, 72; Coleman, *New England Captives*, 1:204–08.

12. Elizabeth Hanson, *God's Mercy Surmounting Man's Cruelty* (Philadelphia, 1729), 34; Coleman, *New England Captives*, 2:163.

13. John Gyles, *Memoirs of Odd Adventures* (Boston, 1736), 4–5; Dolan, 85–93.

14. Alden T. Vaughan and Daniel K. Richter, in "Crossing the Cultural Divide: Indians and New Englanders, 1605–1763," *American Antiquarian Society Proceedings*, 90 (April 16, 1980), 23–99; author's database compiled from the cases documented by Coleman, *New England Captives*, vols. 1 and 2.

15. William Pote, Jr., original ms. journal kept by him 1745–47 during captivity among the French & Indians, Ayer Collection, Newberry Library, Chicago, Ill., 15; Axtell, *Invasion Within*, 291–94; Laurel Thatcher Ulrich, *Good Wives: Image and Reality in the Lives of Women in Northern New England, 1650–1750* (New York: Oxford University Press, 1983), 208–13.

16. Louise Dechêne, *Habitants and Merchants in Seventeenth Century Montreal* (Montreal: McGill-Queens University Press, 1992), 240–49; Trevor Burnard and Ann M. Little, "Where the girls aren't: women as reluctant migrants but rational actors in early America," in *The Practice of U.S. Women's History: Narratives, Intersections, and Dialogues*, ed. Eileen Boris, Jay Kleinberg, and Vicki Ruiz (New Brunswick, N.J.: Rutgers University Press, 2007), 12–29.

17. Peter Moogk, "Manon's Fellow Exiles: Emigration from France to North America before 1763," in *Europeans on the Move: Studies on European Migration, 1500–1800*, ed. Nicholas Canny (Oxford: Clarendon Press, 1994), 236–60; Leslie Choquette, "French and British Emigration to the North American Colonies: A Comparative Overview," *New England/ New France, 1600–1850*, ed. Peter Benes (Boston: Boston University, 1992), 49–59.

18. For evidence of the state's drive to bring more properly trained housewives into Canada, see, for example, the correspondence of Governor Frontenac and Minister Colbert, *Rapport de L'Archiviste de la Province de Québec* (Québec: Ls-A. Proulx, 1927), 7:44, 60, 65–66, 82 (1673–74); and the correspondence of Governor Frontenac and Intendant Bochart Champigny to the Minister, 8:351, 359, 377 (1697–98).

19. Leslie Choquette, "'Ces Amazones du Grand Dieu': Women and Mission in Seventeenth-Century Canada," *French Historical Studies* 17 (1992): 627–55; Clark Robenstine, "French Colonial Policy and the Education of Women and Minorities: Louisiana in the Early Eighteenth Century," *History of Education*

Quarterly 32 (1992): 193–211; Natalie Zemon Davis, "Marie de l'lncarnation: New Worlds," in *Women on the Margins: Three Seventeenth-Century Lives* (Cambridge, Mass.: Harvard University Press, 1995), 63–139.

20. Coleman, *New England Captives*, 1:316–17, 330–31, 356–57, 425–35, 2:44–58, 147,390–91; SC1 45X, Massachusetts Archives Collection, 51:212–13, and 72:13–15, Massachusetts State Archives, Boston; Ann M. Little, "The Life of Mother Marie-Joseph de L'Enfant Jesus, or, How a little English Girl from Wells became a Big French Politician," *Maine History* (Winter 2002), 276–308.

21. Coleman, *New England Captives*, 2: 320–21, 391, 396; Bunker Gay, *A genuine and correct account of the captivity, sufferings & deliverance of Mrs. Jemima Howe, of Hinsdale in New Hampshire* (Boston, 1792), 16–18.

22. Coleman, *New England Captives*, 1:121–29; Choquette, "'Ces Amazones du Grand Dieu'"; Little, "Mother Marie-Joseph."

23. Susanna Johnson, *A Narrative of the Captivity of Mrs. Johnson, together with a Narrative of James Johnson*, 3rd ed. (Windsor, Vt., 1814; reprint, Bowie, Md.: Heritage Books, 1990), 89–90.

24. Coleman, *New England Captives*, 1:255–61; Nathaniel Bouton, ed., *Collections of the New Hampshire Historical Society*, vol 8 (Concord: McFarland & Jenks, 1866), 146–48; Ulrich also cites domestic violence as a reason why Willey might have wanted to remain in Canada, *Good Wives*, 209.

25. Cornelia Hughes Dayton, *Women Before the Bar: Gender, Law, and Society in Connecticut, 1639–1789* (Chapel Hill: University of North Carolina Press, 1995), ch. 3; Nancy Cott, "Divorce and the Changing Status of Women in Eighteenth-Century Massachusetts," *William and Mary Quarterly* 3rd ser., 33 (1976): 586–614; Peter Moogk, *La Nouvelle France: The Making of French Canada—A Cultural History* (East Lansing: Michigan State University Press, 2000), 229–33.

26. Coleman, *New England Captives*, 1:255–61.

27. Evidence taken from Coleman, *New England Captives*, vols. 1 and 2, *passim*. Specific cases from Vol. 1: 234–35, 418–19, 431.

28. Coleman, *New England Captives*, 1:391–93.

29. Mary Storer Papers, Massachusetts Historical Society, Boston, Mass. All letters discussed below are in this collection.

CORNELIA HUGHES DAYTON

Taking the Trade: Abortion and Gender Relations in an Eighteenth-Century New England Village

Some pregnancies end spontaneously, probably because of an abnormality in the fetus or in the way it is implanted in the womb. Colonists made little distinction between spontaneous and induced abortion; no statute attempted to regulate the practice. Efforts to end pregnancies by the use of herbs like savin were generally understood to be efforts to "restore" the regular menstrual cycle. Experienced midwives had impressive records of safe deliveries that are comparable to pre-penicillin twentieth-century experience. Maine midwife Martha Ballard left an extraordinary diary that reveals not only the daily rhythms of her life, but also her skill in delivering some 900 women without losing a mother in childbirth. Ballard, who practiced up until her death in 1812 at age seventy-seven, felt considerable ambivalence toward the assertive young male physicians in her town

Excerpted from "Taking the Trade: Abortion and Gender Relations in an Eighteenth-Century New England Village" by Cornelia Hughes Dayton in *William and Mary Quarterly*, 3rd ser., 48 (1991): 19–49. Notes have been edited and renumbered. Transcripts of the legal documents on which the article is based can be found at http://history.uconn.edu/takingthetrade/.

who had been trained in the use of forceps but did not always have adequate experience to avoid fatal mistakes.*

In the following essay, Cornelia Hughes Dayton carefully reconstructs the narrative of the abortion and death of Sarah Grosvenor in a Connecticut village in 1742. How does Dayton interpret the meaning of abortion for Sarah Grosvenor and her friends? If it was not illegal, why did they seek to keep it secret? In what ways does Dayton think that relations between young women and young men changed in the mid-eighteenth century? How did relations between young people and their parents change? How was the memory of Sarah Grosvenor's death transmitted in the histories of the town?

In 1742 in the village of Pomfret, perched in the hills of northeastern Connecticut, nineteen-year-old Sarah Grosvenor and twenty-seven-year-old Amasa Sessions became involved in a liaison that led to pregnancy, abortion, and death. Both were from prominent yeoman families, and neither a marriage between them nor an arrangement for the support of their illegitimate child would have been an unusual event for mid-eighteenth-century New England. Amasa Sessions chose a different course; in consultation with John Hallowell, a self-proclaimed "practitioner of physick," he coerced his lover into taking an abortifacient. Within two months, Sarah fell ill. Unbeknownst to all but Amasa, Sarah, Sarah's sister Zerviah, and her cousin Hannah, Hallowell made an attempt to "Remove her Conseption" by a "manual opperation." Two days later Sarah miscarried, and her two young relatives secretly buried the fetus in the woods. Over the next month, Sarah struggled against a "Malignant fever" and was attended by several physicians, but on September 14, 1742, she died.[1]

Most accounts of induced abortions among seventeenth- and eighteenth-century whites in the Old and New Worlds consist of only a few lines in a private letter or court record book; these typically refer to the taking of savin or pennyroyal—two common herbal abortifacients. While men and women in diverse cultures have known how to perform abortions by inserting an instrument into the uterus, actual descriptions of such operations are extremely rare for any time period. Few accounts of abortions by instrument have yet been uncovered for early modern England, and I know of no other for colonial North America.[2] Thus the historical fragments recording events in a small New England town in 1742 take on an unusual power to illustrate how an abortion was conducted, how it was talked about, and how it was punished.

We know about the Grosvenor-Sessions case because in 1745 two prominent Windham County magistrates opened an investigation into Sarah's death. Why there was a three-year gap between that event and legal proceedings, and why justices from outside Pomfret initiated the legal process, remain a mystery. In November 1745 the investigating magistrates offered their preliminary opinion that Hallowell, Amasa Sessions, Zerviah Grosvenor, and Hannah Grosvenor were guilty of Sarah's murder, the last three as accessories. From the outset, Connecticut legal officials concentrated not on the act of abortion per se, but on the fact that an abortion attempt had led to a young woman's death.[3]

The case went next to Joseph Fowler, king's attorney for Windham County. He dropped charges against the two Grosvenor women, probably because he needed them as key witnesses and because they had played cover-up roles rather than originating the scheme. A year and a half passed as Fowler's first attempts to get convictions against Hallowell and Sessions failed either before

*Laurel Thatcher Ulrich, *A Midwife's Tale: The life of Martha Ballard, Based on Her Diary, 1785–1812* (New York: Alfred A. Knopf, 1990), ch. 5. See also the ninety-minute film of the same name (produced by Laurie Kahn-Leavitt and directed by Richard P. Rogers for PBS's American Experience series, 1997). The diary is reproduced in its entirety on www.dohistory.org, a website with features that invite interactive analysis and exploration.

grand juries or before the Superior Court on technical grounds. Finally, in March 1747, Fowler presented Hallowell and Sessions separately for the "highhanded Misdemeanour" of to destroy both Sarah Grosvenor's health and "the fruit of her womb."[4] A grand jury endorsed the bill against Hallowell but rejected a similarly worded presentment against Sessions. At Hallowell's trial before the Superior Court in Windham, the jury brought in a guilty verdict and the chief judge sentenced the physician to twenty-nine lashes and two hours of public humiliation standing at the town gallows. Before the sentence could be executed, Hallowell managed to break jail. He fled to Rhode Island; as far as records indicate, he never returned to Connecticut. Thus, in the end, both Amasa Sessions and John Hallowell escaped legal punishment for their actions, whereas Sarah Grosvenor paid for her sexual transgression with her life.

Nearly two years of hearings and trials before the Superior Court produced a file of ten depositions and twenty-four other legal documents. This cache of papers is extraordinarily rich, not alone for its unusual chronicle of an abortion attempt, but for its illumination of the fault lines in Pomfret dividing parents from grown children, men from women, and mid-eighteenth-century colonial culture from its seventeenth-century counterpart.

The depositions reveal that in 1742 the elders of Pomfret, men and women alike, failed to act as vigilant monitors of Sarah Grosvenor's courtship and illness. Instead, young, married householders—kin of Sarah and Amasa—pledged themselves in a conspiracy of silence to allow the abortion plot to unfold undetected. The one person who had the opportunity to play middleman between the generations was Hallowell. A man in his forties, dogged by a shady past and yet adept at acquiring respectable connections, Hallowell provides an intriguing and rare portrait of a socially ambitious, rural medical practitioner. By siding with the young people of Pomfret and keeping their secret, Hallowell betrayed his peers and elders and thereby opened himself to severe censure and expulsion from the community.

Beyond depicting generational conflict, the Grosvenor-Sessions case dramatically highlights key changes in gender relations that reverberated through New England society in the eighteenth century. One of these changes involved the emergence of a marked sexual double standard. In the mid-seventeenth century, a young man like Amasa Sessions would have been pressured by parents, friends, or the courts to marry his lover. Had he resisted, he would most likely have been whipped or fined for the crime of fornication. By the late seventeenth century, New England judges gave up on enjoining sexually active couples to marry. In the 1740s, amid shifting standards of sexual behavior and growing concern over the evidentiary impossibility of establishing paternity, prosecutions of young men for premarital sex ceased. Thus fornication was decriminalized for men, but not for women. Many of Sarah Grosvenor's female peers continued to be prosecuted and fined for bearing illegitimate children. Through private arrangements, and occasionally through civil lawsuits, their male partners were sometimes cajoled or coerced into contributing to the child's upkeep.[5]

What is most striking about the Grosvenor-Sessions case is that an entire community apparently forgave Sessions for the extreme measures he took to avoid accountability for his bastard child. Although he initiated the actions that led to his lover's death, all charges against him were dropped. Moreover, the tragedy did not spur Sessions to leave town; instead, he spent the rest of his life in Pomfret as a respected citizen. Even more dramatically than excusing young men from the crime of fornication, the treatment of Amasa Sessions confirmed that the sexually irresponsible activities of men in their youth would not be held against them as they reached for repute and prosperity in their prime.

The documents allow us to listen in on the quite different responses of young men and women to the drama unfolding in Pomfret. Sarah Grosvenor's female kin and friends, as we shall see, became preoccupied with their guilt and with the inevitability of God's vengeance. Her male kin, on the other hand, reacted cautiously and legalistically, ferreting out information in order to assess how best to protect the Grosvenor family name. The contrast reminds us yet again of the complex and gendered ways in which we must rethink conventional interpretations of secularization in colonial New England.

Finally, the Grosvenor case raises more questions than it answers about New Englanders' access to and attitudes toward abortion. If Sarah had not died after miscarriage, it is doubtful that any word of Sessions's providing her with an abortifacient or Hallowell's operation would have survived into the twentieth century. Because it nearly went unrecorded and because it reveals that many Pomfret residents were familiar with the idea of abortion, the case supports historians' assumptions that abortion attempts were far from rare in colonial America.[6] We can also infer from the case that the most dangerous abortions before 1800 may have been those instigated by men and performed by surgeons with instruments.[7] But both abortion's frequency and the lineaments of its social context remain obscure. . . .

Perhaps the most intriguing question centers on why women and men in early America acted *covertly* to effect abortions when abortion before quickening was legal. The Grosvenor case highlights the answer that applies to most known incidents from the period: abortion was understood as blameworthy because it was an extreme action designed to hide a prior sin, sex outside of marriage.[8] Reading the depositions, it is nearly impossible to disentangle the players' attitudes toward abortion itself from their expressions of censure or anxiety over failed courtship, illegitimacy, and the dangers posed for a young woman by a secret abortion. Strikingly absent from these eighteenth-century documents, however, is either outrage over the destruction of a fetus or denunciations of those who would arrest "nature's proper course." Those absences are a telling measure of how the discourse about abortion would change dramatically in later centuries.

THE NARRATIVE

Before delving into the response of the Pomfret community to Sarah Grosvenor's abortion and death, we need to know just who participated in the conspiracy to cover up her pregnancy and how they managed it. . . .

The chronicle opens in late July 1742 when Zerviah Grosvenor, aged twenty-one, finally prevailed upon her younger sister to admit that she was pregnant. In tears, Sarah explained that she had not told Zerviah sooner because "she had been taking [the] trade to remove it."[9] "Trade" was used in this period to signify stuff or goods, often in the deprecatory sense of rubbish and trash. The *Oxford English Dictionary* confirms that in some parts of England and New England the word was used to refer to medicine. In Pomfret trade meant a particular type of medicine, an abortifacient, thus a substance that might be regarded as "bad" medicine, as rubbish, unsafe and associated with destruction. What is notable is that Sarah and Zerviah, and neighboring young people who also used the word, had no need to explain to one another the meaning of "taking the trade." Perhaps only a few New Englanders knew how to prepare an abortifacient or knew of books that would give them recipes, but many more, especially young women who lived with the fear of becoming pregnant before marriage, were familiar with at least the *idea* of taking an abortifacient.

Sarah probably began taking the trade in mid-May when she was already three-and-a-half-months pregnant.[10] It was brought to her in the form of a powder by Amasa.[11] Sarah understood clearly that her lover had obtained the concoction "from docter hollowel," who conveyed "directions" for her doses through Amasa. Zerviah deposed later that Sarah had been "loath to Take" the drug and "Thot it an Evil," probably because at three and a half months she anticipated quickening, the time from which she knew the law counted abortion an "unlawful measure."[12] At the outset, Sarah argued in vain with Amasa against his proposed "Method." Later, during June and July, she sometimes "neglected" to take the doses he left for her, but, with mounting urgency, Amasa and the doctor pressed her to comply. "It was necessary," Amasa explained in late July, that she take "more, or [else] they were afraid She would be greatly hurt by what was already done." To calm her worries, he assured her that "there was no life [left] in the Child" and that the potion "would not hurt her." Apparently, the men hoped that a few more doses would provoke a miscarriage, thereby expelling the dead fetus and restoring Sarah's body to its natural balance of humors.

Presumably, Hallowell decided to operate in early August because Sarah's pregnancy was increasingly visible, and he guessed that she was not going to miscarry. An operation in which the fetus would be removed or punctured was now the only certain way to terminate the pregnancy secretly.[13] To avoid the scrutiny of Sarah's parents, Hallowell resorted to a plan he had used once before in arranging a private examination of Sarah. Early one afternoon he arrived at the house of John Grosvenor and begged for a room as "he was weary and wanted Rest." John, Sarah's thirty-one-year-old first cousin, lived with his wife, Hannah, and their young children in a homestead only a short walk down the hill but out of sight of Sarah's father's house. While John and Hannah were busy, the physician sent one of the little children to fetch Sarah.

The narrative of Sarah's fateful meeting with Hallowell that August afternoon is best told in the words of one of the deponents. Abigail Nightingale had married and moved to Pomfret two years earlier, and by 1742 she had become Sarah's close friend. Several weeks after the operation, Sarah attempted to relieve her own "Distress of mind" by confiding the details of her shocking experience to Abigail. Unconnected to the Grosvenor or Sessions families by kinship, and without any other apparent stake in the legal uses of her testimony, Abigail can probably be trusted as a fairly accurate paraphraser of Sarah's words.[14] If so, we have here an unparalleled eyewitness account of an eighteenth-century abortion attempt.

This is how Abigail recollected Sarah's deathbed story:

> On [Sarah's] going down [to her cousin John's], [Hallowell] said he wanted to Speake with her alone; and then they two went into a Room together; and then sd. Hallowell told her it was necessary that something more should be done or else she would Certainly die; to which she replyed that she was afraid they had done too much already, and then he told her that there was one thing more that could easily be done, and she asking him what it was; he said he could easily deliver her. But she said she was afraid there was life in the Child, then he asked her how long she had felt it; and she replyed about a fortnight; then he said that was impossible or could not be or ever would; for that the trade she had taken had or would prevent it; and that the alteration she felt Was owing to what she had taken. And he farther told her that he verily thought that the Child grew to her body to the Bigness of his hand, or else it would have Come away before that time. And that it would never Come away, but Certainly Kill her, unless other Means were used.[15] On which she yielded to his making an Attempt to take it away; charging him that if he could percieve that there was life in it he would not proceed on any Account. And then the Doctor openning his portmantua took an Instrument out of it and Laid it on the Bed, and she asking him what it was for, he replyed that it was to make way; and that then he tryed to remove the Child for Some time in vain putting her to the Utmost Distress, and that at Last she observed he trembled and immediately perceived a Strange alteration in her body and thought a bone of the Child was broken; on which she desired him (as she said) to Call in some body, for that she feared she was a dying, and instantly swooned away.

With Sarah's faint, Abigail's account broke off, but within minutes others, who would testify later, stepped into the room. Hallowell reacted to Sarah's swoon by unfastening the door and calling in Hannah, the young mistress of the house, and Zerviah, who had followed her sister there. Cold water and "a bottle of drops" were brought to keep Sarah from fainting again, while Hallowell explained to the "much Surprized" women that "he had been making an Attempt" to deliver Sarah. Despite their protests, he then "used a further force upon her" but did not succeed in "Tak[ing] the Child . . . away." Some days later Hallowell told a Pomfret man that in this effort "to distroy hir conception" he had "either knipt or Squeisd the head of the Conception." At the time of the attempt, Hallowell explained to the women that he "had done so much to her, as would Cause the Birth of the Child in a Little time." Just before sunset, he packed up his portmanteau and went to a nearby tavern, where Amasa was waiting "to hear [the outcome of] the event." Meanwhile, Sarah, weak-kneed and in pain, leaned on the arm of her sister as the young women managed to make their way home in the twilight.

After his attempted "force," Hallowell fades from the scene, while Zerviah and Hannah Grosvenor become the key figures. About two days after enduring the operation, Sarah began to experience contractions. Zerviah ran to get Hannah, telling her "she Tho't . . . Sarah would be quickly delivered." They returned to find Sarah, who was alone

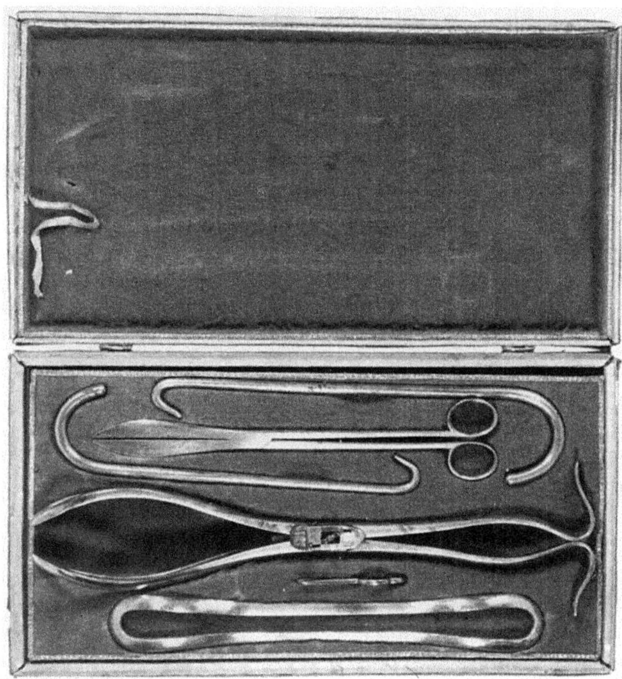

Obstetrical instruments case, ca 1780.
The case includes forceps, a double lever, two double blunt hooks, and a perforator. Professional training in the use of instruments was monopolized by male physicians, giving them an advantage in the medical marketplace of the late eighteenth and nineteenth centuries. The exclusion of midwives from advanced training meant that they were increasingly edged out of birthing rooms or became assistants to better-paid male practitioners. Forceps, invented in the eighteenth century, were used in obstructed births to extract a living fetus. Hooks were used to dismember and remove a fetus that had died. While forceps, if skillfully employed, could be lifesaving, the trend toward overuse increased the risk of infection. (Courtesy of the Smithsonian Institution's Division of Science, Medicine, and Society.)

"in her Father's Chamber," just delivered and rising from the chamber pot. In the pot was "an Untimely birth"—a "Child [that] did not Appear to have any Life In it." To Hannah, it "Seemed by The Scent . . . That it had been hurt and was decaying," while Zerviah later remembered it as "a perfect Child," even "a pritty child." Determined to keep the event "as private as they Could," the two women helped Sarah back to bed, and then "wr[ap]ed . . . up" the fetus, carried it to the woods on the edge of the farmstead, and there "Buried it in the Bushes."

. . . [A]bout ten days after the miscarriage, Sarah grew feverish and weak. Her parents consulted two college-educated physicians who hailed from outside the Pomfret area. Their visits did little good, nor were Sarah's symptoms—fever, delirium, convulsions—relieved by a visit from Hallowell, whom Amasa "fetcht" to Sarah's bedside. In the end, Hallowell, who had decided to move from nearby Killingly to more distant Providence, washed his hands of the case. A few days before Sarah died, her cousin John "went after" Hallowell, whether to bring him back or to express his rage, we do not know. Hallowell predicted "that She woul[d] not live."

Silence seems to have settled on the Grosvenor house and its neighborhood after Sarah's death on September 14. It was two and a half years later that rumors about a murderous abortion spread through and beyond Pomfret village, prompting legal investigation. The silence, the gap between event and prosecution, the passivity of Sarah's parents—all lend mystery to the narrative. But despite its ellipses, the Grosvenor case provides us with an unusual set of details about one young couple's extreme response to the common problem of failed courtship and illegitimacy. To gain insight into both the mysteries and the extremities of the Grosvenor-Sessions case, we need to look more closely at Pomfret, at the two families centrally involved, and at clues to the motivations of the principal participants. Our abortion tale, it turns out, holds beneath its surface a complex trail of evidence about generational conflict and troubled relations between men and women.

THE POMFRET PLAYERS

In 1742 the town of Pomfret had been settled for just over forty years. Within its central neighborhood and in homesteads scattered over rugged, wooded hillsides lived probably no more than 270 men, women, and children.[16] During the founding decades, the fathers of Sarah and Amasa ranked among the ten leading householders; Leicester Grosvenor and Nathaniel Sessions were chosen often to fill important local offices.

Grosvenor, the older of the two by seven years, had inherited standing and a choice farmstead from his father, one of the original six purchasers of the Pomfret territory. When the town was incorporated in 1714, he was elected a militia officer and one of the first selectmen. He was returned to the latter post nineteen times and eventually rose to the highest elective position—that of captain—in the local trainband. Concurrently, he was appointed many times throughout the 1710s and 1720s to ad hoc town committees, often alongside Nathaniel Sessions. But unlike Sessions, Grosvenor went on to serve at the colony level. Pomfret freemen chose him to represent them at ten General Assembly sessions between 1726 and 1744. Finally, in the 1730s, when he was in his late fifties, the legislature appointed him a justice of the peace for Windham County. Thus, until his retirement in 1748 at age seventy-four, his house would have served as the venue for petty trials, hearings, and recordings of documents. After retiring from public office, Grosvenor lived another eleven years, leaving behind in 1759 an estate worth over £600.[17]

Nathaniel Sessions managed a sizable farm and ran one of Pomfret's taverns at the family homestead. Town meetings were sometimes held there. Sessions was chosen constable in 1714 and rose from ensign to lieutenant in the militia—always a step behind Leicester Grosvenor. He could take pride in one exceptional distinction redounding to the family honor: in 1737 his son Darius became only the second Pomfret resident to graduate from Yale College, and before Sessions died at ninety-one he saw Darius elected assistant and then deputy governor of Rhode Island.[18]

The records are silent as to whether Sessions and his family resented the Grosvenors, who must have been perceived in town as more prominent, or whether the two families . . . enjoyed a close relationship that went sour for some reason *before* the affair between Sarah and Amasa. Instead, the signs (such as the cooperative public work of the two fathers, the visits back and forth between the Grosvenor and Sessions girls) point to a long-standing friendship and dense web of interchanges between the families. Indeed, courtship and marriage between a Sessions son and a Grosvenor daughter would hardly have been surprising.

What went wrong in the affair between Sarah and Amasa is not clear. Sarah's sisters and cousins knew that "Amasy" "made Sute to" Sarah, and they gave no indication of disapproving. The few who guessed at Sarah's condition in the summer of 1742 were not so much surprised that she was pregnant as that the couple "did not marry." It was evidently routine in this New England village, as in others, for courting couples to post banns for their nuptials soon after the woman discovered that she was pregnant.

Amasa offered different answers among his Pomfret peers to explain his failure to marry his lover. When Zerviah Grosvenor told Amasa that he and Sarah "had better Marry," he responded, "That would not do," for "he was afraid of his parents . . . [who would] always make their lives [at home] uncomfortable." Later, Abigail Nightingale heard rumors that Amasa was resorting to the standard excuse of men wishing to avoid a shotgun marriage—denying that the child was his.[19] Hallowell, with whom Amasa may have been honest, claimed "the Reason that they did not marry" was "that Sessions Did not Love her well a nough for [he] saith he did not believe it was his son and if he Could Cause her to gitt Red of it he would not Go near her again." Showing yet another face to a Grosvenor kinsman after Sarah's death, Amasa repented his actions and extravagantly claimed he would "give All he had" to "bring Sarah . . . To life again . . . and have her as his wife."

The unusual feature of Amasa's behavior was not his unwillingness to marry Sarah, but his determination to terminate her pregnancy before it showed. Increasing numbers of young men in eighteenth-century New England weathered the temporary obloquy of abandoning a pregnant lover in order to prolong their bachelorhood or marry someone else. What drove Amasa, and an ostensibly reluctant Sarah, to resort to abortion? Was it fear of their fathers? Nathaniel Sessions had chosen Amasa as the son who would remain on the family farm and care for his parents in their old age. An ill-timed marriage could have disrupted these plans and threatened Amasa's inheritance.[20] For his part, Leicester Grosvenor may have made it clear to his daughter that he would be greatly displeased at her marrying before she reached a certain age or until her older sister wed. Rigid piety, an authoritarian nature, an intense concern with being seen as a good household governor—any of these traits in Leicester Grosvenor or Nathaniel Sessions could have colored Amasa's decisions.

Perhaps it was not family relations that proved the catalyst but Amasa's acquaintance with a medical man who boasted about a powder more effective than the herbal remedies that were part of women's lore. Hallowell himself had fathered an illegitimate child fifteen years earlier, and he may have encouraged a rakish attitude in Amasa, beguiling the younger man with the promise of dissociating sex from its possible consequences. Or the explanation may have been that classic one: another woman. Two years after Sarah's death, Amasa married Hannah Miller of Rehoboth, Massachusetts. Perhaps in early 1742 he was already making trips to the town just east of Providence to see his future wife.[21]

What should we make of Sarah's role in the scheme? It is possible that she no longer loved Amasa and was as eager as he to forestall external pressures toward a quick marriage. However, Zerviah swore that on one occasion before the operation Amasa reluctantly agreed to post banns for their nuptials and that Sarah did not object.[22] *If* Sarah was a willing and active participant in the abortion plot all along, then by 1745 her female kin and friends had fabricated and rehearsed a careful and seamless story to preserve the memory of the dead girl untarnished.

In the portrait drawn by her friends, Sarah reacted to her pregnancy and to Amasa's plan first by arguing and finally by doing her utmost to protect her lover. She may have wished to marry Amasa, yet she did not insist on it or bring in older family members to negotiate with him and his parents. Abigail Nightingale insisted that Sarah accepted Amasa's recalcitrance and only pleaded with him that they not "go on to add sin to sin." Privately, she urged Amasa that there was an alternative to taking the trade—a way that would enable him to keep his role hidden and prevent the couple from committing a "Last transgression [that] would be worse then the first." Sarah told him that "she was willing to take the sin and shame to her self, and to be obliged never to tell whose Child it was, and that she did not doubt but that if she humbled her self on her Knees to her Father he would take her and her Child home." Her lover, afraid that his identity would become known, vetoed her proposal.[23]

According to the Pomfret women's reconstruction, abortion was not a freely chosen and defiant act for Sarah. Against her own desires, she reluctantly consented in taking the trade only because Amasa "So very earnestly perswaided her." In fact, she had claimed to her friends that she was coerced; he "would take no denyal." Sarah's confidantes presented her as being aware of her options, shrinking from abortion as an unnatural and immoral deed, and yet finally choosing the strategy consistent with her lover's vision of what would best protect their futures. Thus, if Amasa's hubris was extreme, so too was Sarah's internalization of those strains of thought in her culture that taught women to make themselves pleasing and obedient to men.

While we cannot be sure that the deponents' picture of Sarah's initial recoil and reluctant submission to the abortion plot was entirely accurate, it is clear that once she was caught up in the plan she extracted a pledge of silence from all her confidantes. Near her death, before telling Abigail about the operation, she "insist[ed] on . . . [her friend's] never discovering the Matter" to anyone. Clearly, she had earlier bound Zerviah and Hannah on their honor not to tell their elders. Reluctant when faced with the abortionist's powder, Sarah became a leading co-conspirator when alone with her female friends.

One of the most remarkable aspects of the Grosvenor-Sessions case is Sarah and Amasa's success in keeping their parents in the dark, at least until her final illness. If by July Sarah's sisters grew suspicious that Sarah was "with child," what explains the failure of her parents to observe her pregnancy and to intervene and uncover the abortion scheme? Were they negligent, preoccupied with other matters, or willfully blind? . . .

In terms of who knew what, the events of summer 1742 in Pomfret apparently unfolded in two stages. The first stretched from Sarah's discovery of her pregnancy by early May to some point in late August after her miscarriage. In this period a determined, collective effort by Sarah and Amasa and their friends kept their elders in the dark.[24] When Sarah fell seriously ill from the aftereffects of the abortion attempt and miscarriage, rumors of the young people's secret activities reached Leicester Grosvenor's neighbors and even one of the doctors he had called in. It is difficult to escape the conclusion that by Sarah's death in mid-September her father and stepmother had learned of the steps that had precipitated her mortal condition and kept silent for reasons of their own.

Except for Hallowell, the circle of intimates entrusted by Amasa and Sarah with their scheme consisted of young adults ranging in age from nineteen to thirty-three. Born between about 1710 and 1725, these young people had grown up just as the town attracted enough settlers to support a church, militia, and local market. They were second-generation Pomfret residents who shared the generational identity that came with sitting side by side through long worship services, attending school, playing, and working together at children's tasks. By 1740, these sisters, brothers, cousins, courting couples, and neighbors, in their visits from house to house—sometimes in their own households, sometimes at their parents'—had managed to create a world of talk and socializing that was largely exempt from parental supervision.[25] In Pomfret in 1742 it was this group of young people in their twenties and early thirties, not the cluster of Grosvenor matrons over forty-five, who monitored Sarah's courtship, attempted to get Amasa to marry his lover, privately investigated the activities and motives of Amasa and Hallowell, and, belatedly, spoke out publicly to help Connecticut juries decide who should be blamed for Sarah's death.

That Leicester Grosvenor made no public move to punish those around him and that he avoided giving testimony when legal proceedings commenced are intriguing clues to social changes underway in New England villages in the mid-eighteenth century. Local leaders like Grosvenor, along with the respectable yeomen whom he represented in public office, were increasingly withdrawing delicate family problems from the purview of their communities. Slander, illegitimacy, and feuds among neighbors came infrequently to local courts by midcentury, indicating male householders' growing preference for handling such matters privately.[26] Wealthy and ambitious families adopted this ethic of privacy at the same time that they became caught up in elaborating their material worlds by adding rooms and acquiring luxury goods.[27] . . . But all the fine accoutrements in the world would not excuse Justice Grosvenor from his obligation to govern his household effectively. Mortified no doubt at his inability to monitor the young people in his extended family, he responded, ironically, by extending their conspiracy of silence. The best way for him to shield the family name from scandal and protect his political reputation in the county and colony was to keep the story of Sarah's abortion out of the courts.

THE DOCTOR

John Hallowell's status as an outsider in Pomfret and his dangerous, secret alliance with the town's young adults may have shaped his destiny as the one conspirator sentenced to suffer at the whipping post. Although the physician had been involved in shady dealings before 1742, he had managed to win the trust of many patients and a respectable social standing. Tracking down his history . . . tells us something of the uncertainty surrounding personal and professional identity before the advent of police records and medical licensing boards. It also gives us an all-too-rare glimpse into the fashion in which an eighteenth-century country doctor tried to make his way in the world.

Hallowell's earliest brushes with the law came in the 1720s. In 1725 he purchased land in Killingly, a Connecticut town just north of Pomfret and bordering both Massachusetts and Rhode Island. Newly married, he was probably in his twenties at the time. Seven months before his wife gave birth to their first child, a sixteen-year-old Killingly woman charged Hallowell with fathering her illegitimate child. Using the alias Nicholas Hallaway, he fled to southeastern Connecticut, where he lived as a "transient" for three months. He was arrested and settled the case by admitting to paternity and agreeing to contribute to the child's maintenance for four years.[28]

Hallowell resumed his life in Killingly. Two years later, now referred to as "Dr.," he was arrested again; this time the charge was counterfeiting. Hallowell and several confederates were hauled before the governor and council for questioning and then put on trial before the Superior Court. Although many Killingly witnesses testified to the team's suspect activities in a woodland shelter, the charges against Hallowell were dropped when a key informer failed to appear in court.[29]

Hallowell thus escaped conviction on a serious felony charge, but he had been tainted by stories linking him to the criminal subculture of transient, disorderly, greedy, and manually skilled men who typically made up gangs of counterfeiters in eighteenth-century New England.[30] After 1727 Hallowell may have given up dabbling in money-making schemes and turned to earning his livelihood chiefly from his medical practice. Like two-thirds of the male medical practitioners in colonial New England, he probably did not have college or apprentice training, but his skill, or charm, was not therefore necessarily less than that of any one of his peers who might have inherited a library of books and a fund of knowledge from a physician father. All colonial practitioners, as Richard D. Brown reminds us, mixed learned practices with home or folk remedies, and no doctor had access to safe, reliable pharmacological preparations or antiseptic surgical procedures.[31]

In the years immediately following the counterfeiting charge. Hallowell appears to have made several deliberate moves to portray himself as a sober neighbor and reliable physician. At about the time of his second marriage, in 1729, he became a more frequent attendant at the Killingly meetinghouse, where he renewed his covenant and presented his first two children for baptism. He also threw himself into the land and credit markets of northeastern Connecticut, establishing himself as a physician who was also an enterprising yeoman and a frequent litigant.[32]

These activities had dual implications. On the one hand, they suggest that Hallowell epitomized the eighteenth-century Yankee citizen—a man as comfortable in the courtroom and countinghouse as at a patient's bedside; a man of restless energy, not content to limit his scope to his fields and village; a practical, ambitious man with a shrewd eye for a good deal.[33] On the other hand, Hallowell's losses to Boston creditors, his constant efforts to collect debts, and his farflung practice raise questions about the nature of his activities and medical practice. He evidently had clients not just in towns across northeastern Connecticut but also in neighboring Massachusetts and Rhode Island. Perhaps rural practitioners normally traveled extensively, spending many nights away from their wives and children. It is also possible, however, either that Hallowell was forced to travel because established doctors from leading families had monopolized the local practice or that he chose to recruit patients in Providence and other towns as a cover for illicit activities.[34] Despite his land speculations and his frequent resort to litigation, Hallowell was losing money. In the sixteen years before 1742, his creditors secured judgments against him for a total of £1,060, while he was able to collect only £700 in debts.[35] The disjunction between his ambition and actual material gains may have led Hallowell in middle age to renew his illicit money-making schemes. By supplying young men with potent abortifacients and dabbling in schemes to counterfeit New England's paper money, he betrayed the very gentlemen whose respect, credit, and society he sought.

What is most intriguing about Hallowell was his ability to ingratiate himself throughout his life with elite men whose reputations were unblemished by scandal. Despite the rumors that must have circulated about his early sexual dalliance, counterfeiting activities, suspect medical remedies, heavy debts, and shady business transactions, leading ministers, merchants, and magistrates welcomed him into their houses. . . .

Lacking college degree and family pedigree, Hallowell traded on his profession and his charm to gain acceptability with the elite. In August 1742 he shrewdly removed himself from the Pomfret scene, just before Sarah Grosvenor's death. In that month he moved, possibly without his wife and children, to Providence, where he had many connections. Within five years, Hallowell had so insinuated himself with town leaders such as Stephen Hopkins that fourteen of them petitioned for mitigation of what they saw as the misguided sentence imposed on him in the Grosvenor case.[36]

Hallowell's capacity for landing on his feet, despite persistent brushes with scandal, debt, and the law, suggests that we should look at the fluidity of New England's eighteenth-century elite in new ways.[37] What bound sons of old New England families, learned men, and upwardly mobile merchants and professionals in an expanded elite may partly have been a reshaped, largely unspoken set of values shared by men. We know that the archetype for white New England women as sexual beings was changing from carnal Eve to resisting Pamela and that the calculus of accountability for seduction was shifting blame solely to women.[38] But the simultaneous metamorphosis in cultural images and values defining manhood in the early and mid-eighteenth century has not been studied. The scattered evidence we do have suggests that, increasingly, for men in the more secular and anglicized culture of New England, the lines between legitimate and illegitimate sexuality, between sanctioned and shady business dealings, and between speaking the truth and protecting family honor blurred. Hallowell's acceptability to men like minister Ebenezer Williams and merchant Stephen Hopkins hints at how changing sexual and moral standards shaped the economic and social alliances made by New England's male leadership in the 1700s.

WOMEN'S TALK AND MEN'S TALK

If age played a major role in determining who knew the truth about Sarah Grosvenor's illness, gender affected how the conspiring young adults responded to Sarah's impending death and how they weighed the issue of blame. Our last glimpse into the social world of eighteenth-century Pomfret looks at the different ways in which women and men reconstructed their roles in the events of 1742.

An inward gaze, a strong consciousness of sin and guilt, a desire to avoid conflict and achieve reconciliation, a need to confess—these are the impulses expressed in women's intimate talk in the weeks before Sarah died. The central female characters in the plot, Sarah and Zerviah Grosvenor, lived for six weeks with the daily fear that their parents or aunts might detect Sarah's condition or their covert comings and goings. Deposing three years later, Zerviah represented the sisters as suffering under an intensifying sense of complicity as they had passed through two stages of involvement in the concealment plan. At first, they were passive players, submitting to the hands of men. But once Hallowell declared that he had done all he could, they were left to salvage the conspiracy by enduring the terrors of a first delivery alone, knowing that their failure to call in the older women of the family resembled the decision made by women who committed infanticide.[39] While the pain and shock of miscarrying a five-and-one-half-month fetus through a possibly lacerated vagina may have been the experience that later most grieved Sarah, Zerviah would be haunted particularly by her stealthy venture into the woods with Hannah to bury the shrouded evidence of miscarriage.[40]

The Grosvenor sisters later recalled that they had regarded the first stage of the scheme—taking the trade—as "a Sin" and "an Evil" not so much because it was intended to end the life of a fetus as because it entailed a protracted set of actions, worse than a single lie, to cover up an initial transgression: fornication. According to their religion and the traditions of their New England culture, Sarah and Zerviah knew that the proper response to the sin of "uncleanness" (especially when it led to its visible manifestation, pregnancy) was to confess, seeking to allay God's wrath and cleanse oneself and one's community. Dire were the consequences of hiding a grave sin, so the logic and folklore of religion warned.[41] Having piled one covert act upon another, all in defiance of her parents, each sister wondered if she had not ventured beyond the pale, forsaking God and in turn being forsaken. . . .

. . . [V]isions of judgment and of their personal accountability to God haunted Sarah and Zerviah during the waning days of summer—or so their female friends later contended. Caught between the traditional religious ethic of confession, recently renewed in revivals across New England, and the newer, status-driven cultural pressure to keep moral missteps private, the Grosvenor women declined to take up roles as accusers. By focusing on their own actions, they rejected a portrait of themselves as helpless victims, yet they also ceded to their male kin responsibility for assessing blame and mediating between the public interest in seeing justice done and the private interests of the Grosvenor family. Finally, by trying to keep the conspiracy of silence intact and by allowing Amasa frequent visits to her bedside to lament his role and his delusion by Hallowell, Sarah at once endorsed a policy of private repentance and forgiveness *and* indicated that she wished her lover to be spared eventual public retribution for her death.

Talk among the men of Pomfret in the weeks preceding and following Sarah's death centered on more secular concerns than the preoccupation with sin and God's anger that ran through the women's conversations. Neither Hallowell nor Sessions expressed any guilt or sense of sin, as far as the record shows, *until* Sarah was diagnosed as mortally ill.[42] Indeed, their initial accounts of the plot took the form of braggadocio, with Amasa (according to Hallowell) casting himself as the rake who could "gitt Red" of his child and look elsewhere for female companionship, and Hallowell boasting of his abortionist's surgical technique to Sarah's cousin Ebenezer. Later, anticipating popular censure and possible prosecution, each man "Tried to Cast it" on the other. The physician insisted that "He did not do any thing but What Sessions Importuned him to Do," while Amasa exclaimed "That he could freely be Strip[p]ed naked provided he could bring Sarah . . . To life again . . . , but Doct Hallowell had Deluded him, and Destroyed her."[43] While this sort of denial and buck-passing seems very human, it was the antithesis of the New England way—a religious way of life that made confession its central motif. The Grosvenor-Sessions case is one illustration among many of how New England women continued to measure themselves by "the moral allegory of repentance and confession" while men, at least when presenting themselves before legal authorities, adopted secular voices and learned self-interested strategies.[44]

For the Grosvenor men—at least the cluster of Sarah's cousins living near her—the key issue was not exposing sin but protecting the family's reputation. In the weeks before Sarah died, her cousins John and Ebenezer each attempted to investigate and sort out the roles and motives of Amasa Sessions and John Hallowell in the scheme to conceal Sarah's pregnancy. Grilled in August by Ebenezer . . . , Hallowell revealed that "Sessions had bin Interseeding with him to Remove her Conseption." On another occasion, . . . Hallowell was more specific. He "[did] with her [Sarah] as he did . . . because Sessions Came to him and was So very earnest . . . and offered him five pounds if he would do it." "But," Hallowell boasted, "he would have twenty of[f] of him before he had done."[45] . . .

John and Ebenezer, deposing three or four years after these events, did not . . . explain why they did not act immediately to have charges brought against the two conspirators. Perhaps these young householders were loath to move against a male peer and childhood friend. More likely, they kept their information to themselves to protect John's wife, Hannah, and their cousin Zerviah from prosecution as accessories. They may also have acted, in league with their uncle Leicester, out of a larger concern for keeping the family name out of the courts. Finally, it is probable that the male cousins, partly because of their own complicity and partly because they may have believed that Sarah had consented to the abortion, simply did not think that Amasa's and Hallowell's actions added up to the murder of their relative.

Three years later, yet another Grosvenor cousin intervened, expressing himself much more vehemently than John or Ebenezer ever had. In 1742, John Shaw at age thirty-eight may have been perceived by the younger Grosvenors as too old—too close to the age when men took public office and served as grand jurors—to be trusted with their secret. Shaw seems to have known nothing of Sarah's taking the trade or having a miscarriage until 1745 when "the Storys" suddenly surfaced. Then Hannah and Zerviah gave him a truncated account. Shaw reacted with rage, realizing that Sarah had died not of natural causes but from "what Hollowell had done," and he set out to wring the truth from the doctor. Several times he sought out Hallowell in Rhode Island to tell him that "I could not look upon him otherwise Than [as] a Bad man Since he had Destroyed my Kinswoman." When Hallowell countered that "Amasa Sessions... was the Occasion of it," Shaw's fury grew. "I Told him he was like old Mother Eve When She said The Serpent beguild her, ... [and] I Told him in my Mind he Deserved to dye for it."

Questioning Amasa, Shaw was quick to accept his protestations of sincere regret and his insistence that Hallowell had "Deluded" him. Shaw concluded that Amasa had never "Importuned [Hallowell] ... to lay hands on her" (that is, to perform the manual abortion). Forged in the men's talk about the Grosvenor-Sessions case in 1745 and 1746 appears to have been a consensus that, while Amasa Sessions was somewhat blameworthy "as concerned in it," it was only Hallowell—the outsider, the man easily labeled a quack—who deserved to be branded "a Man of Death." Nevertheless, it was the stories of *both* men and women that ensured the fulfillment of a doctor's warning to Hallowell in the Leicester Grosvenor house just before Sarah died: "The Hand of Justice [will] Take hold of [you] sooner or Later."[46]

THE LAW

The hand of justice reached out to catch John Hallowell in November 1745.... *Something* had caused Zerviah and Hannah Grosvenor to break their silence. Zerviah provided the key to the puzzle, as she alone had been present at the crucial series of incidents leading to Sarah's death. The only surviving account of Zerviah's belated conversion from silence to public confession comes from the stories told by Pomfret residents into the nineteenth century. In Ellen Larned's melodramatic prose, the "whispered" tale recounted Zerviah's increasing discomfort thus: "Night after night, in her solitary chamber, the surviving sister was awakened by the rattling of the rings on which her bed-curtains were suspended, a ghostly knell continuing and intensifying till she was convinced of its preternatural origin; and at length, in response to her agonized entreaties, the spirit of her dead sister made known to her, 'That she could not rest in her grave till her crime was made public.'"[47]

Embellished as this tale undoubtedly is, we should not dismiss it out of hand as a Victorian ghost story. In early modern English culture, belief persisted in both apparitions and the supernatural power of the guiltless victim to return and expose her murderer.[48] Zerviah in 1742 already fretted over her sin as an accomplice, yet she kept her pledge of silence to her sister. It is certainly conceivable that, after a lapse of three years, she could no longer bear the pressure of hiding the acts that she increasingly believed amounted to the murder of her sister and an unborn child. Whether Zerviah's sudden outburst of talk in 1745 came about at the urging of some Pomfret confidante, or perhaps under the influence of the revivals then sweeping Windham County churches, or indeed because of her belief in nightly visitations by her dead sister's spirit, we simply cannot know.[49]

The Pomfret meetinghouse was the site of the first public legal hearing into the facts behind Sarah Grosvenor's death. We can imagine that townsfolk crowded the pews over the course of two November days to watch two prominent county magistrates examine a string of witnesses before pronouncing their preliminary judgment. The evidence, they concluded, was sufficient to bind four people over for trial at the Superior Court: Hallowell, who in their opinion was "Guilty of murdering Sarah," along with Amasa Sessions, Zerviah Grosvenor, and Hannah Grosvenor as accessories to that murder.[50] The inclusion of Zerviah and Hannah may have been a ploy to pressure these crucial, possibly still reluctant, witnesses to testify for the crown. When Joseph Fowler, the king's attorney, prepared a formal indictment in the case eleven months later, he dropped all charges against Zerviah and Hannah. Rather than stand trial, the two women traveled frequently during 1746 and 1747 to the county seat to give evidence against Sessions and Hallowell.

The criminal process recommenced in September 1746. A grand jury empaneled by the Superior Court at its Windham session first rejected a presentment against Hallowell for murdering Sarah "by his Wicked and Diabolical practice." Fowler, recognizing that the capital charges of murder and accessory to murder against Hallowell and Sessions were going to fail before jurors, changed his tack. He presented the grand jury with a joint indictment against the two men not for outright murder but for endangering Sarah's health by trying to "procure an Abortion" with medicines and "a violent manual opperation"; this time the jurors endorsed the bill. When the Superior Court trial opened in November, two attorneys for the defendants managed to persuade the judges that the indictment was faulty on technical grounds. However, upon the advice of the king's attorney that there "appear reasons vehemently to suspect" the two men "Guilty of Sundry Heinous Offenses" at Pomfret four years earlier, the justices agreed to bind them over to answer charges in March 1747.[51]

Fowler next moved to bring separate indictments against Hallowell and Sessions for the "highhanded misdemeanour" of endeavoring to destroy Sarah's health "and the fruit of her womb." This wording echoed the English common law designation of abortion as a misdemeanor, not a felony or capital crime. A newly empaneled grand jury of eighteen county yeomen made what turned out to be the pivotal decision in getting a conviction: they returned a true bill against Hallowell and rejected a similarly worded bill against Sessions.[52] Only Hallowell, "the notorious physician," would go to trial.[53]

On March 20, 1747, John Hallowell stepped before the bar for the final time to answer for the death of Sarah Grosvenor. He maintained his innocence, the case went to a trial jury of twelve men, and they returned with a guilty verdict. The Superior Court judges, who had discretion to choose any penalty less than death, pronounced a severe sentence of public shaming and corporal punishment. Hallowell was to be paraded to the town gallows, made to stand there before the public for two hours "with a rope visibly hanging about his neck," and then endure a public whipping of twenty-nine lashes "on the naked back."[54]

Before the authorities could carry out this sentence, Hallowell escaped and fled to Rhode Island. From Providence seven months after his trial, he audaciously petitioned the Connecticut General Assembly for a mitigated sentence, presenting himself as a destitute "Exile." As previously noted, fourteen respected male citizens of Providence took up his cause, arguing that this valued doctor had been convicted by prejudiced witnesses and hearsay evidence and asserting that corporal punishment was unwarranted in a misdemeanor case. While the Connecticut legislators rejected these petitions, the language used by Hallowell and his Rhode Island patrons is yet another marker of the distance separating many educated New England men at mid-century from their more God-fearing predecessors. Never mentioning the words "sin" or "repentance," the Providence men wrote that Hallowell was justified in escaping the lash since "every Person is prompted [by the natural Law of Self-Preservation] to avoid Pain and Misery."[55]

In the series of indictments against Hallowell and Sessions, the central legal question became who had directly caused Sarah's death. To the farmers in their forties and fifties who sat as jurors, Hallowell clearly deserved punishment. By recklessly endangering Sarah's life he had abused the trust that heads of household placed in him as a physician.[56] Moreover, he had conspired with the younger generation to keep their dangerous activities secret from their parents and elders.

Several rationales could have been behind the Windham jurors' conclusion that Amasa Sessions ought to be spared the lash. Legally, they could distinguish him from Hallowell as not being *directly* responsible for Sarah's death. Along with Sarah's male kin, they dismissed the evidence that Amasa had instigated the scheme, employed Hallowell, and monitored all of his activities. Perhaps they saw him as a native son who deserved the chance to prove himself mature and responsible. They may have excused his actions as nothing more than a misguided effort to cast off an unwanted lover. Rather than acknowledge that a culture that excused male sexual irresponsibility was responsible for Sarah's death, the Grosvenor family, the Pomfret community, and the jury men of the county persuaded themselves that Sessions had been ignorant of the potentially deadly consequences of his actions.

MEMORY AND HISTORY

No family feud, no endless round of recriminations followed the many months of deposing and attending trials that engaged the Grosvenor and Sessions clans in 1746 and 1747. Indeed, as Sarah and Amasa's generation matured, the ties between the two families thickened. . . . In 1775 Amasa's third son, and namesake, married sixteen-year-old Esther Grosvenor, daughter of Sarah's brother, Leicester, Jr.[57]

It is clear that the Grosvenor clan was not willing to break ranks with their respectable yeoman neighbors and heap blame on the Sessions family for Sarah's death. It would, however, be fascinating to know what women in Pomfret and other Windham County towns had to say about the outcome of the legal proceedings in 1747. Did they concur with the jurors that Hallowell was the prime culprit, or did they, unlike Sarah Grosvenor, direct their ire more concertedly at Amasa, insisting that he too was "a Bad man"? Nearly a century later, middle-class New England women would organize against the sexual double standard. However, Amasa's future career tells us that female piety in the 1740s did not instruct Windham County women to expel the newly married, thirty-two-year-old man from their homes.[58]

Amasa, as he grew into middle age in Pomfret, easily replicated his father's status. He served as militia captain in the Seven Years' War, prospered in farming, fathered ten children, and lived fifty-seven years beyond Sarah Grosvenor. His handsome gravestone, inscribed with a long verse, stands but twenty-five feet from the simpler stone erected in 1742 for Sarah.

After his death, male kin remembered Amasa fondly; nephews and grandsons recalled him as a "favorite" relative, "remarkably capable" in his prime and "very corpulent" in old age. Moreover, local story-telling tradition and the published history of the region, which made such a spectacular ghost story out of Sarah's abortion and death, preserved Amasa Sessions's reputation unsullied: the *name* of Sarah's lover was left out of the tale.[59]

If Sarah Grosvenor's life is a cautionary tale in any sense for us in the late twentieth century, it is as a reminder of the historically distinctive ways in which socialized gender roles, community and class solidarity, and legal culture combine in each set of generations to excuse or make invisible certain abuses and crimes against women. The form in which Sarah Grosvenor's death became local history reminds us of how the excuses and erasures of one generation not unwittingly become embedded in the narratives and memories of the next cultural era.

NOTES

1. The documentation is found in the record books and file papers of the Superior Court of Connecticut: *Rex* v. *John Hallowell et al.*, Superior Court Records, Book 9, pp. 113, 173, 175, and Windham County Superior Court Files, box 172, Connecticut State Library, Hartford. Hereafter all loose court papers cited are from *Rex* v. *Hallowell*, Windham County Superior Court Files, box 172, unless otherwise indicated. . . .

2. . . . On the history of abortion practices see . . . Angus McLaren, *Reproductive Rituals: The Perception of Fertility in England from the Sixteenth Century to the Nineteenth Century* (London, 1984), chap. 4; Linda Gordon, *Woman's Body, Woman's Right: A Social History of Birth Control in America* (New York, 1976), pp. 26–41, 49–60. . . .

For specific cases indicating use of herbal abortifacients in the North American colonies, see Julia Cherry Spruill, *Women's Life and Work in the Southern Colonies* (New York, 1972: orig. pub. Chapel Hill, N.C., 1938), pp. 325–26; Roger Thompson, *Sex in Middlesex: Popular Mores in a Massachusetts County, 1649–1699* (Amherst, Mass., 1986), pp. 11, 24–26, 107–8, 182–83. I have found two references to the use of an abortifacient in colonial Connecticut court files.

3. Abortion before quickening (defined in the early modern period as the moment when the mother first felt the fetus move) was not viewed by the English or colonial courts as criminal. No statute law on abortion existed in either Britain or the colonies. To my knowledge, no New England court before 1745 had attempted to prosecute a physician or other conspirators for carrying out an abortion.

On the history of the legal treatment of abortion in Europe and the United States see . . . James C. Mohr, *Abortion in America: The Origins and Evolution of National Policy, 1800–1900* (New York, 1978); Michael Grossberg, *Governing the Hearth: Law and the Family in Nineteenth-Century America* (Chapel Hill, N.C., 1985), chap. 5; and Carroll Smith-Rosenberg, "The Abortion Movement and the AMA, 1850–1880," in *Disorderly Conduct: Visions of Gender of Victorian America* (New York, 1985), pp. 217–244.

4. Indictment against John Hallowell, Mar. 1746/47.

5. The story of the decriminalization of fornication for men in colonial New England is told most succinctly by Carol F. Karlsen, *The Devil in the Shape of a Woman: Witchcraft in Colonial New England* (New York, 1987), pp. 194–96, 198–202, 255. Laurel Thatcher Ulrich describes a late eighteenth-century Massachusetts jurisdiction in *A Midwife's Tale: The*

Life of Martha Ballard, Based on Her Diary, 1785–1812 (New York, 1990), 147–60. . . . A partial survey of fornication prosecutions in the Windham County Court indicates that here, too, the local JPs and annually appointed grand jurymen stopped prosecuting men after the 1730s. The records for 1726–31 show that fifteen men were prosecuted to enjoin child support and twenty-one single women were charged with fornication and bastardy, while only two women brought civil suits for child maintenance. Nearly a decade ahead, in the three-year period 1740–42, no men were prosecuted while twenty-three single women were charged with fornication and ten women initiated civil paternity suits.

6. For a recent summary of the literature see Brief for American Historians as *Amicus Curiae* Supporting the Appellees 5–7, *William L. Webster et al.* v. *Reproductive Health Services et al.*, 109 S. Ct. 3040 (1989).

7. In none of the cases cited in n. 2 above did the woman ingesting an abortifacient die from it. . . .

8. Married women may have hidden their abortion attempts because the activity was associated with lewd or dissident women.

9. Deposition of Zerviah Grosvenor. [All direct quotations from witnesses come from Depositions (see n. 1).] . . . Hallowell's trade may have been an imported medicine or a powder he mixed himself, consisting chiefly of oil of savin, which could be extracted from juniper bushes found throughout New England.

10. So her sister Zerviah later estimated. . . .

11. After she was let into the plot, Zerviah more than once watched Amasa take "a paper or powder out of his pockett" and insist that Sarah "take Some of it." . . .

12. . . . "Unlawful measure" was Zerviah's phrase for Amasa's "Method." Concerned for Sarah's well-being, she pleaded with Hallowell not to give her sister "any thing that should harm her"; Deposition of Zerviah Grosvenor. At the same time, Sarah was thinking about the quickening issue. She confided to a friend that when Amasa first insisted she take the trade, "she [had] feared it was too late". . . .

13. Hallowell claimed that he proceeded with the abortion in order to save Sarah's life. If the powder had had little effect and he knew it, then this claim was a deliberate deception. On the other hand, he may have sincerely believed that the potion had poisoned the fetus and that infection of the uterine cavity had followed fetal death. Since healthy babies were thought at that time to help with their own deliveries, Hallowell may also have anticipated a complicated delivery if Sarah were allowed to go to full term—a delivery that might kill her. . . .

14. Hearsay evidence was still accepted in many eighteenth-century Anglo-American courts. . . . Sarah's reported words may have carried special weight because in early New England persons on their deathbeds were thought to speak the truth.

15. Twentieth-century obstetrical studies show an average of six weeks between fetal death and spontaneous abortion; J Robert Willson and Elsie Reid Carrington, eds., *Obstetrics and Gynecology*, 8th ed. (St. Louis, Mo., 1987), p. 212. Hallowell evidently grasped the link between the two events but felt he could not wait six weeks, either out of concern for Sarah's health or for fear their plot would be discovered.

16. I am using a list of forty heads of household in the Mashamoquet neighborhood of Pomfret in 1731, presuming five persons to a household, and assuming a 2.5 percent annual population growth. See Ellen D. Larned, *History of Windham County, Connecticut* (Worcester, Mass., 1874), vol. I, p. 342, and Bruce C. Daniels, *The Connecticut Town: Growth and Development, 1635–1790* (Middletown, Conn., 1979), pp. 44–51. Pomfret village had no central green or cluster of shops and small house lots around its meeting-house. No maps survive for early Pomfret apart from a 1719 survey of proprietors' tracts. See Larned, *History of Windham County* (1976 ed.), I, foldout at p. 185.

17. . . . Larned, *History of Windham County*, I:200–202, 208–9, 269, 354, 343–44. . . .

18. Larned, *History of Windham County*, I:201, 204, 206, 208–9, 344; Ellen D. Larned, *Historic Gleanings in Windham County, Connecticut* (Providence, R. I., 1899), pp. 141, 148–49. . . .

19. . . . Contradicting Amasa's attempt to disavow paternity were both his investment in Hallowell's efforts to get rid of the fetus and his own ready admission of paternity privately to Zerviah and Sarah.

20. Two years later, in Feb. 1744 (nine months before Amasa married), the senior Sessions deeded to his son the north part of his own farm for a payment of £310. Amasa, in exchange for caring for his parents in their old age, came into the whole farm when his father died in 1771. Pomfret Land Records, III:120; Estate Papers of Nathaniel Sessions, 1771, Pomfret Probate District. On the delay between marriage and "going to housekeeping" see Ulrich, *A Midwife's Tale*, pp. 138–44.

21. Francis G. Sessions, comp., *Materials for a History of the Sessions Family in America* (Albany, N.Y., 1890), p. 60; Pomfret Vit. Rec., I:29. All vital and land records cited hereafter are found in the Barbour Collection, Connecticut State Library.

22. The banns never appeared on the meeting-house door. . . .

23. . . . I have argued elsewhere that this is what most young New England women in the eighteenth century did when faced with illegitimacy. Their parents did not throw them out of the house but instead paid the cost of the mother and child's upkeep until she managed to marry. Dayton, *Women Before the Bar*. ch. 4.

24. In Larned's account, the oral legend insisted that Hallowell's "transaction" (meaning the abortion attempt) and the miscarriage were "utterly unsuspected by any . . . member of the household" other than Zerviah. *History of Windham County*, I:363.

25. The famous "bad books" incident that disrupted Jonathan Edwards's career in 1744 involved a similar group of unsupervised young adults ages twenty-one to twenty-nine. See Patricia J. Tracy, *Jonathan Edwards, Pastor: Religion and Society in Eighteenth-Century Northampton* (New York, 1980),

pp. 160–64. The best general investigation of youth culture in early New England is Thompson's *Sex in Middlesex*, pp. 71–96. . . .

26. Helena M. Wall, *Fierce Communion: Family and Community in Early America* (Cambridge, Mass., 1990); Bruce H. Mann, *Neighbors and Strangers: Law and Community in Early Connecticut* (Chapel Hill, N.C., 1987).

27. . . . For recent studies linking consumption patterns and class stratification see . . . T. H. Breen, "'Baubles of Britain': The American and Consumer Revolutions of the Eighteenth Century," *Past and Present* 119 (May 1988): 73–104. . . .

28. Killingly Land Records, II:139; *Rex* v. *John Hallowell and Mehitable Morris,* Dec. 1726, Windham County Court Records, Book I:43, and Windham County Court Files, box 363. . . .

29. Hallowell was clearly the mastermind of the scheme, and there is little doubt that he lied to the authorities when questioned. . . . The case is found in Charles Hoadley, ed., *Public Records of the Colony of Connecticut,* 15 vols. (Hartford, Conn., 1873), vol. VII, p. 118.

30. The authority on counterfeiting in the colonies is Kenneth Scott . . . *Counterfeiting in Colonial America* [(New York, 1957),] esp. pp. 125, 35, 10, 36. See also Scott's more focused studies, *Counterfeiting in Colonial Connecticut* (New York, 1957) and *Counterfeiting in Colonial Rhode Island* (Providence, R.I., 1960).

For an illuminating social profile of thieves and burglars who often operated in small gangs, see Daniel A. Cohen, "A Fellowship of Thieves: Property Criminals in Eighteenth-Century Massachusetts," *Journal of Social History* XXII (1988):65–92.

31. Richard D. Brown, "The Healing Arts in Colonial and Revolutionary Massachusetts: The Context for Scientific Medicine," in Publications Col. Soc. Mass., *Medicine in Colonial Massachusetts 1620–1820* (Boston, 1980), esp. pp. 40–42. . . .

32. Between 1725 and 1742, Hallowell was a party to twenty land sales and purchases in Killingly. . . .

33. For example, in early 1735 Hallowell made a £170 profit from the sale of a sixty-acre tract with mill and mansion house that he had purchased two months earlier. Killingly Land Rec., IV:26, 36.

34. For a related hypothesis about the mobility of self-taught doctors in contrast to physicians from established medical families see Christianson, "Medical Practitioners of Massachusetts," in Col. Soc. Mass., *Medicine in Colonial Massachusetts,* p. 61. . . .

35. These figures apply to suits in the Windham County Court record books, 1727–42. Hallowell may, of course, have prosecuted debtors in other jurisdictions.

36. The petition's signers included Hopkins, merchant, assembly speaker, and Superior Court justice, soon to become governor; Daniel Jencks, judge, assembly delegate, and prominent Baptist; Obadiah Brown, merchant and shopkeeper; and George Taylor, justice of the peace, town schoolmaster, and Anglican warden. Some of the signers stated that they had made a special trip to Windham to be "Earwitnesses" at Hallowell's trial. . . .

37. For discussions of the elite see Jackson Turner Main, *Society and Economy in Colonial Connecticut* (Princeton, N.J., 1985), esp. pp. 317–66. . . .

38. Laurel Thatcher Ulrich, *Good Wives: Image and Reality in the Lives of Women in Northern New England, 1650–1750* (New York, 1982), pp. 103–5, 113–17.

39. See Ulrich, *Good Wives,* pp. 195–201. . . .

40. Burying the child was one of the key dramatic acts in infanticide episodes and tales, and popular beliefs in the inevitability that "murder will out" centered on the buried corpse. . . . For more on "murder will out" in New England culture, see David D. Hall, *Worlds of Wonder, Days of Judgment: Popular Religious Belief in Early New England* (New York, 1989), pp. 176–78. . . .

41. Hall, *Worlds of Wonder,* pp. 172–78.

42. . . . Abigail Nightingale recalled a scene when Sarah "was just going out of the world." She and Amasa were sitting on Sarah's bed, and Amasa "endeavour[ed] to raise her up &c. He asked my thought of her state &c. and then leaning over her used these words: poor Creature, I have undone you[!]"; Deposition of Abigail Nightingale.

43. . . . For discussions of male and female speech patterns and the distinctive narcissistic bravado of men's talk in early New England, see Robert St. George, "'Heated' Speech and Literacy in Seventeenth-Century New England," in David Grayson Allen and David D. Hall, eds., *Seventeenth-Century New England,* Publications of the Colonial Society of Massachusetts, LXIII (Boston, 1984), pp. 305–15. . . .

44. On the centrality of confession see Hall, *Worlds of Wonder,* pp. 173, 241. . . . On the growing gap between male and female piety in the eighteenth century see Mary Maples Dunn, "Saints and Sisters: Congregational and Quaker Women in the Early Colonial Period," *American Quarterly* XXX (1978): 582–601. . . .

45. Deposition of Ebenezer Grosvenor; Deposition of John Grosvenor.

46. . . . Shaw here was reporting Dr. [Theodore?] Coker's account of his confrontation with Hallowell during Sarah's final illness. . . .

47. Larned reported that, according to "the legend," the ghostly visitations ceased when "Hallowell fled his country." *History of Windham County,* I:363.

48. For mid-eighteenth-century Bristol residents who reported seeing apparitions and holding conversations with them see Jonathan Barry, "Piety and the Patient: Medicine and Religion in Eighteenth Century Bristol," in Roy Porter, ed., *Patients and Practitioners: Lay Perceptions of Medicines in Pre-Industrial Society* (Cambridge, [Eng.,] 1985), p. 157.

49. None of the depositions produced by Hallowell's trial offers any explanation of the three-year gap between Sarah's death and legal proceedings. . . .

50. Record of the Inferior Court held at Pomfret, Nov. 5–6, 1745. . . .

51. Indictment against Hallowell, Sept. 4, 1746; Indictment against Hallowell and Sessions, Sept. 20, 1746: Pleas of Hallowell and Sessions before the adjourned Windham Superior Court,

Nov. [18], 1746; Sup. Ct. Rec., bk. 12, pp. 112–17, 131–33.

52. Sup. Ct. Rec., bk. 12, pp. 173, 175; Indictment against John Hallowell, Mar. 1746/47; *Rex* v. *Amasa Sessions,* Indictment, Mar. 1746/47, Windham Sup. Ct. Files, box 172. See William Blackstone, *Commentaries on the Laws of England* (Facsimile of 1st ed. of 1765–69) (Chicago, 1979), I:125–26, IV:198.

53. Larned, *History of Windham County,* I:363.

54. Even in the context of the inflation of the 1740s, Hallowell's bill of costs was unusually high: £110.2s6d. Sessions was hit hard in the pocketbook too; he was assessed £83.14s.2*d.* in costs.

55. Petition of John Hallowell, Oct. 1747, Conn. Archives, Crimes and Misdemeanors, Ser. I, IV: 108. . . .

56. Note Blackstone's discussion of the liability of "a physician or surgeon who gives his patient a portion . . . to cure him, which contrary to expectation kills him." *Commentaries,* IV:197.

57. Pomfret Vit. Rec., II:67.

58. Carroll Smith-Rosenberg, "Beauty, the Beast and the Militant Woman: A Case Study in Sex Roles and Social Stress in Jacksonian America," *American Quarterly* XXIII (1971):562–84. . . .

59. Sessions, *Sessions Family,* pp. 31, 35; Larned, *History of Windham County,* I:363–64.

DOCUMENTS

Supporting the Revolution

"The ladies going about for money exceeded everything . . ."

This broadside of 1780 announced a women's campaign to raise contributions for patriot soldiers. Organized and led by Esther DeBerdt Reed, wife of the president of Pennsylvania, and by Benjamin Franklin's daughter Sarah Franklin Bache, the campaign was large and effective. "Instead of waiting for the Donations being sent the ladys of each Ward go from dore to dore and collect them," wrote one participant. Collecting contributions this way invited confrontation. One loyalist wrote to her sister, "Of all absurdities, the ladies going about for money exceeded everything; they were so extremely importunate that people were obliged to give them something to get rid of them."* The campaign raised $300,000 in paper dollars in inflated war currency. Rather than let George Washington merge it with the general fund, the women insisted on using it to buy materials for making shirts so that each soldier might know he had received an extraordinary contribution from the women of Philadelphia. The broadside itself is an unusually explicit justification for women's intrusion into politics.

On the commencement of actual war, the Women of America manifested a firm resolution of contribute . . . to the deliverance of their country. Animated by the purest patriotism, they are sensible of sorrow at this day, in not offering more than barren wishes for the success of so glorious a Revolution. They aspire to render themselves more really useful; and this sentiment is universal from the north to the south of the Thirteen United States. Our ambition is kindled by the fame of those heroines of antiquity, who have rendered their sex illustrious, and have proved to the universe, that, if the weakness of our Constitution, if opinion and manners did not forbid us to march to glory by the same paths as the Men, we should at least equal, and sometimes surpass them in our love for the public good. I glory in all that which my sex has done great and commendable. I call to mind with enthusiasm and with admiration, all those acts of courage, of constancy and patriotism, which history has transmitted to us: The people favoured by Heaven, preserved from destruction by the virtues, the zeal and the resolution of Deborah, of Judith, of Esther! The fortitude of the mother of the Macchabees, in giving up her sons to die before her eyes: Rome saved from the fury of a victorious enemy by the efforts of Volumnia, and other Roman Ladies: So many famous sieges where the Women have been seen forgetting the weakness of their sex, building new walls, digging trenches with their feeble hands, furnishing arms to their defenders, they themselves darting the missile weapons on the enemy, resigning the ornaments of their apparel, and their

*Mary Morris to Catharine Livingston, June 10 [1780], Ridley Family Papers, Massachusetts Historical Society, Boston; Anna Rawle to Rebecca Rawle Shoemaker, June 30, 1780, in *Pennsylvania Magazine of History and Biography* 35 (1911): 398.

Excerpted from *The Sentiments of an American Woman* ([Philadelphia]: John Dunlap, 1780).

fortune, to fill the public treasury, and to hasten the deliverance of their country; burying themselves under its ruins; throwing themselves into the flames rather than submit to the disgrace of humiliation before a proud enemy.

Born for liberty, disdaining to bear the irons of a tyrannic Government, we associate ourselves to the grandeur of those Sovereigns, cherished and revered, who have held with so much splendour the scepter of the greatest States, The Batildas, the Elizabeths, the Maries, the Catharines, who have extented the empire of liberty, and contented to reign by sweetness and justice, have broken the chains of slavery, forged by tyrants in times of ignorance and barbarity....

We know that at a distance from the theatre of war, if we enjoy any tranquility, it is the fruit of your watchings, your labours, your dangers.... Who, amongst us, will not renounce with the highest pleasure, those vain ornaments, when she shall consider that the valiant defenders of America will be able to draw some advantage from the money which she may have laid out in these.... The time is arrived to display the same sentiments which animated us at the beginning of the Revolution, when we renounced the use of teas, however agreeable to our taste, rather than receive them from our persecutors; when we made it appear to them that we placed former necessaries in the rank of superfluities, when our liberty was interested; when our republican and laborious hands spun the flax, prepared the linen intended for the use of our soldiers; when [as] exiles and fugitives we supported with courage all the evils which are the concomitants of war....

Sarah Osborn, "The bullets would not cheat the gallows . . ."

Sarah Osborn was eighty-one years old when Congress made it possible for dependent survivors of Revolutionary war veterans to claim their pensions. She testified to her own service as well as to her husband's in the following deposition, sworn before the Court of Common Pleas in Wayne County, New Jersey, in 1837. Osborn's husband was a commissary guard; like many thousands of women, Osborn traveled with him, cooking and cleaning for troops at a time when there was no formal quartermaster corps and in which cleanliness was virtually the only guard against disease. Her account tells of working when the army was at West Point in 1780; of the long expedition south, marching proudly on horseback into Philadelphia, and then continuing to Yorktown. Osborn is the only one of the "women of the army" who has left us a narrative of her experiences. At Yorktown she brought food to soldiers under fire. When she told George Washington that she did not fear the bullets because they "would not cheat the gallows," she was conveying her understanding that her challenge to royal authority was congruent with his; if the soldiers risked being hanged for treason, so would she.

[In the march to Philadelphia in 1781?] Deponent was part of the time on horseback and part of the time in a wagon. Deponent's ... husband was still serving as one of the commissary's guard.... They continued their march to Philadelphia, deponent on horseback through the streets.... Being out of bread, deponent was employed in baking the afternoon and

John C. Dann, Excerpted from The *Revolution Remembered: Eyewitness Accounts of the American Revolution,* ed. (Chicago: University of Chicago Press, 1980), pp. 240–45.

Women like Sarah Osborn, who served in an informal quartermaster corps, were not the only women on or near Revolutionary War battlefields. In 1782, Deborah Sampson, who was already notable in her community of Middleborough, Massachusetts, for her height and strength, adopted men's clothing and the name of Robert Shurtleff. She enlisted for service with the Fourth Massachusetts Regiment. Like many young women from impoverished families, Deborah Sampson had been bound out to domestic service as a young teenager. When her term was up, she taught school briefly in Middleborough and joined the First Baptist Church there. She was expelled from the church before her enlistment. She served with her regiment in New York and possibly in Pennsylvania until she was wounded at a battle near Tarrytown, New York.

After her return to Massachusetts, Sampson married and bore three children. The fame of her exploits persisted. After a fictionalized biography was published by Herman Mann, she went on a wide-ranging speaking tour, perhaps the first American woman to undertake such an enterprise, and applied for the pensions to which her wartime service entitled her. These were awarded slowly and grudgingly, and she died impoverished in 1827. (Joseph Stone, Deborah Sampson (Gannett), 1797, oil on panel. Courtesy of the Rhode Island Historical Society.)

evening... they continued their march... [at Baltimore she] embarked on board a vessel and sailed... until they had got up the St. James River as far as the tide would carry them.... They... marched for Yorktown.... Deponent was on foot.... Deponent took her stand just back of the American tents, say about a mile from the town, and busied herself washing, mending, and cooking for the soldiers, in which she was assisted by the other females; some men washed their own clothing. She heard the roar of the artillery for a number of days.... Deponent's... husband was there throwing up entrenchments, and deponent cooked and carried in beef, and bread, and coffee (in a gallon pot) to the soldiers in the entrenchment.

On one occasion when deponent was thus employed carrying in provisions, she met General Washington, who asked her if she "was not afraid of the cannonballs?"

She replied, "No, the bullets would not cheat the gallows," that "It would not do for the men to fight and starve too."

They dug entrenchments nearer and nearer to Yorktown every night or two till the last. While digging that, the enemy fired very heavy till about nine o'clock next morning, then stopped, and the drums from the enemy beat excessively. Deponent was a little way off in Colonel Van Shaick's or the officers' marquee and a number of officers were present....

The drums continued beating, and all at once the officers hurrahed and swung their hats, and deponent asked them, "What is the matter now?"

One of them replied, "Are not you soldier enough to know what it means?"

Deponent replied, "No."

They then replied, "The British have surrendered."

Deponent, having provisions ready, carried the same down to the entrenchments that morning, and four of the soldiers whom she was in the habit of cooking for ate their breakfasts.

Deponent stood on one side of the road and the American officers upon the other side when the British officers came out of the town and rode up to the American officers and delivered up [their swords, which the deponent] thinks were returned again, and the British officers rode right on before the army, who marched out beating and playing a melancholy tune, their drums covered with black handkerchiefs and their fifes with black ribbands tied around them, into an old field and there grounded their arms and then returned into town again to await their destiny.... The British general at the head of the army was a large, portly man, full face, and the tears rolled down his cheeks as he passed along.

Rachel Wells, "I have Don as much to Carrey on the Warr as maney . . ."

Rachel Wells was probably sixty-five years old when she wrote the following words. She had bought loan office certificates from the state of New Jersey during the Revolution: subsequently she had moved to Philadelphia, but returned to Bordentown, New Jersey, after the war. In an effort to curb speculation, the New Jersey legislature decided that only state residents had a claim on interest payments; Rachel Wells's claim on her money was turned down because she had not been in the state at the war's end in 1783. She appealed directly to the Continental Congress. Although her petition was tabled, it remains—despite its bad spelling—as perhaps the most moving witness to the Revolution left to us by a

Rachel Wells, Petition to Congress, May 18, 1786, Microfilm Papers of the Continental Congress, National Archives, Washington, D.C., microfilm M247, roll 56, item 42, vol. 8, pp. 354–55.

woman. What did Rachel Wells think had been her contribution to the Revolution? What did she think the government owed to her?

To the Honnorabell Congress I rachel do make this Complaint Who am a Widow far advanced in years & Dearly have ocasion of ye Interst for that Cash I Lent the States. I was a Sitisen in ye jersey when I Lent ye State a considerable Sum of Moneys & had I justice dun me it mite be Suficant to suporte me in ye Contrey whear I am now, near burdentown. I Leved hear then . . . but Being . . . so Robd by the Britans & others i went to Phila to try to get a Living . . . & was There in the year 1783 when our assembley was pleasd to pas a Law that No one Should have aney Interest that Livd out of jearsey Stats . . .

Now gentelmen is this Liberty, had it bin advertised that he or She that Moved out of the Stat should Louse his or her Interest you mite have sum plea against me. But I am Innocent Suspected no Trick. I have Don as much to Carrey on the Warr as maney that Sett now at ye healm of government. . . . your asembly Borrowed £300 in gould of me jest as the Warr Comencd & Now I Can Nither git Intrust nor principall Nor Even Security. . . . My dr Sister . . . wrote to me to be thankfull that I had it in my Power to help on the Warr which is well enough but then this is to be Considerd that others gits their Intrust & why then a poor old widow to be put of[f]. . . . I hartely pity others that ar in my Case that Cant Speak for themselves. . . .

god has Spred a plentifull table for us & you gentelmen are ye Carvers for us pray forgit Not the Poor weaklings at the foot of the Tabel ye poor Sogers has got Sum Crumbs That fall from their masters tabel. . . . Why Not Rachel Wells have a Little intrust?

if She did not fight She threw in all her mite which bought ye Sogers food & Clothing & Let Them have Blankets & Since that She has bin obligd to Lay upon Straw & glad of that . . .

ANNETTE GORDON-REED

The Hemings-Jefferson Treaty: Paris, 1789

From 1787 to 1789, Sally Hemings lived in Paris, becoming familiar with the city, learning French, and earning wages. She had been only fourteen years old when she made the Atlantic transit from Virginia, accompanying eight-year-old Polly Jefferson whose father, Thomas, wished his youngest child to join him in France. Three years earlier, Jefferson had taken up his diplomatic post in France, arriving with his teenage daughter Martha (called Patsy) and Sally's older brother James. By the time Polly and Sally joined him, the diplomat was renting an elegant, twenty-four-room house known as the Hôtel de Langeac; it was on the Champs-Elysées at some remove from the city center.

Sally and her brothers were born slaves, the legal property of Virginia planter John Wayles whose daughter Martha became Thomas Jefferson's first and only wife. At the Wayles-Jefferson wedding in 1772, various enslaved Hemingses, including Sally, James, and their mother Elizabeth, were added to Jefferson's human assets. John Wayles was actually Sally's biological father as well as her master; Sally was therefore the half sister of Jefferson's wife. Sally and other Hemings women were at Martha Wayles Jefferson's deathbed in 1782, where Martha, weeping, asked her husband to promise not to remarry and impose a stepmother on their then-living four children. Afterward, the young Sally lived with, and attended, the Jeffersons' youngest daughters; thus, she in effect grew up alongside her nieces. What she thought about this situation, we do not know.

Sally was still a slave girl when she lived in Paris. She remained an enslaved person until several years before her death in 1835. But those who observed her in Paris would not have associated her with the strenuous, debasing, and exhausting field labor that many African-descended women had to endure on New World plantations. She undertook light household duties such as sewing; she accompanied Patsy and Polly on daytime urban promenades and to evening receptions and balls. She wore fine clothes, as circumstances dictated. She did not have her femininity denied her.

Annette Gordon-Reed's essay pivots on a dramatic and private agreement that Sally Hemings and Thomas Jefferson made just before Jefferson was to leave his post and return to Monticello, his beloved Virginia plantation. Being under French law gave the Hemings siblings the opportunity to claim free status; Sally, the teenager, understood it as an extraordinary moment of leverage.

Until very recently, major Jefferson biographers (except for Fawn Brodie) refused to believe that Thomas Jefferson, slave owner, founding father, and two-term president, had a sexual relationship, or, as Gordon-Reed calls it, a long-term, possibly loving concubinage arrangement, with Sally Hemings. Even before there was DNA evidence to support this, Gordon-Reed, a lawyer as well as a scholar, wrote a book carefully laying out the evidence, pro and con. Appalled by decades

Excerpted from chs. 14–17 of *The Hemingses of Monticello: An American Family* by Annette Gordon-Reed (New York: W. W. Norton, 2008). Reprinted by permission of the author and publisher. Notes have been edited and renumbered.

of scholarly obfuscations and willed ignorance about the agency of African Americans, she pointed out the curious disconnect between the popular appeal of the Hemings-Jefferson story in the 1970s and 1980s and the historians' vehement, sometimes irrational denials.*

What do you make of the author's suggestion that for Sally Hemings, being female was more at the core of her identity than being enslaved? Some skeptics will argue that the existence of the 1789 treaty rests on slim evidence—Hemings family lore and an inkwell. How do you assess Gordon-Reed's reasoning?

Postscript to the story told here: the child that Sally Hemings was carrying in 1789 did not survive. Later, at Monticello where they continued their relationship, she gave birth to seven children, five of whom survived infancy. For these children, Thomas Jefferson abided by the terms of the treaty of 1789.

THE HEMINGS-JEFFERSON TREATY: PARIS, 1789

When we think of the young Sally Hemings, . . . we acknowledge that she was born into a cohort—eighteenth-century enslaved black women—whose humanity and femininity were constantly assaulted by slavery and white supremacy. While the experiences typical to that cohort are highly relevant as a starting point for looking at Hemings, they can never be an end in themselves. For Hemings lived in her own skin, and cannot simply be defined through the enumerated experiences of the group—enslaved black females.

Taking account of the larger social context in which Hemings lived is essential. . . . There is . . . no one context to consult in regard to [her] . . . she had the multiple identities that are the normal part of the human makeup. The people and places she encountered gave her multiple personal contexts—the circle of her mother and siblings, her extended family, the larger enslaved community at Monticello, her community in Paris, Jefferson, his white family, and, finally, her own children. Those associations . . . shaped her inner life and outlook. . . .

Sally Hemings . . . spent her first fourteen years in a country that defined her as human chattel. In her fifteenth and sixteenth years, she was in a place [(France)] where a court would . . . transform her status, turning her into a legally recognized free person. Sometime between 1787 and 1789, this teenager learned the difference between law in Virginia and law in France. The power of the former could reenslave her, while the power of the latter could set her free. So she stood poised between the reality of life in the place of her birth and the moment when she had to decide whether to take the step toward freedom in a new land. She could make her journey alone or with her older brother, leaving not only slavery behind but also a large and intensely connected family in Virginia. . .

[The years in Paris were also the time when Hemings became Jefferson's "concubine."] How is it possible to get at the nature of a relationship between a man and a woman like Jefferson and Hemings when neither party specifically writes or speaks to others about that relationship or their feelings? Even written words can be quite deceptive and seldom tell the whole story, for people sometimes choose, for whatever reason, to tell a story of their lives that is rosier, or grimmer, than it actually was. In the absence of words, actions may be quite telling. An event in the life of Hemings's oldest sister Mary that took place at the same time that Hemings was in Paris dealing with Jefferson offers some insight into the varied nature of the veiled relationships between enslaved women and white men. . . .

[Due to mounting family debts, Jefferson was under pressure to hire out some of his slaves. Thus, in the late 1780s] Mary Hemings, Sally's oldest sibling, was hired out to a

*Annette Gordon-Reed, *Thomas Jefferson and Sally Hemings: An American Controversy* (Charlottesville: University Press of Virginia, 1997); Dinitia Smith and Nicholas Wade, "DNA Test Finds Evidence of Jefferson Child by Slave," *New York Times*, Nov. 1, 1998, p. A1.

prosperous merchant named Thomas Bell . . . She moved, along with three of her children—Molly, Joseph, and Betsy—to Bell's home on Main Street [in Charlottesville]. . . .

We do not know the circumstances surrounding the origins of the Bell-Hemings connection: Did he notice her and lease her for the purpose of making her his concubine, or was it something that developed after the leasehold? In either event, things moved quickly, for her children were born soon after she was leased. However matters started, in Mary Hemings we get a rare sense, from her own actions, of an enslaved woman's preferences regarding her choice of mate and the course of her life. Not long after Jefferson returned from Paris, Hemings specifically asked to be sold to Bell. Jefferson complied with her request and gave Nicholas Lewis, still overseeing his affairs, "power to dispose of Mary according to her desire, with such of her younger children as she chose."[1] In an ironic twist on his practice of selling or buying slaves to unite them with family members from other plantations, Jefferson sold Mary Hemings to unite her to her white partner and their children. He knew the couple's situation very well, and he acted in deference not just to the wishes of an enslaved woman but also to the desires of the white father of her children.

Within the extremely narrow constraints of what life offered her—ownership by Thomas Jefferson or ownership by Thomas Bell—Mary Hemings took an action that had enormous, lasting, and, in the end, quite favorable consequences for her, her two youngest children, and the Hemings family as a whole. She found in Bell a man willing to live openly with her, and to treat her and their children as if they were bound together as a legal family. She must have seen that capacity in him during the early stages of their time together. Over the years she would be able to compare notes on her life with a white man with her youngest sister, whom she honored by giving her own youngest daughter the name Sarah (also called Sally), known by the time of her marriage, in the early 1800s, as Sarah Jefferson Bell.[2] . . .

. . . Both Hemings sisters had very firm internal understandings about how they might influence the course of their lives so that they could have what many of the women of their day, black and white, wanted—the ability, during their measured time on earth, to associate with a man who would take care of them and provide the best possible lives for their children with some chance of stability in an unstable world. Mary Hemings experienced firsthand what this instability meant. Although she found a place for herself with Bell, unlike her sister Sally, she experienced one of the harshest aspects of enslaved motherhood. . . . [F]our of her six children were taken from her. The liaison with Bell ensured that any new children she had would be protected. The contingencies of the lives of Sally and Mary Hemings were such that Jefferson and Bell, for whatever reason—their personalities, their feelings about the women involved— supported these sisters' aspirations. As a result both women, in their own way, achieved exactly what they wanted. That their very elemental desires as women were met in the context of slavemaster, black-white relationships is troubling because they mix something that seems almost sacred (the human desire for a secure family life) with something deeply profane (slavery). . . .

The title . . . [of] historian Walter Johnson's *Soul by Souls*[3] captures the enormity of slavery's inhumanity and suggests at least one way to go about illuminating it in the pages of history. Slavery was not just one, enormous act of oppression against a nameless, interchangeable mass of people. It was millions of separate assassinations and attempted assassinations of individual spirits carried out over centuries. When we encounter some of those spirits responding to their circumstances as human beings respond and using whatever means available to them to maintain or assert their humanity in the face of the onslaught, their individual efforts should not be minimized or ignored, because they could never alone have killed off the institution of slavery. That is far too heavy a load to place on people whose burdens in life were already almost unimaginably heavy. . . .

[Paris, 1789:]

James and Sally Hemings had many months to contemplate their possible return to Virginia. Jefferson had, in fact, been preparing to go home long before he received official word that his request for a leave of absence had been granted; he had packed his bags to be ready to go on a moment's notice.[4] The Hemingses, as well as his daughters, were expected to return with him, and were likely as much on tenterhooks as he, for they, too, had to be ready to leave as soon as word arrived. When it was clear that return to America was imminent, Sally Hemings was pregnant, and her pregnancy created a problem that she and Jefferson had to address and sort out. [In a memoir recorded in 1873,] Madison Hemings, [a son of Sally Hemings,] described what happened:

> But during that time my mother became Mr. Jefferson's concubine, and when he was called back home she was *enciente* by him. He desired to bring my mother back to Virginia with him, but she demurred. She was just beginning to understand the French language well, and in France she was free, while if she returned to Virginia she would be re-enslaved. So she refused to return with him. To induce her to do so he promised her extraordinary privileges, and made a solemn pledge that her children should be freed at the age of twenty-one years. In consequence of his promises, on which she implicitly relied, she returned with him to Virginia.[5]

There is much to consider about this very simple, yet powerful, explanation of what happened between Sally Hemings and Thomas Jefferson in France. First, it could only have been a shorthand version of all that actually happened, all the words that passed between these two. . . . The stakes were extremely high for both, but highest for Hemings. She knew all too well what slavery meant, and she lived with the hard knowledge that, were she to return to Virginia, every child from her womb would follow her condition. In this moment and place, she was in the best position she would ever be in to walk away from *partus sequitur ventrem*, [meaning the status of the child follows the status of the mother,] forever. . . .

We cannot know what Hemings thought about abortion for herself or whether the thought of not keeping her baby even crossed her mind. She was away from the network of her mother and female siblings who could counsel her and, as far as we know, without a network of women of color to confide in and discuss a matter so personal. . . .

Hemings's son described his mother as "implicitly" relying on his father, which goes to the mystery at the heart of Sally Hemings's life: Why would she trust Jefferson, and why would she, under any circumstances, return to Virginia with him? Trading immediate freedom for herself and her progeny for a life at Monticello with him and a *promise* of eventual freedom for her children was not an even exchange. There was something in the gap between those two conditions—some desired prospect on the other side of the ocean—that motivated her.

It is all too easy to ignore how being female shaped Hemings's desires and expectations and focus in on the thing that makes her so different from us today: she was born enslaved. By the time they were in France together, Jefferson had already helped set the terms for the development of Hemings's view of herself as a female. As the authority figure at Monticello, he sent a strong message to her when he acted to protect what he considered to be the femininity of Hemings and her female relatives, while failing to show similar concerns for other enslaved women on his plantations. Hemings watched every female go to the fields at harvest time, except her sisters, mother, and whatever white females were at the plantation.[6] She learned from all this that, in Jefferson's eyes, she was a female to be protected from certain things, when most women of her same legal status received no protection at all. . . .

Even without Jefferson's intervention, it is doubtful that Hemings thought being a slave was more at the core of her existence than being female; she could cease to be the one, never the other. Their numbers were still small when she was growing up, but there were free black people in Virginia, and their numbers would grow in the years after she returned to America.[7] The world sent her a very definite and hard message about enslavement at the same time as it conveyed another powerful message about what was to be her role in life as a woman—partner to a man and a mother. Those roles were tenuous because the law did not protect her in either of them. They were not, however, meaningless to her.

Having a child was perhaps the most serious matter that confronted women. Females who faced motherhood during Hemings's time—enslaved, free, black, white, and red—confronted the immediate issue of surviving the ordeal of pregnancy. They knew that even if they survived, at least some of their children would likely die because no society had figured out how to save its children from deadly childhood diseases that are of little import in the developed world today. The death of children was not the only stalker of slave mothers and potential mothers like Hemings. She and other enslaved women faced the added, unspeakable reality that they could be separated from their children by sale. Above all of slavery's depredations, the separation of children from their families crystallized the system's barbarity so clearly that slave owners claimed that it rarely happened or spent endless time talking about how loath they were to do it—just before they did it. . . . [S]eparation from children by sale . . . shaped . . . [enslaved women's] identities as women. Hemings, like other enslaved girls, must have dreamed of a future in which her motherhood would never be blighted by such a moment. . . .

Had Hemings never been in Paris, her choice of mates at Monticello would have been perhaps even more limited than that of other enslaved women on the plantation. Her racial background contributed to her identity and undoubtedly affected her views about who would be attractive as a companion and as father of her children. . . . In slavery and outside of it, members of Hemings's family—female and male—developed a practice of having children with, and marrying when that was available, people who looked something like themselves, which is what most people in the world tend to do.[8] Jefferson probably resembled Hemings more than the average male slave on the plantation did, in terms of hair texture, skin color, and eye color. This is not to say that she would never under any circumstances have welcomed a partner with skin darker than her own or tightly curled hair, as allowances must always be made for the vagaries of attraction. It is human beings we are dealing with, after all, and no one has devised a precise formula or foolproof predictor of personal taste, and black couples and families come in all shades.

Although Hemings was probably not thinking in strictly legal terms about the racial makeup of the child she was carrying in Paris when she was deciding whether to come home with Jefferson, Virginia statutory law on racial categorizations, as Jefferson noted many years later, would make all of her children by him legally white, [for Virginia law provided that a person who was seven-eighths white was to be considered white]. We know Hemings wanted to free her children from slavery, and Jefferson's actions show he wanted that as well. No one has ever said that Hemings thought it important to free them from blackness, too. However, that is exactly the route that three of her four children took when they left both slavery and the black community to live as white people. The one child of hers who did remain in the black community, Madison Hemings, married a woman who was fair-skinned enough that some of their children were able to pass into the white world. We do not know whether the Hemings-Jefferson offspring were raised to do that, but it would not be surprising, particularly given their father's stated values, if that was a part of a plan or at least a very strong hope. . . .

Under the circumstances of Hemings's life, given her society and her family history, what type of man would be most able to end slavery for her children along with all the problems associated with being a person with black skin in America? If not Thomas Jefferson, who? She may have thought him as good a white man as any other, perhaps even better in some ways. That was a judgment to ponder. . . .

Unlike the vast majority of her enslaved cohort back in Virginia, freedom was within . . . [Sally Hemings'] grasp [in Paris], and she ended up using the unique opportunity she possessed, not as an end in itself, but as a starting point for a discussion with the man who wanted to take her home with him. That Jefferson desired that at all, a further contingent element in Hemings's life, gave her leverage under their particular circumstances. Another man might not have cared enough to try to persuade her or would have dared her (and her brother) to do their worst: take their claim to the Admiralty Court. . . .

Hemings had not only her own observations of Jefferson to draw upon; a wealth of family history supplemented her knowledge. Whether she had had time in her young life to learn this fact about him or not, the truth is that few things could have disturbed the very thin-skinned, possessive, and controlling Jefferson more deeply than having persons in his inner circle take the initiative and express their willingness to remove themselves from it. To have this come from a young female, the kind of person he thought was supposed to be under the control of males, whether they were enslaved or not, was likely doubly upsetting. . . . This challenge was a far greater threat to his self-esteem and emotions than to his wallet. He had great confidence in his ability to charm and in his capacity to bring people to his side and keep them there. . . .

[Furthermore,] Hemings knew how Jefferson viewed women, and implicitly understood that if she were paired with an enslaved man [at Monticello] she would have two men over her: her enslaved husband and Jefferson. She would be one step removed from the man who held power over both of them, and Jefferson would have no personal stake in her or the children she bore with another man. . . .

Like other enslaved people when the all too rare chance presented itself, Hemings seized her moment and used the knowledge of her rights to make a decision based upon what she thought was best for her as a woman, family member, and a potential mother in her specific circumstances.

Visitors to the Hôtel de Langeac toasted Jefferson as the "apostle of liberty" and made much of his progressivism in the face of those who wanted to maintain the status quo in society. Imagine the stir if a slave of the "apostle" had shown up at the Admiralty Court in Paris, forced there because he had refused her request for freedom. Jefferson's image, which he so assiduously cultivated throughout his entire public career, would have been left in tatters. . . . To have Jefferson, of all people, act in direct opposition to France's Freedom Principle so that he could keep control over a sixteen-year-old enslaved girl would have been a spectacle for the ages. The word "irony" does not even begin to approach doing the situation justice. If the court had gotten the chance to see her, all would have been revealed instantly. . . . That was an outcome to be avoided at all costs. . . . Aside from whatever he felt for her, the Parisian Admiralty Court and Jefferson's special position and reputation in France gave Sally Hemings latitude to say, "I will go home with you, but only on certain conditions."[9]

Jefferson may have pointed out to Hemings and her brother the potential problems they might face by remaining in Paris. . . . [But] by this time, whatever sense of entitlement [Sally] had as a Hemings had been added to all her experiences to date—traveling across an ocean, . . . learning a new language, . . . and being a handsomely paid employee. The last experience was probably the most important. She worked alongside other French servants at the Hôtel de Langeac and knew she could work elsewhere. The fashion of having African and mixed-race servants gave her an advantage if she sought work as a *femme de chambre*. . . .

And then there was Paris' small community of color. . . . Sally Hemings had a special reason for thinking of this community. She did not likely consider staying in France without thinking of what the future might hold in the way of marriage and companionship. Although only around a thousand *gens de couleur* lived in all of Paris, the vast majority of them, concentrated in a small number of neighborhoods, were males in their late teens and early twenties—exactly suitable for a young woman approaching her seventeenth birthday.[10]

. . . [H]ad Hemings decided to break away from Jefferson and start a new life with her brother, she would have had the chance to be the mother of children who were free at birth and she could have had a legal marriage and the social respectability that would elude her totally in Virginia living with Jefferson. None of her children would have felt compelled to leave her, one another, and their family history behind in order to escape the racism of nineteenth-century America. . . .

. . . With no opportunity for legal marriage, Sally Hemings . . . was operating without the benefit of any written rules. The plan for her life at Monticello with Jefferson . . . depended . . . upon Hemings's ability to hold Jefferson in some serious fashion over the years and, more importantly, the quality of his personal character and his willingness to remain committed to her. It is not all surprising, therefore, that Hemings and Jefferson talked [in Paris] of the very matters that were among the core issues addressed in the basic marriage contract for free couples in the world in which they lived: the treatment of the woman, the man's duties and obligations toward the children, and what the children would receive from the man when they became adults, questions that men and women in every type of society from time immemorial have had to address. That the two would be having sex was implicit in the understanding that Hemings was going to have more children and that provision would be made for them as well as the one about to be born—the particular one that Hemings most wanted: their freedom.

[For the past decade, I have traveled the country, speaking about Hemings and Jefferson. I do not recall a setting where this question was not asked explicitly or implicitly: "Did they love each other?"] The most intimate of situations, the one least likely to be observed by others—sexual compatibility—can . . . be a form of love. But in our Western culture (and some others, to be fair) sex is considered, if not exactly dirty or shameful, a somewhat guilty pleasure that must always be separated from more exalted love. This is especially true when a couple, like Hemings and Jefferson, for reasons of race, status, or gender are not supposed to be together, as if partners who do not have the imprimatur of law, society, and custom could never feel the emotion of love for one another. The invariable charge against such pairs is that they are inauthentic per se, because they are bound together purely for sex, rather than love.

[A] Jefferson great-granddaughter through the Hemings line told a . . . story about Hemings and Jefferson's origins in France when explaining why her great-grandmother gave up the chance for freedom and came back to Virginia, saying, "Jefferson loved her dearly."[11] In other words, she and other family members answered the questions why Hemings trusted Jefferson and came back to Virginia with him, by referencing her confidence in her knowledge of that fact, a confidence that allowed her to take what seems a breathtakingly large risk. . . .

Jefferson wanted Hemings to come back to Virginia with him, so much so that he took to bargaining with her about this. He well knew that in Virginia there were many other women, enslaved and not, who could satisfy any merely carnal impulses as soon as he returned to America. The problem was, however, that they would not actually have been Sally Hemings herself, a requirement that was evidently very important to him. Her siblings and other relatives seemed to have gauged this. . . . [T]heir attitude toward Jefferson after Hemings's return to Virginia is in perfect keeping with the idea that they believed he cared for her. If what had happened between them in France had been along the lines of more typical master-female slave sex, Hemings's expressed desire to stay in the country, especially after she became aware that she was pregnant, would have been exactly what Jefferson needed. He could have left her in Paris with her quite capable older brother, helped the pair financially, . . . thus ridding himself of a potentially embarrassing problem in a way that actually bolstered, instead of hurt, his image. History, and his philosophc friends of the moment, would have recorded that Jefferson (breathing the rarefied air of Enlightenment France) so identified with the Freedom Principle that he let go of two of his own slaves. He would have been a veritable hero.

Instead of doing that, Jefferson insisted on setting up an arrangement with a young woman that he knew could easily result in a houseful of children whose existence would be easily tied to him. . . . During the decades that followed their time in France, . . . this most thin-skinned of individuals persisted on his course, . . . having more children with her who were named in the same fashion as the older ones: for his important and favorite family members and his best friends.[12] . . . Jefferson continued on, guided by his own internal compass and, no doubt, his awareness that the woman being vilified in the press had given up to him a thing whose value he understood: her freedom. He knew very well that these people, really, did not know what, and whom, they were talking about.

If sex had been the only issue, it would have been a far simpler and more practical matter, for himself and his white family when they returned to Monticello, for Jefferson to have installed Hemings in one of his nearby quarter farms . . . and visited her there when the mood hit him. . . . Instead, Jefferson arranged his life at Monticello so that Hemings would be in it every day that he was there, taking care of his possessions, in his private enclave.

What most disturbed contemporary commentators about the arrangement at Monticcllo was not that the master had a slave mistress but that she was not sufficiently hidden away.[13] Hemings was a visible presence in his home when everyone knew that Jefferson had the resources to have her be someplace else. The racism and sexual hysteria this unleashed among white Americans was a thing to behold. . . . Yet, through all the talk during Jefferson's lifetime of his "Congo Harem," "Negro Harem," and "African Harem," only one woman's name emerged: Sally. Jefferson's enemies of the day could list each of Hemings's children, their order of birth and ages, what her duties were at Monticello, but they could never produce the name of another specific woman to be a part of his alleged seraglio.

From her side, it was Hemings who backed down from her decision to stay in France in return for a life at Monticello in which Jefferson would be a very serious presence. . . . [D]uring an almost twenty-year period of childbearing, she conceived no children during Jefferson's sometimes prolonged absences from Monticello as he acted as a public servant, indicating that she had no other sexual partners.[14] That could well have been at his insistence as much as her own personal desires. Still, the expectation of fidelity—on her part at least—suggests something about the nature of their relationship. . . . Hemings's connection to Jefferson, held together totally by whatever was going on between them, was her children's way out of slavery, so long as her children were his, too. She was apparently unwilling to do anything (as in having babies by other men) that might jeopardize that connection and bring the effects of *partus sequitur ventrem* back into her life.

Before Hemings died, she gave one of her sons as heirlooms personal items that had belonged to Jefferson, a pair of his eyeglasses, a shoe buckle, and an inkwell that she had kept during the nine years after his death. These artifacts—things she saw him wear and a thing he used to write words that would make him live in history—were seemingly all that she had left of him. Monticello and virtually all its contents were sold to pay debts or were in the control of his legal white family. These items were quietly passed down in the Hemings family until well into the twentieth century.[15] . . . Hemings's action, which at the very least exhorted her descendants to both remember Jefferson and her connection to him, indicate that she wanted them to know he meant something to her. She had, after all, lived with him for decades, and he had given her valued children whom he had let go to make their way in the world. . . . Jefferson had kept his promises to her.

. . . Working backward to 1789 from either her death in 1835 or Jefferson's death in 1826, one can say that sixteen-year-old Hemings's instincts about how she might best shape her future in the context of her particular circumstances and needs were as sound as her older sister Mary's instincts about Thomas Bell, developing at the same time on another continent. Hemings could not have known this as she treated with Jefferson at the Hôtel de Langeac, but at the end of her life she would be able to say that she got the important things that she most wanted.

Notes

1. TJ to Nicholas Lewis, April 12, 1792, *The Papers of Thomas Jefferson*, ed. Julian P. Boyd et al., 35 vols. to date (Princeton, 1950–), 23:408.

2. Lucia Stanton, "Monticello to Main Street: The Hemings Family and Charlottesville," *Magazine of Albemarle County History* 55 (1997): 100.

3. Walter Johnson, *Soul by soul: Life inside the Antebellum Slave Market* (Cambridge, Mass., 1999).

4. TJ to Andre Limozin, May 3, 1789, *Papers*, 16:86.

5. [Reproduced in] Annette Gordon-Reed, *Thomas Jefferson and Sally Hemings: An American Controversy* (Charlottesville: University Press of Virginia, 1997), 246.

6. Lucia Stanton, *Free Some Day: The African-American Families of Monticello* (Charlottesville, 2000), 105.

7. Philip D. Morgan, *Slave Counterpoint: Black Culture in the Eighteenth-Century Chesapeake and Lowcountry* (Chapel Hill: University of North Carolina Press, 1998), 665–66; "An Act to Authorize the Manumission of Slaves;" *Laws of Virginia*, 1782, chap. 61.

8. Stanton, *Free Some Day*, 106; Lucia Stanton and Dianne Swann Wright, "Bonds of Memory Identity and the Hemings Family," in *Sally Hemings and Thomas Jefferson: History, Memory and Civic Culture*, ed. Jan Ellen Lewis and Peter S. Onuf (Charlottesville, 1999), 170–72.

9. Sue Peabody, *"There Are No Slaves in France": The Political Culture of Race and Slavery in the Ancien Régime* (New York: Oxford University Press, 1996), 101–3.

10. Pierre H. Boulle, "Les Gens de couleur à Paris à la veille de la Révolution" in *L'Image de la Révolution française*, ed. Michel Vovelle. Vol 1 (Paris: Pergamon Press, 1989), 160–61.

11. Stanton and Swann Wright, "Bonds of Memory Identity,"176.

12. Gordon-Reed, *Thomas Jefferson and Sally Hemings*, 196–201.

13. Ibid., 170–71.

14. Ibid., 100–102, 216.

15. Nellie Jones to Stuart Gibboney, July 29, 1938, Aug. 10, 1938; Stuart Gibboney to Nellie Jones, Aug. 1, 1938, Nov. 1, 1938, correspondence in the University of Virginia Library, Accession No. 6636-a-b, Box No. Control Folder, Folder Dates 1735–1961. Nellie Jones was Madison Hemings's granddaughter. She wrote to Gibboney, the then president of the Thomas Jefferson Memorial Foundation, offering to donate mementos that her great-grandmother Sally Hemings had saved and given to their son: a pair of his glasses, an inkwell, and a silver buckle.

LINDA K. KERBER

The Republican Mother and the Woman Citizen: Contradictions and Choices in Revolutionary America

"I expect to see our young women forming a new era in female history," wrote Judith Sargent Murray in 1798. Her optimism was part of a general sense that all possibilities were open in the post-Revolutionary world. The experience of war had given words like *independence* and *self-reliance* personal as well as political overtones; among the things that ordinary people had learned from wartime had been that the world could, as the song played during the British surrender at Yorktown put it, turn upside down. The rich could quickly become poor; wives might suddenly have to manage farms and businesses; women might even, as the famous Deborah Sampson Gannett had done, shoulder a gun. Revolutionary experience taught that it was useful to be prepared for a wide range of unusual possibilities; political theory taught that republics rested on the virtue of their citizens. The stability and competence on which republican government relied required a highly literate and politically sophisticated constituency. Maintaining the republic was an intellectual and educational as well as a political challenge.

Murray herself, born into an elite family in Salem, Massachusetts, had felt the dislocations of the Revolution severely. Widowed, remarried to a Universalist minister of modest means, she understood what it was to be thrown on her own resources. "I would give my daughters every accomplishment which I thought proper," she wrote,

> and to crown all, I would early accustom them to habits of industry and order. They should be taught with precision the art economical; they should be enabled to procure for themselves the necessaries of life; independence should be placed within their grasp. . . . The SEX should be taught to depend on their own efforts, for the procurement of an establishment in life.[1]

The model republican woman was competent and confident. She could resist the vagaries of fashion; she was rational, independent, literate, benevolent, and self-reliant. Nearly every writer who described this paragon prepared a list of role models, echoing the pantheon of heroines admired by the fund-raising women of Philadelphia in 1780 (see pp. 134–135). There were women of the ancient world, like Cornelia, the mother of the Gracchi; rulers like Elizabeth of England and the Empress Catherine the Great of Russia; and a long list of British intellectuals: Lady Mary Wortley Montagu, Hannah More, Mary Wollstonecraft, and the historian Catherine Macaulay. Those who believed in these republican models demanded that their presence be recognized and endorsed and that a new generation of young women be urged to find in them patterns for their own behavior.

The Revolutionary years had brought some women close to direct criticism of political systems. Women had signed petitions, they had boycotted imported tea and textiles, they had made homespun and "felt nationly," as one young woman put it. In some places they had signed oaths of loyalty to patriot or loyalist forces. Rachel Wells bought £300 of government bonds to support the war and had a keen sense of her own contribution: "I did my Posabels every way . . . Ive Don as much to help on this war as Though I had bin a good

This essay has been written for *Women's America*. It is drawn from *Women of the Republic: Intellect and Ideology in Revolutionary America* (Chapel Hill: University of North Carolina Press, 1980), chs. 7 and 9; and *No Constitutional Right to Be Ladies: Women and the Obligations of Citizenship* (New York: Hill & Wang, 1998), introduction and ch. 1

Soger," she told the New Jersey legislature.[2] Women were citizens of the new republic. They could be naturalized; they were required to refrain from treason on pain of punishment; if single, they paid taxes. Women could develop their own agendas; when Abigail Adams wrote the now-famous letter in which she urged her husband and his colleagues in the Continental Congress to "remember the ladies," she urged that domestic violence should be on the republican agenda: "Put it out of the power of our husbands to use us with impunity," she demanded. "Remember all men would be tyrants if they could."[3]

Expressions of women's desire to play a frankly political role were regularly camouflaged in satire, a device that typically makes new ideas and social criticism seem less threatening and more palatable. In 1791, for example, a New Jersey newspaper published a pair of semiserious satires in which women discuss the politics of excise taxes and national defense. "Roxana" expresses a feminist impatience:

> In fifty quarto volumes of ancient and modern history, you will not find fifty illustrious female names; heroes, statesmen, divines, philosophers, artists, are all of masculine gender. And pray what have they done during this long period of usurpation? . . . They have written ten thousand unintelligible books. . . . They have been cutting each other's throats all over the globe.[4]

Some years later, the students at Sarah Pierce's famous school for girls in Litchfield, Connecticut, prepared a "Ladies Declaration of Independence" for the Fourth of July. Alongside the frivolous phrasing is earnest comment on the unfilled promises of the republic. Less than ten years after that, Elizabeth Cady Stanton would use the same technique. "When in the Course of Human Events," the Litchfield declaration begins,

> it becomes necessary for the Ladies to dissolve those bonds by which they have been subjected to others, and to assume among the self styled Lords of Creation that separate and equal station to which the laws of nature and their *own talents* entitle them, a decent respect to the opinions of mankind requires, that they should declare the causes which impel them to the separation.
>
> We hold these truths to be self evident. That all *mankind* are created equal.

The Litchfield women wished to change "social relations." They complained about men who "have undervalued our talents, and disparaged our attainments; they have combined with each other, for the purpose of excluding us from all participation in Legislation and in the administration of Justice."[5]

As these young women understood, American revolutionaries had brilliantly and radically challenged the laws governing the relationship between ruler and ruled, subjects and the king. Republican ideology was antipatriarchal. It voiced the claim of adult men to be freed from the control of kings and political "fathers" in an antique monarchical system. "Is it in the interest of a man to be a boy all his life?" Tom Paine asked in *Common Sense*, the great political manifesto of the era.

But the men who modeled the new American republic after the war remodeled it in their own image. They did not eliminate the political father immediately or completely. George Washington quickly became the "Father of his Country"; at the Governor's Palace in Williamsburg, Virginia, the life-size portrait of George III was quickly replaced by a life-size portrait of George Washington in a similar pose. American revolutionary men understood that two major elements of prerevolutionary social and political life—the system of slavery and the system of domestic relations—directly clashed with the egalitarian principles of the Revolution. But they kept both systems in place. By embedding the three-fifths compromise and the Fugitive Slave Law in the federal Constitution of 1787, the founders actually strengthened and stabilized the system of slavery. And they left virtually intact the old English law governing relations between husbands and wives.

In traditional English practice, at marriage a husband gained access to the body of his wife; it followed that he could easily pressure her into agreement with him on all other matters. A married woman was understood to be "covered" by her husband's civic identity, as though they were walking together under an umbrella that the husband held. There were relatively few constraints on what he could do with her body and her property, though she was nearly always guaranteed the use of one-third of their combined real estate and the ownership of one-third of the moveable property throughout her widowhood. The rules of coverture made it seem logical that fathers be the guardians of the children and that husbands manage the property that wives brought to marriage and earned during it. So long as she was married, she could not make a contract without his permission; she could not make a will until she was a widow. She could not make choices—for example, about to whom a child was to be apprenticed—that challenged the choices made by her husband. The revolutionary republic promised to protect "life, liberty and property," but under the old law a married woman was deprived of her property and had none to protect. Coverture was theoretically incompatible with revolutionary ideology and with the newly developing liberal commercial society. But patriot men carefully sustained it. Recognizing that husbands could easily pressure the electoral choices of married women, legislators concluded not that husbands should be controlled, but that women—unmarried as well as married—should not vote.

Yet the fact of women's citizenship in a democratic republic contained deep within it an implicit challenge to coverture. Patriot men rarely spoke about this issue, but their actions speak for them. In England, the killing of a husband by a wife was *petit treason*, analogous to regicide, although the killing of a wife by a husband was murder. The penalties for *petit treason* were worse than those for murder. The concept was not much enforced in colonial America, but it remained in the statutes. It was the only element of the old law of domestic relations that legislators of the early republic eliminated. Legislators were conscious of what they intended; they carefully retained the concept of *petit treason* for the killing of the master by a slave. With that single exception, neither the Revolutionary government under the Articles of Confederation nor the federal government of the Constitution directly challenged the legal system of coverture.[6] Every free man, rich or poor, white or black, gained something from the system of domestic relations already in place; they had no need to renegotiate it.

The best introduction to the old system of thinking about relations between women and men is to read the treatises on which judges and lawyers relied. They even continued to refer to the body of law of domestic relations by its traditional name, "the law of baron et feme"—not "husband and wife" or "man and woman" but "lord and woman." The same treatises that described the law of baron and feme invariably went on to laws of parent and child, master and servant.

In an era before law schools were attached to universities, and when prospective lawyers "read law" as apprentices in the offices of practitioners, Tapping Reeve conducted perhaps the most respected legal training in the nation. Students came from all over the country to study in his Litchfield, Connecticut, home; among them were Reeve's own brother-in-law Aaron Burr and, years later, John C. Calhoun from South Carolina. There were also future U.S. congressmen and senators, judges and Supreme Court justices. Reeve's treatise on the law of baron and feme, first published in 1816, was reprinted with up-to-date annotations in 1846, a testament to its continued vitality. Reeve offers us pithy accounts of what the early generations of American jurists took to be the common sense of the matter of relations between men and women. Nothing that he wrote would have surprised his contemporaries.

To follow the law of marriage, as Reeve delicately spun out its implications, is to watch the playing out of a stacked deck. Reeve began his book with the forthright statement that "the husband, by marriage, acquires an absolute title to all the personal property of the wife." Husbands also gained extensive power over her real estate; wives gained no advantages "in point of property" from marriage.

Once these asymmetrical property relations were established, personal implications wound their way throughout the law. The husband's control of all property gave him such coercive power over the wife that she could not defy him. Instead of revising the law to remove its coercive elements, jurists simply ensured that the coerced voices would not speak. Husbands were responsible for crimes committed by their wives in their presence or with their approval—except in the case of treason, a crime so severe that responsibility for it overrode obligation to the husband, or in the event that a wife kept a brothel with the husband's knowledge, since keeping a brothel "is an offense of which the wife is supposed to have the principal management."[7] Before married women signed away their right to dower property, judges were supposed to question them privately about whether their husbands had coerced them, although the law offered no protection against continued coercion. A wife could not normally make contracts in her own name; if she did, her husband was bound "to fulfill the contract of his wife, when it is such an one as wives in her rank of life usually purchase. . . . If however, she were to purchase a ship or yoke of oxen, no such presumption would arise, for wives do not usually purchase ships or oxen."[8]

This system of marriage presupposed the husband's right to sexual access to the wife's body. When Reeve explained why it was logical that wives could not enter into contracts, his reason was not only that wives did not control property that could serve as a guarantee; it was that wives could not enter into contracts involving their own labor. "The right of the husband to the person of his wife," Reeve observed, ". . . is a right guarded by the law with the utmost solicitude; if she could bind herself by her contracts, she would be liable to be arrested, taken in execution, and confined in a prison; and then the husband would be deprived of the company of his wife, which the law will not suffer." If a husband were banished from the realm, however, then his wife "could contract, could sue and be sued in her own name; for, in this case, . . . he was already deprived of the company of his wife, and her confinement in prison would not deprive him of his wife to any greater extent than was already the case."[9]

That the system of marriage contradicted the basic tenets of republican thinking was obvious. But women who named the contradictions invited extraordinary hostility and ridicule. Among the most persistent themes was the link of female intellectual activity and political autonomy to an unflattering masculinity. "From all we read, and all we observe, we are authorized in supposing that there is a *sex of soul*," announced the Boston minister John Gardiner. "Women of masculine minds, have generally masculine manners. . . . Queen Elizabeth understood Latin and Greek, swore with the fluency of a sailor, and boxed the ears of her courtiers. . . . Mrs. Macaulay, the author of a dull democratic history, at a tolerably advanced age, married a boy." A "mild, dove-like temper is so necessary to Female beauty, is so natural a part of the sex," reflected Parson Mason Locke Weems wistfully. "A masculine air in a woman frightens us."[10]

When women addressed political issues, the attacks were similar. A good example of this response appears in a newspaper letter written in 1790 by a Marylander who signed himself as "Philanthropos." Warning against literal interpretations of the phrase "All mankind are born equal," "Philanthropos" thought the principle of equality could be "taken in too extensive a sense, and might tend to destroy those degrees of subordination which nature seems to point out," including the subordination of women to men. If women were inept, they were also somehow too effective.

> A Female Orator, in haranguing an Assembly, might like many crafty politicians, keep her *best argument* for last, and would then be sure of the victory—Men would be exposed to temptations too great for their strength, and those who could resist a bribe, offered in the common way, might reasonably yield to what it would be hardly possible for a *man* to refuse.

Selections from Mary Wollstonecraft's *Vindication of the Rights of Woman* were published in the American press shortly after the book was published in London in 1792. She had borne one illegitimate daughter (Fanny Imlay) and lived with William Godwin before marrying him; after marriage she maintained lodgings in another house so that she could be free to write. Once her life history became generally known, it could be used to link intellectual women to political feminism and to aggressive sexuality, as the Federalist writer Timothy Dwight did in his bitter "Morpheus" essays, which ran in a Boston newspaper in 1802. In a dream sequence in "Morpheus," Wollstonecraft has arrived in America and sets out to teach its inhabitants wisdom.

> Women . . . are entitled to all the rights, and are capable of all the energies, of men. I do not mean merely mental energies. If any dispute remained on this subject, I have removed it entirely by displaying, in my immortal writings, all the mental energy of LOCKE and BACON. I intend bodily energies. They can naturally run as fast, leap as high, and as far, and wrestle, scuffle, and box with as much success, as any of the . . . other sex.
>
> That is a mistake (said an old man) . . .
>
> It is no mistake, (said the Female Philosopher).
>
> . . . Why then, (said the senior again), are women always feebler than men?
>
> Because (said MARY) they are educated to be feeble; and by indulgence . . . are made poor, puny,

> baby-faced dolls; instead of the manly women, they ought to be.
>
> *Manly women!* (cried the wag). Wheu! a manly woman is a hoyden, a non descript.
>
> Am I a hoyden (interrupted MARY, with spirit.)
>
> You used to be a strumpet.

Wollstonecraft tells him that she was not a strumpet but a sentimental lover, "too free to brook the restraints of marriage." Her interlocutor responds, "We call them strumpets here, Madam—no offense, I hope," and then argues that when a woman claims the rights of men and the character of a manly woman, she necessarily forgoes what he calls women's "own rights" to "refined consideration." The implication is that Wollstonecraft can be insulted with impunity.

> Still (said the senior) you ought to remember that she is a woman.
>
> *She* ought to remember it (said the young man.)

Thus political behavior, like abstract thought, continued to be specifically proscribed as a threat to sensual attractiveness.

Only the mother who promised to use her political knowledge to serve the republic was spared this hostility. The concept was a variant of the argument for the improved education of women that republicans such as Judith Sargent Murray and Wollstonecraft herself had demanded. It defended education for women not only for their autonomy and self-realization but also so that they could be better wives, rational household managers, and better mothers for the next generation of virtuous republican citizens—especially sons. In a widely reprinted speech, "Thoughts upon Female Education," originally given at the new Young Ladies Academy of Philadelphia, the physician and politician Benjamin Rush addressed the issue directly: "The equal share that every citizen has in the liberty and the possible share he may have in the government of our country make it necessary that our ladies should be qualified to a certain degree, by a peculiar and suitable education, to concur in instructing their sons in the principles of liberty and government." The Republican Mother was an educated woman who could be spared the criticism normally directed at the intellectually competent woman because she placed her learning at her family's service. That she had the leisure and opportunity for study located her solidly in the middle class.

It was commonly believed that republican government was fragile and rested on the presence of virtuous citizens. The Republican Mother was also a Republican Wife.[11] She chose a virtuous man for her husband; she condemned and corrected her husband's lapses from civic virtue; she educated her sons for it. The creation of virtuous citizens required wives and mothers who were well informed, "properly methodical," and free of "invidious and rancorous passions." The word *virtue* was derived from the Latin word for, man, with its connotations of virility. Political action was ideologically marked as masculine; as we have seen, if political voice required independent property holding, it was legally marked masculine as well. Virtue in a woman required another theater for its display. To that end, writers created a mother who had a political purpose and argued that her domestic behavior had a direct political function in the republic.

As one college orator put it,

> Let us then figure to ourselves the accomplished woman, surrounded by a sprightly band, from the babe that imbibes the nutritive fluid, to the generous youth. . . . Let us contemplate the mother distributing the mental nourishment to the fond smiling circle . . . watching the gradual openings of their minds . . . see, under her cultivating hand, reason assuming the reins of government, and knowledge increasing gradually to her beloved pupils. . . . Yes, ye fair, the reformation of a world is in your power. . . . It rests with you to make this retreat [from the corruptions of Europe] doubly peaceful, doubly happy, by banishing from it those crimes and corruptions, which have never yet failed of giving rise to tyranny, or anarchy. While you thus keep our country virtuous, you maintain its independence.[12]

Defined this way, the educated woman ceased to threaten the sanctity of marriage; the intellectual woman need not be masculine.

The ideology of Republican Motherhood was deeply ambivalent. On the one hand, it was a progressive ideology, challenging those who opposed women in politics by the proposal that women could—and should—play a political role through influencing their husbands and raising patriotic children. Within the dynamic relationships of the private family—between husbands and wives, mothers and children—it allocated an assertive role to women. Those who shared the vision of the Republican Mother usually insisted upon better education, clearer recognition of women's economic contributions, and a strong political identification with the republic. This ideology could complement the "fertility transition" under way in the postwar republic, a rapid fall in birthrates that would continue into our own time, and that was first found in urban areas that had experienced commercial and industrial as well as political revolution. Free women, the historian Susan Klepp has recently suggested, "applied egalitarian ideas and a virtuous, prudent sensibility to their bodies and to their traditional images of self as revolutions inspired discussion and debate. . . . On the household level, restricted fertility and high rates of literacy or years of education were persistently linked: the higher the educational attainment of women, the lower fertility rates."[13]

The idea that a mother can perform a political function represents the recognition that a citizen's political socialization takes place at an early age, that the family is a basic part of the system of political communication, and that patterns of family authority influence the general political culture. Most premodern political societies—and even some fairly modern democracies—maintain unarticulated, but nevertheless very firm, social restrictions that seem to isolate the family's domestic world from politics. The willingness of the American woman to overcome this ancient separation brought her into the political community.[14] In this sense, Republican Motherhood was an important and progressive invention congruent with revolutionary politics and the demographic transition. It altered the female domain in which most women had lived out their lives; it justified women's claims for participation in the civic culture. The ideology was strong enough to rout "Philanthropes" and "Morpheus" by redefining female political behavior as valuable rather than abnormal, as a source of strength to the republic rather than an embarrassment. The ideology would be revived as a rallying point for many twentieth-century women reformers, who saw their committment to honest politics, efficient urban sanitation, and pure food and drug laws as an extension of their responsibilities as mothers.

But Republican Motherhood flourished in the context of coverture. The old law of domestic relations hemmed it in at every turn. Republican motherhood could legitimize only a minimum of political sophistication and interest. It was an extension into the republic of conservative traditions, stretching back at least as far as the Renaissance, that put narrow limits on women's assertiveness.[15] Captured by marriage, which not only secured their intimate relations but also their relationship to the public authority, for most of their lives most women had no alternative but to perform the narrow political role they managed to claim for themselves. Just as white planters claimed that democracy in the antebellum South necessarily rested on the economic base of black slavery, so male egalitarian society was said to rest on the moral base of deference among a class of people—women—who would devote their efforts to service by raising sons and disciplining husbands to be virtuous citizens of the republic. The learned woman, who might very well wish to make choices as well as to influence attitudes, was a visible threat to this arrangement. Women were to contain their political judgments within their homes and families; they were not to bridge the world outside and the world within. The Republican Wife was not to tell her husband for whom to vote. She was a citizen but not really a constituent.

Restricting women's politicization was one of a series of conservative choices that Americans made in the postwar years as they avoided the full implications of their own Revolutionary radicalism. By these decisions Americans may well have been spared the agony of the French cycle of revolution and counterrevolution, which spilled more blood and produced a political system more regressive than had the American war. Nevertheless, the impact of these choices was to leave race equality to the mercies of a bloody century that stretched from the Civil War through Reconstruction and lynching into the civil rights movement of our own time. And the impact of these choices was also to leave in place the system by which marriage stood between women and civil society. For most of the history of the United States, deep into the twentieth century, the legal traditions of marriage would be used to deny women citizens juries drawn from a full cross-section of the community, deny them control over their own property and their own earnings, sometimes deny them custody of their children, even deny them their rights as citizens should they marry a foreign man.

The "new era in female history" that Judith Sargent Murray had predicted remained to be created by women, fortified by their memories and myths of female strength during the trials of war, politicized by their resentment of male legislators slighting the issues of greatest significance to women. The promises of the republic remained to be fulfilled; remembering the Revolution helped to keep confidence alive. "Yes, gentlemen," said Elizabeth Cady Stanton to the New York legislature in 1854, "in republican America . . . we, the daughters of the revolutionary heroes of '76 demand at your hands the redress of our grievances—a revision of your State constitution—a new code of laws." Stanton understood that the traditions of coverture positioned domesticity against civic activism, motherhood against citizenship. Not until 1992 did the U.S. Supreme Court rule that as a general principle, "Women do not lose their constitutionally protected liberty when they marry."[16]

Notes

1. Murray's newspaper essays were reprinted in a collected edition, *The Gleaner,* III (Boston, 1798). These comments appear in III, pp. 189; 167–68. See also Sheila L. Skemp, *Judith Sargent Murray: A Brief Biography with Documents* (Boston, 1998).

2. "Rachel Wells Petition for Relief," Nov. 15, 1785, New Jersey Archives, Trenton.

3. Abigail Adams to John Adams, Mar. 31, 1776, *Adams Family Correspondence* (Cambridge, Mass., 1963), I: 370. See Nancy F. Cott, "Passionlessness: An Interpretation of Victorian Sexual Ideology, 1790–1850," *Signs: Journal of Women in Culture and Society* 4 (1978): 219–36.

4. *Burlington* (N.J.) *Advertiser*, Feb. 1, 1791.

5. Miss Pierce's School Papers, 1849, Litchfield His. Soc., Litchfield, Conn.

6. See, for example, "An Act for Annulling the Distinction between the Crimes of Murder and Petit Treason," March 16, 1785, in Asahel Stearns et al., eds., *The General Laws of Massachusetts* . . . I (Boston, 1823), p. 188.

7. Tapping Reeve, *The Law of Baron and Femme, Parent and Child, Guardian and Ward, Master and Servant, and of the Powers of the Courts of Chancery* (New Haven, 1816; Burlington, 1846), ch. v, p. 73.

8. Reeve, ch. vi, pp. 78–79.

9. Reeve, ch. viii, pp. 98–99.

10. *New-England Palladium*, Sept. 18, 1801; Parson Mason Locke Weems, *Hymen's Recruiting Sergeant* (Philadelphia, 1800).

11. Jan Lewis, "The Republican Wife: Virtue and Seduction in the Early Republic," *William and Mary Quarterly* ser. 3, vol. 44 (1987): 689–721.

12. *New York Magazine*, May 1795, pp. 301–5.

13. Susan E. Klepp, "Revolutionary Bodies: Women and the Fertility Transition in the Mid-Atlantic Region, 1760–1820," *Journal of American History* vol. 85 (1998), pp. 916, 915 (I have reversed the order of the sentences).

14. See Gabriel Almond and Sidney Verba, *The Civic Culture* (Princeton, 1963), pp. 377–401.

15. Elaine Forman Crane emphasizes this dimension; *see Ebb-Tide in New England: Women, Seaports, and Social Change, 1630–1800* (Boston, 1998), ch. 6.

16. *Planned Parenthood of Pennsylvania* v. *Casey,* 112 S. Ct. 2791 (1992).

FURTHER READING FOR PART I: EARLY AMERICA, 1600–1820

Overviews

A perceptive survey of the development of early American women's and gender history is Carol F. Karlsen, "Women and Gender," in *A Companion to Colonial America*, ed. Daniel Vickers (Malden, Mass., 2003), 194–235. Carol Berkin offers a short, readable narrative in **First Generations.* Mary Beth Norton compares the gender systems in the New England and Chesapeake colonies in **Founding Mothers and Fathers.* For striking examples of how some colonial women interpreted their own lives, see Anne Firor Scott, "Self-Portraits: Three Women," in *Uprooted Americans: Essays to Honor Oscar Handlin*, ed. Richard Bushman et al. (Boston, 1979).

Bodies and Sexuality

On Algonquian and Iroquoian beliefs about and practices surrounding pregnancy, childbirth, puberty, marriage, and death as recorded by European observers, see James Axtell, ed., *The Indian Peoples of Eastern America: A Documentary History of the Sexes* (New York,

1981). Conflicts between how Algonquins and English viewed marriage are explored in Ann Marie Plane, *Colonial Intimacies: Indian Marriage in Early New England* (Ithaca, N.Y., 2000). For the ways in which colonists understood women's bodies, see Susan Klepp, "Colds, Worms, and Hysteria: Menstrual Regulation in Eighteenth-Century America," in *Regulating Menstruation*, ed. Etienne van de Walle and Elisha Renne (Chicago, 2001). Klepp's book, *Revolutionary Conceptions: Women, Fertility, and Family Limitation in America, 1760–1820* (Chapel Hill, N.C., 2009) examines an important transition in demography and family size. Laurel Thatcher Ulrich's *A Midwife's Tale: The Life of Martha Ballard, Based on Her Diary, 1785–1812* (New York, 1990) offers the deepest look at obstetrical practice and the social context of healing. Rebecca J. Tannenbaum, *The Healer's Calling: Women and Medicine in Early New England* (Ithaca, N.Y., 2002), chronicles women healers in the seventeenth century. Elaine Forman Crane has edited *The Diary of Elizabeth Drinker*, 3 vols. (Boston, 1991), and a single-volume edition, *The Diary of Elizabeth Drinker: The Life Cycle of an Eighteenth-Century Woman* (Boston, 1994); both include extensive comments on Drinker's experience of childbearing and motherhood. Daniel Scott Smith and Michael S. Hindus, "Premarital Pregnancy in America, 1640–1971: An Overview and Interpretation," *Journal of Interdisciplinary History* 5 (1975): 537–70, remains the classic study.

For attitudes toward sexual activity, licit and illicit, see the provocative arguments in Richard Godbeer, *Sexual Revolution in Early America* (Baltimore, Md., 2002), and Clare A. Lyons, *Sex among the Rabble: An Intimate History of Gender and Power in the Age of Revolution, Philadelphia, 1730–1830* (Chapel Hill, N.C., 2006). Like Lyons, Mary E. Fissell explores images and discussions of sex in print culture: "Hairy Women and Naked Truths: Gender and the Politics of Knowledge in *Aristotle's Masterpiece*," *William and Mary Quarterly*, 3rd ser., 60 (2003): 43–74. Kathleen M. Brown offers her own take on the Thomas/Thomasine Hall case in "'Changed . . . into the Fashion of a Man': The Politics of Sexual Difference in a Seventeenth-Century Anglo-American Settlement," *Journal of the History of Sexuality* 6 (1995): 171–93. Another Virginian case study is John Pagan, *Anne Orthwood's Bastard: Sex and Law in Early Virginia* (New York, 2003). A powerful monograph analyzing gender, race, class, work, politics, and masculinity is Kathleen M. Brown, *Good Wives, Nasty Wenches, and Anxious Patriarchs: Gender, Race, and Power in Colonial Virginia* (Chapel Hill, N.C., 1996). Sexual regulation in areas outside the Northeast is analyzed in Jennifer M. Spear, *Race, Sex, and Social Order in Early New Orleans* (Baltimore, Md., 2009); Kirsten Fischer, *Suspect Relations: Sex, Race, and Resistance in Colonial North Carolina* (Ithaca, N.Y., 2002); and the essays in Merril D. Smith, ed., *Sex and Sexuality in* the *Early America* (New York, 1998).

New England's extensive records have been mined by several scholars examining meanings of manhood in the colonial period: Lisa Wilson, *Ye Heart of a Man: The Domestic Life of Men in Colonial New England* (New Haven, Conn., 1999); Anne Lombard, *Making Manhood: Growing Up Male in Colonial New England* (New York, 2003); and R. Todd Romero, "'Ranging Foresters' and 'Women-Like Men': Physical Accomplishment, Spiritual Power, and Indian Masculinity in Early Seventeenth-Century New England," *Ethnohistory* 53 (Spring 2006): 281–329.

Economics and Law

For enslaved women's work, resistance, and community life, a good place to begin is Betty Wood, *Women's Work, Men's Work: The Informal Slave Economies of Lowcountry*

Georgia (Athens, Ga., 1995). David Barry Gaspar and Darlene Clark Hine, eds., *More than Chattel: Black Women and Slavery in the Americas* (Bloomington, Ind., 1996), includes essays on many subjects related to work from the colonial through the antebellum periods. Hilary McD. Beckles, *Natural Rebels: A Social History of Enslaved Black Women in Barbados* (New Brunswick, N.J., 1989) and Jennifer L. Morgan, **Laboring Women,* are among the first book-length studies to focus entirely on African and African-descended women's lives in England's New World colonies. Judith Carney, *Black Rice: The African Origins of Rice Cultivation in the Americas* (Cambridge, Mass., 2001), establishes the centrality of West Africans, particularly women, to the introduction and cultivation of rice in the Americas.

For the gendered division of labor in English households, start with Carole Shammas, *A History of Household Government in America* (Charlottesville, Va., 2002). Julia Cherry Spruill, *Women's Life and Work in the Southern Colonies* (Chapel Hill, N.C., 1996), is rich in descriptive detail and still repays reading. Attention to textile production, needlework, and the fabric and material objects so central to women's daily lives is receiving serious study. See Susan Burrows Swan, *Plain and Fancy: American Women and their Needlework, 1750–1850* (New York, 1977); Marla Miller, *The Needle's Eye: Women and Work in the Age of Revolution* (Amherst, Mass., 2006); and Linda Baumgarten, *What Clothes Reveal: The Language of Clothing in Colonial and Federal America: The Colonial Williamsburg Collection Clothing* (New Haven, Conn., 2002). Laurel Thatcher Ulrich offers a brilliant set of braided case studies in *The Age of Homespun: Objects and Stories in the Creation of an American Myth* (New York, 2001).

Biographies often make clear the economic setting in which women made their way; an especially readable one is Patricia Cleary's study of a shopkeeper (and emigrant from Scotland) whose substantial wealth came from transatlantic trade with England: *Elizabeth Murray: A Woman's Pursuit of Independence in Eighteenth-Century America* (Amherst, Mass., 2000). (Note also the related website.) Urban women's enterprises and survival strategies are explored in Elaine Forman Crane, *Ebb Tide in New England: Women, Seaports, and Social Change, 1630–1800* (Boston, 1998), and Ellen Hartigan-O'Connor, *The Ties That Buy: Women and Commerce in Revolutionary America* (Philadelphia, 2009). For portraits of urban and rural women facing impoverishment and forced into transiency, see Ruth Wallis Herndon, *Unwelcome Americans: Living on the Margin in Early New England* (Philadelphia, 2001). Karin A. Wulf parses the literary circles, commercial enterprises, and poor relief options of never-married women in *Not All Wives: Women of Colonial Philadelphia* (Ithaca, N.Y., 2000). A rich primary source, with a lengthy and insightful set of introductory essays, is *Milcah Martha Moore's Book: A Commonplace Book from Revolutionary America,* ed. Catherine L. Blecki and Karin A. Wulf (University Park, Pa., 1997).

On the law, see Marylynn Salmon, *Women and the Law of Property in Early America* (Chapel Hill, N.C., 1986) and Cornelia Hughes Dayton, *Women before the Bar: Gender, Law, and Society in Connecticut, 1639–1789* (Chapel Hill, N.C., 1995). A recent overview is Holly Brewer, "The Transformation of Domestic Law," in *Cambridge History of Law in America,* ed. Michael Grossberg and Christopher Tomlins, vol. 1 (New York, 2008). Two studies drawing on Virginia court records are Terri L. Snyder, *Brabbling Women: Disorderly Speech and the Law in Early Virginia* (Ithaca, N.Y., 2003), and Linda Sturtz, *Within Her Power: Propertied Women in Colonial Virginia* (2001). Sharon Block offers a comprehensive survey of the mainland colonies' prosecution or neglect of sexual coercion in *Rape and Sexual Power in Early America* (Chapel Hill, N.C., 2006). Domestic violence is explored by several authors in *Over the Threshold: Intimate Violence in Early America*, ed. Christine Daniels and Michael V. Kennedy (New York, 1999). Two women at the heart of a notorious 1820s criminal case—the alleged culprit Ann Carson and the author Mary Clarke—are the focus of Susan Branson, *Dangerous to Know: Women, Crime, and Notoriety in the Early Republic* (Philadelphia, 2008).

Politics

Susan Sleeper-Smith, *Indian Women and French Men: Rethinking Cultural Encounter in the Western Great Lakes* (Amherst, Mass., 2001), positions women as key to diplomacy, as does Juliana Barr, *Peace Came in the Form of a Woman: Indians and Spaniards in the Texas Borderlands* (Chapel Hill, N.C., 2007). A new look at the traffic in women is provided by James F. Brooks, *Captives and Cousins: Slavery, Kinship, and Community in the Southwest Borderlands* (Chapel Hill, N.C., 1996). An important book on the Cherokee is Theda Purdue, *Cherokee Women: Gender and Culture Change, 1700–1835* (Lincoln, Neb., 1998). For the politics of the encounter in the Southwest and along the Pacific coast, see Ramon A. Gutierrez, *When Jesus Came, the Corn Mothers Went Away: Marriage, Sexuality, and Power in New Mexico* (Stanford, Calif., 1991), and Virginia Marie Bouvier, *Women and the Conquest of California, 1542–1840: Codes of Silence* (Tucson, Ariz., 2001). On the politics of conversion in French Canada, see Allan Greer, *Mohawk Saint: Catherine Tekakwitha and the Jesuits* (New York, 2005), and Leslie Choquette, "'Ces Amazones du Grand Dieu': Women and Mission in Seventeenth-Century Canada," *French Historical Studies* 17 (1992): 627–55. A beautifully rich portrait of the founder of the Ursuline convent in Quebec is Natalie Zemon Davis, "New Worlds: Marie de L'Incarnation," ch. 2 of *Women on the Margins: Three Seventeenth-Century Lives* (Cambridge, Mass., 1995). For manhood and military culture across English, French, and Indian contact zones, see Ann M. Little, **Abraham in Arms: War and Gender in Colonial New England.*

Religious and political anxieties were often mingled in early America. For New England, see Jane Kamensky, *Governing the Tongue: The Politics of Speech in Early New England* (New York, 1997) (ACLS Humanities e-book). On witch-hunting, the most sustained analysis of gender as a key factor is *Carol F. Karlsen, *The Devil in the Shape of a Woman.* Elizabeth Reis, *Damned Women: Sinners and Witches in Puritan New England* (Ithaca, N.Y., 1999), makes an interesting argument about why women felt compelled to confess. For additional contexts, see Mary Beth Norton, *In the Devil's Snare: The Salem Witchcraft Crisis of 1692* (New York, 2002), and Elaine G. Breslaw, *Tituba, Reluctant Witch of Salem* (New York, 1996). Most of the surviving pre-Salem primary sources are available in David D. Hall, ed., *Witch-Hunting in Seventeenth-Century New England: A Documentary History, 1638–1693*, 2nd ed. (Boston, 1999). Black women's resistance to Christianity, plus their work patterns, family life, and freedom suits, are chronicled in Catherine Adams and Elizabeth H. Pleck, *Love of Freedom: Black Women in Colonial and Revolutionary New England* (New York, 2010).

Women's part in the political ferment of prerevolutionary mobilization, the war for independence, and the early republic are explored in Mary Beth Norton, *Liberty's Daughters: The Revolutionary Experience of American Women, 1750–1800* (Boston, 1980); Linda K. Kerber, *Women of the Republic: Intellect and Ideology in Revolutionary America* (Chapel Hill,

N.C., 1980); essays in Ronald Hoffman and Peter J. Albert, eds., *Women in the Age of the American Revolution* (Charlottesville, Va., 1989); Cynthia A. Kierner, *Beyond the Household: Women's Place in the Early South, 1700–1835* (Ithaca, N.Y., 1998); and Rosemarie Zagarri, *Revolutionary Backlash: Women and Politics in the Early Republic* (Philadelphia, 2007). Women who were formally or informally part of George Washington's army are analyzed in Holly A. Mayer, *Belonging to the Army: Camp Followers and Community during the American Revolution* (Columbia, S.C., 1996). For biographies, see Edie B. Gelles, *Portia: The World of Abigail Adams* (Bloomington, Ind., 1992; a ACLS Humanities e-book), and Sheila Skemp, *First Lady of Letters: Judith Sargent Murray and the Struggle for Female Independence* (Philadelphia, 2009). For the debate over the relationship of women to the state, see Jan Lewis, "The Republican Wife: Virtue and Seduction in the Early Republic," *William and Mary Quarterly*, 3rd ser., 44 (1987): 689–721; Carroll Smith-Rosenberg, "Discovering the Subject of the Great Constitutional Discussion, 1786–1789," *Journal of American History* 79 (1992): 841–73; Jan Lewis, "'of every age sex & condition': The Representation of Women in the Constitution," *Journal of the Early Republic* 15 (1995): 359–87; and *Linda K. Kerber, *No Constitutional Right to Be Ladies*, ch. 1. The story of New Jersey women having the vote and then losing it is told by Judith Apter Klinghoffer and Lois Elkis, "'The Petticoat Electors': Women's Suffrage in New Jersey, 1776–1807," *Journal of the Early Republic* 12 (1992): 159–93. Catherine Allgor contributes two books on the Washington, D.C., landscape: *Parlor Politics: In Which the Ladies of Washington Help Build a City and a Government* (Charlottesville, Va., 2000), and *A Perfect Union: Dolley Madison and the Creation of the American Nation* (New York, 2006).

Intellect, Ideology, Culture

For open and closed doors to Christian women's preaching and speaking, see Catherine A. Brekus, *Strangers and Pilgrims: Female Preaching in America, 1740–1845* (Chapel Hill, N.C., 1989) and Susan Juster, *Disorderly Women: Sexual Politics and Evangelicalism in Revolutionary New England* (Ithaca, N.Y., 1994). For transatlantic religious networks, see Rebecca Larson, *Daughters of Light: Quaker Women Preaching and Prophesying in the Colonies and Abroad, 1700–1775* (New York, 1999), and Susan Juster, *Doomsayers: Anglo-American Prophecy in the Age of Revolution* (Philadelphia, 2003). For a classic essay, see Mary Maples Dunn, "Saints and Sisters: Congregational and Quaker Women in the Early Colonial Period," in *James, ed., *Women in American Religion*. Laurel Thatcher Ulrich, in **Good Wives*, mines the biblical tropes so familiar to New England immigrant settlers to present nuanced portraits of white women's work, marital, religious, and social lives.

For the very high rates of literacy among white New England women and their schooling opportunities, see E. Jennifer Monaghan, *Learning to Read and Write in Colonial America* (Amherst, Mass., 2005). Margaretta M. Lovell ingeniously brings alive the portrait of a nineteen-year-old Boston gentlewoman in "The Empirical Eye: Copley's Women and the Case of the Blue Dress," ch. 3 of *Art Is a Season of Revolution: Painters, Artisans, and Patrons in Early America* (Philadelphia, 2005). Two early American novels written by women and focusing on the dangers of seduction and the need for female education are available in compact paperbacks, both edited and with introductions by literary scholar Cathy N. Davidson: Susanna Rowson's *Charlotte Temple* (New York, 1987) and Hannah W. Foster's *The Coquette* (New York, 1987). Ruth H. Bloch offers essays on changes in attitudes toward gender, family relations, sexuality, and morality in *Gender and Morality in Anglo-American Culture, 1650–1800* (Berkeley, Calif., 2003). For an innovative study of emotions in early American culture, see Nicole Eustace, *Passion Is the Gale: Emotion, Power, and the Coming of the American Revolution* (Chapel Hill, N.C., 2008).

Asterisks (*) indicate the work's full citation can be found either earlier in this list of works or in the credit lines of an essay by the author excerpted in this volume.

II

The Many Frontiers of Industrializing America

1820–1880

In the nineteenth century, the American economy was transformed by the industrial revolution. Railroads and steamboats linked distant parts of the country and simplified economic interaction, even as the distinctive economies of North and South fostered a political dialogue that became increasingly bitter over the years. In the South, the cotton gin ensured the profitability of the crop and reinforced the system of slave labor. In the North, factories began installing steam-powered spinning and weaving equipment tended by a new class of wage workers. The position of legislators on issues as disparate as tariffs and free speech could be linked to the economic interests and distinctive cultures of their regions. By 1860, institutions that had helped connect the two cultures—political parties, churches, economic networks—had broken down completely. Once the Civil War came, the North's control of modern transportation networks was a crucial ingredient in its success.

It has been relatively easy for historians to see that economic and political developments affected men's lives. The right to vote and hold office was extended to virtually every white man, whether or not he held property; after the Civil War it was extended to black men in many parts of the country. Congress was a national forum for debate among male political leaders; by the 1850s, speeches made there were rapidly diffused to the public by cheap newspapers, printed by newly efficient presses and distributed by railroads throughout the nation. A host of new careers opened to men as politicians, journalists, teachers, capitalists, physicians, and reformers. The expansion of the physical boundaries of the country, by treaty and by war, opened new frontiers and created new opportunities for farmers, merchants, civic promoters, and land speculators.

When we look at these developments through women's eyes, we find that women's lives also changed markedly. The transportation revolution, for example, had special significance for women. Women rarely traveled on their own in the early republic period; long trips meant nights in unfamiliar taverns and lodging houses where accommodations were uncertain and safety could not be assured. The railroad changed that. In the three weeks between January 5 and January 26, 1855, Antoinette Brown and Ernestine Rose spoke at woman suffrage meetings in eleven different counties in upstate New York.

Improvements in the printing technology and distribution of newspapers meant that women as well as men were no longer dependent on local sources of information and political guidance. Even if one's town lacked a temperance society or an abolitionist organization, one could still subscribe to a temperance or abolitionist newspaper, reaching out past the local notables to make contact with a wider political community. Abolitionist newspapers like the *National Anti-Slavery Standard* (which was, for a time, edited by a woman, Lydia Maria Child) and women's rights newspapers like *Una* or the *Revolution* could come straight to a woman's mailbox, enlarging her political world.

The historian David Potter urged us to ask whether established generalizations about the past apply to women as accurately as they apply to men.[1] We often find that they do not. For example, although male as well as female slaves were exploited, women were especially vulnerable to sexual exploitation and to debilitating chronic ailments incidental to childbearing. In free households, female work—including taking in boarders, washing their clothes, and cooking meals for them—might account for as much income as working-class husbands gained from their own employment. If the husband's work was seasonal or erratic, the steady income from taking in boarders could be crucial to the family's survival.

Democracy expanded as suffrage was extended to most white men, but simultaneously constrained as the gap between white men and free black men grew, and with it the gap between white men and all women. As Gerda Lerner has pointed out, many of the new opportunities for men came in a form that closed options for women. When additional men were granted suffrage, for example, "women's political status, while legally unchanged . . . deteriorated relative to the advances made by men."[2] The frontier has traditionally been treated as a metaphor for unbounded opportunity. New scholarship has emphasized the multicultural complexities of frontiers, and their capacity to be sites of tension, rivalry, and violence. The experience of married women in the trans-Mississippi West was likely to be one of hardship encountered at the urging of their husbands, not out of their own initiative and choice.

In the nineteenth century, women pressed at the limits of the ways in which nonvoting citizens could influence the political order. In antislavery petition campaigns, in effective lobbying to persuade legislatures to reform laws dealing with married women's property rights and child custody, in responding to the crisis of the Civil War, in freedwomen pressing charges against former Confederates who tried to intimidate them, in naming alcohol abuse as a leading cause of domestic violence, in inventing new institutions like settlement houses, in campaigning for the vote, women expressed political opinions and sought to shape political events. The lessons they learned in nineteenth-century struggles go a long way toward explaining the many successes they would have in the twentieth.

Notes

1. "American Women and the American Character," (1962) in *History and American Society: Essays of David M. Potter,* ed. Don E. Fehrenbacher (New York: Oxford University Press, 1973), p. 279.

2. Gerda Lerner, "The Lady and the Mill Girl," in *The Majority Finds Its Past: Placing Women in History* (New York: Oxford University Press, 1979), pp. 18–20.

DOCUMENTS

The Testimony of Slave Women

Maria Perkins, "I am quite heartsick . . ."

Because masters understood the connection between literacy and rebelliousness, slaves were rarely taught to read and write. This anguished letter from Maria Perkins is unusual because it was written by an enslaved woman. We do not know whether Perkins's husband Richard managed to persuade his master to buy her and keep the family together. If a trader did buy Maria Perkins or her child, the likelihood of permanent separation was great. Scottsville, mentioned in the letter, is a small town near Charlottesville; Staunton is some forty miles away.

Charlottesville, Oct. 8th, 1852
Dear Husband I write you a letter to let you know my distress my master has sold albert to a trader on Monday court day and myself and other child is for sale also and I want you to let [me] hear from you very soon before next cort if you can I don't know when I don't want you to wait till Christmas I want you to tell dr Hamelton and your master if either will buy me they can attend to it know and then I can go afterwards. I don't want a trader to get me they asked me if I had got any person to buy me and I told them no they took me to the court houste too they never put me up a man buy the name of brady bought albert and is gone I don't know where they say he lives in Scottesville my things is in several places some is in staunton and if I should be sold I don't know what will become of them I don't expect to meet with the luck to get that way till I am quite heartsick nothing more I am and ever will be your kind wife Maria Perkins.

Maria Perkins to Richard Perkins, October 8, 1852, Ulrich B. Phillips Collection, Yale University Library, New Haven.

Rose, "Look for some others for to 'plenish de earth"

Letters like Maria Perkins's are very rare. Most firsthand evidence of the experience of being a slave comes from narratives prepared by ex-slaves after they were free. Some accounts were published by abolitionist societies before the Civil War; some people were interviewed by agents of the Freedmen's Bureau after

Manuscript Slave Narrative Collection, Federal Writers' Project, 1941, vol. 17, Texas Narratives, pt. 4, pp. 174–78, Library of Congress, Washington, D.C.

the war. A large group of elderly ex-slaves was interviewed in the 1930s as part of the Federal Writers' Project. One of these speakers we know only as Rose.

As her moving narrative shows, on the average plantation, the line between "forced breeding" and "strong encouragement" could be a thin one.

What I say am de facts. If I's one day old, I's way over 90, and I's born in Bell Country, right here in Texas, and am owned by Massa William Black. He owns mammy and pappy, too. Massa Black has a big plantation but he has more niggers dan he need for work on dat place, 'cause he am a nigger trader. He trade and buy an sell all de time.

Massa Black am awful cruel and he whip de cullud folks and works 'em hard and feed dem poorly. We'uns have for rations de cornmeal and milk and 'lasses and some beans and peas and meat once a week. We'uns have to work in de field every day from daylight till dark and on Sunday we'uns do us washin'. Church? Shucks, we'uns don't know what dat mean.

I has de correct mem'randum of when de war start. Massa Black sold we'uns right den. Mammy and pappy powerful glad to get sold, and dey and I is put on de block with 'bout ten other niggers. When we'uns gits te de tradin' block, dere lots of white folks dere what come to look us over. One man shows de intres' in pappy. Him named Hawkins. He talk to pappy and pappy talk to him and say, "Dem my woman and chiles. Please buy all of us and have mercy on we'uns." Massa Hawkins say, "Dat gal am a likely lookin' nigger, she am portly and strong, but three am more dan I wants, I guesses."

De sale start and 'fore long pappy a put on de block. Massa Hawkins wins de bid for pappy and when mammy am put on de block, he wins de bid for her. Den dere am three or four other niggers sold befo' my time comes. Den massa Black calls me to de block and de auction man say, "What am I offer for dis portly, strong young wench. She's never been 'bused and will make de good breeder."

I wants to hear Massa Hawkins bid, but him say nothin'. Two other men am biddin' 'gainst each other and I sho' has de worryment. Dere am tears comin' down my cheeks 'cause I's bein' sold to some man dat would make sep'ration from my mammy. One man bids $500 and de auction man ask, "Do I hear more? She am gwine at $500.00." Den someone say, $525.00 and de auction man say, "She am sold for $525.00 to Massa Hawkins." Am I glad and 'cited! Why, I's quiverin' all over.

Massa Hawkins takes we'uns to his place and it am a nice plantation. Lots better am dat place dan Massa Black's. Dere is 'bout 50 niggers what is growed and lots of chillen. De first thing massa do when we'uns gits home am give we'uns rations and a cabin. You mus' believe dis nigger when I says dem rations a feast for us. Dere plenty meat and tea and coffee and white flour. I's never tasted white flour and coffee and mammy fix some biscuits and coffee. Well, de biscuits was yum, yum, yum to me, but de coffee I doesn't like.

De quarters am purty good. Dere am twelve cabins all made from logs and a table and some benches and bunks for sleepin' and a fireplace for cookin' and de heat. Dere am no floor, jus' de ground.

Massa Hawkins am good to he niggers and not force 'em work too hard. Dere am as much diff'ence 'tween him and old Massa Black in de way of treatment as 'twixt de Lawd and de devil. Massa Hawkins 'lows he niggers have reason'ble parties and go fishin', but we'uns am never tooken to church and has no books for larnin'. Dere am no edumcation for de niggers.

Dere am one thing Massa Hawkins does to me what I can't shunt from my mind. I knows he don't do it for meanness, but I allus holds it 'gainst him. What he done am force me to live with dat nigger, Rufus, 'gainst my wants.

After I been at he place 'bout a year, de massa come to me and say, "You gwine live with Rufus in dat cabin over yonder. Go fix it for livin'." I's 'bout sixteen year old and has no larnin', and I's jus' igno'mus chile. I's thought dat him mean for me to tend de cabin for Rufus and some other niggers. Well, dat am start de pestigation for me.

I's took charge of de cabin after work am done and fixes supper. Now, I don't like dat Rufus, 'cause he a bully. He am big and 'cause he so, he think everybody do what him say. We'uns has supper, den I goes here and dere talkin', till I's ready for sleep and den I gits in de bunk. After I's in, dat nigger come and crawl in de bunk with me 'fore I knows it. I says, "What you mean, you fool nigger?" He say for me to hush de mouth. "Dis am my bunk, too," he say.

"You's teched in de head. Git out," I's told him, and I puts de feet 'gainst him and give him a shove and out he go on de floor 'fore he knows what I's doin'. Dat nigger jump up and he mad. He look like de wild bear. He starts for de bunk and I jumps quick for de poker. It am 'bout three feet long and when he comes at me I let him have it over de head. Did dat nigger stop in he tracks? I's say he did. He looks at me steady for a minute and you's could tell he thinkin' hard. Den he go and set on de bench and say, "Jus wait. You thinks it am smart, but you's am foolish in de head. Dey's gwine larn you somethin'."

"Hush yous big mouth and stay 'way from dis nigger, dat all I wants," I say, and jus' sets and hold dat poker in de hand. He jus' sets, lookin' like de bull. Dere we'uns sets and sets for 'bout an hour and den he go out and I bars de door.

De nex' day I goes to de missy and tells her what Rufus wants and missy say dat am de massa's wishes. She say, "Yous am de portly gal and Rufus am de portly man. De massa wants you-uns for to bring forth portly chillen."

I's thinkin' 'bout what de missy say, but say to myse'f, "I's not gwine live with dat Rufus." Dat night when him come in de cabin, I grabs de poker and sits on de bench and says, "Git 'way from me, nigger, 'fore I busts yous brains out and stomp on dem." He say nothin' and git out.

De nex' day de massa call me and tell me, "Woman, I's pay big money for you and I's done dat for de cause I wants you to raise me chillens. I's put yous to live with Rufus for dat purpose. Now, if you doesn't want whippin' at de stake, yous do what I wants."

I thinks 'bout massa buyin' me offen de block and savin' me from bein' sep'rated from my folks and 'bout bein' whipped at de stake. Dere it am. What am I's to do? So I 'cides to do as de massa wish and so I yields.

When we'uns am given freedom, Massa Hawkins tells us we can stay and work for wages or share crop de land. Some stays and some goes. My folks and me stays. We works de land on shares for three years, den moved to other land near by. I stay with my folks till they dies.

If my mem'radum am correct, it am 'bout thirty year since I come to Fort Worth. Here I cooks for white folks till I goes blind 'bout ten year ago.

I never marries, 'cause one 'sperience am 'nough for dis nigger. After what I does for de massa, I's never wants no truck with any man. De Lawd forgive dis cullud woman, but he have to 'scuse me and look for some others for to 'plenish de earth.

SHARON BLOCK

Lines of Color, Sex, and Service: Sexual Coercion in the Early Republic

A long tradition of describing northern society as "free" and southern society as "slave" has had the unfortunate effect of making distinctions seem far more clear in retrospect than they were in experience. Manumission was gradual and grudging in parts of the North where significant numbers of people were held as property. In Massachusetts, New Hampshire, and Vermont, many enslaved took their freedom by walking away from owners or bringing successful freedom suits based on the civil rights promised by the new state constitutions. However, other jurisdictions passed gradual emancipation laws that paid more attention to slave owners' property rights than to human rights. For example, by the 1780 Pennsylvania statute, all enslaved persons living at the time remained in bondage; all children born in the future to enslaved women were declared free but had to serve their mother's owner until the age of twenty-eight. This confusing legal landscape meant that African-descended people experienced a mixture of statuses—enslaved, indentured, free—throughout the first half of the nineteenth century.

Moreover, parental poverty, itinerancy, or perceived idleness could trigger laws allowing local officials to take children and place them in other households as indentured workers. Thus, in the early republic, youths of black, Indian, and white parents were regularly put out to bound labor. Burdened by their work, they were also vulnerable to the power and authority of their masters. This included, as we see in the essay that follows, vulnerability to sexual coercion—a term Sharon Block uses to mark a wider range of experience than is suggested by the simple term *rape.** The essay that follows is based on a close reading of a Pennsylvania court record and on one of the great autobiographies of the nineteenth century, Harriet Jacobs's *Incidents in the Life of a Slave Girl.* Writing under a pseudonym after years as a fugitive, supported in her project by the abolitionist writer and editor Lydia Maria Child, Jacobs herself became invisible to historians. For many years her narrative was treated as fiction. Not until 1987, when historian Jean Fagan Yellin published an edition identifying virtually all the individuals and substantiating virtually all the events, has it been possible to understand the narrative as nonfiction. It is compelling reading.†

In what ways did Rachel Davis and Harriet Jacobs try to avoid the power of their masters? In whom did they find allies? In what ways were the experiences of these young women similar? What difference did slavery make?*

*Sharon Block explains that first names are used for all actors in incidents of sexual coercion because first names more easily distinguish men from women and eliminate confusion in identifying members of the same family.

†Harriet A. Jacobs, *Incidents in the Life of a Slave Girl: Written by Herself,* ed. Jean Fagan Yellin (Cambridge, Mass.: Harvard University Press, 1987): Jean Fagan Yellin, *Harriet Jacobs: A Life* (New York: Basic Civitas Books, 2004).

Excerpted from "Lines of Color, Sex, and Service: Comparative Sexual Coercion in Early America" by Sharon Block in *Sex Love, Race: Crossing Boundaries in North American History,* ed. Martha Hodes (New York: New York University Press, 1999). Reprinted by permission of the author and publisher. Notes have been edited and renumbered.

Rachel Davis was born a free white child in the Pennsylvania mountains in 1790. She was fourteen years old when she became an indentured servant to William and Becky Cress in Philadelphia County. By the time Rachel was fifteen, William had begun making sexual overtures to her. After months of continuing sexual assaults, William's wife, Becky, suspected that her husband was having a sexual relationship with their servant. Ultimately, Becky demanded that Rachel be removed from the house. William continued to visit Rachel at her new home, again trying to have sex with her. In 1807, Rachel's father found out what had occurred and initiated a rape prosecution against William, who was found guilty and sentenced to ten years in prison.[1]

Harriet Jacobs was born an enslaved black child in Edenton, North Carolina, in 1813. In 1825, she became a slave in James and Mary Norcom's household. By the time Harriet was sixteen, James had begun making sexual overtures toward her. After months of continuing sexual assaults, James's wife, Mary, suspected that her husband was having a sexual relationship with their slave. Ultimately, Mary demanded that Harriet be removed from the house. James continued to visit Harriet at her new home, again trying to have sex with her. In 1835, Harriet became a runaway slave, and spent the next seven years a fugitive, hiding in her free grandmother's attic crawlspace.[2]

If we were to focus on the conclusions to these stories, we would frame a picture of the contrasting consequences for masters who sexually coerced black and white women: the master of the white servant was sent to prison, while the black slave imprisoned herself to escape her abuser. But these opposing ends tell only part of the story. Until their conclusions, both women engaged in nearly parallel struggles with masters, mistresses, and unwanted sexual overtures. This contrast between the laborers' similar experiences and their stories' opposing conclusions suggests that the practice of sexual coercion and the classification of the criminal act of rape were differently dependent on status and race.

. . . Rachel had an opportunity for institutional intervention that was unequivocally denied to Harriet. Enslaved women in early America did not have access to legal redress against white men who raped them. While no colonial or early republic statute explicitly excluded enslaved women from being the victims of rape or attempted rape, many mid-Atlantic and Southern legislatures set harsh punishments for black men's sexual assaults on white women, thus implicitly privileging white women as victims of rape.[3] At the same time, enslaved people could only be witnesses against non-white defendants, so an enslaved woman could not testify against a white man who had raped her.[4] Accordingly, no historian has recorded a conviction of a white man for the rape of a slave at any point from 1700 to the Civil War, let alone a conviction of a master for raping his own slave. Rape in early America was a crime whose definition was structured by race.[5]

Even though the early American legal system segregated Rachel Davis and Harriet Jacobs into incomparable categories, their own presentations told nearly parallel stories of sexual coercion. In both women's stories, their masters attempted to control the parameters and meanings of sexual acts. Thus, rape in these situations was not just an act of power, it was also the power to define an act. Servants and slaves could not only be forced to consent, but this force was refigured as consent. At the same time, neither Harriet Jacobs nor Rachel Davis presented herself as an abject victim of her master's will.

Rather than a clear demarcation between the rape of slaves and the rape of servants, these narratives suggest that black and white laboring women interpreted and experienced a master's sexual coercion in strikingly similar ways. The parallels in these two stories, however, stopped at the courtroom door, where a racially based legal system ended the women's comparable negotiations of personal interactions.

CREATING MASTERY: THE PROCESS OF COERCION

How did a master sexually coerce a servant or slave in early America? A master did not have to rely on physical abilities to force his dependents into a sexual act. Instead, he might use the power of his position to create opportunities for sexual coercion, backing a woman into a corner where capitulation was her best option. A servant or enslaved woman often recognized this manipulation and tried to negotiate her way around her master's overtures rather than confront him with direct resistance. But that compromise came at a high price . . . negotiation implied willingness, and a woman's willingness contrasted with the early American legal and social code that rape consisted of irresistible force. Despite its surface counterintuitiveness, it was precisely women's attempts to bargain their way out of sexual assaults that made these sexual encounters seem consensual.[6]

Both Harriet Jacobs and Rachel Davis drew direct links between their status and their masters' sexual assaults on them. Each explained how her master had forced her into situations where he could sexually coerce her without being discovered. Rachel described how William ordered her to hold the lantern for him one night in the stable, where he "tried to persuade me to something." In the most blatantly contrived incident, when they were reaping in the meadow, William "handed me his sickle & bad me to lay it down. He saw where I put it." Later that night, William asked Rachel,

> where I put them sickles. I asked if he did not see—he said no, I must come & show him. I told him I cd go with my sister, or by myself. he said that was not as he bad me. I went. Before we got quite to sickles, he bad me stop—I told him I was partly to the sickles—he bad me stop—I did—he came up & threw me down. . . . I hallowed—he put his hand over my mouth . . . he pulled up my cloathes, & got upon me . . . he did penetrate my body. I was dreadfully injured.

According to Rachel's statement, William had forced her to accompany him into a dark field on a contrived search for a purposefully lost farm implement so that he could rape her. William's authority to control where she went and what she did was integral to his ability to force Rachel to have sex with him.

Harriet Jacobs was even more explicit about the connections between James Norcum's mastery and his ability to force her into sexually vulnerable positions. It seemed to Harriet that he followed her everywhere—in her words, "my master met me at every turn"—trying to force her to have sex with him. As William did with Rachel, James structured Harriet's work so that she was often alone with him. He ordered Harriet to bring his meals to him so that while she watched him eat he could verbally torture her with the consequences of refusing his sexual overtures. Harriet further recalled that "when I succeeded in avoiding opportunities for him to talk to me at home, I was ordered to come to his office, to do some errand." Tiring of Harriet's continued resistance, James ordered his four-year-old daughter to sleep near him, thus requiring that Harriet also sleep in his room in case the child needed attention during the night. James repeatedly used his position as a master who controlled his slave's labor to manipulate Harriet into sexually vulnerable situations.[7] Controlling a woman's daily routine, her work requirements, and her physical presence—in other words, control over her labor and her body—gave men in positions of mastery access to a particular means of sexually coercive behavior.

Each woman also recalled how she had challenged her master's right to force her into a sexual relationship. Rachel recounted how she had "resisted" and "cried" when William tried to pull her into a darkened bedroom after sending the rest of the servants to bed, and how she threatened that she would tell his wife what he was doing. When these forms of resistance did not end his overtures, Rachel tried to carry out her master's orders in ways that might prevent her own sexual vulnerability. Rachel's description of being raped in the dark field began by recollecting that she had suggested that William could find the sickle himself, and then offered to find it on her own or with her sister. Ultimately, William resorted to his position as a master—"he said that was not as he bad me"—and issued a direct order for Rachel to accompany him. Rachel portrayed an interactive relationship with William: she may not have been able to override her master's orders, but she forced him to change their content. Rather than sex in the bedroom while the other children slept and his wife was away, Rachel forced William to order her into the dark field, thereby disrupting his original attempts at a seamless consensual interaction.

Harriet Jacobs's story contained similar efforts to avoid her master's sexual overtures that forced him to refigure his behavior. When Mary Norcum's suspicions made her husband revert to physical gestures instead of words to convey his sexual desires to Harriet, Harriet responded by letting "them pass, as if I did not understand what he meant." When James realized that Harriet could read, he wrote her notes that expressed his sexual intentions. But Harriet repeatedly pretended "'I can't read them, sir.'" Overall, "by managing to keep within sight of people, as much as possible during the day time, I had hitherto succeeded in eluding my master." Harriet forced James into baldly claiming his right for sexual access as a privilege of mastery: according to Harriet, James began constantly "reminding me that I belonged to him, and swearing by heaven and earth that he would compel me to submit to him" because "I was his property; that I must be subject to his will in all things." Like Rachel Davis, Harriet Jacobs engaged in an exchange of maneuvers with her master where each tried to foil the other's plans and counterplans. Despite her master's legal property in her body, Harriet did not portray herself as utterly powerless. By playing into his image of her as too stupid to understand his signs and too illiterate to read his notes, Harriet used her own position as a slave to avoid her master's sexual overtures, forcing him to raise the stakes of his desires toward her.[8]

Because he did not receive unquestioned acquiescence from a servant or slave, a master had to create situations in which his laborers had little choice but to have sexual relations with him. Rachel's attempted refusal to go alone into a dark field with her master and Harriet's feigned ignorance of her master's intentions forced each man to modify his route to sexual interactions. By not consenting to a master's more subtle attempts at sexual relations, a servant or slave might force her master into more overtly coerced sexual acts. Ironically, this compelled a master to enact his laborer's interpretation of his overtures. Rather than the sexual offers that the masters first proposed, the men were forced to use coercion to carry out their sexual plans. Theoretically, a master could coerce through his physical prowess, but most masters did not have to rely exclusively on fists or whips to commit rape. Instead, they could rely on the strength of their mastery.

Beyond the unadorned physical power that could compel a woman into a sexual act, a master had an array of indirect means to force a dependent to have sex with him that simultaneously denied her resistance to him. . . . Harriet characterized her master as "a crafty man, [who] resorted to many means to accomplish his purposes. Sometimes he had stormy, terrific ways, that made his victims tremble; sometimes he assumed a gentleness that he thought must surely subdue." James promised Harriet that if she would give in to him sexually, "I would cherish you. I would make a lady of you." The possibility of a better life that transcended her racial and labor status was more than a bribe to induce Harriet's consent. It created a fiction that Harriet could voluntarily choose to have sexual relations with her master. By switching between the threats of physical harm and the gifts of courtship, James undercut the appearance of a forced sexual interaction. By theoretically allowing space for Harriet's consent to his sexual overtures, James was redefining coercion into consensual sexual relations.[9]

Similarly, William's verbal narration of consensual relations overlay his forceful attempts at sex. While he had Rachel trapped underneath his body, William told her that "he wd have the good will of me." William's modification of the classic legal description of rape as a man having carnal knowledge of a woman "against her will" verbally created a consensual act even as he used force to have sexual relations.[10] In the same incident, William called Rachel by her family nickname, telling her, "Nate you dear creature, I must fuck you." Even while forcing Rachel to have sex with him, William used terms of endearment toward her. William's presentation of an affectionate and therefore consensual sexual relationship with Rachel differentiated his actions from the brutality that early Americans would most easily recognize as rape.

Thus, the process of master–servant and master–slave sexual coercion was not exclusively tied to racial boundaries. Harriet Jacobs's and Rachel Davis's similarly recounted experiences suggest that their sexual interactions were more directly shaped by lines of status and dependency. These patterns would be repeated as masters and their servants or slaves struggled to control public perceptions of what had occurred.

CREATING MASTER NARRATIVES: THE PROCESS OF PUBLICITY

Given these different versions of events, how did families, other household members, and communities interpret evidence of a possibly coercive sexual interaction? How did assaulted women portray what had happened to them? Harriet Jacobs's and Rachel Davis's narratives show that the process of publicizing a master's sexual overtures was again structured by the woman's position as his personally dependent laborer. Words—the power to speak them and the power to construct their meaning—became the prize in a struggle among masters, mistresses, and the assaulted servant or slave.

After attempting sexual overtures toward their laborers, masters had to contend with the possibility that the women would tell others about their masters' behavior. Harriet Jacobs's and Rachel Davis's masters attempted to threaten their laborers into silence about their sexual interactions. Harriet wrote that her master "swore he would kill me, if I was not as silent as the grave."[11] Similarly, William told Rachel that if she told "any body, he wd be the death of me." When Rachel threatened to tell his wife what William had been doing, "he sd if I did, I shd repent." By demanding her silence, each master tried to dictate the parameters of his sexual interactions with his servant or slave without outside interference that might contradict his interpretation or stop his sexual pursuit.

But both women also believed that their masters were afraid of the damage that they could do by publicizing their sexual behavior. Besides his threats of physical violence, William promised Rachel a "gown if she would not tell" what he had done, and on another occasion, "begged [Rachel] not to tell" her new mistress because "it wd be the Ruin of him." Harriet similarly believed that her master "did not wish to have his villainy made public." Instead, he "deemed it prudent to keep up some outward show of decency." From each woman's vantage point, then, her master's concern about his public image again allowed her some room for negotiation: he needed his servant or slave to conceal their sexual interactions. But by not telling anyone about her master's sexual assaults, a woman increased the likelihood that their sexual relationship would not appear to be a rape. This double-edged sword made the servant or slave an unwilling accomplice in the masking of her own sexual coercion.[12]

If pressuring his servant or slave into silence through bribes or threats did not silence her, a master might try to control her description of their sexual interaction. William Cress enacted an elaborate punishment scene that forced Rachel Davis to claim responsibility for anything that may have passed between them. After Rachel's complaints to her mistress prompted Mary to confront her husband about Rachel's allegations, William immediately challenged Rachel. "'Well Rachael,'" William accused, "'what are this you have been scraping up about me?,'" denying even in his question the possibility of his own misdeeds. When Rachel could not present a satisfactory answer, William employed the power of physical correction allowed to him as her master to reform her story. According to Rachel, he "whipt me dreadfully & he said . . . that he never had such a name before. . . . I fell down—he damned me, & bad me beg his pardon. I said I did not know how—he bad me go on my knees . . . he bad me go to house & tell" his wife that she (Rachel) had lied. By whipping Rachel, William attempted to disprove her story of sexual assault: his wife had said that if Rachel's assertions of sexual relations between herself and William "was lies" as William claimed, "he ought to whip" Rachel for her dishonesty. This whipping was not just a punishment unfairly inflicted, it was a punishment that retroactively attempted to define the sexual interactions between a servant and a master. Once subjugated, Rachel was required to deny that William had forced her to have sex with him. Rachel's younger sister, also a servant to William, believed this new version of events: she admitted that "I do remember D[efendant] whipping my sister—it was for telling so many lies." William was using his position as master to rewrite the sexual act that had taken place between them.

Rachel ended her description of this incident by stating that after William had beaten her, "he went to church that day & I showed my back to [my] Sister." Those final words on her master's brutal punishment (a whipping that prevented Rachel from lying on her side for three weeks) revealed the irony of the situation: while William continued to appear as a publicly reverent and virtuous patriarch, Rachel secretly bore the signs of his sins, visible only to those most intimate with her. In the process of sexual coercion, force did not have a solely physical purpose: masters also used force to create an image of consent.

Harriet Jacobs also noted the discrepancy between her master's public image and private behavior, telling her readers how he had preserved his image at her expense. When Harriet's mistress confronted Harriet with suspicions of her husband's sexual improprieties, Harriet swore on a Bible that she had not had a sexual relationship with her master.

When Mary questioned her husband, however, James contradicted Harriet's statements. And just like Rachel's mistress, Harriet's mistress "would gladly have had me flogged for my supposed false oath." But unlike William Cress, James Norcum did not allow Harriet to be whipped because "the old sinner was politic. The application of the lash might have led to remarks that would have exposed him" to his family and community.[13]

In Rachel's and Harriet's narratives, their mistresses—the wives of their abusers—played important roles in the categorization of the sexually abusive relationship. Each woman had to deal with a mistress who ultimately took her displeasure at her husband's sexual relationship out on her servant or slave. Each mistress also used her position of secondary mastery to create a temporary alliance with her servant or slave. Once this alliance outlived its usefulness, it became another tool with which the mistress could assist in redefining or denying the sexual relationship between the master and the slave or servant.

In both women's stories, the masters' wives did not immediately take their hostility at their sexually aggressive husbands out on the objects of their husbands' overtures. When Rachel and William came back from retrieving the "lost" sickle, his wife, Becky, asked "where he had been—he said, after the sickles, with nate (so they called me in family) she sd it was very extraordinary, no body else could go." Perhaps Becky suspected some sort of sexual liaison between her husband and their servant, and her pointed questions let her husband know of her suspicions. When Becky heard William trying to kiss Rachel in the cellar, she "said she had caught him & he wd deceive her no longer," but William denied any wrongdoing and Becky left in tears. These verbal confrontations apparently did not alter William's behavior; he continued to force himself sexually upon Rachel. Finally, Rachel's mistress "saw something was the matter with me, & asked what it was. I told her." After questioning her husband had little visible effect, Becky turned to Rachel to find out about her husband's actions. This temporary alliance brought Rachel some protection from William's retribution, if not from his sexual overtures: when William heard that Rachel had told another relative some of what he had done to her, "he whipt me again, but not so bad—his wife wd not let him & said, he was in Fault."

Similarly, Harriet Jacobs believed that her mistress suspected James's illicit behavior: "She watched her husband with unceasing vigilance; but he was well practised in means to evade it." After Mary heard that her husband planned to have Harriet sleep in his room, she began questioning Harriet, who told her how James had been sexually harassing her. Harriet claimed that Mary, like most slave mistresses "had no compassion for the poor victim of her husband's perfidy. She pitied herself as a martyr." But Harriet also admitted that Mary "spoke kindly, and promised to protect me," ordering Harriet to sleep with her, rather than with James. This protective kindness also allowed Mary to try to obtain the "truth" of Harriet and James's relationship out of Harriet while Harriet slept: "she whispered in my ear, as though it was her husband who was speaking to me, and listened to hear what I would answer." When Harriet did not provide any self-incriminating information, Mary confronted her husband, but Mary's interventions did not end James's sexual overtures toward Harriet.[14]

If mistresses could not personally control their husbands' behavior, how could they stop the sexual relationship between master and laborer that was making a mockery of their marital vows? Theoretically, mistresses could turn to the legal system to petition for a divorce from their husbands. By the early nineteenth century, most states had divorce laws that allowed wives to apply for divorce on the grounds of their husbands' adultery, but women's petitions for divorce were more commonly based on charges of desertion.[15] Furthermore, proving adultery with a slave might be difficult without firsthand witnesses to the sexual interactions, since the slave was limited in her ability to testify against the white man. Married women also had a vested interest in their husbands' social and economic standing. Divorce or incarceration would most probably result in a woman's economic downturn from the loss of her husband's labor.

Ultimately, Rachel Davis's and Harriet Jacobs's mistresses concentrated their energies on removing their laborers from the household. Instead of bringing charges against her husband or applying for a divorce on the grounds of adultery, Becky Cress told Rachel Davis that she must "leave the house." Rachel recalled that "they then hired me out." Rachel's mistress may have ultimately recognized that her husband was (at best) complicit in his sexual relations with Rachel, but she also recognized that she, as his wife, was in a poor position to mandate a reform in his behavior. She could, however, as a mistress, remove the more disposable partner in the sexual relationship, and so she ordered Rachel to leave their home. Whether or not Becky believed Rachel's story of rape, she did not hold Rachel entirely innocent of wrongdoing. At the very least, she spread blame equally between her servant and her husband, with much of the resulting punishment falling on the more vulnerable of the two parties. As Rachel stated, "Before I was hired out, [my mistress] used me very bad & said she would knowck me down if I came to table to eat." Because William was a master—both of Rachel and of his household—his wife could enact only limited direct retribution against him. She could watch his behavior, confront him, and let him know her displeasure, but ultimately, it was easier to remove the object of his overtures than publicly to accuse him of wrongdoing.

Mary Norcum demanded that Harriet Jacobs leave the house once she learned that Harriet was pregnant, believing that conception was proof of their slave's sexual relationship with her husband. Harriet was not the only slave who was reputed to have been kicked out of her house because of a sexual relationship with the master. Recalling a story told to her by her grandmother about another slave, Harriet wrote that "her mistress had that day seen her baby for the first time, and in the lineaments of its fair face she saw a likeness to her husband. She turned the bondswoman and her child out of doors, and forbade her ever to return." In both of these examples, the mistress felt herself in sexual competition with the slave—even if the slave were not a willing competitor for the master's affections.[16]

Thus, while a wife's place in the household hierarchy may have proscribed her options, it did not leave her entirely at her husband's mercy. By forcing her husband to prove his marital loyalty by whipping the laborer for telling untruths about his sexual conduct, each mistress tried to create her own version of household sexual alliances. When mistresses could not force husbands to modify their behavior, these wives turned to regulating their servant's or slave's actions: first, by using them as the source of incriminating information, and later, as a problem that could be eliminated. Mistresses would not permanently join forces with slave or servant women to overthrow the household patriarch; they might want to change their husbands' behavior, but these wives did not wish publicly to condemn or disassociate themselves from their husbands through divorce or other legal action.

The silencing of sexual coercion was more profound in Harriet Jacobs's autobiography than it was in Rachel Davis's court-ordered testimony specifically about rape. Harriet's representation of her conflict with her master centered on the power to create a singular version of reality through the privilege of public speech. Throughout her narrative, Harriet insisted that her master sexually assaulted her only with words, never with his body. She wrote that he "tried his utmost to corrupt the pure principles my grandmother had instilled. He peopled my mind with unclean images." Harriet silenced her own description of her master's actions by calling the sexual degradation of slavery "more than I can describe." Harriet's versions of her master's verbal actions may have stood in for the literally unspeakable physical sexual abuse she suffered at his hands. By describing only James's speech, Harriet turned his possibly physical assaults on her into verbal assaults that no reader could expect her to control.[17]

In a personal letter written a few years before the publication of *Incidents in the Life of a Slave Girl* in 1861, Harriet hinted that she had indeed concealed the extent of James's actions. While she had tried to give a "true and just" account of her life in slavery, she admitted that "there are somethings I might have made plainer I know—Woman can whisper—her cruel wrongs into the ear of a very dear friend—much easier than she can record them for the world to read." In this passage, Jacobs drew a distinction between the private version of her pain and the version she chose to present for public consumption. Victorian womanhood's emphasis on modesty and respectability as well as the established genre of sexual euphemism popularized in sentimental novels probably encouraged Harriet Jacobs to present a sanitized version of her master's assaults on her. But her decision may also have reflected a personal need to distance herself from painful events, and a difficulty in telling others about her suffering that was shared by other victims—black and white—of a master's sexual harassment.[18]

Both Harriet and Rachel first told those closest to them about their masters' unwelcome sexual overtures. Harriet originally hesitated to tell Molly Horniblow, her grandmother and closest living relative, how James was treating her. Harriet "would have given the world to have laid my head on my grandmother's faithful bosom, and told her all my troubles," but James's threats and her own fear of her grandmother's reaction made her stay silent. When Harriet eventually did talk to her grandmother, she told her only some of her difficulties: "I talked with my grandmother about it, and partly told her my fears. I did not dare to tell her the worst." Harriet also told her uncle about some of her suffering. He told another relative that "you don't know what a life they lead her. She has told me something about it, and I wish [her master] was dead, or a better man." Harriet's recollection of interactions with her grandmother and her uncle emphasized that neither relative knew the entire story of her master's abuses. Just as the reader was given a sanitized version in the public transcript of Harriet's life, her hesitancy to confess the full extent of sexual coercion was reiterated in Harriet's personal interactions. Her inability to confess "the worst" of her experiences may have maintained Harriet's image of sexual purity and self-identity, but it was at the cost of denying the full spectrum of her master's assaults on her.[19]

Similarly, Rachel eventually told people close to her—one of her sisters (a servant in another household), her aunt, and her new mistress—about what William was doing to her. She recounted that she was hesitant to tell the whole story even to them. Rachel told her new mistress "something of what passed in the meadow, but not the worst of it. I told my sister Becky . . . the whole of it." Like Harriet's claim that it was easier to tell a close friend than to proclaim one's victimization publicly, Rachel had an easier time confessing her problems to her sister than to her new mistress. When Rachel spoke with her aunt, Elizabeth Ashton, she again refrained from disclosing the full extent of William's coercion. Elizabeth told the court that Rachel had explained how William had isolated her in the cellar, had told her to go to bed with him when his wife was away, had cornered her in the barn, and had forced her to go with him to retrieve the sickle in the meadow. But Rachel stopped short of telling her aunt that William had succeeded in raping her, that his manipulative maneuvers had led to forced sexual intercourse. Elizabeth specified under cross-examination that *"I did not understand from her that he had fully effected his purpose in the meadow."*[20] By minimizing the extent of her master's abuse of her, Rachel created a public version of her master's actions that denied that she had been raped.

The victims of sexual coercion were not the only people who purposefully avoided discussions of sexual assaults. Elizabeth Ashton did not know that William had raped Rachel partly because, as she told the court, "I did not enquire whether he obtained his will in the meadow." When Rachel's sister told her own mistress that "Mr Cress wanted to be gret [great] with her sister Rachael," the mistress replied, "I wanted to hear no more." When this sister eventually told their father what had happened, Jacob Davis recalled that she "did not tell me directly, she did not tell me the worst—I did not think it was so bad." A voluntary conspiracy of silence—from the servant who had difficulty discussing what had happened, to the other women who wanted neither to hear nor tell the full extent of William's abuse of Rachel—worked to deny the sexual coercion that William committed on his servant.

Similarly, Harriet Jacobs's fellow slaves were hesitant to volunteer verbal or physical assistance. Harriet believed that while her friends and relatives knew that she was being sexually abused, they were unable to speak of it. Harriet recalled that "the other slaves in my master's house noticed" her changed behavior as a result of her master's treatment, but "none dared to ask the cause. . . . They knew too well the guilty practices under that roof; and they were aware that to speak of them was an offence that never went unpunished." Harriet's fellow slaves' silence, necessary for their own self-preservation, limited their ability to help Harriet resist their master's overtures. By controlling potential allies, a master enmeshed his original acts of sexual coercion in an ever-widening coercive web that structured his victim's possibilities for support or redress.[21]

By not telling others what had happened to her, Harriet was at the mercy of other people's versions of events. James's wife, Mary, went to the house of Harriet's free grandmother to tell her that Harriet was pregnant with James's baby. Molly Horniblow then turned on Harriet, apparently believing Mary's story that Harriet had consented to the relationship: "'I had rather see you dead than to see you as you now are,'" she told her granddaughter. "'You are a disgrace to your dead mother. . . . Go away . . . and never come to my house, again.'" Because Harriet had consistently denied or downplayed her master's sexual attempts on her, her grandmother believed Mary's story that Harriet had voluntarily had sexual relations with James. Later, Harriet's grandmother learned that Harriet had chosen to become pregnant with another man's baby to try to force her sexually abusive master to leave her alone or sell her. Once her grandmother understood "the real state of the case, and all I had been bearing for years. . . . She laid her old hand gently on my head, and murmured, 'Poor child! Poor child!'" Harriet's inability to speak about her master's sexual coercion temporarily isolated Harriet from the woman who was most able to support her. When Harriet ultimately received her grandmother's forgiveness, she also gained an ally in her fight against her master's sexual demands.[22]

Both Harriet and Rachel believed that an independently powerful figure outside of the household could counterbalance their masters' attempts at dominance. When Rachel's aunt questioned "why she did not go to a Squire to complain" about her master's sexual assaults, Rachel replied "she did not dare—she a bound girl & her father absent." After telling her sister what had happened, her sister "advised her to stay there & be a good girl. . . . I thought nothing could be done, as my father was away." Rachel herself told the court that "I did not know if I went to a Justice, he wd take notice of it. Enough people knew it, but waited till my Father came back." Without a patriarchal figure beside her, Rachel would not directly confront her master, and did not believe herself entitled to legal justice, a belief encouraged (or at least not contradicted) by the women in whom she confided. For Rachel, her father's support was crucial to her ability to receive public redress for her master's sexual assaults on her.

Enslaved women ordinarily did not have access to the protection offered by a patriarchal figure. Harriet Jacobs observed that enslaved men "strive to protect wives and daughter from the insults of their masters. . . . [but] Some poor creatures have been so brutalized by the lash that they will sneak out of the way to give their masters free access to their wives and daughters." Although Harriet Jacobs did not have a waiting patriarchal figure to whom she could turn for protection, supporters outside of the household were still crucial to her limited redress. Harriet repeatedly spoke of her free grandmother's respect in the community, of how James "dreaded" this woman's "scorching rebuke," so that "her presence in the neighborhood was some protection to me." Ultimately, her grandmother's home became a partial refuge from James's pursuit. Harriet also spoke of her white lover's assistance in combating her master's "persecutions" of her through his "wish to aid me." Harriet partly justified her decision to have sexual relations with this man (pseudonymously referred to as "Mr. Sands") because she was "sure my friend, Mr. Sands, would buy me . . . and I thought my freedom could be easily obtained from him." While Harriet could not hope for institutional retribution against her master, she could hope that her new lover would help provide freedom from her master.[23]

Both Harriet Jacobs and Rachel Davis fought similar battles against the veil of silence surrounding their masters' treatment of them. Both were confronted by relatives and neighbors who had limited authority over another household's problems. Both women turned to another powerful figure—father or free grandmother and elite white lover, respectively—to rescue them from their masters' sexual abuse. When Rachel finally told her father about her master's sexual assaults, Jacob Davis successfully encouraged the local legal system to begin a criminal prosecution. But neither Harriet Jacobs's ultimate confession to her grandmother nor her involvement with a white lover could lead to legal intervention. The legal system marked an irreversible disjuncture in the two women's experiences.

EPILOGUE: CREATING RAPE: THE LEGAL PROCESS

Following the process of sexual coercion has led us back to this essay's opening, as Harriet Jacobs's and Rachel Davis's parallel stories reach diametrically opposed conclusions: while Rachel's master was convicted of rape and served a substantial jail sentence, there is no evidence that Harriet's master was ever subject to legal repercussions for his behavior. When a master tried to define coercive sex as consensual sex, both servants and slaves could negotiate with his terms and battle against his actions. But when the legal system defined enslaved women outside the judicial parameters of rape, there was little room for negotiation. The parallels in Harriet Jacobs's and Rachel Davis's stories ended with the legal distinction of criminal behavior. Rachel Davis may not have had easy access to criminal justice—her master was convicted of rape several years after he had first assaulted her. Yet she ultimately received legal protections that were denied to Harriet Jacobs.

We need to understand not only the legal history of rape, but the social history of sexual coercion. By taking seriously the possibility that white and black women in early America could have some experiences in common, we can begin to reassemble the complicated interactions of race, gender, and social and economic status in American history. Certainly the comparative possibilities are not exhausted with these two stories. Historians could compare the sexual experiences of free and enslaved African American women or white and black free servants. Were similar strategies used outside of households, in any relationship between a powerful man and a less powerful woman? In all of these comparisons, we should think carefully about how sex was coerced and how the crime of rape was defined. If we frame our investigations using solely the legal judgment of rape, we not only miss much of the story, we again replace women's experiences—much as their coercers had tried to do—with external categorizations. Instead, by interrogating the multiple and contested meanings of sexual coercion, we can better understand the historical relationships of social and sexual power.

Notes

1. "Commonwealth v. William Cress, Feb. 1808," Pennsylvania Court Papers, 1807–1809, Historical Society of Pennsylvania, Philadelphia, Pa. Unless otherwise noted, all quotations regarding Rachel Davis are from these documents. For the criminal prosecution of William Cress, see "Commonwealth v. William Cress, Philadelphia, Feb. 15, 1808," Pennsylvania Oyer and Terminer Docket, 1778–1827, 261, 262, 263, 265, Pennsylvania Historic and Museum Commission, Harrisburg, Pa.

2. Harriet Jacobs, *Incidents in the Life of a Slave Girl Written by Herself*, ed. Jean Fagan Yellin (1861; reprint, Cambridge, Mass.: Harvard University Press, 1987).

3. For examples of statutes specifying the crime of black-on-white rape, see John D. Cushing, ed., *The Earliest Printed Laws of Pennsylvania 1681–1713* (Wilmington, Del.: Michael Glazier, 1978), 69; B.W. Leigh, ed., *The Revised Code of the Laws of Virginia* (n.p., 1819), 585–86. See also Peter Bardalgio, "Rape and the Law in the Old South: 'Calculated to Excite Indignation in Every Heart,'" *Journal of Southern History* 60 (1994): 756–58.

4. See Thomas D. Morris, "Slaves and the Rules of Evidence in Criminal Trials," *Chicago-Kent Law Review* 68 (1993): 1209–39.

5. For further discussion of the cultural definitions of rape in early America, see Sharon Block, *He Said I Must: Coerced Sex in Early America* (Chapel Hill, OIEAHC at University of North Carolina Press, forthcoming).

6. Much of the following discussion about resistance's reformulation into consent was inspired by Ellen Rooney, "'A Little More than Persuading': Tess and the Subject of Sexual Violence," in *Rape and Representation*, eds. Lynn A. Higgins and Brenda R. Silver (New York: Columbia University Press, 1991), 87–114, and the fictional exploration of twentieth-century household sexual coercion in J. M. Redmann's three-book series culminating in *The Intersection of Law and Desire* (New York: W. W. Norton, 1995).

7. Jacobs, *Incidents*, 28, 27, 31–32. See also p. 41.

8. Ibid., 31, 32, 28, 27.

9. Ibid., 27, 35.

10. Italics added.

11. Jacobs, *Incidents*, 28. See also 32.

12. Ibid., 29.

13. Ibid., 34, 35.

14. Ibid., 31, 33, 34.

15. On divorce in the antebellum South, see Jane Turner Censer, "'Smiling Through Her Tears': Ante-bellum Southern Women and Divorce," *American Journal of Legal History* 25 (1981): 24–47; for Pennsylvania, see Merril D. Smith, *Breaking the Bonds: Marital Discord in Pennsylvania, 1730–1830* (New York: New York University Press, 1991); Thomas Meehan, "'Not Made out of Levity': Evolution of Divorce in Early Pennsylvania," *Pennsylvania Magazine of History and Biography* 92 (1968): 441–64.

16. Jacobs, Incidents, 59, 122.

17. Ibid., 27–28.

18. Harriet Jacobs to Amy Post, June 21, 1857, in Jacobs, *Incidents*, 242. For a discussion of African American women's psychological reactions to systemic sexual exploitation, see Darlene Clark Hine, "Rape and the Inner Lives of Black Women in the Middle West: Preliminary Thoughts on the Culture of Dissemblance," *Signs* 14 (1989), 265–277.

19. Jacobs, *Incidents*, 28, 38, 25.

20. Underlining in original.

21. Jacobs, *Incidents*, 28.

22. Ibid., 56, 57.

23. Ibid., 29, 54–55.

JEANNE BOYDSTON

The Pastoralization of Housework

Having read fiction and advice literature directed to women in the years before the Civil War, in 1966 the historian Barbara Welter identified a pervasive stereotype, which she called the "Cult of True Womanhood." Women were encouraged to cultivate the virtues of domesticity, piety, purity, and submissiveness. Home was referred to as women's "proper sphere" and understood to be a shelter from the outside world in which men engaged in hard work and cutthroat competition. Other historians agreed that men's and women's spheres of activity were separated and suggested that this separation was somehow linked to the simultaneous growth of capitalism and industrialization. Historian Gerda Lerner argued, by contrast, that stressing the shelter of home was a way by which middle-class women distinguished themselves from mill girls, and so maintained class boundaries.

How does Jeanne Boydston describe the relationship between home and work in antebellum America? How does she describe the relationship between women's work and men's work? What does she think were the uses of the ideology of separate spheres? How do the middle-class households described by Boydston differ from the households in which Harriet Jacobs and Rachel Davis lived (pp. 164–173)?

In the colonial period, family survival had been based on two types of resources: the skills of the wife in housewifery, and the skills and property of the husband in agriculture. Both sets of skills involved the production of tangible goods for the family—such items as furnishings, food, and fabrics. Both were likely to involve some market exchange, as husbands sold grain and wives sold eggs or cheese, for example. And both involved services directly to the household. By the early nineteenth century, however, husbands' contributions to their households were focused disproportionately on market exchange—on the cash they brought into the family—while their direct activities in producing both goods and services for the family had vastly decreased.

The meaning of this shift has often been misread, interpreted as an indication that households were no longer dependent on goods and services provided from within but had instead become reliant upon the market for their survival. . . . [But] consumerism was sharply curtailed by the amount of available cash. Choices constantly had to be made: to purchase a new cloak or try to refurbish the old one for another season, to hire a woman to help with the wash or lay aside some money to buy a house. In these patterns of mundane decisions lay the essential economic character of antebellum households: they were in fact "mixed economies"—economic systems that functioned on the bases of both paid and unpaid labor and were dependent upon both. They required paid labor for the cash to purchase some goods and services. Equally, they depended on unpaid labor in the household to process those commodities into consumable form and to produce other goods and services directly without recourse to the cash market. . . .

[The] antebellum era was the last period during which most adult women shared the experience of having been, at some point in their lives, paid household workers. To an extent never repeated, even middle-class wives were likely to have worked as hired "help" in their youth. . . . [It is therefore possible to make a rough calculation] of the cost to a family to replace the unpaid labor of the wife by purchasing it on the market.[1] . . .

In northeastern cities in 1860, a woman hired both to cook and to do the laundry earned between $3 and $4 a week. Seamstresses and maids averaged two-and-a-half dollars a week. On the market, caring for children was at the lower end of the pay scale, seldom commanding more than $2 a week. If we assume that a woman did the full work of a hired cook and child's nurse, and also spent even an hour a day each sewing and cleaning (valued at about three cents an hour apiece), the weekly price of her basic housework would approximate $4.70. Even if we reduce this almost by half to $3 a week (to allow for variations in her work schedule and for the presence of assistance of some sort), taken at an average, this puts the price of a wife's basic housework at about $150 dollars a year.[2] . . .

To this should be added the value of goods a wife might make available within the family for free or at a reduced cost. Among poorer households, this was the labor of scavenging. A rag rug found among the refuse was worth half a dollar in money saved, an old coat, several dollars. Flour for a week, scooped from a broken barrel on the docks, could save the household almost a dollar in cash outlay.[3] In these ways, a wife with a good eye and a quick hand might easily save her family a dollar a week—or $50 or so over the course of the year. In households with more cash, wives found other ways to avoid expenditures. By shopping carefully, buying in bulk, and drying or salting extra food, a wife could save ten to fifty percent of the family food budget . . . this could mean a saving of from 40 cents to over $2 a week. Wives who kept kitchen gardens or chickens . . . could . . . produce food worth a quarter a week (the price of 1/4 bushel of potatoes in New York in 1851).[4]

But there was also the cash that working-class wives brought into the household, by their needlework, or vending, or by taking in boarders, running a grocery or a tavern from her kitchen, or working unpaid in her husband's trade. A boarder might pay $4 a week into the family economy. Subtracting a dollar and a half for food and rent, the wife's labor-time represented $2.50 of that amount, or $130 a year.[5] . . .

The particular labor performed by a given woman depended on the size and resources of her household. . . . Yet we can estimate a general market price of housework by combining the values of the individual activities that made it up: perhaps $150 for cooking, cleaning, laundry, and childrearing; another $50 or so saved through scavenging or careful shopping, another $50 or so in cash brought directly into the household. This would set the price of a wife's labor-time among the laboring poor at roughly $250 a year beyond maintenance. . . . In working-class households with more income, where the wife could focus her labor on money-saving and on taking in a full-time boarder, that price might reach over $500 annually. . . . These shifts in the nature of a wife's work, and in the value of that work, as a husband's income increased seems not to have been entirely lost on males, who advised young men that if they meant to get ahead, they should "get married."[6] . . .

But husbands were not the sole beneficiaries of the economic value of housework, or of its unique invisibility. Employers were enabled by the presence of this sizeable but uncounted labor in the home to pay both men and women wages which were, in fact, below the level of subsistence. The difference was critical to the development of industrialization in the antebellum Northeast.[7] . . . Occasionally, mill owners acknowledged that the wages they paid did not cover maintenance. One agent admitted: "So long as they can do my work *for what I choose to pay them,* I keep them, getting out of them all I can. . . . [H]ow they fare outside my walls I don't know, nor do I consider it my business to know. They must look out for themselves."[8] . . .

Even when employers paid high enough salaries to provide present security for a family, they seldom provided either the income or the job security to ensure a household's well-being against the erratic boom-and-bust cycles of business and the unemployment consequent upon those cycles. . . . Women's unremunerated labor in the household provided the needed "safety net," enabling middle-class families to maintain some degree of both material stability and healthfulness in a volatile economic environment. . . . Put simply, a wife was a good investment for a man who wanted to get ahead.

THE PASTORALIZATION OF HOUSEWORK

The culture of the antebellum Northeast recognized the role of wives in the making of contented and healthy families. Indeed, the years between the War of 1812 and the Civil War were a period of almost unabated celebration of women's special and saving domestic mission. "Grant that others besides woman have responsibilities at home. . . ." wrote the Reverend Jesse Peck in 1857, "[s]till we fully accord the supremacy of domestic bliss to the wife and mother."[9] . . .

As recent historians have recognized, this glorification of wife and motherhood was at the heart of one of the most compelling and widely shared belief systems of the early nineteenth century: the ideology of gender spheres. An elaborate set of intellectual and behavioral conventions, the doctrine of gender spheres expressed a worldview in which both the orderliness of daily social relations and the larger organization of society derived from and depended on the preservation of an all-encompassing gender division of labor. Consequently, in the conceptual and emotional universe of the doctrine of spheres, males and females existed as creatures of naturally and essentially different capacities. As the Providence-based *Ladies Museum* explained in 1825:

> Man is strong—woman is beautiful. Man is daring and confident—woman is diffident and unassuming. Man is great in action—woman i[n] suffering. Man shines abroad—woman at home. Man talks to convince—woman to persuade and please. Man has a rugged heart—woman a soft and tender one. Man prevents misery—woman relieves it. Man has science—woman taste. Man has judgment—woman sensibility. Man is a being of justice—woman of mercy.

These "natural" differences of temperament and ability were presumed to translate into different social roles and responsibilities for men and women. Clearly intended by the order of nature to "shine at home," Woman was deemed especially ill-equipped to venture into the world of nineteenth-century business, where "cunning, intrigue, falsehood, slander, [and] vituperative violence" reigned and where "mercy, pity, and sympathy, are vagrant fowls."[10] . . .

[T]he ideology of gender spheres was partly a response to the ongoing chaos of a changing society—an intellectually and emotionally comforting way of setting limits to the uncertainties of early industrialization. . . . The traits that presumably rendered Woman so defenseless against the guiles and machinations of the business world not only served to confine her to the home as her proper sphere but made her presence there crucial for her family, especially for her husband. Even the most enthusiastic boosters of economic expansion agreed that the explosive opportunism of antebellum society created an atmosphere too heady with competition and greed to engender either social or personal stability. However great his wisdom or strong his determination, to each man must come a time

> when body, mind, and heart are overtaxed with exhausting labor; when the heavens are overcast, and the angry clouds portend the fearful storm; when business schemes are antagonized, thwarted by stubborn matter, capricious man, or an inauspicious providence; when coldness, jealousy, or slander chills his heart, misrepresents his motives, or attacks his reputation; when he looks with suspicion on all he sees, and shrinks from the frauds and corruptions of men with instinctive dread.[11] . . .

Whatever the proclivities or ambitions of individual women, the presumed contrasts between the sexes permitted Woman-in-the-abstract to be defined as the embodiment of all that was contrary to the values and behaviors of men in the marketplace, and thus, to the marketplace itself. Against its callousness, she offered nurturance. Against its ambition, she pitted her self-effacement and the modesty of her needs. Against its materialism, she held up the twin shields of morality and spiritual solace. If business was a world into which only men traveled and where they daily risked losing their souls, then wherever Woman was, was sanctuary. And Woman was in the Home.

The contrast between Man and Woman melted easily into a contrast between "workplace" and "home" and between "work" as Man engaged in it and the "occupations" of Woman in the home. Most writers of prescriptive literature did acknowledge that women were involved in activities of some sort in their households. For example, T. S. Arthur worried that a woman would be unable to keep the constant vigilance required to be a good mother if she also had to attend to "the operations of the needle, the mysteries of culinary science, and all the complicated duties of housekeeping." His language is revealing, however: housework consisted of "mysteries" and "duties"; it was a different order of activity from the labor that men performed. Indeed, some observers cautioned that the wife and mother should deliberately stay clear of employments which might seem to involve her in the economy.... William Alcott was among this group. Noting that a woman "... has duties to perform to the sick and to the well—to the young and to the aged; duties even to domestic animals," Alcott nevertheless cautioned that "[v]ery few of these duties are favorable to the laying up of much property, and some are opposed to it. So that while we commend industry—of the most untiring kind, too—we would neither commend nor recommend strong efforts to lay up property." The advice was not only consistent with, but reflected a critical aspect of the ideology of spheres: to the extent that workers in the household identified themselves with the labor of the marketplace, the function of the home as a place of psychological refuge would be undermined.[12]

Thus, the responsibilities of wives in their households were generally described in the prescriptive literature less as purposeful activities required and ordered by the welfare of their individual families than as emanations of an abstract but shared Womanhood. As Daniel C. Eddy explained:

> Home is woman's throne, where she maintains her royal court, and sways her queenly authority. It is there that man learns to appreciate her worth, and to realize the sweet and tender influences which she casts around her; there she exhibits the excellences of character which God had in view in her creation.

Underscoring the essentially passive nature of women's functions, Eddy concluded: "Her life should be a calm, holy, beautiful walk."[13]

... The consequence of this conflation of ideology with behavior was to obscure both the nature and the economic importance of women's domestic labor. It was not only Woman-in-the-abstract who did not labor in the economy, but also, by extension, individual women. It was not only Woman-in-the-abstract, but presumably, real women who guided the on-going functions of the home through the effortless "emanations" of their very being, providing for the needs of their families without labor, through their very presence in the household. As romantic narrative played against lived experience, the labor and economic value of housework ceased to exist in the culture of the antebellum Northeast. It became work's opposite: a new form of leisure....

William Alcott's description of the wife's labors in *The Young Wife* provides a striking illustration of the pastoralization of housework in descriptions of the antebellum home:

> Where is it that the eye brightens, the smile lights up, the tongue becomes flippant, the form erect, and every motion cheerful and graceful? Is it at home? Is it in doing the work of the kitchen? Is it at the wash-tub—at the oven—darning a stocking—mending a coat—making a pudding? Is it in preparing a neat table and table cloth, with a few plain but neat dishes? Is it in covering it with some of nature's simple but choice viands? Is it in preparing the room for the reception of an absent companion? Is it in warming and lighting the apartments at evening, and waiting, with female patience, for his return from his appointed labor? Is it in greeting him with all her heart on his arrival?[14]

Clearly, Alcott was quite familiar with the types of work performed by women in their own families, and his description is all the more interesting on this account: cooking, baking, washing clothes, mending and darning, serving meals, building fires, attending to lamps—it is a surprisingly accurate catalogue. It is also incomplete, of course. Missing from this picture is the making of the soap that the wash might be done, the lugging and heating of the water, the tiresome process of heating and lifting cast-iron irons, the dusting and sweeping of rooms, the cleaning of the stove, and the making of the stocking and the coat now in need of repair.

Even the domestic tasks which Alcott acknowledges, however, are not to be contemplated as true work, a point which is made explicit in his identification of only the husband's employments as "labor." With "labor," indeed, the wife's activities have no truck, for there is no labor here to perform.... the food appears virtually as a gift of nature, and the compliant fires and lamps seem to light and tend themselves.... All is ordered, and the ordering of it is not only *not* burdensome or tiring, but the certain vehicle of good health and a cheerful disposition. Far from labor, housework is positively regenerating....

The pastoralization of housework, with its emphasis on the sanctified home as an emanation of Woman's nature, required the articulation of a new way of seeing (or, more exactly, of *not* seeing) women as actors, capable of physical exertion. Most specifically, this applied to women as laborers, but the "magical extraction" of physical activity from the concept of Womanhood in fact proceeded in much larger terms and was most apparent in the recurrent celebrations of female "influence." Typically invoked as the female counterpart to the presumably *male* formal political power,[15] the concept of indirect womanly "influence" supplanted notions of women as direct agents, and thus as laborers. [In an article entitled "Woman's Offices and Influences," J. H. Agnew argued that] the contrast between presumably male "power" (physical as well as moral) and female "influence" could be drawn quite explicitly:

> We may stand in awe, indeed, before the exhibition of *power*, whether physical or moral, but we are not won by them to the love of truth and goodness, while *influence* steals in upon our hearts, gets hold of the springs of action, and leads us into its own ways. It is the *inflowing* upon others from the nameless traits of character which constitute woman's idiosyncracy. Her heart is a great reservoir of love, the water-works of moral influence, from which go out ten thousand tubes, conveying the ethereal essences of her nature, and diffusing them quietly over the secret chambers of man's inner being.

Woman does not herself *act*. Rather, she "gets hold of the springs of action." An idiosyncrasy in the human order, she is not so much a physical as an ethereal being. Agnew concluded: "Let man, then, exercise power; woman exercise influence. By this she will best perform her offices, discharge her duties." It is the crowning touch on the pastoralization of housework: the home is not the setting of labor, but of "offices" and "duties." Therefore, what is required for the happy home is not a worker, but rather "a great reservoir of love."[16]

The pastoralization of household labor became a common feature of antebellum literature, both private and published.... [It] shaped much of the fiction of the period. In a piece entitled "The Wife" (published in the *Ladies' Literary Cabinet* in July of 1819 and included in *The Sketch Book* the following year), Washington Irving described the plight of a young couple forced by the husband's disastrous speculations to give up their fashionable life in the city and move to a modest country cottage. One might anticipate numerous headaches and a good deal of hard work in such a move, especially for the wife, but such was not the case for Irving's "Wife." Mary goes out to the cottage to spend the day "superintending its arrangement," but the substance of that process remains a mystery, for the packing and unpacking, cleaning, hanging of curtains, arranging of furniture, putting away of dishes, sorting of clothes, and adjusting of new domestic equipment which one might expect to be required under such circumstances remain undisclosed in the text. Indeed, all we learn is that, when next encountered by the narrator, Mary "'seems in better spirits than I have ever known.'" Transformed into a creature who is far more sylvan nymph than human female, Mary greets her husband and the narrator "singing, in a style of the most touching simplicity.... Mary came tripping forth to meet us; she was in a pretty rural dress of white, a few wild flowers were twisted in her fine hair, a fresh bloom was on her cheek, her whole countenance beamed with smile—I have never seen her look so lovely." To complete the pastoral scene, nature has obligingly provided "'a beautiful tree behind the cottage'" where the threesome picnic on a feast of wild strawberries and thick sweet cream.[17] ...

In both its briefer and its more extended forms in fiction and in exposition, in prescription and in proscription, the pastoralization of housework permeated the culture of the antebellum Northeast. Often, it was expressed simply as a truism, as when the Reverend Hubbard Winslow reminded his Boston congregation that "[t]he more severe manual labors, the toils of the fields, the mechanics, the cares and burdens of mercantile business, the exposures and perils of absence from home, the duties of the learned professions devolve upon man...." [H]e considered women's occupations to be of a "more delicate and retired nature." That same year, the shocked and angered Congregational clergy of Massachusetts drew upon the same assumptions and the same imagery of Womanhood to denounce the abolitionist activities of Sarah and Angelina Grimké. Reminding their female congregants that "the power of woman is in her dependence," the clergy spoke of the "unobtrusive and private" nature of women's "appropriate duties" and directed them to devote their energies to "those departments of life that form the character of individuals" and to embodying "that modesty and delicacy which is the charm of domestic life. . . ."[18]

As we have seen, working class husbands appear to have embraced the view that paid labor was economically superior to unpaid labor. They shared, too, a tendency to pastoralize the labor of their wives. The speeches of early labor activists, for example, frequently invoked both the rhetoric of the ideology of spheres and pastoral images of the household, implying a sharp contrast between "the odious, cruel, unjust and tyrannical system" of the factory, which "compels the operative Mechanic to exhaust his physical and mental powers," with the presumably rejuvenating powers of the home. Discouraging women from carrying their labor "beyond the home," working men called upon women to devote themselves to improving the quality of life within their families. . . . [A]s William Sylvis put it, it was the proper work of woman "to guide the tottering footsteps of tender infancy in the paths of rectitude and virtue, to smooth down the wrinkles of our perverse nature, to weep over our shortcomings, and make us glad in the days of our adversity. . . ."[19]

African-American newspapers of the antebellum Northeast also reflected and reaffirmed the pastoral conventions of women's domestic labor. *The Rights of All* compared women to ornamental creatures of nature, "as various in decorations as the insects, the birds, and the shells. . . ." In 1842, *The Northern Star and Freeman's Advocate* approvingly reprinted an article from the *Philadelphia Temperance Advocate* in which wives were described as deities "who preside over the sanctities of domestic life, and administer its sacred rights. . . ." That this perception ill fit the experiences of those female readers whose home was also their unpaid workplace, as well as those women who worked for money in someone else's home, appears not to have disturbed the paper's editors. Rather than as a worker, Woman was represented as a force of nature—and presumably one intended for man's special benefit: "The morning star of our youth—the day star of our manhood—the evening star of our age."[20]

For both middle-class and working-class men, the insecurities of income-earning during the antebellum period struck at the very heart of their traditional roles as husbands and fathers. Particularly since the late eighteenth century, manhood had been identified with wage-earning—with the provision of the cash necessary to make the necessary purchases of the household. In the context of the reorganization of paid work in the antebellum Northeast, the growing dependency of households on cash, and the roller-coaster business cycles against which few families could feel safe, that identification faced almost constant challenge. And as it was challenged, it intensified.

By the antebellum period, the late-eighteenth century association of manhood with wage-earning had flowered into the cult of the male "breadwinner." A direct response to the unstable economic conditions of early industrialization, this association crossed the lines of the emerging classes, characterizing the self-perceptions and social claims of both laboring and middle-class men.

Among laboring men, the identification of manhood with wage-earning melded easily with the traditional emphasis on the "manliness" of the crafts. . . . General Trades' Union leader Ely Moore warned that the unchecked industrial avarice of employers would create a class of "breadless and impotent" workers. When they struck for higher wages in 1860, the shoemakers of Massachusetts linked the encroachments of capital with an attack upon their manhood; in the "Cordwainers' Song," they called upon each other to "stand for your rights like men" and "Resolve by your fathers' graves" to emerge victorious and "like men" to "hold onto the last!"[21] Gender also provided the language for belittling the oppressor, for working men often expressed their rage—and reaffirmed the importance of their own manhood—by impugning the masculinity of their employers. The "Mechanic" sneered at "[t]he employers and those who hang on their skirts."[22]

In the midst of the upheavals of the antebellum economy, however, it was not only employers who threatened the old artisan definitions of manhood. Because an entire way of life was being undermined, so the dangers seemed to arise from everywhere in the new social order—including from wage-earning women themselves. In fact, women seldom directly imperiled men's jobs. The young women who went to Lowell were entering an essentially new industry. Moreover, in their families and hired out on an individual basis, carding, spinning, fulling, and even, to some extent, weaving had long been a part of women's work. . . .

But if wage-earning women did not directly challenge men's jobs, their very presence in the new paid labor force may have underscored the precariousness of men's position as wage-earners. Particularly given the post-Revolutionary emphasis on the importance of women's remaining in the home to cultivate the private virtues, females who were visible as outworkers and operatives may have seemed to bespeak an "unnaturalness" in society—an inability of wage-earning men to establish proper households. Like the witches of the seventeenth century, wage-earning women became symbols of the threats posed to a particular concept of manhood—in this instance, a concept that identified male claims to authority and power with the status of sole wage-earner. As they grappled with the precariousness of their own positions, laboring-class men focused their anxieties on the women who were their wives, daughters, and sisters, as well as on the men who were their employers.

They expressed these anxieties in two forms. First, wage-earning men complained that women were taking jobs—and thus the proper masculine role—away from men. An 1836 report of the National Trades Union charged that because women's wages were so low, a woman's "efforts to sustain herself and family are actually the same as tying a stone around the neck of her natural protector, Man, and destroying him with the weight she has brought to his assistance." Not uncommonly, working men suggested that women did not really need to work for money and castigated "the girl, or the woman, as the case may be, who being in a condition to live comfortably at home by proper economy" selfishly took work from the truly needy. In 1831, the *Working Man's Advocate* called upon "those females who . . . are not dependent on their labor for a living" to withdraw from paid work so that men might have the jobs.[23]

At the same time, working men organized to call for "the family wage"—a wage packet for the male "breadwinner" high enough to permit his wife and children to withdraw from paid work. As Martha May has pointed out, the family wage "promised a means to diminish capitalists' control over family life, by allowing workingmen to provide independently for their families." But the demand for the family wage also signalled the gendering of the emerging class system, and, in this, the gendering of early industrial culture. Identifying the husband as the proper and "natural" wage-earner, the family wage ideal reinforced a distinctive male claim to the role of "breadwinner." By nature, women were ill-suited to wage-earning, many laboring-class men insisted. The National Trades' Union called attention to Women's "physical organization" and "moral sensibilities" as evidence of her unfitness for paid labor, and the anonymous "mechanic" focused on "the fragile character of a girl's constitution, [and] her peculiar liability to sickness."[24] Presumably, only men had the constitution for regular, paid labor.

It is tempting to see in the antebellum ideology of spheres a simple extension of the Puritan injunction to wives to be keepers at home and faithful helpmates to men. Certainly, the two sets of beliefs were related. The colonists brought with them a conviction that men and women were socially different beings, so created by God and so designated in the order of nature. Both were meant to labor, but they were meant to labor at different tasks. Perhaps even more important, they were meant to occupy quite different stations in social life and to exercise quite different levels of control over economic life. . . . "Labor" may have been a gender-neutral term in colonial culture, but "authority" and "property" were masculine concepts, while "dependence" and "subordination" were clearly feminine conditions. . . .

The origins of the antebellum gender culture were as much in the particular conditions of early industrialization as in the inherited past, however. . . . [T]he specific character of the nineteenth-century gender culture was dictated less by transformations in women's experience than by transformations in men's.

To be sure, the principle of male dominance persisted into the nineteenth century.... Social power in the antebellum Northeast rested increasingly on the ability to command the instruments of production and to accumulate and reinvest profits. From these activities wives were legally barred, as they were from formal political processes that established the ground rules for the development of industrial capitalism. While most men were also eliminated from the contest on other grounds (race, class, and ethnicity, primarily), one had to be male to get into the competition at all....

With the demise of the artisan system, and so of a man's hopes to pass along a trade to his sons, the practical grounds on which a laboring man might lay claim to the role of male head-of-household had altered. Increasingly, it was less his position as future benefactor of the next generation than his position as the provider of the present generation (that is, the "breadwinner") that established a man's familial authority.

For men of the emerging middle class, the stakes were equally high but somewhat different. Many of these were the sons and grandsons of middling farmers, forebears who, while not wealthy, had established their adulthood through the ownership of land, and whose role within the family had been centrally that of the "father." Their power residing in their control of inheritance to the next generation—these were men who might have been described with some degree of accuracy as "patriarchs." But by the second decade of the nineteenth century middling farms throughout much of the Northeast were scarcely capable of supporting the present generation; much less were they sizeable or fertile enough to establish patriarchal control of the family. Simultaneously, the emergence of an increasingly industrialized and urbanized society rendered the inheritance of land a less useful and less attractive investment in the future for sons. Even successful businessmen and professionals experienced diminishing control over their sons' economic futures. A son might still read the law with his father, but new law schools, like medical schools, foreshadowed the time when specialized education, rather than on-the-job training with his father or his father's friends, would offer a young man the best chance for success....

Early industrialization preserved the principle of male dominance, then, but in a new form: the "husband" replaced the "father." Men claimed social authority—and indeed exercised economic control—not because they owned the material resources upon which subsequent generations would be founded, but because they owned the resources upon which the present generations subsisted. More important, they had established hegemony over the definition of those resources. In the gender culture of the antebellum Northeast, subsistence was purchased by wages—and men were the wage-earners.

Early industrialization had simultaneously redefined the paradigm that guided the social and economic position of women. . . . [T]he paradigm of womanhood shifted from "goodwife" to "mother"—that is, from "worker" to "nurturer." . . . [W]hat-ever cultural authority women gained as "mothers" was at the direct cost of a social identity in the terms that counted most in the nineteenth century—that is, as workers. As Caroline Dall noted in 1860, most Americans cherished "that old idea, that all men support all women. . . ." Dall recognized this to be "an absurd fiction," but it was a fiction with enormous social consequences. Even when women did enter paid work, their preeminent social identity as "mothers" (in distinct contrast to "workers") made their status as producers in the economy suspect: the predisposition to consider women "unfit" helped to justify underpaying them.[25]

In all of this, the pastoralization of housework implicitly reinforced both the social right and the power of husbands and capitalists to claim the surplus value of women's labor, both paid and unpaid. It accomplished this by rendering the economic dimension of the labor invisible, thereby making pointless the very question of exploitation: one cannot confiscate what does not exist. Since the ideology of spheres made the non-economic character of housework a simple fact of nature, few observers in the antebellum Northeast felt compelled to argue the point.

The ideology of spheres did not affect all women in the same way, of course. Insisting that the domestic ideal was founded in the nature of Woman (and not in the nature of society), prescriptive writers saw its embodiments everywhere—from the poorest orphan on the streets, to the mechanic's daughter, to the merchant's wife. But their models transparently were meant to be the women of the emerging middle class. It was, after all, in the middle classes that women had presumably been freed from the necessity for labor that had characterized the colonial helpmate; there, that mothers and wives had supposedly been enabled to express their fullest capacities in the service of family formation. In celebrations of middle-class "Motherhood" lay the fullest embodiments of the marginalization of housewives as workers.

But if middle-class women were encased in the image of the nurturant (and nonlaboring) mother, working-class women found that their visible inability to replicate that model worked equally hard against them. As historian Christine Stansell has vividly demonstrated, the inability (or unwillingness) of working-class women to remain in their homes—that is, their need to go out into the streets, as vendors, washerwomen, prostitutes, or simply as neighbors helping a friend out—provided the excuse for a growing middle-class intrusion into working-class households, as reformers claimed that women who could not (or did not wish to) aspire to middle-class standards were defined as poor mothers.[26]

In addition to its specific implications for women, the ideology of spheres, and the pastoralization of housework which lay at the heart of that ideology, both represented and supported larger cultural changes attendant upon the evolution of early industrial capitalism. The transition of industrialization was not purely material: it was ideological as well, involving and requiring new ways of viewing the relationship of labor to its products and of the worker to his or her work. In its denial of the economic value of one form of labor, the pastoralization of housework signalled the growing devaluation of labor in general in industrial America. Artisans were discovering, and would continue to discover, what housewives learned early in the nineteenth century: as the old skills were debased, and gradually replaced by new ones, workers' social claims to the fruits of their labor would be severely undercut. Increasingly, productivity was attributed, not to workers, but to those "most wonderful machines."[27] It was in part against such a redefinition that the craft workers of New York and the shoemakers of Lynn, Massachusetts, struggled.[28]

The denial of the economic value of housework was also one aspect of a tendency, originating much earlier but growing throughout the eighteenth and nineteenth centuries, to draw ever-finer distinctions between the values of different categories of labor, and to elevate certain forms of economic activity to a superior status on the grounds of the income they produced. As with housework, these distinctions were rarely founded on the actual material value of the labor in question. Rather, they were based on contemporary levels of power and wealth, and served to justify those existing conditions. An industrialist or financier presumably deserved to earn very sizeable amounts of money, because in accumulating capital he had clearly contributed more labor and labor of a more valuable kind to society than had, for example, a drayman or a foundry worker. . . .

Finally, the ideology of spheres functioned to support the emergence of the wage system necessary to the development of industrial capitalism. The success of the wage system depends upon a number of factors—among them the perception of money as a neutral index of economic value and the acceptance of the wage as representing a fair "livelihood." The devaluation of housework was a part of a larger process of obscuring the continuation of and necessity for barter-based exchanges in the American economy. In this, it veiled the reliance of the family on resources other than those provided through paid labor and heightened the visibility of the wage as the source of family maintenance.

But how did women respond to the growing devaluation of their contributions as laborers in the family economy? . . . [I]n their private letters and diaries, wives quietly offered their own definition of what constituted the livelihood of their families, posing their own perception of the importance of conservation and stewardship against the cash-based index of the marketplace and easily integrating the family's periodic needs for extra cash into their understanding of their own obligations.

Nevertheless, among the public voices affirming that Woman was meant for a different sphere than Man, and that the employments of Woman in the home were of a spiritual rather than an economic nature, were the voices of many women. In *Woman in America,* for example, Mrs. A. J. Graves declared: "... home is [woman's] appropriate sphere of action; and ... whenever she neglects these duties, or goes out of this sphere ... she is deserting the station which God and nature have assigned to her." Underscoring the stark contrast between Woman's duties in the household and Man's in "the busy and turbulent world," Graves described the refuge of the home in terms as solemn as any penned by men during the antebellum period: "... our husbands and our sons ... will rejoice to return to its sanctuary of rest," she averred, "there to refresh their wearied spirits, and renew their strength for the toils and conflicts of life."[29]

Graves was not unusual in her endorsement of the ideology of spheres and of the pastoralization of housework. Even those women who most championed the continuing importance of women's household labor often couched that position in the language of spheres. No one more graphically illustrates this combination than Catharine Beecher, at once probably the most outspoken defender of the importance of women's domestic labor and one of the chief proponents of the ideology of female domesticity. ... Beecher was clear and insistent that housework was hard work, and she did not shrink from suggesting that its demands and obligations were very similar to men's "business." In her *Treatise on Domestic Economy*, Beecher went so far as to draw a specific analogy between the marriage contract and the wage labor contract:

> No woman is forced to obey any husband but the one she chooses for herself; nor is she obliged to take a husband, if she prefers to remain single. So every domestic, and every artisan or laborer, after passing from parental control, can choose the employer to whom he is to accord obedience, or, if he prefers to relinquish certain advantages, he can remain without taking a subordinate place to any employer.

Nevertheless, Beecher regularly characterized women's work in the home as the occupation merely of administering "the gentler charities of life," a "mission" chiefly of "self-denial" to "lay up treasures, not on earth, but in heaven." This employment she contrasts with the "toils" of Man, to whom was "appointed the out-door labor—to till the earth, dig the mines, toil in the foundries, traverse the ocean, transport the merchandise, labor in manufactories, construct houses ... and all the heavy work. ..."[30]

Beecher's apparently self-defeating endorsement of a view that ultimately discounted the value of women's labor arose from many sources, not the least of which was her own identification with the larger middle-class interests served by the ideology of spheres. Beecher enjoyed the new standing afforded middle-class women by their roles as moral guardians to their families and to societies, and based much of her own claim to status as a woman on the presumed differences between herself and immigrant and laboring-class women. For example, she ended an extended discussion of "the care of Servants" in *The American Woman's Home* with the resigned conclusion that "[t]he mistresses of American families, whether they like it or not, have the duties of missionaries imposed upon them by that class from which our supply of domestic servants is drawn."[31]

But, also like many women in antebellum America, Catharine Beecher was sharply aware of the power difference between males and females. It was a theme to which she constantly returned in her writings, especially in her discussions of women's rights. ... In her *Essay on Slavery and Abolitionism*, Beecher was quite explicit about the reasons why a woman might cloak herself and her positions in the language of dependency and subordination:

> [T]he moment woman begins to feel the promptings of ambition, or the thirst for power, her aegis of defence is gone. All the sacred protection of religion, all the generous promptings of chivalry, all the poetry of romantic gallantry, depend upon woman's retaining her place as dependent and defenceless, and making no claims. ...

It was much the same point that Elizabeth Ellet would later make in her *The Practical Housekeeper:* since men had many more alternatives than women, the smart woman made it her "policy" to create an appearance of domestic serenity.[32]

But it would be a mistake to read women's endorsement of the pastoralization of housework purely as a protective strategy. Women were not immune from the values of their communities, and many wives appear to have shared the perception of the larger society that their work had separated from the economic life of the community and that it was, in fact, not really work at all.

Those misgivings were nowhere more evident than in the letter that Harriet Beecher Stowe wrote to her sister-in-law, Sarah Beecher, in 1850. It was the first opportunity Harriet had had to write since the Stowes had moved to Brunswick, Maine, the spring before. Since her arrival with the children, she explained, she had "made two sofas—or lounges—a barrel chair—divers bedspreads—pillowcases—pillows—bolsters—matresses . . . painted rooms . . . [and] revarnished furniture." She had also laid a month-long siege at the landlord's door, lobbying him to install a new sink. Meanwhile, she had given birth to her eighth child, made her way through the novels of Sir Walter Scott, and tried to meet the obligations of her increasingly active career as an author—all of this while also attending to the more mundane work of running a household: dealing with tradespeople, cooking, and taking care of the children. From delivery bed to delivery cart, downstairs to the kitchen, upstairs to the baby, out to a neighbor's, home to stir the stew, the image of Stowe flies through these pages like the specter of the sorcerer's apprentice.

Halfway through the letter, Stowe paused. "And yet," she confided to her sister-in-law, "I am constantly pursued and haunted by the idea that I don't do anything."[33] It is a jarring note in a letter—and a life—so shaped by the demands of housework. That a skilled and loving mother could impart dignity and a sense of humane purpose to a family otherwise vulnerable to the degradations of the marketplace, Stowe had no doubt. But was that really "work"? She was less certain. In that uncertainty, to borrow Daniel Eddy's words, lay "a world of domestic meaning"—for housewives of the antebellum era, and for women since.

Notes

1. See Luisella Goldschmidt-Clermont, *Unpaid Work in the Household: A Review of Economic Evaluation Methods* (Geneva, 1982).

2. See Edgar Martin, *The Standard of Living in 1860: American Consumption Levels on the Eve of the Civil War* (Chicago, 1942), p. 177; and Faye Dudden, *Serving Women: Household Service in Nineteenth-Century America* (Middletown, Conn., 1983), p. 149.

3. This is calculated on the basis of an average weekly budget for a working-class family of five, as itemized in the New York *Daily Tribune*, May 27, 1851. See also Martin, *Standard of Living*, p. 122.

4. The New York *Daily Tribune*, May 27, 1851.

5. Martin, *Standard of Living*, p. 168.

6. Grant Thorburn, *Sketches from the Note-book of Lurie Todd* (New York, 1847), p. 12.

7. See Alice Kessler-Harris and Karen Brodlin Sacks, "The Demise of Domesticity in America," *Women, Households, and the Economy*, ed. Lourdes Beneria and Catherine R. Stimpson (New Brunswick, N.J., 1987), p. 67.

8. Quoted in Norman Ware, *The Industrial Worker, 1840–1860: The Reaction of American Industrial Society to the Advance of the Industrial Revolution* (New York, 1924; reprinted Gloucester, Mass., 1959), p. 77.

9. Jesse T. Peck, *The True Woman; or, Life and Happiness at Home and Abroad* (New York, 1857), p. 245.

10. *The Ladies Museum*, July 16, 1825, p. 3; Henry Ward Beecher, *Lectures to Young Men, on Various Important Subjects* (Boston, 1846), pp. 87, 91.

11. Peck, *The True Woman*, pp. 242–43.

12. *The Mother's Rule: or, The Right Way and the Wrong Way*, ed. T. S. Arthur (Philadelphia, 1856), p. 261; William A. Alcott, *The Young Wife, or, Duties of Woman in the Marriage Relation* (Boston, 1837), p. 149.

13. Daniel C. Eddy, *The Young Woman's Friend; or the Duties, Trials, Loves, and Hopes of Woman* (Boston, 1857), p. 23.

14. Alcott, *The Young Wife*, pp. 84–85.

15. For an excellent discussion of the concept of female "influence," see Lori D. Ginzburg, *Women and the Work of Benevolence: Morality and Politics in the Northeastern United States, 1820–1885* (New Haven, Conn., 1990).

16. J. H. Agnew, "Women's Offices and Influence," *Harper's New Monthly Magazine* 17:no. 3 (Oct. 1851):654–57, quote on p. 657.

17. Washington Irving, "The Wife," *Ladies Literary Cabinet*, July 4, 1819, pp. 82–84. Quotations are from Washington Irving, *The Sketch Book of Geoffrey Crayon, Gent.* (New York, 1961), pp. 34–36.

18. "Pastoral Letter of the Massachusetts Congregationalist Clergy" (1837) in *Up From the Pedestal: Selected Writings in the History of American Feminism*, ed. Aileen S. Kraditor (Chicago, 1968), pp. 51–52; Reverend Hubbard Winslow, *A Discourse Delivered in the Bowdoin Street Church* (Boston, 1837), p. 8.

19. *The Man*, May 13, 1835; *Life, Speeches, Labors, and Essays of William H. Sylvis*, ed. James C. Sylvis (Philadelphia, 1872), p. 120.

20. *The Rights of All*, June 12, 1829; *The Northern Star and Freeman's Advocate*, Dec. 8, 1842, and Jan. 2, 1843.

21. Moore is quoted in Sean Wilentz, *Chants Democratic: New York City and the Rise of the American Working Class, 1788–1850* (New York, 1986), p. 239. The "Cordwainers' Song" is printed in Alan Dawley, *Class and Community: The Industrial Revolution in Lynn* (Cambridge, Mass., 1976), pp. 82–83.

22. "A Mechanic," *Elements of Social Disorder: A Plea for the Working Classes in the United States* (Providence, R.I., 1844), p. 96.

23. Quoted in John Andrews and W. D. P. Bliss, *A History of Women in Trade Unions*, vol. 10 of *Report*

on Condition of Woman and Child Earners in the United States, Senate Doc. 645, 61st Cong., 2d Sess. (Washington, D.C., 1911; reprint ed. New York, 1974), p. 48; "Mechanic," *Elements of Social Disorder,* p. 45; *Working Man's Advocate,* June 11, 1831.

24. Martha May, "Bread Before Roses: American Workingmen, Labor Unions and the Family Wage," in *Women, Work, and Protest: A Century of U.S. Women's Labor History,* ed. Ruth Milkman (Boston, 1985), p. 4; vol. 6 of *A Documentary History of American Industrial Society,* ed. John R. Commons et al. (New York, 1958), p. 281; "Mechanic," *Elements of Social Disorder,* p. 42.

25. Caroline Dall, *"Woman's Right to Labor"; or, Low Wages and Hard Work* (Boston, 1860), p. 57.

26. Christine Stansell, *City of Women: Sex and Class in New York,* 1789–1860 (New York, 1986), pp. 193–216.

27. The phrase is from the title of Judith McGaw's study, *Most Wonderful Machine: Mechanization and Social Change in Berkshire Papermaking, 1801–1885* (Princeton, 1987).

28. See Wilentz, *Chants Democratic;* and Dawley, *Class and Community,* cited in n. 21 above.

29. Mrs. A. J. Garves, *Woman in America: Being an Examination into the Morals and Intellectual Condition of American Female Society* (New York, 1841), p. 156.

30. Catharine E. Beecher, *A Treatise on Domestic Economy, for the Use of Young Ladies at Home, and at School* (Boston, 1841), p. 26; Beecher, *An Essay on Slavery and Abolitionism, with Reference to the Duty of American Females* (Philadelphia, 1837), p. 128; Catharine E. Beecher and Harriet Beecher Stowe, *The American Woman's Home, or Principles of Domestic Science* (Hartford, Conn., 1975), p. 19.

31. Beecher and Stowe, *The American Woman's Home,* p. 327.

32. Beecher, *Essay on Slavery and Abolitionism,* pp. 101–2; *The Practical Housekeeper; a Cyclopaedia of Domestic Economy,* ed. Mrs. [Elizabeth] Ellet (New York, 1857), p. 17.

33. Harriet Beecher Stowe to Sarah Buckingham Beecher, Dec. 17 [1850], The Schlesinger Library, Radcliffe College, Cambridge, Mass.

DOCUMENT

Working Conditions in Early Factories, 1845

"She complained of the hours for labor being too many . . ."

The textile factories of the first wave of industrialization might not have been built at all had their owners not believed they could count on a steady supply of cheap female labor. The history of industrialization as it affected both men and women needs to be understood in the context of the segmented labor market that women entered. Women were a major part of the first new work force that was shaped into "modern" work patterns: long, uninterrupted hours of labor in a mechanized factory with little or no room for individual initiative.

One of the earliest mill towns was Lowell, Massachusetts, where factory owners began recruiting young, unmarried women to work in six textile mills in 1823. Rural young women already toiled at home at farm labor and also at "outwork," making goods that could be sold for cash. Compared to the work they had done at home, mill work at first seemed to pay well and to offer new opportunities. The Lowell mills developed a system of boardinghouses, which assured families that girls would live in wholesome surroundings. Letters sent home and fiction published by young women in the first wave of employment often testified to their pride in the financial independence that their new work brought.

Work in the mills was strictly segregated by sex: men were supervisors and skilled mechanics; women attended the spinning and weaving machinery. The daily earnings of almost all female workers depended on piece rates—the number of pieces or the output of the particular machine they tended. Their wages ranged from one-third to one-half that of men; the highest-paid woman generally earned less than the lowest-paid man. Employers responded to economic downturns in the 1830s either by lowering wages or by requiring more pieces per day. Mills established stricter discipline: workers who were insubordinate were fired; those who did not fulfill their yearlong contracts were blacklisted. But boardinghouse life meant that the factory women developed strong support networks; when their wages were cut and work hours lengthened in the 1830s, those who lived together came together in opposition to the owners and staged some of the earliest industrial strikes in American history. In 1836, 1,500 women walked

Excerpted from "The First Official Investigation of Labor Conditions in Massachusetts," in *A Documentary History of American Industrial Society*, vol. 8, ed. John R. Commons, Ulrich B. Phillips, Eugene A. Gilmore, Helen L. Sumner, and John B. Andrews (Cleveland, 1910), pp. 133–42.

Women at textile machinery in a New England mill, approximately 1850. Note the poor lighting and the absence of anything to sit on during the long hours at the machines. (Courtesy of George Eastman House.)

out in protest, claiming their inheritance as "Daughters of the Revolution." One manifesto stated: "As our fathers resisted unto blood the lordly avarice of the British ministry, so we, their daughters, never will wear the yoke which has been prepared for us."*

In January 1845, led by the indomitable worker Sarah Bagley, the Female Labor Reform Association organized a petition drive throughout the region, which forced the Massachusetts legislature to hold the first public hearings on industrial working conditions ever held in the United States. On February 13, 1845, Eliza Hemmingway and Sarah Bagley had their chance to testify. What did they think it was important for the legislators to know?

. . . The first petitioner who testified was Eliza R. Hemmingway. She had worked 2 years and 9 months in the Lowell Factories . . . Her employment is weaving—works by the piece. . . . and attends one loom. Her wages average from $16 to $23 a month exclusive of board. She complained of the hours for labor being too many, and the time for meals too limited. In the summer season, the work is commenced at 5 o'clock, a.m., and continued

*Thomas Dublin, *Women at Work: The Transformation of Work and Community in Lowell, Massachusetts, 1826–1860* (New York: Columbia University Press, 1979), p.98.

till 7 o'clock, p.m., with half an hour for breakfast and three quarters of an hour for dinner. During eight months of the year, but half an hour is allowed for dinner. The air in the room she considered not to be wholesome. There were 293 small [oil] lamps and 61 large lamps lighted in the room in which she worked, when evening work is required. These lamps are also lighted sometimes in the morning. About 130 females, 11 men, and 12 children (between the ages of 11 and 14) work in the room with her . . . The children work but 9 months out of 12. The other 3 months they must attend school. Thinks that there is no day when there are less than six of the females out of the mill from sickness. Has known as many as thirty. She herself, is out quite often, on account of sickness. . . .

She thought there was a general desire among the females to work but ten hours, regardless of pay. . . . She knew of one girl who last winter went into the mill at half past 4 o'clock, a.m. and worked till half past 7 o'clock, p.m. She did so to make more money. She earned from $25 to $30 per month. There is always a large number of girls at the gate wishing to get in before the bell rings. . . . They do this to make more wages. A large number come to Lowell to make money to aid their parents who are poor. She knew of many cases where married women came to Lowell and worked in the mills to assist their husbands to pay for their farms. . . .

Miss Sarah G. Bagley said she had worked in the Lowell Mills eight years and a half . . . She is a weaver, and works by the piece. . . . She thinks the health of the operatives is not so good as the health of females who do housework or millinery business. The chief evil, so far as health is concerned, is the shortness of time allowed for meals. The next evil is the length of time employed—not giving them time to cultivate their minds. . . . She had presented a petition, same as the one before the Committee, to 132 girls, most of whom said that they would prefer to work but ten hours. In a pecuniary point of view, it would be better, as their health would be improved. They would have more time for sewing. Their intellectual, moral and religious habits would also be benefited by the change. . . .

On Saturday the 1st of March, a portion of the Committee went to Lowell to examine the mills, and to observe the general appearance of the operatives. . . . [The Committee concluded:] Not only is the interior of the mills kept in the best order, but great regard has been paid by many of the agents to the arrangement of the enclosed grounds. Grass plats have been laid out, trees have been planted . . . everything in and about the mills, and the boarding houses appeared, to have for its end, health and comfort. . . . The [average hours of work per day throughout the year was 11½; the workday was longest in April, when it reached 13½ hours].

CARROLL SMITH-ROSENBERG

The Female World of Love and Ritual: Relations between Women in Nineteenth-Century America

Carroll Smith-Rosenberg's close reading of middle-class girls' and women's diaries and letters to explore the nature of their intense friendships represented a radically new approach when it was published in 1975. It was pioneering in several areas of inquiry that have since become familiar—not just women's and gender history, but the histories of sexuality, family life, and emotions. Note that the essay was published in the pathbreaking, multidisciplinary, community-building women's studies journal *Signs*—and as the opening article in its first issue. As you read it, think about why the essay would have been disconcerting and challenging to many, if not most, members of the historical profession in the 1970s.

The author's work reflected the reinvigorated practices of women's history in the early 1970s, part of the transformation of scholarship and academia wrought by second-wave feminism. But new historical research on gender and sexuality took years to reach publication and constitute a critical mass. College teachers compiling syllabi for courses on women's history coped with a dramatic scarcity of secondary material that they could assign (see pp. 746–751). Unlike the rich resources at our fingertips today, there were no women's history textbooks, syntheses, journals, or websites to consult.

Today, Smith-Rosenberg's nuanced analysis remains a touchstone for scholars' continuing investigation and vigorous debate on the historical existence and meanings of women's same-sex friendships, partnerships, and loves globally.*

The female friendship of the nineteenth century, the long-lived, intimate, loving friendship between two women, is an excellent example of the type of historical phenomena which most historians know something about, which few have thought much about, and which virtually no one has written about.[1] It is one aspect of the female experience which consciously or unconsciously we have chosen to ignore. Yet an abundance of manuscript evidence suggests that eighteenth- and nineteenth-century women routinely formed emotional ties with other women. Such deeply felt, same-sex friendships were casually accepted in American society. Indeed, from at least the late eighteenth through the mid-nineteenth century, a female

*Leila Rupp, *Sapphistries: A Global History of Love between Women* (New York: New York University Press, 2009; Judith M. Bennett, "'Lesbian-like' and the Social History of Lesbianisms," *Journal of the History of Sexuality* 9 (2000): 1–24. For another pioneering integration of sexuality and social history, see Blanche Wiesen Cook, "Female Support Networks and Political Activism: Lillian Wald, Crystal Eastman, Emma Goldman," *Chrysalis* 3 (1977): 43–61.

world of varied and yet highly structured relationships appears to have been an essential aspect of American society. These relationships ranged from the supportive love of sisters, through the enthusiasms of adolescent girls, to sensual avowals of love by mature women. It was a world in which men made but a shadowy appearance.[2]

Defining and analyzing same-sex relationships involves the historian in deeply problematical questions of method and interpretation. This is especially true since historians, influenced by Freud's libidinal theory, have discussed these relationships almost exclusively within the context of individual psychosexual developments or, to be more explicit, psychopathology.[3] Seeing same-sex relationships in terms of a dichotomy between normal and abnormal, they have sought the origins of such apparent deviance in childhood or adolescent trauma and detected the symptoms of "latent" homosexuality in the lives of both those who later became "overtly" homosexual and those who did not. Yet theories concerning the nature and origins of same-sex relationships are frequently contradictory or based on questionable or arbitrary data. In recent years such hypotheses have been subjected to criticism both from within and without the psychological professions. Historians who seek to work within a psychological framework, therefore, are faced with two hard questions: Do sound psychodynamic theories concerning the nature and origins of same-sex relationships exist? If so, does the historical datum exist which would permit the use of such dynamic models?

I would like to suggest an alternative approach to female friendships—one which would view them within a cultural and social setting rather than from an exclusively individual psychosexual perspective. Only by thus altering our approach will we be in the position to evaluate the appropriateness of particular dynamic interpretations. Intimate friendships between men and men and women and women existed in a larger world of social relations and social values. To interpret such friendships more fully they must be related to the structure of the American family and to the nature of sex-role divisions and of male-female relations both within the family and in society generally. The female friendship must not be seen in isolation; it must be analyzed as one aspect of women's overall relations with one another. The ties between mothers and daughters, sisters, female cousins and friends, at all stages of the female life cycle constitute the most suggestive framework for the historian to begin an analysis of intimacy and affection between women. Such an analysis would not only emphasize general cultural patterns rather than the internal dynamics of a particular family or childhood; it would shift the focus of the study from a concern with deviance to that of defining configurations of legitimate behavioral norms and options.[4]

This analysis will be based upon the correspondence and diaries of women and men in thirty-five families between the 1760s and the 1880s. These families, though limited in number, represented a broad range of the American middle class, from hard-pressed pioneer families and orphaned girls to daughters of the intellectual and social elite. It includes families from most geographic regions, rural and urban, and a spectrum of Protestant denominations ranging from Mormon to orthodox Quaker. Although scarcely a comprehensive sample of America's increasingly heterogeneous population, it does, I believe, reflect accurately the literate middle class to which the historian working with letters and diaries is necessarily bound. It has involved an analysis of many thousands of letters written to women friends, kin, husbands, brothers, and children at every period of life from adolescence to old age. Some collections encompass virtually entire life spans; one contains over 100,000 letters as well as diaries and account books. It is my contention that an analysis of women's private letters and diaries which were never intended to be published permits the historian to explore a very private world of emotional realities central both to women's lives and to the middle-class family in nineteenth-century America.[5]

The question of female friendships is peculiarly elusive; we know so little or perhaps have forgotten so much. An intriguing and almost alien form of human relationship, they flourished in a different social structure and amidst different sexual norms. Before attempting to reconstruct their social setting, therefore, it might be best first to describe two not atypical friendships. These two friendships, intense, loving, and openly avowed, began during the women's adolescence and, despite subsequent marriages and geographic separation, continued throughout their lives. For nearly half a century these women played a central emotional role in each other's lives, writing time and again of their love and of the pain of separation. Paradoxically to twentieth-century minds, their love appears to have been both sensual and platonic.

Sarah Butler Wister first met Jeannie Field Musgrove while vacationing with her family at Stockbridge, Massachusetts, in the summer of 1849.[6] Jeannie was then sixteen, Sarah fourteen. During two subsequent years spent together in boarding school, they formed a deep and intimate friendship. Sarah began to keep a bouquet of flowers before Jeannie's portrait and wrote complaining of the intensity and anguish of her affection.[7] Both young women assumed nom de plumes, Jeannie a female name, Sarah a male one; they would use these secret names into old age.[8] They frequently commented on the nature of their affection: "If the day should come," Sarah wrote Jeannie in the spring of 1861, "when you failed me either through your fault or my own, I would forswear all human friendship, thenceforth." A few months later Jeannie commented: "Gratitude is a word I should never use toward you. It is perhaps a misfortune of such intimacy and love that it makes one regard all kindness as a matter of course, as one has always found it, as natural as the embrace in meeting."[9]

Sarah's marriage altered neither the frequency of their correspondence nor their desire to be together. In 1864, when twenty-nine, married, and a mother, Sarah wrote to Jeannie: "I shall be entirely alone [this coming week]. I can give you no idea how desperately I shall want you. . . ." After one such visit Jeannie, then a spinster in New York, echoed Sarah's longing: "Dear darling Sarah! How I love you & how happy I have been! You are the joy of my life. . . . I cannot tell you how much happiness you gave me, nor how constantly it is all in my thoughts. . . . My darling how I long for the time when I shall see you. . . . " After another visit Jeannie wrote: "I want you to tell me in your next letter, to assure me, that I am your dearest. . . . I do not doubt you, & I am not jealous but I long to hear you say it once more & it seems already a long time since your voice fell on my ear. So just fill a quarter page with caresses & expressions of endearment. Your silly Angelina." Jeannie ended one letter: "Goodbye my dearest, dearest lover—ever your own Angelina." And another, "I will go to bed . . . [though] I could write all night—A thousand kisses—I love you with my whole soul—your Angelina."

When Jeannie finally married in 1870 at the age of thirty-seven, Sarah underwent a period of extreme anxiety. Two days before Jeannie's marriage Sarah, then in London, wrote desperately: "Dearest darling—How incessantly have I thought of you these eight days—all today—the entire uncertainty, the distance, the long silence—are all new features in my separation from you, grevious to be borne. . . . Oh Jeannie. I have thought & thought & yearned over you these two days. Are you married I wonder? My dearest love to you wherever and whoever you are."[10] Like many other women in this collection of thirty-five families, marriage brought Sarah and Jeannie physical separation; it did not cause emotional distance. Although at first they may have wondered how marriage would affect their relationship, their affection remained unabated throughout their lives, underscored by their loneliness and their desire to be together.[11]

During the same years that Jeannie and Sarah wrote of their love and need for each other, two slightly younger women began a similar odyssey of love, dependence and—ultimately—physical, though not emotional, separation. Molly and Helena met in 1868 while both attended the Cooper Institute School of Design for Women in New York City. For several years these young women studied and explored the city together, visited each other's families, and formed part of a social network of other artistic young women. Gradually, over the years, their initial friendship deepened into a close intimate bond which continued throughout their lives. The tone in the letters which Molly wrote to Helena changed over these years from "My dear Helena," and signed "your attached friend," to "My dearest Helena," "My Dearest," "My Beloved," and signed "Thine always" or "thine Molly."[12]

The letters they wrote to each other during these first five years permit us to reconstruct something of their relationship together. As Molly wrote in one early letter:

> I have not said to you in so many or so few words that I was happy with you during those few so incredibly short weeks but surely you do not need

> words to tell you what you must know. Those two or three days so dark without, so bright with firelight and contentment within I shall always remember as proof that, for a time, at least—I fancy for quite a long time—we might be sufficient for each other. We know that we can amuse each other for many idle hours together and now we know that we can also work together. And that means much, don't you think so?

She ended: "I shall return in a few days. Imagine yourself kissed many times by one who loved you so dearly."

The intensity and even physical nature of Molly's love was echoed in many of the letters she wrote during the next few years, as, for instance in this short thank-you note for a small present: "Imagine yourself kissed a dozen times my darling. Perhaps it is well for you that we are far apart. You might find my thanks so expressed rather overpowering. I have that delightful feeling that it doesn't matter much what I say or how I say it, since we shall meet so soon and forget in that moment that we were ever separated. . . . I shall see you soon and be content."[13]

At the end of the fifth year, however, several crises occurred. The relationship, at least in its intense form, ended, though Molly and Helena continued an intimate and complex relationship for the next half-century. The exact nature of these crises is not completely clear, but it seems to have involved Molly's decision not to live with Helena, as they had originally planned, but to remain at home because of parental insistence. Molly was now in her late twenties. Helena responded with anger and Molly became frantic at the thought that Helena would break off their relationship. Though she wrote distraught letters and made despairing attempts to see Helena, the relationship never regained its former ardor—possibly because Molly had a male suitor.[14] Within six months Helena had decided to marry a man who was, coincidentally, Molly's friend and publisher. Two years later Molly herself finally married. The letters toward the end of this period discuss the transition both women made to having male lovers—Molly spending much time reassuring Helena, who seemed depressed about the end of their relationship and with her forthcoming marriage.[15]

It is clearly difficult from a distance of 100 years and from a post-Freudian cultural perspective to decipher the complexities of Molly and Helena's relationship. Certainly Molly and Helena were lovers—emotionally if not physically. The emotional intensity and pathos of their love becomes apparent in several letters Molly wrote Helena during their crisis: "I wanted so to put my arms round my girl of all the girls in the world and tell her . . . I love her as wives do love their husbands, as *friends* who have taken each other for life—and believe in her, as I believe in my God. . . . If I didn't love you do you suppose I'd care about anything or have ridiculous notions and panics and behave like an old fool who ought to know better. I'm going to hang on to your skirts. . . . You can't get away from [my] love." Or as she wrote after Helena's decision to marry: "You know dear Helena, I really was in love with you. It was a passion such as I had never known until I saw you. I don't think it was the noblest way to love you." The theme of intense female love was one Molly again expressed in a letter she wrote to the man Helena was to marry: "Do you know sir, that until you came along I believe that she loved me almost as girls love their lovers. *I know I loved her so.* Don't you wonder that I can stand the sight of you." This was in a letter congratulating them on their forthcoming marriage.[16]

The essential question is not whether these women had genital contact and can therefore be defined as heterosexual or homosexual. The twentieth-century tendency to view human love and sexuality within a dichotomized universe of deviance and normality, genitality and platonic love, is alien to the emotions and attitudes of the nineteenth century and fundamentally distorts the nature of these women's emotional interaction. These letters are significant because they force us to place such female love in a particular historical context. There is every indication that these four women, their husbands and families—all eminently respectable and socially conservative—considered such love both socially acceptable and fully compatible with heterosexual marriage. Emotionally and cognitively, their heterosocial and their homosocial worlds were complementary.

One could argue, on the other hand, that these letters were but an example of the romantic rhetoric with which the nineteenth century surrounded the concept of friendship. Yet they possess an emotional intensity and a sensual and physical explicitness that is difficult to dismiss. Jeannie longed to hold Sarah in her arms; Molly mourned her physical isolation from Helena. Molly's love and devotion to Helena, the emotions that bound Jeannie and Sarah together, while perhaps a phenomenon of nineteenth-century society, were not the less real for their Victorian origins. A survey of the correspondence and diaries of eighteenth- and nineteenth-century women indicates that Molly, Jeannie, and Sarah represented one very real behavioral and emotional option socially available to nineteenth-century women.

This is not to argue that individual needs, personalities, and family dynamics did not have a significant role in determining the nature of particular relationships. But the scholar must ask if it is historically possible and, if possible, important, to study the intensely individual aspects of psychosexual dynamics. Is it not the historian's first task to explore the social structure and the world view which made intense and sometimes sensual female love both a possible and an acceptable emotional option? From such a social perspective a new and quite different series of questions suggests itself. What emotional function did such female love serve? What was its place within the hetero- and homosocial worlds which women jointly inhabited? Did a spectrum of love-object choices exist in the nineteenth century across which some individuals, at least, were capable of moving? Without attempting to answer these questions it will be difficult to understand either nineteenth-century sexuality or the nineteenth-century family.

Several factors in American society between the mid-eighteenth and the mid-nineteenth centuries may well have permitted women to form a variety of close emotional relationships with other women. American society was characterized in large part by rigid gender-role differentiation within the family and within society as a whole, leading to the emotional segregation of women and men. The roles of daughter and mother shaded imperceptibly and ineluctably into each other, while the biological realities of frequent pregnancies, childbirth, nursing, and menopause bound women together in physical and emotional intimacy. It was within just such a social framework, I would argue, that a specifically female world did indeed develop, a world built around a generic and unself-conscious pattern of single-sex or homosocial networks. These supportive networks were institutionalized in social conventions or rituals which accompanied virtually every important event in a woman's life, from birth to death. Such female relationships were frequently supported and paralleled by severe social restrictions on intimacy between young men and women. Within such a world of emotional richness and complexity devotion to and love of other women became a plausible and socially accepted form of human interaction.

An abundance of printed and manuscript sources exists to support such a hypothesis. Etiquette books, advice books on child rearing, religious sermons, guides to young men and young women, medical texts, and school curricula all suggest that late eighteenth- and most nineteenth-century Americans assumed the existence of a world composed of distinctly male and female spheres, spheres determined by the immutable laws of God and nature.[17] The unpublished letters and diaries of Americans during this same period concur, detailing the existence of sexually segregated worlds inhabited by human beings with different values, expectations, and personalities. Contacts between men and women frequently partook of a formality and stiffness quite alien to twentieth-century America and which today we tend to define as "Victorian." Women, however, did not form an isolated and oppressed subcategory in male society. Their letters and diaries indicate that women's sphere had an essential integrity and dignity that grew out of women's shared experiences and mutual affection and that, despite the profound changes which affected American social structure and institutions between the 1760s and the 1870s, retained a constancy and predictability. The ways in which women thought of and interacted with each other remained unchanged. Continuity, not discontinuity, characterized this female world. Molly Hallock's and Jeannie Field's words, emotions, and experiences have direct parallels in the 1760s and the 1790s.[18] There are indications in contemporary sociological and psychological literature that female closeness and support networks have continued into the twentieth century—not only among ethnic and working-class groups but even among the middle class.[19]

Most eighteenth- and nineteenth-century women lived within a world bounded by home, church, and the institution of visiting—that endless trooping of women to each other's homes for social purposes. It was a world inhabited by children and by other women.[20] Women helped each other with domestic chores and in times of sickness, sorrow, or trouble. Entire days, even weeks, might be spent almost exclusively with other women.[21] Urban and town women could devote virtually every day to visits, teas, or shopping trips with other women. Rural women developed a pattern of more extended visits that lasted weeks and sometimes months, at times even dislodging husbands from their beds and bedrooms so that dear friends might spend every hour of every day together.[22] When husbands traveled, wives routinely moved in with other women, invited women friends to teas and suppers, sat together sharing and comparing the letters they had received from other close women friends. Secrets were exchanged and cherished, and the husband's return at times viewed with some ambivalence.[23]

Summer vacations were frequently organized to permit old friends to meet at water spas or share a country home. In 1848, for example, a young matron wrote cheerfully to her husband about the delightful time she was having with five close women friends whom she had invited to spend the summer with her; he remained at home alone to face the heat of Philadelphia and a cholera epidemic.[24] Some ninety years earlier, two young Quaker girls commented upon the vacation their aunt had taken alone with another woman; their remarks were openly envious and tell us something of the emotional quality of these friendships: "I hear Aunt is gone with the Friend and wont be back for two weeks, fine times indeed I think the old friends had, taking their pleasure about the country . . . and have the advantage of that fine woman's conversation and instruction, while we poor young girls must spend all spring at home. . . . What a disappointment that we are not together. . . ."[25]

Friends did not form isolated dyads but were normally part of highly integrated networks. Knowing each other, perhaps related to each other, they played a central role in holding communities and kin systems together. Especially when families became geographically mobile women's long visits to each other and their frequent letters filled with discussions of marriages and births, illness and deaths, descriptions of growing children, and reminiscences of times and people past provided an important sense of continuity in a rapidly changing society.[26] Central to this female world was an inner core of kin. The ties between sisters, first cousins, aunts, and nieces provided the underlying structure upon which groups of friends and their network of female relatives clustered. Although most of the women within this sample would appear to be living within isolated nuclear families, the emotional ties between nonresidential kin were deep and binding and provided one of the fundamental existential realities of women's lives.[27] Twenty years after Parke Lewis Butler moved with her husband to Louisiana, she sent her two daughters back to Virginia to attend school, live with their grandmother and aunt, and be integrated back into Virginia society.[28] The constant letters between Maria Inskeep and Fanny Hampton, sisters separated in their early twenties when Maria moved with her husband from New Jersey to Louisiana, held their families together, making it possible for their daughters to feel a part of their cousins' network of friends and interests.[29] The Ripley daughters, growing up in western Massachusetts in the early 1800s, spent months each year with their mother's sister and her family in distant Boston; these female cousins and their network of friends exchanged gossip-filled letters and gradually formed deeply loving and dependent ties.[30]

Women frequently spent their days within the social confines of such extended families. Sisters-in-law visited each other and, in some families, seemed to spend more time with each other than with their husbands. First cousins cared for each other's babies—for weeks or even months in times of sickness or childbirth. Sisters helped each other with housework, shopped and sewed for each other. Geographic separation was borne with difficulty. A sister's absence for even a week or two could cause loneliness and depression and would be bridged by frequent letters. Sibling rivalry was hardly unknown, but with separation or illness the theme of deep affection and dependency reemerged.[31]

Sisterly bonds continued across a lifetime. In her old age a rural Quaker matron, Martha Jefferis, wrote to her daughter Anne concerning her own half-sister, Phoebe: "In sister Phoebe I have a real friend—she studies my comfort and waits on me like a child. . . . She is exceedingly kind and this to all other homes (set aside yours) I would prefer—it is next to being with a daughter." Phoebe's own letters confirmed Martha's evaluation of her feelings. "Thou knowest my dear sister," Phoebe wrote, "there is no one . . . that exactly feels [for] thee as I do, for I think without boasting I can truly say that my desire is for thee."[32]

Such women, whether friends or relatives, assumed an emotional centrality in each other's lives. In their diaries and letters they wrote of the joy and contentment they felt in each other's company, their sense of isolation and despair when apart. The regularity of their correspondence underlies the sincerity of their words. Women named their daughters after one another and sought to integrate dear friends into their lives after marriage.[33] As one young bride wrote to an old friend shortly after her marriage: "I want to see you and talk with you and feel that we are united by the same bonds of sympathy and congeniality as ever."[34] After years of friendship one aging woman wrote of another: "Time cannot destroy the fascination of her manner . . . her voice is music to the ear. . . ."[35] Women made elaborate presents for each other, ranging from the Quakers' frugal pies and breads to painted velvet bags and phantom bouquets.[36] When a friend died, their grief was deeply felt. Martha Jefferis was unable to write to her daughter for three weeks because of the sorrow she felt at the death of a dear friend. Such distress was not unusual. A generation earlier a young Massachusetts farm woman filled pages of her diary with her grief at the death of her "dearest friend" and transcribed the letters of condolence other women sent her. She marked the anniversary of Rachel's death each year in her diary, contrasting her faithfulness with that of Rachel's husband who had soon remarried.[37]

These female friendships served a number of emotional functions. Within this secure and empathetic world women could share sorrows, anxieties, and joys, confident that other women had experienced similar emotions. One mid-nineteenth-century rural matron in a letter to her daughter discussed this particular aspect of women's friendships: "To have such a friend as thyself to look to and sympathize with her—and enter into all her little needs and in whose bosom she could with freedom pour forth her joys and sorrows—such a friend would very much relieve the tedium of many a wearisome hour. . . ." A generation later Molly more informally underscored the importance of this same function in a letter to Helena: "Suppose I come down . . . [and] spend Sunday with you quietly," she wrote Helena ". . . that means talking all the time until you are relieved of all your latest troubles, and I of mine. . . ."[38] These were frequently troubles that apparently no man could understand. When Anne Jefferis Sheppard was first married, she and her older sister Edith (who then lived with Anne) wrote in detail to their mother of the severe depression and anxiety which they experienced. Moses Sheppard, Anne's husband, added cheerful postscripts to the sisters' letters—which he had clearly not read—remarking on Anne's and Edith's contentment. Theirs was an emotional world to which he had little access.[39]

This was, as well, a female world in which hostility and criticism of other women were discouraged, and thus a milieu in which women could develop a sense of inner security and self-esteem. As one young woman wrote to her mother's longtime friend: "I cannot sufficiently thank you for the kind unvaried affection & indulgence you have ever shown and expressed both by words and actions for me. . . . Happy would it be did all the world view me as you do, through the medium of kindness and forbearance."[40] They valued each other. Women, who had little status or power in the larger world of male concerns, possessed status and power in the lives and worlds of other women.[41]

An intimate mother-daughter relationship lay at the heart of this female world. The diaries and letters of both mothers and daughters attest to their closeness and mutual emotional dependency. Daughters routinely discussed their mother's health and activities with their own friends, expressed anxiety in cases of their mother's ill health and concern for her cares.[42] Expressions of hostility which we would today consider routine on the part of both mothers and daughters seem to have been uncommon indeed. On the contrary, this sample of families indicates that the normal relationship between mother and daughter was one of sympathy and understanding.[43]

Only sickness or great geographic distance was allowed to cause extended separation. When marriage did result in such separation, both viewed the distance between them with distress.[44] Something of this sympathy and love between mothers and daughters is evident in a letter Sarah Alden Ripley, at age sixty-nine, wrote her youngest and recently married daughter: "You do not know how much I miss you, not only when I struggle in and out of my mortal envelop and pump my nightly potation and no longer pour into your sympathizing ear my senile gossip, but all the day I muse away, since the sound of your voice no longer rouses me to sympathy with your joys or sorrows. . . . You cannot know how much I miss your affectionate demonstrations."[45] A dozen aging mothers in this sample of over thirty families echoed her sentiments.

Central to these mother-daughter relations is what might be described as an apprenticeship system. In those families where the daughter followed the mother into a life of traditional domesticity, mothers and other older women carefully trained daughters in the arts of housewifery and motherhood. Such training undoubtedly occurred throughout a girl's childhood but became more systematized, almost ritualistic, in the years following the end of her formal education and before her marriage. At this time a girl either returned home from boarding school or no longer divided her time between home and school. Rather, she devoted her energies on two tasks: mastering new domestic skills and participating in the visiting and social activities necessary to finding a husband. Under the careful supervision of their mothers and of older female relatives, such late-adolescent girls temporarily took over the household management from their mothers, tended their young nieces and nephews, and helped in childbirth, nursing, and weaning. Such experiences tied the generations together in shared skills and emotional interaction.[46]

Daughters were born into a female world. Their mother's life expectations and sympathetic network of friends and relations were among the first realities in the life of the developing child. As long as the mother's domestic role remained relatively stable and few viable alternatives competed with it, daughters tended to accept their mother's world and to turn automatically to other women for support and intimacy. It was within this closed and intimate female world that the young girl grew toward womanhood.

One could speculate at length concerning the absence of that mother-daughter hostility today considered almost inevitable to an adolescent's struggle for autonomy and self-identity. It is possible that taboos against female aggression and hostility were sufficiently strong to repress even that between mothers and their adolescent daughters. Yet these letters seem so alive and the interest of daughters in their mothers' affairs so vital and genuine that it is difficult to interpret their closeness exclusively in terms of repression and denial. The functional bonds that held mothers and daughters together in a world that permitted few alternatives to domesticity might well have created a source of mutuality and trust absent in societies where greater options were available for daughters than for mothers. Furthermore, the extended female network—a daughter's close ties with her own older sisters, cousins, and aunts—may well have permitted a diffusion and a relaxation of mother-daughter identification and so have aided a daughter in her struggle for identity and autonomy. None of these explanations are mutually exclusive; all may well have interacted to produce the degree of empathy evident in those letters and diaries.

At some point in adolescence, the young girl began to move outside the matrix of her mother's support group to develop a network of her own. Among the middle class, at least, this transition toward what was at the same time both a limited autonomy and a repetition of her mother's life seemed to have most frequently coincided with a girl's going to school. Indeed education appears to have played a crucial role in the lives of most of the families in this study. Attending school for a few months, for a year, or longer, was common even among daughters of relatively poor families, while middle-class girls routinely spent at least a year in boarding school.[47] These school years ordinarily marked a girl's first separation from home. They served to wean the daughter from her home, to train her in the essential social graces, and, ultimately, to help introduce her into the marriage market. It was not infrequently a trying emotional experience for both mother and daughter.[48]

In this process of leaving one home and adjusting to another, the mother's friends and relatives played a key transitional role. Such older women routinely accepted the role of foster mother; they supervised the young girl's deportment, monitored her health and introduced her to their own network of female friends and kin.[49] Not infrequently women, friends from their own school years, arranged to send their daughters to the same school so that the girls might form bonds paralleling those their mothers had made. For years Molly and Helena wrote of their daughters' meeting and worried over each other's children. When Molly finally brought her daughter east to school, their first act on reaching New York was to meet Helena and her daughters. Elizabeth Bordley Gibson virtually adopted the daughters of her school chum, Eleanor Custis Lewis. The Lewis daughters soon began to write Elizabeth Gibson letters with the salutation "Dearest Mama." Eleuthera DuPont, attending boarding school in Philadelphia at roughly the same time as the Lewis girls, developed a parallel relationship with her mother's friend, Elizabeth McKie Smith. Eleuthera went to the same school and became a close friend of the Smith girls and eventually married their first cousin. During this period she routinely called Mrs. Smith "Mother." Indeed Eleuthera so internalized the sense of having two mothers that she casually wrote her sisters of her "Mamma's" visits at her "mother's" house—that is, at Mrs. Smith's.[50]

Even more important to this process of maturation than their mother's friends were the female friends young women made at school. Young girls helped each other overcome homesickness and endure the crises of adolescence. They gossiped about beaux, incorporated each other into their own kinship systems, and attended and gave teas and balls together. Older girls in boarding school "adopted" younger ones, who called them "Mother."[51] Dear friends might indeed continue this pattern of adoption and mothering throughout their lives; one woman might routinely assume the nurturing role of pseudomother, the other the dependency role of daughter. The pseudomother performed for the other woman all the services which we normally associate with mothers; she went to absurd lengths to purchase items her "daughter" could have obtained from other sources, gave advice and functioned as an idealized figure in her "daughter's" imagination. Helena played such a role for Molly, as did Sarah for Jeannie. Elizabeth Bordley Gibson bought almost all Eleanor Parke Custis Lewis's necessities—from shoes and corset covers to bedding and harp strings—and sent them from Philadelphia to Virginia, a procedure that sometimes took months. Eleanor frequently asked Elizabeth to take back her purchases, have them redone, and argue with shopkeepers about prices. These were favors automatically asked and complied with. Anne Jefferis Sheppard made the analogy very explicitly in a letter to her own mother written shortly after Anne's marriage, when she was feeling depressed about their separation: "Mary Paulen is truly kind, almost acts the part of a mother and trys to aid and *comfort me,* and also to *lighten my new cares.*"[52]

A comparison of the references to men and women in these young women's letters is striking. Boys were obviously indispensable to the elaborate courtship ritual girls engaged in. In these teenage letters and diaries, however, boys appear distant and warded off—an effect produced both by the girl's sense of bonding and by a highly developed and deprecatory whimsy. Girls joked among themselves about the conceit, poor looks or affectations of suitors. Rarely, especially in the eighteenth and early nineteenth centuries, were favorable remarks exchanged. Indeed, while hostility and criticism of other women were so rare as to seem almost tabooed, young women permitted themselves to express a great deal of hostility toward peer-group men.[53] When unacceptable suitors appeared, girls might even band together to harass them. When one such unfortunate came to court Sophie DuPont she hid in her room, first sending her sister Eleuthera to entertain him and then dispatching a number of urgent notes to her neighboring sister-in-law, cousins, and a visiting friend who all came to Sophie's support. A wild female romp ensued, ending only when Sophie banged into a door, lacerated her nose, and retired, with her female cohorts, to bed. Her brother and the presumably disconcerted suitor were left alone. These were not the antics of teenagers but of women in their early and mid-twenties.[54]

Even if young men were acceptable suitors, girls referred to them formally and obliquely: "The last week I received the unexpected intelligence of the arrival of a friend in Boston," Sarah Ripley wrote in her diary of the young man to whom she had been engaged for years and whom she would shortly marry. Harriet Manigault assiduously kept a lively and gossipy diary during the three years preceding her marriage, yet did not once comment upon her own engagement nor indeed make any personal references to her fiancé—who was never identified as such but always referred to as Mr. Wilcox.[55] The point is not that these young women were hostile to young men. Far from it; they sought marriage and domesticity. Yet in these letters and diaries men appear as an other or out group, segregated into different schools, supported by their own male network of friends and kin, socialized to different behavior, and coached to a proper formality in courtship behavior. As a consequence, relations between young women and men frequently lacked the spontaneity and emotional intimacy that characterized the young girls' ties to each other.

Indeed, in sharp contrast to their distant relations with boys, young women's relations with each other were close, often frolicsome, and surprisingly long lasting and devoted. They wrote secret missives to each other, spent long solitary days with each other, curled up together in bed at night to whisper fantasies and secrets.[56] In 1862 one young woman in her early twenties described one such scene to an absent friend: "I have sat up to midnight listening to the confidences of Constance Kinney, whose heart was opened by that most charming of all situations, a seat on a bedside late at night, when all the household are asleep & only oneself & one's confidante survive in wakefulness. So she has told me all her loves and tried to get some confidences in return but being five or six years older than she, I know better. . . ."[57] Elizabeth Bordley and Nelly Parke Custis, teenagers in Philadelphia in the 1790s, routinely secreted themselves until late each night in Nelly's attic, where they each wrote a novel about the other.[58] Quite a few young women kept diaries, and it was a sign of special friendship to show their diaries to each other. The emotional quality of such exchanges emerges from the comments of one young girl who grew up along the Ohio frontier:

> Sisters CW and RT keep diaries & allow me the inestimable pleasure of reading them and in turn they see mine—but O shame covers my face when I think of it; theirs is so much better than mine, that every time. Then I think well now I *will* burn mine but upon second thought it would deprive me the pleasure of reading theirs, for I esteem it a very great privilege indeed, as well as very improving, as we lay our hearts open to each other, it heightens our love & helps to cherish & keep alive that sweet soothing friendship and endears us to each other by that soft attraction.[59]

Girls routinely slept together, kissed and hugged each other. Indeed, while waltzing with young men scandalized the otherwise flighty and highly fashionable Harriet Manigault, she considered waltzing with other young women not only acceptable but pleasant.[60]

Marriage followed adolescence. With increasing frequency in the nineteenth century, marriage involved a girl's traumatic removal from her mother and her mother's network. It involved, as well, adjustment to a husband, who, because he was male came to marriage with both a different world view and vastly different experiences. Not surprisingly, marriage was an event surrounded with supportive, almost ritualistic, practices. (Weddings are one of the last female rituals remaining in twentieth-century America.) Young women routinely spent the months preceding their marriage almost exclusively with other women—at neighborhood sewing bees and quilting parties or in a round of visits to geographically distant friends and relatives. Ostensibly they went to receive assistance in the practical preparations for their new home—sewing and quilting a trousseau and linen—but of equal importance, they appear to have gained emotional support and reassurance. Sarah Ripley spent over a month with friends and relatives in Boston and Hingham before her wedding; Parke Custis Lewis exchanged visits with her aunts and first cousins throughout Virginia.[61] Anne Jefferis, who married with some hesitation, spent virtually half a year in endless visiting with cousins, aunts, and friends. Despite their reassurance and support, however, she would not marry Moses Sheppard until her sister Edith and her cousin Rebecca moved into the groom's home, met his friends, and explored his personality.[62] The wedding did not take place until Edith wrote to Anne: "I can say in truth I am entirely willing thou shouldst follow him even away in the Jersey sands believing if thou are not happy in thy future home it will not be any fault on his part. . . ."[63]

Sisters, cousins, and friends frequently accompanied newlyweds on their wedding night and wedding trip, which often involved additional family visiting. Such extensive visits presumably served to wean the daughter from her family of origin. As such they often contained a note of ambivalence. Nelly Custis, for example, reported homesickness and loneliness on her wedding trip. "I left my Beloved and revered Grandmamma with sincere regret," she wrote Elizabeth Bordley. "It was sometime before I could feel reconciled to traveling without her." Perhaps they also functioned to reassure the young woman herself, and her friends and kin, that though marriage might alter it would not destroy old bonds of intimacy and familiarity.[64]

Married life, too, was structured about a host of female rituals. Childbirth, especially the birth of the first child, became virtually a *rite de passage,* with a lengthy seclusion of the woman before and after delivery, severe restrictions on her activities, and finally a dramatic reemergence.[65] This seclusion was supervised by mothers, sisters, and loving friends. Nursing and weaning involved the advice and assistance of female friends and relatives. So did miscarriage.[66] Death, like birth, was structured around elaborate unisexed rituals. When Nelly Parke Custis Lewis rushed to nurse her daughter who was critically ill while away at school, Nelly received support, not from her husband, who remained on their plantation, but from her old school friend, Elizabeth Bordley. Elizabeth aided Nelly in caring for her dying daughter, cared for Nelly's other children, played a major role in the elaborate funeral arrangements (which the father did not attend), and frequently visited the girl's grave at the mother's request. For years Elizabeth continued to be the confidante of Nelly's anguished recollections of her lost daughter. These memories, Nelly's letters make clear, were for Elizabeth alone. "Mr. L. knows nothing of this," was a frequent comment.[67] Virtually every collection of letters and diaries in my sample contained evidence of women turning to each other for comfort when facing the frequent and unavoidable deaths of the eighteenth and nineteenth centuries.[68] While mourning for her father's death, Sophie DuPont received elaborate letters and visits of condolence—all from women. No man wrote or visited Sophie to offer sympathy at her father's death.[69] Among rural Pennsylvania Quakers, death and mourning rituals assumed an even more extreme same-sex form, with men or women largely barred from the deathbeds of the other sex. Women relatives and friends slept with the dying woman, nursed her, and prepared her body for burial.[70]

Eighteenth- and nineteenth-century women thus lived in emotional proximity to each other. Friendships and intimacies followed the biological ebb and flow of women's lives. Marriage and pregnancy, childbirth and weaning, sickness and death involved physical and psychic trauma which comfort and sympathy made easier to bear. Intense bonds of love and intimacy bound together those women who, offering each other aid and sympathy, shared such stressful moments.

These bonds were often physical as well as emotional. An undeniably romantic and even sensual note frequently marked female relationships. This theme, significant throughout the stages of a woman's life, surfaced first during adolescence. As one teenager from a struggling pioneer family in the Ohio Valley wrote in her diary in 1808: "I laid with my dear R[ebecca] and a glorious good talk we had until about 4[A.M.]—O how hard I do *love* her. . . ."[71] Only a few years later Bostonian Eunice Callender carved her initials and Sarah Ripley's into a favorite tree, along with a pledge of eternal love, and then waited breathlessly for Sarah to discover and respond to her declaration of affection. The response appears to have been affirmative.[72] A half-century later urbane and sophisticated Katherine Wharton commented upon meeting an old school chum: "She was a great pet of mine at school & I thought as I watched her light figure how often I had held her in my arms—how dear she had once been to me." Katie maintained a long intimate friendship with another girl. When a young man began to court this friend seriously, Katie commented in her diary that she had never realized "how deeply I loved Eng and how fully." She wrote over and over again in that entry: "Indeed I love her!" and only with great reluctance left the city that summer since it meant also leaving Eng with Eng's new suitor.[73]

Peggy Emlen, a Quaker adolescent in Philadelphia in the 1760s, expressed similar feelings about her first cousin, Sally Logan. The girls sent love poems to each other (not unlike the ones Elizabeth Bordley wrote to Nellie Custis a generation later), took long solitary walks together, and even haunted the empty house of the other when one was out of town. Indeed Sally's absences from Philadelphia caused Peggy acute unhappiness. So strong were Peggy's feelings that her brothers began to tease about her affection for Sally and threatened to steal Sally's letters, much to both girls' alarm. In one letter that Peggy wrote the absent Sally she elaborately described the depth and nature of her feelings: "I have not words to express my impatience to see My Dear Cousin, what would I not give just now for an hours sweet conversation with her, it seems as if I had a thousand things to say to thee, yet when I see thee, everything will be forgot thro' joy. . . . I have a very great friendship for several Girls yet it dont give me so much uneasiness at being absent from them as from thee. . . . [Let us] go and spend a day down at our place together and there unmolested enjoy each others company."[74]

Sarah Alden Ripley, a young, highly educated woman, formed a similar intense relationship, in this instance with a woman somewhat older than herself. The immediate bond of friendship rested on their atypically intense scholarly interests, but it soon involved strong emotions, at least on Sarah's part. "Friendship," she wrote Mary Emerson, "is fast twining about her willing captive the silken hands of dependence, a dependence so sweet who would renounce it for the apathy of self-sufficiency?" Subsequent letters became far more emotional, almost conspiratorial. Mary visited Sarah secretly in her room, or the two women crept away from family and friends to meet in a nearby woods. Sarah became jealous of Mary's other young friends. Mary's trips away from Boston also thrust Sarah into periods of anguished depression. Interestingly, the letters detailing their love were not destroyed but were preserved and even reprinted in a eulogistic biography of Sarah Alden Ripley.[75]

Tender letters between adolescent women, confessions of loneliness and emotional dependency, were not peculiar to Sarah Alden, Peggy Emlen, or Katie Wharton. They are found throughout the letters of the thirty-five families studied. They have, of course, their parallel today in the musings of many female adolescents. Yet these eighteenth- and nineteenth-century friendships lasted with undiminished, indeed often increased, intensity throughout the women's lives. Sarah Alden Ripley's first child was named after Mary Emerson. Nelly Custis Lewis's love for and dependence on Elizabeth Bordley Gibson only increased after her marriage. Eunice Callender remained enamored of her cousin Sarah Ripley for years and rejected as impossible the suggestion by another woman that their love might some day fade away.[76] Sophie DuPont and her childhood friend, Clementina Smith, exchanged letters filled with love and dependency for forty years while another dear friend, Mary Black Couper, wrote of dreaming that she, Sophie, and her husband were all united in one marriage. Mary's letters to Sophie are filled with avowals of love and indications of ambivalence toward her own husband. Eliza Schlatter, another of Sophie's intimate friends, wrote to her at a time of crisis: "I wish I could be with you present in the body as well as the mind & heart—I would turn your *good husband out of bed*—and snuggle into you and we would have a long talk like old times in Pine St.—I want to tell you so many things that are not *writable*. . . ."[77]

Such mutual dependency and deep affection is a central existential reality coloring the world of supportive networks and rituals. In the case of Katie, Sophie, or Eunice—as with Molly, Jeannie, and Sarah—their need for closeness and support merged with more intense demands for a love which was at the same time both emotional and sensual. Perhaps the most explicit statement concerning women's lifelong friendships appeared in the letter abolitionist and reformer Mary Grew wrote about the same time, referring to her own love for her dear friend and lifelong companion, Margaret Burleigh. Grew wrote, in response to a letter of condolence from another woman on Burleigh's death: "Your words respecting my beloved friend touch me deeply. Evidently . . . you comprehend and appreciate, as few persons do . . . the nature of the relation which existed, which exists, between her and myself. Her only surviving niece . . . also does. To me it seems to have been a closer union than that of most marriages. We know there have been other such between two men and also between two women. And why should there not be. Love is spiritual, only passion is sexual."[78]

How then can we ultimately interpret these long-lived intimate female relationships and integrate them into our understanding of Victorian sexuality? Their ambivalent and romantic rhetoric presents us with an ultimate puzzle: the relationship along the spectrum of human emotions between love, sensuality, and sexuality.

One is tempted, as I have remarked, to compare Molly, Peggy, or Sophie's relationships with the friendships adolescent girls in the twentieth century routinely form—close friendships of great emotional intensity. Helene Deutsch and Clara Thompson have both described these friendships as emotionally necessary to a girl's psychosexual development. But, they warn, such friendships might shade into adolescent and postadolescent homosexuality.[79]

It is possible to speculate that in the twentieth century a number of cultural taboos evolved to cut short the homosocial ties of girl hood and to impel the emerging women of thirteen or fourteen toward heterosexual relationships. In contrast, nineteenth-century American society did not taboo close female relationships but rather recognized them as a socially viable form of human contact—and, as such, acceptable throughout a woman's life. Indeed it was not these homosocial ties that were inhibited but rather heterosexual leanings. While closeness, freedom of emotional expression, and uninhibited physical contact characterized women's relationships with each other, the opposite was frequently true of male-female relationships. One could thus argue that within such a world of female support, intimacy, and ritual it was only to be expected that adult women would turn trustingly and lovingly to each other. It was a behavior they had observed and learned since childhood. A different type of emotional landscape existed in the nineteenth century, one in which Molly and Helena's love became a natural development.

Of perhaps equal significance are the implications we can garner from this framework for the understanding of heterosexual marriages in the nineteenth century. If men and women grew up as they did in relatively homogeneous and segregated sexual groups, then marriage represented a major problem in adjustment. From this perspective we could interpret much of the emotional stiffness and distance that we associate with Victorian marriage as a structural consequence of contemporary sex-role differentiation and gender-role socialization. With marriage both women and men had to adjust to life with a person who was, in essence, a member of an alien group.

I have thus far substituted a cultural or psychosocial for a psychosexual interpretation of women's emotional bonding. But there are psychosexual implications in this model which I think it only fair to make more explicit. Despite Sigmund Freud's insistence on the bisexuality of us all or the recent American Psychiatric Association decision on homosexuality, many psychiatrists today tend explicitly or implicitly to view homosexuality as a totally alien or pathological behavior—as totally unlike heterosexuality. I suspect that in essence they may have adopted an explanatory model similar to the one used in discussing schizophrenia. As a psychiatrist can speak of schizophrenia and of a borderline schizophrenic personality as both ultimately and fundamentally different from a normal or neurotic personality, so they also think of both homosexuality and latent homosexuality as states totally different from heterosexuality. With this rapid dichotomous model of assumption, "latent homosexuality" becomes the indication of a disease in progress—seeds of a pathology which belie the reality of an individual's heterosexuality.

Yet at the same time we are well aware that cultural values can affect choices in the gender of a person's sexual partner. We, for instance, do not necessarily consider homosexual-object choice among men in prison, on shipboard or in boarding schools a necessary indication of pathology. I would urge that we expand this relativistic model and hypothesize that a number of cultures might well tolerate or even encourage diversity in sexual and nonsexual relations. Based on my research into this nineteenth-century world of female intimacy, I would further suggest that rather than seeing a gulf between the normal and the abnormal we view sexual and emotional impulses as part of a continuum or spectrum of affect gradations strongly affected by cultural norms and arrangements, a continuum influenced in part by observed and thus learned behavior. At one end of the continuum lies committed heterosexuality; at the other uncompromising homosexuality; between, a wide latitude of emotions and sexual feelings. Certain cultures and environments permit individuals a great deal of freedom in moving across this spectrum. I would like to suggest that the nineteenth century was such a cultural environment. That is, the supposedly repressive and destructive Victorian sexual ethos may have been more flexible and responsive to the needs of particular individuals than those of mid-twentieth century.

Notes

1. The most notable exception to this rule is now eleven years old: William R. Taylor and Christopher Lasch, "Two 'Kindred Spirits': Sorority and Family in New England, 1839–1846," *New England Quarterly* 36 (1963):25–41. . . . I do not . . . accept the Taylor-Lasch thesis that female friendships developed in the mid-nineteenth century because of geographic mobility and the breakup of the colonial family. I have found these friendships as frequently in the eighteenth century as in the nineteenth and would hypothesize that the geographic mobility of the mid-nineteenth century eroded them as it did so many other traditional social institutions. . . .

2. I do not wish to deny the importance of women's relations with particular men. Obviously, women were close to brothers, husbands, fathers, and sons. However, there is evidence that despite such closeness relationships between men and women differed in both emotional texture and frequency from those between women. . . . I have discussed some aspects of male-female relationships in two articles: "Puberty to Menopause: The Cycle of Femininity in Nineteenth-Century America," Feminist Studies 1 (1973):58–72, and, with Charles Rosenberg, "The Female Animal: Medical and Biological Views of Women in 19th Century America," *Journal of American History* 59 (1973):331–56.

3. See Freud's classic paper on homosexuality, "Three Essays on the Theory of Sexuality," in *The Standard Edition of the Complete Psychological Works of Sigmund Freud*, trans. James Strachey (London: Hogarth Press, 1953), 7:135–72. The essays originally appeared in 1905. . . .

4. . . . [S]ee Charles Rosenberg, "Sexuality, Class and Role," *American Quarterly* 25 (1973):131–53.

5. See, e.g., the letters of Peggy Emlen to Sally Logan, 1768–72, Wells Morris Collection, Box 1, Historical Society of Pennsylvania; and the Eleanor Parke Custis Lewis Letters, Historical Society of Pennsylvania, Philadelphia.

6. Sarah Butler Wister was the daughter of Fanny Kemble and Pierce Butler. In 1859 she married a Philadelphia physician, Owen Wister. The novelist Owen Wister is her son. Jeannie Field Musgrove was the half-orphaned daughter of constitutional lawyer and New York Republican politician David Dudley Field. Their correspondence (1855–98) is in the Sarah Butler Wister Papers, Wister Family Papers, Historical Society of Pennsylvania.

7. Sarah Butler, Butler Place, S.C., to Jeannie Field, New York, Sept. 14, 1855.

8. See, e.g., Sarah Butler Wister, Germantown, Pa., to Jeannie Field, New York, Sept. 25, 1862, Oct. 21, 1863; or Jeannie Field, New York, to Sarah Butler Wister, Germantown, July 3, 1861, Jan. 23 and July 12, 1863.

9. Sarah Butler Wister, Germantown, to Jeannie Field, New York, June 5, 1861, Feb. 29, 1864; Jeannie Field to Sarah Butler Wister, Nov. 22, 1861, Jan. 4 and June 14, 1863.

10. Sarah Butler Wister, London, to Jeannie Field Musgrove, New York, June 18 and Aug. 3, 1870.

11. See, e.g., two of Sarah's letters to Jeannie: Dec. 21, 1873, July 16, 1878.

12. This is the 1868–1920 correspondence between Mary Hallock Foote and Helena, a New York friend (the Mary Hallock Foote Papers are in the Manuscript Division, Stanford University). . . . In many ways these letters are typical of those women wrote to other women. Women frequently began letters to each other with salutations such as "Dearest," "My Most Beloved," "You Darling Girl," and signed them "tenderly" or "to my dear dear sweet friend, good-bye." . . . She was by no means unique. See, e.g., Annie to Charlene Van Vleck Anderson, Appleton, Wis., June 10, 1871, Anderson Family Papers, Manuscript Division, Stanford University; Maggie to Emily Howland, Philadelphia, July 12, 1851, Howland Family Papers, Phoebe King Collection, Friends Historical Library, Swarthmore College; Mary Jane Burleigh to Emily Howland, Sherwood, N.Y., Mar. 27, 1872, Howland Family Papers, Sophia Smith Collection, Smith College; Mary Black Couper to Sophia Madeleine DuPont, Wilmington, Del.: n.d. [1834] (two letters), Samuel Francis DuPont Papers, Eleutherian Mills Foundation, Wilmington, Del. . . . in general the correspondence (1838–49) between Rebecca Biddle of Philadelphia and Martha Jefferis, Chester County, Pa., Jefferis Family Correspondence, Chester County Historical Society, West Chester, Pa.; Phoebe Bradford Diary, June 7 and July 13, 1832, Historical Society of Pennsylvania; . . . the Sarah Alden Ripley Correspondence, Schlesinger Library, Radcliffe College; . . . Anne Sterling Biddle Family Papers, Friends Historical Society, Swarthmore College; Harriet Manigault Wilcox Diary, Aug. 7, 1814, Historical Society of Pennsylvania; . . . Mrs. O. J. Wister and Miss Agnes Irwin, eds., *Worthy Women of Our First Century* (Philadelphia: J. B. Lippincott & Co., 1877), p. 195.

13. Mary Hallock [Foote] to Helena, n.d. [1869–70], n.d. [1871–72], Folder 1, Mary Hallock Foote Letters, . . .

14. Mary Hallock [Foote] to Helena, Sept. 15 and 23, 1873, n.d. [Oct. 1873], Oct. 12, 1873.

15. Mary Hallock [Foote] to Helena, n.d. [Jan. 1874], n.d. [Spring 1874].

16. Mary Hallock [Foote] to Helena, Sept. 23, 1873; Mary Hallock [Foote] to Richard, Dec. 13, 1873. Molly's and Helena's relationship continued for the rest of their lives. . . .

17. . . . [S]ee Barbara Welter, "The Cult of True Womanhood: 1820–1860," *American Quarterly* 18 (Summer 1966):151–74; Anne Firor Scott, *The Southern Lady: From Pedestal to Politics, 1830–1930* (Chicago: University of Chicago Press, 1970), chaps. 1–2; Smith-Rosenberg and Rosenberg.

18. See, e.g., the letters of Peggy Emlen to Sally Logan, 1768–72. . . .

19. See, [e.g.,] Elizabeth Botts, *Family and Social Network* (London: Tavistock Publications, 1957); . . .

20. This pattern seemed to cross class barriers.... See Ann McGrann, Philadelphia, to Sophie M. DuPont, Philadelphia, July 3, 1834, Sophie Madeleine DuPont Letters, Eleutherian Mills Foundation.

21. [See, e.g.,] Harriet Manigault Diary, June 28, 1814, and passim;...

22. [See, e.g.,]... Ann Sterling Biddle Papers, passim,...

23. [See, e.g.,] Phoebe Bradford Diary, Jan. 13, Nov. 16–19, 1832, Apr. 26 and May 7, 1833;...

24. Lisa Mitchell Diary, 1860s, passim, Manuscript Division, Tulane University; . . . Jeannie McCall, Cedar Park, to Peter McCall, Philadelphia, June 30, 1849, McCall Section, Cadwalader Collection, Historical Society of Pennsylvania.

25. Peggy Emlen to Sally Logan, May 3, 1769.

26. For a prime example of this type of letter, see Eleanor Parke Custis Lewis to Elizabeth Bordley Gibson, Passim;...

27. Place of residence is not the only variable significance in characterizing family structure. Strong emotional ties and frequent visiting and correspondence can unite families that do not live under one roof....

28. Eleanor Parke Custis Lewis to Elizabeth Bordley Gibson, Apr. 20 and Sept. 25, 1848.

29. Maria Inskeep to Fanny Hampton Correspondence, 1823–60, Inskeep Collection, Tulane University Library.

30. Eunice Callender, Boston, to Sarah Ripley [Stearns], Sept. 24 and Oct. 29, 1803, Feb. 16, 1805, Apr. 29 and Oct. 9, 1806, May 26, 1810.

31. Sophie DuPont filled her letters to her younger brother Henry (with whom she had been assigned to correspond while he was at boarding school) with accounts of family visiting (see, e.g., Dec. 13, 1827, Jan. 10 and Mar. 9, 1828, Feb. 4 and Mar. 10, 1832).... Mary B. Ashew Diary, July 11 and 13, Aug. 17, Summer and Oct. 1858....

32. Martha Jefferis to Anne Jefferis Sheppard, Jan. 12, 1845; Phoebe Middleton to Martha Jefferis, Feb. 22, 1848....

33. Rebecca Biddle to Martha Jefferis, 1838–49, passim; Martha Jefferis to Anne Jefferis Sheppard, July 6, 1846; Anne Jefferis Sheppard to Rachael Jefferis, Jan. 16, 1865; Sarah Foulke Farquhar [Emlen] Diary, Sept. 22, 1813, Friends Historical Library, Swarthmore College;...

34. Sarah Alden Ripley to Abba Allyn, n.d....

35. Phoebe Bradford Diary, July 13, 1832.

36. Mary Hallock [Foote] to Helena, Dec. 23 [1868 or 1869]; Phoebe Bradford Diary, Dec. 8, 1832; Martha Jefferis and Anne Jefferis Sheppard letters, passim.

37. Martha Jefferis to Anne Jefferis Sheppard, Aug. 3, 1849; Sarah Ripley [Stearns] Diary, Nov. 12, 1808, Jan. 8, 1811....

38. Martha Jefferis to Edith Jefferis, Mar. 15, 1841; Mary Hallock Foote to Helena, n.d. [1874–75?];...

39. Anne Jefferis Sheppard to Martha Jefferis, Sept. 29, 1841.

40. Frances Parke Lewis to Elizabeth Bordley Gibson, Apr. 29, 1821.

41. [See, e.g.,] Mary Jane Burleigh, Mount Pleasant, S.C., to Emily Howland, Sherwood N.Y., Mar. 27, 1872, Howland Family Papers;...

42. [See, e.g.,] Harriet Manigault Diary, Aug. 15, 21, and 23, 1814, Historical Society of Pennsylvania;...

43. Mrs. S. S. Dalton, "Autobiography" (Circle Valley, Utah, 1876), pp. 21–22, Bancroft Library, University of California, Berkeley; Sarah Foulke Emlen Diary, Apr. 1809; Louisa G. Van Vleck, Appleton, Wis., to Charlena Van Vleck Anderson, Göttingen, n.d. [1875],...

44. Abigail Brackett Lyman, Boston, to Mrs. Abigail Brackett (daughter to mother), n.d. [1797], June 3, 1800; Sarah Alden Ripley wrote weekly to her daughter, Sophy Ripley Fisher, after the latter's marriage (Sarah Alden Ripley Correspondence, passim); Phoebe Bradford Diary, Feb. 25, 1833, passim, 1832–33; Louisa G. Van Vleck to Charlena Van Vleck Anderson, Dec. 15, 1873, July 4, Aug. 15 and 29, Sept. 19, and Nov. 9, 1875.... Daughters evidently frequently slept with their mothers—into adulthood (Harriet Manigault [Wilcox] Diary, Feb. 19, 1815; Eleanor Parke Custis Lewis to Elizabeth Bordley Gibson, Oct. 10, 1832). Daughters also frequently asked mothers to live with them and professed delight when they did so.... We did find a few exceptions to this mother-daughter felicity (M. B. Ashew Diary, Nov. 19, 1857, Apr. 10 and May 17, 1858). Sarah Foulke Emlen was at first very hostile to her step-mother (Sarah Foulke Emlen Diary, Aug. 9, 1807), but they later developed a warm supportive relationship.

45. Sarah Alden Ripley to Sophy Thayer, n.d. [1861].

46. [See, e.g.,] Mary Hallock Foote to Helena [Winter 1873] (no. 52); Jossie, Stevens Point, Wis., to Charlena Van Vleck [Anderson], Appleton, Wis., Oct. 24, 1870; Pollie Chandler, Green Bay, Wis., to Charlena Van Vleck [Anderson], Appleton, n.d. [1870]; Eleuthera DuPont to Sophie DuPont, Sept. 5, 1829;...

47. ... Sarah Foulke Emlen Journal, Sarah Ripley Stearns Diary, Mrs. S. S. Dalton, "Autobiography."

48. Maria Revere to her mother [Mrs. Paul Revere], June 13, 1801, Paul Revere Papers, Massachusetts Historical Society. In a letter to Elizabeth Bordley Gibson, Mar. 28, 1847, Eleanor Parke Custis Lewis from Virginia discussed the anxiety her daughter felt when her granddaughters left home to go to boarding school....

49. ... [See, e.g.,] the letters and diaries of three generations of Manigault women in Philadelphia: Mrs. Gabrielle Manigault, her daughter, Harriet Manigault Wilcox, and granddaughter, Charlotte Wilcox McCall.... Mrs. Henry Middleton, Charleston, S.C., to Mrs. Gabrielle Manigault, n.d. [mid 1800s]; Harriet Manigault Diary, vol. 1; Dec. 1, 1813, June 28, 1814; Charlotte Wilcox McCall Diary, vol. 1, 1842, passim. All in Historical Society of Philadelphia.

50. Frances Parke Lewis, Woodlawn, Va., to Elizabeth Bordley Gibson, Philadelphia, Apr. 11, 1821, Lewis Correspondence; Eleuthera DuPont, Philadelphia, to Victorine DuPont Bauday, Brandywine, Dec. 8, 1821, Jan. 31, 1822; Eleuthera DuPont, Brandywine, to Margaretta Lammont [DuPont], Philadelphia, May 1823.

51. [See, e.g.,] Sarah Ripley Stearns Diary, Mar. 9 and 25, 1810; Peggy Emlen to Sally Logan, Mar. and July 4, 1769; . . . Deborah Cope, West Town School, to Rest Cope, Philadelphia, July 9, 1828, Chester County Historical Society, West Chester, Pa.; . . .

52. Anne Jefferis Sheppard to Martha Jefferis, Mar. 17, 1841.

53. [See, e.g.,] Peggy Emlen to Sally Logan, Mar. 1769, Mount Vernon, Va.; . . .

54. Sophie M. DuPont and Eleuthera DuPont, Brandywine, to Victorine DuPont Bauday, Philadelphia, Jan. 25, 1832.

55. Sarah Ripley [Stearns] Diary and Harriet Manigault Diary, passim.

56. [See, e.g.,] Sophie Madeleine DuPont to Eleuthera DuPont, Dec. 1827; Clementina Beach Smith to Sophie Madeleine DuPont, Dec. 26, 1828; Sarah Faulke Emlen Diary, July 21, 1808, Mar. 30, 1809; . . .

57. Jeannie Field, New York, to Sarah Butler Wister, Germantown, Apr. 6, 1862.

58. Elizabeth Bordley Gibson, introductory statement to the Eleanor Parke Custis Lewis Letters [1850s], Historical Society of Pennsylvania.

59. Sarah Foulke [Emlen] Diary, Mar. 30, 1809.

60. Harriet Manigault Diary, May 26, 1815.

61. Sarah Ripley [Stearns] Diary, May 17 and Oct. 2, 1812; Eleanor Parke Custis Lewis to Elizabeth Bordley Gibson, Apr. 23, 1826; . . .

62. Anne Jefferis to Martha Jefferis, Nov. 22 and 27, 1840, Jan. 13 and Mar. 17, 1841; Edith Jefferis, Greenwich, N.J., to Anne Jefferis, Philadelphia, Jan. 31, Feb. 6 and Feb. 1841.

63. Edith Jefferis to Anne Jefferis, Jan. 31, 1841.

64. Eleanor Parke Custis Lewis to Elizabeth Bordley, Nov. 4, 1799. . . .

65. [See, e.g.,] Mary Hallock to Helena DeKay Gilder [1876] (no. 81); n.d. (no. 83), Mar. 3, 1884; Mary Ashew Diary, vol. 2, Sept.–Jan. 1860; . . .

66. [See, e.g.,] Fanny Ferris to Anne Biddle, Nov. 19, 1811; Eleanor Parke Custis Lewis to Elizabeth Bordley Gibson, Nov. 4, 1799, Apr. 27, 1827; . . .

67. Eleanor Parke Custis Lewis to Elizabeth Bordley Gibson, Oct.–Nov. 1820, passim.

68. [See, e.g.,] Emily Howland to Hannah, Sept. 30, 1866; Emily Howland Diary, Feb. 8, 11, and 27, 1880; Phoebe Bradford Diary, Apr. 12 and 13, and Aug. 4, 1833; . . .

69. Mary Black [Couper] to Sophie Madeleine DuPont, Feb. 1827 [Nov. 1, 1834], Nov. 12, 1834, two letters [late Nov. 1834]; Eliza Schlatter to Sophie Madeleine DuPont, Nov. 2, 1834.

70. For a few of the references to death rituals in the Jefferis papers see: Martha Jefferis to Anne Jefferis Sheppard, Sept. 28, 1843, Aug. 21 and Sept. 25, 1844, Jan. 11, 1846, Summer 1848, passim; . . . This is not to argue that men and women did not mourn together. Yet in many families women aided and comforted women and men, men. . . .

71. Sarah Foulke [Emlen] Diary, Dec. 29, 1808.

72. Eunice Callender, Boston, to Sarah Ripley [Stearns], Greenfield, Mass., May 24, 1803.

73. Katherine Johnstone Brinley [Wharton] Journal, Apr. 26, May 30, and May 29, 1856, Historical Society of Pennsylvania.

74. A series of roughly fourteen letters written by Peggy Emlen to Sally Logan (1768–71) has been preserved in the Wells Morris Collection, Box 1, Historical Society of Pennsylvania (see esp. May 3 and July 4, 1769, Jan. 8, 1768).

75. . . . The eulogistic biographical sketch appeared in Wister and Irwin (n. 12 above). . . .

76. See Sarah Alden Ripley to Mary Emerson, Nov. 19, 1823. Sarah Alden Ripley routinely, and one must assume ritualistically, read Mary Emerson's letters to her infant daughter, Mary. Eleanor Parke Custis Lewis reported doing the same with Elizabeth Bordley Gibson's letters, passim. Eunice Callender, Boston, to Sarah Ripley [Stearns], Oct. 19, 1808.

77. Mary Black Couper to Sophie M. DuPont, Mar. 5, 1832. The Clementina Smith–Sophie DuPont correspondence is in the Sophie DuPont Correspondence. The quotation is from Eliza Schlatter, Mount Holly, N.J., to Sophie DuPont, Brandywine, Aug. 24, 1834. . . .

78. Mary Grew, Providence, R.I., to Isabel Howland, Sherwood, N.Y., Apr. 27, 1892, Howland Correspondence, Sophia Smith Collection, Smith College.

79. Helena Deutsch, *Psychology of Women* (New York: Grune & Stratton, 1944), 1: chaps. 1–3; Clara Thompson, *On Women*, ed. Maurice Green (New York: New American Library, 1971).

JAMES C. MOHR

Abortion in America

If we observe nineteenth-century society through women's eyes, surely no experience was as widely shared as the experience of childbirth. The biological act of maternity created powerful bonds among women as they coped with the experience of childbirth. Until the twentieth century, most births took place at home, where the birthing mother was likely to be surrounded by her mother, sisters, and cousins, a midwife and other experienced women, and her woman friends. The "female world of love and ritual" that Carroll Smith-Rosenberg describes "formed across the childbirth bed," writes historian Judith Walzer Leavitt. "When women had suffered the agonies of watching their friends die, when they had helped a friend recover from a difficult delivery, or when they had participated in a successful birthing they developed a closeness that lasted a lifetime." Leavitt finds that these circles of friendly support made significant choices. "The collectivity of women gathered around the birthing bed made sure that birth attendants were responsive to their wishes. They made decisions about when and if to call physicians to births that midwives were attending; they gave or withheld permission for physicians' procedures; and they created the atmosphere of female support in a room that might have contained both women and men." Leavitt argues that when in the twentieth century birthing moved to hospitals, much of this support evaporated; the reforms in hospital practices demanded by feminists since the 1970s have been an effort to reclaim what had been lost.*

During the centuries before reliable fertility control measures made it possible for women to set limits on reproduction, most married women and many unmarried women felt considerable physical and psychological burdens from repeated pregnancies, childbirths, and postpartum recoveries. The cost in terms of time, energy, dreams, and bodies was high. If we observe nineteenth-century society through women's eyes, surely no statistic was as significant as the one that marked the decline in the average number of children borne by each woman. Childbirth was a time of terror.

It is therefore notable that in the early nineteenth century, a sharp decline took place in the birth rates; the decline was particularly marked in urban areas. No innovations in birth control technology appeared in this period; the decline was the result of choices—later age at marriage, abstinence from sexual intercourse—that functioned to limit the number of times women faced childbirth. In the mid-eighteenth century, the average rural woman of free status could expect to face childbirth eight or nine times; by the early nineteenth century, that number had dropped to six and in some urban areas to four. Except for occasional "baby booms," birth rates in the United States have fallen steadily and continue to stabilize in our own time.

*Judith Walzer Leavitt, "Under the Shadow of Maternity: American Women's Responses to Death and Debility Fears in Nineteenth-Century Childbirth," *Feminist Studies* 12 (1986): 129–54.

From chs, 1 and 4 of *Abortion in America: The Origins and Evolution of National Policy* by James C. Mohr (New York: Oxford University Press, 1978). Used by permission of the author and publisher. Notes have been renumbered and edited.

When unsuccessful in avoiding pregnancies, many women attempted to abort them. The methods of the times were dangerous, but until the 1840s, the women were rarely censured by the community if fetal movement had not been felt. As these two sections from James Mohr's comprehensive study suggest, the vigorous attack on abortion after 1840 may well have been a response to the growing willingness of married women to attempt it.

What does the debate on abortion policy reveal about public attitudes toward women and their place in the family and in society? How have attitudes changed since Sarah Grosvenor's time? (See pp. 116–133.)

ABORTION IN AMERICA 1800–1825

In the absence of any legislation whatsoever on the subject of abortion in the United States in 1800, the legal status of the practice was governed by the traditional British common law as interpreted by the local courts of the new American states. For centuries prior to 1800 the key to the common law's attitude toward abortion had been a phenomenon associated with normal gestation known as quickening. Quickening was the first perception of fetal movement by the pregnant woman herself. Quickening generally occurred near the midpoint of gestation, late in the fourth or early in the fifth month, though it could and still does vary a good deal from one woman to another. The common law did not formally recognize the existence of a fetus in criminal cases until it had quickened. After quickening, the expulsion and destruction of a fetus without due cause was considered a crime, because the fetus itself had manifested some semblance of a separate existence: the ability to move. The crime was qualitatively different from the destruction of a human being, however, and punished less harshly. Before quickening, actions that had the effect of terminating what turned out to have been an early pregnancy were not considered criminal under the common law in effect in England and the United States in 1800.[1]

Both practical and moral arguments lay behind the quickening distinction. Practically, because no reliable tests for pregnancy existed in the early nineteenth century, quickening alone could confirm with absolute certainty that a woman really was pregnant. Prior to quickening, each of the telltale signs of pregnancy could, at least in theory, be explained in alternative ways by physicians of the day. Hence, either a doctor or a woman herself could take actions designed to restore menstrual flow after one or more missed periods on the assumption that something might be unnaturally "blocking" or "obstructing" her normal cycles, and if left untreated the obstruction would wreak real harm upon the woman. Medically, the procedures for removing a blockage were the same as those for inducing an early abortion. Not until the obstruction moved could either a physician or a woman, regardless of their suspicions, be completely certain that it was a "natural" blockage—a pregnancy—rather than a potentially dangerous situation. Morally, the question of whether or not a fetus was "alive" had been the subject of philosophical and religious debate among honest people for at least 5000 years. The quickening doctrine itself appears to have entered the British common law tradition by way of the tangled disputes of medieval theologians over whether or not an impregnated ovum possessed a soul.[2] The upshot was that American women in 1800 were legally free to attempt to terminate a condition that might turn out to have been a pregnancy until the existence of that pregnancy was incontrovertibly confirmed by the perception of fetal movement.

An ability to suspend one's modern preconceptions and to accept the early nineteenth century on its own terms regarding the distinction between quick and unquick is absolutely crucial to an understanding of the evolution of abortion policy in the United States. However doubtful the notion appears to modern readers, the distinction was virtually universal in America during the early decades of the nineteenth century and accepted in good faith. Perhaps the strongest evidence of the tenacity and universality of the doctrine in the United States was the fact that American courts pointedly sustained the most lenient implications of the quickening doctrine even after the British themselves had abandoned them. . . .

Because women believed themselves to be carrying inert non-beings prior to quickening, a potential for life rather than life itself, and because the common law permitted them to attempt to rid themselves of suspected and unwanted pregnancies up to the point when the potential for life gave a sure sign that it was developing into something actually alive, some American women did practice abortion in the early decades of the nineteenth century. One piece of evidence for this conclusion was the ready access American women had to abortifacient information from 1800 onward. A chief source of such information was the home medical literature of the era.

Home medical manuals characteristically contained abortifacient information in two different sections. One listed in explicit detail a number of procedures that might release "obstructed menses" and the other identified a number of specific things to be avoided in a suspected pregnancy because they were thought to bring on abortion. Americans probably consulted William Buchan's Domestic Medicine more frequently than any other home medical guide during the first decades of the nineteenth century.[3] Buchan suggested several courses of action designed to restore menstrual flow if a period was missed. These included bloodletting, bathing, iron and quinine concoctions, and if those failed, "a teaspoonful of the tincture of black hellebore [a violent purgative] . . . twice aday in a cup of warm water." Four pages later he listed among "the common causes" of abortion "great evacuations [and] vomiting," exactly as would be produced by the treatment he urged for suppressed menses. Later in pregnancy a venturesome, or desperate, woman could try some of the other abortion inducers he ticked off: "violent exercise; raising great weights; reaching too high; jumping, or stepping from an eminence; strokes [strong blows] on the belly; [and] falls."[4] . . .

Like most early abortion material, Buchan's . . . advice harked back to almost primordial or instinctual methods of ending a pregnancy. Bloodletting, for example, was evidently thought to serve as a surrogate period; it was hoped that bleeding from any part of the body might have the same flushing effect upon the womb that menstrual bleeding was known to have. This primitive folk belief lingered long into the nineteenth century, well after bleeding was abandoned as medical therapy in other kinds of cases, and it was common for abortionists as late as the 1870s to pull a tooth as part of their routine.[5] . . .

In addition to home medical guides and health manuals addressed to women, abortions and abortifacient information were also available in the United States from midwives and midwifery texts.[6] . . .

Herbal healers, the so-called Indian doctors, and various other irregular practitioners also helped spread abortifacient information in the United States during the early decades of the nineteenth century. Their surviving pamphlets, of which Peter Smith's 1813 brochure entitled "The Indian Doctor's Dispensary" is an example, contained abortifacient recipes that typically combined the better-known cathartics with native North American ingredients thought to have emmenagogic properties. For "obstructed menses" Smith recommended a concoction he called "Dr. Reeder's chalybeate." The key ingredients were myrrh and aloes, combined with liquor, sugar, vinegar, iron dust, ivy, and Virginia or seneca snakeroot.[7] A sweet-and-sour cocktail like that may or may not have induced abortion, but must certainly have jolted the system of any woman who tried one. . . .

Finally, and most importantly, America's regular physicians, those who had formal medical training either in the United States or in Great Britain or had been apprenticed under a regular doctor, clearly possessed the physiological knowledge and the surgical techniques necessary to terminate a pregnancy by mechanical means. They knew that dilation of the cervix at virtually any stage of gestation would generally bring on uterine contractions that would in turn lead to the expulsion of the contents of the uterus. They knew that any irritation introduced into the uterus would have the same effect. They knew that rupturing the amniotic sac, especially in the middle and later months of pregnancy, would usually also induce contractions and expulsion, regardless of whether the fetus was viable. Indeed, they were taught in their lecture courses and in their textbooks various procedures much more complex than a simple abortion, such as in utero decapitation and fetal pulverization, processes they were instructed to employ in lieu of the even more horribly dangerous Caesarean section. Like the general public, they knew the drugs and herbs most commonly used as abortifacients and emmenagogues, and also like the general public, they believed such preparations to have been frequently effective.[8] . . .

This placed great pressure on physicians to provide what amounted to abortion services early in pregnancy. An unmarried girl who feared herself pregnant, for example, could approach her family doctor and ask to be treated for menstrual blockage. If he hoped to retain the girl and her family as future patients, the physician would have little choice but to accept the girl's assessment of the situation, even if he suspected otherwise. He realized that every member of his profession would testify to the fact that he had no totally reliable means of distinguishing between an early pregnancy, on the one hand, and the amenorrhea that the girl claimed, on the other. Consequently, he treated for obstruction, which involved exactly the same procedures he would have used to induce an early abortion, and wittingly or unwittingly terminated the pregnancy. Regular physicians were also asked to bring to a safe conclusion abortions that irregulars or women themselves had initiated. . . . And through all of this the physician might bear in mind that he could never be held legally guilty of wrongdoing. No statutes existed anywhere in the United States on the subject of abortion, and the common law . . . considered abortion actionable only after a pregnancy had quickened. No wonder then that Heber C. Kimball, recalling his courtship with a woman he married in 1822, claimed that she had been "taught . . . in our young days, when she got into the family way, to send for a doctor and get rid of the child"; a course that she followed.[9]

In summary, then, the practice of aborting unwanted pregnancies was, if not common, almost certainly not rare in the United States during the first decades of the nineteenth century. A knowledge of various drugs, potions, and techniques was available from home medical guides, from health books for women, from midwives and irregular practitioners, and from trained physicians. Substantial evidence suggests that many American women sought abortions, tried the standard techniques of the day, and no doubt succeeded some proportion of the time in terminating unwanted pregnancies. Moreover, this practice was neither morally nor legally wrong in the eyes of the vast majority of Americans, provided it was accomplished before quickening.

The actual number of abortions in the United States prior to the advent of any statutes regulating its practice simply cannot be known. But an equally significant piece of information about those abortions can be gleaned from the historical record. It concerns the women who were having them. Virtually every observer through the middle of the 1830s believed that an overwhelming percentage of the American women who sought and succeeded in having abortions did so because they feared the social consequences of an illegitimate pregnancy, not because they wanted to limit their fertility per se. The doctor who uncovered the use of snake root as an abortifacient, for example, related that in all of the many instances he heard about "it was taken by women who had indulged in illegitimate love. . . ."[10]

In short, abortion was not thought to be a means of family limitation in the United States, at least on any significant scale, through the first third of the nineteenth century. This was hardly surprising in a largely rural and essentially preindustrial society, whose birthrates were exceeding any ever recorded in a European nation.[11] One could, along with medical student [Thomas] Massie, be less than enthusiastic about such an "unnatural" practice as abortion, yet tolerate it as the "recourse . . . of the victim of passion . . . the child of nature" who was driven by "an unrelenting world" unable to forgive any "deviation from what they have termed virtue."[12] Consequently, Americans in the early nineteenth century could and did look the other way when they encountered abortion. Nothing in their medical knowledge or in the rulings of their courts compelled them to do otherwise, and, as Massie indicated, there was considerable compassion for the women involved. It would be nearly midcentury before the perception of who was having abortions for what reasons would begin to shift in the United States, and that shift would prove to be one of the critical developments in the evolution of American abortion policy.

A final point remains to be made about abortion in the United States during the first decades of the nineteenth century. Most observers appeared to consider it relatively safe, at least by the medical standards of the day, rather than extremely dangerous. . . . This too must have reassured women who decided to risk an abortion before quickening. According to the lecture notes of one of his best students, Walter Channing told his Harvard classes that abortion could be troublesome when produced by external blows, because severe internal hemorrhage would be likely, but that generally considered, "abortion [was] not so dangerous as commonly supposed."[13]

The significance of these opinions lay less in whether or not they were accurate than in the fact that writers on abortion, including physicians, saw no reason to stress the dangers attendant to the process. Far from it. They were skeptical about poisons and purgatives, but appear to have assessed physically induced abortions as medically acceptable risks by the standards of the day, especially if brought on during the period of pregnancy when both popular belief and the public courts condoned them anyhow. Here again was a significant early perception that would later change. That change, like the shift in the perception of who was having abortions for what purposes, would also have an impact on the evolution of American abortion policy. . . .

THE SOCIAL CHARACTER OF ABORTION IN AMERICA 1840–1880

Before 1840 abortion was perceived in the United States primarily as a recourse of the desperate, especially of the young woman in trouble who feared the wrath of an overexacting society. After 1840, however, evidence began to accumulate that the social character of the practice had changed. A high proportion of the women whose abortions contributed to the soaring incidence of that practice in the United States between 1840 and 1880 appeared to be married, native-born, Protestant women, frequently of middle- or upper-class status. The data came from disparate sources, some biased and some not, but in the end proved compelling.

Even before the availability of reliable evidence confirmed that the nation's birthrates were starting to plummet, observers noticed that abortion more and more frequently involved married women rather than single women in trouble. Professor Hugh L. Hodge of the University of Pennsylvania, one of the first physicians in the United States to speak out about abortion in anything approaching a public forum, lectured his introductory obstetrics students in 1839 that abortion was fast becoming a prominent feature of American life. Hodge still considered women trying "to destroy the fruit of illicit pleasure" to be the ones most often seeking abortions, but he alerted his students to the fact that "married women, also, from the fear of labor, from indisposition to have the care, the expense, or the trouble of children, or some other motive" were more and more frequently requesting "that the embryo be destroyed by their medical attendant." Hodge attributed a good deal of this activity to the quickening doctrine, which allowed "women whose moral character is, in other respects, without reproach; mothers who are devoted, with an ardent and self-denying affection, to the children who already constitute[d] their family [to be] perfectly indifferent respecting the foetus in the utero."[14] . . .

Opinion was divided regarding the social status of the women who accounted for the great upsurge of abortion during the middle period of the nineteenth century. While most observers agreed "all classes of society, rich and poor" were involved to some extent, many thought that the middle and upper classes practiced abortion more extensively than the lower classes.[15] The Michigan State Medical Society in 1859 declared that abortion "pervade[d] all ranks" in that state.[16] The Medical Society of Buffalo pointed out that same year "now we have ladies, yes, *educated and refined ladies*" involved as well.[17] On the other hand, court cases revealed at least a sprinkling of lower-class women, servant girls, and the like. . . .

Although the going price for an abortion varied tremendously according to place, time, practitioner, and patient, abortions appear to have been generally quite expensive. Regular physicians testified repeatedly throughout the period that the abortion business was enormously lucrative. Those doctors pledged not to perform abortions bitterly resented men like the Boston botanic indicted for manslaughter in an abortion case in 1851, who posted $8000 bond and returned to his offices, at a time when the average university professor in the United States earned under $2000 per year.[18] . . .

When women turned from regulars to the commercial abortionists, the prices were still not cheap. Itinerants and irregulars generally tried to charge whatever they judged the traffic would bear, which could vary anywhere from $5 to $500. During the 1840s, for example, Madame Restell charged $5 for an initial visit and diagnosis, then negotiated the price of the operation "according to the wealth and liberality of the parties." In a case for which she was indicted in 1846 she asked a young woman about "her beau's circumstances" before quoting a figure, and then tried to get $100 when she found out the man was a reasonably successful manufacturer's representative. The man thought that was too costly, and only after extensive haggling among go-betweens was a $75 fee agreed upon.[19] . . .

Despite the apparent gradual leveling of prices, however, the abortion business remained a profitable commercial venture well into the 1870s. Anthony Comstock, the single-minded leader of a massive anti-obscenity campaign launched in the United States during the 1870s, kept meticulous and extensive records of all of the people he helped arrest while operating as a special agent of the Post Office Department. Between 1872 and 1880 Comstock and his associates aided in the indictment of 55 persons whom Comstock identified as abortionists. The vast majority were very wealthy and posted large bonds with ease. . . .

. . . [A]bortion entered the mainstream of American life during the middle decades of the nineteenth century. While the unmarried and the socially desperate continued to have recourse to it as they had earlier in the century, abortion also became highly visible, much more frequently practiced, and quite common as a means of family limitation among white, Protestant, native-born wives of middle- and upper-class standing. These dramatic changes, in turn, evoked sharp comment from two ideologically opposed groups in American society, each of which either directly or indirectly blamed the other for the shift in abortion patterns. On one side of the debate were the antifeminists, led by regular physicians, and on the other side were the nation's feminists. Both groups agreed that abortion had become a large-scale and socially significant phenomenon in American life, but they disagreed over the reasons why.

Before examining the two chief explanations put forward by contemporaries for the striking shifts in the incidence and the character of abortion in the United States after 1840, two observations may be worth making. First, it is never easy to understand why people do what they do even in the most straightforward of situations; it is nearly impossible to know with certainty the different reasons, rational and irrational, why people in the past might have taken such a psychologically loaded action as the termination of a suspected pregnancy. Second, most participants on both sides of the contemporary debate over why so many American women began to practice abortion after 1840 actually devoted most of their attention to the question of why American women wanted to limit their fertility. This confirmed that abortion was important between 1840 and 1880 primarily as a means of family limitation, but such discussions offer only marginal help in understanding why so many American women turned to abortion itself as a means toward that end.

Cultural anthropologists argue that abortion has been practiced widely and frequently in preindustrial societies at least in part because "it is a woman's method [of limiting fertility] and can be practiced without the man's knowledge."[20] This implies a sort of women's conspiracy to limit population, which would be difficult to demonstrate in the context of nineteenth-century America. Nonetheless, there is some evidence, though it must be considered carefully, to suggest that an American variant of this proposition may have been at least one of the reasons why abortion became such a common form of family limitation in the United States during the period. A number of physicians, as will become evident, certainly believed that one of the keys to the upsurge of abortion was the fact that it was a uniquely female practice, which men could neither control nor prevent. . . .

Earlier in the century observers had alleged that the tract literature and lectures of the women's rights movement advocated family planning and disseminated abortifacient information.[21] In 1859 Harvard professor Walter Channing reported the opinion that "women for whom this office of foeticide, unborn-child-killing, is committed, are strong-minded," and no later writer ever accused them of being weak-minded.[22] . . .

The most common variant of the view that abortion was a manifestation of the women's rights movement hinged upon the word "fashion." Over and over men claimed that women who aborted did so because they cared more about scratching for a better perch in society than they did about raising children. They dared not waste time on the latter lest they fall behind in the former. Women, in short, were accused of being aggressively self-indulgent. Some women, for example, had "the effrontery to say boldly, that they have neither the time nor inclination to nurse babies"; others exhibited "self-indulgence in most disgusting forms"; and many of the women practicing abortion were described as more interested in "selfish and personal ends" or "fast living" than in the maternity for which God had supposedly created them.[23] ... For this reason, some doctors urged that feticide be made a legal ground for divorce.[24] A substantial number of writers between 1840 and 1880, in other words, were willing to portray women who had abortions as domestic subversives. ...

Notwithstanding the possibility that recourse to abortion sometimes reflected the rising consciousness of the women who had them, and notwithstanding the fact that some males, especially regular physicians, were distinctly uneasy about the practice because of what its ultimate effects upon the social position of women might be, the relationship between abortion and feminism in the nineteenth century nevertheless remained indirect and ironical. This becomes evident when the arguments of the feminists themselves are analyzed. One of the most forceful early statements of what subsequently became the feminist position on abortion was made in the 1850s in a volume entitled *The Unwelcome Child.*[25] The author, Henry C. Wright, asserted that women alone had the right to say when they would become pregnant and blamed the tremendous outburst of abortion in America on selfishly sensual husbands. Wright's volume was more interesting than other similar tracts, however, because he published a large number of letters from women detailing the circumstances under which they had sought abortions.

One of Wright's letters was from a woman who had her first abortion in 1841, because her one-year-old firstborn was sick and her husband was earning almost nothing. She "consulted a lady friend, and by her persuasion and assistance, killed" the fetus she was carrying. When she found herself pregnant again shortly thereafter she "consulted a physician. ... He was ready with his logic, his medicines and instruments, and told me how to destroy it. After experimenting on myself three months, I was successful. I killed my child about five months after conception." She steeled herself to go full term with her next pregnancy and to "endure" an addition to her impoverished and unhappy household. When pregnant again she "employed a doctor, to kill my child, and in the destruction of it ... ended my power to be a mother." The woman's point throughout, however, was that abortion "was most repulsive" to her and her recourse to it "rendered [her] an object of loathing to [her]self." Abortion was not a purposeful female conspiracy, but an undesirable necessity forced by thoughtless men. As this woman put it: "I was the veriest slave alive."[26] ...

The attitudes expressed by Wright's correspondents in the 1840s and 1850s became the basis of the official position of American feminists toward abortion after the Civil War. As Elizabeth Cady Stanton phrased it, the practice was one more result of "the degradation of woman" in the nineteenth century, not of woman's rising consciousness or expanding opportunities outside the home.[27] ... The remedy to the problem of abortion in the United States, in their view, was not legalized abortion open to all but *"the education and enfranchisement of women"* which would make abortion unnecessary in a future world of egalitarian respect and sexual discretion.[28] In short, most feminists, though they agreed completely with other observers that abortion was endemic in America by midcentury, did not blame the increase on the rising ambitions of women but asserted with Matilda E. J. Gage "that this crime of 'child murder,' 'abortion,' 'infanticide,' lies at the door of the male sex."[29] The *Woman's Advocate* of Dayton, Ohio, put it even more forcefully in 1869: "Till men learn to check their sensualism, and leave their wives free to choose their periods of maternity, let us hear no more invectives against women for the destruction of prospective unwelcome children, whose dispositions, made miserable by unhappy ante-natal conditions, would only make their lives a curse to themselves and others."[30] ...

Despite the blame and recrimination evoked by the great upsurge of abortion in the United States in the nineteenth century, some of which was directed at women and some at men, it appears likely that most decisions to use abortion probably involved couples conferring together, not just men imposing their wills or women acting unilaterally, and that abortion was the result of diffuse pressures, not merely the rising consciousness of women or the tyrannical aggressions of men. American men and women wanted to express their sexuality and mutual affections, on the one hand, and to limit their fertility, on the other. Abortion was neither desirable nor undesirable in itself, but rather one of the few available means of reconciling and realizing those two higher priorities. And it seems likely that the man and woman agreed to both of those higher priorities in most instances, thus somewhat mooting in advance the question of which one was more responsible for the decisions that made abortion a common phenomenon in mid-nineteenth-century America.[31]

Court records provide one source of evidence for the mutuality of most abortion decisions. Almost every nineteenth-century abortion case that was written up, whether in the popular press, in medical journals, or in the official proceedings of state supreme courts, involved the agreement of both the man and the woman. There is no record of any man ever having sued any woman for aborting his child. . . .

Perhaps the best evidence for the likely mutuality of most abortion decisions is contained in the diary that Lester Frank Ward, who later became one of America's most famous sociologists, kept as a newlywed in the 1860s. Though Ward was unique in writing down the intimate decisions that he and his wife had to make, the couple seemed otherwise typical young Americans, almost as Tocqueville might have described them, anxious for further education and ambitious to get ahead quickly. Both Ward and his wife understood that a child would overburden their limited resources and reduce the probability of ever realizing either their individual goals of self-improvement or their mutual goals as a couple. They avoided pregnancy in pre-marital intercourse, then continued to avoid it after their marriage in August 1862. Not until early in 1864 did Lizzie Ward become pregnant. In March, without consulting her husband, she obtained "an effective remedy" from a local woman, which made her very sick for two days but helped her to terminate her pregnancy. She probably took this action after missing three or four periods; it was still early enough in gestation that her husband did not realize she was pregnant but late enough that lactation had begun. Ward noted in his diary that "the proof" she had been pregnant was "the milk" that appeared after the abortion.[32]

Anti-feminists might have portrayed Lizzie Ward's action as diabolical, a betrayal of duty. Feminists might have viewed it as the only recourse open to a female who wanted both to further her own education and to remain on good terms with an ambitious spouse who would certainly have sacrificed his wife's goals to child-rearing, while he pursued his own. But the decision was really the result of a pre-existing consensus between the two of them. Though Ward had not been party to the process in a legal or direct sense, which may go some distance toward confirming the role of abortion as a more uniquely female method of family limitation than contraception, he was clearly delighted that his wife was "out of danger" and would not be having a child. After this brush with family responsibility, the Wards tried a number of new methods of contraception, which they presumably hoped would be more effective than whatever they had been using to avoid pregnancy before Lizzie had to resort to abortion. These included both "pills" and "instruments." Not until the summer of 1865, after Ward had obtained a decent job in Washington, did the couple have a baby.[33]

Abortion had been for the Wards what it apparently also was for many other American couples: an acceptable means toward a mutually desirable end, one of the only ways they had to allow themselves both to express their sexuality and affection toward each other with some degree of frequency and to postpone family responsibilities until they thought they were better prepared to raise children. The line of acceptability for most Americans trying to reconcile these twin priorities ran just about where Lizzie Ward had drawn it. Infanticide, the destruction of a baby after its birth, was clearly unacceptable, and so was abortion after quickening, though that was a much grayer area than infanticide. But abortion before quickening, like contraception itself, was an appropriate and legally permissible method of avoiding unwanted children. And it had one great advantage, as the Wards learned, over contraception: it worked. As more and more women began to practice abortion, however, and as the practice changed from being invisible to being visible, from being quantitatively insignificant to being a systematic practice that terminated a substantial number of pregnancies after 1840, and from being almost entirely a recourse of the desperate and the socially marginal to being a commonly employed procedure among the middle and upper classes of American society, state legislators decided to reassess their policies toward the practice. Between 1840 and 1860 law-makers in several states began to respond to the increase of abortion in American life.

Notes

1. The quickening doctrine went back to the thirteenth century in England.... On quickening in the common law see Cyril C. Means, Jr., "The Law of New York concerning Abortion and the Status of the Foetus, 1664–1968: A Case of Cessation of Constitutionality," *New York Law Forum* XIV, no. 3 (Fall 1968): 419–426.

2. Ibid., pp. 411–19, and John T. Noonan, Jr., "An Almost Absolute Value in History," in John T. Noonan, Jr., ed., *The Morality of Abortion* (Cambridge, Mass., 1970), pp. 1–59....

3. ... Buchan's volume was published in Philadelphia as early as 1782, where it went through many editions.... This remarkably successful book continued to be reprinted in America through 1850.

4. Buchan, *Domestic Medicine*, pp. 400, 403–4.

5. See, for example, Frederick Hollick, *Diseases of Women, Their Causes and Cure Familiarly Explained: With Practical Hints for Their Prevention, and for the Preservation of Female Health: For Every Female's Private Use* (New York, 1849), p. 150....

6. ... [See] George Ellington, *The Women of New York, or the Under-World of the Great City* (New York, 1869), pp. 399–400.

7. Peter Smith, "The Indian Doctor's Dispensary, Being Father Peter Smith's Advice Respecting Diseases and Their Cure; Consisting of Prescriptions for Many Complaints: And a Description of Medicines, Simple and Compound, Showing Their Virtues and How to Apply Them," [1813] reproduced in J. U. Lloyd, ed., *Bulletin of the Lloyd Library of Botany, Pharmacy and Materia Medica* (1901), Bull. #2, Reproduction Series #2, pp. 46–47.

8. John Burns, *Observations on Abortion: Containing an Account of the Manner in Which It Takes Place, the Causes Which Produce It, and the Method of Preventing or Treating It* (Troy, N.Y., 1808), pp. 73–81....

9. Heber C. Kimball in the *Journal of Discourses*, 26 vols. (Liverpool, 1857), V:91–92.

10. Thomas Massie, "An Experimental Inquiry into the Properties of the Polygala Senega," in Charles Caldwell, ed., *Medical Theses,...* (Philadelphia, 1806), p. 203.

11. ... William Petersen's widely used *Population* (New York, 3rd ed., 1975), p. 15, labels [the U.S. population from 1800 to 1830 as] the "underdeveloped" type and identifies its characteristics as a mixed economy, high fertility rates, falling mortality rates, and very high rates of population growth.

12. Massie, "Polygala Senega," p. 204.

13. John G. Metcalf, student notebooks written while attending Dr. Walter Channing's lectures of midwifery at Harvard Medical School, 1825–1826 (Countway Library, Harvard Medical School), entry for Dec. 27, 1825....

14. Hugh L. Hodge in Francis Wharton and Moreton Stillé, *Treatise on Medical Jurisprudence* (Philadelphia, 1855), p. 270.

15. "Report on Criminal Abortion," *Transactions of the American Medical Association* XII (1859):75.

16. E. P. Christian, "Report to the State Medical Society on Criminal Abortions," *Peninsular & Independent Medical Journal* II:135.

17. "Criminal Abortions," *Buffalo Medical Journal and Monthly Review* XIV (1859):249.

18. *Boston Medical and Surgical Journal* XLIV, no. 14 (May 7, 1851):288.... Worthington Hooker, *Physician and Patient...* (New York, 1849), passim, and especially pp. 405–8. The estimate on income is from Colin B. Burke, "The Quiet Influence" (Ph.D. diss, Washington University of St. Louis, 1973):69, Table 2.19.

19. A Physician of New-York, *Trial of Madame Restell, For Producing Abortion on the Person of Maria Bodine,...* (New York, 1847), pp. 3–4, 10.

20. Kingsley Davis and Judith Blake, "Social Structure and Fertility: An Analytical Framework," *Economic Development and Cultural Change* IV, no. 3 (April 1956):230.

21. Hooker, *Physician and Patient*, p. 93; James Reed, *From Private Vice to Public Virtue: The Birth Control Movement and American Society since 1830* (New York, 1978), chaps. 1–5.

22. Walter Channing, "Effects of Criminal Abortion," *Boston Medical and Surgical Journal* LX (Mar. 17, 1859):135.

23. E. M. Buckingham, "Criminal Abortion," *Cincinnati Lancet & Observer* X (Mar. 1867):141; Channing, "Effects of Criminal Abortion," p. 135; J. C. Stone, "Report on the Subject of Criminal Abortion," *Transactions of the Iowa State Medical Society* I (1867):29; J. Miller, "Criminal Abortion," *The Kansas City Medical Record* I (Aug. 1884):296.

24. [See] H. Gibbons, Sr., "On Feticide," *Pacific Medical and Surgical Journal* (San Francisco) XXI, no. 3 (Aug. 1879):97–111;...

25. Henry C. Wright, *The Unwelcome Child; or, the Crime of an Undesigned and Undesired Maternity* (Boston, 1860). The volume was copyrighted in 1858.

26. Ibid., pp. 65–69.

27. E[lizabeth] C[ady] S[tanton], "Infanticide and Prostitution," *Revolution* I, no. 5 (Feb. 5, 1868):65.

28. Ibid. For the same point reiterated see "Child Murder," in ibid. I, no. 10 (Mar. 12, 1868):146–47....

29. Ibid. I, no. 14 (Apr. 9, 1868):215–16.

30. E. V. B., "Restellism, and the N.Y. Medical Gazette," *Woman's Advocate* (Dayton, Ohio) I, no. 20 (Apr. 8, 1869):16. . . .

31. Carl N. Degler is one of those who have argued persuasively that nineteenth-century American women were very much aware of their own sexuality and desirous, morality books notwithstanding, of expressing it: "What Ought To Be and What Was: Women's Sexuality in the Nineteenth Century," *American Historial Review* LXXIX, no. 5 (Dec. 1974):1467–90.

32. Lester Ward, *Young Ward's Diary,* Bernhard J. Stern, ed. (New York, 1935), p. 140.

33. Ibid., pp. 150, 152–53, 174.

MAUREEN FITZGERALD

Habits of Compassion: Irish American Nuns in New York City

Even before the potato famine of 1845, the population of Ireland was declining, pressed by harsh British policies and the attraction of American opportunity. In the 1840s alone, death and immigration decreased the Irish population by more than 20 percent, and nearly half of all immigrants to the United States in that decade were Irish. And more than half of Irish immigrants were women. They were "the only significant group of foreign-born women who outnumbered men," writes historian Hasia Diner, and "the only significant group of women who chose to migrate in primarily female cliques."*

In the following essay, Maureen Fitzgerald examines the distinctive shape of Irish women's migration and the creative work of the institutions they built. How does Fitzgerald describe the desirability of convent life for Irish American women? How did Irish American nuns "change the nature of convent life even as they embraced it"? How did nuns respond to urban poverty? In what ways did they claim power in the public sphere? How were these ways different from the ways claimed by Protestant women of the same generation?

On Monday morning, August 17, 1896, a simple black hearse pulled by a single horse traveled through the streets of New York City. The hearse carried the body of Sister Mary Irene Fitzgibbon and was followed by four hundred of the three thousand Catholic nuns active in the city.[1] Like Sister Irene, most of the sisters hailed from Irish backgrounds, the children of Irish famine refugees. Thousands of mourners, including Protestants and Jews as well as Catholics, watched from the sidewalks and followed the hearse as it passed by their workplaces and through their neighborhoods, until the procession was estimated at twenty thousand. Secular and Catholic newspapers alike marked her death with prominent articles; the *New York Times*'s headline read simply "Sister Mary Irene Is Dead." The *Times* called her "the most remarkable woman of her age in her sphere of philanthropy," and other non-Catholic newspapers agreed. The *Herald* characterized the massive yet simple procession that marked her death as unprecedented: "Never in the history of New York has such a tribute been paid."[2]

*Hasia Diner, *Erin's Daughters in America: Irish Immigrant Women in the Nineteenth Century* (Baltimore: Johns Hopkins University Press, 1983), p. xiv.

Excerpted from the introduction and ch. 1 of *Habits of Compassion: Irish Catholic Nuns and the Origins of New York's Welfare System, 1830–1920,* by Maureen Fitzgerald (Urbana: University of Illinois Press, 2006). Reprinted by permission of the author and publisher. Notes have been edited and renumbered.

Over the weekend before 3,500 mourners paid their respects at the Foundling Asylum, Sister Irene's crowning achievement, an institution she had founded and then supervised for twenty-seven years. The Foundling Asylum housed an average of six hundred women and 1,800 infants at a time and also provided day care for working mothers, a maternity hospital for poor women, a children's hospital, and a shelter for unwed mothers. With an annual budget of $250,000 derived from *city taxes*, secured initially through Irish Catholic men's control of Tammany Hall, the Foundling Asylum was the largest institution of its kind in the country and the only one in New York City to guarantee care for all children and women who came to its doors, regardless of religion, race or ethnicity, marital status, or ability to pay for care.

The tribute paid to Sister Irene, although remarkable in itself, becomes more so when we consider that Sister Irene Fitzgibbon is virtually unknown to historians of women in the United States. She was but one of approximately two thousand Catholic nuns then active in New York City charities and whose charitable work was dependent primarily or exclusively on public funding. . . .

In the United States between 1830 and 1900, Catholic women established 106 new foundations of women religious and grew to a collective workforce of approximately fifty thousand. In New York City alone, the number of women religious rose from eighty-two in 1848 to 2,846 in 1898, not only increasing their own numbers exponentially but also composing the majority of the church workforce. While men and women joined the church in New York City in relatively equal numbers at mid century, the number of nuns grew to almost triple that of the combined number of priests and brothers by 1898.[3]

Irish and Irish American women, moreover, changed the nature of convent life even as they embraced it. . . . They transform[ed] convents from institutions run by elite women to those composed of and administered by women who had been poor or were from the working class. Convents thus became a primary means through which working class Irish Catholic women gained public power [although not a public voice]. Moreover, convents provided the Irish Catholic working class with the means to articulate and make manifest its political agendas and social vision.

Irish Catholic nuns considered protecting women and children in their group from the ravages of poverty, dislocation, and racial oppression to be central to their work, and they often did so through direct confrontation with Protestant middle-class women. The most derided and vulnerable of Irish Catholic women in nineteenth-century America was the destitute mother with children; she became the archetypal image of a woman whose mothering in poverty necessitated drastic societal intervention. Because they viewed poverty in the nineteenth century, as [many do] today, as a moral problem with roots in particular cultures, Protestant reformers believed that the best strategy for eradicating it was to intervene in motherhood so as to alter the reproduction of moral traits associated with poverty. According to the logic of Protestant reformers, Catholicism either exacerbated or was wholly responsible for the tendency toward dependency, and even alcoholism, evident in the behavioral patterns of the Irish Catholic poor. The sooner children could be removed from the influence of such a mother, community, and religion, the better. . . .

From the early 1850s through the mid-1870s, Protestant elite reformers removed tens of thousands of poor immigrant children from New York City streets and homes and sent them to Protestant homes in the Midwest. . . . The practice of taking urban poor children away from their natural parents rested on the normative belief that the American Protestant nuclear family, guided by the maternal devotion of the American woman, was the only proper setting for child-rearing in the American republic. . . .

A large workforce of Irish Catholic nuns in concert with a city political machine dominated by Irish Catholic men was able in the 1870s and 1880s to construct Catholic institutions that directly offset such programs. Sisters funded these institutions, moreover, through city taxes. In the name of the "parental rights" of the poor, nuns housed tens of thousands of children. . . . By 1885 they directly controlled most of New York City's public child-care system, rearing more than 80 percent of its dependent children while Jews and Protestants controlled 10 percent each. Nuns alone housed fifteen thousand children at a time; perhaps most important, they constructed a "revolving door" policy. They took children into their institutions at the initiation of poor parents, and on a temporary basis only, to be returned when parents themselves thought they were financially able to provide for them.[4] . . .

. . . After the Council of Trent in the early sixteenth century, all Catholic nuns were required to make solemn, lifelong vows and observe papal cloister or enclosure, thereby severely restricting their mobility, rights to property, and ability to transact business or interact directly with the larger populace. These contemplative orders, distinguished from "active" orders by enclosed status and a focus on prayer and meditation, were more likely to exist when and where wealthy women could bring sufficient dowries to convents to fund lifelong seclusion.[5]

In the late eighteenth century . . . Catholic women in Ireland and the United States began to form active "religious institutes" sanctioned by the pope but not regulated by the Vatican until the turn of the twentieth century. Because the women did not call themselves nuns but rather "sisters" or "women religious" and made annual, or what they termed "simple," vows, they were not subject to the same regulation of convent life that governed contemplative orders.[6] Catholic women transformed this opening into a cultural and political mechanism for collective organization and public authority. . . .

Irish Catholic women religious of the early nineteenth century were above all at the center of a nation that existed only in the imaginations of those committed to an Ireland free of British rule. . . . [T]hrough the Penal Laws instituted after Oliver Cromwell's conquest of the island in the seventeenth century, . . . Catholics in Ireland were legally barred from worship in Catholic churches, voting, holding public office, or passing on property to heirs. By 1750 Catholics owned only 5 percent of all the land in Ireland. The . . . [British], moreover, developed ideological rationales for colonization and Protestant rule that linked race to religion. The Irish were judged an inferior race over which dominion was justified because of the strength of Catholic "barbarism" among its people.[7] Although individual Irish people could avoid the worst effects of the Penal Laws by converting to Protestantism, few did. . . .

. . . Consider, for instance, Mother Mary Augustine, born Ellen McKenna, who joined the Sisters of Mercy in New York in 1849, approximately three years after a small contingent of the order had set off from their motherhouse in Dublin to establish themselves in the city. From the earliest days of her childhood McKenna was encouraged by her family to support the development of Catholicism as a gesture of solidarity with other Irish and against British colonialism.[8] . . .

Unlike most of the Irish peasantry who remained Gaelic-speaking, illiterate, and only nominally tied to the institutional church, for instance, Ellen McKenna was sent to school in Waterford at an early age. . . . Ellen McKenna's desire to enter a Catholic sisterhood was not an attempt to leave the world and its strife but rather an effort to play a leading role in shaping nationalist institutional Catholicism. The rise of institutional Catholicism in nineteenth-century Ireland was, perhaps above all, a cultural project in which Irish Catholic nationalists attempted to supplant the institutional structures of British colonialism with institutions of their own. Education and charities, because they decreased dependence on British National Schools and the British Poor Laws, were as central to that [catholic] nationalist vision as the building of parishes. By 1840, although having a workforce of only 1,600 sisters (in a population of eight million), 81 percent of Irish Catholic convents had instituted facilities and programs for the poor, including sick and prisoner visitation, free schools, meal and clothing distribution, houses of industry, and visitation of workhouses among other activities. Of the convents in Ireland, 84 percent ran schools by 1864.[9] . . . Some men in religious orders oversaw the education and care of boys, especially older boys, but charities, as in New York, were to become the almost exclusive province of nuns.

Although from a prosperous family, Ellen McKenna nonetheless experienced the trauma and catastrophe of famine by the mid-1840s, and emigration proved her greatest burden and constant inspiration. When the famine struck just after her father died, she aided the impoverished until the McKennas' own poverty became so great that they were forced to emigrate. Ellen deemed that experience a political "exile" as coerced as a political deportation. And yet she "offered it up" as penance, invoking the forced exile of St. Columba from Ireland:

> Dear St. MacCartin, fearful was the sorrow
> I offered at thy shrine as penance dread
> Upon this day, long, long ago, for Willville
> And home, and hope, to seek strange lands instead
> God, merciful and patient, oh! accept it—
> This hard Columban penance—thus away
> From our sweet motherland, our native country,
> To wear out life. Oh! aid me still, I pray.[10]

Ellen was no longer in Ireland but neither was she about to "wear out life." When her mother died in New York City in 1849, Ellen and her sister, Julia, both joined the Mercy Sisters in New York.

Called Sister Mary Augustine in religious life, Ellen worked immediately in the House of Mercy, the shelter for female famine migrants, where she interacted with thousands of starving Gaelic-speaking women who had fled peasant areas in western Ireland. At every point in her life thereafter she helped move the order into uncharted areas of charitable work, including the establishment of a home for destitute girls in 1860.

As mother superior of the order after the Civil War she also aggressively sought, and won, public funding through Tammany Hall, thereby enabling the order to branch out into work with children on an unprecedented scale. Ireland, however, was never far from her mind, nor were the British, whom she struggled to "forgive" as an act of charity. The continuing migration of the Irish to North America was for her a constant reminder of the deprivation and cultural losses the Irish were forced to endure and the responsibility she felt for reproducing that culture. As she characteristically observed to another Sister of Mercy in 1878, "It grieves me when the children we bring up know little about [St. Patrick] and about St. Brigid, the glory of Irishwomen.[11] . . .

. . . By 1860 the Irish accounted for 1.6 of the 2.2 million Catholics throughout the United States, thereby dwarfing the French, German, and Anglo Catholic communities. The strength of Irish cultural and ecclesiastic power in New York City was premised in part on the proportion of the church's workforce that was Irish. Fifty-nine (55 percent) of 107 male clergy in 1845 were born in Ireland. By 1865, twenty-three of the thirty-two Catholic parishes in New York City were Irish, distinguished from the rest by the English language spoken by priests.[12] The organization of the city's women religious also reflected Irish dominance as the Sisters of Charity, the Sisters of Mercy, and the Sisters of the Good Shepherd, established in New York City in 1817, 1846, and 1859, respectively, became more Irish over time. Each existed outside parish structures, in contrast to others such as the French Holy Cross Sisters and the German Sisters of Notre Dame that were attached, respectively, to French and German parishes. . . .

. . . Without a substantial middle class to foot the bill for churches, charities, and education, and with an ever-growing number of destitute people from peasant backgrounds constituting the laity, the church was poor and resources were scarce. Prioritizing how best to use the resources of the community, especially its labor and funding, was a constant and unresolved tension, and Catholic sisters were often at the center of such battles. . . .

Irish Catholic sisters had to contend with anti-Catholicism of all types, but anti-nun literature and Protestant assumptions about nuns' victimization certainly framed their struggles through the century. . . . [T]he belief that convents were brothels for the use of priests, in which women were tortured and raped, was not limited to a fringe of nativist fanatics. The most popular American version of the immorality of convent life, that contributed by Maria Monk in her *Awful Disclosures of the Hotel Dieu Nunnery of Montreal*, was published originally in 1836 and sold more than three hundred thousand copies by the Civil War, making it second only to *Uncle Tom's Cabin* in antebellum book sales.[13] . . .

Burning convents, avenging "escaped" nuns, and demanding convent inspection laws throughout the United States during the 1850s were all premised on an abhorrence of women's public space, free from male control. . . . Irish Catholic sisters were . . . at the very least inscrutable. Their daily lives, dress, behavior, and value systems did not reflect a "true womanhood" in which domesticity and motherhood rhetorically defined duties to family and nation. Nuns' "delusions" [e]voked . . . pity because their commitment to Catholicism, through which they established independence from individual men, made them literally incomprehensible as women.

Why then would Ellen McKenna choose life in a convent? When asked that question on applications for the Sisters of Mercy in New York, McKenna's cohorts were likely to state that they aspired to life in a sisterhood "for the greater Glory of God."[14] Yet such an assertion reveals relatively little about the reasons for the growth of convent life in nineteenth-century Ireland or why so many Irish women chose that life compared, for instance, to women in other Catholic cultures. . . . They, like Ellen McKenna, were likely to see opportunities and possibilities in the life of a religious that rendered other options less desirable.

At the heart of the choice was a willingness to make vows of chastity, poverty, and obedience. Making such vows seems a simple ritual on its surface, but each was made in the context of larger cultural shifts, and none was ever simple. . . . In the experience of women committed to life in a sisterhood the vows were not discrete but often in conflict. Negotiating their relative weight and balance in any situation or circumstance was at the heart of convent politics. . . .

Catholic women made vows of chastity in direct renunciation of the familial roles as wives, mothers, and daughters. The vows enabled nuns to cast themselves as special women sanctioned by the social and religious culture to live apart from the familial obligations most women were expected to honor. Nuns did not derive status because they were women but because they denied themselves the pleasures and fruits of the female body, especially sex and motherhood. And yet the vows were not only experienced as renunciation but also [paradoxically] as liberation. As Rose-Mary Reuther has [observed,] . . . "Women dedicated to asceticism could count on the support of the Church in making decisions against their family's demands that they marry and bear children."[15] . . .

Church leaders encouraged Irish Catholics to believe that a son or daughter's entrance into the church was a great honor for the family in general, yet Catholic parental resistance was often overt. When the founder of the New York convent of the Sisters of Mercy, thirty-year-old Mary O'Connor, decided to leave Dublin for New York in 1846, her mother beseeched the Dublin male hierarchy to interfere with her daughter's and the Mercy order's decision and convince her to stay in Ireland instead. . . . [From the convent nun's point of view,] conflicts between parents and postulants were expected. . . . [A]pplications for admission to orders asked explicitly if there was parental resistance to the women's entrance. . . . [Convents often denied] entrance to a novice if they believed that aged parents were dependent on that woman's wages or relied on her caretaking for their health. . . .

Among the most important reasons that so many Irish women chose to become women religious was that committing to a life of celibacy was not a radical break from the sexual patterns evident in much of Ireland. . . . The rising rural middling classes increasingly . . . plac[ed] enormous emphasis on consolidating land holdings. Instead of the rampant subdivision characteristic of peasants, only one daughter and one son in each family would be dowered or receive land. . . . Few women in this class could marry in Ireland. . . . Those deemed superfluous, moreover, such as a second or third daughter, understood from an early age that they would not be given a dowry and therefore had few options for marriage. As this pattern accelerated in the aftermath of the famine the proportion of people who remained unmarried in Ireland through most or all of their lives became very high by international standards despite high levels of emigration.[16]

Depopulation, not reproduction, was the organizing principle in gender and sexual relations in postfamine Ireland. One million deaths from starvation and disease and urgent emigration decreased Ireland's population from more than eight million in 1841 to 5.8 million in 1861. By 1921 Ireland's population was at 4.3 million, roughly half the 1841 census. Subdivision and population growth were unthinkable, given their role in making the poor so vulnerable to the potato crop's failure and contributing to what all classes believed was the death of Ireland as they knew it.[17] For many, sex itself was the culprit in Ireland's ruin, and demonizing sexual behavior outside, or even inside, marriage became a critical foundation for Irish Catholic sexual culture.

Thus as the nineteenth century wore on the respectability of all Irish Catholic women was contingent upon maintaining a sexually chaste lifestyle. Unlike American Protestant middle-class culture, however, Irish Catholic dependence on Catholic ascetic tradition worked in tandem with cultural shifts to position mothers and wives on relatively low rungs of a hierarchy of sexual respectability. In the Irish Catholic schema, "virgins" and nuns came first; widows, second; and wives, because of their continuing sexual experience, third. Once a woman lost her status as a virgin in Irish Catholic society, even within marriage, she would never regain it, nor would her position as mother offset the loss of status entailed by heterosexual experience. Protestant women, in contrast, continued to be labeled as sexually "pure" so long as their sexual experience was contained within the institution of marriage. . . .

For nuns, the vow of chastity was never only one of renouncing heterosexuality but always simultaneously a commitment to live in a community of women throughout one's lifetime and according to rules, and with cultural power, governing convent life. Women's ability, desire, and willingness to make a lifelong commitment to live and work with other women provided the social foundation of a sisterhood. Convent rules were often written with proscriptions against "particular friendships," meaning any attachment of particular nuns to each other that might interfere with the general harmony of community life, including exclusive attachments or favoritism, or friendships that led to sexual relations. . . .

Lifelong and very close friendships in convents were not just tolerated but assumed and encouraged. Sometimes two or three natural sisters would join the same sisterhood simultaneously. Women who could count favorite aunts or cousins as role models often followed them into convent life and sometimes into the same convent. Friends often entered convents together. . . . Sisters of Charity Irene Fitzgibbon and Teresa Vincent together founded and administered the Foundling Asylum, their partnership/friendship providing the core of continuity through nearly three decades of work and activism.[18] . . .

The vow of poverty was a complex and even paradoxical one. . . . At base, the vow of poverty was not intended to impoverish women religious but rather to encourage identification with "Christ's poor" in their work and spiritual lives. At times that meant suffering through very real poverty, but at other times women religious risked their work with the poor if they squandered or did not reproduce the wealth they had. Nor did all women religious embrace the same kind of commitment to poverty. Even within orders, poverty was often an unequal experience. . . .

. . . [E]ntrance into a convent allowed women the opportunity to collectivize wealth with other women and apart from men. Some who formed sisterhoods in pre-famine Ireland were very wealthy. . . . Their collectivization of women's wealth made sisterhoods perhaps the most powerful and rich female institutions in pre-famine Ireland. The act of joining a sisterhood moved an individual's wealth to the larger collective, and thus any individual lost their wealth as such. Yet through that action women also removed wealth from the control of men by placing it outside standard patriarchal inheritance structures. When those who dedicated their wealth to the sisterhood died, relatives could not claim an inheritance; the property remained in the hands of the present and future sisterhood.

The premise of sisterhoods' financial autonomy was augmented by the American legal system; nuns maintained feme sole legal status throughout their lifetimes. Married women of the period, who were defined [as] feme covert, or "covered" in marriage, generally did not hold property individually; the property was assumed to become their husbands'. . . .

Nuns, conversely, by virtue of their feme sole status, could and did collectivize wealth, incorporate institutions under exclusively female control, derive revenue from business transactions, sign contracts, and secure loans. No men in the church, furthermore, had either legal or cultural claims to such wealth. Their collective financial and legal power thereby enabled women religious to establish female-run and female-owned public institutions at a time when the most radical woman's rights activists in Protestant America rarely lived apart from marriage or owned property of their own. Catherine Beecher herself, the chief advocate of American marital domesticity, noted in 1843 that Catholic nuns had means to power that she did not. "The rich and noble have places provided as heads of great establishments," she wrote, "where in fact they have a power and station and influence which even ambition might seek." That Catholic nuns lived and worked in the public sphere in all-female enclaves long before such organization was perceived as a social or political possibility for Protestant middle-class women was for Beecher self-evident. As an ambitious unmarried woman who spent her adult lifetime with no clear channels through which to engage her talents and education, Beecher lamented that Protestant culture did not allow her to live and work together with other women in a women's community.[19]

Not all sisters shared equally in that wealth and power. European orders, including those of Irish origin, were divided into lay and choir sisters, the latter the more wealthy postulants. At mid-century, poor women who entered sisterhoods would most likely make vows as a "lay sister." Lay sisters were expected to perform the tasks of domestic servants in convents, thereby freeing the choir sisters for "higher" pursuits. In the American context, however, these distinctions quickly eroded, both because there were so few wealthy women with a requisite choir sister's dowry (approximately five hundred pounds) and because lay sisters actively protested against this caste system. . . .

. . . New York's Mercy lay sisters were successful in gradually winning the abolition of outward indications of class status. In 1878 they were no longer required to wear a distinctive apron that set them apart from choir, and by 1895 community records no longer referred to any single member as choir or lay, even if they were professed as such. Individual work schedules of the New York Mercy Sisters show that while some women worked consistently in high-status or low-status jobs, such as academy teaching or kitchen work, there was often considerable flexibility in work assignments for women over a lifetime. One sister worked alternatively as a first- and fourth-grade teacher in the select school, a kitchen worker, and sewing worker in the boys' home over a ten-year period. Others alternated between sewing, kitchen, teaching, and administrative duties throughout their lifetimes.[20]

Poverty was understood broadly as an ascetic life, denying pleasure and comfort. . . . And yet freedom *from* the world, rather than *in* the world, allowed women public legitimacy in offering a critique of society. . . . As the Irish poor swelled the prisons in New York City and the Sisters of Mercy and Sisters of Charity undertook daily prison visitations, they frequently befriended men and women characterized as irredeemable by native-born Protestants. Catherine Seton, . . . [one of] the Mercy Sisters, became attached to a young man who spent time variously at Sing Sing, the Tombs, and the city penitentiary. After his failed attempt at armed robbery, Mother Seton sent him $5 to aid in his escape and promised to care for his wife and children. When another of her protegés died, she inherited the tools he used for breaking and entering, including jimmies and pistols.[21] That such stories were included in the Mercy Sisters' published annals suggests an unwillingness to accept uncritically the notions of the native-born middle class about exactly what constituted criminality, respectability, or viciousness. In classic Irish fashion it also made for a good, funny story in the midst of tragedy.

For those orders committed to work with the poor in New York City and throughout the United States, financial pressures constantly vied with individual sisterhoods' efforts to keep their work and "mission" focused on those in poverty. . . . In the United States, all charitable sisterhoods had to devise a means of income capable of sustaining both the order itself and its charitable work. The most common strategy was to create an elite school in which tuition was charged and then use that tuition for the convent's upkeep and charities. . . .

Until the mid 1840s, women formed and joined convents in the United States and Ireland with the understanding that women's orders were parallel, separate entities that coexisted with but were not subordinate to local or national male ecclesiastical structures. Convents and monasteries were subordinate to the pope and maintained hierarchies within their respective orders, but most were not subject to the bishops in the dioceses in which they worked. Between their foundation in New York in 1817 and 1846, for instance, New York's Sisters of Charity, like other local convents of the Sisters of Charity, was accountable to their motherhouse at Emmitsburg, Maryland. The motherhouse retained ultimate control of sisters who worked in any specific diocese, and the wishes of local bishops, priests, and laity were considered secondary to the demands and needs of the order at large. Within the motherhouse, a mother general was considered the head officer, followed by assistant mother, bursar, mistress of novices, and various grades of sisters, including professed sisters, novices, and postulants. In each city in which the sisters worked, moreover, internal convent hierarchies were replicated.[22] When nuns established institutions in which they lived apart from the main local convent, particular sisters, usually called sisters superior or head sisters, would be given ultimate charge of the specific institutions. Although the rationalization of the order allowed nuns in localities distant from the motherhouse to govern their own lives and activism in ways responsive to local contexts, they remained ultimately responsible to the motherhouse.

Motherhouse rule was the linchpin in convent autonomy, and through it sisters were able to control the kinds of work they did, their religious lives, and, most important, their ability to make vows of obedience to other women, not to men. Until 1846 the Sisters of Charity did not make vows of obedience to the church at large, but rather to the order to which they belonged, specifically to the mother superior and other female leadership. Obedience, moreover, was interpreted more broadly than simple subordination to specific people. It included the utilization of individual conscience to determine if a superior's actions were in accordance with the larger "mission" or apostolate of each distinctive sisterhood. Dedicating the order and collective lives of nuns to charity, for instance, and to a particular group in poverty—whether orphans, prostitutes, or unwed mothers—meant that those who made vows of obedience were dedicating themselves simultaneously to a religious lifestyle and a lifetime of work. A postulant would learn about the "spirit" or "mission" of the order through intensive study and contemplation of the reasons for the order's foundation, especially through writing by and stories about the founding superior.

When individuals or groups in a community felt that the superiors of an order took action that pitted their obligations to the mission against those to the convent's leadership, community discord could be great enough to induce the majority of professed sisters in the community to impede the reelection or encourage resignation of convent officers. . . .

On an individual level, women religious who rejected the tenor or politics of convent life could simply leave. Despite the dramatic "escapes" so vivid in anti-nun literature, no active orders were "enclosed," and therefore no women within them were barred from leaving at will. Sisters in active orders took yearly "simple vows," not lifelong vows, and therefore could leave convents without a formal repudiation of those vows. In practice, however, the system of novitiate, postulancy, and final profession, which lasted anywhere from three to five years, was expected to weed out those who either did not want to commit to the order for a lifetime or were considered unacceptable by the professed sisters, who would have the final vote in chapter meeting to recommend continuance or expulsion.

On both an individual and collective level, obedience demanded a selflessness that required extraordinary ascetic discipline. As Mother Mckenna advised young Sisters of Mercy about to make their vows in 1873, that sacrifice was intended to benefit both the soul and others in the world:

> . . . I pray God that your heart and soul may be devoted to the poor, sick, and that serving the Lord in His poor, He may make you rich in graces and blessings. . . . Inch by inch this sacrifice is exacted by little trials, more galling than great ones. To say nothing when we would naturally say something sharp; to do simply as we are told, without objection or remonstrance, . . . to seem cheerful when the heart aches, to be kind in return for unkindness, . . .—these efforts will be sacrifices.

Yet Mother Augustine McKenna was also supremely conscious of the need to balance obedience against ambition and assertiveness, particularly when that ambition was in the name of others who needed her help. As the chief architect of the order's work with children, then Sister McKenna wrote out a separate promise to herself and God in 1860 and placed it at the back of the book that held her original vows. She showed it to no one, but other Sisters of Mercy found it and buried it with her. Mother McKenna wrote [in part]:

> In the name of our Lord and Saviour, Jesus Christ, and under the protection of His Immaculate Mother, Mary ever Virgin, I, Sister Mary Augustine, for the love of his Sacred Heart, do resolve,

> but not vow, to suffer all the blame, shame, and humiliation, toil, trial, and trouble, that it may be God's will to permit, in order to establish a home for homeless children. I protest that, in all that concerns it, I rely solely on the assistance of God and the guidance of the Holy Spirit. . . . [23]

[when she wrote this, she knew that her proposal for moving into work with poor children would provoke the archbishop's anger.] As Mother McKenna's resolution suggests, obedience was hardly passivity. . . . Her obedience to the spiritual authorities above was constructed in such a way to ready herself for the worldly battles to come.

And yet few even in the Catholic community understood fully what either Mother McKenna or other sisters did and thought on a regular basis. Indeed, the single most salient political limitation affecting sisters' overall power in nineteenth-century America was their relative lack of public voice. Whereas white, Protestant, middle-class women increasingly legitimated their claims to public power through a set of rational discourses promoting their cause as women or as mothers, nuns were reluctant to promote their causes through public discourse.

The effect of that limitation was both far-reaching and paradoxical. The most powerful women in the church, including the founder of the Foundling Asylum, Sister Irene Fitzgibbon, demanded that they be treated, and nuns under their guidance should treat themselves, as "old shoe[s]."[24] Consistent with an ethic of ascetic selflessness, Sister Irene's pronouncements should not lead historians to assume that these ostensible "old shoes" lacked substantial power. And yet their reluctance to claim that power as such, especially in public and to the larger community, proved decisive in public arenas in which the Catholic hierarchy or Protestant native-borns contested that power. Women religious were thus most vulnerable when discussion of themselves or their work moved to public arenas. Nor did this limitation affect only nuns. Because they were the female leaders in the Irish Catholic community, their unwillingness to spar publicly with Catholic men or Protestant native-borns made the relative power of Irish Catholic women as a group, and the causes they championed, similarly vulnerable to their posture of collective selflessness.

Part of the reason that nuns nave remained virtually invisible in nineteenth-century women's history is that the measures, or signposts, of their public power do not fit the framework constructed for understanding the public power of Protestant middle-class and elite women during the same period. Nuns' strengths were centered in areas of Protestant female reformers' relative weakness. Both white and black Protestant middle-class women derived public power through associational organizations and claims to public voice, especially through their role as mothers. Nuns' effectiveness, however, was based on an ability to live together and organize themselves as large bodies of single women who lived apart from marriage and domesticity. Convents became powerful collectives for activist labor through the sisterhoods' combined labor power in educational and welfare institutions, their centuries-long apprenticeship traditions and systems in nursing, teaching, and charities, their feme sole legal status and accumulation of wealth under exclusively female control, and their freedom from mothering and the direct controls of husbands. It was a form of public organization for welfare work, moreover, that most Protestant women were unable to construct until the turn of the twentieth century.

Indeed, if we concentrate on the spectacular growth of Catholic convents in America through the late nineteenth century, the dominant narrative of Protestant women's work in social reform through the Progressive Era begins to take new shape. Although histories of "women's" constructions of nursing, teaching, and social work rarely acknowledge the influence of Catholic female traditions in these areas, the roots of these "professions" are nonetheless everywhere entwined with the work of nuns. Settlement work in particular is deemed an extraordinary departure from all tradition in that it allowed Protestant women to live together, apart from marriage and within immigrant neighborhoods, and from that base construct charitable programs. The parallels to convent life are so obvious that the compelling question is not whether the convent served as a model for settlement life but why this parallel goes unanalyzed. That such a connection is not thought conspicuously absent is made possible primarily by our construction of frameworks that render nuns historically invisible.

. . . The limits and threats to nuns' power, . . . , were also often distinct from those that threatened Protestant women. Over the course of [the 19th century] nuns' relative power to men in their group was threatened most directly by the rationalization of bishops' authority over religious orders in their dioceses. That process of rationalization, however, was uneven. . . . A critical factor determining whether or for how long nuns could deflect male control . . . was their ability to gain financial independence from the hierarchy. [T]he public funding of nuns' charitable work helped orders delay substantial loss of autonomy until the early twentieth century.

Notes

1. Throughout this work I refer to Catholic women in religious institutes as "women religious," "sisters," and "nuns," thereby reflecting common usage but not canon law, which stipulated that only enclosed women religious be referred to as nuns.

2. *New York Times*, Aug. 17, 1896, 6; *New York Herald Tribune*, Aug. 18, 1896.

3. Mary Ewens, *The Role of the Nun in Nineteenth-Century America* (1971, repr. Salem, N.H.: Ayer Publishers, 1984), 86, 201, 252; *The Catholic Almanac for 1848* (Baltimore: F. Lucas, Jr., 1849), 180–81; *Hoffmann's Catholic Directory, Almanac and Clergy List* (Milwaukee: Hoffmann Brothers, 1898), 98–104.

4. A sizable literature on the availability of this option nationwide makes evident that poor parents used a variety of institutions to rear children temporarily through the Gilded Age period. See especially Patricia Kelleher, "Maternal Strategies: Irish Women's Headship of Families in Gilded Age Chicago," *Journal of Women's History* 13 (Summer 2001): 80; Timothy Hasci, *Second Home: Orphan Asylums and Poor Families in America* (Cambridge: Harvard University Press, 1997); Matthew Crenson, *Building the Invisible Orphanage: A Prehistory of the American Welfare System* (Cambridge: Harvard University Press, 1998).

5. Among the literature on Catholic sisters that has been critical to my understanding of their collective and distinctive histories are Carol K. Coburn and Martha Smith, *Spirited Lives: How Nuns Shaped Catholic Culture and American Life, 1836–1920* (Chapel Hill: University of North Carolina Press, 1999); JoAnn Kay McNamara, *Sisters in Arms: Catholic Nuns through Two Millennia* (Cambridge: Harvard University Press, 1996); and Diane Batts Morrow, *Persons of Color and Religious at the Same Time: The Oblate Sisters of Providence, 1828–1860* (Chapel Hill: University of North Carolina Press, 2002).

6. Two sophisticated studies of Catholic charitics have put the development of Catholic charities in a national context and in relation to the larger welfare system: Mary J. Oates, *The Catholic Philanthropic Tradition in America* (Bloomington: Indiana University Press, 1995), and Dorothy M. Brown and Elizabeth McKeown, *The Poor Belong to Us: Catholic Charities and American Welfare* (Cambridge: Harvard University Press, 1997).

7. Kerby A. Miller, *Emigrants and Exiles: Ireland and the Irish Exodus to North America* (New York: Oxford University Press, 1985), 21–23; William V. Shannon, *The American Irish* (New York: Collier Books, 1963), 21.

8. [Mother Mary Teresa] Austin Carroll, *Leaves from the Annals of the Sisters of Mercy*, 4 vols. (New York: Catholic Publication Society, 1889), 3: 203–13.

9. Caitriona Clear, *Nuns in Nineteenth-Century Ireland* (Dublin: Gill and MacMillan, 1987), 101–105.

10. Carroll, *Leaves from the Annals*, 3:207.

11. Ibid., 3:216.

12. Carol Wittke, *The Irish in America* (Baton Rouge: Louisiana State University Press, 1956), 89; James Olson, *Catholic Immigrants in America* (Chicago: Nelson-Hall, 1987), 29; Jay Dolan, *The Immigrant Church: New York's Irish and German Catholics, 1815–1865* (Baltimore: Johns Hopkins University Press, 1975), 22.

13. Preface to Maria Monk, *Awful Disclosures of the Hotel Dieu Nunnery* (1836, repr. Hamden: Archon Books, 1962), 1.

14. Applications for the Sisters of Mercy of New York, Archives of the Sisters of Mercy, Dobbs Ferry, N.Y. (hereafter ASMNY).

15. Rosemary Ruether, "Mothers of the Church: Ascetic Women in the Late Patristic Age," in *Women of Spirit: Female Leadership in the Jewish and Christian Traditions*, edited by Rosemary Ruether and Eleanor McLaughlin (New York: Simon and Schuster, 1979), 72.

16. K. H. Connell, *The Population of Ireland, 1750–1845* (New York: Oxford University Press, 1950); Robert Kennedy, *The Irish: Emigration, Marriage and Fertility* (Berkeley: University of California Press, 1973); Hasia Diner, *Erin's Daughters in America: Irish Immigrant Women in the Nineteenth Century* (Baltimore: Johns Hopkins University Press, 1983), 6–29.

17. Miller, *Emigrants and Exiles*, 346.

18. Sister Marie De Lourdes Walsh, *The Sisters of Charity of New York, 1809–1959*, 3 vols. (New York: Fordham University Press, 1960), 3: 64–88.

19. Catherine E. Beecher to Sarah Buckingham Beecher, Aug. 20, 1843, reprinted in *The Limits of Sisterhood: The Beecher Sisters on Women's Rights and Woman's Sphere*, edited by Jeanne Boydston, Mary Kelley, and Anne Margolis (Chapel Hill: University of North Carolina Press, 1988), 239–40, 110.

20. "Notes from the Annals of St. Catherine's Convent of Mercy," 1878, ASMNY; *Acts of Chapter, St. Catherine Convent, Madison Avenue, New York*, ASMNY; "Work Schedules," ASMNY.

21. Carroll, *Leaves from the Annals*, 171–72.

22. For the range of elective practices by convents in the United States, see Ewens, *The Role of the Nun*, passim.

23. Mother Mary Augustine McKenna to other Sisters of Mercy, 1873, reprinted in Carroll, *Leaves from the Annals*, 215, 209.

24. Sister Francis Cecilia Conway, "Notes on Foundling," Archives of the Sisters of Charity of New York at Mount St. Vincent. Sister Francis Conway worked with Sister Irene at the Foundling from 1890 to 1896.

SUSAN ZAESKE

Signatures of Citizenship: Debating Women's Antislavery Petitions

As women's activities during the Revolution demonstrate, women participated in politics and public life despite not having the vote. Petitioning legislatures, governors, and town governments had long been a strategy of women who wished to articulate a grievance or ask for relief, often on behalf not directly of themselves but of their family. In the decades before the Civil War, activist women working together presented the U.S. Congress with a radically innovative document: the large-scale collective petition.

The mass petition effort was motivated by the fervent desire some women felt to end slavery. In demanding that Congress hear their voices, abolitionist women had to have thick skins. Petitioning women often found other women hesitant and fearful, and found men scornful, even those political men who were supposed to take such good care of women's interests that they should be content not to have the vote.

The act of petitioning involved more than the silent scribbling of a signature, Susan Zaeske reports. To make a collective petition, someone had to carry it to potential signers and then convince a friend or neighbor or stranger to sign. The person who circulated the petition, who walked house to house in her neighborhood or brought it to church or market, had to be an articulate debater, prepared to meet contempt with patience and reason. As citizens who participate in political campaigns in our own time continually find, seeking political change is itself a politicizing experience.

What criticisms were leveled at women's efforts to petition for antislavery causes? Whose interests—besides those of slaveholders—were undermined by women's political participation? How did women—and their allies, like John Quincy Adams—defend their activities? How is it possible to have a political impact without the vote? (In our own time, young people involved in the environmental movement use some of the strategies that antislavery women devised.) What do you think is the relationship between the women's antislavery petition campaign and subsequent movements for women's rights and for the vote?

Early in February 1834 Louisa, Maria, Abigail, Rosey, and Caroline Dickinson signed their names to a petition addressed to the Senate and House of Representatives of the United States. They were joined by . . . scores of other Ohio women who together prayed Congress to abolish slavery in the District of Columbia. These westerners were among the first women in the United States to collectively petition Congress on a political issue. In so doing they defied the long-standing custom of females limiting their petitioning of Congress to individual prayers regarding personal grievances. During the coming years hundreds of thousands

Excerpted from the introduction and chs. 5 and 6 of *Signatures of Citizenship: Petitioning, Antislavery, and Women's Political Identity* by Susan Zaeske (Chapel Hill: University of North Carolina Press, 2003). Reprinted by permission of the author and publisher. Notes have been edited and renumbered.

of women from throughout the North would join the petition campaign and risk association with the unpopular cause of immediate abolitionism. Maria Weston Chapman, a leader of the petitioning effort, recalled that when antislavery women began to petition Congress, many Americans—male and female alike—were not "wont to witness the appeals kindly." Time and again female petitioners were assailed for leaving their "proper" sphere of the home and abandoning benevolent charitable causes to engage in petitioning and political action in the public arena. Yet antislavery women persevered, . . . seizing the radical potential of one of the few civil rights they were understood to possess—the right of petition—to assert substantial political authority.[1] . . . Large numbers of white and free black American women engaged in collective petitioning of Congress in an attempt to reshape public opinion and influence national policy. . . . [A]bsent the right of suffrage, petitioning provided a conduit for women to assert a modified form of citizenship. Although at the beginning of their involvement in the campaign in 1835 women tended to disavow the political nature of their petitioning, by the 1840s they routinely asserted the right of women to make political demands of their representatives. This change in the rhetoric of female antislavery petitions and appeals, from a tone of humility to a tone of insistence, reflected an ongoing transformation of the political identity of signers from that of subjects to that of citizens. Having encouraged women's involvement in national politics, women's antislavery petitioning created an appetite for further political participation and more rights. After female abolitionists established the right of women to petition Congress collectively on political issues, countless women employed that right to lobby their representatives and agitate public opinion to promote causes such as temperance, antilynching, and ultimately, woman suffrage.

From 1831 to 1863 women publicly expressed their opinion about slavery by affixing approximately 3 million signatures to petitions aimed at Congress. Women's efforts enabled abolitionists to send enough petitions to Congress to provoke debate over the question of slavery, a feat petitioning by men alone had failed to accomplish. . . . Deluged with petitions, in June 1836 the House of Representatives passed a rule immediately tabling all memorials on the subject of slavery. The [gag] rule proved a "godsend" to the struggling antislavery movement, for it linked the popular right of petition with the unpopular cause of immediate abolitionism. Petitioning was intended not only to pressure congressmen but also to rectify public opinion with regard to the sinfulness of slavery. By gathering signatures in family and female social networks as well as through soliciting door-to-door, women discussed the issue of slavery with people who would never go to hear an abolitionist lecturer and who could not read abolitionist tracts. . . .

Although women's petitioning soon became highly controversial, at the outset the philosophy of moral suasion and the tool of petitioning seemed to offer an especially suitable means for women to participate in the abolition movement. Women could use the right of petition—a right that, unlike the ballot, they were generally understood to possess—to apply the force of their supposedly superior morality to reform public opinion with regard to the sin of slavery. Although petitioning was less direct than voting, in the 1830s at least, it was not necessarily considered less powerful. Petitioning was seen as a pure expression of individual moral conscience, as opposed to the vote, which was viewed as tainted with personal interest and party spirit.

Central to comprehending the history of women's antislavery petitioning and its effect on women's political status is an understanding of the nature of the right of petition. At its core a petition is a request for redress of grievances sent from a subordinate (whether an individual or a group) to a superior (whether a ruler or a representative). As a genre of political communication, the petition is characterized by a humble tone and an acknowledgment of the superior status of the recipient.[2]

The supplicatory nature of the right of petition held radical potential for women, for natural law assumed that all subjects (and later all citizens) possessed the right of petition and that rulers (and later representatives) were obliged to receive and respond to petitions regardless of the subject of their prayer. Abolition women relied on the first assumption in order to claim and defend their right to petition amidst an environment in which their political status, like that of free blacks, was undergoing constant renegotiation. In fact, so labile was the political status of certain groups of inhabitants of the republic that state constitutional reform conventions of the 1820s and 1830s revoked free black men's voting rights, rights they had previously possessed and exercised. In 1837 the House of Representatives decided that slaves were not citizens and passed a resolution stating that they had no right of petition. For women, also a group whose political rights were vulnerable, petitioning amounted to an assertion that they possessed the right of petition and that they were citizens, though a type of citizen different from enfranchised men. By assuming the status of petitioners, women, though they lacked the vote, forced a hearing of their requests, for their representatives were obligated, in principle at least, to receive and respond to their grievances. Even when the House repeatedly passed gag rules that immediately tabled all antislavery petitions, through their continued petitioning, women kept alive the slavery question in public discourse. They added to congressional and general public debate, moreover, discussion of women's rights and the nature of female citizenship. . . .

. . . Sarah Grimké, an experienced signature gatherer, complained, "I have sometimes been astonished and grieved at the servitude of women, and at the little idea many of them have of their own moral existence and responsibilities. A woman who is asked to sign a petition for the abolition of slavery in the District of Columbia . . . not infrequently replies, 'My husband does not approve of it.' "[3] . . .

When women affixed their signatures to petitions, making a mark that authorized petitions as statements of their opinions, they threw off the cover of their husbands or fathers and asserted their existence as political individuals. For some women, lending their signature to a petition may have involved rejecting the notion that the signature of their husband, father, or brother adequately represented their opinion. For other women, signing a petition was an act of defiance against the wishes of male protectors, who might have opposed abolitionism or opposed women petitioning or both. It is worth noting, moreover, that throughout the campaign the vast majority of women eschewed the use of marital titles and signed petitions as, for example, Chloe F. Metcalf, Lydia W. Fairbanks, and even Philomela Johnson Jr. rather than Mrs. Metcalf, Mrs. Fairbanks, and Mrs. Johnson. Given that in 1890 Frances E. Willard was still urging women to write their names as individuals rather than as the wives of someone else, the petitioners' decision to drop "Mrs." during the 1830s appears to radically defy gendered signature norms.[4] . . .

Not only signing but also circulating petitions effected a transformation in women's political identities, for it provided practical experience in carrying out a campaign to influence public opinion. Female canvassers developed strategies specially suited to win women's signatures by incorporating women's daily routines and the spaces they inhabited into patterns of circulating petitions. Upper-class antislavery women, for instance, adapted the rituals associated with social visiting to the political activity of circulating antislavery petitions. . . . Middle-class women relied on family and religious networks in addition to other female associations, such as sewing circles, in order to circulate petitions. Hundreds of women of varying class and religious backgrounds went door-to-door seeking signatures from strangers.[5] . . .

Petition circulators also gained experience in practicing their skills of interpersonal persuasion, which involved internalizing arguments they read and heard as well as sharpening their skills of oral argumentation. Such skills are evident in a female signature gatherer's account of her interaction with an older woman who was reluctant to sign a petition. "My *darter* [daughter] says that you want the niggers and whites to marry together," the elder woman reportedly said. Yet when pressed by the petition circulator, the woman admitted that she did not understand abolitionists to condone amalgamation and asked if indeed they did. "Why, no—that's no business of ours," the abolitionist assured her. "We leave all to do as they please with regard to it." The canvasser then explained that the petition simply asked Congress to free slaves in the District of Columbia. After making clear the goal of the petition, the circulator stated, "I suppose you know that the colored people in the District are held as property, bought and sold like beasts, and treated very cruelly. Now what we ask is, that Congress, which 'possesses exclusive jurisdiction' there, should give all those slaves their freedom and place them under the protection of law." The older woman responded in agreement and lamented the fact that her daughter was so mistaken.[6]

Although signature gathering "engendered self-confidence and assertiveness" . . . the resistance they encountered understandably led female abolitionists to regard circulating petitions as an unpleasant duty. . . . Several members of the Providence Rhode Island Female Anti-Slavery Society reported that although they had won many signatures, they found petitioning to be a "self-denying, and unpleasant task."[7] . . .

The burden of petitioning was worsened by denunciations from the press and the pulpit. Clergy and other traditionalists anxious about male political dominance were alarmed to see women encouraging one another to express publicly their opinions separate from those of their husbands. The *Boston Religious Magazine*, the *New York Commercial Advertiser*, and the *Providence Journal* all "sharpened their pens and brightened up their wits" to attack the idea of women circulating and signing petitions to Congress. These newspapers . . . questioned whether women knew anything about slavery and despised the idea that women should meddle with politics. They scolded "female petitioners" for the "impertinence" of "undertaking to teach Congress their duty."[8]

As bad as the editorial condemnations were, they were nowhere near as punitive as those issued by clergymen such as Pastor Albert A. Folsom of the Universal Church in Hingham, Massachusetts. . . . Folsom spelled out the unfortunate consequences that would befall a woman who petitioned with the "clamorous" abolitionists. Such a woman, he said, would begin by seeking "relaxation too often from her domestic obligations." Then she would leave her children and become a slave to her "appetites and passions" while she interested herself "with wonderful zeal in the cause of the Southern negro." Besides suggesting that women petitioners were sexually involved with male slaves for whom they advocated, Folsom predicted that abolition petitioning would poison women's souls, embitter their affections, and exasperate their feelings. "She, who is naturally amiable and modest, . . . is imperceptively transformed into a bigoted, rash, and morose being. . . . Self-sufficiency, arrogance and masculating boldness follow naturally in the train."[9] . . .

Male editors and clergy were not alone in condemning the political activism of antislavery women generated by the petition campaign. Early in 1837 the well-known reformer and female educator Catharine E. Beecher launched her attack on abolitionists and female activism through publication of *An Essay on Slavery and Abolitionism with Reference to the Duty of American Females*, which she wrote in response to Angelina Grimké's *Appeal to the Christian Women of the South*. In the process of encouraging women to petition and take action to abolish slavery, Grimké's *Appeal* advocated a radical expansion of women's role in reform work. Particularly alarming to Beecher was the fact that in carving out a role for women in the abolitionist movement, Grimké had described a model woman as deeply interested in political issues, critical of the clergy, resistant to social norms, confident of her authority to interpret the Bible, unwilling to subordinate herself to men, and defiant of the law. Beecher responded in her *Essay* that the plan of "arraying females" in the abolition movement was "unwise and inexpedient." Engaging in antislavery activity, she feared, would draw women "forth from their appropriate retirement" and thrust them into the "arena of political collision." Once woman entered the political sphere, Beecher predicted, she would be corrupted by power and would lose her "aegis of defence": her moral purity. Consequently she would forfeit "all the sacred protection of religion, all the generous promptings of chivalry, all the poetry of romantic gallantry." Rather than embracing Grimké's model of the active woman, Beecher pleaded with readers to preserve the status of woman by retaining "her place as dependent and defenceless, and making no claims, and maintaining no right but what are the gifts of honour, rectitude and love."[10]

Especially upsetting to Beecher were Grimké's entreaties for women to petition. "Petitions to congress, in reference to the official duties of legislators, seem, IN ALL CASES, to fall entirely without the sphere of female duty," Beecher retorted. The only proper persons to make appeals to rulers, she maintained, were those who appointed rulers: men. Women's role was not to petition legislators but to influence male friends and relatives to address legislators. "But if females cannot influence their nearest friends, to urge forward a public measure in this way, they surely are out of their place, in attempting to do it themselves. . . ."[11]

On one hand, defenders of women's right of petition clung to the argument that female moral superiority rendered women uniquely suited to petition. On the other hand, advocates employed bolder arguments that women possessed a natural and constitutional right of petition and that they were endowed with equal responsibilities and therefore equal rights with man. Angelina Grimké went so far as to argue that the fact that women were denied the right to vote provided no reason to deny them the right of petition. Republican principles demanded that women be heard in some way, she maintained, or Congress would be guilty of taxation without representation. The same reasoning, she implied, also led to the conclusion that women possessed the right to vote. Grimké was not alone in defending women's right to petition and connecting it to the franchise. In the course of defending the right of women to petition against slavery, John Quincy Adams would question, on the floor of the U.S. House of Representatives, the practice of denying women the right to vote.

Although the flood of antislavery petitions that swept into Congress when it convened on December 7, 1837, was sandbagged by a gag [rule,] those pertaining to the annexation of Texas continued to seep onto the floor of the House of Representatives. On March 5, 1838, the House referred all memorials relating to the Texas question to the Committee on Foreign Affairs, which was charged with composing a report about the content of the petitions and the expediency of granting their requests. On June 14 the report was presented by the committee's chairman, Benjamin Howard of Maryland. Annoyed by the preponderance of petitions from females, Howard expressed his "regret" that so many of the memorials were signed by women. It was inappropriate for women to petition their legislators, he said, because females were afforded ample opportunity for the exercise of their influence by approaching their fathers, husbands, and children in the domestic circle and by "shedding over it the mild radiance of the social virtues, instead of rushing into the fierce struggles of political life." By leaving their proper sphere, Howard charged, women were "discreditable, not only to their own particular section of the country, but also to the national character.[12]

Although few northern representatives during the 1830s defended abolitionists' right of petition, especially that of abolitionist women, John Quincy Adams rose to the occasion. "Sir, was it from a son—was it from a father—was it from a husband, that I heard these words?" demanded the former president. "Does this gentleman consider that women, by petitioning this House in favor of suffering and distress, perform an office 'discreditable' to themselves, to the section of the country where they reside, and to the nation?" Adams offered Howard a chance to retract his assertion: "I have a right to make this call upon him. It is to the wives and to the daughters of my constituents that he applies this language." Howard stood his ground. Adams retorted with a four-day harangue defending the propriety of women involving themselves in political matters and of exercising their constitutional right of petition. . . .

. . . John Dickson of New York and Caleb Cushing and Levi Lincoln of Massachusetts, followed Adams's lead in answering attacks on female petitioners. . . . [P]resenting the petition from the 800 ladies of New York, Dickson emphasized the benevolent nature of women's memorializing. "In the Jewish, Greek, and Roman histories," he recalled, "female remonstrance" heard in public councils "were the cause of 'enlargement and deliverance,' of 'light, and gladness, and joy, and honor,' to a despised and an oppressed people." They were, he said, "all-powerful in expanding and extending the principles of charity, humanity, and benevolence, and in breaking the chains of oppression." . . . Dickson characterized female antislavery petitions as motivated not by political gain but by benevolence. "Surely," he hoped more than believed, "the chivalry of this House will never permit it to turn a deaf ear to the remonstrance of ladies, pleading, as they believe, for the wronged and oppressed."[13]

Given the obstreperous attacks southerners leveled against female petitioners, it was necessary for northern members to do much more than deny that antislavery women harbored political motivations. They had to defend the character of female petitioners. As Adams complained, the petitions had been treated with contempt, and "foul and infamous imputations" had been "poured upon a class of citizens as pure and virtuous as the inhabitants of any section of the Union": females. Likewise, Lincoln represented petitioners from his district as "pure, elevated, and [of as high] intellectual character as any in the world, men and women, kind and generous, and of tenderest sympathies, who would no sooner do an injury or an act of injustice to any human being than the most chivalrous or true-hearted of the sons or daughters of the South."[14]

Yet at issue in the arguments over the character of female antislavery petitioners was more than their reputations as women. At issue was their status as citizens. Adams readily apprehended that attacks on the character of female petitioners effectively denied women's right of petition, and he took [Benjamin] Howard to task for representing the exercise of the right of petition as graceful to women as well as to their section of the Union and the nation as a whole. "Now to say, respecting women, that any action of theirs was disgraceful, was more than merely contesting their legal right so to act," Adams averred; "it was contesting the right of the mind, of the soul, and the conscience." This was no "light question," no mere quarrel over the honor of a few women, he emphasized. It concerned "the very utmost depths of the Constitution of the country" and affected "the political rights of one half of the People of the nation."[15]

Throughout the debates . . . , Adams maintained vehemently that there was no legal or constitutional principle linking the right of petition with the character of petitioners. When Adams presented a petition purportedly signed by nine ladies of Fredericksburg, Virginia, Representative Patton, who had lived in that city, assailed Adams for bringing before the House a petition from "mulatto" women of "infamous character." . . . Patton's insinuation that the petition emanated from prostitutes, disclosed Adams, influenced him not a wit in deciding whether or not to present the paper. Rather than worrying over the character of the petitioners, Adams said that he "adhered to the right of petition."

> Where is your law which says that the mean, and the low, and the degraded, shall be deprived of the right of petition, if their moral characters is not good? Where, in the land of freemen, was the right of petition ever placed on the exclusive basis of morality and virtue? Petition is supplication—it is entreaty—it is prayer! And where is the degree of vice or immorality which shall deprive the citizen of the right to supplicate for a boon, or to pray for mercy?[16]

. . . Adams grasped the opportunity . . . to turn the table and question the character of opponents of women's petitions. When in the course of debate Patton disclaimed actually "knowing" the "bad" women who had signed the petition but stated that he "knew of them," Adams said he was glad to hear it, for otherwise he would ask "if they were infamous women, then who was it that had made them infamous?" Not their own color, he judged, but their masters. Adams said he was inclined to believe this because "there existed great resemblances in the South between the progeny of the colored people and the white men who claimed the possession of them. Thus, perhaps, the charge of being infamous might be retorted upon those who made it, as originating from themselves."

Adams's comments threw the House into great agitation, for he had stabbed brutally at the honor of southern gentlemen. Despite the fact that in February 1837 he faced formal censure for casting character aspersions on southerners in return for the imputations against the Fredericksburg women, he persisted in the strategy of questioning the character of representatives who opposed female petitions. Adams shamed representatives who would turn a deaf ear to women's petitions, asking each member to suppose that his own mother was one of the petitioners: "Would you reject and turn the petition out of doors, and say that you would not even hear it read?" "Every member of the House has, or had, a mother," he observed, adding that "in the whole class of human affections, was there one sentiment more honorable, or more divested of earthly alloy, than that which every man must entertain for his mother." . .[17]

. . . [I]n his 1838 speech Adams focused on extending the reach of women's duties to include political affairs. . . . In response to Howard's claim that women had no right to petition Congress on political subjects,

Adams asked rhetorically, "What does the gentleman understand by 'political subjects'?" Adams answered that "every thing which relates to peace and relates to war, or to any other of the great interests of society, is a political subject. Are women to have no opinions or action on subjects relating to the general welfare?" Fellow Massachusetts representative Caleb Cushing bolstered Adams's statements, maintaining that "it seems to me a strange idea to uphold, in this enlightened age, that woman, refined and educated, intellectual woman, is to have no opinion, or no right to express that opinion." . . .[18]

Hoping to take advantage of patriotic sentiments, Adams also invoked heroines of the American Revolution. . . . He called up the example of Deborah Gannett, who had adorned herself in men's clothes, joined the patriot army, and fought for three years until she was wounded. Members of the House were aware of Gannett's feats because within recent memory they had voted to give her husband a military pension based on the services of his wife and had praised her on the grounds that she had "fought and bled for human liberty." After commending Gannett's actions, which involved rushing physically into "the vortex of politics," Adams asked how Howard could conceivably think it wrong for women to petition on a matter of politics. . . .[19]

Although Adams redefined politics to include all subjects relating to the general welfare and adduced numerous historical examples of women's involvement in politics, . . . he recommended a three-pronged test by which one could determine whether it was proper for women to deviate from the custom of remaining distant from politics. When presented with such a circumstance, prescribed Adams, one must inquire "into the motive which actuated them, the means they employ, and the end they have in view." Adams then applied this test to the case at hand, the petitions against annexation of Texas. As for the motive, he said, it was of the "highest order" of purity: "They petition under a conviction that the consequence of the annexation would be the advancement of that which is sin in the sight of God, viz: slavery." The means were appropriate, Adams said, because it was Congress who must decide the question, and it was Congress to whom the women must petition. Echoing a justification offered by the female petitioners themselves, he stated, "It is a petition—it is a prayer—a supplication—that which you address to the Almighty Being above you. And what can be more appropriate to their sex?" As for the end sought by female petitioners, it, too, was virtuous, pure, and of the most exalted character: "to prevent the perpetuation and spread of slavery through America." . . . Adams concluded, "the correct principle is, that women are not only justified, but exhibit the most exalted virtue when they do depart from the domestic circle, and enter on the concerns of their country, of humanity and of their God." Thus Adams repeated the argument employed in the women's appeals, addresses, circulars, and petitions that it was the moral duty of women to speak for those who could not speak for themselves and to help those who could not help themselves. In fact, Adams believed that benevolent activity was a particularly feminine trait: "I say that woman, by the discharge of her duties; has manifested a virtue which is even above the virtues of mankind, and approaches to a superior nature.[20] . . .

. . . Adams characterized Howard as denying women the right of petition because they had no right to vote. Then he asked, "Is it so clear that they have no such right as this last? And if not, who shall say that this argument of the gentleman's is not adding one injustice to another?" In a few short breaths Adams, son of the woman who in 1776 threatened that "the ladies . . . will not hold ourselves bound by any laws in which we have no voice, or representation," went so far as to suggest that women did, in fact, possess the right to vote and that it was an injustice that they were denied the practice of that right. In so doing he embraced a position more radical than that of many women's rights advocates of his time. On the floor of the House of Representatives he questioned the assumption that the Constitution denied women the right to vote. He suggested that the reason women did not vote was custom rather than lack of a right to the franchise. He declared that outright denial of women's right to vote was an injustice, as was the denial of women's right of petition. It would be another eight years before the women of New York petitioned their legislature for the vote, a decade before the National Woman's Rights Convention would assert that women possessed the right of suffrage, and eight decades before an organized movement of women persuaded Congress and the public to adopt the position Adams began to articulate on Friday, June 29, 1838.[21]

Women who had signed petitions were particularly pleased to read Adams's defense of their actions and showered praises upon him. When he returned to Massachusetts after Congress had adjourned, Adams was greeted by expressions of approbation in the form of several celebratory events hosted by women in towns of his congressional district. On September 4, 1838, the ladies of Quincy hosted a formal picnic and ball to honor him for defending their rights. . . . When Adams addressed the group, he thanked the women for their kind celebration and acknowledged the large number of petitions he had received from females of the district. Reviewing scenes from the two most recent sessions of Congress, he recalled that Howard had committed a "violent outrage . . . upon the [female] petitioners, and [an] insult upon the sex." . . . Adams said that he believed questions about the duty of women to participate in public affairs should be left to women's own discretion, and he felt assured "there was not the least danger of their obtruding their wishes upon any of the ordinary subjects of legislation," such as banks, tariffs, and public lands, "all which so profoundly agitate the men of this country." Women, he trusted, were concerned with other kinds of matters. In fact, he believed that "far from being debarred by any rule of delicacy" from petitioning, by the "law of their nature," which rendered them kind, benevolent, and compassionate, women were "fitted above all others" for the exercise of this right.[22] Adams could not bring himself to endorse unlimited exercise by women of the absolute right of petition. Instead he trusted—or perhaps urged—that they would act only on public matters related to woman's moral duty and would take no interest in purely political matters such as banks and tariffs. In other words, Adams expected female moral duty to guide the exercise of women's natural rights.

. . . At the core of the southern case against receiving female petitions was the indictment that the petitions constituted not good works resulting from women's Christian duty but, rather, politically motivated machinations controlled by fanatical ministers and wholly improper actions for women. Conflating notions of female duty with political rights, southerners argued that the women's petitions should be ignored because, having transgressed beyond their proper duties, these women were not respectable, and the House was not obligated to accept petitions from people of questionable character.

Adams remained steadfast in his conviction that women possessed a natural right of petition and perhaps a natural right to vote, yet he linked the exercise of women's civil rights to their duties as women. . . . He construed women's concerns and duties as reaching beyond the household to "every thing which relates to peace and relates to war, or any other of the great interests of society" or "the general welfare."[23] These, he said, were rightly women's concerns. Furthermore, Adams placed these concerns in the category of political subjects, implying that women's duties extended to participation in political affairs. . . . [He was not] willing to abandon the notion that men and women possessed different natures and therefore different duties. But Adams did attempt to use political philosophies associated with women's rights to expand significantly the entailments of women's duty into what many considered the male political realm. . . .

***

Notwithstanding the decline of organized abolition at the state and national levels in 1839, women continued to petition throughout the 1840s, 1850s, and 1860s, sending massive abolition petitions to Congress on the most pressing political issues of the day. . . . By the 1840s they had begun to mix their signatures with those of men; no longer did women accept the notion that men's names should be allowed to stand out because their opinions meant more to representatives. Moreover, the language of women's petitions during this later period dropped deferential overtures characteristic of the memorials of the 1830s and took on a bolder tone. By the 1850s female petitioning had grown so much more acceptable and abolitionist sentiment so much more popular that even its most outspoken critic of the 1830s—Catharine E. Beecher—signed her name at the top of a petition. Acceptance of the propriety of women exercising their right to petition was crucial to the success of the petition campaign to win passage of the Thirteenth Amendment. Finally, after three decades of petitioning and due in large part to the ongoing efforts of women who signed and circulated petitions, abolitionists secured their ultimate goal of emancipating the slaves. In the process of petitioning to end slavery, many women transformed their political identity from humble subjects to national citizens.

Notes

1. Maria Weston Chapman, *Right and Wrong in Massachusetts* (Boston: Henry L. Deveraux, 1840), pp. 11–13.

2. This definition of petitioning is drawn from the *Oxford English Dictionary*.

3. Sarah Grimké, *Letters on the Equality of the Sexes* (1837), in Larry Ceplair, ed., *The Public Years of Sarah and Angelina Grimké: Selected Writings* (New York: Columbia University Press, 1989), p. 239.

4. Frances E. Willard, "A White Life for Two" (1890), in Karlyn Kohrs Campbell, ed. *Man Cannot Speak for Her: Key Texts of the Early Feminists*, Vol. 2 (New York: Praeger, 1989), pp. 335–36.

5. Gerda Lerner, "The Political Activities of Antislavery Women," in *The Majority Finds Its Past: Placing Women in History* (New York: Oxford University Press, 1979), pp. 120–21.

6. *Liberator*, Aug. 4, 1837.

7. Lerner, "Political Activities of Antislavery Women," p. 125.

8. *Emancipator*, Aug. 17, 1837.

9. "A Lecture, Delivered Sunday Evening, by Albert A. Folsom, Pastor of the Universal Church, Hingham, Massachusetts," extracted in *Liberator*, Sept. 22, 1837.

10. Catharine E. Beecher, *An Essay on Slavery and Abolitionism, with Reference to the Duty of American Females* (Philadelphia: Henry Perkins, 1837), pp. 3–6, 97, 101.

11. Ibid., pp. 103–104.

12. John Quincy Adams, *Speech on the Right of the People, Men and Women, to Petition; on the Freedom of Speech and Debate in the House of Representatives of the United States; on the Resolutions of Seven State Legislatures and the Petitions of More than One Hundred Thousand Petitioners, Relating to the Annexation of Texas to this Union. Delivered in the House of Representatives of the United States, in fragments in the morning hour, from the 16th of June to the 7th of July, 1838, inclusive* (Washington, D.C.: Gales and Seaton, 1838), pp. 76–77.

13. *Gales and Seaton's Register of Debates in Congress*, 24th Cong., 1st sess., Feb. 2, 1835, pp. 1131–1132.

14. Ibid., 2d sess., Jan. 9 and Feb. 7, 1837, pp. 1315, 1624.

15. Adams, *Speech on the Right of the People to Petition*, pp. 77–78, 74.

16. *Gales and Seaton's Register of Debates*, 24th Cong., 2d sess., Feb. 6, 1837, pp. 1589, 1596.

17. Ibid., 2d sess., Feb. 9, 1837, p. 1675 and Jan. 9, 1837, p. 1315.

18. Adams, *Speech on the Right of the People to Petition*, pp. 69, 65–66; *Gales and Seaton's Register of Debates*, 24th Cong., 2d sess., Feb. 7, 1837, p. 1645.

19. Adams, *Speech on the Right of the People to Petition*, pp. 70–75.

20. Ibid., pp. 81, 68.

21. Ibid., pp. 65, 77. On the petitions for suffrage directed at the New York legislature, see Jacob Katz Cogan and Lori D. Ginzberg, "1846 Petition for Woman's Suffrage," *Signs* 22 (Winter 1997), pp. 427–439.

22. John Quincy Adams, *Memoirs of John Quincy Adams, Comprising Portions of his Diary from 1795 to 1848*, vol. 10, Charles Francis Adams, ed. (Philadelphia: J.B. Lippincott, 1874–77), pp. 35–37.

23. Adams, *Speech on the Right of the People to Petition*, 69, 65–66.

DOCUMENTS

Claiming Rights I

Sarah and Angelina Grimké: The Connection between Religious Faith, Abolition, and Women's Rights

Sarah and Angelina Grimké were the first, and it seems likely the only, women of a slaveholding family to speak and write publicly as abolitionists. They were the first women agents of the American Anti-Slavery Society to tour widely and to speak to audiences of men and women. They were the first women who, from within the abolitionist movement, defended their rights *as women* to free speech. They were sustained in their work by a deep religious devotion, and their writings are examples of the spirit in which many women's rights advocates developed a wide-ranging critique of the relationship between the state, churches, and families.

The Grimké sisters grew up in Charleston, South Carolina. Their father was a distinguished legislator and judge; although he gave his daughters a traditional female education (lacking Greek, Latin, and philosophy), when he trained his sons for the law he included his daughters in the exercises. Both young women were sensitive to the injustices of slavery; as a young woman Sarah broke the law against teaching slaves to read and Angelina held prayer meetings for the family's slaves. When she was twenty-four years old, Sarah accompanied her father to Philadelphia, where he sought medical treatment; after his death she returned there in 1821 to live among Quakers, who impressed her by their piety, simplicity, and refusal to hold slaves. In 1829 Angelina joined her; both became members of a Quaker meeting. Sarah committed herself to boycott products made in slavery; Angelina joined the Philadelphia Female Antislavery Society. When reformers faced violence from proslavery mobs in the summer of 1835, William Lloyd Garrison wrote strong editorials in the *Liberator* denouncing what he called a "reign of terror." Angelina Grimké responded with a letter complimenting him on his fortitude: "The ground on which you stand is holy ground," she wrote, "never—never surrender it."

Garrison surprised her by printing her letter; thus encouraged to write for a wide audience, Angelina went on to write *An Appeal to the Christian Women of the South*, part of which follows. The pamphlet sold widely in the North and made her reputation, but it was burned in Charleston.

When the American Anti-Slavery Society organized a group of "Agents" to travel and speak on slavery, Angelina and Sarah Grimké were among them. They began in late 1836, speaking to women in private parlors in New York City; by the turn of the year, no private room was big enough and they held their sessions in a Baptist church. They involved themselves in founding women's antislavery societies and organizing women's antislavery petitions to Congress; they published their speeches as pamphlets. In mid-1837 they moved on to Boston, where an intense debate among factions of abolitionists was already under way. Sarah wrote a series of essays that appeared first in newspapers and then as a pamphlet, *Letters on the Equality of the Sexes and the Condition of Women.* Here, we reprint excerpts from two of her letters.

In the summer of 1837, the Congregational ministers of Massachusetts published a "Pastoral Letter" attacking the Grimkés as unwomanly (partly reprinted here, with Sarah Grimké's response). In the past, the two reformers had offered their criticism of slavery in the context of religious faith; now they claimed that as moral individuals, women had as much right to take political positions as men. Though even some of their allies—including Theodore Dwight Weld, whom Angelina would soon marry—sought to dissuade them, they were forthright, as you can see, in their response to the clergymen. The term *feminist* had not yet been invented—it would be devised in the 1910s—but the ingredients of the concept were already present in the ideas of the Grimké sisters.*

ANGELINA GRIMKÉ, APPEAL TO THE CHRISTIAN WOMEN OF THE SOUTH (1836)

. . . Sisters in Christ I feel an interest in *you*, and often has the secret prayer arisen on your behalf, Lord "open thou their eyes that they may see wondrous things out of thy Law"—It is then, because I *do feel* and *do pray* for you, that I thus address you upon a subject about which of all others, perhaps you would rather not hear any thing; but, "would to God ye could bear with me a little in my folly, and indeed bear with me, for I am jealous over you with godly jealousy." Be not afraid then to read my appeal; it is *not* written in the heat of passion or prejudice, but in that solemn calmness which is the result of conviction and duty. It is true, I am going to tell you unwelcome truths, but I mean to speak those *truths in love*, and remember Solomon says, "faithful are the *wounds* of a friend." I do not believe the time has yet come when *Christian women* "will not endure sound doctrine," even on the subject of slavery, if it is spoken to them in tenderness and love, therefore I now address you. . . .

We must come back to the good old doctrine of our forefathers who declared to the world, "this self evident truth that *all* men are created equal, and that they have certain *inalienable* rights among which are life, *liberty*, and the pursuit of happiness." It is even a greater absurdity to suppose a man can be legally born a slave under *our free Republican* Government, than under the petty despotisms of barbarian Africa. If then, we have no right to enslave an African, surely we can have none to enslave an American; if it is a self evident truth that *all* men, every where and of every color are born equal, and have an *inalienable right to liberty*, then it is equally true that *no* man can be born a slave, and no man can ever *rightfully* be reduced to *involuntary* bondage and held as a slave, however fair may be the claim of his master or mistress through will and title-deeds. . . .

But perhaps you will be ready to query, why appeal to *women* on this subject? *We* do not make the laws which perpetuate slavery. No legislative power is vested in *us; we* can do nothing to overthrow the system, even if we wished to do so. To this I reply, I know you do not make the laws, but I also know that *you are the wives and mothers, the sisters and daughters of those who do*; and if you really suppose *you* can do nothing to overthrow slavery, you are greatly mistaken. You can do much in every way: four things I will name. Ist. You can read on this subject. 2d. You can pray over this subject. 3d. You can speak on this subject. 4th. You can *act* on this subject. I have not placed reading before praying because I

*See Gerda Lerner, *The Grimké Sisters from South Carolina: Rebels Against Slavery* (Boston, 1967) and *The Public Years of Sarah and Angelina Grimké: Selected Writings 1835–1839*, ed. Larry Ceplair (New York, 1989). The selections that follow are taken from the Ceplair edition, pp. 37–38, 54–56, 220–23, 268–69, 211, 216.

regard it more important, but because, in order to pray aright, we must understand what we are praying for; it is only then we can "pray with the understanding and the spirit also."

1. Read then on the subject of slavery. Search the Scriptures daily, whether the things I have told you are true. Other books and papers might be a great help to you in this investigation, but they are not necessary. . . .

2. Pray over this subject. When you have entered into your closets, and shut to the doors, then pray to your father, who seeth in secret, that he would open your eyes to see whether slavery is *sinful*, and if it is, that he would enable you to bear a faithful, open and unshrinking testimony against it, and to do whatsoever your hands find to do . . .

3. Speak on this subject. It is through the tongue, the pen, and the press, that truth is principally propagated. Speak then to your relatives, your friends, your acquaintances on the subject of slavery; be not afraid if you are conscientiously convinced it is *sinful*, to say so openly, but calmly, and to let your sentiments be known. If you are served by the slaves of others, try to ameliorate their condition as much as possible; never aggravate their faults, and thus add fuel to the fire of anger already kindled in a master and mistress's bosom. . . .

4. Act on this subject. Some of you *own* slaves yourselves. If you believe slavery is *Sinful*, set them at liberty, "undo the heavy burdens and let the oppressed go free." If they wish to remain with you, pay them wages, if not let them leave you. Should they remain teach them, and have them taught the common branches of an English education; they have minds and those minds, *ought to be improved*. So precious a talent as intellect, never was given to be wrapt in a napkin and buried in the earth. It is the *duty* of all, as far as they can, to improve their own mental faculties, because we are commanded to love God with *all our minds*, as well as with all our hearts, and we commit a great sin, if we *forbid or prevent* that cultivation of the mind in others, which would enable them to perform this duty. Teach your servants then to read & c, and encourage them to believe it is their *duty* to learn, if it were only that they might read the Bible.

But some of you will say, we can neither free our slaves nor teach them to read, for the laws of our state forbid it. Be not surprised when I say such wicked laws *ought to be no barrier* in the way of your duty, and I appeal to the Bible to prove this position. What was the conduct of Shiphrah and Puah, when the king of Egypt issued his cruel mandate, with regard to the Hebrew children? "*They* feared *God*, and did *not* as the King of Egypt commanded them, but saved the men children alive." Did these *women* do right in disobeying that monarch? "*Therefore* (says the sacred text,) God *dealt well* with them, and made them houses."

SARAH M. GRIMKÉ, LETTERS ON THE EQUALITY OF THE SEXES AND THE CONDITION OF WOMEN (1837)

Letter VIII: "On the Condition of Women in the United States"

During the early part of my life, my lot was cast among the butterflies of the *fashionable* world; and of this class of women, I am constrained to say, both from experience and observation, that their education is miserably deficient; that they are taught to regard marriage as the one thing needful, the only avenue to distinction; hence to attract the notice and win the attentions of men, by their external charms, is the chief business of fashionable girls. They seldom think that men will be allured by intellectual acquirements, because they find, that where any mental superiority exists, a woman is generally shunned and regarded as stepping out of her "appropriate sphere," which, in their view, is to dress, to dance, to set out to the best possible advantage her person, to read the novels which inundate the press, and which do more to destroy her character as a rational creature, than any thing else. . . .

There is another and much more numerous class in this country, who are withdrawn by education or circumstances from the circle of fashionable amusements, but who are brought up with the dangerous and absurd idea, that *marriage* is a kind of preferment; and that to be able to keep their husband's house, and render his situation comfortable, is the end of her being. Much that she does and says and thinks is done in reference to this situation; and to be married is too often held up to the view of girls as the sine qua non of human happiness and human existence. . . . I do long to see the time, when it will no longer be necessary for women to expend so many precious hours in furnishing "a well spread table," but that their husbands will forego some of the accustomed indulgences in this way, and encourage their wives to devote some portion of their time to mental cultivation, even at the expense of having to dine sometimes on baked potatoes, or bread and butter. . . .

There is another way in which the general opinion, that women are inferior to men, is manifested, that bears with tremendous effect on the laboring class, and indeed on almost all who are obliged to earn a subsistence, whether it be by mental or physical exertion—I allude to the disproportionate value set on the time and labor of men and of women. A man who is engaged in teaching, can always, I believe, command a higher price for tuition than a woman—even when he teaches the same branches, and is not in any respect superior to the woman. This I know is the case in boarding and other schools with which I have been acquainted, and it is so in every occupation in which the sexes engaged indiscriminately. As for example, in tailoring, a man has twice, or three times as much for making a waistcoat or pantaloons as a woman, although the work done by each may be equally good. In those employments which are peculiar to women, their time is estimated at only half the value of that of men. A woman who goes out to wash, works as hard in proportion as a wood sawyer, or a coal heaver, but she is not generally able to make more than half as much by a day's work. . . .

There is another class of women in this country, to whom I cannot refer, without feelings of the deepest shame and sorrow. I allude to our female slaves. Our southern cities are whelmed beneath a tide of pollution; the virtue of female slaves is wholly at the mercy of irresponsible tyrants, and women are bought and sold in our slave markets, to gratify the brutal lust of those who bear the name of Christians. In our slave States, if amid all her degradation and ignorance, a women desires to preserve her virtue unsullied, she is either bribed or whipped into compliance, or if she dares resist her seducer, her life by the laws of some of the slave States may be, and has actually been sacrificed to the fury of disappointed passion. Where such laws do not exist, the power which is necessarily vested in the master over his property, leaves the defenceless slave entirely at his mercy, and the sufferings of some females on this account, both physical and mental, are intense.

Letter XV: Man Equally Guilty With Woman in the Fall

. . . In contemplating the great moral reformations of the day, and the part which they are bound to take in them, instead of puzzling themselves with the harassing, because unnecessary inquiry, how far they may go without overstepping the bounds of propriety, which separate male and female duties, they will only inquire, "Lord, what wilt thou have us do?" They will be enabled to see the simple truth, that God has made no distinction between men and women as moral beings; that the distinction now so much insisted upon between male and female virtues is as absurd as it is unscriptural, and has been the fruitful source of much mischief—granting to man a license for the exhibition of brute force and conflict on the battle field; for sternness, selfishness, and the exercise of irresponsible power in the circle of home—and to woman a permit to rest on an arm of flesh, and to regard modesty and delicacy, and all the kindred virtues, as peculiarly appropriate to her. Now to me it is perfectly clear, that WHATSOEVER IT IS MORALLY RIGHT FOR A MAN TO DO, IT IS MORALLY RIGHT FOR A WOMAN TO DO; and that confusion must exist in the moral world, until woman takes her stand on the same platform with man, and feels that she is clothed by her Maker with the *same rights*, and, of course, that upon her devolve the *same duties*.

PASTORAL LETTER: THE GENERAL ASSOCIATION OF MASSACHUSETTS TO THE CHURCHES UNDER THEIR CARE

III.—We invite your attention to the dangers which at present seem to threaten the female character with wide spread and permanent injury.

The appropriate duties and influence of women are clearly stated in the New Testament. Those duties and that influence are unobtrusive and private, but the sources of mighty power. When the mild, dependant [sic], softening influence of woman upon the sternness of man's opinion is fully exercised, society feels the effects of it in a thousand forms. The power of woman is in her dependence, flowing from the consciousness of that weakness which God has given her for her protection, and which keeps her in those departments of life that form the character of individuals and of the nation. There are social influences which females use in promoting piety and the great objects of Christian benevolence which we cannot too highly commend. We appreciate the unostentatious prayers and efforts of woman in advancing the cause of religion at home and abroad; in Sabbath schools; in leading religious inquirers to the pastors for instruction; and in all such associated effort as becomes the modesty of her sex; and earnestly hope that she may abound more and more in these labors of piety and love.

But when she assumes the place and tone of man as a public reformer, our care and protection of her seem unnecessary; we put ourselves in self-defence against her; she yields the power which God has given her for protection, and her character becomes unnatural. If the vine, whose strength and beauty is to lean upon the trellis and half conceal its clusters, thinks to assume the independence and the overshading nature of the elm, it will not only cease to bear fruit, but fall in shame and dishonor into the dust. We cannot, therefore, but regret the mistaken conduct of those who encourage females to bear an obtrusive and ostentatious part in measures of reform, and countenance any of that sex who so far forget themselves as to itinerate in the character of public lecturers and teachers. We especially deplore the intimate acquaintance and promiscuous conversation of females with regard to things "which ought not to be named"; by which that modesty and delicacy which is the charm of domestic life, and which constitutes the true influence of woman in society is consumed, and the way opened, as we apprehend, for degeneracy and ruin . . .

SARAH M. GRIMKÉ, RESPONSE TO "THE PASTORAL LETTER . . ."

The motto of woman, when she is engaged in the great work of public reformation should be,—"The Lord is my light and my salvation; whom shall I fear? The Lord is the strength of my life; of whom shall I be afraid?" She must feel, if she feels rightly, that she is fulfilling one of the important duties laid upon her as an accountable being, and that her character, instead of being "unnatural," is in exact accordance with the will of Him to whom, and to no other, she is responsible for the talents and the gifts confided to her. As to the pretty simile, introduced into the "Pastoral Letter," "If the vine whose strength and beauty is to lean upon the trellis work, and half conceal its clusters, thinks to assume the independence and the overshadowing nature of the elm," & c. I shall only remark that it might well suit the poet's fancy, who sings of sparkling eyes and coral lips, and knights in armor clad; but it seems to me utterly inconsistent with the dignity of a Christian body, to endeavor to draw such an anti-scriptural distinction between men and women. Ah! how many of my sex feel in the dominion, thus unrighteously exercised over them, under the gentle appellation of *protection*, that what they have leaned upon has proved a broken reed at best, and oft a spear.

Thine in the bonds of womanhood,

Sarah M. Grimké.

Keziah Kendall, "What I have suffered, I cannot tell you"

We know nothing more about "Keziah Kendall" than what she revealed in this letter, which historians Dianne Avery and Alfred S. Konefsky discovered among the papers of Simon Greenleaf, a prominent Harvard law professor. It has not been possible to locate the author in the usual places—tax lists, land records, church lists. Keziah and her sisters carry the names of Job's daughters; whether the names are real or fictional, the writer assumed that her readers would remember the biblical reference: ". . . in all the land there were no women so fair as Job's daughters; and their father gave them inheritance among their brothers."

Kendall had been dismayed by what she heard at a public lyceum lecture on women's rights given by Greenleaf in early 1839. At a time when the legal disabilities of inherited common law were increasingly being questioned—in Massachusetts, the abolitionists Sarah and Angelina Grimké had only recently delivered a forthright series of lectures on the rights of women—Greenleaf devoted his lecture to the claim that American women were well protected by American law as it stood. He argued that excluding women from politics saved society from "uproar" and impropriety, and that constraints on married women's use of their property was merely a technicality because in a happy marriage all property became part of "a common fund . . . it can make but little difference . . . by whose name it is called." And he insisted that except for "restriction in *political matters*" there were no significant "distinctions between the legal rights of unmarried women, and of men."

Keziah Kendall was unpersuaded, and wrote to demand that Greenleaf offer another lecture, acknowledging the "legal wrongs" of women. What are Kendall's objections to the law as she experienced it? What connections does she draw between paying taxes, voting, and officeholding? Why does she blame Massachusetts property law for her fiancé's death? Why is she worried about her sister's forthcoming marriage?

Keziah Kendall to Simon Greenleaf [1839?] I take the liberty to write to you on the subject of the Lyceum lecture you delivered last Feb but as you are not acquainted with me I think I will introduce myself. My name is Kezia Kendall. I live not many miles from Cambridge, on a farm with two sisters, one older, one younger than myself. I am thirty two. Our parents and only brother are dead—we have a good estate—comfortable house—nice barn, garden, orchard & c and money in the bank besides. Jemima is a very good manager in the house, keeps everything comfortable—sees that the milk is nicely prepared for market—looks after everything herself, and rises before day, winter and summer,—but she never had any head for figures, and always expects me to keep all accounts, and attend to all business concerns. Keranhappuck, (who is called Kerry) is quite young, only nineteen, and as she was a little girl when mother died, we've always petted her, and let her do as she pleased, and now she's courted. Under these circumstances the whole responsibility of our property, not less than twenty five thousand dollars rests upon me. I am not over fond of money, but I

Letter from Keziah Kendall to Simon Greenleaf (undated). Box 3, Folder 10, Simon Greenleaf Papers, Harvard Law School Library. Excerpted from Diane Avery and Alfred S. Konefsky. "The Daughters of Job: Property Rights and Women's Lives in Mid-Nineteenth-Century Massachusetts," *Law and History Review* 10 (Fall 1992): 323–56. Notes have been renumbered and edited.

have worked hard ever since I was a little girl, and tried to do all in my power to help earn, and help save, and it would be strange if I did not think more of it than those who never earned anything, and never saved anything they could get to spend, and you know Sir, there are many such girls nowadays. Well—our milkman brought word when he came from market that you were a going to lecture on the legal rights of women, and so I thought I would go and learn. Now I hope you wont think me bold when I say, I did not like that lecture much. I dont speak of the manner, it was pretty spoken enough, but there was nothing in it but what every body knows. We all know about a widow's thirds,[1] and we all know that a man must maintain his wife, and we all know that he must pay her debts, if she has any—but I never heard of a yankee woman marrying in debt. What I wanted to know, was good reasons for some of those laws that I cant account for. I do hope if you are ever to lecture at the Lyceum again, that you will give us some. I must tell my story to make you understand what I mean. One Lyceum lecture that I heard in C. stated that the Americans went to war with the British, because they were taxed without being represented in Parliament. Now we are taxed every year to the full amount of every dollar we possess—town, county, state taxes—taxes for land, for movables, for money and all. Now I dont want to go representative or any thing else, any more than I do to be a "constable or a sheriff," but I have no voice about public improvements, and I dont see the justice of being taxed any more than the "revolutionary heroes" did. You mention that woman here, are not treated like heathen and Indian women—we know that—nor do I think we are treated as Christian women ought to be, according to the Bible rule of doing to others as you would others should do unto you. I am told (not by you) that if a woman dies a week after she's married that her husband takes all her personal property and the use of her real estate as long as he lives[2]—if a man dies his wife can have her thirds—this does not come up to the Gospel rule. Now the young fellow that is engaged to our Kerry, is a pleasant clever fellow, but he is not quite one and twenty, and I dont s'pouse he ever earned a coat in his life. Uncle told me there was a way for a woman to have her property trustee'd,[3] and I told it to Kerry—but she, poor girl has romantic notions owing to reading too many novels,[4] and when I told her of it, she would not hear of such a thing—"What take the law to keep my property away from James before I marry him—if it was a million of dollars he should have it all." So you see I think the law is in fault here—to tell you the truth I do not think young men are near so careful about getting in debt as girls, and I have known more than one that used their wife's money to pay off old scores. . . . I had rather go to my mantua maker[5] to borrow twenty dollars if I needed it, than to the richest married woman I know.

Another thing I have to tell you—when I was young I had a lover, Jos. Thompson, he went into business in a neighboring town, and after a year or two while I was getting the wedding things—Joe failed, he met with misfortunes that he did not expect,—he could have concealed it from me and married, but he did not—he was honorable, and so we delayed. He lived along here two or three years, and tried all he could to settle with his creditors, but some were stiff and held out, and thought by and by we would marry, and they should get my property. Uncle said he knew if we were married, there were those who would take my cattle and the improvement of my land. Joseph used to visit me often those years, but he lost his spirits and he could not get into business again, and he thought he must go to sea. I begged him not to, and told him we should be able to manage things in time, but he said no—he must try his luck, and at least get enough to settle off old scores, and then he would come here and live and we would make the best of what I had. We parted—but it pleased God he should be lost at sea. What I have suffered, I cannot tell you. Now Joe was no sailor when I engaged with him, and if it had been a thing known that I should always have a right to keep possession of my own, he need never have gone to sea, and we might have lived happily together, and in time with industry and economy, he might have paid off all. I am one that cant be convinced without better reasons than I have heard of, that woman are dealt with by the "gospel rule." There is more might than right in such laws as far as I can see—if you see differently, do tell us next time you lecture. Another thing—you made some reflections upon women following the Anti's. . . . Women have joined the Antislavery societies, and why? women are kept for slaves as well as men—it is a common cause, deny the justice of it, who can! To be sure I do not wish to go about lecturing like the Misses Grimkie, but I have not the knowledge they have, and I verily believe that if I had been brought up among slaves as they were, and knew all that they know, and felt a call from humanity to speak, I should run the venture of your displeasure, and that of a good many others like you.[6] [See pp. 236–237.] I told Uncle that I thought your lecture was a onesided thing—and he said, "why Keziah, Squire Greenleaf is an advocate, not a judge, you must get him to take t'other side next time." Now I have taken this opportunity to ask you to give us a remedy for the "legal wrongs" of women, whenever you have a chance. The fathers of the land should look to these things—who knows but your daughter may be placed in the sad situation I am in, or the dangerous one Kerry is in. I hear you are a good man, to make it certain—do all the good you can, and justify no wrong thing.

Yours with regard
Keziah Kendall.

Notes

1. She is, of course, referring to a widow's dower rights. [See "The Law of Domestic Relations," pp. 57–60.

2. "Kendall" was correct in her understanding of a husband's rights in his wife's personal property if she should die as early as "a week after she's married." But under the common law he would not inherit a life interest in her real estate unless they were parents of a child.

3. This is a reference to the equitable device of placing the woman's property in a trust before marriage for the purpose of avoiding the husband's common law rights in her property as well as protecting it from the husband's creditors. Under the trust agreement, the trustee would be obligated to manage the property for the benefit of the married woman.

4. "Kendall" shared a widely held distrust of romantic novels.

5. In the early republic, mantua makers [i.e., skilled dressmakers] were often economically independent women.

6. "Kendall" is probably referring here to the "Pastoral Letter" issued by the Congregationalist ministers in the summer of 1837 denouncing the public lecturing of the Grimké sisters. [See pp. 236–237.

1. This English print, made between 1785 and 1805, was available for purchase. Anglo-Americans often displayed such prints as we would posters by preserving them in a scrapbook or affixing them to a wall. The multiple architectural features and banners of text were mnemonic (memory-aiding) devices, sending messages of caution and restraint. See how many you can identify! The central figure, whose upper-class status is given away by her fine apparel, is knotting or tatting even as she walks. In the upper left corner, a story unfolds about how indulging in a single vice (drinking) leads to other vices; where is the female protagonist in the final scene? What is the ultimate purpose of women, according to this item of prescriptive literature? (*Keep within Compass*, ca. 1785–1805. Courtesy of the Henry Francis du Pont Winterthur Museum.)

2. This engraving depicts George Washington with the First Regiment of the United States on his way to be inaugurated for his first term as president. Have the women, who fill the public space surrounding Washington and his aides, left the narrow bounds of the compass? They have brought their daughters with them; together they strew his path with flowers. Does the message on the banner acknowledge new political roles for women? (*George Washington on the Bridge at Trenton, New Jersey, 1789.* Courtesy of the Maine Historical Society.)

3. In the antebellum decades, many women embraced reform and benevolence activities, whether through their churches, all-female secular organizations, or ladies' auxiliaries of organizations run by men. They met on planning boards composed of women only, and when they spoke to large gatherings the audience was usually composed of women. By limiting their colleagues to women, they did not compete directly with men, and escaped some—but not all—severe criticism for stepping out of their appropriate sphere of activity. Only a minority of radical women, fiercely devoted to abolishing slavery, resolutely stepped outside the boundaries of the compass to agitate and speak in what critics derided as "promiscuous assemblies," meaning public gatherings that included women and men. (For women's antislavery petitions to Congress, see pp. 224–232.)

A year after its founding in 1837, the Pennsylvania Anti-Slavery Society opened its membership to women. Thereafter, women were integrated into the organization's leadership, as this image of the Executive Committee in 1850 or 1851 makes clear. Many on the committee, including the Motts and Sarah Pugh, were deeply involved in woman's suffrage, as well as belonging to multiple abolition groups. Those standing in the rear, from left to right, are Mary Grew, E. M. Davis, Haworth Wetherfield, Abby Kimber, J. Miller McKim, and Sarah Pugh; those seated, from left to right, are Oliver Johnson, Margaret Jones Burleigh, Benjamin C. Bacon, Robert Purvis, Lucretia Mott, and James Mott. (Phototype reproduction by Frederick F. Gutekunst, Jr. Courtesy of the Sophia Smith Collection, Smith College. For more on the image and its subjects, see "An Anti-Slavery Group of 1850," *Friends' Intelligencer*, Oct, 24, 1896, p. 732. We thank Sherrill Redmon of the Sophia Smith Collection and Christopher Densmore of the Friends Historical Library for their counsel and assistance in finding and identifying this image.)

4. Printing technology improved markedly, and costs were lowered in the nineteenth century. Daily newspapers proliferated, as did magazines. Including illustrations became an important marketing strategy. Here, in the wake of the Civil War, a "female delegation" appears before the House Judiciary Committee to argue that the Fourteenth and Fifteenth amendments provided the constitutional basis for women to vote.

A few decades earlier, women's petitions to Congress were often tabled (see Zaeske, pp. 224–232), and women's bodies were allowed only in the spectator galleries. Women had to go to great lengths to have their voices reach male legislators. For example, in the 1850s, Susan B. Anthony repackaged an 1854 speech that Elizabeth Cady Stanton had given at the New York State Women's Rights Convention as a pamphlet retitled "Address . . . to the Legislature of New York." Copies were placed on the legislators' desks. But not until 1860 did Stanton actually speak in person to the legislature, and it was not until after the Civil War that a standing committee of the U.S. Congress took women's testimony.*

This illustration shows Victoria Woodhull reading a statement on January 11, 1871, to members of the House Judiciary Committee. The room is filled by other women who spoke—Susan B. Anthony and Isabella Beecher Hooker (Harriet Beecher Stowe's sister)—and other women who had come to support them. Elizabeth Cady Stanton is sitting behind Woodhull's left elbow; would you recognize her from the photograph on page 258, taken more than twenty years before? The men in the room included some individuals who supported woman suffrage, among them Albert Gallatin Riddle, a former congressman and leading Washington lawyer. The occasion was timed to coordinate with a national convention, which drew dozens of woman suffrage activists to Washington.

The journalist who reported the occasion used a patronizing tone typical of the era and a wide range of metaphors:

> Miss Victoria C. Woodhull led her women-at-arms into the committee-room of the house. . . . Among the warriors present were . . . Mrs. Stanton, Mrs Beecher Hooker . . . with many lesser lights. Shortly after ten o'clock Miss Victoria C. Woodhull opened the ball . . . Miss Woodhull, who is rather a prepossessing woman, laid aside her alpine hat, pulled out a paper, in which she took far higher ground than has usually been assumed by her coadjutors. Her sex's right of suffrage she claims under the Fourteenth and Fifteenth amendments, showing that women possess the right now, without a Sixteenth Amendment.

He went on to summarize Woodhull's remarks, which in fact initiated a new intellectual strategy for suffragists, and which laid the foundation for the lawsuit that Virginia and Francis Minor would soon bring before the federal courts in Missouri (*Minor* v. *Happersett*, pp. 315–316):

> The Constitution, she avers, makes no distinction of sex; it defines a woman born or naturalized in the United States, and subject to the jurisdiction thereof, to be a citizen, it recognizes the right of citizens to vote, and declares that the right shall not be denied or abridged by the United States, or any state, on account of "race, color, or previous condition of servitude." Women, white and black, belong to races, although to different races. A race of people comprises all the people, male and female. The right to vote cannot be denied on account of race. All people included in the term "race" have a right to vote, unless otherwise prohibited.

Woodhull's innovative reasoning captured one of the ways in which the Fourteenth Amendment would be used in the twentieth and twenty-first centuries to claim civil liberties. Its promise of equal protection to all people was invoked by African Americans challenging segregated schools, by whites and African Americans challenging laws against interracial marriage, and, most recently, by couples claiming the right to same-sex marriage.[†]

During the days that followed, women delegates to the convention lobbied members of Congress "with a ferocity never known before." They tallied their supporters carefully, counted approximately sixty votes on their side from the 243–member House of Representatives, and predicted victory in five years. ("The Feminine Invasion of the Capitol," *Frank Leslie's Illustrated Newspaper* 31, no. 801 (Feb.4, 1871): 347, 349.)

---

[*]"Address by ECS to the Legislature of New York," *The Selected Papers of Elizabeth Cady Stanton and Susan B. Anthony*, vol. 1, ed. Ann Gordon (New York: Rutgers University Press,1997), pp. 240–60.

[†]On school segregation as a denial of equal protection, see *Brown* v. *Board of Education*, 347 U.S. 483 (1954); on the right to marry across lines of color and ethnicity as part of equal protection, see *Loving* v. *Virginia*, 388 U.S. 1 (1967), pp. 767–768; on the right to marriage with a partner of the same sex as a right to equal protection of the law, see *Goodridge* v. *Massachusetts Department of Public Health*, 798 N.R. 2d 941 (Mass. 2003), pp. 773–774.

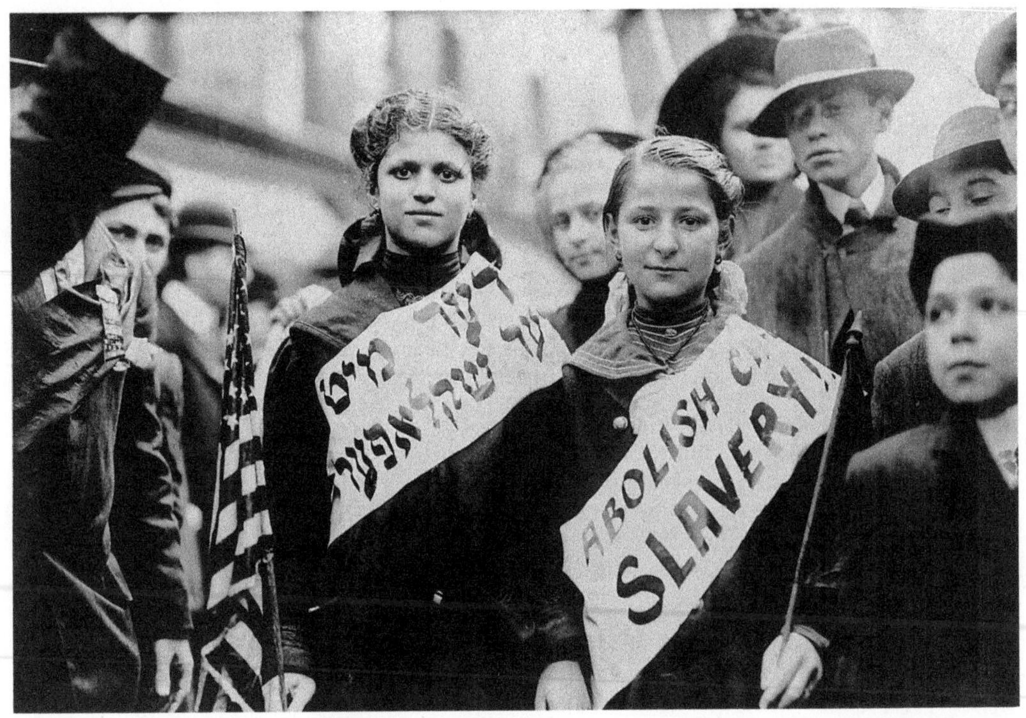

5. Girls have long participated in public demonstrations. This photograph was probably taken at a parade in New York City on May 1, 1909. These girls, wearing Abolish Child Slavery signs in English and Yiddish, are likely to have toiled in garment factories. The movement to abolish child labor was strengthened when women, who had been among its most strenuous supporters, achieved the vote, but not until the Fair Labor Standards Act of 1938 were minimum ages of employment and maximum hours of work set by federal law. ("Protest against Child Labor in a Labor Parade, 1909." Courtesy of George Grantham Bain Collection, LT 10876-2, Library of Congress, Prints and Photographs Division, Washington, D.C., LC-USZ62-22198.)

6. Elizabeth Cady Stanton's daughter Harriot Stanton Blatch led New York City suffragists to adopt the tactic of annual parades as a way of making support for the vote visible. In 1910 some 400 women marched to Union Square, where 10,000 people gathered to hear the speakers; by 1912 it was estimated that there were 10,000 *marchers*. This was a time of transition for the movement from community organizing on a small scale to raising substantial amounts of money for more visible activities such as renting large halls for meetings, publishing and distributing newspapers, and hiring lobbyists and organizers who would make politics their profession. The ability to organize a major parade—which involved building speakers' platforms and hiring bands—was a mark of the maturity and newfound power of the movement. On October 23, 1915, a week before a state referendum on women's suffrage (and almost the 100th anniversary of Elizabeth Cady Stanton's birth), New York suffragists sponsored the parade shown in this dramatic photograph. Well over 25,000 women and 2,500 men marched; at least four times that many watched from sidewalks.

Women had won the right to serve as poll watchers for this special election, to guard against corruption by observing the counting of the ballots. The New York amendment was defeated by the relatively narrow margin of 250,000 votes. ("Suffrage Parade, New York City, October 23,1915." Courtesy of George Grantham Bain Collection, LT 11052-4, Library of Congress, Prints and Photographs Division Washington, D.C.)

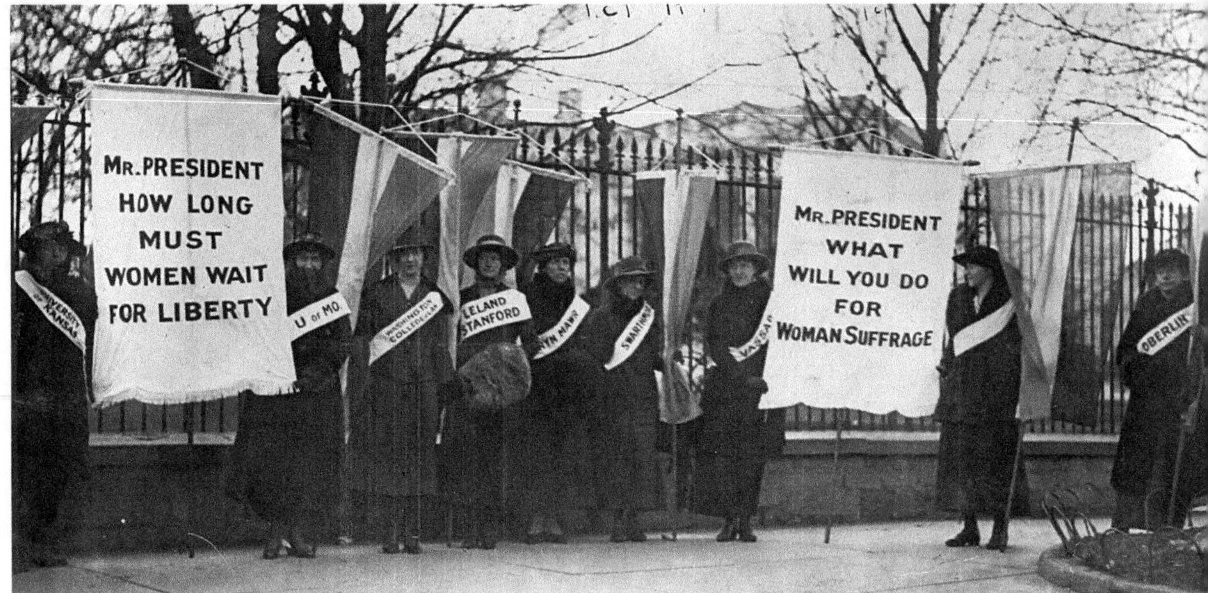

7. In his second successful campaign for the presidency, Woodrow Wilson promised—vaguely—to support woman suffrage. In January 1917, Alice Paul and the National Woman's Party undertook a permanent demonstration—a picket line—in front of the White House, near the gates, to hold the president to his promise. Their silent protest was modeled on the campaigns of British suffragists and may have been the first use of this political strategy in the United States. To provoke continued press attention and to represent the widespread support for the cause, Paul ingeniously arranged for themed days. First came State days—Maryland was first—in which the pickets came exclusively from the given state. On College Day, the one represented in this photograph, thirteen women wore sashes announcing their alma maters. On the afternoon of Wilson's second inaugural, March 4, 1,000 women, in a freezing rain, encircled the White house in one long, marching line, with the pictures and story generating unprecedented press coverage.

In April, with Congress about to declare war and the pickets' banners offering sharp political jibes, the strategy proved divisive among women's rights advocates. Some called the tactic indecorous, insulting to the president, and close to treasonous. Press commentary grew shrill, and the crowds gathered to heckle the "silent sentinels" grew violent; banners were torn to shreds. Arrests followed, in April and on into the fall—not of the attackers but of the pickets for "obstructing sidewalk traffic." These women accepted jail or workhouse terms rather than pay the $25 fine; and on release, they returned defiantly to the picket line.

The cycle of peaceful protest and violent response intensified in August, when the picketers provocatively carried banners mocking "Kaiser Wilson" and highlighting the contradiction between the U.S. policies of criticizing the kaiser for denying democracy in Germany and denying the vote to the half of the U.S. population. In the fall, jailed picketers, including Alice Paul, went on hunger strikes because they had asked for and been denied political prisoner status. Like British suffragists, they were force-fed—an intrusive act that was painful and medically dangerous. All were released in late November, when local officials anticipated (rightly) that the arrests and detentions would be ruled unconstitutional on appeal.

Meanwhile, the pickets of 1917, the private letters that Wilson received from feminists such as Jane Addams and Carrie Chapman Catt, and the exigencies of war led to a presidential change of mind: in early January 1918, Wilson announced his support for the federal woman suffrage amendment then making its way through Congress. In September, he went to the Senate to urge passage there, presenting the matter as critical to the war effort. However, it would take new elections and a newly constituted Senate for the bill to pass, and another year until ratification (see pp. 429–431). ("College Day in the Picket Line, Feb. 1917," National Women's Party Records, Library of Congress, Washington, D.C.,LC-USZ62-31799. See Katherine H. Adams and Michael L. Keene, *Alice Paul and the American Suffrage Campaign* [Urbana: University of Illinois Press, 2007], and the documentary film by Ruth Pollak for the *American Experience* and WGBH, *One Woman, One Vote* [PBS Home Video, 1995; reissued on DVD, 2006], especially the closing episodes.)

8. Women used their vote for a wide range of political expression. The Ku Klux Klan began to recruit women in 1923, not long after the founding of the Klan itself. Many women found the Klan's claims of moral purity appealing; in some localities, Klansmen made themselves useful to white Protestant women by intimidating husbands who engaged in domestic violence. Klanswomen joined in opposing interracial marriage and in linking Catholics, Jews, and African Americans to degeneracy. Believing that immigrants were likely to undermine morality, they supported the exclusion of Asians and the restriction of immigration to Western Europeans. They energetically boycotted anti-Klan business owners and ran for positions on school boards, where they used their influence to fire Catholic and Jewish teachers and distribute Bibles in classes. Within a year of its founding, the Women's Ku Klux Klan claimed more than 250,000 members in each of the forty-eight states. Here they parade proudly down Pennsylvania Avenue in 1928; the U.S. Capitol looms in the background. (Courtesy of the Library of Congress, Prints and Photographs Division, Washington, D.C.)

9. In this photograph, taken sometime between 1935 and 1940, probably in New York City, laundry workers of the International Union, Local 135, strike for better working conditions. The scene reminds us that laundering, as well as domestic service, were often the only jobs open to African American women. Rain or no rain, the picture gives us a sense of workers' standards of how to dress when out in public. Look especially at their feet and heads. (Courtesy of the Library of Congress, Prints and Photographs Division, Washington, D.C.)

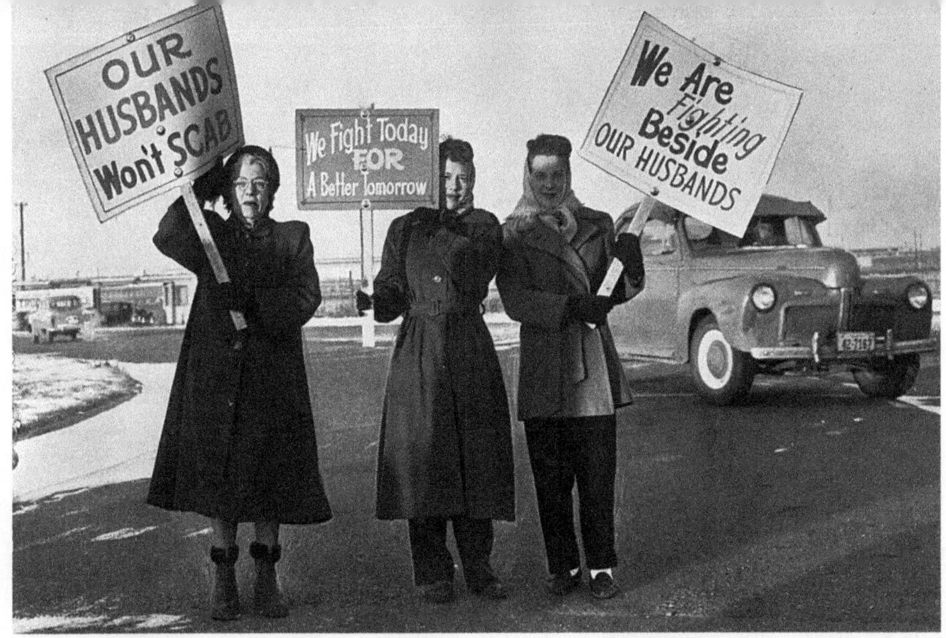

10. During the emergency of World War II, workers in industries that were indispensable to the war effort were forbidden to strike. In the aftermath of the war, industrial relations throughout the nation exploded as workers and management struggled for control over the shop floor and the allocation of profits that resulted from increased productivity. In 1950, tens of thousands of employees of John Deere—a major national manufacturer of heavy farm equipment (tractors, combines, harvesters)—went on strike after failing to reach an agreement on a new United Auto Workers union contract. When John Deere hired strikebreakers, severe violence erupted. Snipers followed union members home from the picket lines; union members began to carry guns for their protection. The company obtained an injunction prohibiting Deere employees from picketing, which nearly ended the strike.

But no injunction could prohibit wives and children of union members from taking over the picket lines. They engaged in this activity with as much vigor as their husbands and fathers had displayed, and made it embarrassing for strikebreakers to cross into work. This photographs was taken from Deere's Des Moines plant, where one of the most bitter struggles took place. A child carried a sign that read "Don't Scab on My Dad." The union survived the bitter three and a half month strike, and rebuilt the union's bargaining strength over the subsequent years.

The families followed a tradition of women who intervened to ensure that strikes would be sustained. In 1937, union wives in Flint, Michigan, formed a supplementary corps—the "Ladies Auxiliary"—to support the workers in a forty-four day sit-in at the General Motors plant. They shamed the police by their presence; they brought food to the strikers, enabling them to stay in the factories longer; and they mobilized their children, who carried signs that read My Daddy Strikes for Us Little Tykes.* An even more bitter 1951 strike by Mexican American miners in New Mexico protested severely dangerous working conditions and wages lower than those of their Anglo coworkers. When an injunction forced the men to end their picket lines, their wives—organized as the Ladies Auxiliary—took their places, leaving the men to care for children and daring the police to use violence against women. The strike became the subject of a notable film, *Salt of the Earth*, filmed on the site of the mine, with a largely nonprofessional cast made up of many of those who had been part of the events, and directed brilliantly by Herbert Biberman, who had been blacklisted and jailed for his Communist sympathies. ("Des Moines, 1950." Courtesy of the State Historical Society of Iowa, Des Moines.)

---

*For the Des Moines strike, see Shelton Stromquist, *Solidarity and Survival: An Oral History of Iowa Labor in the Twentieth Century* (Iowa City: University of Iowa Press, 1993), pp. 208–13. For the Flint strike, see *With Babies and Banners: The Story of the Women's Emergency Brigade*, directed by Lorraine Gray (New Day Films, 1979). For the New Mexico strike and the remarkably feminist implications of the event, see the film *Salt of the Earth* (1954) and Ellen R. Baker, *On Strike and On Film: Mexican American Families and Blacklisted Filmmakers in Cold War America* (Chapel Hill: University of North Carolina Press, 2007).

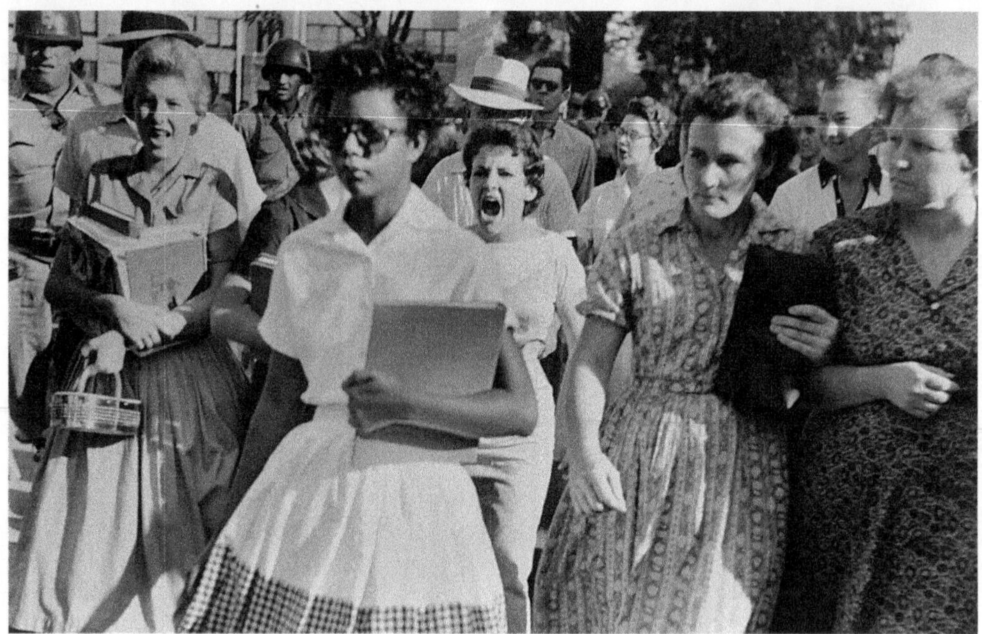

11. Young Elizabeth Eckford faces the gauntlet of racial heckling and hatred at the Court-ordered integration of schools in Little Rock, Arkansas, in 1957. When the Arkansas governor defied the Supreme Court order, President Dwight Eisenhower reluctantly sent in federal troops to enforce it. Even with military protection, the young people who actually integrated public schools had to put up with racist slurs, harassment, and intimidation that required of them daily displays of uncommon courage and self-possession. Summoning up such courage became commonplace for thousands of rank-and-file African Americans, many of them girls and women. Indeed, it was women who carried the civil rights struggle at the grassroots level, often at considerable risk to their physical safety and even their lives. As this picture makes clear, white women were prominent among the harassers. Other white women worked for integration in practice by keeping the schools open. (Photograph by Will Counts.)

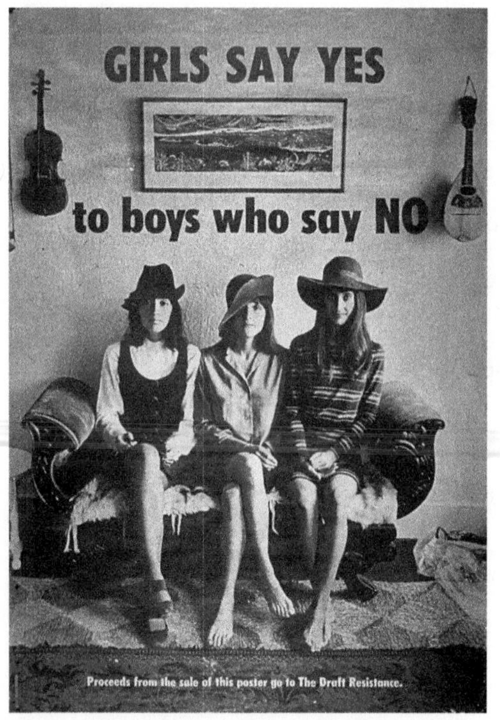

12. This antidraft poster features singer and activist Joan Baez (*far left*) with her sisters, Pauline and Mimi. Proceeds from the poster sales went toward draft resistance for the Vietnam War. At a performance at Madison Square Garden in 1965, Baez told the crowd, "If you feel that to go to war is wrong, then you must say no to the draft. And if young ladies feel it's wrong to kill, then you can say yes to the young men that say no to the draft." In what senses do you think Baez meant women should say yes? Unidentified poster maker, "Girls Say Yes to Boys Who Say No," ca. 1968. Photomechanical lithograph, photograph by Larry Gates. Gift of William Mears. (Courtesy of the National Museum of American History, Smithsonian Institution.)

13. This famous photograph records the ceremonial last mile of the Torch Relay, a feat that ushered in the National Women's Conference in Houston in 1977. The United Nations had declared 1977 International Women's Year (later extending it to a decade), and President Ford had earlier signed legislation spearheaded by Congresswoman Bella Abzug authorizing the expenditure of $5 million to hold a national women's conference as part of the nation's bicentennial observance. Delegates were elected in all fifty states; three First Ladies attended (guess which three); and Maya Angelou read a poem composed for the occasion (one line reads: "We recognize . . . those unknown and unsung women whose strength gave birth to our strength"). The torch, which you see above runner Peggy Kokernot's head, had been carried by a sequence of over 2,000 women runners from Seneca Falls to Texas to symbolize the link between those early feminists who drafted the Declaration of Sentiments and their contemporary counterparts. The complex logistical work behind the relay was undertaken chiefly by the 13,000-member National Association of Girls and Women in Sports. All torchbearers wore bright blue T-shirts with the conference's logo and the relay-inspired slogan, Women on the Move.

The professional photographer who snapped the picture, Diana Mara Henry, recalls: "I was rushing backward as fast as I could in order to get the shot of these proud and happy women energetically marching" to the conference opening.* The mix of women in this front row—by age, ethnic heritage, and national/local prominence—sent a deliberate message about the appeal of feminist principles. Linked arm-in-arm from right to left are Billie Jean King, Susan B. Anthony II (namesake of her great aunt), and Bella Abzug. Next are Houston runners, Sylvia Ortiz, then a college senior, marathon runner Kokernot, and Mechele Cearcy, a high school track star. Next to Cearcy you may recognize Betty Friedan. Rather than an inclusive picture like Henry's, *TIME* chose for its cover a portrait of Peggy Kokernot applauding the proceedings. Why would the magazine editors choose that particular framing?

The Houston conference was a major milestone in second-wave feminist organizing (see pp. 672–690) and nationwide mobilization. The 20,000 persons at the gathering cheered or jeered the 2,000-plus delegates who, plank by plank, voted on a detailed plan of action geared toward achieving the elusive goal of gender equality. Twenty percent of delegates represented the conservative end of the political spectrum, and although they voted in favor of economic rights planks, they vigorously debated and mostly voted against planks on the equal rights amendment, lesbian rights, and abortion. A bipartisan effort mandated and funded by the U.S. Congress to address issues of concern to ordinary women, this sort of conference has never been repeated.

By the late 1970s, there were no longer strict dress codes for women in public; or, if some groups still believed in them, feminists deliberately flouted them. What range of choices in dress, accoutrements, and symbolic items were these women making? (Photograph copyright © 1978 by Diana Mara Henry.)

*Jewish Women's Archive, https://jwa.org/feminism/_html/JWA035.htm.

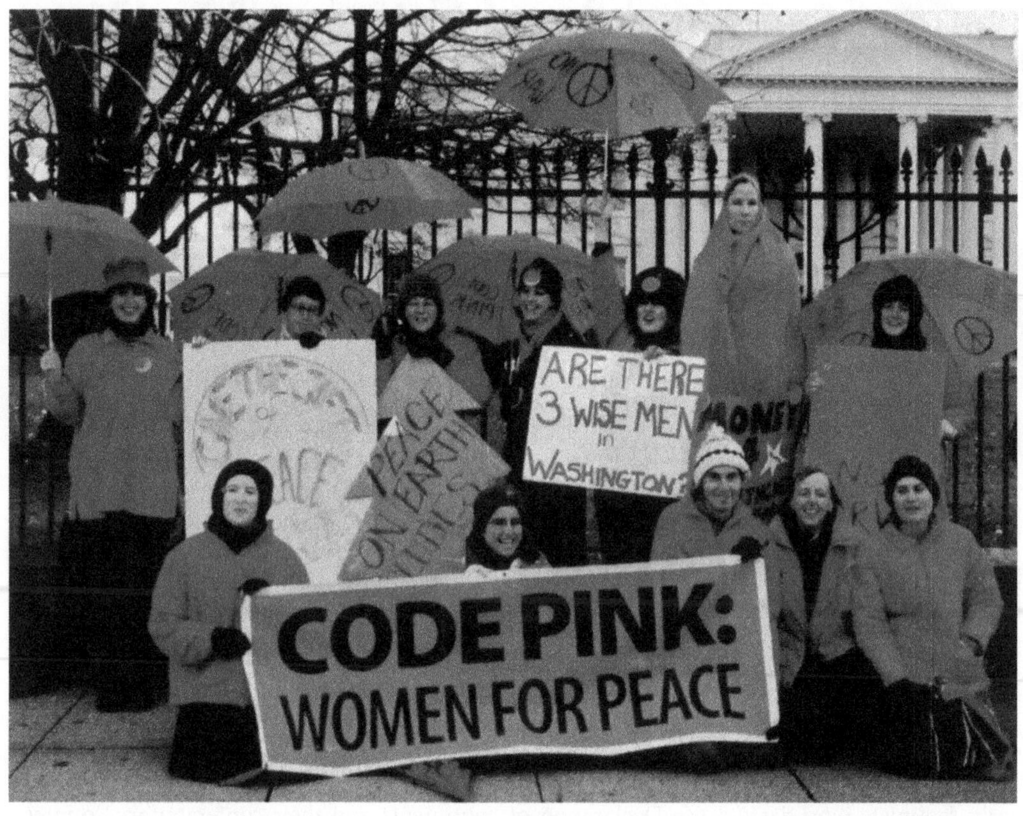

14. On November 12, 2002, a new woman-initiated grassroots group, CODEPINK, began a four-month vigil in front of the White House as a "pre-emptive strike for peace." Since the days of Alice Paul's radical, extended maneuver to post silent sentinels with banners at Woodrow Wilson's gates, protests at the White House fence had become a familiar part of the political scene. But in fall 1995, after the Oklahoma City bombing, this particular stretch—the block with the front of the White House on one side and Lafayette Park on the other—was closed to vehicular traffic as an antiterrorist precaution. Thus, White House picketers lost their ability to interact with the random public represented by drivers and riders in cars. The women who rotated on vigil duty in the winter before the official start of the war in Iraq chose to wear pink jackets and sport pink umbrellas. Ponder what messages they were sending in making that visually arresting choice, and what scenes in U.S. history they may have been conscious of echoing. The vigil culminated on March 8, 2003, International Women's Day, when over 10,000 activists marched in Washington, D.C., to protest U.S. militarism. In an echo of 1917, 25 women, including the feminist writers Alice Walker, Maxine Hong Kingston, and Susan Griffin, and CODEPINK cofounder Medea Benjamin, were arrested for protesting too close to the White House gates. ("Women for Peace." CODEPINK Demonstration at the White House, ca. 2002. Courtesy of CODEPINK.)

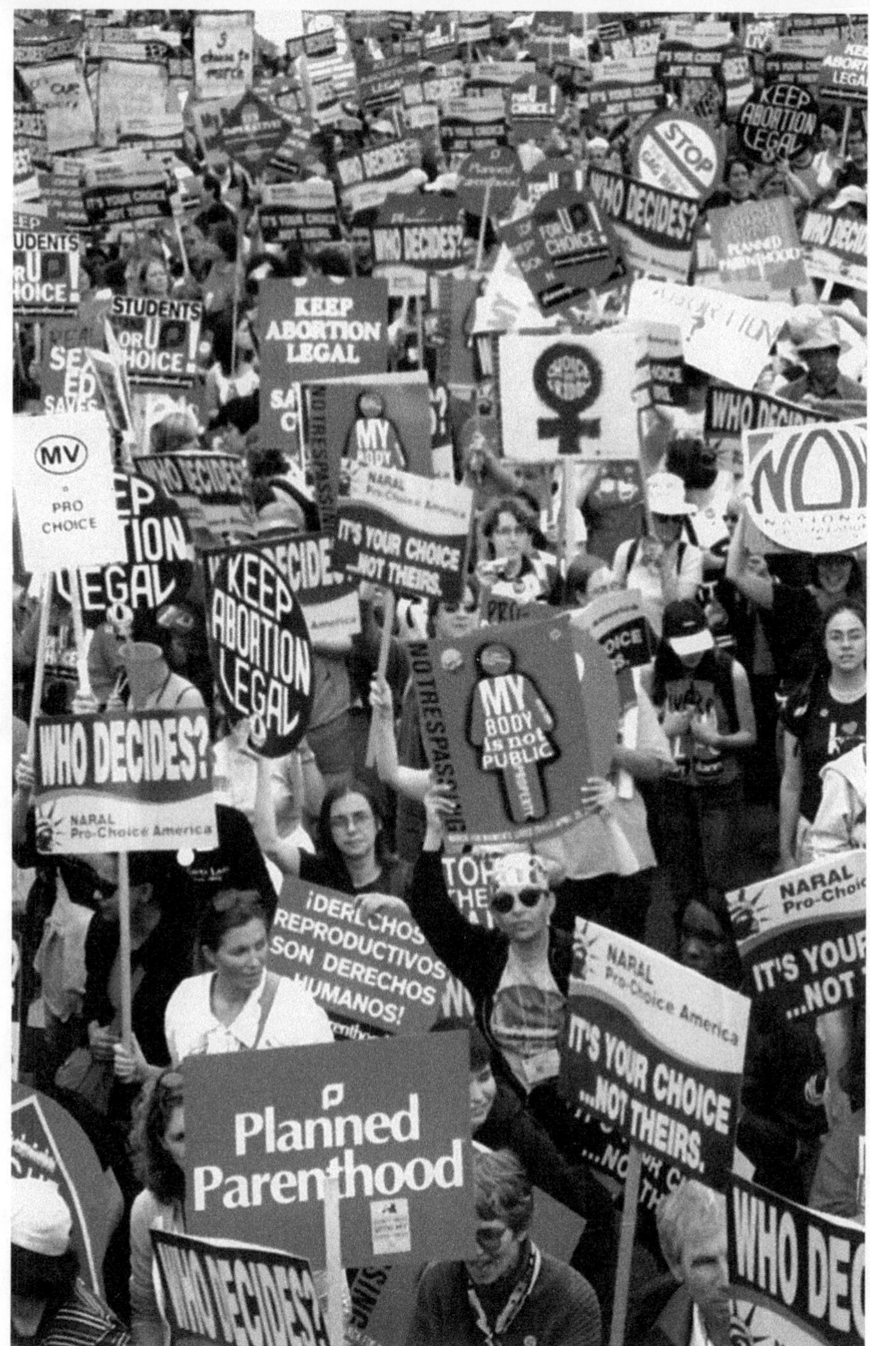

15. Protesters of all kinds continued to believe that one of the best ways to capture the attention of legislators, the president, and the press was to organize marches and rallies in the nation's capital. The next two photographs are freeze frames of tiny subsets of the hundreds of thousands of people who came to Washington on April 25, 2004, to showcase their views on the charged issue of abortion. The occasion was the March for Women's Lives, sponsored by the National Organization for Women (NOW) and other organizations and billed as a mass demonstration for "Choice, Justice, Access, Health, Abortion, and Global Family Planning." The organizers claimed that over 1,150,000 demonstrators filled the National Mall, making it (even if their estimate was high) the largest political rally in U.S. history up to that point. How many different messages can you find on the placards? Assess their rhetorical strategies and put them into debate with the signs held up by counter-demonstrators in the next image. (Photograph by Ramanujam Rajopal, cover of *Peacework Magazine*, May 2004, Creative Commons license, with thanks to the ACLU of Washington.)

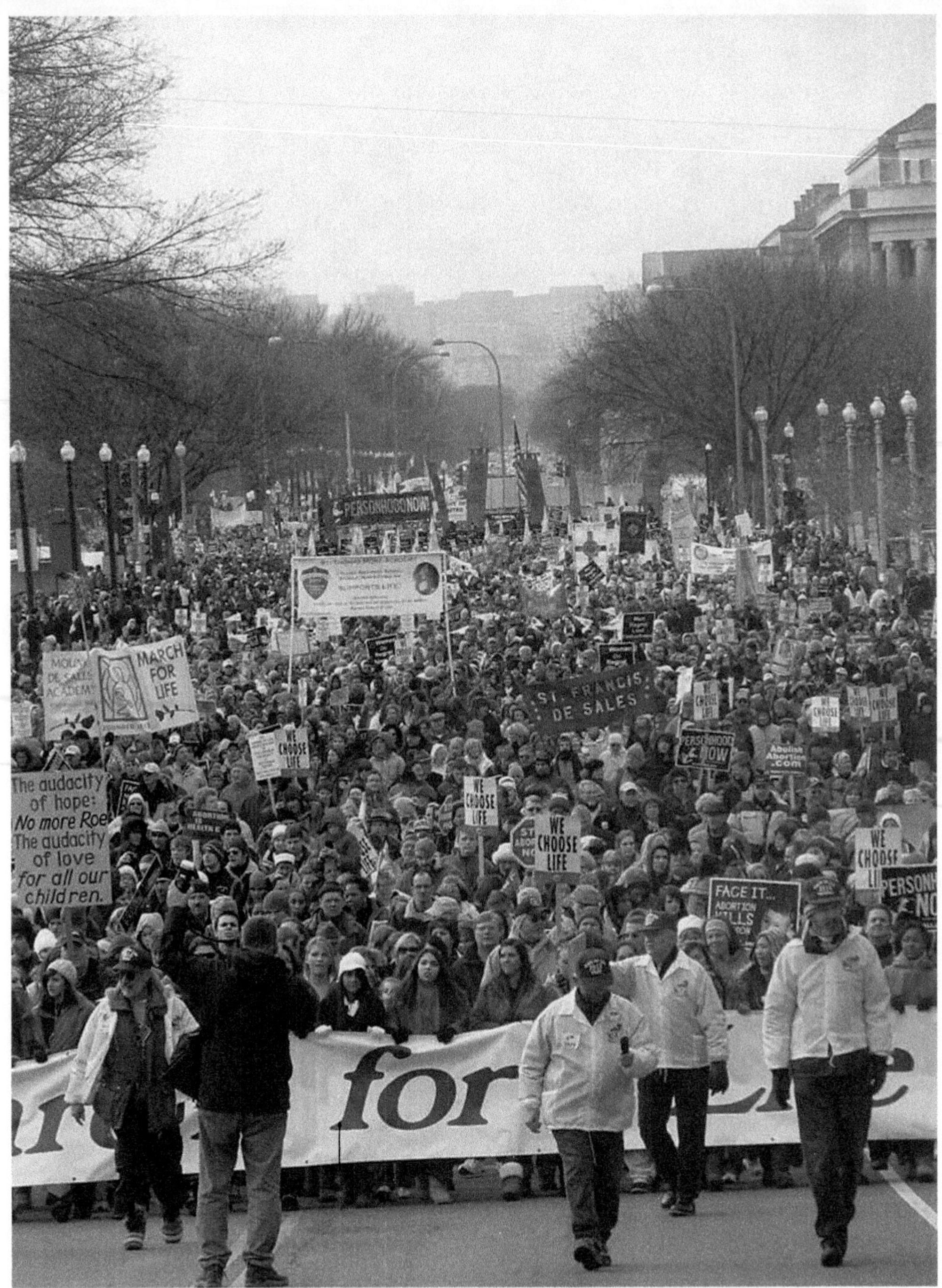

16. After abortion was legalized by the 1973 *Roe* v. *Wade* decision, thousands of women participated in the antiabortion movement. While most antiabortion activists opposed feminism, some argued that their opposition to abortion was a feminist act because it prevented women from making choices they might later regret. Each year on January 22 (the anniversary of the *Roe* decision) participants in the March for Life proceed down Constitution Avenue, past the National Mall, to the Supreme Court. From your knowledge of the contemporary debate, recall signs, slogans, and images used to oppose abortion in addition to those we see from this image taken at the 2010 event. Sincc the early 1990s, we have heard Democratic candidates attempt to bridge the ideological divide by urging "let's keep abortion safe, legal and rare." Do you think a more constructive dialogue is possible? Recently, poll-takers and others have commented that the labels *pro-life* and *pro-choice* no longer capture the thinking of many Americans. Do you agree? (Photograph by John-Henry Westen of LifeSiteNews.com.)

GERDA LERNER

The Meanings of Seneca Falls, 1848–1998

As Keziah Kendall and Sarah and Angelina Grimké had done, many people in the 1830s and 1840s had begun to criticize the way American law and custom defined gender relations. The 1848 Declaration of Sentiments (see pp. 264–266) gathered these complaints into a manifesto and offered an agenda for change that would shape a women's rights movement deep into our own time. But the Declaration itself has its own history, emerging out of the specific social conditions in western New York State, out of political and religious arguments, and out of the personal experiences of the women and men who wrote its words and signed their names to it.

The meticulous research of Judith Wellman has enabled us to know the class position, religious affiliation, kin relations, and political sympathies of many of the signers at Seneca Falls. Two-thirds of the signers were women; the signers' ages stretched from fourteen-year-old Susan Quinn to sixty-eight-year-old George Pryor. Most came with another family member: wives with husbands, mothers with daughters, sisters with brothers. (Daniel Anthony was there, but his daughter Susan would not meet Stanton for another three years.) Seventy percent came from the immediate locality of Seneca Falls and neighboring Waterloo, an area that had seen substantial dislocation from a farm region to a manufacturing town, where a substantial group of men had broken with the Democratic and Whig parties to join the abolitionist Free Soilers, and where dissidents from the Quaker Genesee Yearly Meeting formed their own society of Friends devoted to egalitarian gender relations and abolition. Legislative battles over married women's property acts made women's rights especially visible in New York.*

The Declaration of Sentiments, Stanton's indictment of the relations between men and women in her own society, is still stunning in its energy, its precision, and its foresight. In the essay that follows, written for the quincentenary of the Seneca Falls convention, the distinguished historian Gerda Lerner reflects on the meaning of the Declaration for its time and for our own.

In 1848, according to Karl Marx and Frederick Engels, "a specter [was] haunting Europe—the specter of communism." In that same year, the upstate New York village of Seneca Falls hosted a gathering of fewer than three hundred people, earnestly debating a Declaration of Sentiments to be spread by newsprint and oratory. The Seneca Falls Woman's Rights Convention marked the beginning of the woman's rights movement.

The specter that haunted Europe developed into a mighty movement, embracing the globe, causing revolutions, wars, tyrannies and counterrevolutions. Having gained state power in Russia, China and Eastern Europe, twentieth-century communism, in 1948, seemed more threatening a specter than ever before. Yet, after a bitter period of "cold war," which pitted nuclear nations against one another in a futile stalemate, it fell of its own weight in almost all its major centers.

The small spark figuratively ignited at Seneca Falls never produced revolutions, usurpation of power or wars. Yet it led to a

*Judith Wellman, "The Seneca Falls Woman's Rights Convention: A Study of Social Networks," *Journal of Women's History* 3 (1991): 9–37.

In the familiar photographs, Elizabeth Cady Stanton comes to us as she appeared in her fifties and older—a plump, matronly woman with graying hair and a kindly face. But in 1848, when she wrote the great manifesto that set the agenda for the American women's movement for 150 years, she was thirty-three years old, and the one photograph we have of her from that time shows her to be slight and thin, her dark hair hanging in limp ringlets. She is pictured here with Daniel and Henry; the smallest, Gerrit, was a toddler. Did she look tired because she was the mother of three boys under six? Her future—and ours—lay before her. (Courtesy of Elizabeth Cady Stanton Trust/Coline Jenkins–Sahlin.)

transformation of consciousness and a movement of empowerment on behalf of half the human race, which hardly has its equal in human history.

Until very recently, the Seneca Falls convention of 1848 was not recognized as significant by historians, was not included in history textbooks, not celebrated as an important event in public schools, never mentioned in the media or the press. In the 1950s, the building where it was held, formerly the Wesleyan chapel, was used as a filling station. In the 1960s, it housed a laundromat. It was only due to the resurgence of modern feminism and the advances of the field of Women's History that the convention has entered the nation's consciousness. The establishment of Women's History Month as a national event during the Carter administration and its continuance through every administration since then has helped to educate the nation to the significance of women's role in history. Still, it took decades of struggle by women's organizations, feminist historians and preservationists to rescue the building at Seneca Falls and finally to persuade the National Park Service to turn it into a historic site. . . . This history of "long forgetting and short remembering" has been an important aspect of women's historic past, the significance of which we only understood as we began to study women's history in depth.

Elizabeth Cady Stanton, the great communicator and propagandist of nineteenth-century feminism, has left a detailed account of the origins of the Seneca Falls convention both in her autobiography and in the monumental *History of Woman Suffrage.* The idea for such a meeting originated with her and with Lucretia Mott, when they both attended the 1840 World Anti-slavery Convention in London, at which representatives of female antislavery societies were denied seating and voting rights. Outraged by this humiliating experience, Stanton and Mott decided in London that they would convene a meeting of women in the United States to discuss their grievances as soon as possible. But her responsibilities as mother of a growing family intervened, and Stanton could not implement her plan until 1848, when Lucretia Mott visited her sister Martha Wright in Waterloo, a town near Seneca Falls. There, Stanton met with her, her hostess Jane Hunt and their friend Mary Ann McClintock. Stanton wrote: "I poured out that day the torrent of my long accumulating discontent with such vehemence and indignation that I stirred myself, as well as the rest of the party, to do or dare anything." The five drafted an announcement for a "Woman's Rights Convention" to be held at Seneca Falls on the nineteenth and twentieth of July, and placed the notice in the local paper and the abolitionist press.

The five women who issued the call to the Seneca Falls convention were hardly as naive and inexperienced as later, somewhat mythical versions of the events would lead one to believe. Lucretia Mott was an experienced and highly acclaimed public speaker, a Quaker minister and longtime abolitionist. She had attended the founding meeting of the American Antislavery Society in 1833, which admitted women only as observers. She was a founder of the Philadelphia Female Anti-Slavery Society and its long-term president. The fact that she was announced as the principal speaker at the Seneca Falls convention was a distinct drawing card.

Elizabeth Cady Stanton's "long accumulating discontent" had to do with her struggle to raise her three children (she would later have four more) and run a large household in the frequent absences of her husband Henry, a budding lawyer and Free Soil politican. Still, she found time to be involved in the campaign for reform of women's property rights in New York state, where a reform bill was passed just prior to the convention, and she had spoken before the state legislature.

Martha Wright, Jane Hunt and Mary Ann McClintock were all separatist Quakers, long active in working to improve the position of women within their church. All of them were veterans of reform and women's organizations and had worked on antislavery fairs.

The [region] where they held their convention . . . had for more than two decades been the center of reform and utopian movements, largely due to the economic upheavals brought by the opening of the Erie Canal and the ensuing competition with western agriculture, which brought many farmers to bankruptcy. Economic uncertainty led many to embrace utopian schemes for salvation. The region was known as the "burned-over" district, because so many schemes for reforms had swept over it in rapid succession, from the evangelical revivalism of Charles Grandison Finney, to temperance, abolition, church reform, Mormonism and the chiliastic movement of William Miller, who predicted the second coming of Christ with precision for October 12, 1843 at three A.M. The nearly one million followers of Miller had survived the uneventful passing of that night and the similarly uneventful revised dates of March or October 1844, but their zeal for reform had not lessened.

The men and women who gathered in the Seneca Falls Wesleyan chapel were not a national audience; they all came from upstate New York and represented a relatively narrow spectrum of reform activists. Their local background predisposed them to accept radical pronouncements and challenging proposals. Most of them were abolitionists, the women having been active for nearly ten years in charitable, reform, and antislavery societies. They were experienced in running petition campaigns and many had organized antislavery fund-raising fairs. Historian[s] Nancy Isenberg [and Judith Wellman] who [have] analyzed the origins and affiliations of those attending the convention, showed that many were religious dissidents, Quakers, who just two months prior had separated from their more traditional church and would shortly form their own group, New York Congregationalist Friends. Another dissident group were Wesleyan Methodists who had been involved in a struggle within their church about the role of women and of the laity in church governance. Yet another group came from the ranks of the temperance movement. Among the men in attendance several were local lawyers with Liberty Party or Free Soil affiliations. Also present and taking a prominent part in the deliberations was Frederick Douglass, the former slave and celebrated abolitionist speaker, now editor of the *North Star*.

Far from representing a group of inexperienced housewives running their first public meeting, the majority of the convention participants were reformers with considerable organizational experience. For example, Amy Post and six other women from Rochester who came to Seneca Falls were able to organize a similar woman's rights convention in Rochester just two weeks later. One of the significant aspects of the Seneca Falls convention is that it was grounded in several organizational networks that had already existed for some time and could mobilize the energies of seasoned reform activists.

Most of the reformers attending had family, church and political affiliations in other areas of the North and Midwest. It was through them that the message of Seneca Falls spread quickly and led to the formation of a national movement. The first truly national convention on Woman's Rights was held in Worcester, Massachusetts in 1850. By 1860 ten national and many local woman's rights conventions had been organized.

THE DECLARATION OF SENTIMENTS

The first day of the Seneca Falls meeting was reserved to women, who occupied themselves with debating, paragraph by paragraph, the Declaration of Sentiments prepared by Elizabeth Cady Stanton. Resolutions were offered, debated and adopted. At the end of the second day, sixty-eight women and thirty-two men signed their names to a Declaration of Sentiments, which embodied the program of the nascent movement and provided a model for future woman's rights conventions. The number of signers represented only one third of those present, which probably was due to the radical nature of the statement. . . .

By selecting the Declaration of Independence for their formal model and following its preamble almost verbatim, except for the insertion of gender-neutral language, the organizers of the convention sought to base their main appeal on the democratic rights embodied in the nation's founding document. They also put the weight and symbolism of this revered text behind what was in their time a radical assertion: "We hold these truths to be self-evident: that all men and women are created equal."

The feminist appeal to natural rights and the social contract had long antecedents on the European continent, the most important advocate of it being Mary Wollstonecraft. Her work was well known in the United States, where the same argument had been well made by Judith Sargent Murray, Frances Wright, Emma Willard, Sarah Grimké and Margaret Fuller.

The second fundamental argument for the equality of woman was religious. As stated in the Declaration:

> Resolved, That woman is man's equal—was intended to be so by the Creator, and the highest good of the race demands that she should be recognized as such.

And one of the "grievances" is:

> He [man] has usurped the prerogative of Jehovah himself, claiming it as his right to assign to her a sphere of action, when that belongs to her conscience and her God.

The feminist argument based on biblical grounds can be traced back for seven hundred years prior to 1848, but the women assembled at Seneca Falls were unaware of that fact, because of the nonexistence of anything like Women's History. They did know the Quaker argument, especially as made in her public lectures by Lucretia Mott. They had read Sarah Grimke's *Letters on the Equality of the Sexes*, and several of the resolutions in fact followed her text. They knew the biblical argument by Ann

Lee of the Shakers and they echoed the antislavery biblical argument, applying it to women.

The Declaration departed from precedent in its most radical statement:

> The history of mankind is a history of repeated injuries and usurpations on the part of man toward woman, having in direct object the establishment of an absolute tyranny over her.

The naming of "man" as the culprit, thereby identifying patriarchy as a system of "tyranny," was highly original, but it may have been dictated more by the rhetorical flourishes of the Declaration of Independence than by an actual analysis of woman's situation. When it came to the list of grievances, the authors departed from the text and became quite specific.

Woman had been denied "her inalienable right to the elective franchise"; she had no voice in the making of laws; she was deprived of other rights of citizenship; she was declared civilly dead upon marriage; deprived of her property and wages; discriminated against in case of divorce, and in payment for work. Women were denied equal access to education and were kept out of the professions, held in a subordinate position in Church and State and assigned by man to the domestic sphere. Man has endeavored to destroy woman's self-respect and keep her dependent.

They concluded that in view of the disfranchisement of one-half the people of this country

> . . . we insist that [women] have immediate admission to all the rights and privileges which belong to them as citizens of these United States.

It has been claimed by historians, and by herself, that Stanton's controversial resolution advocating voting rights for women—the only resolution not approved unanimously at the convention—was her most important original contribution. In fact, Sarah and Angelina Grimké had advocated woman's right to vote and hold office in 1838, and Frances Wright had done so in the 1830s. It was not so much the originality, as the inclusiveness of the listed grievances that was important.

The Declaration claimed universality, even though it never mentioned differences among women. Future woman's rights conferences before the Civil War would rectify this omission and pay particular attention to the needs of lower class and slave women.

While grievances pertaining to woman's sexual oppression were not explicitly included in the Declaration of Sentiments, they were very much alive in the consciousness of the leading participants. Elizabeth Cady Stanton had already in 1848 begun to include allusions to what we now call "marital rape" in her letters and soon after the Seneca Falls convention made such references explicit, calling on legislatures to forbid marriage to "drunkards." She soon became an open advocate of divorce and of the right of women to leave abusive marriages. Later woman's rights conventions would include some of these issues among their demands, although they used carefully guarded language and focused on abuses by "drunkards." This was a hidden feminist theme of the mainstream woman's temperance movement in the 1880s and caused many temperance women to embrace woman suffrage. What we now call "a woman's right to her body" was already on the agenda of the nineteenth-century woman's rights movement.

It was the confluence of a broad-ranging programmatic declaration with a format familiar and accessible to reformers that gave the event its historical significance. The Seneca Falls convention was the first forum in which women gathered together to publicly air their own grievances, not those of the needy, the enslaved, orphans or widows. The achievement of a public voice for women and the recognition that women could not win their rights unless they organized, made Seneca Falls a major event in history.

RIGHTS AND EMANCIPATION

. . . It is useful to think of women's demands as encompassing two sets of needs: women's rights and women's emancipation.

Women's rights essentially are civil rights—to vote, to hold office, to have access to education and to economic and political power at every level of society on an equal basis with men. . . . These rights are demanded on the basis of a claim to *equality:* as citizens, as members of society, women are by rights equal and must therefore be treated equally. All of the rights here listed are based on the acceptance of the status quo; . . . These are essentially reformist demands.

Women's emancipation is freedom from oppressive restrictions imposed by reason of sex; self-determination and autonomy. Oppressive restrictions are biological restrictions due to sex, as well as socially imposed ones. Thus, women's bearing and nursing children is a biological given, but the assignment to women of the major responsibility for the rearing of children and for housework is socially imposed.

Self-determination means being free to decide one's own destiny, to define one's own social role. Autonomy means earning one's status, not being born into it or marrying it. . . . It means freedom to define issues, roles, laws and cultural norms on an equality with men. The demands for emancipation are based on stressing women's difference from men, but also on stressing women's difference from other women. They are radical demands, which can only be achieved by transforming society for men and women, equalizing gender definitions for both sexes, assigning the reproductive work of raising the next generation to both men and women, and reorganizing social institutions so as to make such arrangements possible.

Women, just like men, are placed in society as individuals *and* as citizens. They are both equal *and* different. The demand for women's emancipation always includes the demand for women's rights, but the reverse is not true. Generally speaking, women's rights have been won or improved upon in many parts of the world in the past 150 years. Women's emancipation has not yet been won anywhere.

The movement started at Seneca Falls . . . from the start embraced both [concepts]—by demanding legal, property, civil rights; and by demanding changes in gender-role definition and in woman's rights to her own body. As the nineteenth-century movement matured, there developed some tension between advocates of these two different sets of demands, with the mainstream focusing more and more on legal and property rights, while radicals and outsiders, like sex reformers, birth control advocates, and socialist feminists, demanded more profound social changes.

. . . But the same distinctions and tensions . . . have appeared in [the twentieth-century women movement]. One wing focused mainly on women's rights—adoption of ERA, legal/political rights and representation and civil rights for women of different classes, races and sexual orientations. The other wing began as "radical women's liberation" and later branched off into many more specialized groups working on abortion rights; protection of women against violence and sexual harassment; the opening up to women of nontraditional occupations: self-empowerment and the creation of women cultural institutions, ranging from lesbian groupings to women's music festivals and pop culture. The two informally defined wings of the movement often overlapped, sometimes collaborated on specific narrow issues, and recently have worked more and more on bridge-building. The Women's Studies movement has struggled long and hard to bridge the two wings and encompass them educationally. Further, new forms of feminism by women of color or women who define themselves as "different" from the majority in various ways have sprung up and served their own constituencies. Their existence has not weakened the movement, as its critics like to claim, but has strengthened it immensely by grounding it more firmly in different constituencies.

Let us not forget, ever, that when we talk about women's rights we talk about the rights of half the human race. No one expects all men to have the same interests, issues or demands. We should therefore never expect women to have one agenda, one set of issues or demands.

The women's rights demands first raised at Seneca Falls have in the United States been generally achieved for middle-class white women. They have been partially achieved for working-class women and women of color, but progress has been very uneven. . . .

The feminization of poverty and the increasing income gap between the rich and the poor have turned many legal gains won by women into empty shells. An example is the way in which legal restrictions on women's right to choose abortion have fallen more heavily on poor women than on the well-to-do. The uneven availability of child care for working mothers is another example.

The cultural transformation on which demands for woman's emancipation build, has been enormous. Many demands that seemed outrageous 150 years ago are now commonly accepted, such as a woman's right to equal guardianship of her children, to divorce, to jury duty, to acceptance in nontraditional occupations. Female police and fire officers and female military personnel are accepted everywhere without question. Women's participation in competitive sports is another area in which progress has been great, though it is far from complete. Many other feminist demands that seemed outrageously radical thirty years ago have become commonplace today—the acceptance of lesbians as "normal" members of the community; single motherhood; the criminal character of sexual harassment and marital rape. The acceptance of such ideas is still uneven and different in different places, but generally, the feminist program has been accepted by millions of people who refuse to identify themselves as "feminists." What critics decry as the splintering and diffusion of the movement is actually its greatest strength today.

It should also be recognized that the aims of feminism are transformative, but its methods have been peaceful reform, persuasion and education. For 150 years feminists have organized, lobbied, marched, petitioned, put their bodies on the line in demonstrations, and have overcome ancient prejudices by heroic acts of self-help. Whatever gains were won, had to be won step by step, over and over again. Nothing "was given" to women; whatever gains we made we have had to earn. And perhaps the most precious "right" we have won in these two centuries, is the right to know our own history, to draw on the knowledge and experience of the women before us, to celebrate and emulate our heroines and finally to know that "greatness" is not a sexual attribute.

WHAT MEANING DOES SENECA FALLS HOLD TODAY?

- It shows that a small group of people, armed with a persuasive analysis of grievances and an argument based on generally held moral and religious beliefs, can, if they are willing and able to work hard at organizing, create a transformative mass movement. The women who launched a small movement in 1848 had to build, county by county, state by state, the largest grassroots movement of the nineteenth century and then build it again in the twentieth century to transform the right to vote into the right to equal representation.
- Seneca Falls and the movement it spawned show that legal changes can be reversed, unless social and cultural transformations sustain them. Over the past 150 years all of the grievances listed at Seneca Falls have been resolved or at least dealt with, though new inequities and grievances arise in each generation. The "specter that haunted Europe" left some gains, but mostly bloodshed, terror and devastation in its wake, and most of the inequities it sought to adjust are still with us. Feminism has behind it a record of solid gains without the costs of bloody war and revolution.

Although the media and many politicians with monotonous frequency declare feminism to be dead, many of its goals have been accomplished and its momentum, worldwide, is steadily rising. The worldwide movement of women for their emancipation is irreversible. It will continue to live and grow, as long as women anywhere have "grievances" they can proclaim and as long as they are willing and able to organize to rectify them.

DOCUMENTS

Claiming Rights II

Declaration of Sentiments, 1848

The Declaration of Sentiments, Stanton's indictment of the relations between men and women in her own society, is still stunning in its energy, its precision, and its foresight. It challenged many elements of American law and social practice which—thanks to five generations of political activism—no longer exist.

But the Declaration was only the beginning. Out of their vision of a community of equals, out of their discomfort with a social environment that privileged men and undermined women, the men and women at Seneca Falls dedicated themselves to Herculean political work. In one seventeen-day period in 1855 they held sixteen political meetings in fourteen different counties in upstate New York. In 1864, when it seemed possible that an end to slavery might also mean universal equal citizenship, they sent petitions with 100,000 signatures to the Senate and dreamed of getting a million.

They denounced the exclusion of women from learned professions and "nearly all the profitable employments." Male teachers earned $700 a year; women teachers earned $250. Susan B. Anthony would soon be demanding "equal pay for equal work," but there would be no federal equal pay act until 1963.

If Stanton and her Seneca Falls colleagues were to reappear in our own time, what changes would please them? What elements of their agenda would they believe are still alive?

Seneca Falls, New York,
July 19–20, 1848

When, in the course of human events, it becomes necessary for one portion of the family of man to assume among the people of the earth a position different from that which they have hitherto occupied, but one to which the laws of nature and of nature's God entitle them, a decent respect to the opinions of mankind requires that they should declare the causes that impel them to such a course.

We hold these truths to be self-evident: that all men and women are created equal; that they are endowed by their Creator with certain inalienable rights; that among these are life, liberty, and the pursuit of happiness; that to secure these rights governments are instituted, deriving their just powers from the consent of the governed. Whenever any form of government becomes destructive of these ends, it is the right of those who suffer from it to refuse allegiance to it, and to insist upon the institution of a new government, laying its foundation on such principles, and organizing its powers in such form, as to them shall seem most likely to effect their safety and happiness. Prudence, indeed, will dictate that governments long established should not be changed for light and transient

Declaration of Sentiments, in *History of Woman Suffrage,* vol. 1, ed. Elizabeth Cady Stanton, Susan B. Anthony, and Matilda Joslyn Gage (New York: Fowler & Wells, 1881), pp. 70–71. The Declaration and many related documents can be found at the website of The Papers of Elizabeth Cady Stanton and Susan B. Anthony, http://ecssba.rutgers.edu.

causes; and accordingly all experience hath shown that mankind are more disposed to suffer, while evils are sufferable, than to right themselves by abolishing the forms to which they were accustomed. But when a long train of abuses and usurpations, pursuing invariably the same object evinces a design to reduce them under absolute despotism, it is their duty to throw off such government, and to provide new guards for their future security. Such has been the patient sufferance of the women under this government, and such is now the necessity which constrains them to demand the equal station to which they are entitled.

The history of mankind is a history of repeated injuries and usurpations on the part of man toward woman, having in direct object the establishment of an absolute tyranny over her. To prove this, let facts be submitted to a candid world.

He has never permitted her to exercise her inalienable right to the elective franchise.

He has compelled her to submit to laws, in the formation of which she had no voice.

He has withheld from her rights which are given to the most ignorant and degraded men—both native and foreigners.

Having deprived her of this first right of a citizen, the elective franchise, thereby leaving her without representation in the halls of legislation, he has oppressed her on all sides.

He has made her, if married, in the eye of the law, civilly dead.

He has taken from her all right in property, even to the wages she earns.

He has made her, morally, an irresponsible being, as she can commit many crimes with impunity, provided they be done in the presence of her husband. In the covenant of marriage, she is compelled to promise obedience to her husband, he becoming, to all intents and purposes, her master—the law giving him power to deprive her of her liberty, and to administer chastisement.

He has so framed the laws of divorce, as to what shall be the proper causes, and in case of separation, to whom the guardianship of the children shall be given, as to be wholly regardless of the happiness of women—the law, in all cases, going upon a false supposition of the supremacy of man, and giving all power into his hands.

After depriving her of all rights as a married woman, if single, and the owner of property, he has taxed her to support a government which recognizes her only when her property can be made profitable to it.

He has monopolized nearly all the profitable employments, and from those she is permitted to follow, she receives but a scanty remuneration. He closes against her all the avenues to wealth and distinction which he considers most honorable to himself. As a teacher of theology, medicine, or law, she is not known.

He has denied her the facilities for obtaining a thorough education, all colleges being closed against her.

He allows her in Church, as well as State, but a subordinate position, claiming Apostolic authority for her exclusion from the ministry, and, with some exceptions, from any public participation in the affairs of the Church.

He has created a false public sentiment by giving to the world a different code of morals for men and women, by which moral delinquencies which exclude women from society, are not only tolerated, but deemed of little account in man.

He has usurped the prerogative of Jehovah himself, claiming it as his right to assign for her a sphere of action, when that belongs to her conscience and to her God.

He has endeavored, in every way that he could, to destroy her confidence in her own powers, to lessen her self-respect, and to make her willing to lead a dependent and abject life.

Now, in view of this entire disfranchisement of one-half the people of this country, their social and religious degradation—in view of the unjust laws above mentioned, and because women do feel themselves aggrieved, oppressed, and fraudulently deprived of their most sacred rights, we insist that they have immediate admission to all the rights and privileges which belong to them as citizens of the United States.

In entering upon the great work before us, we anticipate no small amount of misconception, misrepresentation, and ridicule; but we shall use every instrumentality within our power to effect our object. We shall employ agents, circulate tracts, petition the State and National legislatures, and endeavor to enlist the pulpit and the press in our behalf. We hope this Convention will be followed by a series of Conventions embracing every part of the country.

The following resolutions were discussed by Lucretia Mott, Thomas and Mary Ann McClintock, Amy Post, Catharine A. F. Stebbins, and others, and were adopted:

WHEREAS, The great precept of nature is conceded to be, that "man shall pursue his own true and substantial happiness." Blackstone in his Commentaries remarks, that this law of Nature being coeval with mankind, and dictated by God himself, is of course superior in obligation to any other. It is binding over all the globe, in all countries, and at all times; no human laws are of any validity if contrary to this, and such of them as are valid, derive all their force, and all their validity, and all their authority, mediately and immediately, from this original; therefore;

Resolved, That such laws as conflict, in any way, with the true and substantial happiness of woman, are contrary to the great precept of nature and of no validity, for this is "superior in obligation to any other."

Resolved, That all laws which prevent woman from occupying such a station in society as her conscience shall dictate, or which place her in a position inferior to that of man, are contrary to the great precept of nature, and therefore of no force or authority.

Resolved, That woman is man's equal—was intended to be so by the Creator, and the highest good of the race demands that she should be recognized as such.

Resolved, That the women of this country ought to be enlightened in regard to the laws under which they live, that they may no longer publish their degradation by declaring themselves satisfied with their present position, nor their ignorance by asserting that they have all the rights they want.

Resolved, That inasmuch as man, while claiming for himself intellectual superiority, does accord to woman moral superiority, it is preeminently his duty to encourage her to speak and teach, as she has an opportunity, in all religious assemblies.

Resolved, That the same amount of virtue, delicacy, and refinement of behavior that is required of woman in the social state, should also be required of man, and the same transgressions should be visited with equal severity on both man and woman.

Resolved, That the objection of indelicacy and impropriety, which is so often brought against woman when she addresses a public audience, comes with a very ill-grace from those who encourage, by their attendance, her appearance on the stage, in the concert, or in feats of the circus.

Resolved, That woman has too long rested satisfied in the circumscribed limits which corrupt customs and a perverted application of the Scriptures have marked out for her, and that it is time she should move in the enlarged sphere which her great Creator has assigned her.

Resolved, That it is the duty of the women of this country to secure to themselves their sacred right to the elective franchise.

Resolved, That the equality of human rights results necessarily from the fact of the identity of the race in capabilities and responsibilities.

Resolved, therefore, That, being invested by the Creator with the same capabilities, and the same consciousness of responsibility for their exercise, it is demonstrably the right and duty of woman, equally with man, to promote every righteous cause by every righteous means; and especially in regard to the great subjects of morals and religion, it is self-evidently her right to participate with her brother in teaching them, both in private and in public, by writing and by speaking, by any instrumentalities proper to be used, and in any assemblies proper to be held; and this being a self-evident truth growing out of the divinely implanted principles of human nature, any custom or authority adverse to it, whether modern or wearing the hoary sanction of antiquity, is to be regarded as a self-evident falsehood, and at war with mankind.

At the last session Lucretia Mott offered and spoke to the following resolution:

Resolved, That the speedy success of our cause depends upon the zealous and untiring efforts of both men and women, for the overthrow of the monopoly of the pulpit, and for the securing to woman an equal participation with men in the various trades, professions, and commerce.

Married Women's Property Acts, New York State, 1848, 1860

Ironically, the first married women's property acts, passed in Mississippi in 1839 and in New York in 1848, were supported by many male legislators out of a desire to preserve the estates of married daughters against spendthrift sons-in-law. Four out of the five sections of the Mississippi act broadened the rights of married women over their own slaves.

Note the limits of the 1848 New York law, and the ways in which women's rights were extended by the 1860 revision. This pattern—of an initial statute that offered married women very modest control over property, followed by subsequent revisions that slowly and very gradually extended their claims—was typical of virtually all states. Under coverture, husbands had property rights in their wives' services, and state legislatures were reluctant to erase these rights. These "services" included the right of "consortium"—understood as including not only housekeeping but also love, affection, companionship, and sexual relations. If a married woman were injured by the negligence of another person, her husband could sue for damages, which included a monetary estimate of the worth of his loss of consortium. A married woman had a right to financial support from her husband but no right to consortium, and if he were injured she had no claim for the loss of his companionship and sexual relations. This imbalance between the sexes in marriage was rarely tested, but when it was—in the case of major accidents—the impact was severe. Not until the early 1950s was a married woman successful in making such a claim (in Washington, D.C., in 1950; in Iowa in 1951) and the states were very slow to recognize it. Feminist lawyers, men and women, pressed the claim throughout the 1970s and 1980s, but not until the 1990s could it be said that all states recognized it.

The nineteenth-century Married Women's Property Acts were narrowly interpreted. For example, although married women were authorized to "carry on any trade or business, and perform any labor or services on her sole or separate account," that authorization was regularly interpreted as applying only when her work was not done on family property. When Mary Ann Brooks, a married woman with a part-time job outside the home, was injured when hit by Adolphus Schwerin's horse and wagon in the early 1870s, she brought suit in her own name for damages. The New York court approved her suit to the limits of her lost wages, but she did not have the right to sue for her inability to perform housework in her own home. For that, Mr. Brooks would have to sue. In some states, when a woman purchased property with her own earnings, she would have to register it in the county courthouse if she wished to assert control over it; if she neglected to register, it could be seized for the payment of her husband's debts, as one Mrs. Odell of Davenport, Iowa, discovered when the piano she had bought with her own money and had shipped at great expense from Chicago was seized when her husband's business went bankrupt.* A married woman could rarely make claims for her earnings within the family; deep into the twentieth century, farm women had no legal claim to the "butter and

**Brooks* v. *Schwerin,* 54 N.Y. 343 (1873); *Odell & Updegraff* v. *Lee & Kinnardet al.,* 14 Iowa 411 (1868).

Laws of the State of New-York, Passed at the Seventy-First Session of the Legislature . . . (Albany, 1848), pp. 307–8; *Laws of the State of New York, Passed at the Eighty-Third Session of the Legislature . . .* (Albany, 1860), pp. 157–59.

egg money" that custom encouraged them to talk about as theirs because they did the hard work of the barn and the chicken coop.

1848

The real and personal property of any female [now married and] who may hereafter marry, and which she shall own at the time of marriage, and the rents issues and profits thereof shall not be subject to the disposal of her husband, nor be liable for his debts, and shall continue her sole and separate property, as if she were a single female. . . .

It shall be lawful for any married female to receive, by gift, grant, devise or bequest, from any person other than her husband and hold to her sole and separate use, as if she were a single female, real and personal property, and the rents, issues and profits thereof, and the same shall not be subject to the disposal of her husband, nor be liable for his debts. . . .

1860

[The provisions of the law of 1848 were retained, and others were added:]

A married woman may bargain, sell, assign, and transfer her separate personal property, and carry on any trade or business, and perform any labor or services on her sole and separate account, and the earnings of any married woman from her trade . . . shall be her sole and separate property, and may be used or invested by her in her own name. . . .

Any married woman may, while married, sue and be sued in all matters having relation to her . . . sole and separate property . . . in the same manner as if she were sole. And any married woman may bring and maintain an action in her own name, for damages, against any person or body corporate, for any injury to her person or character, the same as if she were sole; and the money received upon the settlement . . . shall be her sole and separate property.

No bargain or contract made by any married woman, in respect to her sole and separate property . . . shall be binding upon her husband, or render him or his property in any way liable therefor.

Every married woman is hereby constituted and declared to be the joint guardian of her children, with her husband, with equal powers, rights, and duties in regard to them, with the husband. . . .

DOCUMENT

Photograph of Sojourner Truth

Sojourner Truth's carte de visite

Sojourner Truth (ca.1797–1883) is better known in the twentieth century for words she did not utter—"ar'n't I a woman?"—than for her fierce and exemplary insistence on asserting her rights to express her religious convictions and to speak and act publicly. This portrait, made in a photographer's studio around 1864, depicts the reformer standing, with her hat, shawl, walking stick, and traveling bag, as if on the brink of departing for yet another speaking engagement. It

Entered according to Act of Congress, in the year 1864, by S. T. in the clerk's office of the U.S. District court, for Eastern District of Michigan. (Courtesy Sophia Smith Collection, Smith College, Northampton, Mass.)

is in the genre of *cartes de visite* (visiting cards), which were very popular in the mid-nineteenth century, both among middle-class women making social calls and as forms of publicity used by politicians, writers, and fund-raisers. As the card's inscription explains, Sojourner Truth sold copies of the card to support herself; her biographer Nell Irvin Painter reports that she charged the common market price of 33 cents per card.

She was born into slavery as Isabella in the region north of New York City and south of Albany; her first language was Dutch, and in later life her fluent English would have a Dutch accent. As a child she had four different masters; when she married it was under an 1809 New York State law that recognized slave marriages and the legitimacy of children born to married couples, but Isabella's owner chose her husband for her. When Isabella achieved her freedom six months before New York's gradual emancipation law went into effect on July 4, 1827, she owed no further service, but her five children, born after 1799, remained bound—boys until they reached the age of twenty-eight, girls until they reached twenty-five. As indentured servants, her son would not be free until 1849, her daughters not until 1850 and 1851. Around the time Isabella became free, her owner sold her five-year-old son, Peter, to his brother, who resold the boy to another brother, who resold him yet again to a brother-in-law who took him to Alabama where slavery was permanent and legal. Newly freed, Isabella had the confidence to take the matter to court; with financial and legal support from prominent Quakers and Dutch men for whom she worked, she won her suit and his freedom. Her seven-year-old son returned covered with scars from violent whippings. His sisters remained bound to service.

In 1828 Isabella moved to New York City where she found work as a domestic servant. She joined an unorthodox Methodist church and then a radical religious commune; she made a reputation as a preacher at camp meetings. In 1843 divine inspiration directed her to take the name Sojourner Truth and become an itinerant preacher; she made her way up the Connecticut River Valley to Massachusetts, where she joined the Utopian Northampton Association, an abolitionist commune that had recently been founded by William Lloyd Garrison's sister and brother-in-law, Sarah and George Benson. Garrison himself was a frequent visitor; Frederick Douglass, a former slave and articulate abolitionist, was another. They drew her into abolitionist lecture tours and women's rights meetings. Indeed, she spoke at the first national women's rights convention, in Worcester, Massachusetts, held little more than a year after Seneca Falls and featuring some of the same leading participants, including Elizabeth Cady Stanton.

In 1850 Sojourner Truth dictated her life history to Olive Gilbert, a close friend of Sarah Benson; she paid for its publication and supported herself by selling copies of *The Narrative of Sojourner Truth* wherever she traveled, updating it throughout her long life.

Sojourner Truth spoke the words that would make her famous at a women's rights convention attended by hundreds of women and men in Akron, Ohio, in the summer of 1851. Contemporary newspapers reported various versions of what they agreed was powerful oratory: "I have heard much about the sexes being equal: I can carry as much as any man, and can eat as much too, if I can get it. . . . As for intellect, all I can say is, if a woman have a pint and a man a quart—why cant she have her little pint full? You need not be afraid to give us our rights for fear we will take too much,—for we cant take more than our pint'll hold. . . . I cant read, but I can hear. I have heard the bible and have learned that Eve caused man to sin. Well if woman upset the world, do give her a chance to set it right side up again."

But no contemporary witness noted her speaking the refrain "Ar'n't I a woman?" Historians agree that was added a dozen years later by Frances Dana Gage, a women's rights activist who had been at the Akron meeting, and who wrote a highly dramatized and elaborated version of the event, which underscored Truth's strength and authority. Gage's version was reprinted by Elizabeth Cady Stanton and Susan B. Anthony in the first volume of *The History of Woman Suffrage* (1881) and from there found its way into widespread use. (The current *Wikipedia* entry treats the phrase as if Sojourner Truth, rather than Gage, invented it, although scholars have known differently for nearly two decades.)

Sojourner Truth would live until her mid-eighties. She embraced the Union cause during the Civil War, even before Lincoln embraced emancipation. She went door-to-door in Battle Creek, Michigan (where she had moved in the 1850s), to raise money to support the local African American regiment (in which her grandson was enlisted). She traveled from Michigan to Washington, D.C., making campaign speeches for Lincoln's reelection; she met Abraham Lincoln; she worked to help freedpeople find jobs, and she worked for projects to give former enslaved people free land in Kansas. With all this public activity, Sojourner Truth became famous—the "celebrated colored woman"—and visitors made their way to Battle Creek especially to meet her. Cared for by her children and grandchildren, who lived nearby, she died in Battle Creek in 1883.*

Consider how Sojourner Truth presents herself in the photograph here. What does she hope viewers—in her own time and in ours—will conclude about her?

*Nell Irvin Painter, *Sojourner Truth: A Life, A Symbol* (New York: W. W. Norton, 1996), chs. 18, 26; on speaking Dutch, see p. 7; on the *cartes de visite,* see ch. 20; on the ambivalence of the meeting with Lincoln, see ch. 21. See also Carlton Mabee, *Sojourner Truth: Slave, Prophet, Legend* (New York: New York University Press, 1993).

ROSE STREMLAU

"I Know What an Indian Woman Can Do": Sarah Winnemucca Writes about Rape on the Northern Paiute Frontier

The Comstock lode—a rich vein of silver ore—was discovered by European Americans in the late 1850s in western Nevada, just east of Lake Tahoe and south of Pyramid Lake. Thousands of men trekked to the spot, coming westward over the Oregon Trail and eastward from California. As a consequence, the population of the nearest town, Virginia City, exploded, reaching 30,000 when extraction peaked in 1877. Anglos understood themselves to be seizing opportunity in the rugged wilderness. But far from being "virgin land," the forested mountains and river valleys of the surrounding landscape were the home territory of the Northern Paiutes. As had occurred in so many places in the Americas since 1492, a gender frontier—and a social flashpoint—was created as white settlers quickly outnumbered the locals who had different understandings of gender roles, manliness, and womanliness.

As Rose Stremlau's essay reveals, we know about the reactions of Northern Paiute women to the new dangers and survival challenges they faced because of the writings of one of them, Sarah Winnemucca (1844?–91). Active in lobbying military officers, territorial legislatures, the Interior Department in Washington, and President Hayes to improve conditions for her tribe and to compel governments to keep their promises, Winnemucca was an ardent reformer, a traveling lecturer, and an educator akin to the Grimké sisters. She befriended influential women in the East, securing their help in getting her autobiography published in Boston in 1883. Her biographer, Sally Zanjani, claims it to be "the first book written by an American Indian woman, the first by a Native American west of the Rockies, and the first to describe Paiute culture."[*] But Sarah Winnemucca died discouraged, with her people relegated to woefully inadequate reservation land, and the school she had established in her later years lacking sufficient external funding. If her vision of several such schools flourishing throughout the West had come to pass, the outcomes for many Indian children would have been very different (see Zitkala-Ša, pp. 356–360). Her statue now represents the state of Nevada in the U.S. Capitol Statuary Hall in Washington, D.C.

As you read the essay, ask yourself what skills and systems of knowledge Northern Paiute women needed for everyday living both before and after white settlers infiltrated their homelands. Compare to those of the white colonial goodwives described by Laurel Ulrich (pp. 47–56). Given that Sarah Winnemucca's

[*]*Online Nevada Encyclopedia*, a project of Nevada Humanities, S. V. Sarah Winnemucca," http://www.onlinenevada.org/sarah_winnemucca (accessed Mar. 20, 2009).

Excerpted from Rose Stremlau, "Rape Narratives on the Northern Paiute Frontier: Sarah Winnemucca, Sexual Sovereignty, and Economic Autonomy, 1844–1891," in *Portraits of Women in the American West*, ed. Dee Garceau-Hagen (New York: Routledge, 2005). Reprinted by permission of the author and publisher. Notes have been edited and renumbered.

autobiography is 240 pages long, what insights do we gain by focusing on its stories of sexual violence and intimidation? Is Stremlau's evocation of a rape culture helpful in understanding other places and moments in U.S. history?

In April 1860, while Northern Paiute elders and leaders met in council at Pyramid Lake to determine how best to respond to the non-Indian invasion of their homeland and the destruction of their resource base, Northern Paiute families carried on their day-to-day subsistence work as best they could. Searching for one of their most important food sources, two young Northern Paiute women gathered roots near Williams's Station, a settlers' trading post. Several white men seized the girls, dragged them into a barn, and repeatedly gang raped them. The men . . . held the young women captive, and when the girls' families came searching for them, the men denied having seen them and threatened to shoot whoever continued to scout around their homestead for evidence of the girls. Their posturing was ineffective, however; the Northern Paiute men heard their women's screaming, and they would retaliate.[1]

In Sarah Winnemucca's autobiography, such stories of sexual victimization are as much a part of the Northern Paiute experience as their seasonal hunting and gathering cycle. In particular, Winnemucca described how sexual violence characterized many white men's relations with the Native American women and girls whom they considered racially and culturally inferior and economically marginal. But Winnemucca's life story should not be read as a police blotter detailing individual crimes. Her vivid descriptions of sexual violence suggest how Native people experienced and responded to interracial rape, and her stories of rape point to larger themes in Northern Paiute adaptation. Winnemucca posited that the Northern Paiutes' best chance at survival lay not in assimilation to white culture but in the restoration of their economic autonomy, symbolized by women's ability to work without fear of sexual assault.

Born in approximately 1844 near the Humboldt River in what is today western Nevada, Sarah Winnemucca grew to adulthood in a world turned upside down by rapid, unprecedented change. [Although] the Northern Paiutes had never met an American until the late 1840s, by 1859, non-Indians outnumbered her people in their own homeland. Winnemucca lived her life at an interchange of power relations that would confound even the brightest of us. As a young girl, she keenly perceived that gender roles functioned differently in white society than in her own. From her earliest contacts with Americans, she described a culture infused with masculinity and violence and in which the combination of the two equated to power. As an American Indian woman, Winnemucca had no claim to power in the rough West of non-Indian miners, soldiers, and settlers. But in her culture, she did have power, in part because Northern Paiutes valued the work that women did.

Prior to the non-Indian settlement of the Great Basin, the Northern Paiutes practiced an extremely flexible gendered division of labor that enabled them to adapt rapidly to changes in their environment. Their homeland covered over 70,000 square miles in present-day southeastern Oregon, southwestern Idaho, northwestern Nevada, and northeastern California. Microclimatic variation caused environmental diversity, and across the Great Basin, arid, desert landscapes blended into fertile, lush valleys and waterfronts. These Great Basin hunters and gatherers adapted to their environment by diversifying their sources of food and establishing extended kin relations, which enabled communication and cooperation among groups in times of abundance and need. While lean periods were common, starvation was not, because Native people utilized such a wide variety of natural resources.[2]

The Northern Paiutes migrated from food source to food source in small families and family groups or clusters. Depending on the availability of resources, a married couple or a set of married siblings and their children composed the core of groups that expanded to include a handful of families and then contracted back to the immediate family group. Households joined together for particular communal subsistence activities, especially the pine nut harvest and rabbit drives, or in particularly rich areas, such as near fisheries.

Due to the limited food supplies throughout much of the Great Basin, however, the collective labor of larger groups usually proved a disadvantage over that of an individual or couple. Throughout most of the year, then, families functioned as self-contained units, and the gendered division of labor within families enabled the efficient exploitation of their environment.

Married couples comprised the basic unit of production and social reproduction. Among the Northern Paiutes, marriage was not a private concern between a man and a woman. Instead, married couples produced food and children, and the relationships between husbands and wives also bound kin groups together. Marriage among the Northern Paiutes was a mutually beneficial process rather than an event. When a man visited a woman's home at night and eventually moved his belongings into her home with her consent, the family recognized the couple as married and integrated them into the gendered, adult world of production and reproduction. Marriages ended as informally as they began when husbands moved out of, or were removed from, their wives' homes. . . . [W]hile Great Basin societies lacked the economic, social, political, or religious institutions that bound wives to husbands and ensured the permanence of marital unions, these societies valued the economic and social complementarity that husbands and wives provided each other.[3] . . .

. . . In her autobiography, Winnemucca emphasized the bonds of affection between husbands and wives; reciprocity, it seems, was emotional and physical as well as economic. Many relationships lasted for a lifetime. She explained, "They not only take care of their children together, but they do everything together; and when they grow blind, which I am sorry say is very common, for the smoke they live in destroys their eyes at last, they take sweet care of one another. Marriage is a sweet thing when people love each other."[4]

Married couples divided some tasks and shared others in order to maximize their utilization of local resources. Both spouses' labor was essential to a family's survival, and families formed self-sufficient economic units. Men usually hunted, trapped, and fished, but men also worked alongside their female relatives gathering when the needs of the family demanded it. Individually or in small groups, men stalked large game including deer, pronghorn, and bighorn sheep. Alternately, several hunters sometimes worked together to corral a herd of animals and to net rabbits and other small mammals and fish. Northern Paiute men developed a variety of ways to kill: they shot game with poisoned arrows; tracked them with dogs; prayed and sacrificed for them; ambushed them; enchanted them with spiritual power; netted them; snared them; charged at them in disguises; tricked them into entering traps with noises; and set out fishing lines with specified hooks. Winnemucca explained that because they avoided warfare, Northern Paiute conceptions of masculinity were bound up solely with the skills of hunting and fishing, which provided food for their families.

Women typically gathered plants, roots, and nuts, but they also hunted small animals and fished. Their selective utilization of natural resources and development of many specific subsistence technologies for procuring and processing food suggest that Northern Paiute women were skilled laborers. They developed, transmitted, and continuously perfected systems of knowledge that made edible and palatable piñon nuts, acorns, cattails, rice grass, many species of seeds, camas, swamp onion, biscuit roots, bitterroots, other types of roots, buckberries, wolfberries, other fruits and berries, leaves, stalks, and greens. Women also prepared meat and fish for consumption through a variety of techniques, including roasting and making pemmican. Northern Paiute women did not simply harvest the resources in their environment, however; they manipulated it to produce more abundant harvests in the future. They burned unwanted vegetation, pruned and plucked plants, and broadcast seeds. Just as importantly, they prayed and gave offerings to the spirits of the plants and animals that they consumed to ensure plentiful seasons in the future.[5]

Northern Paiute women may have provided . . . over half of their families' livelihood and perhaps the most important part. Plants provided a significant percentage of nutrients, and nuts provided valuable fat and protein in a diet otherwise prone to deficiencies. Women were accustomed to spending a significant amount of their time gathering away from men's supervision and protection. These women were independent workers unaccustomed to being sexually harassed.

Northern Paiute women's economic contributions accorded them high status as they wielded both spiritual and political power often seen as interrelated. Because of their ability to provide food, women had a political voice. Female and male leaders attained spiritual power in one of three ways: through dreams, through inheritance from a powerful, deceased relative, and through visiting foreign, unknown places. Male and female elders made decisions for family groups, and as Winnemucca explained, "The women know as much as the men do, and their advice is often asked. We have a republic as well as you. The council-tent is our Congress, and anybody can speak who has anything to say, women and all." . . . Notably, Winnemucca went on to explain that women and men sat in different circles in council, but she did not consider this a sign of inferiority. Rather, it was a sign of complementarily and social order.[6]

. . . [M]otherhood also accorded Northern Paiute women status. Whether from the earth or their bodies, women brought forth life, and they were valued for it. Beginning with their first menstruation, young Northern Paiute women underwent a period of seclusion involving fasting, laboring, and bathing in preparation for the roles of wife and mother. Once pregnant, both men and women followed specific taboos intended to insure the well-being of mothers and babies. For men, according to Winnemucca, this included assuming much of women's domestic labor. She wrote: "If he does not do his part in the care of the child, he is considered an outcast. . . . The young mothers often get together and exchange experiences about the attentions of their husbands; and inquire of each other if the fathers did their duty to their children, and were careful of their wives' health." . . . Such complementarity fostered a culture of respect between Northern Paiute men and women, one in which violence had no place.[7]

The sudden, unexpected influx of non-Indians into their homeland compromised the Northern Paiutes' natural resources and rendered their seasonal rounds impossible. While they had obtained horses and European goods by the mid to late eighteenth century, Northern Paiutes did not directly contact Europeans or non-Indian Americans until the early nineteenth century. They paid these trappers and traders little mind until the opening of the Oregon Trail and the discovery of gold in California during the 1840s brought thousands of migrants through the heart of their territory. . . . [I]n 1859, the discovery of gold and silver in Northern Paiute territory along the Virginia Range and the Owyhee Basin attracted thousands of settlers to the area. The Comstock Lode shifted the demographics of their territory within a few months as a minority population of a few hundred whites exploded into a majority of many thousands. As ethnohistorians Martha C. Knack and Omer C. Stewart explain, "Despite the initial trickle of transients, this onslaught of white domination was sudden, complete, and irreversible. The opportunity for natives to respond and resist was nearly gone before they could even comprehend the threat." Seeking rapid profits, these non-Indians destroyed Native hunting and gathering lands; miners cut down groves of piñon trees for shoring and building mine shafts and diverted streams for flumes; ranchers seized grasslands and water; and town dwellers seized timber and the choicest land.[8]

Women's contributions to the family pot may have taken on increasing importance as non-Indians consumed the natural resources most familiar to them, particularly game, and limited the Northern Paiutes' access to other resources, such as fisheries, by locating their settlements near the rivers and lakes. In response, women's skilled gathering of resources with which non-Indians were unfamiliar became vital to Northern Paiute survival. . . .

Northern Paiutes responded to the invasion by trying to maintain their seasonal hunting and gathering cycle, but they did so in different ways; some fled away from non-Indians and onto reservations where they tried to survive by supplementing their traditional food sources with rations and agriculture. Others relocated to the margins of non-Indian communities and combined the seasonal cycle with wage labor. Neither response enabled women to adequately gather, fish, or trap to feed their families. Regardless of their choices and however well they adapted to the new extractive, market-oriented economy of the Great Basin, many Northern Paiutes suffered from a new social ill—chronic starvation.

Most Northern Paiutes could not get far enough away from the newcomers. As early as the 1830s, the Northern Paiutes altered their hunting and gathering cycle by going to the mountains in the summer instead of the valleys where they usually gathered . . . In 1859, as miners flooded into the Great Basin, Northern Paiutes began relocating onto reservations. The Pyramid Lake reservation was established in 1859 and the Malheur in 1873, but poverty stalked the reservations, too. Even under the best of circumstances reservations wanted for funding and capable leadership. Sarah Winnemucca, like her father and many other Great Basin leaders, considered reservations no better than death camps. Unable to continue their seasonal hunting and gathering cycle with the necessary regularity, unprepared to farm, often swindled by the agents charged to care for them, and unsupplied with the rations promised in treaties, Great Basin Indians starved on reservations. Winnemucca wrote her autobiography as a condemnation of the corrupt reservation system, and she recalled a heated exchange between Chief Egan and Agent William Reinhart. Egan begged for the food locked in the agency storehouse: "My children are dying with hunger. I want what I and my people have worked for, that is, we want the wheat." Reinhart replied, "Nothing here is yours. It is all the government's." Like prison camps, reservations condemned Native people, even those who wanted to work to feed their families, to dependency on the government for food. According to Winnemucca, this dependency was emotionally, spiritually, physically, and mentally intolerable to men and women who had been self-sufficient adults just a few years earlier.[9]

Northern Paiutes who settled among non-Indians struggled, too. Forced to adapt and utilize non-Indians as another available resource, Northern Paiutes balanced their seasonal cycle with barter or wage labor in menial jobs. Men cut trees, hauled goods, and tended livestock. Because of the shortage of white women, Indian women easily found domestic work as housekeepers, seamstresses, and laundresses. . . . In the Indian shantytown that bordered Virginia City, Northern Paiute women with their gathering baskets rose early to pick rotting food from non-Indian trash piles. Others waited outside the mines for workers to empty the leftovers from their lunch pails into their baskets. Despite their meager resources. Northern Paiute women continued to provide a significant portion of their families' livelihoods through their adaptation of the subsistence round. Still, whether they lived on the reservations or in towns, Northern Paiute women were vulnerable to poverty and exploitation.[10]

Winnemucca exemplifies how Northern Paiute women put traditional skills to use at non-traditional work as they adapted to survive in the new Great Basin economy. During her early childhood, Winnemucca learned Northern Paiute women's customary domestic and subsistence tasks; she came to understand a woman's role by helping her mother care for her siblings and their household. For example, she prepared food like cattail pollen cakes and practiced crafts like weaving cattails and sagebrush into baskets for gathering and mats for clothing and shelter. As a teenager, her skill at handiwork enabled her to live by selling needlework door-to-door in Virginia City. In her early twenties, she worked as a laundress on the reservation. By her thirties, she had saved enough money to purchase a wagon and team, and when not working as a maid, she hired herself out as a teamster, not an unlikely job for a woman who grew up migrating and moving her home among campsites. In the 1870s, as the speaker of five languages; English, Paiute, Shoshone, Spanish, and Washoe; she translated and taught on the reservation. In the late 1870s, having gained familiarity with the territory through the seasonal round, she scouted for the United States Army. Beginning in the 1870s and through the rest of her life, Winnemucca, member of a chiefly family who had attained power in her own right, served as an ambassador and spokeswoman for her people: she wrote letters, visited American political leaders, gave lectures, and wrote her autobiography to obtain provisions and ensure safe communities for the Northern Paiutes. In the late 1880s, she established and ran a school that educated Northern Paiute children in their own and Anglo-American culture."[11] . . .

Poverty was not the only challenge that Northern Paiute women faced; their work as providers for their families also made them vulnerable to sexual assault. Hunting, gathering, and wage work took women beyond the protection of brothers, fathers, and husbands. In this new world following the non-Indian invasion, women's work became particularly unsafe. The influx of whites brought a disproportionate number of non-Indian men without families to Northern Paiute territory. The mining industry created several new types of communities: only corporations had the assets to transport the equipment necessary to procure minerals from bedrock, and these large mines sparked the establishment of towns, such as Virginia City. Other miners worked alone or in small groups and migrated from base camp to base camp. Mining also attracted supporting industries, such as trading and ranching. Bandits and outlaws roamed the basin looking for easy targets to plunder. Soldiers manned military posts established throughout the territory to protect mining interests and keep the peace between Indians and non-Indians. Many of these new non-Indian communities lacked permanent female residents. Northern Paiutes, who had no standing army or labor system that kept men away from women for long periods of time, noted the preponderance of men without women and families with disapproval.[12] . . .

Newcomers to the Great Basin did not appreciate the Northern Paiutes' egalitarian gender roles, and, often without women of their own, they considered Native women to be subject, sexual resources. While they had never seen a Northern Paiute woman before, many white male newcomers to the Great Basin believed that they were experts on the subject of Indian women. Since the colonial era, Anglo-American culture had adopted the image of the "Indian princess" to symbolize virtue, but Americans associated overt, primitive sexuality with her "darker twin," the "squaw." . . . According to the stereotype, Native women worked like slaves and had sex like animals. Moreover, like their European forebears, Americans claimed sexual access to women, along with other forms of property, as a right of conquest. These beliefs were not limited to men of low status. While recognizing that not all Indian women were "wanton," General Oliver O. Howard, under whom Winnemucca served as a scout and with whom she developed a mutually respectful friendship, commented that he understood why "squaw men" took Indian wives: allegedly the women were compliant and sexually eager.[13]

Some Northern Paiute women utilized their sexuality as another resource that enabled them to survive during this tumultuous period. Many Northern Paiute women, including Sarah Winnemucca and her sister, married white men, perhaps in an effort to broaden their resource base through extending kin ties as Northern Paiutes had always done. Others worked in a nontraditional industry—sex work. Indian women worked as prostitutes in frontier towns across the West during the Gold Rush. Regardless of whether or not particular Indian women actually were working as prostitutes, the predominance of stereotypes about Indian women's sexuality enabled whites to come to the conclusion that they were.[14] . . .

The discovery of Comstock Lode sparked a frenzied competition for resources in the Great Basin and created an environment particularly conducive to violence against American Indian women. Historians of rape have argued that sexual violence often occurs at societal flashpoints, places where diverging groups struggle over power and status. In particular, historians have suggested that men rape women whom they consider racially or culturally inferior and economically dependent. In the Humboldt Sink in the 1850s and 1860s, white men looked down on Northern Paiute women, and their economic vulnerability made them more readily accessible. Dismissed by the American legal system, Northern Paiute women were also not likely to bring charges against rapists.

. . . As whites became increasingly land-hungry, Native people became more defensive and vocal in demanding protection from the army and the federal government. Each resented the other's claim to the land and what grew on it or lay below the surface. Northern Paiute women could not gather roots in the same land that white men mined for silver. When they occupied the land and raped women who came near their camps and posts, these newcomers discouraged women from continuing their subsistence gathering cycle. White men did not simply rape to satisfy sexual urges; they raped Northern Paiute and other Great Basin Indian women to assert their dominance over them and the kinsmen unable to protect them. It worked. The Northern Paiutes were intimidated. Winnemucca explained, "My people have been so unhappy for a long time they now wish to disincrease, instead of multiply. The mothers are afraid to have more children, for fear they shall have daughters, who are not safe even in their mother's presence."[15]

It is historically and morally important to acknowledge that non-Indian men raped Indian women as part of the conquest of the American West. The Anglo-American West bred a *rape culture*, or a "complex of beliefs that encourages male sexual aggression and supports violence against women." Rape cultures equate domination and violence with sexuality, and in rape cultures women experience sexual violence along a continuum of behavior from economic marginalization to rape and murder. Perpetrators in a rape culture assume their behavior is a normal, inevitable aspect of life. While coined by activists working to end rape in contemporary culture, the term *rape culture* is useful to historians because it reminds us that sexual violence is culturally constructed: not all men across time and place have raped women, and when and where men have raped women, they have not committed rape for the same-reasons. Likewise, while they may endure similar physical acts, women experience rape differently in cultures that provide for alternative frameworks for understanding rape other than victimization.[16] That we remember the role of rape in conquest is important, but it is just as important to understand the extent and meaning of Native women's resistance if we want to understand how Native people and their cultures adapted and survived. . . .

. . . While they adopted some aspects of American culture, Northern Paiutes rejected non-Indian redefinitions of sexually appropriate behavior, such as female economic dependence and male sexual aggression. They disapproved of sexually aggressive behavior and labeled men who raped as deviant. Northern Paiutes distinguished among non-Indians based, in part, on their treatment of Native women, and many white men behaved quite badly according to Northern Paiute conceptions of masculinity. Throughout her autobiography, Winnemucca alluded to the ever-present threat posed by "bad white men who might harm us" and noted that she and other Northern Paiute leaders complained about the frequency of sexual assaults to American leaders in the hopes that they would take steps to prevent them.

But Winnemucca and the Northern Paiutes did more than plead to outsiders for assistance; they adapted their own lifestyles to prevent sexual attacks on Northern Paiute women and girls. Because they often experienced sexual violence together as family groups, Northern Paiutes rearranged their domestic relationships to better ensure the safety of female family members. Winnemucca described in detail how her family prevented the gang rape of her sister. During her early childhood, her grandfather, Truckee, moved part of her family cluster to California where he and several of her brothers worked for a rancher. Several white ranch hands repeatedly tried to gang rape Winnemucca's older sister, a young teenager. Each night the family fled their camp as the men came for her sister. Fearing violent retaliation themselves, her kinsmen felt that they could not physically defend the girl. One evening, five men came into their camp, and two entered their darkened tent and closed off the exit behind them. Winnemucca's uncles and brothers attacked the men and scared them off, and the family then boarded with their employers away from the rest of the workers. Finally, after the men asked Truckee for the girl outright—a request he scornfully refused—the family decided the terrified girl would no longer work alongside her mother but would spend her days under the direct supervision of her grandmother in camp and away from the dangers women faced as they worked away from the safety of their base camp. . . . Northern Paiute families experienced sexual violence as a process and a persistent threat instead of as single events.

. . . Northern Paiute families looked to established and newly formed social networks for protection from violence. Above all, . . . Northern Paiute women relied on kin for protection. In her autobiography, Winnemucca offered several examples of Northern Paiute men ensuring the safety of their female relatives. . . . But women also took care of each other. Winnemucca only left her sister-in-law, Mattie, at a military post because she knew her brother would arrive shortly. . . .

Northern Paiutes also relied on some newcomers for protection from others. When traveling, Winnemucca took every opportunity to stay in homes occupied by white women, although this was not always possible because of the gender imbalance of the non-Indian community. . . . [she] also recognized that some white men posed no threat.

When traveling, she commented, "No white women on all the places where we stopped—all men—yet we were treated kindly by all of them, so far."[17]

While fearing common soldiers, the Northern Paiutes sought protection from army officers against miners, settlers, and soldiers. Winnemucca and other Northern Paiute leaders developed close relationships with officers whom they identified as friendly and powerful allies. While scouting for them, Winnemucca accepted the escorts of officers who worried for her safety, but she was more proactive than that: she demanded protection when she felt vulnerable. Perhaps playing into her readers' expectations of feminine vulnerability, she recalled having once pleaded: "Colonel, I am all alone with so many men, I am afraid. I want your protection. I want you to protect me against your soldiers, and I want you to protect my people also."[18]

Unable to always prevent attacks, Northern Paiute women resisted sexual assaults the best they could with the options posed by their cultural worldview. Winnemucca's Anglo-American readers expected women to avoid rape by maintaining a virtuous appearance and reputation, a process that included keeping their bodies fully covered in clothing, appearing in public with appropriate male escorts, and not working outside their homes. While adapting some aspects of their dress, Northern Paiute women did not embrace constrictive gendered expectations of Anglo-American women concerning sexual violence. They continued to work alone or in small groups with other women and without male escort. They continued to gather outside their camps; they had to in order to eat. For Northern Paiute women, to do otherwise, such as send men to gather, made no sense.[19]

When threatened, Northern Paiute women attempted to outrun rapists. Winnemucca recalled an incident that occurred . . . when [she was] traveling with her sister. [N]on-Indian men followed the women. . . . [They] resolved to go down fighting if overtaken:

> Away we went, and they after us like wild men. We rode on till our horses seemed to drop from under us. At last we stopped, and I told sister what to do if the whole three of them overtook us. We could not do very much, but we must die fighting. If there were only two we were all right,—we could kill them; if one we would see what he would do. If he lassoed me she was to jump off her horse and cut the rope, and if he lassoed her I was to do the same. If he got off his horse and came at me she was to cut him, and I would do the same for her. Now we were ready for our work.[20]

In the end, Winnemucca and her sister escaped their would-be rapists. . . .

When unable to outrun perpetrators, . . . Northern Paiute women attacked them or outsmarted them, proving that successful resistance did not necessarily correspond with physical strength. Winnemucca suggested that Northern Paiute women verbally threatened would-be rapists with physical violence and implied that Northern Paiute women were often armed, and thus, that retaliation could hurt. Winnemucca bragged of breaking an offender's nose. The man, a fellow traveler bunked down near her, suggestively laid his hand on her in the middle of the night, and with one straight punch to his face, Winnemucca shunned his proposition. She bloodied his nose and sent him running for the door while she shouted, "Go away, or I will cut you to pieces, you mean man!" Winnemucca sliced another attempted rapist's face with a knife. On a March evening in 1875, Julius Argasse, a white man, either approached Winnemucca on the street or, according to another account, entered her home. Either way Winnemucca refused him with her knife. She was subsequently arrested, but the judge dismissed the charges against her.[21]

When other options for prevention and redress failed, Northern Paiutes and other Great Basin Natives killed rapists. Military doctor George M. Kober recalled a conversation he had with Winnemucca's father in which the chief blamed the ongoing violence on miners and Prospectors who "had no regard for the chastity of Indian women."[22] Winnemucca explained that the rapes of Native women and girls prompted the outbreak of the two Indian wars that she experienced. The Paiute War of 1860 began when the tribe retaliated against the men who kidnapped and raped the two young women who had been gathering roots. Outraged at the treatment of the young women and the men's initial denial of having seen them, the Northern Paiutes killed the four men. Some local whites considered the men upstanding citizens and led a campaign against the Northern Paiutes that resulted in their confinement at Pyramid Lake reservation by the end of the summer. Others, such as settler Richard N. Allen, believed that the Northern Paiutes' retaliation was justified and clearly in response to a wrong committed by these brothers since nearby settlers were unharmed by the Northern Paiutes.[23] . . .

. . . [F]or many Northern Paiutes, distance from non-Indians provided the best protection from violence. The Northern Paiutes' rapid acceptance of reservations must be considered in this context. As Leggins and Egan, two chiefs, explained when the government threatened to open part of their reservation land to non-Indian settlement, "And another thing, we do not want to have white people near us. We know what they are, and what they do to our women and daughters."[24]

While accounts of and allusions to rape permeate her autobiography, Winnemucca revealed little information about the victims. The details she provided suggest that sexual violence threatened all Northern Paiute women. Victims were old and young. Some were women that she did not know while others were family. Winnemucca herself survived sexual violence. Notably, nearly all victims were working, somehow trying to provide food for their families, or in Winnemucca's case, for her people. While she appealed to her readers' belief in women's vulnerability, Winnemucca never questioned the chastity or moral character of victims, and she refused to engage in non-Indian culture's debate over Native sexuality or pander to their stereotypes of Native women. Winnemucca's accounts of rape suggest what experts on contemporary sexual violence confirm: rape is not an act of sexual pleasure reflective of the victim's sexual appeal according to societal standards of beauty; rather it is an act of power, domination, and conquest inseparable from its social, economic, racial, cultural, and gendered context. In other words, sexual violence was intertwined with racial and economic oppression. . . .

. . . While other members of her tribe took up arms against invaders, Winnemucca waged a war of words in defense of Northern Paiute lifeways. Beginning in 1870 with a letter that ended up in the hands of the commissioner of the Bureau of Indian Affairs, Winnemucca repeatedly brought the Northern Paiutes' suffering to the attention of outsiders and demanded redress. . . . At her people's request, Winnemucca wrote letters to influential military and civilian leaders, and then traveled to San Francisco to lecture and to Nevada to lobby politicians. She continued her letter and speaking campaigns following their removal to Malheur and subsequent removals and relocations. Always she pleaded with her readers and listeners for food and land for the Northern Paiutes. In 1880, Winnemucca led a Northern Paiute delegation to Washington, D.C. to meet with Secretary of the Interior Carl Schurz, who directed Indian affairs, in order to obtain the Northern Paiutes' release from their reservations and to secure the allotment of their land into 160-acre plots for each family. Once she returned west and was no longer the subject of stories in eastern newspapers, Schurz failed to deliver on his promises to her. So Winnemucca turned to western newspapers to attack the Bureau of Indian Affairs. In 1883, with the support of Protestant reformers, Winnemucca moved East where she lectured and wrote her autobiography.

Expecting to hear and read titillating accounts of indigenous cultural practices, audiences instead felt their heartstrings pulled by Winnemucca's account of the abuse of Northern Paiute women and girls. By recounting the Northern Paiutes' story, including stories about rape, she generated an enormous amount of sympathy for the Northern Paiutes and aroused anger against the Bureau. Instead of responding to her criticism, the Bureau of Indian Affairs countered with attacks on her character, particularly her chastity. Winnemucca responded by including character references in the conclusion of her autobiography.

Winnemucca's stories of rape did not just generate public sympathy for the Northern Paiutes; they posited solutions to the Northern Paiutes' problems. Historian Miranda Chaytor argues that women's accounts of rape reveal more than the details of their violation because in them, women name the violence, contain it, and identify the people and things that will enable their recovery. When describing rape in the Great Basin, Winnemucca emphasized the vulnerability of women at work. . . . For these women, labor ordered their lives and accorded them status by enabling them to sustain their families. Winnemucca's accounts of rape, therefore, point to what she felt her people had lost that made them so sexually vulnerable—their economic self-sufficiency and autonomy.[25]

. . . During the late nineteenth century, reformers endorsed allotment, or the subdivision of communal land and resources among individual male heads of households, as a means to rapidly assimilate Native Americans into Anglo-American culture. They . . . believed that private land ownership would destroy the extended families that characterized most Native cultures and replace them with patriarchal, nuclear families, complete with a husband in the fields and a wife in the home. . . . Winnemucca lobbied for allotments, . . . not to enable the Northern Paiutes to assimilate but to facilitate the restoration of their economic self-sufficiency. Though she recognized that their seasonal cycle was destroyed, Winnemucca did not believe that it was irreplaceable, and she looked to allotment to restore the economic autonomy of Northern Paiute families through ranching and farming. On allotments, Northern Paiute husbands and wives could work sometimes together and other times apart as they had always done in order to maintain their families in the Northern Paiute way.

Winnemucca spent her final years attempting to prove that Northern Paiute families could survive and even thrive on their own small farms. In 1885, her brother, Natches, purchased a 160-acre ranch, and while Natches farmed, Winnemucca established a school. She taught Northern Paiute children reading, writing, and arithmetic, and the children helped Natches with the farming, and domestic chores. Most importantly, she treated the children kindly according to Northern Paiute custom and schooled them in Northern Paiute culture. The Peabody Institute, named after an eastern donor, was enormously popular with Northern Paiute students and parents, who abhorred the militarized boarding schools that the government forced Indian children to attend. Natches and Winnemucca's ranch and school blossomed for several years until their financial burden and poor health forced them to close in the summer of 1889. Financially and emotionally exhausted, Winnemucca moved to her sister Elma's ranch where she died in 1891.

During her life and since her death, Winnemucca has been the subject of much controversy. Literary and academic audiences honor Winnemucca as the first Native American woman to write her autobiography, *Life among the Piutes*, but many Native people criticize her for her more ambiguous accomplishments, such as scouting for the United States Army and endorsing assimilationist federal policies, particularly allotment. Some Northern Paiutes disown her for her inability to force the federal government to keep its promises to them, and pointing to her notoriety, they dismiss her as a self-serving opportunist. But other Northern Paiutes emphasize her devotion to their sovereignty and culture, generations before whites recognized the value of indigenous ways of life.

Perhaps Winnemucca remains so controversial because she was a leader ahead of her time. In the 1880s, she denounced the disproportionately high incidence of sexual violence against Native American women, and worked to ease their poverty and dramatize the relationship between sexual and economic oppression. Over a century later, the percentage of Native Americans living below the proverty line is over twice that of other Americans, and Native American women still experience sexual abuse in disproportionately high numbers—3.5 times that of other American racial groups. Moreover, unlike other racial groups, someone of another race assaults 90 percent of American Indian rape victims.[26] But Winnemucca also remains controversial because she defied stereotypes of Native American women as sexually lax and available. She personified their power, rooted in cultures that have not totally adopted American culture's attitudes toward women and their sexuality. Through her autobiography, she made Northern Paiute women's power intelligible to white readers during an era when Anglo-Americans were struggling with the question of women's rights themselves; she provided them with an alternative model of gender relations other than male dominance. Winnemucca proclaimed: "I know what an Indian woman can do. . . . My dear reader, I have not lived in this world for over thirty or forty years for nothing, and I know what I am talking bout."[27]

Notes

Hopkins was Winnemucca's married name; we've silently changed it to Winnemucca.

1. Richard N. Allen, *The Tennessee Letters: From Carson Valley, 1857–1869*, David Thompson, compiler (Reno: Grace Dangberg Foundation, 1983), 137–141, 157, 159–160; Myron Angel, *History of Nevada* (Oakland, CA: Thompson and West, 1881; New York: Arno Press, 1973), 150–158.

2. For a description of the Northern Paiute seasonal cycle, see Catherine S. Fowler and Sven Liljeblad, "Northern Paiute," in *The Handbook of North American Indians, Great Basin*, vol. 11, ed. Warren L. D'Azevedo (Washington, DC: Smithsonian Institution, 1986), 435–465; Martha C. Knack and Omer C. Stewart, *As Long as the River Shall Run: An Ethnohistory of the Pyramid Lake Indian Reservation* (Berkeley: University of California Press, 1984), chapter 1.

3. Judith Shapiro, "Kinship," in *The Handbook of North American Indians*, 620–629.

4. Sarah Winnemucca Hopkins, *Life Among the Piutes: Their Wrongs and Claims*, ed. Mrs. Horace Mann (New York: G. P. Putnam and Sons of New York, 1883; reprint, Reno: University of Nevada Press, 1994), 53 (hereafter cited as Winnemucca). Most scholars believe that Winnemucca wrote her autobiography with minimal editing by Mrs. Horace Mann. Sally Zanjani, *Sarah Winnemucca* (Lincoln: University of Nebraska Press, 2001).

5. Fowler, "Subsistence," *in The Handbook of North American Indians*, 64–97; Winnemucca, 50–51.

6 Fowler and Liljeblad, 450–452; Knack and Stewart, 230; and Winnemucca, 52–54.

7. Winnemucca, 45–51.

8. Fowler and Liljeblad; Knack and Stewart, chapter 2.

9. Winnemucca, chapters 5–8; Knack and Stewart, chapters 1–4.

10. Eugene M. Hattori, "'And Some of Them Swear Like Pirates': Acculturation of American Indian Women in Nineteenth Century Virginia City," in *Comstock Women: The Making of a Mining Community*, ed. Ronald M. James and C. Elizabeth Raymond (Reno: University of Nevada Press, 1998), 229–245; Knack and Stewart, chapter 2; Dorothy Nafus Morrison, *Chief Sarah: Sarah Winnemucca's Fight for Indian Rights* (New York: Atheneum, 1980), chapter 6.

11. For detailed accounts of all of Winnemucca's various jobs, see Winnemucca, Morrison, and Zanjani.

12. Winnemucca, 58–59, 231; Knack and Stewart, chapter 2.

13. Rayna Green, "The Pocahontas Perplex: The Images of Indian Women in American Culture," in *Unequal Sisters: A Multicultural Reader in U.S. Women's History*, ed. Ellen Carol DuBois (New York: Routledge, 1990), 15–21, Oliver O. Howard, *My Life and Experiences among Our Hostile Indians* (New York: Da Capo Press, 1972), 214, 222–223, 524–533.

14. Knack and Stewart, 47.

15. Winnemucca, 3–4; Knack and Stewart, chapters 2–8. For accounts of the rape of Indian women during the California Gold Rush, see Albert L. Hurtado, *Indian Survival on the California Frontier* (New Haven: Yale University Press, 1988), chapter 9.

16. Emilie Buchwald, Pamela Fletcher, and Martha Roth, preamble to *Transforming a Rape Culture* (Minneapolis, MN: Milkweed, 1993).

17. Winnemucca, 228.

18. Ibid., 100–104, 167, 178, 188, 231.

19. Hattori, 233–235; Knack and Stewart, chapters 4–5.

20. Winnemucca, 180–182, 228–230.

21. Winnemucca, 231; *Nevada State Journal*, 28 March 1875; *Silver State*, 27 March 1875; Zanjani, 126.

22. George M. Kober, *Reminiscences of George Martin Kober*, M. D., LL. D. (Washington, DC: Kober Foundation of Georgetown University, 1930), 280.

23. Fowler and Liljeblad, 457; Winnemucca, 70–73.

24. Winnemucca, 116.

25. "Husband(ry): Narratives of Rape in the Seventeenth Century," *Gender and History* 7 (1995): 378–407.

26. U.S. Department of Justice, Bureau of Justice Statistics, February 1999 for the period 1992–1996, "http://www/vday.org/ie/index2cfm?articleID+864. United States Department of Commerce, *We the First Americans* (Washington, DC: Government Printing Office, 1993).

27. Winnemucca, 228.

DREW GILPIN FAUST

Enemies in Our Households: Confederate Women and Slavery

The Civil War profoundly disrupted and reshaped American society; more people died in it than in all America's subsequent wars put together. It tested the stability of the Union and the meaning of democracy; Confederates insisted that their vision of a republic, which rested on racial hierarchy and the subordination of blacks, sustained the same claims to self-determination that had been central to the principles of the Revolution of 1776. The war would involve civilians in novel ways.

Because soldiers were recruited as companies from the same locality, it was not impossible for women to dress as men and enlist; buddies kept their secrets. A conservative estimate is that some 400 women joined in this way. A handful of women crossed military lines as spies, some disguising their race or their gender in the process. Thousands more women were recruited as hospital workers in both North and South; late in the war the Union recruited hundreds of freedwomen for this service. The bureaucracy of the federal government was vastly expanded during the war, and the personnel shortage was solved by hiring, for the first time in U.S. history, women to work in the same offices as men doing similar work.

Throughout the nation, familiar patterns of gender relations were disrupted as in the Revolutionary war, but on a far greater and more frightening scale. In the South, as Drew Faust explains, the departure of white men for war meant that white women were challenged to assume authority and to stabilize slavery despite the loss of the usual forms of force that had kept it in place. They discovered that they were living "with enemies in our own households." How they responded to this challenge varied; they were often profoundly transformed by their experiences.

What challenges did elite women face at the beginning of the war? What were some of the ways in which they responded? What allies did they have? What forms of resistance to authority did slaves engage in? How did the disruptions of the war bring into question traditional relations between white women and men?

When slaveholding men departed for battle, white women on farms and plantations across the South assumed direction of the region's "peculiar institution." In the antebellum years white men had borne overwhelming responsibility for slavery's daily management and perpetuation. But as war changed the shape of southern households, it necessarily transformed

Excerpted from ch. 3 of *Mothers of Invention: Women of the Slaveholding South in the American Civil War* by Drew Gilpin Faust (Chapel Hill: University of North Carolina Press, 1996). Reprinted by permission of the author and publisher. Notes have been edited and renumbered.

the structures of domestic authority, requiring white women to exercise unaccustomed—and unsought—power in defense of public as well as private order. Slavery was, as Confederate vice-president Alexander Stephens proclaimed, the "cornerstone" of the region's society, economy, and politics. Yet slavery's survival depended less on sweeping dictates of state policy than on tens of thousands of individual acts of personal domination exercised by particular masters over particular slaves. As wartime opportunity encouraged slaves openly to assert their desire for freedom, the daily struggle over coercion and control on hundreds of plantations and farms became just as crucial to defense of the southern way of life as any military encounter. Women called to manage increasingly restive and even rebellious slaves were in a significant sense garrisoning a second front in the South's war against Yankee domination.[1] . . .

Although white southerners—both male and female—might insist that politics was not, even in the changed circumstances of wartime, an appropriate part of woman's sphere, the female slave manager necessarily served as a pillar of the South's political order. White women's actions as slave mistresses were crucial to Confederate destinies, for the viability of the southern agricultural economy and the stability of the social order as well as the continuing loyalty of the civilian population all depended on successful slave control.

. . . The very meaning of mastery itself was rooted in the concepts of masculinity and male power. From the outset, Confederate leaders were uneasy about the transfer of such responsibility to women. . . .

As support grew in the fall of 1862 for some official draft exemption for slave managers, the *Macon Daily Telegraph* demanded, "Is it possible that Congress thinks . . . our women can control the slaves and oversee the farms? Do they suppose that our patriotic mothers, sisters and daughters can assume and discharge the active duties and drudgery of an overseer? Certainly not. They know better." In October Congress demonstrated that it did indeed know better, passing a law exempting from service one white man on each plantation of twenty or more slaves. But the soon infamous [law] . . . triggered enormous popular resentment, both from nonslaveholders who regarded it as valuing the lives of the elite over their own and from smaller slaveholders who were not included in its scope.[2]

In an effort to silence this threatening outburst of class hostility and at the same time meet the South's ever increasing manpower needs, the Confederate Congress repeatedly amended conscription policy, both broadening the age of eligibility and limiting exemptions. . . . This erosion of the statutory foundation for overseer exemptions greatly increased the difficulty of finding men not subject to military duty who could, as the original bill had phrased it, "secure the proper police of the country." Women across the Confederacy would find themselves unable to obtain the assistance of white men on their plantations and farms.

Conscription policy reveals fundamental Confederate assumptions, for it represents significant choices made by the Confederate leadership, choices that in important ways defined issues of class as more central to Confederate survival than those of gender. . . . White women in slaveowning households found their needs relegated to a position of secondary importance in comparison with the demands of nonslaveholding men. These men could vote, and the Confederacy required their service on the battlefield; retaining their loyalty was a priority. Minimizing class divisions within the Confederacy was imperative—even if ultimately unsuccessful. Addressing emerging gender divisions seemed less critical, because women—even the "privileged" ladies of the slaveowning elite—neither voted nor wrote editorials nor bore arms.[3]

With ever escalating military manpower demands, however, white women came to assume responsibility for directing the slave system that was so central a cause and purpose of the war. Yet they could not forget the promises of male protection and obligation that they believed their due. Women's troubling experiences as slave managers generated a growing fear and resentment of the burdens imposed by the disintegrating institution. Ultimately these tensions did much to undermine women's active support for both slavery and the Confederate cause. And throughout the South eroding slave control and diminishing plantation efficiency directly contributed to failures of morale and productivity on the homefront.

UNPROTECTED AND AFRAID

Women agreed with the Georgia newspaper that had proclaimed them unfit masters. "Where there are so many negroes upon places as upon ours," wrote an Alabama woman to the governor, "it is quite necessary that there should be men who can and will control them, especially at this time." Faced with the prospect of being left with sixty slaves, a Mississippi planter's wife expressed similar sentiments. "Do you think," she demanded of Governor John Pettus, "that this woman's hand can keep them in check?" Women compelled to assume responsibility over slaves tended to regard their new role more as a duty than an opportunity. Like many southern soldiers, they were conscripts rather than volunteers. As Lizzie Neblett explained to her husband, Will, when he enlisted in the 20th Texas Infantry, her impending service as agricultural and slave manager was "a coercive one."[4]

Women's reluctance derived in no small part from a profound sense of their own incapacities. One Mississippi woman complained that she lacked sufficient "moral courage" to govern slaves; another believed "managing negroes . . . beyond my power." "Master's eye and voice," Catherine Edmondston remarked, "are much more potent than mistress'." . . . Slaves themselves frequently seemed to share their mistresses' views of their own incapacities. Ellen Moore of Virginia complained that her laborers "all think I am a kind of usurper & have no authority over them." As war and the promise of freedom encouraged increasing black assertiveness, white women discovered themselves in charge of an institution quite different from the one their husbands, brothers, fathers, and sons had managed before military conflict commenced.[5]

Female apprehensions about slave mastery arose from fears of this very rebelliousness and from a sense of the special threat slave violence might pose to white women. Keziah Brevard, a fifty-eight-year-old South Carolina widow, lived in almost constant fear of her sizable slave force. "It is dreadful to dwell on insurrections," she acknowledged. Yet "many an hour have I laid awake in my life thinking of our danger."[6] . . .

Early in the war, Mary Chesnut, who professed never to have had any fear of her slaves, felt compelled to reconsider her own safety when her cousin Betsey Witherspoon was smothered by her servants. An elderly widow who lived alone with her slaves, Witherspoon was well known as an ineffective and indulgent manager. Her murder underlined both the inadequacies and vulnerabilities of white women as slave masters; her fate was exactly what her South Carolina neighbor Keziah Brevard most feared. Another Carolina widow, Ada Bacot, contemplated Witherspoon's death and the prospects of her own slaves' loyalty with similar dismay. "I fear twould take very little to make them put me out of the way," she wrote.[7] . . .

. . . Reports of individual acts of violence proliferated as well. Ada Bacot was certain the fire in her neighbors' house was set by their slave Abel; Laura Lee was horrified when occupying troops released a Winchester slave convicted of murdering her mistress. In September 1862 the *Mobile Advertiser and Register* noted that a slave had succeeded in poisoning his master; the same month the *Richmond Enquirer* recorded the conviction of one Lavinia for torching her mistress's house.[8] . . .

By the middle years of the war, women had begun publicly to voice their fears, writing hundreds of letters to state and Confederate officials imploring that men be detailed from military service to control the slaves. A group of women living near New Bern petitioned North Carolina Governor Zebulon Vance for exemptions for the few men who still remained at home. "We pray your Excellency to consider that in the absence of all protection the female portion of this community may be subjected to a system of outrage that may be justly denomenated the harrow of harrows more terrable to the contemplation of the virtuous maiden and matron than death." A petition to the Confederate secretary of war from a similar collection of "Ladies of the N.E. beat of Jas[per] County, Miss." sought male protection against an anticipated slave insurrection. If that was impossible, they requested arms and ammunition to defend themselves from "the demonic invasion" so that "we die with honor & innocence sustained."[9]

These women chose different euphemisms to express their anxieties—insult, outrage, "harrow of harrows," dishonor, stain, and molestation—but the theme was undeniably sexual. The Old South had justified white woman's subordination in terms of her biological difference, emphasizing an essential female weakness that rested ultimately in sexual vulnerability. In a society based on the oppression of a potentially hostile population of 4 million black slaves, such vulnerability assumed special significance. On this foundation of race, the white South erected its particular—and particularly compelling—logic of female dependence. Only the white man's strength could provide adequate and necessary protection. The very word *protection* was invoked again and again by Confederate women petitioning for what they believed [was] the fundamental right guaranteed them by the paternalistic social order of the South: "I feel unprotected and afraid," "unable to protect myself," "unable to stand up under her burden without the assistance of some white male to protect her." Denied such assurances of safety, many women would be impelled to question—even if implicitly—the logic of their willing acceptance of their own inferiority. In seeking, like the ladies of Jasper County, Mississippi, to protect themselves, Confederate women profoundly undermined the legitimacy of their subordination, demonstrating that they did not—indeed could not—depend on the supposed superior strength of white men.[10]

Significantly, the "demonic" invaders these Mississippi women most feared were not Yankees but rebellious slaves. In their terror of an insurgent black population, white southern women advanced their own definition of wartime priorities, one seemingly not shared by the Confederate leadership and government. "I fear the blacks more than I do the Yankees," confessed Mrs. A. Ingraham of besieged Vicksburg. . . . Living with slavery in wartime was, one Virginia woman observed, living with "enemies in our own households."[11]

The arrival of black soldiers in parts of the South represented the conjunction and culmination of these fears. Mary Lee of Winchester, Virginia, came "near fainting" when the troops appeared; she felt "more unnerved than by any sight I have seen since the war [began]." These soldiers were at once men, blacks, and national enemies—her gender, racial, and political opposites, the quintessential powerful and hostile Other. Their occupying presence in Winchester reminded her so forcefully of her weakness and vulnerability that she responded with a swoon, an unwanted and unwonted display of the feminine impotence and delicacy she had struggled to overcome during long years of her own as well as Confederate independence.[12]

Yet women often denied or repressed these profound fears of racial violence, confronting them only in the darkest hours of anxious, sleepless nights. Constance Cary Harrison remembered that in the daytime, apprehensions about slave violence seemed "preposterous," but at night, "there was the fear . . . dark, boding, oppressive and altogether hateful . . . the ghost that refused to be laid."[13] . . .

Some women in fact regarded their slaves as protectors, hoping for the loyalty that the many tales of "faithful servants" would enshrine in Confederate popular culture and, later, within the myth of the Lost Cause. Elizabeth Saxon, in a typically rose-colored remembrance of slavery during the war, recalled in 1905 that "not an outrage was perpetrated, no house was burned. . . . [O]n lonely farms women with little children slept at peace, guarded by a sable crowd, whom they perfectly trusted. . . . [I]n no land was ever a people so tender and helpful." The discrepancy between this portrait and the anxieties of everyday life on Confederate plantations underscores how white southerners, both during the war and afterward, struggled to retain a view of slavery as a benevolent institution, appreciated by blacks as well as whites. During the war such "faithful servant" stories served to calm white fears. But examples of persisting white trust and confidence in slaves cannot be discounted entirely, nor can the stories themselves be uniformly dismissed as white inventions. There were in fact slaves who buried the master's silver to hide it from the enemy; there were slaves, like one Catherine Edmondston described, who drew knives to defend mistresses against Yankee troops. Such incidents reinforced white southerners' desire not to believe that men and women they thought they had known intimately—sometimes all their lives—had suddenly become murderers and revolutionaries.[14]

Much of the complexity of wartime relationships between white women and slaves arose because women increasingly relied on slaves' labor, competence, and even companionship at a time when slaves saw diminishing motivation for work or obedience. White women's dependence on their slaves grew simultaneously with slaves' independence of their owners, creating a troubling situation of confusion and ambivalence for mistresses compelled constantly to reassess, to interrogate, and to revise their assumptions as they struggled to reconcile need with fear.... Some slave mistresses, especially in isolated plantation settings, found that in changed wartime households, their closest adult connections were with female slaves. When Rhoda died in April 1862, her owner Anna Green wrote in despair to her sister. "I feel like I have lost my only friend and I do believe she was the most faithful friend I had [even] if she was a servant." Leila Callaway described the death from smallpox of her slave Susanna in almost identical terms. "Next to my own dear family Susanna was my warmest best friend." "I have no one now in your absence," she informed her husband, "to look to for protection." In the disruptions of the South's hierarchies of gender and race, Leila Callaway had invested a black woman with some of the responsibilities—emotional and otherwise—of the absent white man.[15]

... Maria Hawkins keenly felt the absence of her slave protector Moses and wrote to Governor Vance with a variation of the hundreds of letters to southern officials seeking discharge of husbands and sons. Hawkins requested Moses' release from impressment as a laborer on coastal fortifications. "He slept in the house, every night while at home, & protected everything in the house & yard & at these perilous times when deserters are committing depredations, on plantations every day, I am really so much frightened every night, that I am up nearly all night." In Hawkins's particular configuration of gender and racial anxieties, a black male protector was far preferable to no male at all.[16]

THE FRUITS OF THE WAR

Within the context of everyday life in the Confederacy, most women slaveholders confronted neither murderous revolutionaries nor the unfailingly loyal retainers of "moonlight and magnolias" tradition. Instead they faced complex human beings whose desires for freedom expressed themselves in ways that varied with changing means and opportunities as slavery weakened steadily under unrelenting northern military pressure.

Often opportunity was greatest in areas close to Union lines, and slave-owners in these locations confronted the greatest challenges of discipline.... Ada Bacot, widowed South Carolina plantation owner, believed her "orders disregarded more & more every day. I can do nothing so must submit, which is anything but pleasant." When she left Carolina for a nursing post at the Monticello Hospital in Charlottesville, however, she soon discovered "Virginia Negroes are not near so servile as those of S.C." ... When an adolescent slave named William defied her order to clean up the dinner table in the house where she and the other nurses and doctors lodged, she called him to task. But the young slave was "so impertinent that I slaped him in the mouth before I knew what I did." His mother rushed from the kitchen to his defense, provoking Bacot to threaten both slaves with punishment. Unlike many Confederate slave managers, though, Bacot did not live in a world comprised exclusively of women. She turned for aid to the white male doctors who were also residents of the household, and they whipped both irate mother and insolent child.[17]

For many white women this physical dimension of slave control proved most troubling....

Just as "paternalism" and "mastery" were rooted in concepts of masculinity, so violence was similarly gendered as male within the ideology of the Old South. Recourse to physical force in support of male honor and white supremacy was regarded as the right, even the responsibility, of each white man—within his household, on his plantation, in his community, and with the outbreak of war, for his nation. Women slave managers inherited a social order that depended on the threat and often the use of violence. Throughout the history of the peculiar institution, slave mistresses had in fact slapped, hit, and even brutally whipped their slaves—particularly slave women or children. But their relationship to this exercise of physical power was significantly different from that of their men. No gendered code of honor celebrated women's physical power or dominance. A contrasting yet parallel ideology extolled female sensitivity, weakness, and vulnerability. In the prewar years, exercise of the violence fundamental to slavery was overwhelmingly the responsibility and prerogative of white men. A white woman disciplined and punished as the master's subordinate and surrogate. Rationalized, systematic, autonomous, and instrumental use of violence belonged to men.

Ada Bacot surprised herself when she lashed out and slapped young William, and it was in just such moments of rage that many Confederate women embraced physical force. But for the kind of rationalized punishment intended to function as the mainstay of slave discipline, Bacot turned to men. Women alone customarily sought overseers, male relatives, or neighbors to undertake physical coercion of slaves, especially slave men. As white men disappeared to war, however, finding such help became increasingly difficult. . . .

As slaves grew more assertive in anticipation of their freedom, their female managers regarded physical coercion as at once more essential and more impossible. Some white women began to bargain with violence, trying to make slavery seem benign in hopes of retaining their slaves' service, if not their loyalty. Avoiding physical punishment even in the face of insolence or poor work, they endeavored to keep their slaves from departing altogether. . . . [In Texas,] Lizzie Neblett urged her part-time overseer not to beat a slave in response to his insubordination. "I told him not to whip Joe, as long as he done his work well . . . that he might run away & we might never get him & if he never done me any good he might my children." Lizzie worried as well that whipping might provoke violent retaliation against managers who possessed the obvious vulnerability of the Confederacy's white females. Many had, she noted, become "actually affraid to whip the negros."[18]

The Old South's social hierarchies had created a spectrum of legitimate access to violence, so that social empowerment was inextricably bound up with the right to employ physical force. Violence was all but required of white men of all classes, a cultural principle rendered explicit by the coming of war and conscription. Black slaves, by contrast, were forbidden the use of violence entirely, except within their own communities, where the dominant society chose to regard it as essentially invisible. White women stood upon an ill-defined middle ground, where behavior and ideology often diverged.

The Civil War exacerbated this very tension . . . even on the homefront, women felt inadequate; their understanding of their gender undermined their effectiveness. Just as their inability to bear arms left Confederate women feeling "useless," so their inhibitions about violence made many females regard themselves as failures at slave management. As Lizzie Neblett wrote of her frustration in the effort to control eleven recalcitrant slaves, "I am so sick of trying to do a man's business when I am nothing but, a poor contemptible piece of multiplying human flesh tied to the house by a crying young one, looked upon as belonging to a race of inferior beings." The language she chose to describe her self-loathing is significant, for she borrowed it from the vocabulary of race as well as gender. Invoking the objective constraints of biology—"multiplying flesh"—as well as the socially constructed limitations of status—"looked upon as belonging to a race of inferior beings"—she identified herself not with the white elite, not with those in whose interest the war was being fought, but with the South's oppressed and disadvantaged. Increasingly, even though self-indulgently, she came to regard herself as the victim rather than the beneficiary of her region's slave society. Lizzie Neblett's uniquely documented experience with violence and slavery deserves exploration in some detail, for it illustrates not simply the contradictions inherent in female management, but the profound personal crisis of identity generated by her new and unaccustomed role.[19]

TROUBLED IN MIND

When her husband departed for war in the spring of 1863, Lizzie had set about the task of management committed to "doing my best" but was apprehensive both about her ignorance of agriculture and about the behavior she might expect from her eleven slaves. Their initial response to her direction, however, seemed promising. "The negros," she wrote Will in late April, "seem to be mightily stirred up about making a good crop."[20]

By harvest, however, the situation had already changed. "The negros are doing nothing," Lizzie wrote Will at the height of first cotton picking in mid-August. . . . Lizzie harbored few illusions about the long-term loyalty of her own black family. "I dont think we have one who will stay with us."[21]

After a harvest that fell well below the previous year's achievement, Lizzie saw the need for new managerial arrangements. Will had provided for a male neighbor to keep a general supervisory eye over the Neblett slave force, but Lizzie wrote Will in the fall of 1863 that she had contracted to pay a Mr. Meyers to spend three half-days a week with her slaves. "He will be right tight on the negroes I think, but they need it. Meyers will lay down the law and enforce it." But Lizzie emphasized that she would not permit cruelty or abuse.[22]

Controlling Meyers would prove in some ways more difficult than controlling the slaves. His second day on the plantation Meyers whipped three young male slaves for idleness, and on his next visit, as Lizzie put it, "he undertook old Sam." Gossip had spread among slaves in the neighborhood—and from them to their masters—that Sam intended to take a whipping from no man.[23] Will Neblett had, in fact, not been a harsh disciplinarian, tending more to threatening and grumbling than whipping. But Meyers regarded Sam's challenge as quite "enough." When Sam refused to come to Meyers to receive a whipping he felt he did not deserve, Meyers cornered and threatened to shoot him. Enraged, Meyers beat Sam so severely that Lizzie feared he might die. She anxiously called the doctor, who assured her that Sam had no internal injuries and that he had seen slaves beaten far worse.

Lizzie was torn over how to respond—to Meyers or to Sam. "Tho I pity the poor wretch," she confided to Will, "I don't want him to know it." To the other slaves she insisted that "Meyers would not have whipped him if he had not deserved it," and to Will she defensively maintained, "somebody must take them in hand[.] they grow worse all the time[.] I could not begin to write you . . . how little they mind me." She saw Meyers's actions as part of a plan to establish control at the outset: "he lets them know what he is . . . & then has no more trouble." But Lizzie's very insistence and defensiveness suggest that this was not, even in her mind, slave management in its ideal form.[24]

Over the next few days, Lizzie's doubts about Meyers and his course of action grew. Instead of eliminating trouble at the outset, as he had intended, the incident seemed to have created an uproar. Sarah, a cook and house slave, reported to Lizzie that Sam suspected the whipping had been his mistress's idea, and that, when well enough, he would run away until Will came home.[25]

To resolve the volatile situation and to salvage her reputation as slave mistress, Lizzie now enlisted another white man, Coleman, to talk reasonably with Sam. Coleman had been her dead father's overseer and continued to manage her mother's property. In the absence of Will and Lizzie's brothers at the front, he was an obvious family deputy, and he had undoubtedly known Sam before Lizzie had inherited him from her father's estate. Coleman agreed to "try to show Sam the error he had been guilty of." At last Sam spoke the words Coleman sought, admitting he had done wrong and promising no further insubordination.[26]

Two weeks after the incident, Lizzie and Sam finally had a direct and, in Lizzie's view at least, comforting exchange: Meyers had ordered Sam back to work, but Lizzie had interceded in response to Sam's complaints of persisting weakness. Taking his cue from Lizzie's conciliatory gesture and acting as well in accordance with Coleman's advice, Sam apologized for disappointing Lizzie's expectations, acknowledging that as the oldest slave he had special responsibilities in Will's absence. Henceforth, he promised Lizzie, he was "going to do his work faithfully & be of as much service to me as he could. I could not help," Lizzie confessed to Will, "feeling sorry for the old fellow[.] . . . he talked so humbly & seemed so hurt that I should have had him whipped so."[27]

Sam's adroit transformation from rebel into Sambo helped resolve Lizzie's uncertainties about the appropriate course of slave management. Abandoning her defense of Meyers's severity, even interceding on Sam's behalf against her own manager, Lizzie assured Sam she had not been responsible for his punishment, had indeed been "astonished" by it. Meyers, she reported to Will with newfound assurance, "did wrong" and "knows nothing" about the management of slaves. He "don't," she noted revealingly, "treat them as moral beings but manages by brute force." Henceforth, Lizzie concluded, she would not feel impelled by her sense of helplessness to countenance extreme severity. Instead, she promised Sam, if he remained "humble and submissive," she would ensure "he would not get another lick."[28]

The incident of Sam's whipping served as the occasion for an extended negotiation between Lizzie and her slaves about the terms of her power. In calling upon Meyers and Coleman, she demonstrated that, despite appearances, she was not in fact a woman alone, dependent entirely on her own resources. Although the ultimate responsibility might be hers, slave management was a community concern. Pushed toward sanctioning Meyers's cruelty by fear of her own impotence, Lizzie then stepped back from the extreme position in which Meyers had placed her. But at the same time she dissociated herself from Meyers's action, she also reaped its benefit: Sam's abandonment of a posture of overt defiance for one of apparent submission. Sam and Lizzie were ultimately able to join forces in an agreement that Meyers must be at once deplored and tolerated as a necessary evil whom both mistress and slave would strive ceaselessly to manipulate. Abandoning their brief tryouts as Simon Legree and Nat Turner, Lizzie and Sam returned to the more accustomed and comfortable roles of concerned paternalist and loyal slave. Each recognized at last that his or her own performance depended in large measure on a complementary performance by the other.

Lizzie's behavior throughout the crisis demonstrated the essential part gender identities and assumptions played in master-slave relations. . . .

Accustomed to occasional strikes against female slaves, Lizzie called on a male slave to whip the adolescent Tom, then, later, she enlisted a male neighbor to dominate the venerable Sam. Yet even this structured hierarchy of violence was becoming increasingly "disagreeable" to her as she acted out her new wartime role as "chief of affairs." In part, Lizzie knew she was objectively physically weaker than both black and white men around her. But she confessed as well to a "troubled . . . mind," to uncertainties about her appropriate relationship to the ultimate exertion of force upon which slavery rested. As wartime pressures weakened the foundations for the "moral" management that Lizzie preferred, what she referred to as "brute force" became simultaneously more attractive and more dangerous as an instrument of coercion.

Forbidden the physical severity that served as the fundamental prop of his system of slave management, Meyers requested to be released from his contract with Lizzie at the end of the crop year. Early in the agreement, Meyers had told Lizzie that he could "conquer" her slaves, "but may have to kill some one of them." It remained with Lizzie, he explained, to make the decision. In her moments of greatest exasperation, Lizzie was willing to consent to such extreme measures. "I say do it." But with calm reflection, tempered by Will's measured advice, considerations of humanity reasserted their claim. Repeatedly she interceded between Meyers and the slaves, protecting them from whippings or condemning Meyers when he disobeyed her orders and punished them severely. Yet despite her difficulties in managing Meyers and despite her belief that he was "deficient in judgment," Lizzie recognized her dependence on him and on the threat of force he represented. She was determined to "hold him on as long as I can." If he quit and the slaves found that no one was coming to replace him, she wrote revealingly, "the jig will be up." The game, the trick, the sham of her slave management would be over. Without a man—or a man part time for three half-days a week—without the recourse to violence that Meyers embodied, slavery was unworkable. The velvet glove of paternalism required its iron hand.[29]

Violence was the ultimate foundation of power in the slave South, but gender prescriptions carefully barred white women—especially those elite women most likely to find themselves responsible for controlling slaves—from purposeful exercise of physical dominance. Even when circumstances had shifted to make female authority socially desirable, it remained for many plantation mistresses personally unachievable. Lizzie's struggle with her attraction to violence and her simultaneous abhorrence of it embodied the contradictions that the necessary wartime paradox of female slave management imposed. Lizzie begged Will to hire out his slaves or even to "give your negros away and, I'll . . . work with my hands, as hard as I can, but my mind will rest." Lizzie wished repeatedly to die, to be a man, or to give up the slaves altogether—except, tellingly, for "one good negro to wait upon me." White women had reaped slavery's benefits throughout its existence in the colonial and antebellum South. But they could not be its everyday managers without in some measure failing to be what they understood as female. The authority of their class and race could not overcome the dependence they had learned to identify as the essence of their womanhood. [30] . . .

Beginning her duties as slave manager with optimism and enthusiasm, Mary Bell [of Franklin, North Carolina] came ultimately to share with Lizzie Neblett a profound sense of failure and personal inadequacy. As she repeatedly told [her husband], Alf, "unless you could be at home," "unless you were at home," the system would not work. "You say," Mary Bell wrote her husband in December 1864, "you think I am a good farmer if I only had confidence in myself. I confess I have very little confidence in my own judgment and management. Wish I had more. Perhaps if I had I would not get so out of heart. Sometimes I am almost ready to give up and think that surely my lot is harder than anyone else."[31]

A growing disillusionment with slavery among many elite white women arose from this very desire to "give up"—to be freed from burdens of management and fear of black reprisal that often outweighed any tangible benefits from the labor of increasingly recalcitrant slaves. Few slaveowning women had seriously questioned the moral or political legitimacy of the system, although many admitted to the profound evils associated with the institution. Gertrude Thomas noted its "terribly demoralising influence upon our men and boys," and Mary Chesnut's vehement criticisms similarly fixed on the almost unrestricted sexual access slavery gave white men to black women. Yet her concerns, like those of Gertrude Thomas, lay with the impact of these social arrangements on whites and their families rather than on exploited slaves. White southern women readily embraced the racism of their era. Blacks were, Chesnut remarked, "dirty—slatternly—idle—ill smelling by nature." Slaves were unquestionably inferior beings "blest," as one North Carolina woman wrote, "in having a home among Anglo Saxons." Jane Howison Beale of Virginia had no doubt that blacks "were ordained of High Heaven to serve the white man and it is only in that capacity they can be happy useful and respected."[32]

Southern slave mistresses began to convince themselves, however, that an institution that they were certain worked in the interest of blacks did not necessarily advance their own. Confederate women could afford little contemplation of slavery's merits "in the abstract," as its prewar defenders had urged. Slavery's meaning did not rest in the detached and intellectualized realms of politics or moral philosophy. The growing emotional and physical cost of the system to slaveholding women made its own forceful appeal, and many slave mistresses began to persuade themselves that the institution had become a greater inconvenience than benefit. . . . Like Lizzie Neblett, many white women focused on slavery's trials and yearned for the peculiar institution—and all the troublesome blacks constrained within its bonds—magically to disappear . . . . But . . . many women who entertained such fantasies at the same time longed for just "one good negro to wait upon me." For white women, this would be emancipation's greatest cost.[33]

AN ENTIRE RUPTURE OF OUR DOMESTIC RELATIONS

In the summer of 1862 a Confederate woman overheard two small girls "playing ladies." "Good morning, ma'am," said little Sallie to her friend. "How are you today?" "I don't feel very well this morning," four-year-old Nannie Belle replied. *"All my niggers have run away and left me."*[34]

From the first months of the war, white women confronted yet another change in their households, one that a Virginia woman described as "an entire disruption of our domestic relations": the departure of their slaves. Sometimes, especially when Yankee troops swept through an area, the loss was total and immediate. Sarah Hughes of Alabama stood as a roadside spectator at the triumphant procession of hundreds of her slaves toward freedom. Her niece, Eliza Walker, en route to visit her aunt, described the scene that greeted her as she approached the Hughes plantation.

> Down the road [the Bluecoats] . . . came, and with them all the slaves . . . , journeying, as they thought, to the promised land. I saw them as they trudged the main road, many of the women with babes in their arms . . . old and young, men, women and children. Some of them fared better than the others. A negro woman, Laura, my aunt's fancy seamstress, rode Mrs. Hughes' beautiful white pony, sitting [on] the red plush saddle of her mistress. The Hughes' family carriage, driven by Taliaferro, the old coachman, and filled with blue coated soldiers and negroes, passed in state, and this was followed by other vehicles.

With the trusted domestics leading the way, Sarah Hughes's slaves had turned her world upside down.[35]

Usually the departure of slaves was less dramatic and more secretive, as blacks simply stole away one by one or in groups of two or three when they heard of opportunities to reach Union armies and freedom. In Middleburg, Virginia, Catherine Cochran reported, "Scarcely a morning dawned that some stampede was not announced—sometimes persons would awake to find every servant gone & we never went to bed without anticipating such an occurrence." In nearby Winchester, Mary Lee presided over a more extended dissolution of her slave force. Her male slaves were the first to leave in the spring of 1862. Emily and Betty threatened to follow, and Lee considered sending them off to a more secure location away from Federal lines in order to keep from losing them altogether. Having regular help in the house seemed imperative, though, even if it was risky. "I despise menial work," Lee confessed. But she had no confidence she would retain her property. "It is an uncomfortable thought, in waking in the morning, to be uncertain as to whether you will have any servants to bring in water and prepare breakfast. . . . I dread our house servants going and having to do their work." When Betty talked again of leaving in June 1863, Laura Lee, Mary's sister-in-law, locked up the clothes the black woman had packed in anticipation of departure. Laura was determined "not to lose them too, if I could help it." Temporarily thwarted, Betty left for good the next summer, and the Lees lost slave and clothing after all.[36]

By the time of her exile from Winchester in February 1865, Mary Lee was surprised that her household still enjoyed the services of a mother and daughter, Sarah and Emily, who, despite repeated threats and stormy confrontations, had not yet fled to freedom. Mary Lee entertained few illusions about the continuing loyalty of her slaves. Early in the war, she made it clear that "I have never had the least confidence in the fidelity of any negro." Her grief at their gradual disappearance was highly pragmatic; she mourned their lost labor but did not seem to cherish an ideal of master-slave harmony to be shaken by the slaves' choice of freedom over loyalty.[37]

A South Carolina woman, by contrast, became "miserably depressed" when her three most dependable house slaves fled. "If they felt as I do," she explained, "they could not possibly leave me." The Jones family of Georgia, devout Presbyterians, reflected the tenacity of their evangelical proslavery vision in their indignant feelings of betrayal at the departure of their human property. Eva Jones was distraught when three female slaves seized their freedom "without bidding any of us an affectionate adieu." Mary Jones felt deeply wounded by what she regarded as slaves' "ingratitude." Committed to a conception of slavery as a Christian institution founded in reciprocal rights and duties, she could understand blacks' desire for freedom only as an unjust failure to appreciate her dedicated performance of her obligations within the system. "My life long . . . I have been laboring and caring for them, and since the war have labored with all my might to supply their wants, and expended everything I had upon their support, directly or indirectly, and this is their return." Even the shock of the blacks' behavior did not help Mary Jones to understand that her construction of slavery as an institution of mutual benevolence was not shared by her slaves. With their sights set on freedom, the blacks felt no duty to abide by the terms of the system as the white South had defined them.[38] . . .

In their reactions to slaves' departures, women revealed—to themselves as well as to posterity—the extent of their dependence on their servants. In our day of automated housework and prepared foods, it is easy to forget how much skill nineteenth-century housekeeping required. Many slave mistresses lacked this basic competence, having left to their slaves responsibility for execution of a wide range of essential domestic tasks. . . . Many white women felt themselves entirely ignorant about how to perform basic functions of everyday life.[39]

A Louisiana lady who had "never even so much as washed out a pocket handkerchief with my own hands" suddenly had to learn to do laundry for her entire family. Kate Foster found that when her house servants left and she took on the washing, she "came near ruining myself for life as I was too delicately raised for such hard work." . . . Lizzie Carter of Petersburg gained a new understanding of motherhood when she was left without a nurse. "I never knew before the trouble of children," she complained to her sister. Martha

Horne of Missouri remembered after the war that "I had never cooked a meal when the negro women left, and had a hard time learning." . . . When Henrietta Barr's cook departed, she assumed her place in the kitchen. "(Although a confession is humiliating)," she confided to her diary, "I must say I do not in the smallest particular fill the situation as creditably as she did. I certainly do not think my forte lies in cooking."[40]

The forte of the southern lady did not seem to lie in slave management either. These women were beginning to feel they could live neither with slaves nor without them. "To be without them is a misery & to have them is just as bad," confessed Amelia Barr of Galveston. Women already frustrated "trying to do a man's business" and direct slaves now discovered that they often felt equally incompetent executing the tasks that had belonged to their supposed racial inferiors. Like Henrietta Barr, many regarded the situation as "humiliating." "It is such a degradation," Matthella Page Harrison of Virginia wrote as she anticipated the imminent flight of her slaves, "to be so dependent upon the servants as we are."[41]

The concept of female dependence and weakness was not simply a prop of southern gender ideology; in the context of war, white ladies were finding it to be all too painful a reality. Socialized to believe in their own weakness and sheltered from the necessity of performing even life's basic tasks, many white women felt almost crippled by their unpreparedness for the new lives war had brought. Yet as they struggled to cope with change, their dedication to the old order faltered as well. Slavery, the "cornerstone" of the civilization for which their nation fought, increasingly seemed a burden rather than a benefit. White women regarded it as a threat as well. In failing to guarantee what white women believed to be their most fundamental right, in failing to protect women or to exert control over insolent and even rebellious slaves, Confederate men undermined not only the foundations of the South's peculiar institution but the legitimacy of their power as white males, as masters of families of white women and black slaves.

Notes

1. Alexander Stephens, *Southern Confederacy* [Atlanta], March 13, 1861.

2. *Macon Daily Telegraph*, September 1, 1862, quoted in Clarence Mohr, *On the Threshold of Freedom: Masters and Slaves in Civil War Georgia* (Athens: University of Georgia Press, 1986), 221.

3. See *The Statutes at Large of the Confederate States of America, passed at the Third Session of the First Congress* (Richmond: R. M. Smith, 1863), 158, 213–14; James M. Mathews, ed., *The Statutes at Large of the Confederate States of America* (Richmond: R. M. Smith, 1862), 30; *Acts of Congress in Relation to the Conscription and Exemption Laws* (Houston: Texas Book and Job Printing House, 1862), 8 (quotation); *Southern Historical Society Papers 48* (1941): 104; Albert Burton Moore, *Conscription and Conflict in the Confederacy,* (New York: Macmillan, 1924), 83–113.

4. Mrs. B. A. Smith to Governor Shorter, July 18, 1862, Governor's Files, Alabama Dept. of Archives and History, Montgomery, Ala.; hereafter cited as ADAH; A Planter's Wife to Governor John J. Pettus, May 1, 1862, John J. Pettus Papers, Mississippi Dept. of Archives and History, Jackson, Miss.; hereafter cited as MDAH; see also Letitia Andrews to Governor John J. Pettus, March 28, 1863, Pettus Papers, MDAH, and Lizzie Neblett to Will Neblett, April 26, 1863, Lizzie Neblett Papers, Center for American History, University of Texas, Austin, Tex.; hereafter cited as UTA.

5. Lucy A. Sharp to Hon. John C. Randolph, October 1, 1862, Letters Received, Confederate Sec. of War; hereafter cited as LRCSW, S1000, RG 109, reel 72, M437, National Archives, Washington, D.C.; hereafter cited as NA; Sarah Whitesides to Hon. James Seddon, February 13, 1863, LRCSW, RG 109, reel 115, W136, NA; Catherine Edmondston, *Journal of a Secesh Lady: The Diary of Catherine Ann Devereux Edmondston, 1860–1866,* ed. Beth G. Crabtree and James W. Patton (Raleigh: North Carolina Department of Archives and History, 1979), 240; Frances Mitten to editors of the *Christian Index,* July 6, 1864, Thomas Watts, Governor's Papers, ADAH; Martha Fort to George Fort, October 7, 1861, Tomlinson Fort Papers, Special Collections, Woodruff Library, Emory Univ., Atlanta, GA; hereafter cited as EU; Amanda Walker to Secretary of War, October 31, 1862, LRCSW, RG 109, reel 79, W1106, NA.

6. Keziah Brevard Diary, November 28, 1860, April 4, 1861, December 29, 1860, South Caroliniana Library, University of South Carolina, Columbia, S.C.; hereafter cited as SCL.

7. C. Vann Woodward, ed., *Mary Chesnut's Civil War* (New Haven: Yale University Press, 1981), 198–99; Ada Bacot Diary, September 21, 1861, SCL.

8. Laura Lee Diary, March 12, 1862, WM; Bacot Diary, February 27, 1861, SCL; *Mobile Advertiser and Register,* September 11, 1862; *Richmond Enquirer,* September 9, 1862.

9. Nancy Hall et al. to Governor Zebulon Vance, August 11, 1863, Zebulon Vance Papers, North Carolina Division of Archives and History, Raleigh, N.C.; hereafter cited as NCDAH; Miss Lettie Kennedy in behalf of the Ladies of the N.E. beat of Jas. County, Miss., September 15, 1862, LRCSW, RG 109, reel 56, K148, NA. See also Lida Sessums to Governor John J. Pettus, October 8, 1862, Pettus Papers, MDAH.

10. Lucy Watkins to Secretary of War Randolph, October 13, 1862, LRCSW, RG 109, reel 79, M1091, NA; Harriet Pipkin to S. Cooper, Adj Gen. and Insp Gen, series 12 (LR), box 18, H2636, NA; Mary Watts to Hon. James Seddon, May 15, 1863, LRCSW, RG 109, reel 116, W315, NA.

11. W. Maury Darst, "The Vicksburg Diary of Mrs. Alfred Ingraham," May 27, 1863, *Journal of Mississippi History* 44 (May 1982): 171; Catherine Broun Diary, May 11, 1862, Broun Family Papers, Woodson Research Center, Fondren Library, Rice Univ., Houston. Tex.; hereafter cited as RU.

12. Mary Greenhow Lee Diary, April 3, 1864, Winchester-Frederick County Historical Society, Handley Library, Winchester, Va.; hereafter cited as HL.

13. Constance Cary Harrison, "A Virginia Girl in the First Year of the War," *Century* 30 (August 1885): 606.

14. Elizabeth Saxon, *A Southern Woman's War Time Reminiscences* (Memphis: Pilcher, 1905), 33; Eugene D. Genovese, *Roll, Jordan, Roll: The World the Slaves Made* (New York: Pantheon, 1974), 99.

15. Anna Green to Martha Jones, April 16, 1862, Prescott-Jones Papers, Georgia Dept. of Archives and History, Atlanta, GA; hereafter cited as GDAH; Leila Callaway to Morgan Callaway, January 22, 19, 1863, Morgan Callaway Papers, EU.

16. Maria Hawkins to Governor Zebulon Vance, December 11, 1863, Vance Papers, NCDAH.

17. Edmondston, *Journal of a Secesh Lady*, 220; see also Octavia Stephens to Winston Stephens, July 15, 1862, Bryant-Stephens Papers, P.K. Yonge Library, University of Florida, Gainesville, Fla; hereafter cited as UFL; May, "Southern Elite Women," 255; and Bacot Diary, May 3, December 25, 1861, March 17, September 8, 1862, SCL.

18. Lizzie Neblett to Will Neblett, April 15, 1864, August 18, 1863, Neblett Papers, UTA.

19. Ibid., August 28, 1863, Neblett Papers, UTA. For a strikingly similar statement of female incapacity, see Carolina Pettigrew to Charles Pettigrew, June 19, 1862, Pettigrew Family Papers, Southern Historical College, University of North Carolina, Chapel Hill, N.C.; hereafter cited as SHC.

20. Lizzie Neblett to Will Neblett, April 26, 1863, Neblett Papers, UTA.

21. Ibid., August 18, 1863.

22. Ibid., November 17, 1863.

23. Ibid., November 23, 17, 1863.

24. Ibid., November 23, 1863.

25. Ibid., November 29, 1863.

26. Ibid.

27. Ibid., December 6, 1863.

28. Ibid.

29. Ibid., February 12, July 3, June 5, 1864.

30. Ibid., March 20, 1864, letter fragment [1864].

31. Mary Bell to Alfred Bell, November 24, December 16, 1864. See Elizabeth Fox-Genovese, *Within the Plantation Household: Black and White Women of the Old South* (Chapel Hill: University of North Carolina Press, 1988), 142, on women's desire for household slaves.

32. Ella Gertrude Clanton Thomas, *The Secret Eye: The Journal of Ella Gertrude Clanton Thomas, 1848–1889*, ed. Virginia Ingraham Burr (Chapel Hill: University of North Carolina Press, 1990), 236; Mary Chesnut quoted in Elisabeth Muhlenfeld, *Mary Boykin Chesnut: A Biography* (Baton Rouge: Louisiana State University Press, 1981), 109; Mary Brown to John B. Brown, June 20, 1865, W. Vance Brown Papers, NCDAH; Jane Howison Beale, *The Journal of Jane Howison Beale of Fredericksburg, Virginia, 1850–1862* (Fredericksburg: Historic Fredericksburg Foundation, 1979), 43.

33. Lizzie Neblett to Will Neblett, undated letter fragment [1864], Neblett Papers, UTA.

34. Betty Herndon Maury, *The Confederate Diary of Betty Herndon Maury, 1861–1863*, ed. Alice Maury Parmalee (Washington, D.C.: privately printed, 1938), 89.

35. Beale, *Journal*, June 1, 1862, 47; Eliza Kendrick Walker Reminiscences, 117–18, ADAH.

36. Catherine Cochran Reminiscences, March 1862, vol. 1, Virginia Historical Society, Richmond, Va.; hereafter cited as VHS; Mary Greenhow Lee Diary, June 29, July 15, 1862, HL; Laura Lee Diary, June 13, 1863, August 18, 1864, Manuscripts and Rare Books, Swem Library, College at William and Mary. Williamsburg, Va.; hereafter cited as WM. See also Sarah Fitch Poates Diary, July 6, 8, 23, November 1, 1863, Asa Fitch Papers, Dept. of Manuscripts, Library Cornell University, Ithaca, N.Y.; Hereafter cited as CU.

37. Mary Greenhow Lee Diary, March 22, 1862, HL.

38. Emma Mordecai Diary, May 6, 1865, Mordecai Family Papers, SHC; Genovese, *Roll, Jordan, Roll*, 105–6; Robert Manson Myers, ed., *The Children of Pride: A True Story of Georgia and the Civil War* (New Haven: Yale University Press, 1972), 1274, 1287, 1308.

39. On this point, see Fox-Genovese, *Within the Plantation Household*, 115, 128. See also Amanda Worthington Diary, April 25, 1863, MDAH.

40. George C. Rable, *Civil Wars: Women and the Crisis of Southern Nationalism* (Urbana: University of Illinois Press, 1989), 255; Kate Foster Diary, November 15, 1863, Manuscript Dept., Perkins Library, Duke University, Durham, N.C.; hereafter cited as DU; Lizzie Carter to her sister, March 23, 1863, W. Vance Brown Papers, NCDAH; Martha Horne, "War Experiences," in *Reminiscences of the Women of Missouri during the Sixties*, by Missouri Division, United Daughters of the Confederacy (Jefferson City, Mo.: Hugh Stephens, 192–), 43; *The Civil War Diary of Mrs. Henrietta Fitzhugh Barr, 1862–3*, ed. Sally Kiger Winn (Marietta, Ohio: Marietta College Press, 1963), 25. See also Annie Harper Reminiscences, 46, MDAH; Emma Holmes, *The Diary of Miss Emma Holmes, 1861–1866*, ed. John Marszalek (Baton Rouge: Louisiana State University Press, 1979), 467; and Sarah Anne Grover Strickler Diary, August 12, 1862, Manuscripts Dept., Alderman Library, University of Virginia, Charlottesville, Va.; hereafter cited as UVA.

41. Amelia Barr to My Dear Jenny, March 3, [1866?], Amelia Barr Papers, UTA; Lizzie Neblett to Will Neblett, August 8, 1863, Neblett Papers, UTA; Matthella Page Harrison Diary, April 28, 1863, UVA.

Counterfeit Freedom

A. S. Hitchcock, "*Young women particularly flock back & forth . . .*"

Early in the Civil War, before the Emancipation Proclamation, the Union Army occupied the Sea Islands off the coasts of South Carolina and Georgia; plantation owners fled and the army established base camps there. Although the Union forces expected former slaves to continue to work on their old plantations as contract laborers, freedpeople believed that the end of slavery should mean that they could travel freely and that they could choose other ways of supporting themselves.

How did Union officials interpret the movement of women around the islands (which included Beaufort and Hilton Head)? What limited types of work did they posit as appropriate for African American women and men? Note the ways in which black people's efforts at family reunion were criminalized.

A. S. Hitchcock, Acting General Superintendent of Contrabands, to Provost Marshal General of the Department of the South, August 25, 1864

In accordance with a request made by you at this office . . . concerning measures to be instituted to lessen the number of idle & dissolute persons hanging about the central Posts of the Department & traveling to & from between them . . . I write this note. . . .

Had I the control of the negroes the first thing I would endeavor to do, & the thing I think of most importance to be done, is to Keep all the people possible on the farms or plantations at *honest steady* labor. As one great means to this end, I would make it as difficult as possible for them to get to the centres of population. —Young women particularly flock back & forth by scores to Hilton Head, to Beaufort, to the country simply to while away their time, or constantly to seek some new excitement, or what is worse to live by lasciviousness. . . . I would allow no peddling around camps whatsoever. . . . All rationing I would stop utterly, & introduce the poor house system, feeding none on any pretense who would not go to the place provided for all paupers to live. . . . All persons out of the poor house running from place to place to beg a living I would treat as vagabonds, & also all persons, whether in town or on plantations, white or black, who lived without occupation should either go to the poor house or be put in a place where they *must work*—a work house or chain gang, & if women where they could wash iron & scrub for the benefit of the public. . . .

September 6, 1864
GENERAL ORDERS NO. 130

Hilton Head, S.C. . . . The practice of allowing negro women to wander about from one plantation to another, and from one Post or District to another, on Government transports, for no other purpose than to while away their time, or visit their husbands serving in the ranks of the Army, is not only objectionable in every point of view, both to the soldiers and to

Excerpted from *Freedom: A Documentary History of Emancipation, 1861–1867*, ser. 1, vol. 3, ed. Ira Berlin, Joseph P. Reidy, and Leslie S. Rowland, pp. 316–19. Reprinted with the permission of Cambridge University Press.

themselves, but is generally subversive of moral restraint, and must be discontinued at once. All negro women, in future found wandering in this manner, will be immediately arrested, and compelled to work at some steady employment on the Plantations.

Roda Ann Childs, "I was more dead than alive"

In January 1865, before the Civil War was over, Congress and the states in the Union ratified the Thirteenth Amendment, putting an end to slavery and "involuntary servitude, except as punishment for crime whereof the party shall have been duly convicted." Once peace was established, it became clear that the states of the former Confederacy were quite creative in devising systems that maintained racial subordination (for example, broad definitions of what counted as "vagrancy" which, as crimes, could be punished by involuntary servitude). The Civil Rights Act of 1866 was designed to protect freedpeople; it promised "citizens of every race and color . . . full and equal benefit of all laws and proceedings for the security of person and property, as is enjoyed by white citizens. . . ." But the statute had been passed only over the veto of President Andrew Johnson, who denied that the states of the Confederacy had forfeited all civil rights and privileges by their rebellion. The Freedmen's Bureau was charged with protecting the rights of former slaves and assisting their transition to a market economy; it accomplished much, but it was always underfunded and understaffed, and many of its staff members were themselves deeply skeptical of freedpeople.

In a political climate marked by struggle between Congress and the President, the Ku Klux Klan and other vigilantes who wanted to intimidate freedpeople and take vengeance for their own defeat in war seized their opportunity. Not until 1871 did Congress pass the Ku Klux Klan Act, prescribing fines and imprisonment for those who went in disguise to terrorize others. The congressional committee that conducted a traveling inquiry into "the Condition of Affairs in the Late Insurrectionary States" filed a twelve-volume report. Its testimony of violence and intimidation, in excruciating detail, makes it clear that Roda Ann Childs's experience was replicated throughout the South.

Roda Ann Childs made her way to a Freedmen's Bureau agent in Griffin, Georgia, to swear this affidavit; she signed it with her mark. There is no evidence that her case was pursued. What clue does she offer for why she was a target for mob violence?

[*Griffin, GA*] Sept. 25, 1866

Roda Ann Childs came into this office and made the following statement:

"Myself and husband were under contract with Mrs. Amelia Childs of Henry County, and worked from Jan. 1, 1866, until the crops were laid by, or in other words until the main work of the year was done, without difficulty. Then, (the fashion being prevalent among the planters) we were called upon one night, and my husband was demanded; I Said he was not there. They then asked where he was. I Said

Excerpted from *Freedom: A Documentary History of Emancipation, 1861–1876,* ser. 2, ed. Ira Berlin, Joseph P. Reidy and Leslie S. Rowland, p. 807. Reprinted with the permission of Cambridge University Press.

he was gone to the water mellon patch. They then Seized me and took me Some distance from the house, where they 'bucked' me down across a log, Stripped my clothes over my head, one of the men Standing astride my neck, and beat me across my posterior, two men holding my legs. In this manner I was beaten until they were tired. Then they turned me parallel with the log, laying my neck on a limb which projected from the log, and one man placing his foot upon my neck, beat me again on my hip and thigh. Then I was thrown upon the ground on my back, one of the men Stood upon my breast, while two others took hold of my feet and stretched My limbs as far apart as they could, while the man Standing upon my breast applied the Strap to my private parts until fatigued into stopping, and I was more dead than alive. Then a man, Supposed to be an ex-confederate Soldier, as he was on crutches, fell upon me and ravished me. During the whipping one of the men ran his pistol into me, and Said he had a hell of a mind to pull the trigger, and Swore they ought to Shoot me, as my husband had been in the 'God damned Yankee Army,' and Swore they meant to kill every black Son-of-a-bitch they could find that had ever fought against them. They then went back to the house, Seized my two daughters and beat them, demanding their father's pistol, and upon failure to get that, they entered the house and took Such articles of clothing as Suited their fancy, and decamped. There were concerned in this affair eight men, none of which could be recognized for certain.

her
Roda Ann × Childs
mark

TERA W. HUNTER

Reconstruction and the Meanings of Freedom

When the Civil War was ended at Appomattox, a long and complex struggle over its meaning had just begun. The Thirteenth Amendment technically ended slavery, but it left much room for interpretation about the meaning of servitude. It said nothing about equality, leaving resentful southerners to conclude that the North would condone systems of racial hierarchy. Even after the 1868 passage of the Fourteenth Amendment, which provided that "[a]ll persons born or naturalized in the United States . . . are citizens of the United States and of the State wherein they reside," the meanings of "citizenship" remained to be defined.

The aftermath of defeat is an internationally shared phenomenon. How did white southerners understand their defeat? What tensions marked postwar society? What would it mean to "reconstruct" the former Confederacy? Tera Hunter examines the experiences of freedpeople in the city of Atlanta, Georgia—Roda Ann Childs lived not far away. She finds that the process of rebuilding their lives could be quite different for men than for women. What opportunities did African American men have that African American women did not? What strategies might freedwomen use to stabilize their lives? In what ways did freedwomen participate in political life?

The Union victory at Appomattox in the spring of 1865 marked the official end of the war and inspired somber reflection, foot-stomping church meetings, and joyous street parades among the newly free. African Americans eagerly rushed into Atlanta in even greater numbers than before. Between 1860 and 1870, blacks in Atlanta increased from a mere nineteen hundred to ten thousand, more than doubling their proportion in the city's population, from 20 to 46 percent. Women made up the majority of this burgeoning population.[1] . . .

Wherever they came from, virtually all black women were compelled to find jobs as household workers once they arrived in the city. Some had acquired experience in such jobs as house slaves; others had worked in the fields or combined field and domestic chores. Whether or not they were working as domestics for the first time, black women had to struggle to assert new terms for their labor. The Civil War had exposed the parallel contests occurring in white households as the conflict on the battlefield, in the marketplace, and in the political arena unfolded. The war continued on the home front during Reconstruction after the Confederacy's military defeat. . . .

Just as black women and men in Atlanta had to reconstitute their lives as free people and build from the ground up, the city was faced with similar challenges. The legacy of physical desecration left by Sherman's invasion was everywhere. Tons of debris, twisted rails, dislodged roofs, crumbled chimneys, discharged cannon balls, and charred frame dwellings cluttered the streets.[2] Visitors to the city swapped remarks on the distinctive spirit of industry exemplified in the repair and rebuilding. . . . Atlanta aspired to construct a city in the New South in the image of established cities above the Mason-Dixon line.[3]

Excerpted from "Reconstruction and the Meanings of Freedom," ch. 2 of *To 'Joy My Freedom: Black Women's Lives and Labors after the Civil War* by Tera W. Hunter (Cambridge, Mass.: Harvard University Press, 1997). Reprinted by permission of the author and publisher. Notes have been numbered and edited.

The capitalist zeal that impressed outsiders offered few benefits to the average person, however. Overwhelmed contractors could not keep up with demands, which added to housing shortages that sent prices for rents soaring beyond the means of most residents.[4] . . . Some builders took advantage of the shortage to offer makeshift huts and shanties to freedpeople at exorbitant prices.[5] Ex-slaves in more dire straits assembled scanty lodging that consisted of tents, cabins, and shanties made of tin, line, and cloth on rented parcels of land.[6] . . . The cost of food and other consumer goods likewise followed the pattern of scarcity, poor quality, and deliberate price gouging.[7]

The abrupt population growth and the inability of private charities or public coffers to relieve the migrants of want exacerbated postwar privation. Almost everyone in the city, regardless of race, shared the status of newcomer. It was not just African Americans who were migrating to the city in large numbers; so did many whites. In 1860, there were 7,600 whites living in Atlanta, ten years later there were 11,900.[8] White yeoman farmers fled to the city to find wage labor in the wake of the elimination of their rural self-sufficiency. White Northern and foreign industrial workers followed the prosperity promised by the railroad and construction boom.

Women and children, black and white, were particularly noticeable among the destitute sprawled over the desolate urban landscape. The indigent included elderly, single women, widows of soldiers, and wives of unemployed or underemployed men. White women seamstresses who numbered in the thousands during the war were reduced to poverty with the collapse of military uniform manufacturers.[9] Labor agents egregiously contributed to the disproportionate sex ratio among urban blacks by taking away men to distant agricultural fields, leaving the women and children deserted.[10] Those abandoned wandered the streets and scavenged for food, often walking between ten and forty miles per day. "Sometimes I gits along tolerable," stated a widow washerwoman with six children. "Sometimes right slim; but dat's de way wid everybody—times is powerful hard right now."[11]

The municipal government showed neither the capability nor the ambition to meet the needs of the poor. It allocated few resources for basic human services. Yet the Freedmen's Bureau, which was established by the federal government in 1865 to distribute rations and relief to ex-slaves, to monitor the transition to a free labor system, and to protect black rights, proved inadequate also. The bureau was preoccupied with stemming migration, establishing order, and restoring the economy, which led it to force blacks into accepting contracts without sufficient regard for the fairness of the terms. The federals evicted ex-slaves from contraband camps or pushed them further from the center of town to the edges—out of sight and out of mind.[12] Bureau officials urged their agents: "You must not issue rations or afford shelter to any person who can, and will not labor for his or her own support."[13] . . .

Ex-slaves who were evicted from the camps by the end of 1865 were more fortunate than they could appreciate initially. They escaped a smallpox epidemic in the city that devastated the enclaves. One missionary reported a horrifying scene she witnessed in the camps: "Men, women, and children lying on the damp ground suffering in every degree from the mildest symptoms to the most violent. The tents crowded, no fire to make them comfortable, and worse all the poor creatures were almost destitute of wearing apparel."[14] The dead who lay around the sick and suffering were buried in the ground half-naked or without clothes at all. . . .

African-American women and men were willing to endure the adversities of food shortages, natural disasters, dilapidated housing, and inadequate clothing in postwar Atlanta because what they left behind in the countryside, by comparison, was much worse. In the city at least there were reasons to be optimistic that their strength in numbers and their collective strategies of empowerment could be effective. In rural areas, however, their dispersion and separation by miles of uninhabited backwoods left them more vulnerable to elements intent on depriving them of life, liberty, and happiness. Abram Colby, a Republican legislator from Greene County, summed up the motivations for migration by stating that blacks went to Atlanta "for protection." He explained further: "The military is here and nobody interferes with us here . . . we cannot stop anywhere else so safely."[15]

African Americans moved to the city not only in search of safety, but also in search of economic self-sufficiency. Though most ex-slaves held dreams of owning farm land, many preferred to set up households in a city with a more diverse urban economy. In Atlanta they encountered an economy that was quickly recovering from the war and continuing to grow in the direction propelled by military demands and the promise of modernization.[16] . . .

Though the kaleidoscope of industry appeared to offer vast possibilities for workers, African Americans were slotted into unskilled and service labor. Black men filled positions with the railroads; as day workers, they groomed roads, distributed ballast, and shoveled snow off the tracks. As brakemen, they coupled and uncoupled stationary cars and ran along the roof of moving trains to apply the brakes, risking life and limb. Many others worked in rolling and lumber mills, mostly in the lowest-paid positions as helpers to white men. Hotels employed black men as cooks, waiters, porters, bellhops, and barroom workers. A few ex-slaves worked in bakeries, small foundries, the paper mill, and candy factories. Slave artisans were high in number in the antebellum South, but in the postbellum era black men were rarely hired in skilled positions. They were able to benefit from the aggressive physical rebuilding of Atlanta, however, in the construction trades, as painters, carpenters, and brickmasons. Between 1870 and 1880, the proportion of black male shoemakers tripled to constitute the majority of the entire trade. A select few owned small businesses such as barber shops and grocery stores or worked in the professions as teachers and ministers.[17]

The range of job opportunities for black women was more narrow than for men. Black women were excluded from small manufacturing plants that hired white women, such as those that made candy, clothing, textiles, paper boxes, bookbinding, and straw goods. They were confined primarily to domestic labor in private homes as cooks, maids, and child-nurses. A few black women found related jobs in local hotels—a step above the same work performed in private households. Large numbers worked in their own homes in a relatively autonomous craft as laundresses, which had the advantage of accommodating family and community obligations. More desirable, yet less accessible, were skilled jobs outside domestic service as seamstresses or dressmakers. . . . Only a few black women were able to escape common labor and enter the professions as teachers.[18]

Reconstruction of the post-slavery South occurred on many levels. Just as the city's infrastructure had to be rebuilt for daily life to reach a new normalcy, so blacks had to rebuild their lives as free people by earning an independent living. Women's success or frustrations in influencing the character of domestic labor would define how meaningful freedom would be. Slave women had already demonstrated fundamental disagreements with masters over the principles and practices of free labor during the war. This conflict continued as workers and employers negotiated new terms. Even the most mundane and minute details of organizing a free labor system required rethinking assumptions about work that had previously relied on physical coercion. An employer acknowledged the trial-and-error nature of this process: "I had no idea what was considered a task in washing so I gave her all the small things belonging to the children taking out all the table cloths sheets counterpanes & c." The novice employer then decided in the same haphazard manner to pay the laundry worker 30 cents a day. But the laborer asserted her own understanding of fair work. "She was through by dinner time [and] appeared to work steady. I gave her dinner and afterwards told her that I had a few more clothes I wished washed out," the employer explained. "Her reply was that she was tired." The worker and employer held different expectations about the length of the work day and the quantity of the output of labor.[19]

African Americans labored according to their own sense of equity, with the guiding assumption that wage labor should not emulate slavery—especially in the arbitrariness of time and tasks. The experience of an ex-slave named Nancy illustrates this point. As some ex-slaves departed from their former masters' households, the burden of the work shifted to those who remained. Consequently, when the regular cook departed, Nancy's employer added cooking and washing to her previous child-care job, without her consent. Nancy faked illness on ironing days and eventually quit in protest against the extra encumbrance.[20] If workers and employers disagreed on the assignment of specific tasks, they also disagreed on how to execute them. Workers held to their own methods and preferences; employers held to theirs. . . .

If [a worker's] frustrations reached an intolerable level, she could exercise a new privilege as a free worker to register the ultimate complaint: she could quit and seek better terms for her work. Ex-slaves committed themselves to this precept of free labor with a firmness that vexed employers. "We daily hear of people who are in want of servants, and who have had in their employ in the last three or four months, a dozen different ones," stated a familiar news report. "The common experience of all is that the servants of the 'African-persuasion' can't be retained," it continued. "They are fond of change and since it is their privilege to come and go at pleasure, they make full use of the large liberty they enjoy."[21] . . .

African-American women decided to quit work over such grievances as low wages, long hours, ill treatment, and unpleasant tasks. Quitting could not guarantee a higher standard of living or a more pleasant work environment for workers, but it was an effective strategy to deprive employers of complete power over their labor. . . .

Employers did not share the same interpretations of labor mobility, however. They blamed the subversive influence of Yankees and "pernicious" Negroes for inciting "bad" work habits, or they explained quitting as a scientifically proven racial deficiency.[22] Whereas recently freed slaves often worked as much as they needed to survive and no more, white Southerners believed that if they refused to work as hard as slaves driven by fear they were mendicants and vagrants. "When a wench gets very hungry and ragged, she is ready to do the cooking for any sized family," a news report exclaimed. "But after she gets her belly well filled with provender, she begins to don't see the use of working all day and every day, and goes out to enjoy her freedom."[23]

Although many white Southerners resented the presence of the Freedmen's Bureau as the Northern overseer of Reconstruction, they readily sought its assistance to stem the revolving door of domestic workers. "What are persons to do when a 'freedman' that you hire as a nurse goes out at any time & against your direct orders?" one former master queried the bureau. "What must be done when they are hired and do only just what they please? orders being disregarded in every instance," he asked further. A bureau agent responded with an answer to alleviate the employer's frustrations and to teach him a lesson about the precepts of free labor. "Discharge her and tell her she dont suit you," the agent stated simply. "If you have a written contract with them and they quit you without good and sufficient cause—I will use all my power to have them comply," he reassured. But if these words provided comfort, the bureau agent made clear that the operative words were "without good and sufficient cause." He reiterated the employers' obligations and responsibilities to respect the liberties of workers: "You are expected to deal with them as Freemen and Freewomen. Individual exceptions there may be but as a whole where they are well treated they are faithful and work well."[24]

The federal government refused to return to white employers unilateral power to prohibit the mobility of black workers, leading employers to elicit the support of local laws. Quitting work became defined as "idleness" and "vagrancy"—prosecutable offenses. Southern state legislatures began passing repressive Black Codes in 1865 to obstruct black laborers' full participation in the marketplace and political arena. In 1866, the Atlanta City Council responded in a similar vein to stop the movement of household workers: it passed a law requiring employers to solicit recommendations from previous jobs in order to distinguish "worthy" from "worthless" laborers and to make it more difficult for workers to change jobs. Complaints continued long after the law took effect, which suggests its ineffectiveness.[25] . . .

Black women used the marginal leverage they could exercise in the face of conflict between employers to enhance their wages and to improve the conditions of work. When Hannah, "a cook & washer of the first character," was approached by Virginia Shelton in search of domestic help, she bargained for an agreement to match her needs. Hannah wanted to bring along her husband, a general laborer, and expected good wages for both of them. Shelton made an initial offer of $5 per month to Hannah and $10 per month to her husband. But the couple demanded $8 and $15, to which Shelton acceded. Shelton realized that it was worth making compromises with a servant she had traveled a long distance to recruit.[26]

Not all negotiations ended so pleasantly or in the workers' favor, however. . . . Domestic workers often complained of physical abuse by employers following disputes about wages, hours of work, or other work-related matters. . . . Samuel Ellison explained the argument that led to the death of his wife, Eliza Jane. Mrs. Ellison had argued with her employer, Mrs. L. B. Walton, about washing clothes. According to Ellison's husband, "My wife asked Mrs. Walton who would pay her for her washing extra clothes and which she was not bound to do by her contract." Walton's husband intervened and "abused" the laundress for "insulting" his wife. He left the house, returned and began another argument, insisting to Ellison, "shut up you God damn bitch." The fight ended when Walton shot Eliza Jane Ellison to death.[27]

African-American women like Ellison undoubtedly paid a high price for the simple desire to be treated like human beings. Incidents like this one made it apparent that freedom could not be secured through wage labor alone. The material survival of African Americans was critical, but they also needed to exercise their political rights to safeguard it. The political system had to undergo dramatic transformation to advance their interests, but here too they faced many obstacles.

The Ku Klux Klan, an anti-black terrorist organization founded by former Confederate soldiers in 1866, mounted the most bitter opposition to black rights. The KKK quickly became dominated by Democratic Party officials bent on preempting black participation in the electoral arena. The Klan sought to wrest economic and political power from the governing Republicans in order to restore it to the antebellum planter elite and to the Democrats. KKK members victimized Republican politicians like Abram Colby, whom they stripped and beat for hours in the woods. They harassed registered voters and independent landholders, ransacked churches and schools, intimidated common laborers who refused to bow obsequiously to planters, and tormented white Republicans sympathetic to any or all of the foregoing.[28]

African Americans' recalcitrance in commonplace disagreements with employers routinely provoked the vigilantes. Alfred Richardson, a legislator from Clarke County, suggested how labor relations continued to have strong political ramifications. The KKK assisted employers in securing the upper hand in conflicts with wage household workers. "Many times, you know, a white lady has a colored lady for cook or waiting in the house, or something of that sort," Richardson explained. "They have some quarrel, and sometimes probably the colored woman gives the lady a little jaw. In a night or two a crowd will come in and take her out and whip her." The Klan stripped and beat African Americans with sticks, straps, or pistol barrels when all else failed to elicit their compliance.[29]

If the KKK was determined to halt the reconstruction of a free labor system, it was most insistent about eliminating black political power. Though women were denied the right to vote in the dominant political system, they actively engaged in a grass-roots political culture that valued the participation of the entire community. Black women and children attended parades, rallies, and conventions; they voiced their opinions and cast their votes on resolutions passed at mass meetings. In the 1860s and 1870s, women organized their own political organizations, such as the Rising Daughters of Liberty Society, and stood guard at political meetings organized by men to allow them to meet without fear of enemy raids. They boldly tacked buttons on the clothing they wore to work in support of favorite candidates. They took time off from work to attend to their political duties, such as traveling to the polls to make sure men cast the right ballots. White housekeepers were as troubled by the dramatic absences of domestic workers on election day or during political conventions as were the planters and urban employers of men.[30] During an election riot in nearby Macon, a newspaper reported: "The Negro women, if possible, were wilder than the men. They were seen everywhere, talking in an excited manner, and urging the men on. Some of them were almost furious, showing it to be part of their religion to keep their husbands and brothers straight in politics."[31]

Whether they gave political advice and support to the men in their families and communities or carried out more directly subversive activities, black women showed courage in the face of political violence. Hannah Flournoy, a cook and laundress, ran a boardinghouse in Columbus well known as a gathering place for Republicans. When George Ashburn, a white party leader stalked by the KKK, looked to her for shelter she complied, unlike his other supporters in the town. Flournoy promised him, "You are a republican, and I am willing to die for you. I am a republican, tooth and toe-nail."[32] But neither Flournoy nor Ashburn could stop the Klan in its determination to take the life of freedom fighters. After Klansmen killed Ashburn, Flournoy escaped to Atlanta, leaving behind valuable property.

Republican activists like Ashburn and Flournoy were not the only victims of KKK violence. The Klan also targeted bystanders who happened to witness their misdeeds. In White County, Joe Brown's entire family was subjected to sadistic and brutal harassment because Brown had observed a murder committed by the Klan. "They just stripped me stark naked, and fell to beating us," Brown reported later. "They got a great big trace-chain, swung me up from the ground, and swung [my wife] up until she fainted; and they beat us all over the yard with great big sticks." The Klan continued its torture against his mother-in-law and sister-in-law. "They made all the women show their nakedness; they made them lie down, and they jabbed them with sticks." Indiscriminate in violating adults and children, the KKK lined up Brown's young daughters and sons "and went to playing with their backsides with a piece of fishing-pole."[33] . . .

Migrating to Atlanta certainly improved the personal safety of ex-slaves escaping the KKK and sexual assaults, but it did not ensure foolproof protection against bodily harm. Black women risked sexual abuse no matter where they lived. Domestics in white homes were the most susceptible to attacks. A year after the war ended, Henry McNeal Turner and other black men mounted the podium and wrote petitions to demand the cessation of sexual assaults upon black women. Freedom, they insisted, was meaningless without ownership and control over one's own body. Black men took great offense at the fact that while they were falsely accused of raping white women, white men granted themselves total immunity in the exploitation of black women. "*All we ask of the white man is to let our ladies alone,* and they need not fear us," Turner warned. "The difficulty has heretofore been *our ladies were not always at our disposal.*"[34] In Savannah, black men mobilized the Sons of Benevolence "for the protection of female virtue" in 1865.[35] In Richmond, African Americans complained to military authorities that women were being "gobbled up" off the streets, thrown into the jail, and ravished by the guards. In Mobile, black men organized the National Lincoln Association and petitioned the Alabama State Constitutional Convention to enact laws to protect black women from assault by white civilians and the police.[36]

Most whites refused to acknowledge the culpability of white men in abusing black women. "Rape" and "black women" were words that were never uttered in the same breath by white Southerners. Any sexual relations that developed between black women and white men were considered consensual, even coerced by the seductions of black women's lascivious nature. Rape was a crime defined exclusively, in theory and in practice, as perceived or actual threats against white female virtue by black men, which resulted in lynchings and castrations of numbers of innocent black men. But Z. B. Hargrove, a white attorney, admitted with rare candor that the obsession with black men raping white women was misplaced. "It is all on the other foot," as he put it. The "colored women have a great deal more to fear from white men."[37]

Black Atlantans during Reconstruction were subjected to other kinds of physical violence, especially at the hands of white civilians and police. . . . When Mary Price objected to being called a "damned bitch" by a white neighbor, Mr. Hoyt, he brought police officer C. M. Barry to her door to reprimand her. Price's mother, Barbara, pregnant at the time, intervened and spoke to the police: "I replied that I would protect my daughter in my own house, whereupon he pulled me out of the house into the street. Here he called another man and the two jerked and pulled me along [the street] to the guard house and throwed me in there." When a Freedmen's Bureau agent complained to the mayor and city council on the Prices' behalf, the complaint was rebuffed by a unanimous vote acquitting the policeman of all charges against him. Meanwhile, mother and daughter were arrested, convicted for using profane language, and forced to pay $350 each in fines and court costs. Only after it became clear that the Bureau would persist in its efforts to get justice for the Price women did the mayor have a change of heart and fine the offending policeman. Barry was one of the worst officers on the force, and the Freedmen's Bureau eventually forced the city council to fire him, though he was rehired a year later.[38]

African Americans not only had to ward off physical threats; they were also challenged by the existence of perfectly legal abuses that diminished the meaning of freedom. Ex-slaves defined the reconstruction of their families torn asunder by slavery and war as an important aspect of the realization of the full exercise of their civil rights. But former masters seized upon the misery of African Americans, with the assistance of the law, to prolong the conditions of slavery and deny them the prerogative of reuniting their families. The Georgia legislature passed an Apprentice Act in 1866, ostensibly to protect black orphans by providing them with guardianship and "good" homes until they reached the age of consent at twenty-one. Planters used the law to reinstate bondage through uncompensated child labor.[39] Aunts, uncles, parents, and grandparents inundated the Freedmen's Bureau with requests for assistance in rescuing their children, though this same agency also assisted in apprenticing black minors. Martin Lee, for example, a former slave living in Florence, Alabama, wrote to the chief of the Georgia bureau for help in releasing his nephew from bondage. He had successfully reunited part of his extended family, but could not gain the release of his nephew despite the fact that he and the child's mother, Lee's sister, were both willing and able to take custody.[40]

If admitted enemies of black freedom recklessly disregarded the unity of black families through apprenticeships, some of their friends operated just as wantonly. The American Missionary Association (AMA) sometimes impeded parents and relatives who wished to reclaim their children. In 1866, the AMA started an orphanage that operated out of a tent. Soon afterward they opened the Washburn Orphanage in a building to accommodate the large number of homeless black children who were surviving on the streets on scant diets of saltpork and hardtack. But the asylum functioned as a temporary way station for children before apprenticing them out as domestic help to white sponsors. "I succeeded in getting a little girl from the orphans asylum by the name of Mary Jane Peirce," one eager patron of the orphanage exclaimed. "Her father and mother are both dead. She has a step mother and a little step brother." Peirce's new guardian minced no words in disclosing reckless disregard for the reunion of the child's family. "I am glad she will have no outside influence exherted upon her," the guardian admitted.[41] . . .

African Americans persisted in pursuing the reconstitution of family ties, despite the obstacles put in their way. [Rebeca] Craighead [the matron of the asylum,] recognized the persistence of these ex-slaves, yet she showed neither respect nor sensitivity toward the virtues of their ambition. "Somehow these black people have the faculty of finding out where their children are," she acknowledged.[42] Both the uncle, Martin Lee, who used official channels to retrieve his nephew, and the anonymous aunt, who relied on her own resources to "steal" her niece, displayed no small measure of resourcefulness in achieving their aims. Men no less than women, non-kin as well as kin, sought to recreate the family bonds that had been strained or severed by slavery and the Civil War.

Not all missionaries were as insensitive as Craighead; there were others, like Frederick Ayers, who fully appreciated the significance of family to ex-slaves. "The idea of 'freedom' of independence, of calling their wives and their children, and little hut their *own*, was a soul animating one, that buoyed up their spirits," he observed.[43] . . .

Broad understandings of kinship encouraged black women to assume responsibility for needy children other than their natural offspring. Silvey, for example, could hardly survive on the minimal subsistence she earned, yet she extended compassion to the youngsters lost or deserted by other ex-slaves. "She was hard put to it, to work for them all," observed her former owner, Emma Prescott. But "of course, as our means were all limited, we could not supply her enough to feed them. Her life, was anything but ease & it was a pitiful sight."[44] . . .

The most complicated family issues involved romantic relationships between women and men. For generations slaves had married one another and passed on the importance of conjugal obligations, despite the absence of legal protection. Marriages between slaves were long-term commitments, usually only disrupted by forcible separation or the death of a spouse. Emancipation offered new opportunities to reaffirm marital vows and to reunite couples who had previously lived "abroad" in the households of different masters. Even before the last shots of gunfire ending the Civil War, thousands of husbands and wives sought the help of Union officers and

Northern missionaries to register their nuptials and to conduct wedding ceremonies.[45] The significance of formalizing these ties was articulated by a black soldier: "*I praise God for this day!* The Marriage Covenant is at the foundation of all our rights."[46] Putting marriages on a legal footing bolstered the ability of ex-slaves to keep their families together, to make decisions about labor and education, and to stay out of the unscrupulous grasp of erstwhile masters.

The hardships of slavery and war that disrupted families, however, meant that in the postwar period spouses were not always reunited without problems and tensions. Slaves traveled long distances to reunite with spouses from whom they had been separated for years. They wrote love letters and mailed them to churches and to the Freedmen's Bureau, and retraced the routes of labor agents who had taken their partners away.[47] Emotional bonds were sometimes so intense that spouses would choose to suffer indefinitely if they could not be reunited with their lost loved ones. But affections undernourished by hundreds of miles and many years might be supplanted by other relationships. Many ex-slaves faced awkward dilemmas when spouses presumed to be dead or long-lost suddenly reappeared. Ex-slaves created novel solutions for the vexing moral, legal, and practical concerns in resolving marital relations disrupted by forces beyond their control. One woman lived with each of her two husbands for a two-week trial before making a decision. Some men felt obligated to two wives and stayed married to one wife while providing support to the other. In one case, perhaps unique, a wife resumed her relationship with her first husband, while the second husband, a much older man, was brought into the family as a "poor relation."[48]

The presence of children complicated marriages even further. Some spouses registered their marriages with the Freedmen's Bureau or local courts even when their spouses were dead or missing, in order to give legal recognition to their children. When both parents were present and unable to reconcile their differences, child custody became a point of contention. Madison Day and Maria Richardson reached a mutual agreement to separate after emancipation. The love between husband and wife may have changed, but the love that each displayed for their children did not. The Richardsons put the Freedmen's Bureau agent in a quandary in determining who should receive custody. "Neither husband nor wife seem to be in a condition to provide for the children in a manner better than is usual with the freedpeople," the agent noted. "Still both appear to have an affectionate regard for the children and each loudly demands them."[49] . . .

Sheer survival and the reconstruction of family, despite all the difficulties, were the highest priorities of ex-slaves in the postwar period. But the desire for literacy and education was closely related to their strategies for achieving economic self-sufficiency, political autonomy, and personal enrichment. By 1860, 5 percent of the slave population had defied the laws and learned to read and write. Some were taught by their masters, but many learned to read in clandestine sessions taught by other blacks. African Americans all over the South organized secret schools long before the arrival of Northern missionaries. When a New England teacher arrived in Atlanta in 1865, he discovered an ex-slave already running a school in a church basement.[50]

African Americans welcomed the support of New England teachers and the federal government in their education movement. But centuries of slavery had stirred the longing for self-reliance in operating schools and filling teaching staffs, with assistance, but without white control. Ex-slaves enthusiastically raised funds and donated in-kind labor for building, repairing, and maintaining school houses. They opened their spartan quarters to house teachers and shared vegetables from their gardens to feed them. Ex-slaves in Georgia ranked highest in the South in the amount of financial assistance donated to their own education.[51]

The education movement among African Americans in Georgia went hand in hand with the demand for political rights. In January 1865, black ministers formed the Savannah Education Association, which operated schools staffed entirely with black teachers. Despite the efforts of General Davis Tillson, the conservative head of the Freedmen's Bureau, to keep politics out of the organization, African Americans and more liberal white allies infused the group with political objectives. The name was changed to the Georgia Equal Rights and Education Association, explicitly linking equal rights in the political arena with the pursuit of education. The organization became an important training ground for black politicians and laypersons at the grass-roots level and functioned as the state's predecessor to the Republican Party.[52] . . .

African Americans' advocacy of universal public education did not fare well at the city level, because the municipal government was firmly controlled by Democrats and businessmen. William Finch, elected in 1870 as one of Atlanta's first black city councilmen, made universal education a hallmark of his election campaign. Finch attempted, but failed, to galvanize the support of the white working class on this issue. City Hall's cold reception shifted the burden of basic education for blacks to private foundations. Finch did succeed in getting the council to absorb two primary schools run by the AMA. After his short term in office and unsuccessful bid for reelection in December 1871, he continued to be a strong advocate of public education and helped to negotiate a deal in 1872 whereby the city would pay nominal costs for some blacks to receive secondary training at Atlanta University. No publicly funded high school for blacks would be created until a half-century later, however.[53]

Former slaves of all ages were undeterred in their goals to achieve literacy, regardless of the obstacles imposed by municipal and state governments. "It is quite amusing to see little girls eight or ten years old lead up full-grown women, as well as children, to have their names enrolled," remarked a missionary. "Men, women, and children are daily inquiring when the 'Free School' is to commence, and whether all can come[.] There is a large class of married women who wish to attend, if the schools are not too crowded."[54] Household workers figured prominently among this group of older, eager scholars. Their eagerness to learn was not diminished, although often interrupted, by the pressing demands of gainful labor. In fact, these obstacles may have increased the value of education in the eyes of the ex-slaves. Sabbath schools operated by black churches and evening classes sponsored by the Freedmen's Bureau and Northern missionaries afforded alternatives for those who could not sacrifice time during the day. But black women also inventively stole time away from work by carrying their books along and studying during spare moments—even fastening textbooks to backyard fences to glimpse their lessons as they washed clothes.[55]

As parents, working-class adults were especially committed to the education of their children. The story of Sarah J. Thomas, a young woman from Macon, whose mother was a cook and washerwoman, is a poignant illustration. Thomas wrote Edmund Asa Ware, president of Atlanta University, to gain his support in her plans to enroll in the secondary school. "I exspected to come to Atlanta to morrow but I am dissappointed. The reason I can not come to morrow is this. You know how mothers are! I guess about their youngest children *girls* especially," she wrote. Mother Thomas was protective of her daughter and reluctant to send her away alone. "In order that I may *come* Mr. Ware! mother says can she get a place to work there in the family?" she asked. The younger Thomas boasted of her mother's fine skills and reputation and slipped in her salary history. She assured the president, surely swamped by requests for financial aid, that her matriculation depended upon parental supervision, not the need for money. "Mother says she dont mean not the least to work to pay for *my schooling?* father pays for that him self she dont have any thing to do with it she only want to be where she can see me."[56] The young scholar's astute strategizing swayed both her mother and the school's president; she entered Atlanta University and achieved a successful teaching career after graduation in 1875.

Clandestine antebellum activities and values had bolstered the exemplary efforts of African Americans to seek literacy and to build and sustain educational institutions after the war. Ex-slaves took mutual obligations seriously. Their belief in personal development was aided rather than hampered by ideals that emphasized broad definitions of kinship and community. Freedom meant the reestablishment of lost family connections, the achievement of literacy, the exercise of political rights, and the security of a decent livelihood without the sacrifice of human dignity or self-determination. Ex-slave women migrated to Atlanta, where they hoped they would have a better chance of fulfilling these expectations. They were faced with many challenges; uppermost among them were the white residents who were resentful of the abolition of slavery and persisted in thwarting the realization of the true meaning of freedom. Black women continued to struggle, resilient and creative, in pursuing their goals for dignity and autonomy. The character of the contest had already been cast, but the many guises of domination and resistance had yet to be exhausted as life in the New South unfolded.

NOTES

1. . . . Franklin M. Garrett, *Yesterday's Atlanta* (Miami: E. A. Seeman, 1974), p. 38; Eric Foner, *Reconstruction: America's Unfinished Revolution, 1863–1877* (New York: Harper & Row, 1988), pp. 81–82; Leon F. Litwack, *Been in the Storm So Long: The Aftermath of Slavery* (New York: Knopf, 1979), pp. 310–316; U.S. Department of the Treasury, Register of Signatures of Depositors in the Branches of the Freedman's Savings and Trust Company, Atlanta Branch, 1870–1874 (Microfilm Publication, M-544), National Archives (hereafter cited as Freedman's Bank Records). Frederick Ayer to George Whipple, 15 February 1866 (Georgia microfilm reels), American Missionary Association Archives, Amistad Research Center, Tulane University (hereafter cited as AMA Papers).

2. John Richard Dennett, *The South As It Is: 1865–1866,* ed. Henry M. Christman (New York: Viking, 1965), pp. 267–271; Sidney Andrews, *The South Since the War: As Shown by Fourteen Weeks of Travel and Observation in Georgia and the Carolinas* (Boston, 1866; reprint ed., New York: Arno, 1970), pp. 339–340; Don H. Doyle, *New Men, New Cities, New South: Atlanta, Nashville, Charleston, Mobile, 1860–1910* (Chapel Hill: University of North Carolina Press, 1990), p. 31.

3. Rebecca Craighead to [Samuel] Grant, 15 January 1866, Georgia, AMA Papers; Andrews, *South Since the War,* p. 340; Whitelaw Reid, *After the War: A Tour of the Southern States, 1865–1866* (London, 1866; reprint ed., New York: Harper & Row, 1965), p. 355; Doyle, *New Men,* pp. 34–35; Howard N. Rabinowitz, *Race Relations in the Urban South 1865–1890* (New York: Oxford University Press, 1978), pp. 5–17.

4. See James Michael Russell, *Atlanta, 1847–1890: City Building in the Old South and the New* (Baton Rouge: Louisiana State University Press, 1988), pp. 117–128.

5. Frederick Ayers to Rev. George Whipple, 15 February 1866, Georgia, AMA Papers.

6. See Rebecca Craighead to Rev. Samuel Hunt, 30 April 1866, Georgia, AMA Papers; E. T. Ayer to Rev. Samuel Grant, 3 February 1866, Georgia, AMA Papers; Harriet M. Phillips to Rev. Samuel Grant, 15 January 1866, Georgia, AMA Papers; *American Missionary* 13 (January 1869): 4; John T. Trowbridge, *The South: A Tour of Its Battle-Fields and Ruined Cities* (Hartford, 1866; reprint ed., New York: Arno, 1969), p. 453.

7. Frederick Ayers to Rev. George Whipple, 15 February 1866, Georgia, AMA Papers.

8. See Table 1 at the back of the book.

9. Gretchen Ehrmann Maclachlan, "Women's Work: Atlanta's Industrialization and Urbanization, 1879–1929" (Ph.D. diss., Emory University, 1992), p. 29.

10. H. A. Buck to General [Davis Tillson], 2 October 1865, Letters Recd., ser. 732, Atlanta, Ga. Subasst. Comr., Record Group 105: Bureau of Refugees, Freedmen, and Abandoned Lands (hereafter cited as BRFAL), National Archives (hereafter cited as NA), [FSSP A-5153]; Franklin Brown to Gen. Tillson, 30 July 1866, Unregistered Letters Recd., ser. 632, Ga. Asst. Comr., BRFAL, NA, [FSSP A-5327]; clipping from *Augusta Constitutionalist,* 16 February 1866, filed with Lt. Col. D. O. Poole to Brig. Gen. Davis Tillson, 19 February 1866, Unregistered Letters Recd., ser. 632, Ga. Asst. Comr., BRFAL, NA, [FSSP A-5447]. Citations for photocopied documents from the National Archives that were consulted at the Freedmen and Southern Society Project, University of Maryland, conclude with the designation "FSSP" and the project's document control number in square brackets: for example, [FSSP A-5447].

11. Quoted in Trowbridge, *South Tour,* pp. 453–454.

12. Jerry Thornbery, "The Development of Black Atlanta, 1865–1885" (Ph.D. diss., University of Maryland, 1977), pp. 48–53; Edmund L. Drago, *Black Politicians and Reconstruction in Georgia: A Splendid Failure* (Baton Rouge: Louisiana State University Press, 1982), pp. 113–116.

13. Brig. Genl. Davis Tillson to Captain George R. Walbridge, 12 March 1866, Letters Recd., ser. 732, Ga. Subasst. Comr., BRFAL, NA, [FSSP A-5153].

14. Rebecca Craighead to Rev. Samuel Hunt, 15 February 1866, Georgia, AMA Papers; see also F. Ayers to Rev. George Whipple, 15 February 1866, Georgia, AMA Papers.

15. Testimony of Abram Colby, 28 October 1871, in 42nd Congress, 2nd Session, House Report no. 22, pt. 6, *Testimony taken by the Joint Select Committee to Inquire into the Condition of Affairs in the Late Insurrectionary States* (Washington, D.C., 1872), vol. 2, p. 700 (hereafter cited as KKK Hearings). See also testimony of Alfred Richardson, 7 July 1871, KKK Hearings, vol. 1, p. 12.

16. Doyle, *New Men,* pp. 38–48, 151; Jonathan W. McLeod, *Workers and Workplace Dynamics in Reconstruction Era Atlanta* (Los Angeles: Center for Afro-American Studies, University of California), pp. 10–16.

17. McLeod, *Workers and Workplace,* pp. 24–31, 45, 61, 75, 81, 91, 94.

18. Ibid., pp. 77–92, 100–103; Thornbery, "Black Atlanta," pp. 191–225.

19. Entry of 27 May 1865, Ella Gertrude Clanton Thomas Journal, William R. Perkins Library, Duke University (hereafter cited as DU).

20. See entries for May 1865, Thomas Journal, DU.

21. Atlanta *Daily Intelligencer,* 25 October 1865.

22. Emma J. S. Prescott, "Reminiscences of the War," typescript, pp. 49–50, 55, Atlanta History Center (hereafter cited as AHC)

23. Atlanta *Daily New Era,* 27 February 1868.

24. Mr. J. T. Ball to Maj. Knox, 19 March 1866, Unregistered Letters Recd., ser. 2250, Meridian, Miss. Subasst. Comr., BRFAL, NA, [FSSP A-9423].

25. Alexa Wynell Benson, "Race Relations in Atlanta, As Seen in a Critical Analysis of the City Council Proceedings and Other Related Works, 1865–1877" (M.A. thesis, Atlanta University, 1966), pp. 43–44; Foner, *Reconstruction,* pp. 199–202; Theodore Brantner Wilson, *The Black Codes of the South* (University, Ala.: University of Alabama Press, 1965); Rabinowitz, *Race Relations,* pp. 34–35; Atlanta *Daily New Era,* 27 February 1868.

26. Virginia Shelton to William Shelton, 20 August 1866, Campbell Family Papers, DU. See also

Ellen Chisholm to Laura Perry, 27 July 1867, Perry Family Papers, AHC.

27. Affidavit of Samuel Ellison, 16 Jan 1867 BRFAL, NA.

28. Foner, *Reconstruction*, pp. 425–444; see testimony of Abram Colby, 28 October 1871, KKK Hearings, vol. 2, pp. 699–702.

29. Testimony of Alfred Richardson, 7 July 1871, KKK Hearings, vol. 1, pp. 12, 18.

30. Foner, *Reconstruction*, pp. 87, 290–291; Elsa Barkley Brown, "Negotiating and Transforming the Public Sphere: African American Political Life in the Transition from Slavery to Freedom," *Public Culture* 7 (Fall 1994): 107–126; Thomas C. Holt, *Black Over White: Negro Political Leadership in South Carolina during Reconstruction* (Urbana: University of Illinois Press, 1977), pp. 34–35.

31. Macon *Georgia Weekly Telegraph*, 8 October 1872, as quoted in Edmund L. Drago, "Militancy and Black Women in Reconstruction Georgia," *Journal of American Culture* 1 (Winter 1978): 841.

32. Testimony of Hannah Flournoy, 24 October 1871, KKK Hearings, vol. 1, p. 533. On Ashburn's death see Drago, *Black Politicians*, pp. 145, 153.

33. Testimony of Joe Brown, 24 October 1871, KKK Hearings, vol. 1, p. 502.

34. Henry McNeal Turner's emancipation speech, 1 January 1866, Augusta, as quoted in Herbert G. Gutman, *The Black Family in Slavery and Freedom*, 1750–1925 (New York: Pantheon Books, 1977), p. 388. See also Catherine Clinton, "Bloody Terrain: Freedwomen, Sexuality and Violence During Reconstruction," *Georgia Historical Quarterly* 76 (Summer 1992): 318; Atlanta *Weekly Defiance*, 24 February 1883.

35. Eliza Frances Andrews, *The War-Time Journal of a Georgia Girl, 1864–1865*, ed. Spencer Bidwell King, Jr. (Macon, Ga.: Arvidian Press, 1960), p. 349.

36. Gutman, *Black Family*, pp. 387–388.

37. Testimony of Z. B. Hargrove, 13 July 1871, KKK Hearings, vol. 1, p. 83. See also testimony of George B. Burnett, 2 November 1871, KKK Hearings, vol. 2, p. 949. See Jacquelyn Dowd Hall, *Revolt Against Chivalry: Jesse Daniel Ames and the Women's Campaign Against Lynching* (New York: Columbia University Press, 1974).

38. Affidavit of Barbara Price, 15 May 1867, Misc. Court Records, ser. 737, Atlanta, Ga. Subasst. Comr., BRFAL; Bvt. Maj. Fred. Mosebach to Mayor and City Council of Atlanta, 15 May 1867, and Bvt. Maj. Fred. Mosebach to Col. C. C. Sibley, 21 May 1867, vol. 99, pp. 49 and 53–54, Letters Sent, ser. 729, Atlanta, Ga. Subasst. Comr., BRFAL, NA, [FSSP A-5709]. See also James M. Russell and Jerry Thornbery, "William Finch of Atlanta: The Black Politician as Civic Leader," in Howard N. Rabinowitz, ed. *Southern Black Leaders of the Reconstruction Era* (Urbana: University of Illinois Press, 1982), pp. 317, 332.

39. The apprenticeship system was not entirely limited to the conscription of minors; young adults actively providing for themselves were also apprenticed. For example, a turpentine worker with a wife and child was defined as an orphan in North Carolina. See Foner, *Reconstruction*, p. 201.

40. Martin Lee to Mr. Tillson, 7 December 1866, in Ira Berlin et al., "Afro-American Families in the Transition from Slavery to Freedom," *Radical History Review* 42 (Fall 1988): 102–103.

41. Entry of 27 May 1865, Thomas Journal, DU. Evidence from ex-slave narratives suggests a pattern of exploitation of child laborers; they received little or no cash wages. See testimony of Nancy Smith, in George P. Rawick, ed., *The American Slave: A Composite Autobiography* (Westport, Conn.: Greenwood Press, 1941; 1972), *Georgia Narratives*, vol. 13, pt. 3, p. 302 (hereafter cited as WPA Ga. Narr.); testimony of Georgia Telfair, WPA Ga. Narr., vol. 13, pt. 4, p. 5.

42. Rebecca M. Craighead to Bvt. Brig. Gen. J. H. Lewis, 11 May 1866, Ga. Asst. Comr., C-69, 1867, Letters Recd., ser. 631, Ga. Asst. Comr., BRFAL, NA, [FSSP A-415].

43. F. Ayers to Rev. George Whipple, 15 February 1866, Georgia, AMA Papers.

44. Prescott, "Reminiscences of the War," p. 56, AHC. Prescott goes on to reveal that Silvey died penniless, without the help of former owners.

45. Gutman, *Black Family*, pp. 9–23; Berlin et al., "Afro-American Families," pp. 92–93.

46. Corporal Murray, as quoted in J. R. Johnson to Col. S. Lee, 1 June 1866, in Berlin et al., "Afro-American Families," p. 97.

47. For examples of these efforts see Wm. H. Sinclair to Freedmen's Bureau agent at Savannah, Ga., 12 September 1866, Unregistered Letters, ser. 1013, Savannah, Ga. Subasst. Comr., BRFAL, NA, [FSSP A-5762]; R. F. Patterson to Col. D. C. Poole, Letters Recd., ser. 732, Atlanta, Ga. Subasst. Comr., BRFAL, NA, [FSSP A-5704].

48. Gutman, *Black Family*, pp. 418–425.

49. 1st Lt. F. E. Grossmann to the Acting Assistant Adjutant General, 1 October 1866, in Berlin et al., "Afro-American Families," pp. 97–98. Gutman, *Black Family*, pp. 418–425.

50. James D. Anderson, *The Education of Blacks in the South, 1860–1935* (Chapel Hill: University of North Carolina Press, 1988), pp. 4–9, 16; Herbert G. Gutman, "Schools for Freedom: The Post-Emancipation Origins of Afro-American Education," in Herbert G. Gutman, *Power and Culture: Essays on the American Working-Class*, ed. Ira Berlin (New York: Pantheon, 1987), p. 294; Jacqueline Jones, *Soldiers of Light and Love: Northern Teachers and Georgia Blacks 1865–1873 Chapel Hill: University of North Carolina Press, 1980),* p. 59.

51. Gutman, "Schools for Freedom," pp. 286, 294; Jones, *Soldiers of Light and Love*, p. 62; Anderson, *Education of Blacks in the South*, pp. 4–32.

52. Drago, *Black Politicians*, pp. 27–28.

53. Russell and Thornbery, "William Finch of Atlanta," pp. 319, 322; Russell, *Atlanta*, p. 181.

54. Mrs. E. T. Ayers to Rev. Samuel Hunt, 1 September 1866, Georgia, AMA Papers.

55. Jennies Barium to Rev. Samuel Grant, 27 January 1866, Georgia, AMA Papers; Andrews, *South Since the War*, p. 338.

56. Sarah J. Thomas to Mr. [Edmund A.] Ware, 11 October 1869, Edmund A. Ware Papers, Robert W. Woodruff Library, Clarke Atlanta University.

After the Civil War: Reconsidering the Law

Reconstruction Amendments, 1868, 1870

Until 1868, the United States Constitution made no explicit distinctions on the basis of gender. Of qualifications for voters, it said only that "the electors in each State shall have the qualifications requisite for electors of the most numerous branch of the State legislature" (art. 1, sec. 2). Reformers merely needed to persuade each state legislature to change its own rules in order to enfranchise women in national elections.

The word *male* was introduced into the Constitution in section 2 of the Fourteenth Amendment, as part of a complex provision—never enforced—intended to constrain former Confederates from interfering with the civil rights of newly freed slaves. Suffragists were bitterly disappointed at the failure to include sex as a category in the Fifteenth Amendment. But until the test case of *Minor* v. *Happersett* (pp. 315–316), they clung to the hope that the first article of the Fourteenth Amendment would be interpreted broadly enough to admit women to the polls.

Fourteenth Amendment, 1868

1. All persons born or naturalized in the United States, and subject to the jurisdiction thereof, are citizens of the United States and of the State wherein they reside. No State shall make or enforce any law which shall abridge the privileges or immunities of citizens of the United States; nor shall any State deprive any person of life, liberty, or property, without due process of law; nor deny to any person within its jurisdiction the equal protection of the laws.

2. Representatives shall be apportioned among the several States according to their respective numbers, counting the whole number of persons in each State, excluding Indians not taxed. But when the right to vote at any election for the choice of electors for President and Vice-President of the United States, Representatives in Congress, the executive and judicial officers of a State, or the members of the legislature thereof, is denied to any of the male inhabitants of such State, being twenty-one years of age and citizens of the United States, or in any way abridged, except for participation in rebellion, or other crime, the basis of representation therein shall be reduced in the proportion which the number of such male citizens shall bear to the whole number of male citizens twenty-one years of age in such State. . . .

Fifteenth Amendment, 1870

The right of citizens of the United States to vote shall not be denied or abridged by the United States or by any State on account of race, color, or previous condition of servitude. . . .

Coger *v.* The North Western Union Packet Company, *Supreme Court of Iowa, 1873*

A long-established rule of Anglo-American common law is that transportation services licensed by the state are "legally bound to carry all passengers or freight as long as there is enough space, the fee is paid, and no reasonable grounds to refuse to do so exist."* What counts as "reasonable grounds" is open to interpretation. One popular way to evade universal common carrier rules has been to charge different fees for first- and second-class accommodations—thus segregating by economic class—and make only second-class accommodations available to all people of color. The "ladies' car" in railroads or the "ladies' table" on steamships was a popular subterfuge for racial segregation. Throughout the post–Civil War years, African American women challenged their exclusion from ladies' accommodations—often at real physical risk to themselves. (Being thrown off a moving train was the worst of these risks.)

In 1873, Emma Coger, a schoolteacher of mixed race, tried to buy a first-class ticket on a steamboat that crossed the Mississippi from Keokuk, Iowa, to her hometown of Quincy, Illinois. She refused the clerk's offer of a ticket that did not entitle her to meals at the first-class table reserved for ladies traveling alone; she found another passenger, a white man, who purchased a first-class meal ticket on her behalf. When she took a seat at the ladies' table in the cabin, the guard told her to move to the deck or to the pantry, where people of color were to eat. She refused. The captain of the boat appeared, making the same demand; she again refused, and, as the subsequent court record describes it, "he proceeded by force to remove her from the table and the cabin of the boat."

The feisty Emma Coger did not go quietly. As one witness testified, "She swore and abused the captain, saying 'I told you I'd get even with you, you white-livered sons of bitches.' . . . Her conduct was very bad and her language worse. In the struggle, the covering of the table was torn off, dishes broke, and the officer received a slight injury."† Coger was defiant; she sued the steamship company for assault and battery.

Emma Coger hedged her bets. She claimed "she was as white as anybody." A jury trial was held in the Lee District Court. The judge instructed the jury that if Coger's "rights to first-class accommodations were denied her, simply because she has African or negro blood in her veins . . . then the court charges you that the plaintiff is entitled to recover" damages.

Coger won. The steamship company appealed to the Iowa Supreme Court, claiming that the well-known custom on all their boats was that "colored persons could not receive. . . . first class privileges. . . . [Coger] purchased a ticket which entitled her to the rights of a colored person. . . . and gave her no right to meals. . . . Afterward, by fraud, she purchased such a ticket for meals as were sold to white

***West Encyclopedia of American Law*, 2008,
http://legal-dictionary.thefreedictionary.com/Common+carrier.

†Record quoted in Barbara Young Welke, *Recasting American Liberty: Gender, Race, Law, and the Railroad Revolution, 1865–1920* (New York: Cambridge University Press, 2001), pp. 292–93.

Coger v. *The North Western Union Packet Company*, 37 Iowa 145 (1873).

persons. . . . [N]o greater force was used than was necessary to take her, against her resistance, from the table."

Earlier that year, dealing with Myra Bradwell's claim that the Fourteenth Amendment's promise of equal protection should sustain her right to practice law, the U.S. Supreme Court had interpreted the amendment very narrowly. But Iowa Chief Justice Joseph M. Beck had participated in the deliberations of his court when, only a few years before, it had ruled that racially segregated schools were a denial of equal protection of the laws—interpreting the Fourteenth Amendment broadly. Now he wrote the opinion for a unanimous court.

Iowa was unusual. Ten years later, in Tennessee, Ida B. Wells [see pp. 349–355] would have experiences similar to Emma Coger's, but with the opposite result. In 1883, Wells physically resisted her removal from a ladies' car, biting the conductor's hand as he forced her off the train. She sued the railroad company for discrimination; she won in the trial court but lost when the railroad appealed to the Tennessee Supreme Court. (The court offered the opinion that it was Wells who had, by her lawsuit, harassed the railroad.)

The lawsuits courageously brought by Emma Coger, Ida B. Wells, and dozens of other individual African American women in the years after the Civil War tested the claim that the common carriers (railroads, streetcars, steamboats) provided "separate but equal" accommodations to black and white people. Their lawsuits laid the ground for the famous test case challenging separate streetcars for whites and blacks, brought—at no physical risk to themselves—by Homer Plessy and a group of African American professional men in New Orleans at the end of the nineteenth century. In *Plessy* v. *Ferguson*, the U.S. Supreme Court ruled that laws requiring the separation of the races merely reflect social custom and do not label one race as inferior. *Plessy* would not be overturned until the Supreme Court's 1954 decision in *Brown* v. *Board of Education*.

How did the Iowa Supreme Court describe the issues on which it had to decide? On what grounds did they hold for Emma Coger? Contrast this interpretation of the meaning of the Fourteenth Amendment with the U.S. Supreme Court's decision in *Bradwell* (pp. 312–314) and *Minor* (pp. 315–316).

CHIEF JUSTICE JOSEPH BECK, FOR A UNANIMOUS COURT:

"[I]n our opinion, the doctrines and authorities involved in the argument [that Coger is white] are obsolete, and have no longer existence and authority, anywhere within the jurisdiction of the federal constitution, and most certainly not in Iowa. The ground upon which we base this conclusion will be discovered, in the progress of this opinion, to be the absolute equality of all men. We will . . . accept the statement of fact as made by the counsel of [the steamship company], namely, that plaintiff is a woman of color.

In our opinion the plaintiff was entitled to the same rights and privileges while upon defendant's boat, notwithstanding the negro blood, be it more or less, admitted to flow in her veins, which were possessed and exercised by white passengers.

These rights and privileges rest upon the equality of all before the law, the very foundation principle of our government. If the negro must submit to different treatment, to accommodations inferior to those given to the white man, when transported by public carriers, he is deprived of the benefits of this very principle of equality. . . . It may be claimed that as he does not get accommodations equal to the white man he is not charged as great a price. But this does not modify the. . . absurdity and gross injustice of the rule—nay, its positive wickedness. . . .

The decision is planted on the broad and just ground of the equality of all men before the law, which is not limited by color, nationality, religion or condition in life. This principle of equality is announced and secured by the very first words of our State constitution which relate to the rights of the people, in language most comprehensive, and incapable of misconstruction, namely: "All men are, by nature, free and equal." . . . But the doctrine of equality and its application to the rights of [Emma Coger] . . . depend . . . not alone upon the constitution of this State [but also] . . . are recognized and secured by the recent constitutional amendments and legislation of the United States. . . . The persons contemplated by the [Fourteenth] amendment [see p. 309] are: 1. All persons born or naturalized in the United States. . . . These. . . . are secured the right of citizenship of the United States, and protected against abridgment of their privileges and immunities. 2. All persons within the jurisdiction of the States. . . . are protected and secured the equal protection of the laws. [Coger] belongs to both classes of persons, to whom rights are secured and protection extended. . . .

Her money would not purchase for her that which the same sum would entitle a white passenger to receive. . . . [S]he claimed no social privilege, but substantial privileges pertaining to her property and the protection of her person. It cannot be doubted that she was excluded from the table and cabin. . . . because of prejudice entertained against her race, growing out of its former condition of servitude—a prejudice, be it proclaimed to the honor of our people, that is fast giving way to nobler sentiments, and, it is hoped, will soon be entombed with its parent, slavery. . . .

[A] common carrier cannot refuse to transport all persons without distinctions based upon color or nationality. . . . Her dinner ticket gave her a right to dine in the cabin on an equality with other passengers. . . .

Bradwell *v.* Illinois, *1873*

Although she could not practice in the courts until the end of her career, Myra Bradwell was perhaps the most notable female lawyer of the nineteenth century. She read law in the office of her husband, a prominent Chicago attorney and county judge. In 1868 she began to publish the *Chicago Legal News*, a weekly newspaper covering developments in courts and legislatures throughout the country. Because she had received a special charter from the state legislature under which she was permitted to act without the usual legal disabilities of a married woman, she ran the *News* as her own business. She wrote vigorous editorials, evaluating legal opinions and new laws, assessing proposed state legislation, and supporting progressive developments like prison reform, the establishment of law schools, and women's rights. She drafted bills improving married women's rights to child custody and to property, including the Illinois Married Woman's Property Act of 1869. Thanks in part to her own lobbying efforts, Illinois permitted women to own property and to control their own earnings.

It was only logical that Myra Bradwell should seek admission to the bar. Although she passed the entrance tests in 1869, although the Illinois Married Woman's Property Act permitted her to own property, and although the law that gave the state supreme court the power to license attorneys did not explicitly exclude women, her application was rejected by the Illinois Supreme Court on the grounds that she was a married woman, and therefore not a truly free agent. Appealing to the United States Supreme Court, her attorney argued that among the "privileges and immunities" guaranteed to each citizen by the Fourteenth Amendment was the right to pursue any honorable profession. "Intelligence, integrity and honor are the only qualifications that can be prescribed . . . the broad shield of the Constitution is over all, and protects each in that measure of success which his or her individual merits may secure."

The Court's decision came in two parts. Speaking for the majority and citing the most recent decision of the Supreme Court in the slaughterhouse cases, Justice Samuel F. Miller held that the right to practice law in the courts of any particular state was a right that had to be granted by the individual state; it was not one of the "privileges and immunities" of national citizenship. This judgment was supplemented by a concurring opinion, in which Justice Joseph P. Bradley offered an ideological justification for the Court's decision that was based on inherent differences between men and women and that was to be widely used thereafter to defend the exclusion of women from professional careers.

While her case was pending before the U.S. Supreme Court, Bradwell and Alta M. Hulett, another woman who had been refused admission to the bar even though she was otherwise qualified, successfully lobbied for a law that granted freedom of occupational choice to all Illinois citizens, both male and female. The bill was passed in 1872; a year later Alta Hulett was sworn in before the Illinois Bar. Bradwell did not think she should have to beg for admission, and she never formally applied for a license to practice law under the new statute. In the *Chicago Legal News* she observed that "having once complied with the rules and regulations of the court . . . [I] declined to . . . again ask for admission." In 1890, twenty years after her initial application, the Illinois Supreme Court admitted Bradwell to the bar. Two years before her death in 1894 she was admitted to practice before the U.S. Supreme Court, but she never did argue a case there.*

MR. JUSTICE JOSEPH P. BRADLEY:

The claim of the plaintiff, who is a married woman, to be admitted to practice as an attorney and counselor at law, is based upon the supposed right of every person, man or woman, to engage in any lawful employment for a livelihood. The supreme court of Illinois denied the application on the ground that, by the common law, which is the basis of the laws of Illinois, only men were admitted to the bar, and the legislature had not made any change in this respect. . . .

The claim that, under the 14th Amendment of the Constitution, which declares that no state shall make or enforce any law which shall abridge the privileges and immunities of citizens of the United States, and the statute law of Illinois, or the common law prevailing in that state, can no longer be set up as a barrier against the right of females to pursue any lawful employment . . . assumes that it is one of the privileges and immunities of women as citizens to engage in any and every profession, occupation or employment in civil life.

It certainly cannot be affirmed, as a historical fact, that this has ever been established as one of the fundamental privileges and immunities of the sex. On the contrary, the civil law, as well as nature herself, has always recognized a wide difference in the respective spheres and destinies of man and woman. Man is, or should

*See also Frances Olsen, "From False Paternalism to False Equality: Judicial Assaults on Feminist Community, Illinois 1869–1895," *Michigan Law Review* 84 (1986): 1518–43.

Bradwell v. *Illinois*, (83 U.S. 130 (1873).

be, woman's protector and defender. The natural and proper timidity and delicacy which belongs to the female sex evidently unfits it for many of the occupations of civil life. The constitution of the family organization, which is founded in the divine ordinance, as well as in the nature of things, indicates the domestic sphere as that which properly belongs to the domain and functions of womanhood. The harmony, not to say identity, of interests and views which belong or should belong to the family institution, is repugnant to the idea of a woman adopting a distinct and independent career from that of her husband. So firmly fixed was this sentiment in the founders of the common law that it became a maxim of that system of jurisprudence that a woman had no legal existence separate from her husband, who was regarded as her head and representative in the social state; and, notwithstanding some recent modifications of this civil status, many of the special rules of law flowing from and dependent upon this cardinal principle still exist in full force in most states. One of these is, that a married woman is incapable, without her husband's consent, of making contracts which shall be binding on her or him. This very incapacity was one circumstance which the supreme court of Illinois deemed important in rendering a married woman incompetent fully to perform the duties and trusts that belong to the office of an attorney and counselor.

It is true that many women are unmarried and not affected by any of the duties, complications, and incapacities arising out of the married state, but these are exceptions to the general rule. The paramount destiny and mission of woman are to fulfill the noble and benign offices of wife and mother. This is the law of the Creator. And the rules of civil society must be adapted to the general constitution of things, and cannot be based upon exceptional cases. . . .

Comstock Act, 1873

This "Act for the Suppression of Trade in, and Circulation of Obscene Literature and Articles of immoral Use" was passed at the urging of Anthony Comstock, the head of the New York Society for the Suppression of Vice. The first section prohibited the sale of the described materials in the District of Columbia and the territories; subsequent sections prohibited the sending of these materials through the mails or their importation into the United States. Enforcement, as historian Helen Horowitz has explained, was placed in the hands of a newly created "special agent in the United States Post Office with power to confiscate immoral matter in the mails and arrest those sending it."* In the 1870s, many states passed their own versions of the federal law.

The link of "obscene literature and articles of immoral use" reflected contemporary practice. Erotic literature and pornography were often sold in the same shops that sold condoms and other birth control devices; these devices, and substances offering to induce abortion, were often advertised in the pages of pornographic literature. Anthony Comstock included in this category writings on sexual reform and

*Helen Lefkowitz Horowitz, *Rereading Sex: Battles over Sexual Knowledge and Suppression in Nineteenth Century America* (New York: Alfred A. Knopf, 2002), pp. 381ff.

Public Laws of the United States of America, Passed at the Third Session of the Forty-Second Congress (Boston, 1873), p. 598.

free love. The law reflected a belief that both contraception and abortion were acts of interference with the natural order and with God's intentions. No distinction was made between drugs used for abortion and materials used for contraception, or indeed, pornographic pictures that encouraged masturbation; all were treated in the same terms. The law may have begun "as a measure to protect children against erotica" but it included "contraceptive information and materials and advertisements for abortion. . . . it was possible to construe this law as banning printed advocacy of free love."* Note the heavy penalties provided.

Be it enacted . . . That whoever, within the District of Columbia or any of the Territories of the United States . . . shall sell . . . or shall offer to sell, or to lend, or to give away, or in any manner to exhibit, or shall otherwise publish or offer to publish in any manner, or shall have in his possession, for any such purpose or purposes, any obscene book, pamphlet, paper, writing, advertisement, circular, print, picture, drawing or other representation, figure, or image on or of paper or other material, or any cast, instrument, or other article of an immoral nature, or any drug or medicine, or any article whatever, for the prevention of conception, or for causing unlawful abortion, or shall advertize the same for sale, or shall write or print, or cause to be written or printed, any card, circular, book, pamphlet, advertisement, or notice of any kind, stating when, where, how, or of whom, or by what means, any of the articles in this section . . . can be purchased or obtained, or shall manufacture, draw, or print, or in any wise make any of such articles, shall be deemed guilty of a misdemeanor, and on conviction thereof in any court of the United States . . . he shall be imprisoned at hard labor in the penitentiary for not less than six months nor more than five years for each offense, or fined not less than one hundred dollars nor more than two thousand dollars, with costs of court. . . .

Minor *v.* Happersett, *1874*

In 1872 suffragists in a number of places attempted to test the possibilities of the first section of the Fourteenth Amendment. "The power to regulate is one thing, the power to prevent is an entirely different thing," observed Virginia Minor, president of the Woman Suffrage Association of Missouri, and she presented herself at the polls in St. Louis in 1872. When the registrar refused to permit her to register to vote, she and her husband sued him for denying her one of the "privileges and immunities of citizenship"; when they lost the case they appealed to the Supreme Court.

In a unanimous opinion the justices held that if the authors of the Constitution had intended that women should vote, they would have said so explicitly. The decision of the Court meant that woman suffrage could not be developed by way of a quiet reinterpretation of the Constitution but would require an explicit amendment to the Constitution or a series of revisions in the laws of the states.

*Horowitz, *Rereading Sex*, p. 385.

Minor v. *Happersett*, 88 U.S. 162 (1874).

MR. CHIEF JUSTICE MORRISON R. WAITE DELIVERED THE OPINION OF THE COURT:

The question is presented in this case, whether, since the adoption of the fourteenth amendment, a woman, who is a citizen of the United States and of the State of Missouri, is a voter in that State, notwithstanding the provision of the constitution and laws of the State, which confine the right of suffrage to men alone. . . . The argument is, that as a woman, born or naturalized in the United States and subject to the jurisdiction thereof, is a citizen of the United States and of the State in which she resides, she has the right of suffrage as one of the privileges and immunities of her citizenship, which the State cannot by its laws or constitution abridge.

There is no doubt that women may be citizens. They are persons, and by the fourteenth amendment "all persons born or naturalized in the United States and subject to the jurisdiction thereof" are expressly declared to be "citizens of the United States and of the State wherein they reside." But, in our opinion, it did not need this amendment to give them that position . . . sex has never been made one of the elements of citizenship in the United States. In this respect men have never had an advantage over women. The same laws precisely apply to both. The fourteenth amendment did not affect the citizenship of women any more than it did of men . . . Mrs. Minor . . . has always been a citizen from her birth, and entitled to all the privileges and immunities of citizenship.

If the right of suffrage is one of the necessary privileges of a citizen of the United States, then the constitution and laws of Missouri confining it to men are in violation of the Constitution of the United States, as amended, and consequently void. The direct question is, therefore, presented whether all citizens are necessarily voters.

The Constitution does not define the privileges and immunities of citizens. For that definition we must look elsewhere. In this case we need not determine what they are, but only whether suffrage is necessarily one of them.

It certainly is nowhere made so in express terms. The United States has no voters in the States of its own creation. The elective officers of the United States are all elected directly or indirectly by state voters. . . . it cannot for a moment be doubted that if it had been intended to make all citizens of the United States voters, the framers of the Constitution would not have left it to implication. . . .

It is true that the United States guarantees to every State a republican form of government. . . . No particular government is designated as republican, neither is the exact form to be guaranteed, in any manner especially designated. . . . When the Constitution was adopted . . . all the citizens of the States were not invested with the right of suffrage. In all, save perhaps New Jersey, this right was only bestowed upon men and not upon all of them. . . . Under these circumstances it is certainly now too late to contend that a government is not republican, within the meaning of this guaranty in the Constitution, because women are not made voters. . . . If suffrage was intended to be included within its obligations, language better adapted to express that intent would most certainly have been employed. . . .

. . . For nearly ninety years the people have acted upon the idea that the Constitution, when it conferred citizenship, did not necessarily confer the right of suffrage. If uniform practice long continued can settle the construction of so important an instrument as the Constitution of the United States confessedly is, most certainly it has been done here. Our province is to decide what the law is, not to declare what it should be.

We have given this case the careful consideration its importance demands. If the law is wrong, it ought to be changed; but the power for that is not with us. . . . No argument as to woman's need of suffrage can be considered. We can only act upon her rights as they exist. . . .

Page Act, 1875

Named for the California congressman Horace F. Page, who was its most ardent supporter, the Page Act was the nation's first federal regulation of immigration. The legislation was fueled by a mixture of policies: hostility to unscrupulous entrepreneurs who recruited unskilled workers, pressured them into multiyear contracts, brought them to the United States, and then undercut established wages; authentic fears of prostitution rings; and racist hostility to Asians. Knowledge that Chinese families practiced polygamy and foot binding fueled generalizations about immorality and sexual exploitation.

The Page Act gestured in the direction of outlawing contract labor but actually focused on traffic in women. It made the American consular officers in Chinese ports responsible for interrogating all prospective immigrants; in practice, any woman who wished to travel to the United States had to first persuade the consul that she was not a prostitute. Memories of this humiliating experience have been passed down over many generations in some Chinese American families.

The impact of the law was quickly felt. In the two years between 1880 and 1882, some 50,000 Chinese men, but only 220 Chinese women, entered the United States. The much more expansive Chinese Exclusion Acts, the first of which was passed in 1882, barred virtually all but elite Chinese from entering the United States and reiterated the exclusion of prostitutes.

The principle that prospective immigrant women had the additional burden of proving their morality persisted. The 1891 Immigration Act required all pregnant women to prove that they were married. It also provided for the expulsion of immigrants who became a public charge within a year of entry. That time limit was gradually expanded—to two years, then three, then five. In 1910, a new statute provided that alien women who turned to sex work could be deported at any time.

The second gatekeeping mechanism in the Page Act (see the final paragraph) took on renewed vigor in later acts and with the construction of immigrant receiving stations—Ellis Island in New York Harbor in 1892 and Angel Island in San Francisco Bay in 1910. At the latter, Asian immigrant women tended to be detained longer than men, as well as grilled about their sexual character, plans to marry (if single), and ability to support themselves in the United States. See photograph on p. 382.

Be it enacted . . . that in determining whether the immigration of any subject of China, Japan, or any Oriental country, to the United States, is free and voluntary . . . it shall be the duty of the . . . consul of the United States residing at the port from which it is proposed to convey such subjects, in any vessels enrolled or licensed in the United States. . . to ascertain whether such immigrant has entered into a contract or agreement for a term of service within the United States, for lewd and immoral purposes; and if there be such contract or agreement, the said . . . consul shall not deliver the required permit or certificate. . .

Page Act of 1875, 43rd Cong., 2nd sess., ch. 141.

. . . That the importation into the United States of women for the purposes of prostitution is hereby forbidden; and all contracts and agreements in relation thereto, made in advance or in pursuance of such illegal importation and purposes, are hereby declared void; and whoever shall knowingly and willfully import, or cause any importation of, women into the United States for the purposes of prostitution, or shall knowingly or willfully hold, or attempt to hold, any woman to such purposes, in pursuance of such illegal importation and contract or agreement, shall be deemed guilty of a felony, and, on conviction thereof, shall be imprisoned not exceeding five years and pay a fine not exceeding five thousand dollars . . .

. . . That it shall be unlawful for aliens of the following [two] classes to immigrate into the United States, namely, persons who are undergoing a sentence for conviction in their own country of felonious crimes other than political . . . and women "imported for the purposes of prostitution." Every vessel arriving in the United States may be inspected under the direction of the collector of the port at which it arrives, if he shall have reason to believe that any such obnoxious persons are on board. . . .

BARBARA SICHERMAN

Reading *Little Women:* The Many Lives of a Text

Why should girls be learn'd and wise?
Books only serve to spoil their eyes.
The studious eye but faintly twinkles.
And reading paves the way to wrinkles.
—*John Trumbull, 1773*

Although there was much skepticism about whether advanced learning was good for women, the early republic was a time of a transformation of educational opportunity. A virtual revolution in literacy was under way, encouraged by the transition of the economy to a print culture and reinforced by a technology that made printed materials more widely available and injected them into new areas of life. Reading was linked to rationality, upward mobility, and control of one's own life. Although literacy did not increase at the same rate for each class or each sex within each class, what might be called a "literacy gap" between free white men and women gradually closed during the years before the Civil War. As early as the 1780s, 80 percent of the white women of urban New England were literate; they seem to have been the most literate women in the Western world.

The gains were specific to region. The South lagged far behind; as late as 1850 one out of five white women in the South was illiterate. Literacy was denied slaves by law; free blacks lacked both opportunity and institutional support for extended study. Yet urban African Americans quickly narrowed the gap between the races after the Civil War.

In a world in which only a few thousand women were in a college or university in any given year, and in which even high school education was rare, most "higher" education was necessarily self-education. Women shaped their intellectual lives out of their own diary keeping, letter writing, and reading. They chose books that had meaning for their lives. One book came to have more meaning for more women than perhaps any other contemporary publication: Louisa May Alcott's *Little Women.* Barbara Sicherman examines this phenomenon.

What elements of *Little Women* did its first readers respond to? Did the meaning of *Little Women* change over time? What issues in women's lives did it address? How do you account for its continuing popularity? If you have read *Little Women* and viewed one or more of the film versions, what differences of emphasis do you discern?

"I have read and re-read 'Little Women' and it never seems to grow old," fifteen-year-old Jane Addams confided to a friend.[1] Writing in 1876, Addams did not say why she liked *Little Women.* But her partiality was by no means unusual among women, and even some men, of her generation. Louisa May Alcott's tale of growing up female was an unexpected success when it appeared in the fall of 1868. Already a classic when Addams wrote, the book has been called "the most popular girls' story in American literature"; a century and a quarter after publication, there are twenty editions in print.[2]

The early history of this publishing phenomenon is full of ironies. Not the least of them is the author's expressed distaste for the project. When Thomas Niles Jr., literary editor of the respected Boston firm of Roberts Brothers, asked Alcott to write a *"girls' story,"* the author tartly observed in her journal: "I plod away, though I don't enjoy this sort of thing. Never liked girls or knew many, except my sisters, but our queer plays and experiences may prove interesting, though I doubt it."[3] After delivering twelve chapters in June 1868, she claimed that both she and her editor found them *"dull."*[4] Niles assured her that he was "pleased—I ought to be more emphatic & say delighted,—so *please* to consider 'judgement' as favorable"; the following month he predicted that the book would " 'hit.' "[5] Influenced perhaps by the verdict of "some girls" who had pronounced the manuscript " 'splendid!' " Alcott reconsidered while correcting proof: "It reads better than I expected. Not a bit sensational, but simple and true, for we really lived most of it." Of the youngsters who liked it, she observed: "As it is for them, they are the best critics, so I should be satisfied."[6]

The informal "readers' report" was right on target. Published in early October 1868, the first printing (2,000 copies) of *Little Women, or, Meg, Jo, Beth and Amy* sold out within the month. A sequel appeared the following April, with only the designation *Part Second* differentiating it from the original. By the end of the year some 38,000 copies (of both parts) were in print, with another 32,000 in 1870. Nearly 200,000 copies had been printed by Roberts Brothers by January 1888, two months before Alcott's death.[7] Like it or not, with this book Alcott established her niche in the expanding market for juvenile literature.

Perhaps even more remarkable than *Little Women's* initial success has been its longevity. It topped a list of forty books compiled by the Federal Bureau of Education in 1925 that "all children should read before they are sixteen."[8] . . . On a [1976] bicentennial list of the best eleven American children's books, *Little Women, The Adventures of Tom Sawyer,* and *The Adventures of Huckleberry Finn* were the only nineteenth-century titles. Like most iconic works, *Little Women* has been transmuted into other media, into song and opera, theater, radio, and film. A comic strip even surfaced briefly in 1988 in the revamped *Ms.*[9]

Polls and statistics do not begin to do justice to the *Little Women* phenomenon. Reading the book has been a rite of passage for generations of adolescent and preadolescent females of the comfortable classes. It still elicits powerful narratives of love and passion.[10] In a 1982 essay on how she became a writer, Cynthia Ozick declared: "I read 'Little Women' a thousand times. Ten thousand. I am no longer incognito, not even to myself. I am Jo in her 'vortex'; not Jo exactly, but some Jo-of-the-future. I am under an enchantment: Who I truly am must be deferred, waited for and waited for."[11] Ozick's avowal encapsulates recurrent themes in readers' accounts: the deep, almost inexplicable emotions engendered by the novel; the passionate identification with Jo March, the feisty tomboy heroine who publishes stories in her teens; and—allowing for exaggeration—a pattern of multiple readings. Numerous women who grew up in the 1940s and 1950s report that they read the book yearly or more during their teens or earlier; some confide that they continue to read it as adults, though less frequently. Presumably for them, as for Jane Addams, the story did not grow old.

One of many intriguing questions about *Little Women* is how and why the "dull" book, the girls' story by a woman who claimed she never liked girls, captivated so many readers. An added irony is that Alcott, the product of an unconventional upbringing, whose eccentric transcendentalist father self-consciously tested his child-rearing theories on his daughters, took them to live in a commune, and failed utterly as a breadwinner, should write what many contemporaries considered the definitive story of American family life.[12] . . .

EARLY PUBLISHING AND MARKETING HISTORY

Alcott claimed that she kept on with *Little Women* because "lively, simple books are very much needed for girls, and perhaps I can supply the need."[13] . . . She may have regretted being channeled into one type of literature, but she was extremely well paid for her efforts, a source of considerable pride to a woman whose father was so feckless about money.[14]

Juvenile literature was entering a new phase in the 1860s at the very time Alcott was refashioning her career. . . . In contrast to the overtly religious antebellum stories, in which both sexes were expected to be good and domesticated, the new juvenile market was becoming increasingly segmented by gender. An exciting new adventure literature for boys developed after 1850, featuring escape from domesticity and female authority. Seeking to tap into a new market, Niles asked Alcott to write a "girls' story[.]" . . . Although people of all ages and both sexes read *Little Women,* the book evolved for the emerging female youth market, the "young adults" in the transitional period between childhood and adulthood that would soon be labeled adolescence.[15]

These readers had an unusual say in determining Jo's fate. Eager to capitalize on his experiment, Niles urged Alcott to add a chapter "in which allusions might be made to something in the future."[16] Employing a metaphor well suited to a writer who engaged in theatrical performances most of her life, the volume concludes: "So grouped the curtain falls upon Meg, Jo, Beth and Amy. Whether it ever rises again, depends upon the reception given to the first act of the domestic drama, called 'LITTLE WOMEN.'"[17] Reader response to Alcott's floater was positive but complicated her task. Reluctant to depart from autobiography, Alcott insisted that by rights Jo should remain a "literary spinster." But she felt pressured by readers to imagine a different fate for her heroine. The day she began work on the sequel, she observed: "Girls write to ask who the little women marry, as if that was the only end and aim of a woman's life. I *won't* marry Jo to Laurie to please anyone." To foil her readers, she created a "funny match" for Jo—the middle-aged, bumbling German professor, Friedrich Bhaer.[18]

The aspect of the book that has frustrated generations of readers—the foreclosing of marriage between Jo and Laurie—thus represents a compromise between Alcott and her initial audience. Paradoxically, this seeming misstep has probably been a major factor in the story's enduring success. If Jo had remained a spinster, as Alcott wished, or if she had married the attractive and wealthy hero, as readers hoped, it is unlikely that the book would have had such a wide appeal. Rather, the problematic ending contributed to *Little Women's* popularity, the lack of satisfying closure helping to keep the story alive, something to ponder, return to, reread, perhaps with the hope of a different resolution. Alcott's refusal of the conventionally happy ending represented by a pairing of Jo and Laurie and her insistence on a "funny match" to the rumpled and much older professor effectively subvert adolescent romantic ideals. The absence of a compelling love plot has also made it easier for generations of readers to ignore the novel's ending when Jo becomes Mother Bhaer and to retain the image of Jo as the questing teenage tomboy.[19]

At the same time, an adolescent reader, struggling with her appearance and unruly impulses while contemplating the burdens of future womanhood, might find it reassuring that her fictional counterpart emerges happily, if not perhaps ideally, from similar circumstances. For Jo is loved. And she has choices. She turns down the charming but erratic hero, who consoles himself by marrying her pretty and vain younger sister, Amy. Professor Bhaer is no schoolgirl's hero, but Jo believes that he is better suited to her than Laurie. The crucial point is that the choice is hers, its quirkiness another sign of her much-prized individuality.[20] Jo gives up writing sensation stories because her prospective husband considers them unworthy, but she makes it clear that she intends to contribute to the support of their future family.

By marrying off the sisters in the second part, Alcott bowed to young women's interest in romance. The addition of the marriage to the quest plot enabled *Little Women* to touch the essential bases for middle-class female readers in the late nineteenth century. In this regard, it was unusual for its time. . . . The conjunction of quest and marriage plots helps to account for the book's staying power: it is difficult to imagine large numbers of adolescent female readers in the twentieth century gravitating to a book in which the heroine remained single.[21] *Little Women* took off with the publication of the second part in April 1869. A Concord neighbor called it "the rage in '69 as 'Pinafore' was in '68."[22] A savvy judge of the market, Niles urged Alcott to "'Make hay while the Sunshines'" and did everything he could to keep her name before the public.[23] Shortly after the appearance of *Little Women, Part Second,* Roberts Brothers brought out an augmented edition of her first critical success under the title, *Hospital Sketches and Camp and Fireside Stories,* and in succeeding years published *An Old-Fashioned Girl* (1870) and *Little Men* (1871), a sequel to *Little Women*. . . .

Reviewers stressed the realism of her characters and scenes; readers recognized themselves in her work. Thirteen-year-old Annie Adams of Fair Haven, Vermont, wrote *St. Nicholas,* the most prestigious of the new children's magazines, that she and her three sisters each resembled one of the March sisters (she was Jo): "So, you see, I was greatly interested in 'Little Women,' as I could appreciate it so well; and it seemed to me as if Miss Alcott must have seen us four girls before she wrote the story."[24] Girls not only read themselves into *Little Women,* they elaborated on it and incorporated the story into their lives. In 1872 the five Lukens sisters from Brinton, Pennsylvania, sent Alcott a copy of their home newspaper, "Little Things," which was modeled after "The Pickwick Portfolio" produced by the March sisters. Alcott responded with encouragement, asked for further details, and subscribed to the paper . . . She took their aspirations seriously, providing frank, practical advice about magazines, publishers, and authors' fees to these budding literary women.[25]

There was, then, a reciprocal relationship between the characters and home life depicted in *Little Women* and the lives of middle-class American girls. An unusual feature of this identification was the perception that author and heroine were interchangeable. Alcott's work was marketed to encourage the illusion not only that Jo was Alcott but that Alcott was Jo. When Alcott traveled in Europe in 1870, Niles encouraged her to send for publication "'Jo's Letters from Abroad to the March's [sic] at Home'" . . .

Readers responded in kind. An ad for *Little Women* quotes a letter written by "Nelly" addressed to "Dear Jo, or Miss Alcott": "We have all been reading 'Little Women,' and we liked it so much I could not help wanting to write to you. We think *you* are perfectly splendid; I like you better every time I read it. We were all so disappointed about your not marrying Laurie; I cried over that part,— . . . Blurring the lines between author and character, the writer also requested a picture, wished the recipient improved health, and invited her to visit.[26]

The illusion that she was the youthful and unconventional Jo made Alcott a more approachable author. But the conflation of author and character had its risks. Young readers who formed an image of the author as Jo, a teenager for most of the novel, were startled by Alcott's appearance. When the Lukens sisters informed her that some "friends" had been disappointed in her picture, Alcott replied that she could not understand why people insisted Jo was young "when she is said to be 30 at the end of the book . . . After seeing the photograph it is hardly necessary to say that Jo and L.M.A. are *not* one, & that the latter is a tired out old lady of 42."[27]

With the publication of *Little Women, Part Second,* Alcott became a celebrity. Correspondents demanded her photograph and autograph seekers descended on her home while she "dodge[d] into the woods *à la* Hawthorne."[28] . . . Alcott also drew more serious admirers, some of whom, like the Lukens sisters, sought her literary advice. In the 1860s and 1870s authorship was the most respected female vocation—and the best paid. . . .

Alcott was a well-respected writer during her lifetime, an era of relatively inclusive and nonhierarchical definitions of literature. An American literature course taken by Jane Addams at Rockford Female Seminary in 1878–79 covered authors of domestic fiction, Alcott among them.[29] But her literary reputation transcended the category. A review of *Little Men* pronounced: "Even thus early in her brief history as a country and a nation, America can boast a long list of classics—Prescott, Irving, Hawthorne, Longfellow—and Time, the great sculptor will one day carve Miss Alcott's name among them."[30] . . .

A teenage girl contemplating a literary career could dream of becoming a published author who, like Alcott, might produce a beloved and immortal work. At a time when young women were encouraged, even expected, to take part in the literary activities that suffused middle-class domestic life, such success was not beyond imagining. From James S. Hart's [*Manual of American Literature* (1873)], a reader could learn that Alcott began writing for publication at sixteen and, by hard work and perseverance, became both famous and self-supporting by her pen in her late thirties.[31] The real female American success story was Alcott's, not Jo's.

There were, then, many reasons why a young woman seeking a literary career in the 1870s and early 1880s would look to Alcott as a model. Most important was the story that brought pleasure to so many. . . . The contrast with Martha Finley's *Elsie Dinsmore* (1867), a story in which strict obedience is exacted from children—to the point of whipping—is striking. In this first of many volumes, the lachrymose and devoutly religious heroine is put upon by relatives and by her father, who punishes her for refusing to play the piano on the Sabbath. Elsie holds fast to her principles but is otherwise self-abnegating in the extreme: it is difficult to imagine her even trying to have fun. . . .

The fictional world of *Little Women* is strikingly different. Despite the use of John Bunyan's *Pilgrim's Progress* as a framing device, an older Calvinist worldview that emphasized sin and obedience to the deity has been replaced by a moral outlook in which self-discipline and doing good to others come first.[32] Consonant with *Little Women's* new moral tone, so congenial to an expanding middle class, are its informal style and rollicking escapades. Aided by her love of the theater and influenced as well by her youthful idol, Charles Dickens, Alcott was a wonderful painter of dramatic scenes; some were heartbreaking, but many were high-spirited depictions of frolics, games, and theatrical productions.[33] She also had an ear for young people's language: her substitution of dialogue for the long passages of moralizing narrative that characterized most girls' books gave her story a compelling sense of immediacy. So did her use of slang, for which critics often faulted her, but which must have endeared her to young readers. Finally, the beautifully realized portrait of Jo March as tomboy, one of the first of its kind, spoke to changing standards of girlhood. Beginning in the 1860s, tomboys were not only tolerated but even admired—up to a point, the point at which they were expected to become women.[34] Perhaps it was fitting after all that it was Alcott, writing of her idiosyncratic childhood in the 1840s, who identified a new type of American girlhood for the 1870s.[35] . . .

JO AS A LITERARY AND INTELLECTUAL MODEL

Reading Alcott became a necessary ritual for children of the comfortable classes. Growing up at a time and in a class that conferred leisure on its young, children devoted considerable time and energy to literary pursuits. *Little Women* was a way station en route to more adult books. But it was also a text that acquired its own cachet. Alcott was such an accepted part of childhood that even Theodore Roosevelt declared, "at the cost of being deemed effeminate," that he "worshiped" *Little Men, Little Women,* and *An Old-Fashioned Girl.*[36] . . .

Not all of Alcott's early readers focused on Jo; some were taken with the saga of the entire March family, which invited comparisons with their own. Charlotte Perkins Gilman, for example, who grew up in genteel poverty after her father abandoned the family, liked the fact that in Alcott . . . , "the heroes and heroines were almost always poor, and good, while the rich people were generally bad."[37] . . .

Jo March . . . fueled the literary aspirations of M. Carey Thomas, one of Alcott's early readers, during the critical years of early adolescence. In the fall of 1869, the year of *Little Women's* great success, Thomas and her cousin Frank Smith adopted the personae of Jo and Laurie, although as Quakers they should not have been reading fiction at all. At the ages of twelve and fifteen respectively, Thomas and Smith began addressing each other and signing their letters as Jo and Laurie; they meted out other roles to friends and relatives. . . .

When Thomas began a journal in 1870 at age thirteen, she did so in Jo's name. Declaring at the outset: "Ain't going to be sentimental/'No no not for Jo' (not Joe)," she had much in common with Alcott's heroine.[38] Both were "bookworms" and tomboys; both desired independence. Like Jo, Thomas wished to do something "splendid." In early adolescence her ambitions were still diffuse, but they centered on becoming a famous writer, a famous *woman* writer—"Jo (not Joe)." Her life was suffused with literature, with writing as well as reading: in addition to keeping a journal, she wrote poetry, kept a commonplace book, and complied lists of favorite books and poems, some of them annotated. As she gravitated to such champions of aestheticism as Algernon Charles Swinburne and Dante Gabriel Rossetti, by her early twenties she had outgrown Alcott and other writers who upheld morality in their art. But her close friend Bessie King acknowledged the importance of their childhood play in 1879, when Thomas took the audacious step of starting graduate study in Germany: "Somehow today I went back to those early days when our horizon was so limited yet so full of light & our path lay as plain before us. It all came of reading over Miss Alcott's books now the quintescence [sic] of Philistinism then a Bible. . . . Doesn't thee remember when to turn out a 'Jo' was the height of ambition"?[39]

At the time Thomas was so engaged with *Little Women,* she was already a feminist. Sensitive to any gender restriction or slight, whether from people she knew or from biblical or scientific sources, she resolved at fifteen to disprove female inferiority by advancing her own education.[40] Despite its inception as a domestic story, then, Thomas read *Little Women* as a female bildungsroman, as did many women after her. This has in many ways been the most important reading, the one that has made the book such a phenomenon for so many years.

With its secular recasting of *Pilgrim's Progress, Little Women* transforms Christian's allegorical search for the Celestial City into the quintessential female quest plot. In a chapter entitled "Castles in the Air," each of the March sisters reveals her deepest ambition. In its loving depictions of the sisters' struggles to attain their goals (Jo to be a famous writer, Amy an artist, and Meg mistress of a lovely house), *Little Women* succeeds in authorizing female vocation and individuality. Nor did Alcott rule out the possibility of future artistic creativity: although married and managing a large household and school, Jo has not entirely given up her literary dreams, nor Amy her artistic ones. Beth, who has no ambition other than "to stay at home safe with father and mother, and help take care of the family," dies because she can find no way of growing up; her mysterious illness may be read as a failure of imagination, her inability to build castles in the air.[41]

In Jo, Alcott creates a portrait of female creativity that was not traditionally available to women:

> Every few weeks she would shut herself up in her room, put on her scribbling suit, and "fall into a vortex," as she expressed it, writing away at her novel with all her heart and soul, for till that was finished she could find no peace. . . .
>
> She did not think herself a genius by any means; but when the writing fit came on, she gave herself up to it with entire abandon, and led a blissful life, unconscious of want, care, or bad weather, while she sat safe and happy in an imaginary world, full of friends almost as real and dear to her as any in the flesh. Sleep forsook her eyes, meals stood untasted, day and night were all too short to enjoy the happiness which blessed her only at such times, and made these hours worth living, even if they bore no other fruit. The divine afflatus usually lasted a week or two, and then she emerged from her "vortex" hungry, sleepy, cross, or despondent.[42]

Alcott's portrait of concentrated purpose—which describes her own creative practice—is as far removed as it could be from the ordinary lot of women, at least any adult woman. Jo not only has a room of her own; she also has the leisure—and the license—to remove herself from all obligation to others. Jo was important to young women like Thomas because there were so few of her—in literature or in life. . . .

More conventional readers of Thomas's era could find in *Little Women* practical advice on two subjects of growing concern to women: economic opportunities and marriage. Alcott was well qualified to advise on the former because of her long years of struggle in the marketplace. . . . Middle-class women's need to be able to earn a living is a central motif in *Little Women,* as it was in Alcott's life. . . . Mr. March's economic setback, like Bronson Alcott's, forces his daughters into the labor market. Their jobs (as governess and companion) are depicted as mainly unrewarding, although Jo's literary career is described with loving particularity. . . . But although the March sisters marry, Marmee March, who wishes no greater joy for her daughters than a happy marriage, declares that it is better to remain single than to marry without love. Opportunities for self-respecting singlehood and women's employment went hand in hand, as Alcott knew.[43]

If Alcott articulated issues highly pertinent to young women of her era, Jo's continued appeal suggests not only the dearth of fictional heroines to foster dreams of glory but the continued absence of real-life models. Perhaps that is why Simone de Beauvoir was so attracted to *Little Women*, in which she thought she "caught a glimpse of my future self":

> I identified passionately with Jo, the intellectual. . . . She wrote: in order to imitate her more completely, I composed two or three short stories. . . . [T]he relationship between Jo and Laurie touched me to the heart. Later, I had no doubt, they would marry one another; so it was possible for maturity to bring the promises made in childhood to fruition instead of denying them: this thought filled me with renewed hope. . . . [I]n *Little Women* Jo was superior to her sisters, who were either more virtuous or more beautiful than she, because of her passion for knowledge and the vigor of her thinking. . . . I, too, felt I was entitled to consider my taste in reading and my scholastic success as tokens of a personal superiority which would be borne out by the future. I became in my own eyes a character out of a novel.[44]

De Beauvoir found in Jo a model of authentic selfhood, someone she could emulate in the present and through whom she could read—and invent—her own destiny. It was a future full of possibility, open rather than closed, intellectual and literary rather than domestic. By fictionalizing her own life, de Beauvoir could more readily contemplate a career as a writer and an intellectual, no matter how improbable such an outcome seemed to her family. . . . Although de Beauvoir later claimed that she first learned from *Little Women* that "marriage was not necessary," she responded to the romance as well as the quest plot. Her conviction that Jo and Laurie would marry some day and the "renewed hope" this belief gave her suggest the power of wish fulfillment and the reader's capacity to create her own text. There is no textual basis for this belief: Jo and Laurie each marry someone else; each is a parent by the end of the story. De Beauvoir's reading is therefore not just a matter of filling in gaps but of rewriting the text. Her powerful commentary suggests the creativity of the reading experience and the permeability of boundaries between life and art: lives can be fictionalized, texts can be rewritten, art can become life and life art.

Not all women read with the intensity of Thomas or de Beauvoir. But there is considerable evidence that, from the time of her creation until the recent past, Jo March provided for young women of the comfortable classes a model of female independence and of intellectual and literary achievement. This is not the only way of reading *Little Women*, but it constitutes a major interpretive strand, particularly in the twentieth century. Testimony on this point began as soon as the book was published and persists today among women who grew up in the 1940s and 1950s.[45] Thomas, whose love relations were with women, never mentions the marriage plot, but for de Beauvoir, writing in the twentieth century, it was both important and compatible with a quest plot.

INFLECTIONS OF CLASS AND CULTURE

. . . For African American women, in the nineteenth century at least, class rather than race was probably the primary determinant of reading practices. Both Mary Church Terrell, a graduate of Oberlin College, and Ida B. Wells, the slave-born daughter of a carpenter and "a famous cook" who became a journalist and reformer, read Alcott. Terrell claimed that her books "were received with an acclaim among the young people of this country which has rarely if ever been equaled and never surpassed," while Wells observed: "I had formed my ideals on the best of Dickens's stories, Louisa May Alcott's, Mrs. A.D.T. Whitney's, and Charlotte Brontë's books, and Oliver Optic's stories for boys." Neither singled out *Little Women;* both seem to have read Alcott as part of the standard fare of an American middle-class childhood.[46]

For African American writer Ann Petry, [who died in 1997 at the age of 89,] *Little Women* was much more than that. On the occasion of her induction into the Connecticut Women's Hall of Fame, she noted her admiration for women writers who had preceded and set the stage for her—"'Think of Louisa May Alcott.'" *Little Women* was the first book Petry "read on her own as a child." Her comments are reminiscent of those of de Beauvoir and other writers: "I couldn't stop reading because I had encountered Jo March. I felt as though I was part of Jo and she was part of me. I, too, was a tomboy and a misfit and kept a secret diary. . . . She said things like 'I wish I was a horse, then I could run for miles in this splendid air and not lose my breath.' I found myself wishing the same thing whenever I ran for the sheer joy of running. She was a would-be writer—and so was I."[47] . . .

Some working-class women found *Little Women* . . . banal. Dorothy Richardson, a journalist, suggests as much in *The Long Day,* an account of her life among the working class. In an arresting episode, Richardson ridicules the reading preferences of her fellow workers in a paper box factory. The plot of a favorite novel, Laura Jean Libbey's *Little Rosebud's Lovers; or, A Cruel Revenge,* is recounted by one of the workers as a tale of a woman's triumph over all sorts of adversity, including abductions and a false marriage to one of the villains. When Richardson summarizes *Little Women,* a coworker dismisses it: "'[T]hat's no story—that's just everyday happenings. I don't see what's the use of putting things like that in books. I'll bet any money that lady what wrote it knew all them boys and girls. They just sound like real, live people; and when you was telling about them I could just see them as plain as plain could be. . . . I suppose farmer folks likes them kind of stories. . . . They ain't used to the same styles of anything that us city folks are.' "[48]

The box makers found the characters in *Little Women* "real"—an interesting point in itself—but did not care to enter its narrative framework. Though they were not class conscious in a political sense, their awareness of their class position may account at least in part for their disinterest in a story whose heroines, despite economic reverses, had the leisure to pursue their interests in art, music, and literature and could expect to live in suburban cottages, conditions out of reach for most working-class women. Since *their* "everyday happenings" were poverty and exhausting work, the attraction of fictions about working girls who preserved their virtue and came into great wealth, either through marriage or disclosure of their middle- or upper-class origins, is understandable. Such denouements would have seemed just as likely—or unlikely—as a future in a suburban cottage. In the absence, in story or in life, of a female success tradition of moving up the occupational ladder, the "Cinderella tale" of marrying up was the nearest thing to a Horatio Alger story for working-class women.[49]

Reading practices depend on cultural as well as class location. It is a telling commentary on class in America that some Jewish immigrant women, who would be defined as working class on the basis of family income and occupation, not only enjoyed *Little Women* but also found in it a vehicle for envisioning a new and higher status.[50] For them, Alcott's classic provided a model for transcending their status as ethnic outsiders and for gaining access to American life and culture. It was a first step into the kind of middle-class family life rejected by Thomas and de Beauvoir. These immigrants found the book liberating and read it as a success story—but of a different kind.

In *My Mother and I,* Elizabeth G. Stern (1889–1954) charts the cultural distance a Jewish immigrant woman traveled from Russia and a midwestern urban ghetto to the American mainstream: she graduates from college, studies social work marries a professional man, and becomes a social worker and writer.[51] *Little Women* occupies a crucial place in the story. After the narrator comes across it in a stack of newspapers in a rag shop, the book utterly engrosses her: "I sat in the dim light of the rag shop and read the browned pages of that ragged copy of 'Little Women.' . . . [N]o book I have opened has meant as much to me as did that small volume telling in simple words such as I myself spoke, the story of an American childhood in New England. I had found a new literature, the literature of childhood." She had also found the literature of America: "I no longer read the little paper-bound Yiddish novelettes which father then sold. In the old rag shop loft I devoured the English magazines and newspapers." Of the books her teachers brought her from the public library, she writes:

> Far more marvellous than the fairy stories were to me in the ghetto street the stories of American child life, all the Alcott and the Pepper books. The pretty mothers, the childish ideals, the open gardens, the homes of many rooms were as unreal to me as the fairy stories. But reading of them made my aspirations beautiful.
>
> My books were doors that gave me entrance into another world. Often I think that I did not grow up in the ghetto but in the books I read as a child in the ghetto. The life in Soho passed me by and did not touch me, once I began to read.[52] . . .

Stern was not unique in reading *Little Women* as a vehicle for assimilation into American middle-class life or in conflating

"American" and "middle class." More than half a century later, a Jewish male writer explored the novel's appeal as an "American" book:

> [T]o me, a first generation American, raised in an Orthodox Jewish house-hold where more Yiddish was spoken than English, everything about *Little Women* was exotic. It was all so American, so full of a life I did not know but desperately hoped to be part of, an America full of promises, hopes, optimisms, an America where everyone had a chance to become somebody wonderful like Jo March—Louisa May Alcott who (I had discovered that the Marches and the Alcotts were almost identical) did become, with this story book that I adored, world famous.[53]

What had been realistic to the early middle- and upper-middle-class WASP readers of *Little Women* was "exotic" to Jewish immigrants a generation or two later. Could there be a better illustration of the importance of historical location in determining meaning? . . .

One of the Jewish immigrants for whom Alcott's success proved inspiring was Mary Antin, a fervent advocate of assimilation into American life. Alcott's were the children's books she "remember[ed] with the greatest delight" (followed by boys' adventure books, especially Alger's). Antin, who published poems in English in her teens and contemplated a literary career, lingered over the biographical entries she found in an encyclopedia. She "could not resist the temptation to study out the exact place . . . where my name would belong. I saw that it would come not far from 'Alcott, Louisa M.'; and I covered my face with my hands, to hide the silly, baseless joy in it."[54] We have come full circle. Eager to assimilate, Antin responded in ways reminiscent of Alcott's early native-born and middle-class readers who admired her success as an author. Antin, too, could imagine a successful American career for herself, a career for which Alcott was still the model.

CONCLUSION

Not all readers of *Little Women* read the same text. This is literally the case, since the story went through many editions. Not until 1880 did it appear in one volume, illustrated in this case and purged of some of its slang.[55] Since then there have been numerous editions and many publishers. I have been concerned here with the changing meaning of the story for different audiences and with historical continuities as well. For many middle-class readers, early and later, *Little Women* provided a model of womanhood that deviated from conventional gender norms, a continuity that suggests how little these norms changed in their essentials from the late 1860s to the 1960s. Reading individualistically, they viewed Jo as an intellectual and a writer, the liberated woman they sought to become. No matter that Jo marries and raises a family; such readers remember the young Jo, the teenager who is far from beautiful, struggles with her temper, is both a bookworm and the center of action, and dreams of literary glory while helping to support her family with her pen. These readers for the most part took for granted their right to a long and privileged childhood, largely exempt from the labor market. Jewish women who immigrated to the United States in their youth could not assume such a childhood. Nor were those raised in Orthodox Jewish households brought up on an individualistic philosophy. Their school experiences and reading—American books like *Little Women*—made them aware of different standards of decorum and material life that we tend to associate with class, but that are cultural as well. For some of these readers, *Little Women* offered a fascinating glimpse into an American world. Of course we know, as they did not, that the world Alcott depicted was vanishing, even as she wrote. Nevertheless, that fictional world, along with their school encounters, provided a vision of what life, American life, could be.

Can readers do whatever they like with texts? Yes and no. As we have seen, *Little Women* has been read in many ways, depending not only on when and by whom it was read but also on readers' experiences and aspirations. It has been read as a romance or as a quest, or both. It has been read as a family drama that validates virtue over wealth. It has been read as a how-to manual by immigrants who wanted to assimilate into American, middle-class life and as a means of escaping that life by women who knew its gender constraints too well. For many, especially in the early years, *Little Women* was read through the life of the author, whose literary success exceeded that of her fictional persona.

At the same time, both the passion *Little Women* has engendered in diverse readers and its ability to survive its era and transcend its genre point to a text of unusual permeability. . . . Most important, readers' testimony in the nineteenth and twentieth centuries points to *Little Women* as a text that opens up possibilities rather than foreclosing them. With its multiple reference points and voices (four sisters, each distinct and recognizable), its depictions of joy as well as sorrow, its fresh and unlabored speech, Alcott's classic has something for almost everyone. For readers on the threshold of adulthood, the text's authorizing of female ambition has been a significant counterweight to more habitual gender prescriptions.

Little Women is such a harbinger of modern life, of consumer culture and new freedom for middle-class children, it is easy to forget that it was written just a few years after the Civil War, in the midst of Reconstruction and at a time of economic dislocation. For the most part, Alcott left such contemporary markers out of her story, another sign of the text's openness. The Civil War provides an important backdrop and a spur to heroism at home as well as on the battlefield, but it is primarily a plot device to remove Mr. March from the scene. Despite her family's support of John Brown, Alcott does not press a particular interpretation of the war. A final reason *Little Women* has survived so well, despite the chasm that separates Alcott's era from ours, is the virtual absence of references to outside events that would date her story and make it grow old.[56] That way each generation can invent it anew.

Notes

Citations to the Alcott Family Papers (bMS Am 1130.8 and bMS Am 800.23) are by permission of the Houghton Library, Harvard University.

1. Addams to Vallie Beck, March 16, 1876, *The Jane Addams Papers,* edited by Mary Lynn McGree Bryan (Ann Arbor: University Microfilms International, 1984) (hereafter cited as *Addams Papers*), reel 1.

2. Frank Luther Mott, *Golden Multitudes: The Story of Best Sellers in the United States* (New York: Macmillan, 1947), p. 102: *Books in Print,* 1992–93.

3. May 1868, *The Journals of Louisa May Alcott,* edited by Joel Myerson and Daniel Shealy, associate ed. Madeleine B. Stern (Boston: Little, Brown, 1989), pp. 165–66 (hereafter cited as *Journals*). On reading this entry in later years, Alcott quipped: "Good joke."

4. June [1868], Journals, p. 166.

5. Niles to Alcott, June 16, 1868 (#1) and July 25, 1868 (#2), bMS Am 1130.8, Alcott Family Papers, Houghton Library, Harvard University (all citations from Niles's letters are from this collection).

6. August 26 [1868], *Journals,* p. 166. . . .

7. For an account of Alcott's sales through 1909, by which time nearly 598,000 copies of *Little Women* had been printed by Roberts Brothers, see Joel Myerson and Daniel Shealy, "The Sales of Louisa May Alcott's Books," *Harvard Library Bulletin,* n.s., 1 (Spring 1990), esp. pp. 69–71, 86. Sales figures are unreliable for the twentieth century, in part because of foreign sales and the proliferation of editions after the expiration of copyright. Dorothea Lawrence Mann, "When the Alcott Books Were New," *Publishers' Weekly* 116 (September 28, 1929): 1619, claimed sales of nearly three million.

Sales, of course, are only part of the story: library use was high at the outset and remained so.

8. Mann, "When the Alcott Books Were New."

9. See Gloria T. Delamar, *Louisa May Alcott and 'Little Women': Biography, Critique, Publications, Poems, Songs, and Contemporary Relevance* (Jefferson, N.C.: McFarland and Co., 1990), p. 167 and passim.

10. For an intriguing analysis of well-loved texts that takes *Little Women* as a point of departure, see Catharine R. Stimpson, "Reading for Love: Canons, Paracanons, and Whistling Jo March," *New Literary History* 21 (Autumn 1990): 957–76.

11. "Spells, Wishes, Goldfish, Old School Hurts," *New York Times Book Review,* January 31, 1982, p. 24.

12. The classic biography is still Madeleine B. Stern, *Louisa May Alcott* (Norman: University of Oklahoma Press, 1950), which should be supplemented by Stern's extensive criticism on Alcott. See also Sarah Elbert, *A Hunger for Home: Louisa May Alcott and "Little Women"* (Philadelphia: Temple University Press, 1984), and Martha Saxton, *Louisa May: A Modern Biography of Louisa May Alcott* (New York: Avon Books, 1978).

13. June [1868], *Journals,* p. 166.

14. Niles told Alcott that her royalties were higher than any other Roberts Brothers author, including Harriet Beecher Stowe, whom he considered the American writer who could command the highest fees (Alcott possibly excepted). On the redirection of Alcott's career, see Richard H. Brodhead, "Starting Out in the 1860s: Alcott, Authorship, and the Postbellum Literary Field," in *Cultures of Letters: Scenes of Reading and Writing in Nineteenth-Century America* (Chicago: University of Chicago Press, 1993).

15. See Edward G. Salmon, "What Girls Read," *Nineteenth Century* 20 (October 1886): 515–29, and the ad for a series of "Books for Girls" whose intended audience was those "between eight and eighteen. . . . for growing-up girls, the mothers of the next generation." *American Literary Gazette and Publishers' Circular* (ALG) 17 (June 1, 1871): 88.

16. Niles to Alcott, July 25, 1868 (#2).

17. *Little Women* (New York: Random House/Modern Library, 1983), p. 290.

18. November 1, [1868], *Journals,* p. 167; Alcott to Elizabeth Powell, March 20, [1869], in *The Selected Letters of Louisa May Alcott,* edited by Joel Myerson and Daniel Shealy, associate ed. Madeleine B. Stern (Boston: Little, Brown, 1987), p. 125 (hereafter cited as *SL*). Erin Graham, "Books That Girls Have Loved," *Lippincott's Monthly Magazine,* September 1897, pp. 428–32, makes much of Bhaer's foreignness and ungainliness.

19. Jo's standing as a tomboy was recognized—and even respected; an ad for *Little Men* noted that "when a girl, [Jo] was half a boy herself." ALG 17 (May 15, 1871): 49. For girls in early adolescence and/or for lesbian readers, the young Jo may have been the primary romantic interest.

20. A conversation with Dolores Kreisman contributed to this analysis.

21. For an analysis of changes in girls' stories as the heterosexual imperative became stronger, see Martha Vicinus, "What Makes a Heroine?: Nineteenth-Century Girls' Biographies," *Genre* 20 (Summer 1987): 171–87.

22. Frank Preston Stearns, *Sketches from Concord and Appledore* (New York: Putnam, 1895), p. 82.

23. Niles to Alcott, April 14, 1869 (#4).

24. Letter in *St. Nicholas*, February 1878, p. 300.

25. "Little Things," at first handwritten, then typeset on a small press, was part of a national phenomenon. See Paula Petrik, "The Youngest Fourth Estate: The Novelty Toy Printing Press and Adolescence, 1870–1886," in *Small Worlds: Children and Adolescents in America, 1850–1950*, edited by Elliott West and Paula Petrik (Lawrence: University Press of Kansas, 1992), pp. 125–42. Alcott's correspondence with the Lukens sisters, which extended over fourteen years, is reprinted in SL. . . . The Alcott sisters had their own Pickwick Club in 1849.

26. Letter from "Nelly," dated March 12, 1870, reproduced in Delamar, *Louisa May Alcott*, p. 146.

27. Alcott to the Lukens Sisters, October 2, 1874, SL, pp. 185–86. . . .

28. April [1869], *Journals*, p. 171.

29. "American Literature," [1878–79], *Addams Papers*, reel 27, frames 239–95.

30. Undated review of *Little Men* ("Capital" penciled in), bMS Am 800.23, Alcott Family Papers.

31. See, e.g., Louise Chandler Moulton, "Louisa May Alcott," *Our Famous Women* (1883; reprint, Hartford: A. D. Worthington, 1884), pp. 29–52, which was prepared with Alcott's assistance. Reports of Alcott's financial success appeared frequently in the press.

32. *The Ladies' Repository* ([December 1868], p. 472), while finding *Little Women* "very readable," pointedly observed that it was "not a Christian book. It is religion without spirituality, and salvation without Christ."

33. Alcott's depiction of home theatricals drew the wrath of some evangelicals. Niles to Alcott, October 26, 1868 (#3). . . .

34. On tomboys, see Sharon O'Brien, "Tomboyism and Adolescent Conflict: Three Nineteenth-Century Case Studies," in *Woman's Being, Woman's Place: Female Identity and Vocation in American History*, edited by Mary Kelley (Boston: G. K. Hall, 1979), pp. 351–72, which includes a section on Alcott. . . .

35. The Katy books of "Susan Coolidge," pen name of Sarah Chauncey Woolsey, another Roberts Brothers author, are perhaps closest to Alcott's. But even Katy Carr, who begins as another Jo, an ambitious, harumscarum, and fun-loving girl, is severely punished for disobedience; only after suffering a broken back and several years of invalidism does she emerge as a thoughtful girl who will grow into "true womanhood."

36. Roosevelt, *An Autobiography* (1913; reprint, New York: De Capo Press, 1985), p. 17.

37. Gilman, *The Living of Charlotte Perkins Gilman* (1935; reprint, New York: Harper and Row, 1975), p. 35.

38. M. Carey Thomas Journal, June 20, 1870, *The Papers of M. Carey Thomas in the Bryn Mawr College Archives*, edited by Lucy Fisher West (Woodbridge, Conn.: Research Publications, 1982) (hereafter cited as MCTP), reel 1.

39. Elizabeth King Ellicott to Thomas, November 23, [1879], MCTP, reel 39.

40. See Marjorie Housepian Dobkin, ed., *The Making of a Feminist: Early Journals and Letters of M. Carey Thomas* (N.p.: Kent State University Press, 1979), pp. 66–67 and passim.

41. These remarks draw on Sicherman, "Reading and Ambition: M. Carey Thomas and Female Heroism," *American Quarterly* 45 (March 1993): 82–83.

42. *Little Women*, pp. 328–29.

43. On this subject, see Lee Virginia Chambers-Schiller, *Liberty, a Better Husband: Single Women in America: The Generations of 1780–1840* (New Haven: Yale University Press, 1984). In her next book, *An Old-Fashioned Girl*, Alcott ventures much further in envisioning a life of singlehood and lovingly depicts a community of self-supporting women artists.

44. Simone de Beauvoir, *Memoirs of a Dutiful Daughter*, translated by James Kirkup (1949; reprint, Cleveland: World Publishing Co., 1959), pp. 94–95. . . . According to Deirdre Bair, de Beauvoir had read Little Women by the time she was ten. Bair, *Simone de Beauvoir: A Biography* (New York: Summit Books, 1990), pp. 68–71.

45. These conclusions emerge from my reading and from discussions of *Little Women* with more than a dozen women. They were highly educated for the most part and mainly over fifty, but some women under thirty also felt passionately about the book. Most of my informants were white, but see n. 48 below.

46. Mary Church Terrell, *A Colored Woman in a White World* (1940; reprint, New York: Arno Press, 1980), p. 26; Alfreda M. Duster, ed., *Crusade for Justice: The Autobiography of Ida B. Wells* (Chicago: University of Chicago Press, 1970), pp. 7, 21–22. Wells observed that in her early years, she "never read a Negro book or anything about Negroes."

47. *The Middletown Press*, June 1, 1994, p. B1, and Ann Petry to author, letter postmarked July 23, 1994; I am grateful to Farah Jasmine Griffin for the *Middletown Press* reference. *Little Women* continues to play an important role in the lives of some young black women. A high school student in Jamaica, for example, rewrote the story to fit a local setting. And a young, African American academic felt so strongly about *Little Women* that, on learning about my project, she contended with some heat that Aunt March was unfair in taking Amy rather than Jo to Europe; she seemed to be picking up a conversation she had just left off. Comments like these and Petry's suggest the need for research on the interaction between race and class in African American women's reading practices.

48. Dorothy Richardson, *The Long Day: The Story of a New York Working Girl as Told by Herself* (1905; reprint, New York: Quadrangle Books, 1972), pp. 75–86 (quotation, p. 86). . . . *The Long Day*, which purports to be the story of an educated woman forced by circumstances to do manual labor, must be used with caution. It was initially published anonymously, and many scenes read like sensational fiction. Leonora O'Reilly, a feminist trade unionist, was so outraged at the book's condescension and its insinuations that working-class women were immoral that she drafted a blazing indictment. Leonora O'Reilly Papers, edited by Edward T. James, *Papers of the Women's Trade Union League and Its Principal Leaders* (Woodbridge, Conn.: Research Publications, 1981), reel 9.

49. Michael Denning, *Mechanic Accents: Dime Novels and Working-Class Culture in America* (London: Verso, 1987), pp. 197–200, analyzes *Little Rosebud's Lovers* as a "Cinderella tale." He suggests that stories read by the middle class tended to depict working-class women as victims (of seduction and poverty) rather than as triumphant.

50. I have discussed Jewish immigrants at some length because of the abundance of evidence, not because I view them as the only model for an alternative reading of *Little Women*.

51. *My Mother and I* (New York: Macmillan, 1917) is a problematic book. Some contemporaries reviewed it as autobiographical fiction, but recent critics have tended to view it as autobiography. Theodore Roosevelt must have considered it the latter when he lauded it as a "really noteworthy story" of Americanization in the foreword. . . . Moreover, the facts Stern gave out about her early life—including her status as an Eastern European Jewish immigrant—correspond with the narrator's history. Stern's older son, however, maintains that his mother was native born and Protestant and claimed her Jewish foster parents as her biological parents to hide her out-of-wedlock birth. T[homas] Noel Stern, *Secret Family* (South Dartmouth, Mass.: T. Noel Stern, 1988). Ellen M. Umansky, who generously shared her research materials with me, concludes in "Representations of Jewish Women in the Works and Life of Elizabeth Stern," *Modern Judaism* 13 (1993): 165–76: "[I]t may be difficult if not impossible to ever determine which of Stern's literary self representations reflected her own experiences" (p. 174). Sources that appear to substantiate Elizabeth Stern's foreign and Jewish birth are the U.S. Census for 1900 and for 1910, which both list her birthplace as Russia; the certificate of her marriage, which was performed by a prominent Orthodox rabbi in Pittsburgh; and Aaron Levin's will, which lists Stern as his oldest child.

Despite its contested status, I have drawn on *My Mother and I* because Stern's choice of *Little Women* as a critical marker of American aspirations is consistent with other evidence. The narrative's emphasis on the differences between immigrant and American culture comports with representations in less problematic works by Jewish immigrant writers. Moreover, whatever the facts of Stern's birth, she lived with the Jewish Levin family for many years.

52. *My Mother and I*, pp. 69–71.

53. Leo Lerman, "Little Women: Who's in Love with Miss Louisa May Alcott? I Am," *Mademoiselle*, December 1973, reprinted in Madeleine B. Stern, ed., *Critical Essays on Louisa May Alcott* (Boston: G. K. Hall, 1984), p. 113. See also Stephan F. Brumberg, *Going to America, Going to School: The Jewish Immigrant Public School Encounter in Turn-of-the-Century New York City* (New York: Praeger, 1986), pp. 121–22, 141.

54. Mary Antin, *The Promised Land* (Boston: Houghton Mifflin, 1912), pp. 257, 258–59.

55. Elaine Showalter, "*Little Women:* The American Female Myth," chap. 3 in *Sister's Choice: Tradition and Change in Women's Writing* (Oxford: Clarendon Press, 1991), pp. 55–56; Madeleine B. Stern to author, July 31, 1993. The English edition continued to be published in two volumes, the second under the title *Good Wives*.

56. Elizabeth Young, "Embodied Politics: Fictions of the American Civil War" (Ph.D. diss., University of California, Berkeley, 1993), reading *Little Women* in conjunction with *Hospital Sketches*, views it as a "war novel" (p. 108).

DOCUMENT

The Women's Centennial Agenda, 1876

Elizabeth Cady Stanton and Susan B. Anthony,
"Guaranteed to us and our daughters forever"

The capstone of the celebration of the Centennial was a public reading of the Declaration of Independence in Independence Square, Philadelphia, by a descendant of a signer, Richard Henry Lee. Elizabeth Cady Stanton, who was then president of the National Woman Suffrage Association, asked permission to silently present a women's protest and a written Declaration of Rights. The request was denied. "Tomorrow we propose to celebrate what we have done the last hundred years," replied the president of the official ceremonies, "not what we have failed to do."

Led by suffragist Susan B. Anthony, five women appeared at the official reading, distributing copies of their declaration. After this mildly disruptive gesture, they withdrew to the other side of Independence Hall, where they staged a counter-Centennial and Anthony read the following address. Compare it to the Declaration of Sentiments (pp. 264–266) of twenty-eight years before. Note the splendid oratorical flourish of the final paragraph.

July 4, 1876

While the nation is buoyant with patriotism, and all hearts are attuned to praise, it is with sorrow we come to strike the one discordant note, on this one-hundredth anniversary of our country's birth. When subjects of kings, emperors, and czars, from the old world join in our national jubilee, shall the women of the republic refuse to lay their hands with benedictions on the nation's head? Surveying America's exposition, surpassing in magnificence those of London, Paris, and Vienna, shall we not rejoice at the success of the youngest rival among the nations of the earth? May not our hearts, in unison with all, swell with pride at our great achievements as a people; our free speech, free press, free schools, free church, and the rapid progress we have made in material wealth, trade, commerce and the inventive arts? And we do rejoice in the success, thus far, of our experiment of self-government. Our faith is firm and unwavering in the broad principles of human rights proclaimed in 1776, not only as abstract truths, but as the corner stones of a republic. Yet we cannot forget, even in this glad hour, that while all men of every race, and clime, and condition, have been invested with the full rights of citizenship under our hospitable flag, all women still suffer the degradation of disfranchisement.

The history of our country the past hundred years has been a series of assumptions

Excerpted from Susan B. Anthony, Declaration of Rights for Women by the National Woman Suffrage Association, in *History of Woman Suffrage,* vol. 3, ed. Elizabeth Cady Stanton, Susan B. Anthony, and Matilda Joslyn Gage (Rochester, N.Y.: Susan B. Anthony, 1886), pp. 31–34.

and usurpations of power over woman, in direct opposition to the principles of just government, acknowledged by the United States as its foundation. . . .

And for the violation of these fundamental principles of our government, we arraign our rulers on this Fourth day of July, 1876,—and these are our articles of impeachment:

Bills of attainder have been passed by the introduction of the word "male" into all the State constitutions, denying to women the right of suffrage, and thereby making sex a crime—an exercise of power clearly forbidden in article 1, sections 9, 10, of the United States constitution. . . .

The right of trial by a jury of one's peers was so jealously guarded that States refused to ratify the original constitution until it was guaranteed by the sixth amendment. And yet the women of this nation have never been allowed a jury of their peers—being tried in all cases by men, native, and foreign, educated and ignorant, virtuous and vicious. Young girls have been arraigned in our courts for the crime of infanticide; tried, convicted, hanged—victims, perchance, of judge, jurors, advocates—while no woman's voice could be heard in their defense. . . .

Taxation without representation, the immediate cause of the rebellion of the colonies against Great Britain, is one of the grievous wrongs the women of this country have suffered during the century. Deploring war, with all the demoralization that follows in its train, we have been taxed to support standing armies, with their waste of life and wealth. Believing in temperance, we have been taxed to support the vice, crime and pauperism of the liquor traffic. While we suffer its wrongs and abuses infinitely more than man, we have no power to protect our sons against this giant evil. . . .

Unequal codes for men and women. Held by law a perpetual minor, deemed incapable of self-protection, even in the industries of the world, woman is denied equality of rights. The fact of sex, not the quantity or quality of work, in most cases, decides the pay and position; and because of this injustice thousands of fatherless girls are compelled to choose between a life of shame and starvation. Laws catering to man's vices have created two codes of morals in which penalties are graded according to the political status of the offender. Under such laws, women are fined and imprisoned if found alone in the streets, or in public places of resort, at certain hours. Under the pretense of regulating public morals, police officers seizing the occupants of disreputable houses, march the women in platoons to prison, while the men, partners in their guilt, go free. . . .

Representation of woman has had no place in the nation's thought. Since the incorporation of the thirteen original States, twenty-four have been admitted to the Union, not one of which has recognized woman's right of self-government. On this birthday of our national liberties, July Fourth, 1876, Colorado, like all her elder sisters, comes into the Union with the invidious word "male" in her constitution. . . .

The judiciary above the nation has proved itself but the echo of the party in power, by upholding and enforcing laws that are opposed to the spirit and letter of the constitution. When the slave power was dominant, the Supreme Court decided that a black man was not a citizen, because he had not the right to vote; and when the constitution was so amended as to make all persons citizens, the same high tribunal decided that a woman, though a citizen, had not the right to vote. Such vacillating interpretations of constitutional law unsettle our faith in judicial authority, and undermine the liberties of the whole people.

These articles of impeachment against our rulers we now submit to the impartial judgment of the people. To all these wrongs and oppressions woman has not submitted in silence and resignation. From the beginning of the century, when Abigail Adams, the wife of one president and mother of another, said, "We will not hold ourselves bound to obey laws in which we have no voice or representation," until now, woman's discontent has been steadily increasing, culminating nearly thirty years ago in a simultaneous movement among the women of the nation, demanding the right of suffrage. In making our just demands, a higher motive than the pride of sex inspires us; we feel that national safety and stability depend on the complete recognition of the broad principles of our government. Woman's degraded, helpless position is the weak point in our institutions today; a disturbing force everywhere, severing family ties, filling our asylums with the deaf, the dumb, the blind; our prisons with criminals, our cities with drunkenness and prostitution; our homes with disease and death. It was the boast of the founders of the republic, that the rights for which they contended were the rights of human nature. If these rights are ignored in the case of one-half the people, the nation is surely preparing for its downfall. Governments try themselves. The recognition of a governing and a governed class is incompatible with the first principles of freedom. Woman has not been a heedless spectator of the events of this century, nor a dull listener to the grand arguments for the equal rights of humanity. From the earliest history of our country woman has shown equal devotion with man to the cause of freedom, and has stood firmly by his side in its defense. Together they have made this country what it is. Woman's wealth, thought and labor have cemented the stones of every monument man has reared to liberty.

And now, at the close of a hundred years, as the hour-hand of the great clock that marks the centuries points to 1876, we declare our faith in the principles of self-government; our full equality with man in natural rights; that woman was made first for her own happiness, with the absolute right to herself—to all the opportunities and advantages life affords for her complete development; and we deny that dogma of the centuries, incorporated in the codes of all nations—that woman was made for man—her best interests, in all cases, to be sacrificed to his will. We ask of our rulers, at this hour, no special privileges, no special legislation. We ask justice, we ask equality, we ask that all the civil and political rights that belong to citizens of the United States, be guaranteed to us and our daughters forever.

FURTHER READING FOR PART II: THE MANY FRONTIERS OF INDUSTRIALIZING AMERICA, 1820–1880

Bodies and Sexuality

A good starting point is the classic essay by Nancy F. Cott, "Passionless: An Interpretation of Victorian Sexual Ideology, 1790–1850," *Signs* 4 (1978): 219–36. Karen Lystra challenges Cott's influential argument by mining courtship correspondence in *Searching the Heart: Women, Men, and Romantic Love in Nineteenth-Century America* (New York, 1992). For conflict about the meanings of sexuality, see Helen Lefkowitz Horowitz, *Rereading Sex: Battles over Sexual Knowledge and Suppression in Nineteenth-Century America* (New York, 2002). On the sex trade, see Timothy Gilfoyle, *City of Eros: New York City, Prostitution and the Commercialization of Sex, 1790–1920* (New York, 1992); Patricia Cline Cohen, *The Murder of Helen Jewett: The Life and Death of a Prostitute in Nineteenth-Century New York* (New York, 1998); and Anne M. Butler, *Daughters of Joy, Sisters of Mercy: Prostitutes in the American West, 1865–1900* (Urbana, Ill., 1985). Martha Hodes, *White Women, Black Men: Illicit Sex in the Nineteenth Century South* (New Haven, Conn., 1997), is an important reconsideration of race relations; see also the essays in Martha Hodes, ed., *Sex, Love, Race: Crossing Boundaries in North American History* (New York, 1999).

For health and disease in the Slave south, see Sharla M. Fett, *Working Cures: Healing, Health, and Power on Southern Slave Plantations* (Chapel Hill, N.C., 2002), and Sally G. McMillen, *Motherhood in the Old South: Pregnancy, Childbirth and Infant Rearing* (Baton Rouge, La., 1990). The relationship of women to the health reform movement is analyzed by Susan E. Cayleff, *Wash and Be Healed: The Water Cure Movement and Women's Health* (Philadelphia, 1987).

For contrasting interpretations of the birth control movement, see Linda Gordon, **Woman's Body, Woman's Right*, and James Reed, *From Private Vice to Public Virtue: The Birth Control Movement and American Society Since 1830* (New York, 1978). A definitive and highly readable study on birth control techniques and debates is Janet Farrell Brodie, *Contraception and Abortion in Nineteenth-Century America* (Ithaca, N.Y., 1997). For abortion, see James Mohr, **Abortion in America*, and the early chapters of Leslie J. Reagan, **When Abortion Was a Crime*.

On family relations and childbearing, see the works by Degler and Leavitt in the General Reference Works and Overviews. See also Sylvia D. Hoffert, *Private Matters: American Attitudes toward Childbearing and Infant Nurture in the Urban North, 1800–1860* (Urbana, Ill., 1989). For violence inside the family, see Elizabeth H. Pleck, *Domestic Tyranny: The Making of Social Policy against Family Violence from Colonial Times to the Present* (New York, 1987), and the important primary source edited by Ann Taves, *Religion and Domestic Violence in Early New England: The Memoir of Abigail Abbott Bailey* (Bloomington, Ind., 1989). In *The Sea Captain's Wife: A True Story of Love, Race, and War in the Nineteenth Century* (New York, 2006), Martha Hodes chronicles the life and marriages of an often-impoverished, New England–born white woman who ended up marrying into an elite family of color in the British Caribbean. For never-married women, see Lee Chambers-Schiller, *Liberty, A Better Husband: Single Women in America: The Generations of 1780–1840* (New Haven, Conn., 1984).

The social construction of masculinity is drawing more scholarly attention. Start with Amy S. Greenberg, *Manifest Manhood and the Antebellum American Empire* (New York, 2005).

Economics and Law

Dorothy Sterling, ed., *We Are Your Sisters: Black Women in the Nineteenth Century* (New York, 1984), includes many documents on the working lives of black women, slave and free (it also includes documents that have much bearing on politics and ideology). Willie Lee Rose, ed., *A Documentary History of Slavery in North America* (New York, 1976), and John Blassingame, ed., *Slave Testimony: Two Centuries of Letters, Speeches, Interviews and Autobiographies* (Baton Rouge, La., 1977), should also be consulted. Many elderly women who had been enslaved when young were interviewed by the Federal Writer's Project in the 1930s. Selected interviews appear in Ira Berlin et al., eds., *Remembering Slavery: African Americans Talk about Their Personal Experiences of Slavery and Freedom* (New York, 1998).

The pathbreaking study by Deborah Gray White, *Aren't I a Woman?: Female Slaves in the Plantation South* (1985), has been reprinted (New York, 1999) with a new introductory essay by the author. The gripping autobiography of Harriet Jacobs, who when enslaved resisted her so-called master, a persistent sexual predator, and escaped to freedom, is a must-read: *Incidents in the Life of a Slave Girl, Written by Herself*, ed. Jean Fagan Yellin (Cambridge, Mass., 1987; orig. pub. 1860). Read it alongside Yellin's biography, *Harriet Jacobs: A Life* (New York, 2003). For additional insights into women's survival strategies, see Stephanie M. H. Camp, *Closer to Freedom: Enslaved Women and Everyday Resistance in the Plantation South* (Chapel Hill, N.C., 2004).

For ideological representations and social realities of free women's work in the domestic economy, see Jeanne Boydston, **Home and Work*, and Joan Jensen, *Loosening the Bonds: Mid-Atlantic Farm Women, 1750–1850* (New Haven, Conn., 1986). The relationship of women's roles to a developing economy is brilliantly dissected in Mary P. Ryan, *Cradle of the Middle Class: The Family in Oneida County, New York* (Cambridge, Mass., 1981). Important studies of southern women's work are Stephanie McCurry, *Masters of Small Worlds: Yeoman Households, Gender Relations, and the Political Culture of the Antebellum South Carolina Low Country* (New York, 1995), and Brenda E. Stevenson, *Life in Black and White: Family and Community in the Slave South* (New York, 1996). Women's work, legal options, and family lives in urban communities are highlighted in Suzanne Lebsock, *The Free Women of Petersburg: Status and Culture in a Southern Town* (New York, 1984), and Erica Armstrong Dunbar, *A Fragile Freedom: African American Women and Emancipation in the Antebellum City* (New Haven, Conn., 2008). Working-class women's survival strategies and middle-class women reformers' aspirations are at the heart of Christine Stansell, *City of Women: Sex and Class in New York* (New York, 1986). For rural settings, see Nancy Grey Osterud, *Bonds of Community: The Lives of Farm Women in Nineteenth-Century New York* (Ithaca, N.Y., 1991).

Widowhood is an economic category as well as a demographic one; see Lisa Wilson, *Life After Death: Widows in Pennsylvania, 1750–1850* (Philadelphia, 1992), and Kristen E. Wood, *Masterful Women: Slaveholding Widows from the American Revolution through the Civil War* (Chapel Hill, N.C., 2004). For mariners' families, see Lisa Norling, *Captain Ahab Had a Wife: New England Women and the Whalefishery, 1720–1870* (Chapel Hill, N.C., 2000). On domestic work and the maintenance of gendered roles in a frontier context, see Malcolm J. Rohrbaugh, "Duty, Adventure, and Opportunity: Women in the California Gold Rush," in *Days of Gold* (Berkeley, Calif., 1997); John Mack Faragher's two studies, *Women and Men on the Overland Trail* (New Haven, Conn., 1979) and *Sugar Creek: Life on the Illinois Prairie* (New Haven, Conn., 1988); and Paula Petrik, *No Step Backward: Women and Family on the Rocky Mountain Mining Frontier: Helena, Montana, 1865–1900* (Helena, 1987).

On the economic impact of the U.S. absorption of New Mexico on women's relationship to the state, see Deena J. González, *Refusing the Favor: The Spanish-Mexican Women of Santa Fe, 1820–1880* (New York, 1999). For an alternate reading of the interaction of gender, culture, and economics in the region, see Sarah A. Deutsch, *No Separate Refuge: Culture, Class and Gender on an Anglo-Hispanic Frontier in the American Southwest* (New York, 1987).

Classic studies on the impact of industrialization on women are Helen Sumner, *History of Women in Industry in the United States* (Washington, D.C., 1910), and Caroline F. Ware, *The Early New England Cotton Manufacture: A Study in Industrial Beginnings* (1931; repr. New York, 1966). These should be followed by Thomas Dublin, *Women at Work: The Transformation of Work and Community in Lowell, Massachusetts, 1826–1860* (New York, 1979), and Lucy Larcom's classic memoir *A New England Girlhood* (1889; repr. New York, 1961; an on-line book through Project Gutenberg). For another key industrial sector, see Mary H. Blewett, *Men, Women, and Work: Class, Gender, and Protest in the New England Shoe Industry, 1780–1910* (Urbana, Ill., 1988);

For the invention of school teaching as a career for women, see Kathryn Kish Sklar, *Catherine Beecher: A Study in American Domesticity* (New Haven, Conn., 1973), and for the feminization of schooling, Richard M. Bernard and Maris A. Vinovskis, "The Female School Teacher in Antebellum Massachusetts, 1826-1860," *Journal of Social History* 10 (1977): 332–45. See also the important essays on teaching in Anne Firor Scott, *Making the Invisible Woman Visible* (Urbana, Ill., 1984).

For women's entry into the medical professions, see Mary Roth Walsh, *"Doctors Wanted, No Women Need Apply": Sexual Barriers in the Medical Profession, 1835–1975* (New Haven, Conn., 1977). For women physicians as intellectuals, see Susan Wells, *Out of the Dead House: Nineteenth-Century Women Physicians and the Writing of Medicine* (Madison, Wis., 2001).

On developments regarding coverture and married women's property in an important state, see Norma Basch, *In the Eyes of the Law: Women, Marriage, and Property in*

Nineteenth-Century New York (Ithaca, N.Y., 1982). Michael Grossberg expertly analyzes family law, including child custody and adoption, in *Governing the Hearth: Law and the Family in Nineteenth-Century America* (Chapel Hill, N.C., 1985). Two illuminating studies of divorce and men's and women's distinctive marital exit strategies are Hendrik Hartog, *Man and Wife in America: A History* (Cambridge, Mass., 2000), and Norma Basch, *Framing American Divorce: From the Revolutionary Generation to the Victorians* (Berkeley, Calif., 1999). For the South, see Peter Bardaglio, *Reconstructing the Household: Families, Sex, and the Law in the Nineteenth-Century South* (Chapel Hill, N.C., 1995), and Victoria Bynum, *Unruly Women: The Politics of Social and Sexual Control in the Old South, 1840–1865* (Chapel Hill, N.C., 1992). A crucial analysis of the ways in which marriage relations have been grounded in economic relations is offered by Amy Dru Stanley in *From Bondage to Contract: Wage Labor, Marriage and the Market in the Age of Slave Emancipation* (New York, 1998). A compelling case study is found in Melton McLaurin, *Celia, A Slave* (Athens, Ga., 1991), about the trial of a woman charged with murder.

Politics

Northern middle-class women's increasing visibility in benevolence and reform activities is analyzed in the studies by Nancy F. Cott, Carroll Smith-Rosenberg, and Mary P. Ryan cited earlier, and in Nancy A. Hewitt, *Women's Activism and Social Change: Rochester, New York* (Ithaca, N.Y., 1984); Lori D. Ginzberg, *Women and the Work of Benevolence: Morality, Politics, and Class in the Nineteenth-Century United States* (New Haven, Conn., 1990); Anne M. Boylan, *The Origins of Women's Activism: New York and Boston, 1797-1840* (Chapel Hill, N.C., 2002); Barbara Epstein, *The Politics of Domesticity: Women, Evangelism, and Temperance in Nineteenth-Century America* (Middletown, Conn, 1981); and Bruce Dorsey, *Reforming Men and Women: Gender in the Antebellum City* (Ithaca, N.Y., 2006). Estelle Freedman, *Their Sisters' Keepers: Women and Prison Reform in Nineteenth-Century America* (Ann Arbor, Mich., 1981), introduces yet another important reform movement.

Gerda Lerner's classic biography, *The Grimké Sisters from South Carolina: Rebels Against Slavery* (Boston, 1967), shows how a concern for abolition could lead to a concern for women's rights. The connections have been pursued in Jean Fagan Yellin, *Women and Sisters: Antislavery Feminists in American Culture* (New Haven, Conn., 1990); Dorothy Sterling, *Ahead of Her Time: Abby Kelley and the Politics of antislavery* (New York, 1991); Shirley Yee, *Black Women Abolitionists: A Study in Activism, 1828–1860 (1992);* and Julie Roy Jeffrey, *The Great Silent Army of Abolitionism: Ordinary Women in the Anti-Slavery Movement* (Chapel Hill, N.C., 1998). Nancy Isenberg, *Sex and Citizenship in Antebellum America* (Chapel Hill, N.C., 1998), links antislavery reform and political change. Two newer studies of women's mass petitioning campaigns are Susan Zaeske, **Signatures of Citizenship,* and Alissa Portnoy, *Their Right to Speak: Women's Activism in the Indian and Slave Debates* (Cambridge, Mass., 2005). For women's political expression in the absence of social movements, see Elizabeth Varon, *We Mean to Be Counted: White Women and Politics in Antebellum Virginia* (Chapel Hill, N.C., 1998).

African American women's stake in public life is expertly delineated by Martha S. Jones, *All Bound Up Together: The Woman Question in African American Public Culture, 1830–1900* (Chapel Hill, N.C., 2007), and provides context for analyzing Sojourner Truth's career. *The Narrative of Sojourner Truth*, prepared by Olive Gilbert, has been edited by Margaret Washington (New York, 1993). For biographies, see Carlton Mabee,

Sojourner Truth: Slave, Prophet, Legend (New York, 1993), Nell Irvin Painter, *Sojourner Truth: A Life, a Symbol* (New York, 1996) and Margaret Washington, Sojourner Truth's America (Urbana, Ill., 2009).

Ellen Carol DuBois, *Feminism and Suffrage: The Emergence of an Independent Women's Movement in America: 1848-1869* (Ithaca, N.Y., 1978), stresses the radicalism of the demand for suffrage; it should be read with Rosalyn Terborg-Penn, *African-American Women in the Struggle for the Vote, 1850–1920* (Bloomington, Ind., 1998). For American suffragists' international connections, see Leila J. Rupp, *Worlds of Women: The Making of an International Women's Movement* (Princeton, N.J., 1998), and the essays in *Women's Rights and Transatlantic Antislavery in the Era of Emancipation*, ed. Kathryn Kish Sklar and James Brewer Stewart (New Haven, Conn., 2007).

For the background of participants in the Seneca Falls gathering, read Judith Wellman, *The Road to Seneca Falls: Elizabeth Cady Stanton and the First Woman's Rights Convention* (Urbana, Ill., 2004), and Lori D. Ginzberg, *Untidy Origins: A Story of Women's Rights in Antebellum New York* (Chapel Hill, N.C., 2005) . Two new biographical studies are Kathi Kern, *Mrs. Stanton's Bible* (Ithaca, N.Y., 2002), and Lori D. Ginzberg, *Elizabeth Cady Stanton: An American Life* (New York, 2009). Readers will want to browse *The Selected Papers of Elizabeth Cady Stanton and Susan B. Anthony*, vols. 1–5, ed. Ann D. Gordon (New Brunswick, N.J., 1997–2009); Stanton had a wicked wit. Selections from the correspondence between Stanton and Anthony and some of their more notable speeches are conveniently available in Ellen Carol DuBois, ed., *Elizabeth Cady Stanton, Susan B. Anthony: Correspondence, Writing, Speeches* (New York, 1981). Six massive volumes of the basic sources on the suffrage movement have been abridged in **A Concise History of Woman Suffrage*. For challenges to the continued taxation of women without representation, and to the heightened vulnerability of black women to charges of vagrancy, see Linda K. Kerber, **No Constitutional Right to Be Ladies*, chs. 2 and 3.

For politics and gender in the far West, see Albert L. Hurtado, *Intimate Frontiers: Sex, Gender, and Culture in Old California* (Albuquerque, N.M.ex., 1999), and Susan Yohn, A *Contest of Faiths: Missionary Women and Pluralism in the American Southwest* (Ithaca, N.Y., 1995).

There are many memoirs of women's participation in the Civil War, among them Susie King Taylor, *A Black Woman's Civil War Memoirs*, ed. Patricia W. Romero and Willie Lee Rose (New York, 1988). For a northern woman who went south to nurse before she entered the writing career that would make her famous, see Louisa May Alcott, *Hospital Sketches* (New York, 1863); to place Alcott in historical context, see Jane E. Schultz, *Women at the Front: Hospital Workers in Civil War America* (Chapel Hill, N.C., 2004). For the perspective of a southern woman on the home front, see the compelling *Mary Chesnut's Civil War*, ed. C. Vann Woodward (New Haven, Conn., 1981). For treatments of women and the experience of Civil War, see Catherine Clinton and Nina Silber, eds., *Divided Houses: Gender and the Civil War* (New York, 1992); Drew Gilpin Faust, **Mothers of Invention*; Elizabeth D. Leonard, *All the Daring of the Soldier: Women of the Civil War Armies* (New York, 1999); Laura Edwards, *Scarlett Doesn't Live Here Anymore: Southern Women in the Civil War Era* (Urbana, Ill., 2000); and LeeAnn Whites, *Occupied Women: Gender, Military Occupation, and the American Civil War* (Baton Rouge, La., 2009). For northern women and the war, see Jeannie Attie, *Patriotic Toil: Northern Women and the American Civil War* (Ithaca, N.Y., 1998); Judith Ann Giesberg, *Civil War Sisterhood: The*

U.S. Sanitary Commission and Women's Politics in Transition (Boston, 2000); Lyde C. Sizer, *The Political Work of Northern Women Writers and the Civil War, 1850–1872* (Chapel Hill, N.C., 2000); and Nina Silber, *Daughters of the Union: Northern Women Fight the Civil War* (Cambridge, Mass., 2005).

Many compelling gendered interpretations of the Reconstruction era are available. See Noralee Frankel, *Freedom's Women: Black Women and Families in Civil War Era Mississippi* (Bloomington, Ind., 1999); Laura Edwards, *Gendered Strife and Confusion: The Political Culture of Reconstruction* (Urbana, Ill., 1997); two studies by Lee Ann Whites, *The Civil War as a Crisis in Gender: Augusta, Georgia, 1860–1890* (Athens, Ga., 1995), and *Gender Matters: Civil War, Reconstruction, and the Making of the New South* (New York, 2005); Marlie F. Weiner, *Mistresses and Slaves: Plantation Women in South Carolina, 1830–1880* (Urbana, Ill., 1998); Leslie Schwalm, *A Hard Fight for We: Women's Transition from Slavery to Freedom in South Carolina* (Urbana, Ill., 1997); Tera Hunter, *"To 'Joy My Freedom;* and Hannah Rosen, *Terror in the Heart of Freedom: Citizenship, Sexual Violence, and the Meaning of Race in the Postemancipation South* (Chapel Hill, N.C., 2009). For black women's challenge to segregation long before *Plessy* v. *Ferguson,* see Barbara Welke's essay, "When All the Women Were White, and All the Blacks Were Men: Gender, Class, Race and the Road to *Plessy*, 1855–1914," *Law and History Review* 13 (1995): 261–316.

Intellect, Ideology, Culture

Referring to how many women and men took to heart early nineteenth-century prescriptions for gender roles, "The Cult of True Womanhood" was given its name in an essay of the same title by Barbara Welter, *American Quarterly* 18 (1966): 151–74. A very different interpretation of some of the same sources was offered by Gerda Lerner in her classic essay of 1969, "The Lady and the Mill Girl," reprinted in *The Majority Finds Its Past: Placing Women in History* (New York, 1979). Two important books deepened the archival evidence for the social construction of gender in the period: Nancy F. Cott, *The Bonds of Womanhood: "Woman's Sphere" in New England, 1780–1835* (New Haven, Conn., 1977), and Carroll Smith-Rosenberg, *Disorderly Conduct: Visions of Gender in Victorian America* (New York, 1985). All of these should be read alongside subsequent reconsiderations of the concept of separate spheres. See Linda K. Kerber, "Separate Spheres, Female Worlds, Woman's Place: The Rhetoric of Women's History," *Journal of American History* 75 (1988): 9–39, and Leila Rupp et al., "Women's History in the New Millenium: A Retrospective Analysis of Barbara Welter's 'The Cult of True Womanhood, 1820-1860,'" *Journal of Women's History* 14:1 (2002): 149–173. For a recent examination of the way in which understandings of domesticity were used to impose imperial order in the West, see Jane E. Simonsen, *Making Home Work: Domesticity and Native American Assimilation in the American West, 1860–1919* (Chapel Hill, N.C., 2006).

Women's claims to intellectual authority are examined in two important studies by Mary Kelley: *Private Woman, Public Stage: Literary Domesticity in Nineteenth-Century America* (New York, 1984), and *Learning to Stand and Speak: Women, Education, and Public Life in America's Republic* (Chapel Hill, N.C., 2008). For an important journalist and writer, Charles Capper's *Margaret Fuller: An American Romantic Life* (New York, 1992) should be read alongside Fuller's work, conveniently found in Bell Gale Chevigny, ed., *The Woman and the Myth: Margaret Fuller's Life and Writings* (Boston, 1997). Lois Brown has written the first modern biography of the pioneering African American journalist and novelist: *Pauline Elizabeth Hopkins: Black Daughter of the Revolution,* (Chapel Hill, N.C., 2008). Women's cross-dressed performances are analyzed as political and cultural statements in Elizabeth Reitz Mullenix, *Wearing the Breeches: Gender on the Antebellum Stage* (New York, 2000).

Feminist scholarship on Protestant women's piety and its effect on nineteenth-century male clergy was kick-started with Ann Douglas's pioneering 1977 study, *The Feminization of American Culture* (reprinted with a new preface by the author, New York, 1998). William L. Andrews reprints spiritual accounts that span the century in *Sisters of the Spirit: Three Black Women's Autobiographies of the Nineteenth Century* (Bloomington, Ind., 1986). The degree to which members of radical sects and utopian communities challenged conventional gender ideology has attracted much scholarship, including Lawrence Foster, *Women, Family, and Utopia: Communal Experiments of the Shakers, the Oneida Community, and the Mormons* (Syracuse, N.Y., 1991), and Ann Braude, *Radical Spirits: Spiritualism and Women's Rights in Nineteenth-Century America* (Boston, 1989). On the women and men of a Jewish family in Virginia, see Emily Bingham, *Mordecai, An Early American Family* (New York, 2003). The history of nuns in America is beginning to find its historians; see Maureen Fitzgerald, **Habits of Compassion;* Diane Batts Morrow, *Persons of Color and Religious at the Same Time: The Oblate Sisters of Providence, 1828–1860* (Chapel Hill, N.C., 2002); and the journal of Sister Mary Bernard Deggs, *No Cross, No Crown: Black Nuns in Nineteenth-Century New Orleans,* ed. V. M. Gould and C. E. Nolan (Bloomington, Ind., 2001).

Asterisks (*) indicate the work's full citation can be found either earlier in this list of works or in the credit lines of an essay by the author excerpted in this volume.

III

Creating the State in an Industrialized Nation

1880–1945

Between 1880 and 1995, American life was reshaped by an influx of immigrants, rapid technological advances, increasing urbanization, and a growing consumer culture. In the midst of these changes, progressives at the turn of the century and New Dealers during the 1930s worked to redefine the responsibility of the federal government to its citizens. No events contributed more to that redefinition than a crippling economic depression and two world wars.

Historians have customarily acknowledged that women were part of the development of the modern American state. Familiar names in textbooks include Mary Harris ("Mother") Jones, the fiery labor agitator who was a symbol of defiance wherever strikers gathered; Jane Addams, the humanitarian reformer who became a relentless foe of economic exploitation and an equally determined advocate of government regulation; and Eleanor Roosevelt, the brilliantly outspoken and activist First Lady. But women were more than just a few notables or an ancillary group. As progressive reformers and grassroots New Deal advocates, women broadened their sphere of influence from the family-centered world of the home into the formerly male world of politics and government, with significant impact on public policy. As laborers and as the wives and daughters of laborers, women played a key role in the struggle to organize unions that would protect the rights of American workers. Women also endured the economic devastation of the Depression and exerted great effort and ingenuity to hold their families together. As members of the Roosevelt administration, they shared in the search for solutions. During World War II, women filled critical jobs in both the industrial workforce and the armed forces, contributing to an Allied victory. Women, in short, were *active creators* of America's history, not incidental to it.

Including women's experiences does not in itself refocus history. But by valuing the experiences of both sexes, we get a fuller understanding of American life, creating a history in which, as Gerda Lerner suggests, *"both men and women* are the measure of significance."

REBECCA EDWARDS

Pioneers at the Polls: Woman Suffrage in the West

We often think of the western states as pioneering a number of firsts for women, including the vote. Rebecca Edwards dashes the triumphalist story we might hope to tell about legislators' progressive views on gender by revealing the varied political motives and the uneven path that led to woman suffrage in the West. Note the variety of political parties active at the state level and the impulses that fueled the Populist movement.

How did partisan politics overlap with men's arguments for women's enfranchisement? What role did women's activities, individually and collectively, play in the suffrage achievements stretching from 1869 to 1919?

In the United States, the achievement of woman suffrage began on the frontier. The first states to grant women full voting rights were Wyoming, Colorado, Utah, and Idaho; seven of the next eight states that did so were also west of the Mississippi. Before the 19th Amendment passed, giving all American women the ballot, most Western states had already passed referenda or amendments, as had the territory of Alaska. The pattern was so marked that the editors of *The Survey*, commenting on rising pro-suffrage sentiment in 1917, reversed an old slogan, announcing, "Eastward the Star of Suffrage Takes its Way."[1]

Few leaders of the national suffrage movement had expected this pattern to emerge, Their organizations were based in the Northeast. The *Woman's Journal* hailed from Boston, and it carried ward-by-ward accounts of that city's suffrage campaigns beside shorter reports from the distant Plains, Rockies, and Pacific coast. Western suffragists often expressed a sense of isolation from the national movement. Though Susan B. Anthony traveled tirelessly in the West, the area was vast and the priorities of its women often unsettling to her. Meanwhile, such strategists lavished money and attention on New England or on lobbying Congress directly for a federal amendment. For many, the West was a low-stakes laboratory where suffragists could try out new tactics and, in case of victory, advertise the results to voters back east.

The striking regionalism of early suffrage victories has posed a problem for historians. Following the arguments of Frederick Jackson Turner, author of the "frontier thesis," some scholars have suggested that woman suffrage was a by-product of special frontier conditions. Pioneering, they argue, bred a democratic spirit, a strong sense of local community, and more respect (as well as higher wages) for female labor. There is some evidence to support this case, but it leaves important questions unanswered. If Oregon men voted for woman suffrage as a result of their pioneer spirit, why did referenda fail there in 1884, 1900, 1906, 1908, and 1910, before finally winning support in 1912? After reviewing various possible explanations, historian Richard White calls the issue "perplexing." Noting the conditions that led to suffrage in different states, he concludes that "the West's willingness to grant women the vote still ends up as something of a mystery."[2]

Explaining how western women won the vote, in decades when most of their northeastern and southern sisters did not, requires

Excerpted from "Pioneers at the Polls: Woman Suffrage in the West" by Rebecca Edwards in *Votes for Women: The Struggle for Suffrage Revisited*, ed. Jean H. Baker (New York: Oxford University Press, 2002), pp. 90–101. Reprinted with permission of the author and publisher. The notes have been provided by the author expressly for this volume.

careful attention to chronology. Wyoming and Utah territories demand attention first, as odd outliers which granted suffrage more than twenty years earlier than any other place, and a half-century before national suffrage was attained. The next set of victories—in Colorado and Idaho—were the result of specific political conditions in the 1890s. Then, a fourteen-year gap intervened before the next state gave women the ballot. This frustrating period for suffragists provides an important clue in explaining the subsequent blizzard of state-level successes between 1912 and 1919. For woman suffrage in the West, timing was the key.

William H. Bright, the legislator who sponsored woman suffrage in Wyoming, championed the cause for practical (perhaps even cynical) reasons. A southern Democrat, Bright moved to Wyoming to join a gold rush and later became president of the territory's legislature, made up of twenty men. Bright persuaded twelve of these colleagues to vote for his bill. Noting the recent adoption of the 15th Amendment to the Constitution, which enfranchised men irrespective of race or color, he argued that white women's votes would offset those of black men. Along with fellow Democrats, he also sought to twit the territory's governor, John Campbell, who had been appointed by Republicans in Washington. If Campbell vetoed the measure, members of his party might protest, since some radical Republicans favored woman suffrage. If Campbell signed the bill and the spectacle of women voting caused a scandal, blame was sure to fall on him.[3]

Even more important, Bright seems to have borrowed an idea from a handful of congressmen who had recently tried to enfranchise women in the territories. These men sought publicity: they hoped woman suffrage was sensational enough to put remote areas on the map, leading to growth and prosperity. On a related theme, Bright expressed concern over a dearth of women in the West, resulting from the rush of single men to the frontier. In territories like Wyoming—which had a 6-to-l ratio of men to women—wives and mothers were in short supply. Yet in the East, as a result of deaths in the Civil War, it was men who were relatively scarce. Perhaps, Bright argued, suffrage would prompt more women to emigrate, balancing gender ratios and providing the best conditions for the growth of families.

For these reasons, the Wyoming legislature passed the suffrage bill. Governor Campbell signed it in 1869. A few Laramie suffragists had visited the governor to urge his support; otherwise, almost no women's mobilization occurred. The result was nonetheless remarkable. Eastern reformers expressed their surprise and delight at this example of "advanced civilization" and innovation on the frontier. For a brief period, congratulatory telegrams poured in from as far away as Britain and Prussia. Though some Wyoming legislators changed their minds and sought to reverse the measure, Governor Campbell vetoed the repeal and suffrage stayed.[4]

If these events had succeeded in attracting thousands of women to Wyoming, . . . other western legislatures might have followed suit. But as a long-term strategy, woman suffrage served none of the purposes set forth by its sponsors. Meanwhile, a second territory granted women suffrage by a different logic. Utah, founded by Mormon pioneers in the late 1840s, had resisted incorporation into the American nation and fought to remain a haven for members of the Church of Jesus Christ of Latter-Day Saints. The founders of this movement had suffered persecutions further east, culminating in the lynching of their leader Joseph Smith in Missouri. Trekking to the Salt Lake region, church members had relied on one another to build all the elements of a new society. After Utah became a U.S. territory, its leaders tried to shelter their church from the meddling of Congress and non-Mormon territorial governors appointed from Washington.[5]

In these struggles, the most controversial issue was the Mormon practice of plural marriage. According to a doctrine set down by Joseph Smith, some men in the church took more than one wife. As a result, Mormon men were denounced in Congress and the national press as household tyrants whose wives were morally degraded. In December 1869, Congress began debate on a bill that would have disenfranchised any man who expressed his support for polygamy. Mormons were shocked by the attack, and in January 1870, leading women in Salt Lake City organized two protest meetings. Speaking from the pulpit of the Mormon Tabernacle for the first time, women defended the political rights of their "fathers, husbands, and brothers" and their own right to marry whomever and however they pleased. Eliza

Snow, a leading woman of the church, called upon Mormon women "to rise up in the dignity of our calling and speak for ourselves," and one of the meetings endorsed woman suffrage.[6]

Male leaders of the church and Utah Territory had previously been lukewarm or hostile to the idea of women voting. (When asked about women's rights, church leader Brigham Young had joked that women had "the right to ask their husbands to fix up the front yard.") But facing congressional hostility, Mormon men now decided that women could be powerful allies. In February 1870, the territory's legislature extended the full franchise to the women of Utah. Pointing to the recent women's meetings in Salt Lake City, proponents argued that Mormon women would vote to defend the faith. The territory's non-Mormon governor signed the bill into law, apparently hoping the opposite—that Mormon women would use their new power to end polygamy.[7] . . .

. . . [I]n the short term woman suffrage in Utah achieved the Mormons' political goals. It temporarily averted measures to imprison polygamists and disfranchise Mormon men. It also strengthened Mormons' voting majority in Utah, since the few non-Mormons were mainly single men in mining camps. For the next sixteen years, Utah women voted at all elections, demonstrating by overwhelming majorities their support for the policies and candidates selected by men in the church. Only a handful of non-Mormon suffragists in Utah tried to use the ballot to challenge plural marriage, and they did not come close to success.[8]

In the following decade, the tangled history of Utah suffrage took several ironic turns. Mormon women's allegiance to their faith persuaded Republicans in Washington that female voting rights had strengthened the institution of polygamy, rather than undermining it. In 1887, on these grounds, Congress passed a measure disfranchising Utah women—over the combined protests of both Mormon and non-Mormon women in the territory, who had until recently been bitter opponents on the issue of plural marriage. Three years later, amid a barrage of legislation designed to punish polygamists, the church finally abolished plural marriage. Then, as Utah sought statehood in the 1890s, its leaders wrestled over whether or not its proposed state constitution should reinstate female suffrage. To ensure that it did, women mobilized a broad-based, highly visible suffrage movement throughout the territory, twenty-five years *after* they had first won the right to vote. Utah entered the union as a state in 1896 with its women reenfranchised.[9]

In both Wyoming and Utah, the original passage of woman suffrage occurred during Reconstruction. . . . In this era of ferment, during which the nation enfranchised black men, various proposals for extending and strengthening citizenship rights appeared in legislatures and committee rooms around the nation. Political leaders in both Wyoming and Utah followed these debates. . . . Yet the possibilities of Reconstruction must not be overstated, since they did not result in suffrage for women anywhere else. In Kansas, suffragists waged a bitter battle in 1867 that ended in defeat. Voters in Colorado Territory made the same decision ten years later. As the political energies of Reconstruction faded in the 1880s, referenda also failed in Nebraska, Oregon, South Dakota, and Washington Territory.[10] . . .

The result of these developments was to link woman suffrage with Mormonism in the minds of many Americans. After all, Utah was the most populous and prominent place where women had the vote. To the rest of the nation that experiment had brought dubious results. Non-Mormons, most of whom abhorred polygamy, argued that Mormon women were not using the vote wisely. Outside the territory, few suffrage leaders were willing to mount a defense of plural marriage. Only Elizabeth Cady Stanton travelled to Utah and defended Mormon women's right to practice polygamy if they believed it was right and good. (To the mortification of Susan B. Anthony and other colleagues, Stanton observed that husbands took a great deal of time and trouble, and she suggested that sharing one man among several women might be an improvement on conventional marriage arrangements.) Belva Lockwood, a lawyer who ran for U.S. president on the Equal Rights ticket in 1884, was among the few other women's rights leaders who defended Mormonism, reminding U.S. officials that the Constitution guaranteed freedom of religion.[11]

Most other suffrage leaders felt that Mormons' adoption of suffrage—which some believed was a convenient ploy for nefarious purposes—had unfairly associated their movement with an immoral and unpopular religion. Mormon polygamy was unpopular. Newspapers and magazines circulated jokes about the inconvenience of having multiple wives, and editors launched angry diatribes against western "harems" and Mormon women's "enslavement." Furthermore, congressional deliberations over policy in Utah were the most visible woman suffrage debates of the 1880s. Persistent links between woman suffrage and Mormonism placed the national suffrage movement in a difficult position. Movement leaders tended to neglect Utah and heap praise on Wyoming as the model for the nation to emulate. Even after the abolition of plural marriage, the *History of Woman Suffrage*, compiled by leaders of the movement, downplayed the victory in Utah and focused on developments elsewhere.[12]

The second wave of western suffrage victories took place in the 1890s with the rise of a new political movement: Populism. Like Mormons, members of the People's Party, or Populists, as they were called, cast themselves as outsiders and mistrusted the eastern political establishment. . . . [M]any Western Populists believed women would vote to defend their cause. . . . For these men and women, woman suffrage was part of a broader reform agenda that included transforming the American economy and supporting farmers and industrial workers.

In some states the People's Party organized as early as 1890, the year in which Kansas Populists swept to victory. The national party was created on July 4, 1892, from the merger of two organizations: the Farmers' Alliance, dedicated to farmers' rights, and the Knights of Labor, a nationwide labor union. Both these groups included women as organizers and lecturers, and female members participated in grassroots decision-making. Most men in the southern wings of these movements, however, were antagonistic to women's rights, and women there were reluctant to demand the ballot. Westerners were far more vocal in support of woman suffrage, though many men in the movement—and even some women—saw it as a side issue that distracted attention from the Populists' economic program. The Populists' chief goals were a progressive federal income tax, government ownership of railroads and telegraphs, and a looser money supply to ease the burdens of debtors. As a result, and because of southern Populists' reluctance to support the measure, the party never included woman suffrage in its national platform. At best, one of their conventions resolved "that the question of woman suffrage be submitted to the state and territorial legislatures for favorable action."[13]

This opened the way for state Populist coalitions to work for suffrage wherever support existed. By 1894, the *Woman's Journal* noted that Populists had put woman suffrage in their platforms in "nearly every northern State." On the basis of strong Populist endorsements of suffrage, Susan B. Anthony reluctantly began speaking on the party's rostrums in California and elsewhere, hoping the new movement would prove strong enough to give women in some states the right to vote. But in the Northeast and Midwest, the Populist movement was tiny and weak. Everywhere it was fragile, struggling with internal divisions, facing entrenched party loyalties among voters, and rocked by a massive economic depression that struck in 1893.[14]

In only two states, Colorado and Idaho, did the rise of Populism coincide with full suffrage for women. . . . In Colorado, a Populist administration elected in 1892 put a state referendum on the ballot the following year. Two other political parties promptly endorsed it. First were the Prohibitionists, who had long advocated "a temperance ballot," that is, women's right to vote on measures related to the sale of liquor. Second were the powerful Republicans, who had not previously offered much support but now found themselves pressured by the Populist initiative. Though the Colorado suffrage movement had faced earlier defeats, this time woman suffrage passed by the comfortable margin of 55 to 45 percent.[15]

Because of Colorado's larger population, and especially the rapid growth of Denver, its victory was more significant for the national suffrage movement than was the passage of a similar referendum in Idaho in 1896, a year when Populists won power there. Yet the Idaho referendum passed by a much larger margin—almost two to one—with especially high support in the southeastern Mormon counties. As in Colorado, multiple parties endorsed the measure once it was presented, as did most of the state's newspapers. In both states, suffragists had been organized and visible for years before passage and played key roles in campaigning for the referenda and getting out the vote. In addition to the Colorado and Idaho Equal Suffrage Associations, those active in the campaigns included chapters of the Women's Christian Temperance Union, women in labor unions, and prominent female journalists, lawyers, and lecturers, and leaders of reform and literary clubs.[16]

Another similarity between the two states helps to explain why woman suffrage, once it was placed on the ballot, won the endorsement of the Republican and even Democratic parties, most of whose leaders in other states remained strongly opposed to the idea of women voting. The recent, rapid growth of Colorado and Idaho's economies rested on their hardrock mines—in particular, by the 1890s, silver mines. That fact translated into overwhelming political support for "silver coinage," a proposal to increase the money supply by minting silver at a ratio of 16 to 1 to the value of gold (which would have increased silver's relative value). "Silver at a ratio of 16 to 1" was a key demand in almost every Populist platform at both state and national levels. Its popularity was so intense in the Rockies that many Republicans and Democrats also converted to the cause. In both Colorado and Idaho, political leaders urged voters to enfranchise women so they could help work for silver coinage. "A vote for equal suffrage is a vote for silver," proclaimed one Denver newspaper. "The silver states need all the votes they can get," added another Colorado editor.[17] Though the political parties in both states argued over *how* to implement silver coinage, the linkage between that issue and woman suffrage helped to ensure women's victory.

Populist leaders in Colorado rightly claimed credit for introducing their state's suffrage referendum, which pressured other parties to sign on. Yet the results of the initiative were a shock to the new party and especially to Populist Governor Davis Waite. Colorado voters blamed his administration for a devastating depression in 1893, which shut down many of the state's mines and brought the economy to a standstill. Looking for new leadership in 1894, like voters in many other states, Coloradans voted heavily Republican. These voters included a majority of the women whom Populists had worked to enfranchise and whom Waite and others had assumed would owe the party a debt of gratitude. After the election, Waite spoke with bitterness that many Populists in other states backed off their pro-suffrage position. Western urban women, Waite warned, had Republican loyalties and should not be trusted with ballots. "The statements you have made," one Populist wrote to Waite from Minnesota, "have ended woman's suffrage in the People's Party."[18]

If Populist leaders were disillusioned with the results of suffrage, leaders of the suffrage movement were equally frustrated with their political allies. Though some women sought the vote for specific purposes—for example, to pass anti-liquor legislation or Populist economic measures—others advocated it as a basic right of citizens rather than a way to advance such policy goals as silver coinage. Yet partisan alliances were crucial for suffrage victories. In the intense heat of political conflict, men enfranchised women with direct expectations about their future support. Afterward, women's votes brought one of two results. Either party leaders were disappointed by women's independence, as in Colorado, or women's very loyalty, as in Utah, became a point of criticism for opponents. Men in other states concluded that female voters could do little good and much harm. "Oh I have been through the partisan battle," Anthony wrote wearily, "and I don't want to see it again." She began to advocate a strict nonpartisan path.[19]

As the depression ended and the Populist Party faded, it was not easy for suffrage advocates to implement either a partisan *or* a nonpartisan strategy. After 1896, prosperity began to return to most parts of the country and economic debates took on a more comfortable tone. Republicans held the White House as well as majorities in both houses of Congress and claimed credit for the end of hard times. By tacit agreement, Democrats were allowed to exercise "home rule" in southern states, but Republicans dominated the national political scene for over a decade. In these circumstances, the men who held power did not need women's aid, and new political movements had difficulty applying pressure on the dominant party.[20]

Looking back at recent elections, conservative commentators in these years linked woman suffrage to Populism and radicalism in the West, rejecting both. It was widely noted that Colorado and Idaho, which had supported woman suffrage, were hotbeds of Populism, while California had stayed in the Republican column in 1896 and in the same election had defeated a woman suffrage referendum. One Oregon newspaper wrote that suffrage activism in Colorado and Idaho was "the outgrowth of the temporary socialistic spirit that prevails in those states." Between 1871 and 1890, the suffrage movement had suffered from the stigma of Mormon polygamy; in the years between 1897 and 1910, the stigma of radicalism was even worse, and suffragists later referred to this period as "the "doldrums."[21] In retrospect, the victories in Utah, Colorado, and Idaho seemed to have hampered the cause of suffrage in other states.

It is no accident that "the doldrums" ended when new issues and alliances reinvigorated party politics after 1910. Three parties, in fact, challenged Republicans: not only a rejuvenated, reformist Democratic Party, which captured the White House in 1912, but also the Progressive Party (active between 1912 and 1916) and the Socialist Party. Though these groups had different agendas, their followers cooperated in a number of states to work for the passage of woman suffrage and other legislative goals. Socialists played especially key roles in a massive referendum campaign in California, where suffrage had been defeated in 1896 but won by a narrow margin in 1911. The California Women's Socialist Union ignored an international socialist directive forbidding coalitions with nonsocialists and instead cooperated with an array of women's clubs, labor unions, and other groups. They published materials in many languages, organized across class lines, and won enormous support for suffrage, especially among working-class voters in Los Angeles.[22]

There was not an absolute correlation in the early 1910s between the success of woman suffrage and states where men voted in large numbers for socialists or progressives. Some Western states with powerful Socialist movements, such as Oklahoma, did not grant women the vote. Kansas adopted a constitutional amendment for suffrage in 1912, a year when its voters showed little support for new party movements. Nonetheless, as party competition sharpened there were a cascade of victories in the trans-Mississippi West between 1910 and 1914. In addition to California and Kansas, women won the full ballot in Washington (1910), Oregon (1912), Arizona (1912), Montana (1914), Nevada (1917), North Dakota (1917), and Nebraska (1917). Most of these states had strong Socialist or Progressive movements—in some cases both—and in most of them party competition was keen. . . .

In the same years, more complex national patterns emerged and eastern states at last began to swing into the suffrage column. In 1913, Illinois became the first state east of the Mississippi to grant women suffrage and the first to do so by action of the state legislature, rather than by a constitutional amendment submitted to voters. In 1917, the United States entered World War I and members of the National American Woman Suffrage Association (NAWSA) threw themselves enthusiastically into war work, along with many other women's organizations across the United States. Women's patriotic efforts, they believed, would show national leaders that they deserved the vote, and indeed, support for suffrage grew rapidly in the late 1910s, with Democratic President Woodrow Wilson declaring himself in favor at the start of the 1916 campaign.[23]

Meanwhile, the suffrage movement had modernized, taking up effective new tactics of lobbying, advertising, and grassroots organizing. Under the leadership of Carrie Chapman Catt, NAWSA focused its attention on a federal amendment rather than a state-by-state strategy, though Catt was able to formulate her "Winning Plan" partly because of the increasing momentum of state-level victories. In 1917, techniques like those used by Socialist women in California helped win full suffrage for women in New York, which controlled a whopping 45 electoral votes. As Rhode Island, Tennessee, Kentucky, and Maine fell into line, the pattern of western leadership began to break down. Yet victories in the West continued right up to the passage of the 19th Amendment, which in that region was almost an afterthought: west of the Mississippi, only Texas, Arkansas, and New Mexico had not fully enfranchised women already. Montana Congresswoman Jeanette Rankin—the nation's first woman in Congress—had already served her first full term.[24] . . .

The success of suffrage in the West was no mean achievement. It enabled thousands of American women to cast their ballots and participate in campaigns—and a few to serve in elected office—before 1920. By the 1910s, western suffrage helped advance the national cause simply through the rising number of states where women voted, and these voters' growing visibility and clout. In granting women's political rights, the West experienced early all the opportunities and dilemmas that would emerge later nationwide. The West served notice to the nation, early on, that women could be effective organizers in the political arena. Western women showed that they cared deeply about politics and could be strong partisans in the midst of critical campaigns. They seldom united in one party; diverse women had many different priorities and loyalties. And western women showed that they could think for themselves, often straying from the party-line paths that men wanted them to tread.

Notes

1. *The Survey*, June 16, 1917, 258.

2. Richard White, *"It's Your Misfortune and None of My Own": A New History of the American West* (Norman, OK: University of Oklahoma Press, 1991), 359. See also Sandra L. Myres, *Westering Women and the Frontier Experience, 1800–1915* (Albuquerque: University of New Mexico Press, 1982), 233–37.

3. T. A. Larson, "Petticoats at the Polls: Woman Suffrage in Territorial Wyoming," *Pacific Northwest Quarterly* 44 (April 1953): 74–9; Beverly Beeton, *Women Vote in the West: The Woman Suffrage Movement*, 1869–1896 (New York: Garland, 1986), 1–7

4. Larson, "Petticoats at the Polls"; Beeton, *Women Vote in the West*, 8–14.

5. Beeton covers the struggle in Utah (*Women Vote in the West*, chaps. 2–5), as do the articles in Carol Cornwall Madsen, ed., *Battle for the Ballot: Essays on Woman Suffrage in Utah, 1870–1896* (Logan, UT: Utah State University Press, 1997).

6. Lola Van Wagenen, "In Their Own Behalf: The Politicization of Mormon Women and the 1870 Franchise," in Madsen, ed., *Battle for the Ballot*, 66.

7. Ibid., 60–74.

8. Beeton, *Women Vote in the West*, 23–37.

9. Ibid., 63–103; see also Jean Bickmore White, "Woman's Place Is in the Constitution: The Struggle for Equal Rights in Utah in 1895," in Madsen, ed., *Battle for the Ballot*, 221–244.

10. Myres, *Westering Women*, 219, 224–30.

11. Beeton, *Women Vote in the West*, 41–62.

12. Joan Smyth Iversen, "A Debate on the American Home: The Antipolygamy Controversy, 1880–1890," in John C. Fout and Maura Shaw Tantillo, eds., *American Sexual Politics: Sex, Gender, and Race Since the Civil War* (Chicago: University of Chicago Press, 1990), 123–40.

13. Omaha Platform (1892) quoted in Rebecca Edwards, *Angels in the Machinery: Gender in American Party Politics from the Civil War to the Progressive Era* (New York: Oxford University Press, 1997), 105; on the People's Party and women's suffrage generally, see 99–110.

14. *Woman's Journal*, quoted in Edwards, *Angels in the Machinery*, 104; on Kansas, see especially Michael Lewis Goldberg, *An Army of Women: Gender and Politics in Gilded Age Kansas* (Baltimore: The Johns Hopkins University Press, 1997).

15. Beeton, *Women Vote in the West*, 113; see also Carolyn Stefanco, "Networking on the Frontier: The Colorado Women's Suffrage Movement, 1876–1893," in Susan Armitage and Elizabeth Jameson, eds., *The Women's West* (Norman, OK: University of Oklahoma Press, 1987), 265–276.

16. Beeton, *Women Vote in the West*, 104–15.

17. Edwards, *Angels in the Machinery*, 104–5; quotes from *Rocky Ford Enterprise* and *Silver Standard*.

18. Ibid., 106: quotation from Ignatius Donnelly to Davis Waite.

19. Ibid., 109, quotation from Anthony.

20. The analysis of the political realignment of the 1890s in this and the following paragraphs is drawn from Ibid., chaps. 6–7.

21. Ibid., 139, including quote from *Portland Oregonian*.

22. Sherry J. Katz, "A Politics of Coalition: Socialist Women and the California Suffrage Movement, 1900–1911," in Marjorie Spruill Wheeler, ed., *One Woman, One Vote* (Troutdale, OR: New Sage Press, 1995), 245–62.

23. Sara M. Evans, *Born for Liberty: A History of Women in America* (New York: Free Press, 1989), 152–6, 164–72.

24. Ibid., 164–72; for a state-by-state list of suffrage victories see Wheeler, ed., *One Woman, One Vote*, 375–77.

PATRICIA A. SCHECHTER

Ida B. Wells and *Southern Horrors*

Ida B. Wells's 1892 pamphlet *Southern Horrors: Lynch Law in All Its Phases* launched a critical phase of the African American struggle for civil rights. Its statistical refutation of the rape charge against black men that was used to justify lynching is a sociological breakthrough that has stood the test of time and study in the twentieth century. Wells also demonstrates how the concepts of "race" and "rape" were tied to power relations in the administration of justice, in the media, and in everyday life. Finally, Wells expounds the racial and class dimensions of the sexual double standard in ways that connect to contemporary feminist concerns with violence against all women, communities of color, and the poor in the United States and globally.

The insights expressed in *Southern Horrors* reflect Wells's personal and community survival strategy in the New South. Her situation was shaped by both new opportunities and new oppressions facing the first generation of free African Americans who came of age after the Civil War. Wells's parents, who had been slaves in Mississippi, bequeathed to their children a legacy of strong religious faith, pride in wage-earning, and a commitment to education that echoes through the many projects their daughter undertook over her lifetime. Wells's father, James Wells, was a skilled carpenter and a member of the Masons who, after the war, served on the board of Holly Springs local American Missionary Association school, Rust College, which his daughter attended. Wells's mother, "Lizzie" Warrenton Wells, worked as a cook and was a devout Methodist who made sure her children attended church, where she herself learned to read the Bible. After James and Lizzie's untimely deaths in 1878 from a yellow fever epidemic that swept the Delta, sixteen-year-old Ida B. Wells was left to care for her five siblings, earning money by teaching school.

The prospect of better wages and the presence of extended family soon drew Wells to Memphis, Tennessee. There, her intellectual, social, and political horizons expanded in a burgeoning black community notable for its highly accomplished middle-class and elite members. Aspirations for equality nourished community institutions like schools, newspapers, social clubs, literary lyceums, and churches, especially the Baptist and African Methodist Episcopal denominations. In Memphis, Wells found encouragement to turn her intellectual talents into leadership by teaching Sunday school and by pursuing literary activities, especially journalism. Her first newspaper article appeared in 1883 in a Baptist weekly. It explained how Wells had been unfairly ejected from a first-class "ladies" railroad coach and how she fought racial discrimination by taking her case to court. While tens of thousands of educated women joined the paid labor force as school "ma'ams," religious educators, and journalists in the late nineteenth century, these social roles had particular significance for African American women, whose personal, family, and

This essay condenses material from *Ida B. Wells-Barnett and American Reform, 1880–1930* by Patricia A. Schechter (Chapel Hill: University of North Carolina Press, 2001).

community well-being was intimately bound up with their wage-earning, educational activities, and community-betterment work.

As *Southern Horrors* emphatically argues, a white racist backlash followed closely upon the achievements of African Americans after Reconstruction. The result of this backlash was "Jim Crow" segregation, a set of laws designed for the economic deprivation, social marginalization, and political disfranchisement of black people. Jim Crow was established and enforced through systematic violence and terror. Ida B. Wells's eight pamphlets, written between 1892 and 1920, painstakingly document the ways in which African Americans were deprived of their rights through mob and police violence, through negative propaganda campaigns in the media, and through the elimination of economic opportunity and political rights. Few aspects of Jim Crow escaped Wells's sharp scrutiny in the press and eventually, while in Memphis, she caught the negative attention of critics. As the following excerpt explains, she was forced to leave the South as a kind of political exile, first traveling to New York, then to Great Britain, and finally settling in Chicago in 1895. There, she married lawyer and fellow activist Ferdinand L. Barnett (hypenating her name to Wells-Barnett) and raised a family of four children.

Post-exile, Wells-Barnett's writing and activism were sustained through African American community networks and by organizations shared by black and white women reformers, such as the Woman's Christian Temperance Union. Her work with black women's church and club networks nurtured her into a powerful public speaker and political organizer. Between 1892 and 1895, Wells-Barnett organized scores of antilynching committees and women's clubs all over the United States and abroad, and helped inaugurate the National Association of Colored Women (NACW), a group that functioned as the preeminent civil rights organization up to World War I. In 1909, Wells-Barnett cofounded the National Association for the Advancement of Colored People (NAACP), which, in 1917, assumed principal leadership of the antilynching fight in the United States.

The trajectory of Wells-Barnett's civil rights agitation was neither simple nor smooth. Controversy followed her and her work, especially during its first decade. White supremacists in the North and South vilified her in the press, slandering her morals and threatening her with violence for speaking out against lynching. While most African American communities embraced Wells-Barnett as a heroine, there was little consensus about how, exactly, to end lynching or resist Jim Crow. Black leaders were a diverse group ideologically and generationally; regional considerations also came into play as black southerners found themselves more circumscribed than their northern peers. Women's roles were also fundamental to the building of black communities and to resistance work. Though black women's families and communities were dependent upon their contributions, any move on their part into official political and intellectual leadership—especially where interactions with whites were concerned—-usually sparked controversy. Whether in journalism, public speaking, or institutional leadership—as with her Chicago social settlement, the Negro Fellowship League (1909–1919)—Wells-Barnett's initiatives were always double-edged, affording new spaces for community defense and activism while potentially exposing black men as somehow deficient in their protective or leadership roles. For every celebration of her hard work and successes, there were always powerful voices affirming the propriety of male ministers, business leaders, and elected officials leading the civil rights agenda for African Americans. Wells-Barnett remained staunchly committed to equality for black women, however, fighting hard for suffrage rights in Illinois and nationally. After the passage of the Nineteenth Amendment, she eventually ran for public office herself, in 1930.

Wells-Barnett's steadfast commitment to full equality not just for lynching victims but for "every citizen" rings through *Southern Horrors*, lending the text its prophetic, visionary quality; hers is a plea, to quote further from the pamphlet's preface, that "justice be done though the heavens fall." *Southern Horrors* draws on a number of powerful currents in American thought and style to make its case. As a graphic exposé, *Southern Horrors* shares kinship with muckraking journalism, a hallmark of the U.S. press at the turn of the century. Its empirical bent draws on statistical work to be found in the nascent academic field of sociology. *Southern Horrors* also stands in a tradition of radical pamphleteering in U.S. history that includes Tom Paine's *Common Sense* (1776) and David Walker's *Appeal to the Colored People of the Americas* (1829). Like these texts, *Southern Horrors* is peppered with wilting sarcasm and theatrical asides designed to provoke, starting with its title, a mocking send up of "southern honor." Instead of the neat closure of genteel fiction, *Southern Horrors* is full of questions and commands in a kind of call-and-response engagement with the reader, a pattern of expression at the heart of black worship traditions and one designed to work a deep transformation in participants. Finally, *Southern Horrors* ends with a practical list of strategies for "self-help," including education, boycotts, migration, agitation for protective legislation, suing through the courts, and even armed self-defense, to be "used to give that protection which the law refuses to give." Nearly five thousand Americans, almost three-fourths of them black, were lynched in Wells-Barnett's lifetime. Repeated efforts of African American activists to pass federal legislation making lynching a crime were defeated in Congress in 1922, 1937, and 1940.

What are the different kinds of violence or threats of violence that Wells documents in *Southern Horrors*? How is violence linked to issues of sexual, racial, and class privilege? How does Wells compare the social and sexual experiences of black and white women under Jim Crow? In what ways does class shape the social behavior and political strategies of the historical actors Wells describes?

PAMPHLETS BY IDA B. WELLS-BARNETT

Southern Horrors: Lynch Law in All Its Phases (New York: New York Age, 1892).

The Reason Why the Colored American Is Not in the World's Columbian Exposition: The Afro-American's Contribution to Columbian Literature (Chicago: Ida B. Wells, 1893). *United States Atrocities: Lynch Law* (London: Lux Publishing, 1894).

A Red Record: Tabulated Statistics and Alleged Causes of Lynchings in the United States, 1892–1893–1894 (Chicago: Donahue & Henneberry, 1895).

Lynch Law in Georgia (Chicago: Ida B. Wells-Barnett, 1899).

Mob Rule in New Orleans: Robert Charles and His Fight to the Death (Chicago: Ida B. Wells-Barnett, 1900).

The Arkansas Race Riot (Chicago: Ida B. Wells-Barnett, 1920).

CHAPTER I: THE OFFENSE

Wednesday evening May 24th, 1892, the city of Memphis was filled with excitement. Editorials in the daily papers of that date caused a meeting to be held in the Cotton Exchange Building; a committee was sent for the editors of the *Free Speech*, an Afro-American journal published in that city, and the only reason the open threats of lynching that were made were not carried out was because they could not be found. The cause of all this commotion was the following editorial published in the *Free Speech* May 21st, 1892, the Saturday previous.

> Eight negroes lynched since last issue of the *Free Speech*, one at Little Rock, Ark., last Saturday morning where the citizens broke (?) into the penitentiary and got their man; three near Anniston, Ala., one near New Orleans; and three at Clarksville, Ga., the last three for killing a white man, and five on the same old racket—the new alarm about raping white women. The same programme of hanging, then shooting bullets into the lifeless bodies was carried out to the letter.
>
> Nobody in this section of the country believes the old threadbare lie that Negro men rape white women. If Southern white men are not careful, they will over-reach themselves and public sentiment will have a reaction; a conclusion will then be reached which will be very damaging to the moral reputation of their women.

The Daily Commercial of Wednesday following, May 25th, contained the following leader:

> Those negroes who are attempting to make the lynching of individuals of their race a means for arousing the worst passions of their kind are playing with a dangerous sentiment. The negroes may as well understand that there is no mercy for the negro rapist and little patience with his defenders. A negro organ printed in this city, in a recent issue publishes the following atrocious paragraph: "Nobody in this section of the country believes the old thread-bare lie that negro men rape white women. If Southern white men are not careful they will over-reach themselves, and public sentiment will have a reaction; and a conclusion will be reached which will be very damaging to the moral reputation of their women."
>
> The fact that a black scoundrel is allowed to live and utter such loathsome and repulsive calumnies is a volume of evidence as to the wonderful patience of Southern whites. But we have had enough of it.
>
> There are some things that the Southern white man will not tolerate, and the obscene intimations of the foregoing have brought the writer to the very outermost limit of public patience. We hope we have said enough.

The *Evening Scimitar* of same date, copied the *Commercial's* editorial with these words of comment: "Patience under such circumstances is not a virtue. If the negroes themselves do not apply the remedy without delay it will be the duty of those whom he has attacked to tie the wretch who utters these calumnies to a stake at the intersection of Main and Madison Sts., brand him in the forehead with a hot iron and perform upon him a surgical operation with a pair of tailor's shears."

Acting upon this advice, the leading citizens met in the Cotton Exchange Building the same evening, and threats of lynching were freely indulged, not by the lawless element upon which the deviltry of the South is usually saddled—but by the leading business men, in their leading business centre. Mr. Fleming, the business manager and owning a half interest the *Free Speech*, had to leave town to escape the mob, and was afterwards ordered not to return; letters and telegrams sent me in New York where I was spending my vacation advised me that bodily harm awaited my return. Creditors took possession of the office and sold the outfit, and the *Free Speech* was as if it had never been.

The editorial in question was prompted by the many inhuman and fiendish lynchings of Afro-Americans which have recently taken place and was meant as a warning. Eight lynched in one week and five of them charged with rape! The thinking public will not easily believe freedom and education more brutalizing than slavery, and the world knows that the crime of rape was unknown during four years of civil war, when the white women of the South were at the mercy of the race which is all at once charged with being a bestial one.

Since my business has been destroyed and I am an exile from home because of that editorial, the issue has been forced, and as the writer of it I feel that the race and the public generally should have a statement of the facts as they exist. They will serve at the same time as a defense for the Afro-American Sampsons who suffer themselves to be betrayed by white Delilahs.

The whites of Montgomery, Ala., knew J. C. Duke sounded the keynote of the situation—which they would gladly hide from the world, when he said in his paper, *The Herald*, five years ago: "Why is it that white women attract negro men now more than in former days? There was a time when such a thing was unheard of. There is a secret to this thing, and we greatly suspect it is the growing appreciation of white Juliets for colored Romeos." Mr. Duke, like the *Free Speech* proprietors, was forced to leave the city for reflecting on the "honah" of white women and his paper suppressed; but the truth remains that Afro-American men do not always rape (?) white women without their consent.

Mr. Duke, before leaving Montgomery, signed a card disclaiming any intention of slandering Southern white women. The editor of the *Free Speech* has no disclaimer to enter, but asserts instead that there are many white women in the South who would marry colored men if such an act would not place them at once beyond the pale of society and within the clutches of the law. The miscegnation laws of the South only operate against the legitimate union of the races; they leave the white man free to seduce all the colored girls he can, but it is death to the colored man who yields to the force and advances of a similar attraction in white women. White men lynch the offending Afro-American, not because he is a despoiler of virtue, but because he succumbs to the smiles of white women.

CHAPTER II: THE BLACK AND WHITE OF IT

The *Cleveland Gazette* of January 16, 1892, publishes a case in point. *Mrs. J. S. Underwood*, the wife of a minister of Elyria, Ohio, accused an Afro-American of rape. She told her husband that during his absence in 1888, stumping the State for the Prohibition Party, the man came to the kitchen door, forced his way in the house and insulted her. She tried to drive him out with a heavy poker, but he overpowered and chloroformed her, and when she revived her clothing was torn and she was in a horrible condition. She did not know the man but could identify him. She pointed out William Offett, a married man, who was arrested and, being in Ohio, was granted a trial.

The prisoner vehemently denied the charge of rape, but confessed he went to Mrs. Underwood's residence at her invitation and was criminally intimate with her at her request. This availed him nothing against the sworn testimony of a minister's wife, a lady of the highest respectability. He was found guilty, and entered the penitentiary, December 14, 1888, for fifteen years. Some time afterwards the woman's remorse led her to confess to her husband that the man was innocent.

These are her words: "I met Offett at the Post Office. It was raining. He was polite to me, and as I had several bundles in my arms he offered to carry them home for me, which he did. He had a strange fascination for me, and I invited him to call on me. He called, bringing chestnuts and candy for the children. By this means we got them to leave us alone in the room. Then I sat on his lap. He made a proposal to me and I readily consented. Why I did so, I do not know, but that I did is true. He visited me several times after that and each time I was indiscreet. I did not care after the first time. In fact I could not have resisted, and had no desire to resist."

When asked by her husband why she told him she had been outraged, she said: "I had several reasons for telling you. One was the neighbors saw the fellow here, another was, I was afraid I had contracted a loathsome disease, and still another was that I feared I might give birth to a Negro baby. I hoped to save my reputation by telling you a deliberate lie." Her husband horrified by the confession had Offett, who had already served four years, released and secured a divorce.

There are thousands of such cases throughout the South, with the difference that the Southern white men in insatiate fury wreak their vengeance without intervention of law upon the Afro-Americans who consort with their women. A few instances to substantiate the assertion that some white women love the company of the Afro-American will not be out of place. Most of these cases were reported by the daily papers of the South.

In the winter of 1885–6 the wife of a practicing physician in Memphis, in good social standing whose name has escaped me, left home, husband and children, and ran away with her black coachman. She was with him a month before her husband found and brought her home. The coachman could not be found. The doctor moved his family away from Memphis, and is living in another city under an assumed name. . . .

Sarah Clark of Memphis loved a black man and lived openly with him. When she was indicted last spring for miscegenation, she swore in court that she was *not* a white woman. This she did to escape the penitentiary and continued her illicit relation undisturbed. That she is of the lower class of whites, does not disturb the fact that she is a white woman. "The leading citizens" of Memphis are defending the "honor" of *all* white women, *demimonde* included.

Since the manager of the *Free Speech* has been run away from Memphis by the guardians of the honor of Southern white women, a young girl living on Poplar St., who was discovered in intimate relations with a handsome mulatto young colored man, Will Morgan by name, stole her father's money to send the young fellow away from that father's wrath. She has since joined him in Chicago. . . .

The very week the "leading citizens" of Memphis were making a spectacle of themselves in defense of all white women of every kind, an Afro-American, M. Stricklin, was found in a white woman's room in that city. Although she made no outcry of rape, he was jailed and would have been lynched, but the woman stated she bought curtains of him (he was a furniture dealer) and his business in her room that night was to put them up. A white woman's word was taken as absolutely in this case as when the cry of rape is made, and he was freed.

What is true of Memphis is true of the entire South. . . . Frank Weems of Chattanooga who was not lynched in May only because the prominent citizens became his body guard until the doors of the penitentiary closed on him, had letters in his pocket from the white woman in the case, making the appointment with him. Edward Coy who was burned alive in Texarkana, January 1, 1892, died protesting his innocence. Investigation since as given by the Bystander in the *Chicago Inter-Ocean*, October 1, proves: . . . The woman who was paraded as a victim of violence was of bad character; her husband was a drunkard and a gambler. . . . She was compelled by threats, if not by violence, to make the charge against the victim. . . . When she came to apply the match Coy asked her if she would burn him after they had "been sweethearting" so long. . . .

Hundreds of such cases might be cited, but enough have been given to prove the assertion that there are white women in the South who love the Afro-American's company even as there are white men notorious for their preference for Afro-American women.

There is hardly a town in the South which has not an instance of the kind which is well-known, and hence the assertion is reiterated that "nobody in the South believes the old thread-bare lie that negro men rape white women." Hence there is a growing demand among Afro-Americans that the guilt or innocence of parties accused of rape be fully established. They know the men of the section of the country who refuse this are not so desirous of punishing rapists as they pretend. The utterances of the leading white men show that with them it is not the crime but the *class*, Bishop Fitzgerald has become apologist for lynchers of the rapists of *white* women only. . . . But when the victim is a colored woman it is different.

Last winter in Baltimore, Md., three white ruffians assaulted a Miss Camphor, a young Afro-American girl, while out walking with a young man of her own race. They held her escort and outraged the girl. It was a deed dastardly enough to arouse Southern blood, which gives its horror of rape as excuse for lawlessness, but she was an Afro-American. The case went to the courts, an Afro-American lawyer defended the men and they were acquitted.

In Nashville, Tenn., there is a white man, Pat Hanifan, who outraged a little Afro-American girl, and, from the physical injuries received, she has been ruined for life. He was jailed for six months, discharged, and is now a detective in that city. . . . Only two weeks before Eph. Grizzard, who had only been *charged* with rape upon a white woman, had been taken from the jail, with Governor Buchanan and the police and militia standing by, dragged through the streets in broad daylight, knives plunged into him at every step, and with every fiendish cruelty a frenzied mob could devise, he was at last swung out on the bridge with hands cut to pieces as he tried to climb up the stanchions. . . .

At the very moment these civilized whites were announcing their determination "to protect their wives and daughters," by murdering Grizzard, a white man was in the same jail for raping eight-year-old Maggie Reese, an Afro-American girl. He was not harmed. The "honor" of grown women who were glad enough to be supported by the Grizzard boys and Ed Coy, as long as the liasion was not known, needed protection; they were white. The outrage upon helpless childhood needed no avenging in this case; she was black. . . .

CHAPTER III: THE NEW CRY

. . . Thoughtful Afro-Americans with the strong arm of the government withdrawn and with the hope to stop such wholesale massacres urged the race to sacrifice its political rights for the sake of peace. They honestly believed the race should fit itself for government, and when that should be done, the objection to race participation in politics would be removed.

But the sacrifice did not remove the trouble, nor move the South to justice. One by one the Southern States have legally (?) disfranchised the Afro-American, and since the repeal of the Civil Rights Bill nearly every Southern State has passed separate car laws with a penalty against their infringement. The race regardless of advancement is penned into filthy, stifling partitions cut off from smoking cars. . . . The dark and bloody record of the South shows 728 Afro-Americans lynched during the past eight years; . . . and not less than 150 have been known to have met violent death at the hands of cruel bloodthirsty mobs during the past nine months.

To palliate this record (which grows worse as the Afro-American becomes intelligent) and excuse some of the most heinous crimes that ever stained the history of a country, the South is shielding itself behind the plausible screen of defending the honor of its women. This, too, in the face of the fact that only *one-third* of the 728 victims to mobs have been *charged* with rape, to say nothing of those of that one-third who were innocent of the charge. . . .

Even to the better class of Afro-Americans the crime of rape is so revolting they have too often taken the white man's word and given lynch law neither the investigation nor condemnation it deserved.

They forget that a concession of the right to lynch a man for a certain crime, not only concedes the right to lynch any person for any crime, but (so frequently is the cry of rape now raised) it is in a fair way to stamp us a race of rapists and desperadoes. They have gone on hoping and believing that general education and financial strength would solve the difficulty, and are devoting their energies to the accumulation of both. . . .

DOCUMENTS

Claiming an Education

Zitkala-Ša (Gertrude Simmons Bonnin), " . . . this semblance of civilization . . ."

Zitkala-Ša, whose mother was Sioux and father was Anglo-American, sought throughout her life to bridge the cultures of Native Americans and the United States. She was one of the first American Indian women who built an independent career as a writer; her voice, as the following selection from her early writing shows, could be simultaneously eloquent, sentimental, and bitter. Born in 1876, Zitkala-Ša was eight years old when she left her home on the Yankton Sioux Agency in South Dakota for White's Indiana Manual Labor Institute in Wabash, Indiana, a training school funded by Quakers. She continued her education first at a teacher training school close to her home, then at Earlham College, and finally at the New England Conservatory of Music in Boston where she studied the violin.

Throughout her life, Zitkala-Ša worked with her husband, who was an employee of the Bureau of Indian Affairs (BIA), advocating citizenship for Indians, exposing corruption in the BIA, and insisting on the dignity of Indian religions. In this stage of her life, she used her anglicized married name, Gertrude Simmons Bonnin. Bonnin lobbied for the Indian Citizenship Act of 1924; she founded the National Council of American Indians; and she sought to shape the Indian policy of the New Deal years.

When she wrote this memoir of her childhood in 1900 at age twenty-four, Zitkala-Ša had not yet taught at the Carlisle Indian School in Pennsylvania. The experience would strengthen her criticism of the practice of removing native children from their homes. It would also lead her to expose the corruption she found among the school's directors, who received federal money for each child they boarded and whose promotion of "Americanization" could be harsh and cruel. To what extent did her mother anticipate that the experience at the mission school would be difficult? What advantage did the educators think would result from cutting girls' hair? What evidence is there to suggest that she herself was involved in the process of acculturation?

The first turning away from the easy, natural flow of my life occurred in an early spring. It was in my eighth year; in the month of March, I afterward learned. At this age I knew but one language, and that was my mother's native tongue.

From some of my playmates I heard that two paleface missionaries were in our village. They were from that class of white men who wore big hats and carried large hearts, they said. Running direct to my mother, I began to question her why these two strangers were

Excerpted from "Impressions of an Indian Childhood," "The School Days of an Indian Girl," and "An Indian Teacher among Indians" by Zitkala-Ša, *Atlantic Monthly* 85 (January, February, March 1900): 45–47,186–87, 386.

Zitkala-Ša in traditional dress. (Courtesy of the Smithsonian Institution.)

among us. She told me, after I had teased much, that they had come to take away Indian boys and girls to the East. My mother did not seem to want me to talk about them. But in a day or two, I gleaned many wonderful stories from my playfellows concerning the strangers.

"Mother, my friend Judéwin is going home with the missionaries. She is going to a more beautiful country than ours; the palefaces told her so!" I said wistfully, wishing in my heart that I too might go.

Mother sat in a chair, and I was hanging on her knee. Within the last two seasons my big brother Dawée had returned from a three years' education in the East, and his coming back influenced my mother to take a farther step from her native way of living. First it was a change from the buffalo skin to the white man's canvas that covered our wigwam. Now she had given up her wigwam of slender poles, to live, a foreigner, in a home of clumsy logs.

Judéwin had told me of the great tree where grew red, red apples; and how we could reach out our hands and pick all the red apples we could eat. I had never seen apple trees. I had never tasted more than a dozen red apples in my life; and when I heard of the orchards of the East, I was eager to roam among them. The missionaries smiled into my eyes, and patted my head. I wondered how mother could say such hard words against them.

"Mother, ask them if little girls may have all the red apples they want, when they go East," I whispered aloud, in my excitement.

The interpreter heard me, and answered: "Yes, little girl, the nice red apples are for those who pick them; and you will have a ride on the iron horse if you go with these good people."

I had never seen a train, and he knew it.

"Mother, I'm going East! I like big red apples, and I want to ride on the iron horse! Mother, say yes!" I pleaded.

My mother said nothing. The missionaries waited in silence; and my eyes began to blur with tears, though I struggled to choke them back. The corners of my mouth twitched, and my mother saw me.

"I am not ready to give you any word," she said to them. "Tomorrow I shall send you my answer by my son."

With this they left us. Alone with my mother, I yielded to my tears, and cried aloud, shaking my head so as not to hear what she was saying to me. This was the first time I had ever been so unwilling to give up my own desire that I refused to harken to my mother's voice.

There was a solemn silence in our home that night. Before I went to bed I begged the Great Spirit to make my mother willing I should go with the missionaries.

The next morning came, and my mother called me to her side. "My daughter, do you still persist in wishing to leave your mother?" she asked.

"Oh, mother, it is not that I wish to leave you, but I want to see the wonderful Eastern land," I answered. . . .

. . . My brother Dawée came for mother's decision. I dropped my play, and crept close to my aunt.

"Yes, Dawée, my daughter, though she does not understand what it all means, is anxious to go. She will need an education when she is grown, for then there will be fewer real Dakotas, and many more palefaces. This tearing her away, so young, from her mother is necessary, if I would have her an educated woman. The palefaces, who owe us a large debt for stolen lands, have begun to pay a tardy justice in offering some education to our children. But I know my daughter must suffer keenly in this experiment. For her sake, I dread to tell you my reply to the missionaries. Go, tell them that they may take my little daughter, and that the Great Spirit shall not fail to reward them according to their hearts."

Wrapped in my heavy blanket, I walked with my mother to the carriage that was soon to take us to the iron horse. I was happy. I met my playmates, who were also wearing their best thick blankets. We showed one another our new beaded moccasins, and the width of the belts that girdled our new dresses. Soon we were being drawn rapidly away by the white man's horses. When I saw the lonely figure of my mother vanish in the distance, a sense of regret settled heavily upon me. I felt suddenly weak, as if I might fall limp to the ground. I was in the hands of strangers whom my mother did not fully trust. I no longer felt free to be myself, or to voice my own feelings. The tears trickled down my cheeks, and I buried my face in the folds of my blanket. Now the first step, parting me from my mother, was taken, and all my belated tears availed nothing.

Having driven thirty miles to the ferryboat, we crossed the Missouri in the evening. Then riding again a few miles eastward, we stopped before a massive brick building. I looked at it in amazement, and with a vague misgiving, for in our village I had never seen so large a house. Trembling with fear and distrust of the palefaces, my teeth chattering from the chilly ride, I crept noiselessly in my soft moccasins along the narrow hall, keeping very close to the bare wall. I was as frightened and bewildered as the captured young of a wild creature.

The first day in the land of apples was a bitter-cold one; for the snow still covered the ground, and the trees were bare. A large bell rang for breakfast, its loud metallic voice crashing through the belfry overhead and into our sensitive ears. The annoying clatter of shoes on bare floors gave us no peace. The constant clash of harsh noises, with an undercurrent of many voices murmuring an unknown tongue, made a bedlam within which I was securely tied. And though my spirit tore itself in struggling for its lost freedom, all was useless.

A paleface woman, with white hair, came up after us. We were placed in a line of girls who were marching into the dining room. These were Indian girls, in stiff shoes and closely clinging dresses. The small girls wore sleeved aprons and shingled hair. As I walked noiselessly in my soft moccasins, I felt like sinking to the floor, for my blanket had been stripped from my shoulders. I looked hard at the Indian girls, who seemed not to care that they were even more immodestly dressed than I, in their tightly fitting clothes. While we marched in, the boys entered at an opposite door. I watched for the three young braves who came in our party. I spied them in the rear ranks, looking as uncomfortable as I felt. . . .

. . . Late in the morning, my friend Judéwin gave me a terrible warning. Judéwin knew a few words of English; and she had overheard the paleface woman talk about cutting our long, heavy hair. Our mothers had taught us that only unskilled warriors who were captured had their hair shingled by the enemy. Among our people, short hair was worn by mourners, and shingled hair by cowards!

We discussed our fate some moments, and when Judéwin said, "We have to submit, because they are strong," I rebelled.

"No, I will not submit! I will struggle first!" I answered.

I watched my chance, and when no one noticed I disappeared. I crept up the stairs as quietly as I could in my squeaking shoes—my moccasins had been exchanged for shoes. Along the hall I passed, without knowing whither I was going. Turning aside to an open door, I found a large room with three white beds in it. The windows were covered with dark green curtains, which made the room very dim. Thankful that no one was there, I directed my steps toward the corner farthest from the door. On my hands and knees I crawled under the bed, and cuddled myself in the dark corner.

From my hiding place I peered out, shuddering with fear whenever I heard footsteps near by. Though in the hall loud voices were calling my name, and I knew that even Judéwin was searching for me, I did not open my mouth to answer. Then the steps were quickened and the voices became excited. The sounds came nearer and nearer. Women and girls entered the room. I held my breath, and watched them open closet doors and peep behind large trunks. Some one threw up the curtains, and the room was filled with sudden light. What caused them to stoop and look under the bed I do not know. I remember being dragged out, though I resisted by kicking and scratching wildly. In spite of myself, I was carried downstairs and tied fast in a chair.

I cried aloud, shaking my head all the while until I felt the cold blades of the scissors against my neck, and heard them gnaw off one of my thick braids. Then I lost my spirit. Since the day I was taken from my mother I had suffered extreme indignities. People had stared at me. I had been tossed about in the air like a wooden puppet. And now my long hair was shingled like a coward's! In my anguish I moaned for my mother, but no one came to comfort me. Not a soul reasoned quietly with me, as my own mother used to do; for now I was only one of many little animals driven by a herder. . . .

. . . Now, as I look back upon the recent past, I see it from a distance, as a whole. I remember how, from morning till evening, many specimens of civilized peoples visited the Indian school. The city folks with canes and eyeglasses, the countrymen with sunburnt cheeks and clumsy feet, forgot their relative social ranks in an ignorant curiosity. Both sorts of these Christian palefaces were alike astounded at seeing the children of savage warriors so docile and industrious.

As answers to their shallow inquiries they received the students' sample work to look upon. Examining the neatly figured pages, and gazing upon the Indian girls and boys bending over their books, the white visitors walked out of the schoolhouse well satisfied: They were educating the children of the red man! They were paying a liberal fee to the government employees in whose able hands lay the small forest of Indian timber.

In this fashion many have passed idly through the Indian schools during the last decade, afterward to boast of their charity to the North American Indian. But few there are who have paused to question whether real life or long-lasting death lies beneath this semblance of civilization.

Mary McLeod Bethune, *"How the Bethune-Cookman College campus started"*

Mary McLeod Bethune was one of the most distinguished educators of her generation. The daughter of slaves, she received her early education from missionary teachers. Like others of her race who saw education as a key to racial advancement at a time when the white South was indifferent if not hostile to the aspirations of African-Americans, Bethune faced extraordinary obstacles. When she began a little school at Daytona Beach, Florida, in 1904, America was entering an era of reform. Yet even most northern progressives—with the notable exception of women such as Mary White Ovington, one of the founders of the NAACP—shared the racist assumptions of that era, believing that the future of black women, like immigrant women, lay in domestic service. Bethune had larger dreams. Because of her courage, energy, and vision, she was able to keep her little school afloat with her intrepid fund-raising, guiding its growth from grammar school to high school and to what finally became an accredited four-year college. President of the institution from its founding until her resignation in 1942, she remained a trustee of Bethune-Cookman College until her death in 1955. She was an activist and held many important posts within the black community, founding such organizations as the National Association of Colored Women's Clubs and the National Council of Negro Women. A national figure as well, she served in the Roosevelt administration during the 1930s, advising the president on minority affairs. She was also involved in early efforts on behalf of the United Nations. Her many offices and honors, however, never diverted her from her primary purpose—the pursuit of full citizenship rights for all black Americans.*

*See Joyce A. Hanson, *Mary McLeod Bethune and Black Women's Political Activism* (Columbia: University of Missouri Press, 2003).

Excerpted from "Faith That Moved a Dump Heap" by Mary McLeod Bethune, in *Who, The Magazine about People* 1, no. 3 (June 1941): 31–35, 54.

On October 3, 1904, I opened the doors of my school, with an enrollment of five little girls, aged from eight to twelve, whose parents paid me fifty cents' weekly tuition. My own child was the only boy in the school. Though I hadn't a penny left, I considered cash money as the smallest part of my resources. I had faith in a living God, faith in myself, and a desire to serve. . . .

We burned logs and used the charred splinters as pencils, and mashed elderberries for ink. I begged strangers for a broom, a lamp, a bit of cretonne to put around the packing case which served as my desk. I haunted the city dump and the trash piles behind hotels, retrieving discarded linen and kitchenware, cracked dishes, broken chairs, pieces of old lumber. Everything was scoured and mended. This was part of the training to salvage, to reconstruct, to make bricks without straw. As parents began gradually to leave their children overnight, I had to provide sleeping accommodations. I took corn sacks for mattresses. Then I picked Spanish moss from trees, dried and cured it, and used it as a substitute for mattress hair.

The school expanded fast. In less than two years I had 250 pupils. In desperation I hired a large hall next to my original little cottage, and used it as a combined dormitory and classroom. I concentrated more and more on girls, as I felt they especially were hampered by lack of educational opportunities. . . .

I had many volunteer workers and a few regular teachers, who were paid from fifteen

Soon after opening the Daytona Educational and Industrial Institute for Negro Girls, its founder, Mary McLeod Bethune, posed with pupils lining the road leading to its first Daytona Beach building—a four-room cottage. One of the fields nearby, nicknamed Hell's Hole, would soon be purchased by Bethune as the foundation of a genuine campus. At the time, Florida's handful of state-supported public "high" schools for blacks operated only five months a year, in contrast to nine for whites' schools. Bethune, a tireless fund-raiser, chose Daytona Beach, despite the fact that it was home to a Ku Klux Klan chapter, because of two primary factors: it had a fast-growing black population attracted by relatively good jobs, and its wealthy whites, both year-round and summer residents, included some who supported her efforts. (Courtesy of the State Archives of Florida.)

to twenty-five dollars a month and board. I was supposed to keep the balance of the funds for my own pocket, but there was never any balance—only a yawning hole. I wore old clothes sent me by mission boards, recut and redesigned for me in our dress-making classes. At last I saw that our only solution was to stop renting space, and to buy and build our own college.

Near by was a field, popularly called Hell's Hole, which was used as a dumping ground. I approached the owner, determined to buy it. The price was $250. In a daze, he finally agreed to take five dollars down, and the balance in two years. I promised to be back in a few days with the initial payment. He never knew it, but I didn't have five dollars. I raised this sum selling ice cream and sweet-potato pies to the workmen on construction jobs, and I took the owner his money in small change wrapped in my handkerchief.

That's how the Bethune-Cookman college campus started. . . .

As the school expanded, whenever I saw a need for some training or service we did not supply, I schemed to add it to our curriculum. Sometimes that took years. When I came to Florida, there were no hospitals where a Negro could go. A student became critically ill with appendicitis, so I went to a local hospital and begged a white physician to take her in and operate. My pleas were so desperate he finally agreed. A few days after the operation, I visited my pupil.

When I appeared at the front door of the hospital, the nurse ordered me around to the back way. I thrust her aside—and found my little girl segregated in a corner of the porch behind the kitchen. Even my toes clenched with rage.

That decided me. I called on three of my faithful friends, asking them to buy a little cottage behind our school as a hospital. They agreed, and we started with two beds.

From this humble start grew a fully equipped twenty-bed hospital—our college infirmary and a refuge for the needy throughout the state. It was staffed by white and black physicians and by our own student nurses. We ran this hospital for twenty years as part of our contribution to community life; but a short time ago, to ease our financial burden, the city took it over.

Gradually, as educational facilities expanded and there were other places where small children could go, we put the emphasis on high-school and junior-college training. In 1922, Cookman College, a men's school, the first in the state for the higher education of Negroes, amalgamated with us. The combined coeducational college, now run under the auspices of the Methodist Episcopal Church, is called Bethune-Cookman College. We have fourteen modern buildings, a beautiful campus of thirty-two acres, an enrollment in regular and summer sessions of 600 students, a faculty and staff of thirty-two, and 1,800 graduates. The college property, now valued at more than $800,000, is entirely unencumbered.

When I walk through the campus, with its stately palms and well-kept lawns, and think back to the dump-heap foundation, I rub my eyes and pinch myself. And I remember my childish visions in the cotton fields.

But values cannot be calculated in ledger figures and property. More than all else the college has fulfilled my ideals of distinctive training and service. Extending far beyond the immediate sphere of its graduates and students, it has already enriched the lives of 100,000 Negroes.

In 1934, President Franklin D. Roosevelt appointed me director of the division of Negro affairs of the National Youth Administration. My main task now is to supervise the training provided for 600,000 Negro children, and I have to run the college by remote control. Every few weeks, however, I snatch a day or so and return to my beloved home.

This is a strenuous program. The doctor shakes his head and says, "Mrs. Bethune, slow down a little. Relax! Take it just a little easier." I promise to reform, but in an hour the promise is forgotten.

For I am my mother's daughter, and the drums of Africa still beat in my heart. They will not let me rest while there is a single Negro boy or girl without a chance to prove his worth.

PEGGY PASCOE

Ophelia Paquet, a Tillamook Indian Wife: Miscegenation Laws and the Privileges of Property

When Ophelia Paquet's husband died in 1919, the county court recognized her as his widow—the Paquets had been married for thirty years—and appointed Ophelia to administer his estate. As there were no children, Ophelia stood to inherit her late husband's property. It was a just arrangement inasmuch as it was her money that had been used to purchase the land and pay taxes on it. John Paquet, Fred's disreputable brother, thought otherwise. Ultimately the court awarded the estate to him, leaving the sixty-five-year-old widow destitute.

Ophelia's story is a complicated one. It illuminates many issues: the purpose of miscegenation laws, the role of marriage in the transmission of property, the "invisibility" of married women's economic contributions, and the way race can compound gender disadvantage.

In what respects does John Paquet's victory illuminate the convergence of race and class? What parallels does Pascoe draw between the Paquet case and contemporary debates over same-sex marriage? How is the failure to count Ophelia's economic contribution to the marriage related to the "pastoralization" of housework that Jeanne Boydston discussed on pages 174–185?

Although miscegenation laws are usually remembered (when they are remembered at all) as a Southern development aimed at African Americans, they were actually a much broader phenomenon. Adopted in both the North and the South in the colonial period and extended to western states in the nineteenth century, miscegenation laws grew up with slavery but became even more significant after the Civil War, for it was then that they came to form the crucial "bottom line" of the system of white supremacy embodied in segregation.

The earliest miscegenation laws, passed in the South, forbade whites to marry African Americans, but the list of groups prohibited from marrying whites was gradually expanded, especially in western states, by adding first American Indians, then Chinese and Japanese (both often referred to by the catchall term "Mongolians"), and then Malays (or Filipinos). And even this didn't exhaust the list. Oregon prohibited whites from marrying "Kanakas" (or native Hawaiians); South Dakota proscribed "Coreans"; Arizona singled out Hindus; and Georgia prohibited whites from marrying "West" and "Asiatic" Indians.

Many states packed their miscegenation laws with multiple categories and quasi-mathematical definitions of "race." Oregon, for example, declared that "it shall not be lawful within this state for any white person, male or female, to intermarry with any negro, Chinese, or any person having one fourth or more negro, Chinese, or Kanaka blood, or any person having more than one half Indian blood." Altogether, miscegenation laws

From *New Viewpoints in Women's History: Working Papers from the Schlesinger Library 50th Anniversary Conference, March 4–5, 1994,* ed. Susan Ware. Cambridge, Mass.: Arthur and Elizabeth Schlesinger Library on the History of Women in America, Radcliffe College (1994). Condensed and reprinted by permission of the author. Notes have been renumbered and edited.

covered forty-one states and colonies. They spanned three centuries of American history: the first ones were enacted in the 1660s, and the last ones were not declared unconstitutional until 1967.

Although it is their sexual taboos that have attracted most recent attention, the structure and function of miscegenation laws were . . . more fundamentally related to the institution of marriage than to sexual behavior itself. In sheer numbers, many more laws prohibited interracial marriage than interracial sex. And in an even deeper sense, all miscegenation laws were designed to privilege marriage as a social and economic unit. Couples who challenged the laws knew that the right to marry translated into social respectability and economic benefits, including inheritance rights and legitimacy for children, that were denied to sexual liaisons outside marriage. Miscegenation laws were designed to patrol this border by making so-called "miscegenous marriage" a legal impossibility. Thus criminal courts treated offenders as if they had never been married at all; that is, prosecutors charged interracial couples with the moral offense of fornication or other illicit sex crimes, then denied them the use of marriage as a defense.

Civil courts guarded the junction between marriage and economic privilege. From Reconstruction to the 1930s, most miscegenation cases heard in civil courts were ex post facto attempts to invalidate relationships that had already lasted for a long time. They were brought by relatives or, sometimes, by the state, after the death of one partner, almost always a white man. Many of them were specifically designed to take property or inheritances away from the surviving partner, almost always an African American or American Indian woman. By looking at civil law suits like these (which were, at least in appeals court records, more common than criminal cases), we can begin to trace the links between white patriarchal privilege and property that sustained miscegenation laws.

Let me illustrate the point by describing [a] sample case, *In re Paquet's Estate,* decided by the Oregon Supreme Court in 1921.[1] The Paquet case, like most of the civil miscegenation cases of this period, was fought over the estate of a white man. The man in question, Fred Paquet, died in 1919, survived by his 63-year-old Tillamook Indian wife, named Ophelia. The Paquet estate included 22 acres of land, some farm animals, tools, and a buggy, altogether worth perhaps $2500.[2] Fred and Ophelia's relationship had a long history. In the 1880s, Fred had already begun to visit Ophelia frequently and openly enough that he had become one of many targets of a local grand jury which periodically threatened to indict white men who lived with Indian women.[3] Seeking to formalize the relationship—and, presumably, end this harrassment—Fred consulted a lawyer, who advised him to make sure to hold a ceremony which would meet the legal requirements for an "Indian custom" marriage. Accordingly, in 1889, Fred not only reached the customary agreement with Ophelia's Tillamook relatives, paying them $50 in gifts, but also sought the formal sanction of Tillamook tribal chief Betsy Fuller (who was herself married to a white man); Fuller arranged for a tribal council to consider and confirm the marriage.[4] Afterwards Fred and Ophelia lived together until his death, for more than thirty years. Fred clearly considered Ophelia his wife, and his neighbors, too, recognized their relationship, but because Fred died without leaving a formal will, administration of the estate was subject to state laws which provided for the distribution of property to surviving family members.

When Fred Paquet died, the county court recognized Ophelia as his widow and promptly appointed her administrator of the estate. Because the couple had no children, all the property, including the land, which Ophelia lived on and the Paquets had owned for more than two decades, would ordinarily have gone to her. Two days later, though, Fred's brother John came forward to contest Ophelia for control over the property.[5] John Paquet had little to recommend him to the court. Some of his neighbors accused him of raping native women, and he had such an unsavory reputation in the community that at one point the county judge declared him "a man of immoral habits . . . incompetent to transact ordinary business affairs and generally untrustworthy."[6] He was, however, a "white" man, and under Oregon's miscegenation law, that was enough to ensure that he won his case against Ophelia, an Indian woman.

The case eventually ended up in the Oregon Supreme Court. In making its decision, the key issue for the court was whether or not to recognize Fred and Ophelia's marriage, which violated Oregon's miscegenation law.[7] The Court listened to—and then dismissed—Ophelia's argument that the marriage met the requirements for an Indian custom marriage and so should have been recognized as valid out of routine courtesy to the authority of another jurisdiction (that of the Tillamook tribe).[8] The Court also heard and dismissed Ophelia's claim that Oregon's miscegenation law discriminated against Indians and was therefore an unconstitutional denial of the Fourteenth Amendment guarantee of equal protection. The Court ingenuously explained its reasoning; it held that the Oregon miscegenation law did not discriminate because it "applied alike to all persons, either white, negroes, Chinese, Kanaka, or Indians."[9] Following this logic, the Court declared Fred and Ophelia's marriage void because it violated Oregon's miscegenation law; it ordered that the estate and all its property be transferred to "the only relative in the state," John Paquet, to be distributed among him, his siblings and their heirs.[10]

As the Paquet case demonstrates, miscegenation law did not always prevent the formation of interracial relationships, sexual or otherwise. Fred and Ophelia had, after all, lived together for more than thirty years and had apparently won recognition as a couple from many of those around them; their perseverance had even allowed them to elude grand jury crackdowns. They did not, however, manage to escape the really crucial power of miscegenation law: the role it played in connecting white supremacy to the transmission of property. In American law, marriage provided the glue which allowed for the transmission of property from husbands to wives and their children; miscegenation law kept property within racial boundaries by invalidating marriages between white men and women of color whenever ancillary white relatives like John Paquet contested them.[11] . . . Property, so often described in legal sources as simple economic assets (like land and capital) was actually a much more expansive phenomenon, one which took various forms and structured crucial relationships. . . . Race is in and of itself a kind of property.[12] As [legal scholar] Derrick Bell . . . explains, most whites did—and still do—"expect the society to recognize an unspoken but no less vested property right in their 'whiteness.'" "This right," Bell maintains, "is recognized and upheld by courts and the society like all property rights under a government created and sustained primarily for that purpose."[13]

As applied to the Paquet case, this theme is easy to trace, for, in a sense, the victorious John Paquet had turned his "whiteness" (the best—and perhaps the only—asset he had) into property, and did so at Ophelia's expense. This transformation happened not once but repeatedly. One instance occurred shortly after the county judge had branded John Paquet immoral and unreliable. Dismissing these charges as the opinions of "a few scalawags and Garibaldi Indians," John Paquet's lawyers rallied enough white witnesses who would speak in his defense to mount an appeal which convinced a circuit court judge to declare Paquet competent to administer the estate.[14] Another example of the transformation of "whiteness" into property came when the Oregon Supreme Court ruled that Ophelia Paquet's "Indianness" disqualified her from legal marriage to a white man; with Ophelia thus out of the way, John and his siblings won the right to inherit the property.

The second property relationship [is] illuminated by the etymological connection between the words "property" and "propriety." Miscegenation law played on this connection by drawing a sharp line between "legitimate marriage" on the one hand and "illicit sex" on the other, then defining all interracial relationships as illicit sex. The distinction was a crucial one, for husbands were legally obligated to provide for legitimate wives and children, but men owed nothing to "mere" sexual partners: neither inheritance rights nor the legitimacy of children accompanied illicit relationships.

By defining all interracial relationships as illicit, miscegenation law did not so much prohibit or punish illicit sex as it did create and reproduce it. Conditioned by stereotypes which associated women of color with hypersexuality, judges routinely branded long-term settled relationships as "mere" sex rather than marriage. Lawyers played to these assumptions by reducing interracial relationships to interracial sex, then distinguishing interracial sex from marriage by associating it with prostitution. Describing the relationship between Fred and

Ophelia Paquet, for example, John Paquet's lawyers claimed that "the alleged 'marriage' was a mere commercial affair" that did not deserve legal recognition because "the relations were entirely meretricious from their inception."[15]

It was all but impossible for women of color to escape the legacy of these associations. Ophelia Paquet's lawyers tried to find a way out by changing the subject. Rather than refuting the association between women of color and illicit sexuality, they highlighted its flip side, the supposed connection between white women and legitimate marriage. Ophelia Paquet, they told the judge, "had been to the man as good a wife as any white woman could have been."[16] In its final decision, the Oregon Supreme Court came as close as any court of that time did to accepting this line of argument. Taking the unusual step of admitting that "the record is conclusive that [Ophelia] lived with [Fred] as a good and faithful wife for more than 30 years," the judges admitted that they felt some sympathy for Ophelia, enough to recommend—but not require—that John Paquet offer her what they called "a fair and reasonable settlement."[17] But in the Paquet case, as in other miscegenation cases, sexual morality, important as it was, was nonetheless still subordinate to channelling the transmission of property along racial... lines. Ophelia got a judicial pat on the head for good behavior, but John and his siblings got the property.

Which brings me to the third form of property relationship structured by miscegenation laws—and, for that matter, marriage laws in general—and that is women's economic dependence on men. Here the problems started long before the final decision gave John Paquet control of the Paquet estate. One of the most intriguing facts about the Paquet case is that everyone acted as if the estate in question belonged solely to Fred Paquet. In fact, however, throughout the Paquet marriage, Fred had whiled away most of his time; it was Ophelia's basket-making, fruit-picking, milk-selling, and wage work that had provided the income they needed to sustain themselves. And although the deed to their land was made out in Fred Paquet's name, the couple had used Ophelia's earnings, combined with her proceeds from government payments to Tillamook tribal members, both to purchase the property and to pay the yearly taxes on it. It is significant... that, although lawyers on both sides of the case knew this, neither they nor the Oregon Supreme Court judges considered it a key issue at the trial in which Ophelia lost all legal right to what the courts considered "Fred's" estate.

Indeed, Ophelia's economic contribution might never have been taken into account if it were not for the fact that in the wake of the Oregon Supreme Court decision, United States Indian officials found themselves responsible for the care of the now impoverished Ophelia. Apparently hoping both to defend Ophelia and to relieve themselves of the burden of her support, they sued John Paquet on Ophelia's behalf. Working through the federal courts that covered Indian relations and equity claims, rather than the state courts that enforced miscegenation laws, they eventually won a partial settlement. Yet their argument, too, reflected the assumption that men were better suited than women to the ownership of what the legal system referred to as "real" property. Although their brief claimed that "Fred Paquet had practically no income aside from the income he received through the labor and efforts of the said Ophelia Paquet," they asked the Court to grant Ophelia the right to only half of the Paquet land.[18] In the end, the Court ordered that Ophelia should receive a cash settlement (the amount was figured at half the value of the land), but only if she agreed to make her award contingent on its sale.[19] To get any settlement at all, Ophelia Paquet had to relinquish all claims to actual ownership of the land, although such a claim might have given her legal grounds to prevent its sale and so allow her to spend her final years on the property.

It is not even clear that she received any payment on the settlement ordered by the court. As late as 1928, John Paquet's major creditor complained to a judge that Paquet had repeatedly turned down acceptable offers to sell the land; perhaps he had chosen to live on it himself.[20]

Like any single example, the Paquet case captures miscegenation law as it stood at one moment, and a very particular moment at that, one that might be considered the high water mark of American courts' determination to structure both family formation and property transmission along racial dividing lines.

Today, most Americans have trouble remembering that miscegenation laws ever existed . . . [and] are incredulous at the injustice and the arbitrariness of the racial classifications that stand out in [such] . . . cases. [Yet] few . . . notice that one of the themes raised in the Paquet case—the significance of marriage in structuring property transmission—not only remains alive and well, but has, in fact, outlived both the erosion of traditional patriarchy and the rise and fall of racial classifications in marriage law.

More than a generation after the demise of miscegenation laws . . . the drawing of exclusionary lines around marriage [continues]. . . . The most prominent—though hardly the only—victims are lesbian and gay couples, who point out that the sex classifications currently embedded in marriage law operate in much the same way that the race classifications embedded in miscegenation laws once did: that is, they allow courts to categorize same-sex relationships as illicit sex rather than legitimate marriage and they allow courts to exclude same-sex couples from the property benefits of marriage, which now include everything from tax advantages to medical insurance coverage.

Both these modern legal battles and the earlier ones fought by couples like Fred and Ophelia Paquet suggest . . . that focusing on the connections between property and the political economy of marriage . . . offer a revealing vantage point from which to study both the form and power of analogies between race and sex classifications in American law and the relationships between race and gender hierarchies in American history.

Notes

1. The Paquet case can be followed not only by reading the text of the appeals court decision, In re Paquet's Estate, 200 P 911 (Oregon 1921), but also in the following archival case files: *Paquet* v. *Paquet*, file No. 4268, Oregon Supreme Court, 1920; *Paquet* v. *Henkle*, file No. 4267, Oregon Supreme Court, 1920; and Tillamook County Probate file #605, all in the Oregon State Archives; and in *U.S.* v. *John B. Paquet*, Judgment Roll 11409, Register No. 8-8665, March 1925, National Archives and Records Administration, Pacific Northwest Branch.

2. Initial estimates of the value of the estate were much higher, ranging from $4500 to $12,500. I have relied on the figure of $2528.50 provided by court-appointed assessors. See Tillamook Country Probate file #605, Inventory and Appraisement, June 15, 1920.

3. *Paquet* v. *Paquet*, Respondent's brief, November 1, 1920, pp. 2–5.

4. Tillamook County Probate file #605, Judge A.M. Hare, Findings of Facts and Conclusions of Law, February 3, 1920; *Paquet* v. *Paquet*, Appellants Abstract of Record, September 3, 1920, pp. 10–16.

5. *Paquet* v. *Paquet*, Appellants Abstract of Record, September 3, 1920, p. 3.

6. Tillamook County Probate file #605, Judge A. M. Hare, Findings of Fact and Conclusions of Law, February 3, 1920.

7. Court records identify Fred Paquet as being of French Canadian origin. Both sides agreed that Fred was a "pure" or "full-blooded" "white" man and Ophelia was a "pure" or "full-blooded" "Indian" woman. *Paquet* v. *Paquet*, Appellant's First Brief, October 8, 1920, p. 1; *Paquet* v. *Paquet;* Respondent's brief, November 1, 1920, p. 2.

8. The question of legal jurisdiction over Indian tribes was—and is—a very thorny issue. Relations with Indians were generally a responsibility of the U.S. federal government, which, although it advocated assimilating Indian families into white middle-class molds, had little practical choice but to grant general recognition to tribally-determined marriages performed according to Indian custom. In the U.S. legal system, however, jurisdiction over marriage rested with the states rather than the federal government. States could, therefore, use their control over marriage as a wedge to exert some power over Indians by claiming that Indian-white marriages, especially those performed outside recognized reservations, were subject to state jurisdiction. In the Paquet case, for example, the court insisted that, because the Tillamook had never been assigned to a reservation and because Fred and Ophelia lived in a mixed settlement, Ophelia could not be considered part of a recognized tribe nor a "ward" of the federal government. As events would later show, both contentions were inaccurate: Ophelia was an enrolled member of the Tillamook tribe, which was under the supervision of the Siletz Indian Agency; the federal government claimed her as "a ward of the United States." See *U.S.* v. *John B. Paquet*, Bill of Complaint in Equity, September 21, 1923, p. 3.

9. In re Paquet's Estate, 200 P 911 at 913 (Oregon 1921).

10. In re Paquet's Estate, 200 P 911 at 914 (Oregon 1921).

11. Although the issue did not come up in the Paquet case, . . . in miscegenation cases, not only the wife but also the children might lose their legal standing, for one effect of invalidating an interracial marriage was to make the children technically illegitimate. According to the law of most states, illegitimate children automatically inherited from their mothers, but they could inherit from their fathers only if their father had taken legal steps to formally recognize or adopt them. Since plaintiffs could rarely convince judges that fathers had done so, the children of interracial marriages were often disinherited along with their mothers.

12. Derrick Bell, "Remembrances of Racism Past," in Hill and Jones, *Race in America: The Struggle for Equality* (Madison: University of Wisconsin Press, 1992), 78. See also Bell, "White Superiority in

America: Its Legal Legacy, Its Economic Costs," *Villanova Law Review* 33 (1988), 767–779.

13. *Paquet* v. *Henkle*, Respondent's brief, March 14, 1920, p. 6; *Paquet* v. *Henkle*, Index to Transcript, August 25, 1920, p. 3.

14. *Paquet* v. *Paquet*, Respondent's brief, November 1, 1920, p. 7. Using typical imagery, they added that the Paquet relationship was "a case where a white man and a full blooded Indian woman have chosen to cohabit together illictly [sic], to agree to a relation of concubinage, which is not only a violation of the law of Oregon, but a transgression against the law of morality and the law of nature" (p. 16).

15. *Paquet* v. *Paquet*, Appellant's First Brief, October 8, 1920, p. 2.

16. In re Paquet's Estate, 200 P 911 at 914 (Oregon 1921).

17. *U.S.* v. *John B. Paquet*, Bill of Complaint in Equity, September 21, 1923, pp. 4, 6–7.

18. *U.S.* v. *John B. Paquet*, Stipulation, June 2, 1924; *U.S.* v. *John B. Paquet*, Decree, June 2, 1924.

19. Tillamook County Probate file #605, J. S. Cole, Petition, June 7, 1928. Cole was president of the Tillamook-Lincoln County Credit Association.

20. For a particularly insightful analysis of the historical connections between concepts of "race" and "family," see Liu, "Teaching the Differences among Women in a Historical Perspective," *Women's Studies International Forum* 14 (1991): 265–276.

GLENDA GILMORE

Forging Interracial Links in the Jim Crow South

Anna Julia Cooper—an extraordinary woman in her own right—wrote in 1892, "the colored woman of today . . . is confronted by a woman question and a race problem."* Equality of the sexes, Cooper insisted, would mean that black women should not be passive and subordinate in their relationships with black men; and black men should not criticize women's efforts to obtain equal rights. Equality of the sexes, Cooper continued, meant sharing the leadership burden in the struggle against racism. A remarkable group of African American women did just that.

Part of a small but growing black middle class in the South, they were prepared by education, professional training, and voluntary work to be the vanguard of their race. Following the disfranchisement of black men in the 1890s, they emerged not only as community activists, but also as ambassadors to the white community and astute political strategists. Their political skills were put to the test when, during the most racist era in U.S. history, these black women attempted to forge links with elite white women in an interracial movement. At the forefront of the effort was a remarkable North Carolinian, Charlotte Hawkins Brown.

With great sensitivity and insight, Glenda Gilmore illuminates Brown's search for fault lines in the system of white supremacy. She also demonstrates just how Brown manipulated class, gender, and even her own identity in the interests of racial justice. In the end, Brown's generation fell short of their goal

*Anna Julia Cooper, *A Voice from the South by a Black Woman of the South* (Xenia, Ohio: Aldine, 1892), p. 135.

Excerpted from "Forging Interracial Links," ch. 7 of *Gender and Jim Crow: Women and the Politics of White Supremacy in North Carolina, 1896–1920*, by Glenda Elizabeth Gilmore (Chapel Hill: University of North Carolina Press, 1996). Reprinted by permission of the author and publisher. The author has supplied new paragraphs, and renumbered and edited notes.

of racial and sexual equality. The odds against them were overwhelming. In the process, however, they created and nourished a tradition of activism that would emerge with new force and greater success in the 1960s.

Consider Brown's strategy. What were her options? What were the personal costs? Do you agree with Gilmore's characterization of her as a "political genius"?

In the segregated world of the Jim Crow South, laws told black and white people where to eat and where to sit. Undergirding those laws lay a complex web of custom. Its strands separated the races in places beyond the reach of legislation. Custom dictated, for example, which part of the sidewalk belonged to whites and which to blacks. When whites and blacks sometimes occupied the same space, custom demanded that African Americans behave in a subservient manner. Any breach of these codes by a black person could bring an instant response from a white person: a reprimand, a beating, a jail sentence, or even death at the end of a lyncher's rope.

Whites held two unshakable beliefs that gave them the courage and energy to structure such a complicated society, making good on its rules with violence and even murder. First, whites thought that they acted to protect white women from black men's sexual desires. Second, they firmly believed that African Americans should be excluded from the American democratic system. They spoke freely and acted openly against any extension of political rights to blacks. After the turn of the century, restrictive legislation prevented most southern black men from voting and segregation laws crowded the books. White men considered their work done. Henceforth, they thought, African Americans would be a permanent lower caste in southern society: physically separated and politically powerless.

But the white supremacists did not reckon with black women. From behind the borders of segregation and disfranchisement, African American women became diplomats to the white community. They built social service and civic structures that wrested some recognition and meager services from the expanding welfare state. Ironically, as black men were forced from the political sphere, the functions of government expanded, opening a new space for black women to approach officials as good citizens intent on civic betterment.

One of their political strategies was to build contacts with white women. Meager and unequal as they were, these interracial connections often provided black women access to resources for their families, students, and neighbors. Charlotte Hawkins Brown personified such black women across the South who forged invisible careers in interracial politics.

As president of the North Carolina Association of Colored Women's Clubs, Charlotte Hawkins Brown began to direct African American women's formal civic experiences in the state in 1912 and continued to do so for twenty-five years. . . . No black man could claim prominence to equal hers in . . . the state during the period. Brown's work and racialist ideologies illustrate that the decade before woman suffrage constituted a critical period in defining the boundaries of race relations that would remain in place until the post–World War II era.

Charlotte Hawkins Brown's life also provides a parable of the possibilities and the personal costs of interracial cooperation. Her story is so interwoven with myth—fiction that she fashioned to outmaneuver racism—that it is difficult to separate the reality of her experience from the result of her self-creation. The difference between her lived life and her public persona reveals a great deal about her perception of southern whites' racial ideologies and the points at which she saw possibility. Charlotte Hawkins Brown invented herself, repeatedly and with brilliance, but at great personal cost.[1]

According to her account, she was born in Henderson, North Carolina, in 1883 to Caroline Frances Hawkins, the daughter of Rebecca and Mingo Hawkins. Her father was Edmund H. Hight, from "whom fate separated me at birth" and who "belonged to a family that had grown up on the adjoining plantation."[2] Brown characterized her grandmother, Rebecca Hawkins, as a "fair" woman "with blue eyes," the African American sister of her white master, "a great railroad captain whose vision and foresight built up the great Southern Railroad." Brown cast the white master as the Hawkins family's "protector."[3] About the time of my birth, colored people in large numbers were leaving for parts north," she remembered. Charlotte moved with her mother and brother to Cambridge, Massachusetts, where her mother married and the family lived in a large, handsome house near Harvard University.[4] Caroline Hawkins managed a hand laundry in the basement, and Charlotte attended the public schools of Cambridge. Whisked away from the South at an early age, Charlotte was "not conscious of the difference in color and took part in all the activities of my class."[5] She acquired a New England accent, which she kept all of her life.

Charlotte Hawkins's family insisted that she get a practical education and sent her to Massachusetts State Normal School in Salem. Alice Freeman Palmer, the wife of a Harvard professor and the first female president of Wellesley College, was a member of the state board of education that oversaw the school. One day a few months before she entered the normal school, as Charlotte Hawkins was pushing a baby carriage while reading a high school Latin textbook, she chanced to meet Palmer on the street. Hawkins was babysitting to raise money for a silk slip to wear under her new organdy graduation dress, but Palmer assumed that she was an impoverished student, overcoming all odds to get an education. Palmer mentioned Hawkins favorably to the principal of her high school when they next met, and the incident ended. Now, when Hawkins realized that Palmer was an overseer of her normal school, she wrote to her and reminded her of their chance meeting. Palmer responded by paying Hawkins's tuition.[6]

Several months before graduation, Charlotte Hawkins met a supervisor from the American Missionary Association (AMA) on a train. The AMA representative impressed upon Hawkins the needs of the South, and Hawkins left school to accept a position at a one-teacher school in Sedalia, North Carolina, near Greensboro in 1901.[7] The AMA funded the school for two years, then withdrew support. For a year, Hawkins drew no salary, and she and the students survived on what they grew, the produce their parents donated, and a $100 county appropriation. Charlotte Hawkins returned to Cambridge and approached Alice Freeman Palmer for financial help, which Palmer promised to consider when she returned from Europe some months later. Palmer died in Europe, however, and Hawkins decided to name the school in her memory. With continuing county support and private contributions, Palmer Memorial Institute taught practical vocational skills to its students, and Hawkins became active in the North Carolina Teachers Association and in women's club work. In 1911, Hawkins married Edward S. Brown. But the marriage lasted only a few months since Edward said he could not remain in Sedalia and be "Miss Hawkins's husband."[8]

In the South, Brown tells us, she demanded the respect of whites and received it from the "quality people." She insisted upon being addressed as "Miss," "Mrs.," or, after she gained honorary degrees, "Doctor."[9] She refused to be Jim Crowed and reported that several times she was "put out of Pullman berths and seats during all hours of the night." . . . By 1920, with the support of prominent Greensboro whites, Brown built Palmer Memorial Institute into a sprawling complex. She was proud that the most powerful whites in Greensboro served on the Palmer board, including Lula McIver and Julius Cone, head of the huge Cone Mills.[10]

As Brown rendered it, the theme of her life story is challenge met through interracial cooperation. Brown shaped the narrative in two critical ways: she minimized the restrictions of race in her daily life and exaggerated whites' helpfulness at every critical juncture. She obscured the fact that she was illegitimate by making it seem as if her father, Edmund Hight, was separated from the family by slavery. Brown was born in 1883 and had an older brother, demonstrating that her mother had a long-term relationship with Hight. The Hight family continued to live near Henderson throughout the twentieth century. Brown's grandmother, Rebecca Hawkins, may have been the sister of railroad magnate Captain John Hawkins, Jr., but, far from acting as the family's protector, he retained no contact with his black relatives and was a Democrat of the white supremacist persuasion.[11]

Brown mythologized her birth to remind southern whites of slavery's legacy: their shared kinship with African Americans. At the same time, she drew whites as sympathetic figures, the "protectors" of their African American relatives. Such circumstances did exist in the South; they just did not happen to exist within Charlotte's immediate family. As whites created the fictional "good darky" who treasured the interpersonal relationships that sprang from the close association of whites and blacks during slavery, Brown created a fictional "good master" who realized the responsibilities of miscegenation and loved his family, white and black. She used this good master to assuage whites' guilt about slavery and to argue that even slaves and masters achieved interracial understanding. She did not have to fight whites who melded ancestral ties to romantic class mythologies; she could simply join them. She shared their aristocratic roots.

Brown had moved to Cambridge not "about the time of my birth" but at the age of six. Yet she claimed to have no memory of her early life in North Carolina, no firsthand recollection of discrimination against blacks in the South, indeed no racial consciousness while growing up, even though she spent a great deal of time in the South during her childhood, even entire summers. Brown remade herself as a New Englander. When asked how her name should appear on her high school diploma, she instantly dropped her North Carolina name—Lottie Hawkins—for the more genteel sounding "Charlotte Eugenia Hawkins," which she made up on the spot. She spoke in a manner that "combine[d] the mellow tones of the southern Negro and the quick clipped qualities of New England—people turn[ed] around to see who [was] speaking."[12]

By casting herself as a New Englander, Brown attempted to remain above the southern racial structure. In Greensboro, she occupied a place much like that of African diplomats to the United States—she was an exotic but North Carolina's own exotic. If whites accused her of being an outside agitator, Brown could fall back on her North Carolina roots. Then she presented herself as native stock, a female, black Ulysses who fought her way back to the South and to her own people, where she belonged.

The story of the AMA's dispatch of Charlotte Hawkins to the South to save her people competes with another, more complicated parable that Brown merely hinted at and may have consciously avoided dwelling upon. Rather than seeing herself as a New England missionary to a foreign place, Brown may have construed her return to North Carolina as coming to terms with the realities of race in her own life. One night at a Cambridge meeting, she watched magic lantern slides of the race work being done by African Americans in the South. She was particularly struck by two educators, Joseph Price, the founder of Livingstone College, and Lucy Laney, the founder of Haines Institute in Augusta, Georgia. She noted that both Price and Laney were, like herself, very dark skinned. Price and Laney were also brilliant, and their faces on the screen moved Brown to feel that there was a place where she might belong: the South.[13] Brown never acknowledged publicly that she had any personal reason for wanting to leave New England, choosing rather to emphasize the missionary aspect of her return.

As the years passed, accounts of the relationship between Alice Freeman Palmer and Brown made it seem as if Palmer had sent Brown to the South to found the school and that they had enjoyed a close friendship.... Contemporary newspaper accounts, which relied on Brown's own promotional material, reported that Palmer's "efforts" had made the school possible and "until her death she was an ardent supporter of her namesake."[14]

Although Brown did not actually lie about Palmer's interest in her and the school, she embroidered the truth. Brown and Palmer spent less than fifteen minutes together in their lifetimes, and Palmer never promised that she would personally contribute to the school. Instead, Palmer had told Brown upon their second meeting that she was too busy at the moment but that after her return from Europe she would contact friends in Boston to encourage them to support the school. Why, then, when Palmer never returned, did Brown name the school Palmer Memorial Institute? Actually, Brown originally named the school Alice Freeman Palmer Settlement in order to gain support from Palmer's friends in Boston.[15] Palmer, after a brilliant career, had died at a young age and was mourned by her friends, and a memorial to her could prompt contributions....

Around 1910, Brown cannily began to play southern pride against northern dollars when she inspired white leaders in Greensboro to challenge their community to take over the financial support of Palmer.[16] In soliciting southern white support, Brown ... most often called the school Sedalia rather than Palmer.

For example, Brown named the group of students who sang African American spirituals the Sedalia Singers.[17] She understood the white southerners' sense of place, and since her school was the only thing in the crossroads of Sedalia, she did not encroach upon white territory in appropriating the name. The location of Palmer at Sedalia facilitated support from Greensboro whites. It was ten miles outside of the city, surrounded by sparsely populated farmland. Brown never permitted Palmer students to travel alone to Greensboro but instead brought them as a group, with the boys clad in coats and ties and the girls wearing hats and white gloves. Once in the city, they did not mingle with Greensboro's African Americans; rather, Brown negotiated special seating sections for her students at public events.[18]

Although Brown cloaked the curriculum at Palmer in vocational disguises and portrayed it to the press as an industrial school until the late 1930s, the institute offered mostly academic courses from its inception.[19] Booker T. Washington met Brown on a trip to Boston while she was still a student there and pronounced her "the only convert that he made in New England." If he believed her to be a convert, she outfoxed the Wizard himself.[20] . . . Brown never embraced Washington's vocational philosophy past the point of providing for the school's basic needs, but she portrayed the school as industrial, detailing "farm yields" in fund-raising letters.[21] An unidentified Palmer teacher explained the ruse this way: "[Brown] always had a college preparatory class . . . a cultural academic school. All the Negroes had to have that in order to get along in the South." Even though this teacher believed, along with Brown, that African Americans profited most from classical knowledge coupled with reinforcement of middle-class values, support for that sort of training did not exist. So Brown and her teachers positioned Palmer as a "vocational" school. Funding for industrial education "could always get through," the teacher recalled. Despite the vocational exterior, she continued, "you could teach anything you wanted when you got in your school. You came inside your class room and you taught them Latin and French and all the things you knew."[22] Although initially Brown's students were the poor children of the neighborhood, by 1920, Palmer functioned as an academic boarding school that drew students from counties across the state and included secondary grades.[23]

Notwithstanding her vocal cover, at times Brown argued that her approach to "cultural" instruction benefited whites as well as African Americans. She explained, "Recognizing the need of a cultural approach to life, believing absolutely in education through racial contacts, I have devoted my whole life to establish for Negro youth something superior to Jim Crowism." She tried to accomplish this "by bringing the two races together under the highest cultural environment that will increase race pride, mutual respect, confidence, sympathetic understanding, and interracial goodwill."[24]

Why did Brown repeatedly overdraw white understanding and support and minimize the restrictions that her color placed on her? Throughout her life, she operated by a simple rule: it is better to overestimate possibility than to underestimate it. Charlotte Hawkins Brown created a fictional mirror of civility in race relations and held it up to whites as a reflection of their better selves. From slavery, she drew compassion; from the loneliness of Cambridge, racial liberality among her schoolmates; from Alice Freeman Palmer's deferral, a legacy; and from frightened, pinched southern whites, chivalry of a sort. Brown was a political genius, especially suited for interracial work. Her renderings served her own purposes, but she did not . . . delude herself into thinking that they were true. Immune to her own romantic stories, Brown was the consummate pragmatist. So convinced was she of her mission and of her opponent's rigid character, that she could risk the heartbreak of gilding the lily. She expected nothing, received little, and turned that pittance into bounty.

But Charlotte Hawkins Brown was a double agent. When she refused to turn her head toward the "colored" waiting room, she must have felt the stares of its patrons burn into her consciousness. In the decade preceding 1920, Brown immersed herself in social welfare projects and political activity that she kept hidden from whites. After 1920, Brown acquired a national reputation for her interracial work and landed official positions in interracial organizations, success that brought her activities under public scrutiny. Until then, and thereafter when she could, Brown generally said one thing to whites and then did another if it suited her purposes.

Brown's double life left its mark on her.... Living her life as a diplomat to the white community, Brown could never be just Lottie Hawkins. African American women who chose to take up interracial work walked a tightrope that required them to be forever careful, tense, and calculating. One slip would end their careers; they worked without nets.

In Lula Martin McIver, Brown found an exception to her belief that the southern white woman stood at the center of the race "problem." Their first meeting represents a classic case of the Brown treatment. Constantly seeking funds for Palmer Memorial Institute, Brown decided in the spring of 1905 that she must approach prominent white men in Greensboro for support. In Greensboro, Brown had no magic key such as Alice Freeman Palmer's name. Sedalia was a crossroads, Palmer Institute tiny, and Brown unknown. She had no historic connections to white North Carolinians there, no reputation in the black community, no denominational bridge since she had converted to Congregationalism, a faith rare in the South among either African Americans or whites. She had only herself—the New England persona she so carefully cultivated—and courage.

In 1904, she had written a poignant letter to Charles McIver, president of the white women's normal college in Greensboro. It began, "This letter may come to you from a strange source, but it comes from one whose heart is in the educational and moral uplift of our people." It concluded by begging McIver to come to Palmer for a visit. A year later, Brown was still imploring him to the same end, touting the ease of the train ride and signing herself "Very Anxiously Yours."[25] Still McIver did not come. One morning Brown dressed carefully in her customary ankle-length dress, hat, and white gloves and set out to call on him in Greensboro. She had no appointment. Most often Brown did not write or telephone ahead and risk refusal from those she wished to meet but simply appeared on their doorstep. That morning she knocked on the front door of the president's residence and found that he was away. His wife, Lula Martin McIver, invited Brown in, an unusual act in itself. Lula McIver was stunned by Brown's appearance at the door. "Her daring, her enthusiasm, her faith intrigued me," McIver recalled. The two women talked for over an hour and warmed toward each other. Soon, McIver was advising Brown on "the best way to win friends" and on how to raise money among the Greensboro elite for the school.[26]

When Lula McIver opened the door, Brown chanced upon a valuable connection that would prove enduring. Brown sat in the parlor of the state's foremost white female educational advocate. Graduated from the Moravian academy in Salem, Lula Martin had longed to become a doctor like her father. After she learned that the profession was virtually closed to women, she became an outspoken feminist. As an adolescent, she abandoned the Moravians for the Methodists upon reading that the early Moravian settlers chose wives by lottery. In 1885, strong-willed Lula Martin met Charles Duncan McIver, a dedicated young teacher, who supported her feminist ideas and called her a "most sensible" woman. They married in a ceremony that omitted the word "obey," and Lula refused a wedding ring, which she regarded as a "badge of slavery."[27]

The McIvers worked to build North Carolina's white public educational system one school at a time. While Charles traveled throughout the state promoting grade school education, Lula served as his advance team, preceding him to scrub courthouse venues speckled with tobacco juice, to set up chairs, to post flyers, and to raise a crowd. She was delighted when Charles became first president of the state-supported normal school for white women since both felt that educating women would be the key to building an effective public school system. She helped to found the Woman's Association for the Betterment of Public School Houses, and after Charles's death, she accepted a paying position as its field secretary.[28]

The subtleties of Lula McIver's racial ideology are elusive, but at the center of her thinking about race lay the strongly held belief that African Americans deserved a good education. For nearly a half century after they met, McIver continually raised money for Palmer Memorial Institute. Lula McIver attended meetings of black women's clubs in Greensboro. After the early death of Charles McIver in 1909, and to the eternal perplexity of Greensboro whites, each semester Lula McIver invited a male African American student from nearby North Carolina Agricultural and

Technical College to board in the president's residence where she lived until her death. There, surrounded by young white women students, Lula McIver offered an object lesson in race relations.[29]

Both Brown and McIver realized the restrictions on their relationship in the Jim Crow South. For starters, McIver was a woman and thus not powerful in her own right. Moreover, as the normal school's maternal figurehead, she had to act circumspectly since all of her actions reflected upon the school, which was still in the minds of some a dangerous experiment that wasted state money to educate women. Given these restrictions, McIver could do three concrete things for Brown: influence prominent white Greensboro men to support her, introduce leading club women to Palmer's mission, and raise money. She did another intangible and invaluable thing for Brown: Lula McIver publicly referred to Charlotte Hawkins Brown as her friend.[30]

It appears that Lula McIver realized that her husband's influence would be more valuable than her own, and she urged Charles to write an "open letter of endorsement" for Palmer Memorial Institute shortly after she met Brown. Since Charles McIver served on the Southern Education Board, his vote of confidence carried weight in the North as well as the South. The letter went out in June 1905, but Charles McIver admitted in it that he had never been to Palmer.[31] He died four years later. Long after that, Brown named Charles D. McIver as her "first friend" in North Carolina.[32] There is no record that McIver ever made the trip to Sedalia or that Brown ever met him. With Lula McIver's help, Brown appropriated the memory of Charles McIver as she had that of Alice Freeman Palmer.

Local support of Palmer flowered around 1914 when Lula McIver brought a delegation of white women from across the state to visit the school. A member of the delegation wrote an account of the visit that appeared in the *Greensboro Daily Record* and encouraged white women to take an interest in Brown's work. Brown struck just the right note in her solicitation letter: Palmer, she said, "has conducted its work for the past 13 years without seeking very much help from our southern friends." She claimed friendship and a debt come due in the same breath.[33] The 1914 campaign was the beginning of a steady stream of white visitors to the school and financial support from white North Carolinians.[34] In 1917, Lula McIver conducted some of Greensboro's leading white businessmen on a tour of the school. Many of the men who had ignored Brown's previous appeals converted after that visit. E. P. Wharton recalled that Charlotte Brown had called on him around 1903 to obtain support for Palmer and that he was "ashamed of [him]self for losing sight" of Brown's work. He subsequently served for decades as a Palmer trustee. By 1920, the board of Palmer Memorial Institute included a Greensboro attorney, a banker, and an industrial magnate.[35] McIver sought no publicity for a trip she made to Boston with Charlotte Hawkins Brown two years later. There McIver called upon prominent white women, vouched for Brown's success, and asked for contributions to Palmer. When northern white women visited Palmer, they would not spend the night at the black school but stayed instead with Lula McIver.[36]

In 1919, Charlotte Hawkins Brown, with the endorsement of Lula McIver, published a remarkable novel, *Mammy*. On its face, the appearance of *Mammy* places Brown squarely in the accommodationist camp of African Americans, currying favor from whites by invoking the ties of slavery. The story tells of a loving black woman who nurses a white family and raises its children. Then, when the woman becomes old and ill, the family provides no help beyond an occasional visit to her drafty log cabin. Ultimately, they stand by as Mammy goes to the county home. Brown dedicated the book to "my good friend, Mrs. Charles Duncan McIver." She continued, "It is with gratitude I acknowledge her personal interest in the colored members of her household."[37]

What could Brown have hoped to accomplish by the publication of *Mammy?* At the time, she served as president of the statewide Association of Colored Women's Clubs, refused Jim Crow seating, and was secretly organizing a campaign to interest the state's black women in woman suffrage. She had spent almost twenty years building her dignity in North Carolina. It was amazing that she would play the *Mammy* card now. A close reading of Brown's introduction and McIver's response to the dedication indicates that both saw *Mammy* as a tool to promote their agenda: interracial cooperation among women. Mammies represented the one point of contact between southern black and white women, and white women continually bragged about their love for their Mammies. But Brown's *Mammy* is not a tale of love rewarded; it is an indictment of white neglect of African Americans. Brown calls upon white women to remember their duty to black women and redefines that duty in new ways. It is no longer enough to be fond of ol' Mammy; white women must act on that affection.

McIver framed her endorsement of *Mammy* carefully. She said that today's white woman was not the person her mother was, for in her mother's day, there was "understanding and sympathy" between the races. The problem was the separation of the races since there could be no racial harmony without "knowledge of each other's problems and an active interest in solving them." McIver endorsed the concept of "racial integrity" but reminded white southerners that their "task [was the] training of the uncivilized African." Brown must have winced at that remark, but it preceded McIver's most important statement: "I verily believe that to the most intelligent southern white women we must look for leadership in keeping our 'ship of state' off the rocks of racial antagonism." She signed the piece, "Your friend, Lula Martin McIver."[38]

Interracial cooperation, association among black and white women to solve mutual problems, was the solution that *Mammy* endorsed. McIver did not propose that white women individually care for their mammies but that they enter the public sphere and provide leadership. Male sailors had steered the ship of state onto rocky racial shores. It was time for women to man the lifeboats and rescue government from the oppressive racial politics of the white supremacists. In the same month that *Mammy* appeared, the state's white and black women began to do just that by traveling to Memphis, Tennessee, for a formal interracial summit. The state associations of women's clubs and the YWCAs sent forth those first intrepid female navigators.

Most of the black women who traveled to the Memphis interracial summit learned leadership skills in the National Association of Colored Women, but their experience in working with white women had come from two other sources as well: heretofore racially segregated groups that came together on the homefront in World War I and the interracial work of the Young Women's Christian Association (YWCA). During World War I organizational lines between women's groups of both races blurred when the Council of National Defense chose white women from each southern state to head committees to coordinate work on the homefront. In North Carolina, white women set up integrated county councils that included African American and white women, carefully chosen to represent clubs, YWCAs, and denominational social service programs.[39]

The work of the black YWCA centered on another upheaval of the time: African American migration from farm to town. Southern black women believed strongly in the YWCA's ability to reach poor young women who had moved to the city to find work. The national YWCA board determined that any southern African American branch must be supervised by an existing "central" YWCA. "Central" meant white. Once founded, the black YWCA must be overseen by a management committee of three white women and two black women. The rules mandated interracial "cooperation" of a sort. Despite these humiliating restrictions, two southern black women, Mary McCrorey of Charlotte, North Carolina, and Lugenia Burns Hope of Atlanta, founded Ys in their cities.[40]

On the train to Memphis, a group of white men pulled Brown out of the Pullman car and marched her past "southern white women passing for Christians" who were on their way to the Memphis meeting. The white women sat silent as the men forced Brown to the Jim Crow car.[41] Brown probably recognized among the fellow Memphis delegates North Carolina white women whom she had come to know over the past decade. Among them was the wife of the governor, Fanny Bickett. . . .

When Brown rose to address the white women, the frustration of a decade of interracial work erupted, and she shared the humiliation of being ousted from the Pullman car two nights before. She exhorted white women to fight lynching, to recognize the dignity of the African American woman, and to help black women. Brown ended on an ominous note: "You are going to reach out for the same hand that I am reaching out for but I know that the dear Lord will not receive it if you are crushing me beneath your feet."[42] Most of the white women were profoundly moved.

As it happened, the women's Memphis interracial meeting foundered on the spot that Lula McIver had warned of in *Mammy:* the shoal of politics. Two months before the meeting, a federal amendment had mandated woman suffrage and a month after the meeting women would vote for the first time. Just before Brown left for Tennessee, she had been secretly organizing black women in North Carolina to register to vote. One faction of black women would not budge on the issue of suffrage at the Memphis meeting. A full year later, the white and black women still had not agreed on a statement of goals for an interracial movement. Brown, McCrorey, and Hope favored a version that included the controversial demand for protection of African American voting rights. Their language was blunt: "We believe that the ballot is the safe-guard of the Nation and that every citizen in the Nation should have the right to use it. We believe that if there is ever to be any justice before the law, the Negro must have the right to exercise the vote."[43] But the white women balked at the suffrage statement and the condemnation of lynching, both points "which the Negro women dared not leave out."[44] Whites suggested the wording, "We believe that the ballot is the safe-guard of the Nation, and that every *qualified* citizen in the Nation should have the right to use it."[45]

Interracial cooperation led straight into politics. As black and white women inched toward cooperation on a grass roots level, they came face-to-face with larger political forces. With a decade of women's interracial experience behind them, many African American women believed that the time had come to take a firm stand on suffrage. Black women looked to their white allies to support their right to vote, a gesture that underscores the success of interracial cooperation. Yet white women's confusion over black women's suffrage reveals the limits of voluntary interracial work. Upon the passage of woman suffrage, white women involved with interracial social service projects had to chose between gender and race. They could support black women's right to vote as women, or oppose their right to vote as *black* women. Charlotte Hawkins Brown called the question when she used the NACW to organize black women's voter registration drives in urban areas in the fall of 1920. Across the South, other black women did the same thing, reporting back to the National Association for the Advancement of Colored People (NAACP).

In Mobile, Alabama, registrars told black women that they must own property to vote, and when the black juvenile court officer challenged them, court officials fired her.[46] From Birmingham came the news that when a black teacher attempted to register, the registrar "called her an ugly name and ordered her out." Another teacher "answered every question asked her—ex post facto law, habeas corpus proceedings, etc." The frustrated registrar still would not yield and "tore up her card and threw it in her face."[47] Ultimately, in Birmingham, 225 black women succeeded in registering, although 4,500 made the attempt.[48]

It is impossible to judge Charlotte Hawkins Brown's success in the North Carolina registration campaign. Most registration books failed to survive, but those that exist show not only that black women succeeded in urban areas, but that voter registration increased for black men as well. Probably less than 1,000 black women registered in North Carolina that fall.[49] To judge the results of black women's drive for suffrage, however, one must look not just at the few thousand who managed to register in 1920, but at the heritage of interracial work upon which they built and at the example they set for those who followed. The number of black women who voted in 1920 may have been small, but their significance in the South's racial politics was large. For the first time since the nineteenth century in the South, black voters approached the registrars en masse. They assembled as the result of a coordinated, subversive campaign that crossed over the boundaries of voluntary interracial work to reintroduce black civil rights in electoral politics. By their presence at the polls, black women dared whites to use violence and won the dare. In 1921, white supremacy still stood, but black women had found faultlines in its foundations.

NOTES

1. Ceci Jenkins, incomplete notes for "The Twig Bender of Sedalia" ([1946]), unpublished biography of Charlotte Hawkins Brown, reel 1, #12, Brown Collection, Manuscript Collection, Schlesinger Library (SL). See also Stephen Birmingham, *Certain People: America's Black Elite* (Boston: Little, Brown, 1977).

2. "A Biography," reel 1, and "Some Incidents in the Life and Career of Charlotte Hawkins Brown

Growing out of Racial Situations, at the Request of Dr. Ralph Bunche," reel 1, #2, both in Brown Collection, SL.

3. "Some Incidents," 1–2, reel 1, #2, ibid.

4. "A Biography," reel 1, ibid. The language of "A Biography" is closely echoed in Sadie L. Daniel, *Women Builders* (Washington, D.C.: Associated Publishers, 1970), 133–63.

5. "A Biography," 13, reel 1, Brown Collection, SL.

6. On Palmer, see Ruth B. Bordin, *Alice Freeman Palmer: The Evolution of a New Woman* (Ann Arbor: University of Michigan Press, 1993). On the Brown/Palmer relationship, see "A Biography," 16–18, reel 1, and Jenkins, "Twig Bender of Sedalia," reel 1, #7, both in Brown Collection, SL.

7. Daniel, *Women Builders,* 139; "A Biography," 19, reel 1, Brown Collection, SL.

8. Charlotte E. Hawkins to Dr. Buttrick, 31 Aug. 1904, folder 1005, box 111, series 1, subseries 1, General Education Board Collection, RAC. Mary Grinnell to Charlotte Hawkins Brown, 4 Oct. 1910, 8 Feb. 1911; H. F. Kimball to Charlotte Hawkins Brown, 12 June 1911; and J. G. Bright to Charlotte Hawkins Brown, 1 Aug. 1911, all on reel 2, #33; Mary T. Grinnell to Charlotte Hawkins Brown, 6 Aug. 1912, 17 Feb. 1913, reel 2, #34; and Charlotte Hawkins Brown Ebony Questionnaire, 16, reel 1, #11, all in Brown Collection, SL.

9. Brown wrote that it was a "big surprise" that the white people in the South refused to "use the term 'Miss'" when they addressed black women. She continued, "Naturally I was constantly being insulting and insulted which merited for me the name 'Yankee Huzzy.'" See "Some Incidents," 5, reel 1, #2, Brown Collection, SL. Leading whites in Greensboro referred to her as "Dr. Brown" after she received honorary degrees from Wilberforce, Lincoln, and Howard universities. See Junius Scales to Glenda Gilmore, 4 Jan. 1990, in author's possession.

10. Letterhead, Palmer Memorial Institute, C. Hawkins Brown to W. E. B. Dubois [*sic*], to June 1930, W. E. B. Du Bois Papers, reel 33, University of Massachusetts, Amherst.

11. Ruth Anita Hawkins Hughes, *Contributions of Vance County People of Color* (Raleigh: Sparks Press, 1988).

12. Jenkins, "Twig Bender of Sedalia," 1, reel 1, #7, Brown Collection, SL.

13. Ibid., insert B; "Some Incidents," 9, reel 1, #2, Brown Collection, SL.

14. Eva M. Young, "Palmer Memorial Institute Unique," *Charlotte Observer,* 10 Mar. 1940, folder 51, box 94–3, ibid.

15. Jenkins, "Twig Bender of Sedalia," E.F. 16, reel 1, #7, Brown Collection, SL.

16. Ibid., E.F. 16, E.F. 17; "Some Incidents," reel 1, #2, Brown Collection, SL.

17. For an example of the conflation of Sedalia and Palmer Institute, see *Palmer Memorial Institute: The Mission and the Legacy* (Greensboro: Women of Greensboro, [1981]).

18. The description here is from interviews and conversations with Dawn Gilmore, Brooks Gilmore, and Lois MacKenzie, the author's aunt, uncle, and mother, respectively. The author's grandfather, Clyde Manly Gilmore, was Brown's physician, and the author's mother, MacKenzie, was her attorney's secretary in the 1950s.

19. Brown transformed the institute in the late 1930s into a preparatory school for upper-class African Americans. By 1940, the school letterhead read: "The Charm School Idea of the Palmer Memorial Institute, Charlotte Hawkins Brown, President and Promoter." See C. Hawkins Brown to My Dear Friend, 20 Mar. 1940, folder 124, box 112–4, Washington Conservatory of Music Records, Moorland-Spingarn Research Center, Howard University (MRSC).

20. Jenkins, "Twig Bender of Sedalia," insert G, reel 1, #7, Brown Collection, SL.

21. Charlotte Hawkins Brown to Wallace Buttrick, 19 Dec. 1912, folder 1005, box 111, series 1, subseries 1, General Education Board Collection, Rockefeller Archive Center (RAC).

22. "Charlotte Hawkins Brown," Dannett Collection, uncataloged, LC. See also Sylvia G. L. Dannett, *Profiles of Negro Womanhood* (New York: M. W. Lads, 1964–66), 59–63. The notes for Dannett's biographical sketches often do not identify the interviewee and are fragmentary.

23. Map, "Palmer Memorial Institute—Sedalia—Enrol[l]ment—1920–1921," folder 1006, box 111, series 1, subseries 1, General Education Board Collection, RAC.

24. "Some Incidents," reel 1, #2, Brown Collection, SL.

25. Board, 1904, Correspondence G-M, box 14, and C. E. Hawkins to Dr. McIver, 13 Apr. 1905, file Southern Education Board, 1905, Correspondence, E-L, box 15, both in Charles D. McIver Collection, University Archives, Walter Clinton Jackson Library, University of North Carolina, Greensboro (WCJL).

26. Mrs. Charles D. McIver to editor of *Greensboro Daily News,* [ca. 1940], reel 1, #13, and Jenkins, "Twig Bender of Sedalia," reel 1, #7, both in Brown Collection, SL.

27. Rose Howell Holder, *McIver of North Carolina* (Chapel Hill: University of North Carolina Press, 1917), 63–67. See also Virginia T. Lathrop, "Mrs. McIver Believes Greatness of the Past Holds State's Hope for Present and Future," *News and Observer,* 6 Oct. 1940, Clipping File, vol. 94, reel 24, 371–72, North Carolina Collection, University of North Carolina, Chapel Hill (NCC).

28. James Leloudis, "'A More Certain Means of Grace': Pedagogy, Self, and Society in North Carolina, 1880–1920" (Ph.D. diss., University of North Carolina at Chapel Hill, 1989), and Pamela Dean, "Covert Curriculum: Class and Gender in a New South Women's College" (Ph.D. diss., University of North Carolina at Chapel Hill, 1995). On the association, see James Leloudis, "School Reform in the New South: The Woman's Association for the Betterment of Public School Houses in North Carolina, 1902–1919," *Journal of American History* 69 (March 1983): 886–909. See also Lula Martin McIver to Charles L. Coon, 4 Feb. 1909, folder 28, box 2, and Lula Martin McIver to Charles L. Coon, 25 Jan. 1910, folder 29, box 2, both in Coon Papers, Southern Historical Collection, University of North Carolina, Chapel Hill (SHC).

29. Sallie Waugh McBryan to Mrs. McIver, 22 Nov. 1913, file Correspondence, 1909–44, box 141,

Lula Martin McIver Collection, WCJL; "Famous Landmark at WCUNC Razed," *Durham Morning Herald,* 26 Oct. 1952, Clipping File, vol. 94, reel 24, 343–44, NCC.

30. Lula Martin McIver to Charlotte Hawkins Brown, 6 Apr. 1920, reel 2, #41, Brown Collection, SL.

31. Charles D. McIver letter, 5 June 1905, reel 2, #30, Correspondence, 1902–6, ibid.

32. "Award Will Go to Dr. Brown," *Greensboro Daily News,* 10 Apr. 1947, Clipping File, vol. 18, reel 5, 239, NCC.

33. C. Hawkins Brown to My dear Sir [Professor Julius I. Foust], 25 May 1914, file General Correspondence, 1913–15, box 57, Foust Collection, WCJL.

34. Jenkins, "Twig Bender of Sedalia," 77, reel 1, #12, Brown Collection, SL.

35. E. P. Wharton to Charlotte Hawkins Brown, 12 Jan. 1917, reel 2, #37, Jan.–Apr. 1917; Mrs. Charles D. McIver to editor of *Greensboro Daily News,* n.d., reel 1 #13; and Jenkins, "Twig Bender of Sedalia," 78, reel 1, #12, all in Brown Collection, SL.

36. H. F. Kimball to Charlotte Hawkins Brown, 6 Nov. 1916, reel 2, #36, 1916, and "Notes," copy of notebook maintained by Charlotte Hawkins Brown, reel 1, #8, both in Brown Collection, SL; Annie L. Vickery to My Dear Mrs. McIver, 7 Mar. 1917, file Correspondence, 1909–44, box 141, Lula Martin McIver Collection, WCJL.

37. Charlotte Hawkins Brown, *Mammy* (Boston: Pilgrim Press, 1919).

38. Lula Martin McIver to Charlotte Hawkins Brown, 6 Apr. 1920, reel 2, #41, Brown Collection, SL.

39. Laura Holmes Reilley to D. H. Hill, 18 Oct. 1917, file Women's Committee, box 30, North Carolina Council of Defense, World War I Papers, 1903–33, pt. 2, Military Collection, North Carolina Department of Archives and History.

40. Mary J. McCrorey to Mrs. Hope, 7 May 1920; "Mrs. Hope of the Cleveland Meeting, 1920," 29 May 1920; "What the Colored Women Are Asking of the Y.W.C.A."; "To the National Board of the Young Women's Christian Association"; Minutes of the Cleveland Meeting, 1920; "Minutes of the meeting held in the offices of the South Atlantic Field Committee, Richmond, Virginia, 3 July 1920"; and Mary J. McCrorey to Mrs. Hope, 27 Jan. 1921, all in box 5, NU 14-C-5, Y.W.C.A., Neighborhood Union Papers, Special Collections, Robert Woodruff Library, Atlanta University, Atlanta, Georgia. Mary J. McCrorey to Charlotte Hawkins Brown, 2 Apr. 1920, reel 2, #41, Brown Collection, SL.

41. Jacquelyn Dowd Hall, *Revolt against Chivalry: Jessie Daniel Ames and the Women's Campaign against Lynching,* rev. ed. (New York: Columbia University Press, 1987), 93; "Some Incidents," reel 1, #2, Brown Collection, SL.

42. Brown address, folder 1, box 1, ibid.; Hall, *Revolt against Chivalry,* 93–94.

43. "First Draft," section 2, folder 1, box 1, ibid.

44. "Statement of Negro Women in Session, Mar. 26, 1921," folder 1, box 1.

45. Folder 1, box 1, ibid. (emphasis added).

46. W. E. Morton to NAACP, file Voting, 10–30 Nov. 1920, C284, National Association for the Advancement of Colored People Papers, Library of Congress.

47. H. M. Kingsley to NAACP, 9 Nov. 1920, file Voting, 1–9 Nov. 1920, C284, NAACP Papers.

48. Charles McPerson to NAACP, file Voting, 1–9 Nov. 1920, C284, NAACP Papers. For a summary of reports from across the South, see "Disfranchisement of Colored Americans in the Presidential Election of 1920" ([1920]), file Voting, Dec. 1920, C284, NAACP Papers.

49. Glenda E. Gilmore, *Gender and Jim Crow: Women and the Politics of White Supremacy in North Carolina, 1896–1920* (Chapel Hill: University of North Carolina Press, 1996), 219–224.

JUDY YUNG

Unbound Feet: From China to San Francisco's Chinatown

The imbalance of men and women in the largest Chinese community on the West Coast was a source of immense frustration, especially after the Immigration Act of 1924 effectively barred Chinese wives, even those married to U.S. citizens, from entering the country. Pany Lowe, an American-born Chinese man, expressed the feelings of men: "I think most Chinese in this country like have their son go to China get married. Under this new law . . . , can't do this. No allowed marry white girl. Not enough American-born Chinese to go around. China only place to get wife. Not allowed to bring them back. For Chinaman, very unjust."* Although the act was amended in 1930 to allow the entry of women who had been married to U.S. citizens prior to May 26, 1924, the process of gaining entrance was lengthy, costly, and humiliating for most Chinese women. Many men, like Pany Lowe, chose to visit their wives in China rather than subject them to the ordeal of immigration.

Judy Yung's essay traces the experiences of three women from Guangdong Province who arrived in San Francisco in 1922. Two, Wong Ah So and Law Shee Low, came from impoverished villages to join their husbands in arranged marriages. Wong Ah So was in for a major surprise when she discovered her "marriage" was part of a system of enslaving women in forced prostitution to fill what was perceived to be a pressing need in a Chinese bachelor society. The third woman came from a different background with different expectations. Jane Kwong Lee was an urbanized, unmarried "new woman" who came to the United States to further her education. While she would endure many of the same gender and racial restrictions as the other two women, differences in her class and education made her experience—and the opportunities available to her—significantly different from that of other immigrant Chinese women in the 1920s.

Women's emancipation was heralded in San Francisco's Chinatown on the afternoon of November 2, 1902, when Sieh King King, an eighteen-year-old student from China and an ardent reformer, stood before a theater full of men and women and, according to newspaper accounts, "boldly condemned the slave girl system, raged at the horrors of foot-binding and, with all the vehemence of aroused youth, declared that men and women were equal and should enjoy the privileges of equals."[1] Her talk and her views on women's rights were inextricably linked with Chinese nationalism and the 1898 Reform Movement, which advocated that China emulate the West and modernize in order to throw off the yoke of foreign domination. Elevating the status of women to the extent that they could become "new women"—educated mothers and productive citizens—was part of this nationalist effort to strengthen and defend China against further encroachment.

What Sieh King King advocated on behalf of Chinese women—unbound feet, education, equal rights, and public participation—remained at the heart of social change for Chinese women for the next three decades. This was due largely to the continuous influence of nationalism and women's emancipation in China, the reform work of Protestant missionary women in Chinatown, and Chinese women's entry into the urban economy. By 1929, immigrant women had made considerable progress toward freeing themselves of social restrictions and moving into the public arena. Footbinding was no longer practiced, prostitution had been eradicated, and a substantial number of women were working outside the home, educating themselves and their daughters, and playing a more visible role in community affairs. This discussion of the lives of Chinese immigrant women from 1902, when Sieh King King introduced her feminist views in San Francisco, to 1929, the beginnings of the Great Depression, will illustrate how socioeconomic developments in China and the United States facilitated the unbinding of their feet and of their lives.

JOURNEY TO GOLD MOUNTAIN

At the time of Sieh King King's speech, China was still suffering under the stranglehold of Western imperialism and the inept rule of the Manchus. Life for the ordinary Chinese remained disrupted; survival was precarious. Consequently, many able-bodied peasants in Southeast China continued to emigrate overseas where kinfolk had already settled. Despite the Chinese Exclusion Acts and

*Quoted in Judy Yung, *Unbound Feet: A Social History of Chinese Women in San Francisco* (Berkeley: University of California Press, 1995), p. 58.

anti-Chinese hostilities, a good number went to California, the Gold Mountain. As increased numbers of Chinese sojourners became settlers, some found the economic means by which to get married or send for their wives and children from China. American immigration laws and the process of chain migration determined that most Chinese women would continue to come from the rural villages of Guangdong Province, where traditional gender roles still prevailed. Among these women were Wong Ah So and Law Shee Low, who both emigrated as obedient daughters in 1922 to escape poverty at home. Jane Kwong Lee, who also came the same year, was among the small number of urbanized "new women" who emigrated on their own for educational reasons. Together, these three women's stories provide insights into the gender roles and immigration experiences of Chinese women in the early twentieth century.

"I was born in Guangdong Province," begins Wong Ah So's story. "My father was sometimes a sailor and sometimes he worked on the docks, for we were very poor."[2] Patriarchal cultural values often put the daughter at risk when poverty strikes: From among the five children in the family, her mother chose to betroth her, the eldest daughter, to a Gold Mountain man in exchange for a bride price of 450 Mexican dollars.

> I was 19 when this man came to my mother and said that in America there was a great deal of gold. Even if I just peeled potatoes there, he told my mother I would earn seven or eight dollars a day, and if I was willing to do any work at all I would earn lots of money. He was a laundryman, but said he earned plenty of money. He was very nice to me, and my mother liked him, so my mother was glad to have me go with him as his wife.

Out of filial duty and economic necessity, Ah So agreed to sail to the United States with this laundryman, Huey Yow. He had a marriage certificate prepared and told her to claim him as her husband to the immigration officials in San Francisco, although as she admitted later, "I claimed to be the wife of Huey Yow, but in truth had not at any time lived with him as his wife."

In Law Shee Low's case, her family succumbed to poverty after repeated raids by roving bandits in the Chungshan District of Guangdong Province. Conditions became so bad that the family had to sell their land and give up their three servants; all four daughters had to quit school and help at home. Speaking of her arranged marriage to a Gold Mountain man, she said, "I had no choice; we were so poor. We had no food to go with rice, not even soy sauce or black bean paste. Some of our neighbors even had to go begging or sell their daughters, times were so bad. So my parents thought I would have a better future in Gold Mountain."[3] Her fiancé said he was a clothing salesman in San Francisco and a Christian. He had a minister from Canton preside over the first "modern" wedding in his village. Law was eighteen and her husband, thirty-four. Nine months after the wedding, they sailed for America.

Born in 1902 to wealthy parents of the Toishan District, Guangdong Province (her family owned land and her father and uncle were successful businessmen in Australia), Jane Kwong Lee was able to acquire a Western education in the treaty port of Canton. There she was first exposed to American ideas of democracy and women's emancipation. During her last year in school, she was swept up by the May Fourth Movement, in which students agitated for political and cultural reforms in response to continuing foreign domination. At the time of her graduation from middle school, she observed that classmates were either entering technical institutions or getting married. "I thought otherwise," she said. "I enjoyed studying and I wanted to be economically independent. In that sense, it was clear in my mind that I had to have as much formal education as possible."[4]

Although she wanted to become a doctor, medical school was out of the question, as her father's remittances from Australia could no longer support both her and her younger brother's education. Arguing that graduates trained in American colleges and universities were drawing higher salaries in China than local graduates, Jane convinced her mother to sell some of their land in order to pay her passage to the United States. She then obtained a student's visa and sailed for America, planning to earn a doctorate and return home to a prestigious academic post. Jane Kwong Lee's class background, education, and early exposure to Western ideas would lead her to a different life experience in America than Law Shee Low and Wong Ah So, who came as obedient wives from sheltered and impoverished families.

The San Francisco Chinatown that the three women came to call home was different from the slum of "filth and depravity" of bygone days. After the 1906 earthquake and fire destroyed Chinatown, Chinese community leaders seized the opportunity to create a new "Oriental City" on the original site. The new Chinatown, in stark contrast to the old, was by appearance cleaner, healthier, and more modern with its wider paved streets, brick buildings, glass-plated storefronts, and pseudo-Chinese architecture. In an effort to establish order in the community, nurture business, and protect the growing numbers of families, the merchant elite and middle-class bourgeoisie established new institutions: Chinese schools, churches, a hospital, newspapers, and a flurry of civic and political organizations. Soon after the 1911 Revolution in China, queues and footbinding were eliminated, tong wars and prostitution reduced, and more of Chinatown's residents were dressing in Western clothing and adopting democratic ideas. Arriving in San Francisco's Chinatown at this juncture in time gave immigrant women such as Wong Ah So, Law Shee Low, and Jane Kwong Lee unprecedented opportunities to become "new women" in the modern era of Chinatown.

ESCAPING "A FATE WORSE THAN DEATH"

Upon landing in America, Wong Ah So's dreams of wealth and happiness vanished when she found out that her husband, Huey Yow, had in fact been paid $500 by a madam to procure her as a slave.

> When we first landed in San Francisco we lived in a hotel in Chinatown, a nice place, but one day, after I had been there for about two weeks, a woman came to see me. She was young, very pretty, and all dressed in silk. She told me that I was not really Huey Yow's wife, but that she had asked him to buy her a slave, that I belonged to her, and must go with her, but she would treat me well, and I could buy back my freedom, if I was willing to please, and be agreeable, and she would let me off in two years, instead of four if I did not make a fuss.

For the next year, Wong Ah So worked as a prostitute for the madam in various small towns. She was also forced to borrow $1,000 to pay off Huey Yow, who was harassing her and threatening her life. Soon after, she was sold to another madam in Fresno for $2,500. Meanwhile, her family in China continued to write her, asking for money. Even as her debts piled up and she became ill, she fulfilled her filial obligation by sending $300 home to her mother, enclosed with a letter that read in part:

> Every day I have to be treated by the doctor. My private parts pain me so that I cannot have intercourse with men. It is very hard. . . . Next year I certainly will be able to pay off all the debts. Your daughter is even more anxious than her mother to do this. Your daughter will do her part so that the world will not look down upon us.

Then one evening at a tong banquet where she was working, Wong Ah So was recognized by a friend of her father's, who sought help from the Presbyterian Mission Home on her behalf. Ten days later, she was rescued and placed in the care of Donaldina Cameron, the director of the home. As she wrote, "I don't know just how it happened because it was all very sudden. I just know that it happened. I am learning English and to weave, and I am going to send money to my mother when I can. I can't help but cry, but it is going to be better. I will do what Miss Cameron says." A year later, after learning how to read Chinese and speak English and becoming a Christian, Ah So agreed to marry Louie Kwong, a merchant in Boise, Idaho.

Wong Ah So's story harks back to the plight of the many Chinese women who were brought to the United States as prostitutes to fill a specific need in the Chinese bachelor society. By the 1920s, however, the traffic had gone underground and was on the decline due to the Chinese exclusion laws, anti-prostitution legislation, and the efforts of Protestant missionaries. In 1870, the peak year of prostitution, 1,426 or 71 percent of Chinese women in San Francisco were listed as prostitutes. By 1900 the number had dropped to 339 or 16 percent; and by 1910, 92 or 7 percent. No prostitutes could be found in the 1920 census, although English- and Chinese-language newspaper accounts and the records of the Presbyterian Mission Home indicate that organized prostitution continued through the 1920s.[5]

Most well known for her rescue work in Chinatown, Donaldina Cameron was a product of the Social Gospel and Progressive movements, which sought to uplift the "uncivilized"

Chinese women and children wait behind fences at the Immigration Station on Angel Island, near San Francisco. (Courtesy of California Historical Society, FN-18240.)

throughout the world and eradicate political corruption and social vices in the nation's cities. Unable to work effectively among Chinatown bachelors and spurned by white prostitutes, Cameron found her calling among Chinese prostitutes and slave girls. In turn, some Chinese prostitutes, calculating their chances in an oppressive environment with few options for improvement, saw the Mission Home as a way out of their problems. Cameron made it her crusade to free them from "a fate worse than death" by first rescuing them, and then inculcating them with Christian moral values. Numerous accounts in newspapers and religious publications describe in vivid detail the dangerous raids led by Cameron, who was credited with rescuing hundreds of Chinese slave girls during her forty years of service at the Presbyterian Mission Home.[6]

Once rescued, the young women were brought back to the Mission Home to be educated, trained in the domestic arts and industrial skills, and, most importantly, indoctrinated with Victorian moral values. The goal was to regroom them to enter society as Christian women. While some women chose to return to China under Christian escort, others opted to enter companionate marriages, pursue higher education, or become missionary workers. Wong Ah So—a direct beneficiary of the efforts of Protestant missionary women—was among the last to be rescued, Christianized, and married to a Chinese Christian.

IMMIGRANT WIVES AS INDISPENSABLE PARTNERS

Immigrant wives like Law Shee Low also found their lives transformed by the socioeconomic conditions in Chinatown. They did not find streets paved with gold, but practically speaking, they at least had food on the table and hope that through their hard work conditions might improve for themselves and their families. Although women were confined to the domestic sphere within the borders of Chinatown, their contributions as homemakers, wage earners, and culture bearers made them indispensable partners to their husbands in their struggle for economic survival. Their indispensability, combined with changing social attitudes toward women in Chinatown, gave some women leverage to shape gender arrangements within their homes and in the community.

Upon arrival in San Francisco, Law Shee Low moved into a one-room tenement apartment in Chinatown with her husband, where she lived, worked, and gave birth to eleven children, eight of whom survived. While her husband worked in a restaurant that catered to black customers on the outskirts of Chinatown, Law stayed home and took in sewing. Like other immigrant women who followed traditional gender roles, Law believed that the proper place for a woman was at home. As she recalls those days,

> There was no time to feel imprisoned; there was so much to do. We had to cook, wash the clothes and diapers by hand, the floors, and sew whenever we had a chance to sit still. It was the same for all my neighbors. We were all good, obedient, and diligent wives. All sewed; all had six or seven children. Who had time to go out?

Fortunately for Law Shee Low, her husband turned out to be cooperative, supportive, and devoted. Until he developed a heart condition in the 1950s, he remained the chief breadwinner, first cooking at a restaurant, then picking fruit in Suisun [California], sewing at home during the depression, and finally working in the shipyards during World War II. Although he refused to help with housecleaning or childcare, he did all the shopping, cooked the rice, and hung out the wash. In his own way, he showed concern for his wife. "When he was afraid I wasn't eating, he would tell me to eat more. Even though it was an arranged marriage, we got along well. I didn't complain that he went out every day. We hardly talked. Good or bad, we just struggled along as we had work to do."

As far as children were concerned Law Shee Low, like her neighbors, had not known how to interfere with nature. "We didn't know about birth control. We would become pregnant every year without realizing it. Even if we didn't want it, we didn't have the money to go see the doctor." All of Law's children were born at home, with the help of neighbors or the local midwife. Fortunately, her husband wanted children and was more than willing to provide for them all regardless of sex. "Other men would scold their children and beat them. One woman who had four children told me her husband would drag her out of bed and beat her because she didn't want to have any more children. We heard all kinds of sad stories like that, but my husband never picked on me like that."

It was not until her children were older that Law Shee Low went out to work in the sewing factories and to the Chinese movies on Saturdays, but she still did not leave the confines of Chinatown. Prior to that, she went out so seldom that one pair of shoes lasted her ten years. Since their first responsibility was to their families, many immigrant wives like Law found themselves housebound, with no time to learn English or to participate in social activities outside the home. Their husbands continued to be the chief breadwinner, to hold the purse strings, and to be their liaison to the outside world. But in the absence of the mother-in-law, immigrant wives usually ruled the household and assumed the responsibility of disciplinarian, culture-bearer, and of maintaining the integrity of their families. With few exceptions, they were hardworking, frugal, and tolerant, faithful and respectful to their husbands, and self-sacrificing toward their children. As such, they were indispensable partners to their husbands in their efforts to establish and sustain family life in America. And although they presented a submissive image in public, many immigrant women were known to "wear the pants" at home.

Overall, as compared to their predecessors, immigrant women in the early twentieth century were less tolerant of abuses to their persons and more resourceful in upgrading their status, thanks to the influence of the press, the support of Protestant organizations in the community, and a legal system that was sympathetic toward abused women. Although most immigrant wives like Law Shee Low could not read the Chinese newspapers, they were affected by public opinion as filtered through their husbands, neighbors, and social reformers looking after their interests. Law noted that after the 1911 Revolution it was no longer considered "fashionable" to have bound feet, concubines, or slave girls. And as housebound as Law was, she was aware of the mission homes that rescued prostitutes, helped abused women, and provided education for children and immigrant women.

CHINESE WOMEN IN THE LABOR MARKET

Compared to Wong Ah So and Law Shee Low, Jane Kwong Lee had an easier time acclimating to life in America. Not only was she educated, Westernized, English-speaking, and unencumbered by family responsibilities, but she also had the help of affluent relatives who provided her with room and board, financial support, and important contacts that enabled her eventually to strike out on her own.

Arriving in the middle of a school semester and therefore unable to enroll in a college, she decided to look for a job. In spite of her educational background and qualifications, she found that only menial jobs and domestic service were opened to her. "At heart I was sorry for myself; I wished I were a boy," she wrote in her autobiography. "If I were a boy, I could have gone out into the community, finding a job somewhere as many newcomers from China had done." But as a Chinese woman, she had to bide her time and look for work appropriate for her race and gender. Thus, until she could be admitted to college, and during the summers after she enrolled at Mills College, Jane took whatever jobs were open to Chinese women. She tried embroidery work at a Chinatown factory, sorting vegetables in the wholesale district, working as a live-in domestic for a white family, peeling shrimp, sorting fruit at a local cannery, and sewing flannel nightgowns at home.

As was true for European immigrant women, the patterns of work for Chinese women were shaped by the intersection of the local economy, ethnic traditions, language and job skills, and family and child-care needs, but in addition, race was an influential factor. At the time of Jane's arrival, San Francisco was experiencing a period of growth and prosperity. Ranked the eighth largest city in the country, it was the major port of trade for the Pacific Coast and touted as the financial and corporate capital of the West. Jobs were plentiful in the city's three largest economic sectors—domestic and personal service, trade and transportation, and manufacturing and mechanical industries—but they were filled according to a labor market stratified by race and gender, with Chinese men occupying the lowest tier as laborers, servants, factory workers, laundrymen, and small merchants, while Chinese women, handicapped further by gender, worked primarily in garment and food-processing factories for low piece-rate wages. With inadequate child-care services in the community, most seamstresses worked with their children close by or had their babies strapped to their backs.

For Jane Kwong Lee, being Chinese and a woman was a liability in the job market, but because she spoke English, was educated, and had good contacts among Chinese Christians, she was better off than most other immigrant women. She eventually got a scholarship at Mills College and part-time work teaching Chinese school and tutoring Chinese adults in English at the Chinese Episcopal Church in Oakland. After earning her bachelor's degree in sociology, she married, had two children, and returned to Mills College, where she received a master's degree in sociology and economics in 1933. She then dedicated herself to community service, working many years as coordinator of the Chinese YWCA and as a journalist and translator for a number of Chinatown newspapers.

For most immigrant women, joining the labor market proved to be a double-edged sword: On the one hand, their earnings helped to support their families and elevate their socioeconomic status; on the other hand, they became exploited laborers in the factory system, adding work and stress to their already burdensome lives. On the positive side, however, working outside the home offered women social rewards—a new sense of freedom, accomplishment, and camaraderie. They were no longer confined to the home, they were earning money for themselves or the family, and they were making new acquaintances and becoming exposed to new ideas. As Jane Kwong Lee observed, having money to spend made the women feel more liberated in America than in China: "They can buy things for themselves, go out to department stores to choose their own clothes instead of sewing them."

FIRST STEPS TOWARD SOCIAL ACTIVISM

For working-class women like Law Shee Low, family and work responsibilities consumed all their time and energy, leaving little left over for self-improvement or leisure activities, and even less for community involvement. This was not the case for a growing group of educated and professional women like Jane Kwong Lee, who, inspired by Christianity, Chinese nationalism, and Progressivism, took the first steps toward social activism. Prior to the 1911 Revolution in their homeland, Chinese women in America followed the tradition of remaining publicly invisible. They seldom ventured out of their homes except perhaps to shop or go to the Chinese opera, where they sat in a segregated section apart from the men.

The Protestant churches and Chinese YWCA were the first to encourage Chinese women's participation in organized activities outside the home, as evidenced by the small but visible number of them at Sunday services, English classes, meetings, outings, and other church-sponsored programs. Some of the churches also helped organize Chinese women's societies to encourage involvement in Christian activities. Members of these groups met regularly to have lunch or socialize, and paid dues to help support the work of Bible women in their home villages in China.[7]

Aside from Christianity, the intense nationalistic spirit that took hold in the early twentieth century also affected Chinese women in far-reaching ways. Not only did the call for modernization include the need to improve conditions for Chinese women, but reformers also solicited women's active participation in national salvation work. Fundraising for disaster relief and the revolution in China opened up opportunities for women to become involved in the community, develop leadership abilities, and move into the male-dominated public sphere. The Tongmenghui, the revolutionary party founded by Dr. Sun Yat-sen to overthrow the Qing dynasty and establish a republic in China, was the earliest organization to accept women into its ranks. While women in China participated in benefit performances, enlisted in the army, and engaged in dangerous undercover work, women in San Francisco also did their share for the revolutionary effort—making patriotic speeches, donating money and jewelry for the cause, and helping with Red Cross work—sometimes under the auspices of Protestant churches, other times under the banner of the Women's Young China Society.

Although the success of the revolution and the establishment of a republic in China failed to bring peace and prosperity to the country, it did have a lasting impact on the lives of Chinese American women. As Jane Kwong Lee observed, "After the establishment of the Republic of China, Chinese women in this country picked up the forward-looking trend for equality with men. They could go to school, speak in public places, have their feet free from binding, and go out to work in stores and small factories if they needed to work."[8]

Arriving as a liberated woman at the time when she did, Jane did not hesitate to join other women in becoming socially active in the Chinatown community. In her capacity as a community worker at the Chinese YWCA, she made house visits, wrote articles that were published in the local newspapers, and implemented programs that benefited Chinese women in the community. She was particularly known for her loud and forceful speeches that she delivered in Chinese at churches and street corners in support of Christianity and nationalist causes, and before Chinatown organizations on behalf of the Chinese YWCA. Jane also made presentations in English to groups interested in learning more about Chinese culture, and traveled as a Chinese delegate to YWCA functions outside of Chinatown. On one of these occasions, she was so moved by a discussion on racial discrimination that she surprised herself and African Americans at a YWCA meeting by speaking up for them. "I said, you are all equal; nobody is inferior to another."[9]

CONCLUSION

As Sieh King King had advocated in 1902, Chinese women unbound their feet and began to unbind their lives in America during the first three decades of the twentieth century. Most, like Law Shee Low and Wong Ah So, had immigrated for a better livelihood but found themselves exploited as prostitutes or working wives at the bottom of a labor market stratified by race and gender. Some, like Jane Kwong Lee, had come from a privileged background yet still encountered discrimination in the workplace and in the larger American society. But like many other immigrant women before them, they not only persevered and survived, but took advantage of new circumstances to improve their lives and contribute to the well-being of their families and community. Even as immigrant women began to enjoy their new roles as emancipated women, economic depression set in and war loomed large in their homeland. The challenges of the 1930s and 1940s—economic survival and the war effort on two fronts—would lead to even greater dramatic changes in their lives, allowing them to take the first steps toward fuller participation in American society.

Notes

1. *San Francisco Chronicle,* November 3, 1902, p. 7.

2. Wong Ah So's story is taken from "Story of Wong Ah So—Experiences as a Prostitute," *Orientals and Their Cultural Adjustment,* Social Science Source Documents, no. 4 (Nashville: Social Science Institute, Fisk University, 1946), pp. 31–35; and Donaldina Cameron, "The Story of Wong So," *Women and Missions* 2, no. 5 (August 1925):169–72.

3. Law Shee Low's story is based on her interview with Sandy Lee, May 2, 1982; and interview with author, October 20, 1988.

4. Jane Kwong Lee's story is based on her unpublished autobiography, "A Chinese American," in the possession of her daughter Priscilla Holmes.

5. See Lucie Cheng Hirata, "Free, Indentured, Enslaved: Chinese Prostitutes in Nineteenth-Century California," *Signs: Journal of Women in Culture and Society* 5, no. 1 (autumn 1979):3–29. The figures for 1900, 1910, and 1920 are based on my computations from the U.S. National Archives, Record Group 29, "Census of U.S. Population" (manuscript), San Francisco, California.

6. See Peggy Pascoe, *Relations of Rescue: The Search for Female Moral Authority in the American West, 1874–1939* (New York: Oxford University Press, 1990).

7. See Wesley Woo, "Protestant Work among the Chinese in the San Francisco Bay Area, 1850–1920," Ph.D. dissertation, University of California, Berkeley, 1983.

8. Jane Kwong Lee, "Chinese Women in San Francisco," *Chinese Digest* (June 1938):8.

9. Jane Kwong Lee, interview with author, November 2, 1988.

ANNELISE ORLECK

From the Russian Pale to Labor Organizing in New York City

The pale of Jewish settlement was a territory within Russia to which Jews were restricted during the eighteenth and nineteenth centuries and where they were frequently subjected to ferocious outbursts of anti-Semitic violence. Crossing from the pale to the teeming streets of Manhattan's Lower East Side was a frontier crossing of major proportions. Yet two million European Jews who came to the United States between 1880 and 1924 made it across, among them the remarkable young women who are the subjects of Annelise Orleck's lively and informative essay.

Like so many of their fellow immigrants, Rose Schneiderman, Fannia Cohn, Clara Lemlich, and Pauline Newman gravitated to one of the earliest industries to employ women—the garment industry. Based in New York City, the industry had long provided countless married women with piecework to take back to dimly lit tenements, where they often enlisted the help of grandmothers and children. By the turn of the century, much of the work had been transferred to sweatshops and factories that were notorious for their low wages and squalid working conditions. Because so many of the female employees were young single women who presumably regarded their work as a temporary necessity until rescued by marriage, labor leaders usually assumed that the women were virtually unorganizable. Yet between 1909 and 1915, women garment workers in New York as well as in other cities exploded in labor militancy. By 1919, half of all women garment workers belonged to trade unions and many had joined the suffrage struggle as well. The role these four young women played in this process is the focus of Orleck's essay.

What experiences shaped their political consciousness and propelled their activism? As young girls forced to work and forego school and college, how did they educate themselves and for what purpose? Who were their allies and why were these alliances so necessary, yet so unstable? How was the balancing act required of the four with respect to male trade unionists and elite female reformers similar to that required of Charlotte Hawkins Brown, albeit in a different context (see pp. 368–378)? What attracted these young working women to suffrage? What is meant by the term "industrial feminists"?

During the summer of 1907, when New York City was gripped by a severe economic depression, a group of young women workers who had been laid off and were facing eviction took tents and sleeping rolls to the verdant Palisades overlooking the Hudson River. While rising rents and unemployment spread panic among the poor immigrants of Manhattan's Lower East Side, these teenagers lived in a makeshift summer camp, getting work where they could find it, sharing whatever food and drink they could afford, reading, hiking, and gathering around a campfire at night to sing Russian and Yiddish songs. "Thus we avoided paying rent or, worse still, being evicted," Pauline Newman later recalled. "Besides which, we liked living in the open—plenty of fresh air, sunshine and the lovely Hudson for which there was no charge."[1]

Away from the clatter of the shops and the filth of Lower East Side streets, the young women talked into the night, refreshed by what Newman called "the cool of the evening, glorious sunsets, the moon and stars." They shared personal concerns as well as shop-floor gripes—worries about love, about the future, and about the pressing problems of housing and food.

Their cliffside village meant more to Newman and her friends than a summer escape. They had created a vibrant alternative to the tenement life they found so oppressive, and their experience of it had set them to wondering. Perhaps the same sense of joy and comradeship could help workers transcend the drudgery of the garment shops and form the basis for effective organizing.[2]

At season's end, they emerged with strengthened bonds and renewed resolve to organize their communities around issues that the recent depression had brought into sharp relief: the need for stabilized rent and food prices, improved working conditions, and housing for the poor.[3]

The spirit of intimacy and solidarity that pervaded the summer of 1907 would inspire much of Pauline Newman's later organizing. Indeed, it became a model for the vision of change that Newman shared with her fellow Jewish immigrant radicals Fannia Cohn, Rose Schneiderman and Clara Lemlich. The four women moved to political struggle not simply by the need for better wages, hours and working conditions but also, in Newman's words, by a need to ensure that "poverty did not deprive us from finding joy and satisfaction in things of the spirit."[4] This essay examines the early careers of these four remarkable organizers and the role they played in building a militant working women's movement during the first decades of the twentieth century.

For even as girls, these marginally educated immigrants wanted to be more than . . . shop-floor drudges. They wanted lives filled with beauty—with friendships, books, art, music, dance, fresh air, and clean water. "A working girl is a human being," Newman would later tell a legislative committee investigating factory conditions, "with a heart, with desires, with aspirations, with ideas and ideals." That image nourished Newman, Schneiderman, Lemlich, and Cohn throughout their long careers. And it focused them on a single goal: to reshape U.S. society so that "working girls" like themselves could fulfill some of their dreams.[5]

The four women moved through strikingly different cultural milieus over the course of long careers that would carry them in different directions. Still, they each bore the imprint of the shared culture in which they were raised, first in Eastern Europe and then in New York City. That common experience gave them a particular understanding of gender, class, and ethnicity that shaped their later activism and political thought.

All four were born in the Russian-dominated pale of Jewish settlement during the last two decades of the nineteenth century. Rose Schneiderman was born in the Polish village of Saven in 1882; Fannia Cohn was born in Kletsk, Poland, in 1885; Clara Lemlich was born in the Ukrainian village of Gorodok in 1886; and Pauline Newman was born in Kovno, Lithuania, around 1890.[6]

They were ushered into a world swept by a firestorm of new ideas, where the contrasting but equally messianic visions of orthodox Judaism and revolutionary Socialism competed for young minds. The excitement of living in a revolutionary era imbued these young women with a faith in progress and a belief that political commitment gave life meaning. It also taught them, at an early age, that gender, class, and ethnicity were fundamental social categories and essential building blocks for political change. Being born into turbulence does not in itself make a child into a political activist. But the changes sweeping the Russian Empire toward the end of the nineteenth century shaped the consciousness of a generation of Eastern European Jews who contributed, in wildly disproportionate numbers, to revolutionary movements in Russia and to the labor and radical movements in the United States.[7]

The four were exposed to Marxist ideas at a tender age. As Eastern Europe shifted uneasily from feudalism to capitalism in the latter part of the nineteenth century, class analysis became part of the common parlance of young people in Jewish towns and villages. "Behind every other volume of Talmud in those years, there was a volume of Marx," one union organizer recalled of his small Polish town. Clara Lemlich grew up on revolutionary tracts and songs; Fannia Cohn considered herself a committed Socialist by the age of sixteen.[8]

Their awareness of ethnicity was even more keen. As Jews in Eastern Europe, the four learned young that ethnic identity was a double-edged sword. It was a source of strength and solace in their bitterly poor communities, but it also enabled Tsarist authorities to single Jews out and sow seeds of suspicion among their peasant neighbors. Jews living under Russian rule were made painfully aware of their status as permanent "others" in the land where they had lived for centuries. Clara Lemlich's family lived not far from Kishinev, where in 1903 the Tsar's government openly and unabashedly directed an orgy of anti-Jewish violence that shocked the world. In cosmopolitan Minsk, where she had gone to study, Fannia Cohn watched with dismay as the revolutionary populist organization she had joined began mouthing the same anti-Semitic conspiracy theories spewed by the government they despised. Frustration turned to fear when her brother was almost killed in yet another pogrom.[9]

Sex was just as distinct a dividing line as class and ethnicity. Eastern European Jews had observed a strict sexual division of labor for more than a thousand years. But by the late nineteenth century, as political and economic upheaval jolted long-accepted ways of thinking, sex roles too were being questioned. And so the four girls' understandings of gender were informed both by traditional Jewish conceptions of womanhood and by the challenges issued by new political movements.

In traditional Jewish society, mothers were also entrepreneurs. Clara Lemlich, Pauline Newman, and Rose Schneiderman were all raised by mothers who were skilled businesswomen. Jewish mothers' success in this role grew out of and reinforced a belief that women were innately suited to competition in the economic sphere. In contrast to the image of the sheltered middle-class housewife then dominant in the United States, Eastern European Jewish religious tradition glorified strong, economically sophisticated wives and mothers.

But as much as women's entrepreneurship was respected, a far higher premium was placed on study and prayer. And that, religious tradition dictated, could be performed only by men. A woman was expected to be pious, to read the vernacular Yiddish—rather than ancient Hebrew—translation of the Bible, and perhaps to attend women's services at the synagogue. But her primary religious role was as keeper of the home. Formal religious education was offered only to males.[10] Because Eastern European Jewish women had to fight for every scrap of education they received, many began to see education as the key to independence from all masters. This view would strongly influence their political organizing once in the United States.

The four emigrated as part of the mass movement that brought two million Jews from Eastern Europe to the United States between 1881 and 1924. Schneiderman came in 1890, Newman in 1901, Lemlich in 1903, and Cohn in 1904. Like most of their compatriots, they arrived in New York Harbor and settled on Manhattan's Lower East Side, the largest settlement of Eastern European Jews in the United States.[11] The newcomers were tantalized by the exciting diversions that New York life promised: libraries, theater, music, department stores, and amusement parks. But they had neither time nor money to indulge in such pleasures, for all of them soon found themselves laboring long hours to support their families.

At an age when most girls in the United States were still in grade school, immigrant working girls like Newman spent twelve- to fourteen-hour days in the harshest of atmospheres. Their bodies and minds reeled from the shock of the shops: the deafening noise, the brutal pace, and the rebukes of foremen. Some children were able to slough off the hardship with jokes and games. Others, realizing that

Medical Examination at Ellis Island. "The day of the emigrants' arrival in New York was the nearest earthly likeness to the final day of Judgment, when we have to prove our fitness to enter Heaven." The words are those of a sympathetic journalist who shared the anxiety-ridden experience awaiting immigrants at the port of entry, usually Ellis Island. Failing the medical test could mean deportation. (Courtesy of Brown Brothers, Sterling, Pennsylvania.)

they were destined to spend their youth in dank factories rather than in classrooms or schoolyards, grew sullen and withdrawn.

Clara Lemlich, like so many others, was quickly disillusioned by her first job in a New York garment shop: "I went to work two weeks after landing in this country. We worked from sunrise to set seven days a week. . . . Those who worked on machines had to carry the machines on their back both to and from work. . . . The shop we worked in had no central heating, no electric power. . . . The hissing of the machines, the yelling of the foreman, made life unbearable."[12]

Anger drove young women workers like Lemlich and Newman to band together. Untrained and largely unschooled, these young women were drawn to Socialism and trade unionism not because they felt an ideological affinity but because they had a desperate need to improve their working conditions. "I knew very little about Socialism," Lemlich recalled. "[But] the girls, whether Socialist or not, had many stoppages and strikes." Newman too found that for most young women workers, political understanding followed action rather than precipitating it: "We of the 1909 vintage knew nothing about the economics of . . . industry or for that matter about economics in general. All we knew was the bitter fact that, after working seventy and eighty hours in a seven day week, we did not earn enough to keep body and soul together." These assertions reveal much about the political development of the tens of thousands of women garment workers who would soon amaze New York and the nation with their militancy.[13]

Shop-floor culture fed the young women's emerging sense of political identity. Working alongside older men and women who discussed Socialism daily, they began to feel a sense of belonging to a distinct class of people in the world: workers. This allegiance would soon become as important to them as their Judaism. The shops also provided an opportunity for bonding with other women. Slowly, out of their workplace experiences, they began to develop a complex political identity in which class, gender and ethnicity overlapped. Young women workers were moved by the idea of sisterhood. It captured their own experiences in the sex-segregated shops where they worked. The majority of New York's garment workers were little more than girls, and the relationships they forged with factory friends were similar to those of schoolgirls—intense, melodramatic, and deeply loyal. They were teenage confidantes as well as fellow workers, and they relied on shop-floor rapport to soften the harshness of factory life.[14] For young immigrant women trying to build lives in a new land, such bonds were powerful and lasting. From these shop-floor friendships would soon evolve the ties of union sisterhood.[15]

Pauline Newman and her co-workers at the Triangle Shirtwaist Factory literally grew up together. Only twelve when she first came to Triangle, Newman was assigned to a corner known as "the kindergarten," where workers as young as eight, nine, or ten years old trimmed threads from finished garments. They labored, Newman later recalled, "from 7:30 A.M. to 6:30 at night when it wasn't busy. When the season was on we worked till 9 o'clock. No overtime pay." Their only taste of a normal childhood came through the songs and games they invented to help pass the time, the stories they told and the secrets they shared.[16]

By the early twentieth century, New York State had passed laws prohibiting night work for children. But little attempt was made to enforce them. On the rare occasions when an inspector showed up at her factory, Newman remembered, "the employers were always tipped off. . . . 'Quick,' they'd say, 'Into the boxes!' And we children would climb into the big box the finished shirts were stored in. Then some shirts were piled on top of us and when the inspector came—No children." In a way it was fun, Newman remembered. They thought they were playing a game like hide and seek.[17]

But it wasn't really a game. Children who had to help support their parents grew up quickly. Rose Schneiderman was thirteen when her mother begged United Hebrew Charities, an organization run by middle-class German Jews, to find her daughter a "respectable job" at a department store. Retail jobs were deemed more respectable than factory work because the environment was more pleasant and sexual harassment was thought to be less common. Deborah Schneiderman worried that factory work would sully Rose's reputation and make her less marriageable. A job as a fashionable salesgirl, she hoped, would usher

Rose into the middle class. The single mother who had fed her children on charity food baskets and had been forced to place them in orphanages was grimly determined to help them escape poverty.

But then as now, pink-collar jobs paid significantly less than industrial work. Anxious to free her mother from the rigors of maintaining their tenement building, Schneiderman left her job in Ridley's department store for the harsher and more morally suspect conditions of an industrial shop. Making linings for caps and hats, she immediately raised her weekly income from \$2.75 to \$6. As the sole supporter of her family, the sixteen-year-old hoped to work her way up quickly to a skilled job in the cap trade.[18]

Clara Lemlich's family also relied on her wages, particularly because her father was unemployed. She aspired to the skilled position of draper, one of the highest-paid positions a woman could attain in the dressmaking trade. Despite terrible working conditions, many ambitious young women chose garment work over other jobs because it seemed to offer their greatest chance to acquire skills and command high wages. When these hopes were dashed, some young workers grew angry. That anger was fanned and channeled by older women in the shops who were itching to challenge the authority of the bosses.[19]

That is what happened to Rose Schneiderman, who, like many skilled women garment workers, was blocked from advancement by the unofficial gender hierarchy at her factory. Finding that all the highest-paid jobs in her capmaking shop were reserved for men, Schneiderman asked around about ways to break through those barriers. When she approached fellow worker Bessie Braut with her concerns, Schneiderman was initiated simultaneously into trade unionism, Socialism, and feminism. Schneiderman recalled, "Bessie was an unusual person. Her beautiful eyes shone out of a badly pockmarked face and the effect was startling. An outspoken anarchist, she made a strong impression on us. She wasted no time in giving us the facts of life—that the men in our trade belonged to a union and were, therefore, able to better their conditions. She added pointedly that it would be a good thing for the lining-makers to join a union along with the trimmers, who were all women."[20]

Schneiderman, Braut, and several other workers called on the secretary-treasurer of the United Cloth Hat and Cap Makers to request union recognition for their fledgling local of trimmers and lining makers. Within a few days they had enough signatures to win a charter for their local, and Schneiderman was elected secretary.[21]

Surprising even herself, the once-shy redhead soon found she could be an eloquent and fierce advocate for her fellow workers. In recognition of her growing reputation, the capmakers elected her to the Central Labor Union of New York. Deborah Schneiderman was disturbed by the turn Rose's life was taking. She warned Rose that if she pursued a public life she would never find a husband. No man wants a woman with a big mouth, her mother said.[22]

In the flush of excitement at the praise and warmth suddenly coming her way, young Rose did not stop to worry. In organizing, she had found both a calling and a world of friends. She had no intention of turning back. "It was such an exciting time," she wrote later. "A new life opened up for me. All of a sudden I was not lonely anymore. . . . It was the beginning of a period that molded all my subsequent life."[23]

Fannia Cohn, too, chose garment work as her path to a career. And like Schneiderman, Lemlich, and Newman, she found a community there. Unlike the others, however, she did not enter a garment factory looking for work that paid well. She was a comfortable middle-class woman in search of a trade ripe for unionizing.

Cohn arrived in New York in 1904 and moved in with her affluent cousins. There was little about her early days in the United States that was comparable to the hard-pressed scrambling for a living that the Schneidermans, Lemlichs, and Newmans experienced. "My family suggested that I complete my studies and then join the labor movement but I rejected this as I did not want to come into it from 'without' but from 'within.' I realized then that if I wanted to really understand the mind, the aspirations of the workers, I should experience the life of the worker in a shop."[24] In 1905, Fannia Cohn became a sleevemaker. For a year she moved from shop to shop until, in the "white goods" trade, she found the organizing challenge she was looking for.

Shops that manufactured white goods—underwear, kimonos, and robes—were considered particularly hard to organize. Production took place in tiny sweatshops, not large factories, and the manufacturing process had been broken down into small tasks that required little skill. The majority of white goods workers were immigrant girls under the age of fifteen. And because they came from a wide range of backgrounds—Jewish, Italian, Syrian, Turkish, and Greek—it was difficult for them to communicate with each other, let alone organize. As a result, these workers were among the lowest paid in the garment trades.

At twenty, Cohn was an elder in the trade. With her high school education and fluency in three languages, she was seen as a mother figure by many of the adolescents in the shops. She and a handful of older women workers began to operate as mentors, meeting with the girls in each shop and identifying potential leaders. Cohn taught her co-workers to read, write, and speak in public, hoping they would channel those skills into the union struggle. Cohn had already created the role that she would play throughout her career: an educator of younger workers.[25]

Education was a primary driving force in the metamorphosis of all four young women from shop workers to union organizers. From the isolated towns and restive cities of Eastern Europe, where gender, class, and ethnicity stymied Jewish girls' hopes for education, the lure of free public schooling in the United States beckoned powerfully. Having to drop out of school to work was more than a disappointment for many Jewish immigrant girls; it was their first great disillusionment with the dream of America. And they did not give that dream up easily.

"When I went to work," Rose Schneiderman remembered, "I was determined to continue my studies." Her only option was to attend one of the many night schools then open to immigrant workers in New York. Having carried with her from Poland the ideal of education as an exalted, liberating process, she was disgusted by the mediocre instruction she encountered and felt betrayed by teachers who seemed to be patronizing her. "I enrolled and went faithfully every evening for about four weeks. But I found that . . . the instructor seemed more interested in getting one-hundred-percent attendance than in giving one-hundred-percent instruction. He would joke and tell silly stories. . . . I soon realized I was wasting my time." Schneiderman left the evening school but did not stop studying. She asked older co-workers if she could borrow books that she had discussed with them in the shop. In the evenings, she read with her mother at home. Serializations of Emile Zola's *J'Accuse* and other contemporary writings in the Yiddish evening paper *Abendblatt* gave Rose a taste for literature. "I devoured everything I could get my hands on."[26]

Clara Lemlich was an equally avid reader. At the end of each twelve-hour day stitching shirtwaists, she would walk from her factory to the East Broadway branch of the New York Public Library. There she read the library's entire collection of Russian classics. "I was so eager to learn things," she later recalled. When she tired of solitary study, Lemlich joined a free night school on Grand Street. She returned home late each night, ate the dinner her mother had kept warm for her, then slept for just a few hours before rising again for work.[27]

Not surprisingly, young women like Schneiderman, Newman, and Lemlich turned to radical politics to fulfill their desire for a life of the mind. If no other school was available, then what Pauline Newman called "the school of solidarity" would have to do. Membership in the Socialist Party and in unions, tenant organizations, and benevolent societies provided immigrant women with an opportunity to learn and study that most would never have gotten otherwise. And as Newman put it, "Because they were hitherto deprived of any tutorship, they at once became ardent students."[28]

Pauline Newman was just fifteen when she first knocked on the doors of the Socialist Literary Society. Although women were not yet allowed to join, she was permitted to attend classes. The Literary Society was a revelation to the young worker. There she was introduced to the writings of Shakespeare, George Eliot, and Thomas Hardy and personally met writers like Jack London and Charlotte Perkins Gilman, who came to speak there. Gratitude, however, didn't stop her from joining a successful petition drive to admit women to the society.

For Newman—as for Clara Lemlich, who attended Marxist theory classes at the Socialist

Party's Rand School—studying was more than a distraction from work. The "desire to get out of the shop," Newman wrote later, "to learn, to understand, became the dominant force in my life." But unlike many immigrants, who saw schooling as a ladder out of the working class, both she and Lemlich were committed to helping others rise with them. So Newman and Lemlich formed study groups that met during lunch hours and after work to share what they were learning with their friends.[29]

"We tried to educate ourselves," Newman remembered of her co-workers at the Triangle Shirtwaist Factory. "I would invite the girls to my room and we took turns reading poetry in English to improve our understanding of the language." Because they had to steal the time to study, the young women approached everything they read with a heightened sensitivity. And when something they were reading struck a chord of recognition, seemed to reflect on their own lives, the catharsis was not only emotional; it was political.[30]

The evolution of Lemlich's study group illustrates how study often led to union activity. Older workers, who were teaching Lemlich the craft of draping, invited her to join their lunchtime discussion groups to learn more about trade unionism. Soon Lemlich and a group of young women waistmakers formed their own study group. Discussion quickly escalated to action, and they decided to form a union.[31]

Skilled male workers in the shirtwaist trade had been trying to establish a union since 1900. But after five years the union had managed to attract only ten members. The problem, Lemlich told her male colleagues, was that women workers had to be approached by an organizer who understood their particular needs as women. They bristled at the suggestion that this young girl might know more about their business than they did. But years later, one conceded that the failure of the first waistmakers' union was due at least in part to their ham-fisted tactics: "We would issue a circular reading somewhat as follows: 'Murder the exploiters, the blood-suckers, the manufacturers. . . . Pay your dues. . . . Down with the Capitalists!'" Few women or men showed up at their meetings.[32]

During the spring of 1905 the union disbanded and reorganized as Local 25 of the ILGWU, with Clara Lemlich and a group of six

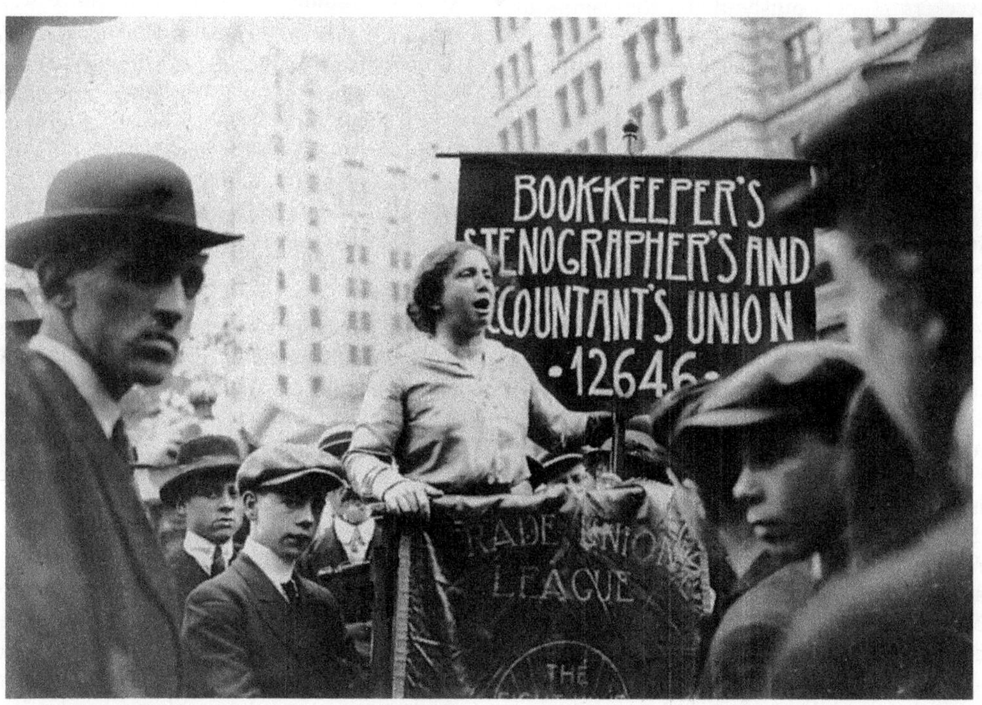

Rose Schneiderman addresses a street rally in New York. (Courtesy of Brown Brothers, Sterling, Pennsylvania.)

young women from her waistmaking shop on the executive board. Taking their cue from Lemlich, the new union used women organizers to attract women workers. Lemlich addressed street-corner meetings in English and Yiddish and found Italian women to address the Italian workers. Soon, like Schneiderman, Newman, and Cohn, she realized that she had found a calling.[33]

In the progressive atmosphere of early-twentieth-century New York City, influential people quickly noticed the militant young working women. Older Socialists, trade unionists, and middle-class reformers offered their assistance. These benefactors helped the young organizers sharpen their arguments, provided financial assistance, and introduced them to politicians and public officials. The protégés recognized the importance of this informal mentoring and would later work to recreate such networks in the unions, schools, and training programs they built for young women workers. Schneiderman, Newman, Lemlich, and Cohn were keenly aware that young working women needed help from more experienced and more powerful allies. But they also worried that the voices of women workers might be outshouted in the clamorous process of building alliances. From these early days, they battled to preserve the integrity of their vision.

Pauline Newman found her first mentors in the Socialist Party, which she joined in 1906 at the age of fifteen. Older women, including former garment worker Theresa Serber Malkiel, took her on as a protégé. Newman quickly blossomed under their tutelage. Before long she was running street-corner meetings. Armed with a sonorous voice and the certitude of youth, she would take "an American flag and a soapbox and go from corner to corner," exhorting the gospel of Socialism in Yiddish and English. "I, like many of my friends and comrades, thought that socialism and socialism alone could and would someday fill the gap between rich and poor," Newman recalled. In a neighborhood crowded with sidewalk proselytizers, this child evangelist became one of the party's most popular street-corner attractions.[34]

In 1908, nine years before New York State gave women the vote, seventeen-year-old Newman was nominated by the Socialist Party to run for New York's Secretary of State. Newman used her campaign as a platform for suffrage. Her speeches were heckled by some Socialist men, and her candidacy provoked amused commentaries in New York City newspapers; some writers snickered at the prospect of a "skirted Secretary of State." It was a largely symbolic crusade, but Newman felt that she got people talking about the idea of women in government. The highlight of the campaign was her whistlestop tour with presidential candidate and Socialist leader Eugene V. Debs on his "Red Special" train.

The Socialist Party opened up a new world to Newman, who, after all, had never graduated from elementary school. Along with Debs, she met future Congressmen Meyer Berger and Morris Hillquit and leading Socialist intellectuals. Newman later wrote about the excitement of discussions that carried over from meetings and went into the night as she and her friends walked through Central Park, arguing till the sun came up. Those nights made her feel part of a historic moment.[35]

While Newman was being nurtured by the Socialist Party, Rose Schneiderman found her mentors in the United Cloth Hat and Cap Makers. At the union's 1904 convention she was elected to the General Executive Board; she was the first woman to win such a high-level post in the American labor movement. During the winter of 1904–5, Schneiderman's leadership skills were tested when owners tried to open up union shops to nonunion workers. The largely immigrant capmaker's union called for a general strike. The 1905 strike was a watershed event in Schneiderman's emerging career. Her role as the only woman leader in the union won attention from the press and lasting respect from male capmakers, including the future president of the union, Max Zaritsky, who became a lifelong friend and admirer.[36]

It also brought her to the attention of the newly formed Women's Trade Union League (WTUL), an organization of progressive middle- and upper-class women reformers founded in 1903 to help working women organize. Schneiderman had misgivings about the group because she "could not believe that men and women who were not wage earners themselves understood the problems that workers faced." But she trusted the League's best-known working-class member, Irish shirtmaker

Leonora O'Reilly. And she could not ignore the favorable publicity that the WTUL won for the strikers. By March 1905, Schneiderman had been elected to the executive board of the New York WTUL. In 1906, the group elected her vice president.[37]

Schneiderman's entrance into the New York WTUL was an important turning point for both her and the organization. Three years after its founding, the WTUL remained dominated by affluent reformers who had dubbed themselves "allies" of the working class. Despite their genuine commitment to trade unionism, League leaders had credibility problems among women workers. Schneiderman had joined the League recognizing that working women lacked the education, the money, and the political clout to organize effectively without powerful allies. Still, she remained ambivalent for a variety of reasons.[38]

The progressive reformers who dominated the League tried to steer workers away from radical influences, particularly the Socialist Party. Yet Schneiderman and O'Reilly, the League's leading working-class organizers, were Socialist Party members and saw unionism as a potentially revolutionary tool. As a result, the pair often felt torn by competing loyalties. Socialists distrusted their work with upper-crust women reformers. Union men were either indifferent or openly hostile to working women's attempts to become leaders in the labor movement. And the League women often seemed to Schneiderman and O'Reilly to act out of a patronizing benevolence that had little to do with real coalition building. The two grew angry at what they saw as attempts by wealthy allies to manipulate them. In January 1906, Leonora O'Reilly announced the first of her many resignations from the League, claiming "an overdose of allies."[39]

There were a few deep friendships between affluent WTUL leaders and working women like Schneiderman, O'Reilly, and Pauline Newman, who joined the League in 1909. Such bonds created hope that intimacy was possible between women of different classes; but cross-class friendships were the exception rather than the rule. Working women like Newman never lost sight of the ways their class background separated them from wealthy reformers. Sisterhood was exhilarating, but outside the WTUL, their lives and political agendas diverged sharply.[40]

Consequently, these women's relations with most wealthy League supporters were marked by deep ambivalence inasmuch as WTUL backers wanted to distance the League from radical working-class activism and to stake out a decidedly middle ground in the struggle for women's rights that was then gathering steam.

Schneiderman tried to counterbalance such influences by encouraging male union leaders to play a more active role in the League, but she had little success. She told them that the WTUL could help the labor movement by successfully organizing women workers, whose low wages might otherwise exert a downward pressure on unionized male wages. A *women's* trade union league was needed, she insisted, because women workers responded to different arguments than did men workers. The League could focus on the particular concerns of women, such as the double shift—having to perform household chores after coming home from long days in the factory. Her suggestions were greeted with indifference.

Addressing the First Convention of American Women Trade Unionists, held in New York on July 14, 1907, Schneiderman reported that she "was very much surprised and not a little disappointed that the attention of men unionists was so small." The truth is, she told her audience, working women needed more than unions. They needed political power. "The time has come," she said firmly, "when working women of the State of New York must be enfranchised and so secure political power to shape their own labor conditions." The convention passed a suffrage resolution, one of the first prosuffrage statements by any organization representing American working-class women.[41]

Schneiderman confronted middle- and upper-class allies with equal frankness. She told the NYWTUL executive board that they were having little success organizing women workers because they approached their task like scholars, not trade unionists. They surveyed conditions in the women's trades, noting which had the lowest salaries, the longest hours, and the worst hygienic conditions. Then they established committees to study the possibilities for unionizing each trade. Finally they went into the shops to explain their findings to the working women. Schneiderman suggested a simpler alternative: take their lead from women workers and respond to requests for aid from women workers who were already trying to organize. It was something they had never thought to do.[42]

Before long, requests for help were pouring in, mostly from immigrant Jewish women. In the dress trade, where Clara Lemlich was working, and in the white goods trade, where Fannia Cohn was organizing, women workers had launched a series of wildcat strikes. "It was not unusual for unorganized workers to walk out without having any direct union affiliation," Schneiderman later recalled.[43]

By 1907, long-simmering anger over speedups, wage cuts, and the requirement that employees pay for their own thread reached a boiling point. Foreshadowing its role in the decades to come, the Women's Trade Union League decided to champion women workers ignored by the male unions. The strike fever soon engulfed Brooklyn, where for two years Fannia Cohn had been struggling against male union leaders' indifference to organize white goods workers. So when three hundred workers in one shop decided to strike in 1908, they bypassed the UGW and called for help from Schneiderman and the WTUL.

Since the ethnic makeup of the Brooklyn white goods trade was far more diverse than any other in the garment industry, this strike raised a new challenge for Schneiderman: how to forge a sense of solidarity between working-class women of many religions and nationalities. Schneiderman decided that the best way to reach immigrant workers was through organizers who literally spoke their language.[44]

She decided to focus first on Italian workers because, after Jews, they comprised the single largest ethnic group in the garment trades. Recognizing the cultural as well as linguistic differences that separated her from Italian immigrant women, Schneiderman tried a strategy she would employ many times over the years to come: to identify and cultivate a leader from within the ranks of the workers. She began working with a Brooklyn priest on ways to approach young Italian women. She also got the League to hire an Italian-speaking organizer who assembled a committee of progressive New York Italians—including prominent women professionals and the editor of a popular evening paper *Bolatino de la Sera*—to popularize trade unionism among Italian women workers.[45]

The strategy proved successful. By 1909 enough workers had enlisted that the ILGWU finally recognized the Brooklyn white goods workers' union. The vast majority of its members were teenage girls; these young women elected their mentor, Fannia Cohn, then twenty-four, to the union's first executive board. Cohn, who stepped off the shop floor to a policy-making position, would remain a paid union official for the rest of her life.[46]

In 1909, Clara Lemlich—then in her twenties and on the executive board of ILGWU Local 25—enlisted Schneiderman's aid in her drive to organize shirt-waist makers. For the past three years, Lemlich had been zigzagging between small shops, stirring up trouble. Her first full-scale strike was at Weisen and Goldstein's Manhattan factory. Like the Triangle Shirtwaist Factory, where Newman worked, Weisen and Goldstein's was considered a model shop. The workrooms were modern and airy—a pleasant contrast to the dark basement rooms where most white goods workers labored. However, the advantages of working in a clean, new factory were offset by the strains of mechanization. In 1907 the workers at Weisen and Goldstein's went on strike to protest speedups.

Older male strikers proved critical to Lemlich's political education. Confused by an argument between workers at a strike meeting, Lemlich asked one to explain the difference between Socialist unionism and the "pure and simple trade unionism" of the American Federation of Labor (AFL). When the meeting ended, the man took Lemlich for a long walk. He explained Socialism in terms she could use with her fellow workers. "He started with a bottle of milk—how it was made, who made the money from it through every stage of its production. Not only did the boss take the profits, he said, but not a drop of that milk did you drink unless he allowed you to. It was funny, you know, because I'd been saying things like that to the girls before. But now I understood it better and I began to use it more often—only with shirtwaists."[47]

Lemlich returned to the picket line with a more sophisticated view of organizing. She became a regular at Socialist Party meetings and began attending classes at the Rand School. Through the Socialist Party she became friends with Rose Schneiderman, Pauline Newman, and other young women organizers. Both individually and in tandem, this group of radical young women organized strikes across the Lower East Side.

In 1909, after being fired from two more shops for leading strikes, Lemlich began working at the Leiserson shop. Brazenly, she marched uninvited into a strike meeting that had been called by the shop's older male elite—the skilled cutters and drapers. Warning them that they would lose if they attempted to strike without organizing the shop's unskilled women, Lemlich demanded their help in organizing women workers. They bridled at her nerve, but ultimately they helped her unionize the women.[48]

Lemlich's reputation as a leader grew rapidly during the fall of 1909 as stories of her bravery spread. During the Leiserson strike, which began that September, she was arrested seventeen times and had six ribs broken by club-wielding police and company guards. Without complaint, she tended to her bruises and returned to the line. By November 1909, when she stepped onto the stage in Cooper Union's Great Hall of the People to deliver the speech that would spark the largest women's strike the nation had yet seen, Lemlich was not the anonymous "wisp of a girl" that news accounts described. She was a battle-scarred veteran of the labor movement, well known among her fellow workers.[49]

Still, it is worth remembering that in this period, the four women activists were just barely adults. Newman, Schneiderman, and Lemlich still lived with their parents. During the Leiserson strike, Lemlich was so fearful that her parents would try to keep her home if they knew about her injuries that she hid her escapades and bruises from them. Later she explained the events to her grandson: "Like rain the blows fell on me. The gangsters hit me.... The boys and girls invented themselves how to give back what they got from the scabs, with stones and whatnot, with sticks.... Sometimes when I came home I wouldn't tell because if I would tell they wouldn't want me to go anymore. Yes, my boy, it's not easy. Unions aren't built easy."[50]

On November 23, 1909, New York City awoke to a general strike of shirtwaist makers, the largest strike by women workers the United States had ever seen. Overnight, between 20,000 and 40,000 workers—most of them teenage girls—silenced their sewing machines to protest the low wages, long hours, and dangerous working conditions. Though the magnitude of the strike amazed nearly everyone, including Schneiderman, Newman, Cohn, and Lemlich, the four knew that this was no spontaneous uprising: they had been organizing feverishly for almost three years and had noted a transformation in the working women they talked to, a growing sense of collective identity matched by an increasing militancy. They had laid the groundwork through a series of smaller strikes and had trained fellow workers to expect and respond to the violent and divisive tactics used by bosses to break the strike.

Despite their effectiveness, the strike was threatened by the escalation of police violence against the young women picketers. Two weeks after the strike call, Schneiderman and Dreier led ten thousand young waistmakers on a march to city hall to demand that Mayor George McClellan rein in the police. He promised an investigation but did little. One month into the strike, there had been 771 arrests, many made with undue force.[51]

WTUL leaders decided to try a different tack. They called a mass meeting of all the young women who had been attacked by police. The press and wealthy supporters were invited. One after another, adolescent girls rose to the stage to tell their stories. Mollie Weingast told a cheering crowd that when an officer tried to arrest her, she informed him that she had a constitutional right to picket. Minnie Margolis demanded that a policeman protect her from physical attack by her boss. When he refused, she took down his badge and precinct numbers. It was, she told the audience, an officer's job to protect her right to protest peacefully. Celie Newman, sixteen, said that police had manhandled her and dragged her into court, where her boss told a judge that she was an anarchist and should be deported. At another meeting earlier that week, seventeen-year-old Etta Ruth said that police had taunted her with lewd suggestions.[52]

Implying that picketers were little better than streetwalkers, employers often resorted to sexual innuendos to discredit the strikers. The workers clearly resented the manner in which middle-class standards of acceptable feminine behavior were used to manipulate them even though they enjoyed none of the advantages of middle-class birth. Then as now, society offered a limited range of cultural images of working-class women. They were either "good" girls who listened docilely to fathers, employers, and policemen, or "bad" women whose aggressive behavior made them akin to prostitutes. By walking on picket lines and going public with their demands, they'd forfeited their claims to femininity and respectability—and thus to protection.[53]

Such women were shown little deference by police and company thugs, who attacked them with iron bars, sticks, and billy clubs. And they received little sympathy in court when they attempted to press charges. One young woman appeared in court with a broken nose, a bruised face, and a head swathed in bandages. Yet the judge dropped her assault charge against police. "You are on strike against God and nature," one magistrate told a worker. Only the League's decision to invite college students and wealthy women onto the picket lines ended the violence. Alva Belmont and Anne Morgan led a contingent of New York's wealthiest women in what newspapers dubbed "mink brigades," which patrolled the dirty sidewalks of the Lower East Side. Fearful of clubbing someone on the Social Register, police grew more restrained.[54]

The socialites' presence generated both money and press for the strikers. The move proved politically wise for the suffrage cause as well, because the constant proselytizing of suffrage zealot Alva Belmont, who often bailed strikers out of jail, got young workers talking about the vote. But rubbing elbows with the mink brigade did not blind workers to the class-determined limits of sisterhood. How far they were from the protected status of more affluent women was made abundantly clear by the violence they encountered at the hands of police and company guards and by the fact that the mink brigades were able to end police brutality simply by joining the picket lines.

Encounters in court and with feminist allies speeded the growth of group consciousness. Telling their stories in court, to reporters, and to sympathetic audiences of college and society women, the strikers grew more confident of their speaking abilities and of their capacity to interpret their world. They became more aware of the distribution of power in the United States. And finally, the violence directed against them intensified their bonds with one another.

For Schneiderman, Newman, and Lemlich, the 1909 shirtwaist uprising sped their maturation as organizers and political leaders. The strike breathed new life into a struggling immigrant labor movement and transformed the tiny ILGWU into a union of national significance. Still, it ended with mixed success for workers. Many won pay increases and union recognition; others did not. And the contracts hammered out by ILGWU negotiators left a devastating legacy, for without consulting the strikers, male union negotiators decided that safety conditions were less important than other issues. Their concessions would come back to haunt the entire labor movement two years later, when the Triangle Shirtwaist Factory burned.[55]

Flames from the volcanic 1909 uprising licked industrial cities from New York to Michigan. Within a matter of weeks, 15,000 women waistmakers in Philadelphia walked off their jobs. The spirit of militancy soon touched the Midwest. In 1910, Chicago women led a strike of 41,000 men's clothing makers. The following year, women workers and the wives of male workers played key roles in a bitter cloakmakers' strike in Cleveland. Meanwhile, in Muscatine, Iowa, young women button makers waged and won a long battle for union recognition. In 1912, corset makers in Kalamazoo, Michigan, launched a campaign for better working conditions that polarized their city and won national press attention. In 1913, a strike of underwear and kimono makers swept up 35,000 young Brooklyn girls and women. Finally, in 1915, Chicago dressmakers capped this period of women's labor militancy by winning recognition of their local union after years of struggle. They elected their organizer, Fannia Cohn, as the first woman vice president of a major American labor union.[56]

Cohn, Rose Schneiderman, Pauline Newman, and Clara Lemlich were at the center of a storm that by 1919 had brought half of all women garment workers into trade unions. Individually and in tandem, the four women participated in all of the major women's strikes between 1909 and 1915, arguably the most intense period of women's labor militancy in U.S. history. This wave of "uprisings" seemed to herald the birth of a working women's movement on a scale never before seen. And it catapulted the four young women into positions of leadership, forcing them, in conjunction with colleagues, to articulate a clearly defined set of goals for the new movement.[57] In the passion and excitement of the years that followed, Schneiderman, Newman, Lemlich, and Cohn would begin to mature as political leaders and to forge a vision of political change that originated in their years on the shop floor. Pauline Newman would later describe this new brand of activism as politics of the 1909 vintage, fermented during a brief era of young women's mass protest. That description expresses the importance of the 1909 strike as both symbol and catalyst for a new working women's politics.

"Industrial feminism," the phrase coined in 1915 by scholar Mildred Moore to describe working women's militancy over the previous six years, evokes the same spirit but focuses more broadly. It simultaneously captures the interaction between women workers and feminist activists and recognizes the profound influence that the shop floor had on shaping working women's political consciousness. Industrial feminism accurately depicts the contours of an emerging political movement that by decade's end would propel the problems and concerns of industrial working women to the center of U.S. political discourse and make them players in the Socialist Party, the suffrage movement, and the politics of progressive reform.[58]

Industrial feminism was not a carefully delineated code of political thought. It was a vision of change forged in an atmosphere of crisis and awakening, as women workers in one city after another "laid down their scissors, shook the threads off their clothes and calmly left the place that stood between them and starvation." These were the words of former cloakmaker, journalist, and Socialist Party activist Theresa Malkiel, a partisan chronicler of women's labor militancy. Once an organizer, later a mentor for Newman, Lemlich, and Schneiderman, Malkiel told readers of the *New York Call* that they should not be surprised by the seemingly sudden explosion of young women workers' discontent. As hard as they might find it to take seriously the notion of a "girl's strike," she warned them, this was no outburst of female hysteria. "It was not . . . a woman's fancy that drove them to it," she wrote, "but an eruption of a long smoldering volcano, an overflow of suffering, abuse and exhaustion."[59]

Common sense, Pauline Newman would later say, dictated the most immediate goals of industrial feminists in the era of women's strikes. Given the dire realities of garment workers' lives, the first order of business had to be to improve their wages, hours, and working conditions. Toward that end the "girl strikers" of 1909–15 followed the most basic tenets of unionism. They organized, struck, and negotiated through their labor unions. But the "long-smoldering volcano" that Malkiel cautioned her readers to heed had been stirred to life by more than dissatisfaction over low wages and poor conditions.

The nascent political philosophy that began to take shape after the 1909 strike was more complex than the bread-and-butter unionism of AFL president Samuel Gompers. Why, young working women reasoned, should unions only negotiate hours and wages? They wanted to build unions that would also offer workers educational and cultural activities, health care, and maybe even a chance to leave the city and enjoy the open countryside.

Such ambitious goals derived largely from the personal experiences of industrial feminist leaders like Cohn, Schneiderman, Lemlich, and Newman. Political activism had enriched the four young women's lives, exposing them to more interesting people than they would have met had they stayed on the shop floor: writers, artists, professors, people with ideas. Through politics they had found their voices and a forum in which to raise them. The personal excitement and satisfaction they found in activism in turn shaped the evolution of their political vision: they wanted to create institutions that would provide some of the same satisfactions to any working woman who joined.

But alone, working women had none of the political or economic clout needed to open up such doors of opportunity. To build a successful movement, the four knew that they would have to win the support of more powerful allies. So they learned to build coalitions. From the time they left the shop floor until the end of their careers, they operated within a tense nexus of union men, progressive middle- and upper-class women, and the working women they sought to organize. These alliances shifted continuously, requiring the four women to perform a draining and politically hazardous balancing act. But each core group contributed an important dimension to the political education of the four organizers.

With their male counterparts and older women in the labor movement, they shared a class solidarity that would always remain at the heart of their politics. Traveling around the country, they met coal miners, loggers, and railroad workers who shared both their experiences of exploitation as laborers and their exhilaration in the economic and political strength that trade unions gave them.

From the middle- and upper-class women who joined them on the picket lines and lent them both financial and strategic support, they learned that trade union activism was not the only way to fight for improved work conditions. These allies would expose Newman, Cohn, Schneiderman, and Lemlich to a world of power and political influence, encouraging them to believe that through suffrage and lobbying, government could be put to work for their benefit.

Finally, as they began to think in terms of forging a national movement, they were forced to develop new techniques to reach women workers of different races, religions, and ethnicities. They learned from the women they sought to organize that just as women workers were best reached by women organizers, so Italian, Polish, and Hispanic immigrants and native-born black and white Protestant women were better reached by one of their own than by Jewish women steeped in the political culture of Eastern Europe and the Lower East Side. Though each of the four women had some success in bridging racial and ethnic divisions, they were forced to acknowledge their limitations. They could not do it all themselves; they had to nurture women shop-floor leaders from different backgrounds.

The work required to remain politically effective in this nexus of often-conflicting relationships yielded some real rewards, both strategically and personally. But sometimes the constant struggling wore on them. Conflicts and tensions were brought into sharp relief as the four exhausted themselves making speeches and giving pep talks to weary workers, when they themselves needed reassurance: although they had achieved recognition by the end of the 1909 strike, Schneiderman, Cohn, Newman, and Lemlich were still poor, uneducated, and young. Newman was only eighteen years old when the strike began, and Lemlich twenty-three. Even the elders in the circle, Cohn and Schneiderman, were only twenty-five and twenty-eight, respectively.

Letters between Newman and Schneiderman from that era reveal their vulnerability to slights and criticisms by male union leaders and female reformers. Life on "the battlefield," as Newman referred to it, was lonely. At an age when other women were contemplating marriage and family, they spent their nights in smoky union halls or the cheap, dingy hotel rooms that unions rented for their organizers. They sometimes questioned their life choices, for the reality of union work was far less glamorous than it had seemed in their shop-floor days. Indeed, Newman would quit several times before decade's end. Ultimately, though, their disillusionment did not drive the four women from the union movement. Instead, it fueled their desire to broaden the vision of U.S. trade unionism. When Schneiderman said "The working woman needs bread, but she needs roses, too," she was speaking from personal experience.[60]

Notes

1. Pauline Newman, "Letters to Hugh and Michael" (1951–69), Box 1, Folder 3, Pauline M. Newman Papers, Schlesinger Library, Radcliffe College, Cambridge, Mass. (hereafter cited as Newman Papers).

2. Ibid.

3. Ibid.; *New York Times*, November 2, 25, December 3, 26, 1907.

4. Newman, "Letters to Hugh and Michael."

5. "The Testimony of Miss Pauline M. Newman," in *Hearings of the New York State Factory Investigating Commission* (Albany: J. B. Lyons Printers, 1915), 2868–71.

6. My estimate of Newman's age is based on evidence suggesting that she was around eighteen years old at the time of the 1909 shirtwaist strike. Newman, like many Jews of her generation, never knew for sure how old she was. Her birthdate was recorded only on the flyleaf of the family Bible. After the Bible was lost in transit, she could only guess at her age.

7. For analyses of the position of Jews in Russian society at the turn of the century, see S. Ettinger, "The Jews at the Outbreak of the Revolution," in *The Jews in Soviet Russia since 1917*, ed. Lionel Kochan, 3d ed. (Oxford: Oxford University Press, 1978), 15–30; see also Salo Baron, *The Russian Jew under Tsars and Soviets* (New York: Macmillan, 1976).

8. Sidney Jonas, interview by author, Brooklyn, N.Y., August 10, 1980; Paula Scheier, "Clara Lemlich Shavelson: Fifty Years in Labor's Front Line," *Jewish Life,* November 1954; Ricki Carole Myers Cohen, "Fannia Cohn and the International Ladies' Garment Workers' Union" (Ph.D. diss., University of Southern California, 1976), 5.

9. Newman, "Letters to Hugh and Michael"; Cohen, "Fannia Cohn," chap. 1; Scheier, "Clara Lemlich Shavelson"; Fannia M. Cohn to "Dear Emma," May 15, 1953, Fannia M. Cohn Papers, Astor, Lenox, and Tilden Foundations, Rare Books and Manuscripts Division, New York Public Library (hereafter cited as Cohn Papers).

In March 1903, gangs organized by Russian police rampaged through the Ukrainian town of Kishinev, killing 51 Jewish men, women, and children, and wounding at least 495 others. Edward H. Judge, *Eastern Kishinev: Anatomy of a Pogrom* (New York: New York University Press, 1992).

10. See Charlotte Baum, Paula Hyman, and Sonya Michel, *The Jewish Woman in America* (New York: NAL/Dutton, 1977), 55–91; Mark Zborowski and Elizabeth Herzog, *Life Is with People* (New York: Schocken, 1962); Jack Kugelmass and Jonathan Bayarin, *From a Ruined Garden: The Memorial Books of Polish Jewry* (New York: Schocken Books, 1985).

11. The Lower East Side continued to receive Jewish immigrants from Eastern Europe into the 1920s. See Ettinger, "Jews at the Outbreak of the Revolution," 19–22; Celia Heller, *On the Edge of Destruction* (New York: Schocken, 1980), 45–55; and Irving Howe, *World of Our Fathers* (New York: Harcourt Brace & Jovanovich, 1976), xix.

12. Clara Lemlich Shavelson to Morris Schappes, March 15, 1965, published in *Jewish Currents* 36, no. 10 (November 1982): 9–11.

13. Clara Lemlich, "Remembering the Waistmakers' General Strike, 1909," *Jewish Currents,* November 1982; Newman, "Letters to Hugh and Michael."

14. Much has been written about the importance of women's colleges to the various social reform movements of the Progressive Era. Stephen Norwood makes a similar argument for high schools. Norwood, *Labor's Flaming Youth: Telephone Workers and Labor Militancy, 1878–1923* (Urbana: University of Illinois Press, 1990).

15. Newman, "Letters to Hugh and Michael"; Pauline Newman, interview by Barbara Wertheimer, New York, N.Y., November 1976; Pauline Newman résumé, n.d., Newman Papers.

16. Pauline Newman, interview by author, New York, N.Y., February 9, 1984; Newman, interview by Wertheimer.

17. Joan Morrison and Charlotte Fox Zabusky, eds., *American Mosaic* (New York: E. P. Dutton, 1980).

18. See Rose Schneiderman, *All for One* (New York: Paul S. Eriksson, 1967), 35–42, and Susan Porter Benson, "The Customers Ain't God: The Work Culture of Department Store Saleswomen, 1890–1940," in *Working Class America,* ed. Michael Frisch and Daniel J. Walkowitz (Urbana: University of Illinois Press, 1983), 185–212.

19. Scheier, "Clara Lemlich Shavelson." See also Susan Glenn, *Daughters of the Shtetl: Work, Unionism and the Immigrant Generation* (Ithaca: Cornell University Press, 1990), 122–31.

20. Schneiderman, *All for One,* 48.

21. Ibid., 48–50.

22. Ibid.

23. Ibid.

24. FMC to Selig Perlman, December 26, 1951, Box 5, Cohn Papers.

25. Information on the problems of organizing the white goods trade is located in Minutes of the Executive Board of the NYWTUL, February 28, August 22, and November 26, 27, 1907, Reel 1, Papers of the New York Women's Trade Union League, Tamiment Institute Library, New York University (hereafter cited as NYWTUL Papers); information on Cohn comes from Cohen, "Fannia Cohn," 11–21.

26. Schneiderman, *All for One,* 39–40.

27. Scheier, "Clara Lemlich Shavelson."

28. Pauline Newman, "The White Goods Workers' Strike," *Ladies' Garment Worker* 4, no. 3 (March 1913):1–4.

29. Scheier, "Clara Lemlich Shavelson"; Pauline Newman, Fragments 1958–61, Box 1, Newman Papers.

30. Newman, interview by Wertheimer; Newman, interview in Morrison and Zabusky, *American Mosaic.*

31. Scheier, "Clara Lemlich Shavelson."

32. Louis Levine [Lewis Lorwin], *The Women's Garment Workers: A History of the International Ladies' Garment Workers' Union* (New York: B. W. Huebsch, 1924), 148–49.

33. This information is pieced together from Scheier, "Clara Lemlich Shavelson"; Dora Smorodin, interview by author, Maplewood, N.J., March 12, 1991; and Levine, *Women's Garment Workers,* 148–49.

34. Newman, interview by Wertheimer; Newman, "Letters to Hugh and Michael."

35. Ibid.

36. Schneiderman, *All for One,* 58–60.

37. Ibid., 73–77; Minutes of the NYWTUL Executive Board, February 24, March 24, 1905. Reel 1, NYWTUL Papers.

38. Nancy Schrom Dye, *As Equals and as Sisters: Feminism, Unionism and the Women's Trade Union League of New York* (Columbia: University of Missouri Press, 1980), 110–22.

39. Ibid.; Minutes of the NYWTUL Executive Board, January 25, 1906, Reel 1, NYWTUL Papers.

40. Newman, interview by Wertheimer; Newman, interview by author, February 9, 1984, New York.

41. See also Alice Kessler-Harris, "Rose Schneiderman," in *American Labor Leaders,* ed. Warren Van Tine and Melvyn Dubofsky (Urbana: University of Illinois Press, 1987), 160–84.

42. Minutes of the NYWTUL Executive Board, February 24, 1905-February 1, 1909, Reel 1, NYWTUL Papers.

43. Schneiderman, *All for One,* 84.

44. Minutes of the NYWTUL Executive Board, February 28, August 22, November 26, 27, 1907, Reel 1, NYWTUL, Papers; Levine, *Women's Garment Workers,* 220.

45. Minutes of the NYWTUL Executive Committee, November 26, 27, 1907, Reel 1, NYWTUL Papers.

46. Levine, *Women's Garment Workers,* 220; Cohen, "Fannia Cohn," 36–43.

47. Scheier, "Clara Lemlich Shavelson."

48. Martha Schaffer, telephone interview by author, March 11, 1989; Joel Schaffer, Evelyn Velson, and Julia Velson, interview by author, Oakland, Calif., September 9, 1992.

49. Scheier, "Clara Lemlich Shavelson."

50. Clara Lemlich Shavelson, interview by Martha and Joel Schaffer, Los Angeles, Calif., February 2, 1974.

51. *New York Call,* November 30, December 4, 5, 6, 7, 8, 29, 1909.

52. *New York Call,* December 5, 7, 8, 1909.

53. *New York Call,* December 29, 1909. For complete coverage of day-to-day events on the picket line, see the *New York Times,* November 5, 6, and 14, 1909, and almost daily from November 23, 1909, through January 28, 1910.

54. Minutes of the New York Women's Trade Union League Membership Meeting, April 20, June 15, 1910, Reel 1, NYWTUL Papers.

55. See Meredith Tax, *The Rising of the Women: Feminist Solidarity and Class Conflict, 1880–1917* (New York: Monthly Review Press, 1980), pp. 230–240. Tax discusses the hierarchical union structure and the ways that union-appointed arbitrators undermined the women workers' control of the strike.

56. For information on the many women's strikes of the period, read the WTUL publication *Life and Labor,* which covered them all in some detail. The progressive magazine *The Survey* (1909–1914) also has good coverage of most of the strikes. See too, Pauline Newman, "The White Goods Workers' Strike," *Ladies' Garment Worker* 4, number 3 (March 1913):1–4; on the Chicago strike see Mari Jo Buhle, *Women and American Socialism, 1870–1920* (Urbana: University of Illinois Press, 1981), 194–198. On the Kalamazoo strike see Karen Mason, "Feeling the Pinch: The Kalamazoo Corset Makers' Strike of 1912," in *To Toil the Livelong Day: America's Women at Work,* ed. Carol Groneman and Mary Beth Norton (Ithaca: Cornell University Press, 1987), 141–60. On the 1915 strike see *Chicago Day Book* cited in Winifred Carsel, *A History of the Chicago Ladies' Garment Workers' Union* (Chicago: Normandie House, 1940).

57. Gladys Boone, *The Women's Trade Union Leagues* (New York: Columbia University Press, 1942), 112–14.

58. Mildred Moore, "A History of the Women's Trade Union League of Chicago" (M.A. thesis, University of Chicago, 1915), cited in Diane Kirkby, "The Wage-Earning Woman and the State: The National Women's Trade Union League and Protective Labor Legislation, 1903–1923," *Labor History* 28, no. 1 (Winter 1987):58–74.

59. Theresa Malkiel, "The Uprising of the 40,000," *New York Call,* December 29, 1909.

60. Pauline Newman, "From the Battlefield—Some Phases of the Cloakmakers' Strike in Cleveland," *Life and Labor,* October 1911.

KATHRYN KISH SKLAR

Florence Kelley and Women's Activism in the Progressive Era

Florence Kelley was a remarkable woman who lived in a period when attempts to address the problems created by industrialization and urbanization generated both the early social sciences and the foundation of the welfare state. Kathryn Sklar, Kelley's biographer, provides in this authoritative and highly informative essay an account of a single individual that also illuminates the pursuit of social justice in which many progressive women of Kelley's generation were involved. Sklar reveals the factors that made it possible for these women to influence public policy even before they were allowed to vote. She also describes the changing political context that limited their influence following the Red Scare at the end of World War I.

What were the influences, personal and intellectual, that shaped Kelley's vision of social reform? What strategies did she employ in pursuit of that vision? What does Sklar mean when she says that Kelley used gender-specific legislation

Written expressly for *Women's America.* A revised version of this essay appears in Rima Lunin Schultz and Adele Hast, eds. *Women Building Chicago, 1790–1990*: A *Biographical Dictionary,* Bloomington: Indiana University Press, 2001.

as a surrogate for class legislation? Precisely how did the Red Scare affect the political agenda of women's organizations? In what respects were at least three of the four significant features of women's power in the Progressive era that Sklar identified highly gendered? As we move into the 1930s and beyond, think about which of the features persist and which do not.

One of the most powerful women in American history deserves to be better known today. Florence Kelley (1859–1932) was well known to her contemporaries as a leading champion of social justice legislation. For most of the 1890s she lived in the nation's leading reform institution, Hull House, a social settlement founded in Chicago by Jane Addams in 1889. Between 1899 and 1932 she served as head of the National Consumers' League in New York City.

Living collectively with other women reformers in Chicago and New York, Florence Kelley was able to make the most of her talents; for four decades she occupied the vanguard of social reform. Her forceful personality flourished in the combative atmosphere generated by her struggles for social justice. Jane Addams's nephew, who resided with Kelley at Hull House, was awed by the way she "hurled the spears of her thought with such apparent carelessness of what breasts they pierced." He thought her "the toughest customer in the reform riot, the finest rough-and-tumble fighter for the good life for others, that Hull House ever knew: Any weapon was a good weapon in her hand—evidence, argument, irony or invective." Nevertheless, he said, those who were close to her knew she was "full of love."[1]

Kelley's career, like that of many of her reform contemporaries, was responding to profound changes in American social and economic life. Rapid industrialization was recasting the economy, massive immigration was reconstituting the working class, and sustained urbanization was making cities the focus of social change.[2] In this context, college-educated women reformers often achieved what men and male-dominated organizations could not.

Florence Kelley's life helps us understand how women reformers accomplished their goals. Her reform career exemplified four significant features of women's power in the Progressive era: their access to higher education; their prominence in early social science; the political autonomy of their separate institutions; and their ability to challenge American traditions of limited government. Having experienced these ingredients of women's power in her own life before 1899, thereafter, as the General Secretary of the National Consumers' League, she integrated them into her strategies for pursuing social justice.[3]

WOMEN'S ACCESS TO HIGHER EDUCATION

When she graduated from Cornell University in 1882, Florence Kelley joined thousands of other young women in her generation who received college educations. Two changes in the 1860s and 1870s enabled white, middle-class women to attend college in sufficient numbers to become a sociological phenomenon. Elite women's colleges, such as Vassar, Smith, and Wellesley, began accepting students between 1865 and 1875, providing equivalents to elite men's colleges such as Harvard, Yale, and Princeton. And state universities, established through the allocation of public lands in the Morrill Act of 1862 and required to be "open for all," gradually made college educations accessible for the first time to large numbers of women in the nation's central and western states. By 1880 women, numbering forty thousand, constituted 33 percent of all enrolled students in higher education.[4] Though a small percentage of all women, they exercised an influence disproportionate to their numbers.

To Cornell Kelley brought a social conscience shaped by her family. Born into an elite Philadelphia family with Quaker and Unitarian political traditions, she grew up against the background of the Civil War and Reconstruction—dramas in which her father and her mother's aunt played major roles. Her father, William Durrah Kelley, one of the founders of the Republican Party, was reelected to fifteen consecutive terms in the U.S. Congress between 1860 and 1890. As a Radical Republican, he advanced the cause of black suffrage and tried to forge a biracial Republican Party in the South. Her mother's aunt, Sarah Pugh, served as president of the Philadelphia Female Anti-Slavery Society almost every year between 1838 and 1870. In the 1860s and 1870s, Pugh accompanied her close friend, Lucretia Mott, to early woman suffrage conventions. To young "Florrie," Sarah Pugh was conscience incarnate, a full-time reformer who lived her beliefs, never wearing slave-made cotton or eating slave-produced sugar.[5]

During six mostly schoolless years before she entered Cornell, Florence systematically read through her father's library, imbibing the fiction of Dickens and Thackeray, Louisa May Alcott and Horatio Alger; the poetry of Shakespeare, Milton, Byron, and Goldsmith; the writings of James Madison; histories by Bancroft, Prescott, and Parkman; and the moral and political philosophy of Emerson, Channing, Burke, Carlyle, Godwin, and Spencer. These readings helped her reach out to her moody and distant father. For that purpose she also began reading government reports at the age of ten and, on trips to Washington, began using the Library of Congress by the time she was twelve.

A darker side of Kelley's childhood was shaped by her mother's permanent depression—caused by the death of five of her eight children before they had reached the age of six. Caroline Bonsall Kelley was a descendant of John Bartram, the Quaker botanist. Orphaned at the age of nine, she was raised in the Pugh family. With the death of her infants, Caroline developed a "settled, gentle melancholy" that threatened to envelop her daughter as long as she lived at home.[6] Florence grew up with two brothers, but no sisters survived. Keenly aware of the high social cost of infant mortality to nineteenth-century families, she developed a rage against human suffering that formed her lifelong career as a reformer.

WOMEN'S PROMINENCE IN EARLY SOCIAL SCIENCE

Like higher education, the newly emerging field of social science served as a critical vehicle by which middle-class women expanded the space they occupied within American civic life between 1860 and 1890. Social science leveled the playing field on which women interacted with men in public life. It offered tools of analysis that enhanced women's ability to investigate economic and social change, speak for the welfare of the whole society, devise policy initiatives, and oversee their implementation. Yet at the same time, social science also deepened women's gender identity in public life and attached their civic activism even more securely to gender-specific issues.[7]

Kelley's early commitment to social science as a tool for social reform built on a generation of women's presence in American social science. Women came with the civic territory that social science embraced. Caroline Dall had been a cofounder of the association in 1865, and other women were especially active in the American Social Science Association's (ASSA) department of education, public health, and social economy, which gave them clear but limited mandates for leadership.

The question of "After college, what?" was as pertinent to Florence Kelley as it was to other women graduates.[8] Barred from admission to graduate study at the University of Pennsylvania because she was a woman, she faced a very limited set of opportunities. First she threw her energies into the New Century Working Women's Guild, an organization that fostered middle-class aid for self-supporting women. She helped found the Guild, taught classes in history, and assembled the group's library. Then, remaining a dutiful daughter, in 1882 she accompanied her brother when his doctor prescribed a winter of European travel to cure temporary blindness. In Europe she encountered M. Carey Thomas, a Cornell acquaintance, who had just completed a Ph.D. at the University of Zurich, the only European university that granted degrees to women. Thomas recommended that Kelley go to Zurich for graduate study.

Initially accompanied by her mother and younger brother, Kelley studied government and law at Zurich between 1883 and 1886. There she promptly befriended exiled socialist students from Russia and Germany. To the shocked amazement of her family and friends, in 1885 she married Lazare Wischnewetzky, a Russian, Jewish, socialist, medical student. She then gave birth to three children in three years.

Cloaked with her new personal identity as a European married woman, she stopped communicating with her family and began to forge a new political identity. Rejecting American public culture because it limited her opportunities for social service and because her father's career revealed so starkly that culture's tolerance of social injustice, she underwent a dramatic conversion to socialism, joined the German Social Democratic Party (SPD), and began to translate the writings of Friedrich Engels and Karl Marx. Outlawed in Germany, the SPD maintained its European headquarters in Zurich, where Kelley met many of its leaders. Since the death of Marx in 1885, Engels had become the chief theoretician of German socialism. Kelley's translation of his 1845 book, *The Condition of the Working Class in England,* is still the preferred scholarly version of that now-classic social science study. This project launched a close but troubled relationship with Engels that persisted until his death in 1895.[9]

When Kelley returned to the United States in 1886 with her small family, she searched without success for a political context capable of sustaining her newfound radicalism. Settling in New York City, within a year she was expelled from the Socialist Labor Party, predominantly a German-speaking immigrant group, for "incessant slander" against party leaders, whom she denounced for failing to recognize the importance of the writings of Marx and Engels.[10] Having reached a political dead-end, Kelley reoriented her use of social science as a vehicle for her activism. She resumed contact with her Philadelphia family and became a self-taught authority on child labor in the United States, as well as a sharp critic of state bureaus of labor, the agencies responsible for monitoring child labor. Writing articles on child labor that deployed both statistical and rhetorical power, she discovered that her most responsive publisher was the Woman's Temperance Publication Association, which printed her lengthy, hard-hitting pamphlet, *Our Toiling Children,* in 1889.

Lazare Wischnewetzky, meanwhile, never having managed to establish a medical practice, began battering her. After enduring this for more than a year, she borrowed money from a friend and fled with her children to Chicago. There she headed for the Woman's Temple, a twelve-story office building and hotel constructed by the Woman's Christian Temperance Union, where she was directed to an even more congenial place—Hull House, the nation's preeminent social settlement founded by Jane Addams and Ellen Gates Starr in 1889.

THE POLITICAL AUTONOMY OF WOMEN'S SEPARATE INSTITUTIONS

"We were welcomed as though we had been invited," Kelley later wrote about her arrival at Hull House. "We stayed."[11] Addams arranged for Kelley's children, Nicholas, Margaret, and John, age seven, six, and five, to live with the family of Henry Demarest Lloyd and his wife, Jessie Bross Lloyd. That winter Kelley cast her lot with Addams and Hull House, remaining until May 1, 1899, when she returned to New York as a figure who had achieved national renown as a reformer of working conditions for women and children.

Chicago and the remarkable political culture of the city's women opened opportunities to Kelley that she had sought in vain in Philadelphia, Germany, and New York. Exploiting those opportunities to the fullest, she drew on the strength of three overlapping circles of politically active women. The core of her support lay with the community of women at Hull House. This remarkable group helped her reconstruct her political identity within women's class-bridging activism, and provided her with an economic and emotional alternative to married family life. Partly overlapping with this nucleus were women trade unionists. By drawing women and men trade unionists into the settlement community, she achieved the passage of pathbreaking legislation. Toward the end of her years in Chicago, she worked with the circle of middle-class and upper-middle-class women who supported Hull House and labor reform.

Florence Kelley's life in Chicago began with her relationship with Jane Addams. Julia Lathrop, another Hull House resident, reported that Kelley and Addams "understood each other's powers" instantly and worked together in a "wonderfully effective way."[12] Addams, the philosopher with a deep appreciation of the unity of life, was better able to construct a vehicle for expressing that unity in day-to-day living than she was capable of devising a diagram for charting the future. And Kelley, the politician with a thorough understanding of what the future should look like, was better able to invoke that future than to express it in her day-to-day existence. Addams taught Kelley how to live and have faith in an imperfect world, and Kelley taught Addams how to make demands on the future.

At Hull House Kelley joined a community of college-educated women reformers who, like Addams and herself, sought work commensurate with their talents. Julia Lathrop, almost twenty years later the first director of the U.S. Children's Bureau, had joined the settlement before Kelley. Alice Hamilton, who arrived in 1897, developed the field of industrial medicine. These four, with Mary Rozet Smith, Jane Addams's life partner, became the settlement's main leaders. In addition to these women, Kelley forged close ties with Mary Kenney, a trade union organizer affiliated with the settlement, who lived nearby with her mother.

Since her father had lost most of his money before his death in 1890, Kelley had to support herself and her children. She first did so by working for the Illinois Bureau of Labor Statistics and the U.S. Department of Labor, collecting data for governmental studies of working conditions. A good example of the empowerment of her Hull House residence lay in her use of data collected for the U.S. Department of Labor, which in 1895 formed the basis of the maps published in *Hull House Maps and Papers*. She and four government "schedule men" collected responses to sixty-four questions on printed schedules from "each house, tenement, and room" in the ward surrounding Hull House.[13] From this data Carroll Wright, head of the Department of Labor, constructed scores of tables. But Kelley and Hull House associates, using only data about nationalities and wages in conjunction with residential information, created color-coded maps that displayed geographic patterns that told more than Wright's charts. Because the maps defined spatial relationships among human groups, they vividly depicted social and economic relationships: the concentration of certain ethnic groups in certain blocks; the relationship between poverty and race; the distances between the isolated brothel district and the rest of the ward; the very poor who lived in crowded, airless rooms in the rear of tenements and those with more resources in the front; and the omniscient observer and the observed. Expressing the democratic relationship among Hull House residents, *Hull House Maps and Papers* listed only "Residents of Hull House" as the volume's editors.

Kelley described the transformative effect of the Hull House community on her personal life in a letter to her mother a few weeks after her arrival. "In the few weeks of my stay here I have won for the children and myself many and dear friends whose generous hospitality astonishes me. It is understood that I am to resume the maiden name and that the children are to have it."[14] By joining a community of women, she had achieved a new degree of personal autonomy.

CHALLENGING TRADITIONS OF LIMITED GOVERNMENT

In the spring of 1892, Kelley used Hull House as a base to exert leadership within an anti-sweatshop campaign that had been launched in 1888 by the Illinois Woman's Alliance, a class-bridging coalition of women's organizations. At mass meetings that attacked the sweatshop system, Kelley shared the podium with Mary Kenney, Henry Demarest Lloyd, and other Chicago notables such as Reverend Jenkin Lloyd Jones, minister at All Souls' Unitarian Church, the most liberal pulpit in Chicago, and with young trade union organizers in the clothing industry such as Abraham Bisno.

Campaigns against sweatshops were widespread in American cities in the 1890s. These efforts targeted "predatory management" and "parasitic manufacturers" who paid such low wages to their workers as to require them to seek support from relief or charity, thereby indirectly providing employers with subsidies that enabled them to lower wages further.[15] Supported by trade unions, these campaigns used a variety of strategies to shift work from tenement sweatshops to factories. In factories, union organizing could more easily succeed in improving working conditions and raising wages to levels necessary to sustain life.

Outcries raised by anti-sweatshop campaigns prompted government inquiries, and in 1893, after intense lobbying in Springfield by Hull House residents and other well-known Chicago women, the passage of path-breaking legislation drafted by Florence Kelley. That year Governor John Peter Altgeld appointed Kelley to a position the new statute created: Chief Factory Inspector of Illinois. Nowhere else in the Western world was a woman trusted to enforce the labor legislation of a city, let alone of a large industrial region the size of Illinois. With eleven deputies, five of whom were required to be women, and a budget of $28,000, for the next three years Kelley enforced the act's chief clauses. The act banned the labor of children under fourteen years of age; it regulated the labor of children age fourteen to sixteen; it outlawed the production of garments in tenements; it prohibited the employment of women and minors for more than eight hours a day; and it created a state office of factory inspection.

The statute's eight-hour clause made it the most advanced in the United States, equaled only by an eight-hour law for all workers in Australia. The limitation of hours, whether through statutes or union negotiations with employers, was the second most important goal of the labor movement between 1870 and 1910, the first being the recognition of the right of workers to form unions. Skilled workers had acquired the eight-hour day for themselves in many trades by the 1890s, but since women were not admitted to most skilled occupations, their hours remained long, often extending to twelve or even fourteen hours a day. In the late 1880s more than 85 percent of female wage earners were between the ages of fourteen and twenty-five and only about 5 percent were married.[16] Excluded from access to skilled jobs and presumed to leave the paid labor force upon marriage, they were crowded into a few unskilled occupations, where they were easily replaced, and employers exploited them by requiring long hours and paying low wages. Statutes that limited women's hours limited this exploitation. How to achieve such reduction of hours without reducing wages was a challenge that Kelley's office met by promoting the formation of unions among affected women workers, thereby helping them negotiate better wages for the hours they worked.

But the reduction of women's hours by statute had other beneficial effects: in many occupations it also reduced the hours of unskilled men, as was the case in garment-making sweatshops. In this and many other occupations, it proved impossible to keep men working longer than the legal limit of the working day for women. Therefore, hours statutes drove sweatshops out of business, since their profits could only be achieved through long hours. In the United States more than in other industrializing nations, the union movement consisted with few exceptions (miners being the chief exception) of skilled workers who shunned responsibility for the welfare of unskilled workers. Therefore, in the United States more than in elsewhere, gender-specific reforms like Kelley's 1893 legislation—undertaken by women for women—also had the effect of aiding all unskilled workers, men as well as women and children. In the United States, where labor movements were not as strong as they were elsewhere, gender-specific reforms accomplished goals that elsewhere were achieved under the auspices of class-specific efforts.[17]

In an era when courts nullified legislative attempts to intervene in the laissez-faire relationship between capital and labor, Kelley's enforcement of this new eight-hour law was inevitably challenged in the courts. In 1895 the Illinois Supreme Court found the eight-hour clause of the 1893 law unconstitutional because it violated women's right to contract their labor on any terms set by their employer. This setback made Kelley determined to change the power of state courts to overturn hours laws for women.

The high tide of Kelley's achievements between 1893 and 1896 ebbed quickly when Altgeld lost the election of 1896. His successor replaced her with a person who did not challenge the economic status quo, and she was unable to find work commensurate with her talents. German admirers came to her rescue. For fifty dollars a month she provided a leading German reform periodical with assessments of recent American social legislation. She also worked in the Crerar Library, a reference library specializing in economic, scientific, and medical topics.

Needing to reach beyond the limits of Hull House activities, Kelley began to work more closely with Ellen Henrotin. Wife of a leading Chicago banker, Henrotin had supported Kelley's legislation in 1892, and spoke vigorously at a rally to defend the law in 1894, urging those in attendance to "agitate for shorter hours for women because it means in the end shorter hours for all workers, men and women."[18] Henrotin's organization in 1893 of thirty women's congresses at the Chicago World's Fair catapulted her into the presidency of the General Federation of Women's Clubs (GFWC; founded 1890) from 1894 to 1898. By 1897 the GFWC served as an umbrella organization for more than five hundred women's clubs, including the powerful Chicago Women's Club. Fostering the creation of over twenty state federations to coordinate those clubs, Henrotin moved the GFWC in progressive directions by establishing national committees on industrial working conditions and national health. In this way she directed the path of what was to become one of the largest grass-roots organizations of American women beyond the minimal goals of good government and civil service reform to the more challenging issues of social inequalities and social justice.

Reflecting her growing awareness of the potential power of women's organizations as a vehicle for her social justice agenda, in 1897 Kelley began to work closely with Henrotin in organizing an Illinois Consumers' League. They built on the example of the New York Consumers' League, which had been founded in 1891 to channel consumers' consciousness toward political action on behalf of workers who made the goods that consumers purchased.

THE NATIONAL CONSUMERS' LEAGUE AND NEW STRATEGIES FOR SOCIAL JUSTICE

Kelley's work with Henrotin helped her make the biggest career step of her life when, in 1899, she agreed to serve as Secretary of the newly formed National Consumers' League, a position she held until her death in 1932. With a salary of $1,500 plus traveling and other expenses, the job offered financial stability and a chance to develop a more radical and more focused women's organization than the GFWC.

When she carried her formidable talents into the National Consumers' League in 1899, women's political culture gained a warrior with formidable rhetorical and organizational skills. She quickly made the National Consumers' League (NCL) into the nation's leading promoter of protective labor legislation for women and children. Between 1900 and 1904 she built sixty-four local consumer leagues—one in nearly every large city outside the South. Through a demanding travel schedule, which required her to spend one day on the road for every day she worked at her desk, Kelley maintained close contact with local leagues, urging them to implement the national organization's agenda and inspiring them to greater action within their states and municipalities. At the age of forty she had finally found a platform that matched her talents and goals.

In New York she lived until 1926 at Lillian Wald's nurses' settlement on Henry Street on Manhattan's Lower East Side. Her children moved east with her. Supported by aid from Jane Addams's life partner, Mary Rozet Smith, Nicholas Kelley graduated from Harvard in 1905 and then from Harvard Law School. Living in Manhattan, he became his mother's closest advisor. In a blow that caused Kelley to spend the rest of that year in retirement in Maine, her daughter Margaret died of heart failure during her first week at Smith College in 1905. After this bereavement Kelley maintained a summer home on Penobscot Bay, Maine, where she retreated for periods of intense work with a secretary each summer. John Kelley never found a professional niche, but remained close to his mother and joined her in Maine each summer.

THE WHITE LABEL CAMPAIGN: NEW WAYS OF EDUCATING MIDDLE-CLASS WOMEN ABOUT INDUSTRIAL WORKING CONDITIONS

The national branch of the Consumers' League was formed in 1898 to coordinate the efforts of previously existing leagues in New York, Brooklyn, Philadelphia, Boston, and Chicago, all of which had conducted campaigns against sweatshops. At a convention of the local leagues called to coordinate their anti-sweatshop efforts, Kelley proposed the creation of a consumers' label as a way of identifying goods made under fair conditions. Her proposal galvanized the convention into creating a national organization "for the express purpose of offering a Consumers' League Label" nationally, recognizing that local efforts against sweatshops could never succeed until all producers were "compelled to compete on a higher level," and agreeing that the label could be a means of achieving that goal.[19] The NCL awarded its label to manufacturers who obeyed state factory laws, produced goods only on their own premises, did not require employees to work overtime, and did not employ children under sixteen years of age. To enforce the label, however, factories had to be inspected. Local leagues had employed their own factory inspectors; Kelley became the league's national inspector.

In determining whether local factories qualified for the label, local league members had to educate themselves about local working conditions. They had to pose and answer questions new to middle-class women, though painfully familiar to union organizers: Did the manufacturer subcontract to home workers in tenements? Were children employed? Were state factory laws violated? Could workers live on their wages, or were they forced to augment their pay with relief or charitable donations? How far below the standard set by the consumers' label were their own state laws? Even more technical questions arose when leagues came into contact with factory inspectors, bureaus of labor statistics, state legislatures, and courts. Should the state issue licenses for home workers? What was the relationship between illiteracy in child workers and the enforcement of effective child labor laws? Was their own state high or low on the NCL's ranked list showing the number of illiterate child workers in each? Should laws prohibit the labor of children at age fourteen or sixteen? Should exceptions be made for the children of widows? How energetically were state factory laws enforced? How could local factory standards be improved? These questions, recently quite alien to middle-class women, now held the interest of thousands of the most politically active among them. This was no small accomplishment. State leagues differed in the degree to which they worked with state officials, but wherever they existed they created new civic space in which women used their new knowledge and power to expand state responsibility for the welfare of women and children workers.

On the road steadily between 1900 and 1907, Kelley inspected workshops, awarded the label to qualified manufacturers, and strengthened local leagues. Her efforts were rewarded by the spectacular growth of NCL locals, both in number and location. The NCL's 1901 report mentioned thirty leagues in eleven states; by 1906 they numbered sixty-three in twenty states.

Flourishing local leagues sustained the national's existence, channeling money, ideas, and the support of other local groups into the national office. At the same time, locals implemented the national's agenda at the state level. Most league members were white, urban, northern, middle-class Protestants, but Jewish women held important positions of leadership. Catholic women became more visible after Cardinal James Gibbons of Baltimore consented to serve as vice president of a Maryland league and Bishop J. Regis Canevin of Pittsburgh encouraged members of that city's Ladies Catholic Benevolent Association to join. Two important reasons for the absence of black women from the NCL's membership and agenda were the league's focus on Northern urban manufacturing, and the residence of 90 percent of the nation's black population in the South, employed primarily in agriculture, in 1900.

10-HOUR LAWS FOR WOMEN: NEW USES OF SOCIAL SCIENCE

The work of educating her constituency being achieved by 1907, Kelley implemented a second stage of league work. With the use of social science data, the NCL overcame legal obstacles to the passage of state laws limiting women's hours. The overturning of Illinois's 1893 law by Illinois's Supreme Court in 1895 made Kelley determined to defend such laws before the U.S. Supreme Court. When an Oregon ten-hour law came before the court in 1907, she threw the resources of the NCL into its defense. This case, *Muller* v. *Oregon,* pitted the NCL and its Oregon branch against a laundry owner who disputed the state's ability to regulate working hours in non-hazardous occupations. For what became known as the "Brandeis Brief," Kelley's Research Director, Josephine Goldmark, gathered printed evidence from medical and other authorities (most of whom were British or European) to demonstrate that workdays longer than ten hours were hazardous to the health of women. Goldmark obtained the services of her brother-in-law, Louis D. Brandeis, a leading Boston attorney, who successfully argued the case on sociological rather than legal grounds, using the evidence that Goldmark had compiled. Thus at the same time that this case cleared the way for state hours laws for women, it also established the court's recognition of sociological evidence, a strategy that sustained the court's ruling against segregated schools in *Brown* v. *Board of Education* in 1954.

In the years immediately following the *Muller* decision, inspired by Kelley's leadership, and supported by other groups, local consumer leagues gained the passage in twenty states of the first laws limiting women's

Two contrasting photographs intended by photojournalist Lewis Hine to reveal the class-based nature of childhood at the turn of the century. Middle-class girls (top) *are pushing a doll made by child laborers and their mother* (bottom). *(Photos courtesy of the Library of Congress. Caption and photoidentification by Miriam Formanek-Brunell,* Made to Play House: Dolls and the Commercialization of American Girlhood, 1830–1930 *[New Haven, Conn.: Yale University Press, 1993], p. 110.)*

working hours. Also responding to the decision, nineteen other states revised and expanded their laws governing women's working hours.

The Supreme Court's 1908 opinion tried to block the possibility of extending such protections to men by emphasizing women's special legal status (they did not possess the same contractual rights as men) and their physiological difference from men (their health affected the health of their future children). Nevertheless, in 1917 Kelley and the NCL again cooperated successfully with the Oregon league in arguing another case on sociological grounds before the U.S. Supreme Court, *Bunting* v. *Oregon*, in which the Court upheld the constitutionality of hours laws for men in non-hazardous occupations. Viewing laws for women as an entering wedge for improving conditions for all working people, Kelley achieved that goal in the progression from *Muller* to *Bunting*. In this as in other aspects of her work with the League, though nominally focused on gender, her reforms had class-wide effects.

THE MINIMUM WAGE CAMPAIGN: NEW USES OF THE POWER OF WOMEN'S ORGANIZATIONS

As early as 1899, Florence Kelley had hoped "to include a requirement as to minimal wages" in the NCL's White Label. Australia and New Zealand had already organized wage boards as part of compulsory arbitration, but the path to an American equivalent did not seem clear until she and other Consumers' League members in 1908 attended the First International Conference of Consumers' Leagues, in Geneva, where they learned about the proposed British wage law of 1909, which that year implemented minimum wages for all workers in certain poorly paid occupations.

Almost immediately on her return, Kelley established her leadership in what became an enormously successful campaign for minimum wage laws for women in the United States. In her campaign she denounced the large profits made in three industries: retail stores, sweatshop garment making, and textile manufacturers. "Low wages produce more poverty than all other causes together," she insisted, urging that "goods and profits are not ends in themselves to which human welfare may continue to be sacrificed."[20]

Kelley argued that minimum wages would raise the standards in women's employment by recognizing their need to support themselves. "So long as women's wages rest upon the assumption that every woman has a husband, father, brother, or lover contributing to her support, so long these sinister incidents of women's industrial employment (tuberculosis, insanity, vice) are inevitable." She urged that "society itself must build the floor beneath their feet."[21]

Minimum wage legislation was much more difficult to achieve than maximum hours laws because, as one of Kelley's allies put it, wage legislation "pierces to the heart the classic claim that industry is a purely private affair."[22] For this reason, Kelley and the NCL were unaided in their efforts by their male-dominated equivalent, the American Association for Labor Legislation (AALL). When Kelley appealed in 1910 to their executive director, John Andrews, he loftily replied: "I question very seriously the wisdom of injecting the minimum wage proposal into the legislative campaign of this year, because I do not believe our courts would at the present time uphold such legislation, and I am afraid it would seriously jeopardize the splendid progress now being made to establish maximum working hours."[23] Two years later the AALL still opposed wage legislation as premature.

Kelley and the NCL were able to move ahead with this pathbreaking legislation because they could mobilize grass-roots support for it at local and state levels. The AALL had no local branches; instead, their power flowed from a network of male academic experts who advised politicians about legislation. If politicians were not ready to move, neither was the AALL. The NCL, by contrast, had in its sixty-four local branches enough political muscle to take the initiative and lead politicians where they otherwise wouldn't have gone.

In 1912 Massachusetts passed the first minimum wage law for women, followed in 1913 by eight additional states: California, Colorado, Minnesota, Nebraska, Oregon, Utah, Washington, and Wisconsin. By 1919 fourteen states and the District of Columbia and Puerto Rico had enacted minimum wage statutes for women. The success of these laws influenced the inclusion of a minimum wage for men *and* women in the Fair Labor Standards Act (FLSA) of 1938. In 1942, when the U.S. Supreme Court approved the constitutionality of the FLSA, the eight-hour day and the minimum wage became part of the social contract for most American workers. The class-bridging activism of middle-class women in the NCL forged the way with these fundamental reforms.

GAINS AND SETBACKS IN THE 1920s

At Henry Street, Kelley continued to benefit from the same consolidation of female reform talents that had sustained her efforts at Hull House in Chicago. The creation of the U.S. Children's Bureau in 1911 sprang from her discussions with Lillian Wald. The Children's Bureau was the only governmental agency in any industrial society that was headed and run by women. Kelley thought that her most important contribution to social change was the passage in 1921 of the Sheppard-Towner Maternity and Infancy Protection Act, which first allocated federal funds to health care. She was instrumental in the creation of the coalition that backed the act's passage, the Women's Joint Congressional Committee, and in the coalition's successful campaign for the bill in Congress. Although limited to a program administered by the Children's Bureau to combat infant and maternal mortality, Kelley thought the Sheppard-Towner Act marked the beginning of a national health care program.[24]

After this high point in 1921, however, the decade brought a series of reversals that threatened to undo most of her achievements. In 1923 the U.S. Supreme Court in *Adkins* v. *Children's Hospital* found Washington, D.C.'s wage law for women unconstitutional. Many state wage boards continued to function during the 1920s and 1930s, however, providing ample evidence of the benefits of the law, but no new wage laws were passed. In 1926, Congress refused to allocate new funds for Sheppard-Towner programs, and responsibility for maternal and infant health returned to state and county levels.[25]

Just as important, by 1922 Kelley's strategy of using gender-specific legislation as a surrogate for class legislation had generated opposition from a new quarter—women who did not themselves benefit from gendered laws. The National Woman's Party (NWP), formed in 1916 by the charismatic leadership of Alice Paul and funded almost entirely by Alva Belmont, created a small coalition consisting primarily of professional women with some wage-earning women who worked in male-dominated occupations. Despite Kelley's strong objections over the damage they would do to gender-specific legislation, including the Sheppard-Towner Act, in 1921 the NWP proposed an Equal Rights Amendment to the U.S. Constitution (ERA). Although mainstream organizations such as the General Federation of Women's Clubs and the League of Women Voters continued to support gender-specific legislation, the NWP's proposed amendment undercut the momentum of such gendered strategies. In the 1920s most wage-earning women opposed the ERA because they stood to lose rather than benefit from it. By the 1970s changes in working conditions and protective labor laws meant that most wage-earning women stood to benefit from the amendment, and many more supported it.[26]

Even more damaging than these reversals, however, were the right-wing attacks launched by hyperpatriots against Kelley and other women reformers during the "red scare" of the 1920s. *The Woman Patriot* exemplified these attacks. Launched in 1916 and published twice a month, before the enactment of the woman suffrage amendment this newsletter was subtitled *Dedicated to the Defense of Womanhood, Motherhood, the Family and the State AGAINST Suffragism, Feminism and Socialism.* After 1920 the newsletter dropped its reference to suffrage, but continued its virulent attacks on the social agenda of women reformers. "SHALL BOLSHEVIST-FEMINISTS SECRETLY GOVERN AMERICA?" their headlines screamed, referring to the Sheppard-Towner Act. When *The Woman Patriot* referred to Kelley as "Mrs. Wischnewtzky" and called her "Moscow's chief conspirator," Kelley urged Addams to join her in a libel suit against them. Addams gently persuaded her to ignore the attacks. Kelley then wrote an impassioned series of autobiographical articles that established her lineage as an inheritor of American ideals and a dedicated promoter of American values.[27]

Attacks on women reformers in the 1920s were in part generated by supporters of American military expansion in the aftermath of World War I, when Kelley and many other women reformers were actively promoting peace and disarmament. For example, *The Woman Patriot* characterized the support that women reformers were giving to disarmament as "an organized internationalist Bolshevist-Feminist plot to embarrass the Limitation of

Armaments Conference." Government employees joined the attack in 1924, when Lucia Maxwell of the Chemical Warfare Department of the Department of War issued a "Spider Web Chart" entitled "The Socialist-Pacifist Movement in America Is an Absolutely Fundamental and Integral Part of International Socialism." Depicting the connections between women's organizations and Congressional lobbying for social legislation and for disarmament, the chart sought to characterize as "pacifist-socialist" most women's organizations in the United States, including the National Consumers' League, the National League of Women Voters, the General Federation of Women's Clubs, the Woman's Christian Temperance Union, the National Congress of Mothers and Parent-Teachers Association, the National Women's Trade Union League, the American Home Economics Association, the American Association of University Women, the National Council of Jewish Women, the Girls' Friendly Society, the Young Women's Christian Association, and the National Federation of Business and Professional Women.[28]

Historians have not measured the effect of these attacks on the political agendas of women's organizations, but after these attacks the agendas of many women's organizations, for example that of the League for Women Voters, shifted from social justice to good government projects, from support for a Child Labor Amendment to the U.S. Constitution to advocacy for a city manager form of governance.[29] Such a shift was in keeping with the demise of the Progressive movement after World War I. But that demise was hastened by the rise of "red scare" tactics in American political culture.

Florence Kelley did not live to see many of her initiatives incorporated into federal legislation in the 1930s. Faced with the collapse of the American economy in the Great Depression of 1929–1939, policymakers drew heavily on the legacy of Progressive reforms initiated between 1890 and 1920. Florence Kelley's legacies, including the minimum wage and maximum hours legislation incorporated in the Fair Labor Standards Act of 1938, were strong enough to survive the reversals of the 1920s. In 1933, with the inauguration of Franklin Delano Roosevelt, Kelley's protégée Frances Perkins became the first woman to serve as a cabinet member. Reflecting the power of women's organizations in shaping a new social contract for American working people, Perkins was appointed Secretary of Labor.[30]

But Kelley's legacy reaches beyond any specific policies. U.S. Supreme Court Justice Felix Frankfurter said in 1953 that the nation owed Kelley an "enduring debt for the continuing process she so largely helped to initiate, by which social legislation is promoted and eventually gets on the statute books."[31] As Kelley shaped it during her long reform career between 1890 and 1930, that process relied heavily on women's organizations and their ability to act independently of the political status quo.

Notes

1. James Weber Linn, *Jane Addams: A Biography* (New York, 1938), 138.
2. For an overview of social change in the Progressive era, see Steven J. Diner, *A Very Different Age: Americans of the Progressive Era* (New York, 1998).
3. For more on Kelley before 1900, see Kathryn Kish Sklar, *Florence Kelley and the Nation's Work: The Rise of Women's Political Culture, 1830–1900* (New Haven, 1995). Specific page references are provided for quotations used below.
4. Mabel Newcomer, *A Century of Higher Education for American Women* (New York, 1959), 37, 46. See also Barbara Miller Solomon, *"In the Company of Educated Women": A History of Women and Higher Education in America* (New Haven, 1985), 62–77.
5. For Kelley's childhood, see Kathryn Kish Sklar, ed., *The Autobiography of Florence Kelley: Notes of Sixty Years* (Chicago, 1986).
6. Sklar, *Autobiography of Florence Kelley,* 30.
7. Kathryn Kish Sklar, "Hull House Maps and Papers: Social Science as Women's Work in the 1890s," in Helene Silverberg, ed., *Gender and American Social Science: The Formative Years* (Princeton, 1998).
8. See Joyce Antler, "After College, What?: New Graduates and the Family Claim," *American Quarterly* 32 (Fall 1980):409–34.
9. See Dorothy Rose Blumberg, "'Dear Mr. Engels': Unpublished Letters, 1884–1894, of Florence Kelley (Wischnewetzky) to Friedrich Engels," *Labor History* 5 (Spring 1964), 103–33.
10. Sklar, *Florence Kelley,* 129.
11. Sklar, *Autobiography of Florence Kelley,* 77.
12. Jane Addams, *My Friend Julia Lathrop* (New York, 1935), 77.
13. Residents of Hull House, *Hull House Maps and Papers* (New York, 1895).
14. FK to Caroline B. Kelley, Chicago, Feb. 24, 1892, Nicholas Kelley Papers, New York Public Library.
15. Kathryn Kish Sklar, "Two Political Cultures in the Progressive Era: The National Consumers' League and the American Association for Labor Legislation," in Linda K. Kerber, Alice Kessler-Harris and Kathryn Kish Sklar, eds., *U.S. History as Women's History: New Feminist Essays* (Chapel Hill, N.C., 1995), 58.

16. U.S. Commissioner of Labor, *Fourth Annual Report, Working Women in Large Cities* (Washington, D.C., 1889), 62–64.

17. For a full argument of this point, see Kathryn Kish Sklar, "The Historical Foundations of Women's Power in the Creation of the American Welfare State, 1830–1930," in Seth Koven and Sonya Michel, eds., *Mothers of a New World: Maternalist Politics and the Origins of Welfare States* (New York, 1993).

18. "Hit at Sweat Shops," *Chicago Tribune*, April 23, 1894; Sklar, *Florence Kelley*, 261.

19. Sklar, *Florence Kelley*, 309.

20. Florence Kelley, "Minimum Wage Boards," *American Journal of Sociology* 17 (Nov. 1911), 303–14.

21. Florence Kelley, "Ten Years from Now," *Survey*, March 26, 1910, 978–81.

22. Sklar, "Two Political Cultures," 60.

23. See, for example, John B. Andrews to Erich Stern, New York, Dec. 14, 1910, American Association for Labor Legislation Papers, Cornell University.

24. See Molly Ladd-Taylor, *Mother-Work: Women, Child Welfare, and the State, 1890–1930* (Urbana, Ill., 1994), 167–96.

25. See J. Stanley Lemons, *The Woman Citizen: Social Feminism in the 1920s* (Urbana, Ill., 1973), 169–76.

26. For the opposition of the progressive mainstream of the women's movement, see Kathryn Kish Sklar, "Why Did Most Politically Active Women Oppose the ERA in the 1920s?" in Joan Hoff-Wilson, ed., *Rights of Passage: the Past and Future of the ERA* (Bloomington, Ind., 1986).

27. *The Woman Patriot*, Vol. 5, no. 29, Nov. 1, 1921, 1. For the complete documents of this correspondence between Kelley and Addams, see Anissa Harper, "Pacifism vs. Patriotism in Women's Organizations in the 1920s: How Was the Debate Shaped by the Expansion of the American Military," in *Women and Social Movements in the United States, 1830–1930*, an Internet website edited by Kathryn Kish Sklar and Thomas Dublin, http://womhist.binghamton.edu. See also Nancy F. Cott, *The Grounding of Modern Feminism* (New Haven, 1987), 243–67.

28. The Spider Web Chart is reproduced in Helen Baker, "How Did the Women's International League for Peace and Freedom Respond to Right Wing Attacks in the 1920s?" in *Women and Social Movements* at http://womhist.binghamton.edu.

29. For example, see the furor aroused within the League of Women Voters over the proposed Child Labor Amendment to the U.S. Constitution in 1924, in Louise M. Young, *In the Public Interest: The League of Women Voters, 1920–1970* (New York, 1989), 97–98.

30. For Perkins see Susan Ware, *Beyond Suffrage: Women in the New Deal* (Cambridge, Mass., 1981), *passim*.

31. Felix Frankfurter, "Foreword," in Josephine Goldmark, *Impatient Crusader: Florence Kelley's Life Story* (Urbana, Ill., 1953), v.

DOCUMENTS

Protecting Women Wage-Workers

Muller *v.* Oregon, *1908*

The farmer's workday was sunrise to sunset. When the first factories were established in the early nineteenth century, they were operated for equally long hours. It was a particular interest of laborers and of Progressive reformers to support enactment of limits on the workday. The ten-hour day was on the agenda of early labor unions, and the federal civil service adopted it shortly after the Civil War. Unable to establish ten-hour days for all workers, twenty states—beginning with Massachusetts in 1874—limited the hours of women's work. Generally, the limit was ten hours per day, sixty-hours per week, with some variations. (In Louisiana the hour limit applied only in factories; in South Carolina only in cotton and woolen mills; and in New Hampshire a day's work could be longer "to make up time lost . . . in consequence of the stopping of the machinery on which the person was dependent for employment.")

In 1905 the United States Supreme Court refused to uphold a state law limiting the hours of bakers to ten hours a day. Ruling in *Lochner* v. *New York* (198 U.S. 45 [1905]), the Court held that such a law was not "a legitimate exercise of the police power of the State, but an unreasonable, unnecessary, and arbitrary interference with the right and liberty of the individual to contract in relation to his labor."

After the *Lochner* decision, Progressives were forced to conclude that it was impractical to support limitations on hours that applied to *all* workers. But it occurred to some that a special case might be made in defense of a limit on working hours for women.

When the constitutionality of the Oregon ten-hour law for women was challenged, Florence Kelley committed the National Consumers League (NCL) to its defense. As Kathryn Kish Sklar has explained (pp. 402–414), NCL's research director, Josephine Goldmark, prepared a pathbreaking brief, of which only 2 pages consisted of traditional abstract legal reasoning, and over 100 pages offered sociological evidence. Her brother-in-law, the future Supreme Court Justice Louis D. Brandeis, argued the case in the U.S. Supreme Court. Goldmark and Brandeis's innovation would come to be known as a "Brandeis brief," and many others would later be modeled on it. (See pp. 431–432.)

In its 1908 *Muller* ruling, a unanimous Supreme Court upheld the constitutionality of the Oregon law, swayed primarily by the case made for women's physical vulnerability. Note that the decision was couched in terms of traditional sex roles. Fifteen years later, only five states lacked maximum hour legislation of some sort, although provisions varied widely.

Protective legislation for women had complex consequences. Obviously an eight-hour workday was vastly preferable to a longer one. But in the absence of a minimum wage, women living at the margin of subsistence found that limitations on the hours they could work cut their income or speeded up their piecework;

some would not have chosen to trade time for money. Maximum hour legislation was often supplemented by restrictions against night work and "heavy" work (the latter often conveniently defined to include well-paying skilled work like iron molding), which further segregated women in the workplace and gave men an advantage in the competition for jobs. There is substantial evidence that male unions understood this when they supported protective legislation.*

Compare the reasoning in *Muller* to that offered in the *Bradwell* case (pp. 312–314) more than thirty-five years before. What were the advantages of pressing the argument of female weakness? What were the disadvantages?

MR. JUSTICE DAVID J. BREWER, WRITING FOR A UNANIMOUS COURT:

. . . It may not be amiss, in the present case, before examining the constitutional question, to notice the course of legislation, as well as expressions of opinion from other than judicial sources. In the brief filed by Mr. Louis D. Brandeis for the defendant . . . is a very copious collection of all these matters. . . .

The legislation and opinions referred to . . . may not be, technically speaking, authorities, and in them is little or no discussion of the constitutional question presented to us for determination, yet, they are significant of a widespread belief that woman's physical structure, and the functions she performs in consequence thereof, justify special legislation restricting or qualifying the conditions under which she should be permitted to toil. . . .

That woman's physical structure and the performance of maternal functions place her at a disadvantage in the struggle for subsistence is obvious. This is especially true when the burdens of motherhood are upon her. Even when they are not, by abundant testimony of the medical fraternity continuance for a long time on her feet at work, repeating this from day to day, tends to injurious effects upon the body, and, as healthy mothers are essential to vigorous offspring, the physical well-being of woman becomes an object of public interest and care in order to preserve the strength and vigor of the race.

. . . Differentiated by these matters from the other sex, she is properly placed in a class by herself, and legislation designed for her protection may be sustained, even when like legislation is not necessary for men, and could not be sustained. It is impossible to close one's eyes to the fact that she still looks to her brother and depends upon him. . . . her physical structure and a proper discharge of her maternal functions—having in view not merely her own health, but the well-being of the race—justify legislation to protect her from the greed as well as the passion of man. The limitations which this statute places upon her contractual powers, upon her right to agree with her employer as to the time she shall labor, are not imposed solely for her benefit, but also largely for the benefit of all. Many words cannot make this plainer. The two sexes differ in structure of body, in the functions to be performed by each, in the amount of physical strength, in the capacity for long continued labor, particularly when done standing, the influence of vigorous health upon the future well-being of the race, the self-reliance which enables one to assert full rights, and in the capacity to maintain the struggle for subsistence. This difference justifies a difference in legislation, and upholds that which is designed to compensate for some of the burdens which rest upon her.

We have not referred in this discussion to the denial of the elective franchise in the State of Oregon, for while it may disclose a lack of political equality in all things with her brother, that is not of itself decisive. The reason runs deeper, and rests in the inherent difference between the two sexes.

For these reasons, and without questioning in any respect the decision in *Lochner* v. *New York*, we are of the opinion that it cannot be adjudged that the act in question is in conflict with the Federal Constitution, so far as it respects the work of a female in a laundry, and the judgment of the Supreme Court of Oregon is Affirmed.

* See *Women in Industry, Decision of the United States Supreme Court in the Case of Curt Muller v. The State of Oregon and Brief by Louis Brandeis, assisted by Josephine Clara Goldmark* (New York: National Consumers League, 1908), pp. 1–8, 16–17; Alice Kessler-Harris, *Out to Work: A History of Wage-Earning Women in the United States* (New York: Oxford University Press 1982), pp. 201–5.

Muller v. *Oregon*, 208 U.S. 412 (1908).

Pauline Newman, "We fought and we bled and we died . . ."

One of the four young garment industry workers whose organizing activities emerged so vividly from the pages of Annelise Orleck's account, Pauline Newman had started out at the Triangle Shirtwaist Factory, which became the scene of one of the great industrial tragedies in New York City's history. Although the factory contained several elevators and two staircases, the eight-story wooden building had no sprinkler system; the doors to the fire escapes were locked to prevent outdoor relaxation. When fire broke out in 1911, 500 employees—many of them young Jewish and Italian women—were trapped behind locked doors. Some on the upper floors jumped to their deaths; others burned or asphyxiated while trapped inside. Altogether, the fire claimed the lives of 146 women. Viewing their charred bodies on the street, one reporter recalled that some of these same women had gone on strike only the year before to demand decent wages, more sanitary working conditions, and safety precautions.

Educational director for the International Ladies' Garment Workers' Union until her death in 1986, Newman conveys in her own words what it was like to be a garment worker in the early twentieth century. What does she feel has been gained by organized labor? What does she feel has been lost over the years?

A cousin of mine worked for the Triangle Shirtwaist Company and she got me on there in October of 1901. It was probably the largest shirtwaist factory in the city of New York then. They had more than two hundred operators, cutters, examiners, finishers. Altogether more than four hundred people on two floors. The fire took place on one floor, the floor where we worked. You've probably heard about that. But that was years later.

We started work at seven-thirty in the morning, and during the busy season we worked until nine in the evening. They didn't pay you any overtime and they didn't give you anything for supper money. Sometimes they'd give you a little apple pie if you had to work very late. That was all. Very generous.

What I had to do was not really very difficult. It was just monotonous. When the shirtwaists were finished at the machine there were some threads that were left, and all the youngsters—we had a corner on the floor that resembled a kindergarten—we were given little scissors to cut the threads off. It wasn't heavy work, but it was monotonous, because you did the same thing from seven-thirty in the morning till nine at night.

Well, of course, there were [child labor] laws on the books, but no one bothered to enforce them. The employers were always tipped off if there was going to be an inspection. "Quick," they'd say, "into the boxes!" And we children would climb into the big boxes the finished shirts were stored in. Then some shirts were piled on top of us, and when the inspector came—no children. The factory always got an okay from the inspector, and I suppose someone at City Hall got a little something, too.

The employers didn't recognize anyone working for them as a human being. You were not allowed to sing. Operators would have liked to have sung, because they, too, had the same thing to do and weren't allowed to sing. We weren't allowed to talk to each other. Oh, no, they would sneak up behind if you were found talking to your next colleague. You were admonished: "If you keep on you'll be fired."

Adapted from "Pauline Newman," in *American Mosaic: The Immigrant Experience in the Words of Those Who Lived It*, ed. Joan Morrison and Charlotte Fox Zabusky (New York: E. P. Dutton, 1980), pp. 9–14.

There was no morgue in New York City large enough to hold the bodies of the young women who had jumped from the burning buildings of the Triangle Shirtwaist Company. They were laid out on a pier for families to identify. (Courtesy of UNITE Archives, Kheel Center for Labor-Management Documentation and Archives, School of Industrial and Labor Relations, Cornell University, Ithaca, New York.)

If you went to the toilet and you were there longer than the floor lady thought you should be, you would be laid off for half a day and sent home. And, of course, that meant no pay. You were not allowed to have your lunch on the fire escape in the summertime. The door was locked to keep us in. That's why so many people were trapped when the fire broke out.

My pay was $1.50 a week no matter how many hours I worked. My sisters made $6.00 a week; and the cutters, they were skilled workers, they might get as much as $12.00. The employers had a sign in the elevator that said: "If you don't come in on Sunday, don't come in on Monday." You were expected to work every day if they needed you and the pay was the same whether you worked extra or not. You had to be there at seven-thirty, so you got up at five-thirty, took the horse car, then the electric trolley to Greene Street, to be there on time. . . .

I stopped working at the Triangle Factory during the strike in 1909 and I didn't go back. The union sent me out to raise money for the strikers. I apparently was able to articulate my feelings and opinions about the criminal conditions, and they didn't have anyone else who could do better, so they assigned me. And I was successful getting money. After my first speech before the Central Trade and Labor Council I got front-page publicity, including my picture. I was only about fifteen then. Everybody saw it. Wealthy women were curious and they asked me if I would speak to them in their homes. I said I would if they would contribute to the strike, and they agreed. So I spent my time from November to the end of March upstate in New York, speaking to the ladies of the Four Hundred [the elite of New York's society] and sending money back. . . .

We didn't gain very much at the end of the strike. I think the hours were reduced to fifty-six a week or something like that. We got a 10 percent increase in wages. I think that the best thing that the strike did was to lay a foundation on which to build a union. There was so much feeling against unions then. The judge, when one of our girls came before him, said to her: "You're not striking against your employer, you know, young lady. You're striking against God," and sentenced her to two weeks on Blackwell's Island, which is now Welfare Island. And a lot of them got a taste of the club. . . .

After the 1909 strike I worked with the union, organizing in Philadelphia and Cleveland and other places, so I wasn't at the Triangle Shirtwaist Factory when the fire broke out, but a lot of my friends were. I was in Philadelphia for the union and, of course, someone from here called me immediately and I came back. It's very difficult to describe the feeling because I knew the place and I knew so many of the girls. The thing that bothered me was the employers got a lawyer. How anyone could have *defended* them!—because I'm quite sure that the fire was planned for insurance purposes. And no one is going to convince me otherwise. And when they testified that the door to the fire escape was open, it was a lie! It was never open. Locked all the time. One hundred and forty-six people were sacrificed, and the judge fined Blank and Harris seventy-five dollars!

Conditions were dreadful in those days. But there was something that is lacking today and I think it was the devotion and the belief. We *believed* in what we were doing. We fought and we bled and we died. Today they don't have to.

You sit down at the table, you negotiate with the employers, you ask for 20 percent, they say 15, but the girls are working. People are working. They're not disturbed, and when the negotations are over they get the increases. They don't really have to fight. Of course, they'll belong to the union and they'll go on strike if you tell them to, but it's the inner faith that people had in those days that I don't see today. It was a terrible time, but it was interesting. I'm glad I lived then.

Even when things were terrible, I always had that faith. . . . Only now, I'm a little discouraged sometimes when I see the workers spending their free hours watching television—trash. We fought so hard for those hours and they waste them. We used to read Tolstoy, Dickens, Shelley, by candlelight, and they watch the *Hollywood Squares*. Well, they're free to do what they want. That's what we fought for.

ELLEN CAROL DUBOIS

The Next Generation of Suffragists: Harriot Stanton Blatch and Grassroots Politics

Campaigns to expand suffrage require that voters who are reasonably content with the status quo be persuaded to welcome new and unpredictable constituencies into the political arena. It is perhaps no surprise that the expansion of suffrage met severe resistance, in the North where there were considerable doubts about the immigrant vote and especially in the South where the franchise had just been restricted to exclude African Americans and, in the process, many poor whites.

The campaign for woman suffrage involved intellectual challenge to established political theory that held a married woman's political interests were represented by her husband. It involved national mass mobilization at a time when even presidential campaigns hardly met that criteria. It required brilliant street theater on a massive scale and, simultaneously, clever and delicate political maneuvering for which women were not noted. Although the accomplishment of woman suffrage in 1920 is well known, the complexity of the work that was required and the high level of political skill that women had to acquire is less appreciated than it deserves to be.

Harriot Blatch, the daughter of Elizabeth Cady Stanton, led the efforts of the Women's Political Union (WPU) to win suffrage for the women of New York State. From 1910 to 1915, the WPU lobbied state legislators to support the suffrage bill. They also targeted public support with parades, suffrage shops, and films. (See Photo Essay: "Women in Public," p. 247.)

Ironically, many suffragists who demanded the vote were deeply skeptical about politics. Believing that women were more pure than men and that politics were corrupt, they insisted that if women had the vote, they would put an end to partisanship. In fact, their views were not so far apart from antisuffragists who resisted the vote precisely because they felt partisan politics would corrupt American womanhood. To their credit, Harriot Blatch and her colleagues understood that acquiring political skills and understanding partisanship were essential to acquiring the vote and, once acquired, using it effectively.

The battle for women's rights had begun in the state of New York, the birthplace of Elizabeth Cady Stanton and the longtime home of Susan B. Anthony. In Seneca Falls, New York, the Declaration of Rights and Sentiments had been rousingly proclaimed in 1848. In Albany, both Stanton and Anthony testified in the 1850s before the New York Senate's Judiciary Committee. There they argued, with some success, for changes in state law to establish women's guardianship rights over their children, grant property and earnings rights to married women, and deliver woman suffrage. In 1915, nearly seventy years later, the struggle, now led by a new generation, had come to focus on woman suffrage. Fittingly, Harriot

Stanton Blatch, Elizabeth Cady Stanton's daughter, led this major effort to win woman suffrage in its home state. But even in the early twentieth century, success was uncertain.

Harriot Stanton, the second daughter and sixth child of Elizabeth Cady and Henry Brewster Stanton, inherited her role as defender of her sex from her mother. She was born in Seneca Falls in 1856, during a period when Elizabeth Cady Stanton was immersed in women's issues and the development of a convention movement to publicize concerns as revolutionary as liberalizing divorce. . . . While other Victorian girls followed their mothers into quiet lives based on family service, Harriot was taught to be assertive and independent. . . . Her mother prepared her daughters to go out into the world not only to make their individual marks on it but also to embody her convictions about women's untapped capacities. . . .

. . . In 1874, [Harriot] enrolled at Vassar, the first all-female college established in the United States. There, she elected an unconventional course of study focused on science, politics, and history. Upon graduation, she became a member of the first generation of women college graduates, one of only a few thousand women in the United States who held a bachelor's degree. . . .

[In 1882,] she met William Blatch, the handsome, accommodating son of a wealthy brewer from Basingstoke, Hampshire, England. Harriot and William married in 1882, and the couple's first child Nora (named after the heroine of Ibsen's *A Doll's House*) was born in England the next year. A second child, Helen, born in 1892, died of whooping cough in 1896. Like her mother but with fewer children, more money, and a compliant husband, Harriot Blatch managed to combine marriage and motherhood with an energetic commitment to reform activities. She joined with veteran British women activists to revive the British suffrage movement. . . . In 1890, she joined the socialist Fabian Society, where she fought for, but failed to win, strong support for women's rights. For two decades as an [expatriate] in Edwardian England, she honed her political skills and updated her mother's feminist convictions, speaking at meetings, writing for suffrage journals, and becoming involved in local politics as a member of the Women's Local Government Society.

In 1902, with her daughter Nora grown and studying engineering at Cornell, and her husband Henry able to retire, Harriot Blatch moved permanently to New York to take up the task she had inherited—leadership of the American suffrage movement. She joined the Women's Trade Union League, a pioneering effort of elite settlement house women and female wage earners joined together to empower, not patronize, working women. There she came to see that to be modern and effective the suffrage movement in the United States must unite women across the classes in a militant effort. She also saw, as other women activists did not, that women's growing interest in electoral politics was crucial to the reinvigoration of the suffrage movement. Like the English suffragist Emmeline Pankhurst, she was committed to forcing the political parties to address the suffrage issue and winning from them the political support necessary to gain victory. . . .

To enact her vision of a militant, democratic suffrage organization based on a coalition of working-class and middle-class working women, Harriot Blatch organized the Equality League of Self-Supporting Women in 1907, renamed the Women's Political Union (WPU) in 1910. Although it gradually moved away from reliance on wage-earning women for its most active participants, the WPU went on to spearhead a political effort to force the New York legislature to pass a bill authorizing a referendum to amend the state constitution to grant women suffrage.

The WPU suffrage campaign, which ran from 1910 to 1915, involved an exhausting and elaborate two-pronged effort: First, both houses of the state legislature had to pass a bill authorizing a referendum on woman suffrage, and then the state's all-male electorate had to approve the referendum. . . . [S]uffragists in New York took hope from a narrowly won suffrage victory in California in October 1911. . . . By 1912, California was the sixth state in which women were voting in the presidential election. Blatch and her followers were determined that New York women would do the same in the next presidential election. . . .

Harriot Blatch had a talent and taste for partisan politics that was unusual in the movement. Although many of the new generation of suffragists were college-trained professionals, Mary Beard, the historian and a close friend, wrote of Blatch that more than others, "she worked steadfastly to root the suffrage movement in politics, where alone it could reach its goal."[1] She certainly had the lineage. Her mother and Susan B. Anthony had immersed themselves in party politics. From them, from her father, and from her years in England, Harriot had come to see that if suffragists were ever to win, they would have to go behind the scenes and engage in precisely the political maneuvering and lobbying that women had traditionally repudiated as the unhappy consequence of the male monopoly of public life. While such openly political methods distressed many older women reformers, they invigorated Harriot.

In one episode, which became a staple of suffrage legend, Harriot and other WPU leaders tracked down a particularly elusive senator. By this time, opposition to suffrage had moved from ridicule to avoidance. "The chase led up and down elevators in and out of the Senate chamber and committee rooms." Finally, they ferreted out his hiding place and cornered him; he could no longer avoid the issue. The WPU account reversed the standard metaphors of gender to emphasize the senator's humiliation at the hands of women. "Of slight build," he was literally overpowered by the suffragists. "With Mrs. Blatch walking on one side with her hand resting ever so slightly on his sleave [*sic*]," the women led him into the committee room and got his vote. "I'll never forgive this," he told Blatch. "Oh yes, you will," she responded, "some day you will be declaring with pride how your vote advanced the suffrage resolution."[2]

The WPU won a similar battle with Robert Wagner, the new Democratic majority leader of the state Senate and one of the most determined opponents of suffrage in the New York legislature. To prevent Wagner from once again employing the delaying legislative tactics of moving to table or returning the referendum resolution to committee for another year, Harriot arranged for three hundred New York City suffragists to go to Albany to pressure him to set a date for a vote. Some fifty or sixty women crowded into the committee room, with the rest gathered in the corridor outside. When Wagner moved to take his place in the chair at the front of the room, the aisle filled with suffragists. "There were no anti-suffragists to rescue him," wrote Harriot later. "There were only all about him, the convinced and ruthless members of the Women's Political Union." He grudgingly agreed to set a date for the state Senate to vote on the suffrage resolution.[3]

In both episodes, the WPU's power rested not only in numbers but also in its willingness to exploit the gendered meanings of power. Wagner yielded because he could not afford to let it be known that he had been physically and politically outmaneuvered by women. The newspapers predictably reported what the women requested, and Wagner graciously granted a date for the Senate vote. But at a time in which accounts of British militant suffragists smashing windows were prominently featured in American papers, the sense of sexual warfare, of women besting men, was close to the surface and hard to overlook.

The Senate debate and vote took place on the date Wagner had guaranteed. Harriot and her followers watched from the gallery. Like good politicians, they had carefully counted their supporters, knew that they had just the right number of votes with not one to spare, and "were full of confidence" that the referendum would carry.[4] Across the hall, the lower house was giving them an unanticipated victory. It looked like the legislative battle might actually be won. But at the last moment a perfidious senator abandoned the public pledge he had given the WPU, shifted his vote, and denied them their victory.

With this undeserved defeat uppermost in her mind, Blatch went to the people. The WPU had organized parades twice before, but the 1912 New York City parade was by far the most carefully organized street demonstration in U.S. suffrage history. The WPU spared no effort at recruiting and educating a large number of marchers and alerting the public to the meaning and significance of the parade. Pledge cards were circulated, committing marchers to take to the streets. Newspapers eagerly covered the clever "stunts" that suffragists devised to advertise the parade: suffragists at the circus, "suffragette hats" for sale at department stores, recruitment booths behind the Public Library.

Harriot was determined that the parade give evidence of a massive, disciplined army of women with which politicians would have to come to terms. She paid great attention to the details of the march, the numbers of marching columns, and the spacing of the lines of marchers. Women were instructed to dress simply, walk erectly, and keep their eyes forward. The spectacle was to be an emotional and sensual evocation of women's power. Opponents, according to Blatch, should be converted through their eyes. "The enemy must see women, marching in increasing numbers year by year out on the public avenues, holding high their banner, Votes For Women." On the appointed day, more than ten thousand took to the streets: women college graduates in their academic gowns, working women by trades and industries, prominent wealthy women, even some men. The president of the national suffrage society marched with a banner that read "Catching Up with China"—a reference to reports that insurgent nationalists in one of China's provincial legislatures had declared women enfranchised. Public demonstrations of this sort were new and a bit daunting to many women. "I marched the whole length," one demonstrator proudly reported to a friend.[5]

In 1912, the emergence of a third national political party, the Progressives, affected the task of getting a suffrage referendum. While Progressive leaders begged women for their support, Blatch was disappointed with the tepid role the party had played in a woman suffrage referendum in Ohio earlier in that year. And former president Theodore Roosevelt, the party's candidate for president in 1912, repeatedly embarrassed himself and his party by sexist declarations that suffragists were "indirectly encouraging immorality."[6] Still, the Progressive Party's support was crucial for the WPU's plans in New York because of the leverage it gave in prying support out of the Republicans, who were struggling to keep voters from bolting to the new party. First the Progressives and then the Republicans endorsed the submission of the suffrage referendum to New York voters at their state conventions. . . . [T]he Democrats followed the other two parties in urging submission of the referendum. Victory, at least in the legislature, was assured. The election of 1912 swept the Democrats . . . into power in the state, and, under the leadership of Woodrow Wilson, into the presidency as well.

There was a last-minute complication when the Republicans added a clause to the referendum subjecting immigrant women, who were citizens by marriage, to special requirements for voting, and the Democrats objected. The issue was a difficult one for Blatch. On the one hand, she had lost her American citizenship by virtue of her marriage to an Englishman and was sympathetic to women whose citizenship was altered by marriage. On the other hand, like her mother decades before, she had her own nativist prejudices, as did many of her middle-class followers. In the end, she decided the issue politically: Keeping the clause would gain the referendum more upstate Republican votes than it would lose downstate Democrats.

Party leaders followed her lead, and in January 1913, both houses passed legislation proposing an amendment to the state constitution striking out the word male and enfranchising citizens over twenty-one "provided that a citizen by marriage should have been an inhabitant of the United States for five years."[7] Blatch had worked three years for this moment, a long time for a single bill. And even with this victory, the most difficult task lay ahead—the winning of the referendum itself. Now the suffrage leaders would have to convince a majority of New York men to vote for woman suffrage.

Harriot Blatch and the leaders of the WPU had no illusions about how difficult this might be. "The task we must accomplish between now and election day 1915 [when the referendum would appear on the ballot] is a Herculean one, compared to that we have just completed," the Executive Committee of the Women's Political Union declared. Harriot had her misgivings about immigrant voters, with their "Germanic and Hebraic attitude toward women," but she counted on the democratic logic of the situation, believing that men who were being allowed to exercise the franchise could be convinced to vote in favor of women's demand to share it. [But a great deal was riding on the New York referendum. "If we win the Empire State all the states will come tumbling down like a deck of cards," she promised.[8]]

To cultivate the voters, the WPU played on its strengths. It based its suffrage advocacy on the proliferating devices of modern mass culture—forms of commercial recreation, methods of advertising, and the pleasures of consumerism. Californians had used billboards, automobile caravans, and suffrage postcards to bring their cause before the electorate in their successful campaign of 1911. New York women had to do the same. ["If we are to reap a victory in 1915, we must cultivate every inch of soil and sow our suffrage seed broadcast in the Empire state," Harriot declared.[9]]

Such an approach conformed to Harriot's view of democracy which, she believed, should be based on the heart rather than the head. Emotions were the key to popular democracy, not reason. "We learned . . . as we toiled in our campaign," she later wrote, "that sermons and logic would never convince. . . . Human beings move because they feel, not because they think."[10] This was not an expression of any special contempt for either women or working-class voters; on the contrary, she considered men (especially politicians) more irrational than women and the rich more prejudiced and conservative than the poor. She believed particularly that changes in women's status and in power relations between the sexes could never be reduced to rational arguments and dispassionate appeals, even to venerable principles of American democracy such as equality and civic virtue.

"Democracy was the keynote" of the grand suffrage ball that the WPU sponsored in January 1913 to inaugurate the referendum campaign. Extensively advertised, it took place in New York City's Seventy-First Street Armory, which was barely large enough for the eight thousand men and women who attended. Rich and poor, working-class and society women alike paid fifty cents to dance the turkey trot and other popular new dances. The event proved, as the WPU put it, "that love of liberty and democracy did not belong to one class or one sex but is deeply rooted in human nature itself."[11] . . .

Given Harriot's appreciation for the role of emotions in mass politics, she was especially intrigued by new technologies of mass communication. "I stand for the achievements of the twentieth century," she declared. "I will make use of . . . anything which civilization places at my command."[12] Lee de Forest, her former son-in-law (Nora's brief marriage to him had ended after a year), was one of the pioneers of modern radio broadcasting. . . . At his invitation, she delivered a radio talk on woman suffrage from the newly opened broadcasting station in downtown Manhattan.

Moving pictures represented another new technology with political possibilities. The WPU arranged for a commercial movie company to produce *The Suffragette and the Man,* a romantic comedy in which the beautiful young heroine, forced to choose between her suffrage principles and her fiancé, first picks principles and then overcomes an anti-suffrage competitor and wins back her lover.

In 1913, the WPU collaborated on a second movie entitled *What 8,000,000 Women Want.* This time the romantic triangle did not involve good and bad men fighting for a heroine's heart but good and bad politics fighting for the hero's soul. Newsreel footage of actual suffrage parades was interspersed with the dramatic action. Harriot played herself and brought to the screen her self-confident authority and her genuine pleasure at conducting the struggle. . . .

[In 1913, as in previous years, the most spectacular suffrage event was the parade organized by the WPU. Each year, the parades had become more stunning affairs, symbolically conveying both the diversity and the unity of modern women.] The 1913 parade was one of the high points of Harriot's suffrage leadership. "We will muster an army fifty thousand strong this year," she predicted. The marchers were arranged by divisions. At the head were two dozen female marshals mounted on horseback and dressed in stylish adaptations of men's evening wear, black cutaways and silk hats with streamers of green, purple, and white, the WPU's colors and those of the movement in England. Leading them, dressed in white and astride a white horse, was Inez Millholland, "the official beauty of the parade." The intention was to provide unforgettable visual images of all kinds of women marching shoulder to shoulder together. "In these times of class wars," Harriot observed, could men really afford "to shut out from public affairs that fine spirit of fellowship" that suffragism represented?[13]

The effectiveness of the parade as political propaganda infuriated antisuffragists, for whom the spectacular aspect of the movement was proof positive of the social and cultural upheaval that votes for women threatened. The antisuffragists charged that the bold stance of the marchers smacked of the deliberate exploitation of "sex appeal." . . . Harriot Blatch found the charges amusing. "Funny idea of sex appeal. Twenty thousand women turn out on a hot day. 87 degrees and march up Fifth Avenue to the blaring music of thirty-five bands; eyes straight to the front; faces red with the hot sun. . . . If it had been mellow moonlight. . . . But a sex appeal set to brass bands! That certainly is a new one."[14] The WPU was determined to finesse the conventional notions of female beauty that had so long restrained women's public activities. . . .

During the legislative lobbying years from 1910 to 1913, Harriot and the WPU had not faced much organizational opposition within the New York suffrage movement. The state suffrage organization was small and ineffective. But once the referendum campaigning began in earnest, the Woman's Political Union, led by the blunt, sometimes undiplomatic Blatch, came into direct conflict with the other great figure of New York suffragism, the moderate, circumspect Carrie Chapman Catt. Within the women's movement, Catt embodied the progressive faith in organizational structure and administrative centralization. In contrast, Harriot celebrated individual initiative, modern invention, and personal freedom. Notwithstanding lofty suffrage rhetoric about the unity of all womanhood and the solidarity of the sex, these two were bound to clash. . . . Catt was always more concerned to unify and reconcile all existing suffragists than to reach out and create new ones. While some activists believed that Blatch was autocratic and high-handed, the ever-diplomatic Catt prized harmony within the movement above all things. Catt's efforts went to creating internal order rather than tackling external obstacles. Unlike Blatch, Catt had little skill or interest in the intricacies of partisan politics and legislative maneuvers.

Catt's plan was to bring all the suffrage societies in New York . . . under one wing, but the Women's Political Union [crucial to her efforts and the richest organization in the state] refused to subsume itself under Catt's leadership. . . . By 1914, it was clear that two parallel suffrage campaigns would be conducted in New York, one by Catt's Empire State Campaign Committee and the other by Harriot Blatch's Women's Political Union. Both raised money for the referendum effort; both sent paid agents around the state; both set up separate offices, sometimes generating considerable conflict among activists in smaller communities in upstate New York. The suffrage movement had survived previous internal divisions and would face others in the future. . . .

In the last six months of the campaign, the WPU flooded the state with publicity-generating gimmicks and stunts. Suffragists played both ends of the gender divide to demonstrate that they could join in traditional male activities as good fellows and at the same time retain their female virtue. On Suffrage Day at the Polo Grounds, New York suffrage organizations competed with each other to sell tickets to a benefit baseball game between the New York Giants and the Chicago Cubs. . . . To counter the anti-suffrage claims that they were bitter women who wanted the ballot as compensation for their inability to find husbands, they even held a series of "married couple days," in which husbands and wives declared their mutual happiness and support of votes for women. . . .

Ten weeks before the end of the campaign, Harriot's single-minded attention to the cause was shattered by the sudden death of her husband, William Blatch, who was accidentally electrocuted. . . . Before leaving [for England to tend to her husband's estate], she took advantage of one benefit of widowhood and resumed her U.S. citizenship. Harriot's decision to leave the country so close to the end of the 1915 campaign is something of a puzzle. She could have postponed the trip a few months. Moreover, England was already at war with Germany, and the transatlantic trip was dangerous. Perhaps she was growing weary of the unrelenting labor of trying to convert New York voters, or perhaps she sensed that she was losing her position as New York's foremost suffragist to Carrie Chapman Catt. . . . By the time she returned in mid-October, the Empire State Campaign Committee . . . had taken over organization of the final suffrage parade. . . .

November 2, 1915, the day toward which Harriot Blatch, Carrie Catt, and thousands of other New York women had been working for years, was the kind of warm, sunny day for which hard-working campaigners pray. When the polls opened at 6 A.M., several thousand suffrage activists were in their places as poll-watchers, guarding against any effort to cheat them of their victory. . . .

By midnight, it was clear that the woman suffrage amendment had been defeated. Out of 1,200,000 votes cast across the state, woman suffrage had been defeated by 190,000 votes, about 16 percent of the total. All the boroughs of New York City voted against woman suffrage as well as fifty-six of the state's sixty-one counties.

Most New York suffragists kept the bitter disappointment they felt to themselves and declared the referendum a moral triumph. "On the whole we have achieved a wonderful victory," Carrie Chapman Catt proclaimed. "It was short of our hopes but the most contemptuous opponents speak with newly acquired respect for our movement."[15] Catt's wing of the campaign announced the day after the election that a second referendum campaign would begin as soon as state law permitted. . . .

Harriot Blatch was one of the few suffrage leaders who dared to react with open anger. She was "disgusted at the conditions which had forced women to campaign in the streets" and humiliated at having to appeal to immigrant men to gain her native-born rights as an American citizen.[16] She vowed she would never make another street-corner speech. Her retreat into this outraged elitism recalled her mother's reaction to her own crushing disappointment at the failure of the Reconstruction constitutional amendments to include women. Blatch also blamed the suffrage forces themselves for the defeat, at least the Catt wing of the movement, which she thought had neglected upstate New York. She believed a second referendum would be a mistake because the antisuffragists would be even better organized for the next round.

In this she was wrong. In 1917, a second voters' referendum was victorious in New York, thus winning an incalculably important political prize in the battle that was intensifying nationwide. Yet Harriot was correct in a larger way. The era of state suffrage referenda was over; with the exception of New York, no other state was won by this method after 1915. From this point on, attention, energy, and political initiative shifted to the federal arena, to the constitutional amendment Elizabeth Cady Stanton and Susan B. Anthony had first introduced and which had been stalled in congressional committee for almost fifty years. In less than five years, the amendment was moved onto the floor, secured a two-thirds vote in the House and three years later in the Senate, and was ratified by three-quarters of the state legislatures to become the law of the land. . . .

Notes

1. "Foreword" by Mary Beard, in Harriot Stanton Blatch and Alma Lutz, *Challenging Years: The Memoirs of Harriot Stanton Blatch* (New York: G. P. Putnam's Sons, 1940), p. vii.

2. Nora de Forest, "Political History of Women's Political Union," reel 1, Harriot Stanton Blatch Papers, Library of Congress, pp. 13–14; *Challenging Years*, pp. 162–63.

3. *Challenging Years*, pp. 163–64.

4. Ibid., pp. 169–70; Women's Political Union 1912–1913 Annual Report, pp. 7–8.

5. *Challenging Years*, p. 180; "Chinese Women Parade for Suffrage," *New York Times*, April 14, 1912, pt. 7, p. 5; Katherine Devereux Blake to Alice Park, n.d., Susan B. Anthony Memorial Collection, Huntington Library, San Marino, CA.

6. "Roosevelt Is for Woman Suffrage," *New York Times*, February 3, 1912, p. 7.

7. "Official Copy of Proposed Amendment," November 2, 1915, Blatch Papers, Library of Congress.

8. "The Referendum Policy of the Women's Political Union," p. 19, reel 1, Blatch Papers, Library of Congress. "Mrs. Blatch Plans Hot Fight to Win New York to Suffrage," *Chicago Tribune*, March 16, 1913. Blatch to Alice Paul, August 26, 1913, reel 4, National Woman's Party Papers: Suffrage Years.

9. Blatch, "Seed Time and Harvest," *Women's Political World*, June 16, 1913, p. 2.

10. *Challenging Years*, p. 192.

11. "Suffragists Tour City to Boom Ball," *New York Daily Mail*, January 11, 1913; "Charity Versus Votes," *Women's Political World*, January 15, 1913, p. 7.

12. "Barnard Girls Test Wireless Phones," *New York Times*, February 26, 1909, p. 7.

13. ". . . with Suffrage Workers," *New York Post*, March 7, 1913; "Eyes to the Front," *New York Tribune*, May 3, 1913; Blatch, "A Reviewing Stand," *Women's Political World*, May 15, 1913, p. 1.

14. "Answers Anti Attack," *New York Times*, May 13, 1913, p. 3.

15. Catt to Mary Grey Peck, December 12, 1912, Catt Papers, Library of Congress.

16. "Mrs. Blatch Pours Out Wrath . . . ," *New York Times*, November 4, 1915, p. 3.

Dimensions of Citizenship I

Mackenzie *v.* Hare, *1915*

The persistent expansion of married women's property acts and the increasing popularity of woman suffrage make it tempting to conclude that the practice of coverture—women's legal and civic subordination to men—steadily dissolved over the course of the nineteenth and early twentieth centuries. But although it is true that some aspects of coverture eroded, others were sustained and even strengthened.

Although Chief Justice Morrison R. Waite had been right when he observed in *Minor* v. *Happersett* (1874) (pp. 315–316) that [t]here is no doubt that women may be citizens," he was wrong when he went on to claim that "sex has never been made one of the elements of citizenship. . . . [M]en have never had an advantage over women." According to the common law and early American practice, white women, like men, became citizens either by birth or by their own choice to be naturalized. But in 1855, following practices established in France by the conservative Code Napoleon (1804) and in Britain in 1844, the U.S. Congress extended the principle of marital unity to provide that "any woman who might lawfully be naturalized under the existing laws, married, or shall be married to a citizen of the United States shall be deemed and taken to be a citizen." That is, foreign women who married male citizens did not need to go through a naturalization process or even take an oath of allegiance. The law did not explain what should happen when a woman with U.S. citizenship married a noncitizen man. For the next fifty years, there was little consistency in how courts dealt with related cases that came before them. Often the principle of "marital unity" prevailed, meaning that women who were American citizens lost their citizenship by marrying a foreign national. In 1907, Congress passed a statute explicitly providing that women take the nationality of their husbands when they marry.

Expatriation—the loss of citizenship—traditionally has been a very severe punishment, usually reserved for cases of treason. If a married woman had to assume the nationality of her husband, she might become the subject of a king or czar in a political system that offered her even less protection than did the United States. She might even become stateless. If Americans claimed to base their political system on the "consent of the governed," could women's "consent" be arbitrarily denied? In time of war, the American woman who married, say, a German national could change her status overnight from a citizen to an alien enemy. President Ulysses S. Grant's daughter lost her citizenship when she married an Englishman in 1874; it required a special act of Congress to reinstate her citizenship when she returned from England as a widow in 1898.

Ethel Mackenzie, who had been born in California, married Gordon Mackenzie, a British subject, in 1909—two years after the passage of the Citizenship

Mackenzie v. *Hare,* 239 U.S. 299 (1915).

Act of 1907. She was active in the woman suffrage movement in California, and when it was successful in 1911 she worked in the San Francisco voter registration drive. It is not surprising that she herself should try to register to vote. When the Board of Election Commissioners denied her application, holding that upon her marriage to a British subject she had "ceased to be a citizen of the United States," she refused to let her husband apply for citizenship and instead challenged the law, claiming that Congress had exceeded its authority. She could not believe that Congress had actually *intended* to deprive her of the citizenship she understood to be her birthright. Why did the Supreme Court deny her claim? What "ancient principle of jurisprudence" did they rely on? Why did the Court think that the marriage of an American woman to a foreign man should be treated differently from the marriage of an American man to a foreign woman?

MR. JUSTICE MCKENNA:

. . . The question . . . is, Did [Ethel Mackenzie] cease to be a citizen by her marriage? . . . [Mackenzie contends] that it was not the intention [of Congress] to deprive an American-born woman, remaining within the jurisdiction of the United States, of her citizenship by reason of her marriage to a resident foreigner. . . . [She is trying to persuade the Court that the citizenship statute was] beyond the authority of Congress. . . . [She offered the] earnest argument . . . that . . . under the Constitution and laws of the United States, [citizenship] became a right, privilege and immunity which could not be taken away from her except as a punishment for crime or by her voluntary expatriation. . . .

[But the Court concludes:] . . . The identity of husband and wife is an ancient principle of our jurisprudence. It was neither accidental nor arbitrary and worked in many instances for her protection. There has been, it is true, much relaxation of it but in its retention as in its origin it is determined by their intimate relation and unity of interests, and this relation and unity may make it of public concern in many instances to merge their identity, and give dominance to the husband. It has purpose, if not necessity, in purely domestic policy; it has greater purpose and, it may be, necessity, in international policy. . . . Having this purpose, has it not the sanction of power?

. . . The law in controversy deals with a condition voluntarily entered into. . . . The marriage of an American woman with a foreigner has consequences . . . [similar to] her physical expatriation. . . . Therefore, as long as the relation lasts it is made tantamount to expatriation. This is no arbitrary exercise of government. . . . It is the conception of the legislation under review that such an act [marriage to a foreign man] may bring the Government into embarrassments and, it may be, into controversies. . . . [Marriage to a foreign man] is as voluntary and distinctive as expatriation and its consequence must be considered as elected.

The decision in *Mackenzie* angered suffragists and energized them; American women needed suffrage to protect themselves against involuntary expatriation and statelessness. The repeal of the Citizenship Act of 1907 was high on the suffragists' agenda, and they returned to it as soon as suffrage was accomplished (see Equal Suffrage [Nineteenth] Amendment). The Cable Act of 1922 provided that "the right of a person to become a naturalized citizen shall not be denied to a person on account of sex or because she is a married woman," but it permitted American women who married foreigners to retain their citizenship only if they married men from countries whose subjects were eligible for U.S. citizenship—that is, not from China or Japan. American-born women who married aliens from China or Japan still lost their citizenship. American-born women who married aliens not from China or Japan were treated as naturalized citizens who would lose their citizenship should they reside abroad for two years.

The Cable Act was extended by amendments well into the 1930s, but some exclusions remained, and the improvements were generally not made retroactive. Thus, as late as the 1950s, some American-born women were denied passports because they had married foreign men before 1922. In 2001, the U.S. Supreme Court upheld a practice of different rules for nonmarital children born abroad. The child born to an unmarried citizen mother and a noncitizen man is a citizen at birth. The child born to an unmarried citizen father and a noncitizen woman can be a citizen only if the father formally legitimizes and financially supports the child before the age of eighteen.*

**Nguyen* v. *Immigration and Naturalization Service*, 533 U.S. 53 (2001). This note draws on Candice Lewis Bredbenner, *A Nationality of Her Own: Women, Marriage and the Law of Citizenship* (Berkeley: University of California Press, 1998).

Equal Suffrage (Nineteenth) Amendment, 1920

When the Fourteenth and Fifteenth amendments (p. 309) failed to provide for universal suffrage, a federal amendment was introduced into the Senate by S. C. Pomeroy of Kansas in 1868 and into the House by George W. Julian of Indiana in March 1869. Historian Ellen DuBois has observed, "Previously the case for suffrage had consistently been put in terms of the individual rights of all persons, regardless of their sex and race. Angered by their exclusion from the Fifteenth Amendment, women's rights advocates began to develop fundamentally different arguments for their cause. They claimed their right to the ballot not as individuals but as a sex. . . . The reason women should vote was not that they were the same as men but that they were different. That made for a rather thorough reversal of classic women's rights premises."*

Arguing for the vote on the basis of women's *difference* from men could be effective in strengthening women's sense of group consciousness, but it also was compatible with racist and nativist arguments that white women needed the vote to counteract the suffrage of black and immigrant men. The old alliance of woman suffrage and abolitionist activism eroded, even though voting rights for black men were increasingly threatened after Reconstruction. The suffrage efforts of 1870 to 1920 continued to display arguments from equality, but younger generations of activists were increasingly likely to emphasize difference—what one activist called "the mother instinct for government."

Woman suffrage was not accomplished easily. One scholar has counted 480 suffrage campaigns between 1870 and 1910, but only seventeen referenda were held, with only two successes. Stanton died in 1902, Anthony in 1906. But a new, younger generation adopted new strategies; Americans were inspired by the militancy of the British suffrage movement; in 1902 Carrie Chapman Catt was simultaneously president of the International Woman Suffrage Alliance and the

*Ellen Carol DuBois, "Outgrowing the Compact of the Fathers: Equal Rights, Woman Suffrage, and the United States Constitution, 1820–1878," *Journal of American History* 74 (1987): 848.

National American Woman Suffrage Association (NAWSA). By 1910 it was clear that a reinvigorated movement was under way, using door-to-door campaigns, street-corner speakers, and poll watchers on election day. For the first time, cross-class suffrage organizations, like New York's Equality League of Independent Women, were mobilizing support for suffrage. Suffragists staged public parades that attracted tens of thousands of supporters.

Although many suffragists had claimed that when women got the vote, there would be no more American endorsements of war, Catt swung NAWSA behind Woodrow Wilson, American support for the Allies, and, eventually, the nation's entry into World War I in April 1917. The more radical National Women's Party (NWP), under the leadership of Alice Paul, staked out a very public position protesting Wilson's failure to explicitly endorse a federal guarantee for women's suffrage. (For the story of the NWP's picketing of the White House in 1917, see p. 248.) Putting aside his states' rights approach, the president publicly endorsed a constitutional amendment in early 1918. One day later, the House of Representatives passed the suffrage amendment, barely achieving the required two-thirds majority. But despite a personal appearance from Wilson, it failed by only two votes to carry the Senate.

As state after state enacted woman suffrage for statewide elections, the number of members of Congress dependent on women's votes increased. With the federal suffrage amendment slated to come before Congress again and again, these men were likely to belive that they had no choice but to support it. In the fall 1918 elections, NAWSA targeted four senators for defeat; two of them failed to be reelected. Moreover, energetic campaigns in the states to elect pro-suffrage candidates to Congress worked. When the amendment came up in the new Congress, Anne F. Scott and Andrew Scott wrote that "224 of those voting yes came from suffrage states, and eighty from nonsuffrage states."* It squeaked by in the Senate. It was ratified by thirty-five states by August 1920; the final state was Tennessee, where, after a bitter struggle, it was ratified by a single vote, just in time to permit women to vote in the elections of 1920.

When Puerto Rican women attempted to register to vote in 1920, however, the U.S. Bureau of Insular Affairs decided that the Nineteenth Amendment did not automatically apply to U.S. territories. Suffragist groups mobilized in Puerto Rico, lobbying throughout the next decade both on the island and in Washington, D.C., with support from the NWP. In 1929 the territorial legislature granted suffrage to women restricted by a literacy requirement; not until 1935 was universal suffrage established in Puerto Rico.

Many southern states had excluded African American men from voting by using literacy tests, poll taxes, and intimidation; in those states black women could vote no more easily than black men, and suffrage was an empty victory. The state of Georgia effectively discouraged white women from voting as well by providing that any woman who did not choose to register to vote did not have to pay the poll tax. This law, which encouraged women—and their husbands—to see voting as an expensive extravagance, was upheld by the U.S. Supreme Court in 1937 (*Breedlove* v. *Suttles*, 302 U.S. 277).

*Anne F. Scott and Andrew MacKay Scott, *One Half the People: The Fight for Woman Suffrage* (Urbana: University of Illinois Press, 1982; orig. publ. Philadelphia: Lippincott, 1975), p. 45.

Section 1. The right of the citizens of the United States to vote shall not be denied or abridged by the United States or by any State on account of sex.

Section 2. Congress shall have power to enforce this article by appropriate legislation.

Adkins *v.* Children's Hospital, *1923*

Minimum wage legislation was the counterpart to maximum hour laws. It was attacked, much as maximum hour legislation had been, as an interference with the right of the employer and employee to contract freely. (See *Muller* v. *Oregon*, pp. 415–416.) But it was also defended; by 1917, twelve states had passed minimum wage laws for women. In 1918, Congress, which had jurisdiction over the District of Columbia, authorized the Wage Board of the District to fix minimum wages for women and children in order to protect them "from conditions detrimental to their health and morals, resulting from wages which are inadequate to maintain decent standards of living."

Then the Ninteenth Amendment was ratified. Children's Hospital, which employed many women at lower than minimum wages, brought a test case against Chairman Jesse C. Adkins and the other members of the Wage Board in 1922; the hospital won in the Court of Appeals for the District of Columbia. Adkins appealed to the U.S. Supreme Court; once again the women of the Consumers League responded, preparing another brief—this one 1,000 pages long—that tried to show the social impact of substandard wages. Justice Louis Brandeis, who had presented the argument in *Muller*, was now sitting on the U.S. Supreme Court, and he did not vote in this case because of his close involvement in laying the groundwork for it. His successor at Harvard Law School, Felix Frankfurter, who had testified before Congress in support of establishing a Minimum Wage Board, now argued before the U.S. Supreme Court on its behalf. He convinced justices William Howard Taft, Oliver Wendell Holmes, Jr., and Edward Sanford that low wages and long hours were linked. In their dissenting opinions they stated that if Congress could regulate one, it could regulate the other. Holmes also observed that the phrase "liberty of contract" did not appear in the Constitution.

The majority of the Court was not persuaded, however. The members of the majority distinguished between maximum hours legislation, which they saw as directly allied to health concerns, and minimum wage legislation, which they thought "simply and exclusively a price-fixing law." The majority also observed that the Nineteenth Amendment obviated the need for protective legislation for women. In taking that position, the justices were endorsing the arguments of Alice Paul and the NWP who had no faith in protective labor legislation and who were lobbying for an equal rights amendment.

Adkins v. *Children's Hospital*, 261 U.S. 525 (1923).

The *Adkins* decision blocked progress in minimum wage legislation for fifteen years, until there was a new president (Franklin D. Roosevelt) and a new approach in Congress. In 1938 the Fair Labor Standards Act established a federal minimum wage for *both* men and women. However, women continued often to be paid less than men for the same jobs. In 1963 the Equal Pay Act prohibited different pay for men and women when their jobs require "equal skill, effort and responsibility and are performed under similar working conditions." The Court has ruled that jobs meriting equal pay must be substantially equal but not necessarily identical. "Dusting is dusting is dusting" said one court in ruling that the pay of maids and janitors must be equal. More recently, the definition of what constitutes "equal skill, effort and responsibility" has been broadened to a public debate over what constitutes "comparable worth."

MR. JUSTICE GEORGE SUTHERLAND:

. . . the ancient inequality of the sexes, otherwise than physical, as suggested in the *Muller Case* has continued "with diminishing intensity." In view of the great—not to say revolutionary—changes which have taken place since that utterance, in the contractual, political and civil status of women, culminating in the Nineteenth Amendment, it is not unreasonable to say that these differences have now come almost, if not quite, to the vanishing point. . . . we cannot accept the doctrine that women of mature age, . . . require or may be subjected to restrictions upon their liberty of contract which could not lawfully be imposed in the case of men under similar circumstances. To do so would be to ignore all the implications to be drawn from the present day trend of legislation, as well as that of common thought and usage, by which woman is accorded emancipation from the old doctrine that she must be given special protection or be subjected to special restraint in her contractual and civil relationships. . . . What is sufficient to supply the necessary cost of living for a woman worker and maintain her in good health and protect her morals is obviously not a precise or unvarying sum. . . . The amount will depend upon a variety of circumstances: the individual temperament, habits of thrift, care, ability to buy necessaries intelligently, and whether the woman lives alone or with her family. . . . It cannot be shown that well paid women safeguard their morals more carefully than those who are poorly paid. Morality rests upon other considerations than wages. . . .

Margaret Sanger, "I resolved that women should have knowledge of contraception. . . ."

The contrast between the high fertility of newly arriving immigrants and the low birth rate among old-stock Americans around the turn of the century prompted such leaders as Theodore Roosevelt to lament "race suicide" and to exhort women of the "proper sort" to perform their maternal functions in the selfless fashion dictated by time and tradition. Viewed through women's eyes,

Margaret Sanger, following her conviction by the New York Court of Appeals in 1918. She and her supporters treated the outcome as a victory because the court allowed physicians to provide contraceptives to married women "to cure or prevent [venereal] disease." (Photograph reprinted by permission of Planned Parenthood® Federation of America.)

however, these population trends looked different, as this selection on the beginnings of the birth control movement dramatically illustrates. Although a few radicals such as Emma Goldman saw contraception as a means of liberating women by restoring to them control over their own bodies and thereby lessening their economic dependence on men, it was Margaret Higgins Sanger whose name would become most closely linked with the crusade for birth control.

The factors that propelled Sanger—a complex personality—to leadership were many. One of eleven children, she helped bury her mother, who died of tuberculosis. Young Margaret, however, was convinced that the sexual demands of her father (who lived to be eighty) were the real cause of her mother's death. A nursing career also shaped Sanger's thinking, as the following account suggests. Arrested under the Comstock Act (pp. 314–315) for publication of a newspaper advocating contraception, she fled in 1914 to England with her husband and three children. There she met the famous British psychologist and sex expert, Havelock Ellis, who further convinced her that sexual experience should be separated from reproduction, enabling couples to enhance the quality of their sexual relationship. Returning to New York, the Sangers continued their activities on behalf of birth control. The opening of the Brownsville clinic in 1916, recounted here, resulted in still further confrontation with authorities, including arrests. The hunger strike of Sanger's sister, Ethel Byrne, a nurse at the clinic, was followed by Sanger's own trial. Convicted of "maintaining a public nuisance," she was sentenced to thirty days in prison. Her lawyer asked for a suspended sentence in exchange for her promise not to break the law again, she announced, "I cannot promise to obey a law I do not respect." Ever the iconoclast and rebel, she gave talks to other inmates on sex hygiene when the prison guards were out of sight. Even after she was released, her attorney pursued an appeal. In January 1918, the New York Court of Appeals upheld her conviction, but interpreted the law in question broadly, allowing physicians to provide contraceptives to *married* women "to cure or prevent [venereal] disease." Sanger appealed unsuccessfully for the right of *nurses* to also provide contraceptives. Still, establishing the right of physicians to deliver birth control was a key breakthrough; it was the foundation of the birth control movement in the twentieth century, and would be a central element in the decision in *Roe* v. *Wade* (see pp. 725–728).

Divorcing William Sanger in 1920, Sanger founded the American Birth Control League in 1921 (in 1942 it was transformed into the Planned Parenthood Federation of America). She soon married William Slee, a wealthy oil man whose resources would be a key source of support for her causes. These included the first doctor-staffed birth control clinic in the United States, a model for hundreds of clinics throughout the nation. Long before medical schools routinely taught the fitting of diaphragms, these clinics, staffed by physicians, made reliable contraceptive services widely available. In 1936 Sanger and her colleagues forced the courts to revisit the Comstock Act: a woman physician in New York ordered a package of diaphragms (also known as pessaries) from Japan; the Customs Bureau seized them as obscene articles. But the U.S. Court of Appeals for the Second Circuit ruled that objects ordered by physicians in good faith were exempted from the punishments of the law (*U.S* v. *One Package*, 86 F.2d 737).

Important financial aid would come in later years from the wealthy feminist Katherine McCormick, who shared Sanger's commitment to research in contraception. In the early 1950s, McCormick provided funds for experiments in endocrinology that led to the development of the birth control pill. At a time when few scientists thought an oral contraceptive was possible, the insistence of Sanger and McCormick that every woman had the right to control her own body helped bring about a major breakthrough in medical technology. In 1960, the year of Sanger's death, "the pill" became available to the public. The timing was propitious, for it coincided with a period of sexual liberation that, while proving in some respects to be a mixed blessing for women, also coincided with new recognition of the intensity of their sexual drive and capacity for sexual pleasure.

Although Sanger saw the development of an oral contraceptive as another victory in a long and difficult struggle for reproductive freedom, others viewed the birth control movement differently. Arguments that limiting family size could not only free women's energies for social reform but prevent the world's poor from producing children they were unable to care for met with opposition from women themselves in the early years of Sanger's crusade. Some feared that birth control would contribute to promiscuity; others feared it would deny women the dignity that was theirs by virtue of motherhood. The Roman Catholic Church was unrelenting in its opposition, maintaining that the use of contraceptives is a sin. Sanger is still being angrily attacked; her contribution to the lives of modern American women remains a matter of political debate. Birth control is not only a technical way of spacing and limiting children so as to benefit both mother and child but is part of a larger debate about the extent to which women should be able to control their own reproductive lives.

AWAKENING AND REVOLT

Early in the year 1912 I came to a sudden realization that my work as a nurse and my activities in social service were entirely palliative and consequently futile and useless to relieve the misery I saw all about me. . . .

It is among the mothers here that the most difficult problems arise—the outcasts of society with theft, filth, perjury, cruelty, brutality oozing from beneath.

Ignorance and neglect go on day by day; children born to breathe but a few hours and pass out of life; pregnant women toiling early and late to give food to four or five children, always hungry; boarders taken into homes where there is not sufficient room for the family; little girls eight and ten years of age sleeping in the same room with dirty, foul smelling, loathsome men; women whose weary, pregnant, shapeless bodies refuse to accommodate themselves to the husbands' desires find husbands looking with lustful eyes upon other women, sometimes upon their own little daughters, six and seven years of age.

In this atmosphere abortions and birth become the main theme of conversation. On Saturday nights I have seen groups of fifty to one hundred women going into questionable offices well known in the community for cheap abortions. I asked several women what took place there, and they all gave the same reply: a quick examination, a probe inserted into the uterus and turned a few times to disturb the fertilized ovum, and then the woman was sent home. Usually the flow began the next day and often continued four or five weeks. Sometimes an ambulance carried the victim to the hospital for a curetage, and if she returned home at all she was looked upon as a lucky woman.

This state of things became a nightmare with me. There seemed no sense to it all, no reason for such waste of mother life, no right to exhaust women's vitality and to throw them on the scrap-heap before the age of thirty-five.

Everywhere I looked, misery and fear stalked—men fearful of losing their jobs, women fearful that even worse conditions might come upon them. The menace of another pregnancy hung like a sword over the head of every poor woman I came in contact with that year. The question which met me was always the same: What can I do to keep from it? or, What can I do to get out of this? Sometimes they talked among themselves bitterly.

"It's the rich that know the tricks," they'd say, "while we have all the kids." Then, if the women were Roman Catholics, they talked about "Yankee tricks," and asked me if I knew what the Protestants did to keep their families down. When I said that I didn't believe that the rich knew much more than they did I was laughed at and suspected of holding back information for money. They would nudge each other and say something about paying me before I left the case if I would reveal the "secret." . . .

I heard over and over again of their desperate efforts at bringing themselves "around"—drinking various herb-teas, taking drops of turpentine on sugar, steaming over a chamber of boiling coffee or of turpentine water, rolling down stairs, and finally inserting slippery-elm sticks, or knitting needles, or shoe hooks into the uterus. I used to shudder with horror as I heard the details and, worse yet, learned of the conditions *behind the reason* for such desperate actions.

. . . Each time I returned it was to hear that Mrs. Cohen had been carried to a hospital but had never come back, that Mrs. Kelly had sent the children to a neighbor's and had put her head into the gas oven to end her misery. Many of the women had consulted midwives, social workers and doctors at the dispensary and asked a way to limit their families, but they were denied this help, sometimes indignantly or gruffly, sometimes jokingly; but always knowledge was denied them. Life for them had but one choice: either to abandon themselves to incessant childbearing, or to terminate their pregnancies through abortions. Is it any wonder they resigned themselves hopelessly, as the Jewish and Italian mothers, or fell into drunkenness, as the Irish and Scotch? The latter were often beaten by husbands, as well as by their sons and daughters. They were driven and cowed, and only as beasts of burden were allowed to exist. . . .

They claimed my thoughts night and day. One by one these women, with their worried, sad, pensive and aging faces would marshal themselves before me in my dreams, sometimes appealingly, sometimes accusingly. I could not escape from the facts of their misery, neither was I able to see the way out of their problems and their troubles. . . .

Finally the thing began to shape itself, to become accumulative during the three weeks I spent in the home of a desperately sick woman living on Grand Street, a lower section of New York's East Side.

Mrs. Sacks was only twenty-eight years old; her husband, an unskilled worker, thirty-two. Three children, aged five, three and one, were none too strong nor sturdy, and it took all the earnings of the father and the ingenuity of the mother to keep them clean, provide them with air and proper food, and give them a chance to grow into decent manhood and womanhood.

Both parents were devoted to these children and to each other. The woman had become pregnant and had taken various drugs and purgatives, as advised by her neighbors. Then, in desperation, she had used some instrument lent to her by a friend. She was found prostrate on the floor amidst the crying children when her husband returned from work. Neighbors advised against the ambulance, and a friendly doctor was called. The husband would not hear of her going to a hospital, and as a little money had been saved in the bank a nurse was called and the battle for that precious life began.

. . . The three-room apartment was turned into a hospital for the dying patient. Never had I worked so fast, so concentratedly as I did to keep alive that little mother. . . .

. . . July's sultry days and nights were melted into a torpid inferno. Day after day, night after night, I slept only in brief snatches, ever too anxious about the condition of that feeble heart bravely carrying on, to stay long from the bedside of the patient. With but one toilet for the building and that on the floor below, everything had to be carried down for disposal, while ice, food and other necessities had to be carried three flights up. It was one of those old airshaft buildings of which there were several thousands then standing in New York City.

At the end of two weeks recovery was in sight, and at the end of three weeks I was preparing to leave the fragile patient to take up the ordinary duties of her life, including those, of wifehood and motherhood. . . .

But as the hour for my departure came nearer, her anxiety increased, and finally with trembling voice she said: "Another baby will finish me, I suppose."

"It's too early to talk about that," I said, and resolved that I would turn the question over to the doctor for his advice. When he came I said: "Mrs. Sacks is worried about having another baby."

"She well might be," replied the doctor, and then he stood before her and said: "Any more such capers, young woman, and there will be no need to call me."

"Yes, yes—I know, Doctor," said the patient with trembling voice, "but," and she hesitated as if it took all of her courage to say it, "what can I do to prevent getting that way again?"

"Oh ho!" laughed the doctor good naturedly, "You want your cake while you eat it too, do you? Well, it can't be done." Then, familiarly slapping her on the back and picking up his hat and bag to depart, he said: "I'll tell you the only sure thing to do. Tell Jake to sleep on the roof!"

With those words he closed the door and went down the stairs, leaving us both petrified and stunned.

Tears sprang to my eyes, and a lump came in my throat as I looked at that face before me. It was stamped with sheer horror. I thought for a moment she might have gone insane, but she conquered her feelings, whatever they may have been, and turning to me in desperation said: "He can't understand, can he?—he's a man after all—but you do, don't you? You're a woman and you'll tell me the secret and I'll never tell it to a soul."

She clasped her hands as if in prayer, she leaned over and looked straight into my eyes and beseechingly implored me to tell her something—something *I really did not know*. . . .

I had to turn away from that imploring face. I could not answer her then. I quieted her as best I could. She saw that I was moved by the tears in my eyes. I promised that I would come back in a few days and tell her what she wanted to know. The few simple means of limiting the family like *coitus interruptus* or the condom were laughed at by the neighboring women when told these were the means used by men in the well-to-do families. That was not believed, and I knew such an answer would be swept aside as useless were I to tell her this at such a time. . . .

The intelligent reasoning of the young mother—how to prevent getting that way again—how sensible, how just she had been—yes, I promised myself I'd go back and have a long talk with her and tell her more, and perhaps she would not laugh but would believe that those methods were all that were really known.

But time flew past, and weeks rolled into months. . . . I was about to retire one night three months later when the telephone rang and an agitated man's voice begged me to come at once to help his wife who was sick again. It was the husband of Mrs. Sacks, and I intuitively knew before I left the telephone that it was almost useless to go.

. . . I arrived a few minutes after the doctor, the same one who had given her such noble advice. The woman was dying. She was unconscious. She died within ten minutes after my arrival. It was the same result, the same story told a thousand times before—death from abortion. She had become pregnant, had used drugs, had then consulted a five-dollar professional abortionist, and death followed.

The doctor shook his head as he rose from listening for the heart beat. . . . The gentle woman, the devoted mother, the loving wife had passed on leaving behind her a frantic husband, helpless in his loneliness, bewildered in his helplessness as he paced up and down the room, hands clenching his head, moaning "My God! My God! My God!"

The Revolution came—but not as it has been pictured nor as history relates that revolutions have come. . . .

After I left that desolate house I walked and walked and walked; for hours and hours I kept on, bag in hand, thinking, regretting, dreading to stop; fearful of my conscience, dreading to face my own accusing soul. At three in the morning I arrived home still clutching a heavy load the weight of which I was quite unconscious.

. . . As I stood at the window and looked out, the miseries and problems of that sleeping city arose before me in a clear vision like a panorama: crowded homes, too many children; babies dying in infancy; mothers overworked; baby nurseries; children neglected and hungry—mothers so nervously wrought they could not give the little things the comfort nor care they needed; mothers half sick most of their lives—"always ailing, never failing"; women made into drudges; children working in cellars; children aged six and seven pushed into the labor market to help earn a living; another baby on the way; still another; yet another; a baby born dead—great relief; an older child dies—sorrow, but nevertheless relief—insurance helps; a mother's death—children scattered into institutions; the father, desperate, drunken; he slinks away to become an outcast in a society which has trapped him.

. . . There was only one thing to be done: call out, start the alarm, set the heather on fire! Awaken the womanhood of America to free the motherhood of the world! I released from my almost paralyzed hand the nursing bag which unconsciously I had clutched, threw it across the room, tore the uniform from my body, flung it into a corner, and renounced all palliative work forever.

I would never go back again to nurse women's ailing bodies while their miseries were as vast as the stars. I was now finished with superficial cures, with doctors and nurses and social workers who were brought face to face with this overwhelming truth of women's needs and yet turned to pass on the other side. They must be made to see these facts. I resolved that women should have knowledge of contraception. They have every right to know about their own bodies. I would strike out—I would scream from the housetops. I would tell the world what was going on in the lives of these poor women. *I would* be heard. No matter what it should cost. *I would be heard*. . . .

I announced to my family the following day that I had finished nursing, that I would never go on another case—and I never have.

I asked doctors what one could do and was told I'd better keep off that subject or Anthony Comstock would get me. I was told that there were laws against that sort of thing. This was the reply from every medical man and woman I approached. . . .

A "PUBLIC NUISANCE"

The selection of a place for the first birth control clinic was of the greatest importance. No one could actually tell how it would be received in any neighborhood. I thought of all the possible difficulties: The indifference of women's organizations, the ignorance of the workers themselves, the resentment of social agencies, the opposition of the medical profession. Then there was the law—the law of New York State.

Section 1142 was definite. It stated that *no one* could give information to prevent conception to *anyone* for any reason. There was, however, Section 1145, which distinctly stated that physicians (*only*) could give advice to prevent conception for the cure or prevention of disease. I inquired about the section, and was told by two attorneys and several physicians that this clause was an exception to 1142 referring only to venereal disease. But anyway, as I was not a physician, it could not protect me. Dared I risk it?

I began to think of the doctors I knew. Several who had previously promised now refused. I wrote, telephoned, asked friends to ask other friends to help me find a woman doctor to help me demonstrate the need of a birth control clinic in New York. None could be found. No one wanted to go to jail. No one cared to test out the law. Perhaps it would have to be done without a doctor. But it had to be done; that I knew.

Fania Mindell, an enthusiastic young worker in the cause, had come on from Chicago to help me. Together we tramped the streets on that dreary day in early October, through a driving rainstorm, to find the best location at the cheapest terms possible . . .

Finally at 46 Amboy Street, in the Brownsville Section of Brooklyn, we found a friendly landlord with a good place vacant at fifty dollars a month rental; and Brownsville was settled on. It was one of the most thickly populated sections. It had a large population of working class Jews, always interested in health measures, always tolerant of new ideas, willing to listen and to accept advice whenever the health of mother or children was involved. I knew that here there would at least be no breaking of windows, no hurling of insults into our teeth; but I was scarcely prepared for the popular support, the sympathy and friendly help given us in that neighborhood from that day to this. . . .

With a small bundle of handbills and a large amount of zeal, we fared forth each morning in a house-to-house canvass of the district in which the clinic was located. Every family in that great district received a "dodger" printed in English, Yiddish and Italian. . . .

Women of every race and creed flocked to the clinic with the determination not to have any more children than their health could stand or their husbands could support. Jews and Christians, Protestants and Roman Catholics alike made their confessions to us, whatever they may have professed at home or in the church. Some did not dare talk this over with their husbands; and some came urged on by their husbands. Men themselves came after work; and some brought timid, embarrassed wives, apologetically dragging a string of little children. . . .

When I asked a bright little Roman Catholic woman what she would say to the priest when he learned that she had been to the Clinic, she answered indignantly: "It's none of his business. My husband has a weak heart and works only four days a week. He gets twelve dollars, and we can barely live on it now. We have enough children."

Her friend, sitting by, nodded a vigorous approval. "When I was married," she broke in, "the priest told us to have lots of children, and we listened to him. I had fifteen. Six are living. Nine baby funerals in our house. I am thirty-six years old now. Look at me! I look sixty."

As I walked home that night, I made a mental calculation of fifteen baptismal fees, nine funeral expenses, masses and candles for the repose of nine little souls, the physical suffering of the mother, and the emotional suffering of both parents; and I asked myself, "Was it fair? Is this the price of Christianity?" . . .

Ethel Byrne, who is my sister and a trained nurse, assisted me in advising, explaining, and demonstrating to the women how to prevent conception. As all of our 488 records were confiscated by the detectives who later arrested us for violation of the New York State law, it is difficult to tell exactly how many more women came in those days to seek advice; but we estimate that it was far more than five hundred. As in any new enterprise, false reports were maliciously spread about the clinic; weird stories without the slightest foundation of truth. We talked plain talk and gave plain facts to the women who came there. We kept a record of every applicant. All were mothers; most of them had large families.

It was whispered about that the police were to raid the place for abortions. We had no fear of that accusation. We were trying to spare mothers the necessity of that ordeal by giving them proper contraceptive information. . . .

The arrest and raid on the Brooklyn clinic was spectacular. There was no need of a large force of plain clothes men to drag off a trio of decent, serious women who were testing out a law on a fundamental principle. My federal arrest, on the contrary, had been assigned to intelligent men. One had to respect the dignity of their mission; but the New York city officials seem to use tactics suitable only for crooks, bandits and burglars. We were not surprised at being arrested, but the shock and horror of it was that a *woman*, with a squad of five plain clothes men, conducted the raid and made the arrest. A woman—the irony of it!

I refused to close down the clinic, hoping that a court decision would allow us to continue such necessary work. I was to be disappointed. Pressure was brought upon the landlord, and we were dispossessed by the law as a "public nuisance." In Holland the clinics were called "public utilities."

When the policewoman entered the clinic with her squad of plain clothes men and announced the arrest of Miss Mindell and myself (Mrs. Byrne was not present at the time and her arrest followed later), the room was crowded to suffocation with women waiting in the outer room. The police began bullying these mothers, asking them questions, writing down their names in order to subpoena them to testify against us at the trial. These women, always afraid of trouble which the very presence of a policeman signifies, screamed and cried aloud. The children on their laps screamed, too. It was like a panic for a few minutes until I walked into the room where they were stampeding and begged them to be quiet and not to get excited. I assured them that nothing could happen to them, that I was under arrest but they would be allowed to return home in a few minutes. That quieted them. The men were blocking the door to prevent anyone from leaving, but I finally persuaded them to allow these women to return to their homes, unmolested though terribly frightened by it all.

. . . The patrol wagon came rattling through the streets to our door, and at length Miss Mindell and I took our seats within and were taken to the police station. . . .

HUNGER STRIKE

Out of that spectacular raid, which resulted in an avalanche of nation-wide publicity in the daily press, four separate and distinct cases resulted:

Mrs. Ethel Byrne, my sister, was charged with violating Section 1142 of the Penal Code, designed to prevent dissemination of birth control information.

Miss Fania Mindell was charged with having sold an allegedly indecent book entitled "What Every Girl Should Know" written by Margaret Sanger.

I was charged with having conducted a clinic at 46 Amboy Street, Brooklyn, in violation of the same section of the Penal Code.

Having re-opened the clinic, I was arrested on a charge of "maintaining a public nuisance," in violation of Section 1530 of the Penal Code.

The three of us were held for trial in the Court of Special Sessions, with bail fixed at $500 each. This meant that our cases would be decided by three judges appointed by the Mayor and not by a jury. . . .

My sister was found guilty, and on January 22 she was sentenced to thirty days in the Workhouse. A writ of habeas corpus as a means of suspending sentence during appeal was refused by Supreme Court Justice Callahan. She spent the night in jail.

Ethel Byrne promptly declared a hunger strike. I knew that she would not flinch. Quiet, taciturn, with a will of steel hidden by a diffident air, schooled by her long training as a professional nurse, she announced briefly that she would neither eat, drink, nor work until her release. Commissioner of Correction Burdette G. Lewis promptly announced that she would be permitted to see no one but her attorney.

While the newspapers were reporting—always on the front page—the condition of the hunger striker, plans were hastened for a monster mass meeting of protest, to be held in Carnegie Hall. Helen Todd acted as chairman, and Dr. Mary Halton was an additional speaker. The hall was crowded by a huge audience of all classes. The women patients of the Brownsville clinic were given places of honor on the platform. The salvos of applause which greeted me showed that intelligent opinion was strongly behind us, and did much to give me the courage to fight with renewed strength for the immediate release of Ethel Byrne.

This meeting was acclaimed by the press as a "triumph of women, for women, by women." The meeting was said to have struck the right note—that of being instructive and persuasive, instead of agitational.

In the meantime, Ethel Byrne's refusal to eat and drink was crowding all other news off the front pages of the New York papers. Her defiance was sharpening the issue between self-respecting citizens and the existing law, which was denounced on every street corner as hypocritical. In the subway crowds, on street-corners, everywhere people gathered, the case was discussed. "They are imprisoning a woman for teaching physiological facts!" I heard one man exclaim. . . .

"It makes little difference whether I starve or not," she replied, through her attorney, "so long as this outrageous arrest calls attention to the archaic laws which would prevent our telling the truth about the facts of life. With eight thousand deaths a year in New York State from illegal operations on women, one more death won't make much difference."

All this served to convince the now panic-stricken Mr. Lewis [Commissioner of Correction in charge of Blackwell's Island] that Mrs. Byrne was different, after all, from the alcoholics and drug addicts who had given him his previous experience, and with whom he had gallantly compared her. When she had gone 103 hours without food, he established a precedent in American prison annals. He ordered her forcibly fed. She was the first woman so treated in this country. . . .

The truth was that Mrs. Byrne was in a critical condition after being rolled in a blanket and having milk, eggs and a stimulant forced into her stomach through a rubber tube. I realized this as soon as I heard that she was "passive under the feeding." Nothing but loss of strength could have lessened the power of her resistance to such authority. Nothing but brutality could have reduced her fiery spirit to acquiescence. I was desperate; torn between admiration for what she was doing and misery over what I feared might be the result.

On January 31st, a committee headed by Mrs. Amos Pinchot, Jessie Ashley and myself went to Albany for the purpose of asking Governor Whitman to appoint a commission to investigate birth control and make a report to the state legislature. Governor Whitman, a wise, fair, intelligent executive and statesman, received us, and listened to our exposition of the economic and moral necessity for birth control; the medical theory behind its justification. He promised to consider appointing the commission. During the interview Miss Jessie Ashley introduced the subject of Mrs. Byrne's treatment on Blackwell's Island and the anxiety we felt about her condition. We tried to make him see the outrage committed by the state in making anyone suffer for so just a cause. The Governor offered Mrs. Byrne a pardon on condition that she would not continue to disseminate birth control information. . . .

When we left Albany that day, I had the promise of a provisional pardon for Mrs. Byrne, but best of all I had in my purse a letter from the Governor to the authorities at Blackwell's Island authorizing me to see her. I was shocked and horrified when, in the late afternoon of February 1st, I saw my sister. She was lying semi-conscious on a cot in a dark corner of the prison cell. . . .

There was not time to inform her of the conditions of her pardon, and moreover she was too ill to face the question. I still believe that I was right in accepting the conditions which the Governor imposed. There was no other course. I saw that she was dangerously ill, that nothing further was to be gained by her keeping on, and that her death would have been a terrible calamity. Her life was what mattered to me, regardless of her future activities. . . .

At any rate, by the time she was released the subject was a burning issue. Newspapers which previously had ignored the case, had to mention a matter important enough to bring the Governor of the State from Albany to New York.

NANCY F. COTT

Equal Rights and Economic Roles: The Conflict over the Equal Rights Amendment in the 1920s

The vote achieved, former suffragists turned their attention to sex-based discrimination in the law. To some, the proper strategy, as in suffrage, seemed to be a constitutional amendment affirming equal rights; men and women would have to be treated under the law as equals and as individuals. In contrast, suffragists who had struggled to pass legislation shortening hours and improving working conditions for women in industry had achieved that goal only because the Supreme Court was prepared to regard women as a special class of workers in need of governmental protection because of their childbearing role. (See *Muller v. Oregon*, pp. 415–416.) An equal rights amendment (ERA) would invalidate sex-based labor laws, they feared, since comparable protection would not be extended to men. The ensuing debate was a critical one creating deep and lasting divisions. Unable to agree on a unified agenda for four decades, veterans of the first women's movement expended energy in internal conflict, thereby diluting their political effectiveness. Not surprisingly women's issues made little headway until the 1960s.

The debate over the ERA was critical not only because of its long-term consequences, but because it highlighted differing views within feminism of the social significance of gender and the meaning of equality. Does equality require that men and women have the "same" rights and be subject to the "same" treatment, or does equality require "different" treatment? How should the law treat the difference created by women's unique reproductive system? With these questions in mind, Nancy Cott carefully assesses the initial debate over the ERA, making clear the assumptions and limitations inherent in the arguments of each side.

THE CONFLICT OVER THE EQUAL RIGHTS AMENDMENT IN THE 1920s

Campaigning for ratification of the Equal Rights Amendment during the 1970s, feminists who found it painful to be opposed by other groups of women were often unaware that the first proposal of that amendment in the 1920s had likewise caused a bitter split between women's groups claiming, on both sides, to represent women's interests. The 1920s conflict itself echoed some earlier ideological and tactical controversies. One central strategic question for the women's rights movement in the late nineteenth century had concerned alliances: should proponents of "the cause of woman" ally with advocates for the rights for freed slaves, with temperance workers, or labor reformers, or a political party, or none of them? At various times different women leaders felt passionately for and against such alliances, not agreeing on what they meant for the breadth of the women's movement and for the priority assigned to women's issues.[1] The 1920s contest over the equal rights amendment reiterated that debate insofar as the National Woman's Party, which proposed the ERA, took a "single-issue" approach, and the opposing women's organizations were committed to maintaining multiple alliances. But in even more striking ways than it recapitulated nineteenth-century struggles the 1920s equal rights conflict also predicted lines of fracture of the later twentieth-century women's movement. The advantages or compromises involved in "multi-issue" organizing are matters of contemporary concern, of course. Perhaps more important, the 1920s debate brought into sharp focus (and left for us generations later to resolve) the question whether "equal rights"—a concept adopted, after all, from the male political tradition—matched women's needs. The initial conflict between women over the ERA set the goal of enabling women to have the same opportunities and situations as men against the goal of enabling women freely to be different from men without adverse consequences. As never before in nineteenth-century controversies, these two were seen as competing, even mutually exclusive, alternatives.

The equal rights amendment was proposed as a legal or civic innovation but the intrafeminist controversy it caused focused on the economic arena. Indeed, the connection between economic and political subordination in women's relation to men has been central in women's rights advocacy since the latter part of the nineteenth century. In the Western political tradition, women were historically excluded from political initiatives because they were defined as dependent—like children and slaves—and their dependence was read as fundamentally economic. Nineteenth-century advocates, along with the vote, claimed women's "right to labor," by which they meant the right for women to have their labor recognized, and diversified. They emphasized that women, as human individuals no less than men, had the right and need to use their talents to serve society and themselves and to gain fair compensation. Influential voices such as Charlotte Perkins Gilman's at the turn of the century stressed not only women's service but the necessity and warrant for women's economic independence. Gilman argued simultaneously that social evolution made women's move "from fireside to factory" inevitable, and also that the move ought to be spurred by conscious renovation of outworn tradition.

By the 1910s suffragists linked political and economic rights, and connected the vote with economic leverage, whether appealing to industrial workers, career women or housewives. They insisted on women's economic independence in principle and defense of wage-earning women in fact. Since the vast majority of wage-earning women were paid too little to become economically independent, however, the two commitments were not identical and might in practice be entirely at odds.[2] The purpose to validate women's existing economic roles might openly conflict with the purpose to throw open economic horizons for women to declare their own self-definition. These tensions introduced by the feminist and suffrage agitation of the 1910s flashed into controversy over the equal rights amendment in the 1920s.

The ERA was the baby of the National Woman's Party, yet not its brainchild alone. As early as 1914, a short-lived New York City group called the Feminist Alliance had suggested a constitutional amendment barring sex discrimination of all sorts. Like the later NWP, the Feminist Alliance was dominated by highly educated and ambitious women in the arts and professions, women who believed that "equal rights" were their due while they also aimed to rejuvenate and reorient thinking about "rights" around female rather than only male definition. Some members of the Feminist Alliance surely joined the NWP, which emerged as the agent of militant and political action during the final decade of the suffrage campaign.[3]

A small group (engaging perhaps 5 percent of all suffragists), the NWP grew from the Congressional Union founded by Alice Paul and Lucy Burns in 1913 to work on the federal rather than the state-by-state route to woman suffrage. Through the 'teens it came to stand for partisan tactics (opposing all Democrats because the Democratic administration had not passed woman suffrage) and for flamboyant, symbolic, publicity-generating actions—large parades, pickets in front of the White House, placards in the Congress, hunger-striking in jail, and more. It gained much of its energy from leftwing radical women who were attracted to its wholesale condemnation of gender inequality and to its tactical adaptations from the labor movement; at the same time, its imperious tendency to work from the top down attracted crucial financial and moral support from some very rich women. When the much larger group, the National American Woman Suffrage Association, moved its focus to a constitutional amendment in 1916, that was due in no little part (although certainly not solely), to the impact of the NWP. Yet while imitating its aim, NAWSA's leaders always hated and resented the NWP, for the way it had horned in on the same pro-suffrage turf while scorning the NAWSA's traditional nonpartisan, educative strategy. These resentments festered into deep and long-lasting personal conflicts between leaders of the two groups.

Just after the 19th Amendment was ratified in August of 1920, the NWP began planning a large convention at which its members would decide whether to continue as a group and, if so, what to work for. The convention, held six months later and tightly orchestrated by chairman Alice Paul, brushed aside all other suggestions and endorsed an ongoing program to "remove all remaining forms of the subjection of women," by means of the elimination of sex discrimination in law.[4] At the outset, NWP leaders seemed unaware that this program of "equal rights" would be much thornier to define and implement than "equal suffrage" had been. They began surveying state legal codes, conferring with lawyers, and drafting numerous versions of equal rights legislation and amendments at the state and federal levels.

Yet the "clean sweep" of such an approach immediately raised a problem: would it invalidate sex-based labor legislation—the laws regulating women's hours, wages, and conditions of work, that women trade unionists and reformers had worked to establish over the past thirty years? The doctrine of "liberty of contract" between employer and employed had ruled court interpretations of labor legislation in the early twentieth century, stymying state regulation of the wages and hours of male workers. State regulation for women workers, espoused and furthered by many women in the NWP, had been made possible only by differentiating female from male wage-earners on the basis of physiology and reproductive functions. Now members of the NWP had to grapple with the question whether such legislation was sex "discrimination," hampering women workers in the labor market. Initially, there was a great deal of sentiment within the NWP, even voiced by Alice Paul herself, that efforts at equal rights legislation should not impair existing sex-based protective labor legislation. However, there was also contrary opinion, which Paul increasingly heeded; by late November 1921 she had come to believe firmly that "enacting labor laws along sex lines is erecting another handicap for women in the economic struggle." Some NWP affiliates were still trying to draft an amendment that would preserve special labor legislation, nonetheless, and continued to introduce equal rights bills with "safeguards" in some states through the following spring.[5]

Meanwhile women leaders in other organizations were becoming nervous and distrustful of the NWP's intentions. Led by the League of Women Voters (successor to the NAWSA), major women's organizations in 1920 formed a national lobbying group called the Women's Joint Congressional Committee. The LWV was interested in eliminating sex discrimination in the law, but more immediately concerned with the extension of sex-based labor legislation. Moreover, the LWV had inherited NAWSA's hostility to Alice Paul. The first president of the LWV, Maud Wood Park, still smarted from the discomfiture that NWP picketing tactics had caused her when she headed the NAWSA's Congressional Committee from 1916 to 1920.[6] Other leading groups in the Women's Joint Congressional Committee were no less suspicious of the NWP. The National Women's Trade Union League since the mid-1910s had concentrated its efforts on labor legislation to protect women workers. Florence Kelley, director of the National Consumers' League, had been part of the inner circle of the NWP during the suffrage campaign, but on the question of protective labor laws her priorities diverged. She had spent three decades trying to get state regulation of workers' hours and conditions, and was not about to abandon the gains achieved for women.[7]

In December 1921, at Kelley's behest, Paul and three other NWP members met for discussion with her and leaders of the League of Women Voters, the National Women's Trade Union League, the Woman's Christian Temperance Union, and the General Federation of Women's Clubs. All the latter objected to the new constitutional amendment now formulated by the NWP: "No political, civil or legal disabilities or inequalities on account of sex, or on account of marriage unless applying alike to both sexes, shall exist within the United States or any place subject to their jurisdiction." Paul gave away no ground, and all left feeling that compromise was unlikely. Each side already thought the other intransigent, though in fact debate was still going on within the NWP.[8]

By mid-1922 the National Consumers' League, the LWV, and the Women's Trade Union League went on record opposing "blanket" equal rights bills, as the NWP formulations at both state and federal levels were called. About the same time, the tide turned in the NWP. The top leadership accepted as definitive the views of Gail Laughlin, a lawyer from Maine, who contended that sex-based labor legislation was not a lamented loss but a positive harm. "If women can be segregated as a class for special legislation," she warned, "the same classification can be used for special restrictions along any other line which may, at any time, appeal to the caprice or prejudice of our legislatures." In her opinion, if "protective" laws affecting women were not abolished and prohibited, "the advancement of women in business and industry will be stopped and women relegated to the lowest, worst paid labor."[9] Since NWP lobbyists working at the state level were making little headway, a federal constitutional amendment appeared all the more appealing. In November 1923, at a grand conference staged in Seneca Falls, New York, commemorating the seventy-fifth anniversary of Elizabeth Cady Stanton's Declaration of Sentiments, the NWP announced new language: "Men and women shall have equal rights throughout the United States and every place subject to its jurisdiction." The constitutional amendment was introduced into Congress on December 10, 1923.[10]

In the NWP view, this was the logical sequel to the 19th Amendment. There were so many different sex discriminations in state codes and legal practices—in family law, labor law, jury privileges, contract rights—that only a constitutional amendment seemed effective to remove them. The NWP took the language of liberal individualism, enshrined in the catchphrase of "equal rights," to express its feminism. As Alice Paul saw it, what women as a gender group shared was their subordination and inequality to men as a whole; the legal structure most clearly expressed this subordination and inequality, and therefore was the logical point of attack. The NWP construed this agenda as "purely feminist," that is, appealing to women as women, uniting women around a concern common to them regardless of the other ways in which they might differ. Indeed, at its founding postsuffrage convention the NWP leadership purposely bypassed issues it saw as less "pure," including birth control, the defense of black women's voting rights in the South, and pacifism, which were predictably controversial among women themselves.

The NWP posited that women could and would perceive self-interest in "purely" gender terms. Faced by female opponents, its leaders imagined a fictive or abstract unity among women rather than attempting to encompass women's real diversity. They separated the proposal of equal rights from other social and political issues and effects. Although the campaign for equal rights was initiated in a vision of inclusiveness—envisioned as a stand that all women could take—it devolved into a practice of exclusiveness. The NWP's "appeal for conscious sex loyalty" (as a member once put it) went out to members of the sex who could subordinate identifications and loyalties of class, ethnicity, race, religion, politics, or whatever else to a "pure" sense of themselves as women differentiated from men. That meant principally women privileged by the dominant culture in every way except that they were female.[11]

In tandem with its lobbying for an equal rights amendment, the NWP presented its opposition to sex-based labor legislation as a positive program of "industrial equality." It championed women wage-earners who complained of "protective" legislation as restrictive, such as printers, railroad conductors, or waitresses hampered by hours limitation, or cleaning women fired and replaced by men after the passage of minimum-wage laws. Only a handful of working-class women rose to support for the ERA, however.[12] Mary Anderson, former factory worker herself and since 1919 the director of the U.S. Women's Bureau, which was founded to guide and assist women workers, threw her weight into the fight against the amendment. Male trade unionists—namely leaders of the American Federation of Labor—also voiced immediate opposition to the NWP aims, appearing at the very first U.S. Senate subcommittee hearings on the equal rights amendment. Male unionists or class-conscious workers in this period put their faith in collective bargaining and did not seek labor legislation for themselves, but endorsed it for women and child workers. This differentiation derived partly from male workers' belief in women's physical weakness and veneration of women's "place" in the home, partly from presumptions about women workers being difficult to organize, and also from the aim to keep women from competing for men's jobs. Male unionists tended to view wage-earning women first as women—potential or actual wives and mothers—and only secondarily as workers. For differing reasons women and men in the labor movement converged in their support of sex-based legislation: women because they saw special protection necessary to defend their stake in industry and in union organizations, limited as it was; men to hold at bay women's demands for equal entry into male-controlled union jobs and organizations.[13]

The arguments against the equal rights amendment offered by trade unionists and by such women's organizations as the League of Women Voters overlapped. They assumed that an equal rights amendment would invalidate sex-based labor laws or, at least, destine them for protracted argument in the courts, where judges had shown hostility to any state regulation of employer prerogatives. They insisted that the greatest good for the greatest number was served by protective labor laws. If sex-based legislation hampered some—as the NWP claimed, and could be shown true, for instance, in the case of women linotypists, who needed to work at night—then the proper tactic was to exempt some occupations, not to eliminate protective laws whole. They feared that state welfare legislation in place, such as widows' pensions, would also be at risk. They contended that a constitutional amendment was too undiscriminating an instrument: objectionable sex discriminations such as those concerning jury duty, inheritance rights, nationality, or child custody would be more efficiently and accurately eliminated by specific bills for specific instances. Sometimes, opponents claimed that the ERA took an unnecessarily federal approach, overriding states' rights, although here they were hardly consistent for many of them were at the same time advocating a constitutional amendment to prohibit child labor.

Against the ERA, spokeswomen cited evidence that wage-earning women wanted and valued labor legislation and that male workers, too, benefitted from limits on women's hours in factories where men and women worked at interdependent tasks. Before hours were legally limited, "we were 'free' and 'equal' to work long hours for starvation wages, or free to leave the job and starve!" WTUL leader Pauline Newman bitterly recalled. Dr. Alice Hamilton, pioneer of industrial medicine, saw the NWP as maintaining "a purely negative program, . . . holding down in their present condition of industrial slavery hundreds of thousands of women without doing anything to alleviate their lot."[14] Trade-unionist and Women's Bureau colleagues attacked the NWP's vision as callously class-biased, the thoughtless outlook of rich women, at best relevant to the experience of exceptional skilled workers or professionals. They regularly accused the NWP of being the unwitting tool (at best) or the paid servant of rapacious employers, although no proof of the latter was ever brought forward. They heard in the NWP program the voice of the ruling class and denounced the equal rights amendment as "class" legislation, by and for the bourgeoisie.[15]

Indeed, at the Women's Bureau Conference on Women in Industry in 1926, the NWP's opposition to sex-based labor legislation was echoed by the president of the National Association of Manufacturers, who declared that the "handful" of women in industry could take care of themselves and were not served by legislative "poultices." In this controversy, the positions also lent themselves to, and inevitably were colored by, male "allies" whose principal concerns dealt less with women's economic or legal protection or advancement than political priorities of their own. At the same conference the U.S. Secretary of Labor appointed by President Coolidge took the side of sex-based protective legislation, proclaiming that "The place fixed for women by God and Nature is a great place," and "wherever we see women at work we must see them in terms of motherhood." What he saw as the great danger of the age was the "increasing loss of the distinction between manliness and true femininity."[16]

Often, ERA opponents who supported sex-based labor legislation—including civic-minded middle-class women, social welfare reformers, government officials, and trade union men—appeared more concerned with workingwomen's motherhood than with economic justice. "Women who are wage earners, with one job in the factory and another in the home have little time and energy left to carry on the fight to better their economic status. They need the help of other women and they need labor laws," announced Mary Anderson. Dr. Hamilton declared that "the great inarticulate body of working women . . . are largely helpless, . . . [and] have very special needs which unaided they cannot attain. . . ."[17] Where NWP advocates had before their eyes women who were eager and robust, supporters of protective legislation saw women overburdened and vulnerable. The former claimed that protective laws penalized the strong; the latter claimed that the ERA would sacrifice the weak. The NWP looked at women as individuals and wanted to dislodge gender differentiation from the labor market. Their opponents looked at women as members of families—daughters, wives, mothers, and widows with family responsibilities—and believed that the promise of "mere equality" did not sufficiently take those relationships into account. The one side tacitly positing the independent professional woman as the paradigm, the other presuming the doubly burdened mother in industry or service, neither side distinguished nor addressed directly the situation of the fastest-growing sector of employed women, in white-collar jobs. At least half of the female labor force—those in manufacturing and in domestic and personal service—worked in taxing, menial jobs with long hours, unpleasant and often unhealthy conditions, very low pay, and rare opportunities for advancement. But in overall pattern women's employment was leaving these sectors and swelling in clerical, managerial, sales, and professional areas. White-collar workers were fewer than 18 percent of all women employed in 1900, but the proportion more than doubled by 1920 and by 1930 was 44 percent.[18]

The relation of sex-based legislation to women workers' welfare was more ambiguous and complicated than either side acknowledged. Such laws immediately benefitted far larger numbers of employed women than they hindered, but the laws also had a negative impact on women's overall economic opportunities, both immediately and in the long term. Sex segregation of the labor market was a very significant factor. In industries monopolizing women workers, where wages, conditions, and hours were more likely to be substandard, protective legislation helped to bring things up to standard. It was in more desirable crafts and trades more unusual for women workers, where skill levels and pay were likely to be higher—that is, where women needed to enter in order to improve their earnings and economic advancement—that sex-based protective legislation held women back. There, as a contemporary inquiry into the issue said, "the practice of enacting laws covering women alone appears to discourage their employment, and thereby fosters the prejudice against them." The segregation of women into low-paid, dead-end jobs that made protective laws for women workers necessary, was thus abetted by the legislation itself.[19]

By 1925, all but four states limited workingwomen's hours; eighteen states prescribed rest periods and meal hours; sixteen states prohibited night work in certain occupations; and thirteen had minimum wage regulations. Such regulation was passed not only because it served women workers, but also because employers, especially large corporate employers, began to see benefits in its stabilization of the labor market and control of unscrupulous competition. Although the National Association of Manufacturers, fixed on "liberty of contract," remained opposed, large employers of women accepted sex-based labor legislation on reasoning about "protection of the race," or could see advantages for themselves in it, or both. A vice-president of Filene's, a large department store in Boston, for instance, approved laws regulating the hours, wages, and conditions of women employees because "economies have been effected by the reduction of labor turnover; by reduction of the number of days lost through illness and accidents; and by increase in the efficiency of the working force as well as in the efficiency of management." He appreciated the legislation's maintaining standards as to hours, wages, and working conditions "throughout industry as a *whole*, thus preventing selfish interests from indulging in unfair competition by the exploitation of women. . . ."[20]

While the anti-ERA side was right in the utilitarian contention that protective laws meant the greatest good to the greatest number of women workers (at least in the short run), the pro-ERA side was also right that such laws hampered women's scope in the labor market and sustained the assumption that employment advantage was not of primary concern to women. Those who advocated sex-based laws were looking at the labor market as it was, trying to protect women in it, but thereby contributing to the perpetuation of existing inequalities. They envisaged wage-earning women as veritable beasts of burden. That group portrait supplanted the prior feminist image of wage-earning women as a vanguard of independent female personalities, as equal producers of the world's wealth. Its advocates did not see that their conception of women's needs helped to confirm women's second-class position in the economy. On the other hand, the ERA advocates who opposed sex-based "protections" were envisioning the labor market as it might be, trying to ensure women the widest opportunities in that imagined arena, and thereby blinking at existing exploitation. They did not admit to the vulnerabilities that sex-based legislation addressed, while they overestimated what legal equality might do to unchain women from the economic stranglehold of the domestic stereotype.

Women on both sides of the controversy, however, saw themselves as legatees of suffragism and feminism, intending to defend the value of women's economic roles, to prevent economic exploitation of women and to open the doors to economic opportunity. A struggle over the very word feminism, which the NWP had embraced, became part of the controversy. For "us even to use the word feminist," contended Women's Trade Union League leader Ethel Smith, "is to invite from the extremists a challenge to our authenticity." Detractors in the WTUL and Women's Bureau called the NWP "ultra" or "extreme" feminists. Mary Anderson considered herself "a good feminist" but objected that "over-articulate theorists were attempting to solve the working women's problems on a purely feministic basis with the working women's own voice far less adequately heard." Her own type of feminist was moderate and practical, Anderson declared; the others, putting the "woman question" above all other questions, were extreme and abstract. The bitterness was compounded by a conflict of personalities and tactics dragged on from the suffrage years. Opponents of the ERA, deeply resenting having to oppose something called equal rights, maligned the NWP as "pernicious," women who "discard[ed] all ethics and fair play," an "insane crowd" who espoused "a kind of hysterical feminism with a slogan for a program."[21] Their critiques fostered public perception of feminism as a sectarian and impracticable doctrine unrelated to real life and blind to injustices besides sex inequality. By the end of the 1920s women outside the NWP rarely made efforts to reclaim the term feminist for themselves, and the meaning of the term was depleted.

Forced into theorizing by this controversy, not prepared as philosophers or legal theorists, spokeswomen on either side in the 1920s were grappling with definitions of women's rights as compared to men's that neither the legal nor economic system was designed to accommodate. The question whether equality required women to have the same rights as men, or different rights, could not be answered without delving into definitions. Did "equality" pertain to opportunity, treatment, or outcome?[22] Should "difference" be construed to mean separation, discrimination, protection, privilege—or assault on the very standard that the male was the human norm?[23]

Opponents of the ERA believed that sex-based legislation was necessary because of women's biological and social roles as mothers. They claimed that "The inherent differences are permanent. Women will always need many laws different from those needed by men"; "Women as such, whether or not they are mothers present or prospective, will always need protective legislation"; "The working mother is handicapped by her own nature."[24] Their approach stressed maternal nature and inclination as well as conditioning, and implied that the sexual division of labor was eternal.

The NWP's approach, on the other hand, presupposed that women's differentiation from men in the law and the labor market was a particular, social-historical, and not necessary or inevitable construction. The sexual division of labor arose from archaic custom, enshrined in employer and employee attitudes and written in the law. The NWP approach assumed that wives and mothers as well as unencumbered women would want and should have open access to jobs and professions. NWP proponents imagined that the sexual division of labor (in the family and the marketplace) would change if women would secure the same rights as men and have free access to wage-earning. Their view made a fragile potential into a necessary fact. They assumed that women's wage-earning would, by its very existence, challenge the sexual division of labor, and that it would provide the means for women's economic independence—although neither of these tenets was necessarily being realized.

Wage-earning women's experience in the 1910s and 1920s, as documented by the Women's Bureau, showed that the sexual division of labor was budged only very selectively and marginally by women's gainful employment. Most women's wages did not bring them economic independence; women earned as part of a plan for family support (as men did, though that was rarely stressed). Contrary to the NWP's feminist visions, in those places in the nation where the highest proportions of wives and mothers worked for pay, the sexual division of labor was most oppressively in place. To every child growing up in the region of Southern textile and tobacco mills, where wives and mothers worked more "jobs" at home and in the factory than any other age or status group—and earned less—the sexual division of labor appeared no less prescriptive and burdensome than it had before women earned wages.[25]

Critiques of the NWP and its ERA as "abstract" or "extreme" or "fanatical" represented the gap between feminist tenets and harsh social reality as an oversight of the NWP, a failure to adjust their sights. Even more sympathetic critics, such as one Southern academic, asked rhetorically, "Do the feminists see in the tired and haggard faces of young waitresses, who spend seventy hours a week of hard work in exchange for a few dollars to pay for food and clothing, a deceptive mask of the noble spirit within?" She answered herself, "Surely it is not an increasing army of jaded girls and spent women that pours every day from factory and shop that the leaders of the feminist movement seek. But the call for women to make all labor their province can mean nothing more. They would free women from the rule of men only to make them greater slaves to the machines of industry."[26] Indeed, the exploitation of female service and industrial workers at "cheap" wages cruelly parodied the feminist notion that gainful employment represented an assertion of independence (just as the wifely duties required of a secretary parodied the feminist expectation that wage-earning would challenge the sexual division of labor and reopen definitions of feminity). What such critics were observing was the distance between the potential for women's wage-earning to challenge the sexual division of labor, and the social facts of gender and class hierarchy that clamped down on that challenge.

Defenders of sex-based protective legislation, trying to acknowledge women's unique reproductive endowments and social obligations, were grappling with problems so difficult they would still be present more than half a century later. Their immediate resolution was to portray women's "difference" in merely customary terms. "Average American women prefer to make a home for husbands and children to anything else," Mary Anderson asserted in defense of her position. "They would rather fulfill this normal function than go into the business world."[27] Keeping alive a critique of the class division of wealth, protective legislation advocates lost sight of the need to challenge the very sexual division of labor that was the root of women's "handicap" or "helplessness." As compared to the NWP's emphasis on the historical and social construction of gender roles, advocates of sex-based protective legislation echoed customary public opinion in proposing that motherhood and wage-earning should be mutually exclusive. They easily found allies among such social conservatives as the National Council of Catholic Women, whose representatives testified against the ERA because it "seriously menaced . . . the unity of the home and family life" and contravened the "essential differences in rights and duties" of the two sexes which were the "result of natural law." Edging into plain disapproval of mothers of young children who earned, protective legislation supporters became more prescriptive, less flexible, than wage-earning mothers themselves, for whom cash recognition of their labor was very welcome. "Why should not a married woman work [for pay], if a single one does?" demanded a mill worker who came to the Southern Summer School for Women Workers. "What would men think if they were told that a married man should not work? If we women would not be so submissive and take everything for granted, if we would awake and stand up for our rights, this world would be a better place to live in, at least it would be better for the women. . . ."[28]

The onset of the Depression in many ways worsened the ERA controversy, for the one side thought protective legislation all the more crucial when need drove women to take any jobs available, and the other side argued that protective legislation prevented women from competing for what jobs there were. In the 1930s it became clear that the labor movement's and League of Women Voters' opposition to the equal rights amendment ran deeper than concern for sex-based legislation as an "entering wedge." The Fair Labor Standards Act of 1938 mandated wages and hours regulation for all workers, and the U.S. Supreme Court upheld it in 1941; but the labor movement and the LWV still opposed the ERA. Other major women's organizations, however—most importantly the National Federation of Business and Professional Women's Clubs and the General Federation of Women's Clubs—and the national platforms of both the Republican [Party] and the Democratic Party endorsed the ERA by 1944.[29]

We generally learn "winners'" history—not the history of lost causes. If the ERA passed by Congress in 1972 had achieved ratification by 1982, perhaps historians of women would read the trajectory of the women's movement from 1923 to the present as a steady upward curve, and award the NWP unqualified original insight. The failure of the ERA this time around (on new, but not unrelated, grounds) compels us to see the longer history of equal rights in its true complexity.[30] The ERA battle of the 1920s seared into memory the fact of warring outlooks among women while it illustrated the inevitable intermeshing of women's legal and political rights with their economic situations. If the controversy testified to the difficulty of protecting women in the economic arena while opening opportunities to them, even more fundamentally the debate brought into question the NWP's premise that the articulation of sex discrimination—or the call for equal rights—would arouse all women to mobilize as a group. What kind of a group were women when their occupational and social and other loyalties were varied, when not all women viewed "women's" interests, or what constituted sex "discrimination," the same way? The ideological dimensions of that problem cross-cut both class consciousness and gender identity. The debate's intensity, both then and now, measured how fundamental was the revision needed if policies and practices of economic and civic life deriving from a male norm were to give full scope to women—and to women of all sorts.

Notes

1. A good introduction to the issue of alliances in the nineteenth-century women's movement, and an essential text on the mid-ninteenth-century split, is Ellen Carol DuBois, *Feminism and Suffrage: The Emergence of an Independent Women's Movement, 1848–1869* (Ithaca, N.Y.: Cornell, 1978).

2. See Leslie Woodcock Tentler, *Wage-Earning Women: Industrial Work and Family Life in the U.S., 1900–1930* (New York: Oxford University Press, 1979), chap. 1, on industrially employed women's wages, keyed below subsistence.

3. On feminists in the final decade of the suffrage campaign, see Nancy F. Cott, *The Grounding of Modern Feminism* (New Haven: Yale University Press, 1987), pp. 23–66.

4. For more detailed discussion of the February 1921 convention, see Nancy F. Cott, "Feminist Politics in the 1920s: The National Woman's Party," *Journal of American History* 71, no. 1 (June 1984).

5. Paul to Jane Norman Smith, Nov. 29, 1921, folder 110, J. N. Smith Collection, Schlesinger Library (hereafter SL). See NWP correspondence of Feb.–Mar. 1921 in the microfilm collection "The National Woman's Party, 1913–1974" (Microfilm Corp. of America), reels #5–7 (hereafter NWP with reel no.), and Cott, *Grounding,* pp. 66–74, 120–25, for more detail.

In Wisconsin, prominent NWP suffragist Mabel Raef Putnam put together a coalition which successfully lobbied through the first state equal rights bill early in 1921. This legislation granted women the same rights and privileges as men *except for* "the special protection and privileges which they now enjoy for the general welfare." . . .

6. Maud Wood Park, *Front Door Lobby,* ed. Edna Stantial (Boston: Beacon Press, 1960), p. 23.

7. Historians' treatments of women's organizations' differing views on the ERA in the 1920s include William N. O'Neill, *Everyone Was Brave* (Chicago: Quadrangle, 1969), pp. 274–94; J. Stanley Lemons, *The Woman Citizen: Social Feminism in the 1920s* (Urbana: University of Illinois Press, 1973), pp. 184–99; William Chafe, *The American Woman: Her Changing Social, Economic and Political Roles* (New York: Oxford University Press, 1972), pp. 112–32; Sheila M. Rothman, *Woman's Proper Place: A History of Changing Ideals and Practices, 1870 to the Present* (New York: Basic Books, 1978), pp. 153–65; Susan Becker, *Origins of the Equal Rights Amendment: American Feminism between the Wars* (Westport, Conn.:

Greenwood Press, 1981), pp. 121–51; Alice Kessler-Harris, *Out to Work: A History of Wage-Earning Women in the U.S.* (New York: Oxford University Press, 1982), pp. 194–95, 205–12; Judith Sealander, *As Minority Becomes Majority* (Westport, Conn.: Greenwood Press, 1983). Fuller documentation of my reading of both sides can be found in Cott, *Grounding*, pp. 122–29 and accompanying notes.

8. "Conference on So-Called 'Equal Rights' Amendment Proposed by the National Woman's Party Dec. 4, 1921," ts. NWTUL Papers, microfilm reel 2. . . .

9. NWP National Council minutes, Dec. 17, 1921, Feb. 14, 1922, Apr. 11, 1922, NWP #114. To the NWP inner circle Laughlin's point was borne out by a 1923 ruling in Wisconsin, where, despite the Equal Rights Bill, the attorney general declined to strike down a 1905 law which prohibited women from being employed in the state legislature. He likened the prohibition to an hours-limitation law, because legislative service required "very long and often unreasonable hours." Alice Paul read his decision as "an extremely effective argument against" drafting equal rights bills with exemptions for sex-based protective legislation. Anita L. Pollitzer to Mrs. Jane Norman Smith, Jan. 5, 1922, folder 110, and Paul to Jane Norman Smith, Feb. 20, 1923, folder 111, J. N. Smith Coll.

10. National Council Minutes, June 19, 1923, NWP #114. Before 1923 the ERA went through scores of drafts, recorded in part F, NWP #116. Versions akin to the suffrage amendment—e.g., "Equal rights with men shall not be denied to women or abridged on account of sex or marriage . . ."—were considered in 1922, but not until 1943 was the amendment introduced into Congress in the form "Equality of rights under the law shall not be denied or abridged by the United States or by any state on account of sex," modeled on the Nineteenth Amendment, which in turn was modeled on the Fifteenth Amendment.

11. Quotation from Edith Houghton Hooker, Editor's Note, *Equal Rights* (the NWP monthly publication), Dec. 22, 1928, p. 365. See Cott, *Grounding*, pp. 75–82.

12. The two most seen on NWP platforms were Josephine Casey, a former ILGWU organizer, suffrage activist, later a bookbinder, and Mary Murray, a Brooklyn Railway employee who had resigned from her union in 1920 to protest its acceptance of laws prohibiting night work for women.

13. Kessler-Harris, *Out to Work*, 200–5; and "Problems of Coalition-Building: Women and Trade Unions in the 1920s," in *Women, Work and Protest*, ed. Ruth Milkman (Boston: Routledge and Kegan Paul, 1985), esp. p. 132.

14. . . . More extensive documentation of the debate can be found in the notes in Cott, *Grounding*, pp. 325–26.

15. Kessler-Harris, *Out to Work*, pp. 189–94, reveals ambivalent assessments of labor legislation by ordinary wage-earning women.

16. Printed release from the National Association of Manufacturers, "Defend American Womanhood by Protecting Their Homes, Edgerton Tells Women in Industry," Jan. 19, 1926, in folder 1118, and ts. speech by James Davis, U.S. Secretary of Labor, Jan. 18, 1926, in folder 1117, Box 71, Mary Van Kleeck Collection, Sophia Smith Collection, Smith College.

17. Mary Anderson, "Should There Be Labor Laws for Women? Yes," *Good Housekeeping*, Sept. 1925. . . .

18. See Valerie K. Oppenheimer, *The Female Labor Force in the U.S.* (Westport, Conn.: Greenwood Press, 1976), pp. 3, 149; Lois Scharf, *To Work and to Wed* (Westport, Conn.: Greenwood Press, 1980), pp. 15–16: Winifred Wandersee, *Women's Work and Family Values 1920–1940* (Cambridge Mass.: Harvard, 1981), pp. 85, 89.

19. Elizabeth F. Baker, "At the Crossroads in the Legal Protection of Women in Industry," *Annals of the American Academy of Political and Social Science* 143 (May 1929):277. . . .

Recently historians have stressed the regressive potential of sex-based protective laws. See . . . Nancy Schrom Dye, *As Equals and as Sisters: Feminism, Unionism and the Women's Trade Union League of New York* (Columbia: University of Missouri Press, 1980), pp. 159–60; Olive Banks, *Faces of Feminism: A Study of Feminism as a Social Movement* (New York: St. Martin's, 1981), p. 115; Judith A. Baer, *The Chains of Protection: The Judicial Response to Women's Labor Legislation* (Westport, Conn.: Greenwood Press, 1978). . . .

20. T. K. Cory to Mary Wiggins, Nov. 10, 1922, folder 378, Consumers' League of Mass. Coll., SL. See n. 16, above.

21. Ethel M. Smith, "What Is Sex Equality and What Are the Feminists Trying to Accomplish?" *Century Monthly Magazine* 118 (May 1929):96. . . . Mary Anderson, *Woman at Work: The Autobiography of Mary Anderson as Told to Mary N. Winslow* (Minneapolis: University of Minnesota Press, 1951), p. 168.

22. There is a valuable discussion of differing meanings for "equality" between the sexes in Jean Bethke Elshtain, "The Feminist Movement and the Question of Equality," *Polity* 7 (Summer 1975): 452–77.

23. This is, of course, the set of issues that has preoccupied feminist lawyers in the 1980s. For a sense of the recent debate, see, e.g., Wendy Williams, "The Equality Crisis: Some Reflections on Culture, Courts, and Feminism," *Women's Rights Law Reporter* 7, no. 3 (Spring 1982):175–200; Nadine Taub, "Will Equality Require More Than Assimilation, Accommodation or Separation from the Existing Social Structure?" *Rutgers Law Review* 37 (1985):825–44; Lucinda Finley, "Transcending Equality Theory: A Way out of the Maternity and the Workplace Debate," *Columbia Law Review* 86, no. 6 (Oct. 1986): 1118–82; and Joan Williams, "Deconstructing Gender," *Michigan Law Review* 87, no. 4 (Feb. 1989):797–845.

24. Florence Kelley, "Shall Women Be Equal before the Law?" (debate with Elsie Hill), *Nation* 114 (Apr. 12, 1922):421. . . .

25. Dolores Janiewski, *Sisterhood Denied: Race, Gender and Class in a New South Community* (Philadelphia: Temple University Press, 1985), pp. 30–32, 127–50; Table 26 (p. 134) shows less than 40% of Durham women above age 12 engaged only in unpaid housework.

26. Guion G. Johnson, "Feminism and the Economic Independence of Woman," *Journal of Social Forces* 3 (May 4, 1925):615; cf. Tentler, *Wage-Earning Women*, esp. pp. 25, 45–46, and Wandersee, *Women's Work*, on motivations and psychological results of women's wage-earning.

27. Mary Anderson quoted in unidentified newspaper clipping, Nov. 25, 1925, in folder 349, Bureau of Vocational Information Collection, SL. Cf. Ethel Smith's objection that the NWP's feminism required that "men and women must have exactly the same things, and be treated in all respects as if they were alike," as distinguished from her own view that "men and women must each have the things best suited to their respective needs, which are not all the time, nor in all things, alike." Smith, "What Is Sex Equality?", p. 96.

28. National Council of Catholic Women testimony at U.S. Congress (House of Representatives) subcommittee of Committee on the Judiciary, hearings, 1925, quoted in Robin Whittemore, "Equality vs. Protection: Debate on the Equal Rights Amendment, 1923–1937" (M.A. thesis, Boston University, 1981), p. 19; mill worker quoted in Mary Frederickson, "The Southern Summer School for Women Workers," *Southern Exposure* 4 (Winter 1977):73. See also Maurine Greenwald, "Working-Class Feminism and the Family Wage Ideal: The Seattle Debate on Married Women's Right to Work, 1914–1920," *Journal of American History* 76, no. 1 (June 1989):118–49.

29. For the history of the NWP in the 1930s and 1940s see Becker, *Origins of the Equal Rights Amendment*. On the initiatives of the National Federation of Business and Professional Women and other groups to forward the equal rights amendment, see Lemons, *Woman Citizen*, pp. 202–4, and the papers of Lena Madesin Phillips and Florence Kitchelt at SL.

30. Jane L. Mansbridge's astute analysis, *Why We Lost the ERA* (Chicago: University of Chicago Press, 1986), is essential reading on the failed 1970s campaign for ratification.

JOAN JACOBS BRUMBERG

Fasting Girls: The Emerging Ideal of Slenderness in American Culture

Although anorexia nervosa is generally considered a modern disease, appetite control has long been an important dimension of female experience. Joan Jacobs Brumberg's pioneering study of anorexia nervosa traces changing cultural pressure on women to control their appetite. Exploring the links between food and femininity in the nineteenth century, Brumberg found that by 1890 thinness had become a way in which young privileged women could distance themselves from their working-class counterparts. More important, food preferences and thin bodies also sent moral and aesthetic messages. The young woman whose frail, delicate frame demonstrated her rejection of all carnal appetites more closely approached the Victorian ideal of femininity than did her more robust counterpart whose heavier physique signaled sexual craving. The twentieth century brought additional pressures to control body weight, according to Brumberg, with the development of scientific nutrition and the standard sizing of clothes. By 1920, fat had become a moral issue. Combined with social changes having to do with food and sexuality occurring in the 1960s, the stage was set for the epidemic of eating disorders evident in the 1980s and 1990s. What evidence is there of the persistence of these disorders in the twenty-first century? What is it that we expect our bodies to convey?

Excerpted from *Fasting Girls: The Emergence of Anorexia Nervosa as a Modern Disease* by Joan Jacobs Brumberg (Cambridge, Mass.: Harvard University Press, 1988). Reprinted by permission of the author.

Within the first two decades of the twentieth century, even before the advent of the flapper, the voice of American women revealed that the female struggle with weight was under way and was becoming intensely personal. As early as 1907 an *Atlantic Monthly* article described the reaction of a woman trying on a dress she had not worn for over a year: "The gown was neither more [n]or less than anticipated. But I . . . *the fault was on me* . . . I was more! Gasping I hooked it together. The gown was hopeless, and I . . . I am fat."[1] . . . By the twentieth century . . . overweight in women was not only a physical liability, it was a character flaw and a social impediment.

Early in the century elite American women began to take body weight seriously as fat became an aesthetic liability for those who followed the world of haute couture. Since the mid-nineteenth century wealthy Americans—the wives of J. P. Morgan, Cornelius Vanderbilt, and Harry Harkness Flagler, for instance—had traveled to Paris to purchase the latest creations from couturier collections such as those on view at Maison Worth on the famed rue de la Paix. The couturier was not just a dressmaker who made clothes for an individual woman; rather, the couturier fashioned "a look" or a collection of dresses for an abstraction—the stylish woman. In order to be stylish and wear couturier clothes, a woman's body had to conform to the dress rather than the dress to the body, as had been the case when the traditional dressmaker fitted each garment.[2] . . .

In 1908 the world of women's fashion was revolutionized by Paul Poiret, whose new silhouette was slim and straight. . . . Almost immediately women of style began to purchase new kinds of undergarments that would make Poiret's look possible; for example, the traditional hourglass corset was cast aside for a rubber girdle to retract the hips.

After World War I the French continued to set the fashion standard for style-conscious American women. In 1922 Jeanne Lanvin's chemise, a straight frock with a simple bateau neckline, was transformed by Gabrielle Chanel into the uniform of the flapper. Chanel dropped the waistline to the hips and began to expose more of the leg: in 1922 she moved her hemlines to midcalf, and in 1926–27 the ideal hem was raised to just below the knee. In order to look good in Chanel's fashionable little dress, its wearer had to think not only about the appearance of her legs but about the smoothness of her form.[3] Women who wore the flapper uniform turned to flattening brassieres constructed of shoulder straps and a single band of material that encased the body from chest to waist. In 1914 a French physician commented on the revised dimensions of women's bodies: "Nowadays it is not the fashion to be corpulent; the proper thing is to have a slight, graceful figure far removed from embonpoint, and *a fortiori* from obesity. For once, the physician is called upon to interest himself in the question of feminine aesthetics."[4]

The slenderized fashion image of the French was picked up and promoted by America's burgeoning ready-to-wear garment industry.[5] Stimulated by the popularity of the Gibson girl and the shirtwaist craze of the 1890s, ready-to-wear production in the United States accelerated in the first two decades of the twentieth century. (See p. 463.) Chanel's chemise dress was a further boon to the garment industry. Because of its simple cut, the chemise was easy to copy and produce, realities that explain its quick adoption as the uniform of the 1920s. According to a 1923 *Vogue,* the American ready-to-wear industry successfully democratized French fashion: "Today, the mode which originates in Paris is a factor in the lives of women of every rank, from the highest to the lowest."[6]

In order to market ready-to-wear clothing, the industry turned in the 1920s to standard sizing, an innovation that put increased emphasis on personal body size and gave legitimacy to the idea of a normative size range. For women, shopping for ready-to-wear clothes in the bustling department stores of the early twentieth century fostered heightened concern about body size.[7] With a dressmaker, every style was theoretically available to every body; with standard sizing, items of clothing could be identified as desirable, only to be rejected on the grounds of fit. (For women the cost of altering a ready-made garment was an "add-on"; for men it was not.) Female figure flaws became a source of frustration and embarrassment, not easily hidden from those who accompanied the shopper or from salesclerks. Experiences in department-store dressing rooms created a host of new anxieties for women and girls who could not fit into stylish clothing. . . .

Ironically, standard sizing created an unexpected experience of frustration in a marketplace that otherwise was offering a continually expansive opportunity for gratification via purchasable goods. Because many manufacturers of stylish women's garments did not make clothing in large sizes, heavy women were at the greatest disadvantage. In addition to the moral [disgrace] of overweight, the standardization of garment production precluded fat women's participation in the mainstream of fashion. This situation became worse as the century progressed. Fashion photography was professionalized, a development that paralleled the growth of modern advertising, and models became slimmer both to compensate for the distortions of the camera and to accommodate the new merchandising canon—modern fashion was best displayed on a lean body.[8]

The appearance in 1918 of America's first best-selling weight-control book confirmed that weight was a source of anxiety among women and that fat was out of fashion. *Diet and Health with a Key to the Calories* by Lulu Hunt Peters was directed at a female audience and based on the assumption that most readers wanted to lose rather than gain weight.... "You should know and also use the word calorie as frequently, or more frequently, than you use the words foot, yard, quart, gallon and so forth. . . . Hereafter you are going to eat calories of food. Instead of saying one slice of bread, or a piece of pie, you will say 100 calories of bread, 350 calories of pie."[9]

Peters' book was popular because it was personal and timely. Her 1918 appeal was related to food shortages caused by the exigencies of the war in Europe. Peters told her readers that it was "more important than ever to reduce" and recommended the formation of local Watch Your Weight Anti-Kaiser Classes. "There are hundreds of thousands of individuals all over America who are hoarding food," she wrote. "They have vast amounts of this valuable commodity stored away in their own anatomy." In good-humored fashion Peters portrayed her own calories counting as both an act of patriotism and humanitarianism:

> I am reducing and the money that I can save will help keep a child from starving . . . [I am explaining to my friends] that for every pang of hunger we feel we can have a double joy, that of knowing we are saving worse pangs in some little children, and that of knowing that for every pang we feel we lose a pound. A pang's a pound the world around we'll say.[10]

But Peters showed herself to be more than simply an informative and patriotic physician. Confessing that she once weighed as much as 200 pounds, the author also understood that heavy women were ashamed of their bulk and unlikely to reveal their actual weight. Peters observed that it was not a happy situation for fat women. "You are viewed with distrust, suspicion, and even aversion," she told her overweight readers. . . .

Peters' book was among the first to articulate the new secular credo of physical denial: modern women suffered to be beautiful (thin) rather than pious. Peters' language and thinking reverberated with references to religious ideas of temptation and sin. For the modern female dieter, sweets, particularly chocolate, were the ultimate temptation. Eating chocolate violated the morality of the dieter and her dedication to her ideal, a slim body. Peters joked about her cravings ("My idea of heaven is a place with me and mine on a cloud of whipped cream") but she was adamant about the fact that indulgence must ultimately be paid for. "If you think you will die unless you have some chocolate creams [go on a] *debauch*," she advised. "'Eat 10 or so' but then *repent* with a 50-calorie dinner of bouillon and crackers." (Italics added.)[11]

Although the damage done by chocolate creams could be mediated by either fasting or more rigid dieting, Peters explained that there was a psychological cost in yielding to the temptation of candy or rich desserts. Like so many modern dieters, Peters wrote about the issue of guilt followed by redemption through parsimonious eating: "Every supposed pleasure in sin [eating] will furnish more than its equivalent of pain [dieting]." But appetite control was not only a question of learning to delay gratification, it was also an issue of self-esteem. "You will be tempted quite frequently, and you will have to choose whether you will enjoy yourself hugely in the twenty minutes or so that you will be consuming the excess calories, or whether you will dislike yourself cordially for the two or three days you lose by your lack of will power." For Peters dieting had as much to do with the mind as with the body. "There is a great deal of psychology to reducing," she wrote astutely.[12] In fact, with the popularization of the concept of calorie counting, physical features once regarded as natural—such as appetite and body weight—were designated as objects of conscious control. The notion of weight control through restriction of calories implied that . . . overweight resulted solely from lack of control; to be a fat woman constituted a failure of personal morality.

The tendency to talk about female dieting as a moral issue was particularly strong among the popular beauty experts, that is, those in the fashion and cosmetics industry who sold scientific advice on how to become and stay beautiful. Many early-twentieth-century beauty culturists, including Grace Peckham Murray, Helena Rubenstein, and Hazel Bishop, studied chemistry and medical specialties such as dermatology. The creams and lotions they created, as well as the electrical gadgets they promoted, were intended to bring the findings of modern chemistry and physiology to the problem of female beauty. Nevertheless, women could not rely entirely on scientifically achieved results. The beauty experts also preached the credo of self-denial: to be beautiful, most women must suffer.

Because they regarded fat women as an affront to their faith, some were willing to criminalize as well as medicalize obesity. In 1902 *Vogue* speculated, "To judge by the efforts of the majority of women to attain slender and sylph-like proportions, one would fancy it a crime to be fat." By 1918 the message was more distinct: "There is one crime against the modern ethics of beauty which is unpardonable; far better it is to commit any number of petty crimes than to be guilty of the sin of growing fat." By 1930 there was no turning back. Helena Rubenstein, a high priestess of the faith, articulated in *The Art of Feminine Beauty* the moral and aesthetic dictum that would govern the lives of subsequent generations of women: "An abundance of fat is something repulsive and not in accord with the principles that rule our conception of the beautiful.[13] . . .

In adolescence fat was considered a particular liability because of the social strains associated with that stage of life. In the 1940s articles with titles such as "What to Do about the Fat Child at Puberty," "Reducing the Adolescent," and "Should the Teens Diet?" captured the rising interest in adolescent weight control.[14] Women's magazines, reflecting the concerns of mothers anxious to save their daughters from social ostracism, for the first time promoted diets for young girls. According to the *Ladies' Home Journal:* "Appearance plays too important a part in a girl's life not to have her grow up to be beauty-conscious. Girls should be encouraged to take an interest in their appearance when they are very young."[15] . . . Adolescent weight control was also promoted by popular magazines hoping to sell products to young women. . . . *Seventeen's* adoption of the cause of weight control confirmed that slimness was a critical dimension of adolescent beauty and that a new constituency, high school girls, was learning how to diet. From 1944 [when it was founded] to 1948, *Seventeen* had published a full complement of articles on nutrition but almost nothing on weight control. Following the mode of earlier home economists and scientific nutritionists, the magazine had presented basic information about food groups and the importance of each in the daily diet; balance but not calories had been the initial focus. In 1948, however, *Seventeen* proclaimed overweight a medical problem and began educating its young readers about calories and the psychology of eating. Adolescent girls were warned against using eating as a form of emotional expression (do not "pamper your blues" with food) and were given practical tips on how to avoid food bingeing. No mention was made of the new "diet pills" (amphetamines) introduced in the 1930s for clinical treatment of obesity. Instead, teenagers were encouraged to go on "sensible" and "well-rounded" diets of between 1,200 and 1,800 calories. By the 1950s advertisements for "diet foods" such as Ry-Krisp were offering assistance as they told the readership "Nobody Loves a Fat Girl."[16] Girls, much as adult women, were expected to tame the natural appetite.

Although adolescent girls were consistently warned against weight reduction without medical supervision, dieting was always cast as a worthwhile endeavor with transforming powers. "Diets can do wonderful things. When dispensed or approved by your physician . . . all you have to do is follow whither the chart leads."[17] The process of metamorphosis from fat to thin always provided a narrative of uplift and interest. "The Fattest Girl in the Class" was the autobiographical account of Jane, an obese girl who, after suffering the social stigma associated with teenage overweight, went on a diet and found happiness.[18] Being thin was tied to attractiveness, popularity with the opposite sex, and self-esteem—all primary ingredients in adolescent culture. Nonfiction accounts of "make-overs" became a popular formula in all the beauty magazines of the postwar period and provided a tantalizing fantasy of psychological and spiritual transformation for mature and adolescent women alike.[19]

The popularization of adolescent female weight control in the postwar era is a prime component of the modern dieting story and a critical factor in explaining anorexia nervosa as we know it today. . . . Since the 1960s the dieting imperative has intensified in two noticeable and important ways. . . . First, the ideal female body size has become considerably slimmer. After a brief flirtation with full-breasted, curvaceous female figures in the politically conservative postwar recovery of the 1950s, our collective taste returned to an ideal of extreme thinness and an androgynous, if not childlike, figure.[20] A series of well-known studies point to the declining weight since the 1950s of fashion models, Miss America contestants, and *Playboy* centerfolds.[21] Neither bosoms, hips, nor buttocks are currently in fashion as young and old alike attempt to meet the new aesthetic standard. A Bloomingdale's ad posits, "Bean lean, slender as the night, narrow as an arrow, pencil thin, get the point?"[22] It is appropriate to recall Annette Kellerman who, at 5 feet 3¾ inches and 137 pounds, epitomized the body beautiful of 1918. Obviously, our cultural tolerance for body fat has diminished over the intervening years.

Second, notably since the middle to late 1970s, a new emphasis on physical fitness and athleticism has intensified cultural pressures on the individual for control and mastery of the body. For women this means that fitness has been added to slimness as a criterion of perfection.[23] Experts on the subject, such as Jane Fonda, encourage women to strive for a lean body with musculature. The incredible popularity among women of aerobics, conditioning programs, and jogging does testify to the satisfactions that come with gaining physical strength through self-discipline, but it also expresses our current urgency about the physical body. Many who are caught up in the exercise cult equate physical fitness and slimness with a higher moral state. . . . Compulsive exercising and chronic dieting have [thus] been joined as twin obsessions. . . . [In the] 1980s clinical reports and autobiographical statements show a clear-cut pattern of anorexic patients who exercise with ritualistic intensity. How much one runs and how little one eats is the prevailing moral calculus in present-day anorexia nervosa. . . .

The proliferation of diet and exercise regimens in the past decade, although an important context for understanding the increase in anorexia nervosa, is not the whole story. For a more complete explanation we must turn to some other recent social changes, keeping in mind that no one factor has caused the contemporary problem. Rather, it is the nature of our economic and cultural environment, interacting with individual and family characteristics, which exacerbates the social and emotional insecurities that put today's young women at increasing risk for anorexia nervosa. Two very basic social transformations are relevant to the problem: one has to do with food; the other, with new expectations between the sexes.

Since World War II, and especially in the last two decades, middle-class Americans have experienced a veritable revolution in terms of how and what we eat, as well as how we think about eating.[24] The imperatives of an expanding capitalist society have generated extraordinary technological and marketing innovations, which in turn have transformed food itself, expanded our repertoire of foods, and affected the ways in which we consume them. Even though much contemporary food is characterized by elaborate processing and conservation techniques that actually reduce and flatten distinctive textures and flavors, the current array of food choices seems to constitute an endless smorgasbord of new and different tastes. [Since] the 1980s an individual in an urban center looking for a quick lunch [has been] able to choose from tacos with guacamole and salsa, hummus and falafel in pita, sushi, tortellini, quiche, and pad thai—along with more traditional "American" fare such as hamburgers. Thirty years ago this diversified international menu was as unknown to most Americans as were many of the food products used to create it. . . . As a consequence of [the expansion of our food repertoire], we are faced with an abundance of food which, in our obesophobic society, necessitates ever greater self-control. . . . It is no wonder, then, that we talk so incessantly about food and dieting.

The food revolution is a matter of ideas and manners as much as technology and markets. . . . In our society food is chosen and eaten not merely on the basis of hunger. It is a commonplace to observe that contemporary advertising connects food to sociability, status, and sexuality. In an affluent society, in particular, where eating appears to involve considerable individual choice, food is regarded as an important analogue of the self.

In the 1960s, for example, many young people in the counterculture gave up goods associated with their bourgeois upbringing and turned instead to a diet of whole grains, unprocessed foods, and no meat. This new diet made a statement about personal and political values and became a way of separating one generation from another. . . . In the 1980s, the extent to which the choice of cuisine dominates and defines the sophisticated life-style [among well-to-do urbanites] is reflected in a recent *New Yorker* cartoon, which shows a young professional couple after a dinner party given by friends. In complete seriousness they say to each other, "We could get close with David and Elizabeth if they didn't put béarnaise sauce on everything."[25] The anorectic is obviously not alone in her use of food and eating as a means of self-definition. There are many others who internalize the dictum "You are what you eat"—or, for that matter, what you don't eat.[26]

Along with the expansion of our food repertoire and our extraordinary attention to food selection, the eating context has changed. Eating is being desocialized. In American society today, more and more food is being consumed away from the family table or any other fixed center of sociability. This process began in the postwar period with the introduction of convenience foods and drive-in restaurants, precursors of the fast-food chains that now constitute a $45-billion-a-year industry. . . . Americans [now] eat everywhere—in the classroom; in theaters, libraries, and museums; on the street; at their desks; on the phone; in hot tubs; in cars while driving. . . . Signs saying "no food and drink," infrequent in other parts of the world, adorn our public buildings, a clear sign of our pattern of vagabond eating.[27]

On college and university campuses, where eating disorders are rampant, the situation is exaggerated. By the early 1970s most undergraduate students were no longer required to take any sit-down meals at fixed times in college dormitories. . . . Typically, students frequent a series of university cafeterias or commercial off-campus restaurants where they can obtain breakfast, lunch, or dinner at any time of the day. Some campus food plans allow unlimited amounts, a policy that fuels the behavior of the bulimic: "I used to go to Contract, eat a whole bunch of stuff, go to the bathroom, throw it up, come back, eat again, throw it up, eat again."[28] In addition, the availability of nearly any kind of food at any time contributes to a pattern of indiscriminate eating. Traditions of food appropriateness—that is, that certain foods are eaten at particular times of the day or in a certain sequence—disappear in this unstructured climate. Thus, an ice-cream cone, a carbonated soft drink, and a bagel constitute an easy popular "meal" that may be eaten at any time of day. Most colleges and the surrounding communities have made provisions to gratify student appetites no matter what the hour. Snack bars and vending machines adorn nearly every free alcove in classroom buildings and residence halls; pizza and Chinese food are delivered hot in the middle of the night.

In a setting where eating is so promiscuous, it is no wonder that food habits become problematic. This is not to say that our universities, on their own, generate eating-disordered students. They do, however, provide fertile ground for those who carry the seeds of disorder with them from home. In the permissive and highly individualized food environment of the post-1970 college or university, overeating and undereating become distinct possibilities.[29]

For those young women with either incipient or pronounced anorexia nervosa, the unstructured college life . . . often accentuates the anorectic's physical and emotional problems. [As one young anorectic explained]:

> I don't know any limits here at all. At home, I have my mom dishing out my food . . . But when I'm here it's a totally different story—I can't tell portion size at all. I always get so afraid afterwards, after eating. Oh my God did I eat that much or this much? So I just pass things up altogether and don't eat.[30]

The anorectic's preoccupation with appetite control is fueled by incessant talk about dieting and weight even among friends and associates who eat regularly. Diet-conscious female students report that fasting, weight control, and binge eating are a normal part of life on American college campuses.[31] . . . In our obesophobic society women struggle with food because, among other things, food represents fat and loss of control. For a contemporary woman to eat heartily, energetically, and happily is usually problematic (and, at best, occasional). As a result, some come to fear and hate their own appetite; eating becomes a shameful and disgusting act, and denial of hunger becomes a central facet of identity and personality. . . .

Among adolescents concerned with the transition to adulthood, an intense concern with appetite control and the body [also] operates in tandem with increasing anxiety over sexuality and the implications of changing sex roles. For sex is the second important arena of social change that may contribute to the rising number of anorectics. There are, in fact, some justifiable social reasons why contemporary young women fear adult womanhood. The "anorexic generations," particularly those born since 1960, have been subject to a set of insecurities that make heterosexuality an anxious rather than a pleasant prospect. Family insecurity, reflected in the frequency of divorce, and changing sex and gender roles became facts of life for this group in their childhood. . . . Although there is no positive correlation between divorced families and anorexia nervosa, family disruption is part of the world view of the anorexic generations. Its members understand implicitly that not all heterosexual relationships have happy endings.

As a consequence of these social changes, some young women are ambivalent about commitments to men and have adopted an ideal of womanhood that reflects the impact of post-1960 feminism. Although they generally draw back from an explicitly feminist vocabulary, most undergraduate women today desire professional careers of their own without forsaking the idea of marriage and a family. A 1985 study of college women by sociologist Mirra Komarovsky reveals that finding one's place in the world of work has become essential for personal dignity in this generation—yet a career without marriage was the choice of only 2 percent of the sample.[32] Convinced that individuality can be accommodated in marriage, these young women are interested in heterosexuality, but admit that "relationships with guys" are difficult even in college. Komarovsky describes conflict over dating rituals (who takes the initiative and who pays), decision making as a couple, intellectual rivalries, and competition for entrance into graduate school. Unlike Mother, who followed Dad to graduate school and supported him along the way, today's undergraduate—whether she is a declared feminist or not—wants her own professional career both as a ticket to the good life and as a protection for herself in case of divorce.

Sexual activity also requires an extraordinary degree of self-protection in the modern world of AIDS. While premarital sex is acceptable (if not desirable), it is an understandable source of worry among female undergraduates. An advertisement in a 1986 issue of *Ms.*, aimed at selling condoms to young women, captured the current ambivalence about the physical side of heterosexuality: "Let's face it, sex these days can be risky business, and you need all the protection you can get. Between the fear of unplanned pregnancy, sexually transmitted diseases, and the potential side effects of many forms of contraception, it may seem like sex is hardly worth the risk anymore."[33] For some students the unprecedented privacy and freedom of modern university life generates as much fear as pleasure. It bears repeating that clinical materials suggest an *absence* [emphasis is the editors'] of sexual activity on the part of anorectics.

Even though feminine dependency is no longer in fashion, these same young women combine traditional expectations with a quest for equity and power. To be brainy and beautiful; to have an exciting $75,000-a-year job; to nurture two wonderful children in consort with a supportive but equally high-powered husband—these are the personal ambitions of many in the present college generation. In order to achieve this level of personal and social perfection, young women must be extremely demanding of themselves: there can be no distracting personal or avocational detours—they must be unrelenting in the pursuit of goals. The kind of personal control required to become the new Superwoman (a term popularized by columnist Ellen Goodman)[34] parallels the single-mindedness that characterizes the anorectic. In sum, the golden ideal of this generation of privileged young women and their most distinctive pathology appear to be flip sides of the same record.

My assertion that the post-1960 epidemic of anorexia nervosa can be related to recent social change in the realm of sexuality [and gender roles] is not an argument for turning back the clock. . . . [H]istorical investigation demonstrates that anorexia nervosa was latent in the economic and emotional milieu of the bourgeois family as early as the 1950s. It makes little sense to think a cure will be achieved by putting women back in the kitchen, reinstituting sit-down meals on the nation's campuses, or limiting personal and professional choices to what they were in the Victorian era. On the basis of the best current research on anorexia nervosa, we must conclude that the disease develops as a result of the intersection of external and internal forces in the life of an individual. External forces such as those described here do not, by themselves, generate psychopathologies, but they do give them shape and influence their frequency.

In the confusion of this transitional moment, when a new future is being tentatively charted for women but gender roles and sexuality are still constrained by tradition, young women on the brink of adulthood are feeling the pain of social change most acutely.[35] They look about for direction, but find little in the way of useful experiential guides. What parts of women's tradition do they want to carry into the future? What parts should be left behind? These are difficult personal and political decisions, and most young women are being asked to make them without benefit of substantive education in the history and experience of their sex. In effect, our young women are being challenged and their expectations raised without a simultaneous level of support for either their specific aspirations or for female creativity in general.

Sadly, the cult of diet and exercise is the closest thing our secular society offers women in terms of a coherent philosophy of the self.[36] This being the case, anorexia nervosa is not a quirk and the symptom choice is not surprising. When personal and social difficulties arise, a substantial number of our young women become preoccupied with their bodies and control of appetite. Of all the messages they hear, the imperative to be beautiful and good, by being thin, is still the strongest and most familiar. Moreover, they are caught, often at a very early age, in a deceptive cognitive trap that has them believing that body weight is entirely subject to their conscious control. Despite feminist influences on the career aspirations of the present college-age generation, little has transpired to dilute the basic strength of this powerful cultural prescription that plays on both individualism and conformity. The unfortunate truth is that even when she wants more than beauty and understands its limitations as a life goal, the bourgeois woman still expends an enormous amount of psychic energy on appetite control as well as on other aspects of presentation of the physical self.

And what of the future? . . .

We can expect to see eating disorders continue, if not increase, among young women in those postindustrial societies where adolescents tend to be under stress. For both young men and young women, vast technological and cultural changes have made the transition to adulthood particularly difficult by transforming the nature of the family and community and rendering the future unpredictable. According to psychologist Urie Bronfenbrenner and others, American adolescents are in the worst trouble: we have the highest incidence of alcohol and drug abuse among adolescents of any country in the world; we also have the highest rate of teenage pregnancy of any industrialized nation; and we appear to have the most anorexia nervosa.[37]

Although the sexually active adolescent mother and the sexually inactive adolescent anorectic may seem to be light-years apart, they are linked by a common, though unarticulated, understanding. For adolescent women the body is still the most powerful paradigm regardless of social class. Unfortunately, a sizable number of our young women—poor and privileged alike—regard their body as the best vehicle for making a statement about their identity and personal dreams. This is what unprotected sexual intercourse and prolonged starvation have in common. Taken together, our unenviable preeminence in these two domains suggests the enormous difficulty involved in making the transition to adult womanhood in a society where women are still evaluated primarily in terms of the body rather than the mind.

Notes

1. "On Growing Fat," *Atlantic Monthly* (Mar. 1907):430–31.

2. Jo Ann Olian, *The House of Worth: The Gilded Age, 1860–1918* (New York: Museum of the City of New York, 1982); Jane Beth Abrams, "The Thinning of America: The Emergence of the Ideal of Slenderness in American Popular Culture, 1870–1930," B.A. thesis, Harvard University, 1983, chap. 2.

3. Michael Batterberry and Ariane Batterberry, *Mirror Mirror: A Social History of Fashion* (New York: Holt, Rinehart and Winston, 1977), pp. 289–97; Diane DeMarly, *The History of Haute Couture, 1850–1950* (New York: Holmes & Meier, 1980), pp. 81–83.

4. P. Rostaine, "How to Get Thin," *Medical Press and Circular* 149 (Dec. 23, 1914):643–44.

5. Stuart Ewen and Elizabeth Ewen, *Channels of Desire: Mass Images and the Shaping of American Consciousness* (New York: McGraw-Hill, 1982), pt. 4; Claudia Kidwell and Margaret C. Christman, *Suiting Everyone: The Democratization of Clothing in America* (Washington, D.C.: Smithsonian Institution Press, 1974).

6. *Vogue* (Jan. 1, 1923):63.

7. Lois W. Banner, *American Beauty* (New York: Random House, 1983), p. 262; Ewen and Ewen, *Channels of Desire*, pp. 193–98.

8. Banner, *American Beauty*, p. 287; Anne Hollander, *Seeing through Clothes* (New York: Viking Press, 1975).

9. Lulu Hunt Peters, *Diet and Health with a Key to the Calories* (Chicago: The Reilly & Britton Company, 1918), pp. 24, 39.

10. Ibid., pp. 12, 104, 110.

11. Ibid., pp. 85, 94.

12. Ibid., pp. 85, 93, 94.

13. "On Her Dressing Table," *Vogue* (Apr. 24, 1902):413; ibid. (July 1, 1918):78.

14. Mildred H. Bryan, "Don't Let Your Child Get Fat!" *Hygeia* 15 (1937):801–3; G. D. Schultz, "Forget That Clean-Plate Bogey!" *Better Homes and Gardens* 21 (Sept. 1942):24.

15. Louise Paine Benjamin, "I Have Three Daughters," *Ladies Homes Journal* 57 (June 1940):74.

16. "You'll Eat It Up at Noon," *Seventeen* (Sept. 1946):21–22; Irma M. Phorylles, "The Lost Waistline," ibid. (Mar. 1948):124; "Overweight?" ibid. (Aug. 1948):184.

17. Ibid.

18. "Fattest Girl in the Class," ibid. (Jan. 1948): 21–22.

19. "Psychology of Dieting," *Ladies' Home Journal* (Jan. 1965):66.

20. Banner, *American Beauty*, pp. 283–85.

21. David M. Garner et al., "Cultural Expectations of Thinness in Women," *Psychology Reports* 47 (1980):483–91.

22. Rita Freedman, *Beauty Bound* (Lexington: Lexington Books, 1986), p. 150.

23. "Coming on Strong: The New Ideal of Beauty," *Time* (Aug. 30, 1983):71–77.

24. William Chafe, *The Unfinished Journey: America since World War II* (New York: Oxford University Press, 1986).

25. *New Yorker* (July 21, 1986):71.

26. "What's Your Food Status Because the Way You Live Has a Lot to Do with the Way You Eat," *Mademoiselle* (Sept. 1985):224–26; "Food as Well as Clothes, Today, Make the Man—As a Matter of Life and Style," *Vogue* (June 1985):271–73.

27. "Severe Growing Pains for Fast Food," *Business Week* (Mar. 22, 1985):225.

28. Greg Foster and Susan Howerin, "The Quest for Perfection: An Interview with a Former Bulimic," *Iris: A Journal about Women* [Charlottesville, Va.] (1986):21.

29. Before they even arrive on campus, during their senior year in high school and the summer before entering college, many girls began to talk about the "freshmen 10 or 15." This is the weight gain predicted as a result of eating starchy institutional food and participating in late-night food forays with friends.

30. Elizabeth Greene, "Support Groups Forming for Students with Eating Disorders," *Chronicle of Higher Education* (Mar. 5, 1986):1, 30.

31. K. A. Halmi, J. R. Falk, and E. Schwartz, "Binge-Eating and Vomiting: A Survey of a College Population," *Psychological Medicine* 11 (1981): 697–706; R. L. Pyle et al., "The Incident of Bulimia in Freshman College Students," *International Journal of Eating Disorders* 2, 3 (1983):75–86.

32. Mirra Komarovsky, *Women in College: Shaping the New Feminine Identities* (New York: Basic Books, 1985), pp. 89–92, 225–300.

33. *Ms.* (Sept. 1986):n.p. The condom is called Mentor.

34. Ellen Goodman, *Close to Home* (New York: Fawcett Crest, 1979).

35. In *Theories of Adolescence* (New York: Random House, 1962), R. E. Muuss wrote: "Societies in a period of rapid transition create a particular adolescent period; the adolescent has not only the society's problem to adjust to but his [or her] own as well" (p. 164).

36. My view of this issue complements ideas presented in Robert Bellah et al., *Habits of the Heart: Individualism and Commitment in American Life* (New York: Harper & Row, 1986).

37. These data are synthesized in Urie Bronfenbrenner, "Alienation and the Four Worlds of Childhood," *Phi Delta Kappan* (Feb. 1986):434.

Photo Essay: Adorning the Body

How women manage their physical appearance is only in part a response to the aesthetics of changing fashions. What women wear and the spirit in which they wear it can code a range of changing judgments about their social role, their political views, and their understanding of their bodies. (Why men's fashion has shifted far more slowly is a question worth pondering.)

As you examine the images that follow, consider the extent to which women's clothing has linked them to the issues that are discussed in the documents and essays. What do you understand to be the relationships between women's bodies and their clothing in different periods of time? In different regions of the country? Among different classes of people?

What personal and political meaning do you find in your own clothing and the clothing that you see around you?

1. Long dresses dragged in muddy ground, signaling that the wearer was not expected to exert herself. By the mid-nineteenth century, as these dresses show, fashionable ball gowns featured wide, heavy skirts over petticoats and impossibly narrow waists. Wearing dresses like these required wearing corsets, often of whalebone, to hold the body rigid and constrict the breathing. ("Fashions for June," *Harper's New Monthly Magazine* 7, no. 37 [June 1853]: 143–44.)

2. Amelia Bloomer did not invent the short skirt and trousers that came to bear her name; known as the "Turkish style," it appeared here and there in the 1840s. Elizabeth Cady Stanton's cousin Elizabeth Miller wore it when she visited Seneca Falls. Stanton envied her ease of movement and began to wear it. Bloomer was the editor of a women's rights journal, the *Lily*, which supported the principle of dress reform. "It seemed proper that I should practise [*sic*] as I preached," she would write years later. "At the outset, I had no idea of fully adopting the style . . . no thought that my action would create an excitement . . . and give to the style my name and the credit due Mrs. Miller. This was all the work of the press. I stood amazed at the furor." Bloomer would wear the costume on her lecture tours throughout the country for the next six years or so; "I found the dress comfortable, light, easy and convenient, and well adapted to the needs of my busy life," she insisted. But Stanton gave up the dress within three years because she found that ridicule deflected attention from her serious arguments about women's right to education, the ballot, and a wide range of work and better pay.*

This was not the first time, nor would it be the last, that critics of women's political positions attacked women's dress rather than debate women's ideas directly. Can you think of occasions in recent years when criticism of women's fashion was also a criticism of women's behavior? (Amelia Bloomer in the "short dress," ca. 1852–1853. Courtesy of the Seneca Falls Historical Society, #1426; http://www.nps.gov/history/history/online_books/wori/images/fig 10.jpg.)

*Dexter Bloomer, *The Life and Writings of Amelia Bloomer* (Boston: Arena, 1985), pp. 67–70.

WOMAN'S EMANCIPATION.
(BEING A LETTER ADDRESSED TO MR. PUNCH, WITH A DRAWING, BY A STRONG-MINDED AMERICAN WOMAN.)

3. Women who adopted the Bloomer costume quickly were subjected to withering scorn, as in this cartoon from *Harper's*, a widely circulated magazine whose editors were certain they had the correct position on what women ought to wear. (See "Fashions for June," p. 460.) What message about women does the cartoon convey? ("Women's Emancipation," *Harper's New Monthly Magazine* 3, no. 15 [Aug. 1851]:424.)

FRANK LESLIE'S
ILLUSTRATED
NEWSPAPER
NEW YORK, JUNE 20, 1874.

4. By 1874 dress reform had more modest goals. At this meeting at the Freeman Place Chapel in Boston, Massachusetts, the speakers do not display the traditional Bloomer costume. Instead of short skirts and trousers, they emphasize the absence of whalebone stays on their undergarments, and hidden bloomers instead of petticoats. Note the dress and headwear of the attentive women in the pews.

Frank Leslie's Illustrated Newspaper was notably friendly to women's reform causes (see its coverage of suffragists before a congressional committee, pp. (244–245). When Frank Leslie died in 1881, his wife and collaborator, Miriam Squier Leslie, had her own name legally changed to Frank Leslie and continued his publishing enterprises for the rest of her life. When she died in 1914, she left her considerable fortune to Carrie Chapman Catt for use in the final stages of the suffrage campaign. (Sketched by E. R. Morse, "The Dress Reform Meeting in Boston," *Frank Leslie's Illustrated Newspaper* 38, no. 77 [June 20, 1874]: 209, 229. For more on the publishers, see Madeleine Stern, *Purple Passage: The Life of Mrs. Frank Leslie* [Norman: University of Oklahoma Press, 1953], and Lynne Vincent Cheney, "Mrs. Frank Leslie's Illustrated Newspaper," *American Heritage* 26, no. 6 [Oct. 1975].)

5. The "Gibson girl" took her name from illustrations by Charles Dana Gibson, whose 1890 image of a tall, elegant woman with an hourglass figure became his signature as an artist. It was widely imitated by other illustrators, and confirmed the style of the first widely mass-produced women's clothing. The "Gibson Girl," one commentator wrote, "looks square at you with intelligent eyes that hide a touch of mischief . . . She is healthy and brave. . . . and she knows as much about golf as French and German."* But, as we shall see, she could not ride a bicycle nor get on and off a streetcar easily. (*Sweetest Story Ever Told*, ca. 1910. Ink over graphite on illustration board. Illustration by Charles Dana Gibson for *Collier's Weekly*, Aug. 13, 1910. Courtesy of the Library of Congress, Prints and Photographs Division, Washington, D.C.)

**Life* 24 (Nov. 15, 1894): 312.

6. Street railways and long-distance railroads were among the benefits of the Industrial Revolution, but, as historian Barbara Welke writes, "[T]he physical act of jumping or stepping from train or streetcar to the ground was qualitatively different for women than the same act undertaken by able-bodied men. Women . . . [were] often burdened by children or by pregnancy" From the years in which the railroad was first invented until the 1920s, fashion details may have changed, but "women's long skirts swept across road and farmyard." Whether hoop skirt, bustle, or Gibson girl look, women's clothing was "long, dark, and cumbersome." At a time when men took pride in jumping on and off railroads and streetcars as they started to move or came to a stop, railroad and streetcar accident reports were "filled with stories of women falling because their skirts caught on a projection or were stepped on by another passenger as they alighted."* What dangers does this woman face? (Photograph courtesy of the Library of Congress, George Grantham Bain Collection, LC-USZ62-91532.)

---

*Barbara Young Welke, *Recasting American Liberty: Gender, Race, Law, and the Railroad Revolution, 1865–1920* (New York: Cambridge University Press, 2001), pp. 55–56. This photograph appears on page 58.

7. The woman on the left, a *mexicana* who perhaps belonged to a family that had settled in New Mexico almost three centuries earlier, is clearly skilled at carrying an *olla* full of water on her head. Photographed in Santa Fe in the mid- or late nineteenth century, she wears the looser, layered clothing long utilized by European women of the laboring classes. The image on the right, taken in a Tucson, Arizona, photography studio probably at the turn of the 1800s, is of a member of a prominent local Mexican American family. The young woman had the privilege of wearing at her wedding the elaborately tailored gown with train, feathered hat, and white gloves that were the height of fashion for elites in the dominant Anglo society.

The twinned practice of wearing an elegant white wedding gown, and staging an elaborate formal wedding was initially restricted to elite Britons and Americans (emulating Queen Victoria's 1840 wedding). By the early twentieth century, urban middle-class couples adopted the "white wedding." It became a widespread practice, supported by burgeoning commercial bridal and related enterprises, only after World War II.* (*Image on left*: Courtesy of the Palace of the Governors / New Mexico History Museum, division of New Mexico Department of Cultural Affairs, negative 3150. *Image on right*: Courtesy of the Arizona Historical Society, Tucson; image #73800, item in the Mexican Heritage Project, donation of Maria Urquides. We are grateful to Elizabeth "Betita" Martínez for identifying and pairing these images in her book, *500 Years of Chicana Women's History/Años de la Mujer Chicana* [New Brunswick, N.J.: Rutgers University Press, 2008], p. 43.)

*Katherine Jellison, introduction to *It's Our Day: America's Love Affair with the White Wedding*, 1945–2005 (Lawrence: University Press of Kansas, 2008).

8. The bicycle offered women the opportunity to travel cheaply and independently in public space; it undermined long-standing assumptions about proper feminine behavior.* Note this woman's clothing and the camera she carries. Almost as soon as the bicycle with two wheels of the same size was invented, women embraced it enthusiastically. Susan B. Anthony observed that "the bicycle had done more to emancipate women than anything else in the world." The bicyclist chose where she would go at the rate she wished to go. On the bicycle, the corset had to be abandoned; shorter skirts, even divided skirts and long bloomers suddenly became a matter of necessity. "If women ride," wrote the reformer Frances E. Willard in 1895, "they must, when riding, dress more rationally than they have been wont to do. If they do this many prejudices as to what they may be allowed to wear will melt away. . . . [T]he comfortable, sensible and artistic wardrobe of the rider will make the conventional style of woman's dress absurd to the eye and unendurable to the understanding." How accurate was Willard's prediction? ("Woman on Bicycle," ca. 1917. Harris & Ewing, photographer. Courtesy of the Library of Congress, Prints and Photographs Division, Washington, D.C.)

*Frances E. Willard, *A Wheel Within a Wheel: How I Learned to Ride the Bicycle* (Chicago: Women's Temperance Union Publishing House, 1895), p. 39.

9. These students were members of a yearlong course entitled "Political and Legal Status of Women" offered to undergraduates at the University of Iowa in 1914 and taught by Frank E. Horak, a young political science professor. The course catalog advertised it as follows:

> A survey of the "woman's rights" or "feminist" movement in general, and a study of the legal rights and political status of women in the United States in particular. In the second semester the course deals with the more important political, politico-economic and politico-social problems which confront women in this and other countries; also with the rules and practices of deliberative meetings.

Notice the students' range of clothing and hairstyles; some were probably old-fashioned even for 1914; others appear comfortable for our own time. Note also the different ways in which the women address the camera. (Courtesy of the State Historical Society of Iowa, Iowa City. We are grateful to curator Mary Bennett for assistance in identifying this photograph.)

10. Congressman T. S. McMillan of Charleston, South Carolina, poses with Miss Ruth Bennett and Miss Sylvia Clavins, who are doing the Charleston on a railing; the U.S. Capitol looms behind them. The short skirts, short hair, and brash behavior marked the women as "flappers." Note the contrast between their clothes and those worn by suffragists demonstrating in front of the White House less than ten years before (see Photo Essay: "Women in Public," p. 248). What difference do you think this change of style made in the lives of women who adopted it? ("Charleston at the Capitol," ca. 1920s. Photo-print by National Photo Company. Courtesy of the Library of Congress, Prints and Photographs Division, Washington D.C.)

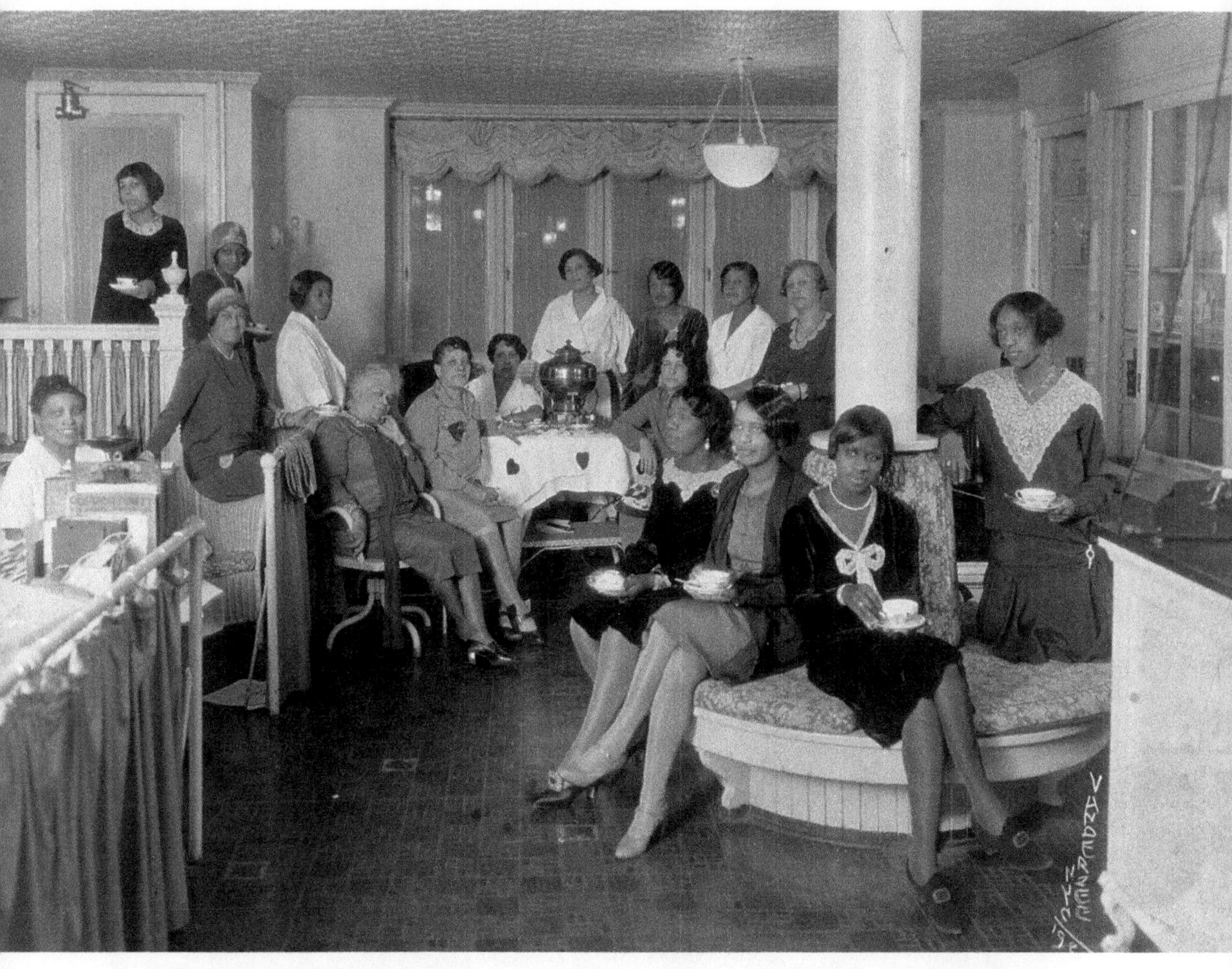

11. Women traditionally devised shampoos and cosmetics for themselves, in their own homes. In the early twentieth century, a number of women entrepreneurs, among them Elizabeth Arden, Helena Rubenstein, and Madam C. J. Walker, invented the concept of the commercial beauty product, made in factories and mass marketed. Walker, who was the daughter of former slaves, was born in 1867; she was probably the first woman self-made millionaire in the nation. In 1905 she developed a scalp-conditioning formula for African Americans. At its peak in the second decade of the century, her business employed some 3,000 people—in a factory in Indianapolis, in hair and manicure salons across the country, and as door-to-door saleswomen. Walker took pride in offering women well-paid alternatives to domestic labor, and in her support for African American philanthropies, especially the antilynching efforts of the NAACP and Bethune-Cookman College (for Bethune-Cookman, see pp. 360–362). She died in 1919. This photography by the distinguished photographer James VanDerZee was taken in her New York salon and offices a decade after Walker's death. How would you describe the hairstyles of these Harlemites, who sported the sophisticated urban look that Madam Walker's products and styling supported? (Courtesy of the Metropolitan Museum of Art, New York © Donna Mussenden VanDerZee.)

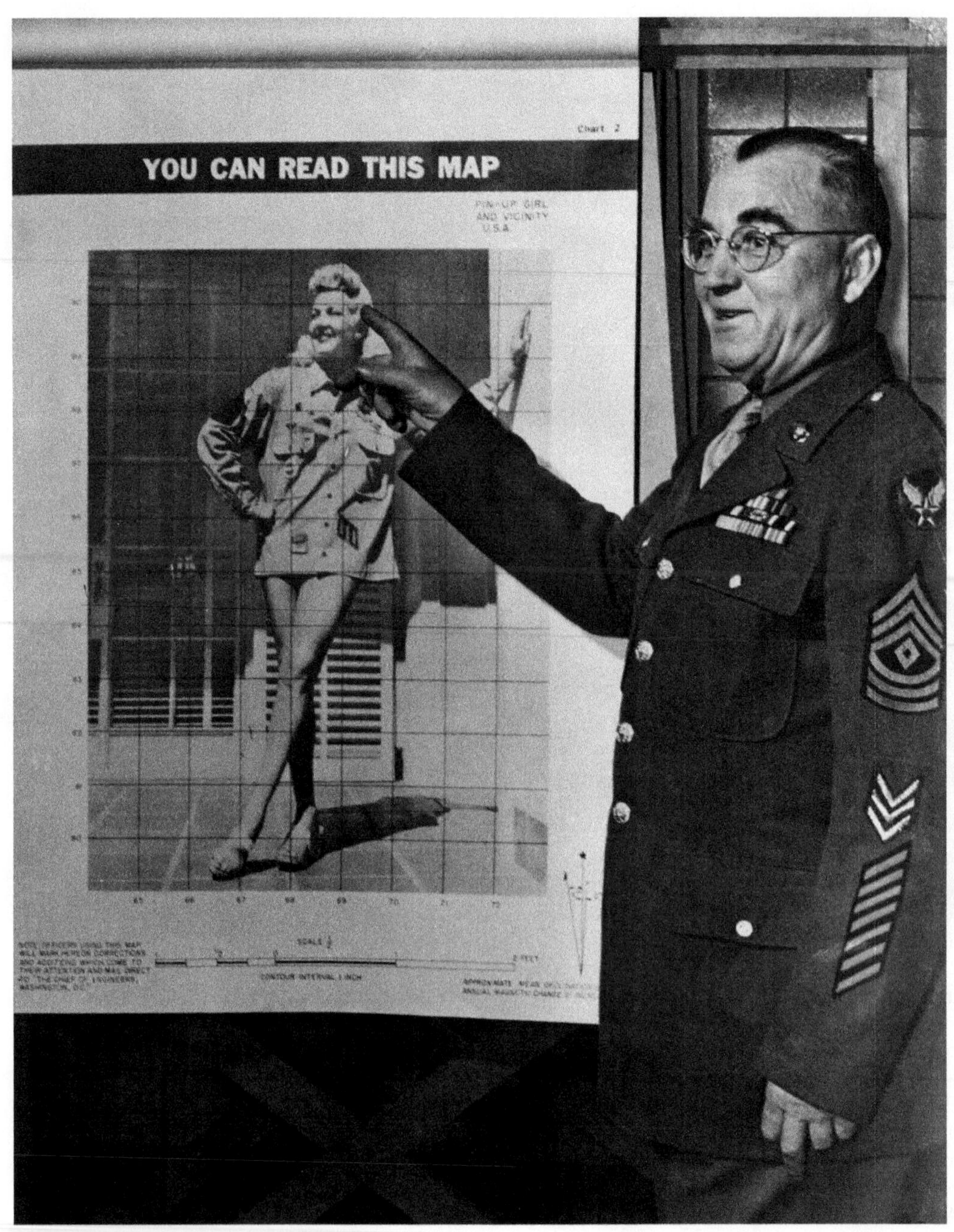

12. An Air Force sergeant uses this image of the movie star Betty Grable (1916–73) to instruct military recruits in the skills of map reading during World War II. The original caption included this line: "The picture of the girl is divided into sections with lines, each of which is numbered, and by checking the lines on it, as on a real map, soldiers can locate any given spot—knowledge which in actual combat can mean the difference between life and death." What messages about women's bodies does this use of her photo—in this pose—convey? (Courtesy Corbis). (For a subtle cultural analysis of the pinup, see Robert B. Westbrook, "'I Want a Girl Just Like the Girl Who Married Harry James': Women and the Problem of Political Obligation in World War II," *American Quarterly* 42 [Dec. 1990]: 587–614.) We are grateful to Robert Westbroook for identifying this photograph.

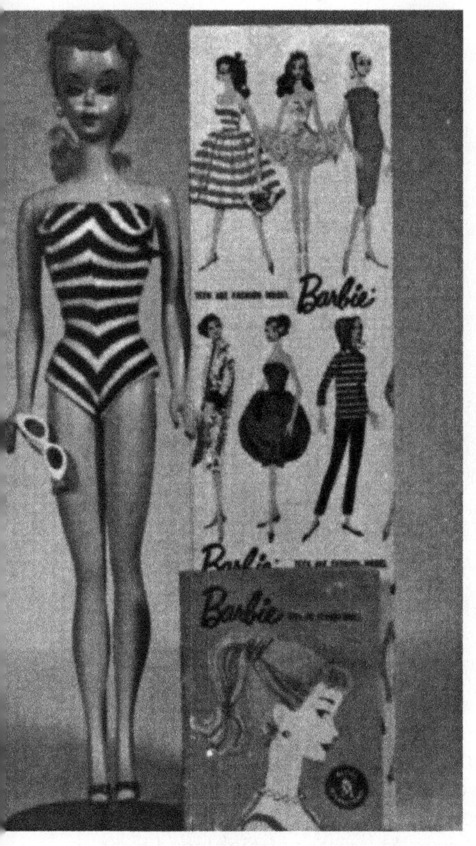

13. Barbie debuted in 1959 after much persistence and research by her creator, Ruth Handler. In the mid-1940s, Handler had founded a small company called Mattel, together with her husband and a partner who soon sold the Handlers his share. Initially housed in their southern California garage, Mattel produced picture frames but soon began to specialize in dollhouse furniture and toys. In 1955 and 1956, Handler had little success in convincing the company's male employees that there was a waiting market for adult-looking dolls aimed at prepubescent girls. She had noticed that her daughter Barbara, having outgrown baby dolls, enjoyed cutting out clothes and accessories from magazines to create adult paper dolls and assign them imaginary grown-up roles and professions. Handler was convinced that a three-dimensional adult doll would help girls become acquainted with the bodily changes they would experience during puberty. On a European family vacation, Handler came upon Lilli, a German-manufactured doll representing a buxom, blond young woman (Lilli had originated in a satirical, adult-oriented newspaper comic strip). The doll could be bought in various outfits, but the clothes were not sold separately. Mattel acquired the patent and rights for the doll, worked with Japanese manufacturers to perfect the vinyl molding phase of production, and hired designers (including women) who embraced Handler's vision of a set of dolls for whom a wide wardrobe and accessories could be purchased.

The first Barbie measured 11.5 inches and was marketed as a "teen-age fashion model" and "a new kind of doll from real life." The purchaser chose between the blond and the brunette versions. *Barbie* (always written in a distinctive script) came in an attractive oblong box illustrated with alluring wardrobe possibilities; inside was a miniature catalog with more details. She cost $3. Note the designers' genius: whereas Lilli's earrings and shoes were molded and painted on, Barbie had bare feet and pierced ears, allowing for endless accessorizing options. The small-waisted, ever smiling, preternaturally young doll soon made its way into the hands of millions of young girls, who were drawn to her long, malleable hair, her ever-expanding wardrobe, her supernatural womanly figure, and her "boyfriend" Ken and their coterie.[*]

During the 1970s, feminists began to ask challenging questions about the relationship between toys such as Barbie, body image, sexism, consumerism, and racial stereotypes. Many of these questions remain unresolved. To what extent do Barbie dolls teach young women to become consumers? Is it sufficient for Mattel simply to change the shade of Barbie's skin to appeal to children of various races and ethnicities? College health and wellness programs often use Barbie as a hook on their websites, pointing out, for example, that a read-life Barbie would be unable to walk given her top-heavy frame. What connections do you think exist between Barbie and eating disorders among adolescents? Between Barbie and the popularity of plastic surgery, diet spa retreats, and tanning salons? If you played with Barbie dolls as a child, what types of scenes did you enact? How did you imagine adulthood through the lens of Barbie? (Photo by Joan Ashabraner. We are grateful to Joan Ashabraner for this image. For a provocative assessment of Barbie threaded with an interview with Ruth Handler, see Susan Stern's 1998 documentary, *Barbie Nation: An Unauthorized Tour* [videorecording, New Day Films].)

---

[*]Marco Tosca, *Barbie: Four Decades of Fashion, Fantasy, and Fun*, trans. Linda M. Eklund (New York: Harry N. Abrams, 1998), pp. 24–33.

14. From the 1600s onward, African American women felt pressure to adopt beauty regimens that made them appear "whiter." Light-skinned people, who often had straighter hair than dark-skinned African Americans, were granted more privileges on plantations during slavery. Throughout the nineteenth and twentieth centuries, many African Americans straightened their hair in order to appear respectable as they sought economic and social rights. By the 1960s, with the civil rights movement ever more visible and the black power movement on the rise, the emphasis on a look that bespoke respectability and conformity began to crumble. Many activist African Americans forged connections with their African past, adopting African styles of dress and hairstyles. Noted civil rights activist Angela Davis popularized the Afro hairstyle when she spoke across the United States. Here, Davis speaks at a street rally in Raleigh, North Carolina, on July 4, 1974. The Afro not only required a fraction of the care of previously popular hairstyles, but it also embodied the recognition that "black is beautiful." Some older African Americans, including religious people and civil rights activists, criticized the Afro as confrontational, fearing that it would limit African Americans' upward social mobility in white-controlled environments. Instead, the model spread to other ethnic groups, helping to make a wider range of hairstyles fashionable. However, as many recent memoirs and blogs by African-descended women have recounted, the "hair wars" in the black family and community have not ended; see the wry commentary of A'Lelia Bundles, who is a great-great granddaughter of Madam C. J. Walker. ("Hair Peace : A 5-Part Manifesto," *The Root*, Mar. 26, 2009, http://www.theroot.com/views/hair-peace-5-part-manifesto?).

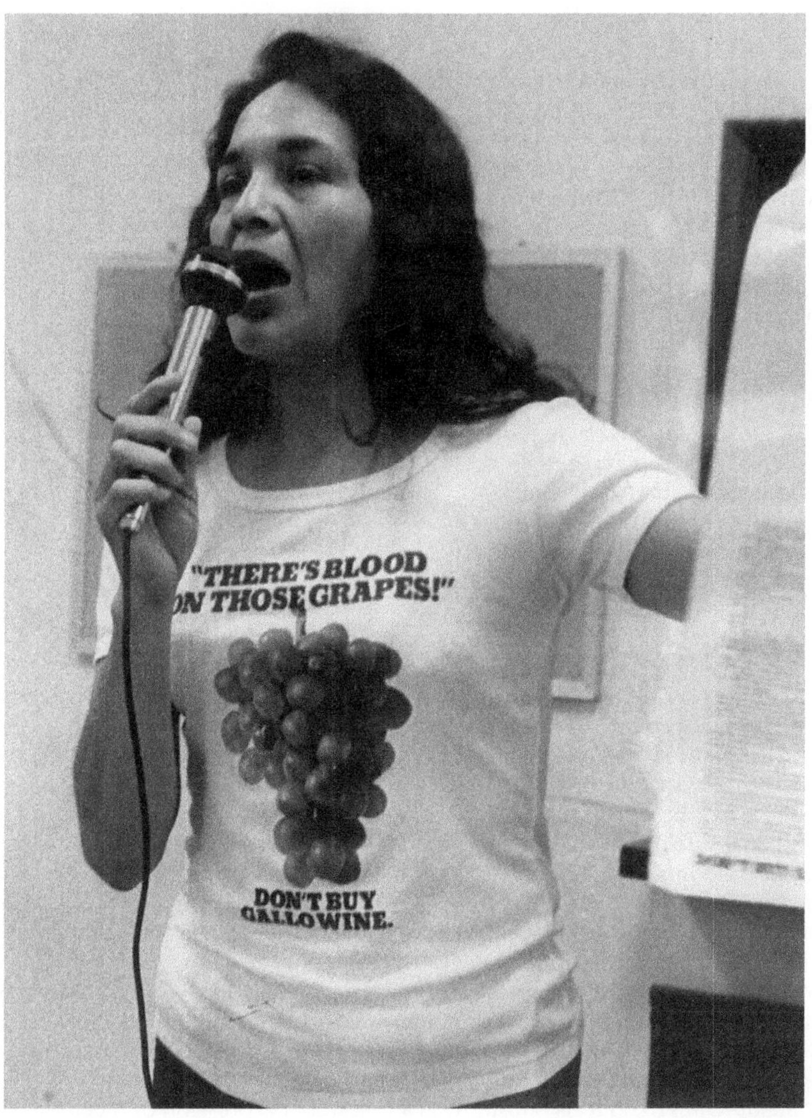

15. Dolores Huerta, a cofounder of the United Farm Workers of America, articulated the grievances of thousands of exploited Mexican and Mexican American farm laborers who toiled in California fields. In this 1973 photograph, Huerta is shown using not only her voice to denounce harsh living conditions and inadequate pay, but also powerful imagery on her T-shirt. Consider how clothing can serve both as a political signal and as a historical artifact. What information does Huerta's T-Shirt Convey? How might you use this photograph as a historical source? ("There's blood on those grapes!" Photograph by Chris Sanchez, likely taken during the Gallo strike, Livingston, California, 1973. Courtesy of the United Farm Workers Collection #273, Walter P. Reuther Library, Wayne State University.)

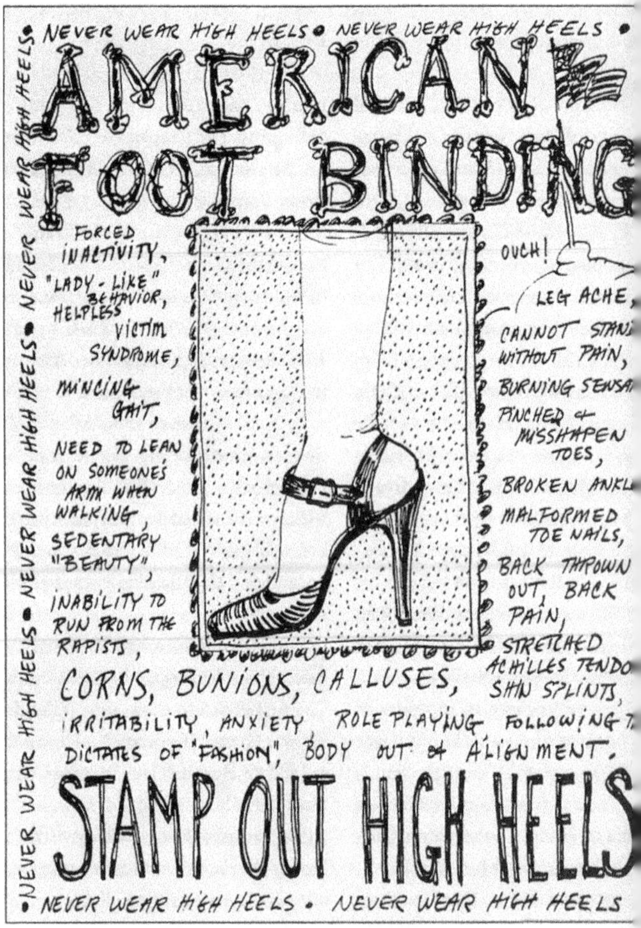

16. Ever since patriot women boycotted elaborate and expensive British imports during the Revolutionary era as a way of expressing their political principles, resistance to fashion trends has been a recurring theme in women's clothing choices. Challenging the fashion industry, women's liberation activists rebelled against uncomfortable and binding clothing. If you view all the photos in this book depicting pre-1970s events (despite Amelia Bloomer and dress reformers), you will see that this rebellion was a very radical gesture. At mid-century, respectable professional dress required nylon stockings held up by girdles or garter belts, making breathing uncomfortable; narrow skirts that prevented running away from danger; and high heels that over the long run shortened muscles and created corns and bunions in the name of looking sexy. (Fifteen times as many women as men develop bunions requiring surgery.) Women who adopted looser, more comfortable clothing risked scorn and even the loss of their jobs. Until Title VII, it was not illegal to treat the display of beauty as a reasonable professional qualification for many lines of work, including flight attendants and executive secretaries. (See the concept of the Bona Fide Occupational Qualification [BFOQ] in the Civil Rights Act 1964, pp. 650–651.) It took two decades, from the mid-1970s to the mid-1990s, before flight attendants—who, it is estimated, walk as much as 225 miles up and down airplane aisles each year—were able to force most airlines to relax rules requiring them to wear shoes with 2 or 2 1/2-inch heels. (Male attendants could always wear loafers.)*

The "Stamp Out High Heels" poster was a grassroots expression of rebellion, addressing issues of health, safety, and cultural conformity. It augured a dramatic shift in sartorial choices. For example, the pants suit may seem dated now, but in the 1970s it was an important wedge for working women, especially in white-collar jobs. Over the past thirty years, the clothes acceptable for women to wear to work and in public have become very diverse—in style, color, fabric, and so on. This diversity, plus the informal, athletic look so prevalent in women's clothes and shoes, owes much to 1970s feminist activism. How many of the claims and slogans featured in the poster do you agree with? ("American Foot Binding: Stamp Out High Heels," poster, Houston, n.d. Courtesy Duke University Library Special Collections, ALFA Collection, Box 12. We are grateful to Rosalyn Baxandall and Linda Gordon, *Dear Sisters: Dispatches from the Women's Liberation Movement* [New York: Basic Books, 2000] p. 40, for identifying this image.)

*See Marc Linder, "Smart Women, Stupid Shoes, and Cynical Employers: The Unlawfulness and Adverse Health Consequences of Sexually Discriminatory Workplace Footwear Requirements for Female Employees," *Journal of Corporation Law* 22 (1996–97): 296–97, 308–12.

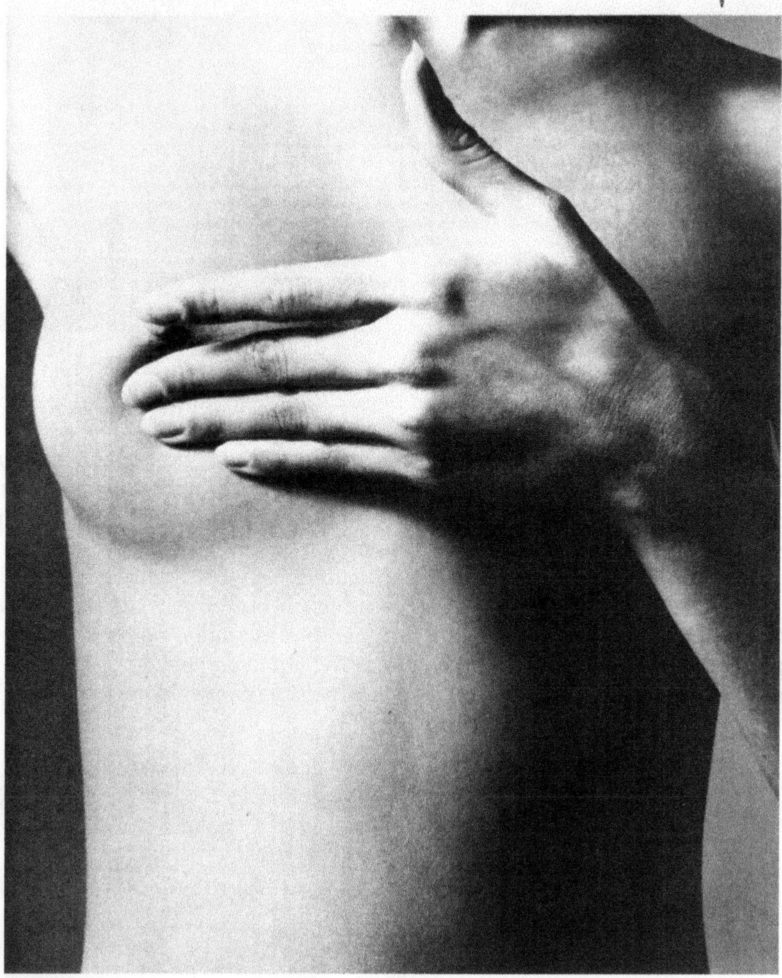

Cancer.
Sometimes you can put your finger on it.
One of the seven warning signals of cancer is a thickening or lump in the breast or elsewhere.
There are six more that you should be aware of. Indigestion or difficulty in swallowing. An obvious change in a wart or mole. A nagging cough or hoarseness. A change in bowel or bladder habits. A sore that does not heal. Unusual bleeding or discharge.
If you notice any one of these warning signals, there's only one thing to do. See your doctor.
We want to wipe out cancer in your lifetime.
Give to the American Cancer Society.

17. Second-wave feminists urged women to take responsibility for their own well-being. As more was understood about breast cancer, it became clear that annual examinations by physicians were not enough to track its appearance; in the 1970s, as today, women are urged to examine their own bodies regularly. Over the years, unclothed women in art and advertising have presented their bodies to the male gaze; in a sharp departure from tradition, the model here is concerned with herself and her own health, encouraging women viewers to knowingly touch their own bodies as an act of self-preservation and self-empowerment. The advertisement appeared in the first issue of *Ms.* magazine. (Photo reprinted by the permission of The American Cancer Society, Inc. for historical purposes only. All rights reserved. See *Ms.* 1, no.1 [July 1972]:35.)

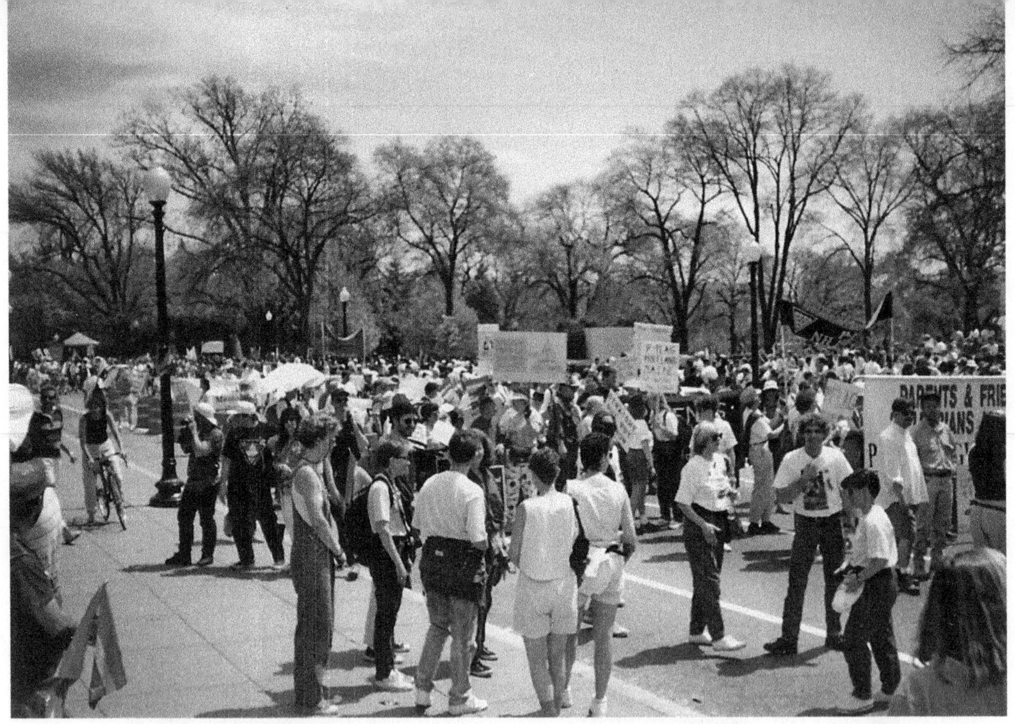

18. In the past fifteen years or so, many men and women have opted for short hair and earrings, and for jeans, T-shirts, and footwear unmarked by sex (sneakers, sandals, flip-flops, boots). Even earlier, starting in the late 1960s, members of older generations could be heard expressing concern about not being able to easily identify the sex of someone they caught a glimpse of. In contrast, those who were part of or close to the cultural shifts away from formal, occasion-driven, and sex-marked dress are comfortable with reading a new set of coded signals. This photograph, it happens, was taken at the Gay Pride parade in Washington, D.C., in 1993, but the androgynous style can be observed in many contemporary American settings. In what ways can these recent transformations be seen as a continuation of past dress reform movements? If you discuss current youths' clothing and body decoration styles with friends and family members born before, say, 1960, do they see the shifts across their lifetimes as revolutionary? (Courtesy of the Nancy V. "Rusty" Barcclo Papers, Iowa Women's Archives, University of Iowa Libraries, Iowa City, Iowa.)

19. Graduation ceremony at a large public university, May 2009. What meanings are conveyed by the footwear of these two women? (Photo by Tom Langdon.)

VICKI L. RUIZ

The Flapper and the Chaperone: Mexican American Teenagers in the Southwest

Over one million Mexicans immigrated to the United States between 1900 and 1930, forming new communities or settling alongside families whose descendants had migrated north decades and centuries before. This essay plunges us into the decisions to be made about dating, dancing, and dressing up by young women growing up Mexican American in western cities and farm towns from the 1920s to the 1940s. Focusing on first-generation teenagers, Vicki Ruiz insists that we see them not as caught between the mores of their Mexican-born Catholic parents and the freedoms of modern America, but rather as navigating "across multiple terrains" simultaneously. Home for most if not all of these young women was located in the *barrios*, dense neighborhoods where Mexican and Mexican American families, businesses, and parishes were clustered.

Ruiz's goal is to uncover the dreams and strategies of young women rather than those of *pachucos* or zoot-suiters, the youthful male subculture that has drawn scholarly attention. What range of sources and methods does she employ? If you were conducting such a study of teenage girls in the 1970s, or during the past decade, what research techniques and documents would be available to you?

In the interwar years, a central figure in cross-sex socializing was the chaperone—*la dueña*. Why do you think adult women and not men were called on to fill the role in Mexican American culture? What cultural messages would be sent if chaperones dogged youthful men's activities, not young women's? Ruiz finds that second-generation women, once married with their own children, tended not to continue the chaperoning tradition. In the 1960s, activist women of Mexican descent embraced the identity of Chicana and, as Ruiz indicates at the close of her essay, issued new challenges to conventional expectations shaped by popular culture, family oligarchy, and men's demands (see Jennie Chavez, pp. 704–705).

Imagine a gathering in a barrio hall, a group of young people dressed "to the nines" trying their best to replicate the dance steps of Fred Astaire and Ginger Rogers. This convivial heterosocial scene was a typical one in the lives of teenagers during the interwar period. But along the walls, a sharp difference was apparent in the barrios. Mothers, fathers, and older relatives chatted with one another as they kept one eye trained on the dance floor. They were the chaperones—the ubiquitous companions of unmarried Mexican-American women. Chaperonage was a traditional instrument of social control. Indeed, the presence of *la dueña* was the prerequisite for attendance at a dance, a movie, or even church-related events. "When we would go to town, I would want to say something to a guy. I couldn't because my

Excerpted from "The Flapper and the Chaperone," ch. 3 of *From Out of the Shadows: Mexican Women in Twentieth-Century America* by Vicki L. Ruiz (New York: Oxford University Press, 1998). Reprinted by permission of the author and publisher. Notes have been edited and renumbered.

mother was always there," remembered Maria Ybarra. "She would always stick to us girls like glue. . . . She never let us out of her sight."[1]

An examination of events like this one reveals the ways in which young Mexican women in the United States between the wars rationalized, resisted, and evaded parental supervision. It offers a glimpse into generational conflict that goes beyond the more general differences in acculturation between immigrants and their children. Chaperonage existed for centuries on both sides of the political border separating Mexico and the United States. While conjuring images of patriarchal domination, chaperonage is best understood as a manifestation of familial oligarchy whereby elders attempted to dictate the activities of youth for the sake of family honor. A family's standing in the community depended, in part, on women's purity. Loss of virginity not only tainted the reputation of an individual, but of her kin as well. For Mexicano immigrants living in a new, bewildering environment filled with temptations, the enforcement of chaperonage assumed a particular urgency.[2] . . .

Confronting "America" began at an early age. Throughout the Southwest, Spanish-speaking children had to sink or swim in an English-only environment. Even on the playground, students were punished for conversing in Spanish. Admonishments, such as "Don't speak that ugly language, you are an American now," not only reflected a strong belief in Anglo conformity but denigrated the self-esteem of Mexican-American children. As Mary Luna stated: "It was rough because I didn't know English. The teacher wouldn't let us talk Spanish. How can you talk to anybody? If you can't talk Spanish and you can't talk English. . . . It wasn't until maybe the fourth or fifth grade that I started catching up. And all that time I just felt I was stupid." Yet Luna credited her love of reading to a Euro-American educator who had converted a small barrio house into a makeshift community center and library. Her words underscore the dual thrust of Americanization—education and consumerism. "To this day I just love going into libraries . . . there are two places that I can go in and get a real warm, happy feeling; that is, the library and Bullock's in the perfume and make-up department."[3] . . .

For Mexican Americans, second-generation women as teenagers have received scant scholarly attention. Among Chicano historians and writers, there appears a fascination with the sons of immigrants, especially as *pachucos*.[4] Young women, however, may have experienced deeper generational tensions as they blended elements of Americanization with Mexican expectations and values. . . .

. . . The recollections of seventeen women serve as the basis for my reconstruction of adolescent aspirations and experiences (or dreams and routines). The women themselves, . . . with two [major] exceptions, . . . are U.S. citizens by birth and attended southwestern schools. All the interviewees were born between 1908 and 1926. Although three came from families once considered middle class in Mexico, most can be considered working class in the United States. Their fathers' typical occupations included farm worker, miner, day laborer, and railroad hand. These women usually characterized their mothers as homemakers, although several remembered that their mothers took seasonal jobs in area factories and fields. The most economically privileged woman in the sample, Ruby Estrada, helped out in her family-owned hardware and furniture store. She is also the only interviewee who attended college. It should be noted that seven of the seventeen narrators married Euro-Americans. Although intermarriage was uncommon, these oral histories give us insight into the lives of those who negotiated across cultures in a deeply personal way and who felt the impact of acculturation most keenly. Rich in emotion and detail, these interviews reveal women's conscious decision-making in the production of culture. In creating their own cultural spaces, the interwar generation challenged the trappings of familial oligarchy.[5]

. . . Within families, young women, perhaps more than their brothers, were expected to uphold certain standards. Parents, therefore, often assumed what they perceived as their unquestionable prerogative to regulate the actions and attitudes of their adolescent daughters. Teenagers, on the other hand, did not always acquiesce in the boundaries set down for them by their elders. Intergenerational tension flared along several fronts.

Like U.S. teenagers, in general, the first area of disagreement between an adolescent and her family would be over her personal appearance. . . . [T]he length of a young woman's tresses was a hot issue spanning class, region, and ethnic lines. During the 1920s, a woman's decision "to bob or not bob" her hair assumed classic proportions within Mexican families. After considerable pleading, Belen Martinez Mason was permitted to cut her hair, though she soon regretted the decision. "Oh, I cried for a month." Differing opinions over fashions often caused ill feelings. One Mexican American woman recalled that as a young girl, her mother dressed her "like a nun" and she could wear "no make-up, no cream, no nothing" on her face. Swimwear, bloomers, and short skirts also became sources of controversy. Some teenagers left home in one outfit and changed into another at school. Once María Fierro arrived home in her bloomers. Her father inquired, "Where have you been dressed like that, like a clown?" "I told him the truth," Fierro explained "He whipped me anyway. . . . So from then on whenever I went to the track meet, I used to change my bloomers so that he wouldn't see that I had gone again."[6] . . . [A] popular ballad chastised Mexican women for applying makeup so heavily as to resemble a piñata. [7]

The use of cosmetics, however, cannot be blamed entirely on Madison Avenue ad campaigns. The innumerable barrio beauty pageants, sponsored by *mutualistas*, patriotic societies, churches, the Mexican Chamber of Commerce, newspapers, and even progressive labor unions, encouraged young women to accentuate their physical attributes. Carefully chaperoned, many teenagers did participate in community contests from La Reina de Cinco de Mayo to Orange Queen. They modeled evening gowns, rode on parade floats, and sold raffle tickets.[8] . . .

The commercialization of personal grooming made additional inroads into the Mexican community with the appearance of barrio beauty parlors. Working as a beautician conferred a certain degree of status—"a nice, clean job"—in comparison to factory or domestic work. As one woman related:

> I always wanted to be a beauty operator. I loved makeup; I loved to dress up and fix up. I used to set my sisters' hair. So I had that in the back of my mind for a long time, and my mom pushed the fact that she wanted me to have a profession—seeing that I wasn't thinking of getting married.[9]

While further research is needed, one can speculate that neighborhood beauty shops reinforced women's networks and became places where they could relax, exchange *chisme* (gossip), and enjoy the company of other women.

During the 1920s, the ethic of consumption became inextricably linked to making it in America. The message of affluence attainable through hard work and a bit of luck was reinforced in English and Spanish-language publications. Mexican barrios were not immune from the burgeoning consumer culture. The society pages of the influential Los Angeles-based *La Opinion*, for example, featured advice columns, horoscopes, and celebrity gossip. Advertisements for makeup, clothing, even feminine hygiene products reminded teenagers of an awaiting world of consumption.[10] . . .

Advertisements aimed at women promised status and affection if the proper bleaching cream, hair coloring, and cosmetics were purchased. Or, as one company boldly claimed, "Those with lighter, more healthy skin tones will become much more successful in business, love, and society." A print ad [in English] for Camay Soap carried by *Hispano America* in 1932 reminded women readers that "Life Is a Beauty Contest." Flapper fashions and celebrity testimonials further fused the connections between gendered identity and consumer culture. Another promotion encouraged readers to "SIGA LAS ESTRELLAS" (FOLLOW THE STARS) and use Max Factor cosmetics.[11] . . .

. . . Mexican women interpreted these visual representations in a myriad of ways. Some ignored them, some redefined their messages, and other internalized them. The popularity of bleaching creams offers a poignant testament to color consciousness in Mexican communities, a historical consciousness accentuated by Americanization through education and popular culture.

Reflecting the coalescence of Mexican and U.S. cultures, Spanish-language publications promoted pride in Latino theater and music while at the same time celebrated the icons of Americanization and consumption. Because of its proximity to Hollywood, *La Opinion* ran contests in which the lucky winner would receive a screen test. On the one hand, *La Opinion* nurtured the dreams of "success" through entertainment and consumption while, on the other, the newspaper railed against the deportations and repatriations of the 1930s. Sparked by manufactured fantasies and clinging to youthful hopes, many Mexican women teenagers avidly read celebrity gossip columns, attended Saturday matinees, cruised Hollywood and Vine, and nurtured their visions of stardom. A handful of Latina actresses, especially Dolores del Rio and Lupe Velez, whetted these aspirations and served as public role models of the "American dream." As a *La Opinion* article on Lupe Velez idealistically claimed, "Art has neither nationalities nor borders".[12]

. . . Mexican-American women teenagers . . . positioned themselves within the cultural messages they gleaned from English and Spanish-language publications, afternoon matinees, and popular radio programs. Their shifting conceptions of acceptable heterosocial behavior, including their desire "to date," heightened existing generational tensions between parents and daughters.

Obviously, the most serious point of contention between an adolescent daughter and her Mexican parents regarded her behavior toward young men. In both cities and rural towns, close chaperonage was a way of life. Recalling the supervisory role played by her "old maid" aunt, María Fierro laughingly explained, "She'd check up on us all the time. I used to get so mad at her." Ruby Estrada recalled that in her small southern Arizona community, "all the mothers" escorted their daughters to the local dances. Estrada's mother was no exception when it came to chaperoning her daughters. "She went especially for us. She'd just sit there and take care of our coats and watch us." Even talking to male peers in broad daylight could be grounds for discipline. Adele Hernández Milligan, a resident of Los Angeles for over fifty years, elaborated: "I remember the first time that I walked home with a boy from school. Anyway, my mother saw me and she was mad. I must have been sixteen or seventeen. She slapped my face because I was walking home with a boy" [13] . . .

Faced with this type of situation, young women had three options: they could accept the rules set down for them; they could rebel; or they could find ways to compromise or circumvent traditional standards. "I was *never* allowed to go out by myself in the evening; it just was not done," related Carmen Bernal Escobar. In rural communities, where restrictions were perhaps even more stringent, "nice" teenagers could not even swim with male peers. According to Ruby Estrada, "We were ladies and wouldn't go swimming out there with a bunch of boys." Yet many seemed to accept these limits with equanimity. Remembering her mother as her chaperone, Lucy Acosta insisted, "I could care less as long as I danced." "It wasn't devastating at all," echoed Ruby Estrada. "We took it in stride. We never thought of it as cruel or mean. . . . It was taken for granted that that's the way it was."[14] . . .

Women in cities had a distinct advantage over their rural peers in that they could venture miles from their neighborhood into the anonymity of dance halls, amusement parks, and other forms of commercialized leisure. With carnival rides and the Cinderella Ballroom, the Nu-Pike amusement park of Long Beach proved a popular hangout for Mexican youth in Los Angeles. It was more difficult to abide by traditional norms when excitement loomed just on the other side of the streetcar line.

Some women openly rebelled. They moved out of their family homes and into apartments. Considering themselves freewheeling single women, they could go out with men unsupervised as was the practice among their Anglo peers. Others challenged parental and cultural standards even further by living with their boyfriends. In his field notes, University of California economist Paul Taylor recorded an incident in which a young woman had moved in with her Anglo boyfriend after he had convinced her that such arrangements were common among Americans. "This terrible freedom in the United States," one Mexicana lamented. "I do not have to worry because I have no daughters, but the poor *señoras* with many girls, they worry".[15]

Those teenagers who did not wish to defy their parents openly would "sneak out" of the house to meet their dates or attend dances with female friends. Whether meeting someone at a drugstore, roller rink, or theater, this practice involved the invention of elaborate stories to mask traditionally inappropriate behavior. In other words, they lied.[16] . . .

. . . [W]hat other tactics did teenagers devise? . . . Alicia Mendeola Shelit recalled that one of her older brothers would accompany her to dances ostensibly as a chaperone. "But then my oldest brother would always have a blind date for me." Carmen Bernal Escobar was permitted to entertain her boyfriends at home, but only under the supervision of her brother or mother. The practice of "going out with the girls," though not [generally] accepted until the 1940s, was fairly common. Several Mexican-American women, often related, would escort one another to an event (such as a dance), socialize with the men in attendance, and then walk home together. In the sample of seventeen interviews, daughters negotiated their activities with their parents. Older siblings and extended kin appeared in the background as either chaperones or accomplices. . . .

. . . [M]any teenage women knew little about sex other than what they picked up from friends, romance magazines, and the local theater. As Mary Luna remembered, "I thought that if somebody kissed you, you could get pregnant." In *Singing for My Echo*, New Mexico native Gregorita Rodríguez confided that on her wedding night, she knelt down and said her rosary until her husband gently asked, "Gregorita, *mi esposa*, are you afraid of me?" At times this naiveté persisted beyond the wedding. "It took four days for my husband to touch me," one woman revealed. "I slept with dress and all. We were both greenhorns, I guess."[17] . . .

Chaperonage . . . exacerbated conflict not only between generations but within individuals as well. In gaily recounting tales of ditching the *dueña* or sneaking down the stairwell, the laughter of the interviewees fails to hide the painful memories of breaking away from familial expectations. Their words resonate with the dilemma of reconciling their search for autonomy with their desire for parental affirmation. . . . [E]very informant who challenged or circumvented chaperonage held a fulltime job, as either a factory or service worker. In contrast, most women who accepted constant supervision did not work for wages. Perhaps because they labored for long hours, for little pay, and frequently under hazardous conditions, factory and service workers were determined to exercise some control over their leisure time.[18] . . .

It may also be significant that none of the employed teenagers had attended high school. They entered the labor market directly after or even before the completion of the eighth grade. Like many female factory workers in the United States, most Mexican operatives were young, unmarried daughters whose wage labor was essential to the economic survival of their families. As members of a "family wage economy," they relinquished all or part of their wages to their elders. According to a 1933 University of California study, of the Mexican families surveyed with working children, the children's monetary contributions constituted 35 percent of total household income. Cognizant of their earning power, they resented the lack of personal autonomy.[19]

Delicate negotiations ensued as both parents and daughters struggled over questions of leisure activities and discretionary income. Could a young woman retain a portion of her wages for her own use? If elders demanded every penny, daughters might be more inclined to splurge on a new outfit or other personal item on their way home from work or, even more extreme, they might choose to move out, taking their paychecks with them. Recognizing their dependence on their children's income, some parents compromised. Their concessions, however, generally took the form of allocating spending money rather than relaxing traditional supervision. Still, women's earning power could be an important bargaining chip. . . .

To complete the picture, we also have to consider the perspective of Mexican immigrant parents who encountered a youth culture very different from that of their generation. For them, courtship had occurred in the plaza; young women and men promenaded under the watchful eyes of town elders, an atmosphere in which an exchange of meaningful glances could well portend engagement. One can understand their consternation as they watched their daughters apply cosmetics and adopt the apparel advertised in fashion magazines. In other words, "If she dresses like a flapper, will she then act like one?" Seeds of suspicion reaffirmed the penchant for traditional supervision. . . .

. . . [P]arents in the barrios of major cities fought a losing battle against urban anonymity and commercialized leisure. The Catholic Church was quick to point out the "dangerous amusement" inherent in dancing, theater-going, dressing fashionably, and reading pulp fiction. Under the section, "The Enemy in the Ballroom," a Catholic advice book warned of the hidden temptations of dance. "I know that some persons can indulge in it without harm; but sometimes even the coldest temperaments are heated by it." Therefore, the author offered the following rules:

> (1) If you know nothing at all . . . about dancing do not trouble yourself to learn (2) Be watchful. . . . and see that your pleasure in dancing does not grow into a passion. . . . (3) Never frequent fairs, picnics, carnivals, or public dancing halls where Heaven only knows what sorts of people congregate. (4) Dance only at private parties where your father or mother is present.

Pious pronouncements such as these had little impact on those adolescents who cherished the opportunity to look and act like vamps and flappers.[20]

Attempting to regulate the social life of young parishioners, barrio priests organized gender-segregated teen groups. In Los Angeles, Juventud Católica Feminina Mexicana (JCFM) had over fifty chapters. In her autobiography *Hoyt Street*, Mary Helen Ponce remembered the group as one organized for "nice" girls with the navy blue uniform as its most appealing feature. . . .

Ponce enjoyed going to "*las vistas*," usually singing cowboy movies shown in the church hall after Sunday evening rosary. . . . The cut-rate features . . . raised money for local activities. . . . In an era of segregated theaters, church halls tendered an environment where Mexicanos and their children could enjoy inexpensive entertainment and sit wherever they pleased. [21] . . .

[P]opular culture offered an alternative vision to parental and church expectations complete with its own aura of legitimacy. . . . Even the Spanish-language press fanned youthful passions. On May 9, 1927, *La Opinion* ran an article entitled; "How do you kiss?" Informing readers that "el beso no es un arte sino una ciencia" [kissing is not an art but rather a science], this short piece outlined the three components of a kiss: quality, quantity, and topography. The modern kiss, furthermore, should last three minutes.[22] Though certainly shocking older Mexicanos, such titillating fare catered to a youth market. . . .

Mexican-American women were not caught between two worlds. They navigated across multiple terrains at home, at work, and at play. They engaged in cultural coalescence. The Mexican-American generation selected, retained, borrowed, and created their own cultural forms. Or as one woman informed anthropologist Ruth Tuck, "Fusion is what we want—the best of both ways."[23] These children of immigrants may have been captivated by consumerism, but few would attain its promises of affluence. Race and gender prejudice as well as socioeconomic segmentation constrained the possibilities of choice. . . .

. . . [W]hat seems most striking is that the struggle over chaperonage occurred against a background of persistent discrimination. During the early 1930s, Mexicans were routinely rounded up and deported and even when deportations diminished, segregation remained. Historian Albert Camarillo has demonstrated that in Los Angeles restrictive real estate covenants and segregated schools increased dramatically between 1920 and 1950. The proportion of Los Angeles area municipalities with covenants prohibiting Mexicans and other people of color from purchasing residences in certain neighborhoods climbed from 20 percent in 1920 to 80 percent in 1946. Many restaurants, theaters, and public swimming pools discriminated against their Spanish-surnamed clientele. In southern California, for example, Mexicans could swim at the public plunges only one day out of the week (just before they drained the pool). Small-town merchants frequently refused to admit Spanish-speaking people into their places of business. "White Trade Only" signs served as bitter reminders of their second-class citizenship.[24]

Individual acts of discrimination could also blunt youthful aspirations. Erminia Ruiz recalled that from the ages of thirteen to fifteen, she worked full-time to support her sisters and widowed mother as a doughnut maker. "They could get me for lower wages." When health officials would stop in to check the premises, the underage employee would hide in the flour bins. At the age of sixteen, she became the proud recipient of a Social Security card and was thrilled to become the first Mexican hired by a downtown Denver cafeteria. Her delight as a "salad girl" proved short-lived. A co-worker reported that $200 had been stolen from her purse. In Erminia's words:

> Immediately they wanted to know what I did with the $200.00. I didn't know what they were talking about so they got . . . a policewoman and they took me in the restroom and undressed me. [Later they would discover that the co-worker's friend had taken the money.] I felt awful. I didn't go back to work.

Though deeply humiliated, Erminia scanned the classified ads the next day and soon combined work with night classes at a storefront business college.[25]. . .

Mexican-American adolescents felt the lure of Hollywood and the threat of deportation, the barbs of discrimination, and the reins of constant supervision. In dealing with all the contradictions in their lives, many young women focused their attention on chaperonage, an area where they could make decisions. The inner conflicts expressed in the oral histories reveal that such decisions were not made impetuously. Hard as it was for young heterosexual women to carve out their own sexual boundaries, imagine the greater difficulty for lesbians coming of age in the Southwest barrios. . . .

. . . Although still practiced in some areas, chaperonage appeared less frequently after World War II. By the 1950s, chaperonage had become more of a generational marker. Typically only the daughters of recent immigrants had to contend with constant supervision. Mexican Americans relegated chaperonage to their own past, a custom that, as parents, they chose not to inflict on their children. Family honor also became less intertwined with female virginity; but the preservation of one's "reputation" was still a major concern.[26] In the poem "Pueblo, 1950," Bernice Zamora captures the consequences of a kiss:

> I remember you, Fred Montoya
> You were the first *vato* to ever kiss me
> I was twelve years old.
> My mother said shame on you,
>
> my teacher said shame on you, and
> I said shame on me, and nobody
> said a word to you.[27]. . .

In challenging chaperonage, Mexican-American teenagers did not attack the foundation of familial oligarchy—only its more obvious manifestation. It would take later generations of Chicana feminists to take on this task.

Notes

1. Interview with Maria Ybarra, December 1, 1990, conducted by David Pérez.

2. For colonial New Mexico, Ramón Gutiérrez convincingly demonstrates how family honor was tied, in part, to women's *vergüenza* (literally, shame or virginity). See Ramón Gutiérrez, "Honor, Ideology, and Class Gender Domination in New Mexico, 1690–1846," *Latin American Perspectives* 12 (Winter 1985): 81–104.

3. Ruth D. Tuck, *Not with the Fist: Mexican-Americans in a Southwest City* (New York: Harcourt, Brace and Co., 1946; rpt. Arno Press, 1974), 185–88; Vicki L. Ruiz, "Oral History and La Mujer: The Rosa Guerrero Story," *in Women on the U.S.-Mexico Border: Responses to Change* (Boston: Allen and Unwin, 1987), 226–27; *interview* with Mary Luna, Volume 20 of *Rosie the Riveter Revisited: Women and the World War I Work Experience*, ed. Sherna Berger Gluck (Long Beach: CSULB Foundation, 1983), 9–10. Bullock's was a major department store in the West. During the 1940s, bilingual education appeared as an exciting experiment in curriculum reform.

4. Mauricio Mazón's *The Zoot Suit Riots* (Austin: University of Texas Press, 1984) and the Luis Valdez play and feature film, *Zoot Suit*, provide examples of the literature on *pachucos*.

5. María Fierro, Rose Escheverria Mulligan, Adele Hernández Milligan, Beatrice Morales Clifton, Mary Luna, Alicia Mendeola Shelit, Carmen Bernal Escobar, Belen Martínez Mason, and Julia Luna Mount grew up in Los Angeles. Lucy Acosta and Alma Araiza García came of age in El Paso and Erminia Ruiz in Denver. Representing the rural experience are María Arredondo and Jesusita Torres (California), María Ybarra (Texas), and Ruby Estrada (Arizona). As a teenager, Eusebia Buriel moved with her family from Silvis, Illinois, to Riverside, California. Nine of these women were born between 1908 and 1919, and eight between 1920 and 1926. This sample includes some who were chaperoned during the 1920s and others who were chaperoned during the thirties and forties. Nine interviews are housed in university archives, seven are part of the *Rosie the Riveter* collection at California State University, Long Beach, California.

6. F. Scott Fitzgerald, "Bernice Bobs Her Hair," *Flappers and Philosophers* (London: W. Collins Sons and Co., Ltd., 1922), 209–46; Martínez Mason interview, 44; interview with Alicia Mendeola Shelit, Volume 37 of *Rosie the Riveter*, 18; Paul S. Taylor, *Mexican Labor in the United States, Volume II* (Berkeley: University of California Press, 1932), 199–200; interview with María Fierro, Volume 12 of *Rosie the Riveter*, 10. [Vicki Ruiz Writes:] Changing clothes at school is not peculiar to our mothers and grandmothers. As a high school student in the early 1970s, I was not allowed to wear the fashionable micro-mini skirts. But I bought one anyway. I left home in a full dirndl skirt with a flowing peasant blouse, but once I arrived at school, I would untie the skirt (which I would then dump in my locker) to reveal the mini-skirt I had worn underneath.

7. Taylor, *Mexican Labor, Vol. II*, vi–vii.

8. Rodolfo F. Acuña, *Community Under Siege: A Chronicle of Chicanos East of the Los Angeles River*,

1945–1975 (Los Angeles: UCLA Chicano Studies Publications, 1984), 278, 407–408, 413–414, 418, 422.

9. Sherna B. Gluck, *Rosie the Riveter Revisited: Women, The War and Social Change* (Boston: Twayne Publishers, 1987), 81, 85.

10. For examples, *see La Opinion*, September 26, 1926; May 14, 1927; June 5, 1927; September 9, 1929; January 15, 1933; January 29, 1938.

11. *La Opinion*, September 29, 1929; *Hispano-America*, July 2, 1932.

12. For examples, *sec La Opinion*, September 23, 24, 27, and 30, 1926; March 2, 1927.

13. Interview with Adele Hernández Milligan, Volume 26 of *Rosie the Riveter*, 17.

14. Escobar interview, 1986; Estrada interview, 11, 13; interview no. 653 with Lucy Acosta conducted by Mario T. García, October 28, 1982 (on file at the Institute of Oral History, University of Texas, El Paso), 17.

15. Paul S. Taylor, "Women in Industry," field notes for his book, *Mexican Labor in the United States, 1927–1930*, Bancroft Library, University of California, 1 box; Richard G. Thurston, "Urbanization and Sociocultural Change in a Mexican-American Enclave" (Ph.D. dissertation, University of California, Los Angeles, 1957).

16. Martínez Mason interview, 30; Ruiz interviews (1990, 1993); Thomas Sheridan, *Los Tucsonenses* (Tucson: University of Arizona Press, 1986), 131–32.

17. Interview with Julia Luna Mount, November 17, 1983, by the author; Fierro interview, 18; Luna interview, 29; Ruiz interview (1993); Gregorita Rodríguez, *Singing for My Echo* (Santa Fe: Cota Editions, 1987), 52; Martínez Mason interview, 62.

18. See Douglas Monroy, "An Essay on Understanding the Work Experiences of Mexicans in Southern California, 1900–1939," *Aztlán* 12 (Spring 1981): 70. Feminist historians have also documented this push for autonomy among the daughters of European immigrants.

19. Heller Committee for Research in Social Economics of the University of California and Constantine Panuzio, *How Mexicans Earn and Live*, University of California Publications in Economics, XIII, No. 1, Cost of Living Studies V (Berkeley: University of California, 1933), 11, 14, 17; Taylor notes; Luna Mount interview; Ruiz interviews (1990, 1993); Shelit interview, 9.

20. Rev. F. X. Lasance, *The Catholic Girl's Guide and Sunday Missal* (New York: Benziger Brothers, 1905), 249–75. I have a 1946 reprint edition passed down to me by my older sister who had received it from our mother.

21. George J. Sanchez, *Becoming Mexican American: Ethnicity, Culture, and Identity in Chicano Los Angeles, 1900–1945* (New York: Oxford University Press, 1993), 167; Mary Helen Ponce, *Hoyt Street* (Albuquerque: University of New Mexico Press, 1993), 258, 266–71.

22. *La Opinion*, May 9, 1927.

23. Tuck, *Not with the Fist*, 134.

24. Rodolfo Acuña, *Occupied America: A History of Chicanos*, 2nd ed. (New York: Harper & Row, 1981), 310, 318, 323, 330–31; Shelit interview, 15; Paul S. Taylor, *Mexican Labor in the United States*, Vol. I (Berkeley: University of California Press, 1930; rpt. Arno Press, 1970), 221–24; Arredondo interview; Ruiz interviews (1990, 1993).

25. Ruiz interview (1993).

26. Acosta interview: Tuck, *Not with the Fist*, 126–27; Thurston, "Urbanization," 109, 117–119; Ruiz interviews (1990, 1993).

27. Bernice Zamora, "Pueblo, 1950," in *Infinite Divisions: An Anthology of Chicana Literature*, eds. Tey Diana Rebolledo and Eliana Rivero (Tucson: University of Arizona Press, 1993), 315.

RUTH SCHWARTZ COWAN

The "Industrial Revolution" in the Home: Household Technology and Social Change in the Twentieth Century

The industrial technology that changed factory work also changed housework; the washing machine replaced the washtub just as the power loom replaced the handloom. Yet the impact of changing household technology on household workers has been little explored. In the following essay, Ruth Schwartz Cowan examines how housework changed with the introduction of a variety of labor-

Excerpted from "The 'Industrial Revolution' in the Home: Household Technology and Social Change in the Twentieth Century" by Ruth Schwartz Cowan, in *Technology and Culture* 17 (1976): 1–23. Notes have been renumbered and edited.

saving appliances and the aggressive use of advertising designed to promote their sale. What emerges is a job that has changed in structure. Less burdensome physically, housework became no less time consuming as new duties were added and the work itself invested with new expectations and greater emotional content. What Cowan describes, in part, is the transition from the nineteenth-century mistress of the household—generally white—who directed a servant's work to the twentieth-century middle-class housewife who, as jane-of-all-trades—laundress, scrub woman, gardener, nursemaid, chauffeur, and cook—was by the 1940s expected to find self-fulfillment in housework. What does this assumption suggest about the role of ideology as well as technology in defining work? Is the job of housework becoming redefined in a way that serves to domesticate the "new woman" rather than liberate her to pursue publicly her talent and abilities? In what sense is the individual housewife more isolated than ever?

When we think about the interaction between technology and society, we tend to think in fairly grandiose terms: massive computers invading the workplace, railroad tracks cutting through vast wildernesses, armies of women and children toiling in the mills. . . . [But] the industrialization of the home was a process very different from the industrialization of other means of production. . . . [What was] the impact of industrialization on families? . . .

What happened . . . to middle-class American women when the implements with which they did their everyday household work changed? Did the technological change in household appliances have any effect upon the structure of American households, or upon the ideologies that governed the behavior of American women, or upon the functions that families needed to perform?

[I have] defined middle-class American women as actual or potential readers of the better-quality women's magazines, such as the *Ladies' Home Journal, American Home, Parents Magazine, Good Housekeeping,* and *McCall's.* Nonfictional material (articles and advertisements) in those magazines [has served] as a partial indicator of some of the technological and social changes that were occurring.

The *Ladies' Home Journal* has been in continuous publication since 1886. A casual survey of the nonfiction in the *Journal* yields the immediate impression that the decade between the end of World War I and the beginning of the depression witnessed the most drastic changes in patterns of household work. Statistical data bear out this impression. Before 1918, for example, illustrations of homes lit by gaslight could still be found . . . ; by 1928 gaslight had disappeared. In 1917 only one-quarter of the dwellings in the United States had been electrified, but by 1920 this figure had doubled (47.4 percent—for rural nonfarm and urban dwellings), and by 1930 four-fifths of all households had been electrified.[1] If electrification had meant simply the change from gas or oil lamps to electric lights, the changes in the housewife's routines might not have been very great (except for eliminating the chore of cleaning and filling oil lamps); but changes in lighting were the least of the changes that electrification implied. Small electric appliances followed quickly on the heels of the electric light, and some of those augured much more profound changes in the housewife's routine.

Ironing, for example, had traditionally been one of the most dreadful household chores, especially in warm weather when the kitchen stove had to be kept hot for the better part of the day; irons were heavy and they had to be returned to the stove frequently to be reheated. Electric irons eased a good part of this burden. They were relatively inexpensive and very quickly replaced their predecessors; advertisements for electric irons first began to appear in the ladies' magazines after the war, and by the end of the decade the old flatiron had disappeared; by 1929 a survey of 100 Ford employees revealed that ninety-eight of them had the new electric irons in their homes.[2]

Data on the diffusion of electric washing machines are somewhat harder to come by; but it is clear from the advertisements in the magazines, particularly advertisements for laundry soap, that by the middle of the 1920s those machines could be found in a significant number of homes. The washing machine is depicted just about as frequently as the laundry tub by the middle of the 1920s; in 1929, forty-nine out of those 100 Ford workers had the machines in their homes. The washing machines did not drastically reduce the time that had to be spent on household laundry, as they did not go through their cycles automatically and did not spin dry; the housewife had to stand guard, stopping and starting the machine at appropriate times, adding soap, sometimes attaching the drain pipes, and putting the clothes through the wringer manually. The machines did, however, reduce a good part of the drudgery that once had been associated with washday, and this was a matter of no small consequence.[3] Soap powders appeared on the market in the early 1920s, thus eliminating the need to scrape and boil bars of laundry soap.[4] By the end of the 1920s Blue Monday must have been considerably less blue for some housewives—and probably considerably less "Monday," for with an electric iron, a washing machine, and a hot water heater, there was no reason to limit the washing to just one day of the week.

Like the routines of washing the laundry, the routines of personal hygiene must have been transformed for many households during the 1920s—the years of the bathroom mania.[5] More and more bathrooms were built in older homes, and new homes began to include them as a matter of course. Before the war most bathroom fixtures (tubs, sinks, and toilets) were made out of porcelain by hand; each bathroom was custom-made for the house in which it was installed. After the war industrialization descended upon the bathroom industry; cast iron enamelware went into mass production and fittings were standardized. In 1921 the dollar value of the production of enameled sanitary fixtures was $2.4 million, the same as it had been in 1915. By 1923, just two years later, that figure had doubled to $4.8 million; it rose again, to $5.1 million, in 1925.[6] The first recessed, double-shell cast iron enameled bathtub was put on the market in the early 1920s. A decade later the standard American bathroom had achieved its standard American form: the recessed tub, plus tiled floors and walls, brass plumbing, a single-unit toilet, an enameled sink, and a medicine chest, all set into a small room which was very often 5 feet square. The bathroom evolved more quickly than any other room of the house; its standardized form was accomplished in just over a decade.

Along with bathrooms came modernized systems for heating hot water: 61 percent of the homes in Zanesville, Ohio, had indoor plumbing with centrally heated water by 1926, and 83 percent of the homes valued over $2,000 in Muncie, Indiana, had hot and cold running water by 1935.[7] These figures may not be typical of small American cities (or even large American cities) at those times, but they do jibe with the impression that one gets from the magazines: After 1918 references to hot water heated on the kitchen range, either for laundering or for bathing, become increasingly difficult to find.

Similarly, during the 1920s many homes were outfitted with central heating; in Muncie most of the homes of the business class had basement heating in 1924; by 1935 Federal Emergency Relief Administration data for the city indicated that only 22.4 percent of the dwellings valued over $2,000 were still heated by a kitchen stove.[8] What all these changes meant in terms of new habits for the average housewife is somewhat hard to calculate; changes there must have been, but it is difficult to know whether those changes produced an overall saving of labor and/or time. Some chores were eliminated—hauling water, heating water on the stove, maintaining the kitchen fire—but other chores were added, most notably the chore of keeping yet another room scrupulously clean.

It is not, however, difficult to be certain about the changing habits that were associated with the new American kitchen—a kitchen from which the coal stove had disappeared. In Muncie in 1924, cooking with gas was done in two out of three homes; in 1935 only 5 percent of the homes valued over $2,000 still had coal or wood stoves for cooking,[9] After 1918 advertisements for coal and wood stoves disappeared from the *Ladies' Home Journal;* stove manufacturers purveyed only their gas, oil, or electric models. Articles giving advice to homemakers on how to deal with the trials and tribulations of starting, stoking, and maintaining a coal or a wood fire also disappeared. Thus it seems a safe assumption that most middle-class homes had switched to the new method of cooking by the time the depression began.

The change in routine that was predicated on the change from coal or wood to gas or oil was profound; aside from the elimination of such chores as loading the fuel and removing the ashes, the new stoves were much easier to light, maintain, and regulate (even when they did not have thermostats, as the earliest models did not).[10] Kitchens were, in addition, much easier to clean when they did not have coal dust regularly tracked through them. . . .

Along with new stoves came new foodstuffs and new dietary habits. Canned foods had been on the market since the middle of the nineteenth century, but they did not become an appreciable part of the standard middle class diet until the 1920s—if the recipes given in cookbooks and in women's magazines are a reliable guide. By 1918 the variety of foods available in cans had been considerably expanded from the peas, corn, and succotash of the nineteenth century; an American housewife with sufficient means could have purchased almost any fruit or vegetable and quite a surprising array of ready-made meals in a can—from Heinz's spaghetti in meat sauce to Purity Cross's lobster à la Newburg. By the middle of the 1920s home canning was becoming a lost art. Canning recipes were relegated to the back pages of the women's magazines; the business-class wives of Muncie reported that, while their mothers had once spent the better part of the summer and fall canning, they themselves rarely put up anything, except an occasional jelly or batch of tomatoes. In part this was also due to changes in the technology of marketing food; increased use of refrigerated railroad cars during this period meant that fresh fruits and vegetables were in the markets all year round at reasonable prices. By the early 1920s convenience foods were also appearing on American tables: cold breakfast cereals, pancake mixes, bouillon cubes, and packaged desserts could be found. Wartime shortages accustomed Americans to eating much lighter meals than they had previously been wont to do; and as fewer family members were taking all their meals at home (businessmen started to eat lunch in restaurants downtown, and factories and schools began installing cafeterias), there was simply less cooking to be done, and what there was of it was easier to do.[11]

Many of the changes just described—from hand power to electric power, from coal and wood to gas and oil as fuels for cooking, from one-room heating to central heating, from pumping water to running water—are enormous technological changes. Changes of a similar dimension, either in the fundamental technology of an industry, in the diffusion of that technology, or in the routines of workers, would have long since been labeled an "industrial revolution." The change from the laundry tub to the washing machine is no less profound than the change from the hand loom to the power loom; the change from pumping water to turning on a water faucet is no less destructive of traditional habits than the change from manual to electric calculating. . . .

What happened to this particular workforce when the technology of [households] . . . was revolutionized? Did structural changes occur? Were new jobs created for which new skills were required? Can we discern new ideologies that influenced the behavior of the workers?

The answer to all of these questions, surprisingly enough, seems to be yes. There were marked structural changes in the workforce, changes that increased the workload and the job description of the workers that remained. New jobs were created for which new skills were required; these jobs were not physically burdensome, but they may have taken up as much time as the jobs they had replaced. New ideologies were also created, ideologies which reinforced new behavioral patterns. . . . Middle-class housewives, the women who must have first felt the impact of the new household technology, were not flocking into the divorce courts or the labor market or the forums of political protest in the years immediately after the revolution in their work. What they were doing was sterilizing baby bottles, shepherding their children to dancing classes and music lessons, planning nutritious meals, shopping for new clothes, studying child psychology, and hand stitching color-coordinated curtains. . . .

The significant change in the structure of the household labor force was the disappearance of paid and unpaid servants (unmarried daughters, maiden aunts, and grandparents fall in the latter category) as household workers—and the imposition of the entire job on the housewife herself. . . . The phenomenon itself is relatively easy to document. Before World War I, when illustrators in the women's magazines depicted women doing housework, the women were very often servants. When the lady of the house was drawn, she was often the person being served, or she was supervising the serving, or she was adding an elegant finishing touch to the work. Nursemaids diapered babies, seamstresses pinned up hems, waitresses served meals, laundresses did the wash, and cooks did the cooking. By the end of the 1920s the servants had disappeared from those illustrations; all those jobs were being done by housewives—elegantly manicured and coiffed, to be sure, but housewives nonetheless.

If we are tempted to suppose that illustrations in advertisements are not a reliable indicator of structural changes of this sort, we can corroborate the changes in other ways. Apparently, the illustrators really did know whereof they drew. Statistically the number of persons throughout the country employed in household service dropped from 1,851,000 in 1910 to 1,411,000 in 1920, while the number of households enumerated in the census rose from 20.3 million to 24.4 million.[12] In Indiana the ratio of households to servants increased from 13.5/1 in 1890 to 30.5/1 in 1920, and in the country as a whole the number of paid domestic servants per 1,000 population dropped from 98.9 in 1900 to 58.0 in 1920. The business-class housewives of Muncie reported that they employed approximately one-half as many woman-hours of domestic service as their mothers had done.[13]

In case we are tempted to doubt these statistics (and indeed statistics about household labor are particularly unreliable, as the labor is often transient, part-time, or simply unreported), we can turn to articles on the servant problem, the disappearance of unpaid family workers, the design of kitchens, or to architectural drawings for houses. All of this evidence reiterates the same point: Qualified servants were difficult to find; their wages had risen and their numbers fallen; houses were being designed without maid's rooms; daughters and unmarried aunts were finding jobs downtown; kitchens were being designed for housewives, not for servants.[14] The first home with a kitchen that was not an entirely separate room was designed by Frank Lloyd Wright in 1934. In 1937 Emily Post invented a new character for her etiquette books: Mrs. Three-in-One, the woman who is her own cook, waitress, and hostess. There must have been many new Mrs. Three-in-Ones abroad in the land during the 1930s.[15]

As the number of household assistants declined, the number of household tasks increased. The middle-class housewife was expected to demonstrate competence at several tasks that previously had not existed at all. Child care is the most obvious example. The average housewife had fewer children than her mother had had, but she was expected to do things for her children that her mother would never have dreamed of doing: to prepare their special infant formulas, sterilize their bottles, weigh them every day, see to it that they ate nutritionally balanced meals, keep them isolated and confined when they had even the slightest illness, consult with their teachers frequently, and chauffeur them to dancing lessons and evening parties.[16] There was very little Freudianism in this new attitude toward child care: Mothers were not spending more time and effort on their children because they feared the psychological trauma of separation, but because competent nursemaids could not be found, and the new theories of child care required constant attention from well-informed persons—persons who were willing and able to read about the latest discoveries in nutrition, in the control of contagious diseases, or in the techniques of behavioral psychology. These persons simply had to be their mothers.

Consumption of economic goods provides another example of the housewife's expanded job description; like child care, the new tasks associated with consumption were not necessarily physically burdensome, but they were time consuming, and they required the acquisition of new skills. Home economists and the editors of women's magazines tried to teach housewives to spend their money wisely. The present generation of housewives, it was argued, had been reared by mothers who did not ordinarily shop for things like clothing, bed linens, or towels; consequently modern housewives did not know how to shop and would have to be taught. Furthermore, their mothers had not been accustomed to the wide variety of goods that were now available in the modern marketplace; the new housewives had to be taught not just to be consumers, but to be informed consumers.[17] Several contemporary observers believed that shopping and shopping wisely were occupying increasing amounts of housewives' time.[18]

[O]bservers also believed that standards of household care changed during the decade of the 1920s. The discovery of the "household germ" led to almost fetishistic concern about the cleanliness of the home. The amount and frequency of laundering probably increased, as bed linen and underwear were changed more often, children's clothes were made increasingly out of washable fabrics, and men's shirts no longer had replaceable collars and snap cuffs.[19] Unfortunately all these changes in standards are difficult to document, being changes in the things that people regard as so insignificant as to be unworthy of comment. . . .

In any event we do have various time studies which demonstrate somewhat surprisingly that housewives with conveniences were spending just as much time on household duties as were housewives without them—or, to put it another way, housework, like so many other types of work, expands to fill the time available. A study comparing the time spent per week in housework by 288 farm families and 154 town families in Oregon in 1928 revealed 61 hours spent by farm wives and 63.4 hours by town wives; in 1929 a U.S. Department of Agriculture study of families in various states produced almost identical results.[20] Just after World War II economists at Bryn Mawr College reported the same phenomenon: 60.55 hours spent by farm housewives, 78.35 hours by women in small cities, 80.57 hours by women in large ones. . . .[21] A recent survey of time studies conducted between 1920 and 1970 concludes that the time spent on housework by nonemployed house wives has remained remarkably constant throughout the period.[22] All these results point in the same direction: mechanization of the household meant that time expended on some jobs decreased, but also that new jobs were substituted, and in some cases—notably laundering—time expenditures for old jobs increased because of higher standards. The advantages of mechanization may be somewhat more dubious than they seem at first glance.

As the job of the housewife changed, the connected ideologies also changed; there was a clearly perceptible difference in the attitudes that women brought to housework before and after World War I.[23] Before the war the trials of doing housework in a servantless home were discussed and they were regarded as just that—trials, necessary chores that had to be got through until a qualified servant could be found. After the war, housework changed: It was no longer a trial and a chore, but something quite different—an emotional "trip." Laundering was not just laundering, but an expression of love; the housewife who truly loved her family would protect them from the embarrassment of tattletale gray. Feeding the family was not just feeding the family, but a way to express the housewife's artistic inclinations and a way to encourage feelings of family loyalty and affection. Diapering the baby was not just diapering, but a time to build the baby's sense of security and love for the mother. Cleaning the bathroom sink was not just cleaning, but an exercise of protective maternal instincts, providing a way for the housewife to keep her family safe from disease. Tasks of this emotional magnitude could not possibly be delegated to servants, even assuming that qualified servants could be found.

Women who failed at these new household tasks were bound to feel guilt about their failure. If I had to choose one word to characterize the temper of the women's magazines during the 1920s, it would be "guilt." Readers of the better-quality women's magazines are portrayed as feeling guilty a good lot of the time, and when they are not guilty they are embarrassed: guilty if their infants have not gained enough weight, embarrassed if their drains are clogged, guilty if their children go to school in soiled clothes, guilty if all the germs behind the bathroom sink are not eradicated, guilty if they fail to notice the first signs of an oncoming cold, embarrassed if accused of having body odor, guilty if their sons go to school without good breakfasts, guilty if their daughters are unpopular because of old-fashioned, or unironed, or—heaven forbid—dirty dresses. In earlier times women were made to feel guilty if they abandoned their children or were too free with their affections. In the years after World War I, American women were made to feel guilty about sending their children to school in scuffed shoes. Between the two kinds of guilt there is a world of difference.

[Several sociological theories predict] that changing patterns of household work will be correlated with at least two striking indicators of social change: the divorce rate and the rate of married women's labor force participation. That correlation may indeed exist, but it certainly is not reflected in the women's magazines of the 1920s and 1930s; divorce and full-time paid employment were not part of the life-style or the life pattern of the middle-class housewife as she was idealized in her magazines. . . .

[A] close analysis of the statistical data corroborates the impression conveyed in the magazines. The divorce rate was indeed rising during the years between the wars, but it was not rising nearly so fast for the middle and upper classes (who had, presumably, easier access to the new technology) as it was for the lower classes. By almost every gauge of socioeconomic status—income, prestige of husband's work, education—the divorce rate is higher for persons lower on the socioeconomic scale—and this is a phenomenon that has been constant over time.[24]

The supposed connection between improved household technology and married women's labor force participation seems just as dubious, and on the same grounds. The single socioeconomic factor which correlates most strongly (in cross-sectional studies) with married women's employment is husband's income, and the correlation is strongly negative; the higher his income, the less likely it will be that she is working.[25] Women's labor force participation increased during the 1920s but this increase was due to the influx of single women into the force. Married women's participation increased slightly during those years, but that increase was largely in factory labor—precisely the kind of work that middle-class women (who were, again, much more likely to have laborsaving devices at home) were least likely to do. . . . [26]

Thus, for middle class American housewives between the wars, the social changes that we can document are not the ones that sociological theories predict; rather, they are changes in the structure of the workforce, in its skills, and in its ideology. These social changes were concomitant with a series of technological changes in the equipment that was used to do the work. What is the relationship between these two series of phenomena? Is it possible to demonstrate causality or the direction of that causality? Was the decline in the number of households employing servants a cause or an effect of the mechanization of those households? Both are, after all, equally possible. . . . Are there any techniques available to the historian to help us answer these questions?

In order to establish causality, we need to find a connecting link between the two sets of phenomena. [One] intervening agent between the social and the technological changes comes immediately to mind: the advertiser—by which term I mean a combination of the manufacturer of the new goods, the advertising agent who promoted the goods, and the periodical that published the promotion. All the new devices and new foodstuffs that were being offered to American households were being manufactured and marketed by large companies which had considerable amounts of capital invested in their production: General Electric, Procter & Gamble, General Foods, Lever Brothers, Frigidaire, Campbell's, Del Monte, American Can, Atlantic & Pacific Tea—these were all well-established firms by the time the household revolution began, and they were all in a position to pay for national advertising campaigns to promote their new products and services. And pay they did; one reason for the expanding size and number of women's magazines in the 1920s was no doubt the expansion in revenues from available advertisers.[27]

Those national advertising campaigns were likely to have been powerful stimulators of the social changes that occurred in the household labor force; the advertisers probably did not initiate the changes, but they certainly encouraged them. Most of the advertising campaigns manifestly worked, so they must have touched upon areas of real concern for American housewives. Appliance ads specifically suggested that the acquisition of one gadget or another would make it possible to fire the maid, spend more time with the children, or have the afternoon free for shopping.[28] Similarly, many advertisements played upon the embarrassment and guilt which were now associated with household work. Ralston, Cream of Wheat, and Ovaltine were not themselves responsible for the compulsive practice of weighing infants and children repeatedly (after every meal for newborns, every day in infancy, every week later on), but the manufacturers certainly did not stint on capitalizing upon the guilt that women apparently felt if their offspring did not gain the required amounts of weight.[29] And yet again, many of the earliest attempts to spread "wise" consumer practices were undertaken by large corporations and the magazines that desired their advertising; mail-order shopping guides, "product-testing" services, pseudoinformative pamphlets, and other such promotional devices were all techniques for urging the housewife to buy new things under the guise of training her in her role as skilled consumer.

Thus the advertisers could well be called the "ideologues" of the 1920s, encouraging certain very specific social changes. . . . Not surprisingly, the changes that occurred were precisely the ones that would gladden the hearts and fatten the purses of the advertisers; fewer household servants meant a greater demand for labor- and time-saving devices; more household tasks for women meant more and more specialized products that they would need to buy; more guilt and embarrassment about their failure to succeed at their work meant a greater likelihood that they would buy the products that were intended to minimize that failure. . . . The advertisers may not have created the image of the ideal American housewife that dominated the 1920s—the woman who cheerfully and skillfully set about making everyone in her family perfectly happy and perfectly healthy—but they certainly helped to perpetuate it. . . .

[Thus,] there is a dynamic interaction between the social changes that married women were experiencing and the technological changes that were occurring in their homes. Viewed this way, the disappearance of competent servants becomes one of the factors that stimulated the mechanization of homes, and this mechanization of homes becomes a factor (though by no means the only one) in the disappearance of servants. Similarly, the emotionalization of housework becomes both cause and effect of the mechanization of that work; and the expansion of time spent on new tasks becomes both cause and effect of the introduction of time-saving devices. For example, the social pressure to spend more time in child care may have led to a decision to purchase the devices; once purchased, the devices could indeed have been used to save time—although often they were not . . . .

The housewife is just about the only unspecialized worker left in America—a veritable jane-of-all-trades at a time when the jacks-of-all-trades have disappeared. As her work became generalized the housewife was also proletarianized: Formerly she was ideally the manager of several other subordinate workers; now she was idealized as the manager and the worker combined. Her managerial functions have not entirely disappeared, but they have certainly diminished and have been replaced by simple manual labor; the middle-class, fairly well-educated housewife ceased to be a personnel manager and became, instead, a chauffeur, charwoman, and short-order cook. The implications of this phenomenon, the proletarianization of a workforce that had previously seen itself as predominantly managerial, deserve to be explored at greater length than is possible here, because I suspect that they will explain certain aspects of the women's liberation movement of the 1960s and 1970s which have previously eluded explanation: why, for example, the movement's greatest strength lies in social and economic groups who seem, on the surface at least, to need it least—women who are white, well-educated, and middle-class.

Finally, instead of desensitizing the emotions that were connected with household work, the industrial revolution in the home seems to have heightened the emotional context of the work, until a woman's sense of self-worth became a function of her success at arranging bits of fruit to form a clown's face in a gelatin salad. That pervasive social illness, which Betty Friedan characterized as "the problem that has no name," arose not among workers who found that their labor brought no emotional satisfaction, but among workers who found that their work was invested with emotional weight far out of proportion to its own inherent value: "How long," a friend of mine is fond of asking, "can we continue to believe that we will have orgasms while waxing the kitchen floor?"

Notes

1. *Historical Statistics of the United States, Colonial Times to 1957* (Washington, D.C., 1960) p. 510.

2. Hazel Kyrk, *Economic Problems of the Family* (New York, 1933), p. 368, reporting a study in *Monthly Labor Review* 30 (1930):1209–52.

3. Although this point seems intuitively obvious, there is some evidence that it may not be true. Studies of energy expenditure during housework have indicated that by far the greatest effort is expended in hauling and lifting the wet wash, tasks which were not eliminated by the introduction of washing machines. In addition, if the introduction

of the machines served to increase the total amount of wash that was done by the housewife, this would tend to cancel the energy-saving effects of the machines themselves.

4. Rinso was the first granulated soap; it came on the market in 1918. . . .

5. I take this account, and the term, from Robert S. Lynd and Helen M. Lynd, *Middletown: A Study in Contemporary American Culture* (New York, 1929), p. 97. . . . The rural situation was quite different from the urban; the President's Conference on Home Building and Home Ownership reported that in the late 1920s, 71 percent of the urban families surveyed had bathrooms, but only 33 percent of the rural families did.

6. The data came from Siegfried Giedion, *Mechanization Takes Command* (New York, 1948), pp. 685–703.

7. *Zanesville, Ohio and Thirty-Six Other American Cities* (New York, 1927), p. 65. Also see Robert S. Lynd and Helen M. Lynd, *Middletown in Transition* (New York, 1936), p. 537. Middletown is Muncie, Indiana.

8. Lynd and Lynd, *Middletown*, p. 96, and *Middletown in Transition*, p. 539.

9. Lynd and Lynd, *Middletown*, p. 98, and *Middletown in Transition*, p. 562.

10. On the advantages of the new stoves, see *Boston Cooking School Cookbook* (Boston, 1916), pp. 15–20; and Russell Lynes, *The Domesticated Americans* (New York, 1957), pp. 119–20.

11. Lynd and Lynd, *Middletown*, pp. 134–35, 153–56.

12. *Historical Statistics*, pp. 16, 77.

13. For Indiana data, see Lynd and Lynd, *Middletown*, p. 169. For national data, see D. L. Kaplan and M. Claire Casey, *Occupational Trends in the United States, 1900–1950*, U.S. Bureau of the Census Working Paper no. 5 (Washington, D.C., 1958), table 6.

14. On the disappearance of maiden aunts, unmarried daughters, and grandparents, see Lynd and Lynd, *Middletown*, pp. 25, 99, 110; Edward Bok, "Editorial," *American Home* 1 (Oct. 1928):15.

15. Emily Post, *Etiquette: The Blue Book of Social Usage*, 5th ed. rev. (New York, 1937), p. 823.

16. This analysis is based upon various child care articles that appeared during the period in the *Ladies' Home Journal, American Home,* and *Parents Magazine.*

17. On consumer education see, for example, "How to Buy Towels," *Ladies' Home Journal 45* (Feb. 1928):134; "Buying Table Linen," *Ladies' Home Journal* 45 (Mar. 1928):43 . . .

18. See, for example, Lynd and Lynd, *Middletown*, pp. 176, 196; and Margaret G. Reid, *Economics of Household Production* (New York, 1934), chap. 13.

19. See advertisement for Cleanliness Institute—"Self-respect thrives on soap and water," *Ladies' Home Journal* 45 (Feb. 1928):107. On changing bed linen, see "When the Bride Goes Shopping," *American Home* 1 (Jan. 1928):370.

20. As reported in Kyrk, p. 51.

21. Bryn Mawr College Department of Social Economy, *Women During the War and After* (Philadelphia, 1945); and Ethel Goldwater, "Woman's Place," *Commentary* 4 (Dec. 1947):578–85.

22. JoAnn Vanek, "Keeping Busy: Time Spent in Housework, United States, 1920–1970" (Ph.D. diss., University of Michigan, 1973).

23. This analysis is based upon my reading of the middle-class women's magazines between 1918 and 1930. For detailed documentation see my paper "Two Washes in the Morning and a Bridge Party at Night: The American Housewife between the Wars," *Women's Studies* 3 (1976):147–72.

24. Robert F. Winch *The Modern Family* (New York, 1952), p. 706; and William J. Goode, *After Divorce* (New york, 1956), p. 4.

25. Juanita Kreps, *Sex in the Marketplace: American Women at Work* (Baltimore, 1971), pp. 19–24.

26. Valerie Kincaid Oppenheimer, *The Female Labor Force in the United States*, Population Monograph Series, no. 5 (Berkeley, 1970), pp. 1–15; and Lynd and Lynd, *Middletown*, pp. 124–27.

27. Lynd and Lynd, *Middletown*, pp. 150, 240–44.

28. See, for example, the advertising campaigns of General Electric and Hotpoint from 1918 through the rest of the decade of the 1920s.

29. The practice of carefully observing children's weight was initiated by medical authorities, national and local governments, and social welfare agencies, as part of the campaign to improve child health which began about the time of World War I.

JACQUELYN DOWD HALL

Disorderly Women: Gender and Labor Militancy in the Appalachian South

In the 1920s, Eleanor Roosevelt and other elite women continued the political activism that reformers and suffragists such as Florence Kelley had initiated. Working-class women had little choice but to continue the labor militancy exemplified by Schneiderman, Newman, Cohn, and Lemlich. (See Orleck, pp. 386–402, and Newman, pp. 417–419.) This was especially true in the South. Unionization had never taken hold in the former states of the Confederacy as it had in heavily industrialized areas of the Northeast and Midwest. Moreover, working conditions had worsened as factory owners introduced new innovations designed to improve productivity. Southern textile mills, as employers of large numbers of poorly paid women, were especially vulnerable to strikes.

Jacquelyn Dowd Hall focuses on one of the many strikes exploding across the South in that tumultuous decade, exploring female activism in an essay that calls into question old stereotypes about southern workers as individualistic, docile, and "hard to organize." In this important study, Hall illuminates the distinctive style of collective action that the women of Elizabethton, Tennessee, employed and the self-concepts and family networks on which that style relied.

In what respects did working conditions resemble those confronting the young immigrant women in New York's garment district about whom Orleck wrote? What were the critical differences? Were the factors that inspired and sustained resistance similar? How does Hall view the actions of Trixie Perry and Texas Bill?

The rising sun "made a sort of halo around the crown of Cross Mountain" as Flossie Cole climbed into a neighbor's Model T and headed west down the gravel road to Elizabethton, bound for work in a rayon plant. Emerging from Stoney Creek hollow, the car joined a caravan of buses and self-styled "taxis" brimming with young people from dozens of tiny communities strung along the creek branches and nestled in the coves of the Blue Ridge Mountains of East Tennessee. The caravan picked up speed as it hit paved roads and crossed the Watauga River bridge, passing beneath a sign advertising the county seat's new-found identity as a "City of Power." By the time Cole reached the factory gate, it was 7:00 A.M., time to begin another ten-hour day as a reeler at the American Glanzstoff plant.[1]

The machines whirred, and work began as usual. But the reeling room stirred with anticipation. The day before, March 12, 1929, all but seventeen of the 360 women in the inspection room next door had walked off their jobs. Now they were gathered at the factory gate, refusing to work but ready to negotiate. When 9:00 A.M., approached and the plant manager failed to appear, they broke past the guards and rushed through the plant, urging their co-workers out on strike. By 1:40 P.M. the machines were idle and the plant was closed.

Excerpted from "Disorderly Women: Gender and Labor Militancy in the Appalachian South" by Jacquelyn Dowd Hall, in *Journal of American History* 73 (1986): 354–82. Notes have been renumbered and edited.

The Elizabethton conflict rocked Carter County and made national headlines. Before March ended, the spirit of protest had jumped the Blue Ridge and spread through the Piedmont. Gastonia, Marion, and Danville saw the most bitter conflicts, but dozens of towns were shocked by an unexpected workers' revolt.[2]

The textile industry has always been a stronghold of women's labor, and women were central to these events. They were noted by contemporaries, sometimes as leaders, more often as pathetic mill girls or as "Amazons" providing comic relief.[3] In historical renditions they have dropped out of sight. The result has been thin description: a one-dimensional view of labor conflict that fails to take culture and community into account.

Elizabethton, of course, is not unusual in this regard. Until recently, historians of trade unionism, like trade unionists themselves, neglected women, while historians of women concentrated on the Northeast and the middle class. There were few scholarly challenges to the assumption that women workers in general and southern women in particular were "hard to organize" and that women as family members exercised a conservative pull against class cohesion. Instances of female militancy were seen and not seen.[4] Because they contradicted conventional wisdom, they were easily dismissed.

Recent scholarship has revised that formulation by unearthing an impressive record of female activism. But our task is not only to describe and celebrate but also to contextualize, and thus to understand. In Elizabethton the preindustrial background, the structure of the work force and the industry, the global forces that impinged on local events—these particularities of time and place conditioned women's choices and shaped their identities. Equally important was a private world traditionally pushed to the margins of labor history. Female friendships and sexuality, cross-generational and cross-class alliances, the incorporation of new consumer desires into a dynamic regional culture—these too energized women's participation. Women in turn were historical subjects, helping to create the circumstances from which the strike arose and guiding by their actions the course the conflict took.

With gender at the center of analysis, unexpected dimensions come into view. Chief among them is the strike's erotic undercurrent, its sexual theme. The activists of Elizabethton belonged to a venerable tradition of "disorderly women," women who, in times of political upheaval, embody tensions that are half-conscious or only dimly understood.[5] Beneath the surface of a conflict that pitted workers and farmers against a new middle class in the town lay an inner world of fantasy, gender ideology, and sexual style.

The melding of narrative and analysis that follows has two major goals. The first is a fresh reading of an important episode in southern labor history, employing a female angle of vision to reveal aspects of the conflict that have been overlooked or misunderstood. The second is a close look at women's distinctive forms of collective action, using language and gesture as points of entry to a culture.

The Elizabethton story may also help to make a more general point. Based as it is on what Michel Foucault has termed "local" or "subjugated" knowledge, that is, perceptions that seem idiosyncratic, naive, and irrelevant to historical explanation, this study highlights the limitations of conventional categories.[6] The women of Elizabethton were neither traditionalists acting on family values nor market-oriented individualists, neither peculiar mountaineers nor familiar modern women. Their irreverence and inventiveness shatter stereotypes and illuminate the intricacies of working-class women's lives.

In 1925 the J. P. Bemberg Company of Barmen, Germany, manufacturer of high-quality rayon yarn by an exclusive stretch spinning process, began pouring the thick concrete floors of its first United States subsidiary. Three years later Germany's leading producer of viscose yarn, the Vereinigte Glanzstoff Fabriken, A.G., of Elberfeld opened a jointly managed branch nearby. A post-World War I fashion revolution, combined with protective tariffs, had spurred the American rayon industry's spectacular growth. As one industry publicist put it, "With long skirts, cotton stockings were quite in order; but with short skirts, nothing would do except sheer, smooth stockings. . . . It was on the trim legs of post-war flappers, it has been said, that rayon first stepped out into big business." Dominated by a handful of European giants, the rayon industry clustered along the Appalachian mountain chain. By World War II, over 70 percent of American rayon production took place in the southern states, with 50 percent of the national total in Virginia and Tennessee alone.[7]

When the Bemberg and Glanzstoff companies chose East Tennessee as a site for overseas expansion, they came to a region that has occupied a peculiar place in the American economy and imagination. Since its "discovery" by local-color writers in the 1870s, southern Appalachia has been seen as a land "where time stood still." Mountain people have been romanticized as "our contemporary ancestors" or maligned as "latter-day white barbarians." Central to both images is the notion of a people untouched by modernity. In fact, as a generation of regional scholars has now made clear, the key to modern Appalachian history lies not in the region's isolation but in its role as a source of raw materials and an outlet for investment in a capitalist world economy.[8]

Frontier families had settled the fertile Watauga River Valley around Elizabethton before the Revolution. Later arrivals pushed farther up the mountains into the hollows carved by fast-falling creeks. Stoney Creek is the oldest and largest of those creek-bed communities. Here descendants of the original settlers cultivated their own small plots, grazed livestock in woods that custom held open to all, hunted and fished in an ancient hardwood forest, mined iron ore, made whiskey, spun cloth, and bartered with local merchants for what they could not produce at home.

In the 1880s East Tennessee's timber and mineral resources attracted the attention of capitalists in the United States and abroad, and an era of land speculation and railroad building began. The railroads opened the way to timber barons, who stripped away the forests, leaving hillsides stark and vulnerable to erosion. Farmers abandoned their fields to follow the march of the logging camps. Left behind, women and children did their best to pick up the slack.[9] But by the time Carter County was "timbered out" in the 1920s, farm families had crept upward to the barren ridge lands or grown dependent on "steady work and cash wages." Meanwhile, in Elizabethton, the county seat, an aggressive new class of bankers, lawyers, and businessmen served as brokers for outside developers, speculated in land, invested in homegrown factories, and looked beyond the hills for their standards of "push, progress and prosperity."[10]

Carter County, however, lacked Appalachia's grand prize: The rush for coal that devastated other parts of the mountains had bypassed that part of East Tennessee. Nor had county farmers been absorbed into the cotton kingdom, with its exploitative credit system and spreading tenancy. To be sure, they were increasingly hard pressed. As arable land disappeared, farms were divided and redivided. In 1880 the average rural family had supported itself on 140 acres of land; by 1920 it was making do on slightly more than 52 acres. Yet however diminished their circumstances, 84.5 percent still owned their own land.[11] The economic base that sustained traditional expectations of independence, production for use, and neighborly reciprocity tottered but did not give way.

The coming of the rayon plants represented a coup for Elizabethton's aspiring businessmen, who wooed investors with promises of free land, tax exemptions, and cheap labor. But at first the whole county seemed to share the boomtown spirit. Men from Stoney Creek, Gap Creek, and other mountain hamlets built the cavernous mills, then stayed on to learn the chemical processes that transformed the cellulose from wood pulp and cotton linters (the short fibers that remain on cotton seeds after longer, spinnable fibers are removed) into "artificial silk." Women vied for jobs in the textile division where they wound, reeled, twisted, and inspected the rayon yarn. Yet for all the excitement it engendered, industrialization in Carter County retained a distinctly rural cast. Although Elizabethton's population tripled (from 2,749 in 1920 to 8,093 in 1930), the rayon workers confounded predictions of spectacular urban growth, for most remained in the countryside, riding to work on chartered buses and trains or in taxis driven by neighbors and friends.

Women made up approximately 37 percent of the 3,213 workers in the mills. Most were under twenty-one, but many were as young as twelve, or more commonly, fourteen. By contrast, the work force contained a large proportion of older, married men. Those men, together with a smaller number of teenage boys, dominated the chemical division, while young women processed the finished yarn.[12]

Whether married or single, town- or country-bred, the men who labored in the rayon plants followed in the footsteps of fathers, and sometimes grandfathers, who had combined farming with a variety of wage-earning occupations. To a greater extent than we might expect, young women who had grown up in Elizabethton could also look to earlier models of gainful labor. A search of the 1910 manuscript census found 20 percent (97/507) of women aged fourteen and over in paid occupations. The largest proportion (29.6 percent) were cooks and servants. But close behind were women in what mountain people called "public work": wage-earning labor performed outside a household setting. For rayon workers from the countryside it was a different story. Only 5.2 percent of adult women on Stoney Creek were gainfully employed (33/638). Nineteen of these were farmers. The rest—except for one music teacher—were servants or washerwomen.[13]

These contrasts are telling, and from them we can surmise two things. The first is that industrialization did not burst upon a static, conflict-free "traditional" world. The women who beat a path to the rayon plants came from families that had already been drawn into an economy where money was a key to survival. The second is that the timber industry, which attracted Carter County's men, undermined its agricultural base, and destroyed its natural resources, created few opportunities for rural women. No wonder that farm daughters in the mills counted their blessings and looked on themselves as pioneers.

Whether they sought work out of family need or for more individualistic reasons, these "factory girls" saw their jobs as a hopeful gamble rather than a desperate last resort, and they remembered the moment with astounding precision. "I'll never forget the day they hired me at Bemberg," said Flossie Cole. "We went down right in front of it. They'd come out and they'd say, 'You and you and you,' and they'd hire so many. And that day I was standing there and he picked out two or three more and he looked at me and he said, 'You.' It thrilled me to death." She worked 56 hours that week and took home $8.16.[14]

Such pay scales were low even for the southern textile industry, and workers quickly found their income eaten away by the cost of commuting or of boarding in town. When the strike came it focused on the issue of Glanzstoff women's wages, which lagged behind those at the older Bemberg plant. But workers had other grievances as well. Caustic chemicals were used to turn cellulose into a viscous fluid that was then forced through spinnerets, thimble-shaped nozzles pierced with tiny holes. The fine, individual streams coagulated into rayon filaments in an acid bath. In the chemical division men waded through water and acid, exposed all day to a lethal spray. Women labored under less dangerous conditions, but for longer hours and less pay. Paid by the piece, they complained of rising production quotas and what everyone referred to as "hard rules."[15]

Women in particular were singled out for petty regulations, aimed not just at extracting labor but at shaping deportment as well. They were forbidden to wear makeup; in some departments they were required to purchase uniforms. Most galling of all was company surveillance of the washroom. According to Bessie Edens, who was promoted to "forelady" in the twisting room, "men could do what they wanted to in their own department," but women had to get a pass to leave the shop floor. "If we went to the bathroom, they'd follow us," Flossie Cole confirmed, "'fraid we'd stay a minute too long." If they did, their pay was docked; one too many trips and they lost their jobs.[16]

Complaints about the washroom may have had other meanings as well. When asked how she heard that a strike was brewing, Nettie Reece cited "bathroom gossip."[17] As the company well knew, the women's washroom, where only a forelady, not a male supervisor, could go, might serve as a communications center, a hub of gossip where complaints were aired and plans were formulated.

The German origins of the plant managers contributed to the tension. Once the strike began, union organizers were quick to play on images of an "imported Prussian autocracy." The frontier republicanism of the mountains shaded easily into post–World War I Americanism as strikers demanded their rights as "natural-born American citizens" oppressed by a "latter day industrialism." In that they had much in common with other twentieth-century workers, for whom the democratic values articulated during the war became a rallying cry for social justice at home. The nationality of the managers helped throw those values into sharp relief.[18]

The strike came on March 12, 1929, led by women in Glanzstoff inspection department, by what one observer called "girls in their teens [who] decided not to put up with the present conditions any longer." The county court immediately issued injunctions forbidding all demonstrations against the company. When strikers ignored the injunctions, the governor sent in the National Guard. The strikers secured a charter from the American Federation of Labor's United Textile Workers union (UTW). Meeting in a place called the Tabernacle, built for religious revivals, they listened to a Baptist preacher from Stoney Creek warn: "The hand of oppression is growing on our people. . . . You women work for practically nothing. You must come together and say that such things must cease to be." Each night more workers "came forward" to take the union oath.[19]

Meanwhile, UTW and Federal Conciliation Service officials arrived on the scene. On March 22 they reached a "gentlemen's agreement" by which the company promised a new wage scale for "good girl help" and agreed not to discriminate against union members. The strikers returned to work, but the conflict was far from over. Higher paychecks never materialized; union members began losing their jobs. On April 4 local businessmen kidnapped two union organizers and ran them out of town. Eleven days later the workers responded with what most observers agreed was a "spontaneous and complete walkout."[20]

This time the conflict quickly escalated. More troops arrived, and the plants became fortresses, with machine guns on the rooftops and armed guardsmen on the ground. The company sent buses manned by soldiers farther up the hollows to recruit new workers and escort them back to town. Pickets blocked narrow mountain roads. Houses were blown up; the town water main was dynamited. An estimated 1,250 individuals were arrested in confrontations with the National Guard.[21]

As far as can be determined, no women were involved in barn burnings and dynamitings—what Bessie Edens referred to as "the rough . . . stuff" that accompanied the second strike. Men "went places that we didn't go," explained Christine Galliher. "They had big dark secrets . . . the men did." But when it came to public demonstrations women held center stage. At the outset "hundreds of girls" had ridden down main street "in buses and taxis, shouting and laughing at people who watched them from windows and doorsteps." Now they blocked the road at Gap Creek and refused soldiers' orders that they walk twelve miles to jail in town. "And there was one girl that was awful tough in the bunch. . . . She said, 'No, by God. We didn't walk out here, and we're not walking back!' And she sat her hind end down in the middle of the road, and we all sat down with her. And the law used tear gas on us! . . . And it nearly put our eyes out, but we still wouldn't walk back to town." In Elizabethton after picket duty, women marched down the "Bemberg Highway . . . draped in the American flag and carrying the colors"—thereby forcing the guardsmen to present arms each time they passed. Inventive, playful, and shrewd, the women's tactics encouraged a holiday spirit. They may also have deflected violence and garnered community support.[22]

Laughter was among the women's most effective weapons. But beneath high spirits the terms of battle had begun to change. Local organizers were hobbled by a national union that lacked the resources and commitment to sustain the strike. Instead of translating workers' grievances into a compelling challenge, the UTW pared their demands down to the bone. On May 26, six weeks after the strike began, the union agreed to a settlement that made no mention of wages, hours, working conditions, or union recognition. The company's only concession was a promise not to discriminate against union members. The workers were less than enthusiastic. According to one reporter, "It took nine speeches and a lot of question answering lasting two and a half hours to get the strikers to accept the terms."[23]

The press, for the most part, greeted the settlement as a workers' victory, or at least a satisfactory resolution of the conflict. Anna Weinstock, the first woman to serve as a federal conciliator, was credited with bringing the company to the bargaining table and was pictured as the heroine of the event. "SETTLED BY A WOMAN!" headlined one journal. "This is the fact that astounds American newspaper editors." "Five feet five inches and 120 pounds of femininity; clean cut, even features"—and so on, in great detail. Little was made of Weinstock's own working-class origins. She was simply a "new woman," come to the rescue of a backward mountain folk. The strikers themselves dropped quickly from view.[24]

From the outside, the conflict at Elizabethton looked like a straightforward case of labor-management strife. But it appeared quite different from within. Everyone interviewed put the blame for low wages on an alliance between the German managers and the "leading citizens" of the town. Preserved in the oral tradition is the story of how the "town fathers" promised the company a supply of cheap and unorganized labor. Bessie Edens put it this way: They told the company that "women wasn't used to working, and they'd work for almost nothing, and the men would work for low wages. That's the way they got the plant here." In this version of events the strike was part of a long-term struggle, with development-minded townspeople on one side and workers, farmers, and country merchants on the other.[25]

Workers' roots in the countryside encouraged resistance and helped them to mobilize support once the strike began. "These workers have come so recently from the farms and mountains . . . and are of such independent spirit," Alfred Hoffman observed, "that they 'Don't care if they do lose their jobs' and cannot be scared." Asked by reporters what would happen if strike activity cost them their jobs, one woman remarked, "I haven't forgotten how to use a hoe," while another said, "We'll go back to the farm."[26] Such threats were not just bravado. High levels of farm ownership sustained cultural independence. Within the internal economy of families, individual fortunes were cushioned by reciprocity; an orientation toward subsistence survived side by side with the desire for cash and store-bought goods.

Stoney Creek farmers were solidly behind the sons and daughters they sent to the factories, as were the small shopkeepers who relied on farmers for their trade. In county politics Stoney Creekers had historically marshaled a block vote against the town. In 1929 Stoney Creek's own J. M. Moreland was county sheriff, and he openly took the strikers' side. A strike leader in the twisting room ran a country store and drove his working neighbors into town. "That's why he was pretty well accepted as their leader," said a fellow worker. "Some of them were cousins and other relations. Some of them traded at his store. Some of them rode in his taxi. All intertwined."[27]

The National Guard had divided loyalties. Parading past the plants, the strikers "waved to and called the first names of the guardsmen, for most of the young men in uniforms [were friends of] the men and girls on strike." Even when the local unit was fortified by outside recruits, fraternizing continued. Nettie Reece, like a number of her girlfriends, met her future husband that way; she saw him on the street and "knew that was mine right there." Some guardsmen went further and simply refused to serve. "The use of the National Guard here was the dirtiest deal ever pulled," one protested. "I turned in my equipment when I was ordered to go out and patrol the road. I was dropped from the payroll two weeks later."[28]

In this context of family- and community-based resistance, women had important roles to play. Farm mothers nurtured the strikers' independence simply by cleaving to the land, passing on to their children a heritage at odds with the values of the new order and maintaining family production as a hedge against the uncertainties of a market economy. But the situation of farm mothers had other effects as well, and it would be a mistake to push the argument for continuity too far. As their husbands ranged widely in search of wage labor, women's work intensified while their status—now tied to earning power—declined. The female strikers of Elizabethton saw their mothers as resourceful and strong but also as increasingly isolated and hard pressed. Most important, they no longer looked to their mothers' lives as patterns for their own.[29]

The summer after the strike, Bessie Edens attended the Southern Summer School for Women Workers, a workers' education project in North Carolina, where she set the group on its ear with an impassioned defense of women's rights:

> It is nothing new for married women to work. They have always worked. . . . Women have always worked harder than men and always had to look up to the man and feel that they were weaker and inferior. . . . If we women would not be so submissive and take every thing for granted, if we would awake and stand up for our rights, this world would be a better place to live in, at least it would be better for the women.
>
> Some girls think that as long as mother takes in washings, keeps ten or twelve boarders or perhaps takes in sewing, she isn't working. But I say that either one of the three is as hard work as

> women could do. So if they do that at home and don't get any wages for it, why would it not be all right for them to go to a factory and receive pay for what they do?

Edens had been the oldest of ten children. She had dreamed of going to nursing school, but her poverty-stricken parents had opposed her plan. At fifteen, she had gone to work as a servant. "Then I'd come back when Momma had a baby and wait on her, and help if she needed me in any way." Asked fifty years later about a daughter's place on a hardscrabble farm, Edens replied: "The girls were supposed to do housework and work in the fields. They were supposed to be slaves."[30]

Bessie Edens was unusual in her articulation of a working-class feminism. But scattered through the life histories written by other students are echoes of her general themes. Read in the context of farm daughters' lives—their first-hand exposure to rural poverty, their yearnings for a more expansive world—these stories reflect the "structure of feeling" women brought to the rayon plants and then to the picket line and union hall.[31] Women such as Edens, it seems, sensed the devaluation of women's handicraft labor in the face of cheap consumer goods. They feared the long arm of their mothers' fate, resented their fathers' distant authority, and envied their brothers' exploits away from home. By opting for work in the rayon plants, they struck out for their own place in a changing world. When low wages, high costs, and autocratic managers affronted their dignity and dashed their hopes, they were the first to revolt.

The Elizabethton story thus presents another pattern in the female protest tradition. In coal-mining communities a rigid division of labor and women's hardships in company towns have resulted, paradoxically, in the notable militancy of miners' wives. By contrast, tobacco factories have tended to employ married women, whose job commitments and associational lives enable them to assume leadership roles in sustained organizing drives. In yet other circumstances, such as the early New England textile mills or the union insurgency of the 1920s and 1930s, single women initiated independent strikes or provided strong support for male-led, mixed-sex campaigns. Where, as in Elizabethton, people were mobilized as family and community members rather than as individual workers, non-wage-earning women could provide essential support. Once in motion, their daughters might outdo men in militancy, perhaps because they had fewer dependents than their male co-workers and could fall back more easily on parental resources, perhaps because the peer culture and increased independence encouraged by factory labor stirred boldness and inspired experimentation.[32]

The fact of women's initiative and participation in collective action is instructive. Even more intriguing is the gender-based symbolism of their protest style. Through dress, language, and gesture, female strikers expressed a complex cultural identity and turned it to their own rebellious purposes.

Consider, for instance, Trixie Perry and a woman who called herself "Texas Bill." Twenty-eight-year-old Trixie Perry was a reeler in the Glanzstoff plant. She had apparently become pregnant ten years before, had married briefly and then divorced, giving her son her maiden name. Her father was a butcher and a farmer, and she lived near her family on the edge of town. Trixie later moved into Elizabethton. She never remarried but went on to have several more children by other men. Texas Bill's background is more elusive. All we know is that she came from out of state, lived in a boardinghouse, and claimed to have been married twice before she arrived in town. These two friends were ringleaders on the picket line. Both were charged with violating the injunction, and both were brought to trial.[33]

Trixie Perry took the stand in a dress sewn from red, white, and blue bunting and a cap made of a small American flag. The prosecuting attorney began his cross-examination:

"You have a United States flag as a cap on your head?"

"Yes."

"Wear it all the time?"

"Whenever I take a notion."

"You are dressed in a United States flag, and the colors?"

"I guess so, I was born under it, guess I have a right to."

The main charge was that Perry and her friend had drawn a line across the road at Gap Creek and dared the soldiers to cross it. Above all they were accused of taunting the National Guard. The defense attorney, a fiery local lawyer playing to a sympathetic crowd, did not deny the charges. Instead, he used the women to mock the government's case. Had Trixie Perry threatened a lieutenant? "He rammed a gun in my face and I told him to take it out or I would knock it out." Had she blocked the road? "A little thing like me block a big road?" What had she said to the threat of a tear gas bomb? "That little old fire cracker of a thing, it won't go off."[34]

Texas Bill was an even bigger hit with the crowd. The defense attorney called her the "Wild Man from Borneo." A guard said she was "the wildest human being I've ever seen." Texas Bill both affirmed and subverted her reputation. Her nickname came from her habit of wearing "cowboy" clothes. But when it was her turn to testify, she "strutted on the stand" in a fashionable black picture hat and a black coat. Besides her other transgressions, she was accused of grabbing a soldier's gun and aiming it at him. What was she doing on the road so early in the morning? "I take a walk every morning before breakfast for my health," Texas replied with what a reporter described as "an assumed ladylike dignity."[35]

Witnesses for the prosecution took pains to contradict Texas Bill's "assumed ladylike dignity." A guardsman complained that she called him a "'God damned yellow son-of-a-bitch,' and then branched out from that." Texas offered no defense: "When that soldier stuck his gun in my face, that did make me mad and I did cuss a little bit and don't deny it." Far from discrediting the strikers, the soldiers' testimony added to their own embarrassment and the audience's delight. In tune with the crowd, the defense attorney "enjoyed making the guards admit they had been 'assaulted' . . . by 16- and 18-year-old girls."[36]

Mock gentility, transgressive laughter, male egos on the line—the mix made for wonderful theater, and proved effective in court as well. The judge reserved maximum sentences for three especially aggressive men; all the women and most of the men were found not guilty or were lightly fined. In the end even those convictions were overturned by the state court of appeals.[37]

Trixie Perry and Texas Bill certainly donned the role of "disorderly woman." Since, presumably, only extraordinary circumstances call forth feminine aggression, women's assaults against persons and property constitute a powerful witness against injustice. At the same time, since women are considered less rational and taken less seriously than men, they may meet less resistance and be punished less severely for their crimes.[38]

But Trixie Perry and Texas Bill were not just out of line in their public acts; they also led unconventional private lives. It was this erotic subtext that most horrified officialdom and amused the courtroom crowd. The only extended discussion of the strike that appears in the city council minutes resulted in a resolution that read in part:

> WHEREAS, it has come to [our] attention . . . that the moral tone of this community has been lowered by reason of men and women congregating in various houses and meeting-places in Elizabethton and there practicing lewdness all hours of the night, in defiance of morality, law and order. . . .
>
> NOW, THEREFORE, BE IT RESOLVED, that the police force of the City arrest and place in the City Jail those who are violating the laws by practicing lewdness within the City of Elizabethton. . . .[39]

Union representatives apparently shared, indeed anticipated, the councilmen's concern. Worried by rumors that unemployed women were resorting to prostitution, they had already announced to the press that 25 percent of the strikers had been sent back to their hillside homes, "chiefly young single girls whom we want to keep off the streets." The townsmen and the trade unionists were thus united in drawing a line between good women and bad, with respectability being measured not only by chastity but by nuances of style and language as well.[40] In the heat of the trial, the question of whether or not women—as workers—had violated the injunction took second place to questions about their status *as women*, as members of their sex. Had they cursed? Had they been on the road at odd hours of the day or night? Was Texas Bill a lady or a "wild man from Borneo"? Fearing that "lewd women" might discredit the organizing drive, the organizers tried to send them home. To protect the community's "moral tone," the city council threatened to lock them up.

There is nothing extraordinary about this association between sexual misbehavior and women's labor militancy. Since strikers are often young single women who violate gender conventions by invading public space customarily reserved for men (and sometimes frequented by prostitutes)—and since female aggressiveness stirs up fears of women's sexual power—opponents have often undercut union organizing drives by insinuations of prostitution or promiscuity. Fearing guilt by association, "respectable" women stay away.[41]

What is impressive here is how Trixie Perry and Texas Bill handled the dichotomy between ladyhood and lewdness, good girls and bad. Using words that, for women in particular, were ordinarily taboo, they refused deference and signaled disrespect. Making no secret of their sexual experience, they combined flirtation with fierceness on the picket line and adopted a provocative courtroom style. And yet, with the language of dress—a cap made of an American flag, an elegant wide-brimmed hat—they claimed their rights as citizens and their place in the female community.

Moreover, that community upheld their claims. The defense attorney chose unruly women as his star witnesses, and the courtroom spectators enthusiastically cheered them on. The prosecuting attorney recommended dismissal of the charges against all the women on trial except Trixie Perry, Texas Bill, and a "hoodlum" named Lucille Ratliffe, on the grounds that the rest came from "good families." Yet in the court transcripts, few differences can be discerned in the behavior of good girls and bad. The other female defendants may have been less flamboyant, but they were no less sharp-tongued. Was Vivian King a member of the UTW? "Yes, and proud of it." Had she been picketing? "Yes, proud of that." What was a young married woman named Dorothy Oxindine doing on Gap Creek at five o'clock in the morning? "Out airing." Did Lena May Jones "holler out 'scab'"? "No, I think the statement made was 'I wouldn't be a scab' and 'Why don't you come and join our organization.'" Did she laugh at a soldier and tell him his gun wouldn't shoot? "I didn't tell him it wouldn't shoot, but I laughed at him . . . and told him he was too much of a man to shoot a lady."[42]

Interviewed over fifty years later, strike participants still refused to make invidious distinctions between themselves and women like Trixie Perry and Texas Bill. Bessie Edens was a settled, self-educated, married woman. But she was also a self-described "daredevil on the picket line," secure in the knowledge that she had a knife hidden in her drawstring underwear. To Edens, who came from a mountain hamlet called Hampton, the chief distinction did not lie between herself and rougher women. It lay between herself and merchants' wives who blamed the trouble on "those hussies from Hampton." When asked what she thought of Trixie Perry and Texas Bill, she answered simply, "There were some girls like that involved. But I didn't care. They did their part."[43]

Nettie Reece, who lived at home with parents who were "pretty particular with [their] daughters," shared Bessie Edens's attitude. After passing along the town gossip about Trixie Perry, she was anxious to make sure her meaning was not misconstrued. "Trixie was not a woman who sold her body," she emphasized. "She just had a big desire for sex. . . . And when she had a cause to fight for, she'd fight." Reece then went on to establish Perry's claim to a certain kind of respectability. After the strike Perry became a hard-working restaurant cook. She was a good neighbor: "If anybody got sick, she was there to wait on them." The children she bore out of wedlock did well in life, and they "never throwed [their mother] aside."[44]

Industrialization, as we know, changed the nature of work, the meaning of time. In Carter County it entailed a shift of economic and political power from the countryside to the town. At issue too were more intimate matters of fantasy, culture, and style.

Implicit in the conflict were two different sexual systems. One, subscribed to by union officials and the local middle class, mandated chastity before marriage, men as breadwinners, and women as housewives in the home. The other, rooted in a rural past and adapted to working-class life, recognized liaisons established without the benefit of clergy or license fees and allowed legitimacy to be broadly construed. It was unfamiliar with—or pragmatic about—prostitution. It circumscribed women's roles without investing in abstract standards of femininity. It was, in short, a society that might produce a Trixie Perry or defend "hussies from Hampton" against the snubs of merchants' wives.

This is not to say that the women of Elizabethton were simply acting on tradition. On the contrary, the strikers dressed the persona of the disorderly woman in unmistakably modern garb. Women's behavior on the witness stand presupposed a certain sophistication: A passing familiarity allowed them to parody ladyhood and to thumb a nose at the genteel standards of the town. Combining garments from the local past with fragments of an expansive consumer culture, the women of Elizabethton assembled their own version of a brash, irreverent Jazz Age style.

By the early 1920s radios and Model Ts had joined railroads and mail-order catalogs as conduits to the larger world. Record companies had discovered hill-country music and East Tennessee's first country-music stars were recording hits that transformed ballad singing, fiddle playing, and banjo picking into one of America's great popular-music sounds. The banjo itself was an Afro-American instrument that had come to the mountains with the railroad gangs. Such cultural interchanges multiplied during the 1920s as rural traditions met the upheavals of industrial life. The result was an explosion of musical creativity—in the hills of Tennessee no less than in New York City and other cosmopolitan centers.[45] Arriving for work in the rayon plants, young people brought with them the useable past of the countryside, but they quickly assimilated the speeded-up rhythms of a changing world.

Work-related peer groups formed a bridge between traditional loyalties and a novel youth culture. Whether married or single, living with parents or on their own, women participated in the strike in same-sex groups. Sisters boarded, worked, and demonstrated together. Girlfriends teamed up in groups or pairs. Trixie Perry and Texas Bill were a case in point. But there were others as well. Nettie Reece joined the union with her parents' approval but also with her whole school girl gang in tow. Ethel and M. C. Ashworth, ages eighteen and seventeen, respectively, came from Virginia to work in the plants. "Hollering and singing [in a] Ford touring car," they were arrested in a demonstration at Watauga Point. Ida and Evelyn Heaton boarded together on Donna Avenue. Evelyn Heaton was hit by a car on the picket line, swore out a warrant, and had the commander of the National Guard placed under arrest. After the strike she was blacklisted, and Ida attended the Southern Summer School.[46]

The sudden gathering of young people in the town nourished new patterns of heterosociability, and the strike's erotic undercurrent surfaced not only in Trixie Perry's "big desire for sex" but also in the behavior of her more conventional peers. The loyalties of the national guardsmen were divided, but their sympathy was obvious, as was their interest in the female strikers. Most of the Elizabethton women were in their teens or early twenties, the usual age of marriage in the region, and the strike provided unaccustomed opportunities for courtship. Rather than choosing a neighbor they had known all their lives, under watchful parental eyes, women flirted on the picket lines or the shop floor. Romance and politics commingled in the excitement of the moment, flowering in a spectrum of behavior—from the outrageousness of Trixie Perry to a spate of marriages among other girls.

What needs emphasis here is the dynamic quality of working-class women's culture—a quality that is sometimes lost in static oppositions between modernism and traditionalism, individualism and family values, consumer and producer mentalities. This is especially important where regional history has been so thoroughly mythologized. Appalachian culture, like all living cultures, embraced continuity and discontinuity, indigenous and borrowed elements.[47] As surely as Anna Weinstock—or Alabama's Zelda Fitzgerald—or any city flapper, the Elizabethton strikers were "new women," making their way in a world their mothers could not have known but carrying with them values handed down through the female line.

Two vignettes may serve to illustrate that process of grounded change.

Flossie Cole's mother, known by everyone on Stoney Creek as "Aunt Tid," was Sheriff Moreland's sister, but that didn't keep her from harboring cardplayers, buckdancers, and whiskey drinkers in her home. Aunt Tid was also a seamstress who "could look at a picture in a catalog and cut a pattern and make a dress just like it." But like most of her friends, Cole jumped at the chance for store-bought clothes: "That first paycheck, that was it . . . I think I bought me some new clothes with the first check I got. I bought me a new pair of shoes and a dress and a hat. Can you imagine someone going to a plant with a hat on? I had a blue dress and black shoes—patent leather, honey, with real high heels—and a blue hat." Nevertheless, before Cole left home in the morning for her job in the rayon plant, Aunt Tid made sure that around her neck—beneath the new blue dress—she wore a bag of asafetida, a strong-smelling resin, a folk remedy to protect her from diseases that might be circulating in the town.[48]

Second, there is visual evidence: a set of sixteen-millimeter films made by the company in order to identify—and to blacklist—workers who participated in the union. In those films groups of smiling women traipse along the picket line dressed in up-to-date clothes.[49] Yet federal conciliator Anna Weinstock, speaking to an interviewer forty years later, pictured them in sunbonnets, and barefooted. "They were," she explained, "what we would normally call hillbillies": women who "never get away from their shacks."[50] This could be seen as the treachery of memory, a problem of retrospection. But it is also an illustration of the power of stereotypes, of how cultural difference is registered as backwardness, of how images of poverty and backwardness hide the realities of working-class women's lives.

The strike, as we know, was defeated. Participants were blacklisted. The Great Depression settled over the mountains, rekindling reliance on older ways of making do. Flossie Cole, for instance, had been new to factory labor, but she was no stranger to women's work. While her brothers had followed their father's lead to the coal mines, she had pursued the two most common occupations of the poorest mountain girls: agricultural labor and domestic service. "We would hire out and stay with people until they got through with us and then go back home. And when we got back home, it was workin' in the corn or wash for people." When Cole lost her job after the strike she went back to domestic service, "back to the drudge house," as she put it.[51]

Young women had poured eagerly into the rayon mills, drawn at least in part by the promise of independence, romance and adventure. As hard times deepened, such motives paled beside stark necessity. Two statistics make the point: The percentage of Carter County women who were gainfully employed held steady through the thirties. But by the end of the period a larger proportion than before worked as servants in other people's homes. When Flossie Cole went "back to the drudge house," she had plenty of company.[52]

Still, despite subsequent hardships, the spirit of the 1920s flickered on. Setting out to explore the strike through oral-history interviews, we expected to find disclaimers or silences. Instead, we heard unfaded memories and no regrets. "I knew I wasn't going to get to go back, and I didn't care," said Bessie Edens. "I wrote them a letter and told them I didn't care whether they took me back or not. I didn't! If I'd starved I wouldn't of cared, because I knew what I was a'doing when I helped to pull it. And I've never regretted it in any way. . . . And it did help the people, and it's helped the town and the country."[53] For those, like Edens, who went on to the Southern Summer School or remained active in the union, the strike was a pivot around which the political convictions and personal aspirations of a lifetime turned. For them, there were intangible rewards: a subtle deepening of individual power, a belief that they had made history and that later generations benefited from what they had done.

The strike, of course, made a fainter impression on other lives. Women's rebelliousness neither redefined gender roles nor overcame economic dependency. Their desire for the trappings of modernity could blur into a self-limiting consumerism. An ideology of romance could end in sexual danger or a married woman's burdensome double day. Still, the women of Elizabethton left a legacy. A norm of female public work, a new style of sexual expressiveness, the entry of women into public space and political struggles previously monopolized by men—all these pushed against traditional constraints even as they created new vulnerabilities. The farm daughters who left home for the rayon plants pioneered a new pattern of female experience, and they created for their post–World War II daughters an environment far different from the one they, in their youth, had known. It would be up to later generations to wrestle with the costs of commercialization and to elaborate a vision that embraced economic justice and community solidarity as well as women's liberation.

Notes

This study began as a collaborative endeavor with Sara Evans of the University of Minnesota, who helped to gather many of the interviews on which I have relied. Rosemarie Hester and Jennifer Dowd also joined me on trips to the mountains, and I benefited from their companionship, ideas, and research. I owe a special debt to Christopher Daly, Lu Ann Jones, Robert Korstad, James Leloudis, and Mary Murphy, with whom I have co-written *Like a Family: The Making of a Southern Cotton Mill World* (Chapel Hill, 1987).

1. Dan Crowe, *Old Town and the Covered Bridge* (Johnson City, Tenn., 1977), pp. 32, 71; Florence (Cole) Grindstaff interview by Jacquelyn Hall, July 10, 1981 (in Hall's possession).

2. For this strike wave, see Tom Tippett, *When Southern Labor Stirs* (New York, 1931); James A. Hodges, "Challenge to the New South: The Great Textile Strike in Elizabethton, Tennessee, 1929," *Tennessee Historical Quarterly* 23 (Dec. 1964):343–57; . . .

3. Contemporary observations include, *Knoxville News Sentinel,* May 17, 1929; Florence Kelley, "Our Newest South," *Survey,* June 15, 1929, pp. 342–44; . . .

4. Anne Firor Scott, "On Seeing and Not Seeing: A Case of Historical Invisibility," *Journal of American History* 71 (June 1984):7–8.

5. Natalie Zemon Davis, *Society and Culture in Early Modern France* (Stanford, 1975), pp. 124–51. . . .

6. Michel Foucault, *Power/Knowledge: Selected Interviews and Other Writings, 1972–1977,* trans. and ed. Colin Gordon (New York, 1980), p. 81.

7. Joseph Leeming, *Rayon: The First Man-Made Fiber* (Brooklyn, 1950), pp. 1–82; Jesse W. Markham, *Competition in the Rayon Industry* (Cambridge, Mass., 1952), pp. 1–38, 97, 186, 193, 209.

8. Bruce Roberts and Nancy Roberts, *Where Time Stood Still: A Portrait of Appalachia* (New York, 1970); William Goodell Frost, "Our Contemporary Ancestors in the Southern Mountains," *Atlantic Monthly* 83 (March 1899):311; Arnold J. Toynbee, *A Study of History,* 2 vols. (New York, 1947), II: 312; . . .

9. For this preindustrial economy, and its transformation, see Eller, *Miners, Millhands, and Mountaineers,* pp. 3–38, 86–127. . . .

10. *Mountaineer,* Dec. 28, Dec. 31, 1887.

11. U.S. Department of the Interior, Census Office, *Report on the Productions of Agriculture as Returned at the Tenth Census* (June 1, 1880) (Washington, 1883), pp. 84–85, 132, 169; U.S. Department of Commerce, Bureau of the Census, *Fourteenth Census of the United States Taken in the Year 1920: Agriculture,* vol. VI, pt. 2 (Washington, [D.C.] 1922), pp. 446–47.

12. Holly, "Elizabethton, Tennessee," pp. 123, 133–38, 156, 198; U.S. Congress, Senate, Committee on Manufactures, *Working Conditions of the Textile Industry in North Carolina, South Carolina, and Tennessee,* 71 Cong., 1 sess., May 8, 9, and 20, 1929, p. 95; Henry Schuettler interview by Hall, n.d. [1981] (in Hall's possession).

13. Thirteenth Census of the United States, 1910, Manuscript Population Schedule, Carter County, Tenn., district 7; ibid., district 15; ibid., district 10; ibid., district 12.

14. Grindstaff interview.

15. *Scraps of Work and Play,* Southern Summer School for Women Workers in Industry, Burnsville, N.C., July 11-Aug. 23, 1929, typescript, pp. 21–22, 24, box 111, American Labor Education Service Records (Martin P. Catherwood Library, New York State School of Industrial and Labor Relations, Cornell University, Ithaca, N.Y.); Bessie Edens interview by Mary Frederickson, Aug. 14, 1975, pp. 1–2, 31–32, Southern Oral History Program Collection, Southern Historical Collection (Wilson Library, University of North Carolina at Chapel Hill) [hereafter SOHP].

16. Edens interview, Aug. 14, 1975, p. 32; Grindstaff interview.

17. Nettie Reece [pseud.] interview by Hall, May 18 and 19, 1983 (in Hall's possession).

18. *Knoxville News Sentinel,* May 13, 1929; *American Bemberg Corporation* v. *George Miller, et al.,* East Tennessee District Supreme Court, Jan. 29, 1930, record of evidence, typescript, box 660 (Tennessee State Library and Archives, Nashville) [hereafter Record of Evidence]. . . .

19. *Knoxville News Sentinel,* Mar. 14, 1929; Christine (Hinkle) Galliher and Dave Galliher interview by Hall, Aug. 8, 1979, pp. 8–9, SOHP; Tom Tippett, "Southern Situation," speech typescript, meeting held at the National Board, May 15, 1929, p. 3, box 25, Young Women's Christian Association Papers, Sophia Smith Collection (Smith College, Northampton, Mass.); Tom Tippett, "Impressions of Situation at Elizabethton, Tenn., May 10, 11, 1929," typescript, p. 1, ibid.

20. *Knoxville News Sentinel,* Mar. 20, Mar. 29, 1929; "Instructions for Adjustment of Wage Scale for Girl Help," Mar. 15, 1929, Records of the Conciliation Service, RG 280 (National Archives); Committee of Striking Workers[,] Members of United Textile Workers of America to the Honorable Herbert Hoover, Apr. 16, 1929, ibid; "Preliminary Report of Commissioner of Conciliation," Apr. 16, 1929, ibid.

21. Dr. J. A. Hardin to Hon. H. H. Horton, May 16, 1929, box 12, Governor Henry H. Horton Papers (Tennessee State Library and Archives); *Knoxville News Sentinel,* May 6, May 10, May 12, May 14, May 19, May 24, 1929.

22. Edens interview, Aug. 14, 1975, pp. 40, 49; Galliher interview, 33; *Knoxville News Sentinel,* Mar. 15, May 16, 1929.

23. *Knoxville News Sentinel,* May 27, 1929; Ina Nell (Hinkle) Harrison interview by Hall, Aug. 8, 1979, p. 2, SOHP; Mary Heaton Vorse, "Rayon Strikers Reluctantly Accept Settlement," press release, May 27, 1929, box 156, Mary Heaton Vorse Papers, Archives of Labor and Urban Affairs (Walter P. Reuther Library, Wayne State University, Detroit, Mich.).

24. "Rays of Sunshine in the Rayon War," *Literary Digest,* June 8, 1929, p. 12; *Charlotte Observer,* June 2, 1929; *Raleigh News and Observer,* May 24, 1929.

25. Edens interview, Aug. 14, 1975, pp. 43–44; Myrtle Simmerly interview by Hall, May 18, 1983 (in Hall's possession); Ollie Hardin interview by Hall and Sara Evans, Aug. 9, 1979 (in Hall's possession); Effie (Hardin) Carson interview by Hall and Evans, Aug. 6, 1979, p. 41, SOHP; Holly, "Elizabethton, Tennessee," 306–7.

26. James Myers, "Field Notes: Textile Strikes in the South," box 374, Archive Union Files (Martin P. Catherwood Library); *Raleigh News and Observer*, Mar. 15, 1929.

27. Hoffmann, "Mountaineer in Industry," 2–5; Robert (Bob) Moreland and Barbara Moreland interview by Hall, July 11, 1981 (in Hall's possession); *Knoxville News Sentinel*, Mar. 15, 1929; Honard Ward interview by Hall, n.d. [1981] (in Hall's possession).

28. *Knoxville News Sentinel*, May 15, 1929; Reece interview; . . .

29. For the argument that precisely because they are "left behind" by the economic developments that pull men into wage labor, woman-centered families may harbor alternative or oppositional values, see Mina Davis Caulfield, "Imperialism, the Family, and Cultures of Resistance," *Socialist Revolution* 4 (Oct. 1974):67–85; . . .

30. Bessie Edens, "Why a Married Woman Should Work," in *Scraps of Work and Play*, pp. 30–31; Edens interview, Aug. 14. 1975, pp. 14, 21, 34–35; Bessie Edens interview by Hall, Aug. 5, 1979 (in Hall's possession); Millie Sample, "Impressions," Aug. 1931, box 9, American Labor Education Service Records.

31. Mirion Bonner, "Behind the Southern Textile Strikes," *Nation*, Oct. 2, 1929, pp. 351–52; "Scraps From Our Lives," in *Scraps of Work and Play*, pp. 5–11; . . .

32. Corbin, *Life, Work, and Rebellion*, pp. 92–93; Louise A. Tilly, "Paths of Proletarianization: Organization of Production, Sexual Division of Labor, and Women's Collective Action," *Signs* 7 (Winter 1981):400–17; . . .

33. *Elizabethton Star*, Nov. 14, 1953, Jan. 31, 1986; Reece interview; Carson interview, 25; Nellie Bowers interview by Hall, May 15, 1983 (in Hall's possession); *Knoxville News Sentinel*, May 17, May 18, 1929.

34. Record of Evidence.

35. *Knoxville News Sentinel*, May 17, 1929.

36. Ibid.; Record of Evidence.

37. *American Bemberg Corporation* v. *George Miller, et al.*, minute books "Q" and "R," Chancery Court minutes, Carter County, Tenn., July 22, 1929 (Carter County Courthouse, Elizabethton, Tenn.); *American Bemberg Corporation* v. *George Miller, et al.*, Court of Appeals, #1, Sept. 5, 1930 (Supreme Court and Courts of Appeal, State of Tennessee, Knoxville).

38. Davis, *Society and Culture in Early Modern France*, pp. 124–51; Laurel Thatcher Ulrich, *Good Wives* (New York, 1982), pp. 191–97.

39. Elizabethton City Council, Minutes, May 23, 1929, Minute Book, vol. 5, pp. 356–57 (City Hall, Elizabethton, Tenn.).

40. *Knoxville News Sentinel*, May 5, 1929; Myers, "Field Notes." . . .

41. See, for instance, Alice Kessler-Harris, "The Autobiography of Ann Washington Craton," *Signs* 1 (Summer 1976):1019–37.

42. *Knoxville News Sentinel*, May 18, 1929; Record of Evidence.

43. Edens interview, Aug. 5, 1979.

44. Reece interview, May 19, 1983.

45. Charles K. Wolfe, *Tennessee Strings: The Story of Country Music in Tennessee* (Knoxville, 1977), pp. 22–90; Barry O'Connell, "Dick Boggs, Musician and Coal Miner," *Appalachian Journal* 11 (Autumn-Winter 1983–84):48.

46. *Miller's Elizabethton, Tenn., City Directory*, 1930; Reece interview; Record of Evidence; *Knoxville News Sentinel*, May 16, May 17, 1929; . . .

47. David E. Whisnant, *All That Is Native and Fine: The Politics of Culture in an American Region* (Chapel Hill, 1983), p. 48.

48. Grindstaff interview; Moreland interview.

49. *Knoxville Journal*, Apr. 22, 1929; sixteen-millimeter film (1 reel), ca. 1929, Helen Raulston Collection, Archives of Appalachia (East Tennessee State University, Johnson City); sixteen-millimeter film (20 reels), ca. 1927–1928, Bemberg Industry Records (Tennessee State Library and Archives). . . .

50. Anna Weinstock Schneider interview by Julia Blodgett Curtis, 1969, pp. 161, 166, 172–3, 177, Anna Weinstock Schneider Papers, box 1 (Martin P. Catherwood Library).

51. Grindstaff interview.

52. Bureau of the Census, *Fifteenth Census of the United States: 1930. Population*, vol. III, pt. 2 (Washington, [D.C.], 1932), p. 909; U.S. Department of Commerce, Bureau of the Census, *Sixteenth Census of the United States: 1940. Population*, vol. II, pt. 6 (Washington, [D.C.], 1943), p. 616.

53. Edens interview, Aug. 14, 1975, p. 50. . . .

LESLIE J. REAGAN

When Abortion Was a Crime: Reproduction and the Economy in the Great Depression

The frequency with which women—especially those who were married, native-born Protestant, and middle- or upper-middle-class—resorted to abortion fueled a movement to criminalize the practice, as James Mohr discussed in Part II. Motivated by a variety of factors that had little to do with the protection of women's health, which was the primary reason advanced by the physicians who led the movement, antiabortionists succeeded in making the practice illegal in the post–Civil War era. Some states did allow physicians to perform therapeutic abortions if the woman's life was threatened by carrying the pregnancy to term. In many states, however, the requirements for getting clearance to perform a therapeutic abortion in a hospital setting made this loophole virtually meaningless, especially when a vigilant district attorney was prepared to pit his interpretation against the physician's.

Leslie Reagan's prizewinning study of the practice and policing of abortion during the century it was criminalized (1867–1973) reveals that, despite the law, millions of abortions were performed during those years—and by no means all by "back-alley" butchers.

"My husband has been out of work for over six months and no help is in sight," wrote one mother to Margaret Sanger and the American Birth Control League; "I can't afford more children." Every year she performed two abortions upon herself, and she reported, "I have just now gotten up from an abortion and I don't want to repeat it again."[1] The disaster of the Great Depression touched all aspects of women's lives, including the most intimate ones, and brought about a new high in the incidence of abortion. As jobs evaporated and wages fell, families found themselves living on insecure and scanty funds. Many working people lost their homes; tenants had their belongings put out on the street. Married couples gave up children to orphanages because they could not support them.

As women pressured doctors for help, the medical practice of abortion, legal and illegal, expanded during the 1930s. Physicians granted, for the first time, that social conditions were an essential component of medical judgment in therapeutic abortion cases. Medical recognition of social indications reveals the ways in which political and social forces shaped medical thinking and practice. A handful of radical physicians, who looked to Europe as a model, raised the possibility of liberalizing the abortion law. . . .

If we move away from the dramatic narratives about abortion produced at inquests or in newspapers, which tell of the deaths and dangers of abortion, and step into the offices of physician-abortionists, a different story can be discerned. Abortion was not extraordinary, but ordinary. The proverbial "back-alley butcher" story of abortion overemphasizes fatalities and limits our understanding of the history of illegal abortion. Case studies of the "professional abortionists" and their practices in the 1930s provide a unique opportunity to analyze the experiences of the tens of thousands of women who went to physician-abortionists. Many women had abortions in a setting nearly identical to the doctors' offices where they received other medical care. These doctors specialized in a single procedure, abortion. They used standard medical procedures to perform safe abortions routinely and ran what may be called abortion clinics. Furthermore, abortion specialists were an integral part of regular medicine, as the network of physicians who referred patients to these physician-abortionists demonstrates. . . .

The Depression years make vivid the relationship between economics and reproduction. Women had abortions on a massive scale. Married women with children found it impossible to bear the expense of another, and unmarried women could not afford to marry. As young working-class women and men put off marriage during the Depression to support their families or to save money for a wedding, marriage rates fell drastically. Yet while they waited to wed, couples engaged in sexual relations, and women became pregnant. Many had abortions.[2]

During the Depression, married women were routinely fired on the assumption that jobs belonged to men and that women had husbands who supported them. Discrimination against married women forced single women to delay marriage and have abortions in order to keep their jobs. One such woman was a young teacher whose fiancé was unemployed. As her daughter recalled fifty years later, "She got pregnant. What were her choices? Marry, lose her job, and bring a child into a family with no means of support? Not marry, lose her job and reputation, and put the baby up for adoption or keep it?" As this scenario makes clear, she had no "choice." Furthermore, it points to the limitations of the rhetoric of "choice" in reproduction: Social forces condition women's reproductive options.[3] . . .

Medical studies and sex surveys demonstrated that women of every social strata turned to abortion in greater numbers during the Depression. Comparative studies by class and race appeared for the first time in the 1930s. Induced abortion rates among white, middle- and upper-class married women rose during the Depression years. The Kinsey Institute for Sex Research, led by Paul H. Gebhard, analyzed data from over five thousand married, white, mostly highly educated, urban women. The researchers found that "the depression of the 1930's resulted in a larger proportion of pregnancies that were artificially aborted." For every age group of women, born between 1890 and 1919, the highest induced abortion rate occurred during "the depth of the depression." White, married women were determined to avoid bearing children during the Depression: They reduced their rate of conception as well.[4] . . . The findings of Kinsey researchers suggest that aborting first pregnancies early in marriage might have been a growing trend, particularly among more educated, urban white women.[5]

Married black women, like their white counterparts, used abortion more during the Depression. . . . Dr. Charles H. Garvin,an esteemed black surgeon from Cleveland, commented in 1932 "that there has been a very definite increase in the numbers of abortions, criminally performed, among the married."[6] . . . In 1935, Harlem Hospital, which cared for mostly poor black patients, opened a separate ward, "The Abortion Service," to treat the women who came for emergency care following illegal abortions. . . .

A study of reproductive histories collected from forty-five hundred women at a New York clinic between 1930 and 1938 suggested that when class was controlled, working-class women, black and white alike, induced abortions at the same rate.[7] . . .

The key difference between black and white women was in their response to pregnancy outside of marriage, not their use of abortion. Unmarried white women who became pregnant were more likely to abort their pregnancies than were African American women in the same situation. Instead, more black women bore children out of wedlock and did so without being ostracized by their families and community. . . .

The tolerance of illegitimacy among African Americans was tempered by class. As African Americans advanced economically, they held their unwed daughters and sons to more rigid standards of chastity. Similarly, by the time the Kinsey Institute interviewed black women in the 1950s, there were clear class differences in the use of abortion by unmarried black women: Those with more education (and presumably more affluence) aborted at a higher rate than those with less education.[8]

. . . A study of working-class women in New York in the 1930s found almost identical abortion rates among Catholic, Jewish, and Protestant women.[9] However, researchers found striking differences in the reproductive patterns followed by women of different religious groups, a finding that seems to reflect class differences. Catholic and Jewish women tended to have their children earlier in their lives and began aborting unwanted pregnancies as they got older; Protestant women tended to abort earlier pregnancies and bear children later.[10] The Kinsey Report found for both married and unmarried white women, the more devout the woman, the less likely she was to have an abortion; the more religiously "inactive" a woman, the more likely she was to have an abortion.[11]

Access to physician-induced abortions and reliance upon self-induced methods varied greatly by class and race. Most affluent white women went to physicians for abortions, while poor women and black women self-induced them. Physicians performed 84 percent of the abortions reported by the white, urban women to Kinsey researchers. Fewer than 10 percent of the affluent white women self-induced their abortions, though black women and poor white women, because of poverty or discrimination in access to medical care, often did so. According to the Kinsey study on abortion, 30 percent of the lower-income and black women reported self-inducing their abortions.[12] . . .

Low-income women's and black women's greater reliance upon self-induced methods of abortion meant that the safety of illegal abortion varied by race and class. . . .

Since poor women and black women were more likely to try to self-induce abortions and less likely to go to doctors or midwives, they suffered more complications. . . . Women reported having no complications after their abortions in 91 percent of the abortions performed by doctors and 86 percent of those performed by midwives. In contrast, only 24 percent of the self-induced abortions were without complications.[13] . . .

As more women had abortions during the Depression, and perhaps more turned to self-induced measures because of their new poverty, growing numbers of women entered the nation's hospitals for care following their illegal abortions. The Depression deepened an earlier trend toward the hospitalization of women who had abortion-related complications in public hospitals. As childbirth gradually moved into the hospital, so too did abortion. . . . One intern at Cook County Hospital recalled that in 1928 she saw at least thirty or forty abortion cases in the month and a half she worked there; or, one woman a day and several hundred women a year entered the hospital because of postabortion complications. In 1934, the County Hospital admitted 1,159 abortion cases, and reported twenty-two abortion-related deaths that year.[14] . . .

Doctors and public health reformers began to realize the importance of illegal abortion as a contributor to maternal mortality. . . . [Obstetrician Frederick J.] Taussig estimated that approximately fifteen thousand women died every year in the United States because of abortion.[15] . . . In hospital wards, doctors saw women with septic infections, perforations of the uterus, hemorrhages, and mutilation of intestines and other organs caused by self-induced abortions or ineptly performed operations.

The hospital atmosphere . . . helped forge a liberal consensus within a section of the medical profession about the horrors of self-induced and poorly performed criminal abortions, together with an acceptance of performing abortions for needy patients or referring them to abortionists. . . .

Most cities had several physicians who "specialized" in abortion, and many small towns had at least one physician-abortionist. . . .

In the mid-1930s one businessman set up a chain of abortion clinics in cities on the West Coast. Doctors Gabler, Keemer, and Timanus, of Chicago, Detroit, and Baltimore respectively, were physician-abortionists who performed abortions for tens of thousands of women during the 1930s. The decades-long existence of these specialty practices points to the tolerance and accessibility of abortion during these years.

Physician-abortionists practiced in a legally and medically gray area. It was not always clear whether they performed illegal abortions or legal, therapeutic abortions. As physicians, the law allowed them to perform therapeutic abortions in order to preserve a woman's life, but abortion was illegal and frowned upon by the profession. What made physician-abortionists different from other doctors was the volume of abortions performed, often to the exclusion of other medical practice. As long as these physicians received referrals from other physicians, practiced safely, and avoided police interference, they might consider the abortions to be therapeutic. Yet any physician who regularly performed abortions also knew that the procedure was criminal and that he or she practiced on a fine line. . . .

It is difficult for the historian to gain access to patient records, and this is particularly true for an illegal procedure. Yet I have uncovered records of abortion patients and have reconstructed, for the first time, the daily practice of an underground abortion clinic and the characteristics of its clientele. Seventy patient records of women who had abortions at a Chicago clinic owned by Dr. Josephine Gabler have been preserved in legal documents. . . . The Gabler clinic (later run by Ada Martin) serves as a case study of a specialty practice and reveals the abortion experiences of many women who found physician-abortionists.[16]

Dr. Josephine Gabler was a major source of abortions for Chicago women and other Midwesterners in the 1930s. She graduated from an Illinois medical school in 1905 and received her Illinois medical license that year. She established herself as a specialist in abortion by the late 1920s, perhaps earlier. Over eighteen thousand abortions were performed at her State Street office between 1932 and 1941.[17] In other words, the clinic provided approximately two thousand abortions a year—about five a day, if it operated seven days a week. Dr. Gabler, and other doctors who worked at the State Street office, provided needed abortion services to women from the entire region, including patients from Illinois, Indiana, Michigan, and Wisconsin. . . .

The Gabler-Martin clinic demonstrates that doctors have been more responsive to the demands of their female patients—even demands for an illegal procedure—than previously suspected. Over two hundred doctors, including some of Chicago's most prominent physicians and AMA members, referred patients to Gabler and Martin for abortions.[18] . . .

When Mrs. Helen B. learned of her pregnancy in 1940, she wanted an abortion. She "finally persuaded" her doctor that she needed an abortion and was given Dr. Josephine Gabler's business card.[19] The use of business cards itself emphasizes the openness of abortion practice in this period. . . .

Gabler and Martin showed their appreciation for referrals—and encouraged their colleagues and allies to keep referring—by paying commissions to those who sent patients. Investigators reported that the payments were usually fifteen dollars each, which was about a quarter of the average fee for abortion. . . .

The other major path to an abortionist's office was through women's personal networks. An abortionist's name and address were critical information, which women shared with each other. In this sample, of the cases where the source of the referral is identifiable, almost a third of the patients found their way to the clinic through friends. . . . Every woman who went to 190 North State Street for an abortion became a potential source of information for others in the same predicament. . . .

In many ways, the experience of getting an abortion at the State Street clinic was like going into any other doctor's office for medical care. Referrals from physicians, note taking by a receptionist, women dressed in white uniforms, instruments and delivery tables, and the instructions for after-care were all typical in a doctor's office—and familiar to women who had previously delivered babies in hospitals. The women received anesthesia and, apparently, a dilation and curettage of the uterus—the same procedure they would have had if they had a legal, therapeutic abortion in the hospital.

Nonetheless, the criminality of abortion made its practice clandestine. Two safeguards designed to shield the people performing abortions made the procedures in Martin's office different from legal, hospital procedures: covering the eyes of patients in order to make identifying the physician-abortionist impossible and warning women not to go to anyone else if they experienced complications. The clinic did not abandon its clients if problems developed following the abortion, but they did not want them going to physicians or local hospitals who might alert authorities.

The majority of women in the State Street patient records were married when they had their abortions. . . . Over half of the married women (thirty-two women, or 57 percent) had children. Over a third of these women had children under two years old. Mothers seemed strongly motivated to avoid having two babies in diapers at once. . . .

A second, and large, group of the married women (twenty-four, or 43 percent) had no children at all. This is not what we would expect; we have learned that married women used birth control and abortion after they had children, not before. . . .

Could they represent a significant number of married couples who intended to have no children at all? Since the records do not say how long they had been married, it is possible that these were abortions of prebridal pregnancies. Perhaps some worried about extramarital affairs. Some may have been college students or married to students. Perhaps they needed an abortion because they could not risk losing their jobs. Probably most who had abortions in the early years of their marriages had children later. Class could shape reproduction in complicated ways. Working women and more affluent college women found it necessary to delay childbearing for different reasons and at different times.

The age range of the State Street patients reflected the diversity of women's reproductive patterns and needs. The ages of the women having abortions in this sample ranged from eighteen to forty-eight years. . . . Their average age was twenty-seven years, but over half were under twenty-five. In 1992, for comparison, most of the women who had abortions were unmarried and under twenty-five years old.[20] . . . The difference is that most of the women in the Martin case records ended their pregnancies within the context of marriage: 80 percent of the Gabler-Martin clinic patients were married; now, 80 percent are unmarried. Today, most of the women who have abortions do so when they are single and finishing high school or college and expect to bear children later.[21] . . .

It is difficult to determine the class of . . . the patients at 190 North State Street, but it seems to have been a mixed group. The records of this office show we cannot assume that working-class women were never able to get safe abortions from physicians. . . . Information about income or the occupation of the woman's husband, if married, was not included in the patient records, but the records show that at least a third of the women worked for wages. . . .

The racial composition of the women who relied upon the abortion services of Dr. Gabler is even more obscure. There is no racial information in the patient records. . . .

Gabler and Martin could provide illegal abortions openly because they paid for protection from the law. Bribery of police and prosecutors underpinned the abortion practice. We only know of the corruption of legal authorities in Chicago because police officer Daniel Moriarity tried to kill Martin in order to silence her.[22] . . .

The office at 190 North State Street where thousands of women obtained abortions from a skilled practitioner was not a rarity.[23] . . .

In Detroit, African American physicians might refer patients to Dr. Edgar Bass Keemer Jr. . . . Throughout his career as an abortionist, which lasted into the 1970s, Keemer served primarily poor women and black women. In thirty-five years, he performed over thirty thousand abortions.[24] . . .

In Baltimore, reputable physicians referred their patients to Dr. George Loutrell Timanus, one of two well-known physician-abortionists in [the city]. Dr. Timanus had a close relationship to Baltimore's white medical elite at Johns Hopkins University, where the faculty taught Timanus's techniques to their students and called him a friend. . . .

Doctors Gabler, Keemer, and Timanus represent a larger pattern of medical involvement in illegal abortion and an expansion of the medical provision of abortions during the 1930s. . . . [Their practices were not temporary, but established; they were not located in back alleys, but on main streets. Dr. Gabler had a business card; Dr. Timanus was listed in the phone book and his office had a sign in front.]

Thousands of women obtained abortions from physicians in conventional medical settings and suffered no complications afterwards. . . . A mixed group of patients—working-class and middle-class women, white and black—reached these trusted physicians. . . .

Notes

1. "Unemployment," *Birth Control Review (BCR)* 5 (May 1931):131.

2. Lois Rita Helmbold, "Beyond the Family Economy: Black and White Working-Class Women During the Great Depression," *Feminist Studies* 13

(Fall 1987):640–641; A. J. Rongy, *Abortion: Legal or Illegal?* (New York: Vanguard Press, 1933), p. 111.

3. Alice Kessler-Harris, *Out to Work: A History of Wage-Earning Women in the United States* (Oxford: Oxford University Press, 1982), pp. 256–257; quotations from typed letter from Charleston, IL 61920, April 20, 1985, "Silent No More" Campaign, National Abortion Rights Action League (NARAL), Chicago.

4. Paul H. Gebhard et al., *Pregnancy, Birth and Abortion* (New York: Harper and Brothers and Paul B. Hoeber Medical Books, 1958), pp. 113–114, 140, table 55. Since much of the data comes from the earlier Kinsey studies on sexuality and this report came out of his institute, hereafter I refer to this book in the text as the Kinsey report or study on abortion.

5. The percentage of first pregnancies aborted in this young generation was no more than 10 percent, but it was more than double the rate of earlier generations of women.

6. Charles H. Garvin, "The Negro Doctor's Task," *BCR* 16 (November 1932):270.

7. Endre K. Brunner and Louis Newton, "Abortions in Relation to Viable Births in 10,609 Pregnancies: A Study Based on 4,500 Clinic Histories," *American Journal of Obstetrics and Gynecology* 38 (July 1939):82–83, 88.

8. Gebhard et al., *Pregnancy, Birth and Abortion*, p. 162. Regina G. Kunzel also finds class difference among African-Americans in their use of maternity homes; Kunzel, *Fallen Women, Problem Girls: Unmarried Mothers and the Professionalization of Social Work, 1890–1945* (New Haven: Yale University Press, 1993), p. 73.

9. Brunner and Newton, "Abortions in Relation to Viable Births," pp. 85, 90.

10. Ibid., p. 87, fig. 4.

11. Gebhard et al., *Pregnancy, Birth and Abortion*, pp. 64–65, 114–118.

12. Ibid., pp. 194–195, 198.

13. Regine K. Stix, "A Study of Pregnancy Wastage," *Milbank Memorial Fund Quarterly* 13 (October 1935):362–363.

14. Dr. Gertrude Engbring in Transcript of *People* v. *Heissler*, 338 Ill. 596 (1930), Case Files, vault no. 44783, Supreme Court of Illinois, Record Series 901, Illinois State Archives, Springfield; Augusta Weber, "Confidential Material Compiled for Joint Commission on Accreditation, June 1964," box 5, "Obstetrics Department—Accreditation 1964," Office of the Administrator, Cook County Hospital Archives. An "Abortion Service" was opened at Harlem Hospital in 1935. Peter Marshall Murray and L. B. Winkelstein, "Incomplete Abortion: An Evaluation of Diagnosis and Treatment of 727 Consecutive Cases of Incomplete Abortions," *Harlem Hospital Bulletin* 3 (June 1950):31.

15. Fred J. Taussig, "Abortion in Relation to Fetal and Maternal Welfare," *American Journal of Obstetrics and Gynecology*, p. 872.

16. This case study is based on patient records and other legal documents discovered in the Transcript of *People* v. *Martin*, 382 Ill. 192 (1943), Case Files, vault no. 51699, Supreme Court of Illinois, Record Series 901.

17. Supplemental Report, Statement of Gordon B. Nash, Assistant State's Attorney, April 23, 1942, in Transcript of *People* v. *Martin*.

18. Of the eighteen doctors named in the patient records, eleven could be identified. (Sometimes only a last name was included on the record.) All eleven were AMA members and eight were specialists of various types.

19. Mrs. Helen B. in transcript of *People* v. *Martin*.

20. "Abortion Surveillance: Preliminary Data—United States, 1992," *Morbidity and Mortality Weekly Report: CDC Surveillance Summaries* 43 (December 23, 1994):930, 932, table I.

21. Recent abortion data show the trend to delaying childbearing. Teenagers make up a smaller proportion of the women having abortions than in the past: in 1972, 33 percent of the women who had abortions were nineteen years old or less; in 1992, teenagers were only 20 percent of the women having abortions, and women twenty-five or older made up 45 percent of the women having abortions. "Abortion Surveillance," p. 932, table I.

22. As a police officer, Moriarity received a little less than $2,500 per year. Quotations in George Wright, "Tells Bribe Behind Killing," *Chicago Daily Tribune*, May 2, 1941, p. 1.

23. Other doctors who appear to have specialized in abortion in Chicago include Dr. William E. Shelton, who may have been involved with Martin ("Dr. William Eugene Shelton," *Daily Tribune*, September 27, 1928; "Loop Physician Held in Abortion Conspiracy Case," *Daily Tribune*, November 21, 1940); Dr. Joseph A. Khamis ("Doctor Accused Second Time as an Abortionist," *Daily Tribune*, August 18, 1942); Dr. Justin L. Mitchell (*People* v. *Mitchell*, 368 Ill. 399); and Dr. Edward Peyser (*People* v. *Peyser*, 380 Ill. 404). All newspaper clippings in Abortionists Files, Historical Health Fraud Collection, American Medical Association, Chicago.

24. Ed Keemer, *Confessions of a Pro-Life Abortionist* (Detroit: Vinco Press, 1980), pp. 13, 18, 27, 29, 89–93.

JACQUELINE JONES

Harder Times: The Great Depression

The chronic scarcity of jobs that characterized the Appalachian South where the Elizabethton strike occurred became a national phenomenon in the 1930s. As the Great Depression tightened its hold on the economy, the plight of America's working people generated protest in the farm belt as well as industrial centers. Government aid eventually alleviated some of the suffering while New Deal legislation and a revitalized labor movement brought improved working conditions. Nevertheless, many workers, agricultural as well as industrial, struggled daily to survive. They remained at the mercy of any employers who would hire them.

African Americans were especially vulnerable. Jacqueline Jones's study of black women reminds us once again of the extent to which race and class shape women's experience. Consider the difference that race made in both the job opportunities available to women in the 1930s and the debate about whether married women should work. Observe how the experience of black domestics demonstrated the power of race and class to override "the bonds of womanhood." Note, too, how the speed-ups generating such dissatisfaction among the textile workers in the 1920s described by Hall (see pp. 493–505) were extended in the 1930s to private household service.

High unemployment rates among their husbands and sons forced many white wives to enter the labor market for the first time in the 1930s.[1] But black men experienced even higher rates of joblessness, causing their wives to cling more desperately to the positions they already had, despite declining wages and deteriorating working conditions. During the Great Depression, most black women maintained only a precarious hold on gainful employment; their positions as family breadwinners depended upon, in the words of one social worker, "the breath of chance, to say nothing of the winds of economic change."[2] Unemployment statistics for the 1930s can be misleading because they do not reveal the impact of a shifting occupational structure on job options for women of the two races. Just as significantly, the relatively high rate of black females' participation in the labor force obscures the highly temporary and degrading nature of their work experiences. Specifically, most of these women could find only seasonal or part-time employment; racial and sexual discrimination deprived them of a living wage no matter how hard they labored; and they endured a degree and type of workplace exploitation for which the mere fact of having a job could not compensate. During the decade, nine out of ten black women workers toiled as agricultural laborers or domestic servants. Various pieces of federal legislation designed to protect and raise the purchasing power of workers (most notably the National Industrial Recovery Act [1933], the Social Security Act [1935], and the Fair Labor Standards Act [1938]) exempted these two groups of workers from their provisions. In essence, then, no more than 10 percent of gainfully employed black women derived any direct benefit from the new federal policies related to minimum wages, maximum hours, unemployment compensation, and social security.[3]

Despite the rapid decline in a wide variety of indicators related to production and economic growth in the early 1930s, and despite the sluggishness of the pre-1941 recovery period, the numbers and kinds of job opportunities for white women expanded, as did their need to help supplement household income. The clerical sector grew (as it had in the 1920s) and would continue to do so in the 1940s, and in the process attracted more and more women into the work force and employed a larger proportion of all white women workers. (The percentage of white women who were gainful workers steadily increased throughout the period 1920 to 1940 from 21.3 to 24.1 percent of all adult females.) Recent historians have stressed the "benefits of labor segregation" for women, arguing that, at least during the early part of the depression decade, unemployment in the male-dominated industrial sector was generally greater than in the female-dominated areas of sales, communications, and secretarial work. But this was a race-specific phenomenon. In a job market segmented by both race and sex, black women had no access to white women's work even though (or perhaps because) it was deemed integral to both industrial capitalism and the burgeoning federal bureaucracy. In 1940 one-third of all white, but only 1.3 percent of all black, working women had clerical jobs. On the other hand, 60 percent of all black female workers were domestic servants; the figure for white women was only 10 percent.[4] . . .

KITCHEN SPEED-UPS: DOMESTIC SERVICE

Contemporary literary and photographic images of a stricken nation showed dejected white men waiting in line for food, jobs, and relief. Yet observers sensitive to the racial dimensions of the crisis provided an alternative symbol—that of a middle-aged black woman in a thin, shabby coat and men's shoes, standing on a street corner in the dead of winter and offering her housecleaning services for 10 cents an hour. If the migrant labor camp symbolized the black agricultural worker's descent into economic marginality, then the "slave markets" in northern cities revealed a similar fate for domestic servants.

"The 'mart' is but a miniature mirror of our economic battle front," wrote two investigative reporters in a 1935 issue of the NAACP's monthly journal, *The Crisis.* A creature of the depression, the slave market consisted of groups of black women, aged seventeen to seventy, who waited on sidewalks for white women to drive up and offer them a day's work. The Bronx market, composed of several small ones—it was estimated that New York City had two hundred altogether—received the most attention from writers during the decade, though the general phenomenon recurred throughout other major cities. Before 1929, many New York domestics had worked for wealthy white families on Long Island. Their new employers, some of them working-class women themselves, paid as little as $5.00 weekly for full-time laborers to wash windows and clothes, iron (as many as twenty-one shirts a shift), and wax floors. The black women earned radically depressed wages: lunch and 35 cents for six hours of work, or $1.87 for an eight-hour day. They had to guard against various ruses that would deprive them of even this pittance—for example, a clock turned back an hour, the promised carfare that never materialized at the end of the day. As individuals they felt trapped, literally and figuratively pushed to the limits of their endurance. A thirty-year-old woman told federal interviewer Vivian Morris that she hated the people she worked for: "Dey's mean, 'ceitful, an' 'ain' hones'; but what ah'm gonna do? Ah got to live—got to hab a place to steh," and so she would talk her way into a job by boasting of her muscle power. But some days groups of women would spontaneously organize themselves and "run off the corner" those job seekers "who persist[ed] in working for less than thirty cents an hour."[5]

Unlike their country cousins, domestics contended directly with white competitors pushed out of their factory and waitressing jobs. The agricultural labor system served as a giant sieve; for the most part, displaced farm families went to the city rather than vying for the remaining tenant positions. The urban economy had no comparable avenues of escape; it was a giant pressure cooker, forcing the unemployed to look for positions in occupations less prestigious than the ones they held formerly or, in the event of ultimate failure, to seek some form of charity or public assistance. A 1937 Women's Bureau survey of destitute women in Chicago revealed that, although only 37 percent of native-born white women listed their "usual occupation" as domestic service, a much greater number had tried to take advantage of employers' preferences for white servants before they gave up the quest for jobs altogether and applied for relief. Meanwhile, the 81 percent of black women who had worked in service had nowhere else to go. Under these circumstances, the mere act of hiring a black woman seemed to some to represent a humanitarian gesture. In 1934 an observer of the social-welfare scene noted approvingly, with unintentional irony, that "From Mistress Martha Washington to Mistress Eleanor Roosevelt is not such a long time as time goes. There may be some significance in the fact that the household of the first First Lady was manned by Negro servants and the present First Lady has followed her example."[6]

The history of domestic service in the 1930s provides a fascinating case study of the lengths to which whites would go in exploiting a captive labor force. Those who employed live-in servants in some cases cut their wages, charged extra for room and board, or lengthened on-duty hours. But it was in the area of day work that housewives elevated labor-expanding and money-saving methods to a fine art. General speed-ups were common in private homes throughout the North and South. Among the best bargains were children and teenagers; in Indianola, Mississippi, a sixteen-year-old black girl worked from 6 A.M. to 7 P.M. daily for $1.50 a week. In the same town a maid could be instructed to do her regular chores, plus those of the recently fired cook, for less pay than she had received previously. (A survey of Mississippi's domestics revealed that the average weekly pay was less than $2.00.) Some women received only carfare, clothing, or lunch for a day's work. Northern white women also lowered wages drastically. In 1932 Philadelphia domestics earned $5.00 to $12.00 for a forty-eight- to sixty-seven-hour work week. Three years later they took home the same amount of money for ninety hours' worth of scrubbing, washing, and cooking (an hourly wage of 15 cents).[7]

The deteriorating working conditions of domestic servants reflected the conscious choices of individual whites who took advantage of the abundant labor supply. Social workers recorded conversations with potential employers seeking "bright, lively" domestics (with the very best references) to do all the cooking, cleaning, laundry, and childcare for very little pay, because, in the words of one Pittsburgh woman, "There are so many people out of work that I am sure I can find a girl for $6.00 a week." Indeed, at times it seemed as if there existed a perversely negative relationship between expectations and compensation. An eighty-three-year-old South Carolina black woman, Jessie Sparrow, resisted working on Sundays because, she told an interviewer in 1937, "when dey pays you dat little bit of money, dey wants every bit your time." A southern white man demonstrated his own brand of logic when he "admitted as a matter of course that his cook was underpaid, but explained that this was necessary, since, if he gave her more money, she might soon have so much that she would no longer be willing to work for him."[8]

The field of domestic service was virtually unaffected by national and state welfare policies. In the 1930s Women's Bureau officials tried to compensate for this inaction with a flurry of correspondence, radio and luncheon-meeting speeches, and voluntary guidelines related to the "servant problem." In her talks on the subject, bureau head Mary Anderson tried to appeal to employers' sense of fairness when she suggested that they draw up job descriptions, guard against accidents in the workplace, and establish reasonable hours and wages. But the few housewives privy to Anderson's exhortations were not inclined to heed them, especially when confronted by a seemingly accommodating "slave" on the street corner. Consequently, black domestic workers in several cities, often under the sponsorship of a local Young Women's Christian Association, Urban League branch, or labor union, made heroic attempts to form employees' organizations that would set uniform standards for service. However, they remained a shifting, amorphous group immune to large-scale organizational efforts. For example, founded in 1934 and affiliated with Building Service Union Local 149 (AFL), the New York Domestic Workers Union had only 1,000 (out of a potential of 100,000) members four years later. It advocated two five-hour shifts six days a week and insisted, "last but not least, no window washing." Baltimore's Domestic Workers Union (in the CIO fold) also welcomed members of both races and remained a relatively insignificant force in the regulation of wages and working conditions. Without adequate financial resources, leaders like New York's

Dora Jones labored to organize women who "still believe in widespread propaganda that all unions are rackets." As a result, efforts by domestics to control wage rates informally through peer pressure or failure to report for work as promised represented spontaneous job actions more widespread and successful than official "union" activity.[9]

During the depression, a long life of work was the corollary of a long day of work. Black women between the ages of twenty-five and sixty-five worked at consistently high rates; they simply could not rely on children or grandchildren to support them in their old age. The Federal Writers Project interviews with former slaves recorded in the late 1930s contain hundreds of examples of women in their seventies and eighties still cooking, cleaning, or hoeing for wages on a sporadic basis in order to keep themselves and their dependents alive. An interviewer described the seventy-seven-year-old widow Mandy Leslie of Fairhope, Alabama, as "a pillar of strength and comfort to several white households" because she did their washing and ironing every week. Living alone, her children gone, this elderly woman boiled clothes in an iron pot heated by a fire, and then rubbed them on a washboard and hung them on lines so they could be ironed the following day. Such was the price exacted from black women for the "strength and comfort" they provided whites.[10]

Notes

1. Lois Scharf, *To Work and to Wed: Female Employment, Feminism, and the Great Depression* (Westport, Conn.: Greenwood Press, 1980), pp. 107–8. . . .

2. Marion Cuthbert, "Problems Facing Negro Young Women," *Opportunity* 14 (Feb. 1936):47–49.

3. U.S. Department of Commerce, Bureau of the Census, *The Labor Force,* Pt. 1, U.S. Summary, p. 90; Mary Elizabeth Pidgeon, "Employed Women Under N.R.A. Codes," United States Department of Labor, Women's Bureau, *Bulletin,* no. 130 (1935); "Women at Work: A Century of Industrial Change," United States Department of Labor, Women's Bureau, *Bulletin,* no. 161 (1939). . . .

4. Alice Kessler-Harris, *Out to Work: A History of Wage-Earning Women in the United States* (New York: Oxford University Press, 1982), pp. 250–72; Ruth Milkman, "Women's Work and Economic Crisis: Some Lessons of the Great Depression," *Review of Radical Political Economics* 8 (Spring 1976):73–97; Winifred D. Wandersee, *Women's Work and Family Values, 1920–1940* (Cambridge, Mass.: Harvard University Press, 1981), pp. 84–102; U.S. Dept. of Commerce, Bureau of the Census, *The Labor Force,* Pt. 1, U.S. Summary, p. 90.

5. Ella Baker and Marvel Cooke, "The Bronx Slave Market," *Crisis* 42 (Nov. 1935):330, 340; Vivian Morris, "Bronx Slave Market," Dec. 6, 1938, Federal Writers Project, Negro Folklore Division (New York), p. 1, Archive of Folk Song, Manuscript Division, Library of Congress, Washington, D.C. . . .

6. Harriet A. Byrne and Cecile Hillyer, "Unattached Women on Relief in Chicago, 1937," United States Department of Labor, Women's Bureau, *Bulletin,* no. 158 (1938); Elmer Anderson Carter, "The Negro Household Employee," *Woman's Press* 28 (July–Aug. 1934):351.

7. John Dollard, *Caste and Class in a Southern Town* (New Haven, Conn.: Yale University Press, 1937), pp. 107–8; Jean Collier Brown, "The Negro Woman Worker," United States Department of Labor, Women's Bureau, *Bulletin,* no. 165 (1938), pp. 3–4, 7; Charles T. Haley, "To Do Good and Do Well: Middle-Class Blacks and the Depression, Philadelphia, 1929–1941" (Ph.D. diss., State University of New York at Binghamton, 1980), p. 59. . . .

8. Harold A. Lett, "Work: Negro Unemployed in Pittsburgh" *Opportunity* 9 (Mar. 1931):79–81; "Women Workers in Indianapolis," *Crisis* 37 (June 1930):189–91; *The American Slave: A Composite Autobiography,* ed. George Rawick, 41 vols., Series 1, Supp. Series 1 and 2 (Westport, Conn.: Greenwood Press, 1972, 1978, 1979), Series 1, *South Carolina Narratives,* pt. IV, vol. 3, p. 146; Hortense Powdermaker, *After Freedom: A Cultural Study in the Deep South* (New York: Viking, 1939), pp. 117–18.

9. "The Domestic Worker of Today," Radio Talk by Miss Mary Anderson, Sept. 21, 1932, Station WJAY, sponsored by Cleveland Parent Teachers Association, Speeches No. 112 (Box 71), Women's Bureau Collection, Department of Labor Archives, Record Group 86, National Archives, Washington, D.C.; Dora Jones quoted in "The Domestic Workers' Union," in *Black Women in White America: A Documentary History,* ed. Gerda Lerner, (New York: Pantheon, 1972), pp. 231–34. On the New York union, see Evelyn Seeley, "Our Feudal Housewives," *The Nation* 46 (May 28, 1938):613–15; on Baltimore, see article reprinted from *Baltimore Afro-American,* Oct. 1936, in *The Black Worker: A Documentary History from Colonial Times to the Present,* vol. 6, *The Era of Post-War Prosperity and the Great Depression, 1920–1936,* eds. Philip S. Foner and Ronald L. Lewis (Philadelphia: Temple University Press, 1981), pp. 184–85; Roderick N. Ryon, "An Ambiguous Legacy: Baltimore Blacks and the CIO, 1936–1941," *Journal of Negro History* 65 (Winter 1980):29. For evidence of the Urban League's efforts in this area, see "Program of Mass Meeting of General House Work Employees, Sept. 21, 1933 (St. Louis)" in Correspondence—Household (Domestic) File, General Correspondence Prior to 1934 (Box 926), Women's Bureau Collection, RG 86, National Archives.

10. Rawick, ed., *American Slave, Alabama Narratives,* vol. 6, p. 251.

DOCUMENT

Struggling to Unionize

Genora Johnson Dollinger, "... Once she understands she is standing in defense of her family—well, God, don't fool around with that woman then"

The 1930s were a period of intense labor organizing. The American Federation of Labor (AFL) had found it could survive in a period of unrestricted immigration (when the supply of unskilled labor was inexhaustible) only by organizing highly skilled workers in particular crafts. The Congress of Industrial Organizations (CIO), as its name implies, tried a different and very difficult approach: organizing all the workers in an entire industry, such as the automobile industry or the electrical industry. To attempt this during the Depression was an enormous challenge. The one advantage organizers had was that President Franklin Roosevelt, unlike his predecessors, refused to use the power of the federal government against the workers, believing they had a right to unionize. His position generated biting criticism in the business community and cost him heavily among more prosperous constituents; however, it brought organized labor solidly into Democratic ranks.

The huge difficulty of the CIO's task, the severe hardships that the workers and their families were suffering, and the preponderance of power which employers had at their disposal—all are illuminated in this powerful account of the famous 1936 strike at General Motors in Flint, Michigan. But that is only part of the story. What Dollinger reveals so powerfully is her own role and that of the women who joined her in the Women's Emergency Brigade.

What propelled Dollinger to assume leadership, and what inspired the women who answered her call to perform such acts of courage? How do you account for the union's response to their actions once victory had been won? What does this suggest about the potential ability of women at the grassroots level, with few resources at their disposal, to help change the course of history?

...When the strike started, my mother—without my father's knowledge—agreed to take care of my two little boys.... I was then relatively free, and immediately went to Roy Reuther and Robert Travis—those were the UAW organizers—and I volunteered to help. I was told to go to the kitchen and peel potatoes, but I said there were plenty of others who could do that, including some of the men. So they gave me a job setting up a press clipping bureau.... I decided anyone sitting with a pair of shears could handle that job, so I organized a sign painting department.... I remember one sign, my own little snow-suited two-year-old holding it high: "My daddy strikes for us little tykes." ...

From Jeane Westin, *Making Do: How Women Survived the '30s* (Chicago: Follett Publishing, 1976), pp. 312–18.

. . . On December 30, the police attempted to break the strike at Fisher 2. . . . People came to watch the police shooting us with rifle bullets, buckshot, and tear gas. We had nothing but rocks and car door hinges, but we picked up the tear gas bombs and heaved them back at the police before they exploded. Men were going down, and fourteen people were shot that night, one seriously. I saw blood flowing.

But before this happened union men had herded all the women to safety—all except me. I said, "I've got just as strong weapons as you've got. You've got no guns, neither have I. I can fight as well as you." I was the only woman too stubborn to leave, so I stayed down there. . . .

At this point Victor [Reuther] privately told some of us, "We may have lost this battle, but we're not losing the war." He seemed to be preparing us for defeat on this night. It was then I asked him: "Victor, can I speak to them?" And he replied, "We've got nothing to lose." He was a fine person, but still I could feel that he didn't think a woman could do much in this situation.

I got up on the sound car—I know it was an electrifying thing . . . a woman's voice calling to the people of Flint after so many hours of fighting . . . and I said, "I'm talking especially to you women out there. You didn't know that mothers"—I meant myself—"are being fired on by the police. The police are cowards enough to fire into the bellies of unarmed men. Aren't they also cowards to fire at mothers of little children? I'm asking you women out there behind the barricades to break through those police lines. Come down here and stand with your brothers, your sons, your sweethearts, your husbands and help us win this fight."

And so help me, I could hardly believe it—one woman started walking toward us. The police grabbed at her and she walked right out of her coat. She marched down, other women following her—the police didn't dare shoot all those women in the back. Then the union men broke through. The battle was over and the union had won.

The women had saved the day. It was then that I realized how much power women had, and I proceeded to organize the Women's Emergency Brigade. . . . We bought red berets and made arm bands with the white letters "EB" for Emergency Brigade. . . .

Listen, I met some of the finest women I have ever come across in my life. When the occasion demands it of a woman and once she understands that she's standing in defense of her family—well, God, *don't fool around with that woman then*. . . .

I saw women stand up under circumstances where big men ran around the corner and hid under a car. I have seen them rise up when I would not have believed they could. . . .

Finally, you know, everything just came to a head. With so many workers' homes without sufficient food and heat in the freezing January temperatures, and powerful General Motors benefiting from the unequal contest . . . well, it came time for a major decision. Plant 4, the largest plant in the Chevrolet division of ten plants, produced all the motors for Chevrolet throughout the country. That plant became our target. . . .

We pretended to strike one of the other Chevrolet plants, Plant 9, which was far removed on the other side of the whole complex and had that action drawing all the company police, city police, and Pinkerton agents . . . a diversionary tactic, you see. The Women's Emergency Brigade was there and they broke the windows to allow air to get in to the tear-gassed union men. Women just played a fantastic role over there at Plant 9.

Now, my husband Kermit's assignment was to shut down Plant 4, the target plant. But I dared not let the brigade know about it because it had to be such a tight secret. The whole union movement had been infiltrated with company spies. After the Plant 9 action, I sent the brigade back to headquarters and with my five lieutenants, walked around the city streets that paralleled the big Chevrolet compound. . . .

We strolled over to Plant 4 which the union men were attempting to shut down. I was very nervous because I knew it was a life and death matter for my husband and the other men inside. By the time we got over there there was a great deal of confusion. . . .

The plant foreman and his hired agents were giving them trouble. . . . The men yelled to us, "My God, we're having an awful time. Don't let anybody come in through the front gate on Chevrolet Avenue." Naturally, that was a big order, so I sent one of my lieutenants to call headquarters. "Tell the brigade to come at once," I told her. And the five of us left strung ourselves across the front gate.

When the city police got word what was happening they came, seventy-five of them, and found us women on the gate. We defied them . . . told them they would have to go in over our dead bodies. . . . Eighty percent had relatives working under those horrible conditions in the plants. "Look," I said, "if you worked in this plant, and you were being driven crazy, and your health was broken down, wouldn't you expect your wife to come down here to see what she could do?"

It threw them off their guard and they began answering my arguments, just long enough. By the time they got provoked and said, "Well, we've got a job to do," and started pushing us, at that point the brigade came down Chevrolet Avenue. There came hundreds of those red berets bobbing up and down with the American flag at their head, singing "Solidarity Forever." The sound of it, from all those voices, just flooded the whole area.

They quickly set up an oval picket line in front of the main gate. This meant the police would have to club and shoot these women, and they had no stomach for that. Then the truck arrived filled with union men, and God, it dawned on me, *we'd saved the gate.*

The union had closed the huge and valuable Plant 4 with another sit-down strike. Soon after, Governor Frank Murphy declared martial law and ordered negotiations started. On February 11th, an agreement was reached recognizing unions in GM plants across the nation. That was a much greater victory than our small, inexperienced union ever expected to win. . . .

It's a measure of the strength of those women of the Red Berets that they could perform so courageously in an atmosphere that was often hostile to them. We organized on our own without the benefit of professional leadership, and yet, we played a role, second to none, in the birth of a union and in changing working families' lives forever.

ALICE KESSLER-HARRIS

Designing Women and Old Fools: Writing Gender into Social Security Law

One historian has called the Social Security Act of 1935 "the most important single piece of social legislation in all American history . . . in terms of historical decisiveness and direct influence upon the lives of individual Americans."* It continues to sustain the modern welfare state, providing the basic foundation for old-age pensions and for unemployment insurance. Its conceptualization of how needy mothers and children could claim government assistance was not replaced for sixty years, and continues to haunt debates over welfare. (President Franklin Delano Roosevelt also hoped to include a national system of health care but could not find congressional support.)

The drive to design the legislation and shepherd it through Congress was led by Frances Perkins, secretary of labor and the first woman cabinet member. It was not easy; anything resembling charity was widely resented. Many compromises were made in order to get enough votes in Congress. Perhaps the most significant was the decision not to conceptualize benefits as entitlement to all citizens. Instead, benefits were linked to payroll taxes paid by employers and employees, who could conclude that they were getting back only what they had put in. The strategy left nearly half the working population—including those who were seasonally or marginally employed—not covered. In the short run, there was a deflationary effect, as money paid into the Social Security Administration was pulled out of circulation. By 1937, efforts to amend the law were under way.

Politicians, economists, and other experts struggled to reform the law. They worked, for the most part, in good faith; they understood themselves to be seeking fairness and equity. They spoke of "the people" or "the worker"; their words were general and generic. But, as historian Alice Kessler-Harris read the minutes of meetings and considered the conversations and arguments, she found that the words they chose inadvertently revealed that the reformers' ideas of fairness rested on their own assumptions about work, family, citizenship, gender, and race. Behind what they would have called "the common sense of the matter" lurked unspoken beliefs: that women are not serious or long-term workers and that African Americans were doomed to marginal employment.

*Kenneth S. Davis, *FDR, the New Deal Years, 1933–1937: A History* (New York: Random House, 1986), p. 437; see also David M. Kennedy, *Freedom from Fear: The American People in Depression and War, 1929–1945* (New York: Oxford University Press, 1999), pp. 257–73.

Excerpted from "Maintaining Self Respect" and "Questions of Equity," chs. 2 and 3 of *In Pursuit of Equity: Women, Men, and the Quest for Economic Citizenship in 20th Century America* by Alice Kessler-Harris (New York: Oxford University Press, 2001). Reprinted by permission of the author and Oxford University Press. Notes have been edited and renumbered.

What were the bureaucrats and legislators trying to accomplish by reforming the social security law? What were they trying to avoid? How did the law reflect their understandings of fairness? How did the new law reflect their view of the appropriate relationship between men and women? Between husbands and wives? Between blacks and whites? Between the citizen and the state? Why were concepts that had lasted since the 1930s attacked at the beginning of the 1970s?

[In the 1930s,] Americans moved from staunch opposition to federal government intervention in the lives of most men (but not women) to eager experiments with government mediation of every kind. Newly adopted social policies had many goals, but among the most dramatic were those connected with earning wages and keeping jobs. . . .

Achieving consensus on issues of who deserved employment and who could languish in uncompensated unemployment required some hard decisions, especially around questions of inclusion and exclusion. For the government to regulate working conditions and monitor benefits for those without jobs, legislators would have to agree on, and administrators determine, eligibility. Someone would have to decide who could be described as a "worker" and who didn't fit the picture; what jobs counted as work and what didn't; how many hours constituted full-time work and how few precluded the activity from being called "work" at all. Innovative programs and policies demanded clarifications and classifications, precisely placing individuals in their relationships to paid and unpaid activities of different sorts. Each categorization opened or closed a door to the status, social rights, and economic security that measured progress toward economic citizenship for someone. Not only did benefits and entitlements rest on symbols of belonging, but so, ultimately, did the identities of workers, as well as their self-respect, political participation, and a newly differentiated set of meanings for crucial concepts like breadwinning, manhood, and citizenship.

The social constraints that guided these decisions had many roots, including most crucially ideologies of race and of American freedom and liberty. Historians are only now beginning to understand the degree to which they reflected a fundamental consensus around issues of race. But the new policies were also deeply embedded in a widespread and widely shared set of assumptions about gender. The Social Security Act of 1935 provides a case in point.

The pressing need of old people in the 1930s was for assistance or relief, not insurance. Advocates ranging from Abraham Epstein, whose American Association for Old Age Security proposed federal grants to the states, to Francis Townsend, whose plan to give everyone over sixty-five two hundred dollars a month to spend at will exceeded all others in popularity, stimulated the public to believe that the federal government could and should help the states solve this problem. Over this, there was little controversy. The very first title of the Social Security Act, Title I, provided states with matching grants to give relief to the needy aged and to care for unemployable old people. It replaced the mostly inadequate state-based programs with uniform federal standards and more generous grants than all but a handful of states had been able to provide. But Old Age Assistance came at a price: it subjected recipients to the indignities of means testing, fostering an unmanly spirit of dependency. . . .

Social insurance advocates sought to circumvent this anxiety with insurance rather than relief: They sought to prevent destitution and "obviate the necessity of public charity" by protecting family breadwinners against the potential hazards of industrial life. . . .

In the United States, the idea of government-subsidized insurance ran counter to the American grain, which reified independence and self-reliance. If there were to be any old age insurance program at all, its designers faced a formidable challenge: to remove aging workers from the labor force (which required that they be adequately supported) while affirming the dignity of pension recipients (which required that the program be self-supporting). To solve the labor force problem, policy makers imagined a program tied to work rather than to citizenship. Deciding which workers would be covered, however, created two classes of citizens: those who participated regularly in the kind of wage work where resolving unemployment seemed most important, and those who did not. In 1930, men made up the vast majority of gainfully employed persons (75 percent of the total); about 12 percent of this number were classified by the census as "Negro." But most African American men did not work in the core industrial sectors, where issues of unemployment and labor force stability mattered most. And while women made up a quarter of all wage earners, their tenuous rights to work led many to assume they had little commitment to wage labor. . . . Despite women's own efforts to seek jobs during the depression, public opinion resolutely condemned wage work for those with husbands and fathers who could support them. Through the depression years, less than 15 percent of married women earned wages. Consciously or not, policy makers imagined a program available to most white wage-earning men that would omit "as a matter of course" most African Americans, by virtue of their positions in the labor market, and most women, whose positions appeared derivative of their marital partners.

Efforts to preserve the dignity of beneficiaries participated in the same gendered imagination. In the battle over unemployment compensation, men fought to maintain a sense of themselves as self-sufficient, independent, free, and capable of providing for their families and especially for the dependent women within them. In the struggle for Old Age Insurance (which we now call Social Security), participants deployed gender in more subtle but equally aggressive ways, not only to promote a conception of fairness that relied on the language of male dignity and female dependence but to ensure adequate support for all the aged. Gendered constructs helped to soothe a public increasingly enamored of government-funded assistance (which seemed to some policy makers an appropriate and to others a short-sighted and short-term solution). And they provided the language of family normalcy that convinced reluctant policy makers who remained skeptical of the capacity of an insurance program to solve employment problems without depending on general taxation. Ultimately, gendered conceptions provided the keystone that maintained public confidence in the core old age program and justified its redistributive goals. By providing economic security in particular ways and to particular people, old age insurance defined a new category of economic citizenship; at the same time . . . it fueled the desires of the excluded for fuller participation. . . .

No sooner had the Social Security Act been signed into law on August 14, 1935, than issues of adequacy began to surface. The bill provided for a 1 percent payroll tax, payable by employers, to be instituted in 1936 and matched by an equivalent contribution from every employee; benefits would not be payable until January 1942. The lag produced a surplus that, in a depression economy, threatened to exercise a deflationary effect. Most important, the exclusions written into the old age insurance provisions of the Social Security Act exempted nearly half the working population, evoking questions about its fairness as well as about its capacity to provide for the aged.[1] Because the program did not provide benefits to those who worked intermittently or for only a few years even when they worked in covered occupations, more than three-fifths of fully employed African Americans were denied coverage. Sixty percent of the excluded workers were female. . . . Probably as many as 85 percent of wage-earning black women were deprived of participation and benefits.[2]

At the same time, powerful popular support continued to build for the state-run, noncontributory old age assistance pensions that provided more generous benefits to the needy aged than those envisioned under Social Security for most contributors. . . . [These fueled] a sense of entitlement to old age pensions as a matter of justice. . . . Everyone knew that even when the insurance program started paying benefits in 1942, they would go at first to only three hundred thousand people, compared to the estimated two million needy elderly who would then be receiving noncontributory assistance.

. . . What was to be done? The solution seemed to be to spend the surplus. But how? And on whom? Despite the sharp and purposeful distinctions between adequacy and equity, the principle was violated by the very first set of amendments, which added old age insurance benefits for wives and widows who had not paid for them. No charitable impulse toward women motivated this act; no concern for their poverty inspired it. Rather, Congress added dependent wives and aged widows in order to shore up the legitimacy of a system in trouble. It did this by enhancing the benefits of already covered (mostly white) males to ensure extra income to those who had aged wives to support and extra insurance to those with young children who survived them. These amendments, adopted in 1939, reinforced the prerogatives, self-images, and citizenship rights of some males while reaffirming racialized conceptions of gender. They redefined equity to incorporate more adequate and appropriate provision for some men, infusing the American system of entitlements with the peculiar imbalance from which it has struggled to release itself since the early 1970s.

In the spring of 1937, the Senate Finance Committee pressured the Social Security Board into creating a federal Advisory Council to suggest remedies. In May, when the new Advisory Council, which J. Douglas Brown agreed to chair, was announced, it consisted of twenty-four members. Six represented employers; six came from the labor movement; and twelve were designated as "public" participants, most of them academics and businessmen. [The public members included three women.][3] . . .

Together with the Social Security Board and several congressional committees, the Advisory Council worked through the following year and a half to recommend basic changes. Their charge from Congress was clear: They had to recommend a permanent way of dealing with ballooning reserves. They were to do this by beginning old age insurance benefits earlier than the originally mandated January 1942 start-up date and by making them larger. They were to explore the possibility of extending benefits to the disabled, to survivors, and to excluded groups. In the end, the council sidestepped the challenge of significantly extending insurance to most of the excluded groups, including the disabled, domestic servants, and agricultural workers and chose to rely instead on a new and expensive package of benefits for aged wives and survivors to reduce the surplus.[4]

The discussions over these alternatives tell us something about how invisible assumptions about men and women informed an entire network of social policy. For when the council moved toward emphasizing expanding benefits to those already covered, it utilized gender to mediate the conflict between adequacy and equity—a conflict in which women played little role but issues of manliness and womanliness assumed paramount importance. . . . The council, as its chairman, Douglas Brown, put it, had adopted "the principle of family protection."

The conversations within the Advisory Council and in Congress clarify the meaning of that principle. The council quickly agreed on pensions for fatherless children—an idea that already had popular support.[5] The Advisory Council adopted the notion rapidly because it promised to significantly reduce the numbers receiving means-tested assistance under both Title I (Old Age Assistance) and Title IV (Aid to Dependent Children) and strengthen the entire Social Security program by providing the illusion that their support was a product of insurance, the provenance of thoughtful and thrifty fathers. . . .

The Advisory Council relied on the same ideas of fairness to provide benefits for the widowed mothers of young children. These widows were to have benefits only as long as their children were young. The sums granted, and the restrictions on them, suggest that insurance for widowed mothers was conceived of as a matter of peace of mind for the husband. The widowed mother was to get three fourths of what her husband's pension would have been. The pension was granted as a matter of need, to enable "the widow to remain at home and care for the children."[6] It was to be reduced or eliminated if her earnings exceeded fifteen dollars a month (a tiny sum, even in 1939), thus encouraging her not to try to earn wages. In the likely event a widow's children reached eighteen before she reached sixty-five, the council recommended that all support end, to be resumed again when she became sixty-five, if in the meantime she had not remarried.[7] A young widow without children lacked any "rights" in her husband's contribution and got no benefits until and unless she grew old without remarrying.

Tying the dignity of men (defined by their capacity to provide) to the virtue of women (their willingness to remain dependent on men and to rear children) proved to be a continuing problem for young and old widows alike. The Social Security Board was fully cognizant of what it called the "widow's gap," noting at congressional hearings that "middle aged widows find it more difficult to become self-supporting." Still, . . . it deferred the annuity of an under-sixty-five widow until she reached that age, on the grounds that "there is some likelihood that the widow may reenter covered employment."[8] Its sympathies for widows whose children were grown could not overcome internalized portraits of the family that fully rationalized its position: "They are likely to have more savings than younger widows and many of them have children who are grown and able to help them until they reach 65 years of age."[9]

The conversations within the council and the provisions finally adopted suggest that old age insurance was never imagined in terms of fair treatment to women—a product of the joint efforts of a marriage partnership. Consistent with the notion of sustaining male provision for the family, and over the objections of some members of the Social Security Board, the council voted to eliminate any annuity to a widow who remarried lest it construct a system that, in the words of one member, constituted widows "a prize for the fellow that has looked for it."[10] It recommended a plan that gave a wife no rights at all in the husband's insurance in consequence of his contributions to it, though demanding that she forfeit everything if she remarried clearly violated the equity principle that promised a return for what had been put in. . . .

. . . Once a woman was no longer dependent on the earnings of a particular male (dead or alive), the council contended, his support for her should cease, "rendering the woman ineligible whether she is the widow of an annuitant or the widow of a worker who dies before 65."[11] As long as she remained dependent on him, the level of the surviving widow's benefits . . . would be tied to the earnings of the deceased male, feeding the illusion that families deprived of a father or husband would nevertheless conceive him in the abstract as a continuing provider. . . .

We have no need to guess at the gendered images that sustained these seemingly arbitrary decisions. They pop up everywhere. For example, halfway through its eighteen months of deliberations, the Advisory Council confronted the question of what allowance to provide to aged widows. Should it be half of what their provider-husbands would have received? Two thirds? Three quarters? After several hours of debate over what proportion of a husband's benefit might appropriately descend to his widow, one member thought to ask a question that had escaped scrutiny: "Why should you pay the widow less than the individual himself gets if unmarried?" "She can look after herself better than he can," shot back the group's actuary.[12] But the question would not die. Two months later the Advisory Council returned to the issue. This time the chairman, prodded by one of its three female members, took up the defense. "A single woman" he suggested, can "adjust herself to a lower budget on account of the fact that she is used to doing her own housework whereas the single man has to go out to a restaurant."[13] By now, though, others had joined the fray. When the argument resumed at the next meeting, Douglas Brown tried to end it by painting a portrait everyone could accept. Lower rates for women made sense, he argued, his patience clearly worn thin,

> on the principle that it is more costly for the single man to live than for the single woman if she is able to avail herself of the home of the child. A woman is able to fit herself into the economy of the home of the child much better than the single man, that is, the grandmother helps in the raising of the children and helps in home affairs, whereas the aged grandfather is the man who sits out on the front porch and can't help much in the home.[14]

Such homely images shaped decisions that influenced the lives of almost everyone. They appeared at sporadic moments of unguarded conversation. Imagining women as irresponsible, the council voted to remove the original act's lump-sum death benefit to widows. "Such settlements," its minutes recorded, "are likely to be used for many other purposes long before her old age." Women could also be greedy and unprincipled. To avoid what it referred to as "deathbed marriages," the council adopted a clause requiring a pair to have been married and living together for at least a year before the husband died or reached sixty for his widow to be eligible for benefits on his account.[15] No benefits accrued to the woman who married a man over the age of sixty, unless she had lived with him for at least a year before he died.

The imagery became more complicated around the question of whether to increase benefits by providing more to every contributor or by enhancing the benefits of married men. Here the council clearly had in mind the normative 1930s household in which wives earned little or nothing, and it wanted to protect the economic well-being of the husbands who supported them. No one noted that its image failed to account for the more than 15 percent of white and at least 33 percent of African American households in which women earned regular wages. Rather, members noted that even the original bill had been criticized by social insurance advocates like Abraham Epstein for its failure to include additional benefits for men with aged wives.... Advisory Council staff members, including Wilbur Cohen and Isadore Falk, ... claimed that old age insurance would be perceived as more fair if it treated married men with greater generosity....

[After considering a number of suggestions for an aged wives' allowance, the Advisory Council] explicitly proposed "that the enhancement of early old-age benefits under the system be attained, not by increasing the amount of benefit now payable to an individual, but by the method of paying to a married annuitant on behalf of an aged wife a supplementary allowance equivalent to fifty percent of the husband's own benefit."[16] ...

None of the three women on the Advisory Council (Theresa McMahon, Elizabeth Wisner, and Josephine Roche, who seems to have been there only rarely) raised a question about gender equity or the rights of women. Neither did political activist and reformer, Mary Dewson, who attended council meetings as a member of the Social Security Board....

We can speculate that under the historical circumstances the proposals of the Advisory Council offered far more security to the families of covered workers than most women could expect to provide through earnings. ... [I]nfluential women social reformers had long since accepted that providing security for the family was the most likely way to safeguard women.... With the exception of McMahon, the women engaged in the Advisory Council's deliberations had been involved in some part of the effort to develop state-run welfare systems, and all were more or less hostile to the efforts of more radical feminists to fight for women's individual rights.... In addition, at least some members of the women's reform network (including perhaps Dewson herself) had become convinced of the need to abandon an earlier strategy of seeking benefits for women only and to focus instead on an integrated system of security. Family benefits would encourage this direction.

If the suggestion to provide dependents' allowances for aging wives appealed to some because it recognized the family responsibilities of men, it appealed to others because it retained equity among covered men by maintaining a relationship between contributions and benefits. This strategy was essential to garnering the votes of southern racists....

[As one council member argued,] "It is impractical to have a level benefit in this country because of the differences between the colored workers of the south and the skilled workers of the north. A single flat figure for everybody would not work."[17] ... [It was important to the council that it not transgress the] relative expectations of income based on occupation or race....

In adopting the program, Congress accepted, with little debate, the relatively rigid definition of the family it demanded. For covered workers, the 1939 amendments provided benefits, without means tests, to fatherless children, widowed mothers of small children, and aged wives and widows. It did not extend benefits to the surviving children of covered women or to aged husbands, aged widowers, or widowed fathers of small children. Thus fatherless children might learn the sweet lesson of continuing parental support beyond the grave, and aging wives would continue to be dependent, though on phantom earnings. But motherless children and aged husbands without resources received quite another lesson in citizenship rights.[18] ...

Three million domestic workers (including two and a quarter million in private households) counted themselves among the women who learned bitter lessons. Like three and a half million agricultural workers, mostly male, they found themselves among the still "uncovered" workers when the 1939 amendments emerged from Congress.[19] In fact, as a group, they had received a slap in the face. Following the Advisory Council's recommendations, Congress incorporated more than a million seamen and bank employees into the old age insurance program. At the same time, it excluded an equal number of mostly female and largely African American workers by eliminating even the few who had crept under the wire. Three hundred thousand domestic workers in clubs, fraternities, and large households and about seven hundred thousand food-processing workers lost their coverage. . . .

When Congress agreed to save the old age insurance system by changing its financing and using the funds generated annually to provide family protection, legislators altered expectations of the Social Security program and provoked a set of new, vaguely anticipated pressures toward universal coverage. Abandoning the idea that each generation of recipients would build a reserve fund that would support its own retirement in favor of a pay-as-you-go system required each generation of working people to subsidize the retirements of its predecessors. The shift turned a program that had originally been perceived primarily as a labor regulation device meant to preserve the dignity of workers who made way for the next generation into something more clearly approximating a promise of economic security freed of its rigid requirement for an equitable return on individual contributions. Adequate insurance for families displaced individual equity as the primary measure of fairness.

The inexorable logic of a system tilted toward adequacy fueled the hopes of policy makers and the excluded that old age insurance could more quickly include everyone and effectively replace the costly and demeaning charity offered by old age assistance. Advisory Council member Paul Douglas warned his colleagues that the changes made there raised the question of why the council could not recommend an "all-inclusive universal system": "If everybody is in from the standpoint of benefits, then everybody is in from the standpoint of contributions, and if there is to be a government subsidy . . . for only the industrial part of the population, it is going to be difficult to have the entire population pay taxes for benefits designed for only half of the population."[20] As Douglas noticed, by enhancing the value of social insurance for some groups of relatively privileged wage earners without extending coverage to significant numbers of additional workers, the program, which was now called Old-Age and Survivors Insurance (OASI), created two classes of citizens. For one of these, the "right to work" had become a more valuable commodity, carrying with it significant economic benefits and social rights for which the other half was indirectly paying. A large proportion of this other half consisted of self-supporting women (black and white) and African Americans of both sexes.

Afterward, the implications of these distinctions became clear. For one thing, some survivors benefited more than others. The family benefits offered under contributory social insurance slowly removed most widows and their children from the public assistance rolls.[21] By 1960, OASDI (disability insurance was added in 1941) covered 93 percent of widows with children. Most of these were the dependents of men who had held covered jobs, leaving only a tiny number of children and their widowed mothers to rely on relief, or what quickly became known as welfare. The result was to produce an invidious distinction between those said to have earned benefits as of right and those for whom benefits remained a matter of public charity. Both systems exercised some controls over the behavior of mothers caring for children, restricting the amount of income a mother could earn before benefits were lost and removing benefits on remarriage, but charitable provision subjected women to stringent moral and supervisory controls as well.[22] At the same time, the promise of more immediate and more reasonable provenance for the aged, anchored in their own virtue and thrift, successfully undermined public support for noncontributory old age assistance schemes, which soon suffered from derogatory labels. Because so many of the poorest and least stable workers could not collect Social Security benefits, these changes also made racial exclusion more visible.

For another, women quickly learned the costs of a gender-segregated labor market, and black women learned the bitterest lessons of all.[23] The poorest-paid workers, invariably women and people of color, appeared to have been multiply disadvantaged. As workers, they would see their intermittent contributions captured by an insurance program that excluded them, to be used to subsidize more stable workers. As consumers, they would pay higher prices as employers factored their share of taxes into the prices of goods and services. As citizens, they were not only deprived of the dignity attached to a contributory program, but they were compelled to support a dual system of noncontributory and contributory relief, producing the apparent injustice of some receiving a demeaning "free" benefit while others received a due return on their investment. . . .

The system's planners had anticipated that some part of the contributions of intermittent workers would be captured and returned to beneficiaries. In their imagination, these workers were single women who would soon marry or married women who, though they worked intermittently, would ultimately reap enhanced benefits earned by their husbands. Policy makers frequently articulated these assumptions. With congressional concurrence, the council agreed on the irrelevance of most women's wage work with respect to this new citizenship right. "A married woman whether she works or no," it decided, "will receive an allowance because of her husband's earning." Its intent could not have been plainer. While "a single woman earns her own benefit rights," it concluded that "a married woman who works will not get advantage . . . of her own earnings, as in any case she will receive the 50% allowance for her husband."[24]

The actual situation was even worse. The council fully expected that married women would work occasionally and that their contributions, as well as the early contributions of single women who then married, would be absorbed by the system and help to sustain its financial health without necessarily yielding any direct benefit to the female contributor. There is no question that this was intentional, done, as Douglas Brown told the House Ways and Means Committee that affirmed the council's recommendations, "in order to control the cost of the system."[25] . . .

While some members of the council deplored its failure to provide equitable treatment to wives who earned wages, suggesting, for example, that "women who work all their lives should have a larger return than those who don't," most symbolically shrugged their shoulders along with Paul Douglas, who declared: "Of course, wives work too." Congress apparently concurred that wives who worked would simply have to sacrifice because, as one put it, "most wives in the long run will build up wage credits on their own account."[26] . . .

The 1939 council that designed this tradeoff also aimed to discourage family members from taking advantage of the insurance program. Fearing inflated claims to benefits by women who falsely maintained they had worked for their husbands, Congress excluded "service performed by an individual in the employ of his spouse." . . . The issue of "forfeited" contributions had lasting resonance, for wives were not the only ones who forfeited their contributions. "Scrubwomen on their knees" fell victim, too, as well as all those who earned less than two hundred dollars a year from a single employer.[27] This hit African Americans particularly hard, as a special 1941 Senate report lamented when it deplored the unfairness to "contributors who fail to qualify because of insufficient employment or low wages. . . . Money thus forfeited by the dispossessed of the act will flow into the insurance fund and from there it will be distributed to workers everywhere."[28]

The architects of the 1939 amendments surely never intended to harm poor women, but the particular ways in which their gendered imagination infused the legislation nevertheless produced negative consequences. In 1940, the male-breadwinner family remained the modal family. Only 15 percent of wives with husbands present earned wages. If countless numbers of others hid the incomes they earned by taking in sewing, laundry, and boarders, still, most white women and men gratefully accepted the derivative benefits offered to wives and widows. Not so for African American women. As the depression deepened throughout the 1930s, racial segregation made wage work an absolute necessity for many black women, regardless of their marital status. At the same time, gender segregation confined more and more women of color to domestic service jobs, most often in private households. Of the two and a quarter million private household workers in the United States in 1940, about 90 percent were women.[29] A little less than half were African Americans. In contrast, men made up 94 percent of agricultural workers. Yet viewed from the perspective of the prospective worker, the figures take on a different cast. Nearly a third of all black workers (1.6 million men and women) and two-thirds of black working women (compared to less than 18 percent of white women workers) were in domestic service.[30] Of the five and a half million African Americans in the labor force in 1935, fully two-thirds were excluded from old age insurance because they belonged to noncovered occupations. No constitutional impediments stood in the way of including them, especially after the Supreme Court sustained the Social Security Act on the grounds of the welfare clause. In contrast to agricultural workers, whom farm interests desperately wanted excluded, and unlike some other groups, such as nonprofits, retail clerks, and the self-employed, no large interest group lobbied to keep domestic workers out of the old age insurance provisions of the new law. Race alone united them.[31] . . .

. . . [The Committee on Economic Security] sent its proposal to Congress with domestic and agricultural workers included. They were eliminated again by the House Ways and Means Committee on the probably specious grounds that their contributions could not buy sufficient benefits and that in any event collecting their taxes and administering benefits would be costly.[32] Agitation to include both groups continued even as the Social Security Act made its way through Congress. Mary Anderson wrote hopefully that she expected, regardless of what happened to the unemployment provisions, that "all workers regardless of occupation will be eligible to share in the old age benefits of the Economic Security Bill."[33]

Her hopes, of course, did not materialize. . . . A racialized conception of gender created the double jeopardy of black women. The policy committees publicly cited putative administrative difficulties that stood in the way of enrolling workers employed in single-person workplaces; in private they admitted the difficulties of offending southern sensibilities. In public, legislators repeatedly sought to protect white housewives, whose ability to handle the paperwork they denigrated; at the same time, they labeled household workers as "girls" and fostered disrespect for the occupation. Over more than a decade, they deployed race to exaggerate the differences between household workers and their employers while seeking to attach to each the special attributes of gender. . . .

Providing benefits for domestics would offer tangible benefits to poorly paid workers, enhance the appearance of fairness, and solve some of the program's financial problems as well. Yet, for many years, pleas to extend coverage to domestic workers, including the recommendation of the Social Security Board, fell on deaf ears. What had made it possible to ignore domestics, argued a piece in the AFL's journal, *American Federationist,* in the fall of 1939, is that they were thought of as different. Ninety percent female, 45 percent African American, with greater proportions married, widowed, deserted, or divorced, and still working in their older years, they simply did not fit the profile of the stable industrial worker for whom social legislation was constructed.[34] Nor did they conform to the restricted images of womanhood within which the 1939 Advisory Council constructed its system of benefits. So they had been left out partly because they were different and mostly because "we have gotten into the habit of excluding them." . . .

Still, for most purposes, most members of Congress and officials of the Social Security Administration continued to support programs that radically distinguished between men and women as contributors. From the perspective of contributors, women's taxes continued to buy far less insurance protection than those of men. . . . From that of beneficiaries, men lacked the protections that their wives had. In 1961, Congress changed the law so that a wife's contributions covered aged husbands and widowers as well. Once again Congress insisted that they demonstrate financial dependency.

. . . The debate rendered voiceless a significant minority of women who believed that if they contributed at the same level as men, their contributions ought to buy their spouses and their children the same protection.

In the 1970s, these women found their voices. The rapidly rising numbers of wage-earning women and of women who did not marry, and the emergence of a dynamic and angry women's movement, soon rendered the discrepancies questionable and led some men and women to wonder if they were discriminatory. "The income security programs of this nation were designed for a land of male and female stereotypes," wrote Representative Martha Griffiths in 1973.[35] A series of court decisions confronted the issue, peaking on March 19, 1975, in the landmark decision of *Weinberger* v. *Wiesenfeld*. Eight justices of the U.S. Supreme Court (the ninth abstaining) agreed that Stephen Wiesenfeld, a widower and lone parent of an infant child, was entitled to Social Security benefits. Wiesenfeld claimed the benefits on the basis of contributions made by his wife, Paula, who had been a schoolteacher before she died in childbirth. But the Social Security Administration had turned him down: widows' benefits were available only to women. Now the Supreme Court demurred. "A father no less than a mother," said the Court, "has a constitutionally protected right to the companionship, care, custody, and management of children he has sired and raised."[36] On this basis, the Court struck down forty years of "archaic and overbroad generalizations," accepting the argument put forth in Wiesenfeld's defense that such generalizations unfairly discriminated against women because their contributions to Social Security did not buy as much as the contributions of men. Wisenfeld's lawyer, Ruth Bader Ginsburg, had done her part to draw a new image of gender to the Court's attention.

The Court's majority decision, written by Justice William J. Brennan, explicitly challenged assumptions about men's and women's wage-earning that underlay the Social Security Act and anchored its old age insurance provisions. As late as 1971, an Advisory Council on Social Security had insisted that men rarely became homemakers after the death of a spouse and that, given their attachment to the workforce, widowed fathers did not require benefits to enable them to provide a home for their children. Acknowledging the truth of the generalization that men had been, and were more likely to be, the principal supporters of their families, Brennan nevertheless argued that this assumption did not "suffice to justify the denigration of efforts of women who do work and whose earnings contribute significantly to families' support." Dismissing the government's claim that benefits were unrelated to contributions, the Court held that statutory rights to benefits were directly "related to years worked and amount earned by a covered employee, and not to the need of the beneficiaries directly." Benefits had to be related to some reasonable classification; they could not be based solely on sex. Wiesenfeld's wife had not only been deprived of the security "a similarly situated male" would have received, she had been "deprived of a portion of her own earnings in order to contribute to the fund out of which benefits would be paid to others." As Justice Lewis Powell put it in a concurring opinion, the statute "discriminates against one particular category of family—that in which the female spouse is a wage-earner covered by social security."[37]

The decision in *Wiesenfeld* was followed by others. An aged widower was entitled to benefits on his wife's earnings whether or not he had been dependent on her, just as a widow was entitled to benefits earned by her husband, the Court declared two years later.[38] . . . With the Department of Health, Education, and Welfare and the Social Security Administration fighting every step, the Court methodically overturned a carefully structured set of images about women's roles in the family. Henceforth, the Court concluded, classifications by gender "must serve important governmental objectives."[39] Imaging women as nonworkers no longer met that test.

Notes

1. Paul H. Douglas, *Social Security in the United States: An Analysis and Appraisal of the Federal Social Security Act* (New York: McGraw-Hill, 1936), estimates that 47 percent of those working would not come under the old age insurance features and thus would require old age assistance.

2. The most careful analysis of the data concludes that 86.69 percent of black female workers and 53.6 percent of black male workers were excluded; F. Davis, "The Effects of the Social Security Act upon the Status of the Negro," Ph.D. diss., University of Iowa, 1939, p. 99, n. 211, and 102, tables 21, 23.

3. "Social Security Advisory Council Is Appointed," typescript of press release, May 10, 1937, File 025: Advisory Council 1937, Box 10, Chairman's Files, RG47, NA2.

4. Typescript, I. S. Falk to the Advisory Council, November 5, 1937, "Benefits for Disabled Persons and Survivors, and Supplemental Allowances for Dependents," ibid., passim.

5. See, for example, Abraham Epstein, *Insecurity: A Challenge to America, a Study of Social Insurance in the United States and Abroad* (New York: Random House, 1938[1933]), part 9.

6. Advisory Council on Social Security, *Final Report*, Senate Document no. 4, 76th Cong., 1st sess., December 10, 1938 (Washington, D.C.: GPO, 1939), p. 18; hereafter, Advisory Council, *Final Report*.

7. Advisory Council Minutes, April 29, 1938, morning session, pp. 8–10 and ff.

8. Advisory Council, *Final Report,* p. 17.

9. House, *Hearings on Social Security Act Amendments of 1939,* p. 6.

10. Advisory Council Minutes, April 29, 1938, second half of morning session, p. 9, A. L. Mowbray of the University of California, Berkeley, speaking.

11. Ibid., pp. 3, 40.

12. Ibid., February 19, 1938, afternoon session, p. 18. The actuary was William Williamson.

13. Ibid., April 29, 1938, first half of morning session, p. 41.

14. Ibid., April 29, 1938, second half of morning session, pp. 5–6.

15. Ibid., first half of morning session, pp. 37–38.

16. Typescript headed "Strictly Confidential," October 22, 1938, File 025, Box 138, Executive Director's Files, Advisory Council on Social Security, RG47, NARA.

17. Jill Quadagno, *The Transformation of Old Age Security: Class and Politics in the American Welfare State* (Chicago: University of Chicago Press, 1988), p. 39, and see ch. 6 on the influence of southern politicians on the old age assistance portion of the Social Security Act.

18. These amendments also included altering the fiscal plan to a pay-as-you-go system, paying benefits on the basis of a wage-averaging device rather than on the basis of accumulated benefits, and expanding the categories of agricultural and domestic workers excluded from coverage. See Edward D. Berkowitz, "The First Social Security Crisis," *Prologue* 15, no. 3 (1983):133–49, for a summary of their full contents.

19. These figures come from the testimony of Sumner Slichter, *Hearings on the Social Security Act Amendments of 1939,* p. 1512. Slichter estimated that eleven million self-employed farmers and others, and about a million employees of nonprofit corporations, also remained uncovered.

20. Advisory Council Minutes, February 19, 1938, afternoon session, p. 20.

21. Gwendolyn Mink, *The Wages of Motherhood: Inequality in the Welfare State, 1917–1942* (Ithaca: Cornell University Press, 1995), p. 175.

22. The best discussion of this issue is in ibid., chs. 6–7.

23. Edward J. McCaffery, *Taxing Women* (Chicago: University of Chicago Press, 1997), ch. 4.

24. Brown, Advisory Council Minutes, February 18, 1938, morning session, p. 14.

25. House, *Hearings on the Social Security Act Amendments of 1939,* p. 1218.

26. Testimony of Sen. Sheridan Downey of California, *Congressional Record—Senate,* July 13, 1939, p. 9012.

27. Downey, *Congressional Record—Senate,* July 13, 1939, p. 9012.

28. *Senate Resolution Preliminary Report, 1941,* p. 8.

29. Thus, though African Americans made up about 10 percent of the labor force, they constituted nearly half of the women in domestic service. Cf. Testimony of Margaret Plunkett, chief, Division of Legislation, Women's Bureau, Department of Labor, U.S. Congress, House, *Hearings before the Committee on Ways and Means, House of Representatives on Social Security Legislation, Amendments to the Social Security Act of 1946,* 79th Cong., 2nd sess. (Washington, D.C.: GPO, 1946), p. 542; hereafter, House, *Hearings on Amendments to the Social Security Act of 1946.* Plunkett also says that 6 percent of agricultural workers were women (p. 545).

30. Figures from Albion Hartwell, "The Need of Social and Unemployment Insurance for Negroes," *Journal of Negro Education* 5 (January 1936), pp. 79–87.

31. This argument appears in the testimony of Edgar G. Brown, director, National Negro Council, Washington, D.C., at U.S. Congress, House, *Hearings on Social Security Act Amendments of 1949,* p. 1878.

32. See the account of this incident in Edwin E. Witte, *The Development of the Social Security Act: A Memorandum on the History of the Committee on Economic Security and Drafting and Legislative History of the Social Security Act* (Madison: University of Wisconsin Press, 1962), pp. 152–53.

33. Mary Anderson, "The Plight of Negro Domestic Labor," *Journal of Negro Education* 5 (January 1936), p. 71.

34. Rae Needleman, "Are Domestic Workers Coming of Age," *American Federationist* 46 (October 1939), pp. 1070–75.

35. Martha W. Griffiths, "Sex Discrimination in Income Security Programs," *Notre Dame Lawyer* 49 (February 1974), p. 534.

36. *Weinberger* v. *Wiesenfeld,* 420 U.S. 636 (1975), p. 652.

37. Ibid., pp. 645, 647.

38. *Califano* v. *Goldfarb,* 97 S.Ct. 1021 (1977), p. 1023. Justice William J. Brennan for the Court.

39. *Califano* v. *Goldfarb,* p. 1028.

BLANCHE WIESEN COOK

Storms on Every Front: Eleanor Roosevelt and Human Rights at Home and in Europe

A woman of limitless energy, compassion, and humanitarian zeal, Eleanor Roosevelt was the most active and controversial First Lady in the nation's history. A fascinating figure, her ability to grow in understanding never ended. She began her adult life as a shy, insecure woman who had imbibed the racism and anti-Semitism of the privileged world to which she was born. She ended her life a feminist and a political champion of civil rights, civil liberties, social justice, and world peace—a woman whose activism was played out on a world stage.

The transformation was well under way by the 1920s. Indeed, it was accelerated when Franklin Delano Roosevelt was paralyzed by polio in 1921 and Eleanor began serving as his representative in the political arena. Long a political activist, she became a shrewd analyst of the political scene. When FDR became president, ER found herself in an increasingly complex political context. She could try to persuade the president in private conversation; she could also use public pulpits of her own. She was the only First Lady ever to write a long-running daily syndicated newspaper column, "My Day." She could choose (or refuse) speaking invitations, and use her opportunities to speak about issues that mattered to her. As the Nazi threat grew, ER found that the State Department insisted on her silence; she would have to find other ways of expressing her commitment to human rights.

Between 9 and 15 November [1938], Jewish homes, schools, hospitals, synagogues, businesses, and cemeteries were invaded, plundered, burned. Kristallnacht, the night of broken glass, was a week of contempt, abuse, destruction.

If anybody doubted the intent of Hitler's words, so clearly revealed in his writings, speeches, and previous outrages, those November days in Germany, Austria, and the Sudetenland shattered any illusion. The violence coincided with Armistice Day, 11 November, when the Allies ended World War I. The defeat of that war was for Hitler to be avenged with new blood, and unlimited terror.

The violence began on 28 October, when Germany expelled thousands of Polish Jews who had lived for decades within the historically changing borders of Germany. Nazis rounded up children and old people on the streets, emptied houses and apartment buildings, allowed people to take nothing with them except 10 marks ($4) and the clothes they wore, shoved them into waiting trucks and trains, and dumped them across the border onto the desolate flats of Poland's borderlands. More than ten thousand Jews were deported in this manner.

Among the deportees was the family of Zindel Grynszpan, whose seventeen-year-old son, Heschel, had previously fled the family

Excerpted and revised by the author from ch. 27 of *Eleanor Roosevelt: The Defining Years, 1933–1938,* by Blanche Wiesen Cook (New York: Viking/Penguin, 1999). Published by permission of the author and publisher. Readers will find ch. 16, "A Silence Beyond Repair," a critical framework for this selection.

home in Hanover to Paris. When he received a letter from his father recounting his family's ordeal, Heschel Grynszpan bought a gun and on 7 November walked to the German embassy in Paris to assassinate the ambassador. Ironically, he was detained by a minor official, Ernst vom Rath, who was himself under investigation by the Gestapo for his opposition to the increasing anti-Semitic violence, and shot him. This murder was the immediate excuse used to launch the well-orchestrated burnings, lootings, and roundups known as Kristallnacht.

Then on 12 November, German Jews were fined a billion marks—$400 million—as penalty for the murder. This "money atonement" was astronomical and rendered it virtually impossible for most Jews to retain sufficient savings to emigrate. Yet another decree ordered the victims to pay for the repair and restoration of their former shops, buildings, and homes—from which they were permanently banished.

These fines had another, more sinister purpose. Hitler had announced: "If there is any country that believes it has not enough Jews, I shall gladly turn over to it all our Jews." Now, if they left, they left penniless. Moreover, most countries had closed their doors, and those who would accept Jews would not accept paupers.

It was a major challenge for FDR, whose policy was to do nothing to involve the United States in European affairs, but who wanted to respond somehow to the thousands of refugees who stood for hours before the U.S. embassy seeking asylum, only to be routinely turned away.

Within days, Jews were stripped of their remaining human rights. They were no longer permitted to drive cars, travel on public transportation, walk in parks, go to museums, attend theaters or concerts. Passports and visas were canceled. They were stateless and impoverished. Charged for the violence and fined for the damage, the Jewish community now owed the Reich, collectively, one billion Reichsmarks. For a time, they were not molested in their homes. But there was nothing to do, no work to be had; no place to pray; no recourse from agony. Many committed suicide; most tried to leave.

For all moral and political purposes, Kristallnacht was the terminal event. Civility in the heart of western Europe lay in ruins, surrounded by broken glass, bloodied streets, desecrated temples, burned Torahs, ripped books of prayer to the one shared God. Hitler's intentions were flagrant, and the whole world was invited to witness. Twenty thousand Jews were removed to concentration camps, which the Anglo-American press named: Dachau near Munich, Oranienburg-Sachsenhausen north of Berlin, Buchenwald near Weimar. . . .

ER's formerly private protests against bigotry were increasingly for public attribution. Although she had resigned in silence from the Colony Club for its discrimination against Elinor Morgenthau, she now canceled a speaking engagement at a country club in Lancaster, Pennsylvania, with a statement of distress that it excluded Jews.

While she counseled complete assimilation and urged Jews to "wipe out in their own consciousness any feeling of difference by joining in all that is being done by Americans" for justice and democracy, she also spoke on behalf of support for refugees in Palestine. . . . On 6 December 1938, ER appealed to fifteen hundred people assembled at the Hotel Astor under the auspices of a national committee for refugees chaired by William Green, president of the American Federation of Labor, to help promote the Léon Blum colony in Palestine for the settlement of one thousand Jewish refugee families. . . .

While ER called for demonstrations of "thought and example," little was done, or said, by FDR's administration to indicate official outrage at Hitler's violence. No message of protest warning of boycott or economic reprisal was sent. Yet history abounds in such protests on behalf of victimized peoples. In 1903 and 1906, Theodore Roosevelt protested against Jewish pogroms in Russia, after Jacob Schiff lobbied for an official U.S. condemnation of the massacre of Jews in Odessa. . . .

FDR sent no similar message to Germany.

FDR did respond to the pitiless carnage and massacre in China. In December 1937, Japan destroyed Nanking in a vicious episode of rape, horror, and death. Half the population, an estimated 300,000 people, were tortured and killed. Whether the details were immediately known to FDR, even of Japan's 12 December sinking of the U.S. gunboat *Panay,* remains controversial. But on 11 January 1938, FDR sent a memo to Cordell Hull and Admiral Cary T. Grayson, head of the

American Red Cross. He called for additional relief funds for the "destitute Chinese civilians" and for medical aid. "I think we could raise $1,000,000 without any trouble at all." On 17 January, the U.S. Red Cross launched an appeal for aid to the Chinese people, initiated by FDR's formal request for such a drive.[1]

No similar appeal was made by FDR to the Red Cross on behalf of Europe's Jews.*

Since he was considered by many the best friend American Jews ever had, FDR's reactions to the European events of 1938 are unexplainable.... Except for Father Charles E. Coughlin, who hailed the violence against "Jewish-sponsored Communism," the press was unanimous in its condemnation....

... FDR agreed to allow all German aliens on visitor visas to remain in the United States for six months "and for other like periods so long as necessary." At the time there were between twelve thousand and fifteen thousand political refugees covered by his order, and "not all Jews, by any means," the president assured the press. "All shades of liberal political thought and many religions are represented."[2]

Anti-Semitism in FDR's State Department increased after Hitler's November atrocities. Breckenridge Long now dedicated himself to keeping refugees out of America. Curiously, FDR continually promoted Breckenridge Long, who had life-and-death control over visas and passports. Nevertheless, in 1938, for the first time, the United States filled its refugee quota.

ER and her asylum-seeking circle faced the urgent refugee crisis in a lonely political environment. Thousands of the earliest refugees who left in 1933 were still wandering Europe seeking safety and political asylum. After 31 January 1933, over 30 percent of Germany's 500,000 Jews had become refugees. After the March 1938 Anschluss, Germany's annexation of Austria, when the Nazis began to expel Austria's 190,000 Jews, the situation became critical. The flight of Czech Jews compounded the problem, and Kristallnacht ignited refugee panic.

FDR expanded his search for underpopulated and suitable lands upon which to place the world's unwanted Jews ... but told his press conference that he had no intention of asking Congress to alter existing immigration quotas....

During her own press conference, ER called for temporary emergency measures to do whatever was possible "to deal with the refugee problem, and at home, for renewed devotion to ... the American way of life." Wary of her husband's strategies, she [rarely criticized] him directly.... "For ourselves, "[she said]," I hope we will do, as individuals, all we can to preserve what is a traditional right in this country—freedom for different races and different religions."...

[From 1938 to 1940, a committee of geographers, scholars, and members of the State Department explored the possibilities of sanctuary for Jews outside the United States, without success. ER was staggered by the contempt for human suffering expressed by the failure of other nations to welcome refugees.] In the bitter time before the burning time there was hope for rescue country by country. But there was no official objection to Hitler's intention to remove Jews from Germany and all his new territories. ER increasingly bypassed State Department restrictions; she worked, often covertly, with private groups and individuals. She campaigned for a less restrictive refugee policy, pursued visas for individuals, and answered and passed on to government officials every appeal sent to her.

Revolted by world events, ER called for entirely new levels of action. Her speeches became more pointed and vigorous, and she spent more time in the company of radical activists, especially members of the American Youth Congress whose ardent views now coincided most completely with her own.

For ER, AYC leaders represented hope for the best of liberal America. Christian theology students, Jewish children of immigrants, black and white activists from the rural South and urban North imagined a nation united for progressive antifascist action.

*During the 1940s, the International Red Cross deflected complaints about its neglect of Jewish needs, given the magnitude of the mounting tragedy, with the explanation that the Red Cross "could not interfere in the internal affairs of a belligerent nation." Blood plasma for U.S. troops was segregated into "white" and "colored," "Christian" and "Hebrew." It was not desegregated until 1954.

A week after Kristallnacht, ER . . . defended the AYC at the annual luncheon of New York's branch of the American Association of University Women and spoke of the need for courage and fearlessness in perilous times. . . . ER's speech was bold: She rejected the current Red Scare tactics which branded the AYC communist and her a dupe or fool: Such name-calling had destroyed democracy in Europe, and she wanted democracy to survive here.

"People whose opinions I respect" had warned her not to attend the AYC convention.

> [But] I didn't think that those youngsters could turn me into a Communist, so I went just the same. . . .
>
> I listened to speeches which you and I could easily have torn to shreds. The Chinese listened while the Japanese spoke; the boy from India spoke with the British delegates. . . . Nobody hissed or left the room. I have been in lots of gatherings of adults who did not show that kind of respect. . . .

She spoke with many delegates, asked what they thought of the Soviet Union; she left convinced that there was interest in communism, but not domination by communists: "We who have training, and have minds that we know how to use must not be swept away" by fear and propaganda. The urgent problems before the United States and the world required scrutiny, debate, honest disagreement, democratic participation, not a wild and fearful flight from controversy. . . .

On 22 November 1938, ER embarked on a dangerous mission when she keynoted the radical biracial Southern Conference on Human Welfare, in Birmingham, Alabama. For the first time since the Civil War, Southern liberals were determined to face the race issue embedded within the region's struggling economy. Since 1890 there had been talk of a "New South," but always before, racial cruelties at the heart of peonage and poverty had been ignored in the interest of white supremacy. . . .

In the aftermath of Kristallnacht, there was a new level of commitment and urgency at the Birmingham meeting. Regional race and anti-union violence was behind the call for the SCHW, first conceived as a civil liberties conference by [pioneering progressive activists] Joseph Gelders and Lucy Randolph Mason. According to Virginia Durr, they wanted to deal with the "terrible things happening" to CIO organizers in Mississippi. Many people were beaten [and run out of town,] crosses were burned. . . .

While the South "led the world" in cotton, tobacco, paper, and other products, it was a disaster area. The average per capita income was half the nation's; the poll tax limited voting rights to 12 percent of the population in eight Southern states, including Virginia; the region's children were being undereducated. The South was hampered by backward and colonial customs; and its entrenched leaders wanted no changes.

The Southern Conference on Human Welfare determined to change the South and challenge segregation. Fifteen hundred delegates, black and white, sat anywhere they wanted Sunday night, 21 November 1938, in the city auditorium of downtown Birmingham. According to Virginia Durr: "Oh, it was a love feast. . . . Southern meetings always include a lot of preaching and praying and hymn singing. . . . The whole meeting was just full of love and hope. It was thrilling. . . . The whole South was coming together to make a new day."[3]

Somebody reported the integrated seating at the opening-night gala, and the next morning the auditorium was surrounded. . . . Every police van in the city and county was there. Policemen were everywhere, inside and out. And there was Eugene "Bull" Connor "saying anybody who broke the segregation law of Alabama would be arrested." Tensions escalated; violence was in the air. The delegates complied and arranged themselves into separate sections.

ER, Mary McLeod Bethune, and Aubrey Williams arrived late that day, out of breath. ER "was ushered in with great applause," looked at the segregated audience—and took her seat on the black side. One of Bull Connor's police officers tapped ER on the shoulder and told her to move. . . .

As if to announce fascism would not triumph here, ER refused to "give in" and placed her chair between the white and black sections. Pauli Murray recalled that ER's demonstration of defiance and courage meant everything to the young people of the South, who now knew they were not alone. Although the national press did not report ER's brave action, the weekly *Afro-American* editorialized: "If the people of the South do not grasp this gesture, we must. Sometimes actions speak louder than words."[4]

ER was given a little folding chair and sat in the middle of whatever meeting hall or church she attended for the rest of the four-day meeting. She said she refused to be segregated, and carried the folding chair with her wherever she went. According to Durr: "Policemen followed us everywhere to make sure the segregation laws were observed, but they didn't arrest Mrs. Roosevelt."

ER's address to the SCHW stirred the packed auditorium:

> We are the leading democracy of the world and as such must prove to the world that democracy is possible and capable of living up to the principles upon which it was founded. The eyes of the world are upon us, and often we find they are not too friendly eyes.

ER emphasized "universal education" in which "every one of our citizens, regardless of nationality, or race," might be allowed to flourish.[5] . . .

The 1938 SCHW adopted thirty-six resolutions, all of which involved the plight of African Americans, and eight of which directly concerned racial issues, including freedom for the four Scottsboro boys who remained in prison; availability of medical services by African American physicians in all public health facilities; more funding for public housing and recreation facilities for African Americans; equal funding for graduate education in state-supported colleges; and—inspired by ER's demonstration—a resolution to support fully integrated SCHW meetings.

Perceived as "one of the gravest sins that a white southerner could commit," that direct assault against tradition created a furor. The antisegregation resolution divided the delegates, some of whom withdrew, and was branded communist, subversive, and un-American. On the other hand, it transformed national assumptions about the unspeakable: White supremacy, and its primary bulwark, segregation, were forevermore on the nation's agenda—put there by an integrated conference, led by Southern New Dealers.[6]

Traditional "race etiquette" was also challenged when Louise Charlton called on Mary McLeod Bethune to speak. (See Bethune pp. 360–362) According to Virginia Durr:

> She said, "Mary, do you wish to come to the platform?" Mrs. Bethune rose. She looked like an African queen. . . . "My name is Mrs. Bethune." So Louise had to say, "Mrs. Bethune, will you come to the platform?" That sounds like a small thing now, but that was a big dividing line. A Negro woman in Birmingham, Alabama, was called Mrs. at a public meeting. . . .

Virginia Durr, wife of Clifford Durr, the assistant general counsel of the Reconstruction Finance Corporation, and sister-in-law of Justice Hugo Black, addressed the meeting to denounce the South's refusal to educate its people and the prevailing ignorance so general throughout the country. The reasons for an uninformed public, she declared, were propaganda and a controlled press dominated by Wall Street. She accused the National Manufacturers Association of being a "huge propaganda machine" intent on the "liquidation of organized labor." . . .

[A week after the SCHW], the Nazi press announced that Germany had embarked upon "the final and unalterably uncompromising solution" to the Jewish question. In the Gestapo's official paper, *Das Schwarze Korps,* on 24 November, the front-page feature announced that it should have been done immediately, brutally, and completely in 1933. But "it had to remain theory" for lack of the "military power we possess today."

> Because it is necessary, because we no longer hear the world's screeching and because, after all, no power on earth can hinder us, we will now bring the Jewish question to its totalitarian solution.[7]

Two weeks after Kristallnacht, accepted without notable "screeching" from any government, Hitler felt sufficiently unrestrained to publish his intentions for all Jews caught in his widening web. First would come pauperization, isolation, ghettoization. They would all be marked for positive identification. Nobody would escape. Then, the starving, bedraggled remnant would become a scrounging, begging scourge. They would be forced to crime, would be an "underworld" of "politico-criminal subhumans," breeders of Bolshevism. At that stage "we should therefore face the hard necessity of exterminating the Jewish underworld. . . . The result will be the actual and definite end of Jewry . . . and its complete extermination."

While the announcement was made two years and eight months before it was actually implemented, the time to protest and resist was at hand. After it was reprinted in the U.S. and European press, many understood the implications of such crude words given the reality of the cruelties under way in Germany, Austria, and Czechoslovakia. Since Kristallnacht, race hatred had triumphed completely and Jews had been removed from all German institutions, doomed to a pariah existence in complete segregation. Jews could no longer dine with Gentiles—not in restaurants, not anywhere; nor could they buy food in the same stores. Nazis established separate stores where Jews were restricted in the purchase of life's staples—milk, bread.

Such laws cast a torchlight on American traditions. ER made the connections: brown shirts, white sheets; the twisted cross, the burning cross. Yet the internal affairs of a nation were deemed sacrosanct, nobody else's business. ER and other citizens no longer agreed with that diplomatic principle.

FDR remained virtually silent about human rights abuses, and did not end trade with Germany, but he began a vigorous rearmament program, emphasizing military planes and naval construction. Immediately after Kristallnacht, on 14 November, he reported to Josephus Daniels, his Wilson-era boss, that he was working on "national defense—especially mass production of planes." By December, he ordered the navy yards to run full-time, "two shifts or even three" wherever possible. It "is time to get action."

While ER approved of all defense programs, she also called for a worldwide educational crusade to address prejudice.... After the SCHW meetings, ER wrote her first articles specifically about Jews and race hatred. One, initially called "Tolerance," was for the *Virginia Quarterly* and attacked the kind of anticommunist hysteria that had resulted in fascist triumph and appeasement throughout so much of Europe. The other, which addressed the mounting hatred against Jews, was dated 25 November 1938....

Untitled, ER's "Jewish article" called for a campaign of understanding to confront "the present catastrophe for Jew and Gentile alike.... In books... schools, newspapers, plays, assemblies we want incessant truth telling about these old legends that divide and antagonize and waste us."

As she struggled to understand "the kind of racial and religious intolerance which is sweeping the world today," ER rejected her former emphasis on assimilation.... Now ER assessed the historic hatred of Jews, their isolation, and forced ghettoization in the Middle Ages, and the ongoing contempt for Jews.... ER now pointed out that even when Jews attempted to assimilate they were condemned for "being too ostentatiously patriotic and of pushing themselves forward as nationals," as in Austria and Germany.

ER was also sensitive to the difficulties assimilated Jews faced among their coreligionists, who resented those who strayed from tradition. Never quite accepted into the majority culture, they were everywhere marginalized.... ER rejected ghettoization and deplored signs that appeared in many American neighborhoods that read "No Dogs or Jews Allowed."

Written from within the veil of her own stereotypes, ER concluded that the future was not up to the Jews.

> The Jew is almost powerless today. It depends almost entirely on the course of the Gentiles what the future holds.... If they perish, we perish sooner or later....

She recalled that as a child her uncle Theodore Roosevelt once said "that when you are afraid to do a thing, that was the time to go and do it. Every time we shirk making up our minds or standing up for a cause in which we believe, we weaken our character and our ability to be fearless." ...

ER challenged Americans to think and act politically, to engage in activist citizenship, to become their best selves. A sense of personal unimportance was encouraged by dictators. Democracy depended on "freedom from prejudice, and public awareness." It required education, economic security, and personal devotion, "a real devotion to freedom.... Freedom is something to guard jealously," but it can never be "freedom for me and not for you."

The bolder ER became, the tougher and more adamant her statements, the higher her public approval rating soared. On 16 January 1939, the *New York Times* published a poll taken by George Gallup regarding America's feelings about ER during 1938. The results were astounding. Two voters in every three voted in her favor (67 percent approved of her conduct, 33 percent disapproved).... According to the poll she had a greater approval rating than FDR.... Given the nature of the controversies ER engaged in and her challenge to work for the transformation of customs and traditions that subjected so many to poverty and powerlessness, America's response indicated a commitment to the very democracy she spoke about so earnestly. ER touched a nerve center in America, and the country would never be the same.

On 10 February 1938, ER [had] commemorated the seventy-fifth anniversary of the Emancipation Proclamation by asserting that while Abraham Lincoln took the "first step toward the abolition of slavery... we still do tolerate slavery in several ways." Her words, addressed to nine thousand people at a meeting sponsored by the National Negro Congress, were electrifying:

> There are still slaves of many different kinds, and today we are facing another era in which we have to make certain things become facts rather than beliefs.

As Europe fell to fascism, ER and her new network of youth and race radicals heralded the greatest changes in America since the betrayal of Reconstruction.

In her 8 December 1938 column, ER criticized liberals, smug partisans, and patriots for celebrating incomplete victories....

"As I listened [to speeches to promote the Leon Blum colony for refugees in Palestine]... I could not help thinking how much all human beings like to fool themselves.... [They] made us feel that... we were more virtuous and fortunate than any other people in the world. Of course, I concede this, and I feel for me it is true, for I have been free and fortunate all my life. While I listened, however, I could not help thinking of some of the letters which pass through my hands.

"Are you free if you cannot vote, if you cannot be sure that the same justice will be meted out to you as to your neighbor,... if you are barred from certain places and from certain opportunities?...

"Are you free when you can't earn enough, no matter how hard you work, to feed and clothe and house your children properly? Are you free when your employer can turn you out of a company house and deny you work because you belong to a union?"

Her thoughts turned to refugees in this country, "of the little girl who wrote me not long ago: 'Why do other children call me names and laugh at my talk? I just don't live in this country very long yet.'" ER concluded:

"There are lots and lots of things which make me wonder whether we ever look ourselves straight in the face and really mean what we say when we are busy patting ourselves on the back...."

With grit, determination, and a very high heart, ER helped launch America's crusade for freedom in the fascist era. She was fortified every day by her new allies, her abiding partnership with FDR, love for the people in her life, and love of the world.

Notes

1. FDR to Cordell Hull, Jan. 11, 1938, in *FDR: His Personal Letters, 1928–1945,* Elliott Roosevelt and Joseph P. Lash, eds. (Millwood, N.Y.: Kraus Reprint, 1970), IV, pp. 744–45; see also Iris Chang, *The Rape of Nanking: The Forgotten Holocaust of World War II* (New York: Penguin, 1997).
2. *New York Times,* Nov. 19, 1938.
3. Linda Reed, *Simple Decency and Common Sense: The Southern Conference Movement, 1938–1945* (Bloomington: Indiana University Press, 1991), pp. 15–16 and passim; Virginia Durr, *Outside the Magic Circle: The Autobiography of Virginia Durr* (Tuscaloosa: Univ. of Alabama Press, 1985).
4. Pauli Murray, *Song in a Weary Throat: An American Pilgrimage* (New York: Harper & Row, 1987), p. 113.
5. For ER's Nov. 22, 1938 speech at the SCHW, see Allida Black, ed., *Courage in a Dangerous World: The Political Writings of Eleanor Roosevelt* (New York: Columbia University Press, 1999).
6. Reed, pp. 46–48.
7. *New York Times,* Nov. 24, 1938; Arthur D. Morse, *While Six Million Died: A Chronicle of American Apathy* (New York: Random House, 1968); Michael Berenbaum, *The World Must Know* (Boston: Little Brown, 1993), p. 35.

VALERIE MATSUMOTO

Japanese American Women during World War II

On no group of U.S. citizens did the war have greater impact than upon Japanese Americans. Fearful of a Japanese fifth column on American shores, military and civilian leaders urged Franklin Roosevelt to issue an executive order removing Americans of Japanese descent on the West Coast to relocation camps inland. Despite the fact that a vast majority of the nearly 120,000 Japanese Americans in the United States were citizens with the same rights and obligations as any other citizen, the president succumbed to pressure and issued Executive Order 9066 in February 1942, which ultimately resulted in the establishment of ten concentration camps, most of which were in remote areas of the West. Forced to leave their homes and businesses at great financial cost, both Japanese-born parents, the Issei, and their American-born children, the Nisei, faced the trauma of removal and the shame of implied disloyalty. Not until 1990 would the nation acknowledge the magnitude of its offense and begin providing financial redress for survivors of the camps.

The following essay explores what life in the camps was like for women and the efforts of younger ones to reconstruct a life after internment.

> The life here cannot be expressed. Sometimes, we are resigned to it, but when we see the barbed wire fences and the sentry tower with floodlights, it gives us a feeling of being prisoners in a "concentration camp." We try to be happy and yet oftentimes a gloominess does creep in. When I see the "I'm an American" editorial and write-ups, the "equality of race etc."—it seems to be mocking us in our faces. I just wonder if all the sacrifices and hard labor on [the] part of our parents has gone up to leave nothing to show for it?
>
> Letter from Shizuko Horiuchi,
> Pomona Assembly Center, May 24, 1942

Overlying the mixed feelings of anxiety, anger, shame, and confusion [of the Japanese Americans who were forced to relocate] was resignation. As a relatively small minority caught in a storm of turbulent events that destroyed their individual and community security, there was little the Japanese Americans could do but shrug and say, "*Shikata ga nai,*" or "It can't be helped," the implication being that the situation must be endured. The phrase lingered on many lips when the Issei, Nisei [second generation], and the young Sansei [third generation] children prepared for the move—which was completed by November 1942—to the ten permanent relocation camps organized by the War Relocation Authority: Topaz, Utah; Poston and Gila River, Arizona; Amache, Colorado; Manzanar and Tule Lake, California; Heart Mountain, Wyoming; Minidoka, Idaho; Denson and Rohwer, Arkansas.[1] Denson and Rohwer were located in the swampy lowlands of Arkansas; the other camps were in desolate desert or semi-desert areas subject to dust storms and extreme temperatures reflected in the nicknames given to the three sections of the Poston Camp: Toaston, Roaston, and Duston.

Pledge of Allegiance, 1942. Dorothea Lange had a keen eye for irony, as in this photograph of Japanese American girls in California a few weeks before they were deported to relocation camps. (Photograph courtesy of the National Archives.)

The conditions of camp life profoundly altered family relations and affected women of all ages and backgrounds. Family unity deteriorated in the crude communal facilities and cramped barracks. The unceasing battle with the elements, the poor food, the shortages of toilet tissue and milk, coupled with wartime profiteering and mismanagement, and the sense of injustice and frustration took their toll on a people uprooted, far from home.

The standard housing in the camps was a spartan barracks, about twenty feet by one hundred feet, divided into four to six rooms furnished with steel army cots. Initially each single room or "apartment" housed an average of eight persons; individuals without kin nearby were often moved in with smaller families. Because the partitions between apartments did not reach the ceiling, even the smallest noises traveled freely from one end of the building to the other. There were usually fourteen barracks in each block, and each block had its own mess hall, laundry, latrine, shower facilities, and recreation room. . . . The even greater lack of privacy in the latrine and shower facilities necessitated adjustments in former notions of modesty. There were no partitions in the shower room, and the latrine consisted of two rows of partitioned toilets "with nothing in front of you, just on the sides."[2] ... A married woman with a family wrote from Heart Mountain:

> Last weekend, we had an awful cold wave and it was about 20° to 30° below zero. In such a weather, it's terrible to try going even to the bath and latrine house.... It really aggravates me to hear some politicians say we Japanese are being coddled, for *it isn't so!!* We're on ration as much as outsiders are. I'd say welcome to anyone to try living behind barbed wire and be cooped in a 20 ft. by 20 ft. room.... We do our sleeping, dressing, ironing, hanging up our clothes in this one room.[3]

After the first numbness of disorientation, the evacuees set about making their situation bearable, creating as much order in their lives as possible. With blankets they partitioned their apartments into tiny rooms and created benches, tables, and shelves as piles of scrap lumber left over from barracks construction vanished; victory gardens and flower patches appeared....

Despite the best efforts of the evacuees to restore order to their disrupted world, camp conditions prevented replication of their prewar lives. Women's work experiences, for example, changed in complex ways during the years of internment. Each camp offered a wide range of jobs, resulting from the organization of the camps as model cities administered through a series of departments headed by European American administrators. The departments handled everything from accounting, agriculture, education, and medical care to mess hall service and the weekly newspaper. The scramble for jobs began early in the assembly centers and camps, and all able-bodied persons were expected to work.

Even before the war many family members had worked, but now children and parents, men and women all received the same low wages. In the relocation camps, doctors, teachers, and other professionals were at the top of the pay scale, earning $19 per month. The majority of workers received $16, and apprentices earned $12. The new equity in pay and the variety of available jobs gave many women unprecedented opportunities for experimentation, as illustrated by one woman's account of her family's work in Poston:

> First I wanted to find art work, but I didn't last too long because it wasn't very interesting ... so I worked in the mess hall, but that wasn't for me, so I went to the accounting department—time-keeping—and I enjoyed that, so I stayed there.... My dad ... went to a shoe shop ... and then he was block gardener.... He got $16.... [My sister] was secretary for the block manager; then she went to the optometry department. She was assistant optometrist; she fixed all the glasses and fitted them.... That was $16.[4]

As early as 1942, the War Relocation Authority began to release evacuees temporarily from the centers and camps to do voluntary seasonal farm work in neighboring areas hard hit by the wartime labor shortage. The work was arduous, as one young woman discovered when she left Topaz to take a job plucking turkeys:

> The smell is terrific until you get used to it.... We all wore gunny sacks around our waist, had a small knife and plucked off the fine feathers.
>
> This is about the hardest work that many of us have done—but without a murmur of complaint we worked 8 hours through the first day without a pause.
>
> We were all so tired that we didn't even feel like eating.... Our fingers and wrists were just aching, and I just dreamt of turkeys and more turkeys.[5]

Work conditions varied from situation to situation, and some exploitative farmers refused to pay the Japanese Americans after they had finished beet topping or fruit picking. One worker noted that the degree of friendliness on the employer's part decreased as the harvest neared completion. Nonetheless, many workers, like the turkey plucker, concluded that "even if the work is hard, it is worth the freedom we are allowed." ...

Like their noninterned contemporaries, most young Nisei women envisioned a future of marriage and children. They—and their parents—anticipated that they would marry other Japanese Americans, but these young women also expected to choose their own husbands and to marry "for love." This mainstream American ideal of marriage differed greatly from the Issei's view of love as a bond that might evolve over the course of an arranged marriage that was firmly rooted in less romantic notions of compatibility and responsibility. The discrepancy between Issei and Nisei conceptions of love and marriage had sturdy prewar roots; internment fostered further divergence from the old customs of arranged marriage. In the artificial hothouse of camp, Nisei romances often bloomed quickly. As Nisei men left to prove their loyalty to the United States in the 442nd Combat Team and the 100th Battalion, young Japanese Americans strove to grasp what happiness and security they could, given the uncertainties of the future. Lily Shoji, in her "Fem-a-lites" newspaper column, commented upon the "changing world" and advised Nisei women: "This is the day of sudden dates, of blind dates on the up-and-up, so let the flash of a uniform be a signal to you to be ready for any emergency.... Romance is blossoming with the emotion and urgency of war."[6]

In keeping with this atmosphere, camp newspaper columns like Shoji's in *The Mercedian, The Daily Tulean Dispatch's* "Strictly Feminine," and the *Poston Chronicle's* "Fashionotes" gave their Nisei readers countless suggestions on how to impress boys, care for their complexions, and choose the latest fashions. These evacuee-authored columns thus mirrored the mainstream girls' periodicals of the time. Such fashion news may seem incongruous in the context of an internment camp whose inmates had little choice in clothing beyond what they could find in the Montgomery Ward or Sears and Roebuck mail-order catalogues. These columns, however, reflect women's efforts to remain in touch with the world outside the barbed wire fence; they reflect as well women's attempt to maintain morale in a drab, depressing environment. "There's something about color in clothes," speculated Tule Lake columnist "Yuri"; "Singing colors have a heart-building effect.... Color is a stimulant we need—both for its effect on ourselves and on others."[7] ...

RESETTLEMENT: COLLEGE AND WORK

Relocation began slowly in 1942. Among the first to venture out of the camps were college students, assisted by the National Japanese American Student Relocation Council, a nongovernmental agency that provided invaluable placement aid to 4,084 Nisei in the years 1942–46.[8] Founded in 1942 by concerned educators, this organization persuaded institutions outside the restricted Western Defense zone to accept Nisei students and facilitated their admissions and leave clearances. A study of the first 400 students to leave camp showed that a third of them were women.[9] Because of the cumbersome screening process, few other evacuees departed on indefinite leave before 1943. In that year, the War Relocation Authority tried to expedite the clearance procedure by broadening an army registration program aimed at Nisei males to include all adults. With this policy change, the migration from the camps steadily increased.[10]

Many Nisei, among them a large number of women, were anxious to leave the limbo of camp and return "to normal life again."[11] ... An aspiring teacher wrote: "Mother and father do not want me to go out. However, I want to go so very much that sometimes I feel that I'd go even if they disowned me. What shall I do? I realize the hard living conditions outside but I think I can take it."[12] Women's developing sense of independence in the camp environment and their growing awareness of their abilities as workers contributed to their self-confidence and hence their desire to leave. Significantly, Issei parents, despite initial reluctance, were gradually beginning to sanction their daughters' departures for education and employment in the Midwest and East. One Nisei noted: "[Father] became more broad-minded in the relocation center.... At first he didn't want me to relocate, but he gave in. . . . He didn't say I could go . . . but he helped me pack, so I thought, 'Well, he didn't say no.'"[13]

The decision to relocate was a difficult one.... Many internees worried about their acceptance in the outside world. The Nisei considered themselves American citizens, and they had an allegiance to the land of their birth.... But evacuation had taught the Japanese Americans that in the eyes of many of their fellow Americans, theirs was the face of the enemy. Many Nisei were torn by mixed feelings of shame, frustration, and bitterness at the denial of their civil rights.... "A feeling of uncertainty hung over the camp; we were worried about the future. Plans were made and remade, as we tried to decide what to do. Some were ready to risk anything to get away. Others feared to leave the protection of the camp."[14]

Thus, those first college students were the scouts whose letters back to camp marked pathways for others to follow. May Yoshino sent a favorable report to her family in Topaz from the nearby University of Utah, indicating that there were "plenty of schoolgirl jobs for those who want to study at the University."[15] Correspondence from other Nisei students shows that although they succeeded at making the dual transition from high school to college and from camp to the outside world, they were not without anxieties as to whether they could handle the study load and the reactions of the European Americans around them. One student at Drake University in Iowa wrote to her interned sister about a professor's reaction to her autobiographical essay, "Evacuation": "Today Mr.—, the English teacher that scares me, told me that the theme that I wrote the other day was very interesting. . . . You could just imagine how wonderful and happy I was to know that he liked it a little bit. . . . I've been awfully busy trying to catch up on work and the work is so different from high school. I think that little by little I'm beginning to adjust myself to college life."[16] . . . Lillian . . . Ota, a Wellesley student, reassured [her interned friends contemplating college:] "During the first few days you'll be invited by the college to teas and receptions. Before long you'll lose the awkwardness you might feel at such doings after the months of abnormal life at evacuation centers."[17] Although Ota had not noticed "that my being a 'Jap' has made much difference on the campus itself," she offered cautionary and pragmatic advice to the Nisei, suggesting the burden of responsibility these relocated students felt, as well as the problem of communicating their experiences and emotions to European Americans.

> It is scarcely necessary to point out that those who have probably never seen a nisei before will get their impression of the nisei as a whole from the relocated students. It won't do you or your family and friends much good to dwell on what you consider injustices when you are questioned about evacuation. Rather, stress the contributions of [our] people to the nation's war effort.[18] . . .

Armed with [such] advice and drawn by encouraging reports, increasing numbers of women students left camp.[19] . . . The trickle of migration from the camps grew into a steady stream by 1943, as the War Relocation Authority developed its resettlement program to aid evacuees in finding housing and employment in the East and Midwest. . . . [But] leaving camp meant [more changes.] Even someone as confident as Marii Kyogoku . . . found that reentry into the European American-dominated world beyond the barbed wire fence was not a simple matter of stepping back into old shoes. Leaving the camps—like entering them—meant major changes in psychological perspective and self-image.

> I had thought that because before evacuation I had adjusted myself rather well in a Caucasian society, I would go right back into my former frame of mind. I have found, however, that though the center became unreal and was as if it had never existed as soon as I got on the train at Delta, I was never so self-conscious in all my life.

Kyogoku was amazed to see so many men and women in uniform and, despite her "proper" dining preparation, felt strange sitting at a table set with clean linen and a full set of silverware.

> I felt a diffidence at facing all these people and things, which was most unusual. Slowly things have come to seem natural, though I am still excited by the sounds of the busy city and thrilled every time I see a street lined with trees, I no longer feel that I am the cynosure of all eyes.[20] . . .

Many relocating Japanese Americans received moral and material assistance from a number of service organizations and religious groups, particularly the Presbyterians, the Methodists, the Society of Friends, and the Young Women's Christian Association. One such Nisei, Dorcas Asano, enthusiastically described to a Quaker sponsor her activities in the big city:

> Since receiving your application for hostel accommodation, I have decided to come to New York and I am really glad for the opportunity to be able to resume the normal civilized life after a year's confinement in camp. New York is really a city of dreams and we are enjoying every minute

> working in offices, rushing back and forth to work in the ever-speeding subway trains, counting our ration points, buying war bonds, going to church, seeing the latest shows, plays, operas, making many new friends and living like our neighbors in the war time. I only wish more of my friends who are behind the fence will take advantage of the many helpful hands offered to them.[21]

The Nisei also derived support and strength from networks—formed before and during internment—of friends and relatives. The homes of those who relocated first became way stations for others as they made the transition into new communities and jobs. In 1944, soon after she obtained a place to stay in New York City, Miné Okubo found that "many of the other evacuees relocating in New York came ringing my doorbell. They were sleeping all over the floor!"[22] Single women often accompanied or joined sisters, brothers, and friends as many interconnecting grapevines carried news of likely jobs, housing, and friendly communities. . . .

For Nisei women, like their non-Japanese sisters, the wartime labor shortage opened the door into industrial, clerical, and managerial occupations. Prior to the war, racism had excluded the Japanese Americans from most white-collar clerical and sales positions, and, according to sociologist Evelyn Nakano Glenn, "the most common form of nonagricultural employment for the immigrant women (Issei) and their American-born daughters (Nisei) was domestic service."[23] The highest percentage of job offers for both men and women continued to be requests for domestic workers. In July 1943, the Kansas City branch of the War Relocation Authority noted that 45 percent of requests for workers were for domestics, and the Milwaukee office cited 61 percent.[24] However, Nisei women also found jobs as secretaries, typists, file clerks, beauticians, and factory workers. By 1950, 47 percent of employed Japanese American women were clerical and sales workers and operatives; only 10 percent were in domestic service.[25] The World War II decade, then, marked a turning point for Japanese American women in the labor force. . . .

[Improved opportunities could not compensate for the] uprooting [of] communities and [the] severe psychological and emotional damage [inflicted upon Japanese Americans by internment.] The vast majority returned to the West Coast at the end of the war in 1945—a move that, like the initial evacuation, was a grueling test of flexibility and fortitude. Even with the assistance of old friends and service organizations, the transition was taxing and painful; the end of the war meant not only long-awaited freedom but more battles to be fought in social, academic, and economic arenas. The Japanese Americans faced hostility, crude living conditions, and a struggle for jobs. Few evacuees received any compensation for their financial losses, estimated conservatively at $400 million, because Congress decided to appropriate only $38 million for the settlement of claims.[26] It is even harder to place a figure on the toll taken in emotional shock, self-blame, broken dreams, and insecurity. One Japanese American woman still sees in her nightmares the watchtower searchlights that troubled her sleep forty years ago.

The war altered Japanese American women's lives in complicated ways. In general, internment and resettlement accelerated earlier trends that differentiated the Nisei from their parents. Although most young women, like their mothers and non-Japanese peers, anticipated a future centered on a husband and children, they had already felt the influence of mainstream middle-class values of love and marriage and quickly moved away from the pattern of arranged marriage in the camps. There, increased peer group activities and the relaxation of parental authority gave them more independence. The Nisei women's expectations of marriage became more akin to the companionate ideals of their peers than to those of the Issei.

As before the war, many Nisei women worked . . . , but the new parity in wages they received altered family dynamics. And though they expected to contribute to the family economy, a large number did so in settings far from the family, availing themselves of opportunities provided by the student and worker relocation programs. In meeting the challenges facing them, Nisei women drew not only upon the disciplined strength inculcated by their Issei parents but also upon firmly rooted support networks and the greater measure of self-reliance and independence that they developed during the crucible of the war years.

Notes

1. Many of the Japanese community leaders arrested by the FBI before the evacuation were interned in special all-male camps in North Dakota, Louisiana, and New Mexico. Some Japanese Americans living outside the perimeter of the Western defense zone in Arizona, Utah, etc., were not interned.

2. Chieko Kimura, personal interview, Apr. 9, 1978, Glendale, Arizona.

3. Shizuko Horiuchi to Henriette Von Blon, Jan. 24, 1943, Henriette Von Blon Collection, Hoover Institution Archives ([hereafter] HIA).

4. Ayako Kanemura, personal interview, Mar. 10, 1978, Glendale, Arizona.

5. Anonymous, *Topaz Times*, Oct. 24, 1942, p. 3.

6. Lily Shoji, "Fem-a-lites," *The Mercedian*, Aug. 7, 1942, p. 4.

7. "Yuri," "Strictly Feminine," *The Daily Tulean Dispatch*, Sept. 29, 1942, p. 2.

8. From 1942 to the end of 1945 the Council allocated about $240,000 in scholarships, most of which were provided through the donations of the church and the World Student Service Fund. The average grant for student for was $156.73, which in that area was a major contribution towards the cost of higher education. Source: National Japanese American Student Relocation Council, Minutes of the Executive Committee Meeting, Philadelphia, Pennsylvania, Dec. 19, 1945.

9. Robert O'Brien, *The College Nisei* (Palo Alto: Pacific Books, 1949), pp. 73–74.

10. The disastrous consequences of the poorly conceived clearance procedure had been examined by Robert Wilson and Bill Hosokawa, *East to America: A History of the Japanese in the United States* (New York: Morrow, 1980), pp. 226–27, and Audrie Girdner and Anne Loftis, *The Great Betrayal: The Evacuation of the Japanese-Americans during World War II* (New York: Macmillan, 1969), pp. 342–43.

11. May Nakamoto to Mrs. Jack Shoup, Nov. 20, 1943, Mrs. Jack Shoup Collection, HIA.

12. Toshiko Imada to Margaret Cosgrave Sowers, Jan. 16, 1943, Margaret Cosgrave Sowers Collection, HIA.

13. Ayako Kanemura, personal interview, Mar. 24, 1978, Glendale, Arizona.

14. Miné Okubo, *Citizen* 13660 (New York: Columbia University Press, 1946), p. 66.

15. *Topaz Times*, Oct. 24, 2942, p. 3.

16. Masako Ono to Atsuko Ono, Sept. 28, 1942, Margaret Cosgrave Sowers Collection, HIA. Prior to the war, few Nisei had college experience: the 1940 census lists 674 second-generation women and 1,507 men who had attended or who were attending college.

17. Lillian Ota, "Campus Report," Trek (Feb. 1943), p. 33.

18. Ota, pp. 33–34.

19. O'Brien, p. 84.

20. Marii Kyogoku, *Resettlement Bulletin* (July 1943), p. 5.

21. Dorcas Asano to Josephine Duveneck, Jan. 22, 1944, Conard-Duveneck Collection, HIA.

22. Miné Okubo, *Miné Okubo: An American Experience*, exhibition catalogue (Oakland: Oakland Museum, 1972), p. 84.

23. Evelyn Nakano Glenn, "The Dialectics of Wage Work: Japanese American Women and Domestic Servants, 1905–1940," *Feminist Studies* 6, no. 3 (Fall 1980):412.

24. Advisory Committee of Evacuees, *Resettlement Bulletin* (July 1943), p. 3.

25. 1950 United States Census, Special Report.

26. Susan M. Hartmann, *The Home Front and Beyond, American Women in the 1940s* (Boston: Twayne Publishers, 1982), p. 126. There is some debate regarding the origins of the assessment of evacuee losses at $400 million. However, a recent study by the Commission on Wartime Relocation and Internment of Civilians has estimated that the Japanese Americans lost between $149 million and $370 million in 1945 dollars, and between $810 million and $2 billion in 1983 dollars. See the *San Francisco Chronicle*, June 16, 1983, p. 12.

BETH BAILEY AND DAVID FARBER

Prostitutes on Strike: The Women of Hotel Street during World War II

On a Sunday afternoon, the nation listened as radio announcers reported the Japanese attack on Pearl Harbor. The date was December 7, 1941. As the military made Hawaii its midpoint stopover in the Pacific, World War II would transform these remote, ethnically diverse islands. For some men returning from combat as well as for those going into it, the place to go in Honolulu was Hotel Street.

Red-light districts of institutionalized military prostitution, legalized and sustained by the active regulation of local authorities and by explicit or informal agreement with the U.S. military, continued to characterize the U.S. military presence in Asia in the second half of the twentieth century—in Korea, where "camptowns" were established outside American bases and remained for decades after the end of the Korean War; in Japan, where the gang rape of a schoolgirl in 1995 poisoned relations between Okinawa and Japan, and between Japan and the United States; and in Vietnam, where the dynamics were captured to some extent in the dramatization of the life of a fictional bar girl in the popular musical *Miss Saigon*.*

Beth Bailey and David Farber focus on the women of Hotel Street, the sex workers who populated its brothels. Note the conditions of work, the complicity and concerns of military authorities, and the conflict between the military and the local police, who acted as agents of the local elite. Note, too, the way the women maneuvered to improve their lives. How did the Hotel Street prostitutes inadvertently undermine Hawaii's racial hierarchy? In what other respects did their strategy foreshadow that of postwar civil rights activists?

Hotel Street was the center of Honolulu's eponymous vice district, through which some 30,000 or more soldiers, sailors, and war workers passed on any given day during most of World War II. . . . On Hotel Street, some of the most complex issues in America's history came together. Systems of race and of gender (complicated by both sex and war) structured individual experience and public policy. At the same time, the story of Hawaii's vice district revolves around the changing role of the State, as it asserted its interests in counterpoint to local elites. For most of the war Hawaii was under martial law, ruled by a military governor. Even if not fully by intention, agents of the federal government—ironically in the form of the military and martial law—emerged as limited guarantors of equality and created openings for social struggle. . . . A critical part of this struggle for power centered on prostitution and its control. . . .

Hotel Street was more than just brothels, but it was the brothels, for most of the men, that gave the district its identity and its dark

*See Saundra Pollock Sturdevant et al., eds., *Let the Good Times Roll: Prostitution and the U.S. Military in Asia* (New York: New Press, 1992); Katharine H. S. Moon, *Sex Among Allies: Military Prostitution in U.S.-Korea Relations* (New York: Columbia University Press, 1997).

magic. During the war years fifteen brothels operated in this section of Chinatown, their presence signaled by neatly lettered, somewhat circumspect signs (" The Bronx Rooms," "The Senator Hotel," "Rex Rooms") and by the lines of men that wound down the streets and alleyways. The brothels were not new; they had developed along with Honolulu's status as a port city, and had, in recent years, served both the growing military population and the plantation workers who came to town on paydays.[1]

Prostitution was illegal in Hawaii. Nonetheless, it existed as a highly and openly regulated system, involving the police department, government officials, and the military. Red-light districts in Honolulu had survived a Progressive Era campaign to close them down, and flourished in the face of the World War II–era May Act until late 1944, when an emerging new political elite succeeded in closing the houses.[2]

Some of the reasons for the brothels' survival are found in Hawaii's multiracial and multicultural society. To many of the people who made up the islands' varied population, prostitution was not a "social evil." And many of the islands' white elite, the "respectable" people who would have provided the necessary pressure to have the brothels closed down, approved of a regulated system of prostitution. The brothels, many believed, kept the predominately lower-class white soldiers and sailors and especially the overwhelmingly male and dark-skinned population of plantation workers [who lived in communities with few women] away from the islands' respectable women, who were, by their definition, white.[3] The head of the Honolulu Police Commission (which was comprised solely of leading white businessmen) said it directly: too many men in and around Honolulu were "just like animals."[4] An editorial in *Hawaii*, a magazine published and supported by the *haole* elite, explained further: "If the sexual desires of men in this predominately masculine community are *going to be satisfied*, certainly not one of us but would rather see them satisfied in regulated brothels than by our young girls and women—whether by rape, seduction or the encouraging of natural tendencies. . . ."[5] The brothels, they thought, helped keep the peace.

The military was pleased with the system, for regulated prostitution kept venereal disease rates relatively low in Hawaii. During World War II, this consideration became especially important. Like any other illness, venereal disease hurt the war effort by cutting into military manpower. At the end of World War I more men left military service with a contagious venereal disease than had been wounded in battle. While the military officials in Hawaii *never* said publicly and directly that they supported regulated vice districts, the military participated fully in the regulation process, putting houses off limits to the men if they broke rules that would compromise venereal disease control, and setting up prophylaxis stations in Honolulu. Each brothel had a sign in its waiting room reminding the men where the "pro" stations were and why it was important for them to make use of the service. The prophylaxis stations were free and open to all—civilian and military—and the Hotel Street stations could handle 1,500 men an hour.[6]

The police department, while to some extent acting on behalf of the *haole* elite, also benefited from the system. Like most police departments, the Honolulu police understood that shutting down the vice district would not end prostitution. Police officials believed that unregulated, dispersed prostitution would more likely be rife with pimps, procurers, and other men who used violence to enforce their criminal order on both the prostitutes and their customers, thus creating much unpleasantness for the police department. In Honolulu, the chief of police personally decided who might open a brothel and who would suffer penalties. The department, according to several sources, received steady payoff money to overlook the varied forms of vice that accompanied the quasi-legal acts of prostitution.[7]

The central charge of the police department was to keep the district orderly and to keep the prostitutes out of sight of respectable Honolulu. The majority of official Honolulu prostitutes were white women recruited through San Francisco. Both police and madams preferred it that way, for women from the mainland had fewer choices but to go along with the system. Each prostitute arriving from the mainland was met at the ship by a member of the vice squad. After she was fingerprinted but before she received her license, she was instructed in the rules that would govern her stay on Hotel Street:

> She may not visit Waikiki Beach or any other beach except Kailua Beach (a beach across the mountains from Honolulu).
>
> She may not patronize any bars or better class cafés.
>
> She may not own property or an automobile.
>
> She may not have a steady "boyfriend" or be seen on the streets with any men.
>
> She may not marry service personnel. She may not attend dances or visit golf courses.
>
> She may not ride in the front seat of a taxicab or with a man in the back seat.
>
> She may not wire money to the mainland without permission of the madam.
>
> She may not telephone the mainland without permission of the madam.
>
> She may not change from one house to another. She may not be out of the brothel after 10:30 at night.[8]

. . . To break these rules was to risk a beating at the hands of the police and possible removal from the islands.

Before the war, few white women served in the houses for more than six months before they returned to the West Coast. The Honolulu service, while lucrative, was not paradise. A few months was often all a woman could take. Some probably earned what money they had hoped for and left the trade. One "sporting girl," writing at the time, said that the police forced prostitutes to leave the islands after about six months "whether the girl's record was up to standard or not . . . [because] she got to know too much in that length of time." Once a prostitute left Hawaii the police prohibited her from returning for a year.[9]

Not all the prostitutes in the Hotel Street district were white. At the Bronx, which was one of the largest houses during the war years, approximately twenty-five prostitutes worked. About half were white women from the mainland and the other half local women. Five of the women were Hawaiian or part Hawaiian. Two were Puerto Rican. The Bronx also had six Japanese prostitutes, which was highly unusual and probably due to Tomi Abe, the Japanese-American woman who ran the Bronx during the war. Most of the madams were white women from the mainland, with names like "Norma Lane," "Peggy Staunton," and "Molly O'Brian." The owners of the buildings in which the brothels operated were almost all Chinese or Chinese American, but almost none were actively involved in running the brothels.[10]

A less fully regulated set of brothels existed across the river—a very narrow river—from the Hotel Street district. Brothels such as the "Local Rooms" were staffed by local women [of color] only, and charged lower prices. Despite their cheaper rates these brothels were much less popular, for their venereal disease rates were astronomical. Men referred to the prostitutes as "white meat" or "dark meat."

During the war, most of the brothels only served white men. Before the war, the brothels had also maintained a color line, but of a more complicated sort. The major Hotel Street brothels used a two-door system, one for whites (almost all of whom were soldiers and sailors) and the other for local men. This segregated system, in a city where segregation was not commonplace, was aimed at the servicemen. Many were Southern, most had been raised with racist beliefs. Some did not like to think of colored men preceding them in the vagina or mouth of a prostitute. Because the district was rough, and the men likely to be drunk and easily moved to violence, segregation was deemed the safest policy.

With the influx of servicemen and war workers following Pearl Harbor, demand for prostitutes soared. With so many white men lining up outside the brothels, the two-door policy was abandoned for the duration and men of color were simply not served. A couple of brothels in the district did not observe a color line and were open to all who could pay. But almost always the men of color had to pay more.

The color line, as far as the white servicemen and war workers saw it, ran only in one direction. While they did not want to share prostitutes with men of color, some white men preferred the "exotic" women.

While the regulated brothels of Hotel Street had been lucrative, thriving businesses through the 1920s and 1930s, the war changed the scale of success. War conditions presented an amazing economic opportunity to the sex workers of Hotel Street. During the war, approximately 250 prostitutes were registered with the Honolulu Police Department—as "entertainers." They paid $1 a year for their licenses, and could make $30,000–$40,000 a year when the average working woman was considered fortunate to make $2,000. The houses took in over $10 million each during the war years, and the twenty-five to thirty madams who ran and/or owned them each took away between $150,000 and $450,000 every year. As a group, the prostitutes and madams of Hotel Street were incredibly successful economically.

But the conditions of sale, "$3 for 3 minutes," suggests how hard they must have worked. Most houses enforced a quota for each woman of 100 men a day, at least twenty days out of every month. The risks of sexually transmitted diseases were extremely high; in 1943,120 professional prostitutes were hospitalized 166 times for a contagious venereal disease. A bad dose put the woman into the hospital—she had to go—for at least two weeks.[11]

Some women could accept the physically brutal and health-threatening conditions. They fixed their attention on the payoff. Others found the life, the numbers of men, and the social contempt degrading. Many sought distance from what they did by shooting morphine or by smoking opium. . . . Opiates gave them back some of the feelings of inviolability their roles as prostitutes worked to take from them.

During the war, even more than before, the women of Hotel Street did their best to exercise as much practical control as they could over their punishing livelihood and over the men who paid them for their services. First of all, the brothels were all owned and operated by women. The prostitutes maximized their economic control by allowing no pimps and there were no behind-the-scenes male owners. Even the doorkeepers at the brothels were women, often powerfully built women of Hawaiian descent. While the brothels existed for men, women controlled access.

The men who wanted sex had to wait in line, sometimes for hours, and in full public view. Because the curfew limited brothel hours, all of this took place only during daylight hours. From souvenir shops and beauty parlors and upstairs windows, the older Chinese women of the district watched and laughed at the lines of white men. Lines were generally quiet, but the shoeshine boys kidded the men who seemed visibly nervous, and quite a few of the men were drunk. But those who fortified themselves with drink faced a further obstacle: the women who kept door at the brothels rejected any man they did not trust to behave properly or to perform quickly. Adeline Naniole, the Hawaiian woman who kept door at the Bronx through part of the war, kept out any man who seemed too drunk. . . . "I don't think you can make business," she would say.[12]

Inside, the system was streamlined for maximum efficiency and control. At the head of the hall that led to the prostitutes' cubicles, a madam stood behind a money booth. Some of the booths were caged; there was no pretense that the houses offered gracious entertainment. The madam collected $3, almost always in singles, and gave the man a token, usually a poker chip. He then waited for an available woman.[13] . . .

Even in the sex act, most men felt little control. That was partly due to the setup: in the interest of time, women rotated from room to room; thus, no time was lost in cleaning up and waiting for the man to dress. When a man's turn came, he went into a cubicle—a regular room divided in half by a flimsy sheet of plywood or wall board that reached only two-thirds of the way to the ceiling. The room was bare except for a single cot, a table with a wash bowl, and a wastebasket. Sometimes, if the maids had been overwhelmed by the pace of business, soiled towels littered the floor. Often the man undressed and waited alone while the prostitute finished up in the cubicle on the other side of the half wall. The man could hear what went on the other side, and he knew that he would be heard in turn.

As time was money, and three minutes was the limit, prostitutes used various strategies to control the sex act itself. After quickly inspecting and washing the man's genitals (as a patron of other brothels described the routine):

> She'd lay on her back and get you on top of her so fast, you wouldn't even know you'd come up there on your own power. She'd grind so that

> you almost felt like you had nothing to do with it. Well, after that, she had you. She could make it go off as quickly as she wanted to. . . .[14]

About a quarter of the men chose fellatio, a fact that worried the senior shore-patrol officer in charge of the district, for he believed that "it is not a far cry from such sex perversions ["buccal coitus," he termed it] to homosexual acts.[15] The women, their minds on the lines outside their doors and always seeking control, seemed to prefer fellatio—it was quicker. For many of the men, sexually inexperienced and fresh from months at sea or long weeks in a battle zone, three minutes was more than enough. As one veteran recalls, "They put it in and they're gone. Sometimes they're gone washing off in the pail. . . .[16]

Despite the impersonal efficiency of the system, it could break down. One regular customer told his favorite, a half-Chinese, half- Mexican prostitute, at the end of a three-minute session, "Judy, you're the bummest fuck I ever had." As he tells it, she was so angry she spent the rest of the night proving him a liar—for free. It meant a lot; he named his daughter after her.[17] . . .

In the houses, men's money bought women's sexual favors; that was undeniable, and to that extent the men commanded and controlled the women. Women's bodies were commodified. Yet the system was structured to emphasize the women's control over the men Standing in line, facing the doorkeeper, taking one's place in the day's quota of 100 anonymous acts: none of those experiences served to confirm a sense of male power or control. . . .

While the prostitutes and madams asserted control within the brothels during the war, it is perhaps more significant that they also attempted to challenge the larger system of controls and regulations within which they lived. After the Pearl Harbor attack the Hotel Street district, like much of the city, was shut down for a few weeks. Soon after the houses reopened, with the troops pouring through Honolulu and the men's pay upped from the prewar scale, the women raised their fee to $5 for three minutes. As they saw it, market conditions had changed.

Word of the price hike immediately reached Frank Steer, at that point an army major who had come to the islands in September 1940 to head the military police. Steer . . . served during the war as provost marshall under the state of martial law imposed on Hawaii after the Japanese attack. Under martial law, he had final authority over matters of vice. . . . Steer had no problem with the existence of brothels, but he did have a problem with the price hike. Raising prices on the fighting men was bad for morale and, as he saw it, unfair. Steer ordered the prices dropped: "The price of meat is still three dollars," he told the madams, and they backed down. They trusted Steer, and they knew he was their ally against the dictates of the police department. But though the prices returned to normal, Hotel Street business would not.

Right after the attack on Pearl Harbor, the women of the houses had rushed to the hospitals and temporary facilities set up for the burned and wounded men. Some of those who came to help were turned away when they admitted their occupations or gave their addresses—the official reason was fear of infection. But more than a few prostitutes nursed the men and did what they could to help. The madams turned over the brothels' living quarters to the overflow of wounded, and for a few days Hotel Street looked like a Red Cross annex.[18]

With their beds filled—and with normal lines of authority disrupted—the women took a chance. They moved out of the district and out of the shadows. They bought and leased houses all around Honolulu—up the rises (mountain slopes), down by the beaches, in fashionable neighborhoods. They told anyone who asked that the district was too risky, that it was a firetrap if the Japanese came back. The explanation was not just a cover; many on the islands believed invasion was imminent. Several prostitutes passed up the promised boom times and joined other women, longtime residents and wives of army and navy officers, who arranged passage on the 20 December special evacuation transport bound for San Francisco.

For several weeks, even as the brothels reopened and long after the wounded had moved out of the prostitutes' living quarters, no one seemed to pay any attention to the women's quiet movement out of the district. The women of Hotel Street, long subject to the dictates of the vice squad, had reason to hope that those days were over.[19]

At first, the women who had moved out of the district attracted little attention; gradually that changed. One businesswoman worked out a lucrative scheme: through an agent, she would buy a house in a fashionable neighborhood and then make clear to her neighbors what her line of work was. The investments paid off handsomely and rapidly, as the neighbors banded together to buy her out—at a premium.[20]

Other women, their minds less on business than on pleasure, simply began to enjoy their earnings. They flouted the rules—rules that had not been officially relaxed—appearing in "respectable" public places, having "wild" parties, doing as they wished. The military police, under martial law holding more authority than the civilian police, let such behavior pass.[21]

The police, especially their chief, William Gabrielson, were outraged at the new order of things. Prostitutes had invaded every neighborhood. Hawaii's carefully calibrated social stratification was being mocked. Mainland whores—white women—were out in public, demonstrating how little difference white skin had to mean in the way of moral superiority or some sort of "natural" right to rule the majority of Hawaii's people of darker hues. Already the hordes of working-class white soldiers, sailors, and war workers had damaged the equilibrium that gave stability to the island's ruling white elite. Now the white prostitutes made a mockery of the whole racist and racialist system. Their too-public presence signaled to all who watched that one set of controls was being challenged. The prostitutes' rejection of hierarchy seemed a foreshadowing of what could happen on a larger scale politically, economically, and culturally after the war. Worse yet, supporting the new laissez-faire approach to the prostitutes was General Emmons, the military governor. . . .

For General Emmons, and for Major Steer, maintaining orderly troops, low rates of venereal diseases, and a reasonably high morale superseded long-range thinking about racial or ethnic boundaries and the elite's postwar control of the islands. . . . The men, judging by the hundreds of thousands of them who went up and down the Hotel Street brothel stairs in the months after the Pearl Harbor attack, wanted prostitutes. The regulated brothels supplied the prostitutes and ensured that they were relatively disease-free (the Hawaii military district had the lowest venereal disease rates in the armed forces). The prostitutes had nursed the wounded and given over their rooms after Pearl Harbor. They had accepted the command not to raise their prices. Many high-ranking military officers believed that "any man who won't fuck, won't fight"; they saw the women of Hotel Street as important to morale and to maintaining a manly spirit among the "boys."[22] All in all, Emmons, Steer, and others who played a role in enforcing martial law believed that keeping the prostitutes safe from needless harassment and hypocritical near-bondage was a commonsense way of keeping the more or less disease-free houses operating smoothly under what were obviously extraordinary conditions.

The matter came to a head quickly. In April of 1942, chief of police Gabrielson ordered his men to evict four prostitutes living together in a house in Waikiki, one of the areas most strictly off-limits to prostitutes in the prewar years. Waikiki before the war was not the bustling tourist center it would become. It was an exclusive resort for the well-to-do, and Jews and people of color knew better than to try to stay in any of its three luxurious hotels. Although a mixture of Hawaii's ethnic/racial groups lived in its residential section, Waikiki was carefully maintained as a respectable area. The war had changed Waikiki: tourism halted for the duration, and servicemen had taken over even one of the exclusive hotels. At least a few of the Hotel Street prostitutes saw an opportunity in wartime Waikiki—for pleasure, if not for profit.

When Gabrielson's man told the women to leave, they complained to Captain Benson of the military police, who seemed well acquainted with their affairs. He told them that the police did not run things anymore, and that his commander did not care where they lived as long as they did not ply their trade outside the Hotel Street district. All this was relayed to Gabrielson, whose angry queries were met with official but vague statements that the military police would take care of such issues in the future.[23]

Gabrielson, angry but thinking strategically, issued Administrative Order No. 83, acknowledging the military control of vice in Honolulu. He then had the memo leaked to the Honolulu *Star-Bulletin*. He wanted to watch the military squirm.

To reiterate what must have slipped many minds in the face of the public and highly regulated system, prostitution was illegal in Honolulu. It was also outlawed through the federal-level May Act, which . . . stated that the federal government would, where local officials were unwilling or unable to do the job themselves, stamp out prostitution aimed at the servicemen. The May Act was not just window-dressing; it was rigorously enforced throughout the country. Though most of the military administration in Hawaii preferred the regulated brothels to what they saw as the alternative, more dangerous system, no one wanted to take the credit for running the brothels and breaking federal law—least of all General Emmons, the military governor of Hawaii. . . .

In a letter to Police Chief Gabrielson . . . Emmons made his position clear:

> I desire to inform you that your understanding regarding the responsibility for vice conditions in the City and County of Honolulu is in error. . . . No directive had been issued to the Police Department in any way limiting its responsibility for any phase of law enforcement. . . . Cancel Administrative Order No. 83.

Chief Gabrielson, with pleasure, resumed control. But the issue had been settled only on the administrative level. The MPs and the vice squad continued to skirmish, with the vice squad trying to round the women up and return them to their living quarters in the quarter, and the MPs undermining those efforts whenever possible. The MPs told the women they were within their rights.

The women of Hotel Street were caught in the middle. They did not want to go back to the prewar order. It was one thing to choose to service 100 men a day, but it was another to abide by rules that denied them their basic freedoms. They framed the issues that way, and they went on strike.[24]

For close to three weeks in June of 1942 a group of prostitutes walked a picket line outside the police department headquarters, which was just a few blocks from the district. The police headquarters also housed Major Steer and his MPs. The women carried placards protesting their treatment and the rules that restricted their freedoms. This strike was not for better pay but for better treatment, for fuller rights of citizenship.

While no documentation of their specific arguments at that time exists, a clear line of reasoning appears in an angry appeal to Honolulu's citizens written by a prostitute in the fall of 1944. In it, she asserted her right to freedom of movement and to adequate police protection, basing her claims on a traditional liberal concept of citizenship. "We pay some of the highest taxes in this town," she wrote. "Where, I ask you, are the beneficial results of our taxes?"

This woman and many of her coworkers believed they were doing vital war work. In addition to the obvious but controversial contributions, the prostitutes had acquitted themselves well after the Pearl Harbor attack and had been willing participants in war-bond drives. One madam had received a special citation from Secretary of the Treasury Henry Morganthau for selling $132,000 in war bonds, most of them, no doubt, to fellow sex workers. The prostitutes believed their good citizenship and patriotism should be recognized as such.[25]

The striking prostitutes gambled that the military police would keep the police department from using force against them and that their military supporters would back them up. What they did took courage, for they had no public allies.

Establishment Hawaii did its best to ignore the strike, and the newspapers carried not a single word about it. General Emmons, however, saw the situation as both embarrassing and serious, and moved quickly to resolve it. . . . Though he had the power under martial law to order the police to do as he wanted, he instead argued his case in what one participant called a "constructive and cooperative" manner. His arguments were simple and straightforward, avoiding the complicated terrains of morality and the political order and focusing instead on the women's working conditions. He said that "the girls are overworked and need periods of rest; that their work is not during daylight hours; that formerly they could go to the Coast for a rest and could be replaced by new girls arriving by steamer; that this is not possible today." Emmons also offered, on behalf of the military, to take over the unpleasant task of ensuring that the women had their regular medical checkups and inspecting the houses for breaches of the sanitary code. The police department, he assured all concerned, would have the right to enforce all other laws and regulations that applied to the women. The police commission and Chief Gabrielson, who really had little choice in the matter, accepted the compromise. The prostitutes ended their strike. Their right to appear in public and to live outside the brothels, while fragile, was won.[26]

Ultimately, the struggle over Hotel Street was not played out in terms of gender, or even with the prostitutes as players. As the prostitutes had seen an opportunity in the context between the military government and the police department, which acted as an agent of the traditional *haole* elite, so too another group saw an opportunity in the divided lines of authority. During the war years a new elite was taking shape, drawn largely from the more liberal range of the *haole* community. By mid-1944, with Hawaii completely out of harm's way and Allied victory seemingly a matter of time, some in Hawaii had begun to look to the future, toward statehood and economic development.

In trying to orchestrate Hawaii's future and maneuver toward statehood, [they] worried about ungovernable prostitutes and regulated brothels. Open prostitution somehow seemed to confirm mainland stereotypes of Hawaii as a primitive, licentious place populated by dark-skinned "natives." . . . One of the [group's] earliest goals was to demolish the unbridled vice district.

The Social Protection Committee of the Honolulu Council of Social Agencies [which] led the way in fighting the regulated brothel system . . . resembled the kind of well-educated, modern reformers who had closed down regulated brothel systems in dozens of American cities during the Progressive Era.[27] On 1 August 1944, the committee issued a bulletin, "Prostitution in Honolulu," that described (in absolutely untitillating prose) the Hotel Street system. The bulletin included a map that showed where every known prostitute in Honolulu lived. The message was clear: the prostitutes live in YOUR neighborhood.[28] . . .

As military control waned, the first phase of the antiprostitution campaign went into effect. All prostitutes were ordered to vacate houses in residential areas and to move back into the district, to the houses in which "they carry on their trade." News of this dictate was carried in the Honolulu newspapers.[29]

One month after the prostitutes had been ordered back into the district, Governor Stainback joined the antiprostitution campaigns, . . . in part, as [a way of] attack[ing] military control [and, in part, as an effort to link] interests with the progressive elite. . . . On 21 September 1944, in one of his first major reversals of military policy, Governor Stainback ordered the regulated brothels shut down. The Social Protection Committee had maneuvered very cleverly, using their greatest weapon: publicity, or at least the threat of publicity. In letters to Admiral Nimitz, Admiral Furlong, and General Richardson, the committee asked whether each supported the system of regulated brothels. The admirals and the general replied, in writing, that they did not support the system. This was, of course, official policy, even though military practice was quite different. When Stainback closed the brothels, the military offered no resistance. A public debate about the issue, in the face of a determined campaign by an influential group of citizens, was not something anyone in the armed forces could weather. The leaders of the Social Protection Committee knew that.[30]

The actual closing of the brothels went smoothly. On 22 September three uniformed members of the vice squad visited the brothels during working hours, between 11 A.M. and 1:30 P.M. The madams had already heard about the governor's order issued the day before and so had the customers. Business had virtually come to a halt in most houses. The vice-squad officers informed the madams that after 2 P.M. any acts of prostitution committed on their premises would subject them to arrest. The prostitutes were told not to practice their trade, in the houses or elsewhere, and to move out of the district as soon as possible.

According to newspaper reports, many of the prostitutes welcomed the end of an era, and not without humor. One greeted the announcement that she could no longer "practice prostitution" with the old witticism, "I don't practice, I'm an expert." Another woman, wearing "an abbreviated red apron, short-short skirt and a pair of cowboy riding boots," gave a loud "whoopie" at the news. Madams took the news in a variety of ways. . . . But in general the[y] seemed to feel they had little about which to complain. One, and probably not the most successful, had voluntarily paid taxes on an income of $383,000 in 1943. . . . No one had expected the wartime boom to last; most prostitutes and madams had only meant to make the most money they could while it lasted. With the new clampdown in effect, some prostitutes left Honolulu as soon as they could arrange transportation back to the mainland. [Others continued to work outside of brothels.] . . .

The struggle of the Honolulu prostitutes, in retrospect, was charged not only by the usual issues surrounding illicit sex trade and lines of authority, but by concerns specific to prestatehood Hawaii. The women who made such claims on the citizens of Hawaii were white women, and their public presence and vocal demands called into question all the associations of race and gender and the ideology of the purity of white women to be defended against the sexual threat of colored races that were implicit and sometimes explicit in underpinning Hawaii's social structure. In the history of prostitution in America, many have justified the "sacrifice" of lower-class women to "protect" the purity of women of the middle and upper classes. The system in Hawaii was in many ways similar, except that race played a crucial role, and the racial lines were more complex in Hawaii than on the mainland. The public struggles—and yes, excesses—of these "impure" white women called the whole ideological system into question.

At least in small part the system had been dependent on the complicity of the white prostitutes. The prostitutes were seen as a means to keep the low-status white service personnel and the plantation workers sexually satisfied It was crucial to the system that the prostitutes not claim any public role in Hawaii. In fact, in exchange for a great deal of money, the prostitutes (despite their white skin) were supposed to accept total pariah status. They were not to live or visit outside the vice district; they were supposed to remain silent and hidden. They could amass capital but they could not exercise their economic power in Hawaii. They were required to return to the mainland. But with their strike and with the aid of the military government, the prostitutes had demanded—and in part had gotten—the rights economic power normally guaranteed in the United States. . . .

The prostitutes' strike was only one small and indirect part of a larger movement toward a more pluralistic postwar society in Hawaii. But it is especially significant because it brought together issues of race and gender in such a way that it worked to undermine the ideology of racial superiority. White prostitutes demanded full rights of citizenship, and while the very public fact of their race had, in some small way, helped to undermine Hawaii's racial hierarchy, their race was not sufficient to guarantee their rights. Instead, the public power they were able to display for a short while in wartime Hawaii depended on the utility the federal authorities found in them.

The prostitutes' temporary victory—their ability to emerge from the dangerous shadows and to operate as legitimate, fully protected war workers—could not have happened without the intervention of the State, in the form of the military government. The concern of the federally authorized participants was not with the rights of prostitutes (though several seemed to have some respect or liking for members of the profession), but with winning the war. [What that] intervention . . . signaled [was] the increased and continuing willingness of the federal government to impose its nationally minded agendas upon local entities. . . . The ways in which socially marginal groups like the prostitutes of Hotel Street could succeed in furthering their struggles by publicly aligning themselves with the relatively autonomous federal government's often mercurial concerns would become an evermore critical characteristic of social change movements in the postwar years.

Notes

1. Herman Gist, interviewed by David Farber, Germantown, Md., Dec. 1989.

2. Barbara Meils Hobson, *Uneasy Virtue: The Politics of Prostitution and the American Reform Tradition* (New York: Basic Books, 1987).

3. Memo from Commissioner Houston to the Honolulu Police Commission, "Abatement of Houses of Prostitution in the City and Country of Honolulu" (n.d. [1 Sept. 1941?]), Lawrence M. Judd papers ([hereafter cited] LJ), Hawaii State Archives (HA).

4. Quoted by James Cummings in a letter to Dr. Theodore Richards, 11 July 1944, "Prostitution" file, Governor Stainback Papers, HA.

5. "Why Talk about Prostitution," *Hawaii* (31 July 1944):5.

6. Eric A. Funnel, "Venereal Disease Control: A Bedtime Story," *Hawaii Medical Journal* (Nov–Dec. 1942): 67–71; Hobson, *Uneasy Virtue.*

7. Frank Steer interviewed by David Farber, Kailua, Oahu, Hawaii, June 1989; Brian Nicol, "Interview with Col. Frank Steer," *Honolulu* (Nov. 1981):83.

8. Jean O'Hara, "My Life as a Honolulu Prostitute," (n.p. [Nov. 1944?]), Hawaii Collection of the University of Hawaii (HC-UH), pp. 15–16.

9. Ibid., pp. 15–18.

10. Letter to Governor Stainback by Senator Alice Kamokila Campbell, 5 Feb. 1945, "Prostitution" folder. Governor Stainback Papers (GS), HA.

11. Social Protection Committee, *Prostitution in Honolulu, Bulletin* 1 (1 Aug. 1944):2–3.

12. Quote from former brothel employee Adeline Naniole, interviewed by Vivian Lee, 2 March 1979, Women Workers in Pineapple, Ethnic Studies Oral History Project, University of Hawaii, p. 769; interviews with Colonel Steer, Herman Gist, and Robert Cowan.

13. Dr. G. Gary Schram, "Suppressed Prostitution," *Honolulu Advertiser* (6 Oct. 1944); interviews with "C" July 1990, by telephone); Herman Gist, Elton Brown (Nov. 1990, by telephone).

14. Ruth Rosen, *The Lost Sisterhood* (Baltimore: Johns Hopkins University Press, 1982), p. 96.

15. Lt. Commander Carl G. Stockholm, "The Effects of Closing Houses of Prostitution on the Navy" (paper given at the Meeting of the Social Protection Committee), 7 Feb. 1945, HC-UH.

16. Elton Brown, telephone interview, Nov. 1990.

17. Ibid.

18. "Hotel Street Harry," *Midpacifican* (15 Aug. 1943):10; Frank Steer interview, June 1989; Peggy Hickok, "In the Midst of War," *Hawaii* (30 June 1942):17.

19. O'Hara, "My Life."

20. "Hotel Street Harry," *Midpacifican* (15 Jan. 1944): 10; Naniole, p. 771; and "Police Clamp Lid on Houses," *Honolulu Advertiser* (24 Sept. 1944):1.

21. O'Hara, p. 41.

22. Elizabeth Fee, "Venereal Disease: The Wage of Sin?" in Kathy Peiss and Christina Simmons, *Passion and Power* (Philadelphia: Temple University Press, 1989), p. 189.

23. 014.12 Civil Authorities, Decimal File 1941–45, RG 338, MGH, National Archives.

24. Colonel Steer's assistant in "Memoranda of Conference with Major Slattery. . . ." May 1945, office of Interior Secretary, Research and Historical Sector, RG338, NA.; J. Garner Anthony, *Hawaii Under Army Rule*, p. 440.

25. O'Hara, "My Life," p. 47.

26. 014.12 Civil Authorities, Decimal File 1941–45, RG 338 MGH, NA.

27. "Prostitution" file, Governor Stainback Papers, HA; Lawrence H. Fuchs, *Hawaii Pono: A Special History* (New York: Harcourt Brace, 1961), p. 279, 28–88; Hobson, *Uneasy Virtue.*

28. Social Protection Committee, "Prostitution in Hawaii" (1 Aug. 1944).

29. "Residential Areas Banned Prostitutes," *Honolulu Advertiser* (20 July 1944).

30. Dr. Charles L. Wilbar Jr., "The Effects of Closing Houses of Prostitution on Community Health," (paper given at the Meeting of the Social Protection Committee), 7 Feb. 1945, 2–3, HC-UH; and "Prostitution" file, GS, HA.

RUTH MILKMAN

Gender at Work: The Sexual Division of Labor during World War II

As the nation, struggling with economic depression, began to fight its second world war in a single generation, unemployment lines quickly vanished. Manpower shortages meant that women would once again move into jobs in industry. They would experience new vocational opportunities; a lessening of discrimination based on marital status, age, and race; and public praise for their

Excerpted from "Redefining 'Women's Work'" and "Demobilization and the Reconstruction of 'Woman's Place' in Industry," chs. 4 and 7 of *Gender at Work: The Dynamics of Job Segregation by Sex During World War II* by Ruth Milkman (Urbana: University of Illinois Press, 1987). Reprinted by permission of the author and the publisher. Notes have been renumbered and edited and figures omitted.

wartime contributions as workers. Using the techniques of advertising, the federal government publicized women's industrial work as patriotic support for the war by personifying the worker as "Rosie the Riveter." In short order, a catchy song circulated, written by Redd Evans and John Jacob Loeb:

> *All the day long, / Whether rain or shine, / She's a part of the assembly line.*
> *She's making history, / Working for victory, / Rosie the Riveter*

A witty Norman Rockwell painting for the cover of the popular magazine the *Saturday Evening Post* made it easy to visualize such a woman.*

The potential provided by the war for refashioning gender roles was enormous, but the results were disappointing. The expectation was that once the men came home, women would happily exchange industrial tools for the broom and mop or new vacuum cleaner and the baby bottle. Polls showed that up to 85 percent of these women needed to continue working and expected that job seniority would entitle them to return after veterans had been absorbed in the work force.

The redefining of "men's jobs" and "women's jobs" precipitated by wartime mobilization and the rapid return to the prewar sexual division of labor is the subject of Ruth Milkman's study. Focusing especially on the auto and electronics industry, she provides unmistakable evidence of the persistence of occupational segregation at a time when the very survival of democracy was at stake. Note how job segregation demonstrates the double meaning of Milkman's title *Gender at Work.* What was the rationale for segregating jobs by sex? What evidence does Milkman provide to suggest that the designation of jobs as "male" or "female" was often arbitrary? Given management's assessment of women's job performance during the war, how does she explain the reversion to old patterns? What factors were involved? What explanation is offered for the fact that black men were able to hold on to wartime gains in industry whereas white and black women were not?

If it is true that occupational sex typing becomes even more important when women's labor force participation increases, what trends do you foresee for the postwar decades given the changes in the pattern of women's labor force participation noted by Jones for the 1930s (pp. 512–515) and by Milkman for the 1940s? How does job segregation help to explain the fact that women have yet to close the earnings gap with men when both are full-time workers?

Conversion to war production involved redefinition of the entire employment structure. Some civilian automobile production jobs were also necessary for the production of tanks, aircraft, engines and ordnance; other war jobs were completely new. The changeover to war production in electrical manufacturing was less dramatic, but also involved shifts in the character and distribution of jobs. Thus, many of the war jobs that had to be filled (in both industries) were not clearly labeled as "women's" or "men's" work, at least at first. . . .

While the government had actively pressured some firms to hire women, it made no effort whatsoever to influence their placement within industry once management complied. The U.S. Employment Service routinely filled employer job openings that called for specific numbers of women and men. Although ceilings

*The cover appeared on May 29, 1943, several months after the song was published. A prizewinning documentary by Connie Field, *The Life and Times of Rosie the Riveter*, was made in 1980.

Frances Green, Reg Kirchner, Ann Waldner, and Blanche Osborne emerging from their four-engine Flying Fortress. *Note that the women followed a long-standing military tradition by naming their airplane. They were among the 1,074 Women's Airforce Service Pilots (WASPs) who flew noncombat missions during World War II. Although 38 died in the line of duty, WASPs were not eligible for military insurance or GI benefits. At the end of the war, the WASPs were disbanded. Not until 1978 were the survivors offered veteran's status. In 2009, when barely 300 of the original 1,000 WASPs were still alive, the WASPs were awarded a Congressional Gold Medal. (Courtesy of the U.S. Army Museum.)*

were imposed on the number of men who could be allocated to each plant, employers had a free hand in placing women and men in particular jobs within this constraint.[1] Although the unions sometimes contested the sexual division of labor after the fact, the initial job assignments were left entirely to management.

Women were not evenly distributed through the various jobs available in the war plants, but were hired into specific classifications that management deemed "suitable" for women and were excluded from other jobs. Some employers conducted special surveys to determine the sexual division of labor in a plant; probably more often such decisions were made informally by individual supervisors.[2] Although data on the distribution of women through job classifications in the wartime auto and electrical industries are sketchy, there is no mistaking the persistence of segregation by sex. A 1943 survey of the auto industry's Detroit plants, for example, found more than one-half of the women workers clustered in only five of seventy-two job classifications. Only 11 percent of the men were employed in these five occupations.[3]

Jobs were also highly segregated in the electrical industry during the war. A 1942 study of electrical appliance plants (most of which had already been converted to military production when surveyed) found women, who were 30 percent of the workers, in only twenty-one job classifications, whereas men were spread across seventy-two of them. Nearly half of the women (47 percent) were employed in a single job category, and 68 percent were clustered in four occupations. Only 16 percent of the men were in these four job classifications.[4] . . .

Job segregation by sex was explicitly acknowledged in many war plants: Jobs were formally labeled "male" and "female." The two largest electrical firms, GE and Westinghouse, continued this practice until the end of the war. And in 45 percent of the auto plants with sexually mixed work forces responding to a survey conducted in mid-1944 by the UAW Women's Bureau, jobs were formally categorized as "male" or "female."[5] Available records suggest that sex segregation also existed elsewhere, even if it was not formally acknowledged. . . .

Segregation appears to be a constant across both industries during the war years. However, in both industries there was considerable plant-to-plant variation in patterns of employment by sex. In the Detroit area, for example, there was a wide range in the proportion of women employed, even among plants manufacturing the same products. In April 1943, women were 29 percent of the workers at the GM Cadillac plant, which was producing engine parts, but women made up 59 percent of the work force at the Excello Corporation's Detroit plant, which made the same product. Similarly, although women were only 2 percent of the workers at Continental Motors, they were 27 percent of those at the Jefferson Avenue plant of the Hudson Motor Car Company. Both plants made aircraft motors.[6] In the electrical industry, too, there was considerable variation of this sort, even among plants owned by the same company and producing similar goods. . . .

Whatever the sexual division of labor happened to be at a given point in time, management always seemed to insist that there was no alternative. When a War Department representative visited an airplane plant where large numbers of women were employed, he was told that the best welder in the plant was a woman. "Their supervisors told me that their work is fine, even better than that of the men who were formerly on those jobs," he reported. "In another plant in the same area, I remarked on the absence of women and was told that women just can't do those jobs—the very same jobs. It is true, they can't do that type of work—as long as the employer refuses to hire and train them."[7]

Although the specifics varied, everywhere management was quick to offer a rationale for the concentration of women in some jobs and their exclusion from others. . . . "Womanpower differs from manpower as oil fuel differs from coal," proclaimed the trade journal *Automotive War Production* in October 1943, "and an understanding of the characteristics of the energy involved was needed for obtaining best results." Although it was now applied to a larger and quite different set of jobs, the basic characterization of women's abilities and limitations was familiar. As *Automotive War Production* put it:

> On certain kinds of operations—the very ones requiring high manipulative skill—women were found to be a whole lot quicker and more efficient than men. Engineering womanpower means realizing fully that women are not only different from men in such things as lifting power and arm reach—but in many other ways that pertain to their physiological and their social functions. To understand these things does not mean to exclude women from *the jobs for which they are peculiarly adapted,* and where they can help to win this war. It merely means using them as women, and not as men.[8]

The idiom of women's war work in the electrical industry closely paralleled that in auto. "Nearly every Westinghouse plant employs women, especially for jobs that require dexterity with tiny parts," reported an article in *Factory Management and Maintenance* in March 1942. "At the East Pittsburgh plant, for instance, women tape coils. The thickness of each coil must be identical to within close limits, so the job requires feminine patience and deft fingers. Another job that calls for unlimited patience is the inspection of moving parts of electric instruments. . . ." Repeatedly stressed, especially in auto, was the lesser physical strength of the average woman worker. "Woman isn't just a 'smaller man,' " *Automotive War Production* pointed out. "Compensations in production processes must be made to allow for the fact that the average woman is only 35 percent muscle in comparison to the average man's 41 percent. Moreover, industrial studies have shown that only 54 percent of woman's weight is strength, as against man's 87 percent, and that the hand squeeze of the average woman exerts only 48 pounds of pressure, against man's 81 pounds."[9]

Accompanying the characterization of women's work as "light" was an emphasis on cleanliness. "Women can satisfactorily fill all or most jobs performed by men, subject only to the limitations of strength and physical requirements," a meeting of the National Association of Manufacturers concluded in March 1942. "However . . . jobs of a particularly 'dirty' character, jobs that subject women to heat process or are of a 'wet' nature should not be filled by women . . . despite the fact that women could, if required, perform them."[10]

The emphasis in the idiom of sex-typing on the physical limitations of women workers had a dual character. It not only justified the sexual divison of labor, but it also served as the basis for increased mechanization and work simplification. "To adjust women's jobs to such [physical] differences, automotive plants have added more mechanical aids such as conveyors, chain hoists, and load lifters," reported *Automotive War Production.* A study by Constance Green found job dilution of this sort widespread in electrical firms and other war industries in the Connecticut Valley as well. "Where ten men had done ten complete jobs, now . . . eight women and two, three, or possibly four men together would do the ten split-up jobs," she noted. "Most often men set up machines, ground or adjusted tools, and generally 'serviced' the women who acted exclusively as machine operators."[11]

Although production technology was already quite advanced in both auto and electrical manufacturing, the pace of development accelerated during the war period. Management attributed this to its desire to make jobs easier for women, but the labor shortage and the opportunity to introduce new technology at government expense under war contracts were at least as important. However, the idiom that constructed women as "delicate" and, although poorly suited to "heavy" work, amenable to monotonous jobs, was now marshaled to justify the use of new technology and work "simplification." At Vultee Aircraft, for example, a manager explained:

> It definitely was in Vultee's favor that the hiring of women was started when production jobs were being simplified to meet the needs of fast, quantity production. . . . Special jigs were added to hold small tools, such as drills, so that women could concentrate on employing more effectively their proven capacity for repetitive operations requiring high digital dexterity.
>
> Unlike the man whom she replaced, she as a woman, had the capacity to withstand the monotony of even more simplified repetitive operations. To have suspended the air wrench from a counterbalanced support for him would have served merely to heighten his boredom with the job. As for the woman who replaced him, she now handles two such counterbalanced, air-driven wrenches, one in each hand.[12] . . .

There was a contradiction in the management literature on women's war work. It simultaneously stressed the fact that "women are being trained in skills that were considered exclusively in man's domain" and their special suitability for "delicate war jobs."[13] These two seemingly conflicting kinds of statements were reconciled through analogies between "women's work" at home and in the war plants. "Note the similarity between squeezing orange juice and the operation of a small drill press," the Sperry Gyroscope Company urged in a recruitment pamphlet. "Anyone can peel potatoes," it went on. "Burring and filing are almost as easy." An automotive industry publication praised women workers at the Ford Motor Company's Willow Run bomber plant in similar terms. "The ladies have shown they can operate drill presses as well as egg beaters," it proclaimed. "Why should men, who from childhood on never so much as sewed on buttons," inquired one manager, "be expected to handle delicate instruments better than women who have plied embroidery needles, knitting needles and darning needles all their lives?"[14] The newsreel *Glamour Girls of '43* pursued the same theme: "Instead of cutting the lines of a dress, this woman cuts the pattern of aircraft parts. Instead of baking cake, this woman is cooking gears to reduce the tension in the gears after use. . . ."[15] In this manner, virtually any job could be labeled "women's work."

Glamour was a related theme in the idiom through which women's war work was demarcated as female. As if calculated to assure women—and men—that war work need not involve a loss of femininity, depictions of women's new work roles were overlaid with allusions to their stylish dress and attractive appearance. "A pretty young inspector in blue slacks pushes a gauge—a cylindrical plug with a diamond-pointed push-button on its side—through the shaft's hollow chamber," was a typical rendition.[16] Such statements, like the housework analogies, effectively reconciled woman's position in what were previously "men's jobs" with traditional images of femininity.

Ultimately, what lay behind the mixed message that war jobs were at once "men's" and "women's" jobs was an unambiguous point: Women *could* do "men's work," but they were only expected to do it temporarily. The ideological definition of women's war work explicitly included the provision that they would gracefully withdraw from their "men's jobs" when the war ended and the rightful owners returned. Women, as everyone knew, were in heavy industry "for the duration." This theme would become much more prominent after the war, but it was a constant undercurrent from the outset.

Before the war, too, women had been stereotyped as temporary workers, and occupational sex-typing had helped to ensure that employed women would continue to view themselves as women first, workers second. Now this took on new importance, because the reserves of "womanpower" war industries drew on included married women, even mothers of young children, in unprecedented numbers. A study by the Automotive Council for War Production noted that of twelve thousand women employed during the war by one large automotive firm in Detroit, 68 percent were married, and 40 percent had children. And a 1943 WPB study found that 40 percent of one hundred fifty thousand women war workers employed in Detroit were mothers. "With the existing prejudice against employing women over forty, the overwhelming majority of these women workers are young mothers with children under 16."[17]

This was the group of women least likely to have been employed in the prewar years. "In this time of pressure for added labor supply," the U.S. Women's Bureau reported, "the married women for the first time in this country's history exceeded single women in the employed group."[18] . . .

Some firms made deliberate efforts to recruit the wives and daughters of men whom they had employed before the war. A 1942 study by Princeton University's Industrial Relations Section reported on the reasons given by employers for this policy: "(1) It increases the local labor supply without affecting housing requirements; (2) it brings in new employees who are already acquainted with the company and who are likely to be as satisfactory employees as their male relatives; and (3) it may help to minimize postwar readjustment since wives of employed men are not looking for permanent employment."[19] Similarly, the Detroit Vickers aircraft plant had a policy of hiring "members of men's families who have gone to forces so that when these men come back there will be less of a problem in getting the women out of the jobs to give them back to the men."[20]

The dramatic rise in married women's employment during the war raised the long-standing tension between women's commitment to marriage and family and their status as individual members of the paid work force to a qualitatively different level. Before the war, the bulk of the female labor force was comprised of unmarried women; young wives with no children; and self-supporting widowed, divorced, and separated women. When married women and mothers went to work during the war, the occupational sex-typing that linked women's roles in the family and in paid work, far from disintegrating, was infused with new energy. . . .

DEMOBILIZATION AND THE RECONSTRUCTION OF "WOMAN'S PLACE" IN INDUSTRY

The war's end generated renewed upheaval in the sexual division of labor. As reconversion brought massive layoffs and then new hiring, the issue of women's position in industry came to the fore. . . . Would there be a return to the "traditional," prewar sexual division of labor as the mobilization-era ideology of "woman's place" in the war effort had promised? Or would the successful wartime deployment of women in "men's jobs" lead to a permanent shift in the boundaries between women's and men's jobs? Or—a third alternative—would completely new, postwar exigencies reshape, or even eliminate, the sexual division of labor?

Reversion to prewar patterns, which ultimately did occur, might appear to have been the only real possibility. Had not the nation been repeatedly assured that women's entrance into industry was a temporary adaptation to the extraordinary needs of war? . . . Such a view is consistent with the prevailing ideology of the demobilization period, but it obscures the significance of the war years themselves. Wartime conditions were indeed transitory, yet the extraordinary period between Pearl Harbor and V-J Day left American society permanently transformed. One legacy of the war years, from which no retreat would be possible, was the increase in female labor force participation. On an individual basis, to be sure, many women faced conflicting pressures after the war—to continue working for pay on the one hand, and to go back to the home on the other. Yet a permanent shift had occurred for women as a social group. Despite the postwar resurgence of the ideology of domesticity, by the early 1950s the number of gainfully employed women exceeded the highest wartime level. And as early as 1948, the labor force participation rate of married women was higher than in 1944, the peak of the war boom. The rise in female employment, especially for married women, would continue throughout the postwar period, and at a far more rapid rate than in the first half of the century. In this respect, far from being a temporary deviation, the war was a watershed period that left women's relationship to work permanently changed.[21]

The crucial issue, then, was not whether women would remain in the work force, but rather which women would do so and on what terms. What would the postwar sexual division of paid labor look like? Would women retain their wartime foothold in basic industries like auto and electrical manufacturing? To what extent would they be able to find work in fields that had been predominantly male before the war? For women who worked for pay, whether by choice or necessity, exclusion from "men's jobs" did not mean the housewifery first celebrated and later decried as the "feminine mystique." Instead, it meant employment in low-wage "female" jobs, especially clerical, sales, and service work—all of which expanded enormously in the postwar decades.

That the war brought a permanent increase in female employment made the demobilization transition particularly consequential. The opportunity was there for incorporating the dramatic wartime changes in women's position in industry into the fabric of a postwar order in which paid work would become increasingly central to women's lives. In the absence of any events affecting the labor market as fundamentally and cataclysmically as the war, there has been no comparable occasion for a wholesale restructuring of the sexual division of labor since the 1940s. The fact that the opportunity the wartime upheaval presented was lost had enormous implications for the entire postwar era.

Why, then, was the potential for an enduring transformation in the sexual division of labor not fulfilled in the 1940s? There are two standard explanations. One focuses on the postwar resurgence of domesticity, both as a practice and as an ideology, and suggests that women war workers themselves relinquished the "men's jobs" they held during the war—either because of the genuine appeal of traditional family commitments or because they were ideologically manipulated. The second explanation, in contrast, suggests that the key problem was the operation of union-instituted seniority systems, and their manipulation by male unionists, to exclude women and to favor returning male veterans in postwar employment.

. . . [B]oth these accounts of the postwar transition, while partially correct, are inadequate. . . . A large body of evidence demonstrates that management took the lead both in purging women from "men's jobs" after the war and in refusing to rehire them (except in traditionally "female" jobs) as postwar production resumed. Management chose this course despite the fact that most women war workers wanted to keep doing "men's work," and despite the fact that refusing to rehire women often violated seniority provisions in union contracts. . . .

I will offer a two-part explanation for management's postwar policy. First, in both auto and electrical manufacturing, the "traditional" sexual division of labor had a historical logic embodied in the structure of each industry, which remained compelling in the demobilization period. At one level, indeed, reconstructing the prewar sexual division of labor was a foregone conclusion from management's perspective. Wartime female substitution was an experiment that employers had undertaken unwillingly and only because there was no alternative. Despite the success with which women were integrated into "men's jobs," the war's end meant an end to the experiment, and management breathed a collective sigh of relief.

But that is only half of the story. The postwar purge of women from men's jobs also reflected management's assessment of labor's position on the issue. For one thing, the CIO's wartime struggles for equal pay for women workers, which narrowed sex differentials in wages considerably, made permanent female substitution less appealing than it might otherwise have been. Moreover, in the reconversion period, male workers displayed a great deal of ambivalence about the postwar employment rights of women war workers, even those with seniority standing. The CIO's official policy was to defend women's job rights in line with the seniority principle, but in practice there was substantial opposition to retaining women in "men's jobs." This, I will suggest, effectively reinforced management's determination to reconstruct the prewar sexual division of labor. . . .

MANAGERIAL POLICY TOWARD WOMEN WORKERS DURING THE WAR—AND AFTER

. . . Why was management so determined to oust women from the positions that they had occupied during the war? Women war workers wanted to keep their jobs, and union seniority policies did not stand in the way of hiring women, yet they were purged. The problem is all the more puzzling in light of contemporary evidence that management was highly satisfied with women war workers' abilities and performance. While initially employers had strenuously resisted replacing men with women in war industries, once having reconciled themselves to the inevitable, they seemed very pleased with the results. Moreover, because sex differentials in wages, although smaller than before, persisted during the war, one might expect management to have seriously considered the possibility of permanent female substitution on economic grounds.

There is no doubt that women's wartime performance proved satisfactory to management. Under the impact of the "manpower" crunch in the seven months following Pearl Harbor, the proportion of jobs for which the nation's employers were willing to consider women rose from 29 to 55 percent. And management praised women's industrial performance extravagantly during the mobilization period. "Women keep piling up evidence that they *can do,* and *do well,* a multitude of jobs," proclaimed the American Management Association in a 1943 report. "The distribution of basic aptitudes between the two sexes does not differ to any appreciable extent. . . . What is needed is *training*—training to develop latent aptitudes, to increase mechanical knowledge and skill, and to overcome any fear of the machine."[22] . . .

. . . In a 1943 National Industrial Conference Board survey of 146 executives, nearly 60 percent stated without qualification that women's production was equal to or greater than that of men on similar work. Similarly, a study by the Bureau of Employment Security of several California war plants found an increase in production per hour of workers of both sexes, and a lowering of costs per hour when women were employed, in every plant studied. The BES study also found that women were easier to supervise, and that labor turnover and accident rates decreased with the introduction of women.[23]

Many traditional management policies toward women workers were revised or eliminated with their successful incorporation into war industry. For example, physical segregation of the sexes was no longer deemed necessary; the belief "that men and women could work satisfactorily side by side" was held by the majority of executives questioned by the magazine *Modern Industry* as early as mid-1942. There were also many efforts to promote women to supervisory posts, especially at the lower levels, although women were almost never given authority over male workers, and there was a lingering conviction that women workers themselves preferred male bosses.[24]

Women workers' wartime performance, then, stood as evidence that they could be successfully incorporated into the industrial labor force. In addition, wage differentials between the sexes persisted during the war years—a consideration that one might expect to have enhanced management's interest in retaining women permanently in the postwar era. The unions, to be sure, had successfully contested sex discrimination in wages in many "equal pay for equal work" cases before the War Labor Board. But although sex differentials were narrowed as a result of these struggles, they were not eliminated. The Conference Board's composite earnings index for twenty-five manufacturing industries registered only a modest increase in the ratio of female to male average hourly earnings, from 61.5 percent in 1941 to 66.4 percent in 1945.[25] . . .

Still, because men and women rarely did "equal work" even during the war, the outcome of successful WLB equal pay cases was to narrow sex differentials in wages, not to eliminate them. And the Board's equal pay policy was not fully enforced, so that even when jobs were identical, or nearly so, women were often paid less than men. The Conference Board found differentials in starting rates paid to men and to "women hired for men's jobs" in nearly half the 148 plants that it surveyed in 1943, well after equal pay "for comparable quality and quantity of work" had become official WLB policy. Of the ninety-two plants in the survey that had systems of automatic progression in wage rates, twenty-five had sex differentials built into the progression systems despite the fact that the WLB had declared this practice improper.[26]

Similarly, a study of women's wages by the New York State Department of Labor found that 40 percent of the 143 plants surveyed had different starting rates for men and women on "men's jobs." When the state's investigators asked employers to account for such differences, most simply referred to "tradition," standard practice, prevailing wage rates, and custom. "It's also cheaper," said one manager.[27] . . .

There were some extra costs associated with the employment of women, to be sure, particularly in previously all-male plants. Women's absenteeism was generally higher than men's, especially if they were married and had domestic responsibilities, although employers succeeded in narrowing or even eliminating the gap in some plants.[28] UAW President R. J. Thomas, summarizing the reasons auto industry employers were reluctant to hire women for postwar jobs, noted other costs associated with expanding or introducing female employment in a plant. "First is that as you know on most jobs equal rates are paid for equal jobs today," he pointed out. "Management doesn't want to pay women equal rates with men. Not only that but in many of these plants additional facilities have to be put in, such as toilet facilities to take care of women. More space has to be taken to give an opportunity of changing clothes and more safety measures have to be instituted. I think it is pretty well recognized that it is an additional expense to a management to have women."[29]

This is an accurate rendition of the reasons auto industry managers themselves adduced for their reluctance to employ women. Yet it is an inadequate explanation for managerial hostility toward female employment. The costs of maintaining special "facilities" for women were largely absorbed by the government during the war, and could hardly have been a major financial consideration in any event. Surely the savings associated with sex differentials in pay would outweigh any expense firms would incur in continuing to maintain such facilities. Indeed, if only the direct economic costs and benefits of female employment are taken into account, one would expect management to have consistently discriminated *in favor of* women and against men in postwar layoffs and rehiring. Particularly in view of the vigorous efforts of employers to increase labor productivity in the reconversion period, management should have preferred to retain women permanently in the "men's jobs" they had just demonstrated their ability to perform.[30]

Industrial employers chose the opposite course, however, defying not only the apparent imperatives of economic rationality, but also the stated preference of women war workers to keep their war jobs and the unions' official policy that layoffs and rehiring be done strictly by seniority. Rather than institutionalizing the wartime incorporation of women into male jobs, management returned to its prewar practices. . . .

THE ROOTS OF MANAGEMENT'S POSTWAR POLICY

In retrospect, then, management's determination to restore the status quo ante seems altogether irrational. Yet from the perspective of employers themselves at the time, it was a foregone conclusion. Management viewed the successful performance of women war workers as, at best, the fortunate outcome of an experiment in which it had participated with great trepidation and only because there was no alternative. To be sure, women had proved better workers than anyone had expected during the war. But now men's jobs were men's jobs once more. The ideology of sex-typing emerged triumphant again, defining the postwar order along prewar lines in both auto and electrical manufacturing.

In part, the explanation for management's postwar policy involves the logic of the sexual division of labor as it had first developed within the auto and electrical industries a half-century earlier. Not only did the traditions of sex-typing established then have a continuing influence in the post–World War II period, but the factors that had originally shaped those traditions remained salient. In auto, wage levels were still high relative to other industries and would continue to increase in the postwar decades. As in the prewar years, automotive management's efforts to boost productivity focused on tightening control over labor, not on reducing pay levels.[31] Under these conditions, female substitution had little to recommend it, and employers continued to indulge the conviction . . . that women simply were not suitable for employment in automotive production jobs.

In electrical manufacturing, too, prewar traditions of sex-typing persisted in the postwar [era]. But in this industry, the prewar sexual division of labor was historically rooted in a logic of feminization linked to labor-intensity and piecework systems. So why should the further extension of feminization during the war have been rolled back? Even in the case of the automobile industry, why was there a permanent departure from prewar tradition in regard to black employment while the sexual division of jobs persisted virtually unaltered? The historical, industry-specific logic of sex-typing seems to constitute only a partial explanation for management's postwar determination to reconstruct the prewar order.

It is tempting to look outside of the industrial setting to the arena of family and social reproduction in seeking a better solution to the conundrum of management's postwar policies. The interest of capital in reconstructing a family structure in which women are responsible for the generational and daily reproduction of the working class, one might argue, ruled out the permanent employment of women in the well-paid manufacturing jobs that they had during the war. In this view, if women—and more significantly, married women—were to be employed outside the home in ever-increasing numbers in the postwar era, it was crucial that they be confined to poorly paid, secondary jobs that would not jeopardize their primary allegiance to family.

The difficulty with this line of argument is in specifying how the presumed interest of collective capital in reconstituting traditional family forms was translated into the actual employer policies with respect to women workers that emerged in this period. The historical record offers no evidence that such familial considerations played a role in shaping managerial policy in the postwar transition.[32] Although the idea that "woman's place is in the home" was pervasive in the postwar period, it was seldom invoked by employers as a justification for restoring the prewar sexual division of jobs. Instead, management tended to define the issue in economic terms and, above all, by reference to women's physical characteristics and supposed inability to perform "men's jobs."

Although it would be extremely difficult to demonstrate that management policy was rooted in conscious concern over social reproduction, there is evidence for a different kind of explanation: that the postwar purge of women from "men's jobs" involved employers' assessment of the implications of their policies toward women for labor relations. The wartime struggles over equal pay indicated that the unions were committed to resisting any effort to substitute women for men in order to take advantage of their historically lower wages. If wage savings could not be garnered from substitution, or if they could only be garnered at substantial political cost, then why attempt to preserve the wartime sexual division of jobs after the war? In addition, given the widespread fear of postwar unemployment, management might reasonably have anticipated that unemployed male workers would be a source of potential political instability, given the working-class cultural ideal of the "family wage" and the obvious ambivalence of male unionists about women's postwar employment rights.

In short, management had good reason to believe that a wholesale postwar reorganization of the sexual division of labor, in defiance of the wartime assurances that women were in "men's jobs" only for the duration, could precipitate widespread resistance from labor. The unions were at the peak of their strength at this time, and at the war's end they were no longer constrained by the no-strike pledge. As one contemporary analyst noted, consideration of labor's reaction figured prominently in employers' postwar policies:

> Employers in plants where women had long been assigned to some jobs were disposed favorably to widening the fields of work open to women, unless the job dilutions had proved complicated and costly. In fact, union men declared that some companies, unless prevented by organized labor, would try to continue to use women on men's work because they could be hired at lower initial base pay, be upgraded more slowly, and would be throughout more docile. With the installation of mechanical aids, which using women had necessitated, already paid for out of war profits, management had frequently no particular reason to oppose keeping women on.... Yet most companies frankly admitted that, given full freedom of choice after the war, if only out of deference to prevailing male opinion in the shops, management would revert to giving men's jobs, so called, only to men. *And employers generally assumed that labor would permit no choice.*[33]

Understanding management's postwar policy in these terms helps explain why, in the auto case, women and blacks were treated differently. Despite their common history of exclusion from most auto jobs in the prewar era, the two groups stood in very different positions at the war's end. Organized feminism was at its nadir in the 1940s, and the labor movement's commitment to sexual equality was limited, so that management had little reason to fear that purging women from the industry would meet with substantial political opposition. In contrast, at least in the North, there was a large and vital black civil rights movement, which enjoyed substantial UAW support and from which management could expect vigorous protests if it pursued racially discriminatory employment policies.[34]

Only a few years earlier, when blacks were first hired in large numbers in Detroit's auto factories during the war mobilization, white workers had been vocal in their opposition, most notably in the numerous hate strikes which erupted in the plants and in the race riot of the summer of 1943.[35] But during the war, Detroit became a stronghold of the civil rights movement. The Motor City had the largest branch of the National Association for the Advancement of Colored People (NAACP) of any city in the nation, with a membership of twenty thousand by 1943, and the UAW had become a strong ally of the NAACP and other civil rights groups. While racial discrimination persisted in the auto industry in regard to promotion to the elite skilled trades, no one contested blacks' claims to semi-skilled jobs in the aftermath of the war.[36]

The sharp regional variation in racial patterns of hiring within the auto industry suggests the critical importance of the political dimension in shaping management's employment policies. Although the proportion of blacks in Detroit's auto plants rose dramatically in the 1940s and 1950s, reaching well over 25 percent of the production work force by 1960, in the nation as a whole the percentage of nonwhite auto workers grew much more modestly, from 4 percent in 1940 to only 9 percent in 1960. The national figures reflect the continuing practice of excluding blacks from employment in southern plants. As a manager at a GM plant in Atlanta told the *Wall Street Journal* in 1957, "When we moved into the South, we agreed to abide by local custom and not hire Negroes for production work. This is no time for social reforming and we're not about to try it."[37]

The situation of women auto workers was entirely different from that of northern blacks. Although the incorporation of women into the industry during the war had not provoked riots or hate strikes, this was primarily because female employment was explicitly understood to be a temporary expedient, "for the duration" only. After the war, women were expected to go "back to the home." There was no parallel expectation regarding black men.

And while women war workers wanted to remain in the auto industry, as we have seen, their preferences (unlike blacks') lacked legitimacy. While black workers had the civil rights movement behind them, there was no mass feminist movement or even popular consciousness of women's job rights at this critical juncture, when the sexual division of labor that would characterize the postwar period was crystallizing. . . .

NOTES

1. U.S. Senate Hearings, *Manpower Problems in Detroit,* 79th Cong. 1st sess., pp. 9–13 (Mar. 1945), pp. 13534, 13638; interview with Edward Cushman.

2. Reference to such a survey made "to determine those operations which were suitable for female operators" is made on pp. 2–3 of the Summary Brief Submitted by Buick Motor Division, Melrose Park, General Motors Corporation, "In the Matter of GMC–Buick, Melrose Park, Ill., and UAW-CIO," 14 June 1943, Walter Reuther Collection, WSU Archives, box 20, folder: "WLB, GM Women's Rates." A survey of this type was also conducted at the Ford Willow Run plant; see the section on "Training of Women" in *Willow Run Bomber Plant, Record of War Effort* (notebook), vol. 2, pt. 2, Jan.–Dec. 1942, p. 30, La Croix Collection, Accession 435, Ford Archives, Dearborn, Michigan, box 15.

3. Computed from data in U.S. Department of Labor, Bureau of Labor Statistics, Division of Wage Analysis, Regional Office no. 8-A, Detroit, Michigan, Dec. 3, 1943, serial no. 8-A-16 (mimeo), "Metalworking Establishments, Detroit, Michigan, Labor Market Area, Straight-Time Average Hourly Earnings, Selected Occupations, July, 1943." UAW Research Department Collection, WSU Archives, box 28, folder: "Wage Rates (Detroit) Bureau of Labor Statistics, 1943–45." . . .

4. Computed from data in "Earnings in Manufacture of Electrical Appliances, 1942," p. 532.

5. Regarding GE and Westinghouse, see U.S. National War Labor Board, *War Labor Reports,* vol. 28, pp. 677–78. . . .

6. See "Summary Employment Status Report for Michigan," Apr. 30, 1943, Records of the U.S. Employment Service, National Archives, Record Group 183, box 181, folder: "Michigan Statewide."

7. Press release of Office of Production Management, Labor Division, Dec. 5, 1941, UAW Research Department Collection, WSU Archives, box 32, folder: "Women Employment 1941."

8. "Engineers of Womanpower," *Automotive War Production* 2 (Oct. 1943):4–5 (emphasis added). . . .

9. "What Women Are Doing in Industry," *Factory Management and Maintenance* 100 (March 1942):63; "Provisions in Plants for Physical Differences Enable Women to Handle Variety of War Jobs," *Automotive War Production* 2 (Sept. 1943):7.

10. "Report of Two Special Meetings on Employing and Training Women for War Jobs," attended by executives from 85 N.A.M. companies from the East and Midwest, Mar. 27 and 30, 1942, in Records of the Automotive Council for War Production, Detroit Public Library, folder: "Manpower: Source Material: New Workers," p. 1.

11. "Provisions in Plants"; Constance Green, "The Role of Women as Production Workers in War Plants in the Connecticut Valley," *Smith College Studies in History* 28 (1946):32. . . .

12. W. Gerald Tuttle, "Women War Workers at Vultee Aircraft," *Personnel Journal* 21 (Sept. 1942):8–9.

13. "Women Work for Victory," *Automotive War Production* 1 (Nov. 1942):4; "Engineers of Womanpower," p. 4.

14. "There's a Job for You at Sperry . . . Today" (pamphlet), Records of UE District 4, UE Archives, University of Pittsburgh folder 877; "Hiring and Training Women for War Work," *Factory Management and Maintenance* 100 (Aug. 1942):73; "Engineers of Womanpower," p. 4.

15. The transcript of this newsreel was made available to me by the Rosie the Riveter Film Project, Emeryville, California.

16. "Engineers of Womanpower," p. 4.

17. "New Workers," *Manpower Reports* 10 (published by the Manpower Division of the Automotive Council for War Production), p. 4; Anne Gould, "Problems of Woman War Workers in Detroit," Aug. 20, 1943, Records of the War Production Board, National Archives, RG 179, box 203, folder: "035.606 Service Trades Divisions, WPB Functions," p. 2.

18. U.S. Department of Labor, Women's Bureau, Special Bulletin no. 20, *Changes in Women's Employment During the War* (1944), p. 18.

19. Helen Baker, *Women in War Industries* (Princeton: Princeton University Press, 1942), p. 15.

20. "Report of Mrs. Betty Sturges Finan on Cleveland Detroit Trip, Feb. 9–17 [1943] inclusive," pp. 3–4, Records of the War Manpower Commission, National Archives, Record Group 211, Series 137, box 977, folder. "Consultants—Betty Sturges Finan." See also "Report of Two Special Meetings," p. 6.

21. See U.S. Bureau of the Census, *Historical Statistics of the U.S.: Colonial Times to 1970* (1975), pp. 131, 133. This claim is considerably more modest than William Chafe's controversial thesis that the wartime changes in female labor force participation make the 1940s a key "turning point in the history of American women." See William H. Chafe, *The American Woman: Her Changing Social, Economic, and Political Role, 1920–1970* (New York: Oxford University Press, 1972), p. 195. . . .

22. Chafe, *The American Woman,* p. 137; American Management Association, Special Research Report no. 2, *Supervision of Women on Production Jobs: A Study of Management's Problems and Practices in Handling Female Personnel* (1943), pp. 8–10 (emphasis in the original).

23. National Industrial Conference Board, "Wartime Pay of Women in Industry," *Studies in Personnel Policy,* no. 58 (1943):27; "Woman's Place," *Business Week* (May 16, 1942):20–22. . . .

24. *Modern Industry,* July 15, 1942, summarized in *Management Review* 31 (Sept. 1942):303–4. Regarding

the use of women as supervisors, see *Supervision of Women on Production Jobs,* pp. 24–27. . . .

25. Computed from data in *The Management Almanac 1946* (New York: National Industrial Conference Board, 1946), p. 77.

26. "Wartime Pay of Women in Industry," pp. 18–19. . . .

27. New York State Department of Labor, Division of Women in Industry, *Women's Wages on Men's Jobs* (1944), p. 26.

28. See New York State Department of Labor, Division of Women in Industry, *Absenteeism in New York State War Production Plants* (1943); National Industrial Conference Board, "The Problem of Absenteeism," *Studies in Personnel Policy,* no. 53 (1943); "Women Workers on War Production," *UAW Research Report* 3 (Mar. 1943):3. . . .

29. *Manpower Problems in Detroit,* pp. 13112–13.

30. See Howell John Harris, *The Right to Manage: Industrial Relations Policies of American Business in the 1940s* (Madison: University of Wisconsin Press, 1982), pp. 66–67, 91–93.

31. Ibid. This is Harris's main thesis.

32. Denise Riley, "The Free Mothers': Pronatalism and Working Women in Industry at the End of the Last War in Britain," *History Workshop* II (Spring 1981):59–118, presents the most convincing case for this argument in regard to the postwar transition for the British case, but she relies on evidence about state policy with virtually none directly from employers.

33. Green, "Role of Women as Production Workers," pp. 64–65 (emphasis added).

34. August Meier and Elliot Rudwick, *Black Detroit and the Rise of the U.A.W.* (New York: Oxford University Press, 1979).

35. Ibid.; Robert C. Weaver, *Negro Labor: A National Problem* (New York: Harcourt, Brace, and World, 1946).

36. Meier and Rudwick, *Black Detroit,* p. 113. See also Karen Anderson, "Last Hired, First Fired: Black Women Workers during World War II," *Journal of American History* 69 (June 1982), especially pp. 86–87, where white male workers' attitudes toward women and blacks are compared.

37. Both the employment figures and the quote are cited in Herbert R. Northrup, Richard L. Rowan, et al., *Negro Employment in Basic Industry,* Industrial Research Unit, Wharton School of Finance and Commerce, University of Pennsylvania (1970), pp. 65–75. The national employment figures are from the U.S. Census, and because (unlike the figures for Detroit) they include both production and nonproduction workers, they overstate the difference between Detroit and the nation as a whole, for the vast majority of nonproduction workers were white in this period. The quote is from the *Wall Street Journal,* Oct. 24, 1957.

FURTHER READING FOR PART III: CREATING THE STATE IN AN INDUSTRIALIZED NATION, 1880–1945

Overviews

The great documentary editions of the papers of notable Americans are an indispensable and fascinating resource for a wide variety of subjects. For this period, try reading through *The Selected Papers of Jane Addams,* ed. Mary Lynn McCree Bryan et al. (Urbana, Ill., 2003, 2008). The two volumes published so far take her life up to 1889; they have bearing on the history of childhood and youth, education, politics, and social reform. Emma Goldman's life and career also touched on many aspects of American politics and ideas; see the documentary edition edited by Candace Falk et al., *Emma Goldman: A Documentary History of the American Years,* 2 vols. [to date] (Urbana, Ill., 2008). For the articulate pioneer of birth control, see *The Selected Papers of Margaret Sanger,* ed. Esther Katz et al. (Urbana, 2007); the first two volumes take her life to 1939.

For single-volume overviews, see William H. Chafe, *The Paradox of Change: American Women in the Twentieth Century* (New York, 1991), and Rosalind Rosenberg, *Divided Lives: American Women in the Twentieth Century* (New York, 1992, 2008). Surveys of specific groups include Karen Anderson, *Changing Woman: A History of Racial Ethnic Women in Modern America* (New York, 1997); Judy Yung, **Unbound Feet: A Social History of Chinese Women in San Francisco*; Vicki L. Ruiz, **From Out of the Shadows: Mexican Women in Twentieth-Century America*; *We Specialize in the Wholly Impossible: A Reader in Black Women's History,* ed. Darlene Clark Hine, Alma King, and Linda Reed (Brooklyn, 1995);

and Joyce Antler, **The Journey Home: Jewish Women and the American Century*. For overviews with a regional focus, see *Writing the Range: Race, Class, and Culture in the Women's West,* ed. Elizabeth Jameson and Susan Armitage (New York, 1997); Christine Anne Farnham, *Women of the American South: A Multicultural Reader* (New York, 1997); and Huping Ling, *Surviving on the Gold Mountain: A History of Chinese American Women and Their Lives* (Ithaca, N.Y., 1998).

Bodies and Sexuality

The medical treatment of women has been much discussed in scholarly articles, so it is worthwhile searching in scholarly databases such as JSTOR and browsing in academic journals such as the *Journal of Women's History* and *the Bulletin of the History of Medicine.* For sexuality, see the essays in *Powers of Desire: The Politics of Sexuality,* ed. Anne Snitow et al. (New York, 1983), and *Passion and Power: Sexuality in History,* ed. Kathy Peiss and Christina Simmons (Philadelphia, 1989).

For book-length studies of birth control, see Andrea Tone, *Devices and Desires: A History of Contraceptives in America* (New York, 2001); James Reed, **From Private Vice to Public Virtue*; Ellen Chesler, *Woman of Valor: Margaret Sanger and the Birth Control Movement in America* (New York, 1992); and Linda Gordon, **Woman's Body, Woman's Right.* On birth control and the black community, see Jessie M. Rodrique, "The Black Community and the Birth Control Movement," in *Passion and Power.*

The practice of medicine by women remained ideologically fraught; see Regina Morantz-Sanchez, *Conduct Unbecoming a Woman: Medicine on Trial in Turn-of-the-Century Brooklyn* (New York, 1999); Carla Bittel, *Mary Putnam Jacobi and the Politics of Medicine in Nineteenth-Century America* (Chapel Hill, N.C., 2009); and Sharon M. Harris, *Dr. Mary Walker: An American Radical,* 1932–1919 (New Brunswick, N.J., 2009.) The new beauty business offered new work and new entrepreneurial opportunities to African American and white women; see Kathy Peiss, *Hope in a Jar: The Making of America's Beauty Culture* (New York, 1998), and Beverly Lowry, *Her Dream of Dreams: The Rise and Triumph of Madame C.J. Walker* (New York, 2003). For a general study of changing standards of beauty, see Lois W. Banner, *American Beauty* (New York, 1983).

Other issues related to bodies and sexuality include homosexuality, domestic violence, venereal disease, infertility, and unwed motherhood. See Regina Kunzel, *Fallen Women, Problem Girls: Unmarried Mothers and the Professionalization of Social Work, 1890–1945* (New Haven, Conn., 1995); Jennifer Terry, *An American Obsession: Science, Medicine, and Homosexuality in Modern Society* (Chicago, 1999); Linda Gordon, *Heroes of Their Own Lives: The Politics and History of Family Violence, Boston, 1880–1960* (New York, 1988), chap. 8; Allan M. Brandt, *No Magic Bullet: A Social History of Venereal Disease in the United States Since 1880* (New York, 1987); Elaine Tyler May, *Barren in the Promised Land: Childless Americans and the Pursuit of Happiness* (Cambridge, Mass., 1995), chs. 1–3; and Julian C. Carter, *The Heart of Whiteness: Normal Sexuality and Race in America, 1880–1940* (Durham, N.C., 2007).

A powerful example of the impact of ideology on understandings of sexuality is Estelle B. Freedman, "The Prison Lesbian: Race, Class, and the Construction of the Aggressive Female Homosexual, 1915–1956," *Feminist Studies* 22 (Summer 1996): 397–423.

Economics and Law

The law shaped women's lives even when individuals were unaware of its impact. The growth of modern states made reliable national identity more significant; married women found themselves vulnerable in ways they could not have predicted. See Candice Bredbenner, *A Nationality of Her Own: Women, Marriage and the Law of Citizenship* (Berkeley, Calif., 1998); Peggy Pascoe, *What Comes Naturally: Miscegenation Law and the Making of Race in America* (New York, 2009); and Barbara Y. Welke, "Law, Personhood and Citizenship in the Long Nineteenth Century: The Borders of Belonging," *The Cambridge History of Law in America,* vol. 2 (New York, 2008). On attitudes toward divorce and the debate on changing divorce laws, see Glenda Riley, *Divorce: An American Tradition* (New York, 1991). On taxation, see Linda K. Kerber, **No Constitutional Right,* ch. 3.

Housework engaged all women, except for the most privileged. See Ruth Schwartz Cowan, **More Work for Mother,* chs. 4–6; Susan Strasser, **Never Done,* chs. 1–12; and Susan Porter Benson, *Household Accounts: Working-Class Family Economies in the Interwar United States* (Ithaca, N.Y., 2007). Farm women had additional burdens, as described in Deborah Fink, *Agrarian Women: Wives and Mothers in Rural Nebraska, 1880-1940* (Chapel Hill, N.C., 1992); Lu Ann Jones, *Mama Learned Us to Work: Farm Women in the New South* (Chapel Hill, N.C., 2002); and Valerie Matsumoto, *Farming the Home Place: A Japanese American Community in California, 1919–1982* (Ithaca, N.Y., 1982). The impact of technology on farm women's work is described in Katherine Jellison, *Entitled to Power: Farm Women and Technology, 1913–1963* (Chapel Hill, N.C., 1993). For the shift to understand housework as a site of consumption, see Janice Williams Rutherford, *Selling Mrs. Consumer: Christine Frederick and the Rise of Household Efficiency* (Athens, Ga., 2003). For changing understandings of the labor of caregiving, see Emily Abel, *Hearts of Wisdom: American Women Caring for Kin, 1850–1940* (Cambridge, Mass., 2000). On the complexity of the immigrant experience, see Suzanne M. Sinke, *Dutch Immigrant Women in the United States, 1880–1920* (Urbana, Ill., 2002).

Whether women worked outside the home and at what jobs depended on economic need and work options as well as family expectations. For a general study, see Leslie Woodcock Tentler, *Wage-Earning Women: Industrial Work and Family Life in the United States, 1900–1930* (New York, 1979). For those finding new opportunities in specific areas, see Patricia A. Cooper, *Once a Cigar Maker: Men, Women, and Work Culture in American Cigar Factories, 1900–1919* (Urbana, Ill., 1987); Jacquelyn Dowd Hall et al., *Like a Family: The Making of a Southern Cotton Mill World* (Chapel Hill, N.C., 1987); Miriam Cohen, *Workshop to Office: Two Generations of Italian Women in New York City, 1900–1950* (Ithaca, N.Y., 1993); and Ardis Cameron, *Radicals of the Worst Sort: Laboring Women in Lawrence, Massachusetts, 1860–1912* (Urbana, Ill., 1993). For the origins of the first workforce in which women and men worked side by side from the Civil War to 1900, see Cindy Sondik Aron, *Ladies and Gentlemen of the Civil Service: Middle Class Workers in Victorian America* (New York, 1987). For new opportunities provided by office work, see Carole Srole, *Transcribing Class and Gender: Masculinity and Femininity in Nineteenth-Century Courts and Offices* (Ann Arbor, Mich., 2009); Margery W. Davies, *Woman's Place Is at the Typewriter: Office Work and Office Workers, 1879–1930* (Philadelphia, 1982); Lisa M. Fine, *The Souls of Skyscrapers: Female Clerical Workers in Chicago, 1890–1930* (Philadelphia, 1990);

and Sharon Strom Hartman, *Beyond the Typewriter: Gender, Class, and the Origins of Modern American Office Work, 1900–1930* (Urbana, Ill., 1992). Susan Porter Benson, *Counter Cultures: Saleswomen, Managers, and Customers in American Department Stores, 1890–1940* (Urbana, Ill., 1986), examines one side of the new economy; Elaine Abelson examines the reverse in *When Ladies Go A-Thieving: Middle-Class Shoplifters in the Victorian Department Store* (New York, 1989).

For efforts to improve the economic well-being of working-class women through unionization, see Annelise Orleck, **Common Sense and a Little Fire*; Nan Enstad, *Ladies of Labor, Girls of Adventure: Working Women, Popular Culture, and Labor Politics at the Turn of the Twentieth Century* (New York, 1999); Susan Levine, *Labor's True Woman: Carpet Weavers, Industrialization, and Labor Reform in the Gilded Age* (Philadelphia, 1984); Nancy Schrom Dye, *As Equals and as Sisters: Feminism, the Labor Movement, and the Women's Trade Union League of New York* (Columbia, Mo., 1980); Elizabeth A. Payne, *Reform, Labor, and Feminism: Margaret Dreier Robins and the Women's Trade Union League* (Urbana, Ill., 1988); Stephen H. Norwood, *Labor's Flaming Youth: Telephone Operators and Worker Militancy,1878–1923* (Urbana, Ill., 1990); as well as selected essays in *Women, Work, and Protest: A Century of U.S. Women's Labor History*, ed. Ruth Milkman (Boston, 1985). On the larger issue of working-class consciousness, see Sarah Eisenstein, *Give Us Bread but Give Us Roses: Working Women's Consciousness in the United States, 1890 to the First World War* (London, 1983), and Nancy A. Hewitt, *Southern Discomfort: Women's Activism in Tampa, Florida, 1880s to 1920s* (Urbana, Ill., 2001). For the compelling story of the workplace fire that prompted many Americans to sympathize with women factory workers, see David Von Drehle, *Triangle: The Fire that Changed America* (New York, 2003).

Prostitution also provided jobs whether women entered such work voluntarily or, as many did, involuntarily, as demonstrated in Ruth Rosen, *Lost Sisterhood: Prostitution in America, 1900–1918* (Baltimore, Md., 1982); Benson Tong, *Unsubmissive Women: Chinese Prostitutes in Nineteenth-Century San Francisco* (Norman, Okla., 1994); and Elizabeth Alice Clement, *Love for Sale: Courting, Treating, and Prostitution in New York City, 1900–1945* (Chapel Hill, N.C., 2006).

How working-class women used their leisure and whether leisure activities contributed to individual and/or collective self-improvement are issues explored by Kathy Lee Peiss, *Cheap Amusements: Working Women and Leisure in Turn-of the-Century New York* (Philadelphia, 1986), and Elizabeth Ewen, *Immigrant Women in the Land of Dollars: Life and Culture on the Lower East Side, 1890-1925* (New York, 1985).

On the role of gender in determining wage inequities, see Alice Kessler-Harris, **In Pursuit of Equity* and **A Woman's Wage*, chs. 1–3. On women and labor unions, see Dorothy Sue Cobble, *Dishing It Out: Waitresses and Their Unions in the Twentieth Century* (Urbana, Ill., 1991); Melinda Chateauvert, *Marching Together: Women of the Brotherhood of Sleeping Car Porters* (Urbana, Ill., 1998); and Elizabeth Faue, *Community of Suffering and Struggle: Women, Men, and the Labor Movement in Minneapolis, 1915–1945* (Chapel Hill, N.C., 1991). On Hispanic women and unionization, see Vicki L. Ruiz, *Cannery Women, Cannery Lives: Mexican Women, Unionization, and the California Food Processing Industry, 1930–1950* (Albuquerque, N. Mex., 1987). For the particular problems facing black women, see Dolores Janiewski, *Sisterhood Denied: Race, Class, and Gender in a New South Community* (Philadelphia, 1985); Elizabeth Clark-Lewis, *"This Work Hada' End": The Transition from Live-in to Day Work* (Memphis, Tenn., 1985); and Phyllis Palmer,

Domesticity and Dirt: Housewives and Domestic Servants in the United States, 1920–1945 (Philadelphia, 1990).

Middle-class women with education discovered new opportunities for employment in a variety of new professions. On nursing, see Barbara Melosh, *The Physician's Hand: Work, Culture, and Conflict in American Nursing* (Philadelphia, 1982); Susan M. Reverby, *Ordered to Care: The Dilemma of American Nursing, 1850–1945* (New York. 1987); and Darlene Clark Hine, *Black Women in White: Racial Conflict and Cooperation in the Nursing Profession, 1890-1950* (Bloomington, Ind., 1989).

For barriers to women in a wide range of scientific work, see Margaret Rossiter, *Women Scientists in America: Struggles and Strategies to 1940* (Baltimore, 1982); in the law, see Virginia G. Drachman, *Sisters in Law: Women Lawyers in Modern American History* (Cambridge, Mass., 1998), and in a wide range of professions, see Stephanie J. Shaw, *What a Woman Ought to Be and to Do: Black Professional Women Workers During the Jim Crow Era* (Chicago, 1995). On the first generation of working women to live alone, see Joanne I. Meyerowitz, *Women Adrift: Independent Wage Earners in Chicago, 1880–1930* (Chicago, 1988). For women as educators, see Ruth Jacknow Markowitz, *My Daughter, the Teacher: Jewish Teachers in the New York City Schools* (New Brunswick, N.J., 1993).

The Great Depression and World War II had very different and decisive impacts on women's economic opportunities. For the 1930s, see Lois Scharf, *To Work and to Wed: Female Employment, Feminism, and the Great Depression* (Westport, Conn., 1980), and Winifred Wandersee, *Women's Work and Family Values, 1920–1940* (Cambridge, Mass., 1981). For World War II, see Leisa D. Meyer, *Creating G.I. Jane: Sexuality and Power in the Women's Army Corps During World War II* (New York, 1996), and Molly Merryman, *Clipped Wings: The Rise and Fall of the Women Air Force Service Pilots (WASPS) of World War II* (New York, 1998). Karen Anderson explores women's work as part of a larger study of women's status during World War II in *Wartime Women: Sex Roles, Family Relations, and the Status of Women during World War II* (Westport, Conn., 1981), as does Susan M. Hartmann in *The Home Front and Beyond: American Women in the 1940s* (Boston, 1982). Job segregation in two key industries is the focus of Ruth Milkman's **Gender at Work.*

Politics

**The Concise History of Woman Suffrage* is a convenient version of the great six-volume compendium edited by Elizabeth Cady Stanton and Susan B. Anthony and their colleagues, and published between 1887 and 1922. There is a growing literature on female political activism in the decades before women could vote. See Katherine H. Addams and Michael L. Keene, *Alice Paul and the American Suffrage Campaign* (Urbana, Ill., 2008), and Rebecca Edwards, *Angels in the Machinery: Gender in American Party Politics from the Civil War to the Progressive Era* (New York, 1997). On white women's clubs, see Karen Blair, *The Clubwoman as Feminist: True Womanhood Redefined, 1868–1914* (New York, 1980); Theodora Penny Martin, *The Sound of Our Own Voices: Women's Study Clubs, 1860–1910* (Boston, 1987); Anne Ruggles Gere, *Intimate Practices: Literacy and Cultural Work in U.S. Women's Clubs, 1880–1920* (Urbana, Ill., 1997). On black women's clubs, see Anne Miess Knupfer, *Toward a Tenderer and a Nobler Womanhood: African American Women's Clubs in Turn-of-the-Century Chicago* (New York, 1996). Leila J. Rupp, *Worlds of Women: The Making of an International Women's Movement* (Princeton, N. J.,1998), examines the entry of women into international politics.

Women's voluntary associations and philanthropy are examined in Priscilla Murolo, *The Ground of Womanhood: Class, Gender, and Working Girls' Clubs, 1884–1928* (Urbana, Ill., 1996); Anne Firor Scott, **Natural Allies*; Elizabeth Hayes Turner, *Women, Culture, and Community: Religion and Reform in Galveston, 1880–1923* (New York, 1997); and Kathleen D. McCarthy, ed., *Lady Bountiful Revisited: Women, Philanthropy, and Power* (New Brunswick, N.J., 1990). McCarthy explores women's philanthropic involvement in the art world in *Women's Culture: American Philanthropy, 1830-1930* (Chicago, 1991). For the unexpected consequences to which reform can lead, see Linda Gordon, *The Great Arizona Orphan Abduction* (Cambridge, Mass., 1999; an ACLS Humanities e-book).

Missionary work provided many opportunities—both philanthropic and spiritual—for U.S. women; a good place to start is Patricia Hill, *The World Their Household: The American Woman's Foreign Mission Movement and Cultural Transformation, 1870–1920* (Ann Arbor, Mich., 1985). See also Karen K. Seat, *"Providence has Freed Our Hands:" Women's Missions and the American Encounter with Japan* (Syracuse, N.Y., 2008). For a woman who displayed remarkable courage amid disaster, see *Terror in Minnie Vautrin's Nanjing: Diaries and Correspondence, 1937–38,* ed. Suping Lu (Urbana, Ill., 2008).

For black women's activism, see Paula Giddings, **When and Where I Enter*; Evelyn Brooks Higginbotham, *Righteous Discontent: The Women's Movement in the Black Baptist Church, 1880–1920* (Cambridge, Mass., 1993); Susan L. Smith, *Sick and Tired of Being Sick and Tired: Black Women's Health Activism in America, 1890–1950* (Philadelphia, 1995); Judith Weisenfeld, *African American Women and Christian Activism: New York's Black YWCA, 1905–1945* (Cambridge, Mass., 1998); and Glenda F. Gilmore, **Gender and Jim Crow*.

The city provided women a new frontier of expanded opportunity and social service; see Sharon Wood, *The Freedom of the Streets: Work, Citizenship and Sexuality in a Gilded Age City* (Chapel Hill, N.C., 2005); Maureen Flanagan, *Seeing With Their Hearts: Chicago Women and the Vision of the Good City, 1871–1933* (Princeton, N. J., 2002); Sarah Deutsch, *Women and the City: Gender, Space, and Power in Boston, 1870–1940* (New York, 2000). On the relationships between social service and the new profession of social work, see Clarke A. Chambers, *Seedtime of Reform: Social Service and Social Action, 1918–1933* (Ann Arbor, 1967), and Robyn Muncy, *Creating a Female Dominion in American Reform, 1890–1935* (New York, 1991). On delinquent girls and the women reformers, see *Regina G. Kunzel, *Fallen Women, Problem Girls*; Ruth M. Alexander, *The "Girl Problem:" Female Sexual Delinquency in New York, 1900–1930* (Ithaca, N.Y., 1995); and Mary F. Odem, *Delinquent Daughters: Protecting and Policing Adolescent Female Sexuality in the United States, 1885–1920* (Chapel Hill, N.C., 1995). On courts and correctional institutions, see Elizabeth J. Clapp, *Mothers of All Children: Women Reformers and the Rise of Juvenile Courts in Progressive-Era America* (University Park, Pa., 1998); Anne M. Butler, *Gendered Justice in the American West: Women Prisoners in Men's Penitentiaries* (Urbana, Ill., 1997); and L. Mara Dodge, *"Whores and Thieves of the Worst Kind": A Study of Women, Crime, and Prisons, 1835–2000* (DeKalb, Ill., 2002).

Female activists and social scientists also had an impact on other social policies, as is demonstrated in Ellen Fitzpatrick, *Endless Crusade: Women Social Scientists and Progressive Reform* (New York, 1990); Theda Skocpol, *The Political Origins of Social Policy in the United States* (Cambridge, Mass., 1992); Molly Ladd-Taylor, *Mother-Work: Women, Child Welfare, and the State, 1890–1930* (Urbana, Ill., 1994); Joanne L. Goodwin, *Gender and the Politics of Welfare Reform: Mother's Pensions in Chicago, 1911–1929* (Chicago, 1997); Linda Gordon, *Pitied but Not Entitled: Single Mothers and the History of Welfare, 1890–1935* (New York, 1994); Gwendolyn Mink, *The Wages of Motherhood: Inequality in the Welfare State, 1917–1942* (Ithaca, N.Y., 1995); Lynne Curry, *Modern Mothers in the Heartland: Gender, Health, and Progress in Illinois, 1900–1930* (Columbus, Ohio, 1999), and S. J. Kleinberg, *Widows and Orphans First: The Family Economy and Social Welfare Policy, 1880–1939* (Urbana, Ill., 2006). On women reformers' continued concern for industrial conditions, see Claudia Clark, *Radium Girls: Women and Industrial Health Reform, 1910–1935* (Chapel Hill, N.C., 1997). These historians make clear that social policies were themselves gendered, particularly with respect to benefits, as women received fewer from the government than did their male counterparts.

The most famous group of reformers were the settlement house women, whose political activism is skillfully probed in Kathryn Kish Sklar's "Hull House in the 1890s: A Community of Women Reformers," *Signs* 10 (1985): 658–77; Allen Davis, *American Heroine: The Life and Legend of Jane Addams* (New York, 1973, and Victoria Bissell Brown, *The Education of Jane Addams* (Philadelphia, 2004). For women reformers in a different context, see Peggy Pascoe, *Relations of Rescue: The Search for Female Moral Authority in the American West, 1874–1939* (New York, 1990).

For an interpretation of the impact of gender on national politics and the involvement of women for and against American empire in the late nineteenth century, see Gail Bederman, *Manliness and Civilization: A Cultural History of Gender and Race in the United States, 1880–1917* (Chicago, 1995); Kristin L. Hoganson, *Fighting for American Manhood: How Gender Politics Provoked the Spanish-American and Philippine-American Wars* (New Haven, Conn., 1998); and Laura Briggs, *Reproducing Empire: Race, Sex, Science, and U.S. Imperialism in Puerto Rico* (Berkeley, Calif., 2002).

For women's involvement in World War I, the place to begin is Kimberly Jensen, *Mobilizing Minerva: American Women in the First World War* (Urbana, Ill., 2008). The peace and socialist movements also attracted dedicated activists. See two studies by Carrie A. Foster: *The Women and the Warriors: The U.S. Section of the Women's International League for Peace and Freedom, 1915–1946* (Syracuse, N.Y., 1995), and *Women for All Seasons: The Story of the Women's International League for Peace and Freedom* (Athens, Ga., 1989). On socialism, see Mary Jo Buhle, *Women and American Socialism, 1870–1920* (Urbana, Ill., 1983). Biographies of radicals include Candace Falk, *Love, Anarchy, and Emma Goldman: A Biography* (New York, 1989); Dee Garrison, *Mary Heaton Vorse: The Life of an American Insurgent* (Philadelphia, 1989); Janice R. MacKinnon and Stephen R. MacKinnon, *Agnes Smedley: The Life and Times of an American Radical* (Berkeley, Calif., 1987); Helen C. Camp, *Iron in Her Soul: Elizabeth Gurley Flynn and the American Left* (Pullman, Wash., 1995). See also Kathleen Kennedy, *Disloyal Mothers and Scurrilous Citizens: Women and Subversion during World War I* (Bloomington, Ind., 1999); and Rhodri Jeffreys-Jones, *Changing Differences: Women and the Shaping of American Foreign Policy, 1917–1994* (New Brunswick, N.J., 1995).

The classic history of suffrage, Eleanor Flexner's *Century of Struggle: The Woman's Rights Movement in the United States* (Cambridge, Mass., 1958), should be supplemented with Anne Firor Scott and Andrew Scott, *One Half the People: The Fight for Woman Suffrage* (Urbana, Ill., 1982); Ellen Carol DuBois, *Harriot Stanton Blatch and the Winning of Woman Suffrage* (New Haven, Conn., 1997); Marjorie Spruill Wheeler, ed., *One Woman, One Vote:*

Rediscovering the Woman Suffrage Movement (Troutdale, Ore., 1995); Jean H. Baker, ed., *Votes for Women: The Struggle for Suffrage Revisited* (New York, 2002); and Suzanne Marilley, *Woman Suffrage and the Origins of Liberal Feminism, 1880–1920* (Cambridge, Mass., 1996). Studies on African American women and suffrage include Rosalyn Terborg-Penn, **African-American Women in the Struggle for the Vote, 1850-1920*, and *African American Women and the Vote, 1837-1935*, ed. Anne D. Gordon with Bettye Collier-Thomas et al. (Amherst, Mass., 1997). For illuminating regional studies, see Marjorie Spruill Wheeler's *New Women of the New South: The Leaders of the Woman Suffrage Movement in the Southern States* (New York, 1993), and Elna Green, *Southern Strategies: Southern Women and the Woman Suffrage Question* (Chapel Hill, N.C., 1997). On antisuffragists, see Susan F. Marshall, *Splintered Sisterhood: Gender and Class in the Campaign against Woman's Suffrage* (Madison, Wis., 1997).

On the Woman's Party, see Christina A. Leonardi, *From Equal Suffrage to Equal Rights: Alice Paul and the National Woman's Party, 1910–1928* (New York, 1986). For women's involvement in other political parties, see Robert J. Dinkin, **Before Equal Suffrage*, and Michael Goldberg, *An Army of Women: Gender and Politics in Gilded Age Kansas* (Baltimore, Md., 1997). On the impact of suffrage, see Kristi Andersen, *After Suffrage: Women in Partisan and Electoral Politics before the New Deal* (Chicago, 1996).

The activities of women in the aftermath of suffrage were first probed in J. Stanley Lemons, *The Woman Citizen: Social Feminism in the 1920s* (Urbana, Ill., 1975). More recent works include Nancy F. Cott, *The Grounding of Modern Feminism* (New Haven, Conn., 1987). For black women's activism, see Jacqueline Anne Rouse, *Lugenia Burns Hope: Black Southern Reformers* (Athens, Ga., 1989); Ula Yvette Taylor, *The Veiled Garvey: The Life and Times of Amy Jacques Garvey* (Chapel Hill, N.C., 2002); and Victoria W. Wolcott, *Remaking Respectability: African American Women in Interwar Detroit* (Chapel Hill, N.C., 2001). On women in partisan politics in the post-suffrage decades, see Catherine E. Rymph, *Republican Women: Feminism and Conservatism from Suffrage Through the Rise of the New Right* (Chapel Hill, N. C., 2006); Jo Freeman, *A Room at a Time: How Women Entered Party Politics* (New York, 2000); and *We Have Come to Stay: American Women and Political Parties, 1880–1960*, ed. Melanie Gustafson et al. (Albuquerque, N. Mex., 1999). For an analysis of how the Get Out the Vote campaigns of the 1920s, prompted by a low turnout of women voters, transformed political culture in the United States, see Liette Patricia Gidlow, *The Big Vote: Gender, Consumer Culture, and the Politics of Exclusion, 1880s to 1920s* (Baltimore, Md., 2004).

On how antisuffragist women morphed into women of the anticommunist right after World War I, see Kim E. Nielsen, *Un-American Womanhood: Antiradicalism, Antifeminism, and the First Red Scare* (Columbus, Ohio, 2001). Women who joined the KKK are the focus of Kathleen M. Blee, *Women of the Klan: Racism and Gender in the 1920s* (Berkeley, Calif., 1991). Glen Jeansonne, *Women of the Far Right: The Mothers' Movement and World War II* (Chicago, 1990), examines conservative women who were isolationists.

Important biographies of activists and/or politicians include Jacquelyn Dowd Hall, *Revolt Against Chivalry: Jessie Daniel Ames and the Women's Campaign Against Lynching* (New York, 1974); Christie Miller, *Ruth Hanna McCormick: A Life in Politics, 1880–1944* (Albuquerque, N. Mex., 1992); Barbara Sicherman, *Alice Hamilton: A Life in Letters* (Cambridge, Mass., 1984); Susan Ware, *Partner and I: Mollie Dewson, Feminism, and New Deal Politics* (New Haven, Conn., 1987); Blanche Weisen Cook, *Eleanor Roosevelt,*

1884–1933, (New York, 1993) and **Eleanor Roosevelt, The Defining Years;* Ingrid Scobie, *Center Stage: Helen Gahagen Douglas, A Life* (New York, 1992); Kathryn Kish Sklar, *Florence Kelley and the Nation's Work* (New Haven, Conn., 1995); Patricia L. Schmidt, *Margaret Chase Smith: Beyond Convention* (Orono, Maine, 1996); Janann Sherman, *No Place for a Woman: A Life of Senator Margaret Chase Smith* (New Brunswick, N.J., 2000); and Joyce Hanson, *Mary McLeod Bethune and Black Women's Political Activism* (Columbia, Mo., 2003).

Intellect, Ideology, Culture

For feminist thought, begin with two studies by Rosalind Rosenberg: *Beyond Separate Spheres: Intellectual Roots of Modern Feminism* (New Haven, Conn., 1982), and *Changing the Subject: How the Women of Columbia Shaped the Way We Think About Sex and Politics* (New York, 2004). For the invention of careers as women historians, and also as historians of women, see Nancy F. Cott, *A Woman Making History: Mary Ritter Beard Through Her Letters* (New Haven, Conn., 1991), and Julie Des Jardins, *Women and the Historical Enterprise in America: Gender, Race, and the Politics of Memory, 1880-1945* (Chapel Hill, N. C., 2003). For the career of a theorist, see Ann J. Lane, *To "Herland" and Beyond: The Life and Work of Charlotte Perkins Gilman* (New York, 1990). To follow an activist who merged ideas with political reform, see Kathryn Kish Sklar and Beverly Wilson Palmer, eds., *The Selected Letters of Florence Kelley, 1869–1931* (Urbana, Ill., 2009). For the career of a novelist, see Peter Conn, *Pearl S. Buck: A Cultural Biography* (New York, 1996). For the career of a photographer, see Linda Gordon, *Dorothea Lange: A Life Beyond Limits* (New York, 2009).

Carroll Smith-Rosenberg, **Disorderly Conduct,* extends its sophisticated and nuanced treatment of gender ideology and social change into the early twentieth century. For perspectives on her work, see "Women's History in the New Millennium: Carroll Smith-Rosenberg's 'The Female World of Love and Ritual' after Twenty-Five Years," *Journal of Women's History* 12 (Autumn 2000): 8–38. On ideology and education, see Helen L. Horowitz, *The Passion and Power of M. Carey Thomas* (New York, 1994), and *Alma Mater: Design and Experience in the Women's Colleges from Their Nineteenth Century Beginning to the 1930s* (New York, 1984). An indispensable overview is Barbara Miller Solomon, *In the Company of Educated Women: A History of Women and Higher Education in America* (New Haven, Conn., 1986). See also Lynn D. Gordon, *Gender and Higher Education in the Progressive Era* (New Haven, Conn., 1990); Devon A. Mihesuah, *Cultivating the Rosebuds: The Education of Women at the Cherokee Female Seminary, 1851–1928* (Urbana, Ill., 1993); and *Yards and Gates: Gender in Harvard and Radcliffe History,* ed. Laurel Thatcher Ulrich (New York, 2004).

Religious organizations often provided the context for women's intellectual and reform activism; see, for example, Evelyn Brooks Higginbotham, *Righteous Discontent: The Women's Movement in the Black Baptist Church, 1880–1920* (Cambridge, Mass., 1993); Eileen Brewer, *Nuns and the Education of American Catholic Women, 1860–1920* (Chicago, 1987); and Carol Coburn, *Spirited Lives: How Nuns Shaped Catholic Culture and American Life, 1836–1920* (Chapel Hill, N.C., 1999).

The racial ideologies of the nineteenth century persisted into the twentieth; see Micki McElya, *Clinging to Mammy: The Faithful Slave in Twentieth-Century America* (Cambridge, Mass., 2007). Such ideologies pursued teachers into classrooms—see Sonya Ramsey, *Reading, Writing, and Segregation: A Century of Black Women Teachers in Nashville* (Urbana, Ill.,

2008)—and into institutions that were supposed to be a relief from work: see Nancy Marie Robertson, *Christian Sisterhood, Race Relations, and the YWCA, 1906–46* (Urbana, Ill., 2007). And they shaped concepts of beauty: see Noliwe M. Rooks, *Hair Raising: Beauty, Culture, and African American Women* (New Brunswick, N.J., 1996).

The intersection of ideology and technology is explored in Virginia Scharff, *Taking the Wheel: Women and the Coming of the Motor Age* (New York, 1991).

Asterisks (*) indicate the work's full citation can be found either earlier in this list of works or in the credit lines of an essay by the author excerpted in this volume.

IV

Struggles against Injustice

1945–2010

On the surface, at least, America of the post–World War II years was a nation of prosperity and opportunity. Indeed, the new atomic age was marked by a greater affluence and heightened consumerism. Enrollment in universities swelled, more and more Americans moved to the suburbs, and the birthrate soared.

But these images mask the reality of life in the United States during an era marked by a cold war. Residential discrimination made the move to the suburbs difficult, if not impossible, for most families of color. Although the domestic ideal cast women as full-time mothers and housewives, most women continued to work outside the home. Fearing domestic subversion, anti-Communists during the McCarthy era purged the government, organized labor, the entertainment industry, and universities of Communists—real and imagined. Labeled as security risks due to their "un-American" identity, gays and lesbians became favored targets of the purges. Like feminists, they were increasingly silenced, as dissent became tantamount to disloyalty.

The election of John F. Kennedy in 1960 promised energy and optimism. The young leader urged his fellow citizens to "ask not what your country can do for you; ask what you can do for your country." Women eagerly answered this call to action. Within a few years, they were on the front lines in the civil rights war in the South. They played key roles in the student movements that rocked college campuses across the nation, challenging everything from restrictive curfews to the narrow focus of the curricula. Women served their nation as nurses and volunteers in Vietnam; at home, they protested against the war. Soon, a feminist consciousness reemerged. Women fought for equal pay for equal work, access to safe and legal abortions, and an end to sexual violence.

By the mid-1980s, however, the time for social reform appeared to be over. The expansive mood of the 1960s disintegrated in the face of anxiety over unemployment, inflation, rising energy costs, and declining productivity. Yet women continued to challenge conventional definitions of womanhood. From the Gulf War in 1990–91, women fought in a gender-integrated military. They continued the battle against sexism and fought to protect their reproductive rights. A new civil rights era emerged in the 1990s, as major corporations implemented domestic partner benefits for same-sex and unmarried couples and, a decade later, courts and state legislatures in a cascade of jurisdictions responded positively to the arguments made by Lambda Legal Defense and Education Fund lawyers that marriage should be open to same-sex couples. In the nation's capital, the number of women in the U.S. House of Representatives leaped to forty-seven in 1992 (from twenty-eight), reaching seventy-two in 2008 and 2009. By the end of the first decade in the twenty-first century, it no longer seemed unusual for a woman to be secretary of state: Madeleine Albright was appointed by President William Jefferson Clinton in 1996; Condoleezza Rice held the post from January 2005 to January 2009; and President Barack Obama named Hillary Rodham Clinton in 2009. Nor did it seem against the odds that a woman would be elected president, given Clinton's success in redefining the profile of a First Lady by winning a Senate seat and making a strong bid for the presidential spot on the 2008 Democratic ticket.

Nevertheless, those who would exploit racial, class, and gender injustice have persisted in their attempts to roll back these gains. This ongoing struggle dramatizes the need for a new generation of feminists—male as well as female—who will forge a better future for all Americans.

DANIEL HOROWITZ

Betty Friedan and the Origins of Feminism in Cold War America

The years immediately after World War II were marked by a resurgent domesticity. The average age at marriage of women dropped sharply—by the end of the 1950s it was twenty. Women's age at the birth of their first child also decreased precipitously; the number of children per family increased sharply. The proportion of women in college fell in comparison to men; many others dropped out of college to marry or because they saw no advantage in increased education.

In 1963 Betty Friedan published *The Feminine Mystique,* a searing indictment of the triviality and frustrations of postwar domesticity (pp. 691–694). She wrote in the voice of an author who located herself in the middle-class suburbs and whose ethnicity was unmarked. But as Daniel Horowitz explains in the essay that follows, Friedan's analysis emerged not only from her experience of suburban life, but also from her experience in left-wing politics and in the labor movement—experiences she did not mention in *The Feminine Mystique.* The execution of Ethel and Julius Rosenberg for spying in 1952 frightened many progressive Jewish organizations lest they be tainted as Communist sympathizers; they would subsequently be inhospitable to reformers from the left.

(For more about Ethel Rosenberg, see the essay by Joyce Antler on pp. 607–616.) The House Un-American Activities Committee investigations that Amy Swerdlow describes on pages 617–630 continued in the late 1950s and early 1960s. Many elements of cold war politics and culture may have contributed to the choices Friedan made as she developed her voice.

In 1951, a labor journalist with a decade's experience in protest movements described a trade union meeting where rank-and-file women talked and men listened. Out of these conversations, she reported, emerged the realization that the women were "fighters—that they refuse any longer to be paid or treated as some inferior species by their bosses, or by any male workers who have swallowed the bosses' thinking."[1] The union was the UE, the United Electrical, Radio and Machine Workers of America, the most radical American union in the postwar period and in the 1940s what historian Ronald Schatz . . . has called "the largest communist-led institution of any kind in the United States."[2] In 1952 that same journalist wrote a pamphlet, *UE Fights for Women Workers,* that the historian Lisa Kannenberg, unaware of the identity of its author, has called "a remarkable manual for fighting wage discrimination that is, ironically, as relevant today as it was in 1952." At the time, the pamphlet helped raise the consciousness of Eleanor Flexner, who in 1959 would publish *Century of Struggle,* the first scholarly history of American women. In 1953–54, Flexner relied extensively on the pamphlet when she taught a course at the Jefferson School of Social Science in New York on "The Woman Question." Flexner's participation in courses at the school, she later

Daniel Horowitz, "Rethinking Betty Friedan and *The Feminine Mystique:* Labor Union Radicalism and Feminism in Cold War America," *American Quarterly* 48 (1998): 1–42. Notes have been renumbered and edited.

said, "marked the beginning of my real involvement in the issues of women's rights, my realization that leftist organizations—parties, unions—were also riddled with male supremacist prejudice and discrimination."[3] The labor journalist and pamphlet writer was Betty Friedan.

In 1973 Friedan remarked that until she started writing *The Feminine Mystique* (1963), "I wasn't even conscious of the woman problem." In 1976 she commented that in the early 1950s she was "still in the embrace of the feminine mystique."[4] Although in 1974 she revealed some potentially controversial elements of her past, even then she left the impression that her landmark book emerged only from her own captivity by the very forces she described. Friedan's portrayal of herself as so totally trapped by the feminine mystique was part of a reinvention of herself as she wrote and promoted *The Feminine Mystique.* Her story made it possible for readers to identify with its author and its author to enhance the book's appeal. However, it hid from view the connection between the union activity in which Friedan participated in the 1940s and early 1950s and the feminism she inspired in the 1960s. In the short term, her misery in the suburbs may have prompted her to write *The Feminine Mystique;* a longer term perspective makes clear that the book's origins lie much earlier—in her college education and in her experiences with labor unions in the 1940s and early 1950s.[5]. . . . Friedan's life provides evidence of. . . . continuity. . . . between the struggle for justice for working women in the 1940s and the feminism of the 1960s. This connection gives feminism and Friedan, both long under attack for a lack of interest in working class and African American women, a past of which they should be proud. . . . Moreover, a new reading of *The Feminine Mystique* sheds light on the remaking of progressive forces in America, the process by which a focus on women and the professional middle and upper middle classes supplemented, in some ways replaced a focus on unions. Finally, an examination of *The Feminine Mystique* reminds us of important shifts in the ideology of the left: from an earlier economic analysis based on Marxism to one developed in the 1950s that also rested on humanistic psychology, and from a focus on the impact of conditions of production on the working class to an emphasis on the effect of consumption on the middle class.

In print and in interviews, Friedan has offered a narrative of her life that she popularized after she became famous in 1963.[6] A full biography might begin in Peoria, where Bettye Naomi Goldstein was born February 4, 1921 and grew up with her siblings and their parents: a father who owned a jewelry store and a mother who had given up her position as a society editor of the local paper to raise a family.[7] My analysis of Friedan's political journey starts with her years at Smith College, although it is important to recognize Friedan's earlier sense of herself as someone whose identity as a Jew, a reader, and a brainy girl made her feel freakish and lonely.[8]

As an undergraduate, she has suggested, her lonely life took a turn for the better. "For the first time," she later remarked of her years in college, "I wasn't a freak for having brains." Friedan has acknowledged that she flourished at Smith, with her editorship of the student newspaper, her election to Phi Beta Kappa in her junior year, and her graduation *summa cum laude* among her most prominent achievements. She has told the story of how Gestalt psychology and Kurt Koffka (one of its three founders) were critical in her intellectual development.[9]

Friedan has described the years between her graduation from Smith in 1942 and the publication of her book twenty-one years later as a time when the feminine mystique increasingly trapped her. In her book and in dozens of speeches, articles, and interviews beginning in 1963, she mentioned a pivotal moment in her life, one that she felt marked the beginning of the process by which she succumbed. She told how, while in graduate school at Berkeley in the year after her graduation from college, the university's offer of a prestigious fellowship forced her to make a painful choice. Her first serious boyfriend, a graduate student who had not earned a similarly generous award, threatened to break off the relationship unless she turned down her fellowship. "I never could explain, hardly knew myself, why" she turned away from a career in psychology, she wrote in 1963. She decided to reject the fellowship because she saw herself ending up as an "old maid college teacher" in part because at Smith, she said, there were so few female professors who had husbands and children.[10]

The feminine mystique, she insisted, had claimed one of its first victims.[11]

After leaving Berkeley, the copy on the dust jacket of *The Feminine Mystique* noted, Friedan did some "applied social-science research" and free-lance writing for magazines. Friedan's biography in a standard reference book quotes her as saying that in the 1940s, "for conscious or unconscious reasons," she worked at "the usual kinds of boring jobs that lead nowhere."[12] This story continues in 1947 with her marriage to Carl Friedan, a returning vet who would eventually switch careers from theater to advertising and public relations. She has told of how she gave birth to three children between 1948 and 1956 and the family moved to the suburbs, with these experiences making her feel trapped. Friedan's picture of her years in the suburbs is not one of contentment and conformity.[13] Though she acknowledged her role in creating and directing a program that brought together teenagers and adult professionals, Friedan portrayed herself as someone who felt "freakish having a career, worried that she was neglecting her children."[14] In an oft-repeated story whose punch line varied, Friedan recounted her response to the census form. In the space where it asked for her occupation, she put down "housewife" but remained guilty, hesitant, and conflicted about such a designation, sometimes pausing and then adding "writer."[15]

Friedan laced *The Feminine Mystique* with suggestions of how much she shared with her suburban sisters. In the opening paragraph, she said that she realized something was wrong in women's lives when she "sensed it first as a question mark in my own life, as a wife and mother of three small children, half-guiltily, and therefore half-heartedly, almost in spite of myself, using my abilities and education in work that took me away from home." Toward the end of the paragraph, when she referred to "a strange discrepancy between the reality of our lives as women and the image to which we were trying to conform," she suggested that she experienced the feminine mystique as keenly and in the same way as her readers. Using the second person plural, she wrote that "all of us went back into the warm brightness of home" and "lowered our eyes from the horizon, and steadily contemplated our own navels." Her work on newspapers, she wrote in *The Feminine Mystique,* proceeded "with no particular plan." Indeed, she claimed that she had participated as a writer in the creation of the image of the happy housewife.[16]

Friedan asserted she embarked on a path that would lead to *The Feminine Mystique* only when, as she read over the responses of her college classmates to a questionnaire in anticipation of their fifteenth reunion in 1957, she discovered what she called "The Problem That Has No Name," the dissatisfaction her suburban peers felt but could not fully articulate. When she submitted articles to women's magazines, Friedan said, editors changed the meaning of what she had written or rejected outright her suggestions for pieces on controversial subjects. Then at a meeting of the Society of Magazine Writers, she heard Vance Packard recount how he had written *The Hidden Persuaders* (1957) after *Reader's Digest* turned down an article critical of advertising. Friedan decided to write her book.[17]

In *"It Changed My Life": Writings on the Women's Movement* (1976), a book that included a 1974 autobiographical article, Friedan suggested some of what she had omitted from earlier versions of her life.[18] Perhaps responding to attacks on her for not being sufficiently radical, she acknowledged that before her marriage and for several years after she participated in radical activities and worked for union publications.[19] She and the friends with whom she lived before marrying considered themselves in "the vanguard of the working-class revolution," participating in "Marxist discussion groups," going to political rallies, and having "only contempt for dreary bourgeois capitalists like our fathers." Without getting much more specific, Friedan noted that right after the war she was "very involved, consciously radical. Not about women, for heaven's sake!" but about African Americans, workers, the threat of war, anti-communism, and "communist splits and schisms." This was a time, Friedan reported briefly, when, working as a labor journalist, she discovered "the grubby economic underside of American reality."[20]

"I was certainly not a feminist then—none of us," she remarked in the mid-1970s, "were a bit interested in women's rights." She remembered one incident, whose implications she said she only understood much later. Covering a strike, she could not interest anyone in the fact that the company and the union discriminated against women. In 1952, she later claimed, pregnant with her second child, she was fired from her job on a union publication and told that her second pregnancy was her fault. The Newspaper Guild, she asserted, was unwilling to honor its commitment to grant pregnancy leaves. This was, Friedan later remembered, as she mentioned her efforts to call a meeting in protest, "the first personal stirring of my own feminism, I guess. But the other women were just embarrassed, and the men uncomprehending. It was my own fault, getting pregnant again, a *personal* matter, not something you should take to the union. There was no word in 1949 for 'sex discrimination.'"[21]

Though in the 1970s Friedan suggested this more interesting version of her life in the 1940s and 1950s, she distracted the reader from what she had said. She began and ended the 1974 piece with images of domestic life. Even as she mentioned participation in Marxist discussion groups, she talked of how she and her friends read fashion magazines and spent much of their earnings on elegant clothes. Describing what she offered as a major turning point in her life, she told of how, after campaigning for Henry Wallace in 1948, all of a sudden she lost interest in political activity. The 1940s and 1950s were a period, she later asserted, when she was fully exposed to what she would label the feminine mystique as she learned that motherhood took the place of career and politics. She gave the impression of herself in the late 1940s as a woman who embraced domesticity, motherhood, and housework, even as she admitted that not everything at the time resulted from the feminine mystique.[22]

In her 1974 article Friedan filled her descriptions of the late 1940s and 1950s with a sense of the conflicts she felt over her new roles, as she surrendered to the feminine mystique with mixed emotions. She reported how wonderful was the time in Parkway Village, Queens, a period when she experienced the pleasure of a spacious apartment, edited the community newspaper, and enjoyed the camaraderie of young marrieds. Yet, having read Benjamin Spock's *Child and Baby Care,* she felt guilty when she returned to work after a maternity leave. With her move to a traditional suburb, she said, the conflicts intensified. She spoke of driving her children to school and lessons, participating in the PTA, and then, when neighbors came by, hiding "like secret drinking in the morning" the book she was working on.[23]

Accomplishing practical, specific tasks around the house and in local politics was "somehow more real and secure than the schizophrenic and even dangerous politics of the world revolution whose vanguard we used to fancy ourselves." Friedan remarked that by 1949 she realized that the revolution was not going to happen in the United States as she anticipated, in part because workers, like others, wanted kitchen gadgets. She reported that she found herself disillusioned with what was happening in unions, in Czechoslovakia, and in the Soviet Union, despite the fact that cries about the spread of Communism merely provided the pretext for attacks on suspected subversives. In those days, she continued, "McCarthyism, the danger of war against Russia and of fascism in America, and the reality of U.S. imperial, corporate wealth and power" combined to make those who once dreamed of "making the whole world over uncomfortable with the Old Left rhetoric of revolution." Using the first person plural as she referred to Margaret Mead's picture in *Male and Female* (1949) of women fulfilled through motherhood and domesticity, Friedan wrote, "we were suckers for that apple." It hardly occurred to any of those in her circle, who themselves now wanted new gadgets, that large corporations profited from marketing household appliances by "overselling us on the bliss of domesticity."[24]

The new information Friedan offered in 1974 did not dislodge the accepted understanding of how she became a feminist . . . [Yet] what the written record reveals of Friedan's life from her arrival at Smith in the fall of 1938 until the publication of *The Feminine Mystique* makes possible a story different from the one she has told. To begin with, usually missing from her narrative is full and specific information about how at college she first developed a sense of herself as a radical.[25] Courses she took, friendships she established with peers and professors, events in the United States and abroad, and her campus leadership all turned Friedan from a provincial outsider into a determined advocate of trade unions as the herald of progressive social change, a healthy skeptic about the authority and rhetorical claims of those in power, a staunch opponent of fascism, a defender of free speech, and a fierce questioner of social privilege expressed by the conspicuous consumption of some of her peers.[26]

What and with whom she studied points well beyond Gestalt psychology and Koffka.[27] Though Friedan acknowledged the importance of James Gibson, she did not mention his activity as an advocate of trade unions.[28] Moreover, her statement that at Smith there were few role models is hard to reconcile with the fact that the college had a number of them; indeed she took courses from both James Gibson and Eleanor Gibson, husband and wife and parents of two children, the first of them born in 1940.[29] As a women's college, and especially one with an adversarial tradition, Smith may well have fostered in Friedan a feminism that was at least implicit—by enabling her to assume leadership positions and by encouraging her to take herself seriously as a writer and thinker.

In the fall of her junior year, Friedan took an economics course taught by Dorothy W. Douglas, Theories and Movements for Social Reconstruction. Douglas was well known at the time for her radicalism.[30] In what she wrote for Douglas, and with youthful enthusiasm characteristic of many members of her generation, Friedan sympathetically responded to the Marxist critique of capitalism as a cultural, economic, and political force.[31]

Friedan also gained an education as a radical in the summer of 1941 when, following Douglas's suggestion, she participated in a writers' workshop at the Highlander Folk School in Tennessee, an institution active in helping the CIO organize in the South. The school offered a series of summer institutes for fledgling journalists which, for 1939 and 1940 (but not 1941), the communist-led League of American Writers helped sponsor. For three years beginning in the fall of 1939, opponents of Highlander had sustained a vicious redbaiting attack, but a FBI investigator found no evidence of subversive activity.[32] In good Popular Front language, Friedan praised Highlander as a truly American institution that was attempting to help America to fulfill its democratic ideals. She explored the contradictions of her social position as a Jewish girl from a well-to-do family who had grown up in a class-divided Peoria, gave evidence of her hostility to the way her parents fought over issues of debt and extravagance, and described the baneful influence of the mass media on American life. Though she also acknowledged that her Smith education did "not lead to much action," she portrayed herself as someone whose radical consciousness relied on the American labor movement as the bulwark against fascism.[33]

At Smith Friedan linked her journalism to political activism. She served as editor-in-chief of the campus newspaper for a year beginning in the spring of 1941. The campaigns she undertook and the editorials she wrote reveal a good deal of her politics. Under Friedan's leadership, the newspaper's reputation for protest was so strong that in a skit a fellow student portrayed an editor, perhaps Friedan herself, as "a strident voice haranguing from a perpetual soap-box.[34] While at Smith, a Peoria paper reported in 1943, Friedan helped organize college building and grounds workers into a union.[35] Under her leadership, the student paper took on the student government for holding closed meetings, fought successfully to challenge the administration's right to control what the newspaper printed, campaigned for the relaxation of restrictions on student social life, censured social clubs for their secrecy, and published critiques of professors' teaching.[36] In response to an article in a campus humor magazine that belittled female employees who cleaned the students' rooms and served them food, an editorial supported the administration's censorship of the publication on the grounds that such action upheld "the liberal democratic tradition of the college."[37]

The editorials written on her watch reveal a young woman who believed that what was involved with almost every issue—at Smith, in the United States and abroad—was the struggle for democracy, freedom, and social justice. Under Friedan's leadership the editors supported American workers and their labor unions in their struggles to organize and improve their conditions. . . . The inequality of power in America, the editorial argued in good social democratic terms, "has to be admitted and dealt with if democracy is to have meaning for 95% of the citizens of this country."[38]

Above all, what haunted the editorials was the spread of fascism and questions about America's involvement in a world war. In April of 1941, the editors made it clear that the defeat of fascism was their primary goal and one that determined their position on questions of war or peace. In the fall of 1941, after the German invasion of the Soviet Union during the preceding summer, the editors increasingly accepted the inevitability of war even as they made it clear that they believed "fighting fascists is only one part of fighting fascism."[39] Some Smith students responded with redbaiting to the newspaper's anti-fascism and reluctance to support intervention wholeheartedly, accusing the editorial board of being dominated by communists, at a time when the Party reached its greatest membership in the years after Pearl Harbor while the United States and the Soviet Union were allies. Though one editor denied the charge of communist influence, like many newspapers at American colleges in these years, on the paper's staff were students attracted to the political analysis offered by radical groups. In the fall of 1940 one columnist argued against lumping communists and Nazis together, remarking that communism was not a "dark terror" but "a precarious scheme worked out by millions of civilized men and women."[40]

When America entered the war in December of 1941, the editors accepted the nation's new role loyally, albeit soberly. The central issue for them was how American students, especially female ones, could "contribute actively to the American cause." . . .

Friedan's experiences at Smith cast a different light on her decision to leave Berkeley after a year of graduate school. The editorials she and her peers had written immediately after Pearl Harbor revealed an impatience to be near the action. A 1943 article in the Peoria paper reported that Friedan turned down the fellowship because "she decided she wanted to work in the labor movement—on the labor press."[41] . . . Off and on from October 1943 until July 1946 she was a staff writer for the Federated Press, a left-wing news service that provided stories for newspapers, especially union ones, across the nation.[42] Here Friedan wrote articles that supported the aspirations of African Americans and union members. She also criticized reactionary forces that, she believed, were working secretly to undermine progressive social advances.[43] As early as 1943, she pictured efforts by businesses, coordinated by the National Association of Manufacturers (NAM), to develop plans that would enhance profits, diminish the power of unions, reverse the New Deal, and allow businesses to operate as they pleased.[44]

At Federated Press, Friedan also paid attention to women's problems. Right after she began to work there, she interviewed UE official Ruth Young, one of the clearest voices in the labor movement articulating women's issues. In the resulting article, Friedan noted that the government could not solve the problem of turnover "merely by pinning up thousands of glamorous posters designed to lure more women into industry." Neither women, unions, nor management, she quoted Young as saying, could solve problems of escalating prices or inadequate child care that were made even more difficult by the fact that "women still have two jobs to do." Action of the federal government, Friedan reported, was needed to solve the problems working women faced.[45]

She paid special attention to stories about protecting the jobs and improving the situation of working women, including married ones with children.

For about six years beginning in July, 1946, precisely at the moment when the wartime Popular Front came under intense attack, Friedan was a reporter for the union's paper *UE News*.[46] At least as early as 1943, when she quoted Young, Friedan was well aware of the UE's commitments to equity for women.[47]

. . . In 1949–50, union activists who followed the recommendations of the Communist Party . . . advocated the automatic granting of several years of seniority to all African Americans as compensation for their years of exclusion from the electrical industry. If the UE pioneered in articulating what we might call affirmative action for African Americans, then before and during World War II it advocated what a later generation would label comparable worth. Against considerable resistance from within its ranks, the UE also worked to improve the conditions of working-class women in part by countering a seniority system which gave advantage to men.[48] After 1949, with the UE out of the CIO and many of the more conservative union members out of the UE, women's issues and women's leadership resumed the importance they had in the UE during World War II, when it had developed, Ruth Milkman has written, a "strong ideological commitment to gender equality."[49]

Beginning in 1946, Friedan [also] witnessed the efforts by federal agencies, congressional committees, major corporations, the Roman Catholic Church, and the CIO to break the hold of what they saw as the domination of the UE by communists. The inclusion of a clause in the Taft-Hartley Act of 1947, requiring union officers to sign an anticommunist affidavit if they wished to do business with the National Labor Relations Board, helped encourage other unions to challenge the UE, whose leaders refused to sign.[50] Internecine fights took place within the UE, part of a longer term fight between radicals and anticommunists in its ranks. . . . Before long, . . . the UE was greatly weakened: in 1949, its connection with the CIO was severed and the newly-formed and CIO-backed IUE recruited many of its members. Membership in UE, numbering more than 600,000 in 1946, fell to 203,000 in 1953 and to 71,000 four years later.[51]

At *UE News,* from her position as a middle-class woman interested in the lives of the working class, Friedan continued to articulate a progressive position on a wide range of issues. She again pointed to concerted efforts, led by big corporations under the leadership of the NAM, to increase profits, exploit labor, and break labor unions.[52] In 1951, she contrasted the extravagant expenditures of the wealthy with the family of a worker who could afford neither fresh vegetables nor new clothes.[53] Friedan also told the story of how valiant union members helped build political coalitions to fight Congressional and corporate efforts to roll back gains workers made during the New Deal and World War II.[54] She drew parallels between the United States in the 1940s and Nazi Germany in the 1930s as she exposed the way HUAC and big business were using every tactic they could to destroy the UE. Friedan hailed the launching of the Progressive Party in 1948.[55] She exposed the existence of racism and discrimination, even when they appeared among union officials and especially when directed against Jews and African Americans. Praising heroic workers who struggled against great odds as they fought monopolies, Friedan, probably expressing her hopes for herself, extolled the skills of a writer "who is able to describe with sincerity and passion the hopes, the struggle and the romance of the working people who make up most of America."[56]

Throughout her years at *UE News,* Friedan participated in discussions on women's issues, including the issue of corporations' systematic discrimination against women. Going to factories to interview those whose stories she was covering, she also wrote about working women, including African Americans and Latinas.[57] In the worlds Friedan inhabited in the decade beginning in 1943, as the historian Kathleen Weigand has shown, people often discussed the cultural and economic sources of women's oppression, the nature of discrimination based on sex, the special difficulties African American women faced, and the dynamics of discrimination against women in a variety of institutions, including the family.[58] Moreover, for the people around Friedan and doubtlessly for Friedan herself, the fight for justice for women was inseparable from the more general struggle to secure rights for African Americans and workers.[59] As she had done at the Federated Press, at *UE News* in the late 1940s and early 1950s she reported on how working women struggled as producers and consumers to make sure their families had enough to live on.[60]

Friedan's focus on working women's issues resulted in her writing the pamphlet, *UE Fights for Women Workers,* published by the UE in June of 1952.[61] She began by suggesting the contradiction in industry's treatment of women as consumers and as producers. "In advertisements across the land," Friedan remarked, "industry glorifies the American woman—in her gleaming GE kitchen, at her Westinghouse laundromat, before her Sylvania television set. Nothing," she announced as she insightfully explored a central contradiction women faced in the postwar world, "is too good for her—unless" she worked for corporations, including GE, or Westinghouse, or Sylvania.[62]

The central theme of the piece was how, in an effort to improve the pay and conditions of working women, the UE fought valiantly against greedy corporations that sought to increase their profits by exploiting women. Friedan discussed a landmark 1945 National War Labor Board decision on sex-based wage discrimination in favor of the UE. Remarking that *"fighting the exploitation of women is men's business too,"* she emphasized how discriminatory practices corporations used against women hurt men as well by exerting downward pressure on wages of all workers. To back up the call for equal pay for equal work and to fight against segregation and discrimination of women, she countered stereotypes justifying lower pay for women: they were physically weaker, entered the work force only temporarily, had no families to support, and worked only for pin money. She highlighted the "even more shocking" situation African American women faced, having to deal as they did with the "double bars" of being female and African American.[63] Friedan set forth a program that was, Lisa Kannenberg has noted, "a prescription for a gender-blind workplace."[64]

The conditions under which she left Federated Press and *UE News* are not entirely clear. In May of 1946, during her second stint at Federated Press, she filed a grievance with the Newspaper Guild, saying she had lost her job in June of 1945 to a man she had replaced during the war. Later she claimed she was "bumped" from her position "by a returning veteran." There is evidence, however, that Friedan had to give up her position to a man who returned to the paper after two years in prison because he refused to serve in the military during what he considered a capitalists' war.[65] Friedan later claimed that she lost her job at the UE during her second pregnancy because the labor movement failed to honor its commitment to maternity leaves. Yet a knowledgeable observer has written that when the union had to cut the staff because of the dramatic drop in its membership, something that resulted from McCarthyite attacks, Friedan "offered to quit so another reporter," a man with more seniority, could remain at *UE News*.[66] Although her experience with unions may have provided a negative spur to her feminism, it also served as a positive inspiration. Friedan was indebted to the UE for major elements of her education about gender equity, sex discrimination, and women's issues.

The reason Friedan left out these years in her life story is now clear. Her stint at the *UE News* took place at the height of the anti-communist crusade, which she experienced at close quarters. When she emerged into the limelight in 1963, the issue of affiliation with communists was wracking SANE, SDS, and the civil rights movement. In the same years, HUAC was still holding hearings, the United States was pursuing an anti-communist war in Vietnam, and J. Edgar Hoover's FBI was wiretapping Martin Luther King, Jr., ostensibly to protect the nation against communist influence. Had Friedan revealed all in the mid-1960s, she would have undercut her book's impact, subjected herself to palpable dangers, and jeopardized the feminist movement, including the National Organization for Women (NOW), an institution she was instrumental in launching. Perhaps instead of emphasizing continuities in her life, she told the story of her conversion in order to heighten the impact of her book and appeal to white middle-class women. Or . . . Friedan may have come to believe a narrative that outlived the needs it originally fulfilled.

Until 1952, almost everything Friedan published as a labor journalist appeared under the name Betty Goldstein, though she had married in 1947. When she emerged as a writer for women's magazines in 1955, it was as Betty Friedan. Aside from indicating her marital status, the change in name was significant. It signaled a shift from an employee for a union paper who wrote highly political articles on the working class to a free-lance writer for mass circulation magazines who concentrated on the suburban middle class in more muted tones [and in the 1950s became a suburbanite herself. In 1957, the Friedans moved into an] eleven-room Victorian house, which they bought with the help of the GI Bill and some money Friedan inherited from her father.[67]

What Friedan wrote for mass circulation women's magazines [during those years] belies her claim that she had contributed to what she later attacked in *The Feminine Mystique*.

Sylvie Murray has demonstrated that Friedan drafted, but was unable to get into print, articles that fully celebrated women's political activism, expressed skepticism about male expertise, and described blue collar and lower middle-class families, not generic middle-class ones. Yet Friedan was able to sell articles that went against the grain of the cold war celebration by criticizing middle-class conformity. . . . Friedan critiqued suburban life by drawing a dismal picture of those who conformed, by offering alternatives to conventional choices, and by exploring the strength of cooperative communities.[68] She drew portraits of American women that opposed the picture of the happy, suburban housewife who turned her back on a career in order to find satisfaction at home.[69] Friedan also portrayed women accomplishing important tasks as they took on traditionally feminine civic roles, thus implicitly undercutting the ideal of the apolitical suburban housewife and mother.[70]

In one particularly revealing piece, Friedan prefigured some of the issues she later claimed she only began to discover when she started to work on *The Feminine Mystique.* In "I Went Back to Work," published in *Charm* in April 1955, she wrote that initially she did not think highly of housework or of housewives and was guilty about what she was doing. Eventually she decided that her commitment to being a good mother was not "going to interfere with what I regarded as my 'real' life." Finding it necessary to be away from home for nine hours a day in order to work, she solved the problem of child care by hiring "a really good mother-substitute—a housekeeper-nurse." In the end, Friedan had no regrets about her decision or apparently about her privileged position. She believed her work outside the home improved her family's situation and acknowledged that her "whole life had always been geared around creative, intellectual work" and "a professional career."[71]

In what ways, then, was Friedan a captive of the feminine mystique? There is no question but that she was miserable in the suburbs. Her emphasis on her captivity may have expressed one part of her ambivalence. Yet, though she claimed that she shared so much with her suburban, white, middle-class sisters in the postwar world, during much of the two decades beginning in 1943 Friedan was participating in left-wing union activity, writing articles that went against the grain of cold war ideology, and living in a cosmopolitan, racially integrated community. During most of the time between her marriage in 1947 and the publication of *The Feminine Mystique,* Friedan combined career and family life. As a woman who worked with her at Federated Press later noted, at the time Friedan and her female colleagues expected to have professional careers.[72] Caution about the predominantly suburban origins of her book is also in order because Friedan's move to suburban Rockland County in 1956 preceded by only a few months her initial work on the survey for her reunion that was so critical to *The Feminine Mystique.*[73]

To be sure, in the postwar world Friedan experienced at first hand the trials of a woman who fought against considerable odds to combine marriage, motherhood, and a career.[74] Yet in critical ways her difficulties did not stem from the dilemmas she described in her book: lack of career and ambition, a securely affluent household, and absence of a political sensibility. Friedan experienced psychological conflicts over issues of creativity in writing and motherhood.[75] Researching and writing her free-lance articles was a laborious process.[76] She had three young children, hardly felt comfortable in the suburbs, had no local institutions to provide a supportive environment for an aspiring writer, and continually faced financial difficulties. Her income from writing articles was unpredictable, a situation exacerbated by the pressure she was under to help support the household and justify the expenses for child care. Tension persisted between the Friedans over a wide range of issues, including who was responsible for earning and spending the family's income. Moreover, she was in a marriage apparently marked by violence.[77]

Friedan was largely right when she said "all the pieces of my own life came together for the first time in the writing" of *The Feminine Mystique.* The skills as a journalist she had developed beginning as a teenager stood her in good stead as she worked to make what she had to say accessible to a wide audience. Her identity as a Jew and an outsider gave her a distinctive perspective on American and suburban life. Her years at Smith boosted her confidence and enhanced her political education. Her life as a wife and mother sensitized her to the conflicts millions of others experienced but could not articulate. Her education as a psychologist led her to understand the gestalt, the wholeness of a situation, and to advocate self-fulfillment based on humanistic psychology. Above all, her work as a labor journalist and activist provided her with the intellectual depth, ideological commitments, and practical experiences crucial to her emergence as a leading feminist in the 1960s.

Why did a woman who had spent so much energy advocating political solutions focus in *The Feminine Mystique* largely on adult education and self-realization and turn social problems into psychological ones? How did a woman who had fought to improve the lives of African Americans, Latinas, and working-class women end up writing a book that saw the problems of America in terms of the lives of affluent, suburban white women?[78]

Even at the time, at least one observer, Gerda Lerner, raised questions about what Friedan emphasized and neglected. Active in the trade union movement in the 1940s, present at the founding meeting of NOW, and after the mid-1960s one of the nation's leading historians of women, in February 1963 Lerner wrote Friedan. "I have just finished reading your splendid book and want to tell you how excited and delighted I am with it. . . . You have done for women," she remarked as she referred to the author who had warned about the destruction of the environment, "what Rachel Carson did for birds and trees." Yet, Lerner continued:

> I have one reservation about your treatment of your subject: you address yourself solely to the problems of middle class, college-educated women. This approach was one of the shortcomings of the suffrage movement for many years and has, I believe, retarded the general advance of women. Working women, especially Negro women, labor not only under the disadvantages imposed by the feminine mystique, but under the more pressing disadvantages of economic discrimination. To leave them out of consideration of the problem or to ignore the contributions they can make toward its solution, is something we simply cannot afford to do. By their desperate need, by their numbers, by their organizational experience (if trade union members), working women are most important in reaching *institutional* solutions to the problems of women.[79]

The dynamics of Friedan's shifts in attention from working-class to middle-class women are not entirely clear. At some point after May 1953, when she followed the proceedings at the UE conference on the problems of women workers, Friedan turned away from working-class and African American women, something that undercut the power of *The Feminine Mystique*. An important question is whether the shift from her UE radicalism and focus on working-class women was a rhetorical strategy designed for the specific situation of *The Feminine Mystique* or part of a longer-term deradicalization. Until her personal papers are fully open and extensive interviewing is carried out, and perhaps not even then, we may not know the dynamics of this change.

NOTES

1. Betty Goldstein, "UE Drive on Wage, Job Discrimination Wins Cheers from Women Members," *UE News*, 16 Apr. 1951, 6. My interview of Friedan in 1987 first brought to my attention the possibility of this alternative story, as did the research my colleague, Helen L. Horowitz, carried out in the late 1980s. The appearance of the article by Joanne Meyerowitz in 1993, cited below, added an important piece of evidence. Because Friedan has denied me permission to quote from her unpublished papers and has not responded to my request that she grant me an opportunity to interview her or to have her respond to my questions, I have not been able to present as full and perhaps as accurate a story as I wished to do.

2. Ronald W. Schatz, *The Electrical Workers: A History of Labor at General Electric and Westinghouse, 1923–60* (Urbana, III., 1983), xiii.

3. Lisa Kannenberg, "The Impact of the Cold War on Women's Trade Union Activism: The UE Experience," *Labor History* 34 (spring-summer 1993): 318; Jacqueline Van Voris, interview with Eleanor Flexner, Northampton, Mass., 16 Oct. 1982, 70–71, Eleanor Flexner Papers, Schlesinger Library, Radcliffe College, Cambridge, Mass. [hereinafter cited as FP-SLRC]; [Eleanor Flexner], "The Woman Question," Syllabus for course at Jefferson School of Social Science, 1953–54, 1, 2, 5. For information on Flexner. I am relying on Ellen C. DuBois, "Eleanor Flexner and the History of American Feminism," *Gender and History* 3 (spring 1991): 81–90. On the Jefferson School, see Annette T. Rubinstein, "David Goldway," *Science and Society* 54 (winter 1990–91): 386–89; Daniel F. Ring, "Two Cultures: Libraries, the Unions, and the 'Case' of the Jefferson School of Social Science," *Journal of Library History* 20 (1985): 287–88.

4. Betty Friedan, "Up From the Kitchen Floor," *New York Times Magazine*, 4 Mar. 1973, 8; Betty Friedan, *"It Changed My Life": Writings on the Women's Movement* (New York, 1976), 304.

5. For evidence of the continuing importance of Friedan and her book, see, for example, Elaine T. May, *Homeward Bound: American Families in the Cold War Era* (New York, 1988), 209–17, 219 and Joanne Meyerowitz, "Beyond the Feminine Mystique: A Reassessment of Postwar Mass Culture, 1946–1958," *Journal of American History* 79 (Mar. 1993): 1455–82. For textbooks, see John M. Faragher et al., *Out of Many: A History of the American People* (Englewood Cliffs, N.J., 1994), 2:865, 943; James A. Henretta et al., *America's History*, 2d ed. (New York, 1993), 2:909, 910, 911, 968; William H. Chafe, *The Unfinished Journey: America Since World War II*, 3d ed. (New York, 1995), 124, 330, 433. A widely-used reader in American women's history contains a selection from Friedan's book, introducing its author as "a suburban housewife": Linda K. Kerber and Jane S. De Hart, *Women's America: Refocusing the Past*, 4th ed. (New York, 1995), 512.

6. For biographical information, in addition to what Friedan has said in print, I am relying on Kathleen Wilson, "Betty (Naomi) Friedan," *Contemporary Authors*, New Revision Series (New York, 1995) 45: 133–36; David Halberstam, *The Fifties* (New York, 1993), 592–98; Marilyn French, "The Emancipation of Betty Friedan," *Esquire* 100 (Dec. 1983): 510, 512, 514, 516, 517; Jennifer Moses, "She's Changed Our

Lives: A Profile of Betty Friedan," *Present Tense* 15 (May–June 1988): 26–31; Lyn Tornabene, "The Liberation of Betty Friedan," *McCall's* 98 (May 1971): 84, 136–40, 142, 146; Paul Wilkes, "Mother Superior to Women's Lib," *New York Times Magazine*, 29 Nov. 1970, 27–29, 140–43, 149–50, 157; Marcia Cohen, *The Sisterhood: The True Story of the Women Who Changed the World* (New York, 1988), 25, 54–71, 83–84, 89–99; Lisa Hammel, "The 'Grandmother' of Women's Lib," *New York Times*, 19 Nov. 1971, 52; Friedan, *Changed My Life*, 5–16; Jacqueline Van Voris, interview of Betty Friedan, New York, N.Y., 17 Apr. 1973, College Archives, Smith College, Northampton, Mass. [hereinafter cited as CA-SC]; Daniel Horowitz, interview of Betty Friedan, Santa Monica, Calif., 18 Mar. 1987. As late as 6 Nov. 1995, the date she sent me a letter denying me permission to quote from her unpublished papers, Friedan reiterated key elements of her story: I am grateful to Rachel Ledford for reporting to me on Friedan's 6 Nov. 1995 talk at the Smithsonian Institution, Washington, D.C. Ironically, two biographies aimed at children provide fuller stories than do other treatments (for instance, they are the only published sources I have been able to locate that make clear that Friedan worked for the UE): Sondra Henry and Emily Taitz, *Betty Friedan: Fighter for Women's Rights* (Hillside, N.J., 1990) and Milton Meltzer, *Betty Friedan: A Voice for Women's Rights* (New York, 1985).

7. This article is based on considerable but hardly exhaustive examination of the available written record. When other researchers examine the Friedan papers (including those to which access is restricted) and are able to carry out extensive interviews, they will be able to offer a fuller exploration of several issues, especially the shifts in Friedan's commitments as a radical at a time of great factionalism, when and how the feminine mystique did or did not trap her, how she interpreted the research on which *The Feminine Mystique* relied, and the pressures Friedan faced from her publisher to shape her 1963 book in certain ways.

8. An examination of what Friedan wrote for her high school paper reveals someone less lonely than she has often portrayed herself: see articles by Friedan in *Peoria Opinion* from the fall of 1936 until the spring of 1938. For one political piece that reveals an early anti-fascism, see Bettye Goldstein, "Long, Coughlin, Roosevelt in 'It Can't Happen Here,'" *Peoria Opinion*, 18 Sept. 1936, 8.

9. Friedan, quoted in Wilkes, "Mother Superior," 140; Betty Friedan, *The Feminine Mystique* (New York, 1963), 12.

10. Friedan, *Feminine Mystique*, 70; Friedan, quoted in Wilkes, "Mother Superior," 140. On the paucity of role models at Smith, see Van Voris, Friedan interview.

11. Horowitz, interview.

12. Dust jacket of 1963 copy of *The Feminine Mystique*, author's possession. See also, "About Betty Friedan . . . ," biographical note accompanying Betty Friedan, "How to Find and Develop Article Ideas," *The Writer* 75 (Mar. 1962), 13.

13. Friedan, quoted in "Betty Friedan," *Current Biography Yearbook 1970*, ed. Charles Moritz (New York, 1971), 146; Betty Friedan, "New York Women: Beyond the Feminine Mystique," *New York Herald Tribune*, 21 Feb. 1965, 7–15, women's liberation, biographics, individuals, box 4, folder 31, clippings on Betty Friedan, Sophia Smith Collection, Smith College [hereinafter referred to as SSC-SC]; Wilkes, "Mother Superior," 141; Friedan, quoted in Wilkes, "Mother Superior," 141; Tornabene, "Liberation," 138; and Friedan, "Kitchen Floor," 8.

14. Tornabene, "Liberation," 138. See Betty Friedan, "The Intellectual Pied Pipers of Rockland County," unpublished paper, written in 1960–61, FP-SLRC, carton 9, folder 347, Friedan Collection, Schlesinger Library, Radcliffe College, Cambridge, Mass. [hereinafter cited as BF-SLRC; unless otherwise noted, the references are to collection 71-62 . . . 81-M23].

15. Rollene W. Saal, "Author of the Month," *Saturday Review*, 21 Mar. 1964, women's liberation, biographies, individuals, box 4, folder 31, SSC-SC; *Hackensack Record*, 2 May 1963, Class of 1942 folders, Betty Goldstein folder, CA-SC; Friedan, "Kitchen Floor," 8.

16. Friedan, *Feminine Mystique*, 9, 20, 66, 70, 186–87.

17. Horowitz, interview: Betty Friedan, "Introduction to the Tenth Anniversary Edition" of *Feminine Mystique* (New York, 1974), 1–5. For early articles with the themes that would emerge in the book, see Betty Friedan, "I Say: Women are *People* Too!" *Good Housekeeping* 151 (Sept. 1960): 59–61, 161–62; Betty Goldstein Friedan, "If One Generation Can Ever Tell Another," *Smith Alumnae Quarterly*, Feb. 1961, 68–70.

18. The 1974 article, which in the book was called "The Way We Were—1949," was originally published with some relatively unimportant differences, but with a more revealing title, as Betty Friedan, "In France, de Beauvoir Had Just Published 'The Second Sex,'" *New York* 8 (30 Dec. 1974–6 Jan. 1975): 52–55. In Horowitz, interview, which covered mainly the years up to 1963, Friedan discussed her move to a radical politics even as she emphasized captivity by the feminine mystique beginning in the Berkeley years. Though Friedan has revealed a good deal about her life, to the best of my knowledge she has not acknowledged in print the full range of reasons she left Berkeley, that she worked for the UE, her authorship of the 1952 pamphlet, and her leadership of the rent strike. Moreover, she has insisted that in the late 1940s and early 1950s, she had interest neither in a career nor in women's problems.

19. I am grateful to Judith Smith for helping me to think through this and other issues.

20. Friedan, *Changed My Life*, 6, 8–9.

21. Friedan, *Changed My Life*, 6, 9, 16; Halberstam, *Fifties*, 593; French, "Emancipation," 510. Horowitz, interview, dates the firing in 1952. In the immediate postwar years, the term "feminist" often referred to women who were Republicans, independent businesswomen, and professionals.

22. Friedan, *Changed My Life*, 5, 6–7, 8–9, 15, 16. She gave 1949 as the turning point because she had been asked to do a piece in 1974 on what had happened a quarter of a century earlier: Horowitz, interview.

23. Friedan, *Changed My Life*, 14–16.

24. Friedan, *Changed My Life*, 12, 16.

25. Cohen, *Sisterhood*, 63 and Wilkes, "Mother Superior," 140 briefly draw a picture of Friedan as a college rebel but to the best of my knowledge, the politics of that rebellion have remained largely unknown.

26. This summary relies on unsigned editorials that appeared under Friedan's editorship, which can be found in *SCAN* [*Smith College Associated News*] from 14 Mar. 1941 to 10 Mar. 1942, p. 2. Although members of the editorial board held a wide range of opinions. I am assuming that as editor-in-chief Friedan had a significant role in shaping editorials. Friedan placed four editorials in her papers: "They Believed in Peace," "Years of Change and Unrest," "Behind Closed Doors," and "Answer No Answer": carton 7, folder 310, BF-SLRC.

27. For the article she published on the basis on her honors thesis, see H. Israel and B. Goldstein, "Operationism in Psychology," *Psychological Review* 51 (May 1944): 177–88.

28. See James J. Gibson, "Why a Union For Teachers?" *Focus* 2 (Nov. 1939): 3–7.

29. I am grateful to Margery Sly, Archivist of Smith College, for providing this information. She has also pointed out that teaching at Smith in Friedan's years were several married, female faculty members who had children and that Harold Israel and Elsa Siipola, two of Friedan's mentors, were married but without children.

30. In 1955 Douglas took the Fifth Amendment before HUAC as she was redbaited, accused of having been a member of a communist teachers union in the late 1930s. I am grateful to Margery Sly and Jacquelyn D. Hall for providing this information on Douglas. See also, Betty Friedan, "Was Their Education UnAmerican?" unpublished article, 1953 or 1954, carton 11, folder 415, BF-SLRC, 3. For Friedan's continued use of Marxist analysis, see Friedan, *It Changed My Life*, 110.

31. Bettye Goldstein, "Discussion of Reading Period Material," paper for Economics 319, 18 Jan. 1941, carton 1, folder 257, BF-SLRC, 1, 2, 4, 8. See also "Questions on *Communist Manifesto*" and "Questions on Imperialism," papers for Economics 319, carton 1, folder 257, BF-SLRC.

32. John M. Glen, *Highlander: No Ordinary School, 1932–1962* (Lexington, Ky., 1988), 47–69. I am grateful to Professor Glen for a letter in which he clarified the timing of the League's sponsorship. Meltzer, *Friedan*, 20 says that Friedan's economics professor pointed her to Highlander but identifies that professor as a male; since the only economics course Friedan took was from Douglas, I am assuming that it was she who urged her student to attend the workshop. Meltzer thinks that is a reasonable assumption: Milton Meltzer, phone conversation with Daniel Horowitz, 24 Sept. 1995.

33. Bettye Goldstein, "Highlander Folk School—American Future," unpublished paper, 1941, carton 6, folder 274, BF-SLRC; Goldstein, "Learning the Score," 22–24.

34. "Epilogue of Failure," *SCAN*, 10 Mar. 1942, 2.

35. "Betty Goldstein, Local Girl, Makes Good in New York," clipping from Peoria newspaper, probably 10 Dec. 1943 issue of *Labor Temple News*, carton 1, folder 86, BF-SLRC.

36. "Behind a Closed Door," *SCAN*, 3 Oct. 1941, 2; "Declaration of Student Independence," *SCAN*, 5 Dec. 1941, 1–2; "SCAN Protests Against Censorship," *SCAN*, 5 Dec. 1941, 1; "A Few Hours More," *SCAN*, 10 Oct. 1941, 2; "Review of Philosophy Courses," *SCAN*, 10 Mar. 1942, 2.

37. "The Tatler Suspension," *SCAN*, 7 Nov. 1941, 2; for the article in question see "Maids We Have Known and Loved," *Tatler*, Oct. 1941, 9, 21. When the administration moved against *SCAN*, over a different incident, the editors changed their minds about the earlier suspension of the *Tatler: SCAN*, 5 Dec. 1941, 1–2.

38. "Education in Emergency," *SCAN*, 15 Apr. 1941, 2; "The Right to Organize," *SCAN*, 21 Oct. 1941, 2; "Comment," *SCAN*, 14 Nov. 1941, 2; Filene's advertisement, *SCAN*, 21 Oct. 1941, 2. Bettye Goldstein, "For Defense of Democracy," *Smith College Monthly* 1 (Oct. 1940): 11, 12, 28 is a passionate defense of democracy and a warning about the possibility of American fascism.

39. "They Choose Peace," *SCAN*, 22 Apr. 1941, 2; for the minority opinion, see "The Case for Intervention," *SCAN*, 2 May 1941, 2; "War Against Fascism," *SCAN*, 24 Oct. 1941, 2. Placing the editorials written on Friedan's watch in the national context of student politics makes clear that after the Nazi-Soviet pact the student movement was more active and radical at Smith than elsewhere. In addition, the commitment of Friedan and her fellow editors to anti-fascism and their reluctance to embrace interventionism fully after the German invasion of the Soviet Union suggests that they dissented from the Communist Party position. On the national context see Robert Cohen, *When The Old Left Was Young: Student Radicals and America's First Mass Student Movement, 1929–1941* (New York, 1993), especially 315–37.

40. J. N., "The Red Menace," *SCAN*, 14 Oct. 1941, 2; Neal Gilkyson, "The Gallery," *SCAN*, 21 Oct. 1941, 2.

41. "Betty Goldstein, Local Girl," Meltzer, *Friedan*, 21 provides explanations for Friedan's decision that do not rely on the standard story.

42. To date her work for the Federated Press, see Betty Friedan, job application for Time Inc., 1 July 1951, carton 1, folder 61, BF-SLRC. For information on the Federated Press, see Doug Reynolds, "Federated Press," *Encyclopedia of the American Left*, ed. Mari Jo Buhle, Paul Buhle, and Dan Georgakas (New York, 1990), 225–27.

43. Betty Goldstein, "Negro Pupils Segregated, Parents Strike; Issue Headed for Courts," Federated Press, 15 Sept. 1943, carton 8, folder 328, BF-SLRC; Betty Goldstein, "Peace Now: Treason in Pious Garb," Federated Press, 16 Feb. 1944, carton 8, folder 328, BF-SLRC; Betty Goldstein, "Well-Heeled 'White Collar League' Seen as Disguised Native Fascist Threat," Federated Press, 16 Mar. 1944, carton 8, folder 328, BF-SLRC.

44. Betty Goldstein, "Big Business Getting Desperate, Promising Postwar Jobs," Federated Press, 19 Nov. 1943, carton 8, folder 328, BF-SLRC; Betty Goldstein, "NAM Convention Pro-War—For War on Labor, New Deal, Roosevelt," Federated Press, 14 Dec. 1943, carton 8, folder 328, BF-SLRC; Betty Goldstein, "Details of Big Business Anti-Labor Conspiracy Uncovered," Federated Press, 11 Feb. 1946,

carton 8, folder 328, BF-SLRC. For the larger story, see Elizabeth A. Fones-Wolf, *Selling Free Enterprise: The Business Assault on Labor and Liberalism, 1945–60* (Urbana, 1994).

45. Betty Goldstein, "Pretty Posters Won't Stop Turnover of Women in Industry," Federated Press, 26 Oct. 1943, and Ruth Young quoted in same, carton 8, folder 328, BF-SLRC.

46. Job application, 1951.

47. For information on women in the UE see Schatz, *Electrical Workers;* Ruth Milkman, *Gender at Work: The Dynamics of Job Segregation by Sex During World War II* (Urbana, 1987); Kannenberg, "Impact"; Lisa A. Kannenberg, "From World War to Cold War: Women Electrical Workers and Their Union, 1940–1955," M.A. thesis, University of North Carolina, Charlotte, 1990. Robert H. Zieger, *The CIO, 1935–1955* (Chapel Hill, N.C., 1995), 253–93 assesses of the role of communists in the CIO, including the UE and discusses the vagueness of the line between sympathy and Party membership in unions like the UE; Ronald L. Filippelli and Mark McCulloch, *Cold War in the Working Class: The Rise and Decline of the United Electrical Workers* (Albany, N.Y., 1994) charts the attack on the UE and discusses the issue of communist presence in the UE.

48. Schatz, *Electrical Workers,* 30, 89, 116–27, 129–30.

49. Milkman, *Gender at Work,* 77–78; see also Kannenberg, "Impact," esp. 311, 315. Nancy B. Palmer, "Gender, Sexuality, and Work: Women and Men in the Electrical Industry, 1940–1955," Ph.D. diss., Boston College, 1995, more skeptical of women's gains in the UE, focuses on how the construction of gender in labor unions, including the UE, limited women's advances: see esp. chap. 4.

50. Zieger, *CIO,* 251.

51. This summary relies on Schatz, *Electrical Workers,* 167–240. The 1946 quote is from Harry Block in Schatz, *Electrical Workers,* 181. For the impact of the attack on UE on women's issues, see Kannenberg, "From World War to Cold War," 95.

52. Betty Goldstein, "NAM Does Gleeful War Dance to Profits, Wage Cuts, Taft Law," *UE News,* 13 Dec. 1947, 4. What follows relies on the more than three dozen articles signed by Betty Goldstein in the *UE News* from the fall of 1946 until early 1952.

53. Betty Goldstein, "A Tale of 'Sacrifice': A Story of Equality in the United States, 1951," *March of Labor,* May 1951, 16–18, carton 8, folder 334, BF-SLRC. This also appeared in *UE News,* 12 Mar. 1951, 6–7.

54. Betty Goldstein, "It'll Take a Strong Union To End Winchester Tyranny," *UE News,* 7 Dec. 1946, 9; Betty Goldstein, "Fighting Together: We Will Win!" *UE News,* 31 May 1947, 5, 8: Betty Goldstein, "Labor Builds New Political Organization To Fight for a People's Congressman," *UE News,* 23 Aug. 1947, 4.

55. Betty Goldstein, "People's Needs Forgotten: Big Business Runs Govt.," *UE News,* 12 May 1947, 5; Betty Goldstein, "In Defense of Freedom! The People Vs. the UnAmerican Committee," *UE News,* 8 Nov. 1947, 6–7; Betty Goldstein, "They Can't Shove the IBEW Down Our Throats," *UE News,* 4 Sept. 1948, 6–7; Betty Goldstein, "UnAmerican Hearing Exposed as Plot By Outsiders to Keep Grip on UE Local," *UE News,* 22 Aug. 1949, 4; Betty Goldstein, "New NAM Theme Song: Labor-Management Teamwork," *UE News,* 9 Jan. 1950, 5; Betty Goldstein, "Plain People of America Organize New Political Party of Their Own," *UE News,* 31 July 1948, 6–7.

56. B. G., review of Sinclair Lewis, *Kingsblood Royal, UE News,* 6 Sept. 1947, 7; B. G., review of the movie "Gentleman's Agreement," *UE News,* 22 Nov. 1947, 11; B. G., review of movie "Crossfire," *UE News,* 9 Aug. 1947, 8–9; Betty Goldstein, "CIO Sold Out Fight for FEPC, T-H Repeal, Rep. Powell Reveals," *UE News,* 17 Apr. 1950, 4; B. G., review of Fielding Burke, *Sons of the Stranger, UE News,* 24 Jan. 1948, 7.

57. These two sentences rely on James Lerner, interview. For treatments of the relationship between communism and women's issues, see Ellen K. Trimberger, "Women in the Old and New Left: The Evolution of a Politics of Personal Life," *Feminist Studies* 5 (fall 1979): 432–61; Van Gosse, "'To Organize in Every Neighborhood, in Every Home': The Gender Politics of American Communists Between the Wars," *Radical History Review* 50 (spring 1991): 109–41; Kannenberg, "From World War to Cold War"; and Kathleen A. Weigand, "Vanguards of Women's Liberation: The Old Left and the Continuity of the Women's Movement in the United States, 1945–1970s," Ph.D. diss., Ohio State University, 1995. For her coverage of Latinas, see Betty Goldstein, "'It's a Union That Fights for All the Workers,'" *UE News,* 3 [?] Sept. 1951, 6–7.

58. Though she does not discuss Friedan's situation, the best treatment of the prominent role of women's issues in radical circles in the 1940s and 1950s is Weigand, "Vanguards." In working on *The Feminine Mystique,* Friedan may have been influenced by writings she may have encountered in the 1940s, such as Mary Inman, *In Women's Defense* (Los Angeles, 1940) and Betty Millard, "Woman Against Myth," *New Masses,* 30 Dec. 1947, 7–10 and 6 Jan. 1948, 7–20. There is evidence that Friedan was well aware of *New Masses.* Under a pseudonym, she published two articles in *New Masses:* Lillian Stone, "Labor and the Community," *New Masses* 57 (23 Oct. 1945): 3–5; Lillian Stone, "New Day in Stamford," *New Masses* 58 (22 Jan. 1946): 3–5. In identifying Friedan as the author, I am relying on a 22 Sept. 1995 conversation with Kathy Kraft, an archivist at the Schlesinger Library and on a letter in carton 49, folder 1783, BF-SLRC.

59. Chinoy, interview.

60. Betty Goldstein, "Price Cuts Promised in Press Invisible to GE Housewives," *UE News,* 1 Feb. 1947, 7; Betty Goldstein, "Union Members Want to Know—WHO Has Too Much Money to Spend," *UE News,* 26 Mar. 1951, 8.

61. [Betty Goldstein], *UE Fights for Women Workers,* UE Publication no. 232, June 1952 (New York, 1952). To authenticate her authorship, I am relying on the following: Horowitz, interview; James Lerner, interview; Betty Friedan, postcard to author, late August, 1995; Meltzer, *Friedan,* 25. Meltzer, who knew Friedan in the 1940s, discusses her work on women's issues at the UE. Friedan may also have written *Women Fight For a Better Life!* (New York, 1953): see Friedan, postcard.

62. [Goldstein], *UE Fights*, 5.

63. [Goldstein], *UE Fights*, 9–18, 26–27, 38.

64. Kannenberg, "Impact," 318.

65. Betty Goldstein to Grievance Committee of Newspaper Guild of New York, 23 May 1946, carton 8, folder 330, BF-SLRC; Friedan, *Changed My Life*, 9; Mim Kelber, phone conversation with Daniel Horowitz, 16 Sept. 1995, identified the man as James Peck; obituary for James Peck, *New York Times* 13 July 1993, B7.

66. Meltzer, *Friedan*, 29. For additional perspectives on Friedan's departure from the *UE News*, see Kelber, conversation and James Lerner, interview. Lerner, who had more seniority than Friedan, worked for the UE for more than 40 years, eventually becoming managing editor of *UE News*. He shared an office with Friedan during her years at *UE News* and has noted that the union protected Friedan's position during her first pregnancy: James Lerner, interview.

67. To date these moves, I am relying on a number of sources, including Betty Friedan to Mrs. Clifford P. Cowen, 5 Aug. 1957, carton 7, folder, 313, BF-SLRC; Friedan, "New York Women"; "About the Author," in "New York Women"; "Friedan," *Current Biography*, 146; *Smith College Bulletin*.

68. Betty Friedan, "Two Are an Island," *Mademoiselle* 41 (July 1955): 88–89, 100–101; Betty Friedan, "Teenage Girl in Trouble," *Coronet* 43 (Mar. 1958): 163–68; Betty Friedan. "The Happy Families of Hickory Hill," *Redbook*, Feb. 1956, 39, 87–90; Stone, Marian and Harold Stone [fictitious names], as told to Betty Friedan, "With Love We Live. . . ." *Coronet* 42 (July 1957): 135–44. For another article on a suburban development that relied on cooperation, see Betty Friedan, "'We Built a Community for Our Children,'" *Redbook*, Mar. 1955, 42–45, 62–63. Friedan's papers contain information on scores of articles that she was working on; this analysis focuses on those actually published. Sylvie Murray's "Suburban Citizens: Domesticity and Community Politics in Queens, New York, 1945–1960," Ph.D. diss., Yale University, 1994 ably contrasts the adversarial politics of Friedan's unpublished pieces with the milder tone of her published ones; on the difficulty of getting into print articles on women who were not middle-class, I am relying on Sylvie Murray, phone conversation with Daniel Horowitz, 9 Oct. 1995.

69. Betty Friedan, "The Gal Who Defied Dior," *Town Journal*, Oct. 1955, 33, 97–98; Betty Friedan, "Millionaire's Wife," *Cosmopolitan*, Sept. 1956, 78–87; Betty Friedan, "New Hampshire Love Story," *Family Circle*, June 1958, 40–41, 74–76. An influential book on the origins of 1960s feminism begins with a discussion of Friedan's magazine articles without seeing how they might connect parts of her career: Sara Evans, *Personal Politics: The Roots of Women's Liberation in the Civil Rights Movement and the New Left* (New York, 1979), 3.

70. Betty Friedan, "Now They're Proud of Peoria," *Reader's Digest* 67 (Aug. 1955): 93–97.

71. Betty Friedan, "I Went Back to Work," *Charm*, Apr. 1955, 145, 200.

72. Kelber, conversation.

73. Parkway Village had some suburban characteristics and was marketed on the basis of its suburban qualities: Murray, conversation. Yet Friedan has made it clear that she was happy there: Friedan, *Changed My Life*, 14. Moreover, being in Parkway Village did not involve inhabiting a single-family home or living individualistically among conformists.

74. Especially crucial but nonetheless elusive is the period from May 1953, when she appears to have ended her union work, and 1955, when her first article appeared in a woman's magazine.

75. Friedan, "How to Find and Develop Article Ideas," 12–15 has some discussion of these conflicts.

76. This becomes clear through an examination of her files on her free-lance work, especially when compared with the files of Vance Packard in the same years.

77. Wilkes, "Mother Superior," 141. On violence in the marriage, see also Tornabene, "Liberation," 138; Cohen, *Sisterhood*, 17–18; Meyer, "Friedan," 608; Myra MacPherson, "The Former Mr. Betty Friedan Has Scars to Prove It," probably 1971, newspaper article from unidentified source, women's liberation, biographies, individuals, box 4, folder 31, clippings on Betty Friedan, SSC-SC.

78. On this problem, see Elizabeth V. Spelman, *Inessential Woman: Problems of Exclusion in Feminist Thought* (Boston, 1988).

79. Gerda Lerner to Betty Friedan, 6 Feb. 1963, box 20a, folder 715, BF-SLRC; quoted with permission of Gerda Lerner. For information on Lerner's participation in the labor movement, the Congress of American Women, and at the founding meeting of NOW, I am relying on Daniel Horowitz, phone conversation with Gerda Lerner, 18 Oct. 1995; Amy Swerdlow, "The Congress of American Women: Left-Feminist Peace Politics in the Cold War," in *U.S. History as Women's History: New Feminist Essays*, ed. Linda K. Kerber, Alice Kessler-Harris, and Kathryn Kish Sklar (Chapel Hill, 1995), 306.

ESTELLE FREEDMAN

Miriam Van Waters and the Burning of Letters

Miriam Van Waters belonged to that elite group of women reformers that included Florence Kelley and Eleanor Roosevelt. She was also part of a transitional generation, having grown up in an era when many educated women seeking public careers rejected marriage and family for a woman-centered existence. The female networks they created enhanced their public as well as private lives, providing professional mentors and allies and personal relationships that were supportive and intimate. Even if the intimacy extended to sexual expression, couples often lived together for extended periods attracting little comment. Prior to the 1920s, many people simply assumed that these were the intense female friendships described in Carroll Smith-Rosenberg's essay "The Female World of Love and Ritual" (pp. 189–204). Tolerance lessened markedly, however, with the pathologizing of homosexuality in the 1920s.

As Estelle Freedman makes clear, Miriam Van Waters was very much aware of the new construction of lesbianism as deviant behavior. As the head of a women's correctional institution and a leading reformer in her field, she was also highly informed about the increasing attention to prison lesbianism. How she understood her own sexuality is the subject of this sensitive and perceptive essay.

Van Waters's problems were compounded by the fact that as a penal administrator, she was on the public payroll during the heyday of domestic containment. In cold war America, lesbianism, like unwed motherhood, represented the dangers of female sexuality and intolerable deviations from the family norm. Used since the 1920s to label and stigmatize nonconforming women, especially feminists, the term *lesbian* in the 1950s came to signify an aggressive deviance that verged on criminality.

Why did Van Waters resist labeling her long-term romantic partnership with Geraldine Thompson as a lesbian relationship? In what sense was class a factor?

On a clear June morning in 1948, the controversial prison reformer Miriam Van Waters made a painful and momentous decision. For months she had been embroiled in a political struggle with conservative state officials who wished to dismiss her as the liberal superintendent of the Massachusetts Reformatory for Women. Local newspapers headlined the claims that Van Waters coddled prisoners, hired ex-inmates, and condoned homosexual behavior in prison. Investigators from the Department of Corrections interrogated her staff and seized inmate files as evidence.

As she sat before a glowing fireplace in her home that June morning, Miriam Van Waters fueled the blaze with some of her most precious possessions. "The Burning of Letters continues," she wrote in her journal that day. "One can have no personal 'life' in this battle, so I have destroyed many letters of over 22 years."

From "'The Burning of Letters Continues': Elusive Identities and the Historical Construction of Sexuality," by Estelle Freedman, in *Journal of Women's History* 9, no. 4 (Winter 1998): 181–200. Reprinted by permission of the author and Indiana University Press. Notes have been renumbered and edited.

Van Waters had met her patron and romantic partner, Geraldine Thompson, twenty-two years earlier. Since the late 1920s they had corresponded almost daily, sharing their thoughts, their activities, and their love during the weeks between their regular visits with one another. All but a few of the daily letters Thompson had addressed to her "Old Sweet," her "Dearest Dearest Love," went up in flames that day. As she burned the letters, Van Waters recorded her sense of loss: "They might have been inspiration, history, joy, style—to me in 'old age.'" Instead, she resolved to keep their message within herself. "The letters are bone and sinew now in my carnage. Doubtless my character has been formed by them."[1] . . .

[To understand] Van Waters's conscious effort to conceal her relationship with Thompson, [we need to understand how Van Waters understood her own sexuality. Did she identify herself as lesbian? What would she have known about same-sex relationships?] . . .

In the early twentieth century, highly-educated women such as Miriam Van Waters might be exposed to published literature that clearly named both male and female homosexuality. Only a generation earlier, even romantic female friends and women who passed as men perceived their experiences within frameworks largely devoid of sexual references. The "female world of love and ritual" mapped by historian Carroll Smith-Rosenberg allowed same-sex attractions to "pass" as sexually innocent, whether they were or not. Beginning in the late nineteenth century, a modern conception of homosexuality emerged, articulated first as a form of gender inversion and later as an expression of erotic desire.[2] Gradually an explicitly sexual language characterized the literature on same-sex relationships. Helen Horowitz' insightful interpretation of M. Carey Thomas provides a good example of the transition. In the 1870s, Thomas' reading of romantic and pre-Raphaelite poets afforded her an initial and asexual framework for understanding passion between women; after the 1890s, however, the Oscar Wilde trial and the availability of works by sexologists such as Richard von Krafft-Ebing allowed Thomas to name sexual acts between women as well. . . .

As a graduate student at Clark University between 1910 and 1913, Van Waters easily discovered the scholarly literature on sexuality. She read Havelock Ellis, Krafft-Ebing, and some Sigmund Freud, as well as the work of her advisor, psychologist G. Stanley Hall. Her own writing recognized the power of sexuality and stressed the importance of sex education and the strategy of channeling youthful energies into recreation and social service. She also became curious about gender identity and same-sex relationships, as a questionnaire she designed reveals. The survey of adolescent girls asked, for example, "did you wish to be a boy?" and was your first "love for some one you knew closely, or for some distant person . . . or for some older woman or girl friend?" A separate questionnaire for teachers asked if "crushes" between girls were "based on mutuality of interest and inclination; or are they more likely to exist between 'masculine,' and excessively 'feminine' types?"[3] The questions suggest Van Waters' interest in whether same-sex attractions correlated with gender identity, an inquiry prompted in part by Ellis' notion of sexual inversion, which associated "mannish" women with lesbianism.

Although Van Waters never conducted this survey, her intellectual curiosity about gender nonconformity and its relationship to homosexuality recurred in her doctoral dissertation, "The Adolescent Girl among Primitive People." At this time she consciously rejected Freudian interpretations of sexuality and adopted Ellis' language of inversion—albeit without the pathological notions of deviant sexuality. Her views also reflected the cultural relativism of Franz Boas. After describing institutionalized gender-crossing among North American Indians, for example, Van Waters concluded that "among primitive peoples, a useful and appropriate life-role is commonly furnished the inverted individual. . . . It is quite possible that modern policy could profitably go to school to the primitive in this regard."[4] Similarly, in an appendix on contemporary American approaches to adolescent delinquents, Van Waters analyzed the case of a cross-dressing young woman accused of being a "white slaver" because she brought girls to her rooms at night. Reluctant to label the girl a "true homosexual," she reported that "it is impossible for her to earn an honest and adequate living while dressed as a woman," and claimed that sympathy for women of the underworld rather than sexual proclivities accounted for her behavior.[5]

During her subsequent career working in juvenile and adult female reformatories, Van Waters retained a liberal tolerance for homosexuality, even as she increasingly incorporated Freudian views of sexual psychopathology. When she discussed the management of "'crushes' and sentimental attachment" among reformatory inmates in her 1925 book, *Youth in Conflict*, she advised that a trained social worker could draw out the girl and replace unhealthy attachments with healthy ones through a beneficial "transference." A harsher passage reflected conservative medical views of sex and gender when she labeled as the most perverse juvenile case she had encountered a narcissistic girl whose "emotional life will be self-centered or flow toward those of her own sex," and who would "never wish to live the biologically normal life."[6]

Despite these published critiques of unhealthy homosexual attachments, as superintendent of the Framingham, Massachusetts, reformatory for women from 1932 to 1957, Miriam Van Waters consistently resisted the labeling of prison relationships as homosexual. Her liberal administration emphasized education, social welfare services, psychiatric counseling, and work opportunities outside prison for the three to four hundred women inmates, the large majority of whom were young, white, Catholic, and working-class. Although the criminological literature then identified black women in prison as the aggressors in interracial sexual relationships, Van Waters and her staff did not draw a racial line around prison homosexuality. Rather, they tried to distinguish between "true homosexuality" and temporary attractions. They believed the former could be detected by the Rorschach test; in the absence of such "positive evidence" they assumed that only the boredom of prison routine stimulated "unnatural" interest in same-sex relationships. Thus an active program of classes and clubs attempted to channel the energies of both black and white prisoners into what the staff considered healthier recreations. Even when staff discovered two women in bed together—of any racial combination—they hesitated to label them as homosexual.

Van Waters' tolerance of prison homosexual liaisons contributed to the conservative assault on her administration in the 1940s. In 1949, when the Commissioner of Corrections dismissed Van Waters from office, he charged:

> That you have known of and failed to prevent the continuance of, or failed to know and recognize that an unwholesome relationship has existed between inmates of the Reformatory for Women which is called the "doll racket" by inmates and some officer personnel; the terms "stud" and "queen" are used with implied meanings, and such association has resulted in "crushes", "courtships", and homosexual practises [*sic*] among the inmates in the Reformatory.[7]

During several months of public hearings, Van Waters successfully defended her policies, in part by minimizing the existence of homosexuality at the reformatory, in part by deferring to psychiatric authorities when asked about homosexual tendencies among inmates. Typical of her strategic evasion was this response to hostile interrogation about whether certain acts or personal styles revealed homosexual tendencies:

> That, sir, is so distinctly a medical and technical question that I would not presume to answer it. One of the first things we are taught is that a homosexual tendency must be distinguished from a homosexual act. A homosexual tendency may be completely repressed and turned into a variety of other expressions, including a great aversion to emotion.[8]

By invoking the power of psychiatry, Van Waters acknowledged the shifting meaning of homosexuality—from an act to an identity. At the same time, she tried to avoid a labeling process that would mark close friends, mannish women, and those who had crushes on other inmates as confirmed homosexuals, a category she reserved for a treatable psychopathological condition that posed problems only when characterized by aggressive sexual behaviors.

Whether consciously or not, Van Waters' testimony represented a form of resistance to the use of accusations of homosexuality to discredit nonconforming women. Rather than sacrifice some "mannish" women or close female friends by calling them either "homosexuals," "latent homosexuals," or "women with homosexual tendencies," she firmly opposed labeling. At the same time, like psychologists of the period, she did so by accepting a definition of true homosexuality as pathology. In the 1950s, partly in response to her reading of the Kinsey Reports, and partly in the wake of the accusations about prison lesbianism during her dismissal hearings, Van Waters' public lectures urged greater tolerance. Homosexuality, she explained, could be "found in all levels of society," in all types of people. Her emphasis, however, was on treatment. Once revealed through use of the Rorschach test, she believed, homosexual tendencies could be reversed with the aid of psychiatry.[9]

In short, for Miriam Van Waters, lesbianism was a curable social problem not unlike alcoholism. Although she initially encountered lesbianism among working-class, immigrant, and black reformatory inmates, she recognized that it occurred within other groups, as well. Rather than emphasizing a heterosexual solution, Van Waters placed great faith in "healthy" female bonding as an alternative to lesbianism. In this sense, whether or not she had internalized modern medical categories, she strategically invoked an earlier discourse of sexually innocent and nurturing female friendships as a corrective to the increasing stigmatization of women's love for women as a form of perversion.

When Superintendent Van Waters evaded the labeling of homosexuality during her dismissal hearings, she also sidestepped implicit questions about her own sexual identity. In her personal life, Van Waters had refused to label her love for a woman as a form of homosexuality, despite her long-term romantic partnership with Geraldine Thompson, a New Jersey philanthropist who was known publicly only as a wealthy benefactor and a supporter of Van Waters' reforms. So, too, she hesitated to assume that other women who appeared to fit the medical definition really were homosexuals, a term she reserved for women's pathological, though curable, sexual aggression toward other women.[10]

What of her internal consciousness of her own sexuality? The private story of Miriam Van Waters' own relationships with women both parallels and contradicts her public pronouncements. Beginning in adolescence, she fell deeply in love with other women and, for the most part, preferred their company to the attentions of male suitors. Never a sexual prude, Van Waters recognized the importance of the erotic, especially within the poetry and fiction she wrote in her late twenties. But she also placed great stock in the power of sublimation for harnessing erotic energy into expression as art, spirituality, or public service. Thus, upon reading Radclyffe Hall's *The Well of Loneliness* in 1929, Van Waters commented in her journal that had Stephen Gordon's parents been more loving, instead of becoming a lesbian Gordon might have "run a girls camp," become a high school counselor, or supervised a juvenile protective agency, all activities remarkably similar to those Van Waters chose.[11]

The detailed introspective journals Van Waters kept as an adult provide further clues about her subjective experience of sexuality, despite the frequently coded and intentionally obscure nature of her writing. Tantalizing passages in Van Waters' journals made little sense to me until late into my research, when I gained access to a cache of personal papers that had not been deposited in the archives. Literally locked away within a rusting trunk and forgotten in an attic, that cache included passionate letters from two of Van Waters' ardent admirers: one set from Hans Weiss, a young Swiss social worker who wished to marry Van Waters; the other, a year's worth of daily letters from Geraldine Thompson, the older, wealthy, married philanthropist whose subsequent correspondence Van Waters burned in 1948. Working with both the journals and the "courtship letters," as I called them, I learned how Van Waters struggled to balance the erotic, the emotional, and the spiritual in each of these relationships.

Despite significant differences between the Weiss and Thompson correspondence—his letters were more erotic, hers more spiritual; he was more emotionally demanding, she longed to be of service to her beloved—I was struck by the consistency in Van Waters' response to her male and female suitors. In each case, she remained publicly silent, restrained in her responses to passion, and conflicted about making any lifelong commitment. The two relationships did present separate challenges to Van Waters' sexuality. The younger, less established Weiss frequently articulated his erotic longings; in response, Van Waters struggled to incorporate physical passion while subsuming it to her ideal of a spiritualized romantic friendship. The older, wealthier, and more powerful Thompson longed for "the Justice of the Peace and church bells" to signify their commitment; in response, Van Waters feared the dependency that could result from their union.[12]

In both cases, the management of passion was a recurrent theme for Miriam Van Waters.

Although her journals were characteristically obscure about sexual experiences, one passage written after a visit with Weiss alluded to an unidentified young "Beloved" with whom she had experienced both a spiritual epiphany and a "yielding to love." In one entry, she recalled a candlelit scene in which her "hands were flung up by a strong clasp of young hands on my wrists—and with another soul—I plunged down a glittering waterfall immeasurably high, and sunk at last—into a pool—where two floated in weariness and content."[13] More typical, however, was her insistence on limiting their intimacy. "As a lover I yield to no one in sustained worship," she wrote in her journal. To Weiss she explained that their spiritual union transcended the need for physical proximity, suggesting that unrequited love could yield the "deepest spiritual gain."[14] By 1930, she had successfully encouraged Weiss to wed someone else; she had already informed him of another, unnamed attraction.

The Thompson courtship, begun during the late 1920s, overlapped with the waning of Van Waters' intimacy with Weiss. Both women valued romantic and spiritual intimacy, and neither wrote explicitly about their sexual experiences. Yet Van Waters left hints about her consciousness of lesbianism and her continuing management of erotic impulses. In 1930, she read an article about Katherine B. Davis' 1929 study of female sexuality, which found that a quarter of unmarried women college graduates acknowledged a sexual component within their intense emotional relationships with other women. Van Waters starred the point that these were normal, not pathological, women, as if to differentiate her experience from the perversions she had earlier identified among juvenile delinquents. As in her relationship with Weiss, however, Van Waters continued to place limits on erotic expression. Thus when Thompson expressed a desire "to 'catch your soul's breath' in kisses," Van Waters questioned the impulse in her journal: "What one calls appetite—satisfaction of warmth needs—hunger needs—is not just that.... In maturity some times in some circumstances—to feed hunger fully—is to lose hunger. There are other ways of quenching the fire—and all must be escaped." Professionally she had recommended channeling youthful sexual energies, whether heterosexual or homosexual. But her personal ideal suggested not simply sublimation but rather that desire could be maintained best by leaving it largely unfulfilled. While staying at Thompson's home, she again alluded to the value of control: "The secret of life is manifested in hunger—it can't safely be quenched—neither by denial, nor complete feeding, nor running away, nor escape—but by a new way."[15]

Whether or not she discovered this "new way" of managing desire, by the time she and Thompson pledged their love at the end of 1930, Van Waters recognized that she had crossed some line. "The object which arouses love—cannot be foreseen or controlled," she wrote in her journal. "All we know is—that same force which engulfs us, and makes us ready for service to husband and children—some times—to some persons—flows out to a man, woman, child, animal, 'cause,' idea." Van Waters did not, however, acknowledge her love publicly nor claim a lesbian identity. When Geraldine longed to "shout about" their love so that her family would "know what life through you is giving me," Miriam counseled discretion.[16] Similarly, when an acquaintance who lived openly with another woman later asked Van Waters in public about the ring she wore—a gift from Thompson—Van Waters seethed at the impudence of this inquiry into her private life. Perhaps her status as a civil service employee, and as the guardian and later adoptive mother of a child, made Van Waters more cautious than her independently wealthy partner, Thompson. Equally likely, Van Waters struggled to reconcile her passion with the psychological construction of lesbianism she had already formed.

Another cryptic journal entry suggests how powerfully that psychological construction influenced her. In a dream, she wrote, she had enjoyed a feeling of "Understanding" that derived in part from "the recent Rorshak [*sic*] and integration." Van Waters used the Rorschach test to detect "innate homosexuality" among inmates; in 1938, a trusted friend administered the test to her and the results made Van Waters feel confident and optimistic. One line in this passage was crossed out heavily in pencil, especially over someone's name, but the entry continued, "Geraldine and I shall learn together."[17] In my reading, the Rorschach test proved to Van Waters that she was not an innate homosexual, thus freeing her of the deviant label and, ironically, granting her permission to integrate her love for Thompson, without adopting a lesbian identity.

Why, then, the burning of letters? Even if Van Waters did not consider herself a lesbian, the world around her was not as thoroughly convinced. Although her close associates insisted to me that the relationship was much too spiritual to have been homosexual, Van Waters' partnership with Geraldine Thompson made her increasingly vulnerable to the insinuations of her political opponents.

In the conformist atmosphere after World War II, accusations of Communism, often conflated with homosexuality, fueled an attack on liberalism. Thus, in 1948, claims that Van Waters tolerated homosexuality at the Massachusetts women's reformatory facilitated her dismissal from office. Aside from the widely publicized claims about the "doll racket" among inmates, rumors about Van Waters' sexuality circulated underground, though never in print. For example, Eleanor Roosevelt—a friend of Thompson and supporter of Van Waters—learned of the whispering campaign when she received several "vile" letters that were so disturbing that she destroyed most of them. Similarly, a hostile postcard sent to supporters referred to Van Waters as "supt. (or Chief Pervert)" of the reformatory.[18] It was at this time that Van Waters burned most of Thompson's correspondence, carefully locking away only that one year of "courtship" letters.

Despite the private insinuations that led her to burn Thompson's letters, Van Waters survived the attempt to fire her. The publicity surrounding prison lesbianism during her hearings, however, contributed to a national preoccupation with homosexuality and to the naming of lesbianism as a social threat. No matter how confident Van Waters may have been that she was not a lesbian, outside observers often assumed that she was. Late in my research, after years of waiting to receive Van Waters' FBI file, I found a 1954 document that seemed to place an official government seal upon Van Waters' identity. While carrying out surveillance on Helen Bryan, a suspected Communist sympathizer with whom Van Waters had a romantic friendship later in life, a local FBI informant read the correspondence between the two women. Shocked by the "unusual" nature of the letters, which contained "numerous repeated terms of endearment and other statements," he came to "the definite opinion that Dr. VAN WATERS and BRYAN are Lesbians."[19] It was to prevent just such a conclusion from being drawn that Van Waters had earlier burned Thompson's letters.

That identity formation is often a social as much as an individual phenomenon is further revealed by a final anecdote from my research on Van Waters, a coda of sorts that brings the story into the 1990s. My book completed, I turned to the task of acquiring permission to quote from sources, including Geraldine Thompson's courtship letters. With trepidation I sent the permission form to Thompson's eldest surviving granddaughter, who soon called to discuss the request. Her initial words, "I will not grant permission," struck further terror in me, until I absorbed the completion of her sentence: "I will not grant permission to repeat any lies; I want the truth." Too much had been concealed in her family, she explained, too much smoothed over. By the end of our conversation, she had told me with confidence that her grandmother had been a lesbian and that she was sure that Thompson and Van Waters were lovers, for they had shared a bed during family vacations. "Do you know what we grandchildren called Miriam when she came to visit?" she asked. "Grammy Thompson's yum-yum." She gladly granted permission to quote when I seemed willing to reveal "the truth."[20] . . .

Van Waters came of age in a transitional moment, when the social possibilities for romantic and sexual love between women increased, but also while medical labeling pathologized these relationships. As an educated, professional woman, exposed to such sexologists as Ellis and Freud, she was both conscious of the erotic and aware of the psychopathic label then attached to same-sex relationships. At the same time, Van Waters was attracted to women; she was able to live outside of heterosexual institutions; and she could and did take advantage of the opportunity to establish a partnership with another woman, even as she fiercely resisted lesbian identification.

Perhaps the fear of losing her job, and her social standing, kept Van Waters from identifying as a lesbian. But her rejection of lesbianism as an identity was not merely self-serving, for she just as fiercely resisted the labeling of working-class prison inmates as lesbians, and during her dismissal hearings in 1949 she more or less placed her class and race privilege on the line to defend these women from such charges. In the end, it was Van Waters' privileges—combined with her distinguished career of service and her upper-class political connections—that protected her from public disgrace. The working-class women she tried to protect would forge their own public lesbian identity, one that equally rejected the pathological discourse of the early twentieth century.

. . . To contemporary feminists, who value our own historically constructed ideal of the openly lesbian sexual subject, Van Waters seems anything but progressive. Yet if we are serious about . . . recognizing women's historical agency, we have to be willing to accept it when beliefs, and possibly behaviors, go against the grain of a "progressive" narrative that embraces categories we have claimed for ourselves. And we must keep in mind that this narrative rests heavily upon a highly class- and race-specific lesbian identity constructed since the 1960s, one that depathologized white, middle-class women's love for women but simultaneously failed to recognize a range of other sources of identity. . . . [Ultimately] Miriam Van Waters' case suggests the ways that some women could simultaneously internalize, resist, manipulate, and ignore the cultural constructions of sexuality in their times. Above all, her story reminds us to look beyond our sources, to read both silences and speech, and, at times, to accept the historical integrity of elusive personal identities.

Notes

1. Miriam Van Waters Journal (hereafter MVW Journal), 16 June 1948, 19 June 1948, and 22 June 1948, file 220v, Anne Gladding-Miriam Van Waters Papers, Schlesinger Library, Radcliffe College (hereafter Gladding-MVW Papers). A handful of surviving letters were scattered through Van Waters' correspondence in the papers she donated to the Schlesinger Library. For a full account of her life, see Estelle B. Freedman, *Maternal Justice: Miriam Van Waters and the Female Reform Tradition* (Chicago: University of Chicago Press, 1996).

2. MVW to parents, 10 October 1911, file 42 (misdated, probably 9 October 1911), MVW Papers; MVW, "Topical Syllabus No. 44 (A) and No. 44 (B) [for teachers], Psychology of Adolescence," 15 November 1911, Box 37, file 464, G. Stanley Hall Papers, Clark University, Worcester, Massachusetts.

3. MVW, "The Adolescent Girl among Primitive People," *Journal of Religious Psychology* 6, no. 4 (1913): 375–421, and 7, no. 1 (1914): 75–120 (esp. pt. 1, 377–78 and pt. 2, 102–5). Her advisor, Alexander Chamberlain, had been Franz Boas' first doctoral student at Clark.

4. MVW, "Adolescent Girl," pt. 2, 108–12.

5. MVW, *Youth in Conflict* (New York: New Republic, 1925), 35–36.

6. McDowell to MVW, 7 January 1949, file 201, MVW Papers.

7. John O'Connor, "Van Waters Rejects Inmate Sex Charge," *Boston Herald*, 1 January 1949, 1.

8. MVW, Boston University lecture transcript, 24 October 1951 (in possession of author).

9. Rumors about Van Waters' sexuality are discussed in MVW to Ethel Sturges Dummer, 26 September 1948, file 825, Ethel Sturges Dummer Papers, Schlesinger Library, Radcliffe College; and in letters from a former inmate to MVW, 1 June 1948, file 195, and from Harry R. Archbald to MVW, 7 February 1949, file 203, both in MVW Papers. For a full discussion of Van Waters' interpretation of lesbian identity and the political response to rumors of her own homosexuality, see Freedman, *Maternal Justice*, esp. chaps. 9, 12, 14, and 15.

10. MVW Journal, 30 March 1929, file 208, Gladding-MVW Papers. MVW's phrasing suggests an ambivalence about the experience of marriage and reproductive, as opposed to social, motherhood: Gordon, she wrote might have been "anything—everything in fact but a stupid wife and mother—Wife she co[uld] have been and mother too."

11. See, for example, Geraldine Thompson (GT) to MVW, 31 October 1930, 4 November 1930, and 14 November 1930, file 261, Gladding-MVW Papers.

12. MVW Journal, 28 June 1928, file 206, Gladding-MVW Papers; compare Hans Weiss' (HW) sweet memory of "what you did for me when you had the tremendous courage of giving yourself to me." HW to MVW, 24 July 1930, file 279, Gladding-MVW Papers.

13. MVW Journal, 19 February 1928, 14 June 1928, file 206, and 23 November 1928, file 208; HW to MVW, 7 August 1930, file 280, all in Gladding-MVW Papers. For complex reasons, Van Waters refused to consider marrying Weiss. Aside from the emotional distance she kept, the formal obstacle to their marriage was his "tremendous longing for a home and for children." He accepted "the cruel reality" that he could not have this with her, for like many professional women, she had chosen career over marriage. Although some women reformers did try to combine the two, having a job and children would be too physically taxing for her and, given her history of tuberculosis, possibly life-threatening. HW to MVW, 19 January 1929, file 276, Gladding-MVW Papers.

14. MVW to Edna Mahan, 20 July 1930, file 253, Gladding-MVW Papers; and Katherine B. Davis, *Factors in the Sex Life of Twenty-Two Hundred Women* (New York: Harper and Row, 1929), 312, 295, 280. The data showed that 28 percent of the women's college graduates and 20 percent of those from coeducational schools recognized sexual components in their relations; in addition, almost equal numbers had enjoyed intense emotional attachments that involved kissing and hugging.

15. GT to MVW, 31 October 1930, file 261, 10 November and 6 November 1930, file 262, all in Gladding-MVW Papers; MVW Journal, 27 September 1930, and 11 June 1931, file 211, Gladding-MVW Papers.

16. MVW Journal, 27 September 1930, and GT to MVW, 13 November 1930, file 262, both in Gladding-MVW Papers.

17. On Rorschach, see, for example, Inmate record, 21 February 1949, file 251, MVW Journal, 11 June 1938, 213v, Gladding-MVW Papers; MVW Journal, vol. 5, 26 June 1938, MVW Papers.

18. Eleanor Roosevelt (ER) letter, 19 December 1948, file 200; GT to Dorothy Kirchwey Brown, 4 January 1949, file 201; ER to GT, n.d., in response to an enclosed letter from GT dated 5 January 1949, all in Box 3820, ER Papers. ER to GT, 13 January 1949, file 8, Friends of Framingham Papers (hereafter FOF Papers), Schlesinger Library, Cambridge, Massachusetts; Miriam Clark Nichols to ER, 18 January 1949, file 8, FOF Papers (the letter was reprinted in *The Civil Service Reporter* [8 February 1949]: 5); George Hooper to Friends of Framingham, 1 January 1949, file 8, FOF Papers.

19. SAC, Boston (100-15782) to Director, FBI (100-206852), "Office Memorandum," Re: Helen Reid Bryan, 20 January 1954, declassified 12 April 1994 pursuant to Freedom of Information Act Request (emphasis in original).

20. Telephone interview with Geraldine Boone, 17 February 1995; and Boone to author, 6 March 1995.

SUSAN K. CAHN

"Mannishness," Lesbianism, and Homophobia in U.S. Women's Sports

Miriam Van Waters, like many white middle-class women who loved other women, chose not to acknowledge her lesbianism. To do so would have meant acknowledging an affiliation with working-class lesbians. Their butch-femme roles and bar culture, like the aggressive prison lesbian, had been so thoroughly pathologized in the 1950s as to seem quite alien to women of a different class and culture. Others made a different choice. Some even tried to organize to gain constitutional rights, but this effort went awry especially in New York City, where the local chapter of the Daughters of Bilitis was discovered to have subsequently been infiltrated with informants who were supplying names to the FBI and CIA. (The group was founded in San Francisco in the mid-1950s to work for social and civil rights for lesbians.) In an era when sexual conformity was seen as essential to national security, it is hardly surprising that *all* women who engaged in any same-sex activity were suspect. Women athletes were particularly vulnerable.

In the following article, Susan Cahn explores the suspicions and the reality behind those suspicions in women's athletics. Note the persistence of concerns about feminine sexuality, whether heterosexual or homosexual, throughout the history of women's sports. What measures did colleges and universities take to protect women's sports from charges of lesbianism? What was the price of such actions? Since those athletes who were lesbian could no more afford to proclaim

Excerpted from "From the 'Muscle Moll' to the 'Butch' Ballplayer: Mannishness, Lesbianism, and Homophobia in U.S. Women's Sports" by Susan K. Cahn, in *Feminist Studies* 19, no. 2 (Summer 1993): 343–68. Reprinted by permission of the publisher. Notes have been edited and renumbered.

their sexual identity publicly than Van Waters, why does Cahn argue that athletics nonetheless afforded them social and psychic space to affirm their identity and find community? Do you agree?

In 1934, *Literary Digest* subtitled an article on women's sports, "Will the Playing Fields One Day Be Ruled by Amazons?" The author, Fred Wittner, answered the question affirmatively and concluded that as an "inevitable consequence" of sport's masculinizing effect, "girls trained in physical education to-day may find it more difficult to attract the most worthy fathers for their children."[1] The image of women athletes as mannish, failed heterosexuals represents a thinly veiled reference to lesbianism in sport. At times, the homosexual allusion has been indisputable, as in a journalist's description of the great athlete Babe Didrikson as a "Sapphic, Brobdingnagian woman" or in television comedian Arsenio Hall's more recent witticism, "If we can put a man on the moon, why can't we get one on Martina Navratilova?"[2] More frequently, however, popular commentary on lesbians in sport has taken the form of indirect references, surfacing through denials and refutations rather than open acknowledgment. When in 1955 an *Ebony* magazine article on African American track stars insisted that "off track, girls are entirely feminine. Most of them like boys, dances, club affairs," the reporter answered the implicit but unspoken charge that athletes, especially Black women in a "manly" sport, were masculine man-haters, or lesbians.[3]

The figure of the mannish lesbian athlete has acted as a powerful but unarticulated "bogey woman" of sport, forming a silent foil for more positive, corrective images that attempt to rehabilitate the image of women athletes and resolve the cultural contradiction between athletic prowess and femininity. As a stereotyped figure in U.S. society, the lesbian athlete forms part of everyday cultural knowledge. Yet historians have paid scant attention to the connection between female sexuality and sport.[4] This essay explores the historical relationship between lesbianism and sport by tracing the development of the stereotyped "mannish lesbian athlete" and examining its relation to the lived experience of mid-twentieth-century lesbian athletes.

I argue that fears of mannish female sexuality in sport initially centered on the prospect of unbridled heterosexual desire. By the 1930s, however, female athletic mannishness began to connote heterosexual failure, usually couched in terms of unattractiveness to men, but also suggesting the possible absence of heterosexual interest. In the years following World War II, the stereotype of the lesbian athlete emerged full blown. The extreme homophobia and the gender conservatism of the postwar era created a context in which longstanding linkages among mannishness, female homosexuality, and athletics cohered around the figure of the mannish lesbian athlete. Paradoxically, the association between masculinity, lesbianism, and sport had a positive outcome for some women. The very cultural matrix that produced the pejorative image also created possibilities for lesbian affirmation. Sport provided social and psychic space for some lesbians to validate themselves and to build a collective culture. Thus, the lesbian athlete was not only a figure of discourse but a living product of women's sexual struggle and cultural innovation.

The athletic woman sparked interest and controversy in the early decades of the twentieth century. In the United States and other Western societies, sport functioned as a male preserve, an all-male domain in which men not only played games together but also demonstrated and affirmed their manhood.[5] The "maleness" of sport derived from a gender ideology which labeled aggression, physicality, competitive spirit, and athletic skill as masculine attributes necessary for achieving true manliness. This notion found unquestioned support in the dualistic, polarized concepts of gender which prevailed in Victorian America. However, by the turn of the century, women had begun to challenge Victorian gender arrangements, breaking down barriers to female participation in previously male arenas of public work, politics, and urban nightlife. Some of these "New Women" sought entry into the world of athletics as well. On college campuses students enjoyed a wide range of intramural sports through newly formed Women's Athletic Associations. Off-campus women took up games like golf, tennis, basketball, swimming, and occasionally even wrestling, car racing, or boxing. As challengers to one of the defining arenas of manhood, skilled female athletes became symbols of the broader march of womanhood out of the Victorian domestic sphere into once prohibited male realms.

The woman athlete represented both the appealing and threatening aspects of modern womanhood. In a positive light, she captured the exuberant spirit, physical vigor, and brazenness of the New Woman. The University of Minnesota student newspaper proclaimed in 1904 that the athletic girl was the "truest type of All-American coed."[6] Several years later, *Harper's Bazaar* labeled the unsportive girl as "not strictly up to date," and *Good Housekeeping* noted that the "tomboy" had come to symbolize "a new type of American girl, new not only physically, but mentally and morally."[7]

Yet, women athletes invoked condemnation as often as praise. Critics ranged from physicians and physical educators to sportswriters, male athletic officials, and casual observers. In their view, strenuous athletic pursuits endangered women and threatened the stability of society. They maintained that women athletes would become manlike, adopting masculine dress, talk, and mannerisms. In addition, they contended, too much exercise would damage female reproductive capacity [interfering with menstruation and causing reproductive organs to harden or atrophy]. And worse yet, the excitement of sport would cause women to lose [sexual] control, . . . unleash[ing] nonprocreative, erotic desires identified with male sexuality and unrespectable women.... These fears collapsed into an all-encompassing concept of "mannishness," a term signifying female masculinity . . .

The public debate over the merits of women's athletic participation remained lively throughout the 1910s and 1920s. On all sides of the issue, however, the controversy about sports and female sexuality presumed heterosexuality. Neither critics nor supporters suggested that "masculine" athleticism might indicate or induce same-sex love. And when experts warned of the "amazonian" athlete's possible sexual transgressions, they linked the physical release of sport with a loss of heterosexual *control*, not of *inclination*.

In the 1930s, however, the heterosexual understanding of the mannish "amazon" began to give way to a new interpretation which educators and promoters could not long ignore. To the familiar charge that female athletes resembled men, critics added the newer accusation that sport-induced mannishness disqualified them as candidates for heterosexual romance. In 1930, an *American Mercury* medical reporter decried the decline of romantic love, pinning the blame on women who entered sport, business, and politics. He claimed that such women "act like men, talk like men, and think like men." The author explained that "women have come closer and closer to men's level," and, consequently, "the purple allure of distance has vamoosed."[8] . . . Although the charges didn't exclusively focus on athletes, they implied that female athleticism was contrary to heterosexual appeal, which appeared to rest on women's difference from and deference to men.

The concern with heterosexual appeal reflected broader sexual transformations in U.S. society. Historians of sexuality have examined the multiple forces which reshaped gender and sexual relations in the first few decades of the twentieth century. Victorian sexual codes crumbled under pressure from an assertive, boldly sexual working-class youth culture, a women's movement which defied prohibitions against public female activism, and the growth of a new pleasure-oriented consumer economy. In the wake of these changes, modern ideals of womanhood embraced an overtly erotic heterosexual sensibility. At the same time, medical fascination with sexual "deviance" created a growing awareness of lesbianism, now understood as a form of congenital or psychological pathology. The medicalization of homosexuality in combination with an antifeminist backlash in the 1920s against female autonomy and power contributed to a more fully articulated taboo against lesbianism. The modern heterosexual woman stood in stark opposition to her threatening sexual counterpart, the "mannish" lesbian.[9]

By the late 1920s and early 1930s, with a modern lesbian taboo and an eroticized definition of heterosexual femininity in place, the assertive, muscular female competitor roused increasing suspicion. It was at this moment that both subtle and direct references to the lesbian athlete emerged in physical education and popular sport. Uncensored discussions of intimate female companionship and harmless athletic "crushes" disappear from the record, pushed underground by the increasingly hostile tone of public discourse about female sexuality and athleticism. Fueled by the gender antagonisms and anxieties of the Depression, the public began scrutinizing women athletes—known for their appropriation of masculine games and styles—for signs of deviance.

Where earlier references to "amazons" had signaled heterosexual ardor, journalists now used the term to mean unattractive, failed heterosexuals. Occasionally, the media made direct mention of athletes' presumed lesbian tendencies. A 1933 *Redbook* article, for example, casually mentioned that track and golf star Babe Didrikson liked men just to horse around with her and not "make love," adding that Babe's fondness for her best girlfriends far surpassed her affection for any man.[10] The direct reference was unusual; the lesbian connotation of mannishness was forged primarily through indirect links of association. . . .

Tentatively voiced in the 1930s, these accusations became harsher and more explicit under the impact of wartime changes in gender and sexuality and the subsequent panic over the "homosexual menace." In a post–World War II climate markedly hostile to nontraditional women and lesbians, women in physical education and in working-class popular sports became convenient targets of homophobic indictment.

World War II opened up significant economic and social possibilities for gay men and women. Embryonic prewar homosexual subcultures blossomed during the war and spread across the midcentury urban landscape. Bars, nightclubs, public cruising spots, and informal social networks facilitated the development of gay and lesbian enclaves. But the permissive atmosphere did not survive the war's end. Waving the banner of Cold War political and social conservatism, government leaders acted at the federal, state, and local levels to purge gays and lesbians from government and military posts, to initiate legal investigations and prosecutions of gay individuals and institutions, and to encourage local police crackdowns on gay bars and street life. The perceived need to safeguard national security and to reestablish social order in the wake of wartime disruption sparked a "homosexual panic" which promoted the fear, loathing, and persecution of homosexuals.[11]

Lesbians suffered condemnation for their violation of gender as well as sexual codes. The tremendous emphasis on family, domesticity, and "traditional" femininity in the late 1940s and 1950s reflected postwar anxieties about the reconsolidation of a gender order shaken by two decades of depression and war. As symbols of women's refusal to conform, lesbians endured intense scrutiny by experts who regularly focused on their subjects' presumed masculinity. Sexologists attributed lesbianism to masculine tendencies and freedoms encouraged by the war, linking it to a general collapsing of gender distinctions which, in their view, destabilized marital and family relations.[12]

Lesbians remained shadowy figures to most Americans, but women athletes—noted for their masculine bodies, interests, and attributes—were visible representatives of the gender inversion often associated with homosexuality. Physical education majors, formerly accused of being unappealing to men, were increasingly charged with being uninterested in them as well. The 1952 University of Minnesota yearbook snidely reported: "Believe it or not, members of the Women's Athletic Association are normal" and found conclusive evidence in the fact that "at least one . . . of WAA's 300 members is engaged."[13]

The lesbian stigma began to plague popular athletics too. . . . The career of Babe Didrikson, which spanned the 1920s to the 1950s, illustrates the shift. In the early 1930s the press had ridiculed the tomboyish track star for her "hatchet face," "door-stop jaw," and "button-breasted" chest. After quitting track, Didrikson dropped out of the national limelight, married professional wrestler George Zaharias in 1938, and then staged a spectacular athletic comeback as a golfer in the late 1940s and 1950s. Fascinated by her personal transformation and then, in the 1950s, moved by her battle with cancer, journalists gave Didrikson's comeback extensive coverage and helped make her a much-loved popular figure. In reflecting on her success, however, sportswriters spent at least as much time on Didrikson's love life as her golf stroke. Headlines blared, "Babe Is a Lady Now: The World's Most Amazing Athlete Has Learned to Wear Nylons and Cook for Her

Huge Husband," and reporters gleefully described how "along came a great big he-man wrestler and the Babe forgot all her man-hating chatter."[14] . . . The challenge for women athletes was not to conquer new athletic feats, which would only further reduce their sexual appeal, but to regain their womanhood through sexual surrender to men.

Media coverage in national magazines and metropolitan newspapers typically focused on the sexual accomplishments of white female athletes, but postwar observers and promoters of African American women's sport also confronted the issue of sexual normalcy. In earlier decades, strong local support for women's sport within Black communities and the racist gender ideologies that prevailed outside Black communities may have weakened the association between African American women athletes and "mannish" lesbianism. Historically, European American racial thought characterized African American women as aggressive, coarse, passionate, and physical—the same qualities assigned to manliness and sport.[15] Excluded from dominant ideals of womanhood, Black women's success in sport could therefore be interpreted not as an unnatural sexual deviation but, rather, as the natural result of their reputed closeness to nature, animals, and masculinity.[16] . . . Moreover, stereotypes of Black females as highly sexual, promiscuous, and unrestrained in their heterosexual passions further discouraged the linkage between mannishness and lesbianism. . . .

Although Black athletes may initially have encountered few lesbian stereotypes . . . circumstances in the broader society eventually pressed African American sport promoters and journalists to address the issue of mannish sexuality. The strong postwar association of sports with lesbianism developed at the same time as Black athletes became a dominant presence in American sport culture. . . . Therefore, while there was no particular correlation between Black women and lesbianism, the association of each with mannishness and sexual aggression potentially linked the two. . . . In the late 1950s, Black sport promoters and journalists joined others in taking up the question of sexual "normalcy." One Black newspaper in 1957 described tennis star Althea Gibson as a childhood "tomboy" who "in later life . . . finds herself victimized by complexes."[17] The article did not elaborate on the nature of Gibson's "complex," but lesbianism is inferred in the linkage between "tomboys" and psychological illness. This connotation becomes clearer by looking at the defense of Black women's sport. Echoing *Ebony's* avowal that "entirely feminine" Black female track stars "like boys, dances, club affairs," in 1962 Tennessee State University track coach Ed Temple asserted, "None of my girls have any trouble getting boy friends. . . . We don't want amazons."[18]

Constant attempts to shore up the heterosexual reputation of athletes can be read as evidence that the longstanding reputation of female athletes as mannish women had become a covert reference to lesbianism. By midcentury, a fundamental reorientation of sexual meanings fused notions of femininity, female eroticism, and heterosexual attractiveness into a single ideal. Mannishness, once primarily a sign of gender crossing, assumed a specifically lesbian-sexual connotation. In the wake of this change, the strong cultural association between sport and masculinity made women's athletics ripe for emerging lesbian stereotypes. This meaning of athletic mannishness raises further questions. What impact did the stereotype have on women's sport? And was the image merely an erroneous stereotype, or did lesbians in fact form a significant presence in sport? . . .

The image of the mannish lesbian athlete had a direct effect on women competitors, on strategies of athletic organizations, and on the overall popularity of women's sport. The lesbian stereotype exerted pressure on athletes to demonstrate their femininity and heterosexuality, viewed as one and the same. Many women adopted an apologetic stance toward their athletic skill. Even as they competed to win, they made sure to display outward signs of femininity in dress and demeanor. They took special care in contact with the media to reveal "feminine" hobbies like cooking and sewing, to mention current boyfriends, and to discuss future marriage plans.[19]

Leaders of women's sport took the same approach at the institutional level. In answer to portrayals of physical education majors and teachers as social rejects and prudes, physical educators revised their philosophy to place heterosexuality at the center of professional objectives. . . . Curricular changes implemented between the mid-1930s and mid-1950s institutionalized the new philosophy. In a paper on postwar objectives, Mildred A. Schaeffer explained that physical education classes should help women "develop an interest in school dances and mixers and a desire to voluntarily attend them."[20] To this end, administrators revised coursework to emphasize beauty and social charm over rigorous exercise and health. They exchanged old rationales of fitness and fun for promises of trimmer waistlines, slimmer hips, and prettier complexions.... Some departments also added coeducational classes to foster "broader, keener, more sympathetic understanding of the opposite sex."[21] Department heads cracked down on "mannish" students and faculty, issuing warnings against "casual styles" which might "lead us back into some dangerous channels."[22] They implemented dress codes which forbade slacks and men's shirts or socks, adding as well a ban on "boyish hair cuts" and unshaven legs.[23]

Popular sport promoters adopted similar tactics. Martialing sexual data like they were athletic statistics, a 1954 AAU poll sought to sway a skeptical public with numerical proof of heterosexuality—the fact that 91 percent of former female athletes surveyed had married.[24] Publicity for the midwestern All-American Girls Baseball League included statistics on the number of married players.... Behind the scenes, teams passed dress and conduct codes. For example, the All-American Girls Baseball League prohibited players from wearing men's clothing or getting "severe" haircuts.[25] That this was an attempt to secure the heterosexual image of athletes was made even clearer when league officials announced that AAGBL policy prohibited the recruitment of "freaks" and "Amazons."[26]

In the end, the strategic emphasis on heterosexuality and the suppression of "mannishness" did little to alter the image of women in sport. The stereotype of the mannish lesbian athlete grew out of the persistent commonsense equation of sport with masculinity. Opponents of women's sport reinforced this belief when they denigrated women's athletic efforts and ridiculed skilled athletes as "grotesque," "mannish," or "unnatural." Leaders of women's sport unwittingly contributed to the same set of ideas when they began to orient their programs around the new feminine heterosexual idea. As physical education policies and media campaigns worked to suppress lesbianism and marginalize athletes who did not conform to dominant standards of femininity, sport officials embedded heterosexism into the institutional and ideological framework of sport. The effect extended beyond sport to the wider culture, where the figure of the mannish lesbian athlete announced that competitiveness, strength, independence, aggression, and physical intimacy among women fell outside the bounds of womanhood. As a symbol of female deviance, she served as a powerful reminder to all women to toe the line of heterosexuality and femininity or risk falling into a despised category of mannish (non-women) women....

[But] was the mannish lesbian athlete merely a figure of homophobic imagination, or was there in fact a strong lesbian presence in sport? When the All-American Girls Baseball League adamantly specified, "*Always appear in feminine attire*... MASCULINE HAIR STYLING? SHOES? COATS? SHIRTS? SOCKS, T-SHIRTS ARE BARRED AT ALL TIMES," and when physical education departments threatened to expel students for overly masculine appearance, were administrators merely responding to external pressure?[27] Or were they cracking down on women who may have indeed enjoyed the feel and look of a tough swagger, a short haircut, and men's clothing? And if so, did mannishness among athletes correspond to lesbianism, as the stereotype suggested? In spite of the public stigmatization, [is it probable that] some women may have found the activities, attributes, and emotions of sport conducive to lesbian self-expression and community formation?

As part of a larger investigation of women's athletic experience, I conducted oral histories with women who played competitive amateur, semiprofessional, and professional sports between 1930 and 1970. The interviews included only six openly lesbian narrators and thirty-six other women who either declared their heterosexuality or left their identity unstated.[28] Although the sample is too small to stand as a representative study, the interviews... and scattered other sources indicate that sport, particularly softball, provided an important site for the development of lesbian subculture and identity in the United States.[29] Gay and straight informants alike confirmed the lesbian presence in popular sport and physical education. Their testimony suggests that from at least the 1940s on, sport provided space for lesbian activity and social networks and served as a path into lesbian culture for young lesbians coming out and searching for companions and community.

Lesbian athletes explained that sport had been integral to their search for sexual identity and lesbian companionship. Ann Maguire, a softball player, physical education major, and top amateur bowler from New England, recalled that as a teenager in the late 1950s,

> I had been trying to figure out who I was and couldn't put a name to it. I mean it was very—no gay groups, no literature, no characters on *Dynasty*—I mean there was just nothing at that time. And trying to put a name to it. . . . I went to a bowling tournament, met two women there [and] for some reason something clicked and it clicked in a way that I was not totally aware of.

She introduced herself to the women, who later invited her to a gay bar. Maguire described her experience at age seventeen:

> I was being served and I was totally fascinated by the fact that, oh god, here I am being served and I'm not twenty-one. And it didn't occur to me until after a while when I relaxed and started realizing that I was at a gay bar. I just became fascinated. . . . And I was back there the next night. . . . I really felt a sense of knowing who I was and feeling very happy. Very happy that I had been able to through some miracle put this into place.[30] . . .

For women like Maguire, sport provided a point of entry into lesbian culture.

The question arises of whether lesbians simply congregated in athletic settings or whether a sports environment could actually "create" or "produce" lesbians. Some women fit the first scenario, describing how, in their struggle to accept and make sense out of lesbian desire, sport offered a kind of home that put feelings and identities into place. For other women, it appears that the lesbian presence in sport encouraged them to explore or act on feelings that they might not have had or responded to in other settings. Midwestern baseball player Nora Cross remembered that "it was my first exposure to gay people. . . . I was pursued by the one I was rooming with, that's how I found out." She got involved with her roommate and lived "a gay lifestyle" as long as she stayed in sport. Dorothy Ferguson Key also noticed that sport changed some women, recalling that "there were girls that came in the league like this . . . yeah, gay," but that at other times "a girl came in, and I mean they just change. . . . When they've been in a year they're completely changed. . . . They lived together."[31]

The athletic setting provided public space for lesbian sociability without naming it as such or excluding women who were not lesbians. This environment could facilitate the coming-out process, allowing women who were unsure about or just beginning to explore their sexual identity to socialize with gay and straight women without having to make immediate decisions or declarations. Gradually and primarily through unspoken communication, lesbians in sport recognized each other and created social networks. Gloria Wilson, who played softball in a mid-sized midwestern city, described her entry into lesbian social circles as a gradual process in which older lesbians slowly opened up their world to her and she grew more sure of her own identity and place in the group.

> A lot was assumed. And I don't think they felt comfortable with me talking until they knew me better. Then I think more was revealed. And we had little beer gatherings after a game at somebody's house. So then it was even more clear who was doing what when. And then I felt more comfortable too, fitting in, talking about my relationship too—and exploring more of the lesbian lifestyle, I guess.[32]

In an era when women did not dare announce their lesbianism in public, the social world of popular sport allowed women to find each other as teammates, friends, and lovers. But if athletics provided a public arena and social activity in which lesbians could recognize and affirm each other, what exactly was it that they recognized? This is where the issue of mannishness arises. Women athletes consistently explained the lesbian reputation of sport by reference to the mannishness of some athletes. . . . Suspected lesbians were said to "act like a man, you know, the way they walked, the way they talked, the things they did."

Such comments could merely indicate the pervasiveness of the masculine reputation of athletes and lesbians. However, lesbian narrators also suggested connections, although more complicated and nuanced, between athletics, lesbianism, and the "mannish" or "butchy" style which some lesbians manifested. None reported any doubt about their own gender identification as girls and women, but they indicated that they had often felt uncomfortable with the activities and attributes associated with the female gender. They preferred boyish clothes and activities to the conventional styles and manners of femininity.

Several spoke of . . . their relief upon finding athletic comrades who shared this sensibility. Josephine D'Angelo recalled that as a lesbian participating in sport, "you brought your culture with you. You brought your arm swinging . . . , the swagger, the way you tilted or cocked your head or whatever. You brought that with you." She explained that this style was acceptable in sports: "First thing you did was to kind of imitate the boys because you know, you're not supposed to throw like a girl." Although her rejection of femininity made her conspicuous in other settings, D'Angelo found that in sport "it was overlooked, see. You weren't different than the other kids. . . . Same likeness, people of a kind."[33]

These athletes were clearly women playing women's sports. But in the gender system of U.S. society, the skills, movements, clothing, and competition of sport were laden with impressions of masculinity. Lesbianism too crossed over the bounds of acceptable femininity. Consequently, sport could relocate girls or women with lesbian identities or feelings in an alternative nexus of gender meanings, allowing them to "be themselves"—or to express their gender and sexuality in an unconventional way. This applied to heterosexual women as well, many of whom also described themselves as "tomboys" attracted to boyish games and styles. As an activity that incorporated prescribed "masculine" physical activity into a way of being in the female body, athletics provided a social space and practice for reorganizing conventional meanings of embodied masculinity and femininity. *All* women in sport gained access to activities and expressive styles labeled masculine by the dominant culture. However, because lesbians were excluded from a concept of "real womanhood" defined around heterosexual appeal and desire, sport formed a milieu in which they could redefine womanhood on their own terms. . . .

However, the connections among lesbianism, masculinity, and sport require qualification. Many lesbians in and out of sport did not adopt "masculine" markers. And even among those who did, narrators indicated that butch styles did not occlude more traditionally "feminine" qualities of affection and tenderness valued by women athletes. Sport allowed women to combine activities and attributes perceived as masculine with more conventionally feminine qualities of friendship, cooperation, nurturance, and affection. Lesbians particularly benefited from this gender configuration, finding that in the athletic setting, qualities otherwise viewed as manifestations of homosexual deviance were understood as inherent, positive aspects of sport.[34] Aggressiveness, toughness, passionate intensity, expanded use of motion and space, strength, and competitiveness contributed to athletic excellence. With such qualities defined as athletic attributes rather than psychological abnormalities, the culture of sport permitted lesbians to express the full range of their gendered sensibilities while sidestepping the stigma of psychological deviance. For these reasons, athletics, in the words of Josephine D'Angelo, formed a "comforting" and "comfortable" place.[35]

Yet lesbians found sport hospitable only under certain conditions. Societal hostility toward homosexuality made lesbianism unspeakable in any realm of culture, but the sexual suspicions that surrounded sport made athletics an especially dangerous place in which to speak out. Physical educators and sport officials vigilantly guarded against signs of "mannishness," and teams occasionally expelled women who wore their hair in a "boyish bob" or engaged in obvious lesbian relationships. Consequently, gay athletes avoided naming or verbally acknowledging their sexuality. Loraine Sumner explained that "you never talked about it. . . . You never saw anything in public amongst the group of us. But you knew right darn well that this one was going with that one. But yet it just wasn't a topic of conversation. Never."[36] Instead, lesbian athletes signaled their identity through dress, posture, and look, reserving spoken communication for private gatherings among women who were acknowledged and accepted members of concealed communities.

Although in hindsight the underground nature of midcentury lesbian communities may seem extremely repressive, it may also have had a positive side. Unlike the bars where women's very presence declared their status as sexual outlaws, in sport athletes could enjoy the public company of lesbians while retaining their membership in local communities where neighbors, kin, and coworkers respected and sometimes even celebrated their athletic abilities. The unacknowledged, indefinite presence of lesbians in sport may have allowed for a wider range of lesbian experience and identity than is currently acknowledged in most scholarship. For instance, among women who did not identify as lesbian but were sexually drawn to other women, sport provided a venue in which they could express their desires without necessarily having articulated their feelings as a distinct sexual identity. The culture of sport provided space for some women to create clearly delineated lesbian identities and communities, at the same time allowing other women to move along the fringes of this world, operating across sexual and community lines without a firmly differentiated lesbian identity.

Women in sport experienced a contradictory array of heterosexual imperatives and homosexual possibilities. The fact that women athletes disrupted a critical domain of male power and privilege made sport a strategic site for shoring up existing gender and sexual hierarchies. The image of the mannish lesbian confirmed both the masculinity of sport and its association with female deviance. Lesbian athletes could not publicly claim their identity without risking expulsion, ostracism, and loss of athletic activities and social networks that had become crucial to their lives. Effectively silenced, their image was conveyed to the dominant culture primarily as a negative stereotype in which the mannish lesbian athlete represented the unfeminine "other," the line beyond which "normal" women must not cross.

The paradox of women's sport history is that the mannish athlete was not only a figure of homophobic discourse but also a human actor engaged in sexual innovation and struggle. Lesbian athletes used the social and psychic space of sport to create a collective culture and affirmative identity. The pride, pleasure, companionship, and dignity lesbians found in the athletic world helped them survive in a hostile society. The challenge posed by their collective existence and their creative reconstruction of womanhood formed a precondition for more overt, political challenges to lesbian oppression which have occurred largely outside the realm of sport.

Notes

1. Fred Wittner, "Shall the Ladies Join Us?" *Literary Digest* 117 (19 May 1934):43.
2. Jim Murray, *Austin American Statesman* (n.d.), Zaharias scrapbook, Barker Texas History Center ([hereafter] BTHC), University of Texas, Austin; Arsenio Hall Show, 1988.
3. "Fastest Women in the World," *Ebony* 10 (June 1955):28.
4. Helen Lenskyj, *Out of Bounds: Women, Sport, and Sexuality* (Toronto: Women's Press, 1986); Yvonne Zipter, *Diamonds Are a Dyke's Best Friend: Reflections, Reminiscences, and Reports from the Field on the Lesbian National Pastime* (Ithaca: Firebrand Books, 1988).
5. J. A. Mangan and Roberta J. Park, eds., *"Fair Sex" to Feminism: Sport and the Socialization of Women in the Industrial and Post-Industrial Era* (London: Frank Cays, 1987).
6. 1904–5 Scrapbooks of Anne Maude Butner, Butner Papers, University of Minnesota Archives, Minneapolis (UMA).
7. Violet W. Mange, "Field Hockey for Women," *Harper's Bazaar* 44 (Apr. 1910):246; Anna de Koven, "The Athletic Woman," *Good Housekeeping* 55 (Aug. 1912):150.
8. George Nathan, "Once There Was a Princess," *American Mercury* 19 (Feb. 1930):242.
9. This is an extremely brief and simplified summary of an extensive literature. For a good synthesis, see Estelle Freedman and John D'Emilio, *Intimate Matters: A History of Sexuality in America* (New York: Harper & Row, 1988), chaps. 8–10.
10. William Marston, "How Can a Woman Do It?" *Redbook* (Sept. 1933):60.
11. John D'Emilio, *Sexual Politics, Sexual Communities: The Making of a Homosexual Minority in the United States, 1940–1970* (Chicago: University of Chicago Press, 1983), pp. 9–53; Alan Berube, *Coming Out Under Fire: The History of Gay Men and Women in World War Two* (New York: Free Press, 1990).
12. Donna Penn, "The Meanings of Lesbianism in Post-War America," *Gender and History* 3 (Summer 1991):190–203; Wini Breines, "The 1950s: Gender and Some Social Science," *Sociological Inquiry* 56 (Winter 1986):69–92.
13. Gopher Yearbook (1952), p. 257, UMA.
14. Paul Gallico, *Houston Post*, 22 Mar. 1960; Pete Martin, "Babe Didrikson Takes Off Her Mask," *Saturday Evening Post* 20 (Sept. 1947):26–27.
15. Paula Giddings, *When and Where I Enter: The Impact of Black Women on Race and Sex in America* (New York: William Morrow, 1984), chaps. 1, 2, 4; Patricia Hill Collins, *Black Feminist Thought: Knowledge, Consciousness, and the Politics of Empowerment* (Boston: Unwin Hyman, 1990), chaps. 4, 8.
16. Elizabeth Lunbeck, "'A New Generation of Women': Progressive Psychiatrists and the

Hyper-sexual Female," *Feminist Studies* 13 (Fall 1987): 513–43.

17. *Baltimore Afro-American*, 29 June 1957.

18. "Fastest Women in the World," pp. 28, 32; *Detroit News* 31 (July 1962):1.

19. Patricia Del Rey, "The Apologetic and Women in Sport," in Carole Oglesby, ed., *Women and Sport* (Philadelphia: Lea & Febiger, 1978), pp. 107–11.

20. Mildred A. Schaeffer, "Desirable Objectives in Post-war Physical Education," *Journal of Health and Physical Education* 16 (Oct. 1945):44–47.

21. "Coeducational Classes," *Journal of Health, Physical Education, and Recreation* 26 (Feb. 1955):18. For curricular changes, I examined physical education records at the universities of Wisconsin, Texas, and Minnesota, Radcliffe College, Smith College, Tennessee State University, and Hampton University.

22. Dudley Ashton, "Recruiting Future Teachers," *Journal of Health, Physical Education, and Recreation* 28 (Oct. 1957):49.

23. The 1949–50 Physical Training Staff Handbook at the University of Texas stated, "Legs should be kept shaved" (p. 16). Box 3R213 of Department of Physical Training for Women Records, BTHC.

24. Roxy Andersen, "Statistical Survey of Former Women Athletes," *Amateur Athlete* (Sept. 1954):10–11.

25. All-American Girls Baseball League (AAGBL) 1951 Constitution, AAGBL Records.

26. Morris Markey, "Hey Ma, You're Out!" (n.d.), 1951 Records of the AAGBL; and "Feminine Sluggers," *People and Places* 8 (1952), AAGBL Records.

27. AAGBL 1951 Constitution, AAGBL Records.

28. The sample included forty-two women, ranging in age from their forties to their seventies, who had played a variety of sports in a range of athletic settings in the West, Midwest, Southeast, and Northeast. The majority were white women from urban working-class and rural backgrounds.

29. Zipter, *Diamonds Are a Dyke's Best Friend;* Lillian Faderman, *Odd Girls and Twilight Lovers: A History of Lesbian Life in Twentieth-Century America* (New York: Columbia University Press, 1991), pp. 154, 161–62.

30. Ann Maguire, interview with the author, Boston, 18 Feb. 1988.

31. Nora Cross (pseudonym), interview with the author, 20 May 1988; Dorothy Ferguson Key, interview with the author, Rockford, Ill., 19 Dec. 1988.

32. Gloria Wilson (pseudonym), interview with the author, 11 May 1988.

33. Josephine D'Angelo, interview with the author, Chicago, 21 Dec. 1988.

34. Joseph P. Goodwin, *More Man Than You'll Ever Be! Gay Folklore and Acculturation in Middle America* (Bloomington: Indiana University Press, 1989), p. 62.

35. D'Angelo interview.

36. Loraine Sumner, interview with the author, West Roxbury, Mass., 18 Feb. 1988.

JOYCE ANTLER

Imagining Jewish Mothers in the 1950s

The wartime alliance between the United States and the USSR melted quickly as the defeat of Germany was followed by a ruthless Soviet occupation of Eastern Europe. The use of the atomic bomb at Hiroshima and Nagasaki in the summer of 1945 was both indication of and cause for heightened mistrust, and failure to develop international control of atomic energy made it worse. By 1948 the former allies had become antagonists. The United States and major Western European nations joined in a mutual defense agreement that anticipated the North Atlantic Treaty Organization (NATO); the USSR and pro-Soviet regimes in Eastern Europe shaped what would eventually become the Warsaw Pact.

Excerpted from ch. 8, with notes modified by the author, of *The Journey Home: Jewish Women and the American Century* by Joyce Antler (New York: Free Press, 1997). Reprinted with the permission of the author and The Free Press, a Division of Simon & Schuster, Inc. Notes have been edited and renumbered. *Yoo Hoo, Mrs. Goldberg*, a documentary by Aviva Kempner, was released in 2009; see www.mollygoldbergfilm.org/home.php.

As historian William Chafe has observed, in this climate "legitimate concerns could easily spill into paranoia."* President Harry S. Truman created a Federal Employee Loyalty Program, appointing a panel authorized to screen for sympathy toward "totalitarian, fascist or subversive" organizations. What counted as sympathy and what counted as subversive were left vague. The House Committee on Un-American Activities (HUAC) was uncompromising—investigating many who had only the vaguest connection with Communist organizations and demanding that witnesses not only account for their own activities but also name others with whom they had associated. If they refused to name others, they were held in contempt of Congress. The only alternative to naming friends and associates was to refuse to answer at all, citing the Fifth Amendment's protection against self-incrimination. When HUAC investigated Communist influence on the entertainment industry, even actors whose programs had no political content could be swept up, as Gertrude Berg would find.

When the Soviet Union tested its first atomic bomb in 1949, the American public was shaken. Early the following year, Klaus Fuchs, a British physicist, was convicted of spying for the Soviet Union. The FBI search for his American collaborators soon found Harry Gold, a Philadelphia chemist, who confessed to his own complicity, and David Greenglass, a machinist, who confessed and also implicated his brother-in-law, Julius Rosenberg. Shortly afterword, Julius's wife, Ethel, was also arrested on suspicion of conspiracy to commit espionage by passing atomic secrets to the Soviets. The evidence against them was fragile, drawn from alleged conversations for which there were no third-party witnesses. But the Rosenbergs' Communist sympathies were invoked at every turn in the trial; they were blamed for the vulnerability of the United States and for making feasible the Communist aggression in Korea. Both Rosenbergs protested their innocence; both were sentenced to death.

An extended series of unsuccessful legal appeals followed; the Rosenberg case became an international cause. The famous Spanish artist Pablo Picasso offered lithograph portraits of the couple as fund-raisers for the costs of their defense; there were mass rallies on their behalf in European and American cities. In June 1953, President Eisenhower refused a last plea for clemency; he explained his decision in a letter to his son John:

> I must say that it goes against the grain to avoid interfering in the case where a woman is to receive capital punishment. . . . [But] in this instance it is the woman who is the strong and recalcitrant character. The man is the weak one. . . . [I]f there would be any commuting of the woman's sentence without the man's then from here on the Soviets would simply recruit their spies from among women.†

Julius and Ethel Rosenberg were executed at Sing Sing prison, New York, on June 19, 1953.

Popular cultural ideas, including images of good mothers, seeped into the ways in which Ethel Rosenberg was judged by the media and the general public. Political anxieties about international relations made radio and television celebrities like Gertrude Berg cautious about the message they sent. And even after the entire European Jewish population had barely survived the Holocaust, Berg and Rosenberg's Jewishness made both vulnerable.

*William Chafe, *The Unfinished Journey: America Since World War II* (New York: Oxford University Press, 1986), p. 98.
†John Lewis Gaddis, *Strategies of Containment: A Critical Appraisal of Postwar American National Security Policy* (New York: Oxford University Press, 1982), p. 138, n. 31.

For most Americans, and not least for American Jews, the postwar period represented a paradoxical time in political as well as popular culture. Recovering from the Depression and World War II, Jews continued their move into the mainstream of American life, enjoying unprecedented economic prosperity and a great increase in opportunities for education, the professions, and business.

Yet troubling signs rippled the smooth surface of Jewish acculturation. Despite its decline, anti-Semitism remained a significant factor in American life, with almost sixty known anti-Semitic organizations operating in 1950. Also ominous was the association of American Jews in the public mind with the menace of communism, an association fostered by the trial and conviction of Ethel and Julius Rosenberg. Although the trial did not trigger the kind of virulent anti-Semitic tirades that many Jewish leaders had feared, the anxiety it caused among Jews suggested that they were perhaps not as at home in America as they had believed.

The polar experiences of American Jews in the 1950s—their spectacular arrival in the American mainstream coupled with lingering fears of anti-Semitism and doubts about Jewish acculturation—are represented by two famous Jewish women of the time: the cherubic, smiling Molly Goldberg, the radio and TV sitcom heroine of the long-running series "The Goldbergs," and the taut, drawn, unsmiling Ethel Greenglass Rosenberg herself.

Although a fictional character, Molly Goldberg was played with such verisimilitude by Gertrude Berg—in fact an American-born, middle-class Jew—that the public easily confused the mythical Molly with her real-life impersonator. Berg, who created the character, lived a very different life from that of Molly Goldberg. Yet Molly/Gertrude was powerful in popular culture precisely because she ostensibly represented reality. Molly's character, tied to Gertrude Berg, not only mobilized the cultural power of a "real" person but, in some sense, became a real person. In much the same way that Molly Goldberg enjoyed a reality independent of Gertrude Berg, so did the media representations of Ethel Greenglass Rosenberg come to dominate public perceptions of the real Ethel. Yet the flesh-and-blood Rosenberg differed as much from the media's Ethel as Gertrude did from Molly.[1]

Second-generation daughters of East European immigrant families, Gertrude Berg and Ethel Rosenberg exemplify the changing aspirations, and the changing representations, of Jewish women in the 1950s. Both women defied convention: Gertrude, by building a media career and directing and producing a long-running hit series, all the while managing her own household and family life; Ethel, by combining a staunch commitment to radical ideology with a conscientious, even obsessive, motherhood. For a generation or more, however, the cultural construction of "Molly" and "Ethel" has left little room for imagining the full historical matrix in which Gertrude and Ethel lived their lives. The potent alliance between media and politics that characterized the Red Scare years obliterated all but the masks of Molly and Ethel.[2]

Molly and Ethel were not the only representations of Jewish women in the politicized culture of the 1950s. Another archetypal middle-class Jewish woman of the decade was "Shirley," a type made famous by Herman Wouk in his 1955 novel, *Marjorie Morningstar*. Selling millions of copies and made into a successful movie starring the popular actress Natalie Wood, the book depicted the transformation of a young, ambitious, "emancipated" Jewish girl into a conventional suburban matron, a Shirley. Rebellious as a youth Marjorie/Shirley matured into "the respectable girl, the mother of the next generation, all tricked out to appear gay and girlish and carefree but with a terrible threatening dullness jutting through"; later Marjorie/Shirley became a regular synagogue goer, active in the Jewish organizations of the town," a model, in fact, of the many thousands of Jewish women who belonged to temple sisterhoods, Hadassah, the National Council of Jewish Women, and similar organizations. While Wouk treats Shirley sympathetically, Mrs. Patimkin, the Shirley-like Jewish mother in Philip Roth's 1959 novella, *Good-bye Columbus*, is portrayed as vain, empty-headed, materialistic. Her daughter, Brenda, demonstrating the worst qualities of 1950s suburban Jewish affluence, joined Marjorie Morningstar as one in a series of indelible images of a new kind of Jewish heroine—assimilated, smoothly confident, flirtatious, beautiful, spoiled. Together with Ethel and Molly, these fictional representations would provide enduring images of Jewish

American womanhood—mothers and daughters, protectors and princesses—that would wield more power and influence than their creators could ever have expected.[3]

Yet these images do not do justice to the varied experiences of Jewish women in postwar America. The activism demonstrated by such groups as the National Council of Jewish Women and the Emma Lazarus Federation of Jewish Women's Clubs (a left-wing group created after the Holocaust by a group of largely Yiddish-speaking women of the immigrant generation) belies the homogeneity of the period and demonstrates that "Molly," "Ethel," and "Shirley" were cultural constructs after all.

. . . "The Rise of the Goldbergs" was one of the most popular serials in radio's golden era, running from 1929 through 1946, and . . . 1949 to 1950. After 1931, the show aired nightly, for some years carried by both the CBS and NBC networks. In 1946, the show (known as "The Goldbergs") made the transition to television, running through 1955. It was revived in the early 1960s as "Mrs. G," a new series about Molly at college. Along the way there were also a comic strip, a syndicated column ("Mamatalks"), a published version of the show's early scripts, a cookbook, a hit Broadway play (*Me and Molly*), two films, and Berg's autobiography, *Molly and Me*. So identified was Gertrude Berg with Molly Goldberg that she signed autographs in the character's name. Yet it was Berg, the consummate professional, who wrote as well as starred in the show's five thousand-plus radio scripts as well as the later television programs.

During the second quarter of the twentieth century, Molly Goldberg became the quintessential representation of the American Jewish mother in popular culture. "Kind-hearted," "humane," "gentle," "gracious," "sympathetic," and "tender"—these were the words typically used in advertisements for the show—Molly Goldberg, like her creator Gertrude Berg, was nonetheless a woman of force and dominance. [Her] genius was to wed the iron qualities of traditional East European Jewish women with a charm and humor that counteracted the threat of their power. During the Depression, when a negative stereotype of the Jewish mother as materialistic and pushy began to appear in the works of Clifford Odets and other Jewish male writers, Berg's Molly had a more positive appeal.[4]

Molly's compassion and the comic elements in her character diverted attention from other, potentially troublesome traits. At best meddlesome and at worst nagging and controlling, Molly got her way in almost every show, but always for the purpose of helping others. Molly's speech, full of malapropisms, reflected her status as an immigrant whose eagerness to adopt American usages was greater than her knowledge: "Come sit on the table, dinner is ready. . . You'll swallow a cup, darling? . . . Throw an eye into the ice-box and give me an accounting. . . ."[5] Molly's generosity and the quaintness of her language—including the famous opening line of the show, "Yoo hoo Mrs. Bloom," which she yelled out the window to her tenement neighbor—endeared her to audiences.

No matter how exaggerated, caricatured, or sentimental the show's characters, to audiences they seemed believable and realistic. Writing in 1951, novelist Charles Angoff praised the show for its realistic representation of "virtually the whole panorama of middle-class Jewish-American life":

> There are the neighbors who borrow from and lend to one another, and who offer advice, whether asked or not . . . there are the sisters and cousins and aunts, with all their jealousies and bickerings and generosities and meddlings . . . the young folk who sometimes think they have "outgrown" their parents but who find that for comfort and counsel there are no substitutes . . . and there is Molly herself, whose heart bleeds for every unmarried girl and starving butcher and lonely grocer, and who is as quick as the proverbial lightning in concocting ideas to get the "right" girl and the "right" man together, to straighten out family squabbles, to help out a reformed thief, to get her own son to invite her to a college affair—in short, Molly the Mixer and the Fixer.

Together these characters presented "neurotic tensions, despair, ecstasy, conniving, kindliness, back-biting . . . the normal life of Bronx and Brooklyn and Manhattan and Chicago and Boston and Philadelphia and San Francisco Jews." Angoff concluded: "I have never heard anyone who knows Jewish life say that 'The Goldbergs' are not true to life. Molly Goldberg, indeed, is so basically true a character that I sometimes think she may become an enduring name in the national literature. She is the prototype of the Jewish mother during the past twenty-five years."[6]

A good part of the praise for "The Goldbergs" was due to its uplifting message about American family life and moral values. Berg once described the, show to a reporter, using Molly's lines: "Jake wants the children to have everything money can buy, and I want them to have everything money can't buy." This philosophical difference formed the core of the show's dramatic conflict, and despite the Goldbergs' upward mobility, it was always resolved in Molly's favor. Listeners found the message of "The Goldbergs" inspirational: ministers composed sermons around the program, and at least one Orthodox rabbi instructed congregants not to turn their radios off on Friday afternoon, so that they could listen to Molly on Shabbos evening "without breaking the law." During wartime, especially, the show received accolades as "a force for decency and the democratic way of life."[7]

Three points stand out regarding the Molly Goldberg character. First, Molly as a Jewish mother was an odd but lovable, generous woman who solved all the problems of her family, neighborhood, and community through her skillful "mixing-in." She was a voluble, talkative busybody, a *balaboste*, but one with a loving heart who could always be trusted to do the right thing.

The second point is that in spite of her ethnicity, which was always prominent (even when the use of dialect subsided), Molly and her children espoused assimilationist values. Over the decades, the audience saw the family leave their Bronx neighborhood, move to the suburbs, and send the children off to college. In this respect, "The Goldbergs" was an accurate representation of the Jewish middle-class's entry into the American mainstream. Despite the family's economic transformation, Molly herself changed very little. Even in the mid-1950s, she looked and sounded like a newly arrived immigrant; in this respect, Molly remained in a television time warp.[8]

The third point is that as the Goldbergs became America's surrogate family, Molly became everybody's mother, a woman who, *because* of her ethnicity (that is, her difference), represented the American ideal of brotherly love and interreligious cooperation. This point was borne out in the huge amount of fan mail Berg received and in the accolades from non-Jewish as well as Jewish organizations.

In order to achieve such wide acceptance in both mainstream and Jewish audiences, Berg made a conscious decision, as she told one reporter, not to bring in

> anything that will bother people . . . unions, politics, fundraising, Zionism, socialism, intergroup relations, I don't stress them. After all, aren't such things second to daily living? The Goldbergs are not defensive about their Jewishness, or especially aware of it. I keep things average. I don't want to lose friends.[9]

Like other situation comedies of the 1950s, "The Goldbergs" portrayed the family as a sea of domestic tranquillity—a "suburban middle landscape," according to one critic—isolated from problems in the larger society. Sitcoms were "Cold War comedies of reassurance," in which politics, "by its telling absence . . . was a contaminating force to be kept beyond the threshold of the private household." In shows like "Leave It to Beaver," "Father Knows Best," "The Adventures of Ozzie and Harriet," "The Donna Reed Show," "I Remember Mama," and "Make Room for Daddy/The Danny Thomas Show," television reinforced values of family togetherness—responsibility, maturity, adjustment, and "enlightened permissiveness."[10] In most of these comedies, it was not the maternal figure but the benevolent patriarch who navigated his family through the shoals of neighborhood life. Yet Molly Goldberg's affable, homespun wisdom, like that of the Norwegian mother in "I Remember Mama" (played by Peggy Wood), was no less authoritative than that of her male counterparts. As women in command of a vast repository of folk wisdom, Berg and Wood steered their families through the special challenges of modern American life, while demonstrating for the television audience that conflict could be easily managed and contained if "normal" family values were upheld.

But this is not the whole story. Gertrude Berg could eliminate controversy from her show, but not from her life. Philip Loeb, who played Molly's husband, Jake, on radio in the late 1940s and took the character to TV in 1949 was a victim of the blacklist in 1950. After a debate with her sponsors (who eventually pulled out), Gertrude Berg succumbed and fired Loeb in 1952; he committed suicide three years later. Comedian Milton Berle reveals in his memoirs that in 1950, when Berg was "fighting the witch-hunters" who had "enough juice to hurt [her] in every way," his sponsors and NBC would not permit Berg to appear on his show, even though she had her own. . . . It is possible that Berg, a member of an actors' group that included many well-known left-wing artists such as Paul Robeson, was herself the target of a blacklist.[11]

The portrait of Molly Goldberg as the ideal Jewish mother of the 1950s may thus have clashed with the reality of Gertrude Berg's own politics; it certainly contrasted with the fact of her career. Married and the mother of two children, Berg had grown up writing skits to amuse the guests at her parents' summer hotel in the Catskills. Even after marriage and motherhood, she was determined to pursue her career as a writer, but the short stories she submitted to popular magazines all came back with rejection slips. Then came her breakthrough in a trial run of "Goldberg" scripts, written for radio. Almost immediately, Berg became a highly successful media entrepreneur. She was no Molly Goldberg, stay-at-home housewife, though she prided herself on her "normal" family life.

Berg's decision to eschew politics and what she described as "defensive" Jewishness reflected a common strategy of leading Jewish organizations of the period. In the late 1940s and the 1950s, these groups embarked on new ventures designed to counteract the forces of bigotry and enhance interreligious and interethnic harmony. Rather than responding exclusively to direct threats to American Jewry, they took action on a panoply of social and cultural concerns, including opposition to McCarthyism and the promotion of civil rights and the ideals of the welfare state. "The Goldbergs," with its exhortation to celebrate human brotherhood and its conscious disregard of difference, mirrored these objectives.

The example of compassionate concern that Molly Goldberg demonstrated to her Christian friends and neighbors was embodied in the postwar program of the National Council of Jewish Women. In 1947, the NCJW introduced a new initiative on "intercultural relations." The initiative, entitled "cultural democracy," exposed the flaws in the idea of the melting pot and championed the free expression of cultural differences. "Something good is lost when people are melted down to a uniform consistency," the NCJW asserted; it was the "diversity of [many] cultures which make the American society strong." According to the NCJW, the prophetic imperative to brotherhood and other Judaic teachings made "the universal concern for all people" a guide for American Jews. But the Council insisted that it was an American as well as a Jewish obligation to eradicate intolerance. . . .

Recognizing prejudice was . . . not sufficient to eradicate it. Council leaders argued that it was crucial to be "'good neighbors,' understanding and respecting our fellow citizens of different racial and religious backgrounds." For this purpose, chapters were instructed to work with other local groups on such issues as eliminating stereotypes and stimulating public interest in building better intercultural understanding. But it was equally important to develop a positive program of action, seeking "economic and social justice" for all people regardless of their race, religion, or national origin.[12] For this reason, the NCJW extended the project on interfaith harmony beyond such local issues as schools, housing, and citizenship to include broad questions of public policy, social legislation, and even international affairs, all of which it considered integral to intercultural work. During the 1950s, the NCJW promoted these objectives through public education and lobbying on behalf of such causes as immigration reform and civil rights.[13]

In 1952, the NCJW launched a related project, the Freedom Campaign, designed to educate the public to the importance of civil liberties and to encourage people in "speaking up for what they believe is right" while "respecting the beliefs of others." Declaring its staunch opposition to communism, the NCJW also declared war on Senator McCarthy and the House Un-American Activities Committee's "campaign of vilification" against "everyone who has ever held an original idea or participated in the activities of a minority group." . . . The Council formed a special alliance with the Young Women's Christian Association (YWCA) in this campaign.[14]

The common ground of racial and religious tolerance that guided NCJW's postwar intercultural effort was specifically acknowledged in 1961, when the council and the YWCA came together again to commemorate the fiftieth anniversary of both organizations' initial commitment to seek public policy protection for working women and children. . . . [They] issued a ten-point "Code of Personal

Commitment," stressing opposition to prejudice, protection of individual liberties, and efforts toward world peace. "I will cultivate objectivity of thought / And will consider new and different points of view," the statement read. "I will recognize my common kinship with all / and remember that whatever happens to anyone happens to me."[15]

Despite the NCJW's freedom campaign and its dedication to protecting the rights of political dissidents and racial, religious, and ethnic minorities, the Council, like Gertrude Berg herself, had little to say about the Rosenberg case or Ethel Rosenberg as a Jewish woman.

Like Gertrude Berg, Ethel Rosenberg aspired to an artistic career, although it was as a singer and actress, rather than a writer, that she hoped to make her mark. An excellent student at Seward Park High School on Manhattan's Lower East Side, Ethel planned to attend college and took college preparatory courses. Graduating in 1931 at the height of the Depression, however, she felt lucky to obtain a clerical job with the National New York Shipping and Packing Company. The Clark House Players, an amateur theater group sponsored by a settlement house around the corner from her home, was the object of most of her enthusiasm over the next few years; she also took acting classes at the Henry Street Settlement and attended lectures by members of several experimental theater companies. At nineteen, Ethel was accepted into the prestigious Schola Cantorum, becoming the choir's youngest member; the group occasionally sang at the Metropolitan Opera House. The following year, singing an operatic solo at a benefit for the International Seamen's Union, Ethel met Julius Rosenberg, who claimed she had the most beautiful voice he had ever heard. They were married three years later.[16]

Ethel pursued her singing and acting interests only sporadically after her marriage. Her independent involvement in political action also declined. Before meeting Julius, she had helped to organize the Ladies Apparel Shipping Clerks Union at her company, serving as the only woman on a four-person strike committee that called a citywide action in which over 10,000 workers participated. Fired for her role in this strike, Ethel brought a complaint before the newly formed National Labor Relations Board; the case was later decided in her favor. By this time, she had found employment as a stenographer with Bell Textile Company. She left this job after Julius found work with the United States Signal Corps, turning her attention to volunteer activities. Among the groups she joined were the women's auxiliary of her husband's union—the Federation of Architects, Engineers, Chemists and Technicians (FAECT)—and, after the start of World War II, the Lower East Side Defense Council.

After the births of her sons—Michael in 1943 and Robert four years later—Rosenberg became increasingly absorbed in family matters. According to one neighbor, she was "literally a mother 24 hours out of 24."[17] But motherhood did not come as easily to Ethel as it did to Molly Goldberg and Gertrude Berg. Beset by physical ailments resulting from chronic scoliosis and the emotional strain of dealing with young children, she grew increasingly concerned about her parenting skills. Setting limits for her children—responding to them with both the generosity and the authority that she felt good parenting entailed—was especially problematic; the importance of these qualities was continually being emphasized in the pages of *Parents Magazine*, which Rosenberg read religiously, and in the vastly popular performances of Gertrude Berg. Seeking guidance, Rosenberg took a course on child psychology at the New School for Social Research and enlisted the help of a social worker at the Jewish Board of Guardians; soon afterward, she began to see a private psychiatrist. Though she deeply loved and respected Julius, he could not alleviate her anxieties about raising their sons. Despite their political radicalism, both accepted the gender role division that allotted breadwinning responsibilities to the husband and child rearing to the wife. "The good mother is the key to proper child rearing," Rosenberg wrote to her lawyer, Manny Bloch, after she had been arrested and imprisoned along with Julius on charges of conspiracy to commit espionage.[18]

In view of Rosenberg's faith in communism, her resorting to psychoanalysis and social work may seem surprising. But Rosenberg's worries as a mother apparently overshadowed any doubts she may have had about succumbing to such capitalist opiates. In the emphasis she placed on child rearing, Rosenberg was in fact not far removed from Molly Goldberg. Whether she read Gertrude Berg's advice column in the 1930s, or listened to any of the Goldberg shows on radio or TV, is unknown, but her idea of what characterized the "good" mother certainly overlapped with Berg's portrayal of Molly as understanding, tolerant, generous—everything Rosenberg's own mother, Tessie Greenglass, was not.

Tessie Greenglass was an unhappy, troubled woman, disappointed in her husband's lack of ambition and inability to move the family out of poverty. Unlike the Goldbergs or the Bergs, the Greenglasses never realized their dream of American success; Tessie's frustrations with this failure were apparently visited on her only daughter. Favoring her three sons, especially the youngest, David, she treated Ethel with disrespect bordering on cruelty; certainly Ethel was abused emotionally (and sometimes physically, since Tessie used corporal punishment on all the children). Despite (or because of) Ethel's excellence at school and her good-girl demeanor at home, she was also the butt of her brothers' jealousy; she was very much the scapegoat of the entire family.[19]

When, years later, David Greenglass accused Ethel and Julius of masterminding the spy ring in which he was allegedly involved at Los Alamos, Rosenberg was not surprised that her mother accepted her brother's story rather than her own. But the extent of her mother's lack of support for her, and for her children, hurt Ethel Rosenberg enormously. When Tessie first visited Rosenberg in prison it was only to scream at her for harming David and to call her a "dirty Communist." After Rosenberg was transferred to solitary confinement at Sing Sing, Tessie did not visit her at all for two years; when she finally did it was only to urge her daughter to confess. Ethel Rosenberg responded angrily, but admitted to her lawyer that she would "still give anything in the world for one kind word from her." Tessie returned two months before Rosenberg's execution to insist again that she affirm her brother's account and admit her guilt. According to the prison official who was present, Rosenberg, enraged, called her mother a "witch" and "yelled and raved to such an extent that she was cautioned by the guard that the interview would be terminated unless she quieted down." That was the last time Rosenberg' saw Tessie.[20]

No doubt Ethel Rosenberg's troubled relationship with her mother accounted in good part for her concerns about her own parenting. But her anxieties about her performance as a mother and her children's emotional well-being were also the product of cultural messages that she, like others with her background and aspirations, absorbed from the surrounding culture. Under the growing influence of child guidance specialists and behavioral psychologists, parenting in the late 1940s and early 1950s became more than ever a matter of expert counseling and knowledge rather than innate capability. During these years, the notion of motherhood as "pathology" was a staple in both the popular and scientific press, with all manner of experts holding mothers accountable for withdrawn, destructive, disturbed, and "deviant" children.[21] If Ethel Rosenberg blamed herself for child-rearing problems—however normal—she was merely reflecting the accepted wisdom. Rosenberg's faith in professional child guidance in fact illuminates why Molly Goldberg was so popular a figure in the postwar period. In representing an earlier time, when parents dominated their children's lives and truly "knew best," sitcoms like "The Goldbergs" provided nostalgic reassurance to a generation increasingly troubled about the viability of a harmonious family life in the context of a pluralistic society. Rosenberg's concern about her own family, and her employment of therapy for herself and counseling for the children, suggests how deeply a part of her generation she was.

In spite of her intense concerns about her children, Ethel Rosenberg's behavior during her trial convinced the jurors and the American public that she was guilty—not because of the evidence, but because she lacked "maternal feeling." That Rosenberg was arrested and tried as a "lever" to force her husband to talk is now well documented. Based wholly on the testimony of her brother David and his wife, Ruth, the case was "not too strong against Mrs. Rosenberg," as one prosecutor acknowledged privately. Such doubts continued after Ethel's conviction and remain today, even though Julius's guilt now appears certain. "Was your wife cognizant of your activities?" prosecutors asked Julius Rosenberg in a questionnaire submitted to him at the Sing-Sing Death House.[22] Given the paucity of evidence regarding her participation in the conspiracy, Ethel Rosenberg's appearance at the trial became all-important.

To the public Ethel Rosenberg's failure to break down under the pressure of her arrest and trial appeared to confirm that she cared more about ideology than about her offspring, and was therefore guilty. Her denial of guilt, along with her repeated reliance on the Fifth Amendment, created the impression, according to one legal scholar, of a "cold, well-composed woman lacking 'normal' feminine characteristics." Because of her failure to lose her composure on the witness stand (both her husband [and] his co-defendant, Morton Sobell, appeared much more uneasy), Rosenberg seemed enigmatic, "unnatural." To the jury foreman she was a "steely, stoney, tight-lipped woman. She was the mastermind. Julius would have spoken if she would have permitted him. He was more human. She was more disciplined." According to another juror, she was certainly guilty—of being a bad mother: "I had two daughters at the time, and it bothered me how they would subject their children to such a thing. I just couldn't understand it."[23]

After the Rosenbergs were convicted and sentenced to death, the image of Ethel as an "unnatural" woman and mother blocked appeals for clemency. FBI director J. Edgar Hoover used the fact of Rosenberg's failure to talk with her own mother for two years as evidence of her evil nature; when Douglas Dillon, then ambassador to France, protested the severity of her sentence compared to those of convicted British spies Klaus Fuchs and Allan Nunn May, Hoover reported that when Tessie Greenglass urged Rosenberg to confess to spare her children, Rosenberg had rebuked her with the words, "Don't mention the children. Children are born every day of the week." Although he had previously opposed the execution of Ethel as well as Julius on the grounds that it would leave two young children orphaned, Hoover changed his mind after receiving the FBI's report that "Ethel was not a good mother after all." President Eisenhower used similar gender-based reasoning in his denial of clemency: "In this instance, it is the woman who is the strong and recalcitrant character, the man who is the weak one." He believed that as the unquestioned "leader in the spy ring," Ethel Rosenberg had renounced all rights to special treatment as a woman and mother of two young children.[24] She was the first American woman to be executed for the crime of conspiracy to commit espionage.

No greater contrast could exist than that between the Molly Goldberg ideal of the 1950s—friendly, garrulous, kindhearted, family-oriented, non-controversial, and nonpolitical—and the public image of Ethel Rosenberg: silent and mysterious, conspiratorial and political, dominating and evil. Blindly loyal to her husband at the cost of abandoning her own children, she seemed, above all—and perhaps most dangerously—a neglectful, uncaring mother. Many Americans who loved Molly Goldberg were deeply shocked by Ethel Rosenberg.

This portrait of Ethel Rosenberg, elaborated in the media, was especially troubling to Jews.[25] In contrast to the Goldbergs, with their seamless adjustment to American society, the Rosenbergs appeared as an alien couple linked to a foreign power; their rejection of mainstream American values, such as those espoused by the Goldbergs and other TV sitcom families, spoke to the dark underside of the American dream and enhanced the presumption of guilt. Moreover, in contrast to the wholesome Goldberg family ("Allow me to ask whether in Jewish families nothing ever goes wrong," one viewer wrote to ask. "Is it always 'Papa darling' and 'Mama darling'? . . . no wrangling, no quibbling?") the Rosenberg family was fatally divided between brothers and sister, mother and daughter.[26] In the early 1950s, when such a family was not yet labeled "dysfunctional," the Rosenbergs seemed not only abnormal but un-American. . . .

That the Molly Goldberg ideal coincided with the aspirations of the real Ethel Rosenberg was no more ironic than the fact that Ethel—a woman excessively concerned about mothering—was portrayed by government officials and the media as a cold, uncaring "monster" of a mother. Ethel's convincing stoicism in the face of her most enormous loss—that of her children—may have been her finest performance.

NOTES

1. For an extended discussion of Molly Goldberg in relation to Ethel Rosenberg, see my "A Bond of Sisterhood: Ethel Rosenberg, Molly Goldberg, and Radical Jewish Women of the 1950s," in Marjorie Garber and Rebecca L. Walkowitz, eds. *Secret Agents: The Rosenberg Case, McCarthyism, and Fifties America* (New York: Routledge, 1995): 197–214.

2. On the politicization of culture during the 1950s, see Stephen J. Whitfield, *The Culture of the Cold*

War (Baltimore: Johns Hopkins University Press, 1991). On women's roles, see Elaine Tyler May, *Homeward Bound: American Families in the Cold War Era* (New York: Basic Books, 1988); Wini Breines, *Young, White, and Miserable: Growing Up Female in the Fifties* (Boston: Beacon, 1992); and Joanne Meyerowitz, ed. *Not June Cleaver: Women and Gender in Postwar America, 1945–1960* (Philadelphia: Temple University Press, 1994).

3. Herman Wouk, *Marjorie Morningstar* (Boston: Little Brown, 1955/1983), 172, 562; Philip Roth, *Goodbye Columbus and Five Short Stories* (Boston: Houghton Mifflin, 1959/1989).

4. B. G. Bienstock, "The Changing Image of the American Jewish Mother," in Virginia Tufte and Barbara Myerhoff, eds. *Changing Images of the Family* (New Haven: Yale University Press, 1979).

5. Charles Angoff, "'The Goldbergs' and Jewish Humor," *Congress Weekly* 18 (March 5, 1951): 13; "The Goldbergs March On," *Life* (April 25, 1949): 59; "The Goldbergs," script, Oct. 3, 1949, Gertrude Berg Papers, Special Collections, Syracuse University, Syracuse, N.Y.

6. Angoff, "'The Goldbergs,'" 12–13. Gertrude Berg cited in Jack Long, "Her Family Is Her Fortune," *American*, n.d., Ill, Gertrude Berg Papers.

7. Joan Jacobs Brumberg, "Gertrude Berg," in Barbara Sicherman and Carol Hurd Green, eds., *Notable American Women—The Modern Period: A Biographical Dictionary* (Cambridge: Belknap Press of Harvard University Press, 1980), 73–74; Sulamith Ish-Kishor, "Interesting People: Gertrude Berg," *Jewish Tribune* (Oct. 10, 1930), 7.

8. Morris Freedman, "The Real Molly Goldberg," *Commentary* 21 (April 1954), 364; also see Donald Weber, *Haunted in the World: Jewish American Culture from Cahan to "The Goldbergs"* (Bloomington: Indiana University Press, 2005); and Glenn D. Smith, *Something on My Own: Gertrude Berg and American Broadcasting, 1929–1956* (Syracuse: Syracuse University Press, 2007).

9. Freedman, "The Real Molly Goldberg," 360.

10. Hal Himmelstein, *Television Myth and the American Mind* (New York: Praeger, 1984), 84–97; David Marc, *Comic Visions: Television Comedy and American Culture* (Boston: Unwin Hyman, 1989), 65; Darrell Y. Hamamoto, *Nervous Laughter: Television Situation Comedy and Liberal Democratic Ideology* (New York: Praeger, 1989), 24–25.

11. Milton Berle, *Milton Berle: An Autobiography* (New York: Delacorte Press, 1974), 293–94.

12. National Council of Jewish Women, "Cultural Democracy—Pattern for America" (mimeograph, Sept. 1947): 5, 4, 11, 9–10, 19, NCJW Papers, Library of Congress, Washington,D.C.

13. National Council of Jewish Women, Committee on Education and Social Action, *Spotlight*,Vols. 5–9, [1949–53], NCJW Papers.

14. *Spotlight*, Vols. 8–9.

15. National Council of Jewish Women and YWCA, Joint Statement, Dec. 6, 1961, NCJW Papers.

16. See Ilene Philipson, *Ethel Rosenberg: Beyond the Myths* (New Brunswick, N.J.: Rutgers University Press, 1988) and Carol Hurd Green, "Ethel Rosenberg," in Sicherman and Green, *Notable American Women*, 601–4.

17. Sheila M. Brennan, "Popular Images of American Women in the 1950s and Their Impact on Ethel Rosenberg's Trial and Conviction," *Women's Rights Law Reporter* 14, No. 1 (Winter 1992): 47.

18. Ethel Rosenberg to Emanuel Bloch, August 31, 1951–Sept. 6, 1951, in Robert Meeropol and Michael Meeropol, *We Are Your Sons: The Legacy of Ethel and Julius Rosenberg* (Boston: Houghton Mifflin, 1975), 101.

19. Philipson, *Ethel Rosenberg*, 28. The testimony of David Greenglass and especially his wife, Ruth Greenglass, played a major role in convicting Ethel. In recent years, David admitted that he made up the story; see Sam Roberts, *Brother: The Untold Story of the Rosenberg Case* (New York: Random House, 2003). Filmmaker Ivy Meeropol, the granddaughter of Ethel and Julius, explores the Greenglass' involvement, and reflects on Ethel's family roles, in her moving documentary, *Heir to an Execution* (2004).

20. Philipson, 345.

21. See, for example, Barbara Ehrenreich and Deirdre English, *For Her Own Good: 150 Years of the Experts' Advice to Women* (New York: Doubleday, 1978), ch. 7.

22. Ronald Radosh and Joyce Milton, *The Rosenberg File: A Search for the Truth* (New York: Holt, Rinehart and Winston, 1973), 417.

23. Brennan, "Popular Images of American Women," 56–59.

24. Fuchs and May received fourteen- and ten-year terms, respectively. Brennan, "Popular Images," 60.

25. See Deborah Dash Moore, "Reconsidering the Rosenbergs: Symbol and Substance in Second Generation American Jewish Consciousness," *Journal of American Ethnic History* 8, No. 1 (Fall 1988): 21–37.

26. Cited by Donald Weber, "Situating Gertrude Berg: *The Goldbergs* and the Construction of Jewish American Identity, 1930–50," in Joyce Antler, ed., *Talking Back: Images of Jewish Women in American Popular Culture* (Hanover, N.H.: University Press of New England, 1998).

AMY SWERDLOW

Ladies' Day at the Capitol: Women Strike for Peace versus HUAC

In the years surrounding World War I, women played a significant role in the peace movement, often justifying their activism in maternalist rhetoric. As mothers and potential mothers, they had a responsibility to save children from the horrors of war. Nearly half a century later, American women would again invoke their role as mothers to urge the end of nuclear testing on behalf of the world's children. The women's peace movement, which Amy Swerdlow explores in the following article, coalesced at a time when the Cuban Missile Crisis had brought the United States and the Soviet Union to the brink of war. It also occurred during a period when virtually any form of political protest was automatically labeled by its critics as "communist inspired." Although the most virulent phase of McCarthyism had subsided by 1962, the machinery of repression was still intact; the women's peace movement was promptly investigated by the HUAC.

Note the prior involvement of some of the woman strikers in radical and liberal causes. Combine this information with Horowitz's point about the persistence of concern about the status of women workers in key unions such as the UE, in the aftermath of World War II (pp. 577–590). Add the growing attention on the part of liberal women to race reconciliation. How does our view of the cold war years change? Does this suggest that some women may have retained a willingness to criticize and subvert dominant power relationships? Might minority women be especially eager to fight injustice?

Note how participants in the peace strike challenged committee tactics by manipulating traditional gender stereotypes. Who were these women? How can their emergence as political activists be explained?

In mid-December of 1962 in the Old House Office Building of the United States Congress, a confrontation took place between a recently formed women's peace movement called Women Strike for Peace (WSP) and the House Committee on Un-American Activities (HUAC). The confrontation took place at a HUAC hearing to determine the extent of Communist party infiltration into "the so-called 'peace movement' in a manner and to a degree affecting the national security."[1] This three-day battle of political and sexual adversaries, which resulted in a rhetorical victory for the women of WSP and a deadly blow to the committee, occurred only twenty-five years ago.[2] It is a moment in the history of peace movements in the United States in which women led the way by taking a more courageous and principled stand in opposition to cold war ideology and political repression than that of their male counterparts.[3] However, in keeping with the historical amnesia which besets both the history of women and radical movements in America, the WSP-HUAC struggle is largely forgotten.[4]

This article seeks to reconstruct the WSP-HUAC confrontation and the reasons it took the form it did. By analyzing the

Amy Swerdlow, "Ladies Day at the Capitol: Women Strike for Peace versus HUAC," was originally published in *Feminist Studies* 8, no. 3 (Fall 1982): 493-520. Reprinted by permission of the publisher and author.

ideology, consciousness, political style, and public demeanor of the WSP women as they defended their right as mothers "to influence the course of government," we can learn a great deal about the strengths and weaknesses of women's movements for social change that build on traditional sex role ideology and on female culture.[5]

WSP burst upon the American political scene on November 1st, 1961, when an estimated fifty thousand women in over sixty cities across the United States walked out of their kitchens and off their jobs in a one-day women's strike for peace. As a radioactive cloud from a Russian nuclear test hung over the American landscape, these women strikers staged the largest female peace action in the nation's history.[6] In small towns and large cities from New York to California, the women visited government officials demanding that they take immediate steps to "End the Arms Race—Not the Human Race."[7] Coming on the heels of a decade noted for cold war consensus, political conformity, and the celebration of female domesticity, this spontaneous women's initiative baffled both the press and the politicians. The women seemed to have emerged from nowhere. They belonged to no unifying organizations, and their leaders were totally unknown as public figures.

The women strikers were actually responding to a call from a handful of Washington, D.C., women who had become alarmed by the acceleration of the nuclear arms race. So disheartened were they by the passivity of traditional peace groups, that they had sent a call to women friends and contacts all over the country urging them to suspend their regular routine of home, family, and job to join with friends and neighbors in a one-day strike to end the nuclear arms race.[8]

The call to strike spread rapidly from Washington through typical female networks: word of mouth and chain letter fashion from woman to woman, from coast to coast, through personal telephone calls, and Christmas card lists. Contacts in Parent Teacher Associations (PTAs), the League of Women Voters, church and temple groups, as well as the established peace organizations such as the Women's International League for Peace and Freedom (WILPF) and the Committee for a Sane Nuclear Policy (SANE), also spread the word.

The nature of the strike in each community depended entirely on what the local women were willing, and able, to do. Some marched, others lobbied local officials, a few groups took ads in local newspapers. Thousands sent telegrams to the White House and to the Soviet embassy, calling upon the two first ladies of the nuclear superpowers, Jacqueline Kennedy and Nina Khrushchev, to urge their husbands on behalf of all the world's children to "stop all nuclear tests—east and west." Amazed by the numbers and composition of the turnout on November 1st, *Newsweek* commented:

> They were perfectly ordinary looking women, with their share of good looks; they looked like the women you would see driving ranch wagons, or shopping at the village market, or attending PTA meetings. It was these women by the thousands, who staged demonstrations in a score of cities across the nation last week, protesting atomic testing. A "strike for peace," they called it and—carrying placards, many wheeling baby buggies or strollers—they marched on city halls and Federal buildings to show their concern about nuclear fallout.[9]

The strikers' concern about the nuclear arms race did not end with the November 1st actions. Within only one year, the one-day strike for peace was transformed by its founders and participants into a national women's movement with local groups in sixty communities and offices in ten cities. With no paid staff and no designated leaders, thousands of women in different parts of the country, most of them previously unknown to each other, managed to establish a loosely structured communications network capable of swift and effective direct action on both a national and international scale.

From its inception, the WSP movement was a non-hierarchical participatory network of activists opposed both to rigid ideologies and formal organizational structure. The WSP women called their format simply "our unorganization." It is interesting to note that the young men of Students for a Democractic Society (SDS), a movement founded in the same year as WSP, more aware of their place in the radical political tradition, more aware of the power of naming, and more confident of their power to do so, named their loose structure "participatory democracy." Eleanor Garst, one of the Washington founders, explained the attractions of the un-organizational format:

> No one must wait for orders from headquarters—there aren't any headquarters. No one's idea must wait for clearance through the national board. No one waits for the president or the director to tell her what to do—and there is no president or director. Any woman who has an idea can propose it through an informal memo system; if enough women think it's good, it's done. Those who don't like a particular action don't have to drop out of the movement; they just sit out that action and wait for one they like. Sound "crazy"?—it is, but it also brings forth and utilizes the creativity of thousands of women who could never be heard from through ordinary channels.[10]

The choice of a loose structure and local autonomy was a reaction to hierarchical and bureaucratic structures of traditional peace groups like WILPF and SANE to which some of the early leaders belonged. These women perceived the WILPF structure, which required that all programmatic and action proposals be cleared with state and national offices, as a roadblock to spontaneous and direct responses to the urgent international crisis.[11] The willingness of the Washington founders to allow each group to act in the way that suited its particular constituency was WSP's greatest strength and the source of the confidence and admiration that women across the country bestowed on the Washington founders. Washington came to be considered the WSP national office not only because it was located in the nation's capital, but also because the Washington group was trusted by all.

There was also another factor militating against a traditional membership organization. Only the year before the WSP strike, Linus Pauling, the Nobel Laureate in physics and opponent of nuclear testing, had been directed by the Senate Internal Security Subcommittee to turn over the names of those who had helped him gather signatures on a scientists' antinuclear petition. The commandeering of membership lists was not an uncommon tactic of political intimidation in the 1950s. Membership lists of radical organizations could therefore be a burden and responsibility. As they served no purpose in the WSP format, it was a sensible strategy to eliminate them. Another benefit was that WSP never had to assess accurately its numerical strength, thus allowing its legend to grow even when its numbers did not.

From its first day onward, WSP tapped a vast reservoir of moral outrage, energy, organizational talent, and sisterhood—female capacities that had been submerged and silenced for more than a decade by McCarthyism and the "feminine mystique." Using standard pressure group tactics, such as lobbying and petitioning, coupled with direct demonstrative action and civil disobedience, executed with imagination and "feminine flair," the WSP women succeeded in putting women's political demands on the front pages of the nation's newspapers, from which they had largely disappeared since the days of the suffrage campaign. WSP also managed to influence public officials and public policy. At a time when peace marchers were ignored, or viewed as "commies" or "kooks," President John F. Kennedy gave public recognition to the women strikers. Commenting on WSP's first antinuclear march at the White House, on January 15, 1962, the president told the nation that he thought the WSP women were "extremely earnest."

> I saw the ladies myself. I recognized why they were here. There were a great number of them, it was in the rain. I understand what they were attempting to say, therefore, I consider their message was received.[12]

In 1970, *Science* reported that "Wiesner (Jerome Wiesner, Pres. Kennedy's Science Advisor) gave the major credit for moving President Kennedy toward the limited Test Ban Treaty of 1963, not to arms controllers inside the government but to the Women Strike for Peace and to SANE and Linus Pauling."[13]

Although WSP, in its first year, was well received by liberal politicians and journalists, the surveillance establishment and the right-wing press were wary. They recognized early what the Rand Corporation described obliquely as the WSP potential "to impact on military policies."[14] Jack Lotto, a Hearst columnist, charged that although the women described themselves as a "group of unsophisticated wives and mothers who are loosely organized in a spontaneous movement for peace, there is nothing spontaneous about the way the pro-Reds have moved in on our mothers and are using them for their own purposes."[15] On the

West Coast, the *San Francisco Examiner* claimed to have proof that "scores of well-intentioned, dedicated women . . . were being made dupes of by known Communists . . . operating openly in the much publicized Women Strike for Peace demonstrations."[16]

That WSP was under Federal Bureau of Investigation (FBI) surveillance from its first public planning meeting in Washington in October 1961, is abundantly evidenced in the forty-three volumes of FBI records on WSP which have been made available to the movement's attorneys under the provisions of the Freedom of Information Act. The records show that FBI offices in major cities, North, East, South, and West—and even in such places as Mobile, Alabama; Phoenix, Arizona; and San Antonio, Texas; not known for WSP activities—were sending and receiving reports on the women, often prepared in cooperation with local "red squads."[17]

Having just lived through the Cuban Missile Crisis of October 1962, WSP celebrated its first anniversary in November with a deep sense of urgency and of heightened political efficacy. But, as the women were making plans to escalate their commitment and their protests, they were stopped in their tracks in the first week of December by HUAC subpoenas to thirteen women peace activists from the New York metropolitan area, as well as Dagmar Wilson of Washington, D.C., the WSP national spokesperson.[18]

It is difficult today to comprehend the emotions and fears such a summons could invoke in individuals and organizations. Lillian Hellman's *Scoundrel Time* gives a picture of the tension, isolation, and near hysteria felt by an articulate and prominent public figure, as she prepared her defense against the committee in 1953.[19] By 1962, cold war hysteria had abated somewhat, as the United States and the USSR were engaged in test ban negotiations, but HUAC represented those forces and those voices in American politics that opposed such negotiations. As a congressional committee, it still possessed the awesome power of an agency of the state to command headlines; cast suspicion; and by labeling individuals as subversives, to destroy careers, lives, and organizations.

The HUAC subpoenas gave no indication of the subject of the hearings, or of their scope. So there was, at first, some confusion about whether it was the WSP connection or other aspects of the subpoenaed women's political lives that were suspect. To add to the confusion, it was soon discovered that three of the women called were not even active in WSP. They were members of the Conference of Greater New York Peace Groups, an organization founded by New Yorkers who had either been expelled from, or who had willingly left, SANE because of its internal red hunt. Of these three women, two had already been named by the committee informers as communists in previous HUAC hearings. One of these women, Elizabeth Moss, had achieved considerable notoriety when she was identified by accused Russian spy William Remington as his mother-in-law and a card-carrying communist. Given these circumstances it was clear that the WSP leadership had some important decisions to make regarding their response to the HUAC hearings. There were two important questions to be faced. First, as WSP had no official membership list, would the movement embrace any woman working for peace even if she were not directly involved in WSP activity? Second, would WSP disavow its members who had past or present communist affiliations, and if WSP did not disavow them, would the movement lose its following and its effectiveness?

The key to WSP unity in the face of the "communist issue" which had divided and disrupted peace, labor, and even civil liberties organizations in the previous decade, was the fact that WSP had previously decided to handle forthrightly and in advance of any attack, the issue of communist inclusion. WSP had, even before the HUAC hearings, decided to reject political screening of its members, deeming it a manifestation of outdated cold war thinking. This decision, the women claimed, was based not on fear or expediency, but on principle. The issue of accepting communists in the movement was brought to the floor of the first national WSP conference in June 1962 by the Los Angeles coordinating council. A prepared statement by the Los Angeles group declared: "Unlike SANE and Turn Toward Peace, WSP must not make the error of initiating its own purges." Treating the issue of communist membership as a question of personal conscience, the Los Angeles group asked, "If there are communists or former communists working in WSP, what difference does that make? We do not question one another about our religious beliefs or other matters of personal conscience. How can we justify political interrogation?" The Los Angeles statement continued, "If fear, mistrust and hatred are ever to be lessened, it will be by courageous individuals who do not hate and fear and can get together to work out tolerable compromises."[20] The argument that "this is a role women would be particularly equipped to play," won over the conference and resulted in the inclusion of a section in the WSP national policy statement which affirmed, "we are women of all races, creeds and political persuasions who are dedicated to the achievement of general and complete disarmament under effective international control."[21]

An emergency meeting of about fifty New York area "key women," along with Dagmar Wilson and other representatives from Washington, was called a few days after the HUAC summonses began to arrive.[22] The first decision made at this meeting was that WSP would live up to the national policy statement that had been arrived at six months earlier and make a reality of the phrase, "We are women of all . . . political persuasions." Following from this decision it was clear that WSP would support and embrace every woman summoned before HUAC, regardless of her past or present affiliations, as long as she supported the movement's campaign against both Russian and American nuclear policies. This meant that in addition to supporting its own women, the three women not active in WSP would also come under the movement's protection if they so desired. They would be given access to the same lawyers as the WSP activists. They would not be isolated or attacked either for their affiliations or for the way they chose to conduct themselves at the hearing. This decision was in sharp contrast to the action taken by SANE in 1960 when it expelled a leading member of its New York chapter after he invoked the Fifth Amendment at a Senate Internal Security Subcommittee hearing, and then refused to tell Norman Cousins, a cochairman of SANE, whether or not he had ever been a communist.[23]

The decision made by the New York and Washington women not "to cower" before the committee, to conduct no internal purges, to acknowledge each woman's right to act for peace and to conduct herself according to the dictates of her conscience was bold for its day. It was arrived at within the movement, by the women themselves, without consultation with the male leaders of traditional peace and civil liberties groups, many of whom disagreed with this WSP policy.[24] It was based not only on the decision to resist the demonology of the cold war, but also on a sense of sisterhood, on feelings of identification with and empathy for the women singled out for attack. Even the subpoenaed women themselves turned for counsel and support more to each other and the WSP leadership than to their families and lawyers. Working together at a feverish pace, night and day for three weeks, writing, phoning, speaking at rallies, the key women seemed to be acting as if they were a family under attack, for which all personal resources, passions, and energies had to be marshaled. But the family, this time, was "the movement" and it was the sisters, not the fathers, who were in charge.

In response to the subpoenas, a massive campaign was organized for the cancellation of the hearings and for support of WSP from national organizations and public figures. An anti-HUAC statement was composed in New York and Washington which spoke so well to the concerns and the consciousness of "the women" that it succeeded in unifying a movement in shock. The WSP statement on the HUAC inquisition was quoted widely by the press, used by local groups in ads and flyers, in letters to editors, and in speeches. "With the fate of humanity resting on a push button," the statement declared, "the quest for peace has become the highest form of patriotism."[25] In this first sentence, the women set the ground rules for their confrontation with the committee: it was going to be a contest over which group was more patriotic. But the test of "Americanism," according to the WSP rules, was the extent of one's dedication to saving America's children from nuclear extinction. Addressing the issue of communism in the movement, WSP declared: "Differences of politics, economics or social belief disappear when we recognize man's common peril . . . we do not ask an oath of loyalty to any set of beliefs. Instead we ask loyalty to the race of man. The time is long past when a small group of censors can silence the voice of peace." These words would be the WSP *leitmotif* in the Washington hearings. The women were saying, once again, as they had throughout their first year, that for them, the arms race, cold war ideology, and cold war politics, were obsolete in the nuclear age, as was the committee itself. This is the spirit Eric Bentley caught and referred to when he wrote: "In the 1960s a new generation came to life. As far as HUAC is concerned it began with Women Strike for Peace."[26]

The WSP strategy against HUAC was innovative. An organizing memorandum from the Washington office declared, "the usual response of protest and public statements is too traditional and ineffectual. . . . Let's Turn the Tables! Let's meet the HUAC challenge in the Good New WSP way!"[27] The "new way" suggested by women all over the country was to insist that WSP had nothing to hide. Instead of refusing to testify, as radicals and civil libertarians had done in the 1950s, large numbers of WSP participants volunteered to "talk." Approximately one hundred women sent wires to Representative Francis Walter, chairman of HUAC, offering to come to Washington to tell all about their movement. The offers were refused by HUAC. But this new WSP tactic pointed up the fact that the committee was less interested in securing information than in exposing and smearing those it chose to investigate. Some WSP groups objected to the free testimony strategy on the grounds that there was a contradiction between denying the right of the committee to exist, and at the same time offering to cooperate with it. But these groups were in a minority. Carol Urner of Portland, Oregon, spoke for all those who volunteered to testify, making it clear that she would not be a "friendly witness." "I could not, of course, divulge the names of others in the movement," she wrote to Representative Walter. "I suppose such a refusal could lead one to 'contempt' and prison and things like that . . . and no mother can accept lightly even the remote possibility of separation from the family which needs her. But mankind needs us too. . . ."[28]

Only three weeks' time elapsed between the arrival of the first subpoenas from HUAC and the date of the Washington hearings. In this short period, the WSP key women managed to develop a legal defense, a national support system for those subpoenaed, and a broad national campaign of public protest against the committee. The women's performance at the hearings was so original, so winning, and so "feminine" in the traditional sense, that it succeeded in capturing the sympathy and the support of large sections of the national media and in strengthening the movement instead of destroying it.

The hearings opened on December 11, 1962, at 10:00 A.M. in the caucus room of the Old House Office Building of the United States Congress in Washington, D.C. Fear, excitement, and exhilaration were in the air as each WSP woman in the audience looked around to see every seat in the room occupied by sisters who had come from eleven states, some from as far as California, in response to a call for their presence from the national leadership. Clyde Doyle, chairman of the subcommittee of HUAC conducting the WSP hearings, opened with a statement of their purpose. Quoting from Lenin, Stalin, Khrushchev, and Gus Hall, he explained:

> Communists believe that there can be no real peace until they have conquered the world. . . . The initiated Communist, understanding his Marxist-Leninist doctrine, knows that a Moscow call to intensify the "fight for peace" means that he should intensify his fight to destroy capitalism and its major bastion, the United States of America.[29]

The WSP women in the audience rose as one as the committee called its first witness, Blanche Posner, a retired schoolteacher who was the volunteer office manager for New York WSP. The decision to rise with the first witness, to stand *with* her, was spontaneous. It was proposed only a few minutes before Posner was called, as a note from an unknown source was circulated around the room. Posner refused to answer any questions about the structure or personnel of WSP. She resorted to the Fifth Amendment forty-four times, as the press pointed out in dozens of news stories covering the first day of the hearings. They also reported the way in which Posner took matters into her own hands, lecturing the committee members as though they were recalcitrant boys at DeWitt Clinton High School in the Bronx, where she had taught. Talking right through the interruptions and objections raised by the chairman and by committeee counsel, Alfred Nittle, Posner declared:

> I don't know, sir, why I am here, but I do know why you are here, I think . . . because you don't

> quite understand the nature of this movement. This movement was inspired and motivated by mothers' love for children. . . . When they were putting their breakfast on the table, they saw not only the wheaties and milk, but they also saw strontium 90 and iodine 131. . . . They feared for the health and life of their children. That is the only motivation.[30]

Each time Posner resorted to the Fifth Amendment, she did it with a pointed criticism of the committee or a quip that endeared her to the women in the hearing room who needed to keep their spirits up in the face of charges that Posner had been identified by an FBI informer as a Communist party member while working in New York City as a schoolteacher. One prize exchange between Nittle and Posner led to particularly enthusiastic applause and laughter from WSP women. Nittle asked, "Did you wear a colored paper daisy to identify yourself as a member of the Women Strike for Peace?" Posner answered, "It sounds like such a far cry from communism it is impossible not to be amused. I still invoke the Fifth Amendment."[31]

Most of the witnesses were called because the committee believed it had evidence to link them with the Communist party through identification by FBI informers or the signing of party nominating petitions. But the strategy backfired with Ruth Meyers, of Roslyn, Long Island. She stepped forward, according to Mary McGrory's report in the *Washington* (D.C.) *Evening Star*, "swathed in red and brown jersey, topped by a steeple crowned red velvet hat," and "she was just as much of a headache to the committee as Posner had been."[32] There was much sparring between Meyers and the committee about the nature and structure of WSP. "Are you presently a member of a group known as Women Strike for Peace?" Nittle asked. "No, sir, Women Strike for Peace has no membership," Meyers answered. Nittle then asked, "You are familiar, I understand, with the structural organization of Women Strike for Peace as evidenced by this plan?" Meyers replied, "I am familiar to the extent of the role that I play in it. I must say that I was not particularly interested in the structure of Women Strike for Peace. I was more involved in my own community activities. . . . I felt that structure, other than the old telephone, has not much of what I was interested in." Nittle then proceeded to deliver what he believed would be the coup de grâce for Meyers. "Mrs. Meyers," he barked, "it appears from the public records that a Ruth Meyers, residing at 1751 East 10th Street, Brooklyn, New York, on July 27, 1948, signed a Communist Party nominating petition. . . . Are you the Ruth Meyers who executed that petition?" Meyers shot back, "No, sir." She then examined the petition carefully, and announced, "I never lived in Brooklyn, and this is not my signature."[33] Although the official transcript does not contain this statement, many, including the author, remember that she added, "My husband could never get me to move there." This female remark brought an explosion of laughter and applause. Meyers also invoked the Fifth Amendment. As she left the witness stand, Meyers received a one-minute ovation for humor, grace, and mistaken identity. In the corridor outside the caucus room in front of the TV cameras, she told reporters that she had never been a Communist. "But I'll never acknowledge the Committee's right to ask me that question."[34]

Another witness, Lyla Hoffman, chose to tell the committee of her past communist affiliation, asserting that she had left the Communist Party, but would not cooperate in naming names or in citing the cause of her resignation. In a statement written after the hearings Hoffman explained, "I felt that it was high time to say, 'What difference does it make what anyone did or believed many years ago? That's not the problem facing humanity today.' But I had to say this in legal terms." She found it very difficult to do so, as the committee was interested only in whether she was a genuine anticommunist or a secret fellow-traveler.[35] Hoffman invoked the Fifth Amendment.

The witnesses that followed Posner, Meyers, and Hoffman, each in her own style, invoked whatever legal and rhetorical strategy her conscience and her situation dictated. They lectured the committee eloquently and courageously on the danger of nuclear holocaust, on women's rights and responsibility to work for peace. In attempting to explain the nonstructured format of WSP, several witnesses suggested that the movement was too fluid and too unpredictable to be comprehended by the masculine mind.

In their most optimistic projections, the WSP women could not have predicted the overwhelmingly favorable press and public response they would receive, and the support and growth for the movement that would result from the HUAC episode. From the outset, the WSP leadership understood that HUAC needed the press to make its tactics of intimidation and punishment work. So, WSP played for the press—as it had done from its founding—and won! The Washington and New York leadership knew that it had two stories; both were developed to the hilt. The first was "motherhood under attack" and the second was the age-old "battle of the sexes." The contest between the sexes, according to the WSP version, involved female common sense, openness, humor, hope and naiveté versus male rigidity, solemnity, suspicion, and dark theories of conspiracy and subversion. The WSP women, in their middle-class, feminine, political style turned the hearings into an episode of the familiar and funny "I Love Lucy," rather than the tragic and scary inquisition of Alger Hiss.

For the first time, HUAC was belittled with humor and treated to a dose of its own moral superiority. Headlines critical of the committee and supportive of WSP were featured on the front pages of prominent newspapers from coast to coast. The *Chicago Daily News* declared: "It's Ladies' Day at Capitol: Hoots, Howls—and Charm; Congressmen Meet Match." Russell Baker's column was headed "Peace March Gals Make Red Hunters Look Silly" and a *Detroit Free Press* story was entitled, "Headhunters Decapitated." A cartoon by Herblock in the *Washington* (D.C.) *Post* of December 13th showed three aging and baffled committee members: One is seated at the hearing table. One is holding a gavel. Another turns to him and says, "I Came in Late, Which Was It That Was Un-American—Women or Peace?"[36] A story in the *Vancouver* (B.C.) *Sun* of December 14 was typical of many other reports:

> The dreaded House Un-American Activities Committee met its Waterloo this week. It tangled with 500 irate women. They laughed at it. Klieg lights glared, television cameras whirred, and 50 reporters scribbled notes while babies cried and cooed during the fantastic inquisition.

Bill Galt, author of the *Vancouver Sun* story, gave a blow-by-blow description of WSP civil disobedience in the Old House Office Building:

> When the first woman headed to the witness table, the crowd rose silently to its feet. The irritated Chairman Clyde Doyle of California outlawed standing. They applauded the next witness and Doyle outlawed clapping. Then they took to running out to kiss the witness. . . . Finally, each woman as she was called was met and handed a huge bouquet. By then Doyle was a beaten man. By the third day the crowd was giving standing ovations to the heroines with impunity.[37]

The hearings were a perfect foil for the humor of Russell Baker, syndicated columnist of the *New York Times.*

> If the House Un-American Activities Committee knew its Greek as well as it knows its Lenin, it would have left the women peace strikers alone. . . . Instead with typical male arrogance it has subpoenaed 15 of the ladies, . . . spent several days trying to show them that women's place is not on the peace march route, and has come out of it covered with foolishness.

Baker, a liberal columnist, understood the committee's purpose and also the "drama of the absurd" that WSP had staged to defeat that purpose. "The Committee's aim was simple enough," Baker pointed out,

> their sleuths studying an organization known as Women Strike for Peace had learned that some of the strikers seemed to have past associations with the Communist Party or its front groups. Presumably if these were exposed, right thinking housewives would give up peace agitation and go back to the kitchen.

The committee had reckoned without female logic, according to Baker:

> How could WSP be infiltrated, witness after witness demanded, when it was not an organization at all? . . . Try as he might, Alfred Nittle, the committee counsel, never managed to break through against this defense.[38]

The *Detroit Free Press* commented: "The House Committee can get away with attacking college students in California, government flunkies who are forced to shrive their souls to save their jobs, and assorted misguided do-gooders. But when it decides to smear an estimated half-million angry women, it's in deep trouble. We wish them nothing but the worst."[39]

Mary McGrory in the *Washington* (D.C.) *Evening Star* played up the difference between the male, HUAC perceptions and those of the female, WSP:

> "Why can't a woman be like a man?" sings Henry Higgins in *My Fair Lady*. That is precisely the question the House Committee on Un-American Activities is asking itself today. . . . The committee is trying to find out if the ladies' group is subversive. All it found out was that their conduct in the caucus room certainly was.

"The leader of the group kept protesting that she was not really the leader at all," McGrory observed. Pointing out that few men would deny being leaders, or admit they didn't know what was going on, Mary McGrory reported that:

> Dagmar Wilson of Washington, when asked if she exercised control over the New York chapter merely giggled and said, "Nobody controls anybody in the Women Strike for Peace. We're all leaders."

Characterizing Wilson's appearance as the "coup de grâce in the battle of the sexes," McGrory noted that the ladies had been using the Congress as a babysitter, while their young crawled in the aisles and noisily sucked their bottles during the whole proceedings. With a mixture of awe and wonder McGrory described how the ladies themselves, as wayward as their babies, hissed, gasped, clapped entirely at will. When several of their number took the Fifth Amendment, to McGrory's surprise, the women applauded, and

> when Mrs. Wilson, trim and beguiling in red wool, stepped up to take the stand, a mother with a baby on one hip worked her way through the crowd and handed her a bouquet of purple and white flowers, exactly as if she were the principal speaker at a ladies' luncheon.

McGrory caught the flavor of Wilson's testimony which was directed not only at the committee, but also at her sisters in the audience. She reported that when Mr. Nittle asked whether the New York chapter had played a dominant role in the group, Wilson replied, "Other cities would be mortified if you said that."

> "Was it," Mr. Nittle wanted to know, "Mrs. Wilson's idea to send delegates to a Moscow peace conference?" "No," said Mrs. Wilson regretfully, "I wish I'd thought of that." When Mr. Nittle pursued the question of whose idea it was to send observers to Moscow, Dagmar Wilson replied, "This is something I find very difficult to explain to the masculine mind."

And, in a sense, it was. "Mr. Nittle pressed forward to the clutch question," one, according to McGrory, "that would bring a man to his knees with patriotic protest: 'I would like to ask you whether you would knowingly permit or encourage a Communist Party member to occupy a leadership position in Women Strike for Peace." Wilson replied:

> Well, my dear sir, I have absolutely no way of controlling, do not desire to control, who wishes to join in the demonstrations and the efforts that women strikers have made for peace. In fact, I would also like to go even further. I would like to say that unless everybody in the whole world joins us in this fight, then God help us.

"Would you knowingly permit or welcome Nazis or Fascists?" asked Mr. Nittle. Mrs. Wilson replied, "if we could only get them on our side."[40] Mr. Doyle then thanked Wilson for appearing and being so helpful. "I want to emphasize," he said,

> that the Committee recognizes that there are many, many, many women, in fact a great great majority of women, in this peace movement who are absolutely patriotic and absolutely adverse to everything the Communist Party stands for. We recognize that you are one of them. We compliment you on your leadership and on your helpfulness to us this morning.

Dagmar Wilson tried to get the last word: "I do hope you live to thank us when we have achieved our goal." But Doyle replied, "Well, we will."[41]

The way in which WSP, a movement of middle-class, middle-aged, white women, mobilized to meet the attack by a feared congressional committee was energetic and bold, politically nontraditional, pragmatic rather than ideological, moralistic and maternal. It was entirely consistent with the already established program, tactics, rhetoric, and image of this one-year-old movement, labeled by the University of Wisconsin's student newspaper as "the bourgeois mother's underground."[42]

Were these courageous women who bowed to traditional notions of female behavior merely using the politics of motherhood for political advantage? Or had they internalized the feminine mystique? It is useful to examine the backgrounds of the WSP women in seeking to understand their use of their own female culture to legitimate a radical critique of national, foreign, and military policies. The WSP key women were mostly in their late thirties to mid forties at the inception of the movement in 1961. Most of them, then, had come into adulthood in the late 1930s and early 1940s. They were students or workers in the years of political ferment preceding World War II. Many had married just before, during, or right after the war. The majority of these women participated in the postwar baby boom, the rise of middle-class affluence, and the privatism and consumerism connected with suburban life. It was during the 1950s that they made their adjustment to family, parenting, community, and consensus politics.

As a movement born out of, and responding to, the consciousness of the 1950s, WSP projected a middle-class and politically moderate image. In an article celebrating WSP's first anniversary, Eleanor Garst, one of WSP's early image makers, proclaimed:

> Breaking all the rules and behaving with incredible disorder and naivete, "the women" continue to attract recruits until the movement now numbers hundreds of thousands.... Furthermore, many of the women behaving in these unaccustomed ways are no odd-ball types, but pillars of the community long courted by civic organizations. Others—perhaps the most numerous—are apolitical housewives who have never before lifted a finger to work for peace or any other social concern.[43]

Although the movement projected an image of political innocence and inexperience, WSP was actually initiated by five women who were already active members of SANE. The women—Dagmar Wilson, Jeanne Bagby, Folly Fodor, Eleanor Garst, and Margaret Russell—had gravitated toward each other because of their mutual distaste for SANE's internal red hunt, which they felt contributed to an escalation, rather than an end to cold war hysteria. Perhaps, more important, they shared a frustration over the slow pace with which the highly structured SANE reacted to international crises. They also resented the reluctance of SANE's male leadership to deal with "mother's issues" such as the contamination of milk by radioactive fallout from nuclear tests.

Dagmar Wilson was forty-five years old, and a political novice when she was moved to call a few friends to her home in the late summer of 1961 to discuss what could be done about the nuclear crisis. At this meeting WSP was born. Wilson was at that time a successful freelance children's book illustrator, the mother of three daughters and wife of Christopher Wilson, a commercial attaché at the British embassy. Wilson had been born in New York City, had moved to Germany as a very young child, and had spent most of her adult years in England where her father, Cesar Searchinger, was a well-known broadcast correspondent for the Columbia Broadcasting System and the National Broadcasting Company.

Wilson came to the United States prior to World War II, held a variety of professional jobs as an artist and teacher, and finally became a freelance illustrator. She worked in a studio at home, so as to be available to her children and to ensure a smooth-running household. Despite the fact that Wilson was so successful an artist that one of her children's books had become a best-seller, she nevertheless identified herself as a housewife.

> My idea in emphasizing the housewife rather than the professional was that I thought the housewife was a downgraded person, and that we, as housewives, had as much right to an opinion and that we deserved as much consideration as anyone else, and I wanted to emphasize . . . this was an important role and that it was time we were heard.[44]

A gifted artist, an intelligent person of good sense, good grace, and charm, Wilson possessed the charisma of those who accurately represent the feelings and the perceptions of their constituency, but excel them in passion and the capacity for creative articulation. Having been most of her life a "nonjoiner" Wilson was, as the *New York Times Magazine* reported in a feature story in May 1962, a "political neophyte."[45] Because Wilson had not been involved in U.S. radical politics of the 1940s, she was free from the self-conscious timidity that plagued those who had been involved in leftist organizations and who feared either exposure or a repetition of the persecution and the political isolation they had experienced in the 1950s.

Among the women who met at Wilson's house to plan the emergency peace action was Eleanor Garst, whose direct, friendly, practical, yet passionate political prose played a powerful role in energizing and unifying the WSP women in their first year. It was she who drafted the call for November 1st, and later helped create most of the anti-HUAC rhetoric.

Garst came from a conservative Baptist background. She recalls that everything in her upbringing told her that the only thing a woman should do was to marry, have babies, care for her husband and babies, and "never mind your own needs." Despite this, Garst was the only one of the inner circle of Washington founders, who in 1961 was a completely self-supporting professional woman, living on her own. She was the mother of two grown children. At the time of the founding of WSP, Garst was employed as a community organizer for the Adams Morgan Demonstration Project, administered by American University, working to maintain integrated neighborhoods in Washington, D.C. She had become a pacifist in her early childhood after reading about war in novels and poems. Her husband, a merchant seaman, refused to be drafted prior to World War II, a decision that he and Eleanor made together without consulting any other pacifists because they knew none. They spent their honeymoon composing an eighty-page brief against peacetime conscription.

After the war, Garst became a professional political worker, writer, and peace activist on the West Coast before coming to Washington. She had been a founder of the Los Angeles SANE and editor of its newsletter. A forceful and easy writer, Garst had already been published in the *Saturday Evening Post, Reporter, Ladies' Home Journal,* and other national publications when she was asked to draft the letter that initiated the successful November 1st strike.

Folly Fodor, a leading figure in the founding group, had come to Washington in 1960 to follow her husband's job with the U.S. Labor Department. She joined SANE on her arrival in Washington and had been elected to the board. Thirty-seven years old at the time of the founding of WSP, Fodor was the mother of two. Folly Fodor was not new to politics. She was the daughter of parents who had been involved in liberal-to-communist political causes and had herself been a leader in political organizations since her youth. As an undergraduate at Antioch College, in Yellow Springs, Ohio, Folly Fodor had become active in the Young People's Socialist League, eventually becoming "head of it," as she put it. In retrospect she believes she spent too much time fighting the communists on campus, and "never did a goddamn thing." Fodor had been chairperson of the Young Democrats of California and as a Democrat she had clandestinely supported Henry Wallace in 1948. During the mid-1950s, after the birth of her second child, Fodor organized a mother's group to oppose nuclear testing. So Fodor, like Garst, was not new to radical causes, to peace activity, or to women's groups. She was ready and eager for a separate women's peace action in the fall of 1961.

Two other women who founded WSP, Jeanne Bagby and Margaret Russell, were also already active in the peace cause at the time of the founding of WSP. Bagby was a frequent contributor to *Liberation* magazine. Together the founders possessed research, writing, organizing, and speaking talents that were not unusual for women active in a variety of community, civic, and church groups in the 1950s. All the founders shared a conviction that the men in the peace movement and the government had failed them and that women had to take things into their own hands.

But what of the thousands of women who joined the founders? What was their social and political background and their motivation to take to the streets in peace protest? Elise Boulding, a sociologist and longtime pacifist activist, who became involved in the WSP communications network right after November 1st, decided to try to find out. During the six months in which Boulding edited the *Women's Peace Movement Bulletin,* an information exchange for WSP groups, she kept asking herself whether the WSP women were really political neophytes as they claimed, or "old pros with a well defined idea of some kind of world social order?" Using the resources of the Institute for Conflict Resolution in Ann Arbor, Michigan, where she was working, and with the help of WSP colleagues in Ann Arbor, she composed a questionnaire that was sent to every eighth name on the mailing lists of forty-five local groups. By the fall of 1962, shortly before the summonses from HUAC, 279 questionnaires had been returned from thirty-seven localities in twenty-two states. According to Boulding, the respondents represented a cross-section of the movement—not only leaders.[46]

Boulding found that the overwhelming majority of the WSP women were well-educated mothers, and that 61 percent were not employed outside the home. But she concluded that the women who went out on strike for peace on November 1, 1961, and stayed on in the movement in the following months, appeared to be a more complex and sophisticated group than the "buggy-pushing housewife" image the movement conveyed. She characterized the early WSP participants as "largely intellectual and civic-minded people, mostly of the middle class"—very much like the Washington founders themselves.[47]

Most of the women strikers had been liberals, radicals, or pacifists in the 1940s. Although few had been political leaders of any kind, they shared the 1940s belief that society could be restructured on humanistic lines through the direct political action of ordinary people. Dorothy Dinnerstein described the psychological process of depoliticization and privatization that many politically active people experienced in the 1950s. Many radicals, according to Dinnerstein, spent the 1950s in a state of moral shock, induced by the twin catastrophes of Stalinism and McCarthyism. They lost their capacity for social connectedness and, "in this condition they withdrew from history—more or less totally, more or less gradually, more or less blindly into intensely personalistic, inward-turning, magically thing-and-place-oriented life." According to Dinnerstein they withdrew their passion from the larger human scene and sought to invest in something less nightmarish, more coherent and mentally manageable.[48] What the WSP women withdrew into, with society's blessing and encouragement, was the domestic sphere, the management of family, children, home, and local community. Many, when their school-aged children no longer required fulltime care, were propelled into the PTAs, League of Women Voters, Democratic party politics, church, synagogue, or cultural activities by their earlier social, political, and humanitarian concerns.

It took the acceleration of nuclear testing by both the capitalist United States and the socialist USSR to convince the WSP women of something they already suspected: that there was no political force in the world acting morally and humanely in the interest of the preservation of life. It took a series of international crises, the example of the civil rights sit-ins, and the Aldermarston antibomb marches in Britain to give the WSP women both the sense of urgency, and of possibility, that are the necessary ingredients for a political movement. Once out in the political arena, the women found that their moral outrage, their real fear for their children's future, and their determination never to be pushed back into the non-political domestic sphere, made them unafraid of a mere congressional committee before which others had quaked.

The women who were drawn to WSP certainly took the job of motherhood seriously. They had willingly chosen to sacrifice careers and personal projects to raise society's children because they had been convinced by the post-Freudians that the making of human beings is a far more important vocation than anything else; and that the making of human beings was a sex-specific vocation requiring the full-time duties of a resident mother.[49] But where the WSP women differed from the majority of their middle-class cohorts was that they saw motherhood not only as a private function, but also as a contribution to society in general and to the future. When they built on their rights and responsibilities to act politically in defense of the world's children, they were invoking not only their maternal consciousness, but their social conscience as well. They were women of heart, emotion, ingenuity, wit, and guile, but they were also serious political thinkers and activists. They chose to rely on their femininity, as most women did in the fifties and early sixties, to create whatever space and power they could carve out for themselves.

The Birmingham (England) Feminist History Group in an article, "Feminism as Femininity in the Nineteen Fifties?" suggests that feminism of the fifties seemed to be more concerned with integrating and foregrounding femininity than in transforming it in a fundamental way.[50] The conduct of WSP before the House Committee on Un-American Activities follows this pattern. The WSP women were not concerned with transforming the ideology of femininity, but rather with using it to enhance women's political power. But in so doing they were transforming that ideology and foreshadowing the feminism that emerged later in the decade.

Very much in the way that the concept of Republican motherhood was used in the late eighteenth century to justify the demand for women's education, and the cult of true womanhood was built upon to project women into the ante-bellum reform movements, WSP used the feminine mystique of the 1950s to legitimize women's right to radical dissent from foreign and military policies. In the repressive political climate of the early 1960s, WSP relied heavily upon sex role stereotypes to legitimize its opposition to cold war policies. But by emphasizing the fact that the men in power could no longer be counted on for protection in the nuclear age, WSP implied that the traditional sex-gender contract no longer worked. And by stressing global issues and international sisterhood, rather than domestic responsibilities, WSP challenged the privatization and isolation of women which was a key element of the feminine mystique. Most important, by performing in relation to HUAC with more courage, candor, and wit than most men had done in a decade of inquisitions, WSP raised women's sense of political power and self-esteem. One of the negative effects for WSP of relying so heavily on the politics of motherhood to project its political message was that it alienated a new generation of younger women who admired the movement's stand for peace, but saw its acquiescence to sex role stereotypes as regressive. In the late 1960s these younger women insisted upon working for peace not as wives, mothers, and sisters, but as autonomous persons.

Sara Evans, in *Personal Politics*, points out that those few young women in the civil rights movement who first raised feminist issues within the movement had to step *outside* the sex role assumptions on which they were raised in order to articulate a radical critique of women's position.[51] For WSP it was obviously different. The founders and leaders of WSP certainly did not step outside the traditional sex role assumptions; rather, they stood squarely upon them, with all their contradictions. By using these contradictions to present a radical critique of man's world, WSP began the transformation of woman's consciousness and woman's role.

Notes

1. U.S. Congress, House, Committee on Un-American Activities, *Communist Activities in the Peace Movement (Women Strike for Peace and Certain Other Groups), Hearings before the Committee on Un-American Activities on H.R. 9944.* 87th Cong., 2d. sess., 1962, p. 2057.

2. Historians and political opponents of HUAC agree that the WSP hearing marked the beginning of the end of the committee's power. Eric Bentley called the WSP-HUAC confrontation, "the fall of HUAC's Bastille." See Eric Bentley, *Thirty Years of Treason* (New York: Viking Press, 1971), p. 951. . . .

3. In May 1960, Senator Thomas Dodd, vice-chairman of the Senate International Security Subcommittee, threatened SANE with congressional investigation if it did not take steps to rid itself of communist infiltrators. SANE responded by voting to exclude all those with communist sympathies. Whole chapters that did not go along with internal red hunts were expelled, as was Henry Abrams, a leading New York activist who refused to tell the Senate committee whether or not he was a communist. Turn Toward Peace also rejected communists or former communists. See Milton S. Katz, "Peace, Politics, and Protest: SANE and the American Peace Movement, 1957–1972" (Ph.D. diss., St. Louis University, 1973), pp. 109–130. . . .

4. The way in which WSP's militant role in the peace movement has been either ignored or trivialized by journalists, peace movement leaders, and historians is illustrated by the following examples. Mary McGrory in her syndicated column described a WSP visit to the White House in the following manner: "This week's Cinderella story has to do with Women Strike for Peace, which after 15 years of drudgery in the skullery of anti-war activity has been invited to the White House" (*New York Post,* 8 Mar. 1977, p. 27). Dave Dellinger, one of the most prominent of the male leaders of the 1960s peace movement, devoted about 10 lines to WSP in a 317-page book on the history of the civil rights and peace movements from 1965 to 1973. He described WSP as a group fearful of engaging in civil disobedience in the 1967 "Mobilization March on the Pentagon." Nowhere in the book did Dellinger mention that nine months earlier 2,500 WSP women broke through police barricades to bang their shoes on the Pentagon doors which had been shut in their faces. See Dave Dellinger, *More Power Than We Know* (Garden City, N.Y.: Anchor Press, 1975). . . .

5. For a symposium on the relationship of feminism, women's culture, and women's politics, see Ellen DuBois, Mari Jo Buhle, Temma Kaplan, Gerda Lerner, and Carroll Smith-Rosenberg, "Politics and Culture in Women's History: A Symposium," *Feminist Studies* 6 (Spring 1980):26–64. . . .

6. The figure of fifty thousand claimed by the Washington founders after November 1st was accepted in most press accounts and became part of the WSP legend. It was based on reports from women in sixty cities and from newspapers across the country. . . .

7. "End the Arms Race—Not the Human Race" was the central slogan of the November 1st "strike": "Help Wanted" flyer, 25 Oct. 1961, Washington, D.C. See WSP Document Collection in custody of the author. (Mimeographed.)

8. "Dear—, Last night I sat with a few friends in a comfortable living room talking of atomic war." Draft of call to strike by Eleanor Garst, Washington, D.C., 22 Sept. 1961. WSP Document Collection. (Mimeographed.)

9. *Newsweek,* 13 Nov. 1961, p. 21.

10. Eleanor Garst, "Women: Middle-Class Masses," *Fellowship* 28 (1 Nov. 1962):10–12.

11. Minutes of the WILPF National Executive Committee stated: "Each branch taking direct action should clear with the National Action Projects Committee. The committee should have, and send out to branches, a list of approved action and a list of the organizations with which we formally cooperate." Women's International League for Peace and Freedom, Minutes of the National Executive Committee meeting of 28–29 Sept. 1961. Swarthmore College Peace Collection, DG 43, Series A-2, Box 18, p. 5.

12. "Transcript of the President's News Conference on World and Domestic Affairs," *New York Times*, 16 Jan. 1962, p. 18.

13. *Science* 167 (13 Mar. 1970):1476.

14. A. E. Wessel, *The American Peace Movement: A Study of Its Themes and Political Potential* (Santa Monica: Rand Corporation, 1962), p. 3.

15. *New York Journal American*, 4 Apr. 1962, p. 10.

16. *San Francisco Examiner*, 21 May 1962, p. 10.

17. The FBI files on WSP are located in the offices of the Washington, D.C., law firm of Gaffney, Anspach, Shember, Klimasi, and Marx. These contain hundreds of documents from security officers in major cities to the director of the FBI and from the directors to the security officers. For instance, as early as 23 Oct. 1961, one week before the November 1st strike, the Cleveland office of the FBI already identified one of the WSP planning groups as communist. (FBI Document 100-39566-8). . . .

18. Those subpoenaed were (in order of appearance) Blanche Posner, Ruth Meyers, Lyla Hoffman, Elsie Neidenberg, Sylvia Contente, Rose Clinton, Iris Freed, Anna Mackenzie, Elizabeth Moss, Ceil Gross, Jean Brancato, Miriam Chesman, Norma Spector, and Dagmar Wilson. Spector never testified; she was excused due to illness. *Hearings before Committee on Un-American Activities*, p. iii.

19. Lillian Hellman, *Scoundrel Time* (Boston: Little, Brown & Co., 1976), p. 99.

20. Los Angeles WISP, Statement I, Ann Arbor Conference, June 9–10, 1962 (WSP Document Collection); . . .

21. "WSP National Policy Statement," *Women Strike for Peace Newsletter*, New York, New Jersey, Connecticut, Summer 1962, pp. 1–2.

22. "Key women" was the name used by WSP for those women who were part of the national and local communications network. They were the ones who were called upon to initiate actions or who called upon others to do so.

23. Katz, "Peace, Politics, and Protest," pp. 122–26.

24. Homer Jack, "The Will of the WISP versus the Humiliation of HUAC," transcript of a talk on Radio Station WBAI, New York, 28 Dec. 1962 (WSP Document Collection).

25. The anti-HUAC statement by WSP was composed by the New York and Washington leadership in their usual collaborative fashion, with no pride or claim of authorship, so it is difficult to know which group wrote what part. It was distributed through official WSP channels via the national office in Washington.

26. Bentley, *Thirty Years of Treason*, p. 951.

27. Women Strike for Peace, Washington, D.C. to "Dear WISP's," 6 Dec. 1962 (WSP Document Collection).

28. Carol Urner to Representative Francis Walter reprinted in the *Women's Peace Movement Bulletin* 1 (20 Dec. 1962):5.

29. *Hearings before Committee on Un-American Activities*, pp. 2064–65.

30. Ibid., p. 2074.

31. Ibid., p. 2085.

32. Mary McGrory, "Prober Finds 'Peacemakers' More Than a Match," *Washington* (D.C.) *Evening Star*, 12 Dec. 1962, p. A-1.

33. *Hearings before Committee on Un-American Activities*, pp. 2095, 2101.

34. McGrory, "Prober Finds 'Peacemakers' More Than a Match," p. A-1.

35. Lyla Hoffman, undated typewritten statement (WSP Document Collection).

36. Thirty-seven favorable news stories, columns and editorials were reprinted in a hastily prepared WSP booklet, published less than two weeks after the hearings. . . .

37. *Vancouver* (B.C.) *Sun*, 14 Dec. 1962, p. 2.

38. "The Ladies Turn Peace Quiz into Greek Comedy," *Detroit Free Press*, 16 Dec. 1962, p. 1.

39. *Detroit Free Press*, 13 Dec. 1962, p. A-8.

40. Mary McGrory, "Nobody Controls Anybody," *Washington* (D.C.) *Evening Star*, 14 Dec. 1962, pp. A-1, A-9.

41. *Hearings before Committee on Un-American Activities*, p. 2201.

42. *Madison* (Wis.) *Daily Cardinal*, 14 Dec. 1962, p. 2.

43. Garst, "Women: Middle-Class Masses," pp. 10–11.

44. Interview with Dagmar Wilson, Leesburg, Va., Sept. 1977.

45. *New York Times Magazine*, 6 May 1962, p. 32.

46. On a WSP activity measure, 38 percent rated themselves as "very active," 10 percent as "active," and 42 percent rated themselves as "not active," or only "slightly active." The profile of the majority of the WSP participants that emerged was indeed that of middle-class, well-educated housewives. . . .

Thirty-eight percent of the women who responded claimed to belong to no other organizations, or at least did not record the names of any organizations in response to questions concerning other community activities. Forty percent of the women were active in a combination of civic, race relations, civil liberties, peace, and electoral political activity. Only 11 percent were members of professional organizations. . . .

47. Ibid., p. 15.

48. Dorothy Dinnerstein, *The Mermaid and the Minotaur: Sexual Arrangements and Human Malaise* (New York: Harper Colophon Books, 1976), pp. 259–62.

49. Ashley Montagu, "The Triumph and Tragedy of the American Woman," *Saturday Review*, 27 (Sept. 1958):14; . . .

50. "Feminism as Femininity in the Nineteen Fifties?" Birmingham (England) Feminist History Group, *Feminist Review*, no. 3 (1979):48–65.

51. Sara Evans, *Personal Politics: The Roots of Women's Liberation in the Civil Rights Movement and the New Left* (New York: Alfred A. Knopf, 1979), p. 23.

CHARLES PAYNE

A Woman's War: African American Women in the Civil Rights Movement

Ask most people who made the civil rights movement happen and the names that come up will be those of male leaders, such as brilliant legal minds: Charles Houston, Thurgood Marshall, and Roy Wilkins, all of the NAACP Legal Defense Fund. Best known is the articulate and charismatic Reverend Martin Luther King, Jr., who reached out to white and black alike with his vision of a beloved community. Other names include Andrew Young and Jesse Jackson, who started out in King's SCLC (Southern Christian Leadership Conference); John Lewis and James Forman of SNCC (Student Nonviolent Coordinating Committee); and James Farmer, who orchestrated the Freedom Rides for CORE (Congress of Racial Equality).

Women's historians found that women played important roles in the movement often at great risk to themselves and their families. Among them were Ella Baker, a veteran organizer who was the founding mother of SNCC; Fannie Lou Hamer, who went from sharecropper to civil rights activist to founding member of the Mississippi Freedom Democratic Party; Septima Clark, who organized citizenship schools for SCLC; Jo Ann Robinson, head of the Women's Political Council, which started the bus boycott that King took over in Montgomery; Diane Nash, organizer of sit-ins and freedom rides for SNCC; and Ruby Doris Smith Robinson, SNCC's executive secretary and a powerful figure in the organization, which was at the vanguard of the movement.

Although historians such as Kathryn Nasstrom* have probed the way memory shapes perceptions of participants' contributions to the civil rights movement, Charles Payne uses a different tactic in order to assess more accurately the role of women. He studies black women in rural Mississippi who were not leaders, but rather grassroots participants. In this selection, he seeks to explain their widespread involvement.

Since their sex seems not to have insulated these women from white violence, and families as well as individuals were the focus of reprisals, why did these women take such risks? Are there factors you would add or expand upon in explaining their motivation? Do you see any similarities with the women of Flint, Michigan, who joined Genora Johnson Dollinger's Emergency Brigade during the CIO's unionizing effort in the 1930s (see pp. 516–518)?†

*See Kathryn Nasstrom, "Down to Now: Memory, Narrative, and Women's Leadership in the Civil Rights Movement in Atlanta, Georgia," *Gender and History* 11 (April 1999): 113–44.

†One point of similarity between the two movements is that the sit-in, which the workers tried successfully for the first time in Dollinger's account, was borrowed by the civil rights movement and used by SNCC demonstrators at lunch counters and other segregated facilities with equal success.

Excerpted from *I've Got the Light of Freedom: The Organizing Tradition and the Mississippi Freedom Struggle* by Charles Payne (Berkeley: University of California Press, 1995). Reprinted by permission of the author and publisher. Notes have been edited and renumbered.

Asked to name all the women they can think of who were associated with the civil rights movement of the 1960s, most audiences are hard-pressed after Rosa Parks and Coretta King. In the South, a few may remember Mrs. Hamer. That so few women are remembered is ironic, to understate it. In the Delta, in the rural South generally, women were in fact much more politically active than men, at least in the early sixties. According to COFO (Council of Federated Organizations) organizers, women took civil rights workers into their homes, of course, giving them a place to eat and sleep, but women also canvassed more than men, showed up more frequently at mass meetings and demonstrations, and more frequently attempted to register to vote. There appears to be no disagreement with Lawrence Guyot's comment that "It's no secret that young people and women led organizationally."[1] Another organizer called the war in the Delta a woman's war.

The greater responsiveness of women represents a departure from the 1950s. Traditional wisdom among political scientists holds that across the Western world men are more politically involved than women.[2] The pattern in Mississippi during the 1950s appears consistent with that. In that especially dangerous period, Black political activism in rural Mississippi seems to have been dominated by men. There were women at all levels of the state NAACP hierarchy, but when they had official positions they tended to have those traditionally assigned to women—hospitality committee, secretary, membership committee—and they did not dominate the membership rolls in the way they would come to dominate many COFO-initiated movements.

The gender-related pattern of participation in the 1960s seems to have been age-specific. That is, among older folks, there is no clear imbalance.... Similarly, there does not seem to be any clear difference between teenage boys and teenage girls. The gender difference appears to be strongest in the years in between, the "settle-aged" years from, roughly, thirty to fifty. In that age range, some of my respondents estimated that women were three or four times more likely to participate than men....

While there was virtually no disagreement among the people I spoke with about the nature of the pattern, there was no consensus at all about what explains it.... These gender differences were not something to which people had given a lot of thought, even though they were aware of them. This is not surprising, given that in 1962 or 1963 gender was not as politicized a social category as it became a few years later.

Joyce Ladner [a Black SNCC veteran and a sociologist] offered an explanation that made sense to several people:

> ... Women in the rural South have a long history of being doers. This is what set them apart from a lot of white women who came into the movement.... If they were employed it was as a maid and not necessarily as major breadwinners in their families. They weren't as beholden to a paycheck. White people considered them less threatening.... Because Southern white men discounted women, period. Because of their strong sexism, they didn't see Black women as much more threatening than they did white women....

Although not mentioned by anyone I interviewed, one factor that probably played some role was SNCC's operating style. Founded by a woman, in its early years, women were always involved in the development of policy and the execution of the group's program.... SNCC organizers were concerned with finding and helping to develop nontraditional sources of leadership. Women obviously represented an enormous pool of untapped leadership potential.... SNCC, despite the traditional expectations of sex roles held by many of its members,[3] was structurally and philosophically open to female participation in a way that many older organizations would not have been.... Still, SNCC's openness to the participation of women does not explain why women were so responsive....

As Joyce Ladner noted, historically, Black women, especially poor Black women in rural areas, have had to fulfill social roles not commonly played by more privileged women. [Acclaimed Black writer] Zora Neale Hurston called southern Black women the mules of the world; they did whatever needed doing. Still, that has not always led to the kind of dominance of political activity that we seem to have [had] in the rural South in the sixties....

The notion that women were less exposed to reprisals than men has a certain plausibility. Southern whites, the argument goes, were less afraid of Black women and thus less likely to initiate either physical violence or economic reprisals against women. Even when economic reprisals were used, the wife's salary was likely to be less important to the family than the husband's. If anyone was going to be fired, better it be the wife. In short, it was simply safer, more cost-effective, for women to participate. . . . [But] the differential-exposure thesis minimizes the very substantial risks that women who joined the movement were running. . . . SNCC's newsletters in 1962 and 1963 suggest that some of the most violent incidents of reprisals took place against women. Women who were even rumored to be a part of the movement lost their jobs. . . . Any woman in Greenwood who contemplated joining the early movement had to be aware of all this. She would have also been aware of the absolutely brutal beating[s] that Annell Ponder, Mrs. Hamer, June Johnson, and Euvester Simpson had received in jail. . . .

Moreover, it is misleading to think of reprisals as being directed against merely the individual who was involved. Anyone who joined the movement placed his or her whole family at risk. . . . The Citizens' Council in particular made it a point to put pressure on the entire family. If anyone in a family was known to be a part of the movement, any adult in that family might have trouble finding work or getting credit. Similarly, the most popular forms of violence in that period—arson, drive-by shootings into homes, and bombings—were reprisals against family units, not just individuals. . . .

When explaining their own decision to join the movement, my respondents constructed answers primarily in terms of either religious belief or pre-existing social networks of kinship and friendship. For many women, both factors seem operative. Thus, Lou Emma Allen was drawn into the movement by her son, a junior-college student. Though she was often afraid, she was sure the Lord would see her through. Lula Belle Johnson got involved after June, her fourteen-year-old daughter, was arrested along with Fannie Lou Hamer and beaten. . . . Susie Morgan was drawn in partly by the activity of her daughters. She prayed and prayed over the decision to join, and finally she could see that it was what the Lord wanted her to do. . . .

The religious issue raises a series of important questions. One line of explanation for the overparticipation of women might go as follows: The movement grew out of the church. Women participate in the church more than men do. (One contemporary estimate is that across all varieties of Black religious activities, women represent seventy-five to ninety percent of the participants.)[4] . . .

This argument is probably more applicable to the urban South. In urban areas, the churches certainly were an early focal point of organizing activity.[5] It is not surprising that there would be a high level of participation by women in the activities of the Southern Christian Leadership Conference, because many of that organization's affiliates were large, urban churches populated largely by women. Their rural counterparts, however, were far less supportive of the movement. In Greenwood, . . . the early movement grew despite the opposition of the church. . . . Nonetheless, if the church as an organization did not lead people into the movement, the religiosity of the population may have been much more important. . . .

Those who joined the movement in its early days could not have known that things would work out as they did. What they knew for certain was that those who joined were going to suffer for it. From the viewpoint of most rural Black southerners in 1962 or 1963, the overwhelming preponderance of evidence must have suggested that the movement was going to fail. Joining a movement under such circumstances may literally require an act of faith. Faith in the Lord made it easier to have faith in the possibility of social change. As the slaves of a century ago, according to Du Bois, saw the fulfillment of Biblical prophecy in the coming of the Civil War, residents of the Delta may have seen the civil rights movement as a sign that God was stirring. . . .

NOTES

1. Howell Raines, *My Soul Is Rested* (New York: Putnam, 1977), p. 241.

2. See Seymour Lipset, *Political Man* (New York: Doubleday, 1960), pp. 189, 193–94. The book, considered a classic, is aptly named; its index contains no entry for "women."

3. Sara Evans, *Personal Politics* (New York: Vintage, 1980). The degree of sexism among men in SNCC has recently become an ongoing controversy, with Black women who participated saying that some white women participants have blown male

chauvinism in the movement out of proportion and that they—Black women—were always able to exercise authority in some rough correspondence to their abilities and desires, and that they ignored or didn't care much about some expressions of chauvinism. See Joyce Ladner, "A Sociology of the Civil Rights Movement: An Insider's Perspective," presented at the annual meeting of the American Sociological Association, August 1988. Ladner points out that while Stokely Carmichael's remark about the position of women in the movement being prone has been much quoted, during his tenure as chair "he encouraged and supported women as project directors and as members of SNCC's Central Committee."

4. Cheryl Gilkes, "Together and In Harness: Women's Traditions in the Sanctified Church," *Signs* 10 (Summer 1985):679.

5. Aldon Morris, *Origins of the Civil Rights Movement* (New York: Free Press, 1984), esp. chs. 1, 4.

DOCUMENTS

Dimensions of Citizenship II

Pauli Murray, "I had entered law school preoccupied with the racial struggle . . . but I graduated an unabashed feminist as well. . . ."

Pauli Murray was a remarkable woman. Born into a family that blended slaves, slave-owning whites, Cherokee Indians, freeborn African Americans—a family whose history she would later celebrate in her book *Proud Shoes*—she grew up an orphan in her grandparents' home in Durham, North Carolina. Bright and energetic but poor, Murray graduated from the city's segregated schools in 1926. In a display of characteristic determination, she applied to Hunter College in New York City. Rejected because she was so poorly prepared, she moved in with a cousin, enrolled in high school in New York, and entered Hunter a year later. The struggle to find work and stay in school in the midst of the Great Depression was so intense, however, that Murray, already suffering from malnutrition, nearly died from tuberculosis. Shortly after her graduation from Hunter in 1933, she found brief sanctuary in Camp Tera, one of the handful of women's camps established by the New Deal as a counterpart to the men's Civilian Conservation Corps, and then as an employee of remedial reading and workers' education projects funded by the WPA (Works Progress Administration).

"World events were breeding a new militancy in younger Negroes like me," she would write. "One did not need Communist propaganda to expose the inescapable parallel between Nazi treatment of Jews in Germany and the repression of Negroes in the American South. Daily occurrences pointed up the hypocrisy of a United States policy that condemned Fascism abroad while tolerating an incipient Fascism within its own borders." In 1938, she applied to the law school at the University of North Carolina at Chapel Hill, attracted by the work of its sociologists on race relations and farm tenancy. Many law school students supported her admission, as did Frank Porter Graham, the president of the university, but state law mandated her rejection because of race.

Torn between her writing and law, Murray threw herself into working for social justice. Her involvement in the unsuccessful struggle to obtain clemency for Odell Waller, a black sharecropper whose right to be tried by a representative jury had been denied because Virginia called to jury service only those who had paid a poll tax, brought her to the attention of Leon Ransom of Howard University Law School in Washington, D.C. When Howard University offered her a scholarship in 1941, she entered law school "with the single-minded intention of destroying Jim Crow."

Excerpted from "Writing or Law School?," "Jim Crow in the Nation's Capital," and "Don't Get Mad, Get Smart" in *Song in a Weary Throat: An American Pilgrimage* (New York: Harper & Row, 1987), pp. 183–85, 205–9, 238–45, 361–62. Reprinted courtesy of the Charlotte Sheedy Agency, Inc.

The following selections from her autobiography include an account of Murray's discovery of sexism amidst her battle with racism during her years at Howard University, and her leadership, eighteen years before the famous sit-ins in Greensboro, North Carolina, of a successful sit-in to desegregate a restaurant in Washington, D.C. Perhaps more than any other single person, Murray linked the civil rights movement with the federal quest for equity for women. After the establishment of New Deal wages and hours legislation, liberals began to recognize that the old protective labor laws (see pp. 415–416) were increasingly "protecting" women from better-paying "men's" jobs, just as the label of "privilege" was sustaining many inequalities, among them unequal access to professions and permissive rather than mandatory jury service (see pp. 647–648).

As early as 1947, Pauli Murray had begun to call discrimination on the basis of sex a system of "Jane Crow." In a biting and deeply personal essay published in *Negro Digest* entitled "Why Negro Girls Stay Single," Murray argued that women suffer "minority status . . . despite their numerical size," and "independently of race, religion or politics." As a staff member of John F. Kennedy's Commission on the Status of Women in 1962, Murray grew firm in her conviction that "Jane Crow" and "Jim Crow" were twin evils. She welcomed the passage of the Civil Rights Act of 1964, with its notable Title VII outlawing employment discrimination on the basis of sex as well as race. With a colleague, Mary Eastwood, she wrote what would become a classic essay, "Jane Crow and the Law." The arguments made there would help make it possible for the Supreme Court to rule in 1971 that discrimination on the basis of sex was discrimination, not privilege (*Reed* v. *Reed*, 404 U.S. 71).

Murray would go on to have an extraordinary legal career as a champion of racial and gender justice, serving on the National Board of the American Civil Liberties Union. In January 1977, she became one of the first women to be ordained as an Episcopal priest. Not long after, she was invited to celebrate her first Holy Eucharist in the Chapel of the Cross in Chapel Hill, the same church where the daughter of a prominent slaveholding family had many years before brought for baptism an infant whose father was her own lawyer brother, and whose mother was her own servant, Harriet. The infant was Pauli Murray's grandmother. On that occasion, "all the strands of my life came together," Murray wrote in an autobiography aptly subtitled "Activist, Feminist, Lawyer, Priest, and Poet." For Pauli Murray, the personal was indeed political.*

Ironically, if Howard Law School equipped me for effective struggle against Jim Crow, it was also the place where I first became conscious of the twin evil of discriminatory sex bias, which I quickly labeled Jane Crow. In my preoccupation with the brutalities of racism, I had failed until now to recognize the subtler, more ambiguous expressions of sexism. In the all-female setting of Hunter College, women were prominent in professional and leadership positions. My awareness of the additional burden of sex discrimination had been further delayed by my WPA experience. Hilda Smith, national director of the WPA Workers' Education Project, was a woman, my local project director and my immediate supervisor were both women, and it had not occurred to me that women as a group received unequal treatment. Now, however, the racial factor was removed in the intimate environment of a

**Song in a Weary Throat* was reprinted by the University of Tennessee Press in 1989 under the title *Pauli Murray: The Autobiography of a Black Activist, Feminist, Lawyer, Priest, and Poet.*

Negro law school dominated by men, and the factor of gender was fully exposed.

During my first year at Howard there were only two women in the law school student body, both of us in the first-year class. When the other woman dropped out before the end of the first term, I was left as the only female for the rest of that year, and I remained the only woman in my class for the entire three-year course. While I was there, not more than two or three women enrolled in the lower classes of the law school. We had no women on the faculty, and the only woman professional on staff was . . . the registrar, who had graduated from the law school many years earlier.

The men were not openly hostile; in fact, they were friendly. But I soon learned that women were often the objects of ridicule disguised as a joke. I was shocked on the first day of class when one of our professors said in his opening remarks that he really didn't know why women came to law school, but that since we were there the men would have to put up with us. His banter brought forth loud laughter from the male students. I was too humiliated to respond, but though the professor did not know it, he had just guaranteed that I would become the top student in his class. Later I began to notice that no matter how well prepared I was or how often I raised my hand, I seldom got to recite. It was not that professors deliberately ignored me but that their freewheeling classroom style of informal discussion allowed the men's deeper voices to obliterate my lighter voice, and my classmates seemed to take it for granted that I had nothing to contribute. For much of that first year I was condemned to silence unless the male students exhausted their arguments or were completely stumped by a professor's question.

My real awakening came several months after school began, when I saw a notice on the official bulletin board inviting "all male students of the First Year Class" to a smoker at the residence of Professor Leon A. Ransom. The exclusion of women from the invitation was so pointed that I went to Dr. Ransom's office to seek an explanation. He told me blandly that Sigma Delta Tau, a legal fraternity limited to male students and members of the legal profession, had established a chapter at the law school and that the purpose of the smoker was to look over first-year men for likely prospects. Through their association with experienced lawyers these young men would enhance their professional development. I had not yet become aware of the sexist bias of the English language, and recalling that the national professional English "fraternity" to which I had been elected while in college included both sexes, I asked Dr. Ransom, "What about us women?"

To my surprise, Dr. Ransom merely chuckled and said that if we women wanted an organization we could set up a legal sorority. Angrily, I said it was ridiculous to speak of a legal sorority for two women, but he did not seem concerned about our plight. I left Dr. Ransom's office feeling both bewildered and betrayed, especially because he was one of the most liberal professors on the university campus and had always treated me as a person. He had encouraged me to come to law school and used his influence to have me awarded a scholarship. Yet he did not seem to appreciate fully that barring women from an organization purporting to promote professional growth had the same degrading effect upon women as compelling us as Negroes to sit in the back of a bus or refusing to admit black lawyers to white bar associations. The discovery that Ransom and other men I deeply admired because of their dedication to civil rights, men who themselves had suffered racial indignities, could countenance exclusion of women from their professional association aroused an incipient feminism in me long before I knew the meaning of the term "feminism." . . .

The fact that an accident of gender exempted me from military service and left me free to pursue my career without interruption made me feel an extra responsibility to carry on the integration battle. Many other Howard University women were feeling a similar responsibility, which was heightened by the dramatic leave-taking of sixty-five Howard men, who marched off campus in a body to report for military duty. We women reasoned that it was our job to help make the country for which our black brothers were fighting a freer place in which to live when they returned from wartime service.

From the nightly bull sessions in Truth Hall a plan of action emerged. . . . It was designed to attract the widest possible support from all segments of the university community, with direct action reserved for the last of a series of steps. My role as student "legal adviser" was to make sure that our proposed actions were within the framework of legality so as not to arouse the official disapproval of the university administration. . . . Although we were engaged in serious business, our planning sessions were fun and challenged our power of imagination. The fact that we were doing something creative about our racial plight was exhilarating and increased our self-esteem. The Direct Action subcommittee attracted some of the leading students on campus, for it was important that those undertaking unorthodox activities maintain academic excellence. Also, we proceeded cautiously, aware that a misstep would compromise our goal. Instead of rushing precipitously into "hostile" territory, a group of students surveyed public eating places in the neighboring, mostly Negro community on Northwest U Street that still catered to the "White Trade Only." One of the most notorious of these lily-white establishments was the Little Palace Cafeteria, located at the busy intersection of Fourteenth and U streets, N.W., and run by a Mr. Chaconas. Because of its strategic location, the Little Palace had long been a source of mortification for countless unsuspecting Negroes, who entered it assuming that at least they would be served in the heart of the Negro section of the city.

The Little Palace Cafeteria was selected as our first target. For a week prior to our move against the cafeteria we held campus pep rallies and drummed up support for our effort through noon-hour broadcasts from the tower of Founder's Library. We decorated hot-chocolate cups and used them around campus as collection cans to solicit the funds we needed for paper, postage, and picket signs. We held a midweek Town Hall meeting and brought in experienced political leaders . . . to lead a forum on civil rights legislation and methods of achieving it. We conducted classes on the legal aspects of picketing and disorderly conduct in the District of Columbia, spent hours in small groups discussing public decorum, anticipating and preparing for the reactions of the black public, the white public, white customers, and white management respectively. We stressed the importance of a dignified appearance, and the subcommittee directed that all participants dress well for the occasion. We also pledged ourselves to exemplary nonviolent conduct, however great the provocation.

Finally, on April 17, a rainy Saturday afternoon, we assembled on campus and began to leave the Howard University grounds in groups of four, about five minutes apart, to make the ten-minute walk to the Little Palace Cafeteria. The demonstration was limited to a carefully selected group of volunteers—less than twenty students—who felt confident they could maintain self-restraint under pressure. As each group arrived, three entered the cafeteria while the fourth remained outside as an "observer." Inside, we took our trays to the steam table and as soon as we were refused service carried our empty trays to a vacant seat at one of the tables, took out magazines, books of poetry or textbooks, notebooks and pencils, and assumed an attitude of concentrated study. Strict silence was maintained. Minutes later the next group arrived and repeated the process. Outside, the observers began to form a picket line with colorful signs reading "Our Boys, our Bonds, our Brothers are Fighting for you! Why Can't We Eat Here?"; "We Die Together—Why Can't We Eat Together?"; "There's No Segregation Law in D.C. What's Your Story, Little Palace?" Two pickets carried posters (prepared for the War Manpower Commission by the Office of War Information) depicting two workers—one black and the other white—working together as riveters on a steel plate. The inscription on the poster read "united we win!"

My heart thumped furiously as I sat at a table awaiting developments. The management was stunned at first, then after trying unsuccessfully to persuade us to leave, called the police. Almost immediately a half-dozen uniformed officers appeared. When they approached us we said simply, "We're waiting for service," and since we did not appear to be violating any law, they made no move to arrest us.

After forty-five minutes had passed and twelve Negro students were occupying most of the tables of the small cafeteria, Chaconas gave up and closed his restaurant eight hours earlier than his normal closing time. Those of us who were inside joined the picket line and kept it going for the rest of the afternoon. Chaconas told reporter Harry McAlpin, who covered the demonstration for the *Chicago Defender:* "I'll lose money, but I'd rather close up than practice democracy this way. The time is not ripe." When Juanita Morrow, a journalism student, interviewed Chaconas several days later, he admitted that he had lost about $180 that Saturday afternoon and evening, a considerable sum for a small business.

Actually, the incident did not arouse the furor we had feared but revealed the possibilities for change. When told why the place was closed and being picketed, a white customer named Raymond Starnes, who came from Charlotte, North Carolina, said, "I eat here regularly, and I don't care who eats here. All I want is to eat. I want the place to stay open. After all, we are all human." Another white bystander, asked what he thought of the students' action, replied, "I think it's reasonable. Negroes are fighting to win this war for democracy just like whites. If it came to a vote, it would get my vote."

When Chaconas opened his place on Monday morning, our picket line was there to greet him, and it continued all day. Within forty-eight hours he capitulated and began to serve Negro customers. We were jubilant. Our conquest of a small "greasy spoon" eating place was a relatively minor skirmish in the long battle to end segregation in the nation's capital—a battle that was ended by a Supreme Court decision ten years later—but it loomed large in our eyes. We had proved that intelligent, imaginative action could bring positive results and, fortunately, we had won our first victory without an embarrassing incident. (One other small restaurant in the area was desegregated that spring before final examinations and summer vacation interrupted our campaign.)

Significantly, the prominent role of women in the leadership and planning of our protest was a by-product of the wartime thinning of the ranks of male students. Twelve of the nineteen Howard University demonstrators at the Little Palace on April 17 were female. . . . Many of those young women who had joined together to defy tradition would continue to make breakthroughs in their respective fields after their college days. . . . The youngest member of that little band of demonstrators, Patricia Roberts, carried the impact of her civil rights experiences from Howard University to the cabinet level of the federal government, [Patricia Roberts Harris served as President Carter's Secretary of Housing and Urban Development from 1977 to '79]. . . .

I had entered law school preoccupied with the racial struggle and single-mindedly bent upon becoming a civil rights attorney, but I graduated an unabashed feminist as well. Ironically, my effort to become a more proficient advocate in the first struggle led directly into the second through an unanticipated chain of events which began in the late fall of my senior year.

One day Dean Hastie called me into his office to discuss what I planned to do after graduation. To my utter surprise, he spoke of the possibility of my returning to teach at the law school after a year of graduate study, and with that possibility in mind he recommended that I apply for a Rosenwald fellowship. For a number of reasons, "graduate study" meant to me "graduate study at Harvard University." At least half of the Howard Law School faculty had studied at Harvard, both Hastie and Ransom held doctorates from its law school, and it had become a tradition at Howard to groom an exceptionally promising law graduate for a future faculty position by sending him to Harvard "to put on the gloss" of a prestigious graduate degree in law. My greatest rival in the preceding class, Francisco Carniero, who had graduated with top honors and as Chief Justice of the Court of Peers, was now completing his year of graduate law there. We had run neck and neck in courses we took together, he topping me by a couple of points in one and I topping him in another.

Naively unaware of Harvard's policy toward women, I was stunned when my schoolmates began kidding me. "Murray," someone said, "don't you know they're not going to let you into Harvard?" Harvard, it became clear, did not admit women to its law school.

Then my hopes were raised by a rumor which circulated around campus that Harvard was opening up to women students. Accordingly, when filling out my application to the Rosenwald Fund, I wrote in the space provided for choice of law school: "I should like to obtain my Master's degree at Harvard University, in the event they have removed their bar against women students. If not, then I should like to work at Yale University or at any other University which has advanced study in the field of labor law." I also wrote to the secretary of Harvard Law School, requesting confirmation or denial of the rumor I had heard. The answer was prompt. On January 5, 1944, the secretary's office wrote back: "Harvard Law School . . . is not open to women for registration."

This verdict was disappointing, of course, but with all the other preoccupations of my senior year, the matter probably would have rested there if I had not won the Rosenwald fellowship or at least if the names of the award winners had not been published nationwide. The announcement, made in late spring, listed me among fifteen white Southerners and twenty-two Negroes (including such notables as E. Franklin Frazier, Adelaide Cromwell Hill, Chester Himes, Rayford W. Logan, Dorothy Porter, and Margaret Walker) who received awards "for creative talent or distinguished scholarship." Mine was the only award in the field of law, and all the news stories reported that I was to do graduate study in labor law at Harvard University.

I was embarrassed to receive congratulatory messages from a number of people who were either unaware of Harvard's restrictive policy or assumed I had broken the barrier. At the same time, some of the men at Howard stepped up their banter, not without a touch of malicious glee. Until then I had been able to lick my wounds in private, but the public disclosure of my dilemma mortified me and presented a challenge I could not pass over lightly. If my schoolmates expected me to dissolve into tears under their stinging gibes, they were disappointed. I simply sat down and wrote a letter of application to Harvard Law School, which was duly processed, and I received a written request for my college transcript and a photograph.

In due course there came from Professor T. R. Powell, who chaired Harvard Law School's Committee on Graduate Studies, a letter that must have been dictated with an impish smirk. As nearly as I can recall, it ran: "Your picture and the salutation on your college transcript indicate that you are not of the sex entitled to be admitted to Harvard Law School." To appreciate the impact of this letter upon me, it is only necessary to remember the similar letter of rejection I had received in 1938 from the dean of the graduate school of the University of North Carolina in Chapel Hill: "Under the laws of North Carolina and under the resolutions of the Board of Trustees of the University of North Carolina, members of your race are not admitted to the University."

The personal hurt I felt now was no different from the personal hurt I had felt then. The niceties of distinction that in one case rejection was based upon custom and involved my sex and in the other was grounded in law and involved my race were wholly irrelevant to me. Both were equally unjust, stigmatizing me for a biological characteristic over which I had no control. But at least in the case of racial rebuffs long experience had taught me some coping mechanisms and I did not feel alone in that struggle. The fact that Harvard's rejection was a source of mild amusement rather than outrage to many of my male colleagues who were ardent civil rights advocates made it all the more bitter to swallow.

The harsh reality was that I was a minority within a minority, with all the built-in disadvantages such status entailed. Because of the considerable snobbery that—even apart from race and sex—existed in the highly competitive field of law, one's initial entry into the profession was profoundly affected by the law school one attended. This was particularly true for anyone who had ambitions to teach law. Since in my case the most common hurdles—lack of funds and a poor scholastic record—did not apply, I felt the injustice of the rejection even more strongly. I knew that however brilliant a record I had made at Howard, among my teaching colleagues I would never be considered on equal academic footing with someone who could boast of Harvard training. I also knew that the school of my second choice, Yale, had suspended its graduate program in law during the wartime emergency. [Professors William H.] Hastie and [Leon] Ransom, my law school mentors, understood my academic dilemma and were quietly supportive of my decision to pursue the Harvard matter further. Dr. [Caroline] Ware, whose great-great-grand-father Henry Ware had been the first dean of Harvard Divinity School and who grew up surrounded by the Harvard tradition, identified with me wholly in my fight. The only one of five generations of Phi Beta Kappas in her family not to take a Harvard degree, she held a Ph.D. from Radcliffe.

Then began the disheartening effort to budge a sluggishly corpulent bureaucracy on which my protests and appeals made about as much impression as a gnat on an elephant's hide. Harvard, being a private institution, was immune from legal attack and thus I had only the force of reason and logic with which to plead my case. A letter to Professor Powell asking what procedure to follow in appealing the law school's policy brought the information that the law school was bound by the rule of the Harvard Corporation not to admit women, and any appeal from that ruling would have to be submitted to the Corporation through its secretary, A. Calvert Smith.

Since my exclusion from Harvard was based solely on gender, my appeal necessarily was strongly feminist in tone:

> I have met a number of women and have heard of many more who wished to attend Harvard and yet were refused. This fight is not mine, but that of women who feel they should have free access to the very best of legal education. . . .
>
> Women are practicing before the Supreme Court, they have become judges and good lawyers, they are represented on the President's Cabinet and greater demand is being made for women lawyers in administrative positions as the men move into the armed forces. They are proving themselves worthy of the confidence and trust placed in them. . . . They are taking an intelligent view toward the political events at home and abroad, and statistics show they are in the majority of the voting population this year. A spot-check on memory would indicate there are only four important places they are not now holding—(1) As graduates of Harvard University, (2) as President of the United States, (3) as a member of the United States Supreme Court, and (4) as workers in the mines. Although [by admitting women] Harvard might lose in the sense of a loss of tradition, it might gain in the quality of the law school student personnel.

Meanwhile, two influential (if wholly unanticipated) male supporters sympathetic to the rights of women materialized. One was President Franklin D. Roosevelt! I had sent copies of the correspondence with Harvard to Mrs. Roosevelt, suggesting that the President might be amused at this attempt to storm the walls of his alma mater, never dreaming it would evoke more than a chuckle on his part. FDR was not merely amused; he actually wrote a letter on my behalf to President James B. Conant of Harvard University.

It would take more than one of that institution's most illustrious graduates to overturn a three-hundred-year tradition of male exclusiveness, however. President Conant's reply, sent on to me by FDR's secretary, only confused the issue. The letter assured President Roosevelt that I was free to do graduate work at Radcliffe, and even sent along a Radcliffe catalogue—never mind the obvious fact that Radcliffe did not offer graduate courses in law. I was flattered that the President of the United States had intervened on my behalf, but I was no nearer my goal. Mrs. Roosevelt was unequivocally in my corner, and wrote me a note saying: "I loved your Harvard appeal."

Lloyd K. Garrison, who was to become a lifelong friend and sponsor, was my second unexpected supporter. Mr. Garrison, former dean of the University of Wisconsin School of Law, was then a member of the National War Labor Board, which he later chaired. He was also a member of the Harvard Board of Overseers. I first met him through an ambitious undertaking of our student organization, the First Annual Court of Peers Dinner, jointly sponsored by the faculty and the Student Guild of Howard University School of Law. Mr. Garrison was our guest speaker, and as chief officer of the Student Guild it was my function to preside over the dinner and sit next to him at the speakers' table.

The great-grandson of abolitionist William Lloyd Garrison, Lloyd K. Garrison bore a striking resemblance to his famous ancestor and had inherited his commitment to human freedom. Unlike the fiery nineteenth-century Garrison, however, Lloyd K. Garrison combined a gentleness of disposition with a tough-minded pragmatism. . . . He was intensely interested in my effort to get into Harvard but warned me that I did not have a chance against the arch-conservative Harvard Corporation. Under the circumstances he encouraged me to follow an alternative plan for graduate study elsewhere, in the meantime pressing my appeal.

A. Calvert Smith informed me that the Harvard Corporation would review my appeal on July 10, by which time I had already applied to Boalt Hall [School] of Law, University of California at Berkeley, one of the few schools in the country whose wartime faculty of distinguished scholars remained relatively intact. On July 12, Mr. Smith wrote me to say that since I was asking, in effect, for a change in the long-established practice of the law school not to admit women, and since the conditions of admission to any department were in general set up by the faculty governing that department, "Whether or not women should be admitted to the Law School is . . . a decision for the Faculty of the Law School." Mr. Smith indicated that since no recommendation from the faculty of the law school was then before the Corporation, "it does not feel itself in a position to take any action on your application."

By sidestepping my appeal, the Harvard Corporation had rid itself temporarily of an annoying question, but it had also called into play a theory about the significance of individual action I had once announced half-seriously to Dr. Ware: "One person plus one typewriter constitutes a movement." If I could not compel admission to Harvard, at least I could raise the issue in such a way that its law school would be unable to avoid it. I was also learning the process of patiently following whatever administrative procedure was available even when there was every reason to believe the result would be futile.

My next letter was addressed to the Faculty of the Harvard Law School, summarizing the correspondence to date and requesting a meeting of the faculty "to reconsider my application and to decide whether it will recommend a change of the policy now in practice." I included a copy of my appeal to the Harvard Corporation and closed on a humorous note:

> [G]entlemen, I would gladly change my sex to meet your requirements but since the way to such change has not been revealed to me, I have no recourse but to appeal to you to change your minds on this subject. Are you to tell me that one is as difficult as the other?

As I had learned in the case of the University of North Carolina, correspondence could accomplish little more than stir up interest among a few key individuals and keep the issue flickering feebly. At the suggestion of Dr. Ware, I wrote to Judge Sarah T. Hughes of the United States District Court of Texas, who also chaired the Committee on Economic and Legal Status of Women. She replied that this was not a matter her committee had considered, but she said, "I shall be glad to discuss the problem at the next meeting which is in September," and asked that I keep her informed. After I left Washington, Dean Hastie wrote: "My best information on the Harvard situation is that the faculty is sharply divided on the matter of admitting women and will probably take the position that no action should be taken while a majority of the permanent faculty are on leave for war work." Lloyd K. Garrison's analysis prepared me for the inevitable. He wrote:

> From what I could pick up in Cambridge, my guesses are:
>
> (1) That the corporation will do nothing unless the Law School takes the initiative in asking that the rules be changed to admit women.
>
> (2) That the Law School will do nothing . . . , certainly not until Dean Landis gets back next fall and probably not then.
>
> (3) That this is due to combination of long tradition, an excessively high enrollment which has become an increasing headache [and]
>
> (4) A touch of some undefinable male egoism, which is, I think, rather particularly strong in and around Boston as compared let us say with the middle west where we take our co-education for granted.
>
> At my last meeting on the Board of Overseers [at Harvard] there was a great debate as to whether women should be admitted to the Medical School and, so I was told (I had to leave the meeting early), the proposal mustered only two votes out of a dozen. . . .

I was in California when the faculty of the Harvard School of Law met on August 7, 1944, and took action on my petition for review. A few days later, Acting Dean E. M. Morgan informed me of their decision. His letter said in part:

> In October, 1942, the Faculty thoroughly considered a proposal to request the University authorities to change the general rule. The first proposition was to admit women only during the emergency. This was almost immediately and unanimously rejected. The second proposal was for a permanent policy admitting women on exactly the same basis as men. This was debated by the Faculty at intervals for about three months, and the views of all members fully considered. There was much difference of opinion, but it was finally unanimously voted that no action looking to a change in the present practice be taken until after the emergency and after the School has returned to normal conditions with its full Faculty in residence. At that time the question will be debated anew. Accordingly it has been necessary to deny all applications for admission by women.
>
> At its meeting on August 7, the Faculty determined to abide by its previous decision.

Having lost my first battle against "Jane Crow," I was somewhat comforted to learn indirectly that the effort was not entirely wasted. That fall when I registered at the University of California's Boalt Hall [School] of Law, I was surprised to discover that news of the Harvard affair had traveled across country, and I was greeted with the remark, "So you're the woman who caused the Harvard Law School faculty to split 7-7 on your application." I also learned later of Harvard's announcement that women would be admitted to its medical school in 1945.

Fortunately, my controversy with Harvard was unresolved when I graduated from Howard in June, and it did not affect the high excitement of the ceremonies. Aunt Pauline came from Durham and Uncle Lewis Murray from Baltimore, each filled with proprietary pride and vying to share the honor of a niece who had "turned out so well." The high point of Aunt Pauline's visit was having tea at the White House with Mrs. Roosevelt. Then on Commencement Day an unexpected recognition electrified the huge outdoor gathering. Harry McAlpin, a reporter for the *Pittsburgh Courier,* captured the mood of the occasion in a story headlined "Flowers from the First Lady." He wrote:

> Flowers—a huge bouquet of them—delivered near the close of the Howard University commencement exercises last Friday, overshadowed all the previous proceedings of the impressive occasion. They were from Mrs. Roosevelt, wife of the President of the United States. They were for brilliant, active, strong-willed Pauli Murray, graduate cum laude of the Howard Law School.

According to McAlpin—no stranger to hyperbole—the arrival of the flowers overshadowed the commencement address . . . [and] the conferring of honorary degree[s]. . . .

Actually, the flowers had been delivered to the law school a half hour before the ceremonies began. When I came in to get my cap and gown, I glanced at them admiringly. . . . When someone finally made me realize it was my name on the card, I removed it, suggesting the flowers be placed on the platform for all the graduates to share. A few minutes later, the sight of University Secretary . . . parading across campus with the spectacularly beautiful display only moments before the academic procession began created an extra touch of excitement and added a special luster to the pageantry of the event. . . .

My intense involvement with the early stirrings of the resurgent feminist movement called on all my professional skills and kept me so busy I had no time to become demoralized. In 1965 and 1966, Title VII was the principal issue that fueled the movement, especially among business and professional women, as we battled against public attitudes ranging from ridicule to disregard of the new law. The Equal Employment Opportunity Commission (EEOC), charged with administration of the statute, was one of the chief offenders in that respect. A warning of what women might expect came shortly after the law went into effect, on July 2, 1965. EEOC Chairman Franklin D. Roosevelt, Jr., declared in his first public statement that "the whole issue of sex discrimination is terribly complicated," and indicated that the Commission had not yet come to grips with most of the problems involved. Along with this lukewarm approach, Chairman Roosevelt announced the appointment of his seven key aides who would head the EEOC staff, giving a further clue to official indifference toward women's issues. All seven appointees to the staff were men, and not one of them had functioned on the President's Commission on the Status of Women or any of its study committees that had canvassed sex-based discrimination in employment. The prevailing attitude of the EEOC staff (with a few exceptions) seemed to be that of its executive director, Herman Edelsburg, who stated some months later at New York University's Annual Conference on Labor that the sex provision of Title VII was a "fluke" and "conceived out of wedlock." The newly appointed EEOC deputy general counsel had recently published a lengthy law review article on Title VII, offering an unduly restrictive interpretation of the sex provision as a prohibited ground of discrimination.

Only two of the EEOC's five commissioners responded sympathetically to representations made by women's groups: Richard Graham, a Republican appointed for a term of one year, who had been given responsibility for reviewing cases of sex discrimination, and Aileen Clarke Hernandez, the lone female member of the Commission, an honors graduate of Howard University and a former official of the International Ladies' Garment Workers' Union, with extensive experience in the administration of the California fair employment practices law. No pressure group existed to press for implementation of women's employment rights under the statute, and members of our feminist network who had fought to keep the word "sex" in Title VII were powerless to do more than sound an alarm. . . .

In the absence of organized group actions, we had to rely upon maximizing our individual efforts. Mary Eastwood and I coauthored a law review article entitled "Jane Crow and the Law: Sex Discrimination and Title VII," setting forth ways in which the Fifth and Fourteenth amendments and the sex provisions of Title VII could be interpreted to accord women equality of rights. We equated the evil of antifeminism (Jane Crow) with the evil of racism (Jim Crow), and we asserted that "the rights of women and the rights of Negroes are only different phases of the fundamental and indivisible issue of human rights." Published in the *George Washington Law Review* in December 1965, at a time when few authoritative legal materials on discrimination against women existed, our article broke new ground and was widely cited.

Goesaert *v.* Cleary, *1948*

In response to the worries of returning World War II veterans over finding jobs in the postwar recession, Michigan's legislature passed a statute prohibiting any woman from serving liquor as a bartender in cities of more than 50,000 unless she was "the wife or daughter of the male owner" of a licensed liquor establishment. (Women could, however, be hired as waitresses.) The statute was justified on the grounds that the presence of a man behind the bar shielded women from drunken violence; we can see it as another version of the protective legislation that had been upheld in *Muller* v. *Oregon* (1908) (pp. 415–416).

Valentine Goesaert's husband had recently died. She and her daughter Margaret wanted to continue to operate their family's tavern in Dearborn, Michigan. The Federal District Court for Michigan denied their claim, observing that the legislature had not been unreasonable: "[T]he legislature may have reasoned that a graver responsibility attaches to the bartender who has control of the liquor supply than to the waitress who merely receives prepared orders of liquor from the bartender for service at a table." The Goesaerts appealed to the U.S. Supreme Court, where they lost again. The decision was 6–3. Note the reasoning of the dissenters as well as the majority.

JUSTICE FELIX FRANKFURTER, WRITING FOR THE MAJORITY:

[The question is: can Michigan forbid females generally] from being barmaids and at the same time make an exception in favor of the wives and daughters of the owners of bars? . . . Beguiling as the subject is, it need not detain us long. To ask whether or not the Equal Protection of the Laws Clause of the Fourteenth Amendment barred Michigan from making the classification the State has made between wives and daughters of owners of liquor places and wives and daughters of non-owners, is one of those rare instances where to state the question is in effect to answer it.

We are to be sure, dealing with a historic calling. We meet the alewife, sprightly and ribald, in Shakespeare, but centuries before him she played a role in the social life in England. . . . The Fourteenth Amendment did not tear history up by the roots, and the regulation of the liquor traffic is one of the oldest and most untrammeled of legislative powers. Michigan could, beyond question, forbid all women from working behind a bar. This is so despite the vast changes in the social and legal position of women. The fact that women may now have achieved the virtues that men have long claimed as their prerogatives and now indulge in vices that men have long practiced, does not preclude the States from drawing a sharp line between the sexes, certainly in such matters as the regulation of the liquor traffic. . . . The Constitution does not require legislatures to reflect sociological insight, or shifting social standards, any more than it requires them to keep abreast of the latest scientific standards.

While Michigan may deny to all women opportunities for bartending, Michigan cannot play favorites among women without rhyme or reason. The Constitution in enjoining the equal protection of the laws upon States precludes irrational discrimination as between persons or groups of persons in the incidence of a law. But the Constitution does not require situations "which are different in fact or opinion to be treated in law as though they were the same." . . . Michigan evidently believes that the oversight assured through ownership of a bar by a barmaid's husband or father minimizes hazards that may confront a barmaid without such protecting oversight. . . . [If it is reasonable,] as we think it is, Michigan has not violated its duty to afford equal protection of the laws. We cannot cross-examine . . . the mind of Michigan legislators nor question their motives . . . we cannot give ear to the suggestion that the real impulse behind this legislation was an unchivalrous desire of male bartenders to try to monopolize the calling. . . .

Justice Wiley Rutledge, dissenting:

. . . This statute arbitrarily discriminates between male and female owners of liquor establishments. A male owner, although he himself is always absent from his bar, may employ his wife and daughter as barmaids. A female owner may neither work as a barmaid herself nor employ her daughter in that position, even if a man is always present in the establishment to keep order. This inevitable result. . . . belies the assumption that the statute was motivated by a legislative solicitude for the moral and physical well-being of women who, but for the law, would be employed as barmaids. Since there could be no other conceivable justification for such discrimination against women owners of liquor establishments, the statute should be held invalid as a denial of equal protection.

Goesaert v. *Cleary*, 335 U.S. 464, 69 S.Ct. 198 (1948).

Hoyt *v.* Florida, *1961;* Taylor *v.* Louisiana, *1975*

When Pauli Murray surveyed the American landscape in 1962 for examples of sex discrimination, jury service was the first contemporary example to which she turned. Jury service was, she thought, the issue that most clearly illustrated widespread "confusion" about whether women had been oppressed by the law and required emancipation, or favored by the law and permitted easy exemption from an onerous duty.

Some members of the founding generation had believed that service on juries is a more significant aspect of citizenship than voting; voting, after all, is complete in a moment, while service on juries requires extended periods of time, debate, and deliberation among the jurors, and ultimately the exercise of judgment, which can result in important consequences—including the death sentence—for an accused fellow citizen. The Constitution promises an "impartial" jury drawn from "the district wherein the crime shall have been committed." The conditions of impartiality are not spelled out; the Constitution promises neither "a jury of one's peers," nor one drawn from a "cross-section" of the community. It is tradition that has linked the concept of the jury with "peers," neighbors, and the community in which the crime is committed and from which the jury is chosen.

When women achieved the vote in Wyoming in 1869 (see Edwards, pp. 342–348), it seemed to follow that they could hold office and serve on juries, but after only a few years, the objection of male voters and officeholders was so severe that the law was changed to exclude them.

In some states, the achievement of jury service followed painlessly on the heels of suffrage. In Iowa, Michigan, Nevada, and Pennsylvania, where statutes defined competent jurors as "all qualified electors . . . of good moral character, sound judgment, and in full possession of the senses of hearing and seeing, and who can speak, write and read the English language," the admission of women to the electorate automatically defined them as competent jurors. When these interpretations were tested in state courts, judges usually upheld them. Not all state courts, however, thought it was obvious that "electors" could be properly construed to mean women as well as men. In 1925 the Illinois Supreme Court ruled that because only men had been voters in 1874 when the jury statute had been passed, the terms "legal voters" and "electors" referred only to male persons. Not until 1939 did the Illinois state legislature permit women to serve on juries.

In most states, new statutes were required. By 1923, eighteen states and the territory of Alaska had arranged for women to serve on juries. But then the momentum ran out; subsequently the issue had to be debated afresh in each state. A few states continued to exclude women completely, but most developed some form of "voluntary" jury service, in which women could be called to serve but could easily decline. In Florida, no women at all served on juries until 1949, when the legislature passed a law providing that women who wished to be eligible could go to their county courthouses and register their willingness to have their names placed in the *venire*, the randomly selected pool from which jurors are selected.

When Gwendolyn Hoyt came to trial in Tampa in 1957, charged with manslaughter for killing her husband, only 218 women of the more than 46,000 women voters in Hillsborough County had registered to serve; the jury commissioner placed only 10 of those women's names in a pool of 10,000 names. It was no surprise that she was tried— and found guilty—by an all-male jury. It took the six-man jury only twenty-five minutes to convict Hoyt of second-degree murder; on January 20, 1958, she was sentenced to imprisonment at hard labor for thirty years.

Hoyt appealed, first to the Florida Supreme Court, and then to the U.S. Supreme Court, which heard the case in 1961. Hoyt claimed temporary insanity, brought on by her suspicions of her husband's infidelity, his rejection of her offer of reconciliation, and her own vulnerability to epilepsy. She believed that women would understand her distress better than would men. But with so few women's names in the large jury pool, they had virtually no chance of being chosen.

Hoyt and her lawyers did *not* claim that a fair jury was required to have women as members. Instead, they claimed that a fair jury would have been drawn at random from a list of names from which women had not been excluded. Hoyt believed that in order to enjoy the *right* to a trial by a jury of her peers, other women would have to be *obliged* to serve on juries.

HOYT v. *FLORIDA*, 1961

MR. JUSTICE JOHN MARSHALL HARLAN:

At the core of appellant's argument is the claim that the nature of the crime of which she was convicted peculiarly demanded the inclusion of persons of her own sex on the jury. She was charged with killing her husband . . . in the context of a marital upheaval involving, among other things, the suspected infidelity of appellant's husband, and culminating in the husband's final rejection of his wife's efforts at reconciliation. It is claimed, in substance, that women jurors would have been more understanding or compassionate than men in assessing the quality of appellant's act and her defense of "temporary insanity." No claim is made that the jury as constituted was otherwise afflicted by any elements of supposed unfairness.

. . . [T]he right to an impartially selected jury assured by the Fourteenth Amendment . . . does not entitle one accused of crime to a jury tailored to the circumstances of the particular

When New York State passed a voluntary jury service law for women in 1937, hundreds of women lined up to register. The New York World Telegram *treated the story as cute: "Women jurors registering in the Hall of Records, and do they like it!" The caption—"They augur no good for love slayers"—predicted that women jurors would not join in the common practice of light sentences for men who had wounded or killed their wives' lovers. Dorothy Kenyon, a feminist attorney who had fought for fifteen years for mandatory jury service, welcomed the new statute as a first step: "This gives a new lease of life to the jury system." In the 1960s, Kenyon and Pauli Murray would lead the efforts of the American Civil Liberties Union to establish equitable jury service throughout the nation. (Courtesy of the Library of Congress.)*

case, whether relating to the sex or other condition of the defendant, or to the nature of the charges to be tried. It requires only that the jury be indiscriminately drawn from among those eligible in the community for jury service, untrammelled by any arbitrary and systematic exclusions. . . . The result of this appeal must therefore depend on whether such an exclusion of women from jury service has been shown.

. . . Florida's [law] does not purport to exclude women from state jury service. Rather, the statute "gives to women the privilege to serve but does not impose service as a duty." It accords women an absolute exemption from jury service unless they expressly waive that privilege. . . . [W]e [cannot] . . . conclude that Florida's statute is . . . infected with unconstitutionality. Despite the enlightened emancipation of women from the restrictions and protections of bygone years, and their entry into many parts of community life formerly considered to be reserved to men, woman is still regarded as the center of home and family life. We cannot say that it is constitutionally impermissible for a State, acting in pursuit of the general welfare, to conclude that a woman should be relieved from the civil duty of jury service unless she herself determines that such service is consistent with her own special responsibilities.

II

. . . Finding no substantial evidence whatever in this record that Florida has arbitrarily undertaken to exclude women from jury service . . . we must sustain the judgment of the Supreme Court of Florida.

JUSTICES WARREN, BLACK, AND DOUGLAS, CONCURRING:

We cannot say from this record that Florida is not making a good faith effort to have women perform jury duty without discrimination on the ground of sex. Hence we concur in the result, for reasons set forth in Part II of the Court's opinion.

Hoyt v. *Florida*, 368 U.S. 57 (1961)

Note that these three justices are careful to uphold the decision of the lower court only "for reasons set forth in Part II of the Court's opinion." What is the difference between the argument in part I and part II? Did granting women the power to avoid jury duty hurt Hoyt's right to a fair trial? If men and women are equal, does a virtually all-male jury *pool* undermine equality? If men and women are equal, does an all-male *jury* undermine equality? Why do you think Justices Warren, Black, and Douglas wrote a separate concurring opinion? To what extent was the Court's opinion based on arguments from equality? On arguments from difference?

When Ruth Bader Ginsburg began to work on the ACLU's Women's Rights Project (see *Frontiero* v. *Richardson*, pp. 723–725), she was committed to persuading the Supreme Court to reverse its decisions on several major cases that had sustained sex discrimination; one of those cases was *Hoyt*. Not until 1975, in a case arising in Louisiana, a state in which women were still required to file a written declaration of their desire to be subject to jury service, was *Hoyt* reversed by the Supreme Court. Billy Taylor, convicted of rape and kidnapping, successfully appealed his conviction on the grounds that women had been systematically excluded from the jury pool. His lawyers drew an analogy between his experience and the Court's decision three years before that a white man was entitled to have a jury from which blacks had not been systematically barred. The majority opinion upheld Taylor's claim. It made extensive use of an opinion written by

Justice William O. Douglas in 1946, relating to jury selection practices in federal courts. What did Douglas mean when he said that "two sexes are not fungible"? Do you agree?

TAYLOR v. *LOUISIANA*, 1975

MR. JUSTICE BYRON R. WHITE:

The Louisiana jury-selection system does not disqualify women from jury service, but in operation its conceded systematic impact is that only a few women, grossly disproportionate to the number of eligible women in the community, are called for jury service. In this case, no women were on the venire from which the petit jury was drawn. . . .

The State first insists that Taylor, a male, has no standing to object to the exclusion of women from his jury. . . . Taylor was not a member of the excluded class; but there is no rule that claims such as Taylor presents may be made only by those defendants who are members of the group excluded from jury service. In [1972] . . . a white man [successfully] challenged his conviction on the ground that Negroes had been systematically excluded from jury service. . . .

We are . . . persuaded that the fair-cross-section requirement is violated by the systematic exclusion of women, who in the judicial district involved here amounted to 53 percent of the citizens eligible for jury service. . . . This very matter was debated in *Ballard* v. *U.S.* [1946]. . . . The . . . view that an all-male panel drawn from various groups in the community would be as truly representative as if women were included, was firmly rejected:

> . . . who would claim that a jury was truly representative of the community if all men were intentionally and systematically excluded from the panel? The truth is that the two sexes are not fungible; a community made up exclusively of one is different from a community composed of both; the subtle interplay of influence one on the other is among the imponderables. . . . The exclusion of one may indeed make the jury less representative of the community than would be true if an economic or racial group were excluded. [Justice William O. Douglas, 1946]

. . . It is untenable to suggest these days that it would be a special hardship for each and every woman to perform jury service . . . it may be burdensome to sort out those who should be exempted from those who should serve. But that task is performed in the case of men, and the administrative convenience in dealing with women as a class is insufficient justification for diluting the quality of community judgment represented by the jury in criminal trials.

Taylor v. *Louisiana*, 419 U.S. 522 (1975).

The decision in *Taylor* addressed only the problem of who is included in the panels from whom jurors are chosen. Not until 1994 did the Supreme Court rule that the Fourteenth Amendment's equal protection clause prohibits the use of peremptory jury challenges on the basis of gender. Overturning a paternity suit in which a woman challenged virtually all the men in the jury pool, leaving an all-female jury to decide on her claims for child support, the majority held "that gender, like race, is an unconstitutional proxy for juror competence and impartiality."*

**J.E.B.* v. *Alabama*, 511 U.S. 127 (1994). For a full treatment of the history of women and jury service, see Linda K. Kerber, *No Constitutional Right to Be Ladies: Women and the Obligations of Citizenship* (New York: Hill & Wang, 1998), ch. 4.

Civil Rights Act, Title VII, 1964

The Civil Rights Act of 1964 was a comprehensive law of enormous significance. It was a complex statute, twenty-eight printed pages long and divided into eleven major sections, or titles. Title I dealt with voting rights; Title III with the desegregation of public facilities; Title V established a Commission on Civil Rights. Title VII defined a long list of practices that would be forbidden to employers and labor unions; obliged the federal government to undertake an "affirmative" program of equal employment opportunity for all employees and job applicants; and created an Equal Employment Opportunity Commission (EEOC) to monitor compliance with the law.

Title VII was notable in that it outlawed discrimination on the basis of sex as well as race. Sex was added to the categories "race, color, religion and national origin" by Congressman Howard Smith, a conservative Democrat from Virginia, who was a vigorous opponent of civil rights legislation. He introduced his motion after urging from Republican supporters of the National Women's Party, who had been lobbying for an equal rights amendment whether or not it would undermine protective labor legislation, and who wanted to equate discrimination on the basis of race with discrimination on the basis of sex. The debate on Smith's motion was filled with misogyny; Smith joked that his amendment would guarantee the "right" of every woman to a husband. But it passed, supported by conservative members who were more comfortable voting for a civil rights bill if there was something in it for white women.

The EEOC, which began to operate in the summer of 1965, anticipated that virtually all of its complaints would come from blacks. The commission was surprised to discover that 25 percent of the complaints received during the first year were from women from a range of racial and ethnic backgrounds, many African American. In the course of responding to these complaints, both the commission and the courts were driven to a more subtle analysis of female job categories and work patterns. Section 703(e) 1 required that employers wishing to restrict a job category to one sex had to show that being male or female was a "bona fide occupational qualification"; it was not enough to say that men or women had traditionally filled any given job.

In the decade that followed, most states developed their own versions of Title VII, establishing laws that prohibited sex discrimination in employment. The federal statute was amended in 1972 and again in 1978; on both occasions the EEOC was given substantial additional powers and responsibilities. The three major areas of EEOC activity are (1) furnishing assistance to comparable state agencies, (2) furnishing advice to employers and labor unions about compliance, and (3) enforcing compliance by conciliation and legal action. In 1978 Congress passed the Pregnancy Discrimination Act, which amplified the definition of sex to include

U.S. Statutes at Large 78 (1964): 253–66. For a discussion of the circumstances of the passage of Title VII, see Jo Freeman, "How 'Sex' Got into Title VII: Persistent Opportunism as a Maker of Public Policy," *Law and Inequality* 9 (1991): 163-84.

pregnancy, childbirth, or related medical conditions. EEOC has been willing to view sexual harassment as a form of sex discrimination but has not endorsed the concept of comparable worth.

Sec. 703.(a) It shall be an unlawful employment practice for an employer—

> (1) to fail or refuse to hire or to discharge any individual, or otherwise to discriminate against any individual with respect to his compensation, terms, conditions, or privileges of employment, because of such individual's race, color, religion, sex, or national origin; or
>
> (2) to limit, segregate, or classify his employees in any way which would deprive or tend to deprive any individual of employment opportunities or otherwise adversely affect his status as an employee, because of such individual's race, color, religion, sex, or national origin.

(b) It shall be an unlawful employment practice for an employment agency to fail or refuse to refer for employment, or otherwise to discriminate against, any individual because of his race, color, religion, sex, or national origin, or to classify or refer for employment any individual on the basis of his race, color, religion, sex, or national origin.

(c) It shall be an unlawful employment practice for a labor organization—

> (1) to exclude or to expel from its membership, or otherwise to discriminate against, any individual because of his race, color, religion, sex, or national origin;
>
> (2) to limit, segregate, or classify its membership, or to classify or fail or refuse to refer for employment any individual, in any way which would deprive or tend to deprive any individual of employment opportunities, or would limit such employment opportunities or otherwise adversely affect his status as an employee or as an applicant for employment, because of such individual's race, color, religion, sex, or national origin; or
>
> (3) to cause or attempt to cause an employer to discriminate against an individual in violation of this section. . . .

(e) Notwithstanding any other provision of this title, (1) it shall not be an unlawful employment practice for an employer to hire and employ employees, for an employment agency to classify, or refer for employment any individual, for a labor organization to classify its membership or to classify or refer for employment any individual, or for an employer, labor organization, or joint labor-management committee controlling apprenticeship or other training or retraining programs to admit or employ any individual in any such program, on the basis of his religion, sex, or national origin in those certain instances where religion, sex, or national origin is a bona fide occupational qualification reasonably necessary to normal operation of that particular business or enterprise. . . .

Sec. 705.(a) There is hereby created a Commission to be known as the Equal Employment Opportunity Commission, which shall be composed of five members, not more than three of whom shall be members of the same political party, who shall be appointed by the President by and with the advice and consent of the Senate. . . .

(g) The Commission shall have power—

> (1) to cooperate with and, with their consent, utilize regional, State, local, and other agencies, both public and private, and individuals; . . .
>
> (3) to furnish to persons subject to this title such technical assistance as they may request to further their compliance with this title or an order issued thereunder;
>
> (4) upon the request of (i) any employer, whose employees or some of them, or (ii) any labor organization, whose members or some of them, refuse or threaten to refuse to cooperate in effectuating the provisions of this title, to assist in such effectuation by conciliation or such other remedial action as is provided by this title;
>
> (5) to make such technical studies as are appropriate to effectuate the purposes and policies of this title and to make the results of such studies available to the public;
>
> (6) to refer matters to the Attorney General with recommendations for intervention in a civil action brought by an aggrieved party under section 706, or for the institution of a civil action by the Attorney General under section 707, and to advise, consult, and assist the Attorney General on such matters. . . .

BETH L. BAILEY

Prescribing the Pill: The Coming of the Sexual Revolution in America's Heartland

In this fascinating bit of historical detective work, Beth Bailey explodes the myth that the advent of the oral contraceptive in 1960 ushered in the Sexual Revolution, freeing women—especially those who were unmarried—to engage in sex without fears of unwanted pregnancies. Bailey tells a different story, one in which use of the new contraceptive is closely linked to concerns about overpopulation and poverty. By narrowing her focus to Lawrence, Kansas, home to the University of Kansas, she provides a clear view of the complex process by which college women gained access to the pill.

Why does Bailey refer to this process as "elite-managed, gradual change"? At what point did young women demand access on their own behalf? Why were their voices virtually mute throughout the 1960s, even though Bailey provides clear evidence that their behavior was changing? Is this silencing on the part of heterosexual young women related in any way to the silencing that Betty Friedan, Miriam Van Waters, or various lesbians imposed on themselves in the postwar era?

American women went "on the pill" in the 1960s. The oral tablets that most Americans called simply "the pill" were approved for contraceptive use by the FDA in 1960. By early 1969, eight and a half million women were using the pill; their numbers had grown by about one million each year from 1961.[1] Every day for three weeks out of their monthly menstrual cycle, millions of women popped the tiny tablet through the foil package that fit into the daisywheel container that somewhat resembled a compact—if one didn't know better. The high hormonal doses of the early oral contraceptives had pronounced side effects, which mimicked pregnancy: breast tenderness, weight gain, some nausea. But the pill was more than 99 percent effective, in no way dependent on the direct cooperation of the woman's partner, and completely separate from the act of sexual intercourse. A great many women were willing to accept some side effects in exchange for freedom from fear of pregnancy. By giving women greater control over their sexual and reproductive lives, this new contraceptive technology helped change the meaning and experience of sex in America.

The great majority of the women who went on the pill in its early years, however, were not the young single women who lived "the revolution." Most were married. . . . Nonetheless, by the mid-1960s the pill symbolized the revolution in sex. . . . In America, talk of the sexual revolution inevitably turned to talk of the pill, and discussions of the pill often centered on its possible effects on America's sexual mores.

Largely because of its symbolic role, the pill frequently appears in discussions (both then and now) as a sort of *deus ex machina*, bringing about the sexual revolution. In 1968

Excerpted from "Prescribing the Pill," ch. 4 of *Sex in the Heartland* by Beth L. Bailey (Cambridge, Mass.: Harvard University Press, 1999). Notes have been renumbered and edited.

a no less distinguished figure than Pearl S. Buck, writing for the mass market in *Reader's Digest,* linked a crisis in sexual morality to the pill: "It is a small object—yet its potential effect upon our society may be even more devastating than the nuclear bomb."[2] ... [But Buck's analogy to the bomb] overlooks a key fact. The pill was not simply a new technology available in the free marketplace of postwar America. It had to be prescribed by a physician.

Doctors, then as now, controlled access to oral contraceptives. And at that time only a small minority of physicians would prescribe birth control pills to women who were not married. Most believed, along with a large majority of the American public, that it was wrong for unmarried women to have sex. Thus, before the pill could play any significant role in the sexual behavior of America's unmarried youth, something had to change. Unmarried women—in large numbers—had to have access to oral contraceptives. How did single women get the pill?

Once again, revolutionary change in Americans' sexual mores and behavior was made possible inadvertently.... The pill did not become available to single women because they raised their voices and demanded the right to sexual freedom and control of their own bodies. Instead, it became available to them as a byproduct of two political movements that were at the heart of sixties liberalism and its attempts to ameliorate the difficult social problems that plagued America and the world.

One of these movements was driven by concern about population growth, both international and domestic, which reached near-panic proportions in the United States during the 1960s and early 1970s. The other, Lyndon Johnson's Great Society, used federal funds and programs to attack the causes and consequences of poverty and racism in the United States. Neither set of efforts, by any stretch of the imagination, was intended to foster a sexual revolution. However, these two movements helped make the pill available to single women, in large part by providing rationales for prescribing contraceptives that did not employ a language of morality....

[In Kansas, population control advocates urged the state senate to] vote on legislation allowing public agencies to distribute information about contraceptives to Kansas citizens. Senate Bill 375 stemmed largely from the intense lobbying efforts of Patricia Schloesser, M.D., head of the state division of maternal and child services, who was motivated by a frightening vision of unrestrained world population growth.... [T]he senate voted unanimously in favor of the measure. The house vote the following April, however, was close enough to require a roll call.... While it was now legal for public institutions to offer birth control and contraceptive information to citizens of Kansas, the legislature had offered no ... funding. Without money for birth control services, the change in law had little practical impact....

Among the most vocal and vehement advocates of birth control in Kansas was the director of Lawrence's public health department, Dr. Dale Clinton.... Like Dr. Schloesser, Clinton believed that the world population explosion was a greater threat to public health than any contagious disease or environmental hazard.... In 1959 the professional organization for public health workers, the 20,000-member American Public Health Association (APHA), had adopted a resolution that called for attention, at "all levels of government," to "the impact of population change on health." And in 1963 the APHA called population growth "one of the world's most important health problems" and began lobbying government officials for action.[3]

[While the population advocates pressed for maximum dissemination of both information about contraceptives and the contraceptives themselves, the Johnson administration pursued a similar strategy as part of a very different objective.] President Johnson pledged in his state of the union address "to seek new ways to use our knowledge to help deal with the explosion in world population and the growing scarcity of world resources." In April [1965], Senator Gruening of Alaska introduced a bill that led to the funding of birth control programs through the Department of Health, Education, and Welfare. Earlier, the Office of Economic Opportunity (OEO) had funneled some money to family planning programs under the "local option" policy that allowed community groups to initiate welfare programs. (Initially the OEO did not allow its funds to be used for contraceptives for unmarried women; that restriction was lifted in 1966.)[4] The federal government's decisions to spend taxpayers' money on public family planning programs were not based on concern about women's reproductive health or a wish to promote sexual freedom. Rather, the funding was a result of the confluence of alarm about the "population problem" and increased federal involvement in programs intended to alleviate the effects of poverty in the United States. Limiting the number of children born to poor women (or allowing poor women to avoid unplanned and unwanted pregnancies) was a priority for these programs.

The political implications of linking Johnson's Great Society (with its strong focus on poverty) and population control were as apparent at the time as they are today. In the early twentieth century, many advocates of birth control had worked closely with the eugenics movement, which sought to limit childbearing among people the eugenicists deemed genetically and racially inferior and so preserve the dominance of white, Anglo-Saxon Americans. Those uncomfortably close links between the birth control movement and the eugenics movement were not so far in the past. . . .

The politics of the Johnson administration's "war on poverty" and welfare programs were complicated at best, and those who attempted to implement policies struggled with opposition from widely divergent sources. In the case of birth control, the administration faced both the suspicions of targeted groups such as poor African Americans *and* voters' reservations about the costs of burgeoning social welfare programs. . . . The American Association of Public Health consistently focused on the dangers of world population growth, an argument that was more compelling to Americans who rejected the idea of "benefits" for the poor and underprivileged. But throughout the 1960s, authors also attempted to demonstrate that contraception for America's poor was fully in keeping with "broadly democratic principles of equal opportunity for all." Birth control, one prominent activist wrote in an attempt to shift the grounds for suspicion, should not be the "special privilege" of the "well-to-do."[5]

Many Americans, however, drew connections between birth control and antipoverty programs that were exactly what government agencies had tried to avoid. For example, when *Good Housekeeping* sampled its 20,000-member "consumer panel" in 1967 on the question "Should Birth Control Be Available to Unmarried Women," its editors discovered that the negative responses (significantly, a strong majority) were based on "moral" arguments, while the affirmative responses were "practical." An Arizona woman wrote: "It would eliminate many dollars in child-welfare payments." A more vehement response came from a woman in the Midwest, who supported birth control for unmarried women because "I deeply resent having to deprive my family of privileges I cannot afford because I have to pay support for others not of my choosing."[6] . . .

Once the Kansas legislature made funding available, Dr. Clinton moved quickly and Lawrence's health department began to offer contraceptive services—something fewer than 20 percent of local health departments in the United States did at that time. Clinton, however, was decidedly uninterested in the professional debate about birth control for the indigent and the related directives. Though the framework provided by state (and eventually federal) guidelines indicated an implicit, but clear, association of these programs with services for the poor, Clinton made it equally clear that his birth control clinic was not "indigent-oriented," nor did he consider it the appropriate site for clinical medicine. He did not intend to focus on the poor, and he did not mean to provide women (of any income level) with health care. Instead, he intended to combat the scourge of unrestrained population growth by offering contraceptives to any and all.

. . . Kansas's laws restricting birth control, in effect from 1870 through 1963, had applied only to public agencies. Even before 1963 a married woman in Lawrence had ready access to birth control if she could afford a private doctor. When the pill became available for contraceptive purposes in 1960, Lawrence doctors had begun prescribing it to married women. . . .

As private doctors in Lawrence were already meeting the needs of their patients, the health department, naturally, would draw from a different constituency. Married women who could afford private doctors were more or less out of the pool. Who was left? Those for whom medical fees were too expensive. . . .

There was also another constituency, one that the state and federal governments had not intended to target: unmarried women. And because of the University of Kansas and Haskell Indian Junior College, Lawrence had a disproportionately high number of young, unmarried women. The Kansas legislature had mandated access to contraceptive information and services only for *married* women 18 years and older. Parental permission was required for women under 18, no matter what their marital status. But the legislature also provided a back door to access: Any woman might receive contraceptives at a public clinic if she was "referred to said center by a licensed physician." Clinton interpreted this law in the broadest terms. He was a licensed physician, legally authorized to make such referrals. Thus, as he made clear in newspaper interviews and public talks, any woman who wanted birth control might receive her referral at the clinic itself, at the time of her appointment. With virtually no exceptions, women seeking contraceptives at the health department came away with the pill.

[At the University of Kansas,] the question was whether the University Health Service should prescribe the pill to unmarried women students. This debate . . . centered around issues of morality. It was precipitated by a 1966 forum on the topic: "Should unmarried undergraduates be given birth control information and/or materials through Watkins Hospital [the student health service]?"

The panelists were three: Rev. Simmons, the campus minister who had helped form the family planning clinic [affiliated with Planned Parenthood] and who focused on sexuality counseling and birth control in his ministry at KU; Father Falteisch, chairman of the moral theology department at St. Louis University and a Roman Catholic priest; and Dr. Raymond Schwegler, director of KU's student health service. According to coverage by the *University Daily Kansan,* Simmons argued that population control was desperately needed. Father Falteisch agreed, and suggested that the Church was moving toward accepting the "responsible use" of contraceptives as legitimate, though not for the unmarried. In the context of 1966 America and their respective churches, both men of the cloth took liberal to progressive positions. The hard line, however, came from the man of medicine.

The *Kansan* described Dr. Schwegler, then about 60 years old, as a "small, white-haired man" with a soft voice, but he certainly never minced words. Watkins would not, Schwegler insisted, give contraceptives to unmarried students "under any circumstances." "I know this is old fashioned, mid-Victorian, and the *Kansan* will cut us to ribbons," he is quoted in the *Kansan* as saying, "but I don't want to do it and my staff backs me completely." Rev. Simmons pushed, arguing that unless premarital intercourse was grounds for expulsion, Schwegler's policy was unfair. Schwegler replied: "We'd have trouble keeping the student population up [if we expelled students for premarital intercourse]. But Watkins will not contribute to the recreational activities of the campus." When a student asked about the possibility of a "rebel doctor," Schwegler deemed it impossible: "All the doctors are handpicked—by me." He continued: "If I had somebody over there who I thought was as far out as some of the teaching faculty, I'd fire him. I want a conservative hospital that can be respected."[7]

The 1966 forum on birth control prompted a flood of letters to the *Kansan.* The letters contained no dire predictions about the earth's future if population growth continued uncontrolled. Instead, students used a language of morality to dispute Schwegler's stance. . . .

The first response to Schwegler published in the *Kansan* was . . . from a graduate student from Iola, Kansas. . . . Noting that the health service did provide the pill to married women, he argued that by so doing the administration had defined the issue as moral, not medical. Thus, he said, the question was, "Who should make the moral decision, the university or the students themselves?" Another graduate student (from Gettysburg, South Dakota) questioned "the irresponsible use of the concept 'morality' as employed primarily by the 'anti-pill' proponents." Morality, he insisted, existed only in a situation in which there was "opportunity for choice." Without "free access" to contraceptives, students were not making a moral—or immoral—choice about premarital intercourse. Instead, their choices were constrained by fear or coercion.

The "anti-pill" faction was represented by only one letter. The writer, a male sophomore from Nebraska, argued that because the university was a "public servant," it must follow the "doctrines of the society." He warned that premarital sex would be likely to increase if

single women could get the pill, for without fear of pregnancy, "restraining factors would be few and far between." Reaching for an analogy, he asked: "If the possibility of punishment for murder were eliminated," would there not be "a substantial increase in the number of murders committed every year?" ...

What was largely missing in this flurry of letters was a statement embracing sexual freedom—an affirmative voice.... [M]ost of the writers shifted the focus away from sex in making their arguments.... While their central claim—that the university should provide contraceptives to unmarried women students—was quite radical, their arguments were not. These were not yet the voices of revolution.

In the forum and in the ensuing debate, there were no arguments centering around the rights of women to control their own bodies. In fact, only two women participated in this public debate, and their names do not appear, effaced in the signatures "Mr. and Mrs. James Cooley" and "Mr. and Mrs. Angus Wright." ... Why didn't women speak out in the paper? After all, the debate was about women's choices—it was not men who might go "on the pill."

Women did not write because the stakes for them were so high. Discussions about morality and the pill in the larger society did not center on the morality of existential choice, but on the immorality of premarital sex. In the February 1967 *Good Housekeeping* poll on unmarried women and the pill, respondents made comments such as: "I truly pity a generation growing up with the morals of alley cats"; and "Making birth control available to unmarried girls to me would mean lowering our moral standards and destroying our culture." These women were not policymakers or experts.... [T]heir voices represent a different sort of authority. These are the voices of mothers—mothers of the sort whose daughters went to state colleges in the Midwest. The *Kansan* was a student paper, but news of a daughter's making public claims about her right to birth control was very likely to travel fast and to travel home.

... Writings in the *Journal of the American College Health Association, School and Society,* and the *Journal of School Health* at the time were equally emphatic about the evils of premarital sex.... The director of the Princeton health service ... warned against prescribing contraceptives to unmarried women, as "the student's unconscious mind might interpret such prescriptions as a signal from 'authority' giving permission for sexual freedom."[8] [A] physician at the Ohio State University health service ... made an unfortunate analogy to sex: "It is all a bit like cars: Some choose a new one and break it in with loving care; others buy from a used car lot—it is just as nice and shiny but you are not sure what problems the previous drivers have left you."[9]

Mass-circulation magazines and professional journals would not have devoted so much space to debates over premarital sex if there had been no audience for them. . . . Nonetheless, these are essentially prescriptive discourses. What of the students themselves?

In the spring semester of 1964 the "Roles of Women" committee of the Associated Women Students (AWS) surveyed its constituency. Presented with descriptions of behavior ("using race as one basis for choosing your associates"; "showing disrespect for those in authority"; "wearing short shorts in town"; "feeling very angry with someone"), students were asked to judge each item. Categories were "morally or ethically right," "generally acceptable," "generally unacceptable," and "morally or ethically wrong." The instructions emphasized that each student should indicate what was right or wrong "for *you.*" More than 1,900 women completed the survey.

Questions about sex provoked the strongest responses. Significantly higher percentages of women students disapproved of "mixed swimming parties in the nude" than of using an exam "which has been illegally obtained." ... [M]ost of the respondents (77 percent of the freshmen and 68 percent of the seniors) rated premarital sex with a fiancé as "morally or ethically wrong," not merely as "generally unacceptable." Even stronger was the students' disapproval of sexual intercourse when the couple was not engaged to be married. A striking 91 percent of both freshmen and seniors labeled it unacceptable or wrong. Only 2 percent of each group deemed premarital sex for those who were not engaged "morally or ethically right."

... In 1967 a student union forum offered three professors addressing the question "Is Free Love a Bargain?" ... This forum was dominated by a professor of English, who accused the audience of coming in search of "some rationalization for the sex you've indulged in." . . . [In] such a climate, with the threat of moral condemnation from peers and authorities alike, few students wished to make public their private decisions about sex.

In 1967, following the "Is Free Love a Bargain?" forum, an unmarried woman finally wrote to the editor of the campus newspaper, claiming her right to both sex and the pill: "I take the pill because I'd rather express my love than repress it. I'm not promiscuous, but once in a while I meet a 'special' guy. I've seen too many girls on campus totally disregard school for several weeks as they suffer anxiety over a missed menstrual period. . . . If a girl takes one chance a year, that's enough to warrant taking the pill." . . . Her letter, which had begun, "I'm a woman and I'm glad," employed a feminist language, emphasizing women's right and capacity to choose. It was a powerful and affirmative statement. But it was unsigned. An editor's note below the letter read: "Contrary to established editorial page policy, we are printing this letter without signature." All letters, no matter how controversial their claims, required signature—except this one. A woman's claiming her right to sex and the pill was understood as a whole different category of risk.

That this woman remained anonymous and was allowed to do so by the *Kansan* editorial board in violation of its policy, that women's voices were so conspicuously silent in the previous year's debate on the pill, that 91 percent of the women students surveyed *said* they believed premarital sex to be "ethically or morally wrong"—all this is strong evidence that it wasn't only the prescriptive voices of adults denying the legitimacy of the culture of youth. Even within student culture, there was a gulf between public claims and private behavior. For the women of KU were having sex. And they were, in increasing numbers, on the pill.

Actually getting the pill could be complicated, however. When a young, single woman sought a prescription for contraceptives in the 1960s, she was making a statement about her sexual status. Virgins didn't need birth control pills unless they did not plan to remain virgins much longer. . . . When a single woman went to a doctor to request any sort of contraceptive device, she risked refusal, embarrassment, even lectures on morality and appropriate behavior. Some women bought cheap rings and tried to pass them off as wedding bands. Others claimed they were coming in for a "premarital exam," with the wedding pending. Still others complained of menstrual cramps or heavy bleeding and came away with the pill, prescribed to "regulate" their periods. But many doctors, especially those in small towns and university communities, saw through such pretexts and often treated young women with suspicion. Single women were not guaranteed, by law or custom, access to birth control.

As women learned through informal networks, alternative newspapers, and the completely mainstream *Journal World*, the quickest, cheapest, and least complicated place to get birth control pills in Lawrence was the public health department. The university student health service refused to "contribute to the recreational activities of the campus," in its director's colorful words, and many students worried about having such information about their sex lives in what were, after all, official university records at the health service. . . . [The Planned Parenthood–affiliated] clinic was open only two nights a month, and simply could not serve large numbers of women. . . .

The number of women obtaining oral contraceptives at the public health department grew dramatically from year to year, and the vast majority of the new patients each year were KU students. The patient load closely followed the academic year. In 1971, for example, there were only 44 new patients in August, but in September, with the beginning of the fall semester, there were 300. That year the Lawrence-Douglas County health department served 8,529 birth control patients and dispensed or prescribed almost 38,000 months of pills. . . . The pill was a wonder drug not simply because of its effectiveness for women but also because of its possible convenience for those who prescribed it. Women went to the health department and walked out a few minutes later "on the pill." Stories of young women who were offered virtual armloads of free pills and told to pass them on to their friends still circulate today. . . .

The Planned Parenthood–affiliated clinic took a very different approach. Prescription of the pill was contingent upon not only a physical examination but also a time-consuming process of education and counseling. . . . The clinic, which had opened in early 1967, closed its doors permanently on the first day of 1970. Though it had been founded to serve low-income residents of Lawrence, the president of its sponsoring group explained, it had been used almost exclusively by KU students (she did not say whether they were married or single). Many of the volunteers were frustrated by what they saw as a misdirection of resources, and upon closing the clinic the directors sent a letter to Dr. Schwegler at the student health service and to the chancellor arguing that the university must take responsibility for its students' birth control needs instead of allowing students to overwhelm community resources needed by and for a different population.[10]

. . . In 1970, after the closing of the Planned Parenthood clinic, a student group approached top-level administrators about the health service's birth control policies. The administrators responded sympathetically, promising that two upcoming vacancies at Watkins would be filled with doctors who would prescribe the pill without using marital status or "morality" as criteria. This never happened. . . . In 1970, 53 percent of American college health services offered no gynecological care to women students, and 72 percent did not prescribe contraceptives (to single *or* married students).[11]

Thus far, the story of the pill in Lawrence, Kansas, has been one of elite-managed, gradual change. . . . Until the 1970s, Lawrence's youth also fit into this model. . . . While thousands of young women went on the pill during the 1960s, public acknowledgment of that private behavior lagged behind. [Although the] pill may have been revolutionary in its results, it was not especially revolutionary in its introduction.

In the early 1970s the women's movement captured the pill, in both its symbolic and its physical manifestations. Women in Lawrence—and not only young women—interrupted the process of gradual change within the paradigms of population control and sexual morality and offered, instead, revolutionary claims about gender equality, cultural authority, and sexual freedom.

By 1972 any woman in Lawrence—married or unmarried—could obtain birth control pills, free if necessary. This had been true, and widely known, for at least five years. But it wasn't simply access to the pill that was at stake. It was the nature of the access, and the meaning attributed to it, that angered some women. In 1972 two different groups of women in Lawrence challenged the medical men who controlled access to the pill.[12] Though the two groups used different methods and different vocabularies . . . both made claims based on the rights and needs of women themselves and not on those of the larger society. In so doing they stepped outside the discourses of morality and of the population problem and centered the debate over access to the pill in a discourse on women, rights, and freedom.

. . . KU's dean of women, Emily Taylor, was a NOW-style feminist who lobbied for political legislation and university policies supporting equal rights for women. Her office had supported a form of liberal feminism on campus, including a commission on the status of women, and had served as a center of action for some women students and administrators throughout her tenure.

On the other end of the continuum, women in Lawrence's large and diverse counterculture had begun to draw connections between the oppression of minorities and the oppression of women. The women of *Vortex* (the most important underground newspaper) published a women's issue in 1970, and soon afterward the *Lavender Luminary*, a lesbian paper, appeared. W.I.T.C.H. (Women's International Terrorist Conspiracy from Hell) emerged briefly as a local group. Consciousness-raising groups formed. In Lawrence, women were talking with other women about their lives, and those conversations would have repercussions in the world they inhabited.

[In February 1972,] a lecture by radical feminist Robin Morgan inspired these two groups of women to unite as the February Sisters. They took over a university building to voice their demands for full health care for women students, a federally funded child care center on campus, an end to discriminatory employment practices at KU, more women in high-level administrative positions, an affirmative action program, and a department of women's studies. . . . When the Sisters emerged from the building early the next morning, they had won commitments from the administration on a substantial portion of their demands, including the women's health program.

[The Sisters] couched their argument in language echoing the American tradition of rights and freedoms. "We, the February Sisters," their proposal for a human sexuality clinic began, in an invocation of the U.S. Constitution. Arguing that "control of her reproductive functions is a fundamental right of every woman," the Sisters insisted: "The University cannot view the action proposal . . . as a request for additional privileges, but rather as a demand to recognize right [*sic*] which have been neglected."[13]

It was not simply the right to access these women claimed. . . . More important, these women were rejecting the frameworks of sexual morality and population control that had governed access to contraceptives for more than a decade. The February Sisters condemned the ways that many Americans used concepts of sexual morality to deny women's autonomy and dignity—a fairly obvious and expected critique—but also criticized the efforts of population control groups. . . . These women understood that rationales for contraception based on population control, no less than those based on morality, left room for comments like the one made by the irritated director of student health, Dr. Schwegler, who said that he did so many pelvic exams he sometimes felt like he worked in a whorehouse. The February Sisters and their allies meant to provide a new framework for prescribing the pill that centered around the needs of women themselves and left no room for such demeaning and disrespectful remarks.[14]

After the actions of the February Sisters in February 1972, Watkins student health center officially began prescribing the pill to unmarried women. Somewhat ironically, the following month the Supreme Court ruled that women could not be denied contraceptives on the basis of marital status.

The struggles over the pill in Lawrence were not yet over, however. Even though Watkins offered contraceptives, students still sought the quick access to birth control and the relative anonymity offered by Dr. Clinton's clinic at the public health department. . . . In August 1972, however, the Kansas State Department of Health cut off funding for Clinton's birth control program. The state agency received its funding from the Department of Health, Education, and Welfare (HEW), and it came with federal mandates [that] committed doctors to follow a specified procedure in prescribing the pill, including performing a complete physical exam, pap smear, visual exam for cancer, tuberculin test, hemoglobin, and urinalysis. Clinton . . . refused to perform these tests. . . . Comprehensive medical services for the indigent were not his mandate, he insisted, and he would continue to provide birth control as before, funding it through donations from patients, not to exceed $1 per woman each month. Dr. Schwegler, the director of KU's student health service, who was also serving as chairman of the public health committee, told the *Journal World* that he was "irritated as a private citizen" over the state health department's action. Clinton prevailed with Lawrence's Board of Health, and his refusal stood. Though the local clinic lost a $12,000 federal grant, it was soon running a $10,000 surplus from donations by birth control patients.[15]

Young women who took the pill Clinton prescribed had sex without fear of pregnancy. They obtained the pill simply by request, without the demeaning act of lying about an impending marriage or the purchase of a cheap gold ring at a drugstore. They were, by and large, grateful. By prescribing the pill, Dr. Clinton inadvertently facilitated the sexual revolution in Lawrence and changed the lives of thousands of young women and their partners. . . .

Notes

1. Elizabeth Rose Siegel Watkins, in "On the Pill: A Social History of Oral Contraceptives in America, 1950–1970" (Ph.D. diss., Harvard University, 1996), pp. 130–131.

2. Pearl S. Buck, "The Pill and the Teen-Age Girl," *Reader's Digest* 92 (April 1968):111, quoted in Watkins, "On the Pill," p. 138.

3. Donald Harting and Leslie Corsa, "The American Public Health Association and the Population Problem," *American Journal of Public Health* 59 (Oct. 1969):1927–29. For a history of population control initiatives, see James Reed, *From Private Vice to Public Virtue* (New York: Basic Books, 1978).

4. Leslie Corsa, "Public Health Programs in Family Planning," *American Journal of Public Health* 56 (Jan. 1966, supplement); Reed, *From Private Vice*, p. 378; Watkins, "On the Pill," pp. 141–142. For statistics on federal funding see "Family Planning

Services," Hearing before the Subcommittee on Public Health and Welfare of the Committee on Interstate and Foreign Commerce, House of Representatives, serial no. 91–70 (Washington: GPO, 1970), pp. 190–193.

5. Mary Calderone, "Health Education for Responsible Parenthood: Preliminary Considerations," *American Journal of Public Health* (Jan. 1964):1735–40.

6. "Should Birth Control Be Available to Unmarried Women?" *Good Housekeeping*, Feb. 1967, p. 14.

7. Will Hardesty, "Birth Control Practices Debated," *University Daily Kansan (UDK)*, Nov. 4, 1966.

8. Willard Dalrymple, M.D., "A Doctor Speaks of College Students and Sex," *Journal of the American College Health Association* 15 (Feb. 1967):286.

9. W. Roy Mason Jr., M.D., "Problems of Married College Students: Health Education Implications," ibid., 14 (April 1966):273–274. Frances K. Harding, M.D., "The College Unmarried Population Explosion," *Journal of School Health* 35 (Dec. 1965):450–457.

10. "Over-Interest Closes County Clinic," *UDK*, Feb. 3, 1970; "Birth Control Clinic Closes," *UDK*, Feb. 5, 1970.

11. The student request was in conjunction with the Commission on the Status of Women at KU, sponsored by the dean of women's office. Information here is from "February Sisters Position Statement on a Health Care Program for Women," Addendum II, in Lorna Zimmer personal files, Lawrence, Kan.; "Women—February First Movement," Women's Studies Program Archives, KU (WSPA); Judy Browder, "Women's Decade of History," WSPA; "Campus Problems for Consideration," Council on Student Affairs files, University of Kansas Archives.

12. There was at least one woman physician in Lawrence, and she had been quoted in the *UDK* refusing to prescribe contraceptives to unmarried women. But in this controversy the divisions that appeared publicly were strictly along gender lines.

13. "February Sisters Position Statement on a Health Care Program for Women," in Zimmer files.

14. Judy Henry, "Groups Urge Birth Control," *UDK*, April 4, 1971. Browder, "Women's Decade," and transcript of "February Sisters Panel Discussion," 1987, statement by Mary Coral, in WSPA.

15. "State Drops Birth Control Funding Here," *Lawrence Daily Journal World (JW)*, Sept. 22, 1972; "Birth Control Funding Possible," *JW*, Sept. 27, 1972; Tim Pryor, "Health Agency Says Changes Due," *JW*, Jan. 10, 1973; Toby MacIntosh, "Policy on Pills is Controversial," *JW*, Feb. 9, 1973.

SUSAN J. DOUGLAS

Why the Shirelles Mattered: Girl Groups on the Cusp of a Feminist Awakening

Worrying about the moral impact of rock 'n' roll on one's teenage children was a conversational staple among white middle-class parents in the 1950s and early 1960s. Concern about the sexual message Elvis's pelvic gyrations sent to viewers was so widespread that when he appeared on *The Ed Sullivan Show*, there were no shots from the waist down of the rock star, who seemed more black than white. What parents did not realize was that their daughters, while Elvis fans, took as their role models of female liberation icons such as the Supremes and the Shirelles, all of whom were, in fact, black. In her insightful essay, Susan J. Douglas explores why the music of these girl groups resonated so intensely with so many American teens. In particular, she examines the meanings of the very mixed messages these teens received about gender and sexuality.

Does Douglas make her case for why the Shirelles and other girl groups "mattered"? Do you agree with her conclusion about their role in the rise of fans' feminist consciousness? What role does the music of today play in the lives of young women?

Excerpted from ch.4 of *Where the Girls Are: Growing Up Female with the Mass Media* by Susan J. Douglas (New York: Times Books, 1994). Reprinted by permission of the publisher. Notes have been edited and renumbered.

OK—here's a test. Get a bunch of women in their thirties and forties and put them in a room with a stereo. Turn up the volume to the "incurs temporary deafness" level and play "Will You Love Me Tomorrow" and see how many know the words—all the words—by heart. If the answer is 100 percent, these are bona fide American baby boomers. Any less, and the group has been infiltrated by impostors, pod people, Venusians. But even more interesting is the fact that non–baby boomers, women both older and younger than my generation, adore this music too, and cling to the lyrics like a life raft.

Why is it that, over thirty years after this song was number one in the country, it still evokes in us such passion, such longing, such euphoria, and such an irresistible desire to sing very loudly off-key and not care who hears us? And it's not just this song, it's girl group music in general, from "He's So Fine" to "Nowhere to Run" to "Sweet Talkin' Guy." . . .

First of all, girl group music was really about us—girls. When rock 'n' roll swiveled onto the national scene in the mid-1950s and united a generation in opposition to their parents, it was music performed by rebellious and sexually provocative young men. Elvis Presley was, of course, rock 'n' roll's most famous and insistently masculine star—in 1956, five of the nine top singles of the year were by Elvis. At the same time, there would be weeks, even months, when no woman or female group had a hit among the top fifteen records.[1] . . .

Then, in December 1960, the Shirelles hit number one with "Will You Love Me Tomorrow"; it was the first time a girl group, and one composed of four black teenagers, had cracked the number one slot.[2] And these girls were not singing about doggies in windows or old Cape Cod. . . . They were singing about whether or not to go all the way and wondering whether the boyfriend, so seemingly full of heartfelt, earnest love in the night, would prove to be an opportunistic, manipulative, lying cad after he got his way, or whether he would, indeed, still be filled with love in the morning. . . . "Will You Love Me Tomorrow" was about a traditional female topic, love, but it was also about female longing and desire, including sexual desire. And, most important, it was about having a choice. . . .

[T]his was new. This was, in fact, revolutionary. Girl group music gave expression to our struggles with the possibilities and dangers of the Sexual Revolution.

What were you to do if you were a teenage girl in the early and mid-1960s, your hormones catapulting you between desire and paranoia, elation and despair, horniness and terror? You didn't know which instincts to act on and which ones to suppress. . . .

For answers—real answers—many of us turned to the record players, radios, and jukeboxes of America. . . .

By the late 1950s, Tin Pan Alley realized that Perry Como, Doris Day, and Mantovani and his orchestra weren't cutting it with the fastest-growing market segment in America, teenagers. . . . Music publishers and producers grasped two key trends: Rock 'n' roll was here to stay, and there was this flourishing market out there, not just boys, but girls, millions of them, ready and eager to buy. . . . At the same time, the proliferation of transistor radios meant that this music could be taken and heard almost everywhere, becoming the background music. . . .

. . . [I]n the aftermath of the Shirelles hit, all kinds of girl groups and girl singers appeared, from the pouf-skirted Angels ("My Boyfriend's Back") to the cute and innocent Dixie Cups to the eat-my-dirt, in-your-face, badass Shangri-Las. . . .

The most important thing about this music, the reason it spoke to us so powerfully, was that it gave voice to all the warring selves inside us struggling, blindly and with a crushing sense of insecurity, to forge something resembling a coherent identity. Even though the girl groups were produced and managed by men, it was in their music that the contradictory messages about female sexuality and rebelliousness were most poignantly and authentically expressed. . . . They sang about the pull between the need to conform and the often overwhelming desire to rebel, about the tension between restraint and freedom, and about the rewards—and costs—of prevailing gender roles. They sang, in other words, about getting mixed messages and about being ambivalent in the face of the upheaval in sex roles. . . .

Some girl group songs, like "I Will Follow Him," allowed us to assume the familiar persona *Cinderella* had trained us for, the selfless masochist whose identity came only from being some appendage to a man. As we sang along with Dionne Warwick's "Walk On By," we were indeed abject martyrs to love, luxuriating in our own self-pity. But other songs addressed our more feisty and impatient side, the side unwilling to sit around and wait for the boy to make the first move. In "tell him" songs like "Easier Said Than Done," "Wishin' and Hopin'," and, of course, "Tell Him," girls were advised to abandon the time-wasting and possibly boy-losing stance of passively waiting for *him* to make the first move. . . . Girls were urged to take up a previously male prerogative—to be active agents of their own love lives and to go out and court the boy. . . .

Girl group songs were, by turns, boastful, rebellious, and self-abnegating, and through them girls could assume different personas, some of them strong and empowering and others masochistic and defeating. . . . The songs were about escaping from yet acquiescing to the demands of a male-dominated society, in which men called the shots but girls could still try to give them a run for their money. . . .

In girl group music, girls talked to each other confidentially, primarily about boys and sex. The songs took our angst-filled conversations, put them to music, and gave them a good beat. Some songs, like "He's So Fine" (doo lang, doo lang, doo lang), picked out a cute boy from the crowd and plotted how he would be hooked. In this song the choice was clearly hers, not his. Songs also re-created images of a clot of girls standing around in their mohair sweaters assessing the male talent and, well, looking over boys the way boys had always looked over girls. . . .

The absolute necessity of female collusion in the face of thoughtless or mystifying behavior by boys bound these songs together, and bound the listeners to the singers in a knowing sorority. . . . And while boys were often identified as the love object, they were also identified as the enemy. So while some of the identities we assumed as we sang along were those of the traditional, passive, obedient, lovesick girl, each of us could also be a sassy, assertive, defiant girl who intended to have more control over her life—or at least her love life. In numerous advice songs, from "Mama Said" to "You Can't Hurry Love," the message that girls knew a thing or two, and that they would share that knowledge with one another to beat the odds in a man's world, circulated confidently.

Other songs fantasized about beating a different set of odds—the seeming inevitability, for white, middle-class girls, of being married off to some boring, respectable guy with no sense of danger or adventure. . . .

Here we come to the rebel category—"Leader of the Pack" . . . and "He's Sure the Boy I Love." Academic zeros, on unemployment, clad in leather jackets, sporting dirty fingernails, and blasting around on motorcycles, the boy heroes in these songs were every suburban parent's nightmare, the boys they loved to hate. By allying herself romantically and morally with the rebel hero, the girl singer and listener proclaimed her independence from society's predictable expectations about her inevitable domestication. There is a role reversal here, too—the girls are gathered in a group, sharing information about their boyfriends, virtually eyeing them up and down, while the rebel heroes simply remain the passive objects of their gaze and their talk. And the girls who sang these songs, like the Shangri-Las, dressed the part of the defiant bad girl who stuck her tongue out at parental and middle-class authority. The Ronettes, whose beehives scraped the ceiling and whose eyeliner was thicker than King Tut's, wore spiked heels and skintight dresses with slits up the side as they begged some boy to "Be My Baby." They combined fashion rebellion with in-your-face sexual insurrection. . . .

While a few girl groups and individual singers were white—the Angels, the Shangri-Las, Dusty Springfield—most successful girl groups were black. Unlike the voices of Patti Page or Doris Day, which seemed as innocent of sexual or emotional angst as a Chatty Cathy doll, the vibrating voices of black teenagers, often trained in the gospel traditions of their churches, suggested a perfect fusion of naivete and knowingness. And with the rise of the civil rights movement, which by 1962 and 1963 dominated the national news, black voices conveyed both a moral authority and a spirited hope for the future. These were the voices of exclusion, of hope for something better, of longing. They were not, like Annette [Funicello] or the Lennon Sisters, the voices of sexual repression, of social complacency, or of homogenized commercialism.

From the Jazz Age to rap music, African American culture has always kicked white culture upside the head for being so pathologically repressed; one consequence, for black women, is that too often they have been stereotyped as more sexually active and responsive than their white-bread sisters. Because of these stereotypes, it was easier, more acceptable, to the music industry and no doubt to white culture at large that black girls, instead of white ones, be the first teens to give voice to girls' changing attitudes toward sex. But since the sexuality of black people has always been deeply threatening to white folks, black characters in popular culture also have been desexualized, the earth-mother mammy being a classic example. The black teens in girl groups, then, while they sounded orgiastic at times, had to look feminine, innocent, and as white as possible. Berry Gordy, the head of Motown, knew this instinctively, and made his girl groups take charm school lessons and learn how to get into and out of cars, carry their handbags, and match their shoes to their dresses.[3] They were trapped, and in the glare of the spotlight, no less, between the old and new definitions of femininity. But under their crinolined skirts and satin cocktail dresses, they were also smuggling into middle-class America a taste of sexual liberation. . . .

The Shirelles paved the way for the decade's most successful girl group, the Supremes, who had sixteen records in the national top ten between 1964 and 1969. But of utmost importance was the role Diana Ross played in making African American beauty enviable to white girls[:] as slim as a rail with those cavernous armpits, gorgeous smile, and enormous, perfectly made-up eyes. . . . The Supremes—who seemed to be both girls and women, sexy yet respectable, and a blend of black and white culture—made it perfectly normal for white girls to idolize and want to emulate their black sisters.

Another striking trend that grew out of the girl group revolution was the proliferation of the male falsetto. From Maurice Williams in "Stay" to . . . Randy and the Rainbows in "Denise" (ooo-be-ooo), and most notably with the Four Seasons and the Beach Boys, boys sang in high-pitched soprano ranges more suited for female than for male sing-along. What this meant was that girls belting out lyrics . . . had the opportunity to assume *male* roles, male subjective stances as they sang, even though they were singing in a female register.

This was nothing less than musical cross-dressing. . . .

While girl group music celebrated love, marriage, female masochism, and passivity, it also urged girls to make the first move, to rebel against their parents and middle-class conventions, and to dump boys who didn't treat them right. Most of all, girl group music—precisely because these were groups, not just individual singers—insisted that it was critically important for girls to band together, talking about men, singing about men, trying to figure them out.

What we have here is a pop culture harbinger in which girl groups, however innocent and commercial, anticipate women's groups, and girl talk anticipates a future kind of women's talk. The consciousness-raising groups of the late sixties and early seventies came naturally to many young women because we'd had a lot of practice. We'd been talking about boys, about loving them and hating them, about how good they often made us feel and how bad they often treated us, for ten years. The Shirelles mattered because they captured so well our confusion in the face of changing sexual mores. And as the confusion of real life intersected with the contradictions in popular culture, girls were prepared to start wondering, sooner or later, why sexual freedoms didn't lead to other freedoms as well. . . .

The Shirelles and the other girl groups mattered because they helped cultivate inside us a desire to rebel. The main purpose of pop music is to make us feel a kind of euphoria that convinces us that we can transcend the shackles of conventional life and rise above the hordes of others who do get trapped. It is the euphoria of commercialism, designed to get us to buy. But this music . . . generated another kind of euphoria as well. For when tens of millions of young girls started feeling, at the same time, that they, as a generation, would not be trapped, there was planted the tiniest seed of a social movement. . . .

Notes

1. See the chart listings in Norm N. Nite, *Rock On Almanac* (New York: Harper & Row, 1989).
2. Charlotte Greig, *Will You Still Love Me Tomorrow?* (London: Virago Press, 1989), p. 33.
3. Ibid., p. 121.

LISA LEVENSTEIN

Hard Choices at 1801 Vine: African American Women, Child Support, and Domestic Violence in Postwar Philadelphia

Drawing lines between the deserving and the undeserving, the worthy poor and the unworthy poor, the independent and the dependent—along with the stigmatizing of the dependent—has been an enduring part of our history. In this essay, Lisa Levenstein explores the efforts of working-class African American women to claim public protection against domestic violence and to seek economic support in the years after World War II. Examining the records of the Philadelphia Municipal Court, she finds that poverty and domestic violence were inextricably entangled in ways that public officials often found difficult to appreciate. The straightforward claims of women citizens for entitlements that the law provided—Aid to Families with Dependent Children, for example—all too easily were translated by judges and social workers into reproach: blame of fathers who could not support their children, blame of women who could not "hold" a husband, blame of mothers who could not care for their children and simultaneously hold a full-time job. Yet African American women continued to turn to the Philadelphia Municipal Court, where they had some real success in persuading judges to recognize their claims and meet their needs.

For their part, legal officials began with the assumption that the wage levels sufficient to enable a single male earner to support his wife and children—the "family wage"—were universally available. They tended to discount the racial discrimination that excluded many African Americans from the secure work force. What other assumptions does Levenstein find that court officials were likely to make when they assessed the charges made by African American women? What risks did African American women take when they turned to the courts? What did they want court officials to understand?

In a Philadelphia criminal courtroom on November 18, 1947, Judge Gay Gordon called Janice Carson, an African American woman in her early twenties, to testify in an assault and battery case that she had brought against her husband. When questioned, Mrs. Carson told the court that she and Vince Carson had had a rocky marriage with constant domestic violence both before and after he served in the army during World War II. The most recent incident had occurred after she told Vince that she was pregnant with their second child: He "beat me and he struck me. . . . He was choking me and he knocked me against a radiator, and the night after that I had a miscarriage."

When Vince Carson took the stand, he admitted that he had beaten Janice. However, he stated that the incident had occurred during an argument "about her allowance" and that he had hit her in self-defense. "She slapped

Excerpted and slightly revised by the author from ch. 2 of *A Movement Without Marches: African American Women and the Politics of Poverty in Postwar Philadelphia* by Lisa Levenstein (Chapel Hill: University of North Carolina Press, 2009). Reprinted by permission of the author and publisher. Notes have been edited and renumbered.

me first, "he testified, "and I just lost thy head and slapped her—" "Your Honor, I never struck him first," interrupted Mrs. Carson. "Everyone knows he fights me." At this point, Judge Gordon intervened in the dispute. "You talk too much," he told Mr. Carson. The judge proceeded to call Mr. Carson a "brute," told him that the "seeds of murder" were planted in his home, and warned him that he would end up in the electric chair one day.

After a few more questions, Judge Gordon turned to Mrs. Carson and asked, "Madam, what do you want me to do with him?" Mrs. Carson explained that although she had separated from Mr. Carson, she still needed his financial support because she had been in poor health since the miscarriage and could not seek employment to support herself and her son. She asked for a "peace bond," a type of bail that would give Mr. Carson freedom and allow him to look for a job as long as he did not beat her. The judge told Mrs. Carson that Mr. Carson belonged in jail, but that he would grant the peace bond. The day after his release, Vince Carson attacked his wife, tore her clothing, and beat her up.[1]

In the years after World War II, working-class African American women like Janice Carson turned to the Philadelphia Municipal Court for economic support and protection from domestic violence . . . The legal system was geared toward preserving two-parent families and limiting the parent financial support that the government provided to poor single mothers through the Aid to Dependent Children (ADC) program. However since judges strongly believed that men needed to fulfill their roles as breadwinners and owed women physical protection and financial support, women could harness the court's biases to work in their favor. Most women won their cases, often obtaining either a small amount of money or limited protection from domestic violence.

Of all the public institutions in the city, it was in the municipal court that the intimate connections between poverty and domestic abuse became most clearly visible. During years when civil rights activists focused on violence outside the home, and well before middle-class feminists would interpret spousal abuse as a political issue, working-class African American women placed the issue of domestic violence squarely on the public stage. Like Mrs. Carson, many viewed their need for protection from violence as integrally linked to their need for financial assistance and struggled because the municipal court separated charges of assault from charges for support. They had to choose between freedom from violence and freedom from hunger, even though gaining one often meant sacrificing the other.

. . . Instituted in early twentieth-century cities throughout the country, municipal courts worked under the assumption that common crimes should be addressed in a comprehensive manner that promoted individual and social rehabilitation. The Philadelphia Municipal Court had been created by the state legislature in 1913 in response to agitation by white middle-class social reformers. . . . Although . . . it was a court of record and had the power to imprision offenders, like most twentieth-century municipal courts, it sought not only to punish, but also to assist, educate, and discipline its clients. Legal authorities conducted thorough investigations of their clients' life circumstances and provided medical testing, counseling, and other social services. To provide specialized attention to different types of cases, the court was divided into five divisions: civil, criminal, domestic relations, juvenile, and misdemeanant. . . . [2]

African American women's legal dealings usually took place in the courthouse that handled domestic and juvenile cases, which they referred to by its address as "1801 Vine." Marcelle Blackwell, who grew up in postwar Philadelphia, described 1801 Vine as the "most famous address in the city of Philadelphia" because of the frequency of women's visits.[3] Opened in 1940, on the eighteenth block of Vine Street, a wide, central thoroughfare for municipal buildings in Philadelphia, its architecture exuded a formality that distinguished it from most other public institutions in the city. The imposing limestone structure had a colonnaded front. Grand front doors opened onto an expansive main hallway with high ceilings, chandeliers, murals, and terrazzo floors. . . . A series of murals throughout the building symbolized the "uplifting" work that the court envisioned itself performing—reuniting families and rehabilitating juvenile delinquents.

. . . Legal rituals underscored the court's function as an institution that enforced the rule of law. Although most trials were conducted without juries, women had to swear before signing petitions or testifying in front of judges, and their statements were carefully recorded by court employees. They interacted mainly with middle-class, often college-educated, interviewers and probation officers who were the foot soldiers of the court's efforts to collect and organize personal and demographic information about clients. . . . In the mid-1950s, African Americans comprised less than one-quarter of the city's population, but black women were half of the plaintiffs in nonsupport cases and two-thirds of the plaintiffs in assault and battery cases. Although African American and white women both experienced domestic violence and nonsupport, black women had less access to alternative resources than did white women and were more likely to take legal action against men.

Women who pressed charges in the municipal court confronted judges whose outlooks exemplified some of the limitations of postwar liberalism in meeting their needs. In the 1950s, the court had fourteen judges, elected by city voters to ten-year terms. All of the judges who worked in the domestic relations court were white men, usually Democrats from Italian American, Polish American, or Jewish backgrounds.[4] Although many of them were active in a range of civic organizations and known for their humanitarianism, they felt little sympathy for the plight of struggling African Americans. Most believed that two-parent families with male breadwinners were superior to other family forms. They looked down on unmarried mothers, particularly those who received welfare, and expressed contempt for fathers who could not adequately support their wives and childen.

Most women who approached the municipal court sought child support or protection from domestic violence. Their suits took three main forms. Unmarried women's suits against the fathers of their children for financial support, called fornication and bastardy, were handled in the women's criminal division, making it ambiguous exactly who legal officals believed should be on trial.[5] In the 1950s, on average, nearly two thousand women pressed these charges each year. The domestic relations court handled married women's financial support cases, usually in the form of nonsupport charges against their husbands. These cases numbered over four thousand each year. . . . Finally, assault and battery charges brought by women against violent men were handled in the criminal division until 1952, when the domestic relations division took control of their adjudication.[6] The court usually handled over six hundred of these cases each year. Although women did not press charges of assault as often as they pressed charges of nonsupport, the large number of assault cases challenges feminist scholarship that has portrayed this period as a time when women rarely used the legal system to prosecute domestic violence.[7]

The rulings in women's assault and battery cases varied widely because judges did not have formal procedures in place for dealing with them. Prior to 1952, the municipal court sent abused women to the magistrates' courts for an initial hearing. Some women settled their cases with the magistrates, securing warnings, peace bonds, and occasionally jail sentences for their husbands. Those not satisfied with the magistrates' hearings could pay a $10 fee to obtain a warrant for their husbands' arrest and press assault and battery charges in the criminal division of the municipal court. During the criminal trials, municipal court judges almost always tried to reconcile couples. However, when reconciliation proved impossible, judges used their own discretion to settle the disputes, finding some men not guilty and requiring others to post peace bonds or go to jail.

. . . The legal system did not address or help remedy the connections between poverty and domestic abuse: women who were financially dependent on their husbands were more vulnerable to abuse, and abuse could reinforce women's poverty by injuring and isolating them. If women with abusive husbands chose to seek support orders, they were left without protection from violence. If they pressed criminal charges and their husbands ended up in jail, they were left without financial support. Faced with this impossible choice, some abused women who relied on men's financial support sought a compromise: They pressed assault charges and then asked judges to give their husbands a warning or put them on probation, hoping that this would allow men to continue earning money while helping curb subsequent episodes of violence. As Mrs. Carson's case illustrates, this strategy could backfire by making men so furious that they continued the abuse.

Nonsupport. . . . cases had far more predictable outcomes. Married women seeking to press nonsupport charges met with an interviewer, usually a woman, who recorded detailed information about their cases and their backgrounds. The interviewer then contacted women's husbands and requested their presence in court. Probation officers investigated men's places of employment to verify their wages and sometimes conducted home visits to inspect couples' living arrangements. Seven to ten days after the women's initial contact with the court, most men came in for their meetings with interviewers. Interviewers spoke individually with the men and then met with the couples together in one or more joint conferences. No matter what interviewers learned about the men's and women's relationships, they tried to convince couples to reconcile. Most women refused and insisted on filing a formal petition for a trial. The cases then joined a line of hundreds of other similar cases waiting for a trial, a backlog caused by the large numbers of women pressing nonsupport charges and the limited number of judges assigned to the cases. On average, it took ten to fourteen weeks before women received hearings. The trials themselves usually lasted less than five minutes because judges were under tremendous pressure to move quickly. Even when men painted unflattering portraits of women's behavior by complaining about their promiscuity, failure to perform domestic chores, or excessive nagging, court policy was formulated so that judges almost always ruled in women's favor and awarded them financial support.[8]

Fornication and bastardy cases, which concerned unmarried couples, involved similar procedures, but were usually settled more quickly. To secure benefits, women had to press charges within two years of the conception of a child. Because the couples were not married, interviewers did not try to persuade them to reconcile. Instead, during the initial meetings and fieldwork inquiries, court workers pressured men to admit paternity and agree to pay child support. Most men recognized that they had a slim chance of winning their cases, acknowledged that they had fathered the child, and agreed to comply with a support order. Fewer than one in ten cases went to trial, and the mothers who testified were usually awarded financial support.

The legal priorities that undergirded the policies favoring reconciliation and men's support of women and children reflected judges' commitment to the family-wage system and to preventing women's dependence on the state. Family-wage ideology envisioned men earning a wage that was sufficient to support a wife and children at home. This ideal was unattainable for most working class African Americans; men could rarely obtain stable, well-paying jobs, and many women with young children were gainfully employed. State authorities recognized that African American women held jobs because African American men's wages were insufficient, but they did not believe that women should be the primary breadwinners for their families or head their own households. Judges claimed that households with married couples and male breadwinners were morally superior to those headed by single mothers. They also preferred two-parent households for fiscal reasons because most married women did not qualify for welfare. The court's Annual Reports noted that interviewers tried to "effect a reconciliation . . . and a reestablishment of wholesome family relationships" to save "the community many millions of dollars" in welfare payments.[9] In cases in which reconciliations proved impossible, judges promoted support orders in order to diminish women's welfare checks. . . .

Women often faulted the court for failing to ensure that they received adequate financial assistance. Many criticized the judges' practice of calculating support orders according to men's wages, which typically awarded them one-third of men's pay. Since most men who came before the court held low-wage jobs, most women received very small stipends. Jessie Redd observed, "When you take a man into court you hardly get enough to pay a baby-sitter."[10] The fact that the court was notoriously slow and inefficient in delivering support checks on time exacerbated the problem. . . . Even more troubling for many women was the court's failure to compensate them for the high rates of male noncompliance. In 1960, 70 percent of the support orders in effect were not being paid.[11]

To address the problem of noncompliance, judges advocated changing men's behavior, a solution that did not take into account

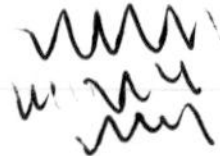

many working-class men's precarious economic circumstances. Annual Reports attributed men's default to willful neglect, charging that men found "devious and sundry" ways to "escape their family obligations." . . . This approach did not take into account how unemployment and low-wage jobs made it difficult for many men—especially African American men—to support families. . . . When there was a sharp increase in the cost of living just after World War II, many men returned to court to get their support orders decreased. That many women returned to have their orders increased for the very same reason illustrates a fundamental problem with court policies that made poor women and children directly dependent on poor men for their livelihood.[12]

Many men charged that they suffered from the court's financial support policies. Those who had remarried, lost their jobs, or had to care for parents or other family members usually found support orders financially burdensome. Particularly in cases involving unmarried mothers, the court's policy of ruling in favor of women was so entrenched that men had little chance of being found innocent even if they did not believe that they had fathered the child. Throughout the postwar period, legal officials engaged in periodic crackdowns on delinquent accounts in which field-workers tracked down men and sometimes even arrested them at their places of employment. Authorities experimented with jail terms and garnished wages; in 1959, 463 men were jailed for nonpayment of support orders. Judges justified the crackdowns by emphasizing that men's avoidance of child support resulted in increased welfare payments to women, claiming that it was "the state and not the wife—who suffers when the husband fails to meet the court order." By laying part of the blame for welfare expenditures on unpaid support orders, judges suggested that African American men contributed to the immorality and fiscal irresponsibility that they associated with ADC.[13]

Working-class African American women insisted that they, not the state, were the victims of men's noncompliance. Thousands of women lived in precarious situations, never assured of receiving financial support because the legal and welfare system forced them to depend on men's irregular contributions. Arlene Starks remarked: "Maybe the next week I'll get a check. Maybe the following week I'll get a check. Now the next two weeks I don't get no check. See, that keeps me off base all the time." Court policies stipulated that men had to default on four consecutive payments before women could issue a complaint at the Department of Accounts. After women reported the nonpayment, probation officers often instructed them to track down men themselves to find the reason for the defaults. . . .

Throughout the 1950s, nearly seven thousand women returned to court each year to complain of men's noncompliance. Many women needed their small support checks so desperately that they returned five to fifteen times over the course of several years when men refused or were unable to pay.[14]

Even when women managed to get their husbands back into court, they did not always receive compensation for missed payments. Several years after Corrine Elkins pressed charges, her husband stopped paying his support order. When she took him back to court, "he was $4,800 in arrears." To Mrs. Elkins's dismay, "The judge dismissed $2,000 of it. He said, 'Well, just get rid of $2,000 of it, and you owe $2,800, and you can pay $5.00 extra each week.'" Knowing that this ruling would have little effect on her husband's behavior, Mrs. Elkins said that she "came to the conclusion, you've got to do things yourself, girl" and started putting in more overtime, working twelve to sixteen hours a day, six or seven days each week. With her arduous schedule and decent city job, Mrs. Elkins could get by without her missed support payments. Most poor mothers could not.[15]

When the court advocated policies that ensured women's financial dependence on men, why did it fail so consistently in enforcing them? First, enforcement procedures were expensive since, as women knew from experience, it could take weeks to track down men and verify their wages. By forcing women to find and discipline men themselves, the court saved money. . . . Second, because welfare administrators decreased women's ADC checks after they pressed nonsupport charges, the state conserved money simply by issuing a support order, regardless of whether or not judges enforced it. Third, as historian Anna R. Igra has argued, in an era in which the "taint of corruption . . . adhered to state spending," the court's financial support policies performed an important symbolic function. By strongly advocating support orders, public authorities . . . could demonstrate both their desire to conserve state monies and their adherence to social norms concerning men's responsibilities to their wives and children.[16]

In most cases, women made carefully calculated decisions about their use of the court. Taking legal action was an ordeal, requiring regular visits to court, several interviews, and a great deal of paperwork. Those with small children found the process particularly difficult. Bell Jackson described a typical visit: "My children and I spent almost six hours in court. I took them at 9:30 that morning and we didn't get out until 3:00 that afternoon . . . I spent my last money getting there, and all that time. And what happened? Nothing, except we discussed why he wasn't staying with us and how come we broke up, which I've been over a lot of times." Prior to initiating such frustrating procedures, women took stock of their circumstances and tried to decide whether the assistance they could receive from the court was worth the costs.[17] . . .

Most ADC recipients tried to avoid going to court because they risked losing money by pressing charges. The fathers of their children usually could not keep up with support orders, and since welfare caseworkers subtracted the dollar amount of support orders from their ADC checks and rarely provided compensation when men defaulted, taking legal action was a potential financial burden, not a help. Women on decent terms with the fathers of their children generally preferred to receive full welfare grants with no court order, supplemented "under the table" with informal gifts from men.

Some women tried to avoid getting involved with the court because of the humiliation that frequently accompanied the process of taking legal action. Pursuing assistance from the court was never publicly maligned in the way that seeking welfare was, but it was still tarnished by its association with low- income Philadelphians. When Hazel Weinberg, a Jewish woman, went to court to press nonsupport charges, she did not return after her first visit because the interviewers were rude and condescending and she found the process "degrading." Many African American women dreaded testifying in court because the judges were well-known for publicly condemning their reliance on ADC and claiming that they neglected their children. Whether or not they received welfare, all black women felt vulnerable to judges' wrath. Joan Park, a financially secure working-class African American woman, explained that she "wouldn't be caught dead in court" because she considered herself an upstanding member of her community and did not want to subject herself to the indignities involved in pursuing legal action.[18]

The women who decided to press nonsupport charges frequently had financial troubles that led them to believe that even a meager court order would make a positive difference in their lives. . . . Ada Morris, a welfare recipient, explained the importance of her small support check to her livelihood: "I sit down on the first of the month . . . and I count my money up—to who I owe. . . . My rent comes first. My gas comes next. My food bill. . . . comes next . . . If I don't get nothing from him—well, I can't pay." For women like Mrs. Morris, who struggled each month to make ends meet, even a small stipend made a difference.[19]

Women who pressed domestic abuse charges tended to come from slightly more financially stable homes than those who pursued nonsupport charges and considered their need for physical protection to be their most pressing concern. They were rarely middle-class, but they were often not completely impoverished either. Although some very poor abused women like Mrs. Carson pressed assault charges, others were either deterred by the $10 fee (until 1952, when the fee was waived) or prioritized financial support over protection from violence. . . .

Most abused women decided to avoid legal action completely. Some lived in an acute state of terror with extremely violent and volatile husbands. They were unable or unwilling to leave their marriages and feared that pressing charges would only make the abuse worse. Charlotte Elkins decided to "hang in there" with her husband while "getting my butt beat" for thirteen years because of the "mental abuse" that accompanied his physical violence. She stated that her husband's verbal and physical assaults made her feel worthless and convinced her that she would be unable to survive on her own. Many women who did not go to court resisted the abuse in other ways, escaping to friends' and relatives' houses, attempting to protect their children, and fighting back. Catherine Sanderson recalled standing up to her husband when he beat her. "I sure would . . . hit him back," she explained. "He wasn't my father." Corrine Elkins never fought back until the night that she decided to leave her husband: "He came home . . . and got crazy, and I went for the kitchen knife . . . and . . . really tried" to kill him.[20]

When women made decisions about their pursuit of legal action, they considered their responsibility for children, access to alternative resources, employment opportunities, and experiences of domestic violence. They also took into account a wide range of facts about their husbands and boyfriends: how much money men made, whether they were abusive or unfaithful, and how involved they were with their children. Most women only pressed financial support charges against men who had jobs because they knew that unemployed men did not have any money to give them. While legal authorities assumed that all African American men who did not provide for their families were irresponsible, African American women had a different and more nuanced definition of nonsupport. Recognizing that racial discrimination made it difficult for the most dedicated husband and father to earn enough to support his wife and children, they did not condemn all men who failed to provide them with financial resources. Instead, most African American women reserved charges of nonsupport for cases in which men deliberately withheld funds from their families, complaining about men squandering their wages on alcohol, other women, or luxury items, instead of rent, food, and clothing for their families. For some married women, the discovery that their husbands had been cheating on them further galvanized them to press nonsupport charges. Unmarried women sometimes responded similarly when they learned that their boyfriends had wives. In other cases, unmarried women may have only had casual contact with the father of their children and pressed charges in court because they had nothing to lose.[21] . . .

Many women who maintained cordial relationships with the fathers of their children found that even the threat of legal action provided them with considerable leverage when negotiating financial support. Because of the strength of their community information networks, women and men who had never set foot in court knew from other people's experiences that women would almost always win financial support cases. Men understood that they would be saddled with a court order and subjected to humiliating treatment from legal authorities, and women knew that men would be angry and would rarely pay regularly. Many women decided that, rather than alienate men by pressing charges, they were better off having men feel indebted to them for not pursuing legal action. The undesirability of legal action gave some leverage to women like Beverly Jordan, who was separated with one child and worked in a coat factory in postwar Philadelphia. Every year, Mrs. Jordan was laid off for two to three months during slow seasons around Christmas and Easter. When this occurred, she would phone her ex-husband and ask for money for food and for her daughter's Christmas present, threatening to take him to court if he did not comply. . . .

In women's dealings with the court, they frequently challenged legal authorities' attempts to collect detailed personal information. Interviewers sought to compile extensive files documenting women's backgrounds and grievances, while field-workers investigated men's earnings and employment records and made home visits to ask about children's school attendance and inspect women's living conditions. Unmarried mothers had to provide detailed descriptions of their relationships with the fathers of their children, the date of the sexual intercourse that produced the child, and accounts of their previous sexual experiences. Many women refused to give court interviewers full access to their private lives, falsifying information or refusing outright to answer questions that they deemed too personal. . . .

One of the only times that interviewers and judges did not attempt to challenge or pry into women's decisions about their private lives was when women withdrew their assault and battery charges against their husbands, which occurred in approximately one-third of all abuse cases. On the witness stand, these women usually minimized the abuse and told judges that they had changed their minds and did not want to press charges. Even when women testified that their husbands had "busted my head open" or stabbed them with knives, if they stated that they wanted to return home with their husbands, judges made no attempt to dissuade them. Most judges feared that if couples separated or the men received jail sentences, the wives would seek public assistance.[23] . . .

. . . Working-class African American women faced problems at every level of the criminal justice system but still refused to give up on the municipal court. Most African Americans in Philadelphia believed that the police department and the courts were racially prejudiced institutions. Yet, building on decades of African American legal assertiveness, women sought to harness a system that they viewed as racist to work on their behalf. Had black women testified against white men, judges' racial prejudices might have served as more of a deterrent to their use of the court. However, since most African American women pressed charges against African American men, they knew that the verdicts would usually be in their favor. Although women did not receive very much money or physical protection from their legal victories, most of them faced such severe problems and had so few alternative sources of support that even the small amount of assistance they secured from the court made a difference. Mrs. Elkins recalled, "In those days, the women didn't really have too much going for them. Except 1801 Vine."

Notes

1. Case 447, November 18, 1947, Philadelphia City Archives, Philadelphia, PA [hereafter PCA].

2. Clarence B. Shenton, *History and Functions of the Municipal Court of Philadelphia* (Philadelphia: Thomas Skelton Harrison Foundation, 1930), 66, 80–81; *Philadelphia Municipal Court Annual Reports* [hereafter PMC-AR], 1949, A19.

3. All interviews were conducted by the author in Philadelphia, PA, between July 1, 1999 and June 27, 2000. Audiotapes are in author's possession. M.B.M. interview.

4. The juvenile division had the court's only black judge, Juanita Kidd Stout, the first African American woman appointed to a court of record in the nation.

5. In the 1940s, Pennsylvania, Maryland, and Massachusetts courts considered fornication and bastardy a criminal action. In eight states, the courts did not allow unmarried women to prosecute the fathers of their children for support at all. Other states heard these cases but dealt with them in civil court. Not until 1963 did the Philadelphia courts begin to hear the cases as civil rather than criminal proceedings.

6. *PMC-AR, 1959,* 318; *PMC-AR, 1964,* 221. Although a few cases of nonsupport each year were brought by husbands against wives, their numbers were very small.

7. Ruth Rosen, *The World Split Open: How the Modern Women's Movement Changed America* (New York: Viking, 2000), 186. Linda Gordon found that poor women's complaints about domestic abuse in social service agencies increased in the 1930s and 1940s, but her account suggests that they rarely approached the legal system; see Linda Gordon, *Heroes of Their Own Lives: The Politics and History of Family Violence: Boston, 1880–1960* (New York: Viking, 1988), 250–60, 280–81.

8. "Municipal Court Judges Decries 'Assembly-Line Justice,'" *Philadelphia Evening Bulletin [hereafter PEB],* February 17, 1957, 1, 6; *PMC-AR, 1950,* 132, 135; "Court Backlog Boosts Aid to Unwed Mothers Here," *PEB,* May 15, 1959, 34.

9. First quotation in *PMC-AR, 1954,* 153; second quotation in *PMC-AR, 1957,* 197.

10. Quoted in "Unwed Mothers Speak Their Piece," *Philadelphia Afro-American,* January 31, 1959,3.

11. "Court Slashes Backlog in Distributing Support Cases," *Philadelphia Inquirer,* January 4, 1959, 14; "In Municipal Court Holidays Bring Added Work . . . Held-up Checks," *Philadelphia Independent,* December 28, 1958, 3; *PMC-AR, 1960,* 21–211.

12. "Wanted: Solomon with an Adding Machine as HCL Plagues Estranged Couples," *PEB,* August 28, 1946, 14.

13. *PMC-AR, 1959,* 196; "Bonnelly Acts to Clear Up Support Cases," *PEB,* March 8, 1959, 3.

14. Starks quoted in Gail Levy and Judith Shouse, "A Concept of Alienation: A New Approach to Understanding the AFDC Recipient," (Master of Social Service Thesis, Bryn Mawr College, 1965), 54; *PMC-AR, 1960,* 210–211; *PMC-AR, 1961,* 215. Similarly in early twentieth-century New York, see Anna R. Igra, "Likely to Become a Public Charge: Deserted Women and the Family Law of the Poor in New York City," *Journal of Women's History* 11:4 (2000): 59–81.

15. C. E. interview. Similarly, see G.J. interview.

16. Anna R. Igra, *Wives Without Husbands: Marriage, Desertion, and Welfare in New York, 1900–1935* (Chapel Hill: University of North Carolina Press, 2007), 44, 97, 122, quotation on 44; Igra, "Likely to Become a Public Charge," 73. On postwar public assistance policy, see *PMC- AR, 1953,* A23; *PMC-AR, 1957,* 201.

17. Quoted in Levy and Shouse, "Concept of Alienation," 81.

18. H. C. interview; J. P. interview.

19. Quoted in Levy and Shouse, "Concept of Alienation," 23.

20. Sanderson quoted in C.S. interview; Elkins quoted in C. E. interview.

21. *PMC-AR, 1944,* A62–A63; *PMC-AR, 1949,* 261; *PMC-AR, 1934,* 276–77; *PMC-AR, 1939,* 1, 310–12; *PMC-AR, 1950,* 173; *PMC-AR, 1957,* 237.

22. M.B.M. interview; J.E.J, interview; Van Dyke interview.

23. *PMC-AR, 1953,* 166. For "busted my head open," see Case 127, February 18, 1948, PCA. For knife wounds, see Case 631 and Case 632, May 22, 1957, PCA. It is not clear from the records whether these cases involved African Americans or whites.

JANE SHERRON DE HART

Second-Wave Feminists and the Dynamics of Social Change

The dissatisfactions that simmered just beneath the surface during the 1950s and early 1960s erupted in the late 1960s into unconcealed anger as small groups of women, many of them movement veterans, gathered to protest their treatment as women. Their actions marked the resurgence of feminism. "As an *ism* [an ideology] *feminism* presupposed a set of principles not necessarily belonging to every woman—nor limited to women," wrote historian Nancy Cott of first-wave feminism.[1] Her observation held. Some men, but not all women, once again embraced its core principles, joining an ongoing struggle to dismantle gender hierarchy.

While this resurgence had many tributaries and flowed into various feminisms, the focus of this essay on what is sometimes referred to as mainstream feminism is of necessity partial. My purpose is to identify the long-term developments that created conditions conducive to the emergence of a mass-based feminist movement as well as the resources these feminists-in-the-making brought with them from other protest movements. The ideological issues these activists wrestled with, the changes they initiated, and the opposition they encountered (especially in their efforts to secure an amendment to the Constitution guaranteeing equal rights for women) also are explored. So, too, is the extent to which, by 1980, the movement's agenda was at the mercy of larger changes in the political climate over which feminists and their allies had little control. How feminism itself changed over the years and what happened to it as a movement are fitting questions to pose about a social movement from which so many women have benefited and with which so few young women seem willing to identify.

Fifty years after gaining the right to vote, women who had been suffragists and women young enough to be their great-granddaughters embarked on a new feminist movement. Referred to as feminism's second wave, to distinguish it from an earlier surge that had occurred around 1910, the goals and membership of this new movement reflected fundamental changes in American life that had developed in the intervening decades, as well as unresolved issues from the past. Medical advances that lengthened life expectancy also provided greater reproductive control; despite the "baby boom" of the postwar years, the nation's birthrate and family size continued to decline; the continuing influx of women, including married women with children, into the workplace produced new patterns of workforce participation among white women; and finally, the restraints of second-class citizenship chafed—even when rationalized as "that's the way things are." These changes alone did not generate a new feminist consciousness. But they enlarged the distance between old gender norms and ideals and new circumstances, creating greater receptivity to feminist perspectives and concerns. What had been regarded as personal problems and grievances could, with a new lens, be seen as political, and thus susceptible to change.

From the outset the new movement was vigorous, diffused, ideologically varied, geographically decentralized, and highly controversial. It was in fact many movements, some predominantly white and middle-class, others comprised largely of women of color, and still others that were low-income and multiracial. The various factions of the movement formed interweaving strands of thought and action. Some of these strands acquired the labels *liberal, radical, socialist,* and, by 1975, *cultural feminism.* Others identified themselves as black, Chicana, Asian American, Native American, or U.S. third world feminists. One cannot make simplistic assumptions about which variant an individual woman might embrace. (For example, Pauli Murray, an African American lawyer and writer, would have been more likely to describe herself as a liberal feminist rather than a black feminist.) Yet divisions and fragmentation between groups should not be overemphasized, obscuring the positive change that arose from their alliances and collective efforts. For example, marking the distinction between liberal feminists and radical feminists by associating the former with advocacy of equal rights and the latter with the belief that male supremacy was the primary form of oppression is an unfair oversimplification.[2] Many equal rights advocates adopted radical feminists' insight into gender oppression, just as they later came to appreciate the insights of feminists of color, who argued that gender was one of several interacting forms of oppression, among them race and class. Liberal feminists could also respond that preempting radicalism for radical feminists only masked the radical potential of liberal feminism. Indeed, as sociologists Myra Marx Ferree and Beth B. Hess have demonstrated in their study of the movement, it was both the "controversies" and the "coalitions" that sustained second-wave feminism.[3]

THE ROOTS OF SECOND-WAVE FEMINISM

At first glance many of the groups associated with this new feminist resurgence seem to have sprouted overnight like mushrooms after a hard rain. But closer investigation reveals deeper roots. Feminism in the African American community reached back to the turn-of-the-century South, where author Anna Julia Cooper first identified the double challenge facing her sisters: "a race problem" and "the woman question." Black women's emphasis on self-definition and empowerment had long suffused their activism on behalf of community development, anti-lynching laws, and civil rights. Furthermore, the existence of a local black and low-income group in New York's Mount Vernon/New Rochelle community, founded in 1960, belied the conventional assumption that second-wave feminism did not exist until the late 1960s. Union women—black and white—had forged their own feminism in the labor movement, especially in the years after World War II. Fighting for equal pay for equal work, their leaders championed equal treatment in the work-place as well as the special needs of working women.[4]

Women of the Old Left, determined to make the Communist Party take seriously "the woman question" in the immediate postwar years, had expanded traditional Marxist understanding of women's oppression as deriving from economic structures. Insisting that social and cultural components were also important and that male domination extended to personal relationships, they forged a new understanding of women's oppression and liberation. When McCarthyism forced their retreat from organized Party activity, some concealed their past affiliations. But they did not hide their commitment to improving women's status in the new organizations they joined, the families they created, and the literary works they produced.[5]

The reformist goals of some key feminists, who sought the inclusion of women in the political and legal system during the 1960s and 1970s, obscure attention from their youthful radicalism. Mary Dublin Keyserling served on President Kennedy's Commission on the Status of Women, and headed the Women's Bureau of the Department of Labor under President Johnson. In both capacities, she pushed for sex to be recognized alongside race in federal civil rights and labor laws. Scarred by an invasive loyalty oath probe during the McCarthy period, she never reflected publicly on how her 1930s participation in Left feminist circles shaped her understanding of sex discrimination. Pauli Murray, a fellow Commission member and leading American Civil Liberties Union lawyer, linked sex and race discrimination well before she advocated for the inclusion of "sex" in the 1964 Civil Rights Act. Participating in Popular Front desegregation and labor campaigns as a student, she could not forget being denied admission first to the law school at the University of North Carolina because she was African American and then to Harvard Law School because she was female. "There exists in the United States a system of discrimination based upon sex which I call 'Jane Crow' because it is so strikingly similar to Jim Crow,' or prejudice based upon race," she wrote in 1947. Slighted as a "menstruating lawyer," Bella Abzug's experience navigating the tricky waters of white supremacy, sexism, and anti-communism that shaped Cold War civil rights and civil liberties cases stayed with her when a Congresswoman in the 1970s. While Abzug spoke openly about her Left feminist past, Betty Friedan, the author of the 1963 bestseller, *The Feminine Mystique*, was not so forthright. A labor journalist in the 1940s and early 1950s, she too had been part of a cross-class, racially integrated feminism that emerged in progressive circles in the aftermath of World War II. Though she represented herself as just another well-educated housewife who voiced discontents of stifling suburban living, her intellectual understanding of the "problem that has no name" took shape well before 1963.[6]

Grassroots organizing provided a rich site for cross-generation transmission of Left feminist ideas and tactics as well. By the late 1960s, Women Strike for Peace activists had become "the mothers of the Movement," supporting New Left activists in their anti-Vietnam War demonstrations. Pioneers of non-hierarchical, participatory democratic organizing, they modeled multi-issue organizing, linking peace to other issues such as health and welfare. Veteran activists sustained gender justice work in local pockets throughout the nation. In Seattle, for example, the approximately twenty-five women who met in the home of a graduate student in 1967 to discuss the formation of an activist women's group ranged in age from fifty-one to eighteen. Among the organizers of the meeting were women whose political past included years of activism in both the Communist Party and the Socialist Workers Party as well as in more recent labor, civil rights, and welfare struggles.[7]

If the roots of this resurgent movement were deep, gnarled, and intertwined, this was not yet apparent in the late 1960s. What was clear was that in a decade when Americans had been thrust into the throes of self-examination by a movement for racial equality, women of diverse experiences were beginning to acquire a feminist consciousness. Although the media and the public did not always differentiate, referring to them collectively as "women's libbers," there were distinct differences between the most visible groups in the vanguard—women's rights advocates and women's liberationists—and within the strands of women's liberationists. The latter included young veterans of the civil rights movement and the New Left who were steeped in commitment to equality and the techniques of protest. Others were young professionals, many of whom were aware of their secondary status in their professions by virtue of the fact that they were women. Women's rights advocates were often more established professionals and veteran activists who had used organizations such as the American Civil Liberties Union (ACLU), the Young Women's Christian Association (YWCA), and the United Auto Workers (UAW) to fight sex-based discrimination. Included, too, were those whose outwardly conformist lives belied an intense awareness of the malaise of domesticity and the untenably narrow boundaries of their prescribed roles. To explore how they came self-consciously to appraise women's condition as one demanding collective action is to explore the process of radicalization that helped to create a new feminist movement.

THE CREATION OF A FEMINIST CONSCIOUSNESS

Although the differences between women's rights advocates and women's liberationists began to blur as the movement matured, initial distinctions were sharp. Women's rights advocates were likely to have been older, to have had professional training or work experience, to have been more inclined to form or join organized feminist groups. Reform oriented, these organizations used traditional pressure group tactics to achieve changes in laws and public policy that would guarantee women equal rights. Emphasis on "rights" meant extending to women in life outside the home the same "rights" men had, granting them the same options, privileges, and responsibilities that men enjoyed. There was little suggestion initially of personal or cultural transformation.

Women's liberationists tended to be younger women, often less highly educated, whose ideology and political style, shaped in the dissent and violence of the 1960s, led them to look at women's predicament differently. Instead of relying upon traditional organizational structure and lobbying techniques, they developed a new style of politics. Instead of limiting their goals to changes in public policy, they embraced a transformation in private, domestic life as well. They sought liberation from ways of thinking and behaving that they believed stunted or distorted women's growth and kept them subordinate to men. Through the extension of their own personal liberation they hoped to remake the male world, changing it as they had changed themselves. For women's liberationists as for women's rights advocates, however, the first step toward becoming feminists demanded a clear statement of women's position in society, one that called attention to the gap between the egalitarian ideal and the actual position of women in American culture. There also had to be a call to action from women themselves, *for* women, *with* women, *through* women. Redefining themselves, they had to make being a woman a political fact; and, as they did so, they had to live with the radical implications of what could only be called a rebirth.

The Making of Liberal Feminists: Women's Rights Advocates

For some women, the process of radicalization began with the appointment of a Presidential Commission on the Status of Women in 1961. Presidents, Democrat and Republican, customarily discharged their political debt to female members of the electorate, especially to those who had loyally served the party, by appointing a few token women, usually party stalwarts, to highly visible posts. John Kennedy was no exception. He was, however, convinced by Esther Peterson, the highest-ranking woman in his administration, that the vast majority of women would be better served if he also appointed a commission charged with investigating obstacles to the full participation of women in society. Peterson, who was assistant secretary of labor and head of the Women's Bureau, believed that the report of such a commission could sensitize the public to barriers to equality just as her own experience as a labor organizer had sensitized her to the particular problems confronting women workers. Citizens thus informed could then be mobilized on behalf of governmental efforts at reform.[8] Accordingly, the commission was appointed with Eleanor Roosevelt serving as chair until her death a year later. Its report, *American Women* (1963), was conservative in tone, acknowledging the importance of women's traditional roles within the home and the progress they had made in a "free democratic society." Acknowledging also that women were an underutilized resource that the nation could ill afford to ignore, the report provided extensive documentation of discriminatory practices in government, education, and employment, along with substantial recommendations for change.[9] Governors, replicating Kennedy's move, appointed state commissions on the status of women. In these commissions hundreds of men and women encountered further evidence of the economic, social, and legal disabilities that encumbered the nation's "second sex." For some, the statistics were old news; for others, they were a revelation.

Aroused by growing evidence of "the enormity of our problem," members of state commissions gathered in Washington in 1966 for the Third National Conference of the Commissions on the Status of Women. Individuals who were coming to know and rely on one another as they pooled their growing knowledge of widespread inequities, they were a network in the making. They were also women who wanted something done. This time they encountered a situation that transformed at least some of those present into activists in a new movement for women's equality. The catalyst proved to be a struggle involving Representative Martha Griffiths and the Equal Employment Opportunity Commission (EEOC), the federal agency in charge of implementing the Civil Rights Act of 1964.

Despite the fact that the law proscribed discrimination on the basis of sex as well as race, the commission refused to take seriously the problem of sexual discrimination. The first executive director of EEOC, believing that "sex" had been injected into the bill by opponents seeking to block its passage, regarded the sex provision as a "fluke" best ignored. Representative Griffiths from Michigan thought otherwise. The inclusion of sex discrimination, while used by civil rights opponents to sabotage the bill, had been initiated by the venerable and elitist National Woman's Party. Support was also strong among women in the

House whom Griffiths had mobilized. While liberals had initially objected, fearing that so encumbering a bill would prevent passage of much-needed legislation on behalf of racial equality, Griffiths had prevailed. Without the sex provision, she had reminded her colleagues, the Civil Rights Act would give black women advantages that white women were denied. A racist formulation that revealed the exclusivity of Griffiths's vision of sisterhood, the appeal worked. Once the bill passed she was determined to see the new law enforced in its entirety. When EEOC failed to do so, she lambasted the agency for its inaction in a biting speech delivered on the House floor only days before the Conference of the Commissions on the Status of Women met.

Griffiths's concern was shared by a group of women working within EEOC. Echoing an argument made the year before by a black trade unionist in the Women's Bureau,[10] they insisted that the agency could be made to take gender-related discrimination more seriously if women had a civil rights organization as adept at applying pressure on their behalf as was the National Association for the Advancement of Colored People (NAACP) on behalf of blacks. Initially the idea was rejected. Conference participants most upset by EEOC's inaction decided instead to propose a resolution urging the agency to treat sexual discrimination with the same seriousness it applied to racial discrimination. When the resolution was ruled inappropriate by conference leaders, they were forced to reconsider. After a whispered conversation over lunch they concluded the time for discussion of the status of women was over. It was time for action. Before the day was out twenty-eight women had paid five dollars each to join the National Organization for Women (NOW), including author Betty Friedan, who happened to be in Washington at the time of the conference.[11]

Friedan's presence in Washington was auspicious; her involvement in NOW, virtually inevitable. By articulating heretofore inarticulated grievances, *The Feminine Mystique* had advanced a process initiated by more dispassionate investigations of women's status and the discriminatory practices which made that status inferior. That process was the collective expression of discontent. It is not surprising that the voices initially heard were those of women who were overwhelmingly white, educated, and middle or upper middle class. College women who regarded themselves the equals of male classmates by virtue of intellect and training were, as Jo Freeman points out, more likely to develop expectations they saw realized by their male peers but not, in most cases, by themselves. The frustrations were even greater for women with professional training. The very fact that many had sought advanced training in fields not traditionally "female" meant that they were less likely to find in traditional gender roles the identity and self esteem such roles provided other women. Moreover, when measuring themselves against fellow professionals who happened to be men, the greater rewards enjoyed by their white male counterparts seemed especially galling. Privileged though they were, such women *felt* more deprived in many cases than did those women who were in reality less privileged. By 1966 this sense of deprivation had been sufficiently articulated and shared and the networks of like-minded women sufficiently developed so that collective discontent could be translated into collective action. The formation of NOW signaled a feminist resurgence.[12]

The three hundred men and women who gathered in October for the organizational meeting of NOW included mainly professionals, some of them veterans of commissions on the status of women as well as a few feminist union activists, notably Dorothy Haener. Adopting bylaws and a statement of purpose, they elected officers, naming Friedan president. Her conviction that intelligent women needed purposeful, generative work of their own was reflected in NOW's statement of purpose, which attacked "the traditional assumption that a woman has to choose between marriage and motherhood on the one hand and serious participation in industry or the professions on the other." Determined that women should be allowed to develop their full potential as human beings, the organization's goal was to bring them into "full participation in the mainstream of American society NOW, exercising all the privileges and responsibilities thereof in truly equal partnership with men." To that end NOW developed a Bill of Rights, adopted at its 1967 meeting, that exhorted Congress to pass an equal rights amendment to the Constitution, called on EEOC to enforce antidiscrimination legislation, and urged federal and state legislators to guarantee equal and unsegregated education. To ensure women control over their reproductive lives, these new feminists called for removal of penal codes denying women contraceptive information and devices as well as safe, legal abortions. To ease the double burden of working mothers, they urged legislation that would ensure maternity leaves without jeopardizing job security or seniority, permit tax deductions for child care expenses, and create public, inexpensive day care centers. To improve the lot of poor women, they urged reform of the welfare system and equality with respect to benefits, including job-training programs.[13]

Not content simply to call for change, NOW leaders, following the lead of equality advocates within the labor movement, worked to make it happen. Using persuasion, pressure, and even litigation, they, with other newly formed women's rights groups such as the Women's Equity Action League (WEAL), launched a massive attack on sex discrimination. By the end of the 1960s NOW members had filed legal suits against newspapers listing jobs under the headings "Help Wanted: Male" and "Help Wanted: Female," successfully arguing that such headings discouraged women from applying for jobs they were perfectly capable of doing. Building on efforts begun in the Kennedy administration such as the passage of the Equal Pay Act, they pressured the federal government to intensify its commitment to equal opportunity. They urged congressmen and labor leaders to persuade the Department of Labor to include women in its guidelines designed to encourage the hiring and promotion of blacks in firms holding contracts with the federal government. They persuaded the Federal Communications Commission to open up new opportunities for women in broadcasting. Tackling the campus as well as the marketplace, WEAL filed suit against more than three hundred colleges and universities, ultimately securing millions of dollars in salary raises for women faculty members who had been victims of discrimination. To ensure that women receive the same pay men received for doing the same work, these new feminists lobbied for passage of a new Equal Employment Opportunity Act that would enable EEOC to fight discrimination more effectively.

NOW also scrutinized the discriminatory practices of financial institutions, persuading them to issue credit to single women and to married women in their own—not their husband's—name. WEAL, in turn, filed charges against banks and other lending institutions that refused to grant mortgages to single women, or in the case of married couples, refused to take into account the wife's earnings in evaluating the couple's eligibility for a mortgage. Colleges and universities that discriminated against female students in their sports programs came under fire, as did fellowship programs that failed to give adequate consideration to female applicants.

While NOW and WEAL attacked barriers in industry and education, the National Women's Political Caucus (NWPC) focused on government and politics. Formed in 1971, the caucus was initiated by Friedan, New York congresswomen Bella Abzug and Shirley Chisholm—both outspoken champions of women's rights—and Gloria Steinem, soon to become founding editor of the new mass-circulation feminist magazine *Ms.* Abzug, a lawyer and veteran activist for peace and civil rights, and Chisholm, the first black woman elected to Congress, were especially concerned about the small numbers of women in government. Accordingly the caucus concentrated on getting women elected and appointed to public office while also rallying support for issues such as the Equal Rights Amendment (see p. 719). Meanwhile, women in the professions, aware of their small numbers and inferior status, began to organize as well. Physicians, lawyers, and university professors fought for equal opportunity in the meetings of such overwhelmingly male groups as the American Medical Association, the American Association of University Professors, and the American Historical Association. Union women also mobilized. In 1974, three thousand women from fifty-eight unions attended the founding convention of the Coalition of Labor Union Women (CLUW), resolving to fight for equality in the workplace and within organized labor.[14]

Collectively such protests served notice that more women were becoming radicalized. The particular combination of events that transformed these women into feminists varied with the individual. A southern legislator, describing the process that brought home the reality of her own second-class citizenship, wrote:

> As a State Senator, I succeeded in getting Mississippi women the right to sit on juries (1968); the opposition's arguments were appalling.

> When women began hiring me in order to get credit, I became upset at the discrimination I saw. After I was divorced in 1970, I was initially denied a home loan. The effect was one of the worst traumas I've suffered. Denial of a home loan to one who was both a professional and a member of the legislature brought things to a head.[15]

Although the number of women who understood what it meant to be the "second sex" was still only a tiny minority, they were nonetheless a minority whose energy, talents, and experience enabled them to work for changes necessary to ensure equal rights. And they were gaining important allies in liberal organizations. The American Civil Liberties Union (ACLU) was a case in point. Best known for its defense of civil liberties, the ACLU put its considerable resources behind a newly created Women's Rights Project, headed by Ruth Bader Ginsburg, then a professor at Columbia School of Law. Her task was to devise a litigation strategy designed to persuade the Supreme Court (of which she is now a member) that gender discrimination in the law was unconstitutional. Since even the liberal Warren Court had been unable to move beyond judicial paternalism and gender stereotypes, the challenge was formidable. But Ginsburg had "high hopes for significant change," as, no doubt, did strategically placed feminists in trade unions, the National Council of Churches, foundations, and other organizations whose support helped legitimate this fledgling movement.[16]

The Making of Women's Liberationists

The process of radicalization that transformed some individuals into liberal feminists occurred simultaneously—but in different fashion and with somewhat different results—among a younger generation of women who initially were also predominantly white and middle class. Many of them veterans of either the civil rights movement or of the New Left, these were the activists who would initially become identified as women's liberationists. Differing in perspective as well as style, they would ultimately push many of their older counterparts beyond the demand for equal rights to recognition that true emancipation would require a far-reaching transformation of society and culture.

The experiences awakening in this 1960s generation a feminist consciousness have been superbly described by Sara Evans in her book, *Personal Politics*.[17] "Freedom, equality, love and hope," the possibility of new human relationships, the importance of participatory democracy—letting the people decide—were, as Evans points out, part of an egalitarian ideology shared by both the southern-based Student Nonviolent Coordinating Committee (SNCC) in its struggle for racial equality and the Students for Democratic Society (SDS) in its efforts to mobilize an interracial organization of the urban poor in northern ghettos. Membership in both organizations—"the movement"—thus reinforced commitment to these ideals among the women who joined. In order to translate ideals into reality, however, young, college-age women who had left the shelter of middle-class families for the hard and dangerous work of transforming society found themselves doing things that they would never have thought possible. Amidst the racial strife of the South, they joined picket lines, created freedom schools, and canvassed for voter registration among blacks, often enduring arrest and jailing. SDS women from affluent suburbs entered decaying tenements and were surrounded by the grim realities of the ghetto. They trudged door-to-door in an effort to reach women whose struggle to survive made many understandably suspicious of intruding strangers. In the process, not only did these young activists achieve a heightened sense of self-worth and autonomy, they also learned the skills of movement building and the nuts and bolts of organizing.

But if being in the movement, brought a new understanding of equality, it also brought new problems. Men who were committed to equality for one group were not necessarily committed to equality for another group. Women in SNCC, as in SDS, found themselves frequently relegated to domestic chores and treated as sex objects, denied most leadership positions, and refused a key voice in the formulation of policy. Moreover, the sexual freedom that had been theirs as part of the cultural revolution taking place in the 1960s soon began to feel more like sexual exploitation as they saw their role in the movement spelled out in the draft resister's slogan: "Girls Say Yes to Guys Who Say No." Efforts to change the situation were firmly rebuffed. When SNCC leader Stokely Carmichael joked that the only "position for women in SNCC is prone," he encapsulated views which, while not his own, reflected all too accurately the feelings of males in the New Left as well as many in SNCC.[18] By 1967, the tensions had become so intense that white women left the movement, propelled, in part, by the ascendancy of black power. They would soon be joined by SDS women aggrieved by their subordinate position within that organization as well as veterans of other New Left and anti-war groups.

White women in SDS and SNCC were not the only women exhibiting a growing awareness of male chauvinism within 1960s social movements. Lesbians too would part company with male activists in the gay liberation movement that erupted in 1969 with the Stonewall Riots in New York City. Women of color engaged in ethnic nationalist movements voiced their discontent about sexual exploitation virtually simultaneously. As sociologist Benita Roth has noted, the "different contexts for doing politics influenced how feminists situated in Black, Chicano/a, and white oppositional communities." If young white women determined to break away from organizations such as SDS to form separate women's liberation groups, women of color were less inclined to sever ties completely from mixed-gender movements like the Black Panthers. Seeing oppressions they experienced as interconnected, these women believed that the fight for racial equality could not be severed from the campaign for gender justice. Because they did not always define their activist work as feminist, only the organizations that most closely resembled white women's liberation groups—such as the National Black Feminist Organization—have gained significant attention.[19]

Becoming part of a women's liberation group and then branching off to create a new one required more time, resources, and racial bridging than many women had to spare. Some opted instead to focus on a particular issue that affected their daily lives, such as welfare or reproductive rights. The National Welfare Rights Organization was a key site of feminist organizing and theory-making during the late 1960s and early 1970s. First meeting locally in groups such as the ANC Mothers Anonymous in Los Angeles, these welfare recipients effectively channeled their shared grievances into clear political and policy goals. In large public demonstrations, in courtrooms, and in legislatures, these activists demanded their right as mothers to a guaranteed income, criticized the criminalization of poor women, and pushed for greater reproductive control.

Another example is JANE, an underground abortion referral network in Chicago created by veterans of the 1960s civil rights and student movements. At first, JANE members connected women with safe doctors, and raised funds to assist low-income women seeking abortions. But by 1969, JANE members had learned how to perform abortions themselves, and set up a clinic known as "the Front," which served 3,000 women per year until 1973.[20]

Radicals all, these insurgents were impatient with liberalism, critical of capitalism, and profoundly suspicious of authority. Skilled in the language of protest and art of organizing, they shared a deep-seated conviction, as had many Old Left feminists, that the personal was political—that is, problems customarily understood as personal and private were often rooted not in the individual but rather in society and in culture. The solutions required were therefore public and political. How the experiences and priorities of this more radical contingent would shape a burgeoning new movement became evident as small women's liberation groups began to spring up spontaneously in major cities and university communities across the country.

STRUCTURE, LEADERSHIP, AND CONSCIOUSNESS-RAISING

Initially, at least, the two branches of mainstream feminism seemed almost to be two different movements, so unlike were they in structure and style. Linked only by newsletters, notices in underground newspapers, and networks of friends, women's liberation groups rejected both traditional organizational structure and leadership. Unlike NOW and the other women's rights groups associated with liberal feminism, they had no central headquarters, no elected officers, no bylaws. There was no legislative agenda and little of the activism that transformed the more politically astute women's rights leaders into skilled lobbyists and tacticians. Instead this younger generation of feminists, organizing new groups wherever they found themselves, concentrated on a kind of personal politics rooted in movement days. Looking back on male-dominated meetings in which, however informal the gathering, a few highly verbal, aggressive men invariably controlled debate and dictated strategy and left less articulate and assertive women effectively excluded, they recalled the technique they had used in organizing the poor. They remembered how they had encouraged those women to talk among themselves until the personal became political, that is, until problems which, at first glance, seemed to be personal were finally understood to be social in cause—rooted in society rather than in the individual—and political in solution. Applying this same process in their own informal "rap groups," women's liberationists developed the technique of "consciousness-raising." Adopted by women's rights groups such as local chapters of NOW, consciousness-raising sessions became one of the most important innovations of mainstream feminism.

The immediate task of the consciousness-raising session was to bring together in a caring, supportive, noncompetitive setting women accustomed to relating most intimately not with other women but with men—husbands, lovers, "friends." As these women talked among themselves, exchanging confidences, reassessing old options, and mentally exploring new ones, a sense of shared problems began to emerge. The women themselves gradually gained greater understanding of how profoundly their lives had been shaped by the constraints of culture. Personal experience with those constraints merged with intellectual awareness of women's inferior status and the factors that made it so. By the same token, new understanding of problems generated new determination to resolve them. Anger, aggression, and frustration formerly turned inward in unconscious self-hatred began to be directed outward, becoming transformed into new energy directed toward constructive goals. If society and culture had defined who women were through their unconscious internalization of tradition, they could reverse the procees, and, by redefining themselves, redefine society and culture. Or, to put it another way, if woman was a *social construct*—the product not so much of biology, but of what people in a particular society and culture believed to be the implications of biology—then women themselves would re-create the construct. At work was a process of discovery so radicalizing that the individuals undergoing it ultimately emerged in a very real sense as different people. Now feminists, these were women with a different understanding of reality—a new "consciousness," a new sense of "sisterhood," and a new commitment to change.

Consciousness-raising was an invigorating and sometimes frightening experience. As one young woman wrote, "This whole movement is the most exhilarating thing of my life. The last eight months have been a personal revolution. Nonetheless, I recognize there is dynamite in this and I'm scared shitless."[21] "Scared" or not, such women could no longer be contained. Veterans of one rap group fanned out, creating others, often with arresting names such as Cell 16, the Furies, Redstockings, Radicalesbians and WITCH (Women's International Terrorist Conspiracy from Hell).

TOWARD A FEMINIST IDEOLOGY: OPPRESSION, SEXISM, AND CHANGE

To explain the significance of the discovery that woman is both a biological being and a social construct *and* that subordination was built into that construct was no simple process. The concept itself was complex. Moreover, some feminists were basically pragmatists. They were eager to talk about what it took to sustain a movement over time, or how to resolve differences; they wanted to discuss critical issues—abortion, child-care, sterilization abuse, an expanded and more participatory welfare—but not the origins of women's oppression. Results, please, not theory, they insisted. Others retorted that results depended on the correct understanding of the problem. Theory mattered. But even among women's liberationists who were more theoretically oriented, ideological perspectives reflected different political stances, experiences, and sexual preferences. Manifestos, position papers, and books began to pile up among these ideologically fractious sisters as liberationists searched for the historical origins of female oppression. Those whose primary loyalty was still to the New Left—soon dubbed "politicos"—attributed women's oppression to capitalism. Others, who would come to be known as socialist-feminists, insisted that both male supremacy and capitalism were responsible for women's subordination and that feminists must be allied with, but apart from, the left. Still other liberationists (often defined as radical feminists) argued that male supremacy, not class or race, was the more fundamental and universal form of oppression and that women as a group constituted an oppressed class.

Feminists of color challenged this notion of gender supremacy as a reflection of whiteness, instead drawing attention to the multiple forms of oppression. In the meantime, however, radical feminists' identification of the family as the basic unit in the system of oppression led to new debates among radical feminists themselves. If marriage as an intersexual alliance divided women, leading them to identify with the oppressor from whom they derived economic advantages rather than each other, ought marriage to be abolished? If so, what new structure should take its place? Pushing the logic of this position, lesbian feminists argued that the ultimate rejection of male domination required not just the rejection of marriage, but the rejection of sexual intimacy with men. Heterosexuality, they insisted, was at the very core of patriarchy. Other feminists disagreed. Family, while a source of gender hierarchy, could also be a site of support. Moreover, collective struggle against male supremacy did not mean rejecting the men with whom one was intimately connected; the challenge ought to be to make them allies.

But the lesbian issue would not go away. Feminists, seeking to desexualize lesbianism, argued that it was a political stance—being a woman-identified woman. Lesbians were quick to reject this position, declaring that who one slept with mattered and that sexual preference was not simply a matter of choice. But did this mean that only women whose sexual preference and behavior involved same-sex partners could be authentic feminists? Surely not, insisted heterosexuals. The more sociologically oriented pointed to sex-based role differentiation as a source of oppression, arguing that work and family roles should be restructured in ways that would encourage greater mutuality and fulfillment for both sexes. Others argued that personality—men and women's psychic identity—were also overly differentiated by sex. Only by merging role and personality characteristics of both sexes within each individual could androgynous men and women be developed and real liberation achieved."[22]

Given the great variety of perspectives and positions even among women's liberationists alone, it is impossible to talk about *a* feminist ideology to which all those who identified with the women's movement subscribed. The ascendancy of radical feminism among women's liberationists in the early 1970s and the eventual embrace of many of their insights by liberal feminists, however, does make it possible to talk about a common conceptual framework shared by mainstream feminists. Most believed that *gender hierarchy* is a primary factor essential to any understanding of why women *as a group* suffer from an unequal distribution of power and resources in a society. They agreed that men have been the dominant sex and that women as a group are subordinate. While not all mainstream feminists were comfortable talking about a *system* of oppression or even using the word "oppression," they were quick to list the many areas where inequities were—and still are—evident.

At the top of the list was the economy. Men, they agreed, are more likely to be economically independent than women because the latter work within the home where their labor has no monetary value and/or outside the home in sex-segregated jobs for wages too meager to ensure economic self-sufficiency. Society and culture also provided numerous examples of the higher status, greater options, and greater power conferred upon men by virtue of their sex. Just as traditional male roles provide access to power and independence, whereas female roles do not, so, feminists pointed out, masculine values define what attributes are admired and rewarded. The very fact that strength, competence, independence, and rationality are considered masculine values, that they are more highly regarded by both sexes, and that they constitute the standard by which mental health is judged these new feminists found revealing indeed. The problem, they insisted, is not simply that the qualities themselves, intrinsically neither "male" or "female," are the product of gender socialization. It is the preference, conscious and unconscious, for whatever society regards as "masculine" that is so persistent and so objectionable—a preference feminists termed *sexism*.

Sexism, they believed, is persistent, pervasive, and powerful. It is internalized by women as well as men. It is most dramatically evident in the programmed-to-please women who search for happiness through submissiveness to men and in the men who use their power to limit women's options and keep them dependent. It is also evident in a more subtle fashion among women who emulate male models and values, refusing to see those aspects of women's lives that are positive and life-affirming, and among men who are unaware of the unconscious sexism permeating their attitudes and actions. Internalized in individuals, sexism is also embedded in institutions—the family, the education system, the media, the economy, politics, law, organized religion, language, and sexual morality.

Given the pervasiveness of sexism, many feminists saw no possibility for real equality short of transformation not only of individuals but also of social institutions and cultural values. Even what was once seen as the relatively simple demand of women's rights advocates for equal pay for equal work no longer looked so simple. What seemed to be a matter of obtaining equal rights *within* the existing system in reality demanded changes that *transform* the system. Involved was:

> a revaluation of women as workers, of women as mothers, of mothers as workers, of work as suitable for one gender and not for the other. The demand implies equal opportunity and thus equal responsibilities. It implies a childhood in which girls are rewarded for competence, risk taking, achievement, competitiveness and independences—just like boys. Equal pay for equal work means a revision in our expectations about women as equal workers and it involves the institutional arrangements to make them so.

"There is nothing small here," a feminist scholar observed.[23] And indeed there was not.

FEMINISM IN ACTION

How feminists chose to enact their new commitment varied. For some the changes consisted largely of private action—relationships renewed, careers resumed. Others, preferring public statements, used flamboyant methods to dramatize their newfound understanding of the subtle ways in which society defined and thereby confined women. As part of the confrontational politics of the 1960s, radical feminists picketed the 1968 Miss America contest, protesting the commercialization of beauty and our national preoccupation with bust size and "congeniality" rather than brain power and character. (In the process they were dubbed "bra burners," despite the fact that no bras were burned.) Activists pushed their way into all-male bars and restaurants as a way of forcing recognition of how these bastions of male exclusivity were themselves statements about "man's world /woman's place." They sat in at the offices of *Ladies' Home Journal* and *Newsweek* protesting the ways in which the media's depiction of women perpetuated old stereotypes at the expense of new realities. Others focused on abortion, mindful that mishandled illegal abortions claimed the lives of an estimated ten thousand women each year. Organizing "speakouts," they talked publicly about their own humiliating and dangerous encounters with the netherworld of abortion, thereby transforming this heretofore taboo and explosive subject into a matter of public debate and an issue of women's rights. Feminist lawyers, no less convinced that forcing a woman to bear a child against her will was a violation of her fundamental rights, used their legal skills to advance the cause of abortion law repeal in the courts.[24]

Feminist legislators, especially black Congresswoman Shirley Chisholm, sponsored legislation to extend minimum wage coverage to domestic workers. Other lawmakers sponsored bills, not always successful, to help housewives to secure some form of economic recognition for work performed, to enable women workers to obtain insurance that would give them the same degree of economic security afforded male coworkers, and to protect them from violence, which is the most blatant form of male oppression.[25]

Trade union feminists, concerned with their dual identity as women and as wage workers, struggled to keep the needs of working women in the forefront. Using affirmative action as a tool for change, women workers critiqued advertisements that divided jobs by gender, challenged gender discrimination in job placement and promotions, and increased public awareness of sex segregated industries. Black feminists, by their own admission "the most pressed down of us all," focused on issues of special concern to many minority women: media depictions of black women, racially coded credit policies, public housing, household workers' rights, and welfare and prison reform. Their sisters on the left in the Third World Women's Alliance, convinced that imperialism as well as sexism, racism, and classism oppressed women, organized demonstrations of solidarity with the women of Cuba and Vietnam. Actions, like voices, differed. Such diversity, however, was basic to the movement.[26]

Feminists collaborated to change the way gender functioned in every aspect of life. They created nonsexist day care centers, wrote and published nonsexist children's books, monitored sex stereotyping in textbooks, lobbied for women's studies programs in high schools and colleges, and founded women's health clinics. They formed rape crisis centers so that rape victims could be treated by caring females; they agitated for more informed, sympathetic treatment on the part of hospital staffs, the police, and the courts. They created shelters for battered women, insisting that physical abuse was not a private family matter but a social problem requiring a public response. On all of these issues, feminists worked across race and class lines at both grassroots and organizational levels, and also formed alliances that bridged generational lines.

The power of coalition-building is evident in the mid 1970s movement that worked to get sexual harassment legally and socially recognized. The term sexual harassment was coined at a 1975 speak out held by Cornell students and staff, who formed Working Women United. After realizing they all had experienced harassment by male supervisors, they sought public acknowledgment that this form of workplace harassment was a widespread phenomenon. They looked to working women's organizations, such as 9 to 5, for inspiration. Moving from Ithaca to New York City, this direct action group became the Working Women United Institute, committed to research, education, and litigation. Feminist lawyers working for the Institute asked the courts to interpret Title VII to include workplace protection against sexual harassment as a guaranteed civil right. Meanwhile, the Alliance Against Sexual Coercion, which brought together veterans of the rape-crisis center network, established a sexual harassment assistance hotline, and trained women's groups on how to help women harassed on the job. Started by ordinary workers who recognized that they should be better treated, the sexual harassment issue engaged diverse groups from socialist feminists to the National Organization for Women.[27]

FEMINISM: THE PUBLIC IMPACT

In a society in which the media, with their hunger for sensationalism, create instant awareness of the more dramatic aspects of social protest movements, feminism burst upon the public consciousness with all the understated visibility of a fireworks display on the Fourth of July. The more radical elements of the movement, with their talk of test tube conception, the slavery of marriage, and the downfall of capitalism, might be dismissed out of hand. But it was hard to ignore 50,000 women parading down New York's Fifth Avenue, the presence of *Ms.* magazine on newsstands, feminist books on the best-seller lists, women in hard hats on construction jobs, or the government-mandated affirmative action programs that put them there. It was harder still to ignore the publicity that accompanied the appointment of women to the Carter cabinet, the enrollment of coeds in the nation's military academies, and the ordination of women to the ministry. A Harris poll of December 1975 reported that 63 percent of the women interviewed favored most changes designed to improve the status of women, although some were quick to insist that they were not "women's libbers." Black women, recognizing that equality is indivisible, viewed feminism even more positively than did their white counterparts, although the feminists among them often preferred their own organizations.[28]

Evidence of changing views was everywhere. The list of organizations lined up in support of ratification of the Equal Rights Amendment included not only such avowedly feminist groups as NOW, WEAL, and NWPC as well as longtime supporters such as the National Woman's Party and the National Federation of Business and Professional Women's Clubs, but also well-established women's organizations such as the General Federation of Women's Clubs, the American Association of University Women, the League of Women Voters, the National Council of Jewish Women, the National Council of Negro Women, and the YWCA.

Even more potent evidence that feminism had "arrived" was the 1977 International Women's Year Conference in Houston. Before more than two thousand delegates from every state and territory in the United States and twenty thousand guests, three First Ladies—Lady Bird Johnson, Betty Ford, and Rosalynn Carter—endorsed the Equal Rights Amendment and the goals of the Houston Conference, their hands holding a lighted torch carried by women runners from Seneca Falls where, in 1848, the famous Declaration of Sentiments had been adopted. Confessing that she once thought the women's movement belonged more to her daughters than to herself, Lady Bird Johnson added, "I have come to know that it belongs to women of all ages." Such an admission, like the presence of these three women on the platform, proclaimed a message about feminists that was boldly printed on balloons throughout the convention hall: "We Are Everywhere."[29]

OPPOSITION TO FEMINISM

For some women the slogan was not a sign of achievement but of threat. Gathered at a counter-convention in Houston were women who shared neither the critique nor the goals of the movement. They were an impressive reminder that social change generates opposition and that opposition to feminism had crystalized in the struggle for ratification of the Equal Rights Amendment. ERA—as the amendment is called—simply stated: "Equality of rights under the law shall not be denied or abridged by the United States or by any State on account of sex." First suggested in 1923 as the logical extension of suffrage, the amendment had long been opposed by those who feared it would be used to strike down laws intended to protect women in the workplace. By the 1960s, those concerns no longer applied. Prodded by NOW, Congress once again turned its attention to a constitutional amendment removing sexual bias from common, statutory, and constitutional law. After a massive lobbying effort by women's rights advocates and their allies, the Senate finally joined the House and sent ERA to the states for ratification by a lopsided vote of eighty-four to eight in 1972. Almost immediately twenty-one states rushed to ratify. Within a year, however, opponents of ratification had begun a counterattack that ultimately stalled the number of ratified states at thirty-five, three short of the needed three-fourths majority when the deadline for ratification expired on June 30, 1982. Opponents even induced some ratifying states to rescind their approval. Early successes indicated a majority of Americans favored ERA—but not a large enough majority.

Opposition to ERA is starkly paradoxical. A constitutional amendment proposed especially to benefit women was opposed by women. The paradox is resolved in part by remembering that many Americans who claim to believe in equality become profoundly apprehensive when the principle is identified with specific governmental policies they consider to be intrusive and unreasonable. When supporters of ERA said that implementation of a constitutional ban on sex discrimination would be left to the Supreme Court, conservatives of both sexes were reminded that this was the same Supreme Court that had not only mandated racial integration, but prohibited prayer in the public schools and struck down bans on birth control, abortion, and pornography. Court-enforced sexual equality, like racial equality, many people believed, would further diminish the power of state and local governments and the right of individuals to live as they chose. As one women wrote her U.S. senator: "*Forced* busing, *forced* mixing, *forced* housing. Now *forced* women! No thank you![30]

Such logic also illuminates antiratificationist charges, mystifying to ratificationists, that ERA would destroy the family. Although ERA supporters correctly pointed out that the amendment had nothing to do with private relationships, social conservatives were not convinced; they had seen what a federal agenda in feminist hands looked like at the International Women's Year Conference in Houston. A meeting subsidized by the U.S. government had endorsed not only women's rights and ERA, but government-sponsored child care, federal funding of abortions for poor women, contraception for minors without parental consent, and gay rights. If Big Brother or, more appropriately, Big Sister, had her way in Washington, women might well be forced to live in the kind of post-ERA world invoked by anti-ERA spokeswoman Phyllis Schlafly—a world in which mothers, no longer financially able to remain at home, would be forced to surrender their children to government-sponsored daycare centers. There childcare personnel would supplant parental authority and family identification with loyalty to the state.

The danger, as anti-ERA women saw it, was not just to family, but to women themselves. Feminists believed that theirs was a struggle for justice and liberation—liberation from economic inequities, social roles, and cultural values that denied rights and limited

autonomy. To require all women to endure constraints dictated not by biology (sex) but by culture (gender) was, from the standpoint of feminists, to deny freedom and self-determination to half the population simply because they were born female. To women who did not believe they were oppressed, feminists' efforts at liberation, especially the rhetoric of radical feminists, appeared *not* as an attack on traditional gender categories, but rather an assault on familiar patterns that provided security, identity, and meaning. Fusing feminism and ERA, an antiratificationist begged her senator not to vote for the amendment, insisting that she did not want to be liberated. "My husband," she wrote, "works for me and takes care of me and our three children, doesn't make me do things that are hard for me (drive in town), loves me and doesn't smoke, drink, gamble, run around or do anything that would upset me. I do what he tells me to do. I like this arrangement. *It's the only way I know how to live.*" Insisted another: "I am a widow, have three children, and work to make ends meet. I am still against ERA. I am a woman—and want to be treated as a woman."[31]

When ERA supporters responded that treating women as individuals legally rather than classifying them by sex had nothing to do with the division of labor between husbands and wives, social etiquette, or the masculinization of women, their reassurances fell on deaf ears. The free-floating anxiety aroused by the enormity of the social change inherent in feminism had acquired concrete focus in ERA. Opponents' predictions of the terrible consequences that would result from ratification of the amendment were not so important as the function such statements served—an indictment of what Schlafly called the "unisex" society and an affirmation of traditional gender categories. For women living in a world in which personal identity, social legitimacy, economic viability, and moral order were rooted in traditional gender categories, calling those categories into question in the name of gender-neutral law meant that feminists must want men and women to be "the same." Finding it difficult to separate gender from sex—to see gender as a social construction—ERA opponents could only conclude that this latest drive for equality was not only absurd ("you can't fool Mother Nature") but dangerous. By rallying women to this danger, Schlafly revealed that the issue was not whether women should stay at home minding the children and cooking the food— Schlafly herself did not do that. The issue was the *meaning* of sexual differences between men and women,

In the early years of the movement, both radical and liberal feminists minimized those differences, believing reproductive control and work in the public sector have made women's lives more like men's. Antifeminists inflated those differences. Their response is a measure both of their belief that women are "eternal in their attributes and unchanged by events" and their anger and distress at changes that had already occurred.[32]

Although supporters managed to persuade Congress to extend the deadline for ratification of ERA from 1979 to 1982, only one state ratified after 1975. By the mid-seventies, the political climate that had sustained the reforms of the sixties had changed. Despite the tall ships and fireworks with which Americans lavishly celebrated the nation's two-hundredth birthday, the wars of Watergate, defeat in Vietnam, economic woes, and finally the Iranian hostage crisis had shaken citizens' confidence. A disaffected and angry segment of white Americans believed that a liberal elite in Washington, engaged in misguided social engineering, had led the country astray politically, and also severed its moral moorings. They ticked off a list of liberal "sins": school busing to achieve racial balance, affirmative action programs and hiring goals that advantaged minorities and women at the expense of white men, a constitutional amendment mandating gender equality, court rulings allowing abortion and forbidding school prayer, and a war on poverty that used hardworking taxpayers' dollars to support people too lazy to work. By the mid-1970s, skillful opinion-mobilizers and politicians welded the people who held these convictions, anxieties, and resentments with older constituencies, forging them all into a resurgent right. Flexing their political muscle in the Republican Party, this New Right was poised to put pro-life candidate Ronald Reagan in the White House in 1980, dropping the party's historic endorsement of ERA. Pro-choice feminists in the Republican Party were, with good reason, alarmed, as were their sisters who bore no allegiance to the GOP. Clearly, feminism's first decade had come to an end; it was time to take stock.

TAKING STOCK

There were gains to be sure. New reproductive freedom came in 1973 with the Supreme Court's liberalization of abortion laws that removed the danger of the illegal, back-alley abortions so long the recourse of desperate women. Sexual preference and practice became less an occasion for denial of civil rights and more a matter of individual choice. Evidence of expanding educational and employment opportunities seemed to be everywhere. Women assumed high-level posts in government, the judiciary, the military, business, and labor. In a new batch of female "firsts," Sandra Day O'Connor assumed a seat on the Supreme Court, NASA's Sally Ride zoomed into space, and Geraldine Ferraro won the vice-presidential slot on the 1984 Democratic ticket. From an expanding population of female college graduates, younger women moved in record numbers into professional school, dramatically changing enrollment patterns in such fields as law, medicine, and business. Their blue-collar counterparts, completing job training programs, trickled into the construction industry and other trades, finding in those jobs the decent wage that had eluded them as waitresses, hairdressers, salesclerks, or domestics. Political participation also increased. Women emerged from years of lobbying for ERA with a new understanding of the political process. (So, too, did their opponents.) More female candidates filed for office and more female politicians worked themselves into positions of power. Revision of discriminatory statutes, while by no means completed, brought a greater measure of legal equality. A heightened public consciousness of sexism ushered in other changes. School officials began admitting boys to home economics classes, girls to shop. Some employers transformed maternity leaves into child-care leaves, making them available to fathers as well as mothers. Liberal religious leaders talked of removing gender-related references from prayer books.

Such gains, while in some cases smacking of tokenism, are not to be minimized. Most required persistent pressure from feminists, from government officials, and often from both. They were by no means comprehensive, however. As in the case of the civil rights movement, the initial beneficiaries of the feminist movement were predominantly middle-class, often highly educated, and relatively young. The increase in the number of single women, the older age at which women married for the first time, the declining birth rate—changes characteristic of the entire female population during the 1970s—were especially characteristic of a younger generation of career-oriented women. But even for these women and their partners, financial as well as personal costs were sometimes high: couples living apart for some portion of the week or year in order to take advantage of career opportunities; married women devoting virtually all of their salaries to domestic and child-care costs, especially during their children's preschool years. Perhaps the personal recognition, independence, and sense of fulfillment associated with career success made the costs "affordable" especially given the alternatives.

The women who stood to gain most from the implementation of feminists' efforts to change the nation's economic and social structure were not those who were young, talented, and educated but those who were less advantaged. Yet by the 1990s the latter could with good reason argue that two decades of feminist activity had left their lives little changed in ways that really count. While the number of women in the work force continued to rise from less than 20 percent in 1920 to just below 70 percent in 2000, working women in the 1970s and 1980s saw the gap between male and female income remain virtually unchanged. By 2003, female workers earned 78 cents for every dollar earned by males, although the gap has narrowed among younger women, who are currently earning more college degrees and MBAs than men. Earnings for women college graduates have increased by 33 percent since 1979, whereas college educated male graduates have increased by only 18 percent.[33] For most women, however, especially older women, the pay gap still persists. Part of the explanation for its persistence lies in pay inequities. More fundamental, however, is the continuation of occupational segregation and the undervaluation of work done by women. The majority of women still cluster in gender-segregated occupations in which wages are artificially low. That women make up more than half of all minimum-wage workers in the United States is, therefore, hardly surprising.[34]

With the dramatic rise in the number of female-headed households—33 percent of all working mothers are their family's breadwinners—the continuation of this occupational ghetto has disturbing implications not only for women workers but also for their children. Female heads of households, often lacking both child-care facilities and skills that would equip them for better-paying jobs if such jobs were available, earn enough to enable less than two-thirds to stay above the poverty level. Their struggle for economic survival is shared by other women, especially older women—widows or divorcees whose years of housework have left them without employment skills. Indeed divorce often contributes to the problem, for with the breaking up of a marriage, the standard of living for most women falls dramatically. The fact that child support, if awarded, is frequently inadequate, unpaid, and uncollectible further exacerbates the economic plight of those women who have custody of their children. Thus, ironic as it may seem, the decade that witnessed the revival of the feminist movement also saw the feminization of poverty. By the end of the 1970s, two out of every three poor persons in the United States were female. At the beginning of the twenty-first century, women remain a disproportionately higher percent of those Americans below the poverty line—a trend that has worsened as the economy deteriorated.[35]

Ironic, too, given the feminist insistence that child-care and household responsibilities should be shared by working spouses, is the persistence of the double burden borne by women working outside the home. Working women continue to do 80 to 90 percent of the chores related to running a household, with husbands and elder children "helping out." For all the talk about the changing structure of family roles, major shifts have occurred slowly, even in households in which women were informed and engaged enough to be familiar with feminist views.[36] Although some fathers have become more involved in parenting, the primary responsibility for children usually remains the mother's.[37] And working mothers still receive little institutional help despite the fact that by 2000, 65 percent of all mothers with children under six worked outside the home.[38] Without a fundamental rethinking of both work and family, women will continue to participate in the labor force in increasing numbers. Many, however, will remain in its lower echelons as marginal members.[39]

In sum, economic and demographic change has been the basis of important changes in attitudes and behavior. As a result, life is more challenging for many women, but the feminization of poverty reminds the nation of its failures. We have yet to see the new social policies necessary to create the egalitarian and humane society envisioned by feminists. Our narrative reminds us that social change is complex and results from the interplay of many factors. Nowhere is this truer than in the women's movement. The swiftness with which a resurgent feminism captured the imagination of millions of American women dramatized the need for change. The inability of feminists to win ratification of ERA dramatized the limits of change. The irony of the polarization, however, was that the failure of ERA did not and could not stop feminism in its tracks and that antifeminist women, in mobilizing to fight the amendment, were themselves assuming a new role whether they acknowledged that fact or not. They organized lobbies, political action committees, and conventions; they also ran for and won public office. Where feminists had led, antifeminists would not be too far behind, defining themselves within the context of change they could not stop.

The rhetoric of liberation that had been so important to the awakening and maturation of women in the 1970s seemed by the 1980s to be less appealing. Women could happily benefit from the achievements of feminism without understanding or embracing its critique. Transformational politics seemed to have given way to a bevy of career women armed with a copy of *Savvy* or *Working Woman,* "dressed for success," and busily playing "games their mothers never taught them" with scant realization, as one observer noted, that "only a decade ago they would never have been allowed to play."[40] Commentators, speculating that feminism had become careerism, pronounced the movement dead.

Although press speculation was off the mark, feminism had changed. By the mid-seventies, radical feminism had given way to cultural feminism. The appeal that alternative institution-building held for cultural feminists in the conservative eighties was understandable. But the kind of celebrating of the female reflected in the search for lost matriarchies and goddess worship seemed to radical and liberal feminists to represent not only female separatism but a retreat from political struggle. Both seemed alien to women whose aim had been to transcend gender, not reaffirm it. Valorization of female difference was also at the heart of still newer varieties of feminism such as eco-feminism: women as natural nurturers were presumed to be uniquely concerned with ecological ruin. If eco-feminism focused on issues that radical and liberal feminists of the 1960s would have regarded as broad human issues rather than distinctively feminist ones, the groups themselves functioned as a sharp reminder that second-wave feminism had always been an ideologically pluralistic, decentralized, and structurally amorphous movement. It is on this youngest generation of feminists that the future of feminism depends. They understand that the battle is not over. Indeed, a resurgent right has made it abundantly clear that older patterns of inequality have not lost their force and that contemporary efforts to secure women's full emancipation can be challenged, slowed, even interrupted. But they cannot be extinguished. To stop struggling is to allow dominance justified by appeals to constructed differences of gender, ethnicity, race, class, and sexual preference to limit our lives and what connects us to each other. Today, the movement continues to expand even in the midst of antifeminist backlash as women continue to make the connection between the personal and political as they confront in their own lives or the lives of others the trauma of sexual harassment, sexual violence, and the reality of the "glass ceiling."

Notes

1. Nancy F. Cott, *The Grounding of Modern Feminism* (New Haven: Yale University Press, 1987). p. 3.

2. Likewise, Marilyn J. Boxer correctly asserts that historians have replicated an artificial dichotomy between socialist feminists and liberal feminists, foreclosing examination of connections and collaborations between these ideologically distinct groups. Boxer, "Rethinking the Socialist Construction and International Career of the Concept 'Bourgeois Feminist,'" *American Historical Review* 112 (February 2007): 131–158.

3. Myra Marx Ferree and Beth B. Hess demonstrate the utility of describing the various movements as strands rather than branches in their volume *Controversy and Coalition: The New Feminist Movement across Four Decades of Change,* 3rd edition (New York: Routledge, 2000), pp. 56–57. . . . Historians remain aware of fragmentation and division among feminists, but find value in exploring points of coalition, which, as Elizabeth Kaminski reminds, "shifts our focus" to the "various opportunities, negotiations, struggles, and successes enacted by people who come together across different points of view and backgrounds to pursue a common goal." Kaminski, "Learning from Coalitions: Intersections and New Directions in Activism and Scholarship" in *Feminist Coalitions: Historical Perspectives on Second-Wave Feminism in the United States,* ed. Stephanie Gilmore (Urbana: University of Illinois Press, 2008), 285–293, p. 285.

4. If one begins dating feminism among African American women with resistance to gendered violence, then enslaved women enacted an early form of feminist resistance and Harriet Jacobs, *Incidents in the Life of a Slave girl: Written by Herself,* ed. Jean Fagan Yellin (Cambridge: Harvard University Press, 1987), becomes a feminist memoir in as much as the narrative reflects Jacobs's consciousness of oppression as a slave and as a woman. Anna Julia Cooper, *A Voice from the South by a Black Woman of the South* (Xenia, Oh.: Aldine, 1892), quote, p. 135. On the distinctive African American feminist tradition, see Patricia Hill Collins, "The Social Construction of Black Feminist Thought," *Signs* 14 (1989):745–73; and idem, *Black Feminist Thought: Knowledge, Consciousness, and the Politics of Empowerment* (New York: Routledge, 1990). On industrial feminism see Annelise Orleck, *Common Sense and a Little Fire: Women and Working-Class Politics in the United States, 1900–1965* (Chapel Hill: University of North Carolina Press, 1991); Nancy F. Gabin, *Feminism in the Labor Movement: Women and the United Auto Workers, 1935–1975* (Ithaca: Cornell University Press, 1990); and Dennis A. Deslippe, *"Rights, Not Roses": Unions and the Rise of Working Class Feminism, 1945–1980* (Urbana: University of Illinois Press, 2000); Dorothy Sue Cobble, *The Other Women's Movement: Workplace Justice and Social Rights in Modern America* (Princeton: Princeton University Press, 2004). . . . Examples of black and low-income women's groups include Mothers Working Along and the Mt. Vernon/New Rochelle group. On the latter, see Rosalyn Baxandall, "Re-visioning the Women's Liberation Movement's Narrative: Early Second Wave African American Feminists," *Feminist Studies* 27 (2001):225–45.

5. "Old Left" refers to those left-wing political organizations such as the Communist Party, Trotskyist organizations such as the Socialist Workers' Party, independent Socialist clubs, and the Freedom Socialist Party, as well as anarchist groups. On the links between the Old Left and new feminists, see Kate Weigand, *Red Feminism: American Communism and the Making of Women's Liberation* (Baltimore: Johns Hopkins University Press, 2001).

6. Daniel Horowitz, *Betty Friedan and the Making of the Feminine Mystique: The American Left, the Cold War, and Modern Feminism* (Amherst: University of Massachusetts Press, 1998). The origins of the feminist movement in the Cold War are also explored extensively in Ruth R. Rosen, *The World Split Open: How the Modern Women's Movement Changed America* (New York: Viking, 2000). . . . Pauli Murray, "Why Negro Girls Stay Single," *The Negro Digest* (July 1947), 4; see also ("Dialogue: Pauli Murray's Notable Connections," *Journal of Women's History* 14, no. 2

(Summer 2002): 54–87. Landon Storrs, "Red Scare Politics and the Suppression of Popular Front Feminism: The Loyalty Investigation of Mary Dublin Keyserling," *Journal of American History* 190, no. 2 (2003): 491–524. Leandra Zarnow, "Braving Jim Crow to Save Willie McGee: Bella Abzug, the Legal Left and Civil Rights Innovation, 1948–1951," *Law & Social Inquiry* 33, issue 4 (fall 2008): 1003–1041.

7. Barbara Winslow, "Old Left/New Left: The Origins and Development of the, Women's Liberation Movement in Seattle, Washington, 1966–1970," paper delivered at the American Historical Association, Seattle, January, 1998. See also Baxandall, "Re-visioning the Women's Liberation Movement's Narrative." Andrea Estepa, "Taking the White Gloves Off: Women Strike for Peace and 'the Movement,' 1963–73" in *Feminist Coalitions: Historical Perspectives on Second-Wave Feminism in the United States*, ed. Stephanie Gilmore (Urbana: University of Illinois Press, 2008), 84–112, p. 96.

8. Cynthia E. Harrison, "A "New Frontier' for Women: The Public Policy of the Kennedy Administration," *Journal of American History* 67 (1980): 630–46.

9. U.S. President's Commission on the Status of Women, *American Women* (Washington, D.C., 1963).

10. Gabin, *Feminism in the Labor Movement*, p. 188.

11. For events leading to the founding of NOW, see Jo Freeman, *The Politics of Women's Liberation: A Case Study of an Emerging Social Movement and Its Relation to the Social Policy Process* (New York: Longman, 1975), pp. 53–55; and Cynthia Harrison, *On Account of Sex; The Politics of Women's Issues, 1945–1968* (Berkeley: University of California Press, 1988), pp. 192–209.

12. Freeman, *Politics of Women's Liberation*, pp. 35–37.

13. National Organization of Women, Statement of Purpose, 1966, reprinted in *Up from the Pedestal*, ed. Aileen S. Kraditor (Chicago: Quadrangle, 1968), pp. 363–64; National Organization of Women, Bill of Rights, 1967, reprinted in *Sisterhood Is Powerful: An Anthology of Writings on the Women's Liberation Movement*, ed. Robin Morgan (New York: Random House, 1970), pp. 512–14.

14. Freeman, *Politics of Women's Liberation*, chap. 3; Maren Lockwood Carden, *The New Feminist Movement* (New York; Russell Sage, 1974), chaps. 8–10; also Gayle Graham Yates, *What Women Want: The Ideas of the Movement* (Cambridge, Mass.: Harvard University Press, 1975), chap. 2; Gabin, *Feminism in the Labor Movement*, p. 226.

15. Quoted in Carolyn Hadley, "Feminist Women in the Southeast," *Bulletin of the Center of the Study of Southern Culture and Religion* 3 (1979):10.

16. Quoted in "Ruth Bader Ginsburg," *1994 Current Biography*, p. 214.

17. Sara Evans, *Personal Politics: The Roots of Women's Liberation in the Civil Rights Movement and the New Left* (New York: Vintage, 1979); see also Evans, "Tomorrow's Yesterday: Feminist Consciousness and the Future of Women," in *Women of America: A History*, ed. Carol Ruth Berkin and Mary Beth Norton (Boston: Houghton Mifflin, 1979), pp. 390–415. The following paragraphs rely heavily on this essay and on Evans's *Personal Politics*.

18. Mary King, one of the authors of the manifesto protesting the treatment of women in SNCC, insists that Carmichael was personally responsive to their concerns if others were not. See Mary King, *Freedom Song* (New York: Morrow, 1987), pp. 45–52. On the treatment of women in the New Left, see Ellen Willis, "Sequel: Letter to a Critic," *Notes from the Second Year* n.v. (1970): 55–58. In a previous article, Willis had argued that the New Left was dominated by men and its theory, priorities, and strategy reflected male interests. See her "Women and the Left," *Notes from the Second Year* n.v. (1970):5–56. See Alice Echols, *Daring to be Bad: Radical Feminism in America, 1965–1975* (Minneapolis: University of Minnesota Press, 1989). . . . For a thoughtful reevaluation of the origins of women's liberation in SDS and SNCC, Winifred Breines, *The Trouble Between Us: An Uneasy History of White and Black Women in the Feminist Movement* (Oxford: Oxford University Press, 2006). For a valuable critique of Breines, Mary Ann Clawson, "Looking for Feminism: Racial Dynamics and Generational Investments in the Second Wave," *Feminist Studies* 34, no. 3 (fall 2008): 526–554.

19. On the early organization of feminists of color, see Esther Ngan-Ling Chow, "The Development of Feminist Consciousness Among Asian American Women," *Gender and Society* 1 (1987): 284–99; William Wei, *The Asian American Movement* (Philadelphia: Temple University Press, 1993); Naomi Barry, "Women's Participation in the Chicano Movement," *Latino Studies Journal* 8 (1997):47–82; Alma Garcia, *Chicano Feminist Thought: The Basic Historical Writings* (New York, Routledge, 1997). Black feminists In SNCC formed a Black Women's Caucus in 1968 to discuss the problems of women in SNCC. Reaching out to non–SNCC, some members of the Black Women's Causes formed an independent feminist group, the Black Women's Alliance. Other SNCC feminists formed a Black Women's Liberation Committee, which was part of SNCC. Benita Roth, *Separate Roads to Feminism: Black, Chicana, and White Feminist Movements in America's Second Wave* (Cambridge: Cambridge University Press, 2004), p. 6. See also, Kimberly Springer, *Living for the Revolution: Black Feminist Organizations, 1968–1980* (Durham, NC: Duke University Press, 2005); and Becky Thompson, "Multiracial Feminism: Recasting the Chronology of Second Wave Feminism," *Feminism Studies* 28, no. 2 (Summer 2002): 337–361 . . . On the exodus of lesbians, see Radicalesbians, "Leaving the Gay Men Behind," in Karla Jay and Allen Young, eds., *Out of the Closets: Voices of Gay Liberation* (New York: Douglas Book Co., 1972).

20. Premilla Nadasen, *Welfare Warriors: The Welfare Rights Movement in the United States* (New York: Routledge, 2005); Anne M. Valk, *Radical Sisters: Second-Wave Feminism and Black Liberation in Washington, D.C.* (Urbana, Ill.: University of Illinois Press, 2008); Felicia Kornbluh, *The Battle for Welfare Rights: Politics and Poverty in Modern America* (Philadelphia: University of Pennsylvania Press, 2007); and Annelise Orleck, *Storming Caesars Palace: How Black Mothers Fought Their Own War on Poverty* (Boston: Beacon Press, 2005). Leslie J. Reagan, *When Abortion Was a Crime: Women, Medicine, and Law in*

the United States, 1867–1973 (Berkeley: University of California Press, 1997), 224–226; and Laura Kaplan, *The Story of JANE: The Legendary Underground Feminist Abortion Service* (New York: Pantheon Books, 1995).

21. Quoted in Evans, 'Tomorrow's Yesterday," p. 407.

22. See *Notes from the Second Year*, (The Redstockings Manifesto and other writing in Robin Morgan, ed., *Sisterhood Is Powerful: An Anthology of Writings from the Women's Liberation Movement* (New York: Random House, 1970); Deborah Babcox and Madeline Belkin, eds. *Liberation Now: Writings from the Women's Liberation Movement* (New York: Dell, 1971); Alexander Bloom and Wini Breines, eds. *'Takin' It to the Streets': A Sixties Render* (New York: Oxford, 1995); Kate Millett, *Sexual Politics* (Garden City, N.Y.: Doubleday, 1970); Shulamith Firestone, *The Dialectic of Sex: The Case for a Feminist Revolution* (New York: Morrow, 1970); Germaine Greer, *The Female Eunuch* (New York: McGraw Hill, 1970); Juliet Mitchell, *Women's Estate* (New York: Vintage, 1971); Evelyn Reed, *Problems of Women's Liberation: A Marxist Approach* (New York: Pathfinder, 1971); Mary Daly, *Beyond God the Father: Toward a Philosophy of Women's Liberation* (Boston: Beacon, 1973); Carolyn Heilbrun, *Toward a Recognition of Androgyny* (New York: Knopf, 1973); and *The Black Woman: An Anthology*, ed. Toni Cade (New York; Signet, 1970).

23. Judith M. Bardwick, *In Transition: How Feminism, Sexval Liberation and the Search for Self-Fulfillment Have Altered America* (New York: Holt, 1979), p. 26.

24. On CWLU, see its newspaper *Womankind*, published between 1970 and 1974, as well as "A Critical History of the CWLU," "CWLU Background History of CWLU, 1968–1976," and Hyde Park Chapter of CWLU, "Socialist Feminism: A Strategy for the Women's Movement," Box 1, Chicago Women's Liberation Union Collection, Chicago Historical Society, Chicago, IL. See also Barbara Ehrenreich, speech at the National Conference on Socialist Feminism, box 2, CWLU Papers.

25. Julie Gallagher, "Waging 'The Good Fight': The Political Career of Shirley Chisholm, 1953–1982," *The Journal of African American History* 92 (2007): 393–416.

26. Black feminists belonged to organizations such as the short-lived National Black Feminist Organization and the National Alliance of Black Feminists. This characterization of black feminists as the most pressed down is from Patricia Haden, Donna Middleton, and Patricia Robinson, "A Historical and Critical Essay for Black Women," in *Voices from Women's Liberation*, ed. Leslie B. Tanner (New York: American Library, 1971), pp. 316–24. For the differing concerns of black feminists, see Carol Kleiman, "When Black Women Rap, the Talk Sure is Different," *Chicago Tribune*, June 1, 1975, sec. 5, p. 13. Information on the Third World Women's Alliance see Box 4, Third World Women's Alliance Papers, Records of the National Conference of Negro Women, Mary McLeod Bethune Museum and Archives, Washington, D.C. Springer, *Living for the Revolution*. For working-class women's activism, see Nancy Maclean, "The Hidden History of Affirmative Action: Working Women's Struggles in the 1970s and the Gender of Class," *Feminist Studies* 25, no. 1 (Spring 1999): 43–78.

27. Carrie N. Baker, *The Women's Movement Against Sexual Harassment* (Cambridge: Cambridge University Press, 2008).

28. Louis Harris, "Changing Views on the Role of Women," *The Harris Survey*, Dec. 11,1975.

29. Caroline Bird and the Members and Staff of the National Commission on the Observance of International Woman's Year, *What Women Want: From the Official Report to the President, the Congress, and the People of the United States* (New York: Simon & Schuster, 1979), p. 68 for Johnson's statement.

30. Violet S. Devieux to Senator Sam J. Ervin, Jr., Mar. 23, 1972, Samuel J. Ervin Papers, #3847 Southern Historical Collection, Library of the University of North Carolina at Chapel Hill. For a fuller analysis of the significance of the struggle over ERA and the debate over feminism, see Donald G. Mathews and Jane S. De Hart, *Sex, Gender, and the ERA: A State and the Nation* (New York: Oxford, 1990).

31. For analysis of these and other anti-ERA women's quotes, see also De Hart, "Gender on the Right: Meanings behind the Existential Scream," *Gender and History* 3 (1991):246–67.

32. This apt characterization is William Chafe's; see *The Paradox of Change* (New York: Oxford, 1991) p. 209.

33. "Highlights of Women's Earnings in 2007," Report 1008 (October 2008), U.S. Bureau of Labor Statistics, U.S. Department of Labor.

34. "Women Still Underrepresented Among Highest Earners," Issues in Labor Statistics, Summary 06–03 (March 2006) U.S. Bureau of Statistics, U.S. Department of Labor.

35. Diane Pearce, "The Feminization of Poverty: Women, Work, and Welfare," *Urban and Social Change Review* 11 (1978):28–36; Barbara Ehrenreich and Francis Fox Piven, "The Feminization of Poverty: When the 'Family Wage System' Breaks Down," *Dissent* 31 (1984):162–70; Leonore J. Weitzman, *The Divorce Revolution and the Unanticipated Consequences for Women and Children in America* (New York: Free Press, 1985); Census Bureau, Historical Poverty Tables, Table 7. Poverty of People, by Sex: 1966 to 2001: http://www.census.gov/hhes/hstpoverty/histpov/histpov7.html.

36. *The American Woman, Status Report - 1988–1989*, ed. Sara E. Rix (New York: W. W. Norton, 1988), p. 151.

37. Arlie Hochshild, *Second Shift: Working Parents and the Revolution at Home* (New York: Viking, 1989).

38. *Statistical Abstracts of the United States*: 2000.

39. Joan Williams, *Unbending Gender: Why Family and Work Conflict and What to Do About It* (New York: Oxford, 2000).

40. *New York Times*, December 12, 1997, p. A3.

DOCUMENTS

Making the Personal Political

Betty Friedan, "The problem that has no name . . . I understood first as a woman . . ."

If the teenagers singing along with the Shirelles were vocalizing more than the usual adolescent discontent, the mothers who worried about their daughters had their own set of frustrations. However, despite some grumbling on the part of adults, mothers seemed no better than their daughters at articulating their discomfort and malaise. It was 1963 when Betty Friedan, identifying herself as a suburban housewife, did the job for them, exposing the triviality and frustrations of a resurgent domesticity. Friedan's indictment, a brief portion of which appears here, was the subject of much controversy. Women who found the gratification associated with child care and housework vastly overemphasized applauded Friedan's forceful articulation of their own dissatisfactions. Other women objected vehemently, insisting that, as wives and mothers and perhaps community activists, they enjoyed a life style that not only benefited both their families and communities, but also provided them personally with freedom, pleasure, and a sense of self-worth. How are we to explain such different responses? Is the housewife described by Friedan foreshadowed in Ruth Schwartz Cowan's article on housework (see pp. 484–492)? Is "the problem" that Friedan identifies a universal one?

The problem lay buried, unspoken, for many years in the minds of American women. It was a strange stirring, a sense of dissatisfaction, a yearning that women suffered in the middle of the twentieth century in the United States. Each suburban wife struggled with it alone. As she made the beds, shopped for groceries, matched slipcover material, ate peanut butter sandwiches with her children, chauffeured Cub Scouts and Brownies, lay beside her husband at night, she was afraid to ask even of herself the silent question—"Is this all?"

For over fifteen years there was no word of this yearning in the millions of words written about women, for women, in all the columns, books and articles by experts telling women their role was to seek fulfillment as wives and mothers. Over and over women heard in voices of tradition and of Freudian sophistication that they could desire no greater destiny than to glory in their own femininity. Experts told them how to catch a man and keep him, how to breast-feed children and handle their toilet training, how to cope with sibling rivalry and adolescent rebellion; how to buy a dishwasher, bake bread, cook gourmet snails, and build a swimming pool with their own hands; how to dress, look, and act more feminine and make marriage more exciting; how to keep their husbands from dying young and their sons from growing into delinquents. They were taught to pity the neurotic, unfeminine, unhappy women who wanted to be poets or physicists or presidents. They

Excerpted from "The Problem That Has No Name," ch. 1 of *The Feminine Mystique* by Betty Friedan (New York: W. W. Norton, 1963).

learned that truly feminine women do not want careers, higher education, political rights—the independence and the opportunities that the old-fashioned feminists fought for. Some women, in their forties and fifties, still remembered painfully giving up those dreams, but most of the younger women no longer even thought about them. A thousand expert voices applauded their femininity, their adjustment, their new maturity. All they had to do was devote their lives from earliest girlhood to finding a husband and bearing children.

By the end of the 1950s, the average marriage age of women in America dropped to 20, and was still dropping, into the teens. Fourteen million girls were engaged by 17. The proportion of women attending college in comparison with men dropped from 47 percent in 1920 to 35 percent in 1958. A century earlier, women had fought for higher education; now girls went to college to get a husband. By the mid-fifties, 60 percent dropped out of college to marry, or because they were afraid too much education would be a marriage bar. Colleges built dormitories for "married students," but the students were almost always the husbands. A new degree was instituted for the wives—"Ph.T." (Putting Husband Through).

Then American girls began getting married in high school. And the women's magazines, deploring the unhappy statistics about these young marriages, urged that courses on marriage, and marriage counselors, be installed in the high schools. Girls started going steady at twelve and thirteen, in junior high. Manufacturers put out brassieres with false bosoms of foam rubber for little girls of ten. And an advertisement for a child's dress, size 3–6x, in the *New York Times* in the fall of 1960, said: "She Too Can Join the Man-Trap Set."

By the end of the fifties, the United States birthrate was overtaking India's. The birth-control movement, renamed Planned Parenthood, was asked to find a method whereby women who had been advised that a third or fourth baby would be born dead or defective might have it anyhow. Statisticians were especially astounded at the fantastic increase in the number of babies among college women. Where once they had two children, now they had four, five, six. Women who had once wanted careers were now making careers out of having babies. So rejoiced *Life* magazine in a 1956 paean to the movement of American women back to the home.

In a New York hospital, a woman had a nervous breakdown when she found she could not breast-feed her baby. In other hospitals, women dying of cancer refused a drug which research had proved might save their lives: Its side effects were said to be unfeminine. "If I have only one life, let me live it as a blonde," a larger-than-life-sized picture of a pretty, vacuous woman proclaimed from newspaper, magazine, and drugstore ads. And across America, three out of every ten women dyed their hair blonde. They ate a chalk called Metrecal, instead of food, to shrink to the size of the thin young models. Department-store buyers reported that American women, since 1939, had become three and four sizes smaller. "Women are out to fit the clothes, instead of vice-versa," one buyer said.

Interior decorators were designing kitchens with mosaic murals and original paintings, for kitchens were once again the center of women's lives. Home sewing became a million-dollar industry. Many women no longer left their homes, except to shop, chauffeur their children, or attend a social engagement with their husbands. Girls were growing up in America without ever having jobs outside the home. In the late fifties, a sociological phenomenon was suddenly remarked: A third of American women now worked, but most were no longer young and very few were pursuing careers. They were married women who held part-time jobs, selling or secretarial, to put their husbands through school, their sons through college, or to help pay the mortgage. Or they were widows supporting families. Fewer and fewer women were entering professional work. The shortages in the nursing, social work, and teaching professions caused crises in almost every American city. Concerned over the Soviet Union's lead in the space race, scientists noted that America's greatest source of unused brainpower was women. But girls would not study physics: It was "unfeminine." A girl refused a science fellowship at Johns Hopkins to take a job in a real-estate office. All she wanted, she said, was what every other American girl wanted—to get married, have four children, and live in a nice house in a nice suburb.

The suburban housewife—she was the dream image of the young American women and the envy, it was said, of women all over the world. The American housewife—freed by science and labor-saving appliances from the drudgery, the dangers of childbirth, and the illnesses of her grandmother. She was healthy, beautiful, educated, concerned only about her husband, her children, her home. She had found true feminine fulfillment. As a housewife and mother, she was respected as a full and equal partner to man in his world. She was free to choose automobiles, clothes, appliances, supermarkets; she had everything that women ever dreamed of.

In the fifteen years after World War II, this mystique of feminine fulfillment became the cherished and self-perpetuating core of contemporary American culture. Millions of women lived their lives in the image of those pretty pictures of the American suburban housewife, kissing their husbands good-bye in front of the picture window, depositing their station wagons full of children at school, and smiling as they ran the new electric waxer over the spotless kitchen floor. They baked their own bread, sewed their own and their children's clothes, kept their new washing machines and dryers running all day. They changed the sheets on the beds twice a week instead of once, took the rug-hooking class in adult education, and pitied their poor frustrated mothers, who had dreamed of having a career. Their only dream was to be perfect wives and mothers; their highest ambition to have five children and a beautiful house, their only fight to get and keep their husbands. They had no thought for the unfeminine problems of the world outside the home; they wanted the men to make the major decisions. They gloried in their role as women, and wrote proudly on the census blank: "Occupation: housewife."

For over fifteen years, the words written for women, and the words women used when they talked to each other, while their husbands sat on the other side of the room and talked shop or politics or septic tanks, were about problems with their children, or how to keep their husbands happy, or improve their children's school, or cook chicken or make slipcovers. Nobody argued whether women were inferior or superior to men; they were simply different. Words like "emancipation" and "career" sounded strange and embarrassing; no one had used them for years. When a Frenchwoman named Simone de Beauvoir wrote a book called *The Second Sex,* an American critic commented that she obviously "didn't know what life was all about," and besides, she was talking about French women. The "woman problem" in America no longer existed.

If a woman had a problem in the 1950s and 1960s she knew that something must be wrong with her marriage, or with herself. Other women were satisfied with their lives, she thought. What kind of a woman was she if she did not feel this mysterious fulfillment waxing the kitchen floor? She was so ashamed to admit her dissatisfaction that she never knew how many other women shared it. If she tried to tell her husband, he didn't understand what she was talking about. She did not really understand it herself. For over fifteen years women in America found it harder to talk about this problem than about sex. Even the psychoanalysts had no name for it. When a woman went to a psychiatrist for help, as many women did, she would say, "I'm so ashamed," or "I must be hopelessly neurotic." "I don't know what's wrong with women today," a suburban psychiatrist said uneasily. "I only know something is wrong because most of my patients happen to be women. And their problem isn't sexual." Most women with this problem did not go to see a psychoanalyst, however. "There's nothing wrong really," they kept telling themselves. "There isn't any problem."

But on an April morning in 1959, I heard a mother of four, having coffee with four other mothers in a suburban development fifteen miles from New York, say in a tone of quiet desperation, "the problem." And the others knew, without words, that she was not talking about a problem with her husband, or her children, or her home. Suddenly they realized they all shared the same problem, the problem that has no name. They began, hesitantly, to talk about it. Later, after they had picked up their children at nursery school and taken them home to nap, two of the women cried, in sheer relief, just to know they were not alone.

Gradually I came to realize that the problem that has no name was shared by countless women in America. As a magazine writer I often interviewed women about problems with their children, or their marriages, or their houses, or their communities. But after a while I began to recognize the telltale signs of this other problem. I saw the same signs in suburban ranch houses and split-levels on Long Island and in New Jersey and Westchester County; in colonial houses in a small Massachusetts town; on patios in Memphis; in suburban and city apartments; in living rooms in the Midwest. Sometimes I sensed the problem, not as a reporter, but as a suburban housewife, for during this time I was also bringing up my own three children in Rockland County, New York. I heard echoes of the problem in college dormitories and semi-private maternity wards, at PTA meetings and luncheons of the League of Women Voters, at suburban cocktail parties, in station wagons waiting for trains, and in snatches of conversation overheard at Schrafft's. The groping words I heard from other women, on quiet afternoons when children were at school or on quiet evenings when husbands worked late, I think I understood first as a woman long before I understood their larger social and psychological implications.

Carol Hanisch, "The protest of the Miss America Pageant . . . told the nation a new feminist movement is afoot. . . ."

Women of Friedan's generation were divided as to whether they saw domesticity as sufficient to their fulfillment or if there truly was "a problem that had no name," and, if so, what it involved. Many young women, who had joined in the protest movements of the 1960s, had no such doubts. The group who gathered in Atlantic City in 1968 to protest the Miss America Pageant instantly caught the eye of the national and world media. Contrary to myth, no bras were burned; however, demonstrators hurled what they called "items of female torture" into a large "Freedom Trash Can," including false eyelashes, hair curlers, girdles, high-heel shoes, Toni home permanents (a sponsor of the pageant), *Playboy* and *Good Housekeeping* magazines, and even some bras. The protesters called for the end of beauty competitions, the pressure to conform to false beauty standards and buy related products, and the elevation of appearance over more important human qualities.

Despite all the media attention and the flood of new members into women's liberation groups, one of the action's originators felt that the basic message had been overshadowed and distorted by some of the protesters' activity, as Carol Hanisch makes clear in this astute analysis.

Were the concerns of the 1968 protesters valid? Are they relevant to today's women? In what sense are they among the body issues Brumberg introduces in "Fasting Girls" (pp. 451–459)? Why does Hanisch consider some of the actions employed by her sister protesters counterproductive? What was the message of the protest that she believed they failed to get across?

The protest of the Miss America Pageant in Atlantic City told the nation that a new feminist movement is afoot in the land.

Due to the tremendous coverage in the mass media, millions of Americans now know there is a Women's Liberation Movement. The action brought many new members into our group and many requests from women outside the city for literature and information. A recurrent theme was, "I've been waiting so long for something like this."

But no action taken in the Women's Liberation struggle will be all good or all bad. We must analyze each step to see what was effective, what was not, and what was downright destructive.

At this point in our struggle, our actions should be aimed primarily at doing two interrelated things: (1) awakening the latent consciousness of women about our own oppression, and (2) building sisterhood. With these in mind, let us examine the Miss America protest.

The idea for the protest came out of the method used first in New York Radical Women of analyzing women's oppression by analyzing our own experiences, called consciousness-raising. One night at a meeting we were watching *Schmearguntz,* a feminist movie which contains flashes of the Miss America Pageant. I found myself remembering the powerful feelings the pageant had evoked in me as a child, an adolescent, and a college student. When I proposed the action to our group, we decided to go around the room with each woman telling how she felt about the pageant. We discovered that many of us who had always put down the contest still watched it. Others had consciously identified with it.

From our communal thinking came the concrete plans for the action. The original planning group agreed that the main point in the demonstration would be that all women are hurt by beauty competition—Miss America as well as ourselves. We opposed the pageant in our own self-interest, e.g., the self-interest of all women.

Yet one of the biggest mistakes of the whole pageant was our anti-womanism. A spirit of every woman "doing her own thing" began to emerge as women not in the original meetings came to the planning meetings. Some just went ahead and did what they wanted to do, even though it was something we had decided against. Because of this egotistic individualism, a definite strain of anti-womanism was presented to the public to the detriment of the action.

Posters that read "Up against the Wall, Miss America," "Miss America Sells It," and "Miss America Is a Big Falsie" hardly raised any woman's consciousness and really harmed the cause of sisterhood. Miss America and all beautiful women came off as our enemy instead of as our sisters who suffer with us.

A more complex situation developed around the decision of a few women to use an "underground" disruptive tactic. The group approved this activity only after its adherents said they would do it anyway as an individual action. We learned there is no such thing as "individual action" in a movement. There is, at this time, no real need to do "underground" actions anyway. We need to reach as many women as possible as quickly as possible with a clear message that has the power of our person behind it. Women need to see other women standing up together and saying these things. That's why draping a women's liberation banner over the balcony and yelling our message was much clearer than spraying a smelly chemical in the audience. The problem of how to enforce group decisions is one we haven't solved.

Another way we came off as anti-woman was our lack of clarity. We didn't say clearly enough that we women are all *forced* to play the Miss America role—not by beautiful women but by men who we have to act that way for, and by a system that has so well institutionalized male supremacy for its own ends. This was not very clear in our guerrilla theater. Women chained to a replica, red, white, and blue bathing-suited Miss America could have been misinterpreted as our blaming beautiful women. Also, crowning a live sheep Miss America sort of said that beautiful women *are* sheep. However, the action did say to some that women are *viewed as* auction-block, docile animals. The grandmother of one of the participants really began to understand the action when she was told about the sheep, and she ended up joining the protest.

There is as great a need for clarity in our language as there is in our actions. The leaflet that was distributed as a press release and flyer was too long, too wordy, too complex, too hippy-yippee-campy. Instead of an "in" phrase like "Racism with Roses," we could have just called the pageant "racist" and everybody would have understood our opposition on that point.

We should avoid the temptation to say everything there is to say about what is wrong with the world and thereby say nothing that a new person can really dig into and understand. Women's liberation itself is revolutionary dynamite. When other issues are interjected, we should clearly relate them to our oppression as women.

We tried to carry the democratic means we used in planning the action into the actual doing of it. We didn't want leaders or spokesmen. It makes the movement not only *seem* stronger and larger if everyone is a leader, but it actually *is* stronger if not dependent on a few. And, of course, many voices are more powerful than one. We must learn how to fight against the media's desire to make leaders—and some women's desire to appoint themselves spokesmen.

The Miss America protest was a zap action, which means using our presence as a group to make women's oppression into a social issue. In such actions we speak to men as a group as well as to women. It is a rare opportunity to talk to men in a situation where they can't talk back. (Men must learn to listen.) Our power of solidarity, not our individual intellectual exchanges will change men.

The reaction of many of the women we talked to about the protest was, "But I'm not oppressed" or "I don't care about Miss America." If more than half the television viewers in the country watch the pageant, somebody cares! While much of the Left was putting us down for attacking something so "silly and unimportant" or "reformist," the Right saw us as a threat and yelled such things as "Go back to Russia" and "Mothers of Mao" at the picket line. Ironically enough, what the Left/Underground press seemed to like best about our action was what was really our worst mistake—our anti-woman signs.

Surprisingly and fortunately, some of the mass media ignored our mistakes and concentrated on our best points. To quote the *Daily News*, "Some women who think the whole idea of such contests is degrading to femininity, took their case to the people. . . . During boardwalk protest, gals say they're not anti-beauty, just anti-beauty contest." Shana Alexander wrote in a *Life* magazine editorial that she "wished they'd gone farther."

The best slogan for the action came up afterward, when Ros Baxandall blurted out on the David Susskind television show that "Every day in a woman's life is a walking Miss America Contest!" But we shouldn't wait for the perfect slogan; we should go ahead to the best of our understanding.

Redstockings, "Male supremacy is the oldest, most basic form of domination."

One radical New York group that formed in 1969 called itself Redstockings. The name was a blending of "bluestocking," which had long been used to refer to women with intellectual and literary interests, with "red," which signaled revolution. In its "Manifesto," the group indicated that "the problem" went far beyond

The Redstockings Manifesto was issued in New York City on July 7, 1969. It appeared as a mimeographed flier, designed for distribution at women's liberation events. It is reprinted by permission of Redstockings. A catalog containing ordering information for this and other documents from the 1960s rebirth years of feminism is available from the Redstocking Women's Liberation Archives for Action Distribution Project, P.O. Box 2625, Gainesville, FL 32602-2625. The catalog is also available on the web at http://www.redstockings.org.

Friedan's resurgent domesticity. Friedan's "problem which had no name" indeed had a name, and that name was male supremacy, the most ancient form of oppression—older even than class oppression. That sexual oppression was the most basic form of oppression would become *the* fundamental tenet for women who became known as radical feminists (today, many prefer the term *gender oppression*).

To what extent were the Redstockings using Marxist theory, substituting women for the working class? What did they believe had prevented women from recognizing their oppression and doing something about it? What was it they wanted to change with respect to men? What did they imply were (and are) the barriers among and between women that have to be overcome to achieve the female solidarity required if women are to be a collective entity—a class prepared to undertake revolutionary action on its own behalf?

REDSTOCKINGS MANIFESTO

I After centuries of individual and preliminary political struggle, women are uniting to achieve their final liberation from male supremacy. Redstockings is dedicated to building this unity and winning our freedom.

II Women are an oppressed class. Our oppression is total, affecting every facet of our lives. We are exploited as sex objects, breeders, domestic servants, and cheap labor. We are considered inferior beings, whose only purpose is to enhance men's lives. Our humanity is denied. Our prescribed behavior is enforced by the threat of physical violence.

Because we have lived so intimately with our oppressors, in isolation from each other, we have been kept from seeing our personal suffering as a political condition. This creates the illusion that a woman's relationship with her man is a matter of interplay between two unique personalities, and can be worked out individually. In reality, every such relationship is a *class* relationship, and the conflicts between individual men and women are *political* conflicts that can only be solved collectively.

III We identify the agents of our oppression as men. Male supremacy is the oldest, most basic form of domination. All other forms of exploitation and oppression (racism, capitalism, imperialism, etc.) are extensions of male supremacy: men dominate women, a few men dominate the rest. All power structures throughout history have been male-dominated and male-oriented. Men have controlled all political, economic and cultural institutions and backed up this control with physical force. They have used their power to keep women in an inferior position. *All men* receive economic, sexual, and psychological benefits from male supremacy. *All men* have oppressed women.

IV Attempts have been made to shift the burden of responsibility from men to institutions or to women themselves. We condemn these arguments as evasions. Institutions alone do not oppress; they are merely tools of the oppressor. To blame institutions implies that men and women are equally victimized, obscures the fact that men benefit from the subordination of women, and gives men the excuse that they are forced to be oppressors. On the contrary, any man is free to renounce his superior position provided that he is willing to be treated like a woman by other men.

We also reject the idea that women consent to or are to blame for their own oppression. Women's submission is not the result of brainwashing, stupidity, or mental illness but of continual, daily pressure from men. We do not need to change ourselves, but to change men.

The most slanderous evasion of all is that women can oppress men. The basis for this illusion is the isolation of individual relationships from their political context and the tendency of men to see any legitimate challenge to their privileges as persecution.

V We regard our personal experience, and our feelings about that experience, as the basis for an analysis of our common situation. We cannot rely on existing ideologies as they are all products of male supremacist culture. We question every generalization and accept none that are not confirmed by our experience.

Our chief task at present is to develop female class consciousness through sharing experience and publicly exposing the sexist foundation of all our institutions. Consciousness-raising is not "therapy," which implies the existence of individual solutions and falsely assumes that the male-female relationship is purely personal, but the only method by which we can ensure that our program for liberation is based on the concrete realities of our lives.

The first requirement for raising class consciousness is honesty, in private and in public, with ourselves and other women.

VI We identify with all women. We define our best interest as that of the poorest, most brutally exploited woman.

We repudiate all economic, racial, educational or status privileges that divide us from other women. We are determined to recognize and eliminate any prejudices we may hold against other women.

We are committed to achieving internal democracy. We will do whatever is necessary to ensure that every woman in our movement has an equal chance to participate, assume responsibility, and develop her political potential.

VII We call on all our sisters to unite with us in struggle.

We call on all men to give up their male privileges and support women's liberation in the interest of our humanity and their own.

In fighting for our liberation we will always take the side of women against their oppressors. We will not ask what is "revolutionary" or "reformist," only what is good for women.

The time for individual skirmishes has passed. This time we are going all the way.

July 7, 1969
REDSTOCKINGS
P.O. Box 748
Stuyvesant Station
New York, N. Y. 10009

Radicalesbians, "What is a lesbian?"

This question mattered in the late 1960s and early 1970s. Was it a label used contemptuously to belittle and isolate radicals like the protesters who had "burned" their bras at the Miss America Pageant? Was the charge a form of rhetorical retaliation to be wielded by opponents against the "man-hating" women who wrote the Redstockings "Manifesto"? Or did it refer to the sexual preferences and behavior of specific women who identified themselves as feminists? Fearing that the presence of the latter would be used by opponents to discredit the growing women's movement, Betty Friedan worried about what she allegedly referred to as the "lavender menace." The "lavender menace" went public in 1970 when a group of lesbians on both coasts stepped forward to demand discussion of homophobia within the emerging feminist movement. In the years to follow, as they increasingly insisted that being a lesbian is fundamentally sexual, not political, and that sexual orientation may not be a matter of choice, the separatist pull became stronger—a phenomenon evident especially among feminists of color,

Radicalesbians, "The Woman-Identified Woman," 1970, Susan O'Malley personal collection; reprinted in *Dear Sisters: Dispatches from the Women's Liberation Movement*, ed. Rosalyn Baxandall and Linda Gordon (New York: Basic Books, 2000).

who castigated the women's liberation movement for its frequent elision of issues of race. In the meantime, a group known as Radicalesbians issued the controversial statement that follows, describing the lesbian as a "woman-identified woman."

Note the reaction to the enduring tendency to equate feminists generally with "unnatural women" or lesbians. Do the authors see lesbianism as a political choice or a biological preference for sexual partners of the same sex? What would be the advantage of viewing lesbianism as a political stance only? What would be the drawbacks of that position? Who would object and why?

What is a lesbian? A lesbian is the rage of all women condensed to the point of explosion. She is the woman who, often beginning at an extremely early age, acts in accordance with her inner compulsion to be a more complete and freer human being than her society—perhaps then, but certainly later—cares to allow her. She may not be fully conscious of the political implications of what for her began as personal necessity, but on some level she has not been able to accept the limitations and oppression laid on her by the most basic role of her society—the female role. The turmoil she experiences tends to induce guilt proportional to the degree to which she feels she is not meeting social expectations, and eventually drives her to question and analyse what the rest of her society more or less accepts. She is forced to evolve her own life pattern, often living much of her life alone, learning usually much earlier than her "straight" (heterosexual) sisters about the essential aloneness of life (which the myth of marriage obscures). For she is caught somewhere between accepting society's view of her—in which case she cannot accept herself, and coming to understand what this sexist society has done to her and why it is functional and necessary for it to do so. Those of us who work that through find ourselves on the other side of a tortuous journey through a night that may have been decades long. The perspective gained from that journey, the liberation of self, the inner peace, the real love of self and of all women, is something to be shared with all women—because we are all women.

It should first be understood that lesbianism, like male homosexuality, is a category of behaviour possible only in a sexist society characterized by rigid sex roles and dominated by male supremacy. Those sex roles dehumanize women by defining us as a supportive/serving caste *in relation to* the master caste of men, and emotionally cripple men by demanding that they be alienated from their own bodies and emotions in order to perform their economic/political/military functions effectively. Homosexuality is a by-product of a particular way of setting up roles (or approved patterns of behaviour) on the basis of sex; as such it is an inauthentic (not consonant with "reality") category. In a society in which men do not oppress women, and sexual expression is allowed to follow feelings, the categories of homosexuality and heterosexuality would disappear.

But lesbianism is also different from male homosexuality, and serves a different function in the society. "Dyke" is a different kind of put-down from "faggot," although both imply you are not playing your socially assigned sex role—are not therefore a "real woman" or a "real man." The grudging admiration felt for the tomboy, and the queasiness felt around a sissy boy point to the same thing: the contempt in which women—or those who play a female role—are held. And the investment in keeping women in that contemptuous role is very great. Lesbian is the word, the label, the condition that holds women in line. When a woman hears this word tossed her way, she knows she is stepping out of line.

Lesbian is a label invented by the Man to throw at any woman who dares to be his equal, who dares to challenge his prerogatives, who dares to assert the primacy of her own needs. To have the label applied to people active in women's liberation is just the most recent instance of a long history; older women will recall that not so long ago, any woman who was successful, independent, not orienting her whole life about a man, would hear this word. For in this sexist society, for a woman to be independent means she *can't be* a woman—she must be a dyke. It says as clearly as can be said: Woman and person are contradictory terms.

And yet, in popular thinking, there is really only one essential difference between a lesbian and other women: that of sexual orientation—which is to say, when you strip off all the packaging, you must finally realize that the essence of being a "woman" is to get fucked by men.

"Lesbian" is one of the sexual categories by which men have divided up humanity. For women, especially those in the movement, to perceive their lesbian sisters through this male grid of role definitions is to accept this male cultural conditioning and to oppress their sisters much as they themselves have been oppressed by men. Are we going to continue the male classification system of defining all females in sexual relation to some other category of people? Affixing the label lesbian not only to a woman who aspires to be a person, but also to any situation of real love, real solidarity, real primacy among women is a primary form of divisiveness among women: It is the condition which keeps women within the confines of the feminine role, and it is the debunking/scare term that keeps women from forming any primary attachments, groups, or associations among ourselves.

Women in the movement have in most cases gone to great lengths to avoid discussion and confrontation with the issue of lesbianism. It puts people uptight. They are hostile, evasive, or try to incorporate it into some "broader issue." They would rather not talk about it. If they have to, they try to dismiss it as a "lavender herring." But it is no side issue. It is absolutely essential to the success and fulfillment of the women's liberation movement that this issue be dealt with. As long as the label "dyke" can be used to frighten women into a less militant stand, keep her separate from her sisters, keep her from giving primacy to anything other than men and family—then to that extent she is controlled by the male culture. Until women see in each other the possibility of a primal commitment which includes sexual love, they will be denying themselves the love and value they readily accord to men, thus affirming their second-class status. As long as male acceptability is primary—both to individual women and to the movement as a whole—the term lesbian will be used effectively against women. Insofar as women want only more privileges within the system, they do not want to antagonize male power. They instead seek acceptability for women's liberation, and the most crucial aspect of the acceptability is to deny lesbianism—i.e., deny any fundamental challenge to the basis of the female.

It should also be said that some younger, more radical women have honestly begun to discuss lesbianism, but so far it has been primarily as a sexual "alternative" to men. This, however, is still giving primacy to men, both because the idea of relating more completely to women occurs as a negative reaction to men, and because the lesbian relationship is being characterized simply by sex, which is divisive and sexist. It must be understood that what is crucial is that women begin disengaging from male-defined response patterns in the privacy of our own psyches; we must cut those cords to the core. For irrespective of where our love and sexual energies flow, if we are male-identified in our heads, we cannot realize our autonomy as human beings.

As the source of self-hate and the lack of real self are rooted in our male-given identity, we must create a new sense of self. As long as we cling to the idea of "being a woman," we will sense some conflict with that incipient self, that sense of I, that sense of a whole person. It is very difficult to realize and accept that being "feminine" and being a whole person are irreconcilable. Only women can give to each other a new sense of self. That identity we have to develop with reference to ourselves, and not in relation to men. As long as women's liberation tries to free women without facing the basic heterosexual structure that binds us in one-to-one relationship with our oppressors, tremendous energies will continue to flow into trying to straighten up each particular relationship with a man, how to get better sex, how to turn his head around—into trying to make the "new man" out of him, in the delusion that this will allow us to be the "new woman." This obviously splits our energies and commitments, leaving us unable to be committed to the construction of the new patterns which will liberate us.

It is the primacy of women relating to women, of women creating a new consciousness of and with each other which is at the heart of women's liberation, and the basis for the cultural revolution. Together we must find, reinforce, and validate our authentic selves. As we do this, we confirm in each other that struggling incipient sense of pride and strength, the divisive barriers begin to melt, we feel this growing solidarity with our sisters. We see ourselves as prime, find our centers inside of ourselves. We find receding the sense of alienation, of being cut off, of being behind a locked window, of being unable to get out what we know is inside. We feel a real-ness, feel at last we are coinciding with ourselves. With that real self, with that consciousness, we begin a revolution to end the imposition of all coercive identifications, and to achieve maximum autonomy in human expression.

Pat Mainardi, The Politics of Housework

"The personal is political": this succinct phrase captured much of the agenda of second wave feminism. Individually, and in consciousness-raising groups, women explored the social and political shape of experiences they had understood to be accidental and private. What had been named personal idiosyncrasy turned out to be intentionally shaped by social and economic pressures, by institutional convenience, and most devastatingly, by male selfishness.

No one captured this insight better than Pat Mainardi, whose essay circulated among the New York Redstockings for more than a year before Robin Morgan published it in *Sisterhood is Powerful: An Anthology of Writings from the Women's Liberation Movement* (New York: Random House, 1970), 447-54. Second-wave feminists called for naming the public pressures that shape what is usually treated as "natural" or "personal choice." Mainardi hit a nerve. She captured the way that reshaping women's lives required reshaping men's lives. She named as selfishness actions that most partners and families treated as "normal" and fulfilling.

What elements of Mainardi's 1970 critique still hit home?

> Though women do not complain of the power of husbands, each complains of her own husband, or of the husbands of her friends. It is the same in all other cases of servitude; at least in the commencement of the emancipatory movement. The serfs did not at first complain of the power of the lords, but only of their tyranny.
>
> —John Stuart Mill
> *On the Subjection of Women*

Liberated women—very different from Women's Liberation! The first signals all kinds of goodies, to warm the hearts (not to mention other parts) of the most radical men. The other signals—HOUSEWORK. The first brings sex without marriage, sex before marriage, cozy housekeeping arrangements ("I'm living with this chick") and the self-content of knowing that you're not the kind of man who wants a doormat instead of a woman. That will come later. After all, who wants that old commodity anymore, the Standard American Housewife, all husband, home and kids? The New Commodity; the Liberated Woman, has sex a lot and has a Career, preferably something that

 See Chicago Women's Liberation Union website, http://www.cwluherstory.org/Classic-Feminist-Writings for the full text and other feminist essays of the period.

can be fitted in with the household chores—like dancing, pottery, or painting.

On the other hand is Women's Liberation—and housework. What? You say this is all trivial? Wonderful! That's what I thought. It seemed perfectly reasonable. We both had careers, both had to work a couple of days a week to earn enough to live on, so why shouldn't we share the housework? So I suggested it to my mate and he agreed—most men are too hip to turn you down flat. You're right, he said. It's only fair. Then an interesting thing happened. I can only explain it by stating that we women have been brainwashed more than even we can imagine. Probably too many years of seeing television women in ecstasy over their shiny waxed floors or breaking down over their dirty shirt collars. Men have no such conditioning. They recognize the essential fact of housework right from the very beginning. Which is that it stinks.

Here's my list of dirty chores: buying groceries, carting them home and putting them away; cooking meals and washing dishes and pots; doing the laundry; digging out the place when things get out of control; washing floors. The list could go on but the sheer necessities are bad enough. All of us have to do these things, or get someone else to do them for us. The longer my husband contemplated these chores, the more repulsed he became, and so proceeded the change from the normally sweet, considerate Dr. Jekyll into the crafty Mr. Hyde who would stop at nothing to avoid the horrors of—housework. As he felt himself backed into a corner laden with dirty dishes, brooms, mops and reeking garbage, his front teeth grew longer and pointier, his fingernails haggled and his eyes grew wild. Housework trivial? Not on your life! Just try to share the burden.

So ensued a dialogue that's been going on for several years. Here are some of the high points: "I don't mind sharing the housework, but I don't do it very well. We should each do the things we're best at." MEANING: Unfortunately I'm no good at things like washing dishes or cooking. What I do best is a little light carpentry, changing light bulbs, moving furniture (how often do you move furniture?). ALSO MEANING: Historically the lower classes (black men and us) have had hundreds of years experience doing menial jobs. It would be a waste of manpower to train someone else to do them now. ALSO MEANING: I don't like the dull, stupid, boring jobs, so you should do them.

"I don't mind sharing the work, but you'll have to show me how to do it." MEANING: I ask a lot of questions and you'll have to show me everything every time I do it because I don't remember so good. Also don't try to sit down and read while I'M doing my jobs because I'm going to annoy hell out of you until it's easier to do them yourself.

"We used to be so happy!" (Said whenever it was his turn to do something.) MEANING: I used to be so happy. MEANING: Life without house work is bliss. No quarrel here. Perfect Agreement.

"We have different standards, and why should I have to work to your standards? That's unfair." MEANING: If I begin to get bugged by the dirt and crap I will say, "This place sure is a sty" or "How can anyone live like this?" and wait for your reaction. I know that all women have a sore called "Guilt over a messy house" or "Household work is ultimately my responsibility." I know that men have caused that sore—if anyone visits and the place is a sty—they're not going to leave and say, "He sure is a lousy housekeeper." You'll take the rap in any case. I can outwait you. ALSO MEANING: I can provoke innumerable scenes over the housework issue. Eventually doing all the housework yourself will be less painful to you than trying to get me to do half. Or I'll suggest we get a maid. She will do my share of the work. You will do yours. It's women's work. . . .

"Housework is too trivial to even talk about." MEANING: It's even more trivial to do. Housework is beneath my status. My purpose in life is to deal with matters of significance. Yours is to deal with matters of insignificance. You should do the housework. . .

Participatory democracy begins at home. If you are planning to implement your politics, there are certain things to remember.

1. He is feeling it more than you. He's losing some leisure and you're gaining it. The measure of your oppression is his resistance.
2. A great many American men are not accustomed to doing monotonous, repetitive work which never issues in any lasting, let alone important, achievement. This is why they would rather repair a cabinet than wash dishes. If human endeavors are like a pyramid with man's highest achievements at the

top, then keeping oneself alive is at the bottom. Men have always had servants (us) to take care of this bottom stratum of life while they have confined their efforts to the rarefied upper regions. It is thus ironic when they ask of women—Where are your great painters, statesmen, etc.? Mme. Matisse ran a millinery shop so he could paint. Mrs. Martin Luther King kept his house and raised his babies.

3. It is a traumatizing experience for someone who has always thought of himself as being against any oppression or exploitation of one human being by another to realize that in his daily life he has been accepting and implementing (and benefiting from) this exploitation; that his rationalization is little different from that of the racist who says, "Black people don't feel pain" (women don't mind doing the shitwork); and that the oldest form of oppression in history has been the oppression of 50 percent of the population by the other 50 percent.
4. Arm yourself with some knowledge of the psychology of oppressed peoples everywhere, and a few facts about the animal kingdom. I admit playing top wolf or who runs the gorillas is silly but as a last resort men bring it up all the time. Talk about bees. If you feel really hostile bring up the sex life of spiders. They have sex. She bites off his head. The psychology of oppressed peoples is not silly. Jews, immigrants, black men and all women have employed the same psychological mechanisms to survive: admiring the oppressor, glorifying the oppressor, wanting to be like the oppressor, wanting the oppressor to like them, mostly because the oppressor held all the power. . . .
5. In a sense, all men everywhere are slightly schizoid—divorced from the reality of maintaining life. This makes it easier for them to play games with it. It is almost a cliché that women feel greater grief at sending a son off to a war or losing him to that war because they bore him, suckled him, and raised him. The men who foment those wars did none of those things and have a more superficial estimate of the worth of human life. One hour a day is a low estimate of the amount of time one has to spend "keeping" oneself. By foisting this off on others, man has seven hours a week—one working day more to play with his mind and not his human needs. Over the course of generations it is easy to see whence evolved the horrifying abstractions of modern life. . . .
6. Keep checking up. Periodically consider who's actually doing the jobs. These things have a way of backsliding so that a year later once again the woman is doing everything. After a year make a list of jobs the man has rarely if ever done. You will find cleaning pots, toilets, refrigerators and ovens high on the list. Use time sheets if necessary. He will accuse you of being petty. He is above that sort of thing (housework). Bear in mind what the worst jobs are, namely the ones that have to be done every day or several times a day. Also the ones that are dirty—it's more pleasant to pick up books, newspapers, etc., than to wash dishes. Alternate the bad jobs. It's the daily grind that gets you down. Also make sure that you don't have the responsibility for the housework with occasional help from him. "I'll cook dinner for you tonight" implies it's really your job and isn't he a nice guy to do some of it for you.
7. Most men had a rich and rewarding bachelor life during which they did not starve or become encrusted with crud or buried under the liner. There is a taboo that says women mustn't strain themselves in the presence of men—we haul around 50 pounds of groceries if we have to but aren't allowed to open a jar if there is someone around to do it for us. The reverse side of the coin is that men aren't supposed to be able to take care of themselves without a woman. Both are excuses for making women do the housework.

I was just finishing this when my husband came in and asked what I was doing. Writing a paper on housework. Housework? he said. Housework? Oh my god how trivial can you get? A paper on housework.

Jennie V. Chavez, "It has taken . . . a long time . . . to realize and speak out about the double oppression of Mexican-American women"

Jennie Chavez, like thousands of young women of color, joined liberation movements in the 1960s and 1970s. In this account of her experience in the Chicano movement, Chavez describes the resistance she faced when, recognizing the double oppression of Mexican American women, she organized "Las Chicanas." Incipient feminists, these women of color recognized early on that gender was not the only factor subordinating women. What insights does she have into power relationships between Mexican Americans and Anglos as well as between men and women within her own ethnic group? Note her disdain for the consumer goods that signal middle-class status. What evidence is there to suggest that Chavez and her Chicana generation had been affected by the sexual revolution of the 1960s? How did males in the movement respond to women asserting themselves? To what does Chavez attribute their machismo? Note the links between Chavez's La Familia and Vicki Ruiz's insights into the family oligarchy experienced by teenagers in the Southwest earlier in the century (pp. 477–484).

As one of the first members of the United Mexican American Students [UMAS] when it got started in 1969 on the UNM [University of New Mexico] campus, I was given special attention, being fairly attractive and flirtatious. But as soon as I started expounding my own ideas the men who ran the organization would either ignore my statement or make a wisecrack about it and continue their own discussion. This continued for two years until I finally broke away because of being unable to handle the situation. I turned to student government. There I was considered a radical racist Mexican militant, yet with the Chicano radicals I was considered a sellout. I was caught in the middle, wanting to help but with neither side allowing me.

The summer of 1970, after the Cambodia crisis, I traveled extensively, "getting my head together," [and formed] Las Chicanas the following December. [The result was that I] caught more shit than I knew existed from both males and females in the movement. Some felt I was dividing the existing UMAS; some were simply afraid of displeasing the men. Some felt that I was wrong and my ideas were "white," and still others felt that their contribution to La Causa or El Movimiento was in giving the men moral support from the kitchen. It took two months of heartbreak on both sides for the organization to be recognized as valid. Now, however, because a few women were willing to stand strong against some of the macho men who ridiculed them, called them white and avoided them socially, the organization has become one of the strongest and best-known in the state.

It has taken what I consider a long time for [Chicanas] to realize and to speak out about the double oppression of the Mexican-American woman. Chicanas traditionally, have been tortilla-makers, baby-producers, to be touched but not heard. In order to someday obtain those middle-class goods (which in my eyes oppress more people than they liberate from "drudgery") our women have not only been working at slave jobs for the white society as housemaids, hotel maids and laundry workers, but have tended also to the wants of a husband and many children—

Excerpted from "Women of the Mexican American Movement" by Jennie V. Chavez, in *Chicana Feminist Thought: The Basic Historical Writings*, ed. Alma M. Garcia (New York: Routledge, 1998), pp. 36–39.

many children because contraceptives have been contrary to the ethnic idea of La Familia (with all its socio-political economic implications).

As the social revolution for all people's freedoms has progressed, so Chicanas have caught the essence of freedom in the air. The change occurred slowly. Mexican-American women have been reluctant to speak up, afraid that they might show up the men in front of the white man—afraid that they may think our men not men. Now, however, the Chicana is becoming as well-educated and as aware of oppression, if not more so, as the Mexican-American male.

The women are changing their puritanical mode of dress, entering the professions of law, business, medicine and engineering. They are no longer afraid to show their intellect, their capabilities and their potential. More and more they oppose the Catholic Church, to which a large majority of our ethnic group belongs, challenging its sexual taboos as well as the idea that all Catholic mothers must be baby-producing factories, and that contraceptives are a sin.

Out of the workshop on "Sex and La Chicana" at the first National Mujeres Por la Raza conference in Houston, Texas came the following resolutions:

(1) that Chicanas should develop a more healthy attitude toward sex and get rid of the misconceptions about its "evil," thus allowing ourselves to be as aggressive as men; (2) that we object to the use of sex as a means of exploiting women and for commercial purposes; (3) that no religious institution should have the authority to sanction what is moral or immoral between a man and a woman.

As the new breed of Mexican-American women, we have been, and probably will continue to be, ridiculed by our men for attempting the acrobatics of equality. We may well be ostracized by La Familia for being vendidos, sell-outs to the "white ideas" of late marriage, postponing or not wanting children and desiring a vocation other than tortilla-rolling, but I believe that this new breed of bronze womanhood, as all women today, will be a vanguard for world change.

Naturally, there are liberated Chicanos who respect and treat women as equals, but they are so few that at this point I still have to generalize. Mexican-American men, as other men of oppressed groups, have been very reluctant to give up their machismo [exaggerated assertion of masculinity] because it has been a last retention of power in a society which dehumanizes and mechanizes them. But now they are comprehending the meaning of carnalismo (brotherhood) in the feminine gender as well . . . a new revolution within a revolution has begun.

"Women in the Asian movement find that . . . stereotypes are still hovering over their heads . . . that [they] must play [the] old role[s] in order to get things done"

Like their Chicana sisters, women in the Asian movement fought against old stereotypes and encountered new ones when they tried to exercise leadership in the Asian movement. They too found that their men were prone to male chauvinism and that as women they had to deal with racism, sexism, and imperialism, and deal with them simultaneously.

On the basis of this document (first published in 1971), compare the stereotypes that exist about women of both ethnic groups in the larger culture. What vision of the future and what strategies do the anonymous authors advocate?

ASIAN WOMEN AS LEADERS

American society is broken up into different levels based on economic income, education, politics, color, and sex. Each level has a prescribed set of rules for action and interplay—roles that are enforced by the levels above. At the bottom of these varying gradations are women of color. Third World women face domination by both racism and sexism (discrimination based on sex). Both racism and sexism are means by which American society controls and oppresses everyone. Everyone is forced to conform to the values and roles established by the dominant group in order to "succeed." For the Asian movement to progress, it must have a clear understanding of sexism, racism, and imperialism; and deal with them simultaneously.

For Asian women in general, the stereotypes or roles have been of two major kinds: either docile, submissive Oriental dolls who will cater to the whims of any man; or the Suzie Wong, sexpot, exotic bitch-body. Between these two are the efficient secretary, sexy stewardess, the good housekeeper and domestic, the girl any guy would like to marry.

Women in the Asian movement find that these stereotypes are still hovering over their heads. Not only these but new stereotypes, too: i.e., Asian men have tried to define for "their women" what it means to be "heavy." Men in the Asian movement also find themselves tied down to stereotypes. Perhaps they may feel that to be a MAN one must have authority and responsibility. In the same light, they will frown on women who take on a lot of responsibility (and the authority that goes along with it), labelling them as "unfeminine." Women then tend to fear this loss of "femininity" and so they do the clerical work and the cleaning up, activities for which intellect is not essential or expected. Women may also fulfill these jobs because they do them best: And why do they do them the best? Because women are never encouraged to do anything else; women's potential abilities as a leader are left untapped and undeveloped. She loses her confidence in being able to handle such responsibility.

The sisters who have achieved a position of authority in the movement are a minority and are still trapped by the stereotypes that society has created. It is a struggle for women to attain the top leadership positions. Women who "make it" into such positions have had to reject the stereotypes already imposed upon them. But because the new definition of "the Asian woman" has not yet evolved, women find themselves in a "limbo." Some find themselves being labelled as Bitches—women who speak out loudly and strongly; who are authoritarian, who boss people around, and command some form of respect. Some must resort to being overly diligent and efficient to prove themselves as worthy of the same leadership positions as the men. Others gain respect by appearing to accomplish work in a multitude of projects but actually only complete a few tasks. And still others attain their leadership positions as token gestures. Some women can gain respect only by putting up with put-downs on other women, i.e., "you're not one of those bird-brained little girls," or "You're as strong as a man!"

Once women do get into leadership positions, they find that their ideas are usurped by the men, who then take credit for the idea as being their own. Women are often heard but not listened to. Many times, the woman must play her old role in order to get things done: "Oh, please, can you help me carry this. It's much too heavy for little old me. . . ."

How can these problems be solved? People must recognize that women are half of the working force in the movement against oppression, exploitation, and imperialism. They are half of the working force in creating the new revolutionary lifestyle. Men and women in the movement must therefore begin to live the ideals and goals they are working for. To do this, they must not let chauvinist acts slide by. People cannot work together effectively if there are hidden tensions or if people let little annoyances build up inside themselves. They must deal with racism or imperialism. They must be able to develop as human beings, not subject to categorizations and stereotypes. Developing as people confident in themselves, in their ideas, they will not be afraid of criticism; they will see the need for criticism, and self-criticism, in order to move forward. The struggle is not men against women nor women against men, but it is a united front striving for a new society, a new way of life.

If I go forward,
Follow me.
Push me if I fall behind.
If I betray you,
If they take me,
Avenge me then in kind.

The Combahee River Collective, "We also find it difficult to separate race from class from sex oppression"

The Combahee River Collective, a black feminist group founded in Boston in 1974, took its name from a guerrilla action planned and led by Harriet Tubman during the Civil War that freed more than 750 South Carolina slaves. The group, which consisted of battle-scarred veterans of the civil rights, New Left, and early women's movements, had done some hard thinking before writing this statement. In it, they stated what they believed to be the limitations of their white feminist sisters as well as their own problems in organizing black feminists.

What were the Collective's specific criticisms of other feminists—radical, liberal, as well as lesbian separatists? Why did they think that black feminism was (and is) so threatening to the black community, especially to black males who identified with black nationalism? What do you regard as their most important insights?

We are a collective of Black feminists who have been meeting together since 1974. During that time we have been involved in the process of defining and clarifying our politics, while at the same time doing political work within our own group and in coalition with other progressive organizations and movements. The most general statement of our politics at the present time would be that we are actively committed to struggling against racial, sexual, heterosexual, and class oppression, and see as our particular task the development of integrated analysis and practice based upon the fact that the major systems of oppression are interlocking. The synthesis of these oppressions creates the conditions of our lives. As Black women we see Black feminism as the logical political movement to combat the manifold and simultaneous oppressions that all women of color face. . . .

1. THE GENESIS OF CONTEMPORARY BLACK FEMINISM

Before looking at the recent development of Black feminism, we would like to affirm that we find our origins in the historical reality of Afro-American women's continuous life-and-death struggle for survival and liberation. Black women's extremely negative relation-

Excerpts from The Combahee River Collective Statement in *Home Girls: A Black Feminist Anthology*, ed. Barbara Smith (Latham, N. Y.: Kitchen Table: Women of Color Press, 1983), pp. 272–82. Reprinted by permission of Barbara Smith.

ship to the American political system (a system of white male rule) has always been determined by our membership in two oppressed racial and sexual castes. As Angela Davis points out in "Reflections on the Black Woman's Role in the Community of Slaves," Black women have always embodied, if only in their physical manifestation, an adversary stance to white male rule and have actively resisted its inroads upon them and their communities in both dramatic and subtle ways. There have always been Black women activists—some known, like Sojourner Truth, Harriet Tubman, Frances E. W. Harper, Ida B. Wells Barnett, and Mary Church Terrell, and thousands upon thousands unknown—who have had a shared awareness of how their sexual identity combined with their racial identity to make their whole life situation and the focus of their political struggles unique. Contemporary Black feminism is the outgrowth of countless generations of personal sacrifice, militancy, and work by our mothers and sisters.

A Black feminist presence has evolved most obviously in connection with the second wave of the American women's movement beginning in the late 1960s. Black, other Third World, and working women have been involved in the feminist movement from its start, but both outside reactionary forces and racism and elitism within the movement itself have served to obscure our participation. In 1973, Black feminists, primarily located in New York, felt the necessity of forming a separate Black feminist group. This became the National Black Feminist Organization (NBFO).

Black feminist politics also have an obvious connection to movements for Black liberation, particularly those of the 1960s and 1970s. Many of us were active in those movements (Civil Rights, Black nationalism, the Black Panthers), and all of our lives were greatly affected and changed by their ideologies, their goals, and the tactics used to achieve their goals. It was our experience and disillusionment within these liberation movements, as well as experience on the periphery of the white male left, that led to the need to develop a politics that was anti-racist, unlike those of white women, and anti-sexist, unlike those of Black and white men.

There is also undeniably a personal genesis for Black feminism, that is, the political realization that comes from the seemingly personal experiences of individual Black women's lives. Black feminists and many more Black women who do not define themselves as feminists have all experienced sexual oppression as a constant factor in our day-to-day existence. As children we realized that we were different from boys and that we were treated differently. For example, we were told in the same breath to be quiet both for the sake of being "ladylike" and to make us less objectionable in the eyes of white people. As we grew older we became aware of the threat of physical and sexual abuse by men. However, we had no way of conceptualizing what was so apparent to us, what we *knew* was really happening.

Black feminists often talk about their feelings of craziness before becoming conscious of the concepts of sexual politics, patriarchal rule, and most importantly, feminism, the political analysis and practice that we women use to struggle against our oppression. The fact that racial politics and indeed racism are pervasive factors in our lives did not allow us, and still does not allow most Black women, to look more deeply into our own experiences and, from that sharing and growing consciousness, to build a politics that will change our lives and inevitably end our oppression. Our development must also be tied to the contemporary economic and political position of Black people. The post–World War II generation of Black youth was the first to be able to minimally partake of certain educational and employment options, previously closed completely to Black people. Although our economic position is still at the very bottom of the American capitalistic economy, a handful of us have been able to gain certain tools as a result of tokenism in education and employment which potentially enable us to more effectively fight our oppression.

A combined anti-racist and anti-sexist position drew us together initially, and as we developed politically we addressed ourselves to heterosexism and economic oppression under capitalism.

2. WHAT WE BELIEVE

Above all else, our politics initially sprang from the shared belief that Black women are inherently valuable, that our liberation is a necessity not as an adjunct to somebody else's but because of our need as human persons for autonomy. This may seem so obvious as to sound simplistic, but it is apparent that no other ostensibly progressive movement has ever considered our specific oppression as a priority or worked seriously for the ending of that oppression. Merely naming the pejorative stereotypes attributed to Black women (e.g., mammy, matriarch, Sapphire, whore, bulldagger), let alone cataloguing the cruel, often murderous, treatment we receive, indicates how little value has been placed upon our lives during four centuries of bondage in the Western hemisphere. We realize that the only people who care enough about us to work consistently for our liberation are us. Our politics evolve from a healthy love for ourselves, our sisters, and our community, which allows us to continue our struggle and work.

This focusing upon our own oppression is embodied in the concept of identity politics. We believe that the most profound and potentially most radical politics come directly out of our own identity, as opposed to working to end somebody else's oppression. In the case of Black women this is a particularly repugnant, dangerous, threatening, and therefore revolutionary concept because it is obvious from looking at all the political movements that have preceded us that anyone is more worthy of liberation than ourselves. We reject pedestals, queenhood, and walking ten paces behind. To be recognized as human, levelly human, is enough.

We believe that sexual politics under patriarchy is as pervasive in Black women's lives as are the politics of class and race. We also often find it difficult to separate race from class from sex oppression because in our lives they are most often experienced simultaneously. We know that there is such a thing as racial-sexual oppression which is neither solely racial nor solely sexual, e.g., the history of rape of Black women by white men as a weapon of political repression.

Although we are feminists and Lesbians, we feel solidarity with progressive Black men and do not advocate the fractionalization that white women who are separatists demand. Our situation as Black people necessitates that we have solidarity around the fact of race, which white women of course do not need to have with white men, unless it is their negative solidarity as racial oppressors. We struggle together with Black men against racism, while we also struggle with Black men about sexism.

We realize that the liberation of all oppressed peoples necessitates the destruction of the political-economic systems of capitalism and imperialism as well as patriarchy. We are socialists because we believe that work must be organized for the collective benefit of those who do the work and create the products, and not for the profit of the bosses. Material resources must be equally distributed among those who create these resources. We are not convinced, however, that a socialist revolution that is not also a feminist and anti-racist revolution will guarantee our liberation. We have arrived at the necessity for developing an understanding of class relationships that takes into account the specific class position of Black women who are generally marginal in the labor force, while at this particular time some of us are temporarily viewed as doubly desirable tokens at white-collar and professional levels. We need to articulate the real class situation of persons who are not merely raceless, sexless workers, but for whom racial and sexual oppression are significant determinants in their working/economic lives. Although we are in essential agreement with Marx's theory as it applied to the very specific economic relationships he analyzed, we know that his analysis must be extended further in order for us to understand our specific economic situation as Black women.

A political contribution which we feel we have already made is the expansion of the feminist principle that the personal is political. In our consciousness-raising sessions, for example, we have in many ways gone beyond white women's revelations because we are dealing with the implications of race and class as well as sex. Even our Black women's style of talking/testifying in Black language about what we have experienced has a resonance that is both cultural and political. We have spent a great deal of energy delving into the cultural and experiential nature of our oppression out of necessity because none of these matters has ever been looked at before. No one before has ever examined the multilayered texture of Black women's lives. An example of this kind of revelation/conceptualization occurred at a meeting as we discussed the ways in which our early intellectual interests had been attacked by our peers, particularly Black males. We discovered that all of us, because we were "smart" had also been considered "ugly," i.e., "smart-ugly." "Smart-ugly" crystallized the way in which most of us had been forced to develop our intellects at great cost to our "social" lives. The sanctions in the Black and white communities against Black women thinkers is comparatively much higher than for white women, particularly ones from the educated middle and upper classes.

As we have already stated, we reject the stance of Lesbian separatism because it is not a viable political analysis or strategy for us. It leaves out far too much and far too many people, particularly Black men, women, and children. We have a great deal of criticism and loathing for what men have been socialized to be in this society: what they support, how they act, and how they oppress. But we do not have the misguided notion that it is their maleness, per se—i.e., their biological maleness—that makes them what they are. As Black women we find any type of biological determinism a particularly dangerous and reactionary basis upon which to build a politic. We must also question whether Lesbian separatism is an adequate and progressive political analysis and strategy, even for those who practice it, since it so completely denies any but the sexual sources of women's oppression, negating the facts of class and race.

3. PROBLEMS IN ORGANIZING BLACK FEMINISTS

During our years together as a Black feminist collective, we have experienced success and defeat, joy and pain, victory and failure. We have found that it is very difficult to organize around Black feminist issues, difficult even to announce in certain contexts that we *are* Black feminists. We have tried to think about the reasons for our difficulties, particularly since the white women's movement continues to be strong and to grow in many directions. In this section we will discuss some of the general reasons for the organizing problems we face and also talk specifically about the stages in organizing our own collective.

The major source of difficulty in our political work is that we are not just trying to fight oppression on one front, or even two, but instead to address a whole range of oppressions. We do not have racial, sexual, heterosexual, or class privilege to rely upon, nor do we have even the minimal access to resources and power that groups who possess any one of these types of privilege have.

The psychological toll of being a Black woman and the difficulties this presents in reaching political consciousness and doing political work can never be underestimated. There is very low value placed upon Black women's psyches in this society, which is both racist and sexist. As an early group member once said, "We are all damaged people merely by virtue of being Black women." We are dispossessed psychologically and on every other level, and yet we feel the necessity to struggle to change the condition of all Black women. In "A Black Feminist's Search for Sisterhood," Michele Wallace arrives at this conclusion:

> We exist as women who are Black who are feminists, each stranded for the moment, working independently because there is not yet an environment in this society remotely congenial to our struggle—because, being on the bottom, we would have to do what no one else has done: We would have to fight the world.[1]

Wallace is pessimistic but realistic in her assessment of Black feminists' position, particularly in her allusion to the nearly classic isolation most of us face. We might use our position at the bottom, however, to make a clear leap into revolutionary action. If Black women were free, it would mean that everyone else would have to be free, since our freedom would necessitate the destruction of all the systems of oppression.

Feminism is, nevertheless, very threatening to the majority of Black people because it calls into question some of the most basic assumptions about our existence, i.e., that sex should be a determinant of power relationships. Here is the way male and female roles were defined in a Black nationalist pamphlet from the early 1970s:

> . . . The man is the head of the house. He is the leader of the house/nation because his knowledge of the world is broader, his awareness is greater, his understanding is fuller and his application of this information is wiser. . . . Women cannot do the same things as men—they are made by nature to function differently. Equality of men and women is something that cannot happen even in the abstract world.[2] . . .

The material conditions of most Black women would hardly lead them to upset both economic and sexual arrangements that seem to represent some stability in their lives. Many Black women have a good understanding of both sexism and racism, but because of the everyday constrictions of their lives, cannot risk struggling against them both.

The reaction of Black men to feminism has been notoriously negative. They are, of course, even more threatened than Black women by the possibility that Black feminists might organize around our own needs. They realize that they might not only lose valuable and hardworking allies in their struggles but that they might also be forced to change their habitually sexist ways of interacting with and oppressing Black women. Accusations that Black feminism divides the Black struggle are powerful deterrents to the growth of an autonomous Black women's movement. . . .

4. BLACK FEMINIST ISSUES AND PROJECTS

During our time together we have identified and worked on many issues of particular relevance to Black women. The inclusiveness of our politics makes us concerned with any situation that impinges upon the lives of women, Third World, and working people. We are of course particularly committed to working on those struggles in which race, sex, and class are simultaneous factors in oppression. We might, for example, become involved in workplace organizing at a factory that employs Third World women or picket a hospital that is cutting back on already inadequate health care to a Third World community, or set up a rape crisis center in a Black neighborhood. Organizing around welfare and daycare concerns might also be a focus. The work to be done and the countless issues that this work represents merely reflect the pervasiveness of our oppression.

Issues and projects that collective members have actually worked on are sterilization abuse, abortion rights, battered women, rape, and health care. We have also done many workshops and educationals on Black feminism on college campuses, at women's conferences, and most recently for high school women.

One issue that is of major concern to us and that we have begun to publicly address is racism in the white women's movement. As Black feminists we are made constantly and painfully aware of how little effort white women have made to understand and combat their racism, which requires among other things that they have a more than superficial comprehension of race, color, and Black history and culture. Eliminating racism in the white women's movement is by definition work for white women to do, but we will continue to speak to and demand accountability on this issue.

In the practice of our politics we do not believe that the end always justifies the means. Many reactionary and destructive acts have been done in the name of achieving "correct" political goals. As feminists we do not want to mess over people in the name of politics. We believe in collective process and a nonhierarchical distribution of power within our own group and in our vision of a revolutionary society. We are committed to a continual examination of our politics as they develop through criticism and self-criticism as an essential aspect of our practice. . . .

As Black feminists and Lesbians we know that we have a very definite revolutionary task to perform and we are ready for the lifetime of work and struggle before us.

Notes

1. Michele Wallace, "A Black Feminist's Search for Sisterhood," *Village Voice*, July 28, 1975, pp. 6–7.

2. Mumininas of Committee for Unified Newark, Mwanamke Mwananchi (The Nationalist Woman), Newark, NJ, 1971, pp. 4–5.

Kay Weiss, "One of the cruelest forms of sexism we live with today is . . . [that] of many doctors"

Critiques of physicians came not only from female patients and medical students, but also from health care workers at every level. Gynecologists and obstetricians who treated women on matters relating to sexual activity, abortion, and childbirth received the severest scrutiny. Many were patronizing, moralistic, and infantilizing in their treatment of female patients. Critics emphasized that the problem was not just the personal shortcomings of individual doctors. Nor was it merely the result of their training. At the heart of the problem was a fundamental devaluation of women that led physicians to feel that it was their responsibility to make health care decisions for their female patients, since women were simply not competent to participate in informed decisions regarding their own health. Medical scientists under the imprimatur of the National Institutes of Health, operating under their own masculinist bias, tested drugs on men and mistakenly assumed the results would apply to women, whom they didn't bother to include in the tests.

Many of these early critiques, like the one that follows, were published and distributed through women's movement networks. In calling for women to take greater responsibility for their own health care, they were forerunners of the classic *Our Bodies, Ourselves.* The book had its origins in 1969 in the discussion of a small group of Boston women who felt frustrated about doctors whom they considered "condescending, paternalistic, judgmental, and non-informative."* (On your next trip to a bookstore, take a look at the book's most recent edition, *Our Bodies, Ourselves for the New Century*, and try to imagine what it would have been like to encounter the text and illustration in the chapters on sexuality and birth control in 1971.)

While these early indictments, including the one that follows, may have verged on exaggeration, they also provide a window into psychotherapy in the age of the feminine mystique. It should come as no surprise that feminists would challenge a sexist psychiatric and psychological establishment that recommended treatment for any woman who displayed mental and physical symptoms suggesting she was not behaving as a "mature adult" who found sexual fulfillment in vaginally induced orgasm and personal fulfillment in marriage and maternity.

In your own experience with the medical community, have most of the problems about which young women complained a quarter of a century ago been remedied as both sexes have come to take greater responsibility for their medical treatment and as more physicians are women? What vestiges linger?

*The Boston Women's Health Book Collective, *The New Our Bodies, Ourselves* (New York: Simon & Schuster, 1984), quoted from the preface of the original edition, xvii.

Kay Weiss, "What Medical Students Learn," KNOW pamphlet #310, Pittsburgh; reprinted in *Dear Sisters: Dispatches from the Women's Liberation Movement,* ed. Rosalyn Baxandall and Linda Gordon (New York: Basic Books, 2000).

One of the cruelest forms of sexism we live with today is the unwillingness of many doctors to diagnose people's diseases with equality. The education of doctors can explain this. [Consider the messages in] the recently revised text *Obstetrics and Gynecology* (1971, 4th edition), which is used this year [1975] in 60 of the nation's medical schools.

SHE'S A CHILD

In *Obstetrics and Gynecology*, women are childlike, helpless creatures with animal-like or "instinctive" natures, who can't get through intercourse, pregnancy, labor or child-raising without "enlightened" physician intervention. The woman in childbirth is just a child herself. Her doctor, even if he is a novice and she is an old pro, is a fount of knowledge while she is "anxious," "fearful," afraid of "getting messy" and may feel "ashamed" and "guilty." The medical student is taught to believe that many symptoms of illness in pregnancy (excessive nausea, headache) are really a result of her "fear of pregnancy" rather than any physical condition he (all medical students and physicians are "he" in *Obstetrics and Gynecology*) need test for. . . .

SHE LOVES RAPE

Many gynecology texts reveal a greater concern with the patient's husband than with the patient herself and tend to maintain sex-role stereotypes in the interest of men and from a male perspective. But *Obstetrics and Gynecology* clearly spells out the attitudes that other texts only imply:

> The normal sexual act . . . entails a masochistic surrender to the man . . . there is always an element of rape.
>
> The traits that compose the core of the female personality are feminine narcissism, masochism, and passivity.
>
> Every phase of a woman's life is influenced by narcissism. Women then love in a different way from men. The woman falls in love with the idea of being loved; whereas the man loves an object for the pleasure it will give. She says, "I am valuable, important, etc. because he loves me. . . ." This type of narcissism finds expression in . . . her interest in clothes, personal appearance, and beauty. Too much feminine narcissism without masochism produces a self-centered woman.
>
> The idea of suffering is an essential part of her life.

SHE FEELS LIKE AN ANIMAL

Women are described in the text alternately as psychopathic and idiotic: "She is likely to feel that she is animal-like . . . to think of the vagina as a 'dirty cavity.' Black patients will think that the source of sexual desires is in the uterus; white patients think that it is in the ovaries. . . . Orgasm represents the woman's ability to accent her own feminine role in life. . . . Menstruation symbolizes her role in life. . . ."

The medical student is persuaded by the authors that women with dysmenorrhea (menstrual dysfunctions including painful uterine contractions) have no organic disease they need test for; these women simply have "personality disorders," "emotional difficulty in the home," or "neurotic predispositions." They need "sex education" and "mental hygiene" . . . if not "intensive psychotherapy." . . . A brief concession is made to the possible physical causes for menstrual pain, but the authors then quickly return to the problem of diagnosis:

> It is important to ascertain how crippling the symptom and how much emotional gain the patient is deriving from it. For example, does the whole household revolve around whether or not the mother is having menstrual cramps? . . .
>
> The adult woman who presents this symptom very often is resentful of the feminine role. Each succeeding period reminds her of the unpleasant fact that she is a woman. . . .

SHE NEEDS A PSYCHIATRIST

. . . Frigidity is defined as "occasional failure to obtain orgasm," placing 99 percent of women in the category of abnormal. If pleasure is only felt from clitoral stimulation, she may be referred to a psychiatrist. . . . Her frigidity may develop because she "resents her husband's preoccupation with his work or his recreational activities." The physician, a "parental figure," should "discover the problem in the patient's personality" and "encourage her to mature sexually."

Twenty-seven gynecology texts written over the past three decades were reviewed by Diana Scully and Pauline Bart in the *American*

Journal of Sociology in January 1973. . . . No text Scully and Bart examined incorporated Kinsey's 1953 findings that orgasm without stimulation "is a physical and physiological impossibility for nearly all females" or Masters and Johnson's 1966 findings that portions of the vagina have no nerve endings and lack sensation and that although orgasm is felt in the vagina, the feeling derives from stimulation of clitoral nerves.

With doctors like these for friends, who needs enemies?

Phyllis Schlafly, "The thoughts of one who loves life as a woman . . ."

Not all well-educated, white middle-class family women with energy and ability to spare reacted to the resurgent domesticity of the cold war years as did Betty Goldstein Friedan, whose book excerpt is the first selection in this document cluster. Phyllis Stewart Schlafly is a case in point. The two had much in common. Separated in age by only three years, both were the first child born to their respective families, the Goldsteins, who were Jewish, and the Stewarts, who were Roman Catholic. Both grew up during the Depression years in Illinois and were valedictorians of their high school classes. Both attended women's colleges, Goldstein choosing prestigious Smith College in Massachusetts and Stewart attending College of the Sacred Heart in Maryville, Illinois, before transferring to Washington University in St. Louis. Excelling in college, both entered graduate school, Goldstein studying for an M.A. in psychology at the University of California, Berkeley, Stewart earning an M.A. in political science at Radcliffe College and Harvard University. (She would later return to Washington University for a law degree.)

Both went on to interesting jobs, Stewart as a congressional researcher in Washington, Goldstein as a journalist in New York City. Both subsequently married, Stewart choosing John Fred Schlafly, Jr., a lawyer and fellow conservative, and Goldstein choosing Carl Friedan, a theatrical producer and later an advertising executive. Both women had children, Schlafly six and Friedan three, whom they reared in suburbia along with the millions of other middle-class families caught up in the resurgent domesticity of the postwar years.

Energetic and intelligent, neither found domesticity sufficient. Friedan continued to write, as did Schlafly, who also became a community volunteer, Republican Party activist, and, in 1952, a congressional candidate, winning her primary but losing in the general election. In the early 1960s, both published first books that became best-sellers— Friedan *The Feminine Mystique* and Schlafly *A Choice Not an Echo,* a political endorsement of conservative Arizona senator Barry Goldwater, the Republican presidential candidate in 1964.

Yet despite these similarities, the personal became political for these two women in ways that would lead them in sharply divergent directions in the years ahead. Friedan's name would become synonymous with a resurgent feminism, Schlafly's with antifeminism. Friedan, as a founder and the first president of the National Organization for Women (NOW), would champion equal rights for

Excerpted from the preface and "Understanding the Difference" of *The Power of the Positive Woman* by Phyllis Schlafly (New Rochelle, N.Y.: Arlington House Publishers, 1977), pp. 9–28.

women. Schlafly, creator and author of the *Phyllis Schlafly Report*, would devote her extraordinary energy as well as formidable organizational and speaking skills to defeat of the Equal Rights Amendment (ERA) (see p. 719). Equality between the sexes, she insisted, would harm rather than help women.

While Schlafly's states' rights stance partially explains her opposition to using the federal government on behalf of sexual equality, more is involved, as is evident in the following document.

The cry of "women's liberation" leaps out from the "lifestyle" sections of newspapers and the pages of slick magazines, from radio speakers and television screens. Cut loose from past patterns of behavior and expectations, women of all ages are searching for their identity—the college woman who has new alternatives thrust upon her via "women's studies" courses, the young woman whose routine is shattered by a chance encounter with a "consciousness-raising session," the woman in her middle years who suddenly finds herself in the "empty-nest syndrome," the woman of any age whose lover or lifetime partner departs for greener pastures (and a younger crop).

All of these women, thanks to the women's liberation movement, no longer see their predicament in terms of personal problems to be confronted and solved. They see their own difficulties as a little cog in the big machine of establishment restraints and stereotypical injustice in which they have lost their own equilibrium. Who am I? Why am I here? Why am I just another faceless victim of society's oppression, a nameless prisoner behind walls too high for me to climb alone? . . .

For a woman to find her identity in the modern world, the path should be sought from the Positive Women who have found the road and possess the map, rather than from those who have not. In this spirit, I share with you the thoughts of one who loves life as a woman and lives love as a woman, whose credentials are from the school of practical experience, and who has learned that fulfillment as a woman is a journey, not a destination.

Like every human being born into this world, the Positive Woman has her share of sorrows and sufferings, of unfulfilled desires and bitter defeats. But she will never be crushed by life's disappointments, because her positive mental attitude has built her an inner security that the actions of other people can never fracture. To the Positive Woman, her particular set of problems is not a conspiracy against her, but a challenge to her character and her capabilities.

The first requirement for the acquisition of power by the Positive Woman is to understand the differences between men and women. Your outlook on life, your faith, your behavior, your potential for fulfillment, all are determined by the parameters of your original premise. The Positive Woman starts with the assumption that the world is her oyster. She rejoices in the creative capability within her body and the power potential of her mind and spirit. She understands that men and women are different, and that those very differences provide the key to her success as a person and fulfillment as a woman.

The women's liberationist, on the other hand, is imprisoned by her own negative view of herself and of her place in the world around her. . . . Someone—it is not clear who, perhaps God, perhaps the "Establishment," perhaps a conspiracy of male chauvinist pigs—dealt women a foul blow by making them female. It becomes necessary, therefore, for women to agitate and demonstrate and hurl demands on society in order to wrest from an oppressive male-dominated social structure the status that has been wrongfully denied to women through the centuries. . . . Confrontation replaces cooperation as the watchword of all relationships. Women and men become adversaries instead of partners. . . . Within the confines of the women's liberationist ideology, therefore, the abolition of this overriding inequality of women becomes the primary goal.

This goal must be achieved at any and all costs—to the woman herself, to the baby, to the family, and to society. Women must be made equal to men in their ability *not* to become pregnant and *not* to be expected to

Phyllis Schlafly demonstrated the domestic ideal by posing cooking her husband's breakfast the morning after her victory in the 1952 Republican congressional primary. She would lose her bid for a congressional seat but continue to be active as a party volunteer. In 1964, she was a strong supporter of Republican presidential candidate Barry Goldwater, and the author of one of the most effective pieces of his campaign literature, A Choice Not an Echo. *The first printing sold more than 600,000 copies and made her national reputation; there were two more printings before election day. In 1967, she lost her bid for the presidency of the National Federation of Republican Women (NFRW). In the early 1970s, the NFRW endorsed the ERA. Independently, Schlafly mobilized women behind conservative issues like free enterprise and support for nuclear weapons development. When she began to publicize her opposition to the ERA, the circulation of* The Phyllis Schlafly Report *bounced quickly from 3,000 to 35,000 and continued to grow. Her organization, the Eagle Forum, took the lead in developing opposition to the ERA and to feminism generally.* (St. Louis Globe-Democrat *photo. Courtesy of The Collections of the St. Louis Mercantile Library at the University of Missouri–St. Louis. Caption courtesy of Catherine Rymph.)*

care for babies they may bring into the world. This is why women's liberationists are compulsively involved in the drive to make abortion and child-care centers for all women, regardless of religion or income, both socially acceptable and government-financed. . . .

If man is targeted as the enemy, and the ultimate goal of women's liberation is independence from men and the avoidance of pregnancy and its consequences, then lesbianism is logically the highest form in the ritual of women's liberation. . . .

The Positive Woman will never travel that dead-end road. It is self-evident to the Positive Woman that the female body with its baby-producing organs was not designed by a conspiracy of men but by the Divine Architect of the human race. Those who think it is unfair that women have babies, whereas men cannot, will have to take up their complaint with God because no other power is capable of changing that fundamental fact. . . . The Positive Woman looks upon her femaleness and her fertility as part of her purpose, her potential, and her power. She rejoices that she has a capability for creativity that men can never have.

The third basic dogma of the women's liberation movement is that there is no difference between male and female except the sex organs, and that all those physical, cognitive, and emotional differences you *think* are there, are merely the result of centuries of restraints imposed by a male-dominated society and sex-stereotyped schooling. The role imposed on women is, by definition, inferior, according to the women's liberationists. . . .

There are countless physical differences between men and women. The female body is 50 to 60 percent water, the male 60 to 70 percent water, which explains why males can dilute alcohol better than women and delay its effect. The average woman is about 25 percent fatty tissue, while the male is 15 percent, making women more buoyant in water and able to swim with less effort. Males have a tendency to color blindness. Only 5 percent of persons who get gout are female. Boys are born bigger. Women live longer in most countries of the world, not only in the United States where we have a hard-driving competitive pace. Women excel in manual dexterity, verbal skills, and memory recall. . . .

Does the physical advantage of men doom women to a life of servility and subservience? The Positive Woman knows that she has a complementary advantage which is at least as great—and, in the hands of a skillful woman, far greater. The Divine Architect who gave men a superior strength to lift weights also gave women a different kind of superior strength. . . . A Positive Woman cannot defeat a man in a wrestling or boxing match, but she can motivate him, inspire him, encourage him, teach him, restrain him, reward him, and have power over him that he can never achieve over her with all his muscle. How or whether a Positive Woman uses her power is determined solely by the way she alone defines her goals and develops her skills.

The differences between men and women are also emotional and psychological. Without woman's innate maternal instinct, the human race would have died out centuries ago. . . . The overriding psychological need of a woman is to love something alive. A baby fulfills this need in the lives of most women. If a baby is not available to fill that need, women search for a baby-substitute. This is the reason why women have traditionally gone into teaching and nursing careers. They are doing what comes naturally to the female psyche. The schoolchild or the patient of any age provides an outlet for a woman to express her natural maternal need. . . . The Positive Woman finds somebody on whom she can lavish her maternal love so that it doesn't well up inside her and cause psychological frustrations. Surely no woman is so isolated by geography or insulated by spirit that she cannot find someone worthy of her maternal love. . . .

One of the strangest quirks of women's liberationists is their complaint that societal restraints prevent men from crying in public or showing their emotions, but permit women to do so, and that therefore we should "liberate" men to enable them, too, to cry in public. The public display of fear, sorrow, anger, and irritation reveals a lack of self-discipline that should be avoided by the Positive Woman just as much as by the Positive Man. Maternal love, however, is not a weakness but a manifestation of strength and service, and it should be nurtured by the Positive Woman. . . .

Another silliness of the women's liberationists is their frenetic desire to force all women to accept the title *Ms* in place of *Miss* or *Mrs.* If Gloria Steinem and Betty Friedan want to call themselves *Ms* in order to conceal their marital status, their wishes should be respected. But most married women feel they worked hard for the *r* in their names; and they don't care to be gratuitously deprived of it. . . .

Finally, women are different from men in dealing with the fundamentals of life itself. Men are philosophers, women are practical, and 'twas ever thus. Men may philosophize about how life began and where we are heading; women are concerned about feeding the kids today. No woman would ever, as Karl Marx did, spend years reading political philosophy in the British Museum while her child starved to death. Women don't take naturally to a search for the intangible and the abstract. . . . Where man is discursive, logical, abstract, or philosophical, woman tends to be emotional, personal, practical, or mystical. Each set of qualities is vital and complements the other. Among the many differences explained in [Amaury] de Riencourt's book, [*Sex and Power in History*], are the following:

> Women tend more toward conformity than men—which is why they often excel in such disciplines as spelling and punctuation where there is only one correct answer, determined by social authority. Higher intellectual activities, however, require a mental independence and power of abstraction that they usually lack, not to mention a certain form of aggressive boldness of the imagination which can only exist in a sex that is basically aggressive for biological reasons.
>
> To sum up: The masculine proclivity in problem solving is analytical and categorical; the feminine, synthetic and contextual. . . . Deep down, man tends to focus on the object, on external results and achievements; woman focuses on subjective motives and feelings. If life can be compared to a play, man focuses on the theme and structure of the play, woman on the innermost feelings displayed by the actors.

De Riencourt provides impressive refutation of two of the basic errors of the women's liberation movement: (1) that there are no emotional or cognitive differences between the sexes, and (2) that women should strive to be like men. . . . An effort to eliminate the differences by social engineering or legislative or constitutional tinkering cannot succeed, which is fortunate, but social relationships and spiritual values can be ruptured in the attempt. . . .

DOCUMENTS

Dimensions of Citizenship III

Equal Rights Amendment, 1972

An equal rights amendment, with wording slightly different from that passed by Congress in 1972, was sponsored in 1923 by the National Woman's Party. It seemed to party members the logical corollary to suffrage. But that amendment was vigorously opposed by the League of Women Voters and other progressive reformers, lest it undermine the protective legislation for which they had fought so hard. A key question raised was what impact the amendment, if passed, would have on a military draft (see *Rostker* v. *Goldberg*, p. 738).

An equal rights amendment was introduced regularly in Congress virtually every year thereafter, but it received little attention until after World War II. In 1950 and 1953, it was passed by the Senate but ignored by the House.

By 1970 much protective legislation had been applied to both men and women. It was possible to support an equal rights amendment without risking the undoing of labor law reforms. The hope that the Supreme Court would apply the Fourteenth Amendment's "equal protection of the laws" clause to cases involving discrimination on the basis of sex as firmly as it applied the clause to cases involving racial discrimination had not been fulfilled. When the current Equal Rights Amendment was introduced in 1970, it was endorsed by a wide range of organizations, some of which had once opposed it; these organizations included groups as disparate as the United Automobile Workers and the Woman's Christian Temperance Union. Its main sponsor in the House was Martha Griffiths of Michigan; in the Senate, Birch Bayh of Indiana.

The ERA was passed by Congress on March 22, 1972, and sent to the states for ratification. There was much initial enthusiasm; within two days six states had ratified. But the pace of ratification slowed after 1975, and only thirty-five of the needed thirty-eight states had ratified it by 1978. (Four state legislatures voted to rescind ratification, although the legality of that move was open to question.) In October 1978 Congress extended the deadline for ratification to June 30, 1982; the extension expired with no additional ratifications. The amendment was reintroduced in Congress in 1983 but has not been passed. Compare the language here to that of the Fifteenth Amendment (p. 309) and Title VII of the 1964 Civil Rights Act (pp. 650–651).

Section 1. Equality of rights under the law shall not be denied or abridged by the United States or by any State on account of sex.

Section 2. The Congress shall have the power to enforce, by appropriate legislation, the provisions of this article.

Section 3. The amendment shall take effect two years after the date of ratification.

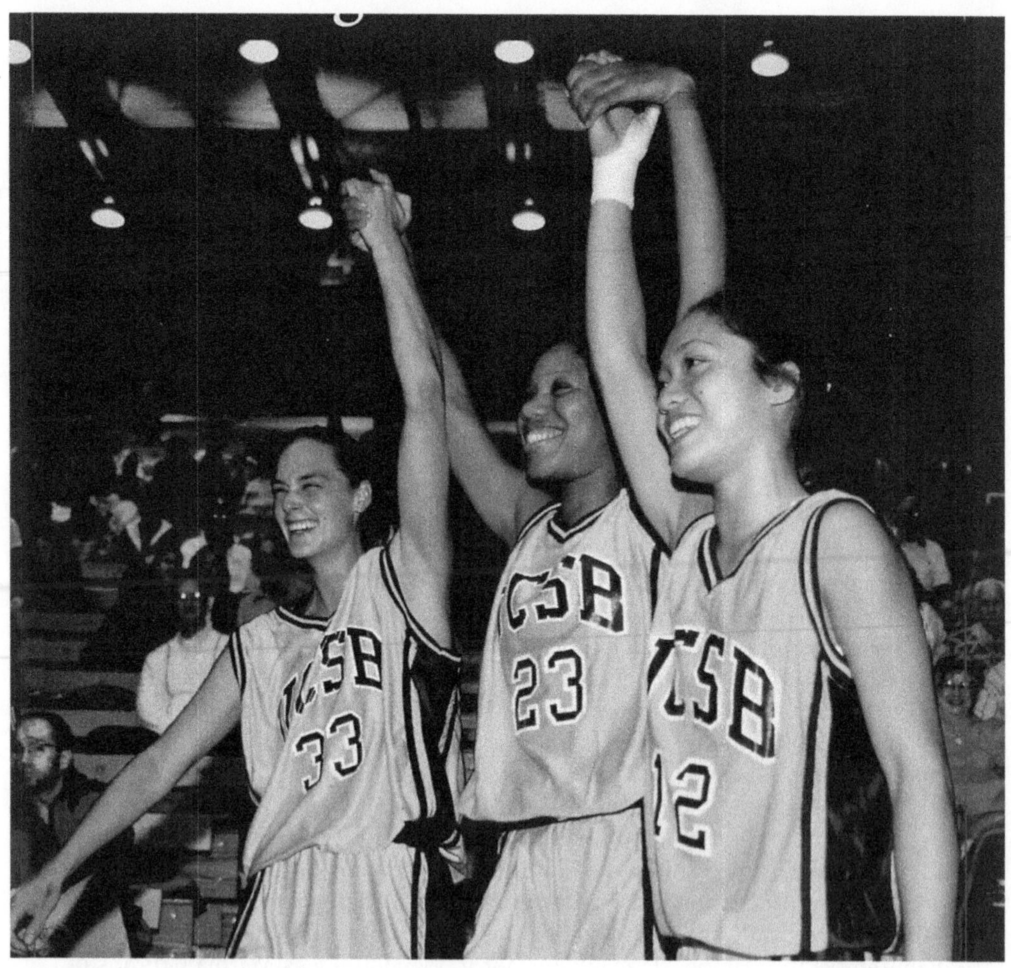

By the turn of the twenty-first century, diversity in admissions and more equitable funding for women's athletics had made new opportunities for women to hone their skills and overcome challenges, as these players at the University of California attest. (Photo courtesy of the Department of Athletics, University of California, Santa Barbara.)

Title IX, Education Amendments of 1972

In 1972, women received 9 percent of the M.D. degrees awarded by universities in the United States, 7 percent of the law degrees, and 15 percent of the doctoral degrees. Women were 2 percent of college varsity athletes. It was common practice to encourage women students into specialties marked as appropriate for women: teaching rather than scientific research, for example, or nursing rather than medicine. It was estimated that colleges offered athletic scholarships to 50,000 men, while women athletes received fewer than 50. It was usual practice for the travel expenses of men's athletic teams to be paid for from student fees (paid by both women and men), while women's teams received 0.5 percent of schools' athletic dollars. Women's teams often had to raise their own travel funds, sometimes from bake sales and raffles. Title IX of the Education Amendments to the Civil Rights Act, passed in 1972, was brief but far-reaching.

No person in the United States shall, on the basis of sex, be excluded from participation in, be denied the benefits of, or be subjected to discrimination under any education program or activity receiving Federal financial assistance. . . .

Each Federal department and agency which is empowered to extend Federal financial assistance to any education program or activity, by way of grant, loan, or contract . . . is authorized and directed to effectuate the provisions of . . . this title with respect to such program or activity by issuing rules, regulations, or orders of general applicability which shall be consistent with achievement of the objectives of the statute. . . .

Title IX has proved to be a powerful tool in the fight for gender equity because it affects a wide range of educational opportunities and services. Title IX forbids sex discrimination in admissions policies (outlawing the common practice of using separate standards for men and women); in career training and vocational programs (which had previously been largely segregated by sex); and in employment. Title IX also forbids discrimination against pregnant or parenting students and requires schools to provide an environment that is free of sexual harassment.

The most widely discussed consequence of Title IX, however, has been its transformative effect on high school and undergraduate athletic programs. In the years since the passage of Title IX, the number of women participating in National Collegiate Athletic Association (NCAA) intercollegiate athletics has risen from approximately 32,000 in 1971 to roughly 178,000 in 2007–8, an increase of over 450 percent. (The number of men in intercollegiate athletics has also risen at the rate of 38 percent, from 173,000 to 240,000 athletes.) At the high school level, the change is even more striking: over three million girls participated in high school sports in 2007–8, compared with fewer than 300,000 in 1971–72, an increase of nearly 1,000 percent. (During the same time period, high school boys' participation in sports rose by approximately 15 percent.) Thus, contrary to the widespread misperception that Title IX has decreased the opportunities for males to participate in sports, the number of male athletes has continued to increase and, most significantly, so has the funding for men's sports. At Division I schools (with major football and basketball teams), although the number of men's teams has declined, the amount of money spent on men's athletics is still almost twice as much as the money spent on women's athletics. Between 1995–96 and 2004–5, Division I schools increased their spending on men's football by approximately $2.45 million per team, while the average funding increase for women's teams (except basketball) was about $135,000 per team.

Title IX is enforced by the Department of Education's Office of Civil Rights. Enforcement has been gradual. Not until 1975 were there full federal regulations applying to secondary schools and colleges and universities, and these have continued to evolve over time. The Title IX regulations governing athletic programs require that the total amount of athletic financial assistance awarded to men and women be proportionate to their respective participation rates in intercollegiate athletic programs. They require that male and female athletes receive equivalent—not identical—benefits, treatment, services, and opportunities. Title IX does *not* require that all teams be coeducational, that the same number of teams be provided for men and women, or that men's teams be cut in order for the institution to come into compliance with the law.

In 2002, the U.S. secretary of education established the Commission on Opportunity in Athletics. At issue were the measures of fairness. After more than a year of intense public debate, the commission announced its wholehearted support for the goal of gender equity in sports, while suggesting that schools be offered more flexible terms of establishing their compliance with Title IX. In 2005, the Department of Education agreed to one modification, but it has continued to rely on the "three-prong test" established in 1979. This test requires schools to show either that the ratio of male and female athletes is about equal to the ratio of all male and female undergraduates; that they have a "history and continuing practice" of expanding opportunities for women; or that they are "fully and effectively accommodating the interests and abilities" of women on campus. More than three-quarters of colleges and universities are in comfortable compliance with Title IX, having added women's teams and continued to support men's teams. It is Division I schools, which reserve substantial numbers of slots for revenue-producing sports (even at the expense of cutting men's minor sports), that have found it most difficult to meet Title IX's expectations.

Recent reports confirm several arguments that women have made about Title IX's effects on intercollegiate sports programs. Both men's and women's participation levels in college athletics have increased since the passage of Title IX. College and universities have responded to Title IX by increasing women's participation rather than decreasing men's participation. Men's sports continue to receive funding and athletic opportunities out of proportion to their representation in the college population; 57 percent of undergraduates are women, yet they receive only 42 percent of the athletic participation opportunities. In addition, the NCAA's 2007–8 report on sports participation shows that male athletic participation in intercollegiate sports—both the numbers of athletes and the number of teams—has reached an all-time high.

Argument continues about what constitutes equitable treatment. Is it fair for men to hold the majority of athletic scholarships (an imbalance largely due to the size of men's football and basketball teams)? Is it fair for a university to support a women's varsity rowing team but not a men's varsity rowing team? What is the proper relationship between women's sports and men's sports? Between women's sports and men's "minor" sports? Perhaps most significantly, what is the wise relationship between expenditures on athletics and expenditures on academic programs?

Most recently, students and their parents began using Title IX to fight sexual harassment at school and during school-sponsorcd activities. In 1999 the Supreme Court responded to the appeal of the fifth-grade girl who had been subjected to explicit sexual teasing by a classmate. He attempted to touch her breasts and genital area, he told her "I want to get into bed with you," and he rubbed his body against her in the hallway. Her grades plummeted as she lost the ability to concentrate on her studies. Although she and her mother complained repeatedly to teachers and the principal, no action was taken. The Court ruled that school districts may be liable for damages when administrators are indifferent to repeated and known acts of student-to-student sexual harassment, during school hours and on school grounds (*Davis* v. *Monroe County Board of Education*, 119 S.Ct. 1661). The case raised the question of responsibility of schools to provide a harassment-free environment (see *Meritor Savings Bank* v. *Mechelle Vinson* et al., pp. 741–742). In the face of successful Title IX sexual assault lawsuits brought by women at several universities in 2007, more colleges and universities are adopting policies and procedures intended to protect students from all forms of unwelcome sexual conduct, although schools continue to struggle to find effective ways of enforcing these policies.*

*This note was prepared with information from reports and press releases issued in 2007 and 2008 by the National Collegiate Athletic Association (NCAA), the National Federation of State High School Associations (NFHS), the Women's Sports Foundation, the National Coalition for Women and Girls in Education, and the ACLU Women's Rights Projects, which are available on their websites.

Frontiero *v.* Richardson, *1973*

Sharron A. Frontiero was an Air Force officer who was dismayed to discover that she could not claim dependent's benefits for her husband on the same terms that her male colleagues could for their wives. She and her husband brought suit, claiming that statutes requiring spouses of female members of the uniformed services to receive more than half of their support from their wives to be considered dependents, while all spouses of male members were treated as dependents, violated the due process clause of the Fifth Amendment and the equal protection clause of the Fourteenth Amendment.

Until 1971, the Supreme Court had never ruled that discrimination on the basis of sex was a violation of the equal protection clause of the Fourteenth Amendment. So long as a legislature had a "reasonable" basis for making distinctions between men and women, discriminatory laws were upheld. Between 1971 and 1975, in a stunning series of decisions, the Supreme Court placed the burden of proof that discrimination on the basis of sex was reasonable on those who tried to discriminate. Ruth Bader Ginsburg was a thirty-eight-year-old law professor working with the American Civil Liberties Union (ACLU) in 1971 when the Court accepted her argument that an Idaho law requiring that fathers, rather than mothers, always be preferred as executors of their children's estates was unconstitutional (*Reed* v. *Reed*, 404 U.S. 71 [1971]).

The ACLU set up a Women's Rights Project in 1972 with Ginsburg at its head to follow up on the implications of the *Reed* decision. Ginsburg wrote the brief and managed the argument in *Frontiero;* it was one of a brilliant series of cases that she argued in the early 1970s. With her colleagues, she helped persuade the Court that a wide range of discriminatory practices were illegal. Her career as a litigator would lead to her appointment as a judge on the U.S. Court of Appeals in 1980 and, in 1993, to her appointment to the U.S. Supreme Court.

The Supreme Court ruled in favor of the Frontieros in a complex decision that used statistical information about woman's place in the work force in a manner reminiscent of the Brandeis Brief (see Sklar, p. 409). Speaking for three of his colleagues Justice William J. Brennan, Jr., prepared a historically based argument, explaining the distance American public opinion had traveled since the *Bradwell* case (see pp. 312–314). He drew analogies between discrimination on the basis of race, which the court subjected to strict scrutiny, and discrimination on the basis of sex.

In concurring with Brennan's opinion, three justices observed that although they agreed with the Frontieros in this particular case, they were not yet persuaded that sex ought to be regularly treated as a "suspect category." Only when—or if—the Equal Rights Amendment were passed could the Court be sure that the public agreed that discrimination on the basis of sex ought to be evaluated as critically as discrimination on the basis of race. Note that the facts in *Frontiero* relate to discrimination against the husband of the wage earner, not directly against a woman. It is the family of the wage earner that is discriminated against. A similar case, also argued by Ginsburg, is *Weinberger* v. *Weisenfeld* (420 U.S. 636 [1975]), in which the husband of a dead woman successfully demanded survivor's benefits equal to those available to widows. Ginsburg and her colleagues stressed that both men and women benefited from gender-blind equal treatment under the law.

MR. JUSTICE WILLIAM J. BRENNAN, JR., DELIVERED THE OPINION OF THE COURT:

The question before us concerns the right of a female member of the uniformed services to claim her spouse as a "dependent." . . .

At the outset, appellants contend that classifications based upon sex, like classifications based upon race, alienage, and national origin, are inherently suspect and must therefore be subjected to close judicial scrutiny. We agree. . . .

There can be no doubt that our Nation has had a long and unfortunate history of sex discrimination. Traditionally, such discrimination was rationalized by an attitude of "romantic paternalism" which, in practical effect, put women, not on a pedestal, but in a cage. Indeed, this paternalistic attitude became so firmly rooted in our national consciousness that, 100 years ago, a distinguished Member of this Court was able to proclaim. . . . "The natural and proper timidity and delicacy which belongs to the female sex evidently unfits it for many of the occupations of civil life." . . .

It is true, of course, that the position of women in America has improved markedly in recent decades. Nevertheless, it can hardly be doubted that, in part because of the high visibility of the sex characteristic, women still face pervasive, although at times more subtle, discrimination in our educational institutions, in the job market, and perhaps most conspicuously, in the political arena. . . .

Moreover, since sex, like race and national origin, is an immutable characteristic determined solely by the accident of birth, the imposition of special disabilities upon the member of a particular sex because of their sex would seem to violate "the basic concept of our system that legal burdens should bear some relationship to individual responsibility. . . . " And what differentiates sex from such non-suspect statuses as intelligence or physical disability, and aligns it with the recognized suspect criteria, is that the sex characteristic frequently bears no relation to ability to perform or contribute to society. . . .

. . . over the past decade, Congress has itself manifested an increasing sensitivity to sex-based classification. In Tit[le] VII of the Civil Rights Act of 1964, for example, Congress expressly declared that no employer, labor union, or other organization subject to the provisions of the Act shall discriminate against any individual on the basis of "race, color, religion, *sex*, or national origin." Similarly, the Equal Pay Act of 1963 provides that no employer covered by the Act "shall discriminate . . . between employees on the basis of sex." . . .

With these considerations in mind, we can only conclude that classifications based upon sex, like classifications based upon race, alienage, or national origin, are inherently suspect, and must therefore be subjected to strict judicial scrutiny. Applying the analysis mandated by that stricter standard of review, it is clear that the statutory scheme now before us is constitutionally invalid. . . .

MR. JUSTICE LEWIS F. POWELL, JR., WITH WHOM THE CHIEF JUSTICE AND MR. JUSTICE HARRY A. BLACKMUN JOIN, CONCURRING IN THE OPINION:

I agree that the challenged statutes constitute an unconstitutional discrimination against servicewomen . . . but I cannot join the opinion of Mr. Justice Brennan, which would hold that all classifications based upon sex . . . are "inherently suspect and must therefore be subjected to close judicial scrutiny." . . . The Equal Rights Amendment, which if adopted will resolve the substance of this precise question, has been approved by the Congress and submitted for ratification by the States. If this Amendment is duly adopted, it will represent the will of the people accomplished in the manner prescribed by the constitution. . . . It seems to me that this reaching out to pre-empt by judicial action a major political decision which is currently in process of resolution does not reflect appropriate respect for duly prescribed legislative processes.

Frontiero v. *Richardson*, 411 U.S. 677 (1973).

Roe *v.* Wade, *1973;* Planned Parenthood of Southeastern Pennsylvania *v.* Casey, *1992;* Carhart *v.* Gonzales, *2007*

The Comstock Act had been echoed by a series of anticontraception and antiabortion laws throughout the country. By 1900, James Mohr observes, "Every state in the Union had an antiabortion law of some kind on its books . . . except Kentucky, where the state courts outlawed the practice anyway."* (See Leslie Reagan's essay, pp. 506–511.)

*James C. Mohr, *Abortion in America: The Origins and Evolution of National Policy, 1800–1900* (New York: Oxford University Press, 1978), pp. 229–30.

In 1962 the ethics of abortion became a pressing problem when it was revealed that thalidomide, a drug extensively used in Europe and occasionally in the United States, resulted in the birth of thousands of babies with phocomelia (deformed or missing arms and legs). Sherri Finkbine, an Arizona woman who had taken the drug, demanded a legal abortion. Although her own doctors supported her, the county medical society refused to approve the procedure, and, lacking confidence that she and her doctors would be granted immunity from prosecution, she fled to Sweden, where abortion was legal. Believing that other women should not have to discover the dangers of thalidomide the way she did, Sherri Finkbine told her story to local newspapers, and the news traveled quickly across the nation.

Her plight, and her challenge to hospital practice, helped to shift public opinion, both within the medical profession, which would subsequently be instrumental in advocating liberalization of abortion legislation, and among women's groups, which began to articulate dismay that women were generally denied access to safe abortion services. Estimates of the number of illegal abortions performed each year before 1973 range from 200,000 to 1,200,000; it is estimated that 200 women died each year as a result. Abortion was virtually the only medical procedure to which middle-class women did not have access. The issue was less intense for black women's groups; working-class minority women lacked a wide range of medical services, and abortion was only one among many which they needed. Thus, at the beginning of the reinvigorated women's movement of the late 1960s, black and white women were divided about the place that access to legal abortion should hold in their list of priorities for legal change.

Some physicians, like those who had approved Sherri Finkbine's request for a therapeutic abortion, sought to liberalize antiabortion laws, arguing that medical practitioners were best situated to judge when an abortion was appropriate. They were joined by a grassroots movement of women throughout the country who argued that current abortion statutes undermined their own constitutional right to equal protection of the laws. It was not equal protection, they insisted, when women with financial resources—like Sherri Finkbine—could find safe abortions and poor women could not, nor when women could not make their own fundamental decisions whether to carry and bear a child. The severe social stigma to which unmarried pregnant women were subjected deprived them of dignity. Before the *Roe* decision was handed down, a number of advances for reproductive rights occurred on the state level. In Connecticut over 800 women, joined as plaintiffs in a case popularly known as "Women versus Connecticut," convinced the state supreme court to declare the state's severe law unconstitutional; in 1969 the California Supreme Court held the California abortion law unconstitutional because it violated "the fundamental right of the woman to choose whether to bear children," citing the U.S. Supreme Court's decisions in *Griswold* (see pp. 768–769) and *Loving* (see pp. 767–768). Women activists also filed lawsuits in New Jersey, Rhode Island, Pennsylvania, and Massachusetts. In Iowa the Young Women's Christian Association supported abortion reform as early as 1966; women legislators took the lead in introducing reform bills, and a statewide organization largely composed of women—the Iowa Association for Medical Control of Abortion—lobbied vigorously for reform.** In 1970, Alaska, Hawaii, New York, and Washington legalized abortion.

Texas law continued to prohibit abortion except for the purpose of saving the mother's life. In 1970, Norma McCorvey, a single pregnant woman, known as Jane Roe to protect her privacy, brought a class action suit challenging the constitutionality of that law as a violation of her right to liberty as guaranteed by the due process clause of the Fourteenth Amendment.

The Supreme Court's 7–2 decision in *Roe* v. *Wade* marked a sharp change from long-established practice. As the opening lines of the majority decision make clear, the justices were aware they were making a sensitive and important decision.

On what constitutional grounds does Justice Blackmun base the Supreme Court's reasoning? Where does he find the right of privacy? (See Fourteenth Amendment, p. 309). What limits does the Court place on the exercise of that right?

**Amy Kesselman, "Women Versus Connecticut: Conducting a Statewide Hearing on Abortion," in *Abortion Wars: A Half Century of Struggle*, ed. Rickie Solinger (Berkeley: University of California Press, 1998), pp. 42–67; *People* v. *Dr. Leon Belous*, 458 P.2d 194 (1969); James C. Mohr, "Iowa's Abortion Battles of the Late 1960s and Early 1970s: Long-term Perspectives and Short-term Analyses," *Annals of Iowa* 50, 1, 3rd ser. (Summer 1989): 63–89.

ROE v. *WADE*, 1973

MR. JUSTICE HARRY A. BLACKMUN DELIVERED THE OPINION OF THE COURT:

We forthwith acknowledge our awareness of the sensitive and emotional nature of the abortion controversy, of the vigorous opposing views, even among physicians, and of the deep and seemingly absolute convictions that the subject inspires. One's philosophy, one's experiences, one's exposure to the raw edges of human existence, one's religious training, one's attitudes toward life and family and their values, and the moral standards one establishes and seeks to observe, are all likely to influence and to color one's thinking and conclusions about abortion.

In addition, population growth, pollution, poverty, and racial overtones tend to complicate and not to simplify the problem.

Our task, of course, is to resolve the issue by constitutional measurement, free of emotion and of predilection. We seek earnestly to do this....

The principal thrust of the appellant's attack on the Texas statutes is that they improperly invade a right, said to be possessed by the pregnant woman, to choose to terminate her pregnancy. Appellant would discover this right in the concept of personal "liberty" embodied in the Fourteenth Amendment's Due Process Clause; or in personal, marital, familial and sexual privacy said to be protected by the Bill of Rights . . . or among those rights reserved to the people by the Ninth Amendment....

It perhaps is not generally appreciated that the restrictive criminal abortion laws in effect in a majority of States today are of relatively recent vintage. Those laws, generally proscribing abortion or its attempt at any time during pregnancy except when necessary to preserve the pregnant woman's life, are not of ancient or even of common-law origin. Instead, they derive from statutory changes effected, for the most part, in the latter half of the nineteenth century.... At common law, at the time of the adoption of our Constitution, and throughout the major portion of the nineteenth century . . . a woman enjoyed a substantially broader right to terminate a pregnancy than she does in most states today....

When most criminal abortion laws were first enacted, the procedure was a hazardous one for the woman. This was particularly true prior to the development of antisepsis.... Abortion mortality was high. . . . Modern medical techniques have altered this situation. Appellants . . . refer to medical data indicating that abortion in early pregnancy, that is, prior to the end of the first trimester, although not without its risk, is now relatively safe. Mortality rates for women undergoing early abortions, where the procedure is legal, appear to be as low as or lower than the rates for normal childbirth. Consequently, any interest of the State in protecting the woman from an inherently hazardous procedure . . . has largely disappeared. . . . The State has a legitimate interest in seeing to it that abortion, like any other medical procedure, is performed under circumstances that insure maximum safety for the patient....

The Constitution does not explicitly mention any right of privacy. In a line of decisions, however . . . the Court has recognized that a right of personal privacy, or a guarantee of certain areas or zones of privacy, does exist under the Constitution. . . . This right . . . whether it be founded in the Fourteenth Amendment's concept of personal liberty . . . or . . . in the Ninth Amendment's reservation of rights to the people, is broad enough to encompass a woman's decision whether or not to terminate her pregnancy. . . . We . . . conclude that the right of personal privacy includes the abortion decision, but that this right is not unqualified and must be considered against important state interests in regulation. . . .

. . . the State does have a important and legitimate interest in preserving and protecting the health of the pregnant woman . . . and . . . it has still *another* important and legitimate interest in protecting the potentiality of human life. These interests are separate and distinct. Each grows in substantiality as the woman approaches term, and, at a point during pregnancy, each becomes "compelling."

With respect to the State's important and legitimate interest in the health of the mother, the "compelling" point, in the light of present medical knowledge, is at approximately the end of the first trimester. This is so because of the now-established medical fact . . . that until the end of the first trimester mortality in abortion may be less than mortality in normal childbirth. It follows that . . . for the period of pregnancy prior to this "compelling" point, the attending physician, in consultation with his patient, is free to determine, without regulation by the State, that in his medical judgment, the patient's pregnancy should be terminated.

. . . For the stage subsequent to approximately the end of the first trimester, the State, in promoting its interest in the health of the mother, may, if it chooses, regulate the abortion procedure in ways that are reasonably related to maternal health.

For the stage subsequent to viability, the State in promoting its interest in the potentiality of human life may, if it chooses, regulate, and even proscribe, abortion except where it is necessary, in appropriate medical judgment, for the preservation of the life or health of the mother.

Our conclusion . . . is . . . that the Texas abortion statutes, as a unit, must fall. . . .

Roe v. *Wade*, 410 U.S. 113 (1973).

In the years before 1973, when abortion was generally illegal, commonly performed in the private offices of doctors and unlicensed practitioners without emergency medical support, and generally without anesthesia, death from abortion was substantial. In 1985, it was estimated that only two deaths occurred from illegal abortion and only six deaths resulted from legal abortion.

The issues that were raised by *Roe* v. *Wade* have not been fully settled and are not likely to be easily resolved, touching as they do on basic religious and ethical beliefs. Because only women become pregnant, and because there is no obvious parallel to pregnancy in male experience, arguments about abortion are less easily made on the equal treatment grounds that served women's rights activists well in *Frontiero* (see *Frontiero* v. *Richardson*, pp. 723–725) and other similar cases. Advocates generally ask what equal treatment would mean for men and women, who are differently situated in relation to abortion.

Abortion is an issue of concern to men as well as to women. It is an issue on which women and men hold a wide variety of views. Among the questions raised are:

1. What are the limits of a woman's right to make her own reproductive decisions?
2. Should the unborn be afforded legal rights?
3. What rights does the father have? In 1976 the Supreme Court held that a state could not require a married woman to get her husband's consent before having an

abortion (*Planned Parenthood* v. *Danforth,* 428 U.S. 52 [1976]). Is the husband's claim of a role in an abortion decision a reinstatement of the old law of coverture?

4. What rights does the community have to set general policy? What are the appropriate limits of government intervention? The state may not require a woman to conceive a child; can the state require a woman to bear a child?
5. Will any of these rights change as improvements are made in the technology for the discovery of birth defects and genetic abnormalities, for the implantation of embryos, and for caring for premature infants at earlier ages?

In the 1980s, a number of states tested what boundaries would be considered reasonable limits on the abortion rights sustained in *Roe*. In 1980, the Supreme Court upheld the "Hyde Amendment" by which Congress refused to fund even medically necessary abortions for indigent women (*Harris* v. *McRae,* 448 U.S. 297). This decision was not the focus of massive public protest, and it was replicated in the laws of many states. An effort to defeat the Hyde Amendment failed in Congress in 1993, but some states did revise their practice, covering some abortions for indigent women, usually in the case of rape or incest.

Missouri legislators developed further the position that the state could deny any form of public support or facilities for the performance of abortions. A 1986 law prohibited the use of public employees and facilities to perform or assist abortions not necessary to save the life of the mother and also prohibited the use of public funds for counseling a woman in abortion decisions not necessary to save her life. It included a preamble that claimed that the life of each human being begins at conception and a provision that required that medical tests of fetal viability—tests whose efficacy was disputed—be performed before any abortion on a fetus estimated to be twenty weeks or more in gestation. Since 97 percent of all late abortions (done at an estimated sixteen-week gestational age) were performed at a single hospital in Kansas City that, although private, received public aid and was located on public property, the practical impact of the law was great.

In deciding *Webster* v. *Reproductive Health Services* in July 1989, by a 5–3 vote, the Supreme Court majority claimed that the conclusions of *Roe* had not been changed.* Missouri law left a pregnant woman free to terminate her pregnancy so long as neither public funds nor facilities were used for it; this was, the Court majority said, a "value judgment" favoring childbirth over abortion. But the majority raised a general question about *Roe.* "[T]he rigid Roe framework," wrote Chief Justice Rehnquist in the majority opinion, "is hardly consistent with the notion of a Constitution cast in general terms, as ours is, and usually speaking in general principles, as ours does. The key elements of the *Roe* framework—trimesters and viability—are not found in the text of the Constitution or in any place else one would expect to find a constitutional principle . . . the result has been a web of legal rules that . . . [resemble] a code of regulations rather than a body of constitutional doctrine." Justice Anthony Scalia concurred, adding that

***William L. Webster, Attorney General of Missouri* v. *Reproductive Health Services,* 109 S. Ct. 3040 (1989).

in his view, *Roe* should have been overturned; abortion is, he thought, a field in which the Court "has little proper business since the answers to most of the cruel questions posed are political and not juridical." He was appalled at efforts to bring the pressure of public opinion to bear on the decisions of the Court, notably the March on Washington of some 200,000 people that had been sponsored by pro-choice groups shortly before the *Webster* case was argued in April 1989.

Justice Harry A. Blackmun, who had written the Court's opinion in *Roe,* now wrote a bitter dissent for the minority. He denied that Rehnquist's opinion left *Roe* "undisturbed." Rather it challenged a large body of legal precedent that had established a "private sphere of individual liberty," which although not explicitly specified in the Constitution had long been taken to have been implied by the Fourth Amendment guarantee against unreasonable searches. The right to privacy had been invoked in the 1960s when the Court protected the sale and use of birth control devices; the *Webster* decision, Blackmun feared, bypassed "the true jurisprudential debate underlying this case: . . . whether and to what extent . . . a right to privacy extends to matters of childbearing and family life, including abortion." Justice John Paul Stevens argued that the preamble's claim that life begins at conception was a religious view, and to write it into law was to ignore First Amendment requirements for the separation of church and state. Finally, Blackmun argued that the state had a distinct interest in maintaining public health, and that as safe and legal abortions became more difficult to get, an increase in deaths from illegal abortions could be predicted. "For today," he concluded, "the women of this Nation still retain the liberty to control their destinies. But the signs are evident and very ominous, and a chill wind blows."

The Court's decision in *Webster* left many questions open. If states could deny public funds for abortions, what other limitations was it reasonable for state legislatures to impose? Was it reasonable to require a waiting period? Was it reasonable to require minors to get the consent of one parent? of both parents?

In 1988 and 1989 Pennsylvania amended its Abortion Control Act of 1982 extensively, requiring a twenty-four-hour waiting period and the provision of "certain information" twenty-four hours before the abortion is performed. Minors were required to have the consent of one parent, and married women to have notified their husbands, although it was possible for a court to waive that requirement and all requirements could be waived in the event of a "medical emergency." Because most of the justices had made public substantial reservations about the decision in *Roe,* it seemed to many observers not unreasonable to predict that the Court would uphold the entire Pennsylvania statute and, possibly, overturn *Roe* v. *Wade.* Instead, a plurality organized by Justices Sandra Day O'Connor, Anthony Kennedy, and David Souter, joined by Harry Blackmun and John Paul Stevens, wrote a complex opinion that began with a ringing affirmation of *Roe.* But O'Connor, Kennedy, and Souter also made it clear that they shared Rehnquist's skepticism of the trimester framework of *Roe.* How does the plurality think the principle of equal protection of the laws should be applied in abortion decisions?

Note the comments on coverture at the end of the plurality opinion; why did court find it useful to refer to *Bradwell* v. *Illinois* (pp. 312–314) and *Hoyt* v. *Florida* (pp. 647–648)? The final statement in the selection marks the first explicit recognition by the Court of the end of coverture. Why do the dissenting justices think *Roe* should be overturned?

PLANNED PARENTHOOD OF SOUTHEASTERN PENNSYLVANIA v. *CASEY*, 1992

JUSTICES O'CONNOR, KENNEDY, SOUTER:
(WITH WHOM JUSTICES BLACKMAN AND STEVENS JOIN)

Liberty finds no refuge in a jurisprudence of doubt. Yet 19 years after our holding that the Constitution protects a woman's right to terminate her pregnancy in its early stages . . . that definition of liberty is still questioned. . . . After considering the fundamental constitutional questions resolved by *Roe,* principles of institutional integrity, and the rule of *stare decisis* [the principle that decisions of previous courts should be let stand unless there is overwhelming reason to change them], we are led to conclude this: the essential holding of *Roe* v. *Wade* should be retained and once again reaffirmed. . . . Constitutional protection of the woman's decision to terminate her pregnancy derives from the Due Process Clause of the Fourteenth Amendment. It declares that no State shall "deprive any person of life, liberty, or property, without due process of law." . . . It is a premise of the Constitution that there is a realm of personal liberty which the government may not enter. We have vindicated this principle before. Marriage is mentioned nowhere in the Bill of Rights and interracial marriage was illegal in most States in the 19th century, but the Court was no doubt correct in finding it to be an aspect of liberty protected against state interference by the substantive component of the Due Process Clause in *Loving* v. *Virginia* 388 U.S. 1 (1967). . . .

Men and women of good conscience can disagree, and we suppose some always shall disagree, about the profound moral and spiritual implications of terminating a pregnancy, even in its earliest stage. Some of us as individuals find abortion offensive to our most basic principles of morality, but that cannot control our decision. Our obligation is to define the liberty of all, not to mandate our own moral code. . . .

Our law affords constitutional protection to personal decisions relating to marriage, procreation, contraception, family relationships, child rearing, and education. . . . These matters, involving the most intimate and personal choices a person may make in a lifetime, choices central to personal dignity and autonomy, are central to the liberty protected by the Fourteenth Amendment. At the heart of liberty is the right to define one's own concept of existence, of meaning, of the universe, and of the mystery of human life. Beliefs about these matters could not define the attributes of personhood were they formed under compulsion of the State. The woman's right to terminate her pregnancy before viability is the most central principle of *Roe* v. *Wade.* It is a rule of law and a component of liberty we cannot renounce.

On the other side of the equation is the interest of the State in the protection of potential life. The *Roe* Court recognized the State's "important and legitimate interest in protecting the potentiality of human life." . . . That portion of the decision in *Roe* has been given too little acknowledgment and implementation by the Court in its subsequent cases. . . . Though the woman has a right to choose to terminate or continue her pregnancy before viability, it does not at all follow that the State is prohibited from taking steps to ensure that this choice is thoughtful and informed. Even in the earliest stages of pregnancy, the State may enact rules and regulations designed to encourage her to know that there are philosophic and social arguments of great weight that can be brought to bear in favor of continuing the pregnancy to full term. . . . We reject the trimester framework, which we do not consider to be part of the essential holding of *Roe.* . . . Measures aimed at ensuring that a woman's choice contemplates the consequences for the fetus do not necessarily interfere with the right recognized in *Roe* . . . not every law which makes a right more difficult to exercise is, ipso facto, an infringement of that right. . . .

. . . We . . . see no reason why the State may not require doctors to inform a woman seeking an abortion of the availability of materials relating to the consequences to the fetus. . . . Whether the mandatory 24-hour waiting period is . . . invalid because in practice it is a substantial obstacle to a woman's choice to terminate her pregnancy is a closer question. [We do not agree with the District Court] that the waiting period constitutes an undue burden. . . . [From Part D: We have already established the precedent, and] we reaffirm today, that a State may require a minor seeking an abortion to obtain the consent of a parent or guardian, provided that there is an adequate judicial bypass procedure. . . .

. . . Pennsylvania's abortion law provides, except in cases of medical emergency, that no physician shall perform an abortion on a married woman without receiving a signed statement from the woman that she has notified her spouse that she is about to undergo an abortion. The woman has the option of providing an alternative signed statement certifying that her husband is not the man who impregnated her; that her husband could not be located; that the pregnancy is the result of spousal sexual assault which she had reported [or that she fears bodily harm from him]. A physician who performs an abortion on a married woman without receiving the appropriate signed statement will have his or her license revoked, and is liable to the husband for damages.

. . . In well-functioning marriages, spouses discuss important intimate decisions such as whether to bear a child. But there are millions of women in this country who are the victims of regular physical and psychological abuse at the hands of their husbands. . . . Many may have a reasonable fear that notifying their husbands will provoke further instances of child abuse [or psychological abuse]. . . .

. . . [A]s a general matter . . . the father's interest in the welfare of the child and the mother's interest are equal. Before birth, however, the issue takes on a very different cast. It is an inescapable biological fact that state regulation with respect to the child a woman is carrying will have a far greater impact on the mother's liberty than on the father's. [That is why the Court has already ruled that when the wife and husband disagree on the abortion decision, the decision of the wife should prevail.]

. . . There was a time, not so long ago, when a different understanding of the family and of the Constitution prevailed. In *Bradwell* v. *Illinois* [pp. 312–314], three Members of this Court reaffirmed the common-law principle that "a woman had no legal existence separate from her husband." . . . Only one generation has passed since this Court observed that "woman is still regarded as the center of home and family life," with attendant "special responsibilities" that precluded full and independent legal status under the Constitution (*Hoyt* v. *Florida* [pp. 647–648]). These views, of course, are no longer consistent with our understanding of the family, the individual, or the Constitution. . . . [The Pennsylvania abortion law] embodies a view of marriage consonant with the common-law status of married women but repugnant to our present understanding of marriage and of the nature of the rights secured by the Constitution. Women do not lose their constitutionally protected liberty when they marry.

CHIEF JUSTICE REHNQUIST, WITH WHOM JUSTICE WHITE, JUSTICE SCALIA, AND JUSTICE CLARENCE THOMAS JOIN:

The joint opinion . . . retains the outer shell of *Roe* v. *Wade* . . . but beats a wholesale retreat from the substance of that case. We believe that *Roe* was wrongly decided, and that it can and should be overruled consistently with our traditional approach to *stare decisis* in constitutional cases. We would . . . uphold the challenged provisions of the Pennsylvania statute in their entirety. . . . [B]y foreclosing all democratic outlet for the deep passions this issue arouses, by banishing the issue from the political forum that gives all participants, even the losers, the satisfaction of a fair hearing and an honest fight, by continuing the imposition of a rigid national rule instead of allowing for regional differences, the Court merely prolongs and intensifies the anguish.

We should get out of this area, where we have no right to be, and where we do neither ourselves nor the country any good by remaining.

Planned Parenthood of Southeastern Pennsylvania v. *Casey*, 505 U.S. 833 (1992).

The U.S. Supreme Court began its opinion in *Casey* by scorning "a jurisprudence of doubt." In 2000 it reaffirmed its support of the principles of *Roe* v. *Wade*, and struck down another state abortion statute, this one a Nebraska law forbidding a specific procedure that physicians called "Dillation and Evacuation" and opponents called "partial birth abortion" (*Stenberg* v. *Carhart*, 530 U.S. 914 [2000]. But within a few years, Congress overrode that decision by passing a federal "partial birth abortion ban." The four Nebraska physicians who had challenged the state statute now challenged the federal version—not least on the grounds that it did not contain an exception for the health of the mother. Now the U.S. Supreme Court denied their challenge despite the strong opposition of the American College of Obstetricians and Gynecologists, which found the procedure necessary and proper in certain cases.

In *Carhart* v. *Gonzales* (550 U.S. 124 [2007]), the Supreme Court agreed with Congress that the procedure was distinctively "brutal and inhumane," and that Congress and the Court could bar it "in furtherance of its legitimate interests in regulating the medical profession." Although the majority, in an opinion written by Justice Anthony Kennedy, acknowledged that "we find no reliable data to measure the phenomenon," it announced that "it seems unexceptionable to conclude some women come to regret their choice to abort the infant life they once created and sustained. . . . Severe depression and loss of esteem can follow." For the mother's own good, he wrote that "[t]he law need not give abortion doctors unfettered choice in the course of their medical practice. . . ." Justice Kennedy acknowledged early on that "the principles set forth in the joint opinion in *Planned Parenthood of Southeastern Pa.* v. *Casey*. . . did not find support from all those who join [in this] opinion," but he asserted that they reaffirmed "*Roe*'s essential holding."

Justice Ruth Bader Ginsburg—who was joined in dissent by Justices Stevens, Souter, and Breyer—took the unusual step of reading her emphatic dissent from the bench. She began by restating *Roe*'s promise, emphasizing not only "the right of the woman to choose to have an abortion before viability and to obtain it without undue interference from the State," but also that the State's "legitimate interests . . . in protecting . . . the life of the fetus that may become a child" were limited by its interests "in protecting *the health of the woman*" [her emphasis]. The Court, Ginsburg asserted, was now "retreating from prior rulings that abortion restrictions cannot be imposed absent an exception safeguarding a woman's health." She was deeply critical of the reasoning on which Congress had based the "partial birth abortion ban" statute: "Congress claimed that there was a medical consensus that the banned procedure is never necessary . . . and that 'there is no credible medical evidence that partial-birth abortions are safe or are safer than other abortion procedures.' But the congressional record includes . . . statements from nine professional associations, including the American College of Obstetrics and Gynecology, the American Public Health Association, and the California Medical Association, attesting that intact D&E carries meaningful safety advantages over other methods . . . the physicians who testified that intact D&E is never necessary to preserve the health of a woman had slim authority for their opinions. They had no training for, or personal experience with the intact D&E procedure. . . ." Relying on misleading information, "the Court deprives women of the right to make an autonomous choice, even at the expense of their safety."

As the Court had recognized in *Casey* fifteen years before, Ginsburg observed, "at stake in cases challenging abortion restrictions is a woman's 'control over her [own] destiny.'" She cited the lines from the *Hoyt* decision that had been quoted in *Casey*:

"There was a time, not so long ago, when women were regarded as the center of home and family life, with attendant special responsibilities that precluded full and independent legal status under the Constitution." In the *Casey* decision, the Court made clear that these views "are no longer consistent with our understanding of the family, the individual, or the Constitution." Women, it is now acknowledged, have the talent, capacity, and right no participate equally in the economic and social life of the Nation. Their ability to realize their full potential, the Court [had] recognized, is intimately connected to "their ability to control their reproductive lives" Thus, legal challenges to undue restrictions on abortion procedures do not seek to vindicate some generalized notion of privacy; rather they center on a woman's autonomy to determine her life's course, and thus to enjoy equal citizenship stature.

What difference would it have made if, in 1973, the majority had grounded its defense of women's right to choose not in privacy rights but in equal protection and equal rights claims?

"We were the first American women sent to live and work in the midst of guerrilla warfare. . . ."

The American ships and planes that went to Vietnam carried women as well as men. There were approximately 10,000 military women and more than 13,000 Red Cross women, as well as smaller numbers of women foreign service officers, staff of the U.S. Agency for International Development, and employees of the United Service Organizations (USO). In 1980, Congress authorized a memorial to be built "in honor and recognition of the men and women of the Armed Forces of the United States who served in Vietnam." The competition for the design of the memorial was won by twenty-one-year-old Maya Lin, an undergraduate architecture student at Yale. The memorial stands today in Washington, visited by millions of people each year. They leave offerings as at a shrine: flowers, photographs, mementos.

The design of the memorial—whose black granite walls bear the names of 58,000 Americans who died, including 8 women—was controversial from the beginning. Many veterans groups insisted on a more traditional, representational design. In 1984 an additional statue that depicted three soldiers was placed in a grove of trees nearby. When the additional statue failed to include the figure of a woman, women veterans began to urge the addition of another statue honoring the women who had served.

In 1988 Congress authorized a statue recognizing women, to be constructed on federal property at the Vietnam Veterans Memorial from funds (like those of the other memorials) raised from private donations. The comments that follow were made at hearings conducted by Senator Dale Bumpers of Arkansas, chair of the Senate Subcommittee on Public Lands, National Parks, and Forests.

U.S. Senate Committee on Energy and Natural Resources, *Vietnam Women's Memorial.* Hearing before the Subcommittee on Public Lands, National Parks, and Forests to consider S. 2042, February 23, 1988, 100th Cong., 2nd Sess.

Each of the veterans had complex memories of their experience in Vietnam, twenty years before. How do the women explain the meaning of their service? How is Robert Doubek's testimony affected by concerns about class, race, and gender?

Both Karen Johnson's testimony and the arguments of the Supreme Court in *Rostker* v. *Goldberg* (pp. 738–740) address the issue of whether men and women have an equal obligation to serve in the military. Do you think men and women have an equal obligation to serve in the military in time of war, as Karen Johnson believes? Does that obligation extend to service in combat? Does the exclusion of women from combat suggest that American society attaches greater value to women's lives than men's? What other factors might also be relevant in explaining the exclusion of women from combat? (For more on these issues, see Elizabeth Hillman's essay, pp. 754–763.)

STATEMENT OF DONNA-MARIE BOULAY, CHAIRMAN, VIETNAM WOMEN'S MEMORIAL PROJECT

Mr. Chairman, people who serve in wars have unique experiences. War was never meant to be. War makes death. Day after day, even hour after hour, we lived and worked amidst the wounded, the dead, and the dying.

I arrived in Vietnam at the end of February 1967. A few days later I was assigned to triage for the first time. The medevac helicopters brought twelve soldiers into our emergency room. Ten were already dead. Two were bleeding to death.

Mr. Chairman, our daily duty was to care for the badly wounded, the young men whose legs had been blown off, whose arms had been traumatically amputated, whose bodies and faces had been burned beyond recognition.

We eased the agony of a young marine, his legs amputated, his wounds dangerously infected. We worked hard to stop the bleeding of a sailor who had been shot in his liver. He died three days after, in immense pain.

We cared for a young Army lieutenant from New York named Pat who had been admitted with a badly mangled leg and later evacuated to Japan, like many of the other seriously wounded soldiers we treated. I do not know whether Pat's leg was saved. I hope so. Pat was a good soldier.

Mr. Chairman, "Pat" is not short for "Patrick." Pat is a nurse. Patty was a nurse. She was stationed at the 24th Evacuation Hospital in Long Binh.

We were the first American women sent to live and work in the midst of guerrilla warfare. The month-long Tet offensive was especially frightening. The Viet Cong blew up the ammunition dump down the street, causing a wall in our unit to collapse on some patients.

VC snipers shot at us. The North Vietnamese Army artillery roared throughout the nights. Those of us not at work huddled in our bunkers, wondering if we would survive until dawn.

At work, listening to the thundering sounds around us, we tried to keep our hands from shaking, the fear out of our voices and off of our faces, so that the wounded would not see or hear it.

Women served in Vietnam in many capacities. We served as personnel specialists, journalists, clerk-typists, intelligence officers, and nurses. There was no such thing as a generic woman soldier, as there was no such thing as a generic male soldier. Men served as mechanics, engineers, pilots, divers, and infantrymen.

The design of the men's statue at the Veterans Memorial was selected, according to Frederick Hart, the sculptor, because they "depict the bonds of men at war and because the infantry bore the greatest burden."

Mr. Chairman, we are proposing that the design for the women's statue be that of a nurse who served in Vietnam. The statue of a nurse is so compatible with the existing trio of figures because the nurses' experience so closely parallels the experience of the infantrymen—the intensity, the trauma, the carnage of war.

The statue design which we are proposing is an easily recognizable symbol of healing and hope, consistent with the spirit and the experience of the Vietnam Veterans Memorial. . . .

STATEMENT OF KAREN K. JOHNSON, LITTLE ROCK, AR

I was born in Petersburg, Virginia. My father was in the military. He was killed in France on November the 11th, 1944.

I was raised in Oklahoma. I graduated from college in 1964 and explored the military as a career and joined the Army in 1965.

My family was very patriotic because of the trials and tribulations that we had to go through because of being raised without a father. Considering that everyone in my family had experienced all that patriotism, when I said that I was going to join the Army it was not a new thought, even though I was the first woman to have joined.

My family felt that all Americans owed their country any sacrifice needed for the national good, regardless of their race or sex, that patriotism should be a blind emotion, and it should be accepted by our country without any thought or qualm as to who offered such patriotism.

Consequently, after I served in Germany from 1966 to 1968, when my country asked me to go overseas again to Vietnam, I went. I served in Vietnam from July of 1970 to March of 1972, for a total of 20 months in country.

When I tell people these facts, they always ask me, was I a nurse, that I did not see any combat, and that I must have volunteered. When I tell them that I was awarded a Bronze Star, they ask me what for.

For 18 years I have answered these questions with several long-winded explanations which were really an apology for my Vietnam service, because I was not a nurse and I was not a combat soldier, and there were many others who had served who the public much better understood their service in their traditional roles.

I have kept silent on what I did in Vietnam because it was easier than making the apologies or trying to educate my listener. I know now that I have done many Vietnam veterans a great disservice by my silence. Thanks to the support of the Arkansas Vietnam Veterans, my husband and my grandchildren, I have made my last apology, felt my last twinge of embarrassment, and I will not remain silent to the detriment of my comrades in arms.

I am a veterans' veteran and I am proud of it. I was not a nurse. I saw very little full-fledged combat, and when my country called I went willingly. I see no disgrace in answering such a call or in volunteering to serve in the United States Army.

I served as the Command Information Officer of the United States Army, Vietnam Headquarters, located at Long Binh. However, my job entailed finding out what Army troops were doing, photographing those troops, writing news reports, and printing the internal publications to keep the troops informed.

I could not do that from Long Binh. I traveled all over Vietnam. Wherever there were Army troops, I went, too. I have flown in attack helicopters, been shot at in jeeps, and I went over the Hay Van Pass in several convoys.

Whatever it took to get the news out to the troops is what I and my staff did, and we did it very well. "Uptight Magazine," one of our publications, was awarded the Thomas Jefferson Award for the outstanding military publication in its field, an award that was given to me by "Time Magazine."

Our office published a twice-daily news bulletin, a weekly Long Binh paper, the weekly "Army Reporter," "Uptight Magazine Quarterly"; and "Tour 364," the history of the war, was updated every six months so that troops rotating home had a written history of their service. We were also responsible for the free distribution of "Stars and Stripes" to ensure that every U.S. military personnel serving in Vietnam had daily access to a newspaper.

There were a lot of obstacles to resolve to make all of this happen. My staff made it happen every day for 20 months, in 12 hour shifts, seven days a week, including Christmas, when we worked harder because we were responsible for making Operation Jingle Bells work so that the troops could see Bob Hope.

I am here today to tell you that I am very proud of that staff, and especially of Spec. 5 Steven Henry Warner, who gave his life so the American soldier could be the best informed and most motivated soldier in the world. I do not believe they would want me to apologize for our service or the fact that Steve Warner gave his life as a journalist and not as a combat soldier.

If there is any apology owed, it is the one I owe my staff for not standing up for them for the last 18 years because I did not like the questions my admission to being a Vietnam veteran elicited because I was a woman, something not well understood by the American public.

Their service and mine should be given equal recognition with all who served, not diminished because of the non-traditional position I held.

I come before you today to ask you to legislate equal dignity for the women who served their country by answering the call to arms. The Vietnam Women's Memorial would do much to give women veterans a new sense of self-respect and it will make a strong public statement that bias, prejudice, or ignorance of the sacrifices that women veterans have made for their country will no longer be tolerated.

Today the flag that covered my father's casket when he was put to final rest in 1948 lies in front of me, because I have always wanted him to be proud of me, his only child. And I believe he would be proudest of me today when I say, after 18 long years of silence: I was an American soldier; I answered my country's call to arms; and I am an American veteran, a title I should be able to share with equal dignity with all who have served before me and will serve after me. . . .

STATEMENT OF ROBERT W. DOUBEK . . .

Mr. Chairman, my name is Robert W. Doubek of Washington, D.C. I am a Vietnam veteran. I am employed in the private sector. I was a founder of the Vietnam Veterans Memorial Fund. I served as its Executive Director and Project Director. I was responsible for building the memorial. I did the work. In recognition of my achievement, I was nominated for a Congressional Gold Medal which was a bill passed by the Senate on November 14, 1985.

The fact is that women are not represented by the Vietnam Veterans Memorial. The fact is also that the memorial does not represent anyone. It is not a legislative body. It is a symbol of honor, and as such, it is complete as a tribute to all who served their country in the Vietnam War.

It is a basic rule of common sense that mandates that something which is not broken should not be fixed. The genius of the wall is its equalizing and unifying effect. All veterans are honored, regardless of rank, service branch, commission, sex, or any other category. The names of the eight women casualties take their rightful places of honor. To ensure that this fact is never overlooked, the inscription on the first panel of the wall states that the memorial is in honor of the men and women of the Armed Forces. The reason I know this is because I was instrumental in drafting the inscription.

In 1982, politics required that we add a figurative sculpture as a more specific symbol of the Vietnam veteran. Even with the heroic and dangerous service rendered by other combatants such as Air Force and Navy pilots, Navy swiftboat crews, and the life saving efforts of nurses, helicopter pilots and medics, there was only one possible choice of what category would be literally depicted to symbolize the Vietnam veteran, and that could only be the enlisted infantrymen, grunts. They account for the majority of names on the wall; they bore the brunt of the battle. The fact is all grunts were men.

The addition of a statue of a woman or of any other category, for that matter, would reduce the symbolism of the existing sculpture from honoring or symbolizing the Vietnam veterans community as a whole to symbolizing only enlisted infantrymen. This in turn would open a Pandora's box of proliferating statuary toward the goal of trying to depict every possible category. The National Park Service has already received requests for a statue to literally depict Native Americans and even for scout dogs, and in fact, I want to say that the figure for Native American casualties was 225.

The addition of a statue solely on the basis of gender raises troubling questions about proportion. Is gender of such overriding importance among veterans that we should have a specific statue to women who suffered eight casualties, and none for the Navy which suffered over 2,500, nor for the Air Force which suffered over 2,400? Is gender of such importance to outweigh that some 90 percent of the women who served in Vietnam in the military were officers [nurses were commissioned officers], while over 87 percent of all casualties were enlisted? . . . Approval . . . would set the precedent that strict literal depiction of both genders is an absolute requirement of all military related memorials. What about the new Navy memorial? Will Congress mandate an additional figure at the Iwo Jima Memorial?

STATEMENT OF COL. MARY EVELYN BANE, USMC (RETIRED), ARLINGTON, VA

Mr. Chairman, my name is Mary Evelyn Bane. I live in Arlington, Virginia, and I have lived in the Washington metropolitan area for a total of almost 19 nonconsecutive years. I retired in 1977 from a 26-year career in the United States Marine Corps in the grade of colonel. I never served in Vietnam, only a few women Marines did, and they were in Saigon, but I was in active service during the entire period of the war there. My career was in personnel management and, like most Marine officers, I had a variety of assignments and experiences, including two tours at our famous or infamous Parris Island training recruits, and an assignment with the Joint Staff in France. All of my male Marine colleagues did serve in Vietnam, many of them more than once, and some of their names are on the Vietnam Veterans Memorial.

I am opposed to the installation of a statue of a woman at the site of the VVM for both artistic and philosophical reasons, artistically, because it is at odds with the design as well as the theme of the memorial. . . . [and] philosophically simply because I am a woman. This may seem unfathomable to the statue's proponents, but perhaps I can explain. From the beginning of my chosen career in what most will agree is a macho outfit, I tried hard to be the best Marine I was capable of being. When I was commissioned, fewer than 1 percent of the officers in the Marine Corps were female. Women were assigned to women's billets, and restricted to a handful of occupational specialties considered appropriate for women. Over the years, through the combined efforts of many, many people, of which I am happy to say I am one, the concept of how women could and should serve their country has changed. The huge increase in the military's population required by the Vietnam War hastened the changes.

Nevertheless, in 1973 when I, then a lieutenant colonel, was assigned as the Marine Corps member of a Department of Defense ad hoc group studying the recruitment and processing of non-prior service personnel, the Civil Service GS-15 chair of the group complained to the Commandant of the Marine Corps that he had not appointed a real Marine.

My point here is that sex is an accident of birth. I chose to be a Marine and worked hard at it, and spent a career combatting discrimination based on sex. I feel every service person should be recognized for what he or she accomplished as a soldier, sailor, Marine or airman. The Vietnam Veterans Memorial recognizes American military members for their service in Vietnam, irrespective of sex, rank, service, race, or occupational specialty. To single out one of these criteria for special recognition in the form of a statue on the site of the Vietnam Veterans Memorial would not only violate the integrity of the design, but would be discriminatory.

Rostker *v.* Goldberg, *1981*

Classical republican tradition linked political identity with property holding and military obligation. In the United States, the obligations of male citizens include military service; the obligations of female citizens do not. Although women had been employed by the army and navy as nurses, not until World War II were they involved in military service in substantial numbers. Women's sections of the army, navy, and air force accepted volunteers under strict regulations that excluded them from combat duty, limited the numbers who could be accepted and the rank to which they could rise (until 1967 no woman could serve in a command position), and offered fewer fringe benefits than were received by servicemen of the same rank (see *Frontiero* v. *Richardson*, pp. 723–725). Partly in response to the Vietnam War, many of these restrictions were eased; in 1976 women were admitted to West Point, Annapolis, and the Air Force Academy.

When President Jimmy Carter recommended the resumption of peacetime selective service registration in 1980, he proposed registering women as well as men. The president and his supporters on the Armed Services Committees of the Senate and the House sought to separate the issue of registration, the actual draft, and the use of women in combat. They argued that decision on whether women would actually be drafted (and, if so, whether mothers would be exempted) and whether women would be placed in combat positions could be left for future debate. They also argued that registration did not necessarily mean that one would be drafted, for men who planned to request exemption as conscientious objectors were still required to register.

Opponents insisted that the issues were linked: if the sexes were treated equally in registration, it would be impossible to reject equity in future treatment. Since the primary goal of Selective Service was to identify combat-ready men, opponents also argued that if women were not used in combat there was no need to register them. In the course of debate contrasting ideas of the role of women in American society were expressed.* This debate overlapped with the debate on the Equal Rights Amendment, taking place at the same time; probably the single most effective argument used by opponents of the ERA was that it would involve women in the draft. In the end, Congress approved registration for men but not for women.

The Military Selective Service Act of 1980 was challenged by a group of men who argued that they had been denied the equal protection of the laws guaranteed by the Fifth Amendment. The Carter administration was now placed in the odd position of having to defend the statute it had opposed.

Note the reasoning of the Supreme Court and its emphasis on the exclusion of women from combat positions. (The vote was 6–3.) Although the argument was not offered in *Rostker*, some men have argued that if women are drafted but not placed in combat positions, the likelihood that any specific man would be assigned to a noncombat job diminishes, and men are therefore placed at greater risk for combat assignments. Moreover, some men in similar situations, such as police or prison guards, have demanded the exclusion of women on the grounds that women cannot back men up effectively in physical confrontation; thus, giving women equal opportunity to become prison guards actually increases the risks to men. Yet another perspective is offered by the legal historian Leo Kanowitz, who argues that "the equanimity with which men's exclusive liability for military service is regarded by the general population, even during times of violent combat . . . [suggests] the philosophy that a man's life is less precious than that of a woman." Do you agree?

*See the *Congressional Record*, June 10, 1980. For extended comment, see Linda K. Kerber, *No Constitutional Right to Be Ladies: Women and the Obligations of Citizenship* (New York: Hill & Wang, (1998), ch. 5.

MR. JUSTICE WILLIAM H. REHNQUIST DELIVERED THE OPINION OF THE COURT:

The question presented is whether the Military Selective Service Act . . . violates the Fifth Amendment to the United States Constitution in authorizing the President to require the registration of males and not females. Whenever called upon to judge the constitutionality of an Act of Congress—"the gravest and most delicate duty that this Court is called upon to perform," . . . the Court accords "great weight to the decisions of Congress."

. . . This case is quite different from several of the gender-based discrimination cases we have considered in that . . . Congress did not act "unthinkingly" or "reflexively and not for any considered reason." . . . The question of registering women for the draft not only received considerable national attention and was the subject of wide-ranging public debate, but also was extensively considered by Congress in hearings, floor debate, and in committee. Hearings held by both Houses of Congress in response to the President's request for authorization to register women adduced extensive testimony and evidence concerning the issue. . . . the decision to exempt women from registration was not the "accidental byproduct of a traditional way of thinking about women. . . ."

Women as a group, however, unlike men as a group, are not eligible for combat. The restrictions on the participation of women in combat in the Navy and Air Force are statutory. . . . The Army and Marine Corps preclude the use of women in combat as a matter of established policy. . . . The existence of the combat restrictions clearly indicates the basis for Congress' decision to exempt women from registration. The purpose of registration was to prepare for a draft of combat troops. Since women are excluded from combat, Congress concluded that they would not be needed in the event of a draft, and therefore decided not to register them. . . . This is not a case of Congress arbitrarily choosing to burden one of two similarly situated groups, such as would be the case with an all-black or all-white, or an all-Catholic or all-Lutheran, or an all-Republican or all-Democratic registration. Men and women, because of the combat restrictions on women, are simply not similarly situated for purposes of a draft or registration for a draft. . . . The Constitution requires that Congress treat similarly situated persons similarly, not that it engage in gestures of superficial equality.

MR. JUSTICE BYRON WHITE, DISSENTING:

I assume . . . that excluding women from combat positions does not offend the Constitution . . . [but] I perceive little, if any, indication that Congress itself concluded that every position in the military, no matter how far removed from-combat, must be filled with combat-ready men.

MR. JUSTICE THURGOOD MARSHALL, DISSENTING:

The Court today places its imprimatur on one of the most potent remaining public expressions of "ancient canards about the proper role of women." It upholds a statute that requires males but not females to register for the draft, and which thereby categorically excludes women from a fundamental civic obligation.

Rostker v. *Goldberg*, 453 U.S. 57 (1981).

Meritor Savings Bank *v.* Mechelle Vinson et al., *1986*

The term "sexual harassment" was unknown before the mid-1970s. One legal scholar has written, "the term was invented by feminist activists, given legal content by feminist litigators and scholars, and sustained by a wide-ranging body of scholarship generated largely by feminist academics." Another legal scholar observes "[f]or the first time in history, women have defined women's injuries in a law."*

Consider Part 1 of Section 703 of Title VII of the Civil Rights Act of 1964 (pp. 650–651). The authors of the statute were defining economic injuries, and for more than a decade the Equal Employment Opportunity Commission supported only economic claims of sex discrimination. But working women had long put up with behavior that, beginning in the 1970s, they began to say was also sex discrimination: supervisors who referred to all women as "whores," whether or not in joking tones; workplaces that had cheesecake or frankly pornographic calenders on the walls; and, worst of all, covert or explicit pressure to have sex with supervisors or employers for fear of losing their jobs if they refused.

Legal scholar Catharine MacKinnon gave names to two forms of sexual harassment: (1) "quid pro quo": when sexual submission to a supervisor becomes, either implicitly or explicitly, a condition of employment; and (2) "offensive working environment": when the conduct of a supervisor, co-employee, or client unreasonably interferes with an individual's work or creates an intimidating and hostile workplace. By the late 1970s, many behaviors that men had described as flirting, and that women had "put up with" because they saw no alternative, could be named and challenged. In 1980, the EEOC published an official set of guidelines describing behavior it would challenge as sexual harassment, even if the actors claimed they were merely flirting or "joking around."

In 1986, a unanimous Supreme Court for the first time formally recognized sexual harassment as a violation of Title VII. Catharine MacKinnon was one of the attorneys for Mechelle Vinson, an African American woman who had been hired in 1974 as a teller-trainee by a vice president of Meritor Savings Bank and was steadily promoted for four years until she became assistant branch manager. During those four years, she had a sexual relationship with the man (Mr. Taylor) who had hired her. . . . However, when she tried to decline his attentions, he exposed himself to her, and even forcibly raped her.

Vinson claimed that she had been the victim of both "quid pro quo" and offensive environment forms of sexual harassment. Vinson told the court "that because she was afraid of Taylor she never reported his harassment to any of his supervisors and never attempted to use the bank's complaint procedure." But

*Martha Chamallas, "Writing About Sexual Harassment: A Guide to the Literature," *UCLA Women's Law Journal* 4 (1993): 37–38; Catharine MacKinnon, *Feminism Unmodified: Discourses on Life and Law* (Cambridge, Mass.: Harvard University Press, 1987), p. 105; Vicki Schultz, "Reconceptualizing Sexual Harassment," *Yale Law Journal* 107 (1998): 1683–1805.

when she was fired for what the bank claimed was excessive use of sick leave, she sued the bank, claiming sexual harassment and asking for punitive damages. The bank claimed that "any sexual harassment by Taylor was unknown to the bank and engaged in without its consent or approval."

A unanimous Court agreed with Vinson. What analogies do they see with race discrimination? Why do they hold Meritor Bank guilty as well as Mr. Taylor? Taylor argued that Vinson wore sexually provocative clothing. How much responsibility do you think the victim of sexual harassment should be expected to take for avoiding the harassment?

JUSTICE WILLIAM REHNQUIST:

This case presents important questions concerning claims of workplace "sexual harassment" brought under Title VII of the Civil Rights Act of 1964 . . . [Vinson] argues . . . that unwelcome sexual advances that create an offensive or hostile working environment violate Title VII. Without question, when a supervisor sexually harasses a subordinate because of the subordinate's sex, that supervisor "discriminate[s]" on the basis of sex. [Meritor Bank] does not challenge this proposition. It contends instead that in prohibiting discrimination with respect to "compensation, terms, conditions, or privileges" of employment, Congress was concerned with what petitioner describes as "tangible loss" of "an economic character," not "purely psychological aspects of the workplace environment."

We reject petitioner's view. First, the language of Title VII is not limited to "economic" or "tangible" discrimination. The phrase "terms, conditions, or privileges of employment" evinces a congressional intent "to strike at the entire spectrum of disparate treatment of men and women" in employment. . . . As the Court of Appeals for the Eleventh Circuit wrote . . . in 1982: "Sexual harassment which creates a hostile or offensive environment for members of one sex is every bit the arbitrary barrier to sexual equality at the workplace that racial harassment is to racial equality. Surely a requirement that a man or woman run a gauntlet of sexual abuse in return for the privilege of being allowed to work and make a living can be as demeaning and disconcerting as the harshest of racial epithets."

. . . [W]e reject the . . . view that the mere existence of a grievance procedure and a policy against discrimination, coupled with respondent's failure to invoke that procedure, must insulate petitioner from liability. . . . the bank's grievance procedure apparently required an employee to complain first to her supervisor, in this case Taylor. Since Taylor was the alleged perpetrator, it is not altogether surprising that respondent failed to invoke the procedure and report her grievance to him. . . . [W]e hold that a claim of "hostile environment" sex discrimination is actionable under Title VII. . . .

Meritor Savings Bank v. *Mechelle Vinson et al.*, 477 U.S. 57 (1986).

A wave of attention to sexual harassment in the workplace took place after the fall of 1991, when hearings on the nomination of Clarence Thomas to the Supreme Court were interrupted by the charges of Anita Hill that he had sexually harassed her a decade earlier. Ironically, their encounter had taken place within the EEOC itself, where Thomas had been director and Hill had been a lawyer on his staff. In response, Thomas charged that he was himself victimized by the media attention. Adrienne Davis and Stephanie Wildman observe, "in a stunning sleight of hand, [Thomas] managed to convince all involved, including the Senate, that white racism, rather than a Black woman, had accused him of harassment."* Thomas's nomination to the Supreme Court was confirmed by the Senate.

Over the years since the *Meritor* decision, increasing numbers of workers have filed sexual harassment complaints, and a massive body of doctrine has developed on the details of the law's protection. In 1998 the Supreme Court ruled that harassment based on an employee's homosexuality could constitute sex discrimination, and that male-on-male harassment could be a cause of action (*Oncale v. Sundowner Offshore Services, Inc.*). The definition of an "offensive working environment" remains under debate. Legal theorist Vicki Schultz has proposed:

> Many of the most prevalent forms of harassment are actions that are designed to maintain work—particularly the more highly rewarded lines of work—as bastions of masculine competence and authority. Every day, in workplaces all over the country, men uphold the image that their jobs demand masculine mastery by acting to undermine their female colleagues' perceived (or sometimes even actual) competence to do the work. The forms of such harassment are wide-ranging. They include characterizing the work as appropriate for men only; denigrating women's performance or ability to master the job; providing patronizing forms of help in performing the job; withholding the training, information, or opportunity to learn to do the job well; engaging in deliberate work sabotage; . . . isolating women from the social networks that confer a sense of belonging . . . much of the time, harassment assumes a form that has little or nothing to do with sexuality but everything to do with gender.†

Have you or your family members or friends encountered some of these forms of harassment, or others?

*Adrienne D. Davis and Stephanie M. Wildman, "The Legacy of Doubt: Treatment of Sex and Race in the Hill-Thomas Hearings," *Southern California Law Review* 65 (1992): 1367.

†Schultz, p. 1687.

Violence against Women Act, 1994, 2000, 2005

The Violence against Women Act (VAWA) was part of the comprehensive Violent Crime Control and Law Enforcement Act, passed in 1994. It was pathbreaking in establishing a new right: "All persons within the United States shall have the right to be free from crimes of violence motivated by gender." Congress was persuaded that the states fail to treat violent assaults against women as seriously as they treat other forms of violent assault. As one member of the Senate observed, "Typically we do not ask whether the victim of a barroom brawl is a real victim; we do not comment that the victim deserved to be hit; we do not inquire whether there was resistance or whether the victim said 'no' persistently enough."

VAWA provided funding to states for criminal law enforcement against perpetrators of violence. It also created (based on the commerce clause of the Fourteenth Amendment) a new federal civil rights remedy for victims of violence resulting from "animus based on the victim's gender." It defined domestic violence and sexual assault as potential infractions of the victim's civil rights. It overrode the inadequate remedies that persist in many states (for example, several states exempted cohabiting companions from rape laws). A victim of a violent crime motivated by the victim's gender was permitted to bring a civil lawsuit in federal or state court, seeking money damages or an injunction.

(a) PURPOSE.—Pursuant to the affirmative power of Congress to enact this subtitle under section 5 of the Fourteenth Amendment to the Constitution, as well as under section 8 of Article I of the Constitution, it is the purpose of this subtitle to protect the civil rights of victims of gender motivated violence and to promote public safety, health, and activities affecting interstate commerce by establishing a Federal civil rights cause of action for victims of crimes of violence motivated by gender.

(b) RIGHT TO BE FREE FROM CRIMES OF VIOLENCE.—All persons within the United States shall have the right to be free from crimes of violence motivated by gender (as defined in subsection (d)).

(c) CAUSE OF ACTION.—A person (including a person who acts under color of any statute, ordinance, regulation, custom, or usage of any State) who commits a crime of violence motivated by gender and thus deprives another of the right declared in subsection (b) shall be liable to the party injured, in an action for the recovery of compensatory and punitive damages, injunctive and declaratory relief, and such other relief as a court may deem appropriate.

(d) DEFINITIONS.—For purposes of this section—

(1) the term "crime of violence motivated by gender" means a crime of violence committed because of gender or on the basis of gender, and due, at least in part, to an animus based on the victim's gender; and

(2) the term "crime of violence" means—

(A) an act or series of acts that would constitute a felony against the person or that would constitute a felony against property if the conduct presents a serious risk of physical injury to another, and that would come within the meaning of State or Federal offenses described in section 16 of title 18, United States Code, whether or not these acts have actually resulted in criminal charges, prosecution, or conviction and whether or not those acts were committed in the special maritime, territorial, or prison jurisdiction of the United States; and

(B) includes an act or series of acts that would constitute a felony described in subparagraph (A) but for the relationship between the person who takes such action and the individual against whom such action is taken.

U.S. Statutes at Large 108: 1796.

Not long after VAWA was passed, Christy Brzonkala charged that she had been raped by two college football players in her dorm during her first semester at Virginia Polytechnic Institute. The athletes were not suspended from school, even though they'd boasted about what they'd done and had been found guilty of "abusive conduct" by the university's judicial committee. Virginia Tech sentenced one of the players to two semesters' suspension, but upon appeal the provost set the suspension aside, calling it excessive punishment.

Brzonkala dropped out of school, fearing its dangers, and sued Virginia Tech, claiming damages equal to what the school earned from the Sugar Bowl, in which the athletes played. In May 2000, the U.S. Supreme Court upheld an appeals court ruling that Congress had reached too far in its interpretation of a right to regulate interstate commerce. The Court invalidated the part of the VAWA that permitted victims of rape, domestic violence, and other crimes "motivated by gender" to sue their attackers in federal court.*

**U.S.* v. *Morrison*, 529 U.S. 598 (2000).

Congress acted quickly: Within a few months it had reauthorized all but the contested section of VAWA. It provided more than $3 billion to fight violence against women: (1) $1 billion over five years to help prosecutors track down domestic abusers; (2) $875 million to expand shelters for battered women; (3) $95 million over two years to protect foreign women brought into the country by the international sex trade; and (4) $140 million to stop violent crimes against women on college campuses. The amount of money required is itself an indictment of the extent to which gender-motivated crimes, international trafficking in women, and the conditions on college campuses are major threats to women. (For trafficking, see Resnik, pp. 781–792). This last point is particularly chilling to those of us who study and work on college campuses. From your own experience on campuses, what programs and strategies to increase awareness of violence against women and to prevent it are in place, and which to your mind are most effective?

DOCUMENTS

Making Women's Studies

"Over its long history—since Judith Sargent Murray began to draft her essays in 1776," the distinguished historian Anne Firor Scott has observed, "women's history developed in close association with women's activism, and has itself affected that activism, providing the inspiration and encouragement for many efforts to broaden women's world. . . . Also from the beginning, women's history followed a separate track from the grand narratives of the American past created by male historians."* Anne Firor Scott was one of the first scholars to offer a course in U.S. women's history. As you see from her brief memoir, it was prompted by one student's foresight and initiative. Whether there were enough easily available documents and published scholarship to sustain a course was not a frivolous question. Anne Scott answered it with a nine-page syllabus,which we condense here. That course, and others in women's history (among them, Annette Baxter's at Barnard, Natalie Zemon Davis and Jill Conway's at the University of Toronto, Carl Degler's at Stanford, Gerda Lerner's at Sarah Lawrence†) prompted dozens and then hundreds of others, as syllabi were passed around privately and then published by the shortlived KNOW, Inc. The courses in turn prompted an explosion of research—

*Anne Firor Scott, "Unfinished Business," *Journal of Women's History* 8 (1996):111,118.

Women's History syllabus, University of Washington Summer Session, 1971; Mary Aikin Rothschild Papers, Sophia Smith Collection, Smith College, Northampton, Mass. We are grateful to Mary Rothschild and to archivist Maida Goodwin for making this rare original copy available to us.

Anne Firor Scott's major books include *The Southern Lady: From Pedestal to Politics, 1830–1930* (Chicago: University of Chicago Press, 1970); *The American Woman: Who Was She*? (Englewood Cliffs, N.J.: Prentice-Hall, 1971); with Andrew M. Scott, *One Half the People: The Fight for Woman Suffrage* (Philadelphia: Lippincott, 1976; reissue, Urbana: University of Illinois Press, 1991); *Making the Invisible Woman Visible* [essays] (Urbana, 1984); *Natural Allies: Women's Associations in American History* (Urbana, 1991); ed., *Unheard Voices: The First Historians of Southern Women* (Charlottesville, Va., 1993); ed., *Pauli Murray and Caroline Ware: Forty Years of Letters in Black and White* (Chapel Hill: University of North Carolina Press, 2006). Among her reflections on the state of the field of women's history is "Unfinished Business," *Journal of Women's History* 8, no. 2 (1996): 111–20. An extended interview with her appears in the History News Network: http://hnn.us/roundup/entries/30623.html.

†For Gerda Lerner on "The Meanings of Seneca Falls," see pp. 257–263. Lerner's major books include *The Grimké Sisters from South Carolina: Rebels Against Slavery* (Boston, 1967); *Black Women in White America: A Documentary History (New York, 1972); The Female Experience: An American Documentary* (Indianapolis, 1977); *The Majority Finds Its Past: Placing Women in History* (New York, 1979); *The Creation of Patriarchy* (New York, 1986); *The Creation of Feminist Consciousness: From the Middle Ages to Eighteen-Seventy* (New York, 1993); *Why History Matters: Life and Thought* (New York, 1997); *Fireweed: A Political Autobiography* (Philadelphia, 2002); and *Living With History/Making Social Change* (Chapel Hill, 2009). An extended interview with Gerda Lerner conducted by Lee Formwalt appeared in the *OAH Newsletter* (Organization of American Historians) in November 2006 and is available on-line: http://www.oah.org/pubs/nl/2006nov/lerner.html. For more on Lerner's life and career, see the interview conducted by Kathryn Kish Sklar for the Jewish Women's Archives: http://jwa.org/encyclopedia/article/lerner-gerda.

in term papers by students, in master's theses and doctoral dissertations, and in the work of senior scholars, including Anne Firor Scott's own.

None of the interpretative essays in this volume had been written at the time of the early courses in women's history. Note the improvisatory spirit of Anne Firor Scott's first course. Consider the differences between Anne Scott's 1971 syllabus and the table of contents of the book you are holding in your hands.

ANNE FIROR SCOTT TO LINDA K. KERBER, MAY 17, 2009 E-MAIL COMMUNICATION:

In 1971 I was promoted to full professor at Duke University, and—with *The Southern Lady* in print—I announced to the department that I would introduce a two semester course to be called "The Social History of American Women." The plan was approved.

In the spring I went to the annual meeting of the Organization of American Historians and was on the program to critique two papers; . . . as usual I worked hard to make the critique both respectful and tough. At the end a member of the audience came up and introduced himself as chairman of the History Department at the University of Washington. He said he understood my husband was coming to Seattle for summer school—the Seattle folks were trying to lure him to their institution—and that he wondered if I would be willing to teach a course in the history of American women. I thought he must have been bowled over by my critique. I said I would be delighted.

When I got to Seattle in June I met a very pregnant graduate student named Mary Aikin [now Mary Aikin Rothschild, Professor Emerita, Arizona State University], who told me that she had noticed Andy's appointment, had "stormed in" (her words) to the chair of history and said, "We can't miss this chance, we must ask Anne Scott to teach a course." The chair said, "Who is Anne Scott?" Mary tried to enlighten him. He said, "We have no money." She said, "I will find the money." It happened that she was good friends with a Dean Bell who was in charge of experimental programs, and so she got a commitment from him to pay for my class. All this had happened before the department chair went to the OAH and was the reason he . . . asked me to come (NOT that he had been bowled over by my critique, though he said it was impressive).

There was very little secondary literature, so I scoured the library for first hand accounts—biographies and autobiographies—of women. Fourteen people showed up [for the course]. I sent them off to read the books I had turned up. They were enthusiastic, worked VERY hard, and had a fine time discussing what they were finding. . . . There are some underlined and capitalized statements in my journal about how well it was all going, and of course it gave me a head start for the fall.

I suspect that was one of the first courses in women's history to be offered in the 70s. (There had been one in the 1930s.) But my students say that I bootlegged women's history into the two-semester introductory American history course which I taught from 1961 until I retired. Sara Evans, for example, has said many times that I got her started when she was 18. So it is hard to pinpoint any date.

The Search for the American Woman: Anne Firor Scott's First Women's History Syllabus, University of Washington Summer Session, 1971

This syllabus has been edited. Each class assignment included long lists of recommended reading: we have reproduced in full only two of these assignments here. Discussion questions have been moved to the beginning of the day's assignments.

THE SEARCH FOR THE AMERICAN WOMAN GIS 468 MTWTh 10:50
Anne Firor Scott Balmer 309

The goal of this course will be to sketch a preliminary outline of the history of American women based on a wide variety of primary and secondary materials. Since secondary works are few, members of the class will be asked to work in primary sources and to contribute what they learn to the general discussion. We will look for data to help us formulate some generalizations about: (1) the social role of women in different times and places; (2) the economic roles which women have assumed at different times; (3) the prevailing ideas about woman's nature; (4) the nature of marriage and the family at different points in the past.

Each assignment sheet will list a large number of possible sources, most of which should be available in the Library. Each student will be expected to choose one source to examine, and will be asked to hand in—at the beginning of each class period—a single sheet about 8x10 giving the source and identifying one or two main ideas drawn from it. On this basis, discussion will proceed each day.

Each student will write one short paper (10 pages) on any one of the daily discussion topics which interests him most. These papers are due August 9.

The following books are for purchase by all members of the class:

Eleanor Flexner, Century of Struggle [1959]
Aileen Kraditor. Up From the Pedestal [1968]
Anne F. Scott, The American Woman: Who Was She?. [1971]

In addition, the following books are on reserve: [twenty-six titles, among them:]

Jane Addams, Twenty Years at Hull House
Jane Addams, My Friend Julia Lathrop
Mary Anderson, Woman at Work
Mary Beard, America Through Woman's Eyes
Mary Beard, Woman as a Force in History
Mary S. Benson, Woman in 18th Century America
Jessie Bernard, Academic Women
Alice Stone Blackwell, Lucy Stone
Sophonisba Breckenridge, Woman in the 20th Century
Helen B. Campbell, Prisoners of Poverty
Carrie Chapman Catt and N. R. Shuler, Woman Suffrage and Politics
Jennie June Croly, History of the Woman's Club Movement
Barbara Cross (ed.) Educated Woman in America
Margaret Fuller, Woman in the 19th Century
Alice Hamilton, Exploring the Dangerous Trades
Eugene Hecker, A Short History of Women's Rights
Phebe Mitchell Kendall, Marie Mitchell: Life, Letters and Journal
Mary E. Massey, Bonnet Brigades
Mary Gray Peck, Carrie Chapman Catt
Julia Cherry Spruill, Woman's Life and Work in the Southern Colonies
E. C. Stanton, S. B. Anthony and I. Harper, History of Woman Suffrage (6 vols.)

ASSIGNMENT I WOMAN IN THE WESTERN TRADITION

How many distinctive life styles and how many different views of "women's place" can we find by a quick check through some of the documents of the western tradition, beginning with the Greeks and coming down to the 17th century when the American colonies began to be peopled? As you read, look for answers to the following questions:

1. In what way do the women contribute to the economic life of the community?
2. Is there any evidence that women played a role in politics?
3. What does the legal status of women seem to be in this case?
4. Is woman's development helped or hindered by the prevailing social and cultural expectation? What is that expectation?
5. Are women being educated? How?
6. Is it possible to find out anything about women generally or are only the upper class visible in the source?
7. Do women have any special religious role in this society?
8. Does any picture of marriage patterns or mother-child relationship emerge from this reading?
9. Do you find any information about female/male sexuality? If so, how?
10. If you are reading a fictional work, in what ways do you feel it represents that society? Is it overdrawn/underdrawn to make a point?
11. If you read 2 or more sources for the same period, does the picture of women differ? If so, how? Why? Do you find myths and realities?

POSSIBLE SOURCES: (The student should feel free to find others on his own.) [Twenty-six sources listed; among them:]

Plato, Republic (Book V of the Jowett translation, Chp. XV and XVI of the Cornford translation) Lysistrata
H. F. Kitto, The Greeks, pp. 236–252
F. A. Wright, translator and editor, Select Letters of St Jerome, "Letter to Laeta," 403 A.D., pp. 338–371
Eileen Power, Medieval People, Chapters 3 and 4
Chaucer, The Canterbury Tales
Jacob Burckhardt, The Civilization of the Renaissance in Italy, pp. 279–282; 272–274
Chilton Lathan Powell, English Domestic Relations
Alice Clark, Working Life of Women in the 17th Century
Rousseau, Emile, Book V. "Sophy or the Woman"
Margaret Mead, Sex and Temperament in Three Societies

ASSIGNMENT II WOMEN IN COLONIAL AMERICA

The questions in the first assignment can be adapted to this one. In addition, every member of the class should read Chapter I of Century of Struggle, paying special attention to the notes. [list of twenty-nine possible sources follows]

ASSIGNMENT III WOMEN IN THE 19TH CENTURY: AN OVERVIEW

Note: Look again at the questions on Assignment I, and see if there are others you would like to ask.

Everyone should read and be prepared to discuss Part I and Part II of Century of Struggle. Again, pay close attention to her footnotes and follow up on any points of special interest to you.

ASSIGNMENT IV WOMEN IN THE 19TH CENTURY: EDUCATION

Everyone should also read: Anne F. Scott, American Woman: Who Was She? Chap. 3, and Aileen Kraditor, Up From the Pedestal, Section on Education. Find out what you can about the history of women at the University of Washington.

POSSSIBLE SOURCES: [list of twenty possible sources follows]

ASSIGNMENT V WOMEN AND REFORM

Questions:

1. Is there anything peculiarly feminine about the kinds of reform movements or the kinds of methods women have used?
2. Is there a discernible relationship between the reform in which women engage and their concerns about their own role?

POSSIBLE SOURCES: [twenty titles follow]

ASSIGNMENT VI HOME AND MOTHER: IMAGE AND REALITY

Pick up clues about family life from any biography or autobiography that you read for other purposes. Consider the social consequences of colored women to America in the 19th and 20th centuries.

- B. Welter, "The Cult of True Womanhood, 1820–860," American Quarterly XVIII (Summer 1966)
- Anne L. Kuhn, The Mother's Role in Childhood Education
- Herbert R. Brown, The Sentimental Novel in America
- Helen Papashivily, All the Happy Endings
- W. Wasserstrom, Heiress of All the Ages
- Catherine M. Sedgewick, Home (Microfilm)
- Catherine M. Sedgewick, Means and Ends
- Lydia Sigourney, Letters to Mothers
- Horace Bushnell, Christian Nurture
- ———, Woman Suffrage: The Reform Against Nature
- Barbara Cross The Educated Woman in America pp. 3–13,51–101
- John Abbott, The Mother At Home, or Principals of Christian Duty
- Donald Meyer, Positive Thinkers (chapter on women, Mary Baker Eddy)
- Mary Bushnell Cheney, Life and Letters of Horace Bushnell
- Catherine E. Beecher and H. B Stowe, The American Woman's Home
- Catherine E. Beecher, A Treatise on Domestic Economy
- Catherine E. Beecher, "How to Redeem Woman's Profession from Dishonor," Harper's New Monthly Magazine XXX (1865) pp. 710–716
- Ronald Hogeland, "The Female Appendage" Civil War History, July 1971
- Harriet Beecher Stowe, Pink and White Tyranny
- Wm. McLoughlin, The Meaning of Henry Ward Beecher
- Charlotte Perkins Gilman, The Home
- Godey's Ladies Book
- E. Franklin Frazier, The Negro Family in the United States, pp. 34–42
- William R. Taylor, Cavalier and Yankee
- Louise Hall Tharp, The Peabody Sisters of Salem
- Mary E. Livermore, Autobiography
- Oscar Handlin, Race and Nationality in American Life (chapter, "The Horrors")
- Richard Sennett, Families Against the City
- Elsie Clews Parsons, The Family
- Papers and Proceedings of the American Sociological Society, III (Chicago, 1909—whole series of articles on American family life

ASSIGNMENT VII TWENTIETH CENTURY FEMINISM AND THE SEXUAL REVOLUTION

I. Biography and Autobiography

- Rheta Childe Dorr, Woman of Fifty
- Margaret Sanger, Autobiography
- Mabel Dodge Luhan, Autobiography
- Mary Gray Peck, Carrie Chapman Catt
- The Living of Charlotte Perkins Gilman
- Margaret Mead, ed., Anthropologist at Work
- Mary Anderson, Woman at Work
- Harriot Stanton Blatch, Challenging Years
- Virginia Gildersleeve, Many a Good Crusade
- Ellen Glasgow, Woman Within
- Alice Hamilton, Exploring the Dangerous Trades
- Josephine Goldmark, Impatient Crusader
- Anna Howard Shaw, The Story of a Pioneer
- Peggy Lamson, Few Are Chosen
- Vida Scudder, On Journey
- The Letters of Edna St. Vincent Millay
- Mary Church Terrell, A Colored Woman in a White World

II. Specific discussions of problems of women [thirty-nine titles; among them:]

- Rheta Childe Dorr, What Eight Million Women Want
- Margaret Sanger, Woman and the New Race
- Anna Garlin Spencer, Woman's Place in Social Culture

Frieda Kirchwey, Our Changing Morality

Elsie Clews Parsons, The Old Fashioned Woman

Ida M. Tarbell, The Business of Being a Woman

Havelock Ellis, Men and Women

Helen Deutsch, The Psychology of Women

Mirra Komarovsky, Women in the Modern World: Their Education and Their Dilemmas

Betty Friedan, The Feminine Mystique

Robin Morgan, Sisterhood is Powerful

Kate Millett, Sexual Politics

III. Periodical Articles [Fourteen articles; among them:]

"Women's Work After the War," The New Republic, Jan. 25, 1919

Mary Van Kleeck, "Woman and Machines," Atlantic Monthly, Feb. 1921

Talcott Parsons, "Age and Sex in the Social Structure of the United States," American Sociological Review, vol. 7, pp. 604–616

"American Woman's Dilemma," Life, June 16, 1947

"Why Women Quit," Business Week, Oct. 16, 1943

Lotte Bailyn, "Career and Family Orientations of Husbands and Wives in Relation to Marital Happiness," Human Relations vol. 23, No. 2 (1970), pp. 97–113

The two great social movements of the mid-twentieth century exerted an unprecedented impact on American higher education. As college students moved into political action for civil rights and, subsequently, for women's liberation, they were startled by the absence of these issues in their own studies—in history, sociology, literature, political science. Hungry for their history, African American students and their allies demanded that colleges and universities include African American experience in the curriculum; women's liberation activists followed suit. College and university faculties, accustomed to defining what was appropriate for students to learn, were generally slow to appreciate the compliment that was being paid, and instead were often shocked, hostile, even furious, denigrating the knowledge that the students demanded. Women's studies programs—like the African American studies programs initiated in the early 1970s—(both of which now thrive) were typically the result of protracted negotiations; in a extreme cases these came about only after sit-ins, hunger strikes, and other disruptive protests. The documents that follow trace some of the intense and sometimes nasty debate at Harvard University, one of the last major research universities to institute a degree in women's studies.

Founding the Committee for Women's Studies at Harvard University, 1986

1970s
STUDENTS ESTABLISH AN AD HOC COMMITTEE FOR WOMEN'S STUDIES TO LOBBY FOR A CONCENTRATION IN THE FIELD

By the mid-1970s, as the Boston area women's movement fragmented, Radcliffe student activists—liberal feminists, radical feminists, socialist feminists, Third World feminists, and Marxist-Leninists—joined together to fight for women's studies at Harvard. Part of the forgotten story of the student movement of the 1970s, the Committee for Women's Studies aimed to create a Women's Studies Department along the lines of the embattled Afro-American Studies Department and to infuse women's scholarship and experience into the entire Harvard curriculum. The egregious exclusion of all but a few distinguished women from Harvard's faculty and the invisibility of women in our studies kept us focused on the task at hand. We had a multi-pronged strategy, from educational forums to leaflets and petitions to negotiating with the administration. At the time, as an art student, I saw my main contribution to the Committee for Women's Studies as designing educational and polemical materials. As a historian today looking back, I can discern in my participation in the Committee for Women's Studies the beginnings of my longstanding research interests in feminism, gender, and race. I still carry with me lessons learned about respecting the political, social, and cultural differences among us, the painful personal costs of racism and homophobia, and the importance of taking a stand in the supposed ivory tower of academia.

—Yaël Simpson Fletcher

1978
FACULTY COUNCIL ESTABLISHES A COMMITTEE ON WOMEN'S STUDIES TO ENCOURAGE THE DEVELOPMENT OF DEPARTMENTAL COURSES IN THE FIELD

The Faculty Committee will not recommend establishing a department or a concentration in women's studies, Edward L. Keenan '57, dean of the Graduate School of Arts and Sciences and chairman of the Faculty Committee, said yesterday. The standing committee that would be created would primarily concern itself with encouraging departments to offer courses in women's studies, and would probably not offer courses on its own, Keenan said.

—*Harvard Crimson,* May 24, 1978

A graduate student said she thought it was unfortunate that someone could go through Harvard and "not know a single thing about one woman in the world."

—*Harvard Crimson*, Feb. 9, 1979

1986
HARVARD FACULTY DEBATES WOMEN'S STUDIES

A month after a leading British historian [Olwen Hufton] accepted the University's first joint tenured position in Women's Studies, the field is on the verge of becoming an official Harvard concentration. . . . As the vote approaches, however, the idea that was first advanced more than eight years ago remains a subject of disagreement among professors.

"Courses taught by women under Women's Studies have been a vehicle for feminist

Excerpted from *Yards and Gates: Gender in Harvard and Radcliffe History,* ed. Laurel Thatcher Ulrich (New York: Palgrave Macmillan, 2004), pp. 299–302.

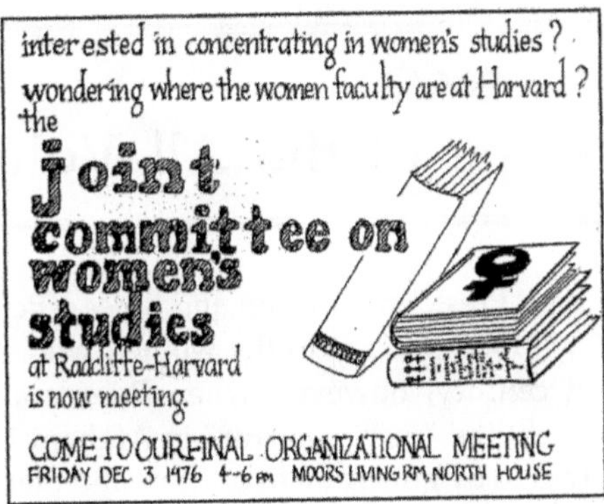

Poster advocating a concentration in Women's Studies, 1970s. (Yaël Simpson Fletcher.)

propaganda," Harvey C. Mansfield, Jr., Professor of Government, said yesterday.

"It may disrupt the process of integration of Women's Studies courses with other disciplines," said Steven E. Ozment, professor of history and associate dean for undergraduate education. "It's like trying to bottle sunlight," said Ozment. "The experience of women is so broad that it may be impossible for a set core of courses to define it."

"I think Women's Studies would be the best 350th gift that Harvard would get," said Assistant Professor of History, Catherine Clinton.

—All from the *Harvard Crimson*, Oct. 23, 1986

With only one dissenting voice, the Faculty of Arts and Sciences voted yesterday to create an undergraduate degree-granting program in Women's Studies. . . . "I am delighted," said Women's Studies Committee Chairman Susan R. Suleiman, professor of Romantic and comparative literature. "This is a really important and historic day for Harvard and I am gratified by the reaction of my colleagues who have shown they are not unresponsive to the needs of students."

—*Harvard Crimson*, Nov. 19, 1986

Harvard is the latest of some 450 schools, including the seven other Ivy League colleges, to adopt women's studies, a field first recognized in the late 1960s and now considered at the cutting edge of many scholarly disciplines. . . . The approval yesterday followed several years of work by a faculty committee and a petition signed last spring by 2,104 students, nearly one-third of Harvard's undergraduates.

—*Boston Globe*, Nov. 19, 1986

ELIZABETH L. HILLMAN

The Female Shape of the All-Volunteer Force

During the Vietnam War, President Johnson and other officials referred to our "boys in uniform" without apology to the women who also served in that war. By the twenty-first century, however, when President George W. Bush deployed U.S. troops to fight the "war on terror" in Afghanistan and Iraq, these troops were always referred to by government officials and members of the media as "our brave men and women in uniform." In the span of thirty short years, the participation of women in the military rose dramatically; by early 2009, women were 14.3 percent of the armed forces. No longer invisible, servicewomen are now consistently acknowledged as critical members of the U.S. military.

In this essay, Elizabeth Hillman explains how women came to figure crucially in recruitment, and how the military has responded to this dramatic demographic shift within its ranks. What factors account for the "feminization" of the armed services? Why have military leaders supported affirmative action? What have been the benefits and the costs of women's enhanced presence in the U.S. military? Why have many women found military service appealing?

Because of the numbers and influence of women in the ranks, the U.S. military took on a distinctively female shape in the last decades of the twentieth century. In every service, at nearly every rank and grade, in virtually every unit and at every installation, servicewomen reported for duty alongside men. As early as the 1970s, military and political leaders knew that the military could not meet its personnel needs without drawing on the female labor force. And the need for women in uniform has not let up since. The tremendous demand for military resources in the post-Vietnam era, coupled with women's push for equal opportunity, has drawn women into the military in transformative numbers. In spite of the resistance of military institutions, the post-Vietnam armed forces have become "feminized" in many key respects. "Female" issues such as promoting healthy families, ending sexual harassment, and preventing sexualized torture command the attention of military task forces and congressional committees. "Feminine" skills including compromise, negotiation, and communication are among the skills most critical to successful peacekeeping operations and even to military interrogation. And women themselves are essential cogs in the military manpower machine.

But this new gender balance, this "feminization," has caught military and political leaders off guard. The United States has not reconceived military service as a civic duty of and career opportunity for both women and men, nor has it made the military workplace safe for women. Instead, military and civilian leaders have restricted women's opportunities and reinvented a "warrior" culture of aggression and male coming-of-age.[1] Despite the integration of women and racial minorities into most of the armed forces, the U.S. military remains one of the only American institutions that can legally discriminate on the basis of sex.

In the last three decades, observers in and out of uniform have debated the wisdom and consequences of women's military service. But none can dispute the new gender demographics of the post-Vietnam U.S. military. Those demographics reveal a startling and

"The Female Shape of the All-Volunteer Force" by Elizabeth L. Hillman, ch. 8 of *Iraq and the Lessons of Vietnam, or, How Not to Learn from the Past*, ed. Lloyd C. Gardner and Marilyn B. Young (New York: New Press, 2007). Reprinted by permission of New Press and the author. Notes have been edited and renumbered.

largely ignored truth: with the end of forcible service for men, women rescued the all-volunteer force from devastating shortfalls in the number and quality of recruits. As the Vietnam War ended, the Selective Service Act was allowed to expire. When the last draft call went out in 1973, women made up less than 2 percent of the U.S. military. Ten years later, the female presence in the ranks had increased five times over. By September 2005, women were 16 percent of the American armed forced.[2] Without them, the military would have suffered not only a shortage of personnel, but also a striking drop in the education levels and test scores of new recruits.

Much as the officials and consultants of the Vietnam era failed to appreciate the degree to which women and racial minorities would become essential military personnel, the architects of the early twenty-first century military transformation have failed to reckon with the consequences of women's heightened military participation. One of the lessons that the military has forgotten since the Vietnam War is that women saved the all-volunteer force. That rescue came at great cost—to servicewomen, to the military, and to the United States.

THE ALL-VOLUNTEER FORCE: WOMEN AS SAVING GRACE

In 2003, the University of Michigan won a battle in the courts to preserve its ability to consider race in student admissions decisions. It won by arguing that diversity was a compelling objective of state educational policy.[3] A turning point in that case was the amicus curiae [friend of the court] brief signed by twenty-nine retired generals and admirals, including notable military leaders such as Admiral William T. Crowe, chairman of the Joint Chiefs of Staff from 1985 to 1989; General Norman Schwarzkopf, commander of allied forces in the Gulf War of 1991; and General Wesley Clark, supreme allied commander in Europe from 1997 to 2000. Their brief, quoted at some length in Justice Sandra Day O'Connor's opinion for the Supreme Court, stressed the negative consequences of racial disparities in the Vietnam-era armed forces and declared that affirmative action was essential to maintaining a diverse, well-qualified military. That amicus brief was a direct outgrowth of the military's role as a model of successful racial integration. Active-duty as well as retired military leaders routinely invoke the rhetoric of equal opportunity in the strongest possible language.[4] The armed forces of the early twenty-first century embrace diversity as a positive good as thoroughly and publicly as any American institution.

But thirty years ago, the experts who were asked to prepare the nation for the end of conscription did not see diversity as a possibility, much less a goal. During the Vietnam War, the Department of Defense had relied on forced service, not volunteers, to fill many of the least desirable and most dangerous military occupations. The risks and hardships of serving in the Army's ground forces rather than in the more technical, less martial forces of the air and sea services persuaded many young men to enlist in the Navy or Air Force rather than wait for a draft notice and end up in the infantry. After the war, military planners and civilian government officials underestimated the degree to which the end of the draft would also end this incentive to volunteer. They also misjudged the extent of American youth's disenchantment with military service. As a result, they anticipated almost no change in the gender or racial demographics of military service in a volunteer military.[5]

The most influential expert assessment was the report prepared by the Gates Commission in 1970. Chartered by President Nixon to develop a plan to end the draft and named for its chair, Thomas S. Gates, a former secretary of defense, the commission unanimously recommended that conscription be ended. The commission's report ignored women entirely, mentioning female service only in the context of alternatives to a volunteer force. Instead, the report stressed the importance of increasing military pay, describing "the first indispensable step" toward a successful volunteer force as removing "the present inequity in the pay" of servicemen. This emphasis on financial incentives reflected the influence of commissioners such as economists Alan Greenspan and Milton Friedman, but the commission's failure to discuss even the possible recruitment of women was nonetheless a remarkable omission.[6] Military leaders knew—and had known since at least World War II, when more than 350,000 women served in military uniforms—that women could be relied upon to fill gaps in military staffing. A 1966 Pentagon task force had studied the use of women to meet the personnel needs of the war in Vietnam, and in 1967 Congress had lifted the 2 percent ceiling on female enlistments.[7] In addition, the commissioners themselves had identified the structural factors—the evolution in military occupations and the skills that those occupations required—that soon led to many more women in uniform. The commission noted the trend toward more technical and bureaucratic military jobs, documenting how the proportion of military occupations involving ground combat had fallen from 25 percent in 1945 to 10 percent by 1974. This meant that an increasing number of military positions could be filled by servicewomen without even reaching the question as to whether women should be subjected to combat situations. The commission also identified the quality of recruits as a major concern for an all-volunteer force, a problem that could logically be addressed by broadening the potential pool of recruits to include women. But the commission failed to connect the dots when it came to women. The demographics of the commission itself were part of the problem: only one of fifteen commissioners, and none of the thirty-one senior staff and research leads, was a woman.[8]

The experts' botched forecast was apparent almost immediately. As soon as the draft ended, the numbers and quality indicators of male volunteers fell and the Department of Defense scrambled to recruit women. By 1972, Secretary of Defense Melvin R. Laird was establishing a task force, to prepare contingencies for the use of women if the draft ended, and by 1978, the Carter administration was explicitly directing the Pentagon to increase the number of servicewomen.[9] A 1977 Brookings Institution study recommended recruiting women because it was less expensive and would reduce the pressure for more men.[10] Fifteen years after the draft ended, the number of women in uniform had increased from 1.5 percent to more than 9 percent. Women's scores on military aptitude tests shored up the military's quality indicators as well as its overall numbers.[11] In fiscal years 1974 to 1976, for example, 88 percent of the women who joined the Army were high school graduates, as compared to only 52 percent of the men; in the first decade of the volunteer force, 92 percent of all women enlistees had high school diplomas, compared to only 70 percent of male enlistees. One scholar bluntly wrote, "It is widely acknowledged that women were the saving grace of the volunteer concept during the 1970s."[12]

After the 1970s, women continued to enlist in larger numbers than initially expected, spurred in part by changes in military personnel policies. In order to attempt to recruit more men, the military increased pay and benefits and recognized the need to support military families and service members' dependents. These changes in military policy created economic and social incentives that made recruiting and retention of skilled, reliable servicemen possible. But they also made a military career more attractive to women, especially those who lacked significant economic opportunities in the civilian sector. The military eliminated restrictions on assignments that prevented women from serving in many military occupations and relaxed restrictions that forced pregnant women to be discharged and limited the number of dependent children of recruits. These trends combined to make the armed forces a viable career choice for those seeking economic security and educational support. By the late 1990s, the number of military personnel who served for more than four years had increased significantly, one of many indicators of an increasingly career-oriented force.[13]

This sea change in military demographics made women the fastest-growing segment of veterans in the early twenty-first century. In 1983, Congress established a Secretary of Veterans' Affairs Advisory Committee on Women Veterans. In 1994, a Center for Women Veterans was established in the Department of Veterans Affairs after legislation championed by Representative Maxine Waters of California.[14]

In addition to missing the gender implications of the volunteer force, government planners also underestimated the rate at which African Americans would enlist in a volunteer military. The percentage of African Americans in the military nearly doubled in the first decade after the end of the draft. This concurrent increase in minority and female participation led to a dramatic rise in the number of African American women in the service; by 1986, black women were 43 percent of Army enlisted women and 30 percent of the entire female force.[15] In 2005, women constituted 16 percent of the military workforce and 48 percent of the overall civilian workforce. African American women, however, accounted for 28 percent of the female military presence despite being only 13 percent of the female civilian labor force. In the Army, this overrepresentation of African American women was especially pronounced: black women made up 39 percent of female Army personnel on active duty in 2004.[16] In recent years, the Congressional Black Caucus Veterans Braintrust has paid particular attention to the needs of the fast-growing population of African American female veterans. In many respects, African American women were at the center of the demographic transformation triggered by the end of the Vietnam War. Their experience crystallizes the role and treatment of women in the volunteer force: they helped to save the volunteer army by enlisting in disproportionately high numbers but their opportunities for military success were circumscribed by discrimination and harassment.

WOMEN VOLUNTEERS: FITS, STARTS, AND PROGRESS

Once in uniform, women were assigned, evaluated, and promoted in ways that reflected cultural assumptions about female capability. Military laws and policies structured the work environments of servicewomen and reinforced a gender hierarchy that affected civilian as well as military women. Within that hierarchy, sexual harassment and assault became a feature of the military workplace and threatened the lives and health of women around domestic and foreign military bases. Because the volunteer force needed female servicemembers, and because women needed the career stability and economic opportunities that military service offered, the ranks of servicewomen steadily grew. But the emphasis on male authority and aggressiveness that predominated in many quarters of military service left women unprotected from discrimination and abuse. Women made great strides toward becoming full participants in military service. Their success, however, came against a backdrop of continued restrictions and a repetitious debate about whether or not they belonged in the service at all.

When the Vietnam War ended, servicewomen had already won the support of many commanders and political leaders. The Defense Department Advisory Committee on Women in the Services, established by Secretary of Defense George C. Marshall in 1951 to aid in the recruitment of women during the Korean War, monitored the progress of women's service and recommended solutions to recurring problems.[17] The promotion and recruiting restrictions that had prevented women from either attaining high rank or reaching a significant proportion of the force were already gone, and by 1972, the Air Force, Army, and Navy Reserve Officer Training Corps (ROTC) programs were all open to women.[18] Admiral Elmo Zumwalt, the Navy's maverick chief of naval operations from 1970 to 1974, opened many previously closed naval occupational specialties to women during his tenure. The Air Force led the way in accommodating women's reproductive lives by allowing women with children to enlist and permitting waivers of the Department of Defense's automatic discharge policy for pregnant women. Civil courts, responding to new pressure for civil rights and expanding notions of legal equality, had also begun to push the armed forces to treat women fairly. Sharron Frontiero, who served in the Air Force, found that her male colleagues automatically got dependents' benefits for their wives, but in order for her to get dependent's allowances for her husband, she had to prove that she provided more than 50% of his financial support. She challenged this practice, and in 1973, the Supreme Court struck down sex discrimination in the distribution of military benefits.[19] Still, in 1972, just before the draft ended, only 42,000 women served in the military, and more than 90 percent were assigned to jobs classified as medical, dental, or clerical in nature.[20]

The advent of the volunteer force brought sharp increases not only in servicewomen's numbers (more than 100,000 women were serving in 1976 and more than 150,000 by 1979) but also in their opportunities. By 1976, the percentage of women in those "feminine" military classifications had dropped to 60 percent, and by 1983, it was down to 55 percent, with increasing numbers of women assigned to fields such as intelligence, supply, and equipment repair.[21] Congress opened the elite national service academies to women in 1976, and the courts continued to nudge the military in the direction of equitable gender policies, holding in 1976 that the Marine Corps' policy of mandatory discharge of pregnant Marines violated the Constitution and ordering the Navy to open additional ships to women in 1978.[22] By 2005, women accounted for about one-sixth of the active and reserve forces. They were most outnumbered in Marine Corps, where female marines were but 5 percent of the force, but they made up nearly a quarter of both Army and Air Force reserves.[23]

Progress toward equal opportunity across gender lines was not a steady march, however. As the number of servicewomen grew, gender-based restrictions on military assignments remained in place. Military leaders limited the changes wrought by women's military presence by preserving some positions as male-only. They argued that the risks involved, the physical capabilities required, or the military facilities available (such as berthing capacity on ships) would make women's presence in these positions a detriment to military effectiveness. This debate centered on the issue of the appropriateness and practicability of assigning women only to noncombat jobs. Proponents of women in combat argued that the restrictions protected masculine privilege, not female bodies, while opponents pointed to the history of male participation in war fighting and the vital importance of bonding ("unit cohesion") in guaranteeing performance under fire. The Supreme Court upheld the all-male Selective Service system in 1981 on the grounds that women were not eligible for combat, demonstrating the importance of this military personnel policy.[24]

The patchwork of combat exclusion rules that evolved as Congress and the president negotiated with the services revealed widespread resistance to the full inclusion of female service members. Identifying combat positions was not a simple task; some military occupational specialties were opened, closed, and reopened to women as opinions shifted about their suitability for women. Lawrence J. Korb, a scholar of military affairs and an assistant secretary of defense from 1981 to 1985, once described the "combat-exclusion policy" as "the worst of all possible worlds for female military personnel" because it limited women's advancement but failed to protect them from the risks of dangerous service. The arguments for and against permitting women to serve in combat positions were endlessly recycled during the first three decades of the volunteer force.[25]

Still, the trend was clearly in the direction of opening doors to women. Most military jobs are now performed by both men and women. In 1988, the Department of Defense opened about 30,000 new positions to service women by setting a single standard (called the "risk rule") to be used in evaluating sex-based restrictions on assignments. The service of military women in the invasion of Panama in 1989 and the Persian Gulf War in 1990 and 1991 led to more pressure to lift sex-based restrictions on assignments. Combat aviation opened to women in 1993, and a 1994 policy change rescinded the "risk rule" in favor of a ban on the assignment of women to units below the brigade level with a primary mission of engaging in direct ground combat. Servicewomen have acted as peacekeepers in Haiti, enforced no-fly zones in Iraq, flown combat missions in Kosovo, died in terrorist attacks on the USS *Cole* in 2000 and at the Pentagon in 2001, and been wounded alongside men in Afghanistan and Iraq in the first U.S. wars of the twenty-first century.[26]

Thirty years into the volunteer force, women shoulder the burdens of military duty but have yet to ascend to the highest ranks of military institutions. In 2005, there were 43 female flag or general officers as compared to 874 male such officers, a female representation of less than five percent, and only one woman stood among the 173 men at the two highest grades. The wide gap between women's representation at the top and the bottom of the military hierarchy reflects more than the time lag between accession to duty and late-career promotions.[27]

The vestiges of the combat exclusion policy keep women off the fastest tracks to military promotion. In 2005, sex-based restrictions on women's assignments placed 15 to 20 percent of military positions off-limits for women, most of them in the infantry and special forces. Women are excluded from 178 enlisted specialties (5 percent of all available specialties) and 17 officer specialties (1 percent of those available). Servicewomen remain concentrated in health care and administrative occupations. Although these combat exclusions cannot eliminate female casualties, they have placed disproportionately more servicemen than women in harm's way. Even in the ongoing war in Iraq, which has brought female military casualties and deaths to the front pages of U.S. newspapers, servicewomen account for only 1 percent of deaths and 2 percent of the wounded.[28] For those who served short terms in the conscript army of the Vietnam War, avoiding combat had been a way to stay alive; for those who make careers in the volunteer military, avoiding combat is still a safer way to go, but it has also become a professional liability. Women are "underrepresented in tactical operations, the area that yields two-thirds of the general and flag officers of the Services." Women are also a smaller percentage of service academy graduates than men, partly because so many women are directly commissioned as nurses but also because women's presence at the academies has been carefully monitored by officials unwilling to permit too many women to populate the ranks of elite cadets and midshipmen. Women of all races have lower promotion and retention rates than men, though the data vary across race lines. White women tend to leave the military before attaining high rank, while African American women—notwithstanding a widespread perception among white servicemen that minorities are favored in selection for promotions—are promoted at lower rates than the members of any other demographic category. Every service except the Air Force still includes photographs in the packets considered by promotion boards, furthering the perception that race and gender are taken into account—as pluses or minuses in the promotion process.[29]

Family responsibilities also contribute to women's underrepresentation at the highest levels of military service. Although most senior servicemen are married, husbands—and children—are scarce for women at high ranks as compared to men. At the relatively senior ranks of O–5 and O–6 (that is, lieutenant colonels and colonels in the Army, Air Force, and Marine Corps and commanders and captains in the Navy), 90 percent of men but only 55 percent of women are married. Ninety-four percent of military spouses are women. Even with such relatively low rates of marriage, servicewomen routinely identify family issues such as child care among their primary concerns about continued military service.[30]

Women's family responsibilities were of great concern to those who opposed the integration of women into the military infrastructure. But fears about women missing too much time for medical reasons and maternity, including pregnancy-related disabilities, have proven unfounded. Most studies of gender differences in performance point out that men miss more time for disciplinary matters such as drug and alcohol abuse than women miss for medical leave. After all, the demands of family push servicemen as well as women away from the sacrifices that a military career requires.[31]

THE VOLUNTEER FORCE TODAY

Women's military opportunities have opened up dramatically since the Vietnam War, and women were critical in keeping the volunteer army afloat after the draft ended. But women's appearance in the volunteer military was not enough to meet the armed forces' relentless need for more people, more expertise, and more money. Servicewomen mitigated, but did not end, the constant pressure to recruit. The military's failure to promote gender equity in assignment and promotion policies and its inability to build a culture in which women were valued and respected as much as men have created additional problems for the volunteer force. Though the gender transformation of the volunteer military answered the question of whether women should serve, doubts about the proper extent of that service have persisted in American public discourse. In the post-9/11 military, the debate continues over women's military participation, even in the face of rising demands for military personnel and declining success in recruiting.[32]

Thirty years into the volunteer military, the United States has invested enormous resources in recruiting military personnel. In fiscal year 2003, the Department of Defense spent $455 million on special incentives such as enlistment bonuses, college funds, and loan repayments. In addition to these incentive programs, the United States has repeatedly increased military pay since the Vietnam era, responding to studies that stressed higher pay as a primary means of recruiting high-quality personnel. These financial incentives are necessary because current military personnel policies prohibit so many potential recruits from enlisting. According to the Department of Defense, at least half of U.S. youth between the ages of 16 and 21 are not qualified to enlist, mostly because of "physical and mental deficits" such as asthma, obesity, illegal drug use, or the use of prescription antidepressants. Potential recruits are also disqualified for failure to meet educational, aptitude, or moral character standards (measured by criminal convictions and evidence of "asocial behavior"). A recruit can also be disqualified for having too many children; if unmarried, no dependent children are allowed, and if married, a recruit may have no more than two dependent children. Waivers to these requirements are permitted and are more likely during times of greatest need; in 2005, the GAO reported that waivers for physical disabilities appeared to be increasing, while waivers for character failings were declining. The military's policy prohibiting service by men and women who are unable—or refuse—to hide their gay or lesbian sexual orientation also limits the pool of available military recruits. The constant need for more personnel both taxes resources and undermines morale.[33]

The twenty-first-century U.S. military also faces an uphill battle in retaining high-quality personnel because of the conditions under which many service members work and live. One recent study described the strain that the post-9/11 military actions have placed on the volunteer military as "unprecedented" because of lengthy, frequent deployments and "exposure to nontraditional, hostile combat conditions." These conditions have contributed to declining interest among male high school students in military service, a shift that is especially evident among African American young men since fiscal year 2002. As a result of these trends, the military has little choice but to recruit women to help to fill its ranks.[34]

The women who heed the call to join, as well as the civilian women who live or work with service members, must reckon with not only limits on advancement but also a climate of sexual harassment, assault, and violence.[35] Some of the abuse endured by military and civilian women at the hands of servicemen takes place at home, where the stresses of military life can explode into family violence. The pressures of military service are often worst at the bottom of the military hierarchy, where financial pressures are greatest and where the wives of young enlistees often find their career opportunities limited by their husbands' service. Military families often face "separations, serious financial pressures, isolation from family and peer support systems, and frequent moves," all of which increase the risk of family violence. Military training and combat experience may also increase the risk of domestic violence. The Department of Defense has responded to public outcry and congressional mandates by establishing programs to discourage and track spousal and child abuse in military families, but the problem is far from resolved.[36]

Abuse of women also takes place in military workplaces, partly because of continued resistance to the integration of the volunteer force. Women and racial minorities struggle with being excluded, tested, and harassed more often than white men, who still dominate the ranks, constituting 58 percent of the 2005 military. Servicewomen routinely hear denigrating comments about female capabilities, rebuff unwanted sexual advances, are physically harassed, and must face down assumptions that they are promoted because of, not in spite of, their gender and/or race. The parade of military sexual harassment and assault scandals in the 1990s and first few years of the 2000s demonstrated that sexualized abuse had become a part of military service.[37] Servicewomen are also disproportionately censured under the "don't ask/don't tell" policy, and fear of being called a lesbian deters women from reporting unwanted sexual advances and assaults. The military's zero-tolerance response to this epidemic of abuse has led some servicemen to avoid allegations of sexual harassment by avoiding women entirely, a reaction that further isolates servicewomen and limits their advancement. As a 2005 task force on sexual harassment and assault at the U.S. service academies described the situation: "Although progress has been made, hostile attitudes and inappropriate actions toward women, and the toleration of these by some . . . continue to hinder the establishment of a safe and professional environment."[38]

In 2006 [as I write], even with the help of women enlistees, the volunteer force faces constant challenges to meet its personnel needs. Despite their willingness to serve, women have not been able to rescue the U.S. military from the threat posed by the end of conscription, nor have they changed its fundamental nature. Their service has not ended the insular nature of military service, lessened the rigidity of military culture, or restored the luster of military service to attract and keep the best and brightest. They have not transformed the military's social and political order into the entrepreneurial, risk-taking environment that Secretary of Defense Donald Rumsfeld called for. And neither has their presence forestalled the sexual violence so often committed by U.S. service members.

Perhaps the most telling example of the success and limits of the gender integration of the volunteer force is the appearance of women at the center of the first major military scandal of the twenty-first century. Although the sexual harassment and torture of detainees in the post-9/11 wars was perpetrated by both women and men, the public faces of the American torturers indisputably belonged to two Army women, a private and a general: the derisive smile and dangling cigarette of Specialist Lynndie R. England, a young female enlistee photographed while pointing at naked detainees, and the stern visage of Brigadier General Janis Karpinski, the Army Reserve officer in charge of the prison at Abu Ghraib during the most publicized incidents of prisoner abuse.[39] Other women were also key figures in the debacle, including dozens of enlisted military police and nonmilitary interrogators. Lieutenant Colonel Diane E. Beaver, the staff judge advocate for a joint task force at Guantanamo Bay, wrote a key legal brief recommending the use of more aggressive interrogation techniques in 2002. Major General Barbara Fast, the highest-ranking woman to serve in Iraq, was the intelligence chief for the U.S. military ground commander and oversaw the interrogation centers at Abu Ghraib during 2003 and 2004. Not all of these women were punished for their roles in the scandal, but several were, most notably Karpinski, who was reprimanded and demoted, and England, who was sentenced to three years' confinement and dishonorably discharged. Servicewomen's successful integration into the intelligence, military police, and legal career fields put them at the center of detainee operations in Iraq and made them relatively easy to blame for the military's maltreatment of detainees and mismanagement of detention facilities.[40]

Whoever bears ultimate responsibility for the crimes that took place in American detention facilities in the post-9/11 wars, Lynndie England has joined the rogues' gallery of U.S. service members punished for their failures in wartime. That gallery used to be exclusively male, featuring the troubled Eddie Slovik, executed during World War II for desertion; the unfortunate Claude Batchelor, a trumpet player turned infantryman who was court-martialed after the Korean War for collaborating with Communists while imprisoned in North Korea; and the notorious William Calley, convicted but barely punished for leading the horrifying massacre at My Lai. The addition of women to such a dubious military legacy suggests that women bear the impossible burdens of wartime service no more nobly or easily than men.

Notes

1. See Judith A. Youngman, "Whatever Happened to the Citizen Soldier?" in *Women in Uniform: Exploding the Myths, Exploring the Facts* (Washington, DC: Women's Research and Education Institute, 1998); Laura Miller, "Not Just Weapons of the Weak: Gender Harassment as a Form of Protest for Army Men," *Social Psychology Quarterly* 60 (1997), pp. 32–51.

2. *Military Personnel: Reporting Additional Service member Demographics Could Enhance Congressional Oversight*, General Accounting Office Report to Congressional Requesters, September 2005 (hereafter GAO report), pp. 10–11; see also chart, p. 38.

3. *Grutter* v. *Bollinger*, 539 U.S. 306 (2003).

4. Defense Equal Opportunity Council, *Report of the Task Force on Discrimination and Sexual Harassment*, vol. I, Washington, DC, May 1995, p. i.

5. Martin Binkin and Mark J. Eitelberg, "Women and Minorities in the All-Volunteer Force," in *The All-Volunteer Force After a Decade: Retrospect and Prospect*, ed. William Bowman et al. (New York: Pergamon-Brassey's, 1986), p. 74.

6. *The Report of the President's Commission on an All-Volunteer Force* (New York: Collier/Macmillan, 1970).

7. Binkin and Eitelberg, "Women and Minorities in the All-Volunteer Force," p. 82.

8. *The Report of the President's Commission on an All-Volunteer Force*, pp. 43, 18. The only female commissioner was Dr. Jeanne Noble, a professor of education and vice president of the National Council of Negro Women, who in 1962 had become one of the first African American women to receive tenure at New York University.

9. Binkin and Eitelberg, "Women and Minorities in the All-Volunteer Force," p. 83.

10. Carolyn Becraft, "Women and the Military: Bureaucratic Policies and Politics," in *Women in the Military*, ed. E.A. Blacksmith (New York: II.W. Wilson, 1992), p. 9.

11. Lawrence Korb, "The Pentagon's Perspective," in *Who Defends America? Race, Sex, and Class in the Armed Forces*, ed. Edwin Dorn (Washington, DC: Joint Center for Political Studies, 1989), pp. 24–25.

12. Martin Binkin, *America's Volunteer Military: Progress and Prospects* (Washington, DC: Brookings Institution, 1984), pp. 7–8, 48.

13. Office of the Under Secretary of Defense Personnel and Readiness, *Career Progression of Minority and Women Officers* (Washington, DC: 1998) (hereafter Career Progression report), p. 10.

14. See the research compiled by the Women's Research and Education Institute, available at www.wrei.org, which uses Bureau of Labor Statistics to document the rising number of women veterans.

15. Binkin and Eitelberg, "Women and Minorities in the All-Volunteer Force," p. 82; *Who Defends America?*, p. 48.

16. GAO report, pp. 3, 42.

17. Laura L. Miller, "Feminism and the Exclusion of Army Women from Combat," in *Women in the Military*, ed. Rita James Simon (New Brunswick, NJ: Transaction, 2001), p. 109. See also the DACOW1TS Web site at http://www.dtic.mil/dacowits (visited July 29, 2006).

18. For a chronology of significant dates, see Captain Lory Manning, *Women in the Military: Where They Stand*, 5th ed. (Washington, DC: Women's Research and Education Institute, 2005), pp. 4–9.

19. *Frontiero* v. *Richardson*, 411 U.S. 677 (1973).

20. Binkin and Eitelberg, "Women and Minorities in the All-Volunteer Force," p. 85.

21. It is important to remember that these aggregate figures describe a volunteer military that was not a monolith but instead a collection of service branches and subcultures. The almost entirely male Marine Corps shares little in mission or tradition, for instance, with the technocratic Air Force, which is nearly one-fifth female.

22. *Crawford* v. *Cushman*, 538 F.2d 1114 (1976); *Owens* et al. v. *Brown*, 455 F.Supp. 291 (1978).

23. GAO report, p. 38.

24. Rostker v. Goldberg, 453 U.S. 57 (1981). See pp. 738–740.

25. Becraft, "Women and the Military," pp. 11–15; Korb, "The Pentagon's Perspective,"p. 25. For a useful overview of the issues surrounding women in combat, see *Female Soldiers: Combatants or Noncombatants*, ed. Nancy Loring Goldman (Westport, CT: Greenwood Press, 1982). In 2005, the arguments looked much the same as in 1982. See, e.g., "G.I. Jane, Again,". *National Review* 57, no. 10 (June 6, 2005), pp. 22–24 (Army's restrictions on women in combat and debating the efficacy of such restrictions); "Women Already See Combat," *USA Today*, May 25, 2005; M.C. Devilbiss, *Women and Military Service: A History, Analysis, and Overview* (Maxwell Air Force Base, AL: Air University Press, 1990); Linda Grant DePauw, *Battle Cries and Lullabies* (Norman: University of Oklahoma Press, 1998).

26. On the integration of women into combat aviation, see Captain Alice W.W. Parham, "The Quiet Revolution: Repeal of the Exclusionary Statutes in Combat Aviation—What We Have L.earned from a Decade of Integration," 12 *William and Mary Journal of Women and the Law* 377 (2006); Korb, "The Pentagon's Perspective," p. 25.

27. Department of Defense, *Active Duty Military Personnel*, September 30, 2005, available at the Office of the Secretary of Defense (OSD) Web site, http://www.defenselink.mil/osd/; Susan Hosek et al., *Minority and Gender Differences in Officer Career Progression* (Santa Monica, CA: Rand, 2001), pp. 2–3.

28. GAO report, pp. 38–39, 45, 121.

29. *Career Progression* report, pp. viii, 24, 18, 58, 75–76.

30. Karen Houppert, *Home Fires Burning: Married to the Military—for Better or Worse* (New York: Ballantine, 2005), p. xix.

31. Korb, "The Pentagon's Perspective," p. 25. See also Elizabeth Lutes Hillman, *Defending America: Military Culture and the Cold War Court-Martial* (Princeton, NJ: Princeton University Press, 2005), pp. 70–79.

32. See, e.g., Rowan Scarborough, "Iraq War Muddles Role of Women," *Washington Times*, October 17, 2005, p. A4; Jodi Wilgoren, "A Nation at War: Women in the Military: A New War Brings New Role for Women," *New York Times*, March 28, 2003, p. Bl; Rowan Scarborough, "Army Affirms Its Ban on Women in Combat," *Washington Times*, January 19, 2005, p. A1.

33. The Gates Commission report was the first such study; the most recent is the Government Accounting Office's *Military Personnel: DOD Needs to Improve the Transparency and Reassess the Reasonableness, Appropriateness, Affordability, and Sustainability of Its Military Compensation System*, GAO-05-798 (Washington, DC: July 19, 2005), which points out that military pay is but 70 percent of comparable civilian pay scales; GAO report, pp. 4, 68–76.

34. James Hosek, Jennifer Kavanaugh, and Laura Miller, *How Deployments Affect Service Members* (Santa Monica, CA: Rand, 2006), p. xiii; GAO report, pp. 80, 67, 4; "Problem for Navy: Too Few Hands on Deck," *New York Times*, February 2, 1999, pp. Al, 17.

35. Notwithstanding this grim picture, the primary targets of military sexual violence are civilian rather than military women. Cynthia Enloe's work reveals the stark dimensions of the military's long and tragic history of participating in human sex trafficking and prostitution around the world. Cynthia Enloe, *Does Khaki Become You? The Militarization of Women's Lives* (Boston: South End Press, 1983), pp. 18–45; *Bananas, Beaches, and Bases: Making Feminist Sense of International Politics* (Berkeley: University of California Press, 1990), pp. 81–90; *The Morning After: Sexual Politics at the End of the Cold War* (Berkeley: University of California Press, 1993), pp. 142–160. In the ongoing war in Iraq, the secondary targets of sexual violence seem to be the male enemy, particularly captured irregulars thought to be terrorists and considered "high- value" detainees.

36. See, e.g., Margaret C. Harrell, *Invisible Women: Junior Enlisted Army Wives* (Santa Monica, CA: Rand, 2000); James Hosek et al., *Married to the Military: The Employment and Earnings of Military Wives Compared with Those of Civilian Wives* (Santa Monica, CA: Rand, 2002), and *Battle Cries on the*

Homefront: Violence in the Military Family, ed. Peter J. Mercier and Judith D. Mercier (Springfield, IL: Charles C. Thomas, 2000). See also the Miles Foundation Web page,http://hometown.aol.com/milesfdn/myhomepage/ (accessed July 26, 2006).

37. GAO report, p. 40; Career Progression report, Chapter 7; see Linda Bird Francke, *Ground Zero: The Gender Wars in the Military* (New York: Simon & Schuster, 1997).

38. See Aaron Belkin and Geoffrey Bateman, eds., *Don't Ask/Don't Tell: Debating the Gay Ban in the Military* (Boulder.CO: Lynne Rienner, 2003); Human Rights Watch, *Uniform Discrimination: The 'Don't Ask, Don't Tell' Policy of the U.S. Military* (January 2003), http://www.hrw.org/reports/2003/usa0103/ (accessed July 24, 2006) (especially section titled "Impact on Women"); Servicemembers Legal Defense Network statistics on the disproportionately high discharge rate for servicewomen accused of being lesbians, http://www.sldn.org/binary-data/SLDN_ARTICLES/pdf_file/351 .pdf (accessed July 10,2006); *Report of the Defense Task Force on Sexual Harassment and Violence at the Military Service Academies* (Washington, DC: Department of Defense, June 2005), executive summary.

39. See, e.g., Karen J. Greenberg and Joshua L. Dratel, eds., *The Torture Papers: The Road to Abu Ghraib* (New York: Cambridge University Press, 2005).

40. James W. Smith III, "A Few Good Scapegoats: The Abu Ghraib Courts-Martial and the Failure of the Military Justice System," 27 *Whittier Law Review* 671 (2006).

DOCUMENT

The Changing Workplace

Susan Eisenberg, "Entering construction . . . was a little like falling in love with someone you weren't supposed to"

For women trying to escape traditionally "female" jobs that carried low pay, a new alternative was better-paying "male" jobs. Since the expulsion of Rosie the Riveter in the aftermath of World War II, electricians, plumbers, welders, carpenters, and machinists had been almost entirely male and white. But with the passage of the Civil Rights Act in 1964 and executive orders promoting affirmative action, women gained access to jobs in the construction industry. Making sexual harassment illegal eventually helped. Nevertheless, despite these major pressures on the construction industry from the federal government, the number of women in the construction industry has remained pitifully small in subsequent decades—9.7 percent in 2008.*

For Susan Eisenberg and the other women who entered the trades in the 1970s and stuck it out, the experience has been both challenging and rewarding. Her account shows how being pregnant on the job added a new dimension to the challenges. Above all, Eisenberg's is a story of enormous pride in her work and her young daughter's pride in a mother who builds buildings.

Like many of the first women in their locals I've met across the country, I started in 1978, when affirmative action guidelines were mandated. I graduated four years later in the first apprenticeship class of IBEW Local 103 (Boston), to include women. Of the six women who started together, five of us graduated, a higher percentage than the men in our class. We owed that largely to the support, information-sharing, and prodding we gave each other. . . .

I remember, particularly in those first years, the enormous encouragement I felt from women on the outside, as though I represented them as well. Not only friends, but strangers, too. Women driving past my jobsite who would notice me and honk and give me a raised fist. The neighbor who rode to work on the same early morning bus and always cheered me on. The older black woman I met once in the bathroom of a remodel job, who had noticed my tool pouch on the sink and told me about her own unfulfilled ambitions of a job in the skilled trades, and how she had taught herself radio electronics from books. I felt indebted and privileged that I was able to

*U.S. Department of Labor, Bureau of Labor Statistics, Report 1011, *Women in the Labor Force: A Databook* (2008 ed.), p. 227.

live out a dream of generations of women who had been locked out. . . .

My initial experience in union construction was my worst. In the first shop that I worked for, the journeymen were extremely hostile and unwilling to train me. There was even a foreman I worked under who tried to get me injured. Fortunately, I was laid off, and went to work for another shop where my experience was just the opposite. I was able to work on small jobs with some good mechanics who took me seriously and gave me a chance to learn the trade. They taught me how to mount boxes, pull and connect wires, and lay out the circuitry from a panel in an electric closet to the receptacles and lights in a room. After a lot of insisting, I got a chance to do the bigger and heavier work: wiring motors; cutting, threading, and bending pipe; mounting equipment. I learned how to climb and carry ladders, use power tools, and maneuver myself around the debris and dangers on a construction site.

Even though the work and its newness were exhilarating, I also found myself often overcome with anger, depression, or the feeling that I was in over my head. Working outside in a New England winter, or even by the water in the fall, is cold. And there were a lot of times I just had to grit my teeth and plunge across fear to do what I was asked: climb a crane, walk across a beam, work on scaffolding.

The hardest part of the job for me to get used to, though, was the talk on a construction site. Not the swearing—which guys often apologized for when I hadn't even noticed it—but jokes about beating up wives, racist and anti-Semitic slurs, degrading remarks about each other's girlfriends or some woman who happened to pass by, and comments about each others' personal lives that I found incredibly cruel. . . . On one remodel job, a residence for elders, one of the electricians joked about pulling the fire alarm and raping all the women residents . . . When I tried to say why a comment like that wasn't funny, he suggested that I could rape all the men. . . . I had to learn to harden myself, to expect little support from coworkers in group conversations, and to be selective about who and what was worth responding to. It quickly became clear that responding to all the comments I found offensive would guarantee not being heard. . . .

I worked into the sixth month of my first pregnancy without telling anyone except the general foreman and a woman elevator installer that I was pregnant. I told most people on the day I stopped working. . . . [S]ince I wore baggy clothes to work (what I called my maternity overalls) and since no one expected to see a pregnant woman on a construction sight—they didn't. I presented myself as I always had—as an electrician there to work and earn a paycheck. . . .

Not talking about my pregnancy exaggerated the feeling I often have in construction of feeling split in two. At coffee break, I would be intently aware of the kicking in my womb while having a conversation about the Red Sox. It also meant making a clear pact with myself to ask for help when I needed it or refuse to do things I felt I shouldn't do—that I would put health and safety ahead of ego. . . .

Driving around Boston, I love pointing out to my daughter and son "the jobs we worked together." It brings back the times when I felt like I carried a delicious secret: lying on a plank across an open airshaft on the roof of a building, tying in a fan motor, talking to the baby-in-utero. It gave me a powerful appreciation for the changes we have brought about. "We built that, Susie?" my daughter asks as we drive by a big hotel. "You bet!" I tell her.

DOCUMENTS

Rethinking Marriage

Loving *v.* Virginia, *1967*; Griswold *v.* Connecticut, *1965*; Defense of Marriage Act, *1996*; Goodridge *v.* Massachusetts Department of Public Health, *2003*

Although marriage is generally understood to be the most private of matters, it has been subjected to regulation by colonies and the states since the founding era. The national government has also been deeply involved in defining which marriages would be legally recognized. It has enacted laws in areas ranging from polygamy, to immigration policy, to the family structures that would be eligible for social security and aid to dependent children. As World War II ended, pressures for legislative change grew. American military personnel successfully claimed the right to bring spouses into the United States more easily than established quotas permitted. Federal laws that made Asians ineligible for citizenship proved embarrassing when China was a U.S. ally during World War II; the exclusion of Chinese was ended in 1943. American military personnel stationed in Japan during the Occupation repeatedly challenged the rule that Asians were ineligible for citizenship. Acts passed in 1945 and 1946, which cautiously facilitated the entry of foreign fiancées and spouses regardless of race, were responses to this situation. And the joint income tax, devised in 1948, offered substantial advantages to married couples that unmarried individuals did not (and still do not) enjoy.*

The democratic, inclusive rhetoric of a war against fascism made American practices of segregation increasingly anomalous and an international embarrassment. Among the civil rights that increasing numbers of citizens claimed was the right to marry the person of their choice despite state laws defining interracial marriage between whites and others as miscegenation. (Generally, these statutes permitted interracial marriage among other groups.) At the close of World War II, the laws of thirty states barred interracial marriage. Challenges built state by state. Although the California Supreme Court struck down that state's miscegenation statute in 1948† and thirteen other legislatures repealed their laws, bans continued to be enforced with serious penalties in sixteen other states.

*Carolyn Jones, "Split Income and Separate Spheres: Tax Law and Gender Roles in the 1940s," *Law and History Review*, 6 (Fall 1988): 259–310.
†*Perez* v. *Sharp*, 32 Cal 2d. 711 (1948)

Virginia's law made it illegal for "any white person in the state to marry any save a white person, or a person with no other admixture of blood than white and American Indian." (The link between whiteness and Native Americans was arranged in order to include all those white Virginians who proudly claimed descent from Pocahontas.) In 1958, two Virginians, Mildred Jeter, who was black, and Richard Loving, who was white, married in a ceremony in Washington, D.C. When they returned to Virginia to live, they were indicted for violating Virginia's ban on interracial marriages. They were found guilty and sentenced to one year in jail, which would be suspended if they left the state and did not return for twenty-five years. The aptly named Lovings moved to Washington, D.C., and challenged the conviction; eventually their case reached the U.S. Supreme Court. Richard Loving said to his attorney, "Tell the Court I love my wife, and it is just unfair that I can't live with her in Virginia."

How did the state of Virginia defend its practice? On what grounds did the Supreme Court declare the miscegenation law illegal? How did the Court describe "freedom to marry"?

LOVING v. *VIRGINIA*, 1967

CHIEF JUSTICE EARL WARREN WROTE THE OPINION FOR A UNANIMOUS COURT:

. . . the State [of Virginia] argues that the meaning of the Equal Protection Clause [of the Fourteenth Amendment, see p. 247] . . . is only that state penal laws containing an interracial element as part of the definition of the offense must apply equally to whites and Negroes in the sense that members of each race are punished to the same degree. Thus the State contends that, because its miscegenation statutes punish equally both the white and the Negro participants in an interracial marriage, these statutes, despite their reliance on racial classifications, do not constitute an invidious discrimination based upon race. . . .

Because we reject the notion that the mere "equal application" of a statute containing racial classifications is enough to remove the classifications from the Fourteenth Amendment's proscription of all invidious racial discriminations, we do not accept the State's contention. . . . There is patently no legitimate overriding purpose independent of invidious racial discrimination which justifies this classification. The fact that Virginia prohibits only interracial marriages involving white persons demonstrates that the racial classifications must stand on their own justification, as measures designed to maintain White Supremacy. . . . There can be no doubt that restricting the freedom to marry solely because of racial classification violates the central meaning of the Equal Protection Clause.

These statutes also deprive the Lovings of liberty without due process of law in violation of the Due Process Clause of the Fourteenth Amendment. The freedom to marry has long

Loving v. *Virginia*, 388 U.S. 1 (1967).

been recognized as one of the vital personal rights essential to the orderly pursuit of happiness by free men.

Marriage is one of the "basic civil rights of man," fundamental to our very existence and survival. To deny this fundamental freedom on so unsupportable a basis as the racial classifications embodied in these statutes . . . is surely to deprive all the State's citizens of liberty without due process of law. . . . Under our Constitution, the freedom to marry or not marry, a person of another race resides with the individual and cannot be infringed by the state.

These convictions must be reversed. It is so ordered.

Meanwhile, debate over the appropriate limits of contraception—dating at least from the Comstock Act (see p. 314–315)—continued in the postwar era. Long after were legal in other states, Connecticut continued to forbid their use. Seeking to test the statute, the Planned Parenthood League (PPL) of Connecticut established a center in New Haven where a physician offered counsel and prescriptions to married couples. It opened on November 1, 1961; within ten days it had served seventy-five patients. But on the tenth day, detectives arrived to arrest its volunteer physician, Dr. C. Lee Buxton, who was the chairman of the Yale Medical School's department of obstetrics and gynecology, and Estelle Griswold, the executive director of the PPL. They were quickly convicted and fined. They appealed their conviction. When their case reached the U.S. Supreme Court, they won on a 7–2 decision.

Note the discussion of marital privacy in Justice Douglas's opinion. Why did Justice Stewart disagree?

GRISWOLD v. *CONNECTICUT*, 1965

JUSTICE WILLIAM O. DOUGLAS WROTE THE MAJORITY OPINION:

. . . The association of people is not mentioned in the Constitution nor in the Bill of Rights . . . [but] specific guarantees in the Bill of Rights have penumbras, formed by emanations from those guarantees that help give them life and substance. Various guarantees create zones of privacy.

The right of association contained in the penumbra of the First Amendment is one. . . . The Third Amendment in its prohibition against the quartering of soldiers "in any house" in time of peace without the consent of the owner is another facet of that privacy. The Fourth Amendment explicitly affirms the "right of the people to be secure in their persons, houses, papers, and effects, against unreasonable searches and seizures." . . . We deal with a right of privacy older than the Bill of Rights—older than our political parties, older than our school system. Marriage is a coming together for better or for worse, hopefully enduring, and intimate to the degree of being sacred. It is an

Griswold v. *Connecticut*, 381 U.S. 479 (1965). See Mary L. Dudziak, "Just Say No: Birth Control in the Connecticut Supreme Court Before Griswold v. Connecticut," *Iowa Law Review* 75 (May 1990): 915–39.

association that promotes a way of life, not causes; a harmony in living, not political faiths, a bilateral loyalty, not commercial or social projects. Yet it is an association for as noble a purpose as any involved in our prior decisions.

JUSTICE BYRON WHITE, CONCURRING

In my view this Connecticut law as applied to married couples deprives them of "liberty" without due process of law . . . the liberty entitled to protection under the Fourteenth Amendment includes the right "to marry, establish a home and bring up children." . . . These [prior] decisions affirm that there is a "realm of family life which the state cannot enter" without substantial justification.

JUSTICE POTTER STEWART, DISSENTING

Since 1879 Connecticut has had on its books a law which forbids the use of contraceptives by anyone. I think this is an uncommonly silly law. As a practical matter, the law is obviously unenforceable . . . as a philosophical matter, I believe the use of contraceptives in the relationship of marriage should be left to personal and private choice, based upon each individual's moral, ethical and religious beliefs. . . . But we are not asked in this case to say whether we think this law is unwise, or even asinine. We are asked to hold that it violates the United States Constitution. And that I cannot do. . . .

What provision of the Constitution, then, does make this state law invalid? The Court says it is the right of privacy "created by several fundamental constitutional guarantees." With all deference I can find no such general right of privacy in the Bill of Rights, in any other part of the Constitution. . . . It is the essence of judicial duty to subordinate our own personal views, our own ideas of what legislation is wise and what is not. If, as I should surely hope, the law before us does not reflect the standards of the people of Connecticut, the people of Connecticut can freely exercise their true Ninth and Tenth Amendment rights to persuade their elected representatives to repeal it. That is the constitutional way to take this law off the books.

Griswold v. *Connecticut* limited its decision to married couples, recognizing for them a zone of privacy in their intimate relations into which the state could not intrude. Not until 1972 did the Supreme Court rule that unmarried people also have a right to contraceptives. That decision, as historian Nancy F. Cott has observed, "pronounced a historic reversal, since it denied the state's right to distinguish between citizens of differing marital status." The Court recognized "the right of the individual, married or single, to be free from unwarranted governmental intrusion into matters so fundamentally affecting a person as the decision whether to bear or beget a child."* That decision made

**Eisenstadt* v. *Baird*, 405 U.S. 438 (1972). Nancy F. Cott, *Public Vows: A History of Marriage and the Nation* (Cambridge, Mass.: Harvard University Press 2000) pp. 198–99

state practice congruent with the sexual revolution that characterized American society in the 1960s and 1970s, sustained by new developments in contraceptive technology, notably the widely available birth control pill. (See Beth Bailey pp. 652–660.)

But the Supreme Court was not prepared to recognize intimate privacy for same-sex couples. From the 1970s to early twenty-first century, gay men and lesbians challenged criminal sodomy laws, usually written in generic terms but enforced only against gay couples, which denied intimate privacy. In 1986 the Atlanta police, acting on a tip, entered the apartment of Michael Hardwick and found him in bed with another man. When they were arrested for violating Georgia's sodomy statutes, they claimed—unsuccessfully—that their constitutional right to equal protection of the laws had been violated. Chief Justice Warren Burger observed, "Decisions of individuals relating to homosexual conduct have been subject to state intervention throughout the history of Western civilization." The vote was 5-4; voting with the majority was Justice Lewis Powell, who stated publicly several years later that the decision was one he regretted.*

In the aftermath of *Bowers* v. *Hardwick,* gay men and lesbians argued with increasing conviction that they were marked as criminals for behavior covered by the protections of privacy when engaged in by heterosexuals. They argued that they too fulfilled one of the major social reasons for the practice of marriage—the choice of committed relationships rather than transient ones. Lesbians and gay men also identified ways in which the status of marriage gave privileges and rights to heterosexual couples, including tax advantages in the form of joint-income tax returns; the ability to share health insurance coverage (often paid for in part by employers); and rights related to the acquisition and inheritance of property, awards of child custody, and companionship as next of kin when partners were hospitalized or dying. And they resented the stigma of being marked as criminals.

By the late twentieth century, these claims developed a dynamism of their own. The number of states that had laws criminalizing sodomy declined substantially, and virtually none enforced these laws against private consensual heterosexual conduct. The European Court of Human Rights sustained the right of homosexual adults to engage in intimate, consensual conduct. As this book goes to press, same–sex marriages are valid in Belgium, Canada, the Netherlands, Norway, South Africa, Spain, and Sweden. Same-sex couples may obtain state benefits under various forms of partnership in many other nations, including Denmark, France, Germany, Iceland, New Zealand, and the United Kingdom.

In 1993, the Hawaii Supreme Court held that although it was not prepared to say that the claim of gay men and lesbians to same-sex marriage was a fundamental right "rooted in the traditions and collective conscience of our

***Bowers* v. *Hardwick,* 478 U.S. 186 (1986).

people," it did agree that by limiting the rights and benefits that were associated with marriage to heterosexual couples, the state had established a sex-based classification, reserving "a multiplicity of rights and benefits" for a single class of people, and therefore presumed to be unconstitutional unless it could be justified by "compelling state interests." The logic of the decision established twenty years before in *Frontiero* v. *Richardson* (see pp. 723–725) that illegality must turn on the act, not the gender of the actor—opened the door to claims on behalf of same-sex partnerships. In 2000, Vermont extended the rights and protections of marriage to same-sex couples who had established a "civil union."

In 2003, the U.S. Supreme Court heard arguments in *Lawrence* v. *Texas*, a case with many similarities to *Bowers*. Acting on what turned out to be a false report of a disturbance, Houston police entered John Lawrence's apartment and found him in bed with Tyron Garner. Lawrence and Garner challenged the Texas law that criminalized private homosexual intimacy. Writing for the majority in a sweeping 6–3 decision, Justice Anthony Kennedy placed the matter in the center of constitutional understandings of liberty: "As the Constitution endures, persons in every generation can invoke its principles in their own search for greater freedom." The protection against intrusion should be broadly understood; liberty is traditionally the protection from unwarranted government intrusions into a dwelling or other private places. In our tradition the state is not omnipresent in the home. Liberty is also the right to "an autonomy of self that includes freedom of thought, belief, expression, and certain intimate conduct. [This case] involves liberty of the person both in its spatial and more transcendent dimensions. . . . To say that the issue in *Bowers* was simply the right to engage in certain sexual conduct demeans the claim [of John Lawrence]. . . just as it would demean a married couple were it to be said marriage is simply about the right to have sexual intercourse . . . [this] personal relationship . . . is within the liberty of persons to choose without being punished as criminals."

The Court explicitly overturned *Bowers*. It recognized that the decision in *Bowers* had relied on historical misunderstandings and overstatements. The Court was persuaded that laws directed specifically against homosexual conduct are of a relatively recent vintage; in the nineteenth century, laws against sodomy criminalized heterosexual as well as homosexual conduct and were enforced generally only when the activity was public or involved a minor or the victim of assault. "It was not until the 1970s that any state singled out same-sex relations for criminal prosecution." And the Court pointed to changing international understandings: "the right the petitioners seek has been accepted as an integral part of human freedom in many other countries."*

Many people, however, were deeply dismayed by these moves toward treating marriage as malleable. Polls in 2000 showed strong popular support for the extension of health insurance, Social Security benefits, and insurance rights to

**Lawrence* v. *Texas*, 539 U.S. 558 (2003).

same-sex partners. But strong majorities—as high as two-thirds—opposed "marriage." Hawaii voters, who supported the extension of benefits, also overwhelmingly supported a constitutional amendment to bar same-sex marriages. Predicting that once a single state recognized same-sex marriage, gay and lesbian couples would travel there to solemnize their relationship and then return to their home states to live (much as couples had made use of Nevada's "quickie" divorce laws in the 1940s and 1950s), Congress quickly passed the Defense of Marriage Act in 1996. It was a brief statute with two major parts.

AN ACT TO DEFINE AND PROTECT THE INSTITUTION OF MARRIAGE, 1996

. . . No State, territory or possession of the United States, or Indian tribe, shall be required to give effect to any public act, record, or judicial proceeding of any other State, territory possession or tribe respecting a relationship between persons of the same sex that is treated as a marriage under the laws of such other State, territory, possession or tribe, or a right or claim arising from such relationship . . .

In determining the meaning of any Act of Congress, or of any ruling, regulation, or interpretation of the various administrative bureaus and agencies of the United States, the word "marriage" means only a legal union between one man and one woman as husband and wife, and the word "spouse" refers only to a person of the opposite sex who is a husband or a wife.

U.S. Statutes at Large, 110:2419

DOMA, as the Defense of Marriage Act came to be known, was echoed by a successful movement to enact similar state statutes and to amend state constitutions. The movement strengthened over the next decade. Twenty-nine states now have constitutional provisions that restrict marriage to heterosexuals; another thirteen states have statutes that do the same.

Yet challenges to limiting marriage to heterosexuals also grew in number and in intensity. In November 2003, the Supreme Judicial Court of Massachusetts decided by a 4–3 vote that barring same-sex couples from "access to the protections, benefits and obligations of civil marriage" "arbitrarily" deprives them "of membership in one of our community's most rewarding and cherished institutions. That exclusion is incompatible with the constitutional principles of respect for individual autonomy and equality under law" and "violates the Massachusetts Constitution." To those who would offer civil unions as the equivalent of marriage, and who thought that the constitutional claim was merely a semantic quibble over language, Chief Justice Margaret Marshall and her colleagues in the majority invoked the decision of the U.S. Supreme Court in *Brown* v. *Board of Education*: a separate but equal institution is inherently unequal.

GOODRIDGE v. *MASSACHUSETTS DEPARTMENT OF PUBLIC HEALTH*, 2003

CHIEF JUSTICE MARSHALL:

Marriage is a vital social institution. The exclusive commitment of two individuals to each other nurtures love and mutual support; it brings stability to our society. For those who choose to marry, and for their children, marriage provides an abundance of legal, financial, and social benefits. In return it imposes weighty legal, financial, and social obligations. The question before us is whether, consistent with the Massachusetts Constitution, the Commonwealth may deny the protections, benefits, and obligations conferred by civil marriage to two individuals of the same sex who wish to marry. We conclude that it may not. The Massachusetts Constitution affirms the dignity and equality of all individuals. It forbids the creation of second-class citizens. In reaching our conclusion we have given full deference to the arguments made by the Commonwealth. But it has failed to identify any constitutionally adequate reason for denying civil marriage to same-sex couples.

We are mindful that our decision marks a change in the history of our marriage law. . . .

In Massachusetts, civil marriage is, and since pre-Colonial days has been, precisely what its name implies: a wholly secular institution. No religious ceremony has ever been required to validate a Massachusetts marriage . . . Civil marriage anchors an ordered society by encouraging stable relationships over transient ones. It is central to the way the Commonwealth identifies individuals, provides for the orderly distribution of property, ensures that children and adults are cared for and supported whenever possible from private rather than public funds, and tracks important epidemiological and demographic data.

Marriage also bestows enormous private and social advantages on those who choose to marry . . . the decision whether and whom to marry is among life's momentous acts of self-definition. . . . The benefits accessible only by way of a marriage license are enormous . . . "hundreds of statutes" are related to marriage and to marital benefits. With no attempt to be comprehensive, we note that some of the statutory benefits conferred by the Legislature on those who enter into civil marriage include, as to property: joint Massachusetts income tax filing; tenancy by the entirety (a form of ownership that provides certain protections against creditors and allows for the automatic descent of property to the surviving spouse without probate); extension of the benefit of the homestead protection (securing up to $300,000 in equity from creditors) to one's spouse and children; automatic rights to inherit the property of a deceased spouse who does not leave a will. . . .

Where a married couple has children, their children are also directly or indirectly, but no less auspiciously, the recipients of the special legal and economic protections obtained by civil marriage . . . [including] the greater ease of access to family-based State and Federal benefits that attend the presumptions of one's parentage.

It is undoubtedly for these concrete reasons, as well as for its intimately personal significance, that civil marriage has long been termed a "civil right." See, e.g., *Loving* v. *Virginia*. . . .

The Department [of Health] . . . argues that broadening civil marriage to include same-sex couples will trivialize or destroy the institution of marriage as it has historically been fashioned. Certainly our decision today marks a significant change in the definition of marriage as it has been inherited from the common law, and understood by many societies for centuries. But it does not

Goodridge v. *Massachusetts Department of Public Health*, 798 N.R. 2d 941 (Mass. 2003).

disturb the fundamental value of marriage in our society.

Here, the plaintiffs seek only to be married, not to undermine the institution of civil marriage. They do not want marriage abolished. They do not attack the binary nature of marriage, the consanguinity provisions, or any of the other gate-keeping provisions of the marriage licensing law. Recognizing the right of an individual to marry a person of the same sex will not diminish the validity or dignity of opposite-sex marriage, any more than recognizing the right of an individual to marry a person of a different race devalues the marriage of a person who marries someone of her own race. If anything, extending civil marriage to same-sex couples reinforces the importance of marriage to individuals and communities. That same-sex couples are willing to embrace marriage's solemn obligations of exclusivity, mutual support, and commitment to one another is a testament to the enduring place of marriage in our laws and in the human spirit.

The Goodridge decision set off, one historian observed, "a rolling act of civil disobedience" as mayors in San Francisco, Portland, Oregon, and other cities issued marriage licenses. But the decision was also met with a firestorm of protest: every one of these non-Massachusetts marriages were nullified by state courts while at the same time DOMA statutes and constitutional amendments seemed to block same-sex marriage in other jurisdictions. The issue continued to be hotly debated throughout the nation in state and federal elections. Civil unions were embraced in Vermont. Prompted by a 2006 state supreme court ruling in New Jersey that same-sex couples are entitled to the same benefits and protections as opposite-sex couples, the legislature authorized civil unions. New Hampshire, Maine, and Vermont legalized same-sex marriage in 2009.

Whatever position supporters or opponents take, the terms of marriage are now increasingly recognized as not only a private matter but also a civil rights issue. In October 2008, the Connecticut Supreme Court ruled that equal protection of the law requires equal access to marriage. The California Supreme Court had made a similar ruling a few months before, but California voters interrupted with an initiative (Proposition 8 on the fall 2008 state ballot) to add a state constitutional amendment barring such marriage, and in the spring of 2009, the California Supreme Court ruled that the initiative was a valid exercise of the voters' right to amend the Constitution.

Meanwhile, the American Foundation for Equal Rights initiated a challenge to Proposition 8 in the *federal* courts, on behalf of Kristin Perry and Sandra Stier, and another same-sex couple who had been denied marriage licenses, claiming that they had been denied the equal protection of the law promised in the Fourteenth Amendment. The trial was held in the U.S. District Court for the Northern District of California in January, 2010; as this book goes to press Judge Vaughn R. Walker has not yet made a ruling. His ruling was appealed to the U.S. Court of Appeals for the Ninth Circuit, and unless the voters of California repeal Proposition 8, to the U.S. Supreme Court. The first two witnesses to testify at length in *Perry* v. *Schwarzenegger* were historians. Nancy Cott, author of *Public Vows: A*

History of Marriage and the Nation (2000), whose essay on equal rights appears on pp. 441–451 of this book, testified that the history of marriage has changed over time and that it has been a secular, not religious, institution in the United States. Chauncey, author of *Gay New York: Gender, Urban Culture, and the Making of the Gay Male World, 1890–1940* (1994), testified to the long history of discrimination against gay men and lesbians in the United States. Their testimony can be followed on the transcripts posted by the Equal Rights Foundation (http://www.equalrightsfoundation.org/our-work/hearing-transcripts). Start with page 181 of Day 1 for Cott's testimony; page 356 for Chauncey's).

In April 2009, the Iowa Supreme Court became the first court to overturn a DOMA statute unanimously, ruling that limiting marriage to heterosexuals is a violation of the Iowa state constitution's equal protection clause and the constitutional separation of powers.* To rule otherwise, they said, would be a denial of the court's "constitutional mandate to protect the free exercise of religion in Iowa," and also its general responsibility to "proceed as civil judges, far removed from the theological debate of religious clerics." They observed that they were instructed by the Iowa Code § 595A.1 that "provides that 'Marriage is a civil contract' and then regulates that civil contract . . . we give respect to the views of all Iowans on the issue of same-sex marriage—religious or otherwise—by giving respect to our constitutional principles. These principles require that the state recognize both opposite-sex and same-sex civil marriage." The court invoked its own strong history of sustaining civil rights: roughly a century before the U.S. Supreme Court made its rulings, public school segregation, the denial of equal access to public accommodations, and the definition of interracial marriage as miscegenation had all been declared to be denials of equal protection of the laws in Iowa. And the court took note of Iowa's recognition of women's equality: it was the first state to admit a woman to the practice of law and to its public university on the same terms as male students.

In July 2009, the Massachusetts attorney general sued the United States, and the federal Departments of Health and Human Services and of Veterans Affairs, charging that the federal Defense of Marriage Act challenged states' rights to regulate marriage, and, by denying same-sex partners Social Security survivors' payments, the right to file taxes jointly, and access to Medicaid protection, and by denying the spouses of all veterans the right to burial at veterans' cemeteries, DOMA denied Massachusetts citizens equal protection of the laws.

As you consider the current debates over the meanings of the protections, benefits, and obligations of marriage, compare and contrast contemporary understandings with those that characterized marriage in the United States at the time of the founding of the nation in the late eighteenth century; in 1920, when women gained the vote; and at the close of World War II. Consider the changing traditions of coverture over the years. Consider the extent to which marriage relations are part of the social security system and other contemporary

**Varnum* v. *Brien*, 763 N. W. 2d 862 (Iowa 2009).

entitlements. (See Alice Kessler-Harris, pp. 519–529, and *Frontiero* v. *Richardson*, pp. 723–725).

For reasonably up-to-date summaries of the rapidly changing marriage laws in the various states, consult the website of the National Conference of State Legislatures: www.ncsl.org/programs/cyf/samesex.htm.

DOCUMENT

Embracing Global Feminism

The United Nations Charter of 1948 committed it to promote and encourage respect for human rights "without distinction as to race, sex, language and religion." A Commission on Human Rights, with a Subcommission on the Status of Women, was constructed as part of the UN's Economic and Social Council (ECOSOC); shortly afterward, the subcommission broke off to be an independent Commission on the Status of Women (CSW), reporting directly to the Economic and Social Council. Whether constituted as subcommission or commission, members found it almost impossible to get the attention of ECOSOC, or to persuade the UN that women's infirmities really deserved international attention. The shrill insistence of the Soviet Union that it had already solved all of women's problems meant that it was almost impossible to make critical assessments of women's status independently of cold war rivalries.

Yet the CSW did engage in significant advocacy, even though the press paid almost no attention to it and most male politicians, inside and outside the UN, were dismissive. For example, that some of the language of the Universal Declaration of Human Rights is gender-neutral is due to CSW insistence. At the time of its founding, nearly one-third of UN member nations did not allow women to vote; the CSW moved its 1950 meeting to Lebanon to call international attention to the denial of democracy there and elsewhere. (French women could not vote until 1945, and women in French Algeria not until 1958, on the eve of their own independence; Swiss women did not get the right to vote or stand for election until 1971. In 2009, women in Saudi Arabia lacked the right to vote, and neither men nor women could vote in the United Arab Emirates. In Lebanon, where all men over twenty-one—whatever their education—are required to vote, women over twenty-one may now choose to vote, but only if they have an elementary education, which is not required of men.)* The CSW identified and sought to publicize weaknesses in women's literacy, education, employment, and the integrity of their citizenship. (For the vulnerability of married women's citizenship in the United States earlier in the century, see *Mackenzie* v. *Hare*, pp. 427–429.) By 1979 the UN adopted—at the CSW's urging—a Convention on the Elimination of All Forms of Discrimination Against Women, which recognized women's rights in family life as well as in the public sector. The United States refused to sign this convention, and as this volume goes to press, has remained adamant in its refusal.

Identifying 1975–85 as the UN Decade for Women, the UN convened three major international conferences—1975 in Mexico City, 1980 in Copenhagen, and

*Data on women's voting from CIA World Factbook, available at https://www.cia.gov/library/publications/the-world-factbook/fields/2123.html.

"Women's Rights Are Human Rights" (speech, First Lady Hillary Clinton, United Nations Fourth World Conference on Women, Plenary Session, Beijing, China, September 5, 1995). The full text and a short video clip of this speech are available at http://www.americanrhetoric.com/speeches/hillaryclintonbeijingspeech.htm. The full text and full audio file of the speech are available at http://www.5wcw.org/docs/Clinton_speech.html.

1985 in Nairobi. All three generally focused on economic development. A fourth was held a decade later, in 1995 in Beijing, on the heels of the UN Conference on Human Rights held at Vienna in 1993, at which it had been clear that it was not easy to find international consensus on women's entitlements. The Declaration that emerged from Vienna specified that "the human rights of women and of the girl-child are an inalienable, integral, and indivisible part of universal human rights"; it named as a target "gender-based violence and all forms of sexual harassment and exploitation, including those resulting from cultural prejudice and international trafficking"; but it omitted provisions on reproductive rights because they had run afoul of religious arguments about what constituted freedom.*

At Beijing, as at the conferences that had preceded it, the number of official delegates was swamped by the enormous numbers of women who surrounded the conference with meetings of their own. These meetings were sponsored by hundreds of women's non-governmental organizations (NGOs), notably from underdeveloped countries which demanded improvements in the status of women that could be measured by international law. The conference itself was an expression of post–cold war confidence, and the invitation to Hillary Clinton, wife of the then president of the United States, to offer a major speech recognized the international power of the United State and Clinton's own longstanding commitment to women's rights. The speech was expected to attract international attention.

In her memoir, Clinton describes the care she and her "speech team"—which included Madeleine Albright, then the U.S. permanent representative to the United Nations (President Bill Clinton would appoint her secretary of state in 1997)—lavished on the wording. "Although I had delivered thousands of speeches, I was nervous," Hillary Clinton wrote. "I felt passionately about the subject, and I was speaking as a representative of my country. . . . If nothing came out of the conference, it would be viewed as another missed opportunity to galvanize global opinion on behalf of . . . the cause of women's rights. . . . I wanted the speech to be simple, accessible and unambiguous in its message that women's rights are not separate from, or a subsidiary of, human rights. . . . Pushing the envelope in this speech meant being clear about the injustice of the Chinese government's behavior. The Chinese leadership had blocked non–governmental organizations from holding their NGO forum at the main conference in Beijing. They forced NGOs devoted to causes ranging from prenatal care to microlending to convene at a makeshift site in the small city of Huairou, forty miles north, where there were few accommodations or facilities. Although I didn't mention China or any other country by name, there was little doubt about the egregious human rights violators to whom I was referring."†

As you read this speech, note the women's vulnerabilities that are named. Compare the list that Hillary Clinton constructs with the list of demands for reform in the 1848 Seneca Falls Declaration of Sentiments. Do you think it is useful to describe women's rights as human rights? What difference does it make? Does the impact or emphasis of the speech seem to change in any way when you listen to the audio version?

*Vienna Declaration and Programme of Action, UN World Conference on Human Rights, June 14–25, 1993, A/Conf 157/23, Sec. I, par. 18.

†Hillary Rodham Clinton, *Living History* (New York: Simon & Schuster, 2003), pp. 303–5. In 2009 Hillary Clinton was appointed secretary of state by President Barack Obama.

Hillary Clinton, "Women's Rights Are Human Rights," 1995

I would like to thank the Secretary General for inviting me to be part of this important United Nations Fourth World Conference on Women. This is truly a celebration—a celebration of the contributions women make in every aspect of life: in the home, on the job, in the community, as mothers, wives, sisters, daughters, learners, workers, citizens and leaders.

It is also a coming together, much the way women come together every day in every country. . . . Whether it is while playing with our children in the park, or washing clothes in a river, or taking a break at the office water cooler, we come together and talk about our aspirations and concerns. And time and again, our talk turns to our children and our families. However different we may appear, there is far more that unites us than divides us. We share a common future, and we are here to find common ground so that we may help bring new dignity and respect to women and girls all over the world, and in so doing bring new strength and stability to families as well.

By gathering in Beijing, we are focusing world attention on issues that matter most in our lives—the lives of women and their families: access to education, health care, jobs and credit, the chance to enjoy basic legal and human rights and to participate fully in the political life of our countries.

There are some who question the reason for this conference. . . . There are some who wonder whether the lives of women and girls matter to economic and political progress around the globe. . . .

The great challenge of this conference is to give voice to women everywhere whose experiences go unnoticed, whose words go unheard. Women comprise more than half the world's population, 70% of the world's poor, and two-thirds of those who are not taught to read and write. We are the primary caretakers for most of the world's children and elderly. Yet much of the work we do is not valued—not by economists, not by historians, not by popular culture, not by government leaders.

At this very moment, as we sit here, women around the world are giving birth, raising children, cooking meals, washing clothes, cleaning houses, planting crops, working on assembly lines, running companies, and running countries. Women also are dying from diseases that should have been prevented or treated. They are watching their children succumb to malnutrition caused by poverty and economic deprivation. They are being denied the right to go to school by their own fathers and brothers. They are being forced into prostitution, and they are being barred from the bank lending offices and banned from the ballot box.

Those of us who have the opportunity to be here have the responsibility to speak for those who could not. As an American . . . I want to speak up for mothers who are fighting for good schools, safe neighborhoods, clean air, and clean airwaves; for older women, some of them widows, who find that, after raising their families, their skills and life experiences are not valued in the marketplace; for women who are working all night as nurses, hotel clerks, or fast food chefs so that they can be at home during the day with their children; and for women everywhere who simply don't have time to do everything they are called upon to do each and every day.

Speaking to you today, I speak for them, just as each of us speaks for women around the world who are denied the chance to go to school, or see a doctor, or own property, or have a say about the direction of their lives, simply because they are women. . . . We need to understand there is no one formula for how women should lead our lives. That is why we must respect the choices that each woman makes for herself and her family. Every woman deserves the chance to realize her own God-given potential. But we must recognize that women will never gain full dignity until their human rights are respected and protected.

Our goals for this conference, to strengthen families and societies by empowering women to take greater control over their own destinies, cannot be fully achieved unless all governments—here and around the world—accept their responsibility to protect and promote internationally recognized human rights. The international community has long acknowledged and recently reaffirmed at Vienna that both women and men are entitled to a range of protections and personal freedoms, from the right of personal security to the right to determine freely the number and spacing of the children they bear. No one should be forced to remain silent for fear of religious or political persecution, arrest, abuse, or torture.

Tragically, women are most often the ones whose human rights are violated. Even now, in the late 20th century, the rape of women continues to be used as an instrument of armed conflict. Women and children make up a large majority of the world's refugees. And when women are excluded from the political process, they become even more vulnerable to abuse. I believe that now, on the eve of a new millennium, it is time to break the silence. It is time for us to say here in Beijing, and for the world to hear, that it is no longer acceptable to discuss women's rights as separate from human rights.

These abuses have continued because, for too long, the history of women has been a history of silence. Even today, there are those who are trying to silence our words. But the voices of this conference . . . must be heard loudly and clearly: It is a violation of *human* rights when babies are denied food, or drowned, or suffocated, or their spines broken, simply because they are born girls; . . . when women and girls are sold into the slavery of prostitution for human greed—and the kinds of reasons that are used to justify this practice should no longer be tolerated; . . . when women are doused with gasoline, set on fire, and burned to death because their marriage dowries are deemed too small; . . . when individual women are raped in their own communities and when thousands of women are subjected to rape as a tactic or prize of war; . . . when a leading cause of death worldwide among women ages 14 to 44 is the violence they are subjected to in their own homes by their own relatives; . . . when young girls are brutalized by the painful and degrading practice of genital mutilation; . . . [and] when women are denied the right to plan their own families, and that includes being forced to have abortions or being sterilized against their will.

If there is one message that echoes forth from this conference, let it be that human rights are women's rights and women's rights are human rights once and for all. And among those rights are the right to speak freely—and the right to be heard.

Women must enjoy the rights to participate fully in the social and political lives of their countries, if we want freedom and democracy to thrive and endure. . . .

In my country, we recently celebrated the 75th anniversary of Women's Suffrage. It took 150 years after the signing of our Declaration of Independence for women to win the right to vote. It took 72 years of organized struggle, before that happened, on the part of many courageous women and men. It was one of America's most divisive philosophical wars. But it was a bloodless war. Suffrage was achieved without a shot being fired. . . . We have seen peace prevail in most places for a half century. We have avoided another world war. But we have not solved older, deeply-rooted problems that continue to diminish the potential of half the world's population.

. . . As long as discrimination and inequities remain so commonplace everywhere in the world, as long as girls and women are valued less, fed less, fed last, overworked, underpaid, not schooled, subjected to violence in and outside their homes—the potential of the human family to create a peaceful, prosperous world will not be realized.

Let this conference be our—and the world's—call to action. Let us heed that call so we can create a world in which every woman is treated with respect and dignity, every boy and girl is loved and cared for equally, and every family has the hope of a strong and stable future. . . .

God's blessing on you, your work, and all who will benefit from it.

JUDITH RESNIK

Sisterhood, Slavery, and Sovereignty: Transnational Women's Rights Movements from 1840 through the Beginning of the Twenty-first Century

In this essay, Judith Resnik reminds us that feminist human rights activists in our own time are part of a long tradition that stretches back at least to the antislavery suffragists of the nineteenth century.

There are striking parallels. Today's challenge to labor trafficking—increasingly described as slavery—is the continuation of the nineteenth century's abolition movement. The U.S. State Department currently estimates that over 80 percent of internationally trafficked workers are women and girls, driven into substandard service jobs and sex work.* Another continuation of the nineteenth-century woman suffragists' efforts to expand women's political agency is the current campaign to ratify the UN Convention on the Elimination of All Forms of Discrimination Against Women (CEDAW). Resnik considers the parallels between these movements over time, and wonders why it is that the United States seems to find it easier to take a leading role in attacking trafficking than to support the reforms outlined in CEDAW.

As Hillary Clinton's 1995 speech in Beijing made clear (pp. 777–780), feminist activists in the United States increasingly understand themselves to be part of an international struggle for human rights. They also recognize that their relative successes in the United States not only can be credited to their own doing but also reflect some real advantages that they enjoyed compared to women in some other nations: the absence of a powerful and conservative state religion; the absence of a dictatorial regime; and the relative ease with which grassroots movements could accomplish legal change. The United Nations Development

*Office to Monitor and Combat Trafficking in Persons, *Trafficking in Persons Report*, June 4, 2008, http://www.state.gov/g/tip/rls/tiprpt/2008/105376.htm (accessed June 10, 2009).

Excerpted from "Sisterhood, Slavery, and Sovereignty: Transnational Antislavery Work and Women's Rights Movements in the United States During the Twentieth Century" by Judith Resnik, ch. 2 of *Women's Rights and Transatlantic Antislavery in the Era of Emancipation*, ed. Kathryn Kish Sklar and James Brewer Stewart (New Haven, Conn.: Yale University Press, 2007). This essay was revised by the author for *Women's America* and reprinted by permission of Yale University Press and the author. Notes have been edited and renumbered. This essay builds on Judith Resnik, "Categorical Federalism: Jurisdiction, Gender, and the Globe," *Yale Law Journal* 111 (2001): 619–80, and on "Law's Migration: American Exceptionalism, Silent Dialogues, and Federalism's Multiple Ports of Entry," *Yale Law Journal* 115 (2006): 1564–1670.

Program recently recognized that "gender inequality is one of the most significant obstacles to human development throughout the world."*

What specific parallels does Resnik find between the campaign for woman suffrage in the nineteenth century and the campaigns for the U.S. ratification of CEDAW now? What parallels does she find between attacks on slavery in the nineteenth century and efforts to end trafficking now? What do you think are the most important differences between the campaigns against trafficking and those to support the ratification of CEDAW?

Over the past century, transnational women's rights groups used the term "slavery" as they addressed violence against women and sought to redefine war crimes under international law, to organize legal opposition to trafficking in persons, and to change the understanding of the scope of human rights. These efforts succeeded at the local, national, and international levels.

During the last three decades of the twentieth century, for example, the United States became active in transnational efforts to stem trafficking in women, expressly described as a form of slavery. By the late twentieth century, the United States had taken a leadership role in pressuring other nations to stem trafficking in persons. Yet the United States has been slow to join other transnational human rights efforts. The long road to women's voting rights in the nineteenth and early twentieth centuries in the United States parallels the country's more recent hesitation to ratify and apply domestically the U.N. Convention on the Elimination of All Forms of Discrimination Against Women, often referred to as CEDAW . . . .

What explains the differences in U.S. responses? Contemporary anti-trafficking, anti-sexual slavery activists have coupled concerns about women's vulnerability with images of harms coming from abroad. Supporters of anti-trafficking laws do so based on their commitment to enabling all humans to be free from forced labor and from sexual exploitation, but these efforts also attract advocates who are influenced by protectionist, puritanical, and nativist impulses. In contrast, domestic support for transnational movements—such as CEDAW and other human rights initiatives that propose profound reorderings of gender and race hierarchies—is more difficult to muster. In such instances, lawmakers in the United States have repeatedly responded by protesting against "foreign" influences. Sometimes, such objections are couched in the language of federalism. Objectors claim that the federalist form of the U.S. government imposes a special constraint on the national government, limiting its capacity to embrace international accords such as CEDAW.

The contemporary human rights movement needs to acknowledge its own roots in anti-slavery and in women's rights projects of centuries past. . . . Consider the many times that meetings have been held to make new claims of right and the many individuals who have crossed boundaries to join those efforts.[1] One such example is of recent vintage. In March of 2001, the International Bar Association (IBA), led for the first time in its history by a woman, convened its first-ever World Woman Lawyer Conference in London, England. For that event, travelers from North America to London followed the same route that North American women had taken 160 years earlier to another "first-ever" event—the World Anti-Slavery Conference, organized by the British Foreign Anti-Slavery Association. At that time, anti-slavery organizations in Britain were sex-segregated, while some of their counterparts in the United States were not. Women were among the delegates sent from the various local state-based societies but were not seated. The all-male World Anti-Slavery Conference debated the question of admitting women delegates and then voted them out.[2]

We know, however, that although these women were excluded, their work could not be. The 1840 conference was built on efforts of women and men working on both sides of the Atlantic, in Calcutta, Sierra Leone, and the Cape of Good Hope. During the 1820s and 1830s, around the world, women campaigned against slavery, sometimes in independent organizations (such as The Female Society of

*UN Development Program (UNDR), *Arab Human Development Report, 2005*, "http://arabstates.undp.org/contents/file/ArabHumanDevelopRep2005En.pdf".

Birmingham, England) and other times working in "auxiliary" institutions, the women's wings of men's associations.[3]

From the perspective of those in the United States, the 1840 World Anti-Slavery Conference was an important moment for domestic movements on slavery and on sisterhood. It was there that Lucretia Mott (a delegate from Pennsylvania) and Elizabeth Cady Stanton (whose husband, Henry, was a delegate from Massachusetts) first met. In their exclusion from that meeting, they understood that they had something in common as women. As Mott wrote in her diary, "[We] resolved to hold a convention as soon as we returned home, and form a society to advocate the rights of women."[4] Coupled with the many other meetings and activities, the encounter in England led to the 1848 Convention at Seneca Falls.

Women's activities in both the movements against slavery and for women's equality have served as paradigms for much subsequent emancipatory work.[5] Women—in groups ranging from sewing circles and religious communities to communes and legal action committees—have drawn together to forward an array of projects. The commonality sometimes stemmed from shared experiences of exclusion and marginalization in groups run by men. Women often responded by creating women-centered organizations, seeking to change laws and practices both within their own townships and around the world. Some of the societies, clubs, caucuses, and associations have been segregated by race; many were class-based, but some cut across these lines. Repeatedly, controversies erupted about their focus and composition.

American legal literature on transnational human rights work tends to place the beginnings of nongovernmental organizations (NGOs) in the early 1960s by citing the formation of some of the great international human rights organizations.[6] But I suggest conceptualizing the early women's groups as the original NGOs. Long before that name became popular in the development literature, women were engaged in collective action to restructure civil society. Such groups were nongovernmental not by choice but by necessity. Until all too recently, women could not vote, run for office, become lawyers, serve in the military or as jurors, or, if married, contract or hold property in their own names. Yet, lacking juridical voice, women nevertheless voiced their views through the means then available, often inventing organizations that had small numbers but grand aspirations.

From my own discipline of law comes several examples. In 1886, a handful of women formed the Equity Club, the first national organization of women lawyers in the United States. That organization lasted only a short time, but was soon followed by another, the National Association of Women Lawyers, formed in 1899 and continuing today as a part of the National Conference of Women's Bar Associations. In the late 1970s, a group of women judges created the National Association of Women Judges, which helped prompt an International Association of Women Judges, that by 2000 was comprised of thirty-four national associations and more than four thousand members in eighty-five nations. . . .

Recall that the 1840 World Anti-Slavery-Conference's goal was the abolition of slavery. Yet, 160 years later, in 2001, . . . the International Court for the Former Territories of Yugoslavia (ICTY), constituted by the United Nations and sitting in The Hague, issued a ruling on sexual slavery. As the *New York Times* put it, that decision was the first time that "an international tribunal [had] prosecuted and condemned sexual slavery" as a crime against humanity.[7] The presiding judge—Judge Florence Mumba of Zambia—gave the decision for the three-judge bench. . . . The ruling included hundreds of factual findings supporting its conclusion that the repeated rapes of women held as hostages and terrorized by their captors violated international legal norms.

The contrast between 2001 and 1840 is in many respects stark. In 1840, women were not permitted to sit as delegates at the World Anti-Slavery Conference. But at the tribunal at The Hague in 2001, a woman prosecutor acting on behalf of the United Nations presented evidence about war crimes against women, and another woman served as a presiding judge. The perpetrators were found guilty. The outcome recognized sexual slavery *as* a war crime, thereby changing the meaning *of* war crimes.

But it is the continuity between 2001 and 1840 that is central to my thesis. First, a trial on sexual slavery could not have happened but for movements and meetings akin to those formed in earlier centuries as sisterhoods came together in opposition to slavery. Second, the celebration of women holding powerful positions today must be tempered by the knowledge that, despite all those meetings and the resultant lawmaking, many women remain subjected to practices still fairly called slavery and requiring new lawmaking efforts to eliminate them.[8] Third, controversy remains about such reforms. Although the United States has been deeply involved in and supportive of the ICTY as well as of anti-trafficking legislation, this country has refused to join another international tribunal, the International Criminal Court (ICC), whose charge includes responding to war crimes targeted at women. The United States also has refused to ratify CEDAW, a treaty aimed specifically at intervening to generate substantive equality for women.[9] Fourth, as in the nineteenth century, feminists in the twenty-first century debate priorities as their differing experiences of class, race, nationality, and ethnicity influence their understandings of the risks and benefits of various efforts at reform.

These priorities have been discussed in many venues. In the late 1940s, for example, the United Nations created a Commission on the Status of Women (CSW). . . . Its establishment marked both a recognition of specific challenges related to achieving women's equality and a conceptual and practical division between work styled "human rights" and programs denominated "women's rights." Through the Universal Declaration of Human Rights and several covenants (both general and specific to women) and through a series of Women's Conferences identified by where they took place (Mexico City, Nairobi, Copenhagen, Vienna, Beijing), the United Nations has broadened its understanding of women's equality. . . .

What constitutes equality and how to obtain government assistance to bring it about are the questions. . . . Conflicts about priorities among women, diverse on many dimensions, made convergence on certain agendas difficult. Yet the issue of violence offered a sad commonality, for violence pervades the lives of women of all races, ethnicities, sexualities, nationalities, and classes. By the 1980s, many civil rights advocates had come to understand that violence was itself a form of subordination of women.

In 1979, the U.N. General Assembly promulgated the Convention on the Elimination of All Forms of Discrimination Against Women. CEDAW requires signatory states to take "in the political, social, economic, and cultural fields, all appropriate measures, including legislation, to ensure the full development and advancement of women, for the purposes of guaranteeing them the exercise and enjoyment of human rights and fundamental freedoms on a basis of equality with men." In 1992, in General Recommendation 19, the expert committee charged with overseeing CEDAW's implementation detailed how violence directed at women because of their gender or disproportionately affecting women constituted a form of discrimination to be redressed by signatory states.[10]

Given CEDAW's mandate that states take "all appropriate measures to eliminate discrimination," CEDAW encourages "temporary special measures aimed at accelerating de facto equality between men and women." Not only is affirmative action appropriate, but the definition of what constitutes inequality differs from that in current American constitutional law, which requires proof of discriminatory intent; CEDAW's focus is on purpose and effect rather than intentionality.[11] As of 2006, more than 180 countries have ratified the basic provisions of CEDAW, albeit sometimes with reservations limiting obligations on particular aspects. . . . Although President Jimmy Carter signed CEDAW for the United States in 1980, subsequent administrations have either not succeeded in convincing Congress to ratify CEDAW or opposed its ratification.[12]

In addition to shaping CEDAW, women's networks have also helped international tribunals to recognize that enslaving women to provide sexual services to armed forces violates international norms of war. Those groups influenced the writing of the Statute of Rome, which, while creating the world's first ongoing International Criminal Court (ICC), was also "the first international treaty to recognize a range of acts of sexual and gender violence as among the most serious crimes under international law."[13]

The ICC recognizes women in three roles: as victims, witnesses, and decision-makers. Within its definition of "crimes against humanity" (knowingly making a "widespread or systematic attack directed against any civilian population"), the Court's enabling statute specifies harms to women, including "[r]ape, sexual slavery, enforced prostitution, forced pregnancy, enforced sterilization, or any other form of sexual violence of comparable gravity." Another such crime, enslavement, is explained with specific reference to trafficking in "persons, in particular women and children." The crime of persecution is defined as "against any identifiable group or collectivity on political, racial, national, ethnic, cultural, religious, gender . . . or other grounds . . . ."

Further, the ICC recognizes that women testifying about such situations may need specific services. The Court's statute and rules create a Victims and Witnesses Unit whose staff must have expertise in crimes involving sexualized violence. Further, the rules provide "principles of evidence in cases of sexual violence" that prohibit the inference of consent from conduct, words, or silence in coercive environments, and that make inadmissible a victim's prior or subsequent sexual history.

Moreover, the statutory framework aims to put women into the governance structure of the ICC, which is "the first time principles of female participation have been incorporated explicitly in an international treaty of this nature." The text requires that countries, empowered to nominate judges and prosecutors, seek the "fair representation" of both women and men. Moreover, such judges and prosecutors should have expertise in issues including "violence against women or children.[14]

The debate producing these provisions was intense. Representatives of the Vatican, as well as of some countries that are identified with Catholicism or Islam, raised concerns that proposed language about "forced pregnancy" could be grounds for seeking rights to abortion. . . . Another tension was whether the term "gender" recognized the rights of gay men and lesbians. The compromise resulted in a provision that, for "the purpose of this Statute," the term gender referred "to the two sexes, male and female, within the context of society. The term 'gender' does not indicate any meaning different from the above. "Whether the addition of the phrase "within the context of society" could be read to leave open the possibility of inclusion of sexual orientation as a form of impermissible persecution is a question, but that formulation was the "only definition" that certain states were willing to support.[15]

Slavery can also be found in another recent international document—the U.N. Convention Against Transnational Organized Crime—supplemented by two protocols, one to "Prevent, Suppress, and Punish Trafficking in Persons, Especially Women and Children" and the other addressed to "The Smuggling of Migrants." . . . As of 2006, more than 110 countries had signed, and more than ninety had completed their internal ratification processes to become parties to these protocols.[16]

The United States has been a leader in anti-trafficking initiatives. In addition to supporting international work within the framework of the U.N. protocols, the United States has enacted domestic law, the Trafficking Victims protection Act (TVPA) of 2000, which created an interagency task force chaired by the Secretary of State to monitor and combat trafficking by facilitating "cooperation among countries of origin, transit, and destination" to prevent and prosecute traffickers. Further, Congress obliged the President to undertake "international initiatives to enhance economic opportunity for potential victims" by funding programs "in foreign countries to assist" victims of trafficking to reintegrate or resettle. In addition, Congress imposed "minimum standards" on other countries to prompt efforts to combat trafficking and announced that the United States would not "provide nonhumanitarian, nontrade-related foreign assistance" to governments that had neither met the standards nor made "significant efforts" to do so.

Under the legislation, the Secretary of State must report about other countries' compliance, and the President has the discretion to withhold various forms of aid. Congress made "victims of a severe form of trafficking" eligible in limited circumstances for certain benefits such as legal assistance (otherwise unavailable under U.S. law). In 2003, the reauthorization of the TVPA created a new civil remedy enabling individual victims of trafficking to bring lawsuits for damages against perpetrators. Congress has also imposed new criminal penalties on traffickers. In 2008, Congress returned to the topic in legislation named after the English abolitionist William Wilberforce, and provided additional services to both adult and child victims of trafficking by making them eligible for more government benefits and able, in certain circumstances, to remain in the United States.[17]

The various forms of recognition provided to women by international and domestic laws should be read both as a radical advancement and as a limited improvement. . . . Women have not only gained recognition as rights holders; women have changed the meaning of what counts as rights. As explained by the U.N. Declaration on the Elimination of Violence Against Women, violence is a "manifestation of historically unequal power relations between men and women, which has led to domination over and discrimination against women by men and to the prevention of the full advancement of women." Violence is a "crucial social mechanism by which women are forced into a subordinate position compared with men."

But despite the many documents and provisions, international bodies and domestic governments have repeatedly failed to address a variety of injuries. A notable example is the challenge brought by "comfort women," tens of thousands of whom were detained in Korea and required to provide sexual services to Japanese soldiers during World War II. Responding as had members of earlier generations of women who were unable to obtain redress through formal channels, a group of late twentieth-century activists created their own means by inventing an ad hoc court. There, they held a trial with international jurists and legal experts who rendered what they termed a judgment, detailing the illegality of the practices and holding Japan responsible.[18]

Such extraordinary efforts to underscore harms against women are paralleled by sadly ordinary events throughout the world, many of which go unredressed. As is detailed by a 2000 UNICEF survey, *Domestic Violence Against Women and Girls*, violence against women remains "one of the most pervasive of human rights violations, denying women and girls equality, security, dignity, self-worth, and their right to enjoy fundamental freedoms." As the report explains, most countries have laws prohibiting such violence but violations are common . . . . Although the "family is often equated with sanctuary . . . [for many] it is also a place that imperils lives, and breeds some of the most drastic forms of violence perpetrated against women and girls."[19]

Further, violence is but one marker of women's inequality. For every one man who is illiterate around the world, two women are. Seventy percent of world's poor are women, and women are "less nourished than men, less healthy, more vulnerable to physical violence and sexual abuse."[20] Moreover, the ratification of CEDAW was accompanied by a notably high number of reservations, bespeaking a constrained willingness from many countries to subscribe to all of CEDAW's parameters. Indeed, several of the countries that have ratified CEDAW are identified with very oppressive conditions for women. In short, despite the many textual commitments to equality and the laws now existing at all levels of government, millions around the world continue to face inequality in all its ugly forms.

These many harms continue to prompt questions for advocates about what priorities to pursue . . . Another U.S. domestic effort is the Violence Against Women Act (VAWA), which Congress passed in 1994 and which authorized millions of dollars for programs to train police and to provide shelters for victims. VAWA also created new civil and criminal provisions to ease interstate enforcement of protection orders. Included was a "Civil Rights Remedy" permitting victims of "gender motivated violence" to bring actions for damages in federal courts.[21]

Congress . . . enacted VAWA under its constitutional authority to regulate interstate commerce and to ensure equal protection of the laws. But VAWA was also the subject of debate within civil rights communities. While the legislation was pending, NGOs and commentators voiced concerns that men of color would bear the brunt of the criminal sanctions, that women with few material resources would have little ability to use the civil remedies, and that immigrant women would be unable to obtain relief without jeopardizing their status in the country.

After enactment, objections of a different kind . . . came to the fore about whether the federal government had the power to give victims access to federal redress. Oppositions to equality efforts have long been couched in terms of authority—and what in law is sometimes referred to as "jurisdiction." In the nineteenth century, for example, opponents of civil rights had argued the permissibility of slavery and of male control over women, including the power of husbands to "chastise" their wives. Further, went their claim, even if such laws should be revised, states, rather than the national government, had exclusive authority over such "domestic" matters as the relationship between master and slave and between husband and wife. Opponents of emancipation for slaves had similar attitudes: they resented rights movements from abroad and argued that foreign critics of slavery ought to stay out of America's affairs, which they could not understand.

Even after the Civil War, as women pursued the vote, a parallel objection was made that the national government should not and could not interfere with state decision-making. When women tried to rely on the Fourteenth and Fifteenth Amendments to vote, they were rebuffed by the Supreme Court, which concluded that state law governed that right. And, during the New Deal, as proposals surfaced to respond to economic emergencies, national policies gave states primary authority over forms of poverty identified with women, children, and people of color, but located more federal control over wage work, identified with white men.[22]

The word "federalism" does not appear in the U.S. Constitution, and the word was not used in Supreme Court opinions until the late 1930s. Moreover, the term did not become a synonym for discussions of states' rights until a few decades thereafter. Further, state law has not, historically, had unfettered reign over relationships within families; the federal legal regime has dealt repeatedly with "domestic relations." For example, after the Civil War, Congress insisted that newly freed slaves had the right to marry. Congress also regulated the marriage of members of Indian tribes and "whites," and it prohibited Mormons from marrying more than one person at a time. During the twentieth century, . . . Congress enacted legislation determining the parameters of family units for federal tax, bankruptcy, pension, social benefits, and immigration law. . . .

Yet, twentieth-century opponents of VAWA relied on what was, by then, called "federalism" rather than "states' rights." They argued that Congress had gone beyond its constitutional powers under the Commerce Clause and the Fourteenth Amendment because (they claimed) violence against women was an aspect of criminal, tort, and family law that belonged to the states, rather than a problem over which the federal government had power because it was intertwined with the economy and equality.

A bare majority of five in the U.S. Supreme Court agreed, deeming aggression against women to be "non-economic, violent criminal conduct" that Congress could not redress by authorizing victims to pursue damage actions in federal courts against private persons. Such division of state and federal authority was justifiable, according to the Court, because "the Constitution requires a distinction between what is truly national and what is truly local."[23]

Just as objections to VAWA were predicated on arguments about states' rights and jurisdiction, so too have objections to joining certain kinds of transnational human rights work been framed in terms of jurisdiction. States' rights is one set of prerogatives; adherence to gender roles is another. In a 2001 Heritage Foundation publication entitled *How U.N. Conventions on Women's and Children's Rights Undermine Family, Religion, and Sovereignty*, that objection was explicit. This report argued that . . . CEDAW undervalued the nuclear family by encouraging mothers to "leave their children in the care of strangers" to enter "the workforce." Complaining that the "United Nations has become the tool of a powerful feminist-socialist alliance that has worked deliberately to promote a radical restructuring of society," the monograph called on Congress to devote time and resources to protect against the dangers that the United Nations poses to the sovereignty of the United States.[24]

Objections to the United States joining the International Criminal Court (ICC) are also advanced on sovereignty grounds. Although representatives from the United States were deeply involved in the 1990s in shaping the ICC Statute and President William Clinton signed the treaty at the end of December of 2000, the Bush administration . . . posited the ICC as a particular threat to this country's prerogatives. Congress concurred in 2002 by legislating against involvement in and cooperation with the ICC and by requiring that American armed forces involved in peacekeeping be immunized from extradition to and prosecution at the ICC.[25]

What are the possible explanations for the contrast between the U.S. hesitancy to embrace CEDAW and the ICC, and its simultaneous willingness to welcome transnational and national lawmaking focused on forms of slavery experienced by women? . . . The refusal to ratify CEDAW and the ICC can be ascribed to a general reluctance to subject decisions made under the aegis of the U.S. to review by multi-national bodies. Further, keeping one's distance from CEDAW while embracing anti-trafficking work can be understood to cohere in that both responses reflect anxieties about "foreign" influences affecting norms about women's roles domestically. . . . Action against the "White Slave Trade" and legislation such as the 1908 Mann Act authorizing prosecution of those transporting women across state lines "for immoral purposes" were inspired by "distinct strains of anti-urbanism, of xenophobia and opposition to continued large-scale immigration, and even of anti-Semitism."[26] . . . As late as 1960, a case involving a Mann Act prosecution prompted a discussion by the Supreme Court about the purpose of the Mann Act to "protect women who were weak from men who were bad."[27]

Such laws were not only aimed at protecting women but also at enforcing attitudes about the moral propriety of certain forms of sexual behavior. Parallels come from recent provisions in the U.S. Trafficking Victims Protection Act, providing funding for anti-trafficking work but requiring that recipients of grants affirm that their programs do not "promote, support, or advocate the legalization or practice of prostitution."[28] Anti-trafficking laws continue to incorporate concerns about foreign influences, mobile women, female sexual predators, and disruption of families. . . . In the 1990s, anti-trafficking legislation succeeded, in part because of the many awful examples of trafficked people and in part through appeal to concerns about the vulnerability of women to men and of the United States to foreign influences—both of which resonate with groups identified with conservative political and religious agendas.[29]

In contrast, efforts to obtain ratification of CEDAW have foundered because CEDAW proposes an understanding of women's lives that moves further afield from conventional conceptions of both women and the law in the United States. CEDAW defines discrimination to include any "distinction, exclusion, or restriction made on the basis of sex" that produces an inequality in any field, "political, economic, social, cultural, [and] civil." Pursuant to that mandate, the inquiries made of countries are far-reaching, seeking accounts of how gender affects the delivery of health care and family planning, safety, education employment, recreation and sports, government benefits, and political power. . . .

Under CEDAW, the United States—like nations around the world—would have to report to a committee of twenty-three experts about the ways in which the country was or was not fulfilling these mandates. Further, CEDAW's openness to affirmative-interventions and its definition of discrimination based on the effects of actions rather than disproof of the intent of the actors are arguably broader than interpretations of the U.S. Constitution. . . . Even some of the federal statutes that reach private conduct do not do as much as provisions in some other countries. For example, the federal Family and Medical Leave Act makes national provisions for rights of leave from wage workplaces but, unlike laws in some countries, does not require such leaves to be paid either through public subsidies or through work benefits packages.

In short, CEDAW aspires to reorganize internal norms of behavior and prompt new interventions, while anti-trafficking laws express condemnation of practices such as forced labor and forced sex that have become abhorrent worldwide. The political distance maintained by the government of the United States from CEDAW and the country's embrace of anti-trafficking laws stem from the contrast between CEDAW's co-venturing with foreigners to create new norms and the TVPA's work with other countries to police extant norms, certain views about American identity, and the borders of the United States. Positioning women as vulnerable, raced, sexed, ethnicized, and in need of protection came more easily to U.S. lawmakers than did inviting women to explore roles never held before and developing plot lines not yet imagined. . . .

Reflect then on more than one hundred and fifty years of transnational human rights efforts. Women have long understood the utility of a mixture of local, national, and transnational organizing. That utility has been amplified through the diminished clarity of physical boundaries represented by the term "globalization" and through the creation of more federations (such as the European Union) and regional alliances. Current market and political conditions promote interest in forms of governance that regulate transactions outside and beyond the nation-state.

That interest, in turn, has generated new opportunities for women to advance equality claims. . . . For example, although the United States has not ratified CEDAW, the City of San Francisco has made it a part of its own domestic law, implemented through requiring reports on the roles women play in departments ranging from Public Works to Probation. Dozens of other cities have called for ratification, just as many had promulgated anti-apartheid legislation and have embraced international protocols to stem global warming.

In earlier centuries, women did not have the opportunity to participate in many organizations and, hence, from necessity, crafted their own. What experiences of the twentieth century teach is that even when women gain entry into more organizations, they need to make such entities responsive to women's concerns by continuing to work in groups constituted around gender. . . . Federations and globalization thus offer yet more opportunities, multiplying the tracks to pursue, the number of meetings to attend, and the complexity of forging successful, focused, and collegial organizations. In all the many sites of work, women need to insist on the relevancy of gender even as they bemoan its centrality.

NOTES

1. See generally Hilary Charlesworth and Christine Chinkin, *The Boundaries of International Law: A Feminist Analysis* (Manchester University Press, 2000); Charlotte Bunch, "Women's Rights as Human Rights: Toward a Re-Vision of Human Rights," 12 *Human Rights Quarterly* 486 (1990).

2. See Kathryn Kish Sklar, "Women Who Speak for the Entire Nation: American and British Women at the World Anti-Slavery Convention, London, 1840," in *The Abolitionist Sisterhood: Women's Political Culture in Antebellum America*, 301, 308-12 (Jean Fagan Yellin and John C. Van Horne, eds. Cornell University Press, 1994). The admission of women to some anti-slavery societies in the United States was one of the reasons for the breaking apart of the American Anti-Slavery Society. See Clare Taylor, *British and American Abolitionists: An Episode in Transatlantic Understanding* 13 (Edinburgh University Press, 1974); Beth A. Salerno, *Sister Societies: Women's Antislavery Organizations in Antebellum America* (Northern Illinois Press, 2005).

3. See Elizabeth Heyrick, "Immediate, Not Gradual Abolition; or An Inquiry into the Shortest, Safest, and Most Effective Means of Getting Rid of West Indian Slavery," at http://dlxs.library.cornell.edu/m/mayantislavery/browse_H.html (follow hyperlink for "Immediate, not gradual abolition"). Heyrick's influence in the United States is detailed in Salerno, 20–23.

4. See Sklar, 302 (quoting Mott).

5. See Leila J. Rupp, *Worlds of Women: The Making of an International Women's Movement* (Princeton University Press, 1997).

6. See Michael H. Posner and Candy Whittome, "The Status of Human Rights NGOs," 25 *Columbia Human Rights Law Review* 269, 270 (1994).

7. The decision, *Prosecutor v. Kunarac, Kovac, and Vukovic*, Case Nos. IT-96-23 and IT-96-23/I, Int'l Crim. Trib. for Former Yugoslavia, Trial Chamber I (Feb. 22, 2001) (at http://www.un.org/icty/kunarac/trialc2/judgement/jun-tj010222e.pdf), was affirmed in 2002 by a five-judge appellate court. See International Criminal Tribunal for the Former Yugoslavia (ICTY) (Appeals Chamber) (June 12, 2002) (at http://www.un.org/icty/kunarac/appeal/judgement/kun-aj020612e.pdf). The tribunal had before and has since tried cases of rape under the legal definition of "torture." See Marlise Simons, "3 Serbs Convicted in Wartime Rapes," *New York Times*, Feb. 23, 2001, Al.

The ICTY was a pathbreaking institution, with justices coming from many different countries and a staff of more than 1,200 from more than seventy countries. Court proceedings are conducted through simultaneous translations in several languages and are televised except when security requires otherwise. The United Nations has since established tribunals for Rwanda, East Timor, and Sierra Leone. The statute establishing the International Criminal Court, discussed later in this chapter, recognized rape under certain circumstances as constituting a crime against humanity.

8. See, e.g., "Protocol to Prevent, Suppress, and Punish Trafficking in Persons, Especially Women and Children, Supplementing the United Nations Convention Against Transnational Organized Crime," Nov. 15, 2000, S. Treaty Doc. No. 108-16, 40 L.L.M. 335 (entered into force Dec. 25, 2003) at http://www.ohchr.org/English/law/protocoltraffic.htm.

9. Convention on the Elimination of All Forms of Discrimination Against Women, 1249 U.N.T.S. 20378 (entered into force Sept. 3, 1981) (hereinafter CEDAW), available at http://www.un.org/womenwatch/daw/cedaw/cedaw.htm (last visited Mar. 3, 2009) (stating that 185 states have ratifications, accessions and successions of CEDAW). See generally Arvonne S. Fraser, "The Convention on the Elimination of All Forms of Discrimination Against Women (The Women's Convention)," in *Women, Politics, and the United Nations* 77-94 (Anne Winslow ed. Greenwood Press, 1995).

10. Comm. on the Elimination of All Forms of Discrimination Against Women, Report of the Comm. on the Elimination of All Forms of Discrimination Against Women, General Recommendation No. 19, U.N. Doc. A/47/38 (Feb. 19, 1993). In addition, in 1994, the U.N. Commission on Human

Rights created the Office of Special Rapporteur on Violence Against Women. See United Nations Commission on Human Rights, Res. 1994/45 (March 4, 1994) at http://www.ohchr.org/English/issues/women/rapporteur.

11. A comparative analysis is provided by Ruth Bader Ginsburg and Deborah Jones Merritt in "Affirmative Action, an International Human Rights Dialogue," 21 *Cardozo Law Review* 253 (1999).

12. The Clinton administration proposed adoption with a series of "reservations, understandings, and declarations." See Malvina Halberstam, "United States Ratification of the Convention on the Elimination of All Forms of Discrimination Against Women," 31 *George Washington Journal of International Law and Economics* 49, 55 (1997). Even when states have ratified CEDAW, the record of compliance is uneven. Some state parties have failed to file reports and others have provided stale information.

13. Cate Steains, "Gender Issues," in *The International Criminal Court: The Making of the Rome Statute: Issues, Negotiations, Results* 357–64, 378 (Roy S. Lee, ed., Boston: Kluwer Law International, 1999). See also Rhonda Copelon, "Gendered War Crimes: Reconceptualizing Rape in Time of War," in *Women's Rights, Human Rights: International Feminist Perspectives* 197–214 (Julie Peters and Andrea Wolper eds, Routledge, 1995); Theodor Meron, "Rape as a Crime Under International Humanitarian Law," 87 *American Journal of International Law* 424 (1993).

14. Rome Statute of the International Criminal Court, July 17, 1998, Arts. 36 (8) (a) (iii) and 54 (b), U.N. Doc. A/CONF. 183/9, 37 I.L.M. 1002 (1998), available at http://untreaty.un.org/cod/icc/statute/romefra.htm.

15. Steains, 370–74.

16. Protocol to Prevent, Suppress and Punish Trafficking in Persons, Especially Women and Children, Supplementing the United Nations Convention Against Transnational Organized Crime, art. 3(a), Dec. 12, 2000, G.A. Res. 55/25, U.N. Doc. A/55/383 (2000), available at http://www.unodc.org/unodc/en/treaties/CTOC/countrylist-traffickingprotocol.html (status as of Oct. 26, 2008). For the list of nations that have ratified the Protocol, go to the website. See also Janie Chuang, "Redirecting the Debate over Trafficking in Women: Definitions, Paradigms, and Contexts," 11 *Harvard Human Rights Journal* 65 (1998).

17. William Wilberforce Trafficking Victims Protection Reauthorization Act of 2007, Pub. L. No. 110-457, 122 Stat. 5044 codified as amended at 22 U.S.C. § 7101 et seq. The phrase "severe forms of trafficking" is defined as "sex trafficking in which a commercial sex act is induced by force, fraud, or coercion, or in which the person induced to perform such an act" is under eighteen, and the activity entails "the recruitment, harboring, transportation, provision, or obtaining of a person for labor or services, through the use of force, fraud, or coercion for the purpose of subjection to involuntary servitude, peonage, debt bondage, or slavery." (22 U.S.C. § 7102 (8)).

18. See Christine M. Chinkin, "Women's International Tribunal on Japanese Military Sexual Slavery," 95 *American Journal of International Law* 335 (2001).

19. UNICEF, Domestic Violence Against Women and Girls, 6 *Innocenti Digest*, June 2000, at http://www.unicef-icdc.org/publications/pdf/digest6e.pdf.

20. Martha C. Nussbaum, *Women and Human Development: The Capabilities Approach* (Cambridge University Press, 2000). Literacy data can be found in the Gender-Related Development Index in United Nations Development Program, *Human Development Report* 138–41 (Oxford University Press, 1999).

21. Violence Against Women Act, Pub. L. No. 103-322, 108 Stat. 1796 (1994) (recodified at 42 U.S.C. § 13981). For more analysis see Judith Resnik, "Reconstructing Equality: Of Justice, Justicia, and the Gender of Jurisdiction," 14 *Yale Journal of Law and Feminism* 393 (2003).

22. See Judith Resnik, "Categorical Federalism: Jurisdiction, Gender, and the Globe," 111 *Yale Law Journal* 619 (2001); Reva B. Siegel, "The Rule of Love: Wife Beatings as Prerogative and Privacy," 105 *Yale Law Journal* 2117 (1996); *Minor v. Happersett*, 88 U.S. 162, 171 (1875).

23. *United States v. Morrison*, 529 U.S. 598, 617–618 (2000). The *Morrison* ruling overturned only one provision within VAWA, its Civil Rights Remedy. The rest of VAWA's provisions remained and were reauthorized and funded thereafter.

24. Patrick F. Fagan, "How U.N. Conventions on Women's and Children's Rights Undermine Family, Religion, and Sovereignty," Heritage Foundation, Backgrounder No. 1407, (2001), at http://www.heritage.org/Research/Reports/2001/02/BG1407es-How-UN-Conventions-On-Womens visited 5/25/10.

25. See the American Service Members Protection Act of 2002, Tit. II, Pub. L. No. 107-206, 116 Stat. 820 (codified at 22 U.S.C. §§ 7401-33 (pocket part, 2003)).

26. Alexander M. Bickel and Benno C. Schmidt, Jr., *The Judiciary and Responsible Government, 1910–1921* at 229 (Part I of Volume IX of *The History of the Supreme Court of the United States,* which is part of the Oliver Wendell Holmes Devise, 1984).

27. *Wyatt* v. *United States*, 362 U.S. 525, 530 (1960).

28. Trafficking Victims Protection Reauthorization Act of 2003 at § 7, Pub. L. No. 108-193, 117 Stat. 2875, 2886 (2003) (recodified at 22 U.S.C. § 7110(g)(2) (2006)).

29. See, e.g. Tony Carnes, "'Odd Couple' Politics: Evangelists, Feminists Make Common Cause Against Sex Trafficking," 44 *Christianity Today*, Issue 3 (March 6, 2000); Statement of Rep. Christopher Smith, "Fighting the Scourge of Trafficking in Women and Judge," 147 Cong. Rec. E2179-02 (Nov. 29, 2001).

FURTHER READING FOR PART IV: THE STRUGGLE AGAINST INJUSTICE 1945–2010

Overviews

Recent overviews of this remarkable period in women's history are Ruth Rosen, *The World Split Open: How the Modern Women's Movement Changed America* (New York, 2000); Estelle Freedman, *No Turning Back: The History of Feminism and the Future of Women* (New York, 2002); Sara Evans, *Tidal Wave: How Women Changed America at Century's End* (New York, 2003); and Gail Collins, *When Everything Changed: The Amazing Journey of American Women From 1960 to the Present* (New York, 2009). On economic equality, Alice Kessler-Harris, **In Pursuit of Equity*, is indispensable.

Bodies and Sexuality

On the development of homosexual subcultures, see John D'Emilio, *Sexual Politics, Sexual Communities: The Making of a Homosexual Minority in the U.S., 1940–1970* (Chicago, 1983); Allan Berube, *Coming Out Under Fire: Gay Men and Women in World War II* (New York, 1990), and Lillian Faderman, *Odd Girls and Twilight Lovers: A History of Lesbian Ljfe in Twentieth-Century America* (New York, 1991). Recent scholarship in gay and lesbian history that shows how homosexuals began making a place for themselves in the public sphere includes Martin Meeker, *Contacts Desired: Gay and Lesbian Communication and Community, 1940s–1970s* (Chicago, 2006), and Marcia M. Gallo, *Different Daughters: A History of the Daughters of Bilitis and the Rise of the Lesbian Rights Movement* (New York, 2006). On transsexuals, see Joanne Meyerowitz, *How Sex Changed: A History of Transsexuality in the United States* (Cambridge, Mass., 2002). On the relationship between sexuality and citizenship rights, see Margot Canaday, *The Straight State: Sexuality and Citizenship in Twentieth-Century America* (Princeton, 2009).

For the historically contingent quality of biological experience, see Lara Freidenfelds, *The Modern Period: Menstruation in Twentieth-Century America* (Baltimore, 2009) and Linda M. Blum, *At the Breast: Ideologies of Breastfeeding and Motherhood in the Contemporary United States* (Boston, 1999). For changing practices of childbirth, see Judith Walzer Leavitt, *Make Room for Daddy: The Journey from the Waiting Room to the Birthing Room* (Chapel Hill, N.C., 2009). For the postwar pressure to bear children, see Elaine Tyler May, *Barren in the Promised Land: Childless Americans and the Pursuit of Happiness* (New York, 1995). On single pregnancy, see Rickie Solinger, *Wake Up Little Susie: Single Pregnancy and Race Before Roe v. Wade* (New York, 1992). On the pill and the sexual revolution, see Beth Bailey, **Sex in the Heartland*.

On abortion and fetal politics, see Rosalind Pollack Petchesky, *Abortion and Woman's Choice: The State, Sexuality, and Reproductive Freedom* (New York, 1984) and Leslie J. Reagan, **When Abortion Was a Crime*. On the constitutional history of abortion rights, see David Garrow, *Liberty and Sexuality: The Right to Privacy and the Making of Roe* v. *Wade* (New York, 1994). On the abortion debate, see Kristin Luker, *Abortion and the Politics of Motherhood* (Berkeley, Calif., 1984), and Faye Ginsburg, *Contested Lives: The Abortion Debate in an American Community* (Berkeley, Calif., 1998). On the related issues of abortion and sterilization, see Rebecca M. Kluchin, *Fit to be Tied: Sterilization and Reproductive Rights in America, 1950–1980* (New Brunswick, N.J., 2009), and Johanna Schoen, *Choice* *and Coercion: Birth Control, Sterilization, and Abortion in Public Health and Welfare* (Chapel Hill, N.C., 2005).

For how women changed the health care system, see Sandra Morgen, *Into Our Own Hands: The Women's Health Movement in the United States, 1969–1990* (New Brunswick, N.J., 2002); David P. Cline, *Creating Choice: A Community Responds to the Need for Abortion and Birth Control, 1961–1973* (New York, 2006); Jennifer Nelson, *Women of Color and the Reproductive Rights Movement* (New York, 2003); Iris Ofelia López, *Matters of Choice: Puerto Rican Women's Struggle for Reproductive Freedom* (New Brunswick, N.J., 2009); and the review essay by Johanna Schoen, "Women, the Health Professions, and the State," *Journal of Women's History* 16 (2004): 215–25. On how the women's health movement created transnational women's networks, see Kathy David, *The Making of Our Bodies, Ourselves: How Feminism Travels Across Borders* (Durham, N.C., 2007).

Eating disorders and preoccupation with aging began earlier in the century, as is demonstrated in Joan Jacob Brumberg's studies, **Fasting Girls* and *The Body Project: An Intimate History of American Girls* (New York, 1997). See also Lois Banner, *In Full Flower: Aging Women, Power and Sexuality: A History* (New York, 1992), and Susan Bordo, *Unbearable Weight: Feminism, Western Culture, and the Body* (Berkeley, Calif., 1993).

On women's pursuit of beauty, see Elizabeth Haiken, *Venus Envy: A History of Cosmetic Surgery* (Baltimore, Md., 1999), and Jill Fields, *An Intimate Affair: Women, Lingerie, and Sexuality* (Berkeley, Calif., 2007). On how ethnicity and race shape ideas of beauty, see Sarah Banet-Weiser, *The Most Beautiful Girl in the World: Beauty Pageants and National Identity* (Berkeley, Calif., 1999), and Maxine Leeds Craig, *Ain't I a Beauty Queen? Black Women, Beauty, and the Politics of Race* (New York, 2003).

On sexuality and popular culture in the 1950s and 1960s, see Susan J. Douglas, **Where the Girls Are*; and Alice Echols, *The Scars of Sweet Paradise: The Life and Times of Janis Joplin* (New York, 1999). For essays that explore the sexual politics of the 1990s, see Lisa Duggan, *Sex Wars: Sexual Dissent and Political Culture* (New Brunswick, N.J., 1995).

Economics and Law

On new occupations for women, see Susan Eisenberg, *We'll Call You If We Need You: Experiences of Women Working Construction* (Ithaca, N.Y., 1998); Carol Chetkovich, *Real Heat: Gender and Race in the Urban Fire Service* (New Brunswick, N.J., 1997); Susan Hagen and Mary Carouba, *Women at Ground Zero: Stories of Courage and Compassion* (New York, 2002); and Margaret A. Weitekamp, *Right Stuff, Wrong Sex: America's First Women in Space Program* (Baltimore, Md., 2004).

A major factor opening up new occupational categories for women was affirmative action, which was initiated during the 1960s and early 1970s. Although discrimination in the professions continued, as is made clear in such studies as Mary Beth Walsh's **"Doctors Wanted, No Women Need Apply,"* affirmative action had an ameliorating impact, as is demonstrated in Margaret W. Rossiter, *Women Scientists in America: Before Affirmative Action, 1940–1972* (Baltimore, Md., 1995).

Title VII was a powerful legal tool in women's fight for employment rights. See Nancy MacLean, *Freedom Is Not Enough: The Opening of the American Workplace* (Cambridge, Mass., 2006), ch. 4; Marjorie A. Stockford, *The Bellwomen: The Story of the Landmark AT&T Sex Discrimination Case* (New Brunswick, N.J., 2004); and, for the first case to test the legality of sex-based affirmative action plans under Title VII, Melvin I.

Urofsky, *Affirmative Action on Trial: Sex Discrimination in Johnson* v. *Santa Clara* [1987], (Lawrence, Kans., 1997). For a case that sought, unsuccessfully, to show that a major national retail chain discriminated against women in its hiring practices, see Alice Kessler-Harris, "Equal Employment Opportunity Commission v. Sears, Roebuck and Company: A Personal Account," *Radical History Review* 35 (April 1986): 57–79. Women expanded the legal definition of fairness to include freedom from sexual harassment. See Augustus B. Cochran III, *Sexual Harassment and the Law: The Mechelle Vinson Case* (Lawrence, Kans., 2004).

On women's demands for equal rights in the workplace and their involvement with labor unions, see Dennis A. Deslippe, *"Rights, Not Roses:" Unions and the Rise of Working Class Feminism, 1945–1980* (Urbana, Ill., 2000); Dorothy Sue Cobble, *The Other Women's Movement: Workplace Justice and Social Rights in Modern America* (Princeton, N.J., 2004); Nancy F. Gabin, *Feminism in the Labor Movement: Women and the United Auto Workers, 1935–1975* (Ithaca, N.Y., 1990); and Carmen Teresa Whalen, "Sweatshops Here and There: The Garment Industry, Latinas, and Labor Migrations," *International Labor and Working-Class History* 61 (April 2002): 45–68. Kathleen Barry, *Femininity in Flight: A History of Flight Attendants* (Durham, N.C., 2007), traces the evolution of the image of workers once known as stewardesses as well as their activism.

The wage gap associated with gender-based occupational segregation continues to be severe; its consequences ripple throughout society. See Alice Kessler-Harris, **A Woman's Wage*; Kessler-Harris, **In Pursuit of Equity*; and Linda M. Blum, *Between Feminism and Labor: The Significance of the Comparable Worth Movement* (Berkeley, Calif., 1991).

For the reconstruction of welfare in the late twentieth century, see Premilla Nadasen, *Welfare Warriors: The Welfare Rights Movement in the United States* (New York, 2005), and Felicia A. Kornbluh *The Battle for Welfare Rights: Politics and Poverty in Modern America* (Philadelphia, 2007). For perspectives from two cities, see Annelise Orleck, *Storming Caesar's Palace: How Black Mothers Fought Their Own War on Poverty* (Boston, 2005)—on Las Vegas; and *Lisa Levenstein, *A Movement Without Marches*—on Philadelphia.

Influential studies of working women that reveal the ongoing problems they face include Arlie Hochshild, *The Second Shift: Working Parents and the Revolution at Home* (New York, 1989), and Joan Williams, *Unbending Gender: Why Family and Work Conflict and What To Do About It* (New York, 2000). On child care, see Sonya Michel, *Children's Interests/Mothers' Rights: The Shaping of America's Child Care Policy* (New Haven, Conn., 1999). On the military services, see Linda Bird Francke, *Ground Zero: The Gender Wars in the Military* (New York, 1997) and Helen Benedict, *The Lonely Soldier: The Private War of Women Serving in Iraq* (Boston, 2009).

On women and jury service, see Linda K. Kerber, **No Constitutional Right*, ch. 4. On women in the legal profession, see Cynthia Fuchs Epstein, *Women in Law*, 2nd ed. (Urbana, Ill., 1993; orig. pub. 1981), and Fred Strebeigh, *Equal: Women Reshape American Law* (New York, 2009). For working women's use of the law, see Clara Bingham and Laura Leedy Gansler, *Class Action: The Story of Lois Jenson and the Landmark Case that Changed Sexual Harassment Law* (New York, 2002). For marriage in American culture, see Kristin Celello, *Making Marriage Work: A History of Marriage and Divorce in the Twentieth-Century United States* (Chapel Hill, N.C. 2009).

Politics

Although the 1950s have traditionally been considered a period in which female activism was largely dormant and women were caught up in a resurgent domesticity, more recent studies have suggested a much more complex reality. See, for example, *Not June Cleaver: Women and Gender in Postwar America, 1945–1960,* ed. Joanne Meyerowitz (Philadelphia, 1994). For women active in the peace movement during the 1950s, see Amy Swerdlow, *Women Strike for Peace: Traditional Motherhood and Radical Politics in the 1960s* (Urbana, Ill., 1993). For women in the civil rights movement, see *The Montgomery Bus Boycott and the Women Who Started It: The Memoir of Jo Ann Gibson Robinson,* ed. David Garrow (Knoxville, Tenn., 1987); Charles Payne, **I've Got the Light of Freedom;* Cynthia Griggs Fleming, *Soon We Will Not Cry: The Liberation of Ruby Doris Smith Robinson* (Lanham, Md., 1998); Chana Kai Lee, *For Freedom's Sake: The Life of Fannie Lou Hamer* (Urbana, Ill., 1999); Gerald Horne, *Race Woman: The Lives of Shirley Graham Du Bois* (New York, 2000); Debra L. Schultz, *Going South: Jewish Women in the Civil Rights Movement* (New York, 2001); Barbara Ransby, *Ella Baker and the Black Freedom Movement: A Radical Democratic Vision* (Chapel Hill, N.C., 2003); and Christina Green, *Our Separate Ways: Women and the Black Freedom Movement in Durham, North Carolina* (Chapel Hill, N.C., 2005). Women are among the courageous activists profiled in Raymond Arsenault, *Freedom Riders: 1961 and the Struggle for Racial Justice* (New York, 2006). Important autobiographies include Anne Moody, *Coming of Age in Mississippi* (New York, 1968), and Elaine Brown, *A Taste of Power: A Black Woman's Story* (New York, 1992), which recounts her years in the Black Panthers.

On women's direct influence on international relations, see Edward P. Crapol, *Women and American Foreign Policy: Lobbyists, Critics, and Insiders* (Wilmington, Del., 1992), and Rhodri Jeffreys-Jones, *Changing Differences: Women and the Shaping of American Foreign Policy, 1917–1994* (New Brunswick, N.J., 1995). On less obvious ways in which gender affects foreign relations, see also Emily Rosenberg's reflections on "Gender" in "A Round Table: Explaining the History of American Foreign Relations," *Journal of American History* 77 (June 1990): 116–24, and Mire Koikari, *Pedagogy of Democracy: Feminism and the Cold War in the U.S. Occupation of Japan* (Philadelphia, 2008). For women and military obligation, see Linda K. Kerber, **No Constitutional Right,* ch. 5. An aspect of international relations not often considered, but in which women are involved, is the experience of war brides, as is demonstrated in Ji-Yeon Yuh, *Beyond the Shadow of Camptown: Korean Military Brides in America* (New York, 2002). For trafficking in women and its relationship to U.S. foreign policy, a good place to begin is with *Trafficking in Women and Children in East Asia and Beyond: A Review of U.S. Policy: Hearing before the Subcommittee on East Asian and Pacific Affairs of the Committee on Foreign Relations* (Washington, D.C., 2003; PDF version available at http://purl.access.gpo.gov/GPO/LPS39399).

Biographies and autobiographies remain a fine way of capturing both actors and their times. For a range of careers, see Kathryn S. Olmsted, *Red Spy Queen: A Biography of Elizabeth Bentley* (Chapel Hill, N.C., 2002), and Katherine Graham, *Personal History* (New York, 1997). Mary Beth Rogers' *Barbara Jordan: American Hero* (New York, 1998) offers a look at one of the most remarkable women in American politics in the twentieth century.

On the role of key liberal organizations and the women who belong to them in promoting feminism, see Susan M. Hartmann, *The Other Feminists: Activists in the Liberal Establishment* (New Haven, Conn., 1998). On the changing activism of women within the Republican Party, see Catherine E. Rymph, **Republican Women.*

For the roots of feminist resurgence, see Kathleen Anne Weigand, *Red Feminism: American Communism and the Making of Women's Liberation* (Baltimore, Md., 2000); Leila Rupp and Verta Taylor, *Survival in the Doldrums: The American Women's Rights Movement, 1945 to the 1960s* (New York, 1987); Cynthia Harrison, *On Account of Sex: The Politics of Women's Issues, 1945–1968* (Berkeley, Calif., 1988); and Sara Evans, *Personal Politics: The Roots of Women's Liberation in the Civil Rights Movement and the New Left* (New York, 1979). On the rise and demise of radical feminism, see Alice Echols, *Daring to Be Bad: Radical Feminism in America, 1965–1975* (Minneapolis, 1989).

For comprehensive studies of second-wave feminism, see Ruth Rosen, **The World Split Open*; Estelle B. Freedman, **No Turning Back*; and Sara M. Evans, **Tidal Wave.* On black and Chicana feminism, see Patricia Hill Collins, *Black Feminist Thought: Knowledge, Consciousness, and the Politics of Empowerment* (New York, 1990); Kimberly Springer, *Living for the Revolution: Black Feminist Organizations, 1968–1980* (Durham, N.C., 2005); *Chicana Feminist Thought: The Basic Historical Writings*, ed. Alma M. Garcia (New York, 1997); and Benita Roth, *Separate Roads to Feminism: Black, Chicana, and White Feminist Movements in America's Second Wave* (New York, 2004).

The women's movement politicized issues that had been previously thought of as private. For a history of the early grassroots movement against domestic violence, see Susan Schechter, *Women and Male Violence: The Visions and Struggles of the Battered Women's Movement* (Boston, 1982); on lawyers' work on this issue, see Elizabeth M. Schneider, *Battered Women and Feminist Lawmaking* (New Haven, Conn., 2000). On sexual harassment, see Carrie N. Baker, *The Women's Movement Against Sexual Harassment* (New York, 2008).

For international perspectives on the U.S. women's movement, see Lee Ann Banaszak, ed., *The U.S. Women's Movement in Global Perspective* (Lanham, Md., 2006), and Kathy Davis, **The Making of Our Bodies, Ourselves.* On the equal rights amendment and the politicization of women during the ratification struggle, see Donald G. Mathews and Jane Sherron De Hart, *Sex, Gender, and the ERA: A State and the Nation* (New York, 1990), and David Kyvig, *Explicit and Authentic Acts: Amending the U.S. Constitution, 1776–1995* (Lawrence, Kans., 1996), ch. 17. Despite the failure of the ERA, American law changed substantially in the twentieth century, as shown by Fred Strebeigh, *Equal: Women Reshape American Law* (New York, 2009). On new approaches to analyzing the complexity of the women's movement, see Stephanie Gilmore, ed., *Feminist Coalitions: Historical Perspectives on Second-Wave Feminism in the United States* (Urbana, Ill., 2008), and Anna Enke, *Finding the Movement: Sexuality, Contested Spaces, and Feminist Activism* (Durham, N.C., 2007).

Intellect, Ideology, and Culture

Women brought scholarly focus to the study of women's lives as they created women's history and women's studies departments across the academy. See Marilyn Jacoby Boxer, *When Women Ask the Questions: Creating Women's Studies in America* (Baltimore, Md., 1998) and Rosalind Rosenberg, *Changing the Subject: How Women of Columbia Shaped the*

Way We Think about Sex and Politics (New York, 2004). For psychoanalysis and psychology, see Mari Jo Buhle, *Feminism and Its Discontents: A Century of Struggle with Psychoanalysis* (Cambridge, Mass., 1998). On women's lives within the academy, see Margaret Rossiter, **Women Scientists in America*; Bonnie G. Smith, *The Gender of History: Men, Women, and Historical Practice* (Cambridge, Mass., 1998); Eileen Boris, ed., *Voices of Women Historians: The Personal, the Political, the Professional* (Bloomington, Ind., 1999); and Deborah Gray White, ed., *Telling Histories: Black Women Historians in the Ivory Tower* (Chapel Hill, N.C., 2008). For an important Supreme Court ruling on equal rights in publicly supported universities, see Philippa Strum, *Women in the Barracks: The VMI Case and Equal Rights* (Lawrence, Kans., 2002).

For the impact of the new domesticity and pro-natalism during the years after World War II, see Elaine Tyler May's *Homeward Bound: American Families in the Cold War Era* (New York, 1988). Ruth Feldstein traces the widespread notion that bad mothering led to a host of social problems in *Motherhood in Black and White: Race and Sex in American Liberalism, 1930–1965* (Ithaca, N.Y., 2000). For the intersection of ideology, sexuality, and sports, see Susan E. Cayleff, *Babe: The Life and Legend of Babe Didrikson Zaharias* (Urbana, Ill., 1995), and Susan K. Cahn, *Coming on Strong: Gender and Sexuality in Twentieth-Century Women's Sports* (Cambridge, Mass., 1994). On women and conservative ideology, see Rebecca Klatch, *Women of the New Right* (Philadelphia, 1987), and Donald T. Critchlow, *Phyllis Schlafly and Grassroots Conservativism: A Woman's Crusade* (Princeton, N.J., 2005). See also Kathleen M. Blee, *Inside Organized Racism: Women in the Hate Movement* (Berkeley, Calif., 2002).

On the early critiques of the resurgent feminism of the late 1960s, see Midge Decter, *The New Chastity and Other Arguments Against Women's Liberation* (New York, 1972); George Gilder, *Sexual Suicide* (New York, 1973); and Phyllis Schlafly, *The Power of the Positive Woman* (New York, 1977). More recent critics are of a younger generation, such as Katie Roiphe, *Last Night in Paradise: Sex and Morals at the Century's End* (New York, 1997) and Wendy Shalit, *A Return to Modesty: Discovering the Lost Virtue* (New York, 2000), who argue that contemporary young women desire a return to more "traditional" standards of gender and sexuality. On the tension between second- and third-wave feminists see Astrid Henry, *Not My Mother's Sister: Generational Conflict and Third-Wave Feminism*, (Bloomington, Ind., 2004).

For cultural histories that focus on women's lives, see Sherrie A. Inness, *Disco Divas: Women, Gender, and Popular Culture in the 1970s* (Philadelphia, 2003); Katherine Jellison, *It's Our Day: America's Love Affair with the White Wedding, 1945–2005* (Lawrence, Kans., 2008); Miriam Forman-Brunnell, *Babysitter: An American History* (New York, 2009); Laura Browder, *Her Best Shot: Women and Guns in America* (Chapel Hill, N.C., 2006); Noralee Frankel, *Stripping Gypsy: The Life of Gypsy Rose Lee* (New York, 2009); and Jennifer Scanlon, *Bad Girls Go Everywhere: The Life of Helen Gurley Brown* (New York, 2009).

Asterisks (*) indicate the work's full citation can be found either earlier in this list of works or in the credit lines of an essay by the author excerpted in this volume.

Further Reading and Resources

PRINT SOURCES

General Reference Works and Overviews

All those interested in women and gender in U.S. history should become acquainted with *Notable American Women,* a five-volume biographical encyclopedia published between 1971 and 2004, which includes excellent short biographies and a brief bibliography for many of the women appearing in this book. It rewards browsing as well as dipping in for research. See *Notable American Women, 1607–1950: A Biographical Dictionary,* ed. Edward T. James, Janet Wilson James, and Paul Boyer, 3 vols. (Cambridge, Mass., 1971); *Notable American Women: The Modern Period,* ed. Barbara Sicherman and Carol Hurd Green (Cambridge, Mass., 1980); and *Notable American Women: Completing the Twentieth Century,* ed. Susan Ware (Cambridge, Mass., 2004). Other useful encyclopedias are *Black Women in America: An Historical Encyclopedia,* ed. Darlene Clark Hine, 2 vols. (Brooklyn, N.Y., 1993); *Jewish Women in America: An Historical Encyclopedia,* ed. Paula Hyman and Deborah Dash Moore, 2 vols. (New York, 1997); *Encyclopedia of Lesbian, Gay, Bisexual and Transgender History in America,* ed. Marc Stein, 3 vols. (New York, 2004); and *Amazons to Fighter Pilots: A Biographical Dictionary of Military Women,* ed. Reina Pennington (Westport, Conn., 2003). An unusual atlas is Sarah Opdycke, *The Routledge Historical Atlas of Women in America* (New York, 2000). Data on recent developments are found in Women's Action Coalition, *WAC Stats: The Facts About Women,* 2nd ed. (New York, 1993).

Sara M. Evans has written a sprightly one-volume synthesis of U.S. women's history, *Born for Liberty: A History of Women in America* (New York, 1989, 1997). Listed here, rather than in the chronological sections that follow, are highly important, topical studies that cover broad sweeps of time. We enumerate them here so as to avoid frequent repetitions, and we use as a frame the broad, topical categories of our bibliography. **Bodies and Sexuality**: John D'Emilio and Estelle Freedman, *Intimate Matters: A History of Sexuality in America* (New York, 1988, 1997); Judith Walzer Leavitt, *Brought to Bed: Childbearing in America, 1750–1950* (New York, 1986); Linda Gordon, *Woman's Body, Woman's Right: Birth Control in America* (New York, 1977; most recent edition published as *The Moral Property of Women,* Urbana, Ill., 2002); Carl N. Degler, *At Odds: Women and the Family in America from the Revolution to the Present* (New York, 1980); David Peterson Del Mar, *What Trouble I Have Seen: A History of Violence Against Wives* (Cambridge, Mass., 1998); Anthony E. Rotundo, *American Manhood: Transformations in Masculinity from the Revolution to the Modern Era* (New York, 1993). **Economics and Law**: Jacqueline Jones, **Labor of Love, Labor of Sorrow: Black Women, Work, and the Family from Slavery to the Present*; Gerda Lerner, ed., *Black Women in White America* (New York, 1972); Ruth Schwartz Cowan, *More Work for Mother: The Ironies of Household Technology from the Open Hearth to the Microwave* (New York, 1983); Susan Strasser, *Never Done: A History of American Housework* (New York, 1982); Alice Kessler-Harris, *Out to Work: A History of Wage Earning Women in the United States* (New York, 1982); Claudia Goldin, *Understanding the Gender Gap: An Economic History of American Women* (New York, 1989); Alice Kessler-Harris, *A Woman's Wage: Historical Meanings and Social Consequences* (Lexington, Ky., 1991); Ava Baron, ed., *Work Engendered: Toward a New History of American Labor* (Ithaca, N.Y., 1991); Eileen Boris and Cynthia

R. Daniels, eds., *Homework: Historical and Contemporary Perspectives on Paid Labor at Home* (Urbana, Il., 1989); Regina Morantz-Sanchez, *Sympathy and Science: Women Physicians in American Medicine* (New York, 1985). On law, see Nancy F. Cott, *Public Vows: A History of Marriage and the Nation* (Cambridge, Mass., 2000); Sandra Van Burkleo, *"Belonging to the World:" Women's Rights and American Constitutional Culture* (New York, 2001). **Politics:** Paula Giddings, *When and Where I Enter: The Impact of Black Women on Race and Sex in America* (New York, 1984); *The Concise History of Woman Suffrage*, ed. Mari Jo Buhle and Paul Buhle (Urbana, Ill., 1978); Linda K. Kerber, *No Constitutional Right to Be Ladies: Women and the Obligations of Citizenship* (New York, 1998); Anne Firor Scott, *Natural Allies: Women's Associations in American History* (Urbana, Ill., 1991); Glenna Matthews, *The Rise of Public Woman: Woman's Power and Woman's Place in the United States, 1630–1970* (New York, 1994); Robert J. Dinkin, *Before Equal Suffrage: Women in Partisan Politics from Colonial Times to 1920* (Westport, Conn., 1995). **Intellect, Ideology, Culture**: Annette Kolodny, *The Land Before Her: Fantasy and Experience of the American Frontier, 1630–1860* (Chapel Hill, N.C., 1984); Linda K. Kerber, Alice Kessler-Harris, and Kathryn Kish Sklar, eds., *U.S. History as Women's History: New Feminist Essays* (Chapel Hill, N.C., 1995); Janet Wilson James, ed., *Women in American Religion* (Philadelphia, 1980); Rosemary Radford Reuther and Rosemary Keller, eds., *Women and Religion in America*, 3 vols. (New York, 1981–86).

Note that when a work is preceded by an asterisk (*), the full citation will be found either earlier in this list of works or in the credit lines of an essay by the author excerpted in *Women's America*.

WEBSITES

Listed here is a sampling of the on-line sites that we and other instructors and students have found valuable. Most of these have a Related Links page that will lead you to other trusted sites of interest. Do your own exploring while at the same time discussing with your peers and instructor what criteria to use to evaluate the reliability and value of particular sites (e.g., always check the identity of the creators and sponsors). Note that state historical societies, state archives, and major libraries and repositories of original historical material often have extremely informative websites, including finding aids for women's history collections.

General

American Women's History: A Research Guide
http://frank.mtsu.edu/~kmiddlet/history/women/wh-intro.html

BlackPast.org: Remembered & Reclaimed, An Online Reference Guide to African American History
http://www.blackpast.org

Center for American Women and Politics
http://www.cawp.rutgers.edu/

Center for History and New Media
http://chnm.gmu.edu/about/
A gateway to digital exhibits, tools, and projects

Documenting the American South
http://docsouth.unc.edu

Ethnic America, Ethnic Voices
http://www.digitalhistory.uh.edu/historyonline/ethnic_am.cfm

GLBTQ: An Encyclopedia of Gay, Lesbian, Bisexual, Transgender & Queer Culture
http://www.glbtq.com/subject/literature_a-b.html

History Matters: The U.S. Survey Course on the Web
http://historymatters.gmu.edu/
A gateway to web resources, plus other tools; type *women* into the search box to get an annotated list of useful sites

In Motion: The African-American Migration Experience (slave trade through twentieth-century)
http://www.inmotionaame.org/home.cfm?
Jewish Women's Archive: A Comprehensive Historical Encyclopedia
http://jwa.org/encyclopedia
The Library of Congress, American Memory: Women's History
http://memory.loc.gov/ammem/browse/ListSome.php?category=Women%27s%20History
National Library of Medicine, National Institutes of Health
http://www.nlm.nih.gov/hmd/
National Museum of the American Indian
http://www.nmai.si.edu/searchcollections/home.aspx
National Women's History Museum's CyberMuseum of exhibits
http://www.nwhm.org/exhibits/index.html
North American Women's Letters and Diaries, Colonial to 1950
http://solomon.nwld.alexanderstreet.com/ (subscription required)
Sophia Smith Collection: Women's History Archives at Smith College
http://www.smith.edu/libraries/libs/ssc/index.html
Women and Social Movements in the U.S., 1600–2000
http://womhist.alexanderstreet.com/ (part is open access, part by library subscription)
Women Working, 1800–1930
http://ocp.hul.harvard.edu/ww/
Women's Legal History Biography Project
http://www.law.stanford.edu/library/womenslegalhistory/

1600–1820

The Atlantic Slave Trade and Slave Life in the Americas: A Visual Record
http://hitchcock.itc.virginia.edu/Slavery/index.php
Colonial House: Interactive History (based on the PBS series)
http://www.pbs.org/wnet/colonialhouse/history/
DoHistory
http://www.dohistory.org
Interactive, analytical site based on the book and film *A Midwife's Tale*, with a searchable version of the late eighteenth-century diary, and a History Toolkit
The Elizabeth Murray Project:
http://salticid.nmc.csulb.edu/cgi-bin/WebObjects/eMurray2.woa/wa/select/
Documentrary archive relating to a Boston shopkeeper in the 1750s
New Jersey History Partnership: The American Revolution
http://www.njhistorypartnership.org/home_page.html
The Pocahontas Archive
http://digital.lib.lehigh.edu/trial/pocahontas
Salem Witch Trials Documentary Archive and Transcription Project
http://etext.virginia.edu/salem/witchcraft
Virtual Jamestown
http://www.virtualjamestown.org
Includes databases on indentured servants and eighteenth-centrury runaway servant ads

1820–1880

Born in Slavery: Slave Narratives from the Federal Writers' Project, 1936–1938
http://lcweb4.loc.gov/ammem/snhtml/
Includes photographs
Center for Lowell History: Mill Life, *The Lowell Offering*
http://library.uml.edu/clh/index.html

Civil War Women: Primary Sources on the Internet
http://library.duke.edu/specialcollections/bingham/guides/cwdocs.html
Denver Public Library, Photograph gallery of Native American Women and Life
http://www.photoswest.org/exhib/gallery4/leadin.htm
Digital Schomburg: African American Women Writers of the 19th Century
http://digital.nypl.org/schomburg/writers_aa19/toc.html
Documenting the American South
http://docsouth.unc.edu
The Elizabeth Cady Stanton and Susan B. Anthony Papers Project
http://ecssba.rutgers.edu/index.html
Godey's Lady's Book Online
http://www.history.rochester.edu/godeys/
Harriet Jacobs Paper Project
http://harrietjacobspapers.org
The Valley of the Shadow: Two Communities in the American Civil War
http://valley.vcdh.virginia.edu
Western New York Suffragists: Winning the Vote
http://www.winningthevote.org/
Women's Rights National Historical Park (at Seneca Falls)
http://www.nps.gov/wori/historyculture/index.htm

1880–1945

America in the 1930s
http://xroads.virginia.edu/~1930s/front.html
Clash of Cultures in the 1910s and 1920s: The New Woman
http://ehistory.osu.edu/osu/mmh/clash/NewWoman/newwomen-page1.htm
The Emma Goldman Papers
http://sunsite3.berkeley.edu/goldman/
Florence Kelley in Chicago, 1891–1899
http://florencekelley.northwestern.edu/
HEARTH: Home Economics Archive
http://hearth.library.cornell.edu/h/hearth/index.html
Jane Addams Hull-House Museum
http://www.uic.edu/jaddams/hull/
Japanese American Relocation Digital Archives
http://www.calisphere.universityofcalifornia.edu/jarda/
The Margaret Sanger Papers Project
http://www.nyu.edu/projects/sanger/
See especially Documents Online
New Jersey History Partnership: The Progressive Era, including Alice Paul's Attic
http://www.njhistorypartnership.org/home_page.html
The Rutgers Oral History Archives
http://oralhistory.rutgers.edu/home.html
Transcripts of hundreds of interviews about military service and home-front experiences in World War II and more recent conflicts
"A Summons to Comradeship:" World War I and II Posters and Postcards
http://digital.lib.umn.edu/warposters/warpost.html
Tenement Museum, New York City
http://www.tenement.org/
The Triangle Factory Fire
http://www.ilr.cornell.edu/trianglefire/

Votes for Women: Selections from the NAWSA collection, 1848–1921
http://memory.loc.gov/ammem/naw/nawshome.html
The WASPs: Women Pilots of WWII
http://www.npr.org/templates/story/story.php?storyId=881741
Thirty-minute radio documentary by Joe Richman (2002)

1945–2010

Ad*Access
http://http://library.duke.edu/digitalcollections/adaccess
Database of American and Canadian ads, about 7,000 images, covering five product categories: Beauty and Hygiene, Radio, Television, Transportation, and World War II propaganda, dated between 1911 and 1955
Black American Feminisms, A Multidisciplinary Bibliography
http://www.library.ucsb.edu/subjects/blackfeminism/
The Chicago Women's Liberation Union (CWLU History)
http://www.cwluherstory.org/2.html
Documents from the Women's Liberation Movement
http://scriptorium.lib.duke.edu/wlm
The Feminist Chronicles, 1853–1993 (a digitized 1993 book)
http://feminist.org/research/chronicles/chronicl.html
Gifts of Speech: Women's Speeches from Around the World
http://www.giftsofspeech.org/
Most date from 1990 onward, but also included are nineteenth-century suffragists and Emma Goldman's 1917 antiwar speeches
Making Face, Making Soul, a site by, for and about Chicanas
http://www.chicanas.com/huh.html
No Turning Back: The Feminist Resource Site
http://noturningback.stanford.edu/resources.html
Links to resources accompanying Estelle Freedman's 2003 book, *The History of Feminism and the Future of Women*
The 3rd WWWave
http://www.3rdwwwave.com/
Voices of Civil Rights: online exhibition
http://www.loc.gov/exhibits/civilrights/cr-exhibit.html
Women's Studies/Women's Issues: Resource Sites
http://userpages.umbc.edu/~korenman/wmst/links.html
List of trusted, academically-oriented websites; see especially Women of Color and Women-Related Web Sites Arts and Humanities (History)

FILMS

A number of films both complement and supplement *Women's America*. This list is not comprehensive; it includes films, new and old, that we, our students, and our colleagues have found interesting and informative.

Many fine films from many different producers are aired on the *American Experience* series of the Public Broadcasting Service (PBS). The website for PBS, www.pbs.org, has a webpage for each film, often with a transcript, sometimes with interviews, often with documents.

The American Social History Project has prepared a number of short documentaries that emphasize the perspective of working people on the great events of U.S. history. Those that focus on women's experience include *Daughters of Free Men*, about the Lowell Mill workers, and *Heaven Will Protect the Working Girl*, about immigrant life in the city at the turn of the twentieth-century See the American Social History Project website: http://ashp.cuny.edu/ashp-documentaries/.

A Midwife's Tale (1998, 88 min., color) presents a delicate enactment of the book of the same name by Laurel Thatcher Ulrich. A rare account of a woman's life in northern New England in the years of the early republic. Produced by Laurie Kahn-Leavitt. PBS Video, http://www.pbs.org/wgbh/amex/midwife/.

Hearts and Hands: A Social History of Nineteenth Century Women and Quilts (1987, 63 min., color) is a beautifully crafted and absorbing documentary that explores the lives of anonymous and notable women as they intersected with the major movements and events of the nineteenth century. See the companion book, *Hearts and Hands: The Influence of Women and Quilts on American Society* by Pat Ferrero, Elaine Hedges, and Julie Silber. available from New Day Films, www.newday.com/films/Hearts_and_Hands.html.

Anna Deavere Smith narrates *Hawaii's Last Queen,* a biography of Lili'uokalani written and produced by Vivian Ducat. Lili'uokalani resisted the authority of American sugar growers as long as she could, but in 1893 she was forced to surrender her throne to the United States; annexation took place in 1898. The film is part of the PBS *American Experience* series; enriching materials can be found on the PBS website: http://uww.pbs.org/wgbh/amex/hawaii/program.html.

Ida B. Wells: A Passion for a Justice (1990, 53 min., color) examines the personal and intense career of slave-bom African American journalist and activist Ida B. Wells, from her militant opposition to lynchings and discrimination to her determined support for the NAACP and the women's suffrage movement. This excellent film is particularly effective at showing how her activism was shaped by both her sex and race. Produced by William Greaves, California Newsreel: Film and Video for Social Change, http://newsreel.org/nav/title.asp?tc=CN0166.

The Women of Hull-House (1992, 18 min., b/w, color) describes the work of Florence Kelley, Julia Lathrop, Grace and Edith Abbott, and founders Jane Addams and Ellen Gates Starr, and the thirteen-building complex that served as a focal point for education, urban research, and social reform in Chicago during the early twentieth century. Jane Addams's Hull House Museum, the University of Illinois at Chicago, 800 South Halsted Street, Chicago, IL 60607-7017.

The filmmakers describe Emma Goldman as a "notorious lecturer, fearless and merciless publisher." In *Emma Goldman* a 90-minute film by Mel Bucklin, produced for PBS's *American Experience*, Goldman's life is traced in photographs, documents, and interviews with historians. A DVD is available from PBS. The transcript, primary sources, and suggestions for further reading can be found on the PBS website: http://www.pbs.org/wgbh/amex/goldman/filmmore/fd.html .

One Woman, One Vote (1995, 1 hr., 46 min., b/w) documents the seventy-year battle for woman suffrage, which finally culminated in the ratification of the Nineteenth Amendment to the Constitution in 1920. This splendid film portrays the movement's leaders, among them Susan B. Anthony, Elizabeth Cady Stanton, Lucy Stone, and Alice Paul, who dedicated much of their lives to the suffrage struggle. Interspersed are useful comments from historians. PBS Video, www.pbs.org.

Beginning in 1911, *You May Call Her Madam Secretary* (1986, 58 min., b/w, color) follows New Dealer Frances Perkins from teaching to settlement house work to FDR's cabinet as secretary of labor, documenting effectively the continuity between Progressivism and the New Deal. Vineyard Video Productions, http://www.vineyardvideo.org/francesperkins.shtml.

Based on Alice Lynch's account of the labor movement in the 1930s, *Union Maids* (1976, 50 min., b/w) depicts the personal experiences of three women who were labor organizers in Chicago during this period. Film by Julia Reichert, James Klein, and Miles Mogulescu, distributed by New Day Films, http://www.newday.com/films/Union_ Maids.html.

A portrayal of the Bryn Mawr Summer School, which flourished between 1921 and 1938, *The Women of Summer* (1975, 55 min., color) documents the effort to expose blue-collar women to humanistic study in such a way as to empower them to go back to their own communities as leaders. Duplicated in the South, these summer schools for women workers were part of the worker's education movement. Their impact on some of the alumnae is conveyed in archival footage, oral histories, and clips of many of the women leaders who served to link Progressivism and the New Deal. Film by Suzanne Bauman and Rita Heller, Film-Makers Library, http://filmakers.com/index.php?a=filmDetail&filmID=106.

The story of the Women's Emergency Brigade, *With Babies and Banners* (1979, 45 min., color) by Lyn Goldfarb, is an account of women's critical role in the General Motors sit-down strike in Flint, Michigan, in 1937, which was the key to the success of the Congress of Industrial Organizations' drive for industrial unionism. New Day Films, http://www.newday.com/films/With Babies_and_Banners.html.

Including rare home movies and voice recordings of Eleanor Roosevelt, as well as recollections of friends, relatives, colleagues, and historians (including Blanche Wiesen Cook; see pp. 530–36), *Eleanor Roosevelt* is a 2–1/2 hour biographical film by Sue Williams. It was produced for the American Experience series and is available on the PBS website: http://www.pbs.org/wgbh/amex/eleanor/.

The Life and Times of Rosie the Riveter (1980, 65 min., color), by Connie Field, presents the powerful and moving reminiscences of five women who welcomed the challenges and higher pay provided by new jobs in industry during World War II and details their loss of opportunities at the war's end when women were told to return home. Clarity Educational Productions, http://www.clarityfilms.org/rosie/index.html.

Never Turn Back: The Life of Fannie Lou Hamer (1983, 58, min., color) is an informative and powerful documentary that follows the career of black activist Fannie Lou Hamer from her early life as a sharecropper in Sunflower County, Mississippi, to national prominence as a civil rights leader and founding member of the Mississippi Freedom Democratic Party in the 1960s. Rediscovery Productions, 1-800-242-2946.

Polyethylene, a plastic developed for use in weapons, was molded into a new form of food container by Earl Tupper in 1945; Brownie Wise was a saleswoman who devised the new strategy of selling them in the context of home "parties" in which housewives made profit and Tupperware saleswomen changed the history of marketing. *Tupperware*! a film by Laurie Kahn-Leavitt (2005), is part of the PBS *American Experience* series. A DVD is available from PBS, and the transcript, primary sources, and further reading can be found on the PBS website: http://www.pbs.org/wgbh/amex/tupperware/.

Barbie Nation: An Unauthorized Tour, a film by Susan Stern (1998), traces the history of the doll from its invention in 1957 by Ruth Handler for her family's plastic business and as a response to her daughter's fascination with adult paper dolls, to its spread as a cultural artifact and sometimes ironic icon. Available from Bernal Beach Films, http://www.barbienation.com/index.html.

Focusing solely on Mexican American and Chicana women, *Adelante, Mujeres* (1992, 30 min., b/w, color) provides a brief history from colonial Mexico to the present. Women are presented in their work and family roles and as community and union activists. Made by the National Women's History Project, distributed by Women Make Movies, http://www.wmm.com/filmCatalog/pages/c27O.shtml.

Chisholm, '72: Unbought and Unbossed, a film by Shola Lynch (2004), follows Shirley Chisholm, the first African American woman elected to Congress (in 1968, from New York City). The film follows her across the country in her presidential campaign. The filmmakers have included archival footage and interviewed a wide range of her colleagues and other feminist activists. First aired on PBS's *Point of View* series and available from www.pbs.org.

Eyes on the Prize: Fighting Back (1986, 60 min., color) examines the explosive integration of the public schools in Little Rock, Arkansas, and the courage of the young black girls who had to go past angry white mobs to enter the schools. PBS Video, http://www.pbs.org/wgbh/amex/eyesontheprize/about/fd.html.

INDEX

E

F

G

H

M

N

O

S

V

W

Y

Z